Chapter	WHAT HAPPENS IN THE BRAIN?	HOW WE DEVELC		
11 Motivation	Hunger: What Happens in the Brain? Sex: What Happens in the Brain?	Achievement: How We Develop	Hunger: How We Differ Sex: How We Differ Achievement: How We Differ	Hunger and Eating Disorders: When Things Go Wrong Sex: When Things Go Wrong Affiliation: When Things Go Wrong
12 Emotion	Emotion: What Happens in the Brain?	Emotion: How We Develop	The Range of Emotional Experience: How We Differ	Disorders of Emotion: When Things Go Wrong
13 Personality	Personality: What Happens in the Brain?	Freud's Psychosexual Stages: How We Develop How Much Do Genetic Factors Contribute to Personality? How We Develop	Personality: How We Differ	Personality Disorders: When Things Go Wrong
14 Social Psychology	Social Functioning: What Happens in the Brain?	Attitudes: How We Develop	Roles, Gender, and Social Skills: How We Differ Conformity and Culture: How We Differ	Disorders of Social Functioning: When Things Go Wrong
15 Stress, Coping, and Health	Physiological Responses to Stress: What Happens in the Brain?	Life Changes: How We Develop	Individual Responses to Stress: How We Differ	Posttraumatic Stress Disorder: When Things Go Wrong
16 Psychological Disorders	The Neuroscience Model: What Happens in the Brain? How Do Neuroscientists Explain Depression? What Happens in the Brain? How Do Neuroscientists Explain Generalized Anxiety Disorder? What Happens in the Brain? How Do Neuroscientists Explain Obsessive-Compulsive Disorder? What Happens in the Brain? How Do Neuroscientists Explain Schizophrenia? What Happens in the Brain?	The Developmental Psychopathology Model: How We Develop	The Socio-cultural Model: How We Differ How Do Socio-cultural Theorists Explain Somatoform Disorders? How We Differ	Throughout
17 Treatment of Psychological Disorders	Biological Treatments: What Happens in the Brain?	Psychodynamic Therapies: How We Develop	Who Seeks Treatment? How We Differ	Throughout

Psychology Around Us

Canadian Edition

Ronald Comer
Princeton University

Elizabeth Gould
Princeton University

Nancy Ogden
Mount Royal University

Mike Boyes
University of Calgary

WILEY

John Wiley & Sons Canada, Ltd.

Library and Archives Canada Cataloguing in Publication

Psychology around us / Ronald Comer . . . [et al.].—Canadian ed.
Includes bibliographical references and index.
ISBN 978-0-470-67889-3
1. Psychology—Textbooks. I. Comer, Ronald J.
BF121.P8326 2012 150 C2011-907675-6

Production Credits

VICE-PRESIDENT AND PUBLISHER	Veronica Visentin
ACQUISITIONS EDITOR	Rodney Burke
SENIOR MARKETING MANAGER	Patty Maher
EDITORIAL MANAGER	Karen Staudinger
PRODUCTION MANAGER	Tegan Wallace
DEVELOPMENTAL EDITOR	Leanne Rancourt
MEDIA EDITOR	Channade Fenandoe
EDITORIAL ASSISTANTS	Laura Hwee and Sara Tinteri
COVER DESIGN	Joanna Vieira
INTERIOR DESIGN	Adrian So
TYPESETTING	Macmillan Publishing Solutions
PHOTO RESEARCHER	Rachel Irwin
COVER PHOTO	© Shutterstock/Victor Newman
PRINTING AND BINDING	COURIER

Printed and bound in the United States of America
1 2 3 4 5 CP 16 15 14 13 12

WILEY

John Wiley & Sons Canada, Ltd.
6045 Freemont Blvd.
Mississauga, Ontario L5R 4J3

Visit our website at: www.wiley.ca

To our children

Lindsey, Sean, and William

E.G.

Jon and Jami

Greg and Emily

R.C.

Michael, Daniel, Danielle, David, Emily, and Katie

N.O. and M.B.

About the Authors

Ronald Comer has taught in Princeton University's Department of Psychology for the past 35 years and has served as Director of Clinical Psychology Studies for most of that time. He has received the President's Award for Distinguished Teaching at the university. Comer also is the author of the textbooks *Abnormal Psychology*, now in its seventh edition, and *Fundamentals of Abnormal Psychology*, now in its sixth edition, and the coauthor of *Case Studies in Abnormal Psychology*. He is the producer of various educational videos, including *The Introduction to Psychology Video Library Series*. In addition, he has published journal articles in clinical psychology, personality, social psychology, and family medicine.

Elizabeth Gould has taught in Princeton University's Department of Psychology for the past 12 years. A leading researcher in the study of adult neurogenesis, she has published numerous journal articles on the production of new neurons in the adult mammalian brain. Gould has been honored for her breakthrough work with a number of awards, including the 2006 NARSAD Distinguished Investigator Award and the 2009 Royal Society of the Arts Benjamin Franklin Medal. She serves on the editorial boards of *The Journal of Neuroscience, Neurobiology of Learning and Memory, Biological Psychology*, and *Cell Stem Cell*.

Nancy Ogden has taught at Mount Royal University in the Department of Psychology for the past 20 years. She has previously published another Canadian introductory psychology textbook. Ogden has twice received the Teaching Excellence Award. She works and publishes in the areas of social and emotional development in children and adolescents and their families, and also does research in areas pertaining to the development of study strategy information in undergraduates.

Mike Boyes has taught at the University of Calgary in the Department of Psychology for 25 years. He has previously published another Canadian introductory psychology textbook. Boyes received the University of Calgary Student Union Teaching Award. He works and publishes in the areas of cognitive and social development in children and adolescents, as well as in programs aimed at eliminating family violence. He also studies attention management among novice and experienced drivers.

Brief Contents

Contents

To the Instructor

Psychology is all around us. If ever there was subject matter that permeates our everyday lives, it is psychology. Behaviour occurs everywhere, and mental processes affect all that we do; therefore the study of individual behaviour and mental processes can help shed light on a wide range of events and issues.

Psychology Around Us, Canadian Edition, helps open students' minds to the notion that psychology is indeed around them every day and that its principles are immediately applicable to a whole host of life's questions. It also features classroom-proven pedagogy to keep students engaged and help them master the material.

Between the four authors of this text, we have taught a wide variety of psychology courses for about 100 years combined. Throughout those years, we have always been struck by how differently students react to various areas within psychology. For example, students are fascinated by instances of "memory gone bad" yet take for granted that people can remember in the first place. Students are interested in the role of neurotransmitters in mood disorders and schizophrenia, but fail to see the point of learning about specific neurotransmitters in the neuroscience chapter. Students are captivated by failures in attention (ADHD), thought (schizophrenia), communication (autism), or coping (posttraumatic stress disorder), yet almost nonchalant about the fact that people mostly attend, think, communicate, and cope quite well.

Our textbook is dedicated to helping students appreciate that *both* normal and abnormal behaviour are fascinating, energizing, and exciting, and we are committed to demonstrating for students the relevance and interconnectedness of all areas of psychology. The textbook aims to encourage students to examine not only what they know about human behaviour but how they know it, and seeks to open students up to an appreciation of psychology outside of the classroom.

About the Text

As instructors and researchers, we (the authors) are passionate about the study of psychology and genuinely fascinated by behaviour, thought, and emotion and the way they interact. When we teach a course, we consider ourselves successful if we have engaged our students in the rigorous study of psychology while simultaneously transferring our passion for the subject. These same criteria of success should be applied to a textbook in psychology: It should broaden the reader's knowledge about the field and, at the same time, move, excite, and motivate the student. To achieve this goal, our textbook includes a range of features—some traditional, others innovative.

In some ways this book is radically different than any other book on the market. What makes it so different? Take a look at the brief table of contents on page vii. Go ahead . . . we'll wait. Did you see the differences? You may have noticed a few things, but probably nothing that you would consider "radical." That's because this book is not so different that it will require you to change the way you traditionally teach your course. What's different is on the *inside*. While each topic is still covered in its own separate chapter, the integrated nature of psychology permeates every chapter. How can students get a full appreciation of memory without discussing the vital role of the hippocampus, or how memory develops, or Alzheimer's disease? This is probably how you teach your course, and ***Psychology Around Us, Canadian Edition,*** is the first book available that is truly integrated—that actually brings all of these elements together into one, complete discussion of any given topic of psychology.

This integration is accomplished by offering a thorough presentation of the nature, explanations, applications, and research (including key Canadian research) of each topic, but also includes sections on neuroscience, development, dysfunctions, and individual differences that illustrate how each of these key areas is tied to other areas of psychology. These sections serve to engage students for the duration of the course and present psychology as a united and integrated discipline . . . students truly get to see "the big picture."

For example, most of today's textbooks offer a detailed chapter on neuroscience early in the book and detailed chapters on psychological disorders late in the textbook. In between are chapters on other subfields of psychology—from sensation, perception, language, and thought, to emotion, personality, and social behaviour. These middle chapters focus on the nature, explanations, and applications of each subfield, but they typically do not explore how the *brain functions* or what *dysfunctions* may occur in each area.

In other textbooks it is left to the reader to remember the structure and function of the brain from an earlier chapter and see its implications for the material at hand, or to place the current material on hold and tie it weeks later to subsequent chapters on related psychological disorders and treatments. No wonder some students are impatient to "get to the psychology!" They are not set up from the outset to appreciate the full range of the field.

Special Pedagogical Tools

Tying It Together

To achieve our goal of showing students how psychology is indeed all around us, and to bring our textbook in line with the course curricula of most professors, we have structured each of the chapters in our textbook in a very particular way—with a cross-sectional presentation. Every chapter on a substantive area of psychology includes **Tying It Together** sections on the *development, brain function, individual differences, and dysfunctions* that occur in that realm of mental life. These sections, entitled **How We Develop, What Happens in the Brain?, How We Differ,** and **When Things Go Wrong,** are all earmarked with an icon so students can readily integrate the material into what they already know. Material from these sections is then summarized at the end of the chapter in a **Tying It Together** summary.

Your Brain and Behaviour

Many introductory psychology students consider the study of neuroscience to be difficult and at times irrelevant to the study of human behaviour. In recent years, however, neuroscience has been tied to virtually every subfield of psychology. Remarkable brain imaging studies, in conjunction with animal studies, have helped us to identify the neural mechanisms of everyday experience. Accordingly, ***Psychology Around Us, Canadian Edition,*** incorporates neuroscience information into chapters where it has traditionally been absent, such as social psychology and consciousness.

In addition, the text offers a key teaching feature that helps bring neuroscience directly into the lives of readers: Exciting and accessible two-page layouts appear throughout the book illustrating the link between the brain and behaviour when people are performing such common activities as eating pizza, learning to play a video game, acquiring a second language, giving a speech in public, or running a marathon. These layouts, which include neuroimages and findings from both human studies and relevant animal experiments, draw students into the brain and provide them with up-to-date information about the neural mechanisms at work during their everyday experiences. And to make sure they have a firm understanding of the concepts, each feature includes questions that allow students to test their knowledge (answers are available with the Before You Go On answers on the book companion site or *WileyPLUS*). Regardless of their background in neuroscience, students come away intrigued by material that has traditionally been considered difficult.

Additional Features

Chapter-Opening Vignettes

Every chapter begins with a vignette that shows the power of psychology in understanding a range of human behaviours. This theme is reinforced throughout the chapter, celebrating the extraordinary processes that make the everyday possible.

Guided Learning

A **Learning Objective** for each chapter section identifies the most important material for students to understand while reading that section. These learning objectives also serve as the driving principle in *WileyPLUS*.

Following each section is a **Before You Go On** feature that helps students check their mastery of the important items covered. **What Do You Know?** questions prompt students to stop and review the key concepts just presented. **What Do You Think?** questions encourage students to think critically on key questions in the chapter. Answers to all of the What Do You Know? questions are available online, through *WileyPLUS*, or through a unique QR code found within each section, making studying familiar and accessible to today's tech-savvy students.

Special Topics on Psychology Around Us

Each chapter highlights interesting news stories, current controversies in psychology, and relevant research findings that demonstrate psychology around us.

- The **Psychology Around Us** boxes highlight how psychology affects us in our everyday lives, in every way, with examples from Canada and around the world.
- The **Things Students Want to Know** boxes answer questions that Canadian introductory psychology students frequently ask.
- The **Practically Speaking** box emphasizes the practical application of everyday psychology.

Thorough Coverage

Psychology Around Us, Canadian Edition, contains 17 chapters that cover all the topics of psychology in depth. Instead of combining chapters on motivation and emotion, or stress and emotion, or even psychological disorders and their treatment, each topic is given full coverage in its own, separate chapter. This gives you ultimate flexibility in determining how much time you want your students to devote to each topic. If you only want to cover emotion briefly, then simply assign the relevant pages from that chapter; but if you want to cover emotion in depth, you have a full chapter at your disposal that contains detailed and integrated coverage of the topic.

Helpful Study Tools . . .

- **Key Terms** are listed at the end of each chapter with page references.
- **Marginal Definitions** define the key terms discussed in the text.
- **Marginal Notes** present interesting facts and quotes throughout the chapter.

Chapter Summary

The end-of-chapter summary reviews the main concepts presented in the chapter with reference to the specific Learning Objectives. It provides students with another opportunity to review what they have learned as well as to see how the key topics within the chapter fit together.

Resources

Psychology Around Us, Canadian Edition, is accompanied by a host of resources and ancillary materials designed to facilitate a mastery of psychology.

Powerful Media Resources

WileyPLUS is an innovative, research-based online environment for effective teaching and learning.

WileyPLUS builds students' confidence because it takes the guesswork out of studying by providing students with a clear roadmap: what to do, how to do it, whether they did it right. Students will take more initiative so you'll have greater impact on their achievement in the classroom and beyond.

Instructor Resources

Instructor Resources can be found within the ***Psychology Around Us, Canadian Edition,*** *WileyPLUS* course and on the text's companion website, www.wiley.com/go/comer.

Concept Videos

The ***Psychology Around Us*** series of Concept, or "lecture-launcher," Videos help bring lectures to life and, most importantly, captivate students. They help demonstrate that psychology is all around us and that thought and behaviour, from the everyday to the abnormal, is truly fascinating. Averaging about five minutes in length, this collection of videos covers a range of relevant topics.

Each video is a high-quality excerpt from various agencies or independent video libraries chosen from a televised news report, documentary, lab study, or the like, and illustrating a particular lecture point, bringing the topic to life in exciting ways.

In addition, the video package has been produced by Ron Comer and other leading university educators whose extensive teaching, video, and psychology backgrounds enable them to develop video materials that address the lecture needs and goals of teachers and students.

The large selection of clips in this package focus on topics ranging from the split-brain phenomenon to conformity and obedience, emotions of fear or disgust, sensations of taste and smell, infant facial recognition, gender orientation, and brain development.

The videos are accompanied by an extensive *Instructor's Guide*. This guide offers a description of each module in the package, its length and source, features of special interest, and relevant textbook/lecture topics.

The video program is readily accessible and easily integrated into any introductory psychology course through the ***Psychology Around Us, Canadian Edition,*** *WileyPLUS* course. If instructors choose not to use any or all of the videos in the classroom they have the option of assigning videos to students for viewing outside of class. Instructors can also use the prepared quizzes that test understanding of the video's content and relevance.

Psychology Around Us Video Lab Activities

Psychology Around Us, Canadian Edition, offers a series of 15 active learning projects that students can conduct on their own. Traditionally, such exercises have been presented in book form, with *written* exercises guiding students through paper-and-pencil tasks. Today students can *interact* with computerized exercises, become more engaged by video and animated material, and receive immediate feedback about the effects and accuracy of their choices.

These lab activities use extensive video material to drive student learning. The combination of video footage and digital interactive technology brings the lab exercises to life for students, actively engaging the students and helping them to better process the lesson at hand. The kinds of video material included in the *Video Lab Activities* range from laboratory footage about the brain to videos of everyday events to psychology documentary excerpts.

For example, one video lab exercise on *Memory Manufacturing and Eyewitness Testimony* unfolds as a cluster of video-digital lab exercises on memory. They guide the student to also explore (1) pre-event and post-event memory interference, (2) childhood memory limits, (3) snapshot memories, and (4) the creation of false memories.

Like the Concept Videos, the Video Labs are accessible through the ***Psychology Around Us, Canadian Edition,*** *WileyPLUS* course. Should instructors so choose they have the option of assigning the Videos Labs to students for completion outside of class; the student's work is then viewable by the instructor in *WileyPLUS*'s Gradebook section.

Instructor's Manual

Prepared by Rajiv Jhangiani, *Capilano University*

This *Instructor's Manual* is designed to help instructors maximize student learning and encourage critical thinking. It presents teaching suggestions for every chapter using the book's objectives as well as including ideas for lecture classroom discussions, demonstrations, and videos. This manual will also share activity-based applications to everyday life.

PowerPoint Presentations

Prepared by Susan McBride, *Langara College*

Every chapter contains a *PowerPoint Presentation* with a combination of key concepts, figures and tables, and problems and examples from the textbook. The instructor's version also includes notes for additional discussion points or activities you can use during your lecture.

In addition, each PowerPoint Presentation comes with a "media-enriched" version that contains links to all of the concept videos available for that chapter. Using these presentations in your class means that the rich array of videos discussed above are simply a mouse-click away.

TestBank

Prepared by Cheryl Techentin, *Mount Royal University,* and **David R. Cann,** *Mount Royal University*

The *Test Bank* contains over 200 questions per chapter with a variety of question types—multiple choice, true/false, short answer, and essay, and each chapter also has one terminology question and one diagram-labelling question. The Test Bank is available in two Word® document formats (one that is organized by Learning Objective, so you can ensure your tests have complete coverage of each chapter, and one organized by question type, for those who only want a specific type of question on their tests), as a Computerized Test Bank, or through Respondus®, which allows you to upload the test bank into your learning management system (e.g., Blackboard). The questions are available to instructors to create and print multiple versions of the same test by scrambling the order of all questions found in the Word version of the test bank. This allows users to customize exams by altering or adding new problems.

Chapter Quizzes

Prepared by Wendy Bourque, *University of New Brunswick* and *St. Thomas University*

This resource offers 20 questions per chapter that students can use to test their knowledge of the chapter content.

Clicker Questions

Prepared by Wendy Bourque, *University of New Brunswick* and *St. Thomas University*

This resource offers 10-15 questions per chapter that can be used with a variety of person response (or "clicker") systems.

Student Resources

Student Resources can be found within the ***Psychology Around Us, Canadian Edition,*** *WileyPLUS* course and on the text's companion website, www.wiley.com/go/comer.

Online Study Tools

Psychology Around Us, Canadian Edition, provides students with a website containing a wealth of support materials to develop their understanding of class material and increase their ability to solve problems in the classroom. On this website students will find Chapter Quizzes for every chapter that will allow them to assess their understanding of chapter concepts. In addition, students have access to Interactive Flash Cards, Chapter Summaries, Learning Objectives, Web Resources, and more!

Acknowledgements

The writing of this text has been a group effort involving the input and support of many individuals. We, Nancy and Mike, owe an enormous debt of gratitude to the people at Wiley Canada for their encouragement, support, and assistance in guiding and developing the production of this text. We would like to thank those whom we worked with most closely, in particular Rodney Burke, Acquisitions Editor, who was not only the visionary for the project but who also served as the glue that bound the entire team, and Leanne Rancourt, Developmental Editor, who was supportive, perceptive, and thoughtful and whose clear and insightful navigation kept us on course. Her insights and high expectations have made this text infinitely stronger.

We are extremely thankful to the entire editorial and production team, who guided us through the challenging steps of developing this book, including Veronica Visentin, Vice-President and Publisher; Carolyn J. Wells, Vice-President of Higher Education Marketing; Patty Maher, Senior Marketing Manager; Karen Staudinger, Editorial Manager; Kyle Fisher, Sales Manager; Channade Fenandoe, Media Editor; and Laura Hwee and Sara Tinteri, Editorial Assistants. Our thanks also goes to Tegan Wallace, Production Manager; Lynda Jess, Publishing Services Assistant; Adrian So for the interior design concept; and Joanna Vieira for the design of the cover. We appreciate the efforts of Janice Dyer, our copyeditor; Laurel Hyatt, our proofreader; Rachel Irwin, our photo and permissions editor; and Belle Wong, our indexer.

As well, we would like to thank George Alder both for his significant contributions to Chapter 2 and for the single-handed creation of Appendix A, which introduces students to statistics and their importance in psychology research. George can explain theories and concepts about research and statistics in ways that are uniquely comprehensible to students, and we know that the book is stronger because of his involvement. Evelyn Field developed and wrote the section on Evolutionary Psychology in Chapter 4, and we would like to thank her for sharing her expertise and for her cogent writing. Like George, Evelyn is skilled at drawing students into material that is typically viewed as "dry" or "uninteresting," and we are confident that students will gain not only in understanding from her work but that they will benefit by having their interest sparked as well. Finally, we would like to thank our research assistant, Daniel Cryderman, for his contributions to the text. He uncomplainingly searched for and acquired hundreds of citation sources, worked tirelessly on the manuscript, and created answers for all of the Before You Go On questions. On a personal note, we would also like to thank our families, friends, and colleagues for their encouragement and support.

Finally, a very special thank you goes out to the faculty members who have contributed to the development of this text, its art program, its digital resources, and its powerful supplemental program. We would particularly like to thank Wendy Bourque, David Cann, Rajiv Jhangiani, Susan McBride, and Cheryl Techentin for their extraordinary and creative work. To the reviewers and editorial advisory board members who gave their time and constructive criticism, we offer our heartfelt thanks. We are deeply indebted to the following individuals and trust they will recognize their significant contributions throughout the text.

Editorial Advisory Board Members

Ben Dyson, *Ryerson University*
Lynne Honey, *Grant MacEwan University*
Trudy Kwong, *Mount Royal University*
Colleen MacQuarrie, *University of Prince Edward Island*
Heather Schellinck, *Dalhousie University*
Doug Symons, *Acadia University*
Claire Vanston, *Capilano University*

Reviewers

George Alder, *Simon Fraser University*
Wendy Bourque, *University of New Brunswick*
John Conklin, *Camosun College*
Leora Dahl, *Okanagan College*
Ben Dyson, *Ryerson University*
Carla Gunn, *University of New Brunswick*
Sandra Hessels, *Huron University College at Western*
Mark Holder, *University of British Columbia*
Lynne Honey, *Grant MacEwan University*
Rajiv Jhangiani, *Capilano University*
Jacqueline Kampman, *Thompson Rivers University*
Trudy Kwong, *Mount Royal University*
Laura Loewen, *Okanagan College*
Colleen MacQuarrie, *University of Prince Edward Island*
Rick Maddigan, *Memorial University*
Susan McBride, *Langara College*
Rick Mehta, *Acadian University*
Blaine Mullins, *University of Alberta*
Tim Parker, *University of Alberta, Augustana Campus*
Heather Schellinck, *Dalhousie University*
Harry Strub, *University of Winnipeg*
Doug Symons, *Acadia University*
Claire Vanston, *Capilano University*

To the Student

How to Use This Book

The features in this book promote your reading comprehension, reflection, problem-solving skills, and critical-thinking skills. These skills are key to success in the course and in your life beyond. Let's walk through the pedagogical features that will help you learn the material in this book.

CHAPTER 14

Social Psychology

CHAPTER OUTLINE

- Social Cognition: Attitudes
- Social Cognition: Attributions
- Social Forces
- Social Relations
- Social Functioning *What Happens in the Brain?*
- Disorders of Social Functioning *When Things Go Wrong*

SOCIAL PSYCHOLOGY AT THE STANLEY CUP FINALS

On June 15, 2011, the Vancouver Canucks lost to the Boston Bruins in game seven of the Stanley Cup final. During the Vancouver home games, thousands of fans gathered in the streets around the arena and watched the games on large screens (as people had done during the Winter Olympics). Following previous games (all Vancouver wins), the crowds had been boisterous but controlled. Following the seventh-game loss, some members of the crowd began to get out of hand. Bottles were tossed at the big screens, porta-potties were tipped over, and the first of what would eventually be a total of 17 cars (including two police cars) were turned over and set ablaze. Fights broke out and 140 people were reported injured, including nine police officers. Transit in the area was shut down, and people attending a musical (*Wicked*) at a nearby theatre were told to wait in the theatre for several hours until the riot subsided. Rioters moved through downtown Vancouver, smashing windows and looting stores. Eventually the rioters were dispersed at about midnight.

At the time of this writing, about 100 people had been arrested in relation to the riot. However, that number is likely to increase as there was also a *virtual* riot: social media videos and photos taken on cell phones were posted in the days following the disturbance. The various sites asked that anyone recognizing a rioter provide his or her name so that it could be passed along to the police and additional rioters could be charged. It has been suggested that the actions of the social media "mob" demanding charges and justice were in some ways similar to the actions of the mob of rioters, but debate on that comparison continues.

The actions of people in and after such events are of particular interest to social psychologists. Many "rioters" were otherwise regular citizens, and yet they behaved in uncharacteristic ways during the riot. Social psychologists study the social forces involved in this sort of behaviour.

The British poet John Donne's famous words, "No man is an island," highlight the interconnectedness of humankind. We live in a world of approximately 7 billion people, and each and every day we influence and are influenced by others. Social psychologists devote themselves to the study of human interconnectedness. Unlike many areas of psychology that focus on areas of individual difference, such as personality, social psychology is based on the belief that "it is not so much the kind of person a man is, as the kind of situation in which he finds himself that determines how he will act" (Milgram, 2004, p. 101).

We might think of social psychology in a general way as the scientific study of how people are affected by other people. This informal definition covers considerable territory. Many aspects of an individual's functioning may be affected by others—thoughts, feelings, and behaviours may

Chapter-Opening Vignettes

Every chapter begins with a vignette that shows the power of psychology in understanding a range of human behaviours. This theme is reinforced throughout the chapter, celebrating the extraordinary processes that make the everyday possible.

Guided Learning

Chapter Learning Objectives summarize what you should be able to do once you have studied the chapter. You can use the learning goals in two ways. First, study them before reading the chapter to get an overall picture of how the concepts in the chapter are related to each other and what you will be learning. Then, after reading the chapter, use the learning objectives to review what you have learned, either individually or in peer study groups. You can improve learning and retention without significantly increasing study time.

What Is a Science?

LEARNING OBJECTIVE 1

List two core beliefs of science, and describe the steps in the scientific method.

Before we look at psychology in particular, take a moment to try to answer the general question, what is a science? You might answer by listing types of sciences, such as chemistry, biology, or physics. You might envision a white-coated person in a lab somewhere, mixing strangely bubbling chemicals or lecturing students about where to start an incision on the frog in the tray in front of them. Such things are only *sometimes* associated with science. Two characteristics that all sciences share, however, are similar principles, or beliefs,

Helpful Study Tools . . .

Following each section is a Before You Go On feature that helps you check your mastery of the important items covered. **What Do You Know?** questions ask you to stop and review the key concepts just presented. **What Do You Think?** questions encourage you to think critically about key questions in the chapter. Answers to all of the What Do You Know? questions are available online, through *WileyPLUS*, or through a unique QR code found within each section that leads you directly to the answers.

Before You Go On

What Do You Know?

1. What is learning?
2. What happens in synapses during habituation? What happens during sensitization?

What Do You Think?

Give an example from your own life of a time when you experienced non-associative learning.

This text is designed to intersect at precise points with side notes that are placed in the page margins—interesting and relevant psychology facts, contemporary news stories, historical points, material from movies, and the like. In addition, interspersed with the text material at just the right points on each page are elements such as relevant, exciting boxes, current controversies in psychology, research surprises, and perfectly selected photos, all from Canada and around the world.

PRACTICALLY SPEAKING Addictions: Living out of Control

Reducing harm. Vancouver's Coastal Health Service opened a safe injection site near Vancouver's Downtown Eastside in 2003. It offers clean needle and supervision of injections by heroin users, as well as support and referrals for treatment.

Many people struggle with addiction problems. According to some clinical theorists, addictions are not only about alcohol and substance abuse; they may also cover dependencies such as food, the Internet, gambling, caffeine, shopping, sex, and exercise, to name a few (Page & Brewster, 2009; Stein, 2008). Addictive patterns do not suddenly appear; they are usually long-standing and may be rooted in various psychological problems. Whereas it takes time for individuals to lose control of their life to a dependency, it also takes time, motivation, commitment, discipline, and often the help of a professional treatment program to regain control and recover from an addiction. There are no quick fixes for recovery.

How do you know whether you or someone close to you is experiencing an addiction? This is a complex issue that typically requires careful clinical assessment for a definitive answer. Nevertheless, there are some straightforward questions that you can use to determine whether professional attention is in order. For example, is the person unable to meet responsibilities at home, school, or the office? Has the person tried to stop the repeated behaviour but cannot, and continues to engage in it despite the apparent dangers?

Although most clinicians agree that there is no substitute for careful clinical assessment and treatment of addictions, some have developed basic detection devices that can help get the ball rolling. For example, a brief tool to detect alcohol addiction is known as the CAGE questionnaire. It asks these questions: (1) Has the person ever felt that he or she should CUT DOWN on the drinking? (2) Has the person ever been ANNOYED by people criticizing the drinking?

Key Terms are listed at the end of each chapter with page references.

Margin Definitions define the key terms discussed in the text.

Margin Notes present interesting facts and quotes throughout the chapter.

At the *level of the person*, psychologists analyze how the *content* of mental processes—including emotions, thoughts, and ideas—form and influence behaviour. To use a computer analogy, this level relates to the software rather than the mechanical functioning, or hardware, of the brain. The level of the person includes many of the things that people think of first when they discuss psychology—ideas such as consciousness, intelligence, personality, and motivation. Although internal biological structures of the brain allow such person-level processes to occur, we cannot understand the processes unique to each individual, such as personality or motivation, without also studying this content.

"Everything that irritates us about others can lead us to an understanding of ourselves."
—*Carl Jung, psychiatrist and philosopher*

Psychologists must also look beyond the individual at the *level of the group*. This perspective acknowledges that humans are shaped by their social environment and that this environment varies over time. A *group* can be made up of friends, family members, or a large population. Often a large group shares a culture, a set of common beliefs, practices, values, and history that are transmitted across generations. The groups to which people belong or perceive themselves to belong can influence their thoughts and behaviours in fundamental ways (Prinstein & Dodge, 2008).

culture a set of shared beliefs and practices that are transmitted across generations.

When they conduct research, psychologists may focus on a single level of analysis.

Seeing the "Big Picture" in Psychology

Tying It Together

Psychology is an integrated discipline. Everything is connected to everything else—your ability to react with fear or excitement is tied to neuroscience and your past development, for example. Every chapter on a substantive area of psychology in this text not only offers a thorough presentation of the nature, explanations, and applications of that area, but also includes sections on the *development, brain function, individual differences*, and *dysfunctions* that occur in that realm of mental life. Your success in this course will depend on how well you can integrate this information meaningfully. The more often you review your prior knowledge and connect it with new knowledge, the more automatic and refined learned knowledge and skills become.

Intelligence — WHAT HAPPENS IN THE BRAIN?

LEARNING OBJECTIVE 5

Describe how brain size, number of neurons, processing speed, brain activity, and cortical thickness relate to intelligence.

So far in this chapter, we have explored several important questions concerning the nature, measurement, and sources of intelligence. We now add another question: what happens in the brain when we exhibit intelligence? Have researchers, for example, detected relationships between specific brain activities or specific brain structures and intelligence? To answer this question, let's look at four areas of investigation: brain size, brain speed, brain activity, and cortical thickness (Reynolds et al., 2008; Vernon et al., 2000).

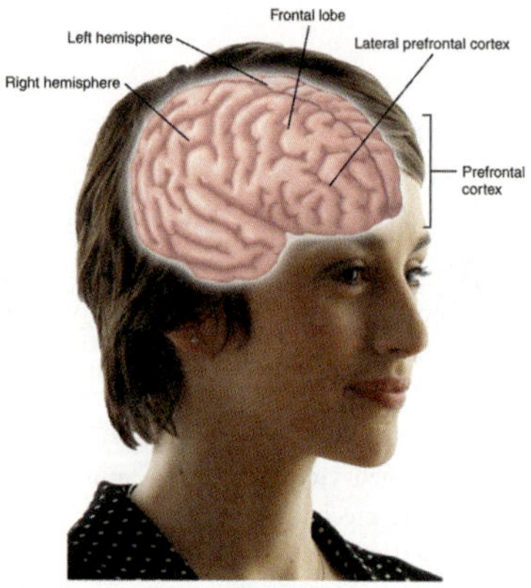

Brain Size, Number of Neurons, and Intelligence

Researchers have been exploring correlations between brain size and intelligence since the mid-nineteenth century (Ash & Gallup, 2008; Galton, 1948, 1888). Philippe Rushton has done some work here as well (Rushton, 2009). Initially, limi-

Prenatal and Postnatal Learning — HOW WE DEVELOP

LEARNING OBJECTIVE 7

Summarize the types of learning that occur before we are born and during early postnatal life.

Several studies suggest that non-associative learning can occur before we are even born. Fetuses show habituation and sensitization to smells and other sensory stimuli (Faas et al., 2000). In one set of studies, for example, infants who had been prenatally exposed to garlic—through their mothers' digestion—showed evidence, after they were born, of recognizing the garlic odour. They did not try to avoid the smell, as babies new to garlic typically do (Mennella, Johnson, & Beauchamp, 1995). Habituation studies of newborns also show that they can distinguish between new and familiar sights and sounds. Even very soon after birth, babies typically stop moving for a brief time when they are exposed to a new visual or auditory stimulus. This response suggests that they have already become accustomed, or habituated, to "old" sights and sounds (Slater & Morrison, 1991). They have learned to recognize them.

We are also capable of basic associative learning before birth. One team of researchers reported classical conditioning of human fetuses. Recall from Chapter 5 that hearing is partially developed before birth. These researchers paired specific music (initially a neutral stimulus) with relaxation exercises done by the mother. The maternal relaxation exer-

Early olfactory learning. In this study, infants are exposed to bottles containing smells of their mothers, their fathers, and other people. In such research undertakings, babies consistently show highest preference for the smell of their mothers and second highest for that of their fathers.

Hearing — WHEN THINGS GO WRONG

There are many conditions that lead to abnormalities in the auditory system. Some cause either partial or total deafness, the loss of hearing. Abnormalities in the auditory system can also add unwanted auditory perceptions.

deafness loss or lack of hearing.

Deafness Deafness has a variety of causes. It can be genetic or caused by infection, physical trauma, or exposure to toxins, including overdose of common medications such as aspirin.

Since speech is an important mode of communication for humans, deafness can have dramatic consequences for socialization. This is particularly a concern for children, because young children need auditory stimulation to develop normal spoken language skills. For this reason, physicians try to identify auditory deficits at an early life stage. Parents can then make choices among different options to help their children with deafness. Some deaf individuals learn to use sign language and other methods of communication that rely on the senses other than hearing. Research over the past years has made progress in the construction of cochlear implants that help individuals with deafness to hear sounds (Sharma et al., 2009). Although this work is developing at a rapid pace, there remain many deaf people who are not helped by cochlear implants (Battmer et al., 2009). This is one reason why many individuals and families choose to avoid them. Some in the deaf community also believe that hearing is not necessary to lead a productive and fulfilling life. For them, the potential benefits of implants may not outweigh the potential risks of surgery required to place them in the cochlea (Hyde & Power, 2006).

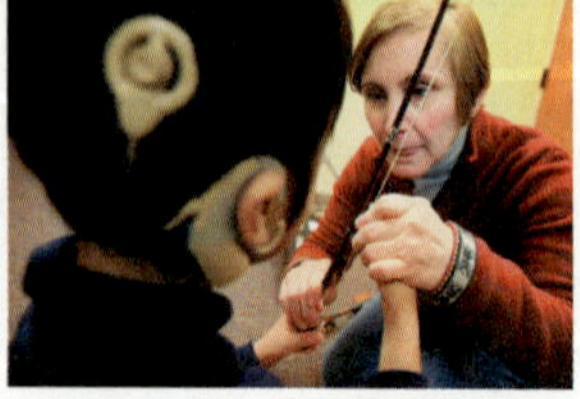

A world of new possibilities. After undergoing successful cochlear implant surgery, this 4-year-old child practises the violin under the instruction of his music teacher at the Memphis Oral School for the Deaf.

Extremes in Intelligence — HOW WE DIFFER

LEARNING OBJECTIVE 6

Discuss mental retardation and giftedness.

Earlier in the chapter, we mentioned that intelligence, as measured by IQ tests, follows a normal distribution—that is, a distribution shaped like a bell curve. At either end of this curve are a small number of people who score either much lower or much higher than the people who make up the large middle. At the lower end are people who are diagnosed with mental retardation, and at the higher end are those who are intellectually gifted (**Figure 10-9**).

Making music. A young man with Down syndrome is the percussionist in a community orchestra (left), while a child prodigy sings opera to an appreciative audience at a school for the arts (right).

Mental Retardation (Intellectual Disability)

Most individuals demonstrate sufficient levels of intelligence to survive on their own and to manage their daily lives. But the intellectual and adaptive functioning of some people is well below that of most other people. These individuals are said to display mental retardation, a combination of general intellectual functioning that is well below average and poor adaptive behaviour (APA, 2000). That is, in addition to having an IQ score of 70 or below, many of these individuals experience great difficulty in areas such as communication, home living, self-direction, work, and safety (APA, 2000). Some psychologists now prefer the term *intellectual disability* to mental retardation, so we will use the terms interchangeably in our discussion (National Center on Birth Defects and Developmental Disabilities, 2005).

mental retardation term describing individuals who display general intellectual functioning that is well below average and, at the same time, poor adaptive behaviour.

Your Brain and Behaviour

It's our hope that you will come to see the fascination of psychology and develop a passion for this field of study. One example of how we demonstrate this to you is a regular feature throughout the textbook—a two-page spread called *Tying It Together: Your Brain and Behaviour.* Centring on a common everyday activity, these lively spreads clarify the remarkable brain events that help give life to the activity and serve as awe-inspiring reminders that psychology is everywhere.

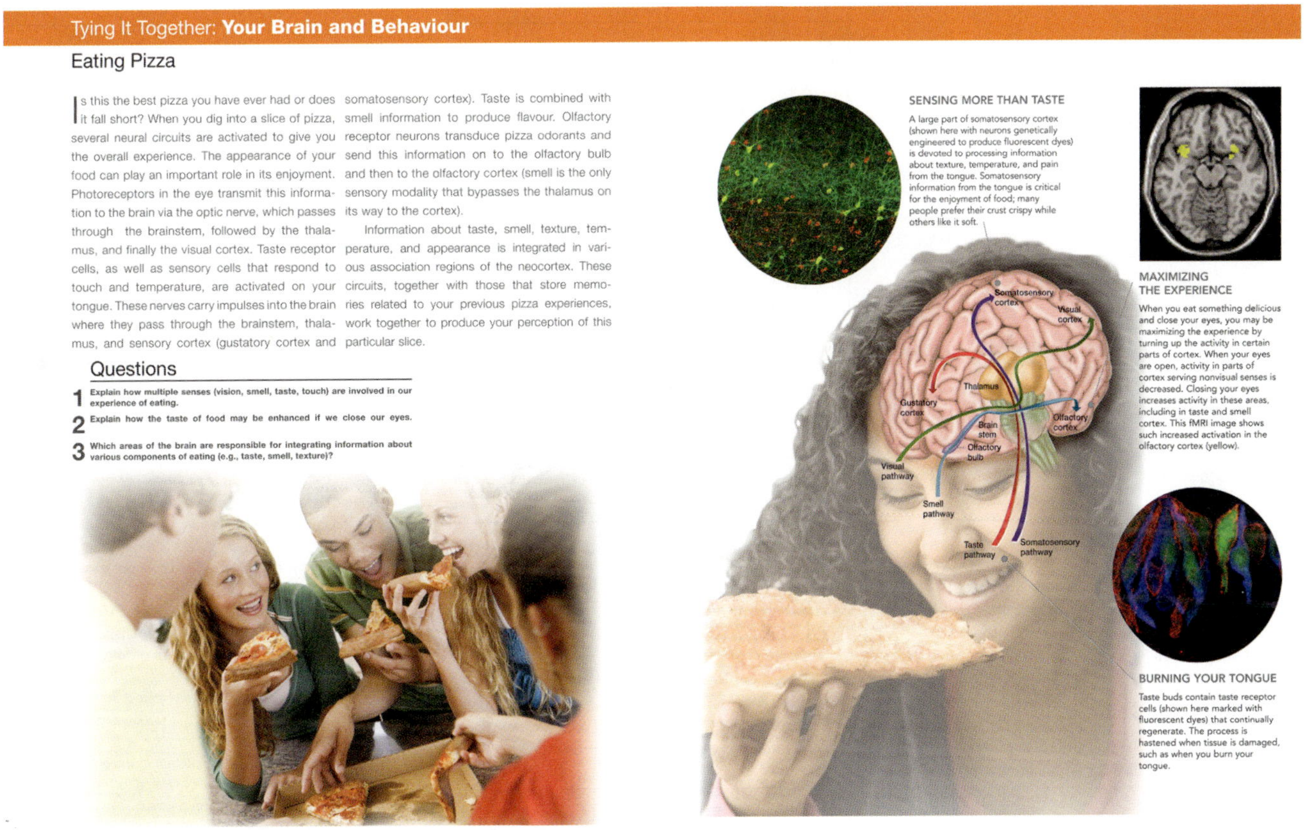

Tying It Together: **Your Brain and Behaviour**

Eating Pizza

Is this the best pizza you have ever had or does it fall short? When you dig into a slice of pizza, several neural circuits are activated to give you the overall experience. The appearance of your food can play an important role in its enjoyment. Photoreceptors in the eye transmit this information to the brain via the optic nerve, which passes through the brainstem, followed by the thalamus, and finally the visual cortex. Taste receptor cells, as well as sensory cells that respond to touch and temperature, are activated on your tongue. These nerves carry impulses into the brain where they pass through the brainstem, thalamus, and sensory cortex (gustatory cortex and somatosensory cortex). Taste is combined with smell information to produce flavour. Olfactory receptor neurons transduce pizza odorants and send this information on to the olfactory bulb and then to the olfactory cortex (smell is the only sensory modality that bypasses the thalamus on its way to the cortex).

Information about taste, smell, texture, temperature, and appearance is integrated in various association regions of the neocortex. These circuits, together with those that store memories related to your previous pizza experiences, work together to produce your perception of this particular slice.

Questions

1 **Explain how multiple senses (vision, smell, taste, touch) are involved in our experience of eating.**

2 **Explain how the taste of food may be enhanced if we close our eyes.**

3 **Which areas of the brain are responsible for integrating information about various components of eating (e.g., taste, smell, texture)?**

SENSING MORE THAN TASTE

A large part of somatosensory cortex (shown here with neurons genetically engineered to produce fluorescent dyes) is devoted to processing information about texture, temperature, and pain from the tongue. Somatosensory information from the tongue is critical for the enjoyment of food; many people prefer their crust crispy while others like it soft.

MAXIMIZING THE EXPERIENCE

When you eat something delicious and close your eyes, you may be maximizing the experience by turning up the activity in certain parts of cortex. When your eyes are open, activity in parts of cortex serving nonvisual senses is decreased. Closing your eyes increases activity in these areas, including in taste and smell cortex. This fMRI image shows such increased activation in the olfactory cortex (yellow).

BURNING YOUR TONGUE

Taste buds contain taste receptor cells (shown here marked with fluorescent dyes) that continually regenerate. The process is hastened when tissue is damaged, such as when you burn your tongue.

Review Main Concepts

Chapter Summary

Each chapter ends with a summary and list of key terms aimed at representing the scope and emphasis of a relatively large amount of material in an efficient and concise form. The end-of-chapter summary reviews the main concepts presented in the chapter with reference to the specific Learning Objectives. It provides you with another opportunity to review what you have learned as well as to see how the key topics within the chapter fit together. You can write your own summary first, as a review strategy, and then check your work against the text summary to self-evaluate your understanding of the big picture in each chapter.

Summary

What Is Psychology?

LEARNING OBJECTIVE 1 Define psychology, and describe the goals and levels of analysis psychologists use.

- Psychology is the study of mental processes and behaviour.
- The goals of psychology are to *describe*, *explain*, *predict*, and *control* behaviour and mental processes. Psychologists vary in the degree to which they focus on some of these goals more than others.
- The study of psychology must occur at multiple levels, including the level of the *brain* (the biological activity associated with mental processes and behaviour), the level of the *person* (the content of mental processes), and the level of the *group* (social influences on behaviour).

Psychology's Roots in Philosophy

LEARNING OBJECTIVE 2 Describe the influences of early myths and ancient Greek philosophies on psychology.

gists and describe their major theories and research methods.

- The development of psychology has been strongly influenced by shifts in the social environment and development of new technology.
- The first psychology laboratory was founded in Leipzig, Germany, by physiologist Wilhelm Wundt. Wundt was interested in human consciousness and will, which he studied through small, structured activities that could be easily watched and replicated.
- Structuralism, a school of thought developed by one of Wundt's students, relied upon the use of introspection, the careful observation of human perception. The goal of the structuralists was to find the smallest building blocks of consciousness.
- William James established the first psychology laboratory in the United States at Harvard and helped shift the field's focus to the functions of mental events and behaviours, forming a school of thought known as

- Gestalt psychologists studied human tendencies to perceive pattern rather than dividing consciousness into its smallest parts. They focused on putting together the "parts," or individual sensations, to create a "whole" or perception that went beyond the sum of the parts.

Twentieth-Century Approaches

LEARNING OBJECTIVE 4 Summarize the major principles of the psychoanalytical, behaviourist, humanistic, cognitive, and neuroscience approaches to psychology.

- Over the years, different fields of psychology emerged, with different ideas about what was the appropriate area of study for human psychology. Some of the most influential fields were the psychoanalytic, behaviourist, humanistic, cognitive, and neuroscience schools of thought.
- Sigmund Freud's psychoanalytical theory focused on the importance of unconscious mental processes.
- Behaviourists believed strongly that psychology should restrict its focus to the careful study of observable behaviours.
- Humanistic psychologists reacted against the mechanical portrayals of people by the behaviourists, and emphasized individuals' potential for growth and self-actualization.
- Cognitive psychologists reignited interest in the study of mental processes, comparing the workings of the mind to the workings of computers.
- Biological science, including interest in the workings of the brain and in our genetic inheritance, is the major influence on neuroscience approaches.

Psychology Today

LEARNING OBJECTIVE 5 Describe the three major branches of psychology and summarize key trends in psychology.

- The theoretical and cultural diversity of the field of psychology has increased dramatically over recent years.
- There are three key branches of psychology: academic, applied, and clinical/counselling.
- Across the three branches and many specialty areas in psychology, psychologists are united by their shared values. Psychologists generally agree that psychology is *theory-driven*, *empirical*, *multilevel*, and *contextual*.
- Currently, psychology appears to be developing as a science in response to a growing diversity throughout the field, advances in *technology* (such as brain scanning), and the development of *new schools* such as positive

Key Terms

academic psychology 26
applied psychology 27
behaviour 6
behavioural genetics 22
behaviourism 18
client-centred therapy 21
clinical and counselling psychology 28
cognitive neuroscience 30
cognitive psychology 21
collectivist 30
consciousness 12
cross-cultural psychology 21
cultural psychology 21
cultural universality 23
culture 7
evolutionary psychology 22
functionalism 13
Gestalt psychology 14
humanistic psychology 19
individualistic 30
information processing 21
introspection 12
mental processes 6
neuroscience 22
psychoanalytic theory 16
psychology 5
reinforcement 19
response 18
social neuroscience 31
sociobiologists 22
stimuli 18
structuralism 12
unconscious 16
voluntarism 12

Video Lab Activities

These activities use extensive video material to drive student learning. The combination of video footage and digital interactive technology brings the lab exercises to life. In actively engaging with the material you will better process the concepts. The kinds of video material included in the Video Lab Exercises range from laboratory footage about the brain to videos of everyday events to psychology documentary excerpts. These activities are accessible via *WileyPLUS*.

Psychology Around Us

Memory Manufacturing and Eyewitness Testimony

"This Is a Stick-up!"

Memory plays a big role in our lives and in psychology. Generally, most people believe that they can remember things pretty well. Indeed, retrieving past memories, including "buried" memories, is a major part of daily functioning. Similarly, in the criminal justice system, the memories of eyewitnesses are heavily relied upon and lead to many convictions. BUT are our memories as accurate as we like to believe? Should we have great confidence in our recollections of recent everyday events, let alone our adult memories of childhood events, the recollections of eyewitnesses, and the like?

As you are working on this online exercise, consider the following questions...

- What do you think this lab exercise says about the accuracy of our memories?
- What implications might this lab exercise hold for the field of psychology's assumptions, techniques, and interpretations?
- How might this contrived situation differ from a real-life event? Does this contrivance help account for the accuracy or inaccuracy of your memories? Pro or con?

View this in Action WILEY PLUS www.wileyplus.com

Video Lab Exercise

Tying It Together Summary

This section pulls together **fascinating and relevant facts and concepts** from the chapter's integrated sections on development, brain functioning, dysfunctions, and individual differences. Used in combination with the Chapter Summary, Tying It Together will help keep you focused on psychology's "big picture."

Hopefully, by understanding the rationale for the pedagogical elements in this text, you will become more motivated to use them while you study. We hope you enjoy using this book as much as we enjoyed writing it for you!

TYING IT TOGETHER

The study of social psychology is closely connected to the study of all other areas of psychology. Throughout this chapter, we have stressed how social functioning interfaces with psychology's various subfields, including our highlighted sections on brain function, individual differences, abnormal functioning, and development. To remind you of how social psychology is tied to other psychology subfields and issues, we have selected some interesting points from throughout the chapter.

WHAT HAPPENS IN THE BRAIN?

- There has been so much research on the brain's role in social functioning that there is now a branch of neuroscience called *social neuroscience*.
- The prefrontal cortex, much larger in humans than most animals, houses many of the structures important in social functioning.
- High levels of aggression have been linked with a combination of high testosterone activity and low serotonin activity.

HOW WE DIFFER

- Females and males who act outside their society's gender roles may face harsh reactions.
- Studies show that, on average, women in North America are more socially skilled than men.
- People who are trusting and outward-looking and who form secure attachments in their relationships are more likely to perform altruistic behaviours.
- Both men and women are aggressive, but males are, on average, more likely to engage in direct, physical, and verbal aggression. Female aggression is more likely, on average, to be relational, such as snubbing someone.

WHEN THINGS GO WRONG

- Around 7 out of every 100 people in North America experience social anxiety disorder. Another 1 or 2 percent have avoidant personality disorders.
- In contrast, at least 2 percent of the population display dependent personality disorder.
- As many as 1 in every 150 individuals may have autism or an autism-like disorder.

HOW WE DEVELOP

- Part of our socialization as children involves learning our society's norms. Once learned, our norms can influence our behaviour for life.
- Childhood socialization can lead us to develop long-lasting attitudes, including stereotypes and prejudice.
- Although autism is sometimes referred to as a childhood disorder, it is in fact a lifespan disorder for most individuals.

Psychology Around Us

CHAPTER 1

Psychology: Yesterday and Today

CHAPTER OUTLINE

FACEBOOK "FRIENDS"

How many friends do you have on Facebook? Are they your friends or are they "friends?" Are Facebook friends the same as "real" friends? Are there consequences to the way people share information on Facebook that could actually be changing how we think about friendship and other important human relationships?

Psychologists have studied friendship for many years, but additional research may be needed to better understand how Facebook friendships are similar to and different from more traditional friendship. Ninety-eight percent of Canadian 16- to 24-year-olds were on the Internet in 2009, placing them among the most connected in the world. Most (96 percent) use a home computer, and even more have access to computers through their schools or libraries (Statistics Canada, 2010). Moreover, 88 percent of Canadian teens say that they participate in online social networking. This new social phenomenon is providing many opportunities for fascinating psychological research.

For example, do the ways in which we use Facebook challenge our assumptions about what is private and what is public in our friendships and other relationships? It may be hilarious to share pictures from that crazy party you were at last weekend with your friends on your Facebook page, but what happens if a prospective employer sees the pictures and has doubts about your seriousness as a potential employee? Or what if one of your relatives (your mother?) finds out that you were out at a party when you told her that you were tired and were staying home that night? Or what if your boyfriend or girlfriend sees a tagged picture of you on another friend's Facebook site and thinks you were getting a bit too cozy with someone else? How does our use of Facebook influence our "real world" relationships?

A study by Amy Muise, Emily Christofides, and Serge Desmariais (2009) at the University of Guelph suggests that more Facebook use leads to more jealousy in close relationships. They found that people in relationships who reported spending more time looking at each other's Facebook pages also reported experiencing more feelings of jealousy based on what they were seeing on their partner's Facebook page. In essence, this research suggests that if your partner sees things on your Facebook page (or someone else's Facebook page) that are somewhat ambiguous, he or she may react with jealousy.

Social networks like Facebook are also changing other aspects of our relationships. For example, do online contact opportunities help us get started in new relationships? A study by Robert Stephure and Susan Boon at the University of Calgary and Stacey MacKinnon at UPEI carried out in 2009 shows that those who use online contacts to start a relationship process (dating, etc.) are more likely to be older (middle aged and beyond). Younger Canadians also make use of social media within their relationships, but they seem to move more easily back and forth between their real and virtual lives. Think about your own experiences. What are some of the ways in which you use social media in and around your friendships and other relationships?

American anthropologist Ilana Gershon, in her book *The Breakup 2.0: Disconnecting over New Media* (2010), demonstrated that university students see clear roles for social media in their "real world" relationships. For example, students reported that Facebook might best be seen as a place for initiating *casual* relationships, while texting moves relationships up to another level of seriousness. Texting, in turn, may lead to cell phone calls, and ultimately to a face-to-face date. In addition, Gershon's students indicated that they would sometimes fake information on their own Facebook page by exaggerating some claims and minimizing others to make themselves look better. However, despite this they also said they tended to trust what others had posted on their own Facebook pages.

So, social media are providing psychologists with new areas to extend their relationship research, while at the same time showing us ways in which social media may actually be changing some of the basic components of how we manage our relationships. Some observers see the increased use of online social media in our relationships as evidence of the increasing detachment and moral deterioration of society. Others see it as merely a technology-aided extension of tendencies people have always expressed. Are the ways in which we use social media in our relationships within the normal range of human experience, or is it changing us and the nature of our relationships? These are the types of questions that the science of psychology is set up to answer. But they're not the only questions.

Online friendships.
Psychologists study all kinds of mental processes and behaviours, including new ones like using social media.

While psychology can help us try to understand new behaviour, like having hundreds of Facebook "friends," it also helps us to understand far more common things that we all do. Why do people use Facebook or Myspace in the first place, for example? Psychology can provide some insights. As you read this book, you'll see that all the topics we examine contribute not only to our understanding of unusual or problematic behaviours, but also to things that happen all around us, every day.

We'll discuss human development, examining how we mature and what shapes us as we age. Maybe the ease of online communication helps some otherwise shy children gain early confidence and establish more and better social relationships. We'll look at motivation and emotion, getting some ideas about why people do things and how we experience our feelings. What drives people to spend hours every day on the Internet, for example? We'll look at theories of intelligence, including one that suggests that the kind of intelligence needed to hack into websites and steal social insurance numbers is different from the kind of intelligence needed to empathize with people such as parents who have lost a child. Along the way, our goal is to help you gain insight not only into the attention-grabbing and sometimes bizarre things that can go wrong, but also into the often-overlooked but miraculous things that usually go right. We've also included several "Things Students Want to Know" boxes that are based on questions that come up regularly in our own classes. As well, we have included several "Practically Speaking" boxes that we hope will help you to use what you learn to make even more things go right in your own life.

Every journey begins with a first step, and in this chapter, the first step is to learn what psychology is. After that, we'll discuss where psychology originated and how it developed. Finally, we'll learn more about psychology today, including what psychologists do, where they do it, and what's new and changing in what they do. ■

THINGS STUDENTS WANT TO KNOW

Students ask great questions. As you learn about psychology, you will probably start to wonder what psychology has to say about issues that are important to you, or whether something you have heard about human behaviour is actually supported by psychological research. We will include some of those questions in these boxes as we move through the book. Here are a few to start us off:

Do you "analyze" students based on the questions they ask and how they ask them? The simple answer is no. Most people assume that all psychologists are therapists, when in fact clinical psychology is but one specialty in a field that includes cognitive, social, developmental, and sports psychology, among many others. So usually the only analyzing we do involves our efforts to provide an answer to your questions.

Is it true that the nature versus nurture debate was solved years ago? No, in fact it is still very much alive in psychology.

Do we produce any new neurons after childhood? Actually, current research indicates that new neurons continue to be formed throughout life, even in old age.

I have heard that as we age and when we drink our neurons die. Is that true? In normal non-pathological aging, there is little or no loss of neurons, though excessive amounts of alcohol will eventually have negative effects on your brain.

What Is Psychology?

LEARNING OBJECTIVE 1

Define psychology, and describe the goals and levels of analysis psychologists use.

People have probably been curious about the inner workings of the mind since they first began to communicate their ideas to others and to recognize that other people have thoughts and emotions that are separate from their own. Today, the science of studying *mental processes* and *behaviour* is known as **psychology**. The term also refers to the application of

psychology the study of mental processes and behaviours.

PSYCHOLOGY AROUND US More than a Train Ride

Andrea looked around the train. She noticed a child watching his mother expectantly, while the mother stared out the train window, looking tired and distracted. She saw a man bobbing his head ever so slightly to the sound of whatever was playing on his iPod. And she observed a woman who looked sad and downcast.

Andrea also noticed that all of these passengers shared certain behaviours. For example, no one made eye contact. If someone happened to catch Andrea's eye, the passenger would quickly cast his or her eyes down, like pulling a hand from a hot stove. When someone sat down next to an already seated passenger, the passenger always seemed to move his or her body—sometimes a little, sometimes a lot, but always immediately. Was there meaning in these patterns, Andrea wondered, or was each person on the train making an individual choice?

Chances are that you, like Andrea, often find yourself reflecting on why people—including you—think and act as they do. You may wonder, for example, why you can't seem to settle down and start your research paper. You may be curious about why a friend of yours is attracted to someone you find repulsive. You may sense that a family member is depressed and may try to think of ways you can help. All of us, in short, have an interest in how the human mind works.

that knowledge to various realms of human life, including mental dysfunction, education, and business.

mental processes activities of our brain when engaged in thinking, observing the environment, and using language.

behaviour observable activities of an organism, often in response to environmental cues.

Mental processes describe the activity of our brains when we are engaged in thinking, observing the environment, and using language. Mental processes include complex experiences such as joy, love, and even the act of lying. During psychology's early history, the primary method for exploring internal mental processes was to observe outward **behaviour**, our observable actions, and make inferences, or guesses, about what was happening in the mind. Since psychology became an experimental science in the nineteenth century, however, psychological researchers have sought more direct ways to examine mental processes. In fact, the advent of brain imaging and other forms of technology has enabled scientists to uncover fascinating connections between behaviour and mental processes and to move toward a more comprehensive view of how mental processes occur in various individuals and situations.

When psychologists study mental processes and behaviour, they generally have one of four goals in mind:

- ***Description.*** Psychologists seek to *describe* very specifically the things that they observe. As you read this book, you'll see that psychologists have described phenomena ranging from how babies learn to talk to how we fall in love, how we make decisions, and more.
- ***Explanation.*** Telling what, where, when, and how is sometimes not enough. A key goal for many psychologists is to answer the question of "Why?" As we'll see in Chapter 2, psychologists have developed hypotheses and theories to *explain* a huge variety of events, from why we get hungry to why we either like or don't like parties.
- ***Prediction.*** Psychologists also seek to *predict* the circumstances under which a variety of behaviours and mental process are likely to occur. You'll learn later in this book, for example, about research that predicts the conditions under which we are most likely to offer help to a stranger in need.
- ***Control.*** We often encounter situations in which we want to either limit or increase certain behaviours or mental processes—whether our own or those of others. Psychology can give students advice on controlling their own behaviours that ranges from how to limit unhealthy stress or how to increase what you remember from a class.

In order to describe, explain, predict, or control mental processes and behaviours, we need to recognize the many influences on them. All our thoughts and actions, down to the simplest tasks, involve complex activation and coordination of a number of levels—the levels of the *brain*, the *individual*, and the *group*. As you will see throughout this textbook, no psychological process occurs solely at one of these levels. Analyzing how the brain, the individual, and the group influence each other reveals much about how we function—insights that might be overlooked if we were to focus on only one of these levels alone (see **Table 1-1**).

> "Man is the only animal for whom his own existence is a problem which he has to solve."
> —*Erich Fromm, psychologist and philosopher*

At the *level of the brain*, psychologists consider the brain cell activity that occurs during the transmission and storage of information. They also focus on the design of the brain, including the chemicals and tissues that it is composed of and the genes that guide its formation. As we'll see later in this chapter, technological advances in the fields of molecular biology and brain imaging have made it possible to study how brain structure and activity differ from person to person and situation to situation. For example, a psychologist studying the brain can now look at what parts of the brain are activated by the administration of a drug (whether prescribed or illegal), or the brain changes that accompany anxiety and depression (Damsa et al., 2009).

At the *level of the person*, psychologists analyze how the *content* of mental processes—including emotions, thoughts, and ideas—form and influence behaviour. To use a computer analogy, this level relates to the software rather than the mechanical functioning, or hardware, of the brain. The level of the person includes many of the things that people think of first when they discuss psychology—ideas such as consciousness, intelligence, personality, and motivation. Although internal biological structures of the brain allow such person-level processes to occur, we cannot understand the processes unique to each individual, such as personality or motivation, without also studying this content.

> "Everything that irritates us about others can lead us to an understanding of ourselves."
> —*Carl Jung, psychiatrist and philosopher*

Psychologists must also look beyond the individual at the *level of the group*. This perspective acknowledges that humans are shaped by their social environment and that this environment varies over time. A *group* can be made up of friends, family members, or a large population. Often a large group shares a **culture**, a set of common beliefs, practices, values, and history that are transmitted across generations. The groups to which people belong or perceive themselves to belong can influence their thoughts and behaviours in fundamental ways (Prinstein & Dodge, 2008).

culture a set of shared beliefs and practices that are transmitted across generations.

When they conduct research, psychologists may focus on a single level of analysis. It is important to recognize, however, that activity does not take place only at one level or another. During even our most everyday activities, we are operating at all three levels at once. The levels also interact. Brain activity is detectable only with special instruments, like microscopes or neuroimaging machines, but is nevertheless affected by other levels, even by our broad cultural contexts. Similarly, barely noticeable changes in the biology of our brains can cause major changes in our general state of being or how we respond to others.

Let's go back for a moment to our earlier discussion of virtual relationships on Facebook. If psychologists set out to understand behaviour involved in virtual relationships, they could examine it at various levels. Operating at the level of the brain, they could

TABLE 1-1 The Levels of Analysis in Psychology

Level	What Is Analyzed	Example: Using Social Media
The brain	How brain structure and brain cell activity differ from person to person and situation to situation	What are the patterns of brain activation as people interact with "friends" online?
The person	How the content of the individual's mental processes form and influence behaviour	Are there personality factors that influence how much people use different types of social media? Can online social support or crisis resources improve people's decision-making and quality of life?
The group	How behaviour is shaped by the social and cultural environments	What features of social networking sites, such as relative anonymity, ease of access, and lack of face-to-face contact, increase or decrease users' feelings of belonging and connectedness?

Source: Adapted from Gardner, 1993

explore patterns of brain activation in Facebook users to see what brain changes occur when they go online or seek to link to or interact with others. At the level of the person, psychologists could explore questions of intelligence and personality to see whether there are certain characteristics related to the type and extent of Facebook use. Finally, at the level of the group, psychologists might examine how anonymity buffers Facebook groups if they bend general standards of polite behaviour, or how users' participation on Facebook strengthens bonds to other users and decreases (or perhaps increases) their broader sense of connection to the population at large. As you'll see throughout this book, the notion of multiple levels of analysis has played an important role in the development of psychological theories (Fodor, 2007, 2006, 1968).

Having examined what psychologists study and how they do it, let's next consider how psychology got its start, how historical and societal factors have affected the way psychologists study the mind and behaviour, and how psychologists have shifted their energies among the different goals and levels of analysis throughout psychology's history. We will then consider where the field of psychology is today and where it may be going tomorrow.

Before You Go On www.wiley.com/go/comer

What Do You Know?

1. How is behaviour different from mental processes? How are they the same?
2. What are the three levels of analysis in psychology?

What Do You Think?

What would be the focus of each of the four goals of psychology when studying the use of Facebook and other social media? How would the questions and actions of a psychologist who seeks to describe social media use differ from those of someone who wants to limit children's and adolescents' use levels, for example?

SCAN TO GET THE ANSWERS

Psychology's Roots in Philosophy

LEARNING OBJECTIVE 2

Describe the influences of early myths and ancient Greek philosophies on psychology.

Before the development of science as we know it today, humans attempted to explain the natural environment through *myths*, tales that often gave human qualities to natural events. A lack of game to hunt might be the result of a lack of respect having been shown to local animals, for example. In order to control both natural and human behaviour, people of past times also developed a number of magical ceremonies and rituals. Some theorists today believe that these methods for influencing and understanding events were the first forms of religious practice, and that such practices reflect an innate human need to understand and make sense of people and the natural world. In fact, according to such theorists, the science of today is somewhat similar to primitive myths in that it represents our attempts to describe, explain, predict, and control our reality (Waterfield, 2000).

Rituals. Many ceremonies and celebrations developed as a way to understand the natural and human world. Here a group of Coast Salish dancers dance in celebration of a land claim agreement in 2006.

Although they focused on supernatural, life-giving forces, the early rudimentary belief systems contributed to the explosion of intellectual curiosity and information that occurred in the fourth and fifth centuries B.C.E. It was around that time that the great thinkers of ancient Greece began moving beyond supernatural explanations. Instead, they tried to find ways to determine the nature of reality and the limitations of human awareness of reality. To accomplish these difficult goals, they engaged in open, critical discussions of each other's ideas. Such intellectual dialogue created a flow of ideas, and new ideas of any nature were both respected and challenged. In such open forums, students and non-intellectuals could challenge prevailing doctrines and even their instructors.

The history of psychology (and most other sciences) starts with the history of philosophy, as the Greeks' efforts came to be called. *Philosophy* is defined as the study of knowledge and reality. The ancient philosophers' method of introducing problems and then questioning proposed solutions is at the core of today's modern scientific method, which we will discuss in greater detail in Chapter 2. The freedom of thought found in Greek society emphasized that theories, ideas about the way things work, are never final, but rather are always capable of improvement. Today's psychologists still take that view.

Discussing the problem. Ancient Greek society valued the ongoing development of ideas through thought and discussion. Today psychologists and clinicians continue to support the ongoing development of knowledge, though with a more scientific approach.

Hippocrates (ca. 460–377 B.C.E.), a Greek physician, actually produced one of the first psychological theories, suggesting that an individual's physical and psychological health is influenced by *humours*. He believed that these four bodily fluids (blood, phlegm, yellow bile, and black bile) collectively determined a person's character and well-being and predicted the individual's responses to various situations. He also correctly identified the brain as the organ of mental life. Hippocrates tested his theories with direct observation and at least some dissections. Because of such efforts, academic study became rooted firmly in detailed scientific methods of study.

PSYCHOLOGY AROUND US Almost Human

Have you ever turned your iPod or Zune to shuffle and thought, "That's exactly the mix I want to hear right now—my iPod really understands me"? No? Just us? Well, this idea is part of a long standing human characteristic called anthropomorphism. The Greek philosopher Xenophanes coined this term to describe the human tendency to project our mental and emotional characteristics onto non-human objects. Many thinkers before and even during the time of Xenophanes were interested in how myths could explain natural phenomena. But Xenophanes was more interested in why people used myths in the first place—why they saw gods as expressing the qualities of human beings, for example. Nowadays, we see anthropomorphism at work not only when we think about past gods or our MP3 players, but also when we treat action figures, avatars, and dolls as real beings, when we connect with our pets, and when we curse at our laptops.

Most psychologists believe that anthropomorphism helps us gain some sense of control over our environment. Occasionally, this need for control can take on pretty extreme forms. Famous hotel owner Leona Helmsley left $12 million in her will to her dog Trouble. A German woman, Eija-Ritta Berliner-Mauer, "married" the Berlin Wall in 1979 and mourned "his" fall in the 1990s. And an American woman, Erika La Brie, "married" the Eiffel tower in 2008, becoming Erika La Tour Eiffel.

Other Greek philosophers, such as Socrates (ca. 470–399 B.C.E.) and Plato (ca. 427–347 B.C.E.), believed that "truth" lies in the mind and is highly dependent upon our perceived, or subjective, states. Socrates looked for concepts that are the "essence" of human nature and searched for elements that various concepts have in common. He tried, for example, to identify *why* something—anything—is beautiful, and what essential factors an object must possess in order to be beautiful. His student, Plato, believed that certain ideas and concepts are pure and signify an ultimate reality. Plato believed that we could use reasoning to uncover these core ideas deeply imbedded in every human soul. The ideas of these two philosophers represented early studies of mental states and processes.

Hippocrates' psychological theory. This medieval manuscript illustrates the psychological effects of the humours proposed by the Greek physician. The illustration on the left demonstrates the melancholia produced by black bile, while the one on the right depicts the joyous, musical, and passionate personality produced by blood.

Similarly, Aristotle (ca. 384–322 B.C.E.), the most famous thinker of the Greek period, made key contributions to the foundations of psychology. His writings represent some of the first important theories about many of the topics discussed throughout this book, such as sensations, dreams, sleep, and learning (Lorusso, 2010), although, at the same time, he mistakenly believed that the brain was an organ of minor importance. Aristotle was one of the first to promote empirical, or testable, investigations of the natural world. He looked inward at sensory experiences and also scrutinized his environment carefully, searching for the basic purpose of all objects and creatures. In his studies, he formed ideas about how living things are hierarchically categorized, concluding—centuries before Charles Darwin—that humans are closely related to animals.

Psychology's Roots in Physiology and Psychophysics

Besides philosophical musings on the nature of the human experience, others were interested in the physical parts of the human being—in how the senses worked and in how information was managed within the brain. The area of psychophysics, pioneered by Johannes Muller, sought to understand just how humans process sensory information. Psychophysics looked at questions like how much sound or light must be present before we notice it, and how much sound or light must be added to an initial signal before we notice the change. Herman Von Helmholtz, a student of Muller's, was the first to measure the speed of a nerve impulse and determined that nerve impulses occur over time rather than instantaneously. This finding led to the understanding that thought and movement are linked, but are not the same thing. While he was not particularly interested in psychology, Von Helmholtz's work laid a part of the foundation for modern physiological psychology and neuroscience (Benjamin, 2007).

Gustav Fechner published a book summarizing this work in 1860, called *Elements of Psychophysics*. In the book, Fechner (1860/1966) lays out many of the methods and study techniques that would come to be used by those working in the emerging field of psychology, who we will talk about next.

Before You Go On

www.wiley.com/go/comer

What Do You Know?

3. What do the earliest myths have in common with today's scientific studies?
4. Greek philosophers who believed reasoning would uncover ideals or core ideas were focused on which aspect of psychology?
5. How did the Greek philosopher Hippocrates explain mental processes and behaviour? How did his research methods influence today's study of psychology?

SCAN TO GET THE ANSWERS

What Do You Think?

What advantages do you think a scientific approach has for explaining behaviour and mental processes compared to a supernatural approach?

The Early Days of Psychology

LEARNING OBJECTIVE 3

Name important early psychologists and describe their major theories and research methods.

Approximately 2,000 years after they lived, the philosophies of the ancient Greeks re-emerged to influence European thinkers during the Renaissance period of the 1400s through the 1600s. In the centuries both during and after the Renaissance, European society underwent a scientific revolution. A spiritual worldview, which had dominated for several centuries, was increasingly replaced by a view of the world based on mathematics and mechanics. By 1800, both the universe and human beings were believed to be machines subject to fixed natural laws. The roles of magic and mysticism in science essentially disappeared (Leahey, 2000).

Charles Darwin (1809–1882). The theories by the English naturalist about human evolution shifted scientific attention toward human origins and behaviour.

Although mysticism declined as a form of explanation for human nature, there remained great confusion and disagreement regarding human motives and origins. In the latter part of the nineteenth century, Charles Darwin proposed the theory of evolution, making the radical suggestion that all life on Earth was related and that human beings were just one outcome of many variations from a common ancestral point. Darwin also suggested natural selection as the mechanism through which some variations survive over the years while others fall out of existence. Natural selection proposes that although all kinds of variations can be passed down from parent to offspring, some variations are *adaptive*—better suited to an organism's environment. These adaptive variations help the organism to thrive. On the other hand, less-adaptive variations reduce the ability of an organism to survive. Darwin's theories about man's evolution from the ape shifted scientific interest toward an understanding of the origins of humans and our behaviour.

Social and technological developments during the 1800s also helped set the stage further for the science of psychology. Improvements in transportation, communication, and education allowed information to flow more freely to more levels of society than ever before, leading to a rise of popular interest in science.

William Shakespeare (1564–1616), Original Psychologist

"To be, or not to be," from Shakespeare's play *Hamlet*, is the famous line uttered by the play's main character to indicate his psychological struggle with suicide as a way to end his mental suffering. Hamlet's father is murdered by his uncle, who then marries Hamlet's mother. After Hamlet learns of his uncle's brutality from a ghostly vision, he struggles with the ethical and moral contradictions of how to avenge his father's murder. *Hamlet* is arguably Shakespeare's greatest tragedy. Through the story, both the characters of *Hamlet* and the audience explore the themes of suicide, revenge, incest, moral corruption, and mental dysfunction.

One aspect of Shakespeare's genius was his ability to portray the mental lives of his characters in disturbing and realistic detail. Through his keen observations of the human condition, he examined the intricacies of mental disturbances and individuals' struggles with self-knowledge, themes that did not fully emerge in psychological science until the late nineteenth and early twentieth centuries.

Indeed, Shakespeare's unique understanding of mental dysfunction predated Western psychology by almost 300 years. Through the characters in his plays, he presented many of the classic symptoms associated with contemporary psychological maladies, including sociopathy (*Richard III*), alcoholism (*Henry V*), anxiety (*Macbeth*), depression (*King Lear* and *Hamlet*), dementia (*Hamlet*), epilepsy (*Julius Caeser*), obsessive compulsive patterns (*Macbeth*), palsy (*Troilus and Cressida*), eating disturbances (*Henry IV Parts I & II* and *The Merry Wives of Windsor*), and paranoia (*Coriolanus, Othello, Hamlet, Macbeth,* and *Richard III*), to name a few (Cummings, 2003). Altogether, the Bard speculated on the nature and causes of behaviour in at least 20 of his 38 plays and many of his sonnets.

The Founding of Psychology

In this atmosphere, psychology emerged as a distinct scientific field of investigation. As we have observed, prior to the late nineteenth century, psychology was virtually indistinguishable from the study of philosophy. In 1879, however, the physiologist Wilhelm Wundt (1832–1920) opened a laboratory in Leipzig, Germany, dedicated exclusively to the study of psychology. As a natural scientist, Wundt believed that the experimental methods of other sciences were the best way to study the mind and behaviour, so he established a program that trained students to perform such experiments in psychology. James Mark Baldwin believed that Wundt was on the right track and established the first psychology lab in the British Empire in Toronto in 1890 (Pantalony, 1997). Psychology's emphasis on rigorous, scientific experimentation continues to this day, as we'll see in Chapter 2.

consciousness personal awareness of ongoing mental processes, behaviours, and environmental events.

voluntarism belief that much of behaviour is motivated and that attention is focused for an explicit purpose.

Wundt exposed research participants to simple, standardized, repeatable situations and then asked them to make observations, an approach similar to ones used in the study of physiology. One of Wundt's most famous experiments, for example, involved a clock and pendulum. Wundt found that when determining the exact location of the pendulum at a specific time, his observations were always off by 1/10 of a second. He believed that he had found evidence that humans have a limited attention capacity and that it requires 1/10 of a second to shift focus from one object to another (Wundt, 1883).

The father of experimental psychology. Wilhelm Wundt works with colleagues in his laboratory at the University of Leipzig, one of the first laboratories devoted exclusively to psychological research.

Wundt studied the content and processes of **consciousness**, the behaviours and mental processes that we're aware are happening. In his laboratory, he was particularly interested in studying the idea of *will* and how it influences what individuals choose to attend to in their environments. He believed that much of behaviour is motivated and that attention is focused for an explicit purpose. Wundt called this branch of investigation **voluntarism**.

Later, Wundt also went on to form theories about emotion and the importance of historical and social forces in human behaviour. His ideas about cultural psychology are in fact appreciated today for their early recognition that an individual's social context must also be taken into account to fully explain his or her mental processes and behaviour (Benjamin, 2007, 1997).

Beyond his own direct contributions to the new field of psychology, Wundt also served as teacher and mentor to many students who went on to shape the future of psychology. G. Stanley Hall was one of the first Americans to visit Wundt's lab. Hall would go on to found the first American psychology laboratory at Johns Hopkins University in 1883. James McKeen Cattell was the first American to earn his doctorate with Wundt, and would go on to establish psychology labs at the University of Pennsylvania and Columbia University. Directly and indirectly, Wundt did much to shape the emerging science of psychology.

structuralism the belief that the mind is a collection of sensory experiences and that its study should focus on mental processes rather than explanation of the mechanisms underlying those processes.

introspection a method of psychological study endorsed by Wundt and his followers involving careful evaluation of mental processes and how they expand simple thoughts into complex ideas.

Structuralism: Looking for the Components of Consciousness

One of Wundt's students, Edward Titchener (1867–1927), expanded upon his ideas and formed the school of **structuralism** in the United States. Titchener's goal was to uncover the structure, or basic elements, of the conscious mind, much like looking at the parts that make up a car engine or bicycle, or the individual bricks in a complicated Lego sculpture.

To study the conscious mind, the structuralists relied heavily on a method originated by Wundt, called **introspection**, which literally means "looking inward." This method involved the careful observation of the details of mental processes and how they expand simple thoughts into complex ideas. If shown a house made of Lego, for example, an introspecting structuralist would describe the smooth, shiny texture of each brick, the colour of the brick, the tiny gap between it and the adjoining bricks, and so forth.

Introspection of a Harsher Kind

Today, when we talk about being "introspective," an elusive, often mysterious process of turning inward comes to mind. For example, author Shashi Deshpande (1988) says that when we try to introspect, "the real picture, the real you never emerges.... Ten different mirrors show you ten different faces."

So how could such an elusive and mysterious process further the cause of science, as it did for Edward Titchener and other structuralists early in the twentieth century? Well, they were using a different kind of introspection—one that was more concrete and at times harsher. Psychologists Duane Schultz and Sydney Schultz (1987) describe one of the techniques of introspection used in Titchener's lab: "Graduate students [in his lab] were made to swallow a stomach tube in the morning and keep it in place throughout the day. Apparently, many of them vomited at first..., before they gradually got used to it. In between their lectures and other activities they would report to the lab where hot water would be poured down the tube, and the subjects would introspect on the sensations they were experiencing. The process would be repeated with iced water" (1986, p. 91). And you thought your courses were unpleasant!

Toward the end of the 1800s, arguments began to emerge against the use of introspection as an experimental technique. Skeptics pointed out that scientists using introspection often arrived at diverse findings, depending on who was using the technique and what they were trying to find. The school of structuralism also came under attack for its failure to incorporate the study of animals and to examine issues of abnormal behaviour.

The major concern many psychologists had with structuralism, however, was its emphasis on gathering knowledge for its own sake without any further agendas such as a desire to apply our knowledge of the mind in practical ways. Recall the four goals of psychology discussed earlier. The goal of the structuralists was to use introspection to *describe* observable mental processes rather than to *explain* the mechanisms underlying consciousness or to try to *control* such mechanisms. They believed that speculation about unobservable events had no place in the scientific study of psychology. Ultimately, even Titchener himself acknowledged the need to understand the purpose of human thought and behaviour rather than to merely describe it.

Although many of structuralism's principles did not survive, its propositions that psychologists should focus largely on observable events and that scientific study should focus on simple elements as building blocks of complex experience have lived on in certain modern schools of thought.

Functionalism: Toward the Practical Application of Psychology

William James (1842–1910), one of the most important early psychologists (and philosophers), was instrumental in shifting attention away from the structure of mental content to the purposes and functions of our mental processes. James set up the first psychology laboratory in the United States at Harvard University and wrote one of the first important psychology texts, *Principles of Psychology*. James believed that mental events and overt behaviours have functions (Hoffman, 2010). Thus, James's approach was called **functionalism**. To use our earlier analogy, functionalists were less interested in describing the parts of a car engine or bicycle, and more interested in what the engine or bicycle could do under a variety of conditions.

functionalism the belief that mental processes have purpose and focus of study should be on how the mind adapts those purposes to changing environments.

Functionalists viewed the mind as an ever-changing stream of mental events rather than the more or less static set of components that the structuralists were seeking. For this reason, James and his colleagues were also interested in understanding how the mind adapts and functions in a changing environment.

Functionalism did not rely primarily on a single research method, such as introspection. It used a variety of methods, and it also highlighted differences among individuals rather than similarities. And unlike structuralism, functionalism emphasized the need for research to include animals, children, and persons with mental disorders in order to

William James. The influential psychologist and philosopher investigated the purposes and functions of our mental processes. His book, *Principles of Psychology*, took 12 years to write and was 1,200 pages in length.

understand both normal and abnormal psychological functioning (Richardson, 2006; Keller, 1973).

The shift from structuralism to functionalism was apparent in an early experiment on how humans locate sound. Participants in the experiment were asked to point to the location of a sound (Angell, 1903). A structuralist would have asked each participant to provide an introspective report of his or her conscious experience of the sound. Functionalists, however, were more concerned with issues like how accurately participants could point in the direction in which the sound was physically located.

Although it never really became a formal school of psychology, functionalism helped to focus psychologists' attention on what the mind can and does accomplish. Spurred by the emphasis of functionalists on providing applicable and concrete information, psychology began to tackle socially relevant topics. Researchers William Lowe Bryan and Noble Harter (1897), for example, performed a famous investigation regarding how quickly telegraph operators could learn necessary typing skills. Their findings were used to improve training for railroad telegraphers, and the study is now widely regarded as one of the first to have a significant social and commercial impact. Functionalism also marked the beginning of exploration into socially important issues, such as learning and education, and indeed, *educational psychology* remains a significant area of research in the field today.

Gestalt Psychology: More than Putting Together the Building Blocks

Gestalt psychology the field of psychology arguing that we have inborn tendencies to structure what we see in particular ways and to structure our perceptions into broad perceptual units.

While opponents of structuralism in North America were raising concerns that structuralism did not examine the uses of consciousness, other psychologists in Germany were questioning in a more basic way the structuralist idea that consciousness can be reduced to basic mental elements. **Gestalt psychology** is based on the idea that we have inborn tendencies to impose structure on what we see, and these tendencies cause us to perceive things as broad "perceptual units" rather than as individual sensations. Indeed, the word *Gestalt* is of German origin, meaning "whole" or "form." The school subscribed to the idea that "the whole is greater than the sum of its parts."

Facial recognition. Even babies younger than 3 months of age can piece together the component parts of a face and recognize it as a whole object. In particular, they can recognize the familiar face of their mother.

For example, when you watch TV you see complete pictures, when in fact each picture is made up of thousands of small dots, called *pixels*. If you get close enough to the screen, you can see the picture break down, but our brains still favour integrating those dots into a cohesive whole. Similar findings have been gathered regarding our tendency to group eyes, noses, and mouths into recognizable human faces. Children 3 months of age or younger show a preference for human faces, but only when the component parts of faces are arranged correctly in a facial orientation (Turati et al., 2010; Morton & Johnson, 1991).

Gestaltists developed over 100 perceptual principles to describe how the brain and sensory systems perceive environmental stimuli. Some of the Gestalt laws are shown in **Figure 1-1**. Gestaltists also viewed learning as tied to perception—the recognition and identification of stimuli that come through our senses. (We will discuss perception in Chapter 5.) They believed that problem solving occurs when a person develops a sudden and complete insight into a solution—indeed, they believed that problems remain in an unsolved state until such points of insight occur.

PSYCHOLOGY AROUND US "Music Is My religion."

This famous line is attributed to the legendary guitarist and songwriter Jimi Hendrix. Clearly, for Hendrix, music is a phenomenon whose wholeness is greater than the sum of its parts. Music is defined, fairly simply, as an arrangement of sounds that produces a continuous and unified auditory experience. Its elements include melody, tone, harmony, rhythm, pitch, and timbre. But, of course, music is much, much more than the sum of these elements.

Like Hendrix, many musicians and songwriters have described music's broad, special, and almost mystical powers. Billy Joel said, "Music in itself is healing." Ray Charles claimed, "Music [is] a necessity for me—like food or water." Bono asserted that "Music can change the world because it can change people." And Paul Simon proclaimed that "Music is forever."

And let's not forget the impact of music on scholars, scientists, and everyone else. Physicist Albert Einstein once said, "I often think in music. I live my daydreams in music. I see my life in terms of music.... I get most joy in life out of music."

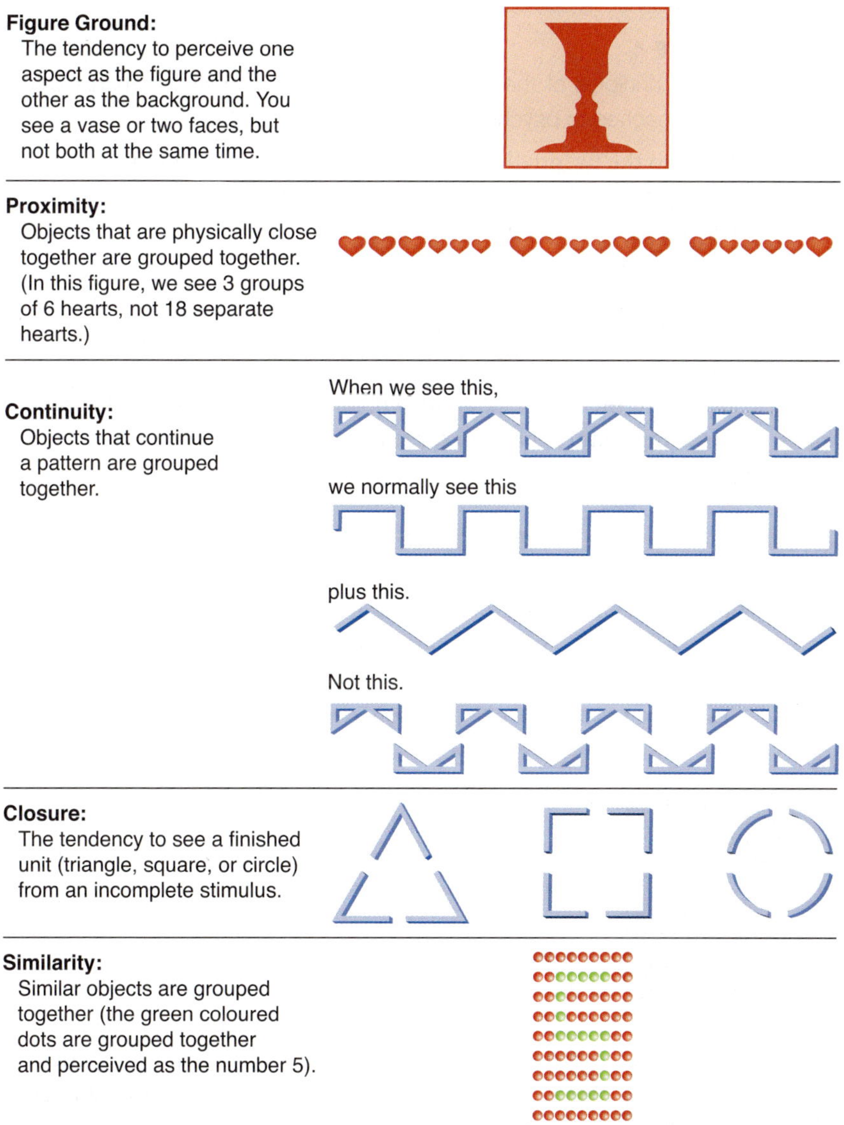

FIGURE 1-1 Gestalt laws. Gestalt psychologists studied how we perceive stimuli as whole forms or figures rather than individual lines and curves.

Together with the functionalists, the Gestalt school helped guide psychology away from the study of parts and toward a broader view of the human mind and functioning. Many of its concepts and the importance of the study of perception are still present in modern psychology.

Before You Go On

www.wiley.com/go/comer

What Do You Know?

6. What is introspection, and which early school of psychologists relied most heavily upon it?
7. What is the main difference in approach between functionalism and structuralism?
8. What did the Gestalt psychologists study?

SCAN TO GET THE ANSWERS

What Do You Think?

Which early school of psychology most closely resembles the way you view the human mind? Why?

Twentieth-Century Approaches

LEARNING OBJECTIVE 4

Summarize the major principles of the psychoanalytical, behaviourist, humanistic, cognitive, and neuroscience approaches to psychology.

From the late 1800s into the twentieth century, psychology continued to grow as a science. In the years leading up to World War I and through World War II, there was tremendous growth in the field of psychology. The number of psychologists rapidly expanded, and popular interest in psychology grew to unprecedented levels.

As more people became interested in the field, more viewpoints on behaviour and mental processes continued to emerge. Several twentieth-century schools of thought had major influence on the field, including the psychodynamic approach, the behaviourist approach, the humanistic approach, the cognitive approach, and the sociobiological approach. Next we'll explore the defining features of all of these approaches.

unconscious hypothesized repository of thoughts, feelings, and sensations outside human awareness, thought in some theories to have a strong bearing on human behaviour.

psychoanalytic theory psychological theory that human mental processes are influenced by the competition between unconscious forces to come into awareness.

Psychoanalysis: Psychology of the Unconscious

Wundt, Titchener, and the structuralists, James and the functionalists, and the Gestaltists held very different views about how the mind is structured and how it should be studied. But they were all alike in one way: they all focused on consciousness, behaviours and mental processes that we are aware are happening. And, as you will see in Chapter 6, their early endeavours into the conscious experience remain an area of considerable study in psychology today. Other theorists, however, eventually came along and focused largely on mental processes of which we are unaware, those that happen in the unconscious mind.

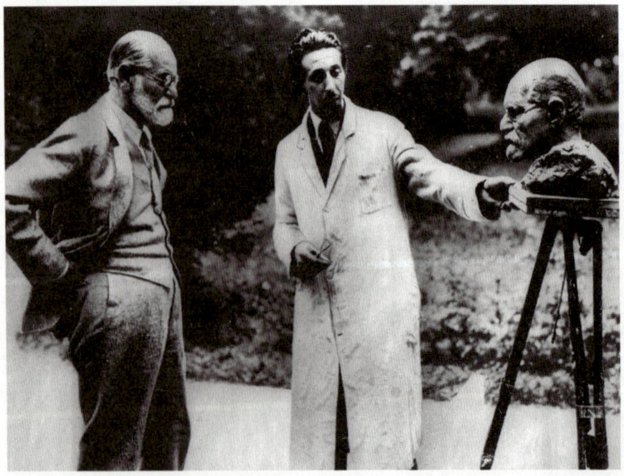

Eye to eye. Sigmund Freud, founder of psychoanalytic theory, examines a sculptured bust of himself at his village home in 1931.

Sigmund Freud (1856–1939), a Viennese neurologist, suggested that many of our thoughts and feelings exist beyond the realm of awareness, in the unconscious. Freud did not conduct experimental studies of laboratory participants. He built his theory instead on information from patients he saw in his medical practice. Based on his detailed observations of these people's cases, Freud came to believe that the mind is a complex interaction of those thoughts and memories that exist at different levels of awareness, some conscious and some unconscious. He saw mental life as a competition among forces that strive to reach the upper levels of awareness. Freud's theory was developed over decades and is called the psychoanalytic theory.

Freud further believed that childhood experiences help set the stage for later psychological functioning by contributing to effective or ineffective interactions among conscious and unconscious forces. According to Freud, certain developmental milestones must be achieved successfully in order for a person to achieve emotional adjustment. He also was interested in how children unconsciously adopt social and moral norms from their parents and, in turn, develop a conscious awareness of what constitutes acceptable and unacceptable expressions of their internal desires. Freud suggested that these conscious standards lead to unavoidable tensions between our unconscious, primal needs and our conscious, social or moral restraints. According to Freud, the back-and-forth tension within and between the conscious and unconscious mind is what shapes personality, helps produce abnormal behaviours in some cases, and governs virtually all behaviour.

> "Freud: If it's not one thing, it's your mother."
> —*Robin Williams, comedian*

In fact, Freud and his followers saw the conscious mind as a thin mask over a deep unconscious mental world, a world that contains impulses and urges that cannot be expressed freely given the constraints of a person's social environment. Let's return again to our consideration of users of social media. Freud would likely view the activities of the heaviest users of social media as driven by feelings of anxiety that arise in face-to-face interactions. He would also be interested whether the ways in which people use social media are related to increases or decreases in levels of anxiety or psychological adjustment.

PSYCHOLOGY AROUND US Unconscious Shoplifting?

A counsellor reports a case involving Ellen, a middle-aged school principal arrested for shoplifting in a supermarket. "[Ellen] claimed to have no memory of having shoplifted.... But the supermarket had video tapes of her having stolen...items on at least three separate occasions....

"[It] was apparent that something deeper was going on with her.... [O]n a rational level, it would have been [silly] for her to have jeopardized her career and reputation by engaging in petty larceny. [Ellen's motivations] would therefore have had to be unconscious....

"Let us consider her background for clues. To begin with, she has been emotionally overwrought for over a year. In addition to the...pressures, concerns and anxieties [of] being a principal at a Christian-based high school, she has been caring for her sister and her best friend, both of whom are dying of cancer. Ellen has had no one to turn to for support in these matters....

"[Perhaps,] exhausted from her role as caretaker...she has been psychologically longing...to be taken care of by someone else. Although it may sound strange, I believe that Ellen had, in essence, projected the role of nurturing mother on to the supermarket....

"[A] mother gives freely, without expecting anything in return. Therefore, it wouldn't make any sense to pay the mother. Rationally, all this is absurd. But we are not rational beings, especially when under some real psychological stress.

"It, therefore, makes sense that Ellen would have no awareness of having shoplifted on those occasions...." (Dilloff, 2010)

As we shall see later in the textbook, psychoanalytic notions typically have not held up well when subjected to rigorous scientific study. For evidence, Freud relied on anecdotes and case histories of remarkable changes in his patients. Researchers have not been able to find much support for his claims when they test them with larger groups of people (Nicholls, 2010; Wallerstein, 2006). The lack of research support, as well as philosophical differences, prevented many of his contemporaries from accepting Freud's theories. William James, the functionalist, for example, rejected the psychoanalytic notion of the unconscious. To him, conscious ideas were not a product of underlying machinery; what was observed in the conscious mind was the complete experience.

Nevertheless, to this day, psychoanalysis remains an influential theory of mental functioning and personality in the field of psychology. Clearly, Freud's theory increased the applications of psychology to many new aspects of everyday life. It stirred interest in motivation, sexuality, child development, dreams, and abnormal behaviour—all topics we will discuss later in this book. Freud's use of discussion as a therapeutic technique helped lead to the creation of psychiatry and clinical psychology as influential therapeutic methods, and these methods continue to thrive.

Although many of Freud's ideas have been challenged, they certainly marked a turning point in the understanding of human nature. Psychoanalytic theory was among the first psychological theories to provide a comprehensive view of human nature, and it helped make psychology relevant to more people than ever before.

Behaviourism: Psychology of Adaptation

behaviourism a branch of psychological thought arguing that psychology should study only directly observable behaviours rather than abstract mental processes.

stimuli elements of the environment that trigger changes in our internal or external states.

response the way we react to stimuli.

In addition to theories about the conscious and the unconscious mind, a third area of psychology, called **behaviourism**, emerged in the early part of the twentieth century. This school of thought was founded on the belief that psychology should study only behaviours that are directly observable rather than abstract mental processes.

Early behaviourists tended to focus on the relationships between **stimuli**—things that trigger changes in our internal or external states—and **responses**—the ways we react to stimuli. As you'll read in Chapter 7 on Learning, these behaviourists developed a number of influential ideas about how responses produce consequences and how those consequences in turn affect an organism's future responses to stimuli.

Behaviourism originated in North America and Russia. In North America, animal research was growing in popularity, while in Russia, Ivan Pavlov's (1849–1936) discovery of a phenomenon that came to be called *conditioning* linked various animal behaviours to events in the animals' environments (Bitterman, 2006; Bauer, 1952). Pavlov, a physiologist, observed that dogs salivated when his lab assistants brought them food. Later, he noticed that the dogs also salivated when the lab assistants appeared—even when they brought no food. The dogs had been *conditioned*—that is, they had learned—to associate one stimulus (food) with another (lab assistants) and to respond in the same way to both. You will read more about Pavlov's work in Chapter 7. Such successful studies of non-human behaviour called into question the methods being used to investigate human behaviour. Even though animals could not introspect, scientists seemed to be learning a great deal by observing their behaviour.

The box! B.F. Skinner developed the so-called "Skinner box" to help him investigate how consequences reinforce behaviour. Here he uses the box to train a rat to press a lever for a food reward.

Edward Thorndike (1874–1949), who was technically a functionalist, helped transition the field of psychology toward behaviourism by proposing that animal findings could help explain human behaviour. As behaviourism proved increasingly fruitful and popular, tensions grew between investigators who used introspection and those who relied on observation.

John Watson (1878–1958) is generally credited with pioneering the school of behaviourism. He agreed with Thorndike that animals could be useful in guiding our understanding of human psychology, and he sharply disagreed with psychoanalysis and with the notion of unobservable mental processes. As we'll discuss in Chapter 7, he was able to extend Pavlov's animal work to young children, and he essentially launched modern psychological theory by demonstrating that children could be conditioned by researchers to fear various objects and situations.

B.F. Skinner (1904–1990), who emerged as the leading behaviourist after World War II, helped expand behaviourism's perspective by acknowledging that internal, mental processes may indeed be at work in some situations, such as when an animal runs to get food. But even here, Skinner argued, empirical—observable—information should be gathered first, and then theories about causation could be formulated from that. That is, even when behaviourists acknowledged that internal mental processes were probably at work, they held that their primary job was to describe empirical phenomena, not to explain them. For example, when observing the behaviour of a monkey who is attempting to obtain food, a behaviourist might describe how the animal distinguishes a particular food from other stimuli, how it approaches the food, and what steps it takes to obtain it—observations meant to reveal how particular responses come to be associated with the food stimulus.

An idea central to behaviourism is that the consequence resulting from a particular behaviour serves to either increase or decrease the likelihood that an individual will perform that same behaviour again in the future. If the consequence of a given behaviour is rewarding, it is regarded as **reinforcing**, and the individual will be more likely to repeat the behaviour down the road. A behaviour is *positively* reinforcing when it brings about a desired outcome (such as food or a prize), and *negatively* reinforcing when it helps an organism avoid undesirable outcomes. For example, procrastination may be negatively reinforcing to the extent that it helps people avoid the pain of actually sitting down to do their homework. Remember, if a behaviour is either positively or negatively reinforcing, we are more likely to do it again later.

reinforcement a learning process in which the consequence resulting from a behaviour will increase or decrease the likelihood that the behaviour will occur again.

The term *negative reinforcement* is sometimes confused with *punishment*, but the latter is really a very different factor in behaviour. Unlike negative reinforcements, *punishments* render behaviours less likely to be repeated. Denying a child his dessert for not eating his broccoli is a punishment, whereas stopping yelling at him about eating his broccoli when he eats it is negatively reinforcing.

The principles of behaviourism became widely used in advertising and in helping businesses address personnel problems. As behaviourism grew in popularity, its principles were applied to numerous industries as well as to courts, schools, and even the military. During this period, researchers also placed great emphasis on the development of controlled scientific methods that might establish psychology once and for all as a true science. Given the appeal of its objective and controlled methods of investigation, behaviourism reached considerable prominence in the academic field, and it continues to have a strong influence on psychology today. Indeed, most of today's experimental studies continue to adhere to rigorous research standards similar to those laid down by behaviourists.

The real teachers. Behaviourists use principles of conditioning, reinforcement, and modelling to teach animals various behaviours in laboratory settings. However, like this young Bonoba chimpanzee, animals (and humans) usually learn behaviours in their natural environments where their parents and other important figures inadvertently apply learning principles.

Behaviourism was not embraced by all, however. Some psychologists criticized John Watson and other prominent behaviourists for popularizing and, in their view, cheapening psychology. In 1929, for example, psychologist Joseph Jastrow wrote that behaviourism's portrayal in popular magazines and newspapers undermined psychology's role as a valid science (Jastrow, 1929). Similarly, other psychologists raised questions about the merits of this area of psychology.

In addition, over time, the behaviourists themselves began to disagree with each other and to divide into competing schools of thought. In the 1960s, for example, the Alberta-born psychologist Albert Bandura (1925–) demonstrated that children often seem to learn not by conditioning or clear rewards and punishments, but by *social observation*, or *modelling*. Bandura and other psychologists also showed that people could learn without any apparent change in their overt behaviour, a phenomenon that suggested individual changes might reflect some kind of internal representations and mental processes. With these and related developments, pure behaviourism (that is, behaviourism with no attention to mental processes, such as beliefs or thoughts) began to lose some of its influence.

Humanistic Psychology: A New Direction

By the 1950s and 1960s, psychoanalytic and behaviourist theories were at opposite ends of the psychology spectrum, one focusing exclusively on mental processes and the other exclusively on behaviour. The 1960s were a particularly troubled time socially and economically in North America. It was also a time when heated debates took place regarding the relationship between people and authority figures and when questions were raised about essential human rights. In this atmosphere, **humanistic psychology** emerged as an alternative theory that sought to give greater prominence to the special and unique features

humanistic psychology theory of psychology that sought to give greater prominence to special and unique features of human functioning.

Humanistic pioneer. Carl Rogers was the founder of client-centred therapy, which promotes an equal relationship between therapists and clients and helps clients to achieve their full potential.

of human functioning than to the mechanistic principles that characterized psychoanalysis and behaviourism.

Founding humanistic theorists Carl Rogers (1902–1987) and Abraham Maslow (1908–1970) rejected the approach of behaviourists. They felt that behaviourists looked at humans just as they looked at animals, largely regarding people as machines that could be predicted and controlled but giving little or no weight to consciousness and other distinctly human characteristics. Humanism, in contrast, focused on the potential of individuals and highlighted each person's subjectivity, consciousness, free will, and other special human qualities. According to humanistic psychologists, all people have the potential for creativity, positive outlook, and the pursuit of higher values. They claimed that if we can fulfill our full potential, we will inevitably lead a positive life of psychological growth.

Maslow, in fact, proposed that each of us has a basic, broad motive to fulfill our special potential as human beings, which he called the drive for *self-actualization.* He suggested that anyone who achieved this broad motive would indeed lead a positive and fulfilling life. Maslow's hierarchy of human needs summarized his theory and is shown in **Figure 1-2**.

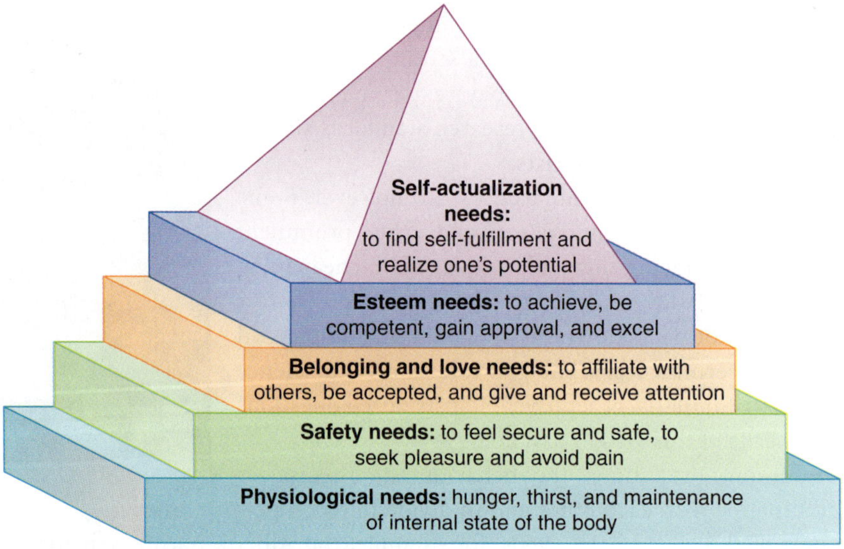

FIGURE 1-2 Maslow's hierarchy of needs. Maslow prioritized our numerous needs and believed that we must satisfy basic physiological and safety needs first. Only then can we progress up the hierarchy and achieve self-actualization.

Top Self-Actualizers

Maslow believed that only around 2 percent of all people achieve full self-actualization. Such people might be rich or poor, famous or unknown, and from just about any walk of life. To help clarify the notion of self-actualization, however, he listed famous individuals whom he believed were self-actualizers. His list included Albert Einstein, Eleanor Roosevelt (American first lady), Frederick Douglass (American social reformer), Abraham Lincoln, Thomas Jefferson, Jane Addams (first American woman to receive the Nobel Peace Prize), William James, Albert Schweitzer (physician and humanitarian), Walt Whitman (American poet and essayist), Mohandus Ghandi (Indian spiritual and political activist and leader), Martin Luther King, Jr., and George Washington. Why might Maslow have considered these people to be fully self-actualized? What well-known people in today's world might be considered fully self-actualized?

Carl Rogers developed a humanistic alternative to the psychoanalytic approach to psychotherapy, which he called client-centred therapy. According to Rogers, therapists should respect their clients as equals. The therapist establishes a trusting and warm relationship with the client by "mirroring" feelings and conveying unconditional support and positive regard for the client. This very human approach to therapy played an important role in the establishment of the fields of clinical and counselling psychology after World War II.

client-centred therapy an approach to therapy founded by Carl Rogers, based on the notion that the client is an equal and positive gains are made by mirroring clients' thoughts and feelings in an atmosphere of unconditional positive regard.

In certain respects, the humanists were not actually seeking to prove behaviourists and psychoanalysts wrong, but rather to complete their ideas. They believed that behaviourism was too limited to the objective realm, and that psychoanalysis failed to acknowledge the free will and autonomy of individuals. The goal of humanists, in contrast, was to jolt people from a psychological rut and to help them realize their innate and grand potential. Although humanism did not ultimately have as great an impact on psychology as the schools of behaviourism and psychoanalysis, it sparked a greater appreciation of human consciousness and helped to establish a balance between the prevailing views of psychology. Perhaps most importantly, the movement triggered an increased interest in mental processes.

Cognitive Psychology: Revitalization of Study of the Mind

In the years after World War II, a new school of psychology emerged whose goal was to measure mental processes effectively. The famous psychologist George A. Miller has recalled that period as a time when "cognition [mental process] was a dirty word because cognitive psychologists were seen as fuzzy, hand-waving, imprecise people who really never did anything that was testable" (Baars, 1986, p. 254). While serving as president of the American Psychological Association in 1960, the Canadian psychologist Donald Hebb (1904–1985) urged the psychological community to apply the rigorous experimental standards seen in behavioural studies—that is, controlled and objective methods—to the study of human thought.

In 1967, Ulric Neisser, a student of Miller's, published the influential text *Cognitive Psychology* in which he described *cognition* as "all the processes by which .... sensory input is transformed, reduced, elaborated, stored, recovered, and used" (Neisser, 1967, pg. 4). Neisser went on to define cognitive psychology as the study of information processing, the means by which information is stored and operates internally.

cognitive psychology the field of psychology studying mental processes as forms of information processing, or the ways in which information is stored and operated in our minds.

information processing the means by which information is stored and operates internally.

Cognitive psychologists compared the human mind to a computer, likening mental processes to the mind's *software* and the human nervous system to the system's *hardware*. Early cognitive psychologists reasoned that if modifying software can control the "behaviour" of computers, identifying and modifying mental processes can control human behaviour. Cognitive psychology soon became the dominant model of the mind.

Under this engineering model, cognitive psychologists focused their attention on the *functioning* of cognitive mechanisms rather than on their content. Cognitive researchers were able to observe the "inputs" and "outputs" of the mental system through carefully controlled experimentation, and then to theorize about the internal mechanisms that must underlie such mental functioning.

Cognitive psychology continues to influence contemporary theory and research into memory, perception, and consciousness, among other areas that we will discuss in this text. The rigorous experimental standards established by cognitive scientists continue to define current methods for studying how information is stored and manipulated by the brain across different situations. Moreover, at the core of a relatively new field called cultural psychology is an interest in how cognitive processing may vary across different populations due to the influences of their distinct socio-cultural environments. While cultural psychology looks to see how human thought and action might vary across cultures, cross-cultural psychology uses cognitive experimental methods to help distinguish mental processes that are *universal* or common to all humans from those that are shaped by particular variables in the social and physical environment (Jensen, 2011).

cultural psychology the study of how cognitive processing varies across different populations.

cross-cultural psychology the study of what is generally or universally true about human beings regardless of culture.

Psychobiology/Neuroscience: Exploring the Origins of the Mind

Interest in the biological basis of psychological phenomena can be traced through the work of Hippocrates, Aristotle, Pavlov, and even Freud. Thus, it is not surprising that eventually a distinct area of psychology, called *psychobiology*, emerged. Psychobiology attempted to explain psychological functions by looking primarily at their biological foundations (Gariepy & Blair, 2008; Hergenhahn, 2005). In particular, psychobiology explored brain structure and brain activity and the ways they might be related to individual behaviours and group dynamics. The term *psychobiology* has fallen into disuse, although this subfield of psychology has continued to grow. It is now referred to as **neuroscience.**

neuroscience the study of psychological functions by looking at biological foundations of those functions. Previously known as psychobiology.

Early psychobiology gained momentum with the advancement of scientific and medical techniques. Karl Lashley (1890–1958), one of the most influential psychobiologists, based his work on the study of animal neurological functioning. He used surgical techniques to destroy certain areas in the brains of animals and then observed the effects of such destruction on memory, learning, and other cognitive processes. Lashley found that the tissues within certain areas of the brain were often linked to particular cognitive functions. His ultimate goal was to pinpoint all areas of the brain responsible for memory, learning, and other higher functions. He was never able to fully accomplish this goal, and it continues to be a major interest in contemporary research.

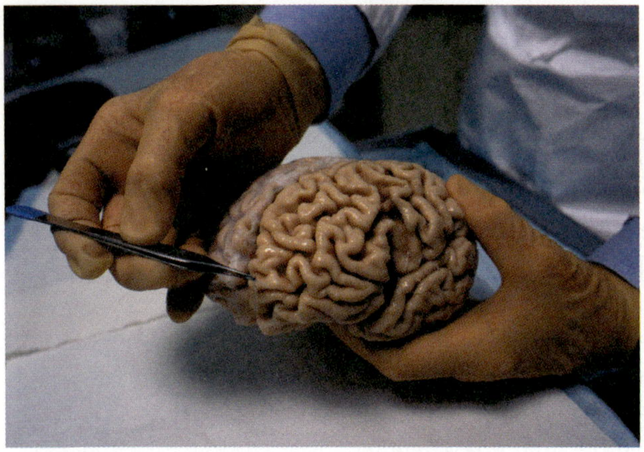

Studying the human brain. Neuroscientists examine brain structure and brain activity to determine how they are related to behaviour. Here a researcher dissects the brain of a former patient with dementia as part of a study to learn more about memory and memory disorders.

Roger Sperry (1913–1994), a researcher who was influenced greatly by Lashley, pioneered *split-brain* research on animals. Sperry and his colleagues severed the connections responsible for relaying information between the left and right hemispheres, or halves, of the brain. They found that even after the brain is split surgically, the two hemispheres of animals can often function and learn independently. Later investigators found similar results when they studied human beings who had undergone a similar split-brain surgery to stop severe seizures from spreading from one side of the brain to the other (Gazzaniga, 2010, 2005). Split-brain research on both animals and humans made it possible to study the separate functioning of the brain's hemispheres, which, as we'll see in Chapter 4, remains a popular topic in contemporary psychology.

A number of psychological subfields have been influenced by the field of neuroscience, as well as by Darwin's early work on evolution. **Behavioural genetics**, for example, studies the influence of genes on cognition and behaviour. This is not a completely new field. Early in the twentieth century, and even during the rise of behaviourism, a number of animal researchers used evolutionary principles to help explain human behaviour.

behavioural genetics a subfield of psychology looking at the influence of genes on human behaviour.

sociobiologists theorists who believe humans have a genetically innate concept of how social behaviour should be organized.

evolutionary psychology a field of study believing that the body and brain are products of evolution and that genetic inheritance plays an important role in shaping the complete range of thoughts and behaviours.

Similarly, **sociobiologists**, as they were initially called, theorized that humans have an innate concept of how social behaviour should be organized. In 1975, Harvard biologist Edward O. Wilson, a specialist on ants, brought great attention to this view with his book *Sociobiology: The New Synthesis*. He and other sociobiologists suggested that humans are genetically more predisposed than other organisms to learn language, create culture, protect territory, and acquire specific societal rules and regulations. Sociobiologists did not claim that genetic influences are necessarily more important than environmental factors, such as parenting or the mass media. Rather, they proposed that our social behaviour is the result of biological *and* cultural influences. One sociobiologist, David Barash (1979, p. 45), commented, "For too long social science and biological science have pursued 'nothing but' approaches. Sociobiology may just help redress that imbalance."

The subfield of sociobiology is now part of a still broader subfield called **evolutionary psychology**. Evolutionary psychologists continue to hold that the body and brain are

TABLE 1-2 The Major Perspectives in Psychology Today

Perspectives	Major emphases
Psychoanalytic	Interactions between the conscious and unconscious mind govern virtually all behaviour; childhood experiences set the stage for later psychological functioning.
Behaviourist	Only observable behaviour can be studied scientifically. Perspective focuses on stimulus-response relationships and the consequences for behaviour.
Humanist	People can be helped to realize their full and grand potential, which will inevitably lead to their positive psychological growth.
Cognitive	Mental processes are studied using an information processing model (inputs/outputs).
Neuroscience/Psychobiological	Psychobiological functions are explained primarily in terms of their biological foundations.
Evolutionary	Behaviour and mental processes are explained in terms of evolution, inheritance, and adaptation.

largely products of evolution and that inheritance plays an important role in shaping thought and behaviour (see **Table 1-2**). The laws of evolutionary psychology are thought to apply to all organisms and to all kinds of mental functions and behaviours (not only social ones), just as the laws of physics apply to all bodies in space.

Sociobiology. Psychologists are interested in what stays the same and what varies across cultures within human families.

Evolutionary psychology has become one of the most popular topics in contemporary psychology (Confer et al., 2010; Buss, 2009, 2005, 1999). Evolutionary psychologists suggest that some behaviours and mental processes are more effective than others at solving problems of living—namely, those that help people to survive and reproduce. These successful strategies are passed on to people's children, as well as taught to others, and they eventually become important parts of each individual's inborn makeup. We'll look at evolutionary psychology in detail in Chapter 4.

One goal of evolutionary psychologists is to identify **cultural universality**, human behaviours and practices that occur across all cultures. Just as behaviourists study animal behaviour to identify simple actions that form the basis of more complex human behaviours, evolutionary psychologists believe that uncovering universal human behaviours will help identify inborn functions common to all humans. Theoretically, such

cultural universality behaviours and practices that occur across all cultures.

Did Our Ancestors Prefer Blondes?

One of the criticisms of evolutionary psychology is that it is fairly easy—and often inaccurate—to produce theories about how certain current behaviours, traits, or emotions may have evolved from earlier times. Evolutionary psychologist Matthew Rossano, for example, writes, "It is quite tempting to observe a current behaviour and construct an evolutionary story [a 'just so' story] about how that behaviour evolved for some adaptive purpose.

"One of the best examples of this comes from the neuroscientist V. S. Ramachandran, who became so frustrated with what he considered to be the excess of unsubstantiated 'just so' stories in evolutionary psychology that he made one up himself and called it 'Why do gentlemen prefer blondes?' He proceeded to weave an imaginative tale about how, in our evolutionary history, fair-skinned females would have been preferable as mates because indicators of health, fertility, and sexual fidelity would have been more clearly visible than on their darker complexioned counterparts. He had no evidence, of course—just a plausible story. Much to his amazement, the article was accepted for publication! Critics of evolutionary psychology contend [that 'just so'] stories have proliferated in the field, straining the credibility of the discipline.

"On the other hand, this criticism is often used unfairly to smear the entire field of evolutionary psychology as nothing but 'just so' stories" (Rossano, 2002, pp. 44–45).

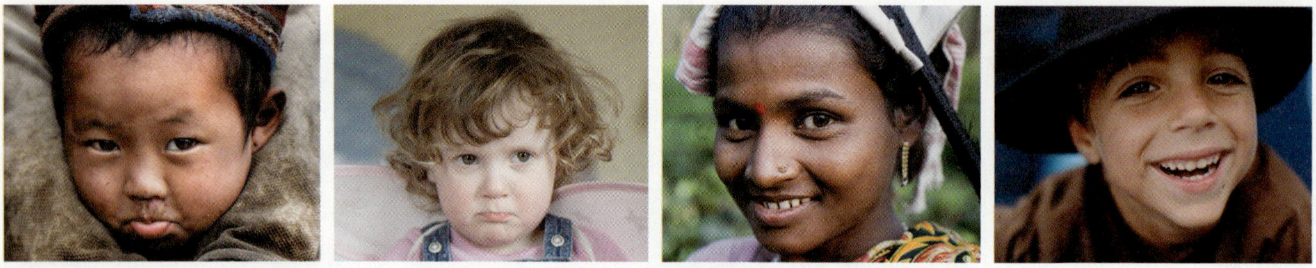

That certain look. Facial expressions of sadness (left two photos) and happiness (right two photos) are universal across all cultures. Are these commonalities related to our evolutionary history?

knowledge will answer important questions about the relative impact of biological factors and life experiences on our development.

Throughout this book, we'll be observing a number of common practices displayed by people across cultures, such as using specific facial expressions to express emotions, displaying a fear of snakes, telling stories, and giving gifts (Chomsky, 2005; Brown, 1991). But are such commonalities the direct result of evolutionary forces? Have these behaviours and reactions been passed on from generation to generation largely because they remain highly adaptive? In fact, two evolutionary biologists, Stephen Jay Gould and Richard Lewontin (1979), did not think so. They argued that some of the traits and behaviours seen across cultures are no longer evolutionarily advantageous and instead may be *by-products* of behaviours that served adaptive functions a long time ago. Initially, for example, the human smile may have represented a submissive baring of teeth often seen in animals, designed to ward off attacks by enemies. Over many, many years, however, it has come to be used in human social environments to signal the presence of a friend, or to signal humour.

Although it can be difficult and at times misleading to identify evolutionary roots for today's behaviours, the study of genetics and inheritance continues to play an important role in psychology. Indeed, many investigations conducted over the past two decades have established the importance of genetic influences on human development. We'll see later in this book, for example, that studies of twins who were separated at birth and reared in different families often find that the twins continue to share many characteristics (Segal, 2010). The verdict on evolutionary psychology may still be out, but few of today's psychologists question the contribution of genetic factors to mental functioning and behaviour.

Before You Go On

www.wiley.com/go/comer

What Do You Know?

9. Which theorist is most closely associated with psychoanalytic theory—the theory that unconscious conflicts, rooted in childhood, affect much of our behaviour?
10. According to behaviourist theorists, what are the various reinforcement principles, and what impact does each have on behaviour?
11. What did humanist theorist Abraham Maslow suggest is the ultimate goal of human beings?
12. What are cognitions?
13. What is the main idea of evolutionary psychology?

SCAN TO GET THE ANSWERS

What Do You Think?

Which of the theories presented here depend largely on biological principles? Which of the theories seem to be based more on environmental explanations? And which appear to rely on an interaction of factors? Do you find one theory to be more plausible than the others? Why?

Psychology Today

LEARNING OBJECTIVE 5

Describe the three major branches of psychology and summarize key trends in psychology.

In the contemporary field of psychology, we can recognize the influence of various schools of thought that date back to the days of Greek philosophers. The psychological orientations we have discussed in this chapter, such as functionalism, behaviourism, and cognitive science, have not disappeared, but rather continue to develop and interact with one another. Indeed, today there is broad recognition that psychology must be as diverse as the humans whose behaviour it attempts to explain (Sternberg & Grigorenko, 2001).

More detailed information is available now than ever before about how the brain functions, and this information has in fact served to emphasize the importance of analyzing human thought and behaviour at a variety of levels. Brain imaging studies have, for example, been used to test behavioural principles, identifying which areas of the brain are activated when a behaviour is performed or when an outcome is better (or worse) than expected (Aguirre, 2010). Similarly, cognitive psychologists and biologists have examined psychoanalytic notions, such as the proposal that our unconscious minds hold memories that might be too anxiety-provoking for our conscious minds. Recent investigations have, for example, linked real memories to one pattern of brain activity and false memories to another (Garoff-Eaton, Slotnick, & Schacter, 2006).

As the diversity of the field has increased, so too has the need for there to be communication among its various voices. Indeed, Canada's nearly 19,000 psychologists (Statistics Canada, 2006) are represented in various professional organizations, including the Canadian Psychological Association (4,500 members), the Canadian Society for Brain, Behaviour and Cognitive Science (500 members), and the American Society for Neuroscience (38,000 members), which collectively address the interests and needs of more than 50 different specialities in psychology. **Figure 1-3** shows the variety of fields of study in psychology today.

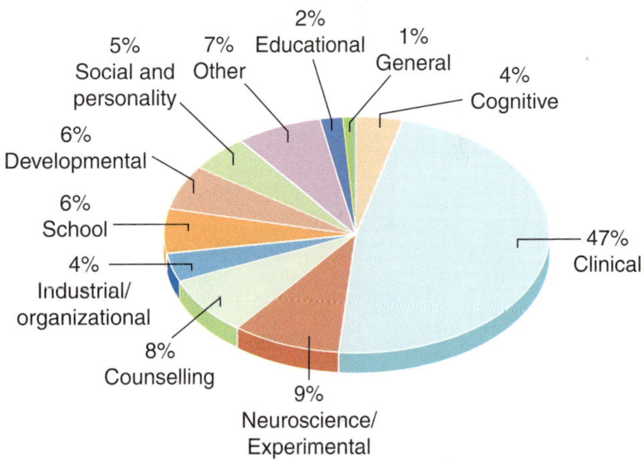

FIGURE 1-3 **Percentage of recent doctorates awarded in each subfield of psychology.** Psychologists today have a wide variety of areas to pursue.

PSYCHOLOGY AROUND US Choosing Wisely

As she comes closer to graduation, Jasmine, a psychology major, is beginning to worry more and more about what she is going to do after university. She is certain that she wants to go to graduate school in psychology, but she isn't sure she is particularly interested in clinical work. For one thing, she tends to get irritated when friends assume that just because she's a psychology major, she's interested in their problems or has good advice for them.

At first, Jasmine was interested in understanding how issues like race and class influence clinical disorder rates in urban communities. But, as she moved through her major, she became less interested in these broader social influences and more interested in studying the impact of biological and developmental factors on individual stress levels and on the emergence of psychological problems, particularly in poor communities. Recently, she has been gathering information about Ph.D. programs in clinical psychology. Still, she isn't sure that clinical psychology is the right fit for her. And she's not sure how to go about getting all the answers she's looking for.

Because psychology today is so wide-ranging, Jasmine's decision about her future in this field is more complicated and confusing than it would have been just 25 years ago. At the same time, as she considers this important decision, she'll find that she has more options for an exciting and fulfilling career in psychology than she ever might have imagined.

Branches of Psychology

There are currently three key branches of psychology: *academic psychology*, *clinical and counselling psychology* (including clinical, counselling, and clinical neuropsychology), and *applied psychology* (the rest, including school, rehabilitation, industrial/organizational, health, and forensic psychology). **Figure 1-4** shows these three branches of psychology as well as the subfields within them. Psychologists from all three branches share an interest in mental processes and behaviour. They differ in the amount of emphasis they each place on the psychology of individuals, the discovery of general principles of psychology, and the application of psychological knowledge to groups of people. **Figure 1-5** summarizes the range of settings in which academic, applied, and clinical and counselling psychologists work.

academic psychology a branch of psychology focusing on research and instruction in the various areas or fields of study in psychology.

Academic Psychology When Wilhelm Wundt founded psychology as a discipline distinct from philosophy in 1879, his goal was to examine human nature. He did not focus on questions of how psychology could be applied or used outside the laboratory. Today, the branch of psychology known as **academic psychology** carries on Wundt's mission. Academic psychology involves research and instruction on a wide variety of psychological topics.

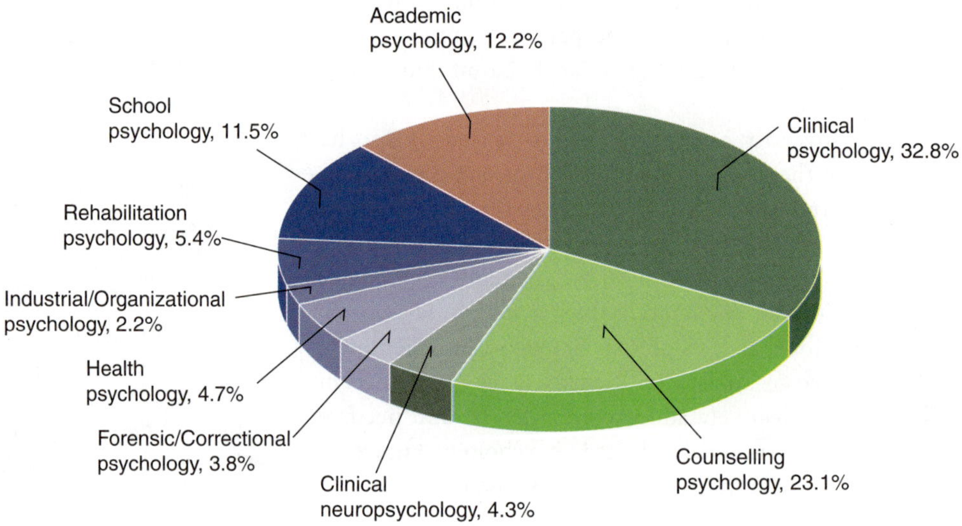

FIGURE 1-4 Which branches of psychology do psychologists work in? Percentage of psychologists in each branch of psychology (based on data from the College of Ontario Psychologists, 2010).

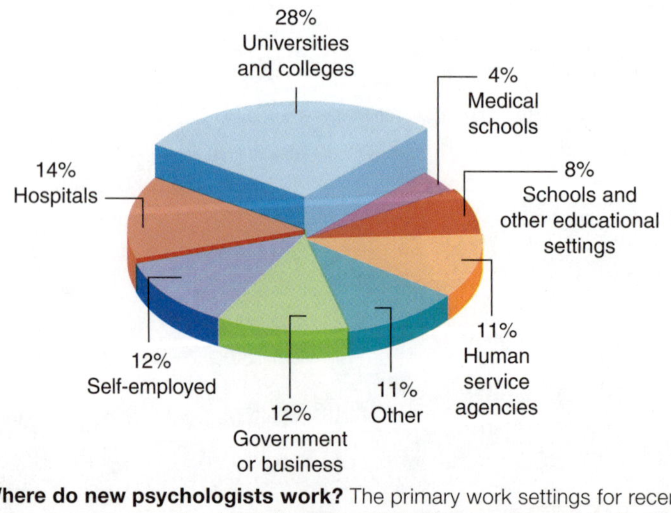

FIGURE 1-5 Where do new psychologists work? The primary work settings for recent Ph.D. graduates in psychology are post-secondary institutions, hospitals, the government, businesses, and human service agencies.

Academic psychologists typically work at colleges and universities, where they often divide their time between teaching and conducting research in their particular fields of interest. A *developmental psychologist*, for example, may teach courses on child development while also researching how children think and behave. The efforts of academic researchers have resulted in a large body of psychological knowledge, and, for the most part, the chapters throughout this textbook reflect their considerable work and findings.

PRACTICALLY SPEAKING What Can You Do with a Psychology Degree?

Psychology's wide influence. Psychologist Daniel Kahneman (left) is awarded the 2002 Nobel Prize in Economics. He did much of the work that earned the prize while at the University of British Columbia.

Psychology is the study of behaviour and mental life. Students who major in psychology gain a broad understanding of what makes people "tick" from a wide range of perspectives, including developmental, social, clinical, and biological. They also acquire a body of knowledge and set of skills that help qualify them for a broad range of career choices.

If people want to become psychologists, they will find that an undergraduate degree in psychology prepares them to pursue graduate degrees in any number of psychology subfields, including clinical, health, cognitive, social, neuroscience, organizational, educational, and sports psychology. Alternatively, being an undergraduate major in psychology can help open the door to graduate study in many other fields, such as law, business management, economics, and medicine.

Even if graduate study is not for you, an undergraduate degree in psychology can lead to interesting jobs and careers. Psychology majors are typically viewed by prospective employers as well-qualified to work in fields that require people skills, as well as having good analytical, research, and writing abilities. "But," you might say, "just about every job deals with people." Yes, that's the point.

An undergraduate degree in psychology particularly qualifies individuals for entry-level jobs in people-oriented careers such as communications, marketing, human resources, sales, and business. Beyond people skills, the analytic, research, and writing skills of psychology majors enhance their eligibility for human-service, legal, and law-enforcement jobs, including positions as paralegals and corrections officers. Furthermore, the same skills may make individuals good candidates for careers in general business, marketing research, management consulting, computer game design, and investment banking.

In short, psychology is related to so much in our world that a degree in this discipline can lead to work and careers in more areas and fields than you might imagine. Keep in mind, for example, that psychologists Daniel Kahneman (2002) and Herbert Simon (1978) are Nobel Laureates in *economics*, while the neuroscientists Eric Kandel (2000), Rita Levi-Montalcini (1986), and Roger Sperry (1981) won their Nobel Prizes in *medicine* and *physiology*.

Applied Psychology Although Wilhelm Wundt intended for psychology to pursue "pure" scientific knowledge, many of his students went on to apply their knowledge to a variety of disciplines (Hergenhahn, 2005). Functionalism, founded by William James, marked the first formal branch of applied psychology. As you'll recall, this orientation was influenced by evolutionary theory and focused on applying psychological principles to social issues. Today, the branch of psychology called **applied psychology** involves the application of psychological principles to help solve practical problems in education, marketing, and other fields (Davey, 2011). Lawyers may consult with psychologists to help determine who to select for a jury. Advertisers may consult with psychologists to conduct research to determine how best to market products to teenagers. Throughout this book, we will examine a wide range of research developments, both those with immediate

applied psychology the branch of psychology applying psychological principles to practical problems in other fields, such as education, marketing, or industry.

practical applications and those that simply further our insights about the human mind and behaviour.

Applied psychologists have earned either a master's degree, which requires two years of graduate study, or a Ph.D. (doctorate of philosophy). Many applied psychologists specialize in a broad traditional academic field, such as developmental or social psychology, and use their expertise further to help guide decisions and work outside of academic settings. There are also a number of specialized programs of study within applied psychology. *Sports psychologists*, for example, may provide guidance to athletes or teams, helping them overcome feelings of anxiety or frustration or teaching them to focus their energy more effectively.

clinical and counselling psychology the study of abnormal psychological behaviour and interventions designed to change that behaviour.

Clinical and Counselling Psychology **Clinical and counselling psychology** help individuals to cope more effectively or to overcome abnormal functioning. Actually, there are several different types of mental-health practitioners.

- *Clinical psychologists* generally provide *psychotherapy*, which involves helping people to modify thoughts, feelings, and behaviours that are causing them distress or inhibiting their functioning. They also may administer and interpret psychological tests to provide further information relevant to treatment. Many clinical psychologists earn a Ph.D. degree awarded by a university graduate program, which typically requires training in therapeutic practices and in the conduct and interpretation of research. Some clinical psychologists earn a Psy.D. (doctorate of psychology) degree. This degree is awarded by graduate programs that place less emphasis on research and greater emphasis on psychotherapy and psychological testing. As well, clinical psychologists who wish to practise psychotherapy in Canada must be registered with their provincial College of Psychologists, which establishes and oversees practice guidelines and the ethics of clinical practice.

The couch! Sigmund Freud's signature therapy procedure was to have patients lie on a couch and say whatever came to mind, while he took notes behind them. This wax recreation of the neurologist and his office is on display at a museum in Berlin, Germany.

- *Counselling psychologists* and *psychiatric social workers* also provide psychotherapy for people with psychological problems. These professionals may also help individuals and families deal with issues tied to relationships, careers, child-rearing, and other important areas of functioning. In addition, some social workers provide aid to families through social service systems that are available in a community. Counselling psychologists earn a Ph.D. or Psy.D. in their field, while social workers earn either an M.S.W. (masters of social work) or D.S.W. (doctorate of social work) degree from a school of social work.

- *Psychiatrists*, who may also provide guidance and therapy to individuals, are professionals who attend medical school and earn an M.D. (doctorate of medicine). Psychiatrists generally have less training in psychological research and testing than clinical psychologists, but they have medical knowledge and the ability to prescribe medications for abnormal emotional states or behaviour problems, a professional privilege that is not granted to clinical or counselling psychologists or social workers in Canada.

Canadian psychologists are not able to prescribe drugs for their clients. In the United States, only New Mexico and Louisiana currently grant prescription privileges to psychologists who receive special pharmacological training. The U.S. territory of Guam also grants such privileges to psychologists.

Shared Values

Although the three branches of psychology—academic, applied, and clinical and counselling—have different goals and ways of meeting those goals, they do share important values that guide their work. Many of those values will shape our discussions throughout this textbook, so let's take a look at them here.

- *Psychology is theory-driven.* If you're going to explain human behaviour, you have to have a theory. We will describe the elements of a good theory in Chapter 2. Psychologists have developed theories, or potential answers, for many key questions: Do mental processes exist? What are the relative roles of biological inheritance and environmental influence in shaping human psychology? How do we explain deviant behaviour, such as bullying? Each school of psychology provides ideas to help answer such questions. And every branch of psychology uses its potential answers to guide research or improve psychological interventions.
- *Psychology is empirical.* From its very start, what separated psychology from other human disciplines, such as philosophy, was its emphasis on controlled observations and experimentation. Psychology finds more use and value in ideas that receive strong empirical, or research, support, than in ideas, even seemingly compelling ones, that cannot be supported with evidence from systematic testing.
- *Psychology is multi-level.* As we discussed at the beginning of this chapter, to understand the complete picture of human mental processes and behaviour, psychologists must account for what is happening at the levels of the brain, the person, and the group. Although certain theories place more emphasis on one level than another, all of the levels are indeed operating to influence whatever mental process or behaviour we may be observing. Thus, in chapters throughout this textbook, we will be presenting evidence about what happens at each of these three levels.
- *Psychology is contextual.* As recently as 25 years ago, the thought of Internet social networks—actually, even the thought of the Internet—was unimaginable to most people. As the history of psychology shows, however, technological advances have had a strong influence on the development, rise, and fall of particular theories. Without the computer, for example, the field of cognitive psychology would have been described very differently. In fact, technological and other societal changes force us to look at human behaviour from new perspectives that broaden our awareness. All of this means that some of the theories you're studying today may eventually go the way of structuralism—influential but dramatically changed in nature. This is the way that science progresses.

Current Trends in Psychology

The values of psychology—theory-driven, empirical, multi-level, and contextual—work together to drive constant progress and change in the field. Today, those values, as well as larger social developments, are shaping several trends in psychology. In particular, the field is growing more diverse, continuing to profit from technological advances, and continuing to give birth to new schools of thought.

Growing Diversity Early in the history of psychology, few women or members of racial minority groups were able to obtain the advanced education and professional status necessary to contribute to the field. As psychology itself has grown more diverse, however, so have psychologists. Psychology now has more women earning graduate degrees than does any other science. Indeed, 70.5 percent of psychologists in Canada are women (Statistics Canada, 2006). In addition, 16 percent of newly earned Ph.D.s are awarded to minority group members, compared to 7 percent 30 years ago (APA, 2009).

Mary Wright became the first female president of the Canadian Psychological Association in 1968, 30 years after that organization was formed.

Growing diversity among psychologists has overlapped with an increased interest in the diversity of the people they study, treat, and influence. *Cultural psychology* has, for example, become an important area of investigation. As we observed earlier, this field of study seeks to uncover mental processes that exist across all cultures, as well as important cultural differences.

Growth of women Ph.D.s in psychology. Over a 30-year period, the increase in the percentage of women earning Ph.D.s has been dramatic, especially in the clinical, developmental, and counselling fields (Gathercoal et al., 2010; Cynkar, 2007).

collectivist a culture whose members focus more on the needs of the group and less on individual desires.

individualistic a culture that places the wants or desires of the person over the needs of the group.

Cultural psychologists often focus on differences between *collectivist* cultures and *individualistic* cultures. Members of **collectivist** cultures emphasize the needs of the group and subsume individual desires to those of the family or peer group. In contrast, **individualistic** cultures stress the needs of persons over those of the group. One study of differences between these two types of cultures examined positive emotions, such as happiness. Individuals from Eastern cultures, which tend to be more collectivist, and Western cultures, which tend to be more individualistic, appear to hold different beliefs about the sources of happiness. When asked to talk about events that make them feel happy, Chinese research participants focused on interpersonal interactions and evaluations from others, while Western participants pointed to personal achievement and self-evaluation (Lu & Shih, 1997).

Research has also indicated that even within a broad culture, subcultures may differ with regard to happiness. Studies have shown, for example, that positive emotions, such as strong self-acceptance are, on average, a bit lower among individuals from southern parts of the United States than among those from the West or Midwest. Some researchers have hypothesized that these lower levels of well-being and self-acceptance may reflect a subculture that is relatively more concerned with showing hospitality and respecting tradition than with fostering positive self-concepts and promoting personal growth (Markus et al., 2004). Given psychology's growing interest in these and related differences among people and between groups, we have included throughout the textbook sections called "How We Differ." These sections examine how memory, emotions, social values, and the like differ from situation to situation, person to person, and group to group.

Advances in Technology As we observed earlier, technological shifts also contribute to shifts in psychological theory. The development of computers in the 1950s and 1960s contributed to the cognitive psychology revolution. Technology has continued to change the face of science and psychology in more recent years. Innovations such as brain imaging and effective pharmacological, or drug, treatments for mental disorders have revealed a great deal about human mental processes and behaviour. As you'll see in Chapter 4, for example, the development of brain-imaging technology has made it possible for researchers to directly observe activity in the brain.

cognitive neuroscience the study of mental processes and how they relate to the biological functions of the brain.

In fact, in recent years a new area of psychological study and theory has emerged: **cognitive neuroscience** focuses not only on mental processes, but also on how mental processes interact with the biological functions of the brain. That is, what happens in the brain when we are remembering something, making a decision, or paying attention to

Notable Women in Psychology

The early history of psychology consists mainly of the work of men, as was typical of most fields. Still, from early on women were very much involved in shaping psychology, and their contributions should also be noted. Today the majority of our undergraduate and graduate students in psychology are women. Here are but a few of the field's female pioneers (Keates and Stam, 2009).

- The work of Mary Whilton Calkins (1863–1930) was noteworthy for her emphasis on the self, consciousness, emotions, and dreams, which stood in stark contrast to John Watson's behaviourist movement at the time. Calkins was the first woman president of the American Psychological Association (APA).
- Leta Hollingsworth (1886–1939) was best known for her studies of "mentally deficient" and "mentally gifted" individuals, and for her views on gender differences in mental functioning. She was one of the first theorists of her time to challenge the notion that women were biologically inferior, arguing instead that women were victims of a male-dominated social order.
- Magda Arnold (1903–2002) is generally thought of as the "mother of modern emotion theory" (Keates & Stam, 2009). She received her Ph.D. at the University of Toronto in 1942. Her book *Emotion and Personality* (1960) consolidated her position as a leader in emotion research.
- Mary Ainsworth (1913–1999) was also a University of Toronto graduate, obtaining her Ph.D. in 1939. She is internationally known for her work on mother–infant attachment and for the development of the Strange Situation method of assessing attachment in toddlers.
- Mary Wright (1915–) is best known for her work on the history of Canadian psychology. She also wrote of the history of the development of the Canadian Psychological Association. She was elected the first woman president of the CPA in 1968.
- Brenda Milner (1918–) has been a pioneer in the study of memory and other cognitive functions in humans. She was the first to investigate how damage to the brain's hippocampus affects memory through her study of a famous amnesia patient known as H.M. in the research literature.

something? One goal of cognitive neuroscientists is to link specific mental processes to particular brain activities. Similarly, a field called **social neuroscience** has emerged, which seeks to link social functioning to particular brain activities. Recent studies have, for example, found that there is a network of nerve cells in the brain that is activated when we show empathy, our ability to understand the intentions of others.

social neuroscience the study of social functioning and how it is tied to brain activity.

Cognitive and social neuroscience are currently among psychology's more active areas of theory and research. Given the enormous growth and impact of such areas, we have also included throughout the book a section called "What Happens in the Brain?" In these sections, you'll learn about the neuroscience of memory, emotions, social behaviour, and the like. You'll discover, for example, what happens in the brain when you are learning new material before an important test, and then again when you get together with friends to celebrate the completion of that test.

The development of imaging tools, computer technology, and a number of biological techniques has also helped enhance our understanding and treatment of mental dysfunction in recent years. These tools have enabled researchers to look directly at the brains of disturbed persons while they are feeling sad or anxious, hearing voices, or recalling repressed memories. Such studies have helped reveal that depression, for example, is related not only to traumatic childhood experiences, significant losses in life, and feelings of helplessness, but also to abnormal activity of key chemicals in the brain. Given such wide-ranging insights, we also have included in most chapters a section called "When Things Go Wrong." We discuss in these sections what happens when normal psychological processes, such as memory, emotional coping, social engagement, and the like, go astray.

At first glance, psychology's intensified focus on the brain may make it appear that technology and biology are dominating contemporary psychology. However, it is unlikely that psychology will ever be overtaken by biology. Indeed, recent findings in cognitive neuroscience and other areas suggest that our insights about mental functions (and dysfunctions) and about behaviour are most complete when the different branches of the field intersect and cooperate. In clinical psychology, for example, it is now clear that many mental disorders are best understood and treated when explanations and techniques from different schools of thought are combined.

One important area of psychology that has intersected with other areas of the field for many years is developmental psychology, the study of how we change over the course of our lives. Developmental psychology has both incorporated and contributed to research in areas such as our use of language, our emotions, our personalities, and the structure of our brains. We emphasize the cross-fertilization of development and other areas by including in most chapters a section called "How We Develop."

New Schools of Thought As we saw earlier, historical schools of thought in psychology sow the seeds for related but new ideas. We can see, for example, influences of the functionalists, who were interested in applying psychological research, and the humanists, who were interested in helping people achieve their highest potential, when we look at a relatively new movement in the field called *positive psychology*. Positive psychology gives special focus to more upbeat features of human functioning, including happiness, meaning in life, and character strengths, as well as increased attention to how those features of positive living might be developed more readily (Baumgardner & Crothers, 2009; Seligman & Csikszentmihalyi, 2000).

Happiness seems to have become a buzz word of the twenty-first century. It has been embraced particularly by the popular media, fuelling a self-help industry that claims to give people tools for achieving emotional well-being. This heightened interest in positive functioning has been used to help market nutritional advice, as seen, for example, in the book *The Good Mood Diet: Feel Great While You Lose Weight* (Kleiner & Condor, 2007), and has appeared even in fields not associated primarily with psychology, as in the book *The Architecture of Happiness* (Botton, 2006). The field of positive psychology has tried to devote scholarly discussion and scientific study to happiness and its positive counterparts. In fact, an estimated 150 psychology departments in the United States now offer courses in positive psychology (Senior, 2006).

Accentuating the positive. Residents of a small Spanish village cry out in joy as they are drenched with 30 tons of water during a water festival. Positive psychologists study the impact that happiness and positive emotions have on human functioning.

A growing body of research does indeed suggest that positive emotions can have a profound impact on development and behaviour. As you'll see in a later chapter, when we discuss stress, coping, and health, a number of studies have found that having a positive outlook promotes *resilience*, the ability to bounce back in the face of adversity (Garbarino, 2011). Similarly, studies indicate that positive emotions may boost the functioning of our immune systems. Research even suggests that our emotions help influence how well we resist common colds (Cohen et al., 2008, 2003)!

In Chapter 12, on emotions, we'll also consider a line of research that suggests that each of us has a particular "set-point" on our happiness thermometer, a relatively stable level of well-being that we may carry with us to each situation in our lives. We may depart from that set-point for short periods of time, but many of us return to our particular level of happiness within weeks or months of a destabilizing event (Headey, 2008).

In Chapter 17, we'll see that some psychologists have even developed a new form of therapy, called *positive psychotherapy.* This type of therapy does not target specific symptoms of mental dysfunction, but rather focuses on increasing the positive emotions and sense of engagement and meaning experienced by clients (Seligman et al., 2006). According to proponents of positive psychology, certain techniques and behaviours can be of particular help to people in their efforts to achieve happiness or return to happiness after unpleasant events.

What Changes and What Remains Constant? Since the early years of Greek philosophy, theorists have attempted to determine how the human mind operates and whether there are universal laws that govern mental processes and behaviours. Those questions remain at the forefront of contemporary psychology as today's neuroscientists, cultural theorists, and other psychologists try to determine how the mind and body are related, whether there are knowable universal truths about mental processes and human behaviours, and whether such truths are best understood through the perspective of the brain, the individual, or the group, or a particular combination of the three. It is not likely that psychology can ever provide complete answers to these complex questions. However, striving to uncover even partial answers has already uncovered a wealth of information about how human beings function and has produced a range of compelling theories and research findings.

Socrates' approach to teaching involved leading students through their assumptions and logic by asking them specific, precise questions. This approach, called the Socratic method, remains an important part of a clinical psychologist's therapeutic practice to this day.

As you read about these theories and findings throughout this textbook, you will do well to keep asking yourself a question raised by Carl Jung (1875–1961), one of the field's most famous clinical theorists: "How much truth [is] captured by this [particular] viewpoint?" Ideas move in and out of vogue, and what is accepted today as a useful or accurate outlook might not be seen the same way tomorrow.

Both historical and social forces determine the focus of scientific energy. Psychology, perhaps more than any other field, struggles constantly to achieve a proper balance between popular trends and interests, societal influences, and scientific objectivity (Leahey, 2000, p. 544). Although fads and fashions will likely continue to exert some influence on the development of psychology in the coming years, it is important to recognize that such fads hardly comprise the substance of the field. Moreover, we must always keep in mind the limitations of psychology (or of any discipline) in answering the basic questions of human existence. As we noted at the beginning of this chapter, scientific knowledge serves as a *means* for exploring such questions rather than an end.

Before You Go On

www.wiley.com/go/comer

What Do You Know?

14. What are the three major branches of psychology?
15. What is cultural universality, and what kinds of psychologists are interested in it?
16. What is the focus of positive psychology?

What Do You Think?

Which branch of psychology most appeals to you as a potential profession? Why?
What kinds of things do you think would be important for positive psychologists to study?

SCAN TO GET THE ANSWERS

Summary

What Is Psychology?

LEARNING OBJECTIVE 1 Define psychology, and describe the goals and levels of analysis psychologists use.

- Psychology is the study of mental processes and behaviour.
- The goals of psychology are to *describe*, *explain*, *predict*, and *control* behaviour and mental processes. Psychologists vary in the degree to which they focus on some of these goals more than others.
- The study of psychology must occur at multiple levels, including the level of the *brain* (the biological activity associated with mental processes and behaviour), the level of the *person* (the content of mental processes), and the level of the *group* (social influences on behaviour).

Psychology's Roots in Philosophy

LEARNING OBJECTIVE 2 Describe the influences of early myths and ancient Greek philosophies on psychology.

- Early explanations of human behaviour were rooted in superstition and magic.
- Later, philosophers, beginning with the ancient Greeks, tried to develop more objective theories of human consciousness and reality.
- The work of such early philosophers as Hippocrates, Socrates, Plato, and Aristotle contributed to the later formation of psychology as a natural science.

The Early Days of Psychology

LEARNING OBJECTIVE 3 Name important early psychologists and describe their major theories and research methods.

- The development of psychology has been strongly influenced by shifts in the social environment and development of new technology.
- The first psychology laboratory was founded in Leipzig, Germany, by physiologist Wilhelm Wundt. Wundt was interested in human consciousness and will, which he studied through small, structured activities that could be easily watched and replicated.
- Structuralism, a school of thought developed by one of Wundt's students, relied upon the use of introspection, the careful observation of human perception. The goal of the structuralists was to find the smallest building blocks of consciousness.
- William James established the first psychology laboratory in the United States at Harvard and helped shift the field's focus to the functions of mental events and behaviours, forming a school of thought known as functionalism.
- Gestalt psychologists studied human tendencies to perceive pattern rather than dividing consciousness into its smallest parts. They focused on putting together the "parts," or individual sensations, to create a "whole" or perception that went beyond the sum of the parts.

Twentieth-Century Approaches

LEARNING OBJECTIVE 4 Summarize the major principles of the psychoanalytical, behaviourist, humanistic, cognitive, and neuroscience approaches to psychology.

- Over the years, different fields of psychology emerged, with different ideas about what was the appropriate area of study for human psychology. Some of the most influential fields were the psychoanalytic, behaviourist, humanistic, cognitive, and neuroscience schools of thought.
- Sigmund Freud's psychoanalytical theory focused on the importance of unconscious mental processes.
- Behaviourists believed strongly that psychology should restrict its focus to the careful study of observable behaviours.
- Humanistic psychologists reacted against the mechanical portrayals of people by the behaviourists, and emphasized individuals' potential for growth and self-actualization.
- Cognitive psychologists reignited interest in the study of mental processes, comparing the workings of the mind to the workings of computers.
- Biological science, including interest in the workings of the brain and in our genetic inheritance, is the major influence on neuroscience approaches.

Psychology Today

LEARNING OBJECTIVE 5 Describe the three major branches of psychology and summarize key trends in psychology.

- The theoretical and cultural diversity of the field of psychology has increased dramatically over recent years.
- There are three key branches of psychology: academic, applied, and clinical/counselling.
- Across the three branches and many specialty areas in psychology, psychologists are united by their shared values. Psychologists generally agree that psychology is *theory-driven*, *empirical*, *multilevel*, and *contextual*.
- Currently, psychology appears to be developing as a science in response to a growing diversity throughout the field, advances in *technology* (such as brain scanning), and the development of *new schools* such as positive psychology.

Key Terms

CHAPTER 2

Similarly, in the hypothetico-deductive approach, psychologists set out to create controlled observations that will prove or disprove their hypotheses. In many cases, research results do indeed disprove their hypotheses. Psychologists may then reject or modify their theories and generate new hypotheses for further testing. Through repetition of this process, theories evolve over time to become more and more accurate explanations of human thought and behaviour. This approach is outlined in **Figure 2-1**.

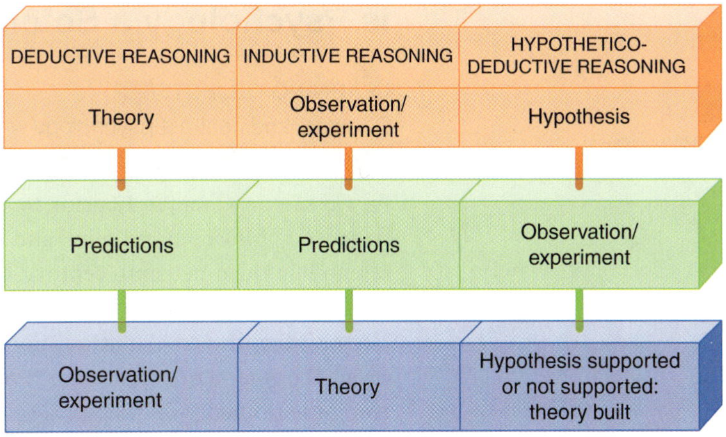

FIGURE 2-1 Reasoning and the scientific method. Several different kinds of reasoning may be used as scientists carry out their work. Most psychological researchers use the hypothetico-deductive approach.

As we discussed at the beginning of the chapter, many people have ideas about whether watching violence on TV causes people to exhibit more violent behaviour. To produce a scientific theory about the effects of televised aggression and violence, a person would need to step outside his or her personal beliefs to avoid bias. A scientific approach would involve the steps described below:

- *Make observation.* We might first examine what child viewers do after watching a TV program containing violence. For example, do they exhibit aggressive behaviour in a free-play opportunity after watching *Hockey Night in Canada* broadcast in which there were a number of on-ice fights? That is, do they engage in behaviours that suggest increased levels of aggression and violence?
- *Develop hypotheses.* After making such observations, we would generate hypotheses about what led to the behaviour we observed. If viewers acted more aggressively, for example, did the on-ice fights and/or aggressive play cause viewers to think of their fellow human beings in a more negative light? Or were the viewers simply modelling themselves after the players? Whatever our explanation, we would generate a falsifiable hypothesis to test. One hypothesis, for example, might be that viewers change their behaviour to be more like the people they see playing in the hockey game.
- *Test hypotheses.* As we'll see in this chapter, there are several kinds of research studies we could conduct to see if this hypothesis can be disproved.
- *Build a theory.* If the hypothesis is, indeed, disproved, we might modify or even throw it out and develop and test a new hypothesis. If our hypothesis that people who watch *Hockey Night in Canada* change their behaviour to be more like the players in the game is not disproved, we might test it further. We might, for example, decide to study the viewers of a variety of televised sporting events (e.g., curling, figure skating, or mixed martial arts). If the results continue to support our hypothesis, the hypothesis can become a theory. A theory, in turn, can become a framework to generate additional hypotheses.

Before You Go On

www.wiley.com/go/comer

What Do You Know?

1. What are the two core beliefs of a science?
2. What is the difference between inductive and deductive reasoning?
3. What is the difference between a hypothesis and a theory?
4. What is the hypothetico-deductive method?

What Do You Think?

Based on what you know about the scientific method, do you think psychology is a science in the same way chemistry, biology, and physics are sciences?

SCAN TO GET THE ANSWERS

Is Psychology a Science?

LEARNING OBJECTIVE 2

Compare and contrast psychology with other natural sciences, such as biology, chemistry, and physics, and with pseudosciences, such as astrology.

As we saw in Chapter 1, prior to the nineteenth century, psychology was a field based largely on philosophy, religion, and even mysticism. With a rise in the popularity of animal research in the nineteenth century, however, scientists began to develop an increased interest in physiology and how human actions are tied to innate biological functions. Charles Darwin's theories on evolution, along with advances in the field of biology, raised questions about the interactions between humans and our environments. Given such roots, many credit the influence of biological science for shifting psychology from a philosophy toward becoming a science (Hergenhahn, 2005).

Although psychology is now defined as a natural science that uses experimental methods to study mental processes and behaviour, it does differ from the physical sciences, such as biology, in key ways, including how it pursues scientific goals and its role in influencing personal and social values.

Goals of Psychology

As we saw in Chapter 1, all sciences share the goals of describing, explaining, predicting, and controlling the phenomena they study. However, the emphasis each field places on these goals may vary. One key difference between psychology and the physical sciences, for example, is in the area of description. A core goal of many physical sciences is to isolate and describe the smallest elements that contribute to a larger whole. Biologists look at how a cell contributes to the overall functioning of an organism, for example. Chemists and physicists examine how atoms and subatomic particles make up the structure of, well, everything. Although psychology also attempts to isolate fundamental elements of behaviour and mental processes, psychologists face an additional task because behaviour is determined by many such factors simultaneously.

The basic factors that affect behaviour can be temporary or permanent fixtures in a person's life. The atomic structure of gold, for example, is the same in all gold all over the world, but a complex behaviour, such as reading this textbook, cannot be broken down into a standard set of elements that work the same for every person. The reading behaviour of a student might be influenced by a temporary factor, such as anticipation of an upcoming exam, which does not affect the reading behaviour of non-students. The idea behind psychological research is both to *isolate* the relative contribution of such factors and to think about how these factors *come together* to influence human behaviour.

Multiple influences. Behaviour is complex and is determined by many factors operating simultaneously. What factors—temporary, permanent, or both—might be influencing this man to take a dip in the ocean on a cold day?

Psychologists face an additional challenge because much of what they study does not have a clear and observable physical reality like the basic units of study in other scientific fields. With the help of special tools, scientists in those fields can observe even the tiniest bits of matter, including atoms and DNA. Of course, this is also true of psychology *to some degree*. Behaviours, sensations, or physiological responses, for example, can be directly observed, measured, and explained. In his review of science, the great German philosopher Immanuel Kant suggested that when studying phenomena such as these, psychology is

Thoughts versus behaviours. Thoughts cannot be observed directly, but behaviours can. Thus psychologists can be more certain about the romantic feelings of the woman on the right than those of the woman on the left.

indeed empirical and very close to a "real" science (Kant, 2003). Other psychologists, such as the behaviourist B. F. Skinner, also advocated this view of psychology, and in fact, as we saw in Chapter 1, many behaviourists have stated that, as scientists, psychologists should study *only* what is directly observable.

On the other hand, as Kant himself observed, many of the processes that form the basis of psychology cannot be observed or described directly. We have no microscopes or tests that will allow us to see a thought or an emotion, for example, with the same clarity as a cell. Granted, good scientific work and sound experimental study have enabled us to look at many of the ways thoughts and feelings can influence behaviours, and psychologists are always seeking out new ways of objectively defining these and other elusive features of mental functioning. But direct observation continues to be a difficult task in the field of psychology.

Values and the Application of Psychology

Psychology is also distinct from other scientific fields inasmuch as it deals in major ways with issues associated with values, morality, and personal preference—issues that historically were addressed exclusively by spiritual and political leaders. Like all scientists, psychologists try to provide society with useful information that has practical applications. But people are particularly inclined to use psychological information to decide issues that overlap with philosophy, religion, the law, and other such realms of life. For example, on its website (www.cpa.ca), the Canadian Psychological Association offers policy statements based on psychological research on topics ranging from the death penalty (studies show it does not reduce homicide rates), bullying (research shows solutions require relationship changes), and physical punishment of children (it is an ineffectual way of controlling a child's behaviour and it models aggressive behaviour for the child).

Happy birthday! Yangyang, a female goat cloned by Chinese scientists in 2000, wears a wreath at her 6th birthday party. Advances in genetic research and genetic engineering hold much promise, but it is important to consider the ethical implications.

Of course, other sciences also influence the values and ethics of human beings to various degrees. The field of genetic research, for example, was pioneered by biological scientists who were looking for better farming practices. However, some early geneticists soon came to believe that selective breeding could be applied to humans to increase the likelihood of desired offspring. Their research contributed to a field eventually known as *eugenics*. Eugenics influenced not only many people's personal childbearing decisions, but also contributed to policies of governments and social agencies in some locations that required forced sterilization surgery for people deemed unfit to reproduce (Whitaker, 2002).

Angus McLaren, (1990) of the University of Victoria history department, points out that Alberta established a eugenics board in 1927 to rule on involuntary sterilizations; it was not disbanded until 1972. Indeed, eugenics has often been associated with racism and homophobia.

Today, the field of genetic research sparks concerns and debate about food practices, stem cell research, human cloning, and other such issues. Every scientific field must wrestle with questions of how to ethically apply the knowledge it discovers about the world, but few more so than the field of psychology. In addition, few sciences are as plagued as psychology is with popular imitations and misrepresentations of their work.

Misrepresentation of Psychology

It is natural for people to seek guidance periodically on how to live their lives. And psychologists certainly do not shy away from helping people with their problems, as evidenced by the thriving areas of clinical and counselling psychology and other applied disciplines described in Chapter 1. Ultimately, however, science—even psychology—cannot answer fundamental and subjective questions about human nature.

People who claim to do so are misrepresenting the science of psychology with *pseudopsychology* (Leahey, 2005). Pseudopsychology, or *pop psychology*, is not based on the scientific method, yet it takes on the appearance of science. Pseudopsychologists often have hidden goals, such as the goal of promoting certain moral or religious values (Hergenhan, 2005).

"Do you believe in UFOs, astral projections, mental telepathy, ESP, [and] clairvoyance . . . ? Uh, if there's a steady paycheck in it, I'll believe anything you say."

—*Dialogue from the 1984 movie* Ghostbusters

A fundamental difference between pseudopsychology and psychology is that psychology does not claim to address all human issues, whereas pseudoscientists argue that psychological principles can provide the answers to all of life's major questions (Leahey, 2005).

PSYCHOLOGY AROUND US Psychology . . . Not!

Astrology is a good example of pseudopsychology. It uses Zodiac "signs" to predict one's future and give advice about one's relationships and decisions. Astrology's guiding principle is that all human beings have particular personality traits that are based on the alignment of planets on the dates of their births. Moreover, astrologers believe that those celestial-based traits determine how people will react to events and interact with others. The predictions, connections, and claims of astrology have no scientific foundation. Most of them cannot, by definition, be tested and falsified, while others have consistently failed to receive any support. Yet the methods and tests used in astrology bear some resemblance to psychological personality tests. Thus, astrologers often adopt the terminology and topics of psychology, confusing many individuals—including many astrologers themselves—into believing that their field is scientifically based.

Clearly, psychologists must maintain a difficult balance. On the one hand, it is important to encourage the human drive to seek guidance and derive meaning about how to live effectively. On the other hand, psychology must distance itself from pseudoscience to maintain its status as a natural, empirically-based science. As one researcher wrote, "Mainstream psychologists have a problem differentiating themselves from what they regard as a pseudoscience without seeming dogmatically intolerant" (Hergenhahn, 2005, p. 532).

Making Psychology More Popular

Stan Coren

Within many scientific disciplines, there are charismatic researchers and practitioners who are able to describe their complex topics so that almost anyone can understand the concepts. These individuals present facts about science in ways that engage the public's imagination. As a result, some of them become well-known figures in the popular media, such as in mass-market books, magazines, television, and radio. Psychology too has its share of such individuals.

Fraser Mustard is a physician who, during a long career at McMaster University, was involved in establishing its unique problem-focused approach to medical training. Since retiring, he has become internationally known for his work on the "Early Years study" and as an advocate for the critical importance of the first six years of life in establishing children's intellectual potential and future achievements (McCain & Mustard, 1999). His work has lead to the expansion of many early education programs, improving developmental outcomes for Canadian children.

Another well-known researcher is psychologist Brenda Milner, Ph.D., who trained under another well-known Canadian cognitive psychologist, Donald Hebb. Milner specializes in brain functioning (frontal lobes and lateralization). As well, she has pioneered work into spatial memory and language using recently developed brain imaging techniques. Milner has been recognized for her work by being made a member of the Royal Society of Canada and the National Academy of Science (in the United States), as well as winning the Swiss international Balzan Prize for Cognitive Neurosciences.

And then, of course, there are the celebrity practitioners—professionals who are very well known to the public as book authors or from work on radio and television. Some of these practitioners are well trained and have appropriate professional credentials. Stan Coren, a cognitive psychologist at the University of British Columbia, has written one of the most used textbooks on sensation and perception (Coren, Ward, & Enns, 2004). As well, he has written widely-read books on handedness (1993), the effects of sleep deprivation on everyday life (1996), and many books on the intelligence, behaviour, and role of dogs (1997, 1998, 2003, 2006a, 2006b, 2008a, 2008b, 2010a, 2010b), in addition to hosting a Life Channel show on dog behaviour call Good Dog!

But a word to the wise. For each Coren, who is well qualified, there are many more celebrity practitioners who do not have proper training or appropriate credentials in their supposed areas of expertise, including some of the media's most popular TV and radio advisors. Before listening too closely, it is always best to check the qualifications of a psychologist or other professional who is dispensing advice on radio, television, or the Web.

Before You Go On

www.wiley.com/go/comer

What Do You Know?

5. What are the four goals of psychology?
6. What is the main difference between psychology and pseudopsychology?

What Do You Think?

Why do you think that pseudopsychology appeals to so many people even though it is not based on science and does not reflect the truth?

SCAN TO GET THE ANSWERS

How Do Psychologists Conduct Research?

LEARNING OBJECTIVE 3

List steps in the research process and key characteristics of descriptive and experimental psychological research methods.

Let's go back to the controversy over TV aggression and violence. Suppose that you frequently watch *Hockey Night in Canada*. Let's say that after viewing the broadcast, you notice that you drive a bit more aggressively. You wonder whether all people who watch this particular broadcast become more aggressive than those people who do not. How would you, as a psychological researcher, study this question?

Observation. Watching rats run through mazes is only a very small part of how psychologists conduct research.

As we described earlier, the scientific method begins with observation. So, after noting your own reaction, you may decide to observe other viewers. Maybe you get together with some friends or sit in a common area when the game is on, and you watch how everyone interacts with each other during and after the show—though you will have to be aware of influences other than the game if the setting is a bar and everyone is drinking!

State a Hypothesis

After you've made such observations, you need to generate a prediction; this is your research hypothesis (see **Figure 2-2**). As we have noted, a hypothesis defines what you think will happen and states your prediction in a way that can be tested and found to be either true or false. Your hypothesis might be: watching *Hockey Night in Canada* typically increases viewers' aggressive behaviour.

variable condition, event, or situation that is studied in an experiment.

Notice in your hypothesis that you are saying that one thing results in another thing. The two things are called *variables*. A **variable** is a condition or event or situation—it can really be many things. A condition or event that is thought to be a factor in changing

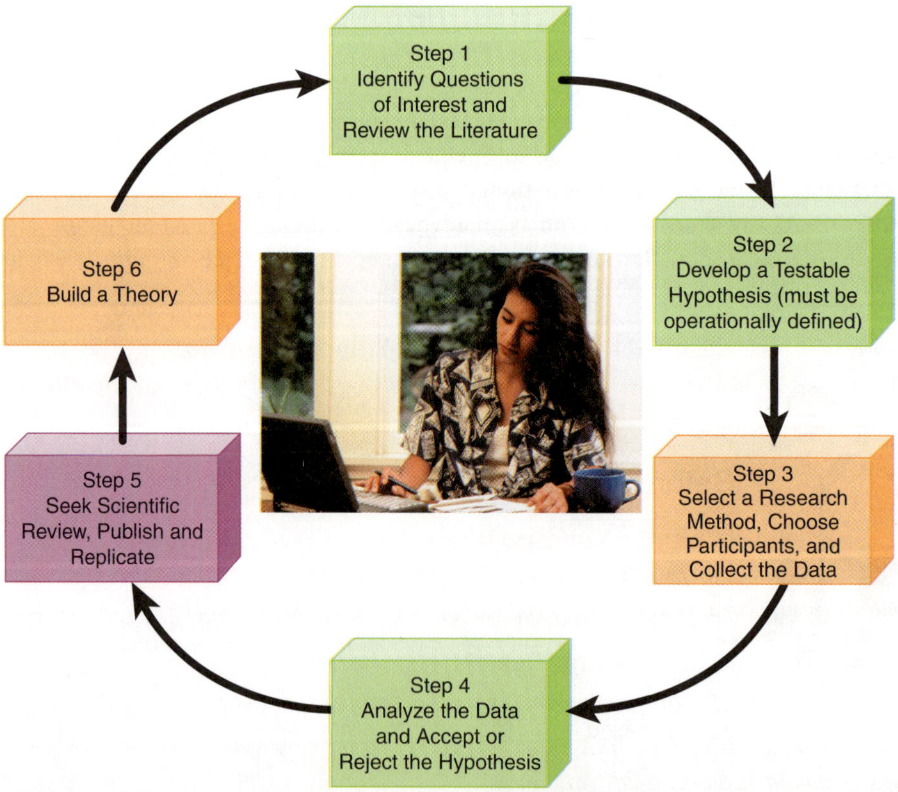

FIGURE 2-2 How do psychologists conduct research? Psychologists follow certain steps and confront a number of choice points as they study questions about mental processes and behaviours.

another condition or event is known as an **independent variable**. We call it the independent variable because it is the one the researcher sets loose to see what changes it will cause. In this study, watching or not watching *Hockey Night in Canada* is an independent variable. A researcher could change this variable to see how it affects aggressive behaviour. Aggressive behaviour would be a **dependent variable**, the condition or event you expect to change as a result of varying the independent variable. It is the dependent variable because if our hypothesis is correct then people's scores on this variable will "depend" on their exposure to the independent variable. How about another example? If you wanted to see if drinking an energy drink would help you read more pages of your textbook in an hour of studying, you could read for an hour without any energy drink, drink one energy drink and read for an hour, then drink a second energy drink and read for another hour. You could count the number of pages you read in each of the three hours. So in this study, what is the independent variable? (It is the amount of energy drink consumed). What is the dependent variable? (If you thought "pages read," you are right).

independent variable condition or event that is thought to be a factor in changing another condition or event.

dependent variable condition or event that you expect to change as a result of variations in the independent variable.

In addition to defining these variables, you also have to **operationalize** the variables—develop very precise definitions of the independent and dependent variables that allow you to measure and test them (McGrath, 2011). In this case, you might define the independent variable as the length of time viewers watch the game. As a researcher, you may require the participants in your study to watch part of a game, a whole game, or even several hockey games. In our other example above, we operationalized stimulant drink use as zero, one, or two cans, but we could have operationalized it as zero, half, one, one-and-a-half, or two cans (note that you are not supposed to drink more than two cans of energy drink).

operationalize to develop a working definition of a variable that allows you to test it.

While it may be relatively easy to create an operational definition of watching, it is harder to operationalize the dependent variable in this study, aggressive or violent behaviour. You might have participants fill out a questionnaire asking about their feelings of anger or hostility and their intentions for managing a number of hypothetical situations (such as being cut off in traffic). If you did this, however, you would not know for sure that the attitudes and intentions stated on the questionnaire reflect aggressive behaviour. People may think a lot about behaving aggressively without actually doing so. Thus, you might prefer to have participants in your study demonstrate some kind of actual aggressive behaviour. You could, for example, set up a situation in which each participant spends 30 minutes playing an online game involving potential aggression or violence against one or more other study participants. Even here, however, you would not be sure that your operational definition of aggressive behaviour is on target. You might not be measuring "true-life" behaviour; the participants might be altering their research behaviour because they know they are being watched.

There are yet other ways researchers could operationally define aggressive behaviour—perhaps involving verbal aggression or self-criticism. Each definition would have advantages and disadvantages, and each would have implications for the conclusions the researchers can draw. In our other example, we counted pages read as our dependent variable, but can you think of any problems with that? One possible issue might occur if after two energy drinks people read a lot more pages but do not later recall much of what they read. This would suggest a problem with your operationalization if the dependent variable you were interested in was studying success.

Choose Participants

Once you have identified your variables, you need to select the people who will participate in your study. It generally isn't feasible for researchers to go out into the world and study the entire population of people whose behaviour interests them. Indeed, a population of interest could sometimes include everybody in the whole world. Even when psychologists are not interested in the entire human population, their populations of interest may be very large groups, such as all Canadians, adults, teenagers, children, men, or women. In your hockey violence study, the population of interest includes everyone who watches *Hockey Night in Canada* and everyone who doesn't.

sample the group of people studied in an experiment, used to stand in for an entire group of people.

random selection identifying a sample in such a way that everyone in the population of interest has an equal chance of being involved in the study.

Because they cannot usually study an entire population, researchers must obtain a subset, or **sample**, from their population of interest (McGrath, 2011). This subset stands in for the population as a whole. Population sampling of this kind is used very frequently. Political pollsters, for example, interview samples of the voting population to predict which candidate will win a national, provincial, or civic election.

In most instances, researchers prefer to obtain their samples through **random selection**. Random selection is simply a fancy term for choosing your participants in such a way that everybody in the population of interest has an equal chance of becoming part of the sample. That way, you can minimize *sampling biases*—that is, you will not inadvertently select a group that is especially likely to confirm your hypothesis (such as people who watch *Hockey Night in Canada* while drinking in a rowdy sports bar). If you include only your pro-aggressive hockey friends in your sample, the study probably will yield very different results than if you include only people opposed to showing hockey violence. Indeed, neither sample would be fully representative of the population at large.

Proper sampling. Which of the people in this photo should be included in a study? All of them and others too, if a researcher wants to draw conclusions about the entire population. Only some of them, if the researcher seeks to understand just children, just adults, just women, or other subgroups.

Truly random selection can be elusive. The members of your population who do not watch *Hockey Night in Canada* includes, for example, 3-year-olds, who probably are not interested in the game and probably are not capable of making the same kinds of choices about aggressive behaviour that 25- or 45-year-old persons might make. Thus, you may decide to narrow your sample to include adolescents or adults only. Of course, such a choice would mean that your findings will be relevant to adolescents or adults only, rather than to the entire human population. Researchers in psychology often try to choose samples that make their results relevant to the broadest possible segments of their populations of interest.

PSYCHOLOGY AROUND US Wrong Sample, Wrong Conclusion

Although this is an example based on American history, it is a good example. In 1936, in the midst of the Depression, President Franklin Delano Roosevelt ran for re-election against Kansas governor Alfred Landon. Landon ran on a platform of cutting government spending, and he seemed to be a heavy favourite.

Back in those days, the *Literary Digest* was America's most popular magazine. It predicted that Landon would win, based on the largest number of people to ever reply to a poll: 2.4 million! In fact, the Digest had correctly called the winner in every presidential election since 1916.

But as you may know, Landon did not win the 1936 election. The *Digest's* prestige suffered and, partly because of this, it went bankrupt a few years later. The magazine had predicted that Roosevelt would get only 44 percent of the vote, when in fact he wound up with winning a total of 62 percent of the vote!

What went wrong? Simple. The *Literary Digest* picked its sample incorrectly. The magazine mailed 10 million questionnaires using addresses from the phone book and club membership lists. By doing so, it tended to miss poor voters who did not have phones and did not join clubs (only one household in four had a phone at that time). Poor people were overwhelmingly in favour of Roosevelt, but few of their voices were represented in the *Digest* poll. Hence, "sampling bias" created a sample that was non-representative.

A new polling organization run by George Gallup used "random" methods of selection in that same election and predicted that Roosevelt would win with 56 percent of the vote—close enough to help launch the famous and still-going-strong Gallup Polling (Squire, 1988).

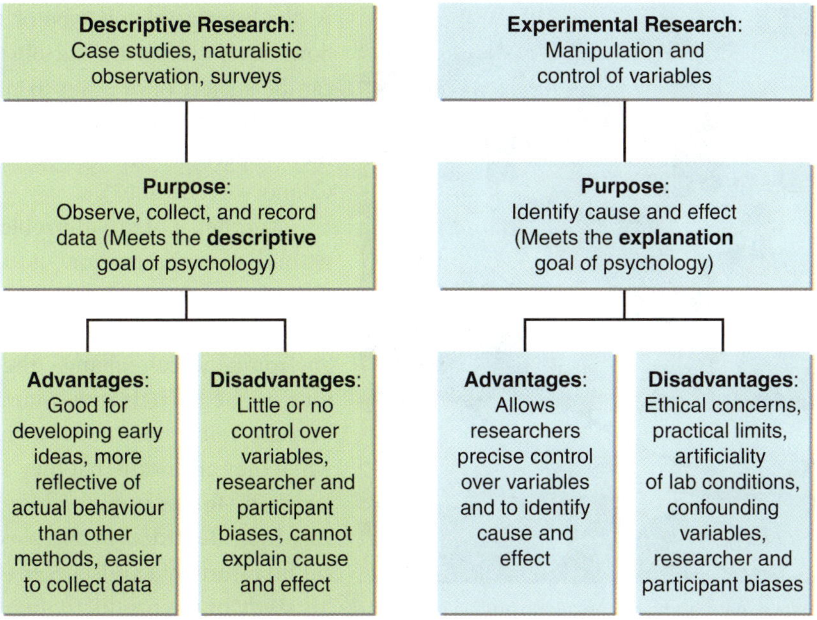

FIGURE 2-3 **Descriptive versus experimental research.** Because descriptive methods and experimental methods each serve particular purposes and have different advantages and disadvantages, psychological research includes both kinds of approaches.

Pick a Research Method

Researchers have several options when designing studies to test their hypotheses (McGrath, 2011). Research methods differ in their goals, samples, and the ability of researchers to generalize their results to a population. Most of the methods we describe next, including case studies, naturalistic observation, and surveys, are known as descriptive research methods. They allow researchers to pursue the goal of description: to determine the existence (and sometimes the strength) of a relationship between the variables of interest. In addition to such descriptive methods, we will also describe *experiments*, which allow researchers to explain the *causes* of behaviour (see **Figure 2-3**).

descriptive research methods studies that allow researchers to demonstrate a relationship between the variables of interest, without specifying a causal relationship.

case study study focusing on a single person.

Case Studies A case study focuses on a single person. Medical and psychological practitioners who treat people with problems often conduct case studies to help determine whether therapeutic interventions affect their client's symptoms (Lee, Mishna, & Brennenstuhl, 2010). A case study can be a good resource for developing early ideas about phenomena. One disadvantage of a case study, however, is that it can be affected greatly by *researcher bias*, which occurs when researchers see only what they expect to see in their studies. Some clinician/researchers may, for example, note only the healthy behaviours of persons after they have provided treatment to those individuals. Another disadvantage of case studies is that researchers cannot confidently generalize to other situations from the study of a single person (Lee et al., 2010). Suppose, for example, that you conduct a case study to test your hypothesis that watching *Hockey Night in Canada* increases aggressive behaviour: you closely observe one man who watches such a game, and you find that he later reports himself to be non-violent and gentle, even when frustrated by the behaviour of other drivers while driving. Your case study observation might indicate that your hypothesis is worthy of further research, but without comparison participants, it is impossible to say much about other viewers of the game. You would not know whether this person's behaviour after watching the game is the norm or an exception.

naturalistic observation a study in which researchers directly observe people in a study behaving as they normally do.

Naturalistic Observation In naturalistic observations, researchers watch as unobtrusively as possible while people behave as they normally do. Researchers often make naturalistic observations of children in schools or daycare centres. Perhaps as a researcher you could go into participants' homes over multiple weeks and see whether they watch hockey games at all. You could then observe whether those people who watch games engage in more aggressive behaviour and whether those who don't watch behave less aggressively. Naturalistic observations have the advantage of being more reflective of actual human behaviour than most other research designs.

A first-hand look. Unlike case studies or surveys, naturalistic observations enable researchers to directly observe people in their natural settings. Here, for example, a psychologist observes a preschool classroom through a one-way mirror.

A disadvantage of this type of research, however, is that naturalistic observations can be subject once again to researcher bias—observers may notice only what they expect to see (Goodwin, 2011; Connor-Greene, 2007).

Another potential problem with naturalistic observation is that the mere presence of a researcher or even a video camera in an otherwise natural environment can change the behaviour of the participants. Many people become nicer or more considerate when they are aware that they are being watched, for example. This problem was first identified in the psychological literature by Landsberger (1958) in his study of the productivity of factory workers. In his studies, he found that the workers' productivity increased whenever changes to the workplace were implemented, regardless of what type of change was imposed. Landsberger suggested that this increase in productivity occurred because the workers were motivated to perform better because they knew that they were being observed. This phenomenon has since been termed the **Hawthorne effect** (Goodwin, 2011) because the study was conducted at the Hawthorne plant of Western Electric near Chicago.

Hawthorne effect people who are being observed in studies or at their workplace will improve or change some of their behaviour simply because they are being watched or studied, not in response to an experimental manipulation.

Many of the potential problems with naturalistic observation can actually be effectively addressed. Multiple observers can be used to control for individual observer bias. Observers can be used who are not informed about the specific hypothesis under investigation, thus limiting the opportunities for bias to affect their observations. Observers can spend a lot of time in the setting they wish to observe so that they become an accepted part of the setting and their presence does not disrupt usual behaviour. As we will see in later chapters, some of psychology's most important studies were descriptive studies involving naturalistic observation.

Surveys A third descriptive approach, frequently used in psychological research, is the **survey**. In a survey, researchers ask people a series of questions. Researchers can conduct surveys using in-person, telephone, or email interviews, or they may ask the questions via a written questionnaire. To test your aggressive behaviour hypothesis, for example, you might design a questionnaire that asks people about their *Hockey Night in Canada* watching habits and about their aggressive attitudes, and use their answers to determine whether or not a relationship exists between the two variables.

survey study in which researchers give participants a questionnaire or interview them.

The advantage of a survey approach is that surveys allow researchers to obtain information that they might not be able to gather using case studies or naturalistic observations. It might be hard, for example, to tell whether a person in a case study is avoiding aggressive behaviour because he or she wishes to do the right thing, or whether the individual is avoiding aggressive behaviour to get some kind of reward. A survey can help pin down such issues. Another reason surveys are sometimes favoured by psychologists is that they can also provide data that enable researchers to measure how strong the relationship is between two variables of interest.

Surveys do suffer some disadvantages, however (McGrath, 2011). Their data can be unreliable because people frequently answer in ways that are socially acceptable rather than in ways that are reflective of their true attitudes, a problem known as *participant bias*. Thus, people in your *Hockey Night in Canada* study may describe themselves on a survey as less aggressive than they actually are because they know that being aggressive is considered a socially inappropriate trait. Similarly, participants in a survey study may be unaware of just how aggressive they are. Although subject bias obviously is a common concern for survey researchers, it can also occur in experiments and other types of research as well, as we shall soon see.

Another problem is that survey data cannot tell us the *direction* of the relationship between variables. Do people who watch *Hockey Night in Canada* a lot become more aggressive, or are highly aggressive people drawn to watch *Hockey Night in Canada* a lot? A survey cannot help you answer this question. Despite these concerns, a lot of very informative descriptive research is conducted in psychology.

Experiments If you want to know what *causes* what, you have to design an experiment (McGrath, 2011). An **experiment** is a controlled observation in which researchers manipulate levels of one variable—the independent variable—and then observe any changes in another variable—the dependent variable—that result from their manipulation.

experiment controlled observation in which researchers manipulate the presence or amount of the independent variable to see what effect it has on the dependent variable.

experimental group group that is exposed to the independent variable.

control group group that has not been or will not be exposed to the independent variable.

One way of experimentally testing your *Hockey Night in Canada* hypothesis in this kind of study would be to divide your sample into two groups: an **experimental group** and a **control group**. An experimental group is the one exposed to the independent variable. In our example, the experimental group would consist of people who are instructed to watch *Hockey Night in Canada*. A control group, in contrast, consists of people who are similar to those in the experimental group but who are not exposed to the independent variable—for example, people not instructed to view *Hockey Night in Canada*. By comparing the aggressive behaviour of the two groups after one group watches *Hockey Night in Canada* and the other does not, you might conclude with some degree of confidence that differences in aggressive behaviour are caused by exposure to *Hockey Night in Canada*. You could also create a more complex experiment, in which multiple experimental groups watch varying amounts of hockey or where some watch games that contain many fights and hard checks, while others watch less violent games. You could then compare them with the non-watching control group participants to determine whether the amount of hockey viewing or the type of games being watched affects levels of aggressive behaviour.

Many psychology experiments involve different levels of the independent variable of interest, as such higher levels of design complexity better match the real world reality we are trying to study. For example, we could also set up our study so that the experimental groups either watched a little or a lot of more or less violent hockey. This sort of design allows us to look for *interaction effects*. It may be that watching a small amount of violent hockey has no effect on aggressive behaviour, while watching a lot of it does increase aggressive behaviour. This sort of interaction effect could be observed and reported using this sort of more complex experimental design.

The composition of experimental and control groups needs careful attention. In our example, no one in the control group watches *Hockey Night in Canada* (see **Figure 2-4**) and none will be instructed to do so for the study. But what about the experimental group? Should you include people who have watched the broadcast previously? Or should you begin with a group of participants who—like the control group—have never, ever watched the broadcast, and then expose the experimental group to a marathon of *Hockey Night in Canada* broadcasts? Either approach is acceptable, but the two approaches may lead to different conclusions.

Other kinds of differences—past or present—between the experimental and control groups may also influence the results of an experiment. Researchers may use *random assignment* to make sure that everyone in their sample has an equal chance of being in either the control or experimental group (Remler & Van Ryzin, 2011). Even then, however, researchers still run the risk that the groups will differ in some important

FIGURE 2-4 The experimental design. Key features of experimental designs are independent and dependent variables and random assignment of experimental and control groups.

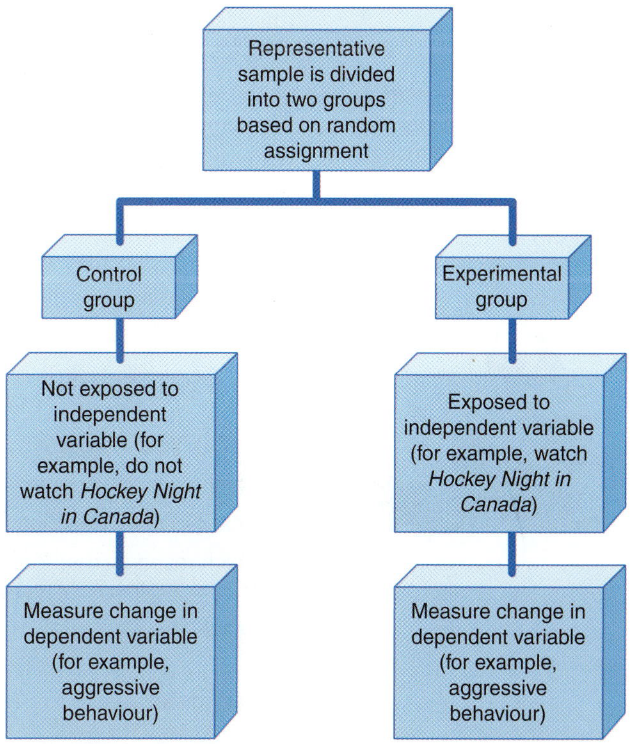

ways. Suppose that you randomly assign your *Hockey Night in Canada* viewing participants to each of your groups, but nevertheless wind up with more males in one group and more females in the other group. Such an unintended group difference may affect the participants' subsequent aggressive behaviours and so may lead you to draw incorrect conclusions. Some researchers pre-interview or give questionnaires to participants in both the experimental and control groups to make sure that the groups are comparable to one another. Their goal is to help guarantee that whatever effects emerge in the study are caused by the experimental manipulation of the independent variable and are not attributable to other, pre-existing variables, such as income level. If the groups are fairly large, random assignment will largely take care of these group membership concerns.

Experimental answer. Do complex visual images stimulate babies? To answer this causal question, experimenters showed swirling designs to one group of babies (experimental group) and bland designs to another group (control group). Babies in the experimental group typically attend to their designs longer than do those in the control group, suggesting that complex images do indeed attract the attention of babies.

In addition, experimenters must be careful when deciding what tasks will be performed by participants in the control group. Researchers often have the participants in a control group engage in an activity of some kind, just to make sure that the changes seen in the experimental participants are indeed due to the impact of the independent variable and not the result of the experimental participants being particularly active during the study. You might, for example, have your control group participants view another sporting event that is engaging but less violent. You could, for example, show soccer or basketball games to the control group. If afterwards the experimental participants still demonstrate more aggressive behaviour than the control participants, you can be more certain that the hockey game is in fact responsible.

Finally, experimenters must be careful to avoid bias in their studies. Once again, they must avoid subject bias and researcher bias—sources of bias that we discussed earlier. In addition, they must set up their studies so that they do not unintentionally convey to participants the outcome that they (the experimenters) expect to see, an undesired effect known as a *demand characteristic*. If a researcher were to tell participants in the experimental group of the *Hockey Night in Canada* study that their answers to an assertiveness and aggressiveness questionnaire will indicate how much *Hockey Night in Canada* contributes to problematic real-life behaviour, the researcher might be creating a demand characteristic that is encouraging those participants to understate their aggressive inclinations. For this reason, many studies, particularly pharmaceutical ones, are designed so that the persons who administer the study or who evaluate the behaviour of participants are unaware of the hypotheses of the study (Remler & Van Ryzin, 2011). Indeed, a number of studies use a specialized method known as a **double-blind procedure**, in which neither the participant nor the researcher knows which group—experimental or control—the participant is in. This information is sealed and only revealed after the data for the study have been collected (Wender et al., 2011). Double-blind studies help keep researchers from observing or creating what they want to observe and participants from intentionally acting in ways that confirm a researcher's hypothesis.

double-blind procedure study in which neither the participant nor the researcher knows what treatment or procedure the participant is receiving.

Before You Go On

www.wiley.com/go/comer

What Do You Know?

7. Which variable is controlled or manipulated by an experimenter?
8. What are three descriptive research methods used in psychology?
9. Which research method allows research to say that one variable causes another?

What Do You Think?

What would you conclude if people's aggressive behaviour increased after a single exposure to *Hockey Night in Canada*? How would that conclusion be different if aggressive behaviour only increased after a marathon viewing of *Hockey Night in Canada*?

SCAN TO GET THE ANSWERS

How Do Psychologists Make Sense of Research Results?

LEARNING OBJECTIVE 4

Tell what information is conveyed by statistics, including correlation coefficients, means, and standard deviations, and explain how psychologists draw conclusions about cause and effect.

Once researchers obtain results from an experiment or descriptive study, what do they do with them? Can they simply eyeball their findings and say that there's a relationship between this and that variable, or that the two groups under study are different? No, scientists cannot depend just on impressions or logic. If they tried, they would have no way of knowing whether a relationship found between variables or a difference between groups actually matters.

Psychologists use *statistics* to describe and measure relationships between variables. Scientists use many statistical analyses to look at the differences and similarities between groups (Goodwin, 2011). We won't go into a lot of depth about statistics here (for more details see Appendix A at the end of this text). We will, however, give you a few tips to help you understand the research findings you'll be reading about in this book and elsewhere. We will discuss correlations, which describe the relationships between variables, and then go on to discuss the statistical tests researchers use to determine how likely it is that their results are occurring simply by chance. Then, we will examine how researchers use the statistical results to decide whether or not their hypothesis has been supported and to guide the next steps in the research process.

Correlations: Measures of Relationships

A predictable relationship between two or more variables is called a correlation (for more detailed information on correlation, see page 706 of Appendix A). To describe correlations, especially in descriptive studies, psychologists use a statistic called a correlation coefficient.

A correlation coefficient can range from −1.00 to +1.00. The number itself and the positive or negative sign in the correlation coefficient each convey different information.

The positive or negative sign tells you the direction of the relationship. When scores on both variables get bigger together, the relationship is known as a positive correlation. In our example, we predicted a positive correlation between *Hockey Night in Canada* watching and aggressive behaviour: as watching increases, so will aggressive behaviour. If we had suggested that aggressive behaviour does not increase, but actually drops, as people watch more and more televised hockey (perhaps because viewing hockey could serve to release and thus reduce aggressive urges), then we would be predicting a negative correlation. When the variables are negatively correlated, higher scores on one variable are related to lower scores on another variable. **Figure 2-5** shows various such relationships.

In addition to looking at the positive or negative sign, we must consider the value of the number in the correlation coefficient. The number tells the size, or strength, of the relationship between variables—that is, how well we can predict one variable if we know the other. The larger the number, the stronger the relationship. Thus, a correlation coefficient of 0 means that there is no linear relationship between the two variables. Knowing a person's score on one variable tells you nothing about the person's score on the other. The farther a correlation coefficient gets from 0 in either the positive or negative direction, the stronger the relationship between the two variables. A high positive correlation coefficient means that scores on the two variables under examination typically rise and fall together, and a high negative correlation coefficient means that a rise in one of the variables usually is accompanied by a fall in the other. A correlation of −1.00 or +1.00 is known as a perfect correlation, one in which the variables' scores are always perfectly related. One score always rises or falls in direct proportion to the changes in the other variable.

correlation predictable relationship between two or more variables.

correlation coefficient statistic expressing the strength and nature of a relationship between two variables.

positive correlation relationship in which, on average, scores on two variables increase together.

negative correlation relationship in which, on average, scores on one variable increase as scores on another variable decrease.

perfect correlation one in which two variables are exactly related, such that low, medium, and high scores on both variables are always exactly related.

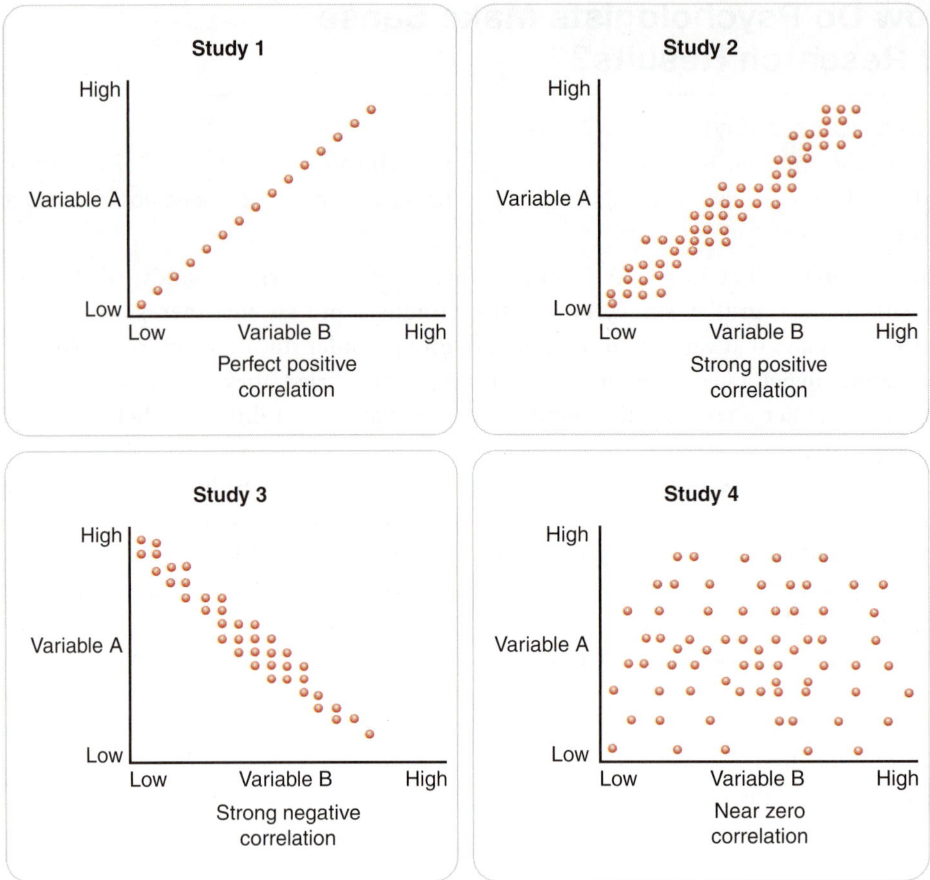

FIGURE 2-5 Graphing correlations. If we were to plot each participant's score on Variable A and Variable B on a graph, we would see that the variables display a perfect positive correlation in Study 1, strong positive correlation in Study 2, strong negative correlation in Study 3, and near zero correlation in Study 4.

Again, it is important to keep in mind that in correlation coefficients, the positive and negative sign and the number itself provide two different pieces of information. A correlation with a negative coefficient is not weaker than one with a positive coefficient. In fact, the relationship may be stronger if, for example, the negative correlation is −0.7 and the positive correlation is +0.2. A negative correlation of −0.7 would mean that the two variables are quite strongly related in such a way that low scores on one variable very often are associated with high scores on the other (see **Figure 2-6**).

+1.00	Perfect positive relationship
+.88	Very strong positive relationship
+.62	Strong positive relationship
+.38	Moderate positive relationship
+.12	Weak positive relationship
0.00	No relationship
−.12	Weak negative relationship
−.38	Moderate negative relationship
−.62	Strong negative relationship
−.88	Very strong negative relationship
−1.00	Perfect negative relationship

FIGURE 2-6 How to read a correlation coefficient. The sign of the coefficient tells us the direction and the number tells us the magnitude, or strength, of the relationship between two variables.

In psychology, really exciting relationships are often reflected by a correlation coefficient of 0.3 and above. This is far from a perfect correlation, largely because relationships between behaviours, thoughts, and emotions can be so complex and because so many other variables may also be at work in such relationships. Nevertheless, 0.3 or above typically means that the two variables in question do indeed have some kind of predictable relationship.

Correlations offer lots of useful information, particularly when we are interested in the scientific goal of prediction (Girden & Kabacoff, 2011). The correlation coefficient tells us just how well we can use one piece of information about someone, such as how much the person watches televised hockey, to predict his or her behaviour in another realm, in this case aggressive behaviour. One key piece of information correlations do *not* tell us, however, is *causality* (Remler & Van Ryzin, 2011). That is, they do not shed light on whether or not a change in one variable actually causes the change in the other (see **Figure 2-7**). As we mentioned earlier, only experimental studies and experimental analyses can tell us whether causality is at work.

You may have already made the connection, but the descriptive approach to psychological research described earlier in this chapter is also called correlational research, as

PSYCHOLOGY AROUND US Don't Be Fooled

Every month, it seems, new studies tie happiness to certain kinds of jobs. One study, for example, found that people who work as clergy, firefighters, physical therapists, architects, special education teachers, and airplane pilots tend to be happier than other workers (GSS, 2007). Meanwhile, people who work as service station attendants, roofers, machine operators, labourers, hotel maids, and kitchen workers were found to be less happy than most other workers.

So what can we conclude from such studies? Not all that much, it turns out. Most important, we cannot conclude, despite the exclamations of news anchors and popular magazines, that certain jobs *produce* more (or less) happiness than others.

The problem is that the findings from studies of jobs and happiness usually are correlational. As such, they don't tell us what *causes* the relationship. In fact, jobs and happiness may be correlated for any one of three reasons:

1. Certain jobs do in fact cause more happiness, the preferred interpretation of news anchors and magazines. That is, working as a firefighter may in fact make you particularly happy in life, while working as a service station attendant may make you particularly unhappy.
2. Happiness may cause people to seek certain jobs. Perhaps happy people are more likely than unhappy people to seek work as clergymen, special education teachers, or airline pilots.
3. Job choice and level of happiness may each be caused by a third variable, such as financial security. Perhaps lack of money causes certain people to be unhappy and, independently, causes those same people to work as machine operators, hotel maids, and kitchen workers.

Of course, it may well be that some jobs are more satisfying and produce more happiness than others. It's just that we need more correlational studies to nail down that causal relationship.

it often involves looking at the relationships among variables using correlation statistics. Researchers using these approaches to their data are appropriately cautious about drawing conclusions about causality when using correlations. However, they also know that over a number of studies, correlations can help us narrow down the causal factors that could be at work in the situations we are studying. For example, Andrew Harrell at the University of Alberta (Harrell, 1981) found that general tolerance for violence was more strongly positively correlated with verbal hostility while watching hockey than was frequency of exposure to hockey. This suggests that just watching hockey or lots of hockey may not be a significant causal factor in increasing aggressiveness, unless the people involved are already tolerant of violence. So correlational research can and does help us narrow down the causal possibilities in the behaviour we are studying.

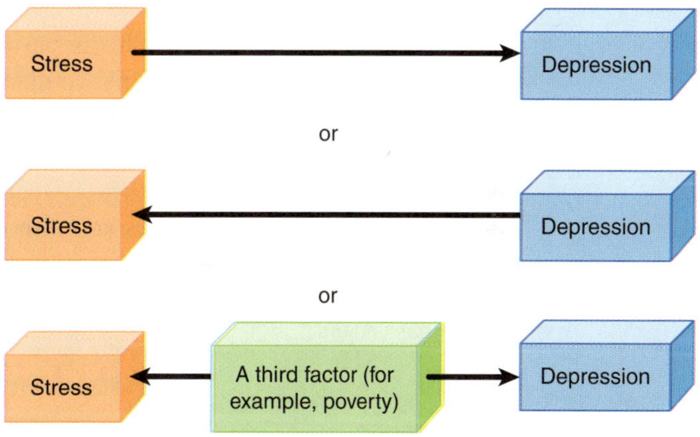

FIGURE 2-7 Correlation versus causation. Research has found a strong correlation between stress and clinical depression. However, this correlation does not tell us whether stress causes depression, depression causes stressful events, or other factors, such as poverty, produce both stress and depression.

Experimental Analyses: Establishing Cause and Effect

If you want to examine differences between groups and determine the cause of such differences, you have to do a particular kind of statistical analyses. Collectively, these are called *experimental analyses* because they are associated with experiments. Researchers sometimes divide experimental analyses into two categories: *descriptive statistics*, which describe or summarize the data gathered from a study, and *inferential statistics*, which tell researchers what they can conclude, or infer, more broadly from their results (for more information, see pages 709–712 in Appendix A).

In order to describe differences between the scores of experimental groups and control groups, researchers calculate the *mean* and *standard deviation* of each group. The **mean** is the arithmetic average of the scores of all participants in a group. This is the same average you've been calculating since Grade 4 math class. Big differences between the mean—the

mean arithmetic average of a set of scores.

Correlation versus causality. The repeated co-occurrence of two events (correlation) does not necessarily mean that one is causing the other. Children who eat ice cream, for example, tend to have bike accidents. It may be that eating ice cream while riding causes young bikers to have more accidents. Or, it may be that parents typically treat their children to ice cream whenever they have accidents. Or, perhaps hot summer days lead to increases in both ice cream eating and bike riding.

average score—of an experimental group and the mean of a control group may indeed suggest big differences between the participants in the groups.

standard deviation statistical index of how much scores vary within a group.

To be certain of this, however, researchers also look at the **standard deviation**, an index of how much the participants' scores *vary* from one another within each group. Suppose, for example, you have ten control-group participants who watch a soccer game and then obtain scores of 4, 5, 4, 6, 5, 4, 4, 7, 5, and 6 on an aggressiveness scale, and ten experimental-group participants who watch *Hockey Night in Canada*, then obtain scores of 1, 2, 12, 11, 5, 9, 4, 1, 3, and 2. Each group would have a mean score of 5 aggressiveness points. Unless you also examine the standard deviations for both groups (1.05 for the control group and 4.20 for the experimental group), you might not realize that there are more extreme reactions in the *Hockey Night in Canada* group than in the other group (see **Figure 2-8**).

Aggressiveness

Soccer game		*Hockey Night in Canada*
4		1
5		2
4		12
6		11
5		5
4		9
4		4
7		1
5		3
6		2
5 ←	*Mean*	→ *5*
1.05 ←	*Standard deviation*	→ *4.20*

FIGURE 2-8 **Variability and the standard deviation.** Although these two sets of data have the same mean, or average, score of aggressiveness in our fictitious study, viewers of *Hockey Night in Canada* are much more varied in their aggressiveness scores (high standard deviation) than are viewers of soccer (low standard deviation).

After determining the mean and standard deviation of each group, researchers can compare the two groups. Psychologists typically compare means using statistical procedures known as *t-tests* (for two groups) or *analyses of variance* (for two or more groups). These procedures look both at the mean differences and at the variance within the groups, as well as at the size of the groups. The statistical procedures are known as significance tests because they measure whether the differences found between groups are *statistically significant*.

In statistics, the word *significant* has a slightly different meaning from most people's everyday use of the same word. A test of statistical significance tells us how likely it is that the differences found between groups are due to experimental manipulations rather than due to chance. Such tests indicate this likelihood by calculating a *probability statistic*. If a test of statistical significance yields a probability statistic of

$p < .05$, it means that if researchers were to conduct the same study 100 times, they would, by chance alone, get the same result found in the current study less than 5 percent of the time, if there really were no difference between the populations from which the samples were obtained. In other words, there's an extremely low probability that the result found in the current study occurred simply as a random act of chance. Most likely, it occurred because of a real difference between the two groups of subjects in the study. By convention, when a test of statistical analysis yields a probability of less than .05 ($p < .05$), psychological researchers conclude that the difference they have found between groups in their study is statistically significant—there is likely to be a real difference that is due to the manipulations carried out in the study.

Analyzing the results. A big part of conducting good research is knowing how to properly handle the numbers gathered and the findings they represent.

Keep in mind that the numerical difference between group means and the probability statistic says nothing about how big an effect you're seeing in your study. Let's say that participants who watch *Hockey Night in Canada* later display a higher mean aggressiveness score than do those who watch soccer, and that the probability statistic is less than 0.01 ($p < .01$). This does not necessarily mean that the hockey viewers have become much more aggressive than the non-viewers. It just means that there's less than 1 chance in 100 that you obtained that result by chance. If you want to know how big the effect of watching hockey is, you need to calculate yet another statistic, known as *effect size*, which describes the strength of the relationship between two variables. If you were to find a large effect size in your study, it would suggest that watching hockey strongly increases aggressive behaviour (for more information, see pages 711–712 in Appendix A).

Using Statistics to Evaluate and Plan Research

If you get a result like this—a difference between groups that is very unlikely to have occurred by chance—does it mean you have fully supported your hypothesis and should sit back and toast your success? Well, not yet. Scientists need to be sure. They need to go back and test their hypotheses some more. It is only through **replication**, taking the data from one observation and expanding on it to see if it holds up under multiple conditions and in multiple samples, that we can determine whether what we hypothesize is correct. Over time, replication enables hypotheses to become theories and theories to become laws.

replication repeated testing of a hypothesis to ensure that the results you achieve in one experiment are not due to chance.

Another important part of science is to use different research methods to explore the same research question (McGrath, 2011). If researchers use several approaches, including surveys, experimentation, and independent observations, and obtain the same results, they can be more certain that their hypotheses are accurate and have confidence about incorporating those hypotheses into theories.

As we described earlier in our discussion of the scientific method, a theory is also a framework to generate additional hypotheses. If your hypothesis about *Hockey Night in Canada* proves correct, and people on average report themselves to be more aggressive and exhibit more aggressive behaviours on experimental tasks after watching hockey, you have reason to continue your line of research. You can conduct the same experiment with other sports shows, such as football or boxing, and see whether the hypothesis continues to hold up for all kinds of aggressive or violent sports. You may also decide to look at other forms of social behaviour besides aggressiveness, such as empathy or sense of fair play. If you continue to replicate these results with other sports and other social behaviours, you are effectively supporting the theory that watching *Hockey Night in Canada* in fact contributes to increased aggressive behaviour within Canadian culture. A Nobel Prize (or perhaps the Order of Canada) is inevitable.

PRACTICALLY SPEAKING Tips on Reading a Scientific Journal Article

As a psychology student, particularly if you major in psychology, you will most likely read journal articles for some of your required classes. Initially, this task may seem overwhelming. The authors of journal articles tend to use unfamiliar language, condense complex concepts into a small space, and make assumptions about the reader's knowledge of their topic. However, you can turn this task into something interesting and worthwhile by following a few simple steps.

When you read a research paper, try to understand the scientific contributions the authors are making. You should read the paper critically and not assume that the authors are always correct.

You do not need to read the paper sequentially to get the gist of it. First, you might read the abstract, the introduction, and the conclusions. Next, look through the references to determine whose work is at the root of the current research. After this first read-through, try to summarize the article in one or two sentences.

Then, go back and read the entire paper from beginning to end. Study the figures, re-read parts that are difficult to understand, and look up unfamiliar words. Make notes in the margins or on separate sheets of paper. And answer the following questions as you work:

- **Title:** What does this tell you about the problem?
- **Abstract:** What does this general overview tell you about the current paper?
- **Introduction:** What are the authors' assumptions, important ideas, and hypotheses?
- **Methods:** Do the methods seem to effectively test the authors' hypotheses?
- **Related work:** How does the current work relate to past work? What is new or different about the current study?
- **Conclusions:** What were the study's results, and do they make sense? What were the study's limitations? What do the authors propose for future research? How does the study contribute to a better understanding of the problem?

You also may choose to outline, summarize, or keep more detailed notes, especially if you are using the article for a term paper.

Before You Go On

www.wiley.com/go/comer

What Do You Know?

10. What two pieces of information does a correlation coefficient give about the relationship between variables?
11. What do the mean and standard deviation tell you about scores of a group?
12. What do *t*-tests tell experimenters?

What Do You Think?

What are some examples of positive and negative correlations that you have observed in everyday life?

SCAN TO GET THE ANSWERS

What Ethical Research Guidelines Do Psychologists Follow?

LEARNING OBJECTIVE 5

Tell what ethical steps psychologists take to protect the rights of human research participants.

Today, psychological research must be designed with the goal of protecting the participants (human or animal) involved with the study. Psychology researchers are bound by the same broad ethical principles that govern doctors and other clinicians. The Code of Ethics of the Canadian Psychological Association states it clearly: "psychologists have a higher duty of care to members of society than the general duty of care that all members of society have to each other" (Canadian Code of Ethics for Psychologists, 2000).

Research ethics in Canada are guided by a joint statement on the ethics of research involving human participants created by the three main research grant agencies: the Medical Research Council of Canada (MRC), the Natural Science and Engineering Research Council of Canada (NSERC), and the Social Sciences and Humanities Research Council of Canada (SSHRC). To ensure that researchers follow proper ethical practices, **research ethics boards (REBs)** provide oversight in academic and other research settings across the world. Any institution (university, private corporation, government agency, or medical school) conducting research involving human participants is expected to appoint an REB, which consists of a mixture of researchers from inside and outside the field. REBs examine research proposals and rule on the potential risks and benefits of each study's procedures (CIHR, NSERC, SSHRC, 1998). If the risk or discomfort associated with a proposed study is deemed to outweigh the potential scientific benefit from the study, then the undertaking

research ethics board (REB) research oversight group that evaluates research to protect the rights of participants in the study.

PSYCHOLOGY AROUND US A Notorious Project

Between 1957 and 1964, a psychiatrist named Donald Cameron working at Allen Memorial Institute at McGill University worked under a contract with the American Central Intelligence Agency (CIA) as part of a larger project called MKULTRA (Collins, 2002; Klein, 2007). As part of that project, Cameron administered LSD (a drug that influences brain neurochemistry and produces hallucinations) and electroconvulsive therapy (ECT, a shock delivered to the brain that induces epileptic seizures) to mental patients who had entered the institute with relatively minor mental health issues, such postpartum depression or anxiety disorders.

Linda Macdonald was one of those participants. In 1963 she checked into a Canadian institution to be treated for fatigue and depression. Six months later, she couldn't read, write, cook a meal, or make a bed. She did not remember her husband, her five children, or any of the first 26 years of her life. During her stay, Ms. Macdonald was given massive doses of various drugs, put into a drug-induced sleep for 86 days, given more than 100 electroconvulsive treatments, and exposed to "psychic driving," a technique in which repetitive taped messages were played for her 16 hours a day. The purpose was not to treat this woman's depression, but to gather information about the causes and effects of brainwashing (Davis, 1992; Powis, 1990).

During this project, the drugs and ECT were administered without the patients' consent and were not primarily intended to treat their conditions. Instead, they were used to examine the drug's and ECT's potential effectiveness as interrogation or mind control techniques. The patients sustained permanent damage as a result of their treatments, including loss of identity or loss of speech, and loss of memory. When this work was made public by the TV show *the fifth estate* in 1985, it was discovered that the Canadian government was aware of the research. The patients were unable to sue the CIA for their treatment, but they did eventually receive a $100,000 payment from the Canadian government.

These sorts of horror stories illustrate the potential for serious harm in some psychological studies. Participants need to be clearly informed about just what they are getting into, and that they have the right to refuse or discontinue involvement in research at any point. It also shows the need for a set of strict guidelines regarding the ethical treatment of research participants and the ethical design and conduct of psychological experiments.

is rejected. REBs generally require that psychologists studying human participants take the following steps to protect human participants:

informed consent requirement that researchers give as much information as possible about the purpose, procedures, risks, and benefits of the study so that a participant can make an informed decision about whether or not to participate.

- *Obtain informed consent.* **Informed consent** from participants requires that researchers give as much information as possible about the purpose, procedures, risks, and benefits of a study, so participants can make informed decisions about whether they want to be involved in the study (Nagy, 2011). If participants include children, researchers must obtain informed consent from both the parents or caregivers and the child.
- *Protect participants from harm and discomfort.* In addition to medical or physical risks, such as those faced by the patients in Cameron's experiments, researchers must avoid putting participants in situations that could cause them undue emotional stress, for example.
- *Protect confidentiality.* Researchers must have in place, and explain to participants, careful plans to protect information about the identities of participants and the confidentiality of their research responses.
- *Participation must be voluntary.* Researchers must make it clear that participants have the right to decide not to participate in the study and that their decision will in no way affect their treatment or involvement in a related class or any other activity. Further, participants have the right to end their participation at any point or to decline to answer any particular questions during the study.
- *Provide complete debriefing.* In some cases, if participants were to have full knowledge about the purposes and goals of a study before it began, their responses during the study might be influenced by that knowledge. Researchers often try to balance giving participants enough information before a study to protect their rights, yet withholding information that may affect participants' responses. Thus, at the end of a study, researchers are required to offer a **debriefing** to participants—an information session during which they reveal any information that was withheld earlier.

debriefing supplying full information to participants at the end of their participation in a research study.

In addition to ruling on the costs and benefits of the study, research ethics boards also assess other issues. They look, for example, at the compensation individuals receive

Consent has its limits. To protect children who participate in studies, researchers must also obtain informed consent from their parents or caregivers.

for their participation (to make sure that participants are not tempted to participate in potentially dangerous studies by high levels of compensation), and they determine whether particular groups (such as men, women, or members of minority ethnic groups) are singled out unnecessarily.

As a result of these ethical guidelines, several of the older "classic" psychological studies we will discuss later in this book would not be approved by a university REB. See if you can identify which studies these are and why when we discuss them.

> "The purpose of psychology is to give us a completely different idea of the things we know best."
>
> —*Paul Valery, French poet and essayist*

The ethical research guidelines we have discussed so far cover research with human beings. However, as you may already know, or will find out shortly (in Chapter 4), a lot of research in psychology involves the use of animals as participants. Animal rights advocates point out that animals are especially vulnerable research participants, since they cannot give their consent to be part of a study. They also argue that animals may be exposed to more extreme risks than humans, for sometimes unclear benefits.

Psychologists take their ethical obligations towards animal research participants very seriously. The Canadian Council on Animal Care (1989) has crafted a set of ethical guidelines for research involving animals and works to ensure that the guidelines are followed. Its code includes the following points:

- "The use of animals in research, teaching, and testing is acceptable ONLY if it promises to contribute to understanding of fundamental biological principles, or to the development of knowledge that can reasonably be expected to benefit humans or animals."
- Animals should be used only if the researcher's best efforts to find an alternative have failed.

Facts and Figures on Animal Research

As will be clear as we move through this book, research in psychology is conducted with both human and animal participants. Research involving animals has been the focus of scrutiny and debate in recent years. The importance of animal research to our psychological understanding means that we need to clarify some important facts and figures about animal research (CCAP, 1989).

1. The welfare of animal subjects is of great interest and concern not only to animal activists, but also to animal researchers, government agencies, scientific organizations, and the public.
2. Around 8 percent of psychological research involves the use of animals; 90 percent of the animals used are rodents and birds (mostly rats and mice); only 5 percent are monkeys and other primates.
3. Every regulated institution that conducts animal research must be certified by the Canadian Council on Animal Care, which carefully reviews and oversees all such studies at their institution. The CCAC ensures that each study follows all ethical, legal, and humane guidelines, and the council pays close attention to such issues as the prevention or alleviation of animal pain, alternatives to the use of animals, and the clinical and scientific importance of the study.
4. In surveys (Hagelin, Carlsson, & Hau, 2003), 75 percent of the public say that they can accept animal research as long as it is for scientific purposes—though this level of agreement varies from 29 percent to 100 percent depending on the study. Most respondents even approve of experiments that bring some pain to animals when those investigations are seeking a cure for childhood leukemia, AIDS, or other significant problems.

- Those using animals should employ the most humane methods on the smallest number of appropriate animals required to obtain valid information.
- Other parts of the code seek to limit pain or distress, ensure proper recovery periods, and ensure general humane treatment of animal participants.

All such guidelines—for both animal and human research undertakings—help ensure not only more ethical procedures, but better science as well.

Before You Go On

www.wiley.com/go/comer

What Do You Know?

13. What does a research ethics board do?
14. What is informed consent and how does it relate to debriefing?

What Do You Think?

Are ethical standards different for psychology than those for other sciences? Should they be?

SCAN TO GET THE ANSWERS

Summary

What Is a Science?

LEARNING OBJECTIVE 1 List two core beliefs of science, and describe the steps in the scientific method.

- Science is an approach to knowing the world built on the core principles that (1) the universe operates according to certain natural laws, and (2) these laws are discoverable and testable.
- Science is founded upon the scientific method, a process that moves from making controlled, direct observations to generating progressively broader conclusions and tests and attempting to disprove hypotheses.

Is Psychology a Science?

LEARNING OBJECTIVE 2 Compare and contrast psychology with other natural sciences, such as biology, chemistry, and physics, and with pseudosciences, such as astrology.

- Psychology shares with every science the primary goals of describing, explaining, predicting, and controlling the objects of study. The goals of psychology differ from those of other sciences because the search for elements of mental processes and behaviour is complicated by constantly shifting human factors.
- Psychology also shares more similarity with the fields of religion and philosophy than many sciences do because psychological findings are more often associated with values, morality, and personal preference.
- Psychology is different from pseudopsychology. Although the latter also attempts to answer fundamental questions about human nature and behaviour, it has no basis in the scientific method.

How Do Psychologists Conduct Research?

LEARNING OBJECTIVE 3 List steps in the research process and key characteristics of descriptive and experimental psychological research methods.

- Psychological research is rooted in first generating a hypothesis, or prediction, about the relationship between two or more variables based on observations.
- Psychologists conduct research with a sample, a small group meant to represent the larger population of interest. The best means of selecting a sample is random selection, a procedure in which everyone in the population has an equal chance of being selected to be in the sample.
- Descriptive research methods include case studies, naturalistic observations, and surveys.
- Case studies are in-depth observations of a single individual.
- Naturalistic observation involves observing people in settings outside of laboratories where their behaviour occurs naturally.

- Surveys may be conducted in interviews or with questionnaires.
- Only experiments allow researchers to draw conclusions about cause-and-effect relationships.
- All research methods have advantages for particular uses and all are subject to various drawbacks. Researchers must plan carefully to avoid subject bias, researcher bias, and demand characteristics.

How Do Psychologists Make Sense of Research Results?

LEARNING OBJECTIVE 4 Tell what information is conveyed by statistics, including correlation coefficients, means, and standard deviations, and explain how psychologists draw conclusions about cause and effect.

- Correlations allow us to describe and measure relationships between two or more variables. A *correlation coefficient* tells the direction and size of a correlation.
- Researchers use the mean and standard deviation to describe and summarize their results.
- Researchers use *p values* to determine the statistical significance of results. *Effect size* tells how strong the relationship is between variables.
- Replication of experiments and repeated study of the same predictions using different methods help hypotheses become theories.

What Ethical Research Guidelines Do Psychologists Follow?

LEARNING OBJECTIVE 5 Tell what ethical steps psychologists take to protect the rights of human research participants.

- Today, oversight boards called research ethics boards (REBs) help to protect human rights.
- Psychological researchers must obtain informed consent from human participants, protect them from harm and discomfort, protect their confidentiality, and completely debrief them at the end of their participation.
- The use of animal participants in research has also raised ethical concerns. An oversight council called the Canadian Council on Animal Care (CCAC) works to protect animals' needs and comfort in experiments.

Key Terms

biases 40
case study 49
control group 51
correlation 53
correlation coefficient 53
debriefing 60
deductive reasoning 39
dependent variable 47
descriptive research methods 49
double-blind procedure 52
empirical 40
experiment 51
experimental group 51
Hawthorne effect 50
hypothesis 40
hypothetico-deductive reasoning 40
independent variable 47
inductive reasoning 40
informed consent 60
mean 55
naturalistic observation 49
negative correlation 53
operationalize 47
perfect correlation 53
positive correlation 53
random selection 48
replication 57
research ethics board (REB) 59
sample 48
standard deviation 56
survey 50
theories 40
variable 46

CHAPTER 3

Human Development

CHAPTER OUTLINE

COULD YOU GROW UP WITHOUT PARENTS?

What is your earliest memory? According to Carole Peterson and her colleagues at Memorial University in St. John's, Newfoundland (2005), most people's earliest memory is usually something that happened when they were around 3 years old, and it is usually a family event involving parents, siblings, or other family members. The birth of siblings is often remembered as young as 2 years of age, perhaps because it is more significant. Beyond a significant event or two, however, we recall little of our earliest years.

Given that we can remember basically none of our first years, how important can our early experiences actually be for our development as individuals? How important is it to have one or more attentive parents looking after us and making sure that all of our physical, social, and emotional needs are being met? Psychologists are pretty sure parents *are* important, but can we examine this question experimentally? Not ethically.

However, what if we found a large number of infants and children who, for varying amounts of time—from weeks to months to years—were living in conditions where there was only one person caring for up to 18 children at a time, where each child spent 18 to 20 hours a day in a crib without any human contact whatsoever, even being fed by bottles propped on pillows. How do you think children raised in such deprived circumstances would turn out as they grew up? Elinor Ames, a retired developmental psychologist and researcher at Simon Fraser University in Burnaby, B.C., discovered a natural opportunity to study just such an occurrence. In the early 1990s, as a result of social policies, a great many infants in Romania were given to state-run orphanages. The infants lived in the impoverished conditions described above. Once word of their situation got out internationally, many people, including many Canadians, tried to adopt Romanian orphans to help them escape the isolation and deprivation that characterized their lives. A number of Canadian families were successful, and many Romanian orphans joined families in Canada. Ames studied the progress of a number of these orphans (Chisholm, Carter, Ames, Morison, & Sara, 1995; Morison, Ames, Chisholm, & Kim, 1995; Fisher, Ames, Chisholm, & Savoie, 1997).

How did things work out? For some (about one-third of the children), things turned out well. These children were more likely to have been adopted before 4 months of age than were the two-thirds of children who did not fare as well. All of the children were somewhat developmentally delayed (behind where other infants their age would be) when they first arrived, but many (two-thirds) made up their relative developmental delays within the first six months. Some of the developmental problems encountered were a

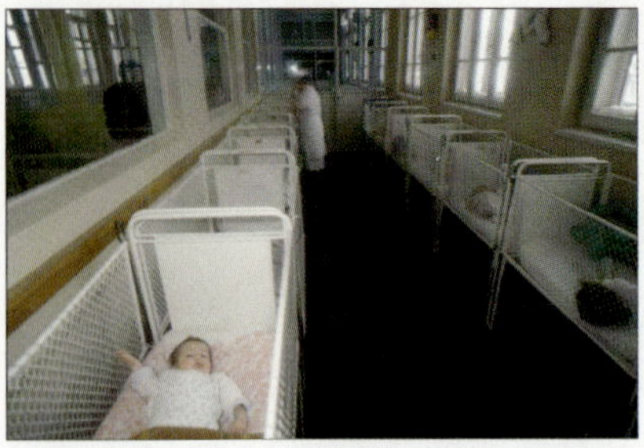

Romanian orphanages. Children in these Romanian orphanages were often left in cribs by themselves all day, without any human contact. What effects do you think this would have on a child's development?

refusal of solid food, and some did not seem to know when to stop eating (they had never been given more than they could eat at a single meal before). Many of them took longer than usual to develop basic social skills, and about one-third of them continued to have trouble getting along socially with peers into grade school. Children in this group also tended to show indiscriminately friendly behaviour toward strangers (Ames & Chisholm, 2001). And unfortunately, some of the orphans continue to struggle today.

Most of the Romanian orphans now in Canada are doing relatively well, but Ames's research shows us that the parental (or caregiver) attention we get—which was *not* provided by the Romanian orphanages—plays an important role in the development of basic social skills, even if we don't remember it at all.

developmental psychology the study of changes in behaviour and mental processes over time and the factors that influence the course of those constancies and changes.

If you were charting the development of vulnerable infants, what would you focus on? Unlike other fields in psychology, which often focus on what a person is like at a particular moment in his or her life, **developmental psychology** is interested in how our behaviour and mental processes change over time and how various factors influence the characteristics that change and those that remain relatively stable. In the case of the Romanian children adopted by Canadian families, developmental psychologists might wonder whether variables such as age of adoption, extent of pre-adoption neglect, and level of stimulation provided by the adoptive parents might play a role in their developmental outcomes.

In addition to noticing similarities between groups of people, developmental psychologists are interested in differences between individuals. For example, would being adopted into a family that initially speaks a language other than Romanian affect a child's cognitive or emotional and social development? This question would be relevant to many, if not all, of the orphans. However, assessing whether the number of other children or the age of the other children in the family would make a difference to a given child's developmental outcome is more specific to a given individual.

Thinking about the development of Romanian orphans is interesting, but so is considering our own origins. What happened to make you into the woman or man that you have become? Was it genes? Parents? Friends? Or perhaps other, more individualized factors, led to you being where you are right at this moment. Do changes occur because of biological factors or because of our experiences? Are we all destined to turn into copies of our mothers or fathers (and would that be a good or a bad thing)?

Unfortunately, development is too complex and depends on too many influences that steer the course of our lives in one direction or another for developmental psychologists to state with precision what causes us to be the way we are (Jensen, 2011). Instead, they try to identify several general factors that work together to influence how we grow and change over the lifespan.

It's worth noting that the terms *developmental psychology* and *child psychology* have often been treated interchangeably. However, a revolution has occurred over the last few years, and developmental psychologists now acknowledge that developmental changes do not stop when we leave childhood (see **Table 3-1**).

TABLE 3-1 Developmental Stages Over the Lifespan

Stage	Approximate Age
Prenatal	Conception to birth
Infancy and toddlerhood	Birth to 2 years
Early childhood	2–6 years
Middle childhood	6–12 years
Adolescence	12–20 years
Emerging adulthood	20–25 years
Young adulthood	25–45 years
Middle adulthood	45–60 years
Later adulthood	60 years to death

In fact, *lifespan developmental psychology* involves the study of the entire course of human life, from conception to death. For instance, in the Lifespan Development program at the University of Victoria, researchers look at how individual, genetic, social, and historical forces influence the entire course of development, or at least those parts of it that are of particular interest to individual researchers. As we will see later in this chapter, a trend toward a longer human lifespan and a growing interest in the lifespan developmental perspective has also given rise to fields of study such as *gerontology* and the *psychology of aging* (Overton & Lerner, 2010).

"We worry about what a child will become tomorrow, yet we forget that he is someone today."
—*Stacia Tauscher, author*

We will also need to talk about how things go wrong, an area in which another revolution has been brewing. A new field of study called *developmental psychopathology* has provided a way to help us think closely about the factors over the course of a lifetime that contribute to one person becoming an empathic law-abiding citizen, and another becoming a self-absorbed criminal. ■

Understanding How We Develop

LEARNING OBJECTIVE 1

Understand the key debates underlying research and theory in child development.

Before we discuss what happens in development, it's useful to consider some of the key issues that concern developmental psychologists. These issues are often foundations for theory, research, and clinical work, but they are not always directly tested. As you read through the rest of the chapter, you may want to think about how the theories we will discuss later fit with these big ideas about human development.

What Drives Change? Nature and Nurture

A key historic debate in human development is how much of our growth, personality, and behaviour is influenced by *nature,* our genetic inheritance, and how much is influenced by *nurture,* a term that encompasses the environment around us as well as our experiences as we grow.

Scientists who take a strong view of the influence of genetics or biology on development are said to view development *endogenously* (Porges & Carter, 2010). That is, they look at development as biologically programmed to happen sequentially, a process known as **maturation**. Other scientists believe that our experiences have a greater influence on how we develop.

maturation the unfolding of development in a particular sequence and time frame.

Thinking back to the Romanian orphans we talked about at the beginning of the chapter, what do you see as the main influence accounting for the difficulties some of them experienced here in Canada? Clearly, while nature may play a role, there is a lot of nurture involved in the difficulties the orphans experienced, both in Romania and in Canada, and in the things that their new Canadian parents were able to do to help them catch up developmentally to their peers.

Nature versus nurture. How much of our growth, personality, and development is attributed to our genetic inheritance or the environment we grow up in is still a key debate in human development.

It is not as easy, however, to attribute the characteristics of people in general to either nature or nurture exclusively. In the real world, our traits and behaviours are almost always influenced by an interaction between such factors. It is better to think of development as an inevitable and ongoing interaction between nature *and* nurture. However, in spite of the clear evidence that nature and nurture work together, some researchers continue to have robust debates about whether nature or nurture factors are more important. You will see that the so-called nature–nurture issue applies not only to specific questions about development, but also to ideas about intelligence (discussed in Chapter 10), social behaviour (Chapter 14), and pretty much all of the psychological disorders that we discuss throughout this text and in Chapter 16.

Qualitative versus Quantitative Shifts in Development

Throughout this chapter, whether we are referring to physical development, social development, or cognitive development, you will notice that we talk a lot about **stages**. A stage is a developmental point or phase within which children, adolescents, or adults think, experience emotions, or behave in particular ways. Stages usually involve *discontinuous* development with clear qualitative differences in thinking or behaviour.

stage a distinct developmental phase in which organisms behave, think, or respond in a particular way that is qualitatively different from the way they responded before.

It is important to understand what is meant by quantitative and qualitative change. *Quantitative change* involves gradual increases in thinking or behaviour. In contrast, when we talk of *qualitative change*, it is not just that we are bigger, faster, or more coordinated, but that we are *different* in some way. For example, a caterpillar can grow little by little into a bigger caterpillar—a quantitative change—but when the caterpillar becomes a butterfly, there has been a qualitative change.

There have been some arguments among developmental researchers about whether or not stages represent qualitative shifts in the growth of individuals (MacNamara, Button, & Collins, 2010; see **Figure 3-1**). Qualitative (stage) theorists would argue that once we acquire language, for example, we think of the world in a different way because we are able to give things names and even to think about things that don't have a concrete reality. Without the word "love," they argue, it would be hard to conceive of the various things that love means, because one cannot point to love or sense it in a direct way (at least not the same way you do a ball or a favourite toy). In the same way, being able to logically organize your mental categories makes for a qualitative difference in how you think about the world.

(a) Qualitative development (b) Quantitative development

FIGURE 3-1 Do stages represent qualitative or quantitative shifts in development? (a) Some theorists believe that individuals make qualitative, discontinuous jumps in development as they move from stage to stage. (b) Others think that development is a steady continuous process.

On the other hand, what looks like qualitative differences at a distance may not appear so upon closer inspection. If you were to walk around an elementary school, you might be struck by the differences you see in the students from one grade level to another. On the other hand, those apparent qualitative differences might actually look like more gradual quantitative differences if you worked at the school and saw the children slowly grow and acquire new skills over the course of a whole academic year. Many theorists believe the individual variations in developmental timing indicate that development often represents more of a quantitative shift. According to these theorists, development is the result of an ongoing acquisition of new information and new experiences. What may seem like big, sudden developmental changes actually are the result of a gradual accumulation of many small changes, often so small that they are hard to notice. For example, theorists and researchers in the quantitative camp believe that walking comes as a result of a series of small developmental changes, including the steady growth of our muscles until they can hold our body weight and the development of our brains until they can control physical coordination (Lloyd et al., 2010).

Quantitative theorists have an easier time accounting for individual differences in the timing of milestones, but a harder time explaining why most people go through similar sequences of development during similar times of life, despite considerable variations in their experiences. As we will see, human development involves both qualitative and quantitative processes.

PSYCHOLOGY AROUND US Around the World

The documentary *Babies* (2010) follows four babies from the day they are born until the day they take their first steps: Ponjiao from Namibia, Bayarjargal from Mongolia, Mari from Japan, and Hattie from the United States. The movie includes no narration. It just shows how each baby develops in response to his or her particular environment.

Not surprisingly, the child-rearing practices in these four countries are very different. Bayarjargal's farmer parents tie him to a post in their yurt (a tent-like home) and leave him alone for much of the day to fend for himself (and be tormented by his brother). Ponjiao plays with sticks and usually shares his mother's lap with another child. Mari, an only child, soaks in all of her parents' attention. Yet the movie suggests that Bayarjargal and Ponjiao are in the process of becoming more active and independent than the wealthier and more closely watched Hattie and Mari.

The filmmakers invite the audience to think about questions like, what makes for a happy, well-adjusted baby? Should parents take a more active, closely observant role in watching over their children, or will that result in children who are overly dependent and less willing to step out on their own? Does a lack of resources necessarily lead to poor developmental outcomes? And . . . just why are babies so darned cute?

Do Early Experiences Matter? Critical Periods and Sensitive Periods

Related to the question of stage theories versus continuous theories of development is the question of whether there are critical periods in development. A **critical period** is a point in development when the organism is extremely sensitive to a particular kind of environmental input that can either encourage or discourage the development of certain brain functions (Anderson et al., 2011). If the environmental input does not occur at a specific point in time, or if a noxious substance or experience is encountered, development will be thrown off track (hence, the term *critical*). For example, an early critical period theorist, Konrad Lorenz (2002, 1971, 1970), found that goslings will forever connect with whatever goose-sized moving stimuli they see most often during the first 36 hours of their lives. In Lorenz's work, he was able to get certain goslings to think of him (or more specifically, his boots) as their mother. He used the term *imprinting* to describe the development of this attachment—the goslings imprinted upon Lorenz. The results are clear in the photo on the next page.

critical periods points in development when an organism is extremely sensitive to environmental input, making it easier for the organism to acquire certain brain functions and behaviours.

Psychologists have long been curious about whether critical periods operate in the lives of human beings. Of course, it would be unethical for researchers to deprive human beings of their usual early experiences to see what would happen, but cases

The followers. Ethology pioneer Konrad Lorenz lead these baby geese into viewing him as their mother by being sure he (or more specifically, his boots) was the first approximately goose-size being they saw when they hatched. For geese, the first 36 hours after birth is a critical learning period during which they become imprinted to their mother—or a mother substitute, in this case.

All is not lost. Early deprivation, such as that experienced by these young children at a Vietnamese orphanage, can result in severe psychological disabilities. Moving the children to more positive and stimulating settings, however, can help many of them to recover at least partially.

of human deprivation—extreme poverty or death of one's parents, for example—do sometimes occur naturally. By studying the histories of children in these adverse situations, researchers have learned that serious psychological disabilities may result from early deprivation (Pollak et al., 2010; Rutter et al., 2010). At the same time, however, other studies have found that subsequent changes in environmental input (for example, removing deprived children from their early negative environments and placing them in more positive ones) can help the children recover partially or, in some cases, completely (Sheridan et al., 2010).

Because individuals can recover at least partially even after deprivation during key time periods in their lives, most of today's psychologists and biologists believe that critical periods are better defined as *sensitive periods*, times when individuals are especially receptive to environmental input, but not rigidly so (Baird, 2010; Michel & Tyler, 2005). Terri Lewis and Daphne Maurier at McMaster University (2005) have studied infants and young children with cataracts and shown that critical and sensitive periods in early life are particularly influential in the development of the visual system. They found that timing for specific aspects of vision varied, with the sensitive period for motion detection being much shorter than those for acuity and peripheral vision. For more complex cognitive and social development, however, theorists today are less inclined to believe that particular environmental experiences are essential during a critical period; instead, they view sensitive periods as largely *experience-driven*, flexible, and with less well-defined boundaries than a critical period (Armstrong et al., 2006).

Before You Go On

www.wiley.com/go/comer

What Do You Know?

1. How do quantitative theories of development differ from qualitative theories of development?
2. What is the difference between a critical period and a sensitive period?

What Do You Think?

Do you see biological or environmental factors as playing more of a major role in your own development?

SCAN TO GET THE ANSWERS

How Is Developmental Psychology Investigated?

LEARNING OBJECTIVE 2

Describe and discuss the advantages and disadvantages of cross-sectional and longitudinal designs for researching development.

PSYCHOLOGY AROUND US "Oh, No! Not the Pencil!"

Any researcher looking to study children immediately runs into trouble. Because children typically lack insight into what factors motivate their behaviour, questionnaires and interviews are often of limited use. Instead, many researchers opt for "impact" studies. Here, they set children up in certain predicaments and see how they handle the unexpected turn of events.

One common impact study looks at how children control and hide their emotions. The researcher asks a child to rank a set of prizes from undesirable to incredibly desirable. The prizes may include pencils, candy, gum, special toys, and the like. Then, the experimenter has the child work through a series of tasks, all the while implying that the favourite prize will be waiting at the end. Finally, at the very end of the session, the experimenter pulls a fast one and presents the child with the prize that had been rated most undesirable. You can imagine the child's disbelief when he or she finally receives the gift from the bottom of their wish list.

Of course, that disbelief is what enables the researcher to observe how the child copes with disappointment. Does the child try to cover up his or her true feelings? Does he or she have an emotional meltdown? (If it makes you feel better, the child usually gets his or her chosen prize at the very end of the experiment.)

As we've noted, developmental psychologists are interested in learning about changes that happen as we age. But how do they go about measuring those changes?

Not all developmental research involves setting up its child participants, like that described in the Psychology Around Us box. Nevertheless, working with children requires researchers to devise a research design that will allow them to assess how individuals change (or remain the same) over time, regardless of what we hope to assess developmentally. One approach is to use the **cross-sectional design**. In this approach, researchers compare groups of different-aged people to one another at a single point in time (Memmert, 2011). For example, they might compare a group of 60-year-olds to a group of 30-year-olds on a memory task to see how memory changes over time. The benefit of the cross-sectional approach is that it's easy and straightforward, as well as convenient, for both researchers and participants.

cross-sectional design a research approach that compares groups of different-aged people to one another.

The big problem with the cross-sectional approach is that it assumes that any changes found in a study are the result of age. Researchers must remember to also consider other factors that might influence their results. Let's say that the task used to measure memory differences between the two age groups mentioned above is computer-based. If the 30-year-olds perform better on the memory task, the researchers might conclude that the results are due to age-related changes in memory. But the findings could be related more to the fact that 30-year-olds are more familiar with and less intimidated by computer technology than some 60-year-olds are.

These sorts of historical differences are called *cohort effects*. A *cohort* is any group of people born at about the same time. As a result of when they were born, the development of people in a particular cohort will be affected by the cultural and historical changes to which they were exposed. Wars, recessions, natural disasters, famines, and anything else that provides particular cohorts with unique experiences or challenges can influence development. If the two groups in your cross-sectional study come from different cohorts, then you cannot be sure whether the differences you see are due to development or cohort differences. For example, several years ago the provincial government in Alberta cut educational funding by reducing the number of hours of kindergarten education that children would be provided with. If we were comparing the development of Alberta children in grades 1 and 3, we might miss the fact that the better school performance of the grade 3 children is at least partially a cohort effect of their longer kindergarten experience, and not entirely due to developmental differences.

Another drawback of cross-sectional research is that it does not provide much explanation of how or when age-related changes may have occurred. For example, if in the memory study researchers find that older participants demonstrate memory declines, the researchers wouldn't know whether the declines occurred suddenly or accumulated gradually over the past 30 years.

longitudinal design a research approach that follows the same people over a period of time by administering the same tasks or questionnaires and seeing how their responses change.

For these reasons, many developmental researchers prefer to use a **longitudinal design** (see **Figure 3-2**). This design allows researchers to follow the same group of people over a long period of time, administering the same tasks or questionnaires to them at different points in their lives to see how their responses change. We will discuss one of the most famous of these longitudinal studies in Chapter 10 when we talk about a long-term longitudinal study of extremely intelligent people (Jolly et al., 2011; Feldhusen, 2003).

The main benefit of longitudinal research is that researchers can be reasonably confident that the observed changes are a function of time and developmental experiences. Unfortunately, longitudinal studies require considerable time and money—the study you'll read about in Chapter 10 went on for 85 years! Moreover, many participants in longitudinal studies drop out of the studies over the course of their lives because they move away, lose interest, become ill, or even die (see **Table 3-2**).

cohort-sequential design blended cross-sectional and longitudinal research, designed to look at how individuals from different age groups compare to one another and to follow them over time.

Seeking to obtain the advantages and avoid the drawbacks of cross-sectional and longitudinal designs, some developmental researchers design studies that combine the two. A **cohort-sequential design** looks at how age groups compare to one another at various points in the research, but also takes a longitudinal approach to see how those differences vary over time (deHaan, Prinzie, & Dekovic, 2010). In a way it is like a series of mini-longitudinal studies, with the end of one study lining up with the start of the next. For example, to compare patterns in alcohol use, one study followed children from three age groups for four years (Duncan, Duncan, & Strycker, 2006). One group was followed from ages 9 to 12, another from ages 11 to 14, and another from ages 13 to 16. By using this design, the researchers could measure any differences between the groups that persisted over time. However, because of the age overlap among groups over time, they could also look at differences that might result from age.

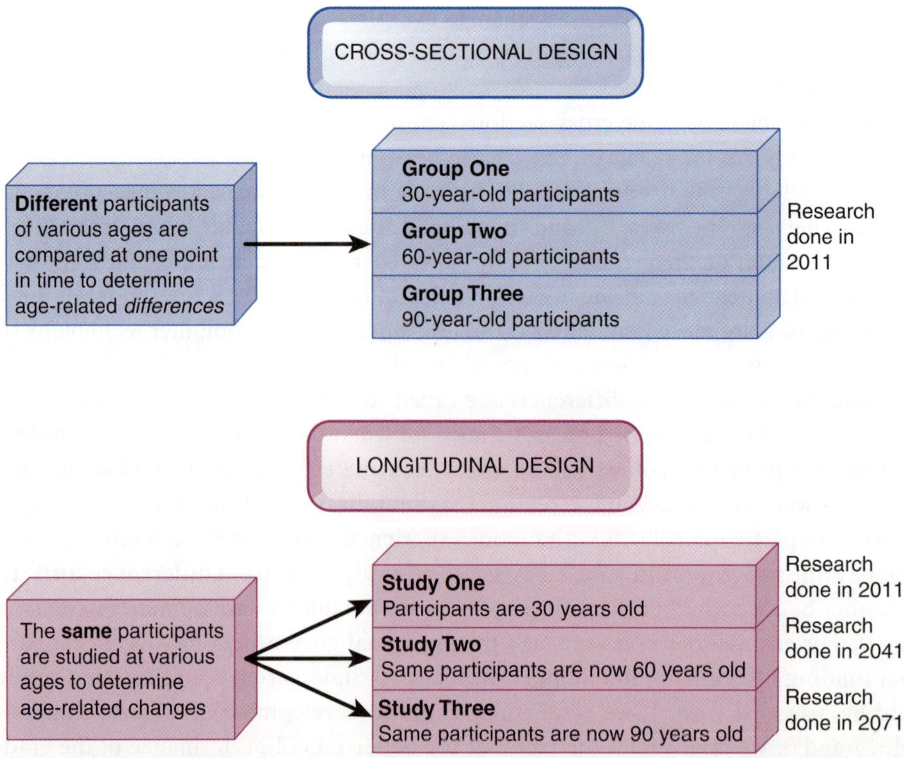

FIGURE 3-2 Cross-sectional versus longitudinal research design. Cross-sectional research studies different participants of various ages at one point in time to examine age-related differences. Longitudinal research studies the *same* participants over a longer period of time to determine age-related changes.

TABLE 3-2 Comparison of Cross-sectional and Longitudinal Research Designs

	Cross-sectional Design	Longitudinal Design
Advantages	• Easy and straightforward • Convenient for both researchers and participants	• Gives reasonably reliable information about age changes • Gives information about the stability or instability of traits • Gives information about the effects of early experiences
Disadvantages	• Cohort effects are difficult to separate • Does not explain how or when changes may have occurred	• Requires considerable time and money • Many participants drop out over the course of study • Cohort effects are not studied as all participants come from the same cohort

Before You Go On

www.wiley.com/go/comer

What Do You Know?

3. What is the main advantage of using a longitudinal design instead of a cross-sectional design?

What Do You Think?

If a researcher today finds differences between a group of 20-year-olds and a group of 70-year-olds, what historical, social, and cultural factors might have contributed to those differences?

SCAN TO GET THE ANSWERS

Before We Are Born

HOW WE DEVELOP

LEARNING OBJECTIVE 3

Discuss patterns of genetic inheritance and describe stages and potential problems during prenatal development.

An enormous amount goes into shaping human development during the **prenatal period**, the nine months or so stretching from conception to birth. Growth during this period happens incredibly quickly. Our biological parents are the starting point for our development by contributing parts of their own genetic inheritance. We will see that the contributions from a mother and a father can form a variety of combinations—some matching exactly, some differing completely.

prenatal period the period of development stretching from conception to birth.

In the Beginning: Genetics

Genes are the most basic building blocks of our biological inheritance (Kagan, 2010). Each gene is composed of a specific sequence of **deoxyribonucleic acid**, or **DNA**, molecules. DNA and genes are arranged in strands called **chromosomes**, found in each cell of our bodies. We each have 23 pairs, or 46 total, chromosomes. Twenty-three chromosomes are contributed by each of our biological parents, and the resulting combination is called our **genotype**, which broadly refers to a person's genetic inheritance. A person's **phenotype** is the observable manifestation of that genotype, the physical and psychological characteristics that are on display in each individual.

It is difficult to determine a person's genotype solely on the basis of his or her phenotype—appearance or behaviour. Consider the ability to roll your tongue. Tongue rolling is genetically determined; either you are born with the ability or you will never have it (McDonald, 2010; Fry, 1988). If you can roll your tongue, you display a tongue-rolling phenotype. Without further information, however, we cannot say exactly what your genotype is. Variations of the same gene, such as the gene for tongue rolling, are called **alleles**. If both parents contribute the same allele, then the person is **homozygous** for the trait—that is, he or she has two matching alleles of the same gene. If you can roll your tongue, you *may* be homozygous for the tongue-rolling gene.

genes basic building blocks of our biological inheritance.

deoxyribonucleic acid (DNA) molecules in which genetic information is enclosed.

chromosomes strands of DNA; each human being has 46 chromosomes, distributed in pairs.

genotype a person's genetic inheritance.

phenotype the observable manifestation of a person's genetic inheritance.

allele variation of a gene.

homozygous both parents contribute the same genetic material for a particular trait.

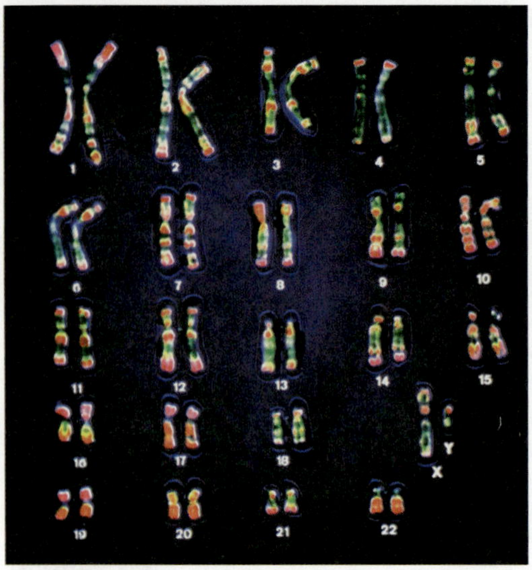

Magical pairs. A person's entire genetic inheritance is contained in 23 pairs of chromosomes, with each parent contributing one chromosome to each pair. Here we see an individual's chromosomes stained with dyes and photographed under a microscope.

To roll or not to roll. In this family, the father can roll his tongue (a dominant trait), while the mother cannot (a recessive trait). As a result, their son displays a tongue-rolling phenotype, which is rooted in a heterozygous tongue-rolling genotype.

It turns out, however, that people can still roll their tongues if they inherit a tongue-rolling allele from one of their parents and a non-rolling allele from the other. In such instances, individuals have the observable phenotype of tongue rolling, but their genotype is **heterozygous**, a combination of two different alleles. Thus, if you can roll your tongue, you are displaying a tongue-rolling phenotype, and this phenotype may reflect either a homozygous or a heterozygous genotype (see **Figure 3-3**).

heterozygous parents contribute two different alleles to offspring.

Genotype :	Homozygous		Heterozygous		Homozygous	
Parent Contributions :	Mother: tongue rolling allele	Father: tongue rolling allele	Mother: tongue rolling allele	Father: non-tongue rolling allele	Mother: non-tongue rolling allele	Father: non-tongue rolling allele
Phenotype :	Tongue rolling trait will be expressed		Tongue rolling trait will be expressed		Tongue rolling trait will not be expressed	

FIGURE 3-3 Genotype versus phenotype. Individuals who are able to roll their tongues may have either a homozygous or a heterozygous genotype for tongue rolling. In contrast, people who cannot roll their tongues must have a homozygous genotype for non-tongue rolling.

Depending on the trait in question, any of three different phenotypes can result when a person has a heterozygous combination of different alleles (adapted from Truett et al., 1994):

- One possibility is that the trait either will be expressed in its entirety or will not be expressed at all. This is the case with heterozygous tongue rolling. If you have one "rolling" allele and one "non-rolling" allele, you will be able to roll your tongue. Tongue rolling is a **dominant trait**, a trait that is expressed in your phenotype regardless of whether your genotype is homozygous or heterozygous for the trait. A **recessive trait**, on the other hand, is one that is expressed in your phenotype only when you are homozygous for that trait. The inability to roll your tongue is recessive. You must have two matching "non-rolling" alleles to be prevented from rolling your tongue.
- For some traits, a person with a heterozygous pair of alleles may show a *mixture* of genetic coding. For example, children of couples who have different racial backgrounds can have features associated with the backgrounds of both parents, such as blended skin colour or eye shape.
- For yet other traits, persons with a heterozygous pair of alleles may express *both* of the parents' genes in their phenotype. This outcome is called **codominance**. An example of codominance is found in blood type. If one parent has blood Type A and the other parent has Type B, the child can express both in the form blood Type AB.

dominant trait a trait that is expressed in a phenotype, no matter whether the genotype is homozygous or heterozygous for the trait.

recessive trait a trait that is only expressed if a person carries the same two genetic alleles (e.g., is homozygous for the trait).

codominance in a heterozygous combination of alleles, both traits are expressed in the offspring.

The thing that makes the study of genetics particularly challenging is that only a few of our traits are **discrete traits**, the product of a single gene pair. Instead, most human traits are **polygenic traits**, ones that involve the combined impact of multiple genes. It is especially likely that traits affecting our behaviour are polygenetic.

discrete trait a trait that results as the product of a single gene pairing.

polygenic trait a trait that manifests as the result of the contributions of multiple genes.

One example of a relatively simple genetic trait is something called PKU (phenolketonuria). This condition is a recessive genetic condition. Infants born with it lack an enzyme called phenylalanine hydroxylase. Without that enzyme they cannot break down an amino acid called phenylalanine. Over time, phenylalanine can build up in the system and cause problems with brain development, potentially leading to an intellectual disability, brain damage, and/or seizures. The good news is that if detected with a simple screening test at birth, PKU can be controlled with diet and no negative developmental effects need occur (James et al., 2006).

As we will see, however, our environment plays a very strong role in determining our development, beginning before we are even born.

PSYCHOLOGY AROUND US Lefties

During the Middle Ages, people who were left-handed were believed to be possessed by the Devil. In later centuries, doctors thought left-handedness was linked with criminal behaviour. Of course, we no longer believe that left-handers are evil. We now know, too, that left-handedness unfolds in the womb. In fact, fetuses show a preference for which hand they keep nearer their mouth.

Researchers have recently found that handedness is, at least partly, a genetically inherited preference. Still, our environment plays a role in how we express that preference. More than a few children, for example, have learned to be "righties" in response to their parents' disapproval of their natural left-handedness. Further complicating matters is the fact that handedness usually is displayed along a continuum. We may prefer one hand over another, but it may not be an absolute preference. We may even shift hands between tasks.

What does appear to be clear from biological evidence is that handedness is linked with brain lateralization, or brain asymmetry. As you will see later in this book, the two halves of the human brain are not exactly alike—that is, they're asymmetrical. In addition, each half has primary control over certain functions. It turns out that lefties and righties differ in which hemisphere controls their particular handedness.

All that said, larger questions remain. Why should there be a connection between brain asymmetry and handedness? Why are our brains asymmetrical in the first place? What about those lefties who learn to become righties?

Birth Order Effects: What's Real?

What is your birth order within your family? Are you a first-born? An only child? A second-born? A third-born? Have you ever explained yourself or others by referring to birth order? "Oh, I'm the middle child, so I just don't feel like I belong." Or perhaps, "he is spoiled and acts out because he's an only child." In reality, the effect of birth order on personality is hotly debated by psychologists, and most of these "effects" may not be strongly supported by research data. In 1996, scientist and scholar Frank Sulloway published the book *Born to Rebel* in which he argued that first-borns tend to be more responsible, while later-borns tend to be more rebellious. He further hypothesized that later-borns tend to be more open to experience and more agreeable than first-borns, and, at the same time, less neurotic, less extraverted, and less conscientious (Jefferson, Herbst, & McCrae, 1998).

Although Sulloway's book was widely praised at first, many psychologists eventually questioned his methodology and noted inconsistencies in his data. Most notably, in 2000, the journal *Politics and the Life Sciences* attempted to publish a special issue devoted to a discussion of Sulloway's book.

The issue was to include articles and commentaries from a number of scholars who rejected or questioned Sulloway's work (Townsend, 2000, p. 135). The debate became so heated that, according to the journal's editor, Sulloway threatened legal action and the publication of the issue was delayed for four years, eventually appearing in 2004.

Scientists typically subject research to peer review, in which an article is read by fellow scientists and intensely scrutinized and revised before it is published. Books, however, do not always have to go through this process, which was one of the criticisms levelled against Sulloway's research (Townsend, 2000). In contrast to Sulloway's findings, a peer-reviewed article that examined over 1,000 birth order studies concluded that birth order does not influence personality in a clear and consistent way (Jefferson et al., 1998).

Research findings on birth order and other areas, such as intelligence and physical features, show somewhat stronger correlations. It has been found, for example, that first-borns tend to score about three points higher on IQ tests compared to second-borns. Similarly, children born earlier in a family are, on average, taller and weigh more than those born later (Kluger, 2007). Canadian researcher Jennifer Davis, as part of her doctoral dissertation at McMaster University (eventually peer reviewed and published; Davis, 1997) showed that first-borns were more driven to attain social status, and that drive decreased as one's place in the birth order within the family decreased.

Despite the fact that birth order studies have not consistently produced clear or compelling findings, the topic remains very popular in the public domain. Indeed, in recent years, *Time* and other newsmagazines have presented several cover stories on the relationship between birth order and psychological and social functioning, an indicator that even though many psychologists believe birth order to be a subject unworthy of research, the public's fascination with the topic continues to grow (Kluger, 2007).

Prenatal Development

zygote a single cell resulting from successful fertilization of the egg by sperm.

Prenatal development begins with *conception*, when a sperm fertilizes an egg, resulting in the creation of a single cell, called a **zygote**. The first two weeks after conception is known as the *germinal stage*. During the first 36 hours of this stage, the single cell zygote divides and becomes two cells. These two cells then divide to become four, those four divide and become eight, and so on. As its cells keep multiplying, the zygote moves up through the mother's Fallopian tube (where it was first fertilized) to her uterus. After the fourth day following conception, the zygote is now referred to as the *blastocyst*. About a week after fertilization, the blastocyst implants itself to the side of the uterus. The other major transition that occurs during the germinal stage is the formation of a nutrient-rich structure called the **placenta**, which attaches to the wall of the uterus. The placenta allows the circulatory system of the mother to interact with the circulatory system of the embryo to exchange oxygen and nutrients through the umbilical cord.

placenta a nutrient-rich structure that serves to feed the developing fetus.

The second stage of the prenatal period is the *embryonic stage* (2 to 8 weeks). Most of the major systems of the body, such as the nervous and circulatory systems, as well as the basic structure of the body, begin to take shape during this stage. It is during this stage that the new organism is most vulnerable to influences that can lead to **miscarriage**, discharge from the uterus before it is able to function on its own, or to the development of defects. Given such possibilities, new parents often wait until the pregnancy has passed well into the last stage, or *fetal stage*, before announcing it (see **Figure 3-4**).

miscarriage discharge of the fetus from the uterus before it is able to function on its own.

The fetal stage lasts from the end of the embryonic stage until the birth of the baby (9 to 40 weeks). The fetus has several characteristics, including a developing muscular and skeletal system, that lead to a sudden ability to move. Especially during the last three months, the fetus' brain begins to grow at a remarkable pace (Dobbing & Sands, 1973). Organs that began to emerge in the embryonic stage now start to function independently, and the fetus begins to hiccup, see, hear, and sleep. All of these functions contribute to the fetus' eventual ability to function independently of the mother.

Prior to Birth — WHEN THINGS GO WRONG

The fetus is vulnerable to any number of problems immediately following conception. As you will see throughout the book, many disorders are inherited from the parents. Some

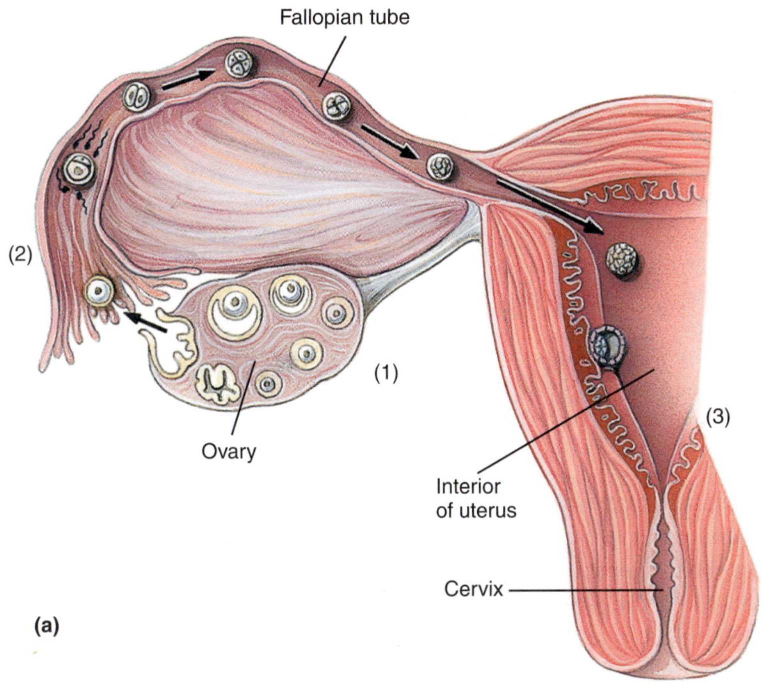

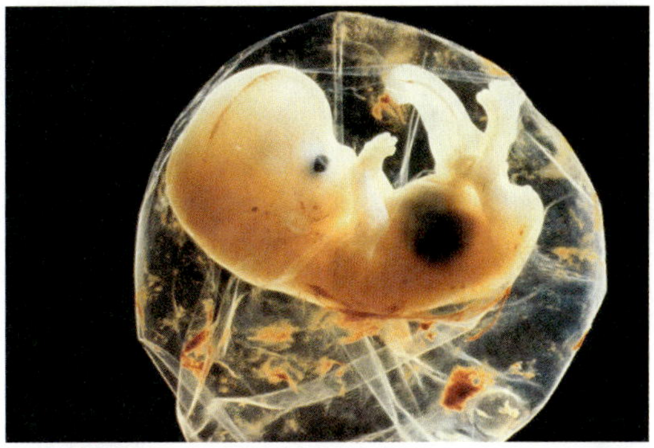

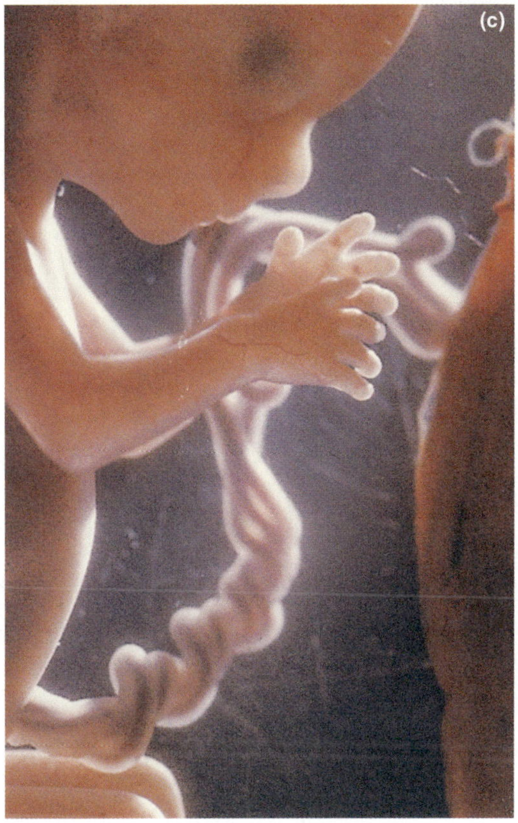

FIGURE 3-4 Prenatal development. ***(a) Germinal period: From ovulation to implantation:*** After the egg leaves the ovary (1), it travels to the opening of the Fallopian tube (2) where it is fertilized and becomes a zygote. About a week later, the zygote reaches the uterus, implants itself in the wall of the uterus (3), and triggers the formation of the nutrient-rich placenta. ***(b) Embryonic stage:*** Once the zygote is implanted it grows rapidly. By 8 weeks, many external body structures and internal organs have been formed. Notice that the head grows faster than the rest of the body. At this stage, the embryo is vulnerable to miscarriage. ***(c) Fetal stage:*** From 8 weeks to birth, the fetus continues to enlarge rapidly and the basic structures undergo substantial change.

of these disorders, such as sickle-cell anemia, cystic fibrosis, or phenylketonuria (PKU), are linked to recessive genes, whereas others, such as MAfan syndrome or Huntington disease, are caused by dominant genes. Still other disorders are linked to chromosomal problems. In Chapter 10, for example, when we talk about intelligence, we will also talk about *Down syndrome*, a pattern caused by the presence of an extra chromosome in the twenty-first chromosome pair.

In addition to genetic and chromosomal problems, a number of environmental agents, called **teratogens**, can negatively influence development during the prenatal period. There are a great number of factors (diseases, toxins, drugs, hormones, etc.) that can interfere with typical prenatal development. The nature and extent of their impact upon the developing fetus vary depending on a number of factors, including the dose of the teratogen, the timing and extent of exposure, and the age of the organism (zygote, embryo, or fetus). Below we list just a few of teratogens along with their potential effects (Shepard & Lemire, 2004):

teratogens any environmental agent that causes damage during gestation.

- Rubella (also known as three-day measles)—over half of the infants exposed during the embryonic period suffer from serious defects such as deafness, intellectual disability, and a number of internal system defects (Eberhart-Phillips, Frederick & Baron, 1993). Infants exposed in the fetal period show fewer physical defects, but are at increased risk of mental illness in adulthood (Brown & Susser, 2002).
- Some other diseases that exert a teratogenic effect are syphilis, genital herpes, and AIDS.
- Smoking at any point in the pregnancy increases the likelihood of a miscarriage or the baby being born low birth weight. Smoking tobacco in pregnancy is also related

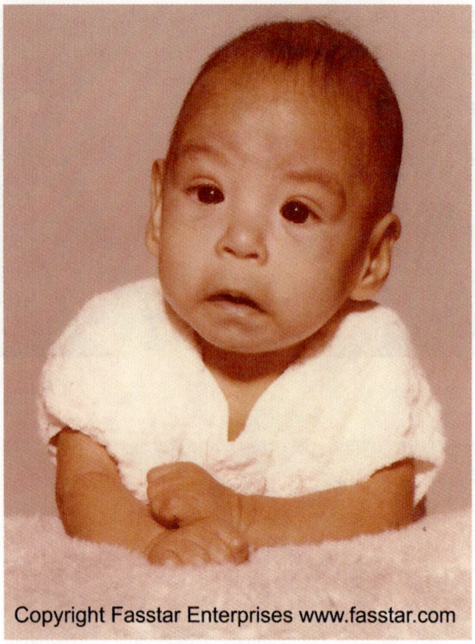

Fetal alcohol syndrome. Caused by early prenatal exposure to alcohol, FAS presents several characteristic facial features.

to other postnatal risks, including premature birth, sudden infant death syndrome, and asthma (Jaakkola & Gissler, 2004).

- Alcohol affects prenatal development at any point in pregnancy, but especially when brain growth is most rapid early in gestation. Drinking alcohol during pregnancy can result in fetal alcohol syndrome (FAS) or fetal alcohol spectrum disorder (FASD), in which neurons do not all end up where they are needed to form the neural networks in the brain. This results in characteristic facial deformities as well as other physical deformities and intellectual disabilities (Caley et al., 2008).
- Heroin use in pregnancy causes babies to be born with low birth weight and addicted to heroin; they must go through withdrawal (Steinhausen, Blattman, & Pfund, 2007).

Pregnant women should avoid risks, such as smoking or ingesting alcohol and other substances, both legal and illegal, all of which have been linked to birth defects. Even soft cheeses and deli meats can pose certain risks because of the possibility of contracting listeria (during the Maple Leaf tainted deli meat recall of 2008, as many as 10 Canadian adults died from ingesting these meats before the exact cause of the problem was identified), a bacterium that can put the fetus at significant risk (CDC, 2010; Guevara, 2008; Stehlin, 1996).

Before You Go On

www.wiley.com/go/comer

What Do You Know?

4. What are the possible phenotypic outcomes from a heterozygous genotype?
5. What are some differences between first-borns and later-borns?
6. What are teratogens and what do their effects depend upon?
7. What are the three stages of prenatal development, and what happens at each stage?

SCAN TO GET THE ANSWERS

What Do You Think?

Given that teratogens are considered to be any environmental agent that can cause damage to the developing organism, what other factors, other than those identified above, could be considered teratogenic? (Hint: physical injury to the mother that affects the developing zygote, embryo, or fetus.)

Infancy

HOW WE DEVELOP

LEARNING OBJECTIVE 4

Summarize the major physical, cognitive, and emotional developments that take place during infancy.

Families of newborns often think that their infants basically sleep, eat, drool, and excrete. While it's true that in adult terms a baby's capabilities are limited, if you look a bit closer you will be amazed at what they can already do.

Physical Development

Compared to some other species, human infants are still relatively "unfinished" at birth and remain dependent on their caregivers for longer than virtually all other species on our planet. Our key senses develop fully during our first months and we learn to walk after about a year or so, but our brains—although they also show amazing development during infancy—are not fully developed until we are teenagers or young adults.

Two patterns are apparent in babies' growth and development, both pre- and postnatal. First, growth follows a **proximodistal** pattern. That is, parts closer to the centre of the body grow and develop sooner than parts at the outer edges (the extremities) (Logsdon, 2011). Second, growth follows a **cephalocaudal pattern**, from head to foot. You have probably noticed, for example, that the heads of infants are much larger in proportion to their bodies than the heads of toddlers or adolescents.

proximodistal pattern a pattern in which growth and development proceed from the centre to the extremities.

cephalocaudal pattern a pattern in which growth and development proceed from top to bottom.

What Happens in the Body During Infancy? The senses of taste, smell, and touch are all highly developed at birth. A baby can distinguish the scent of his or her mother's milk from another woman's milk (Porter & Winberg, 1999) and can make fine distinctions between various tastes after only a few days out of the womb (Tatzer, Schubert, Timischl, & Simbruner, 1985).

Other senses are less developed. Hearing is still immature and affected by fluid from the mother's womb that continues to fill space in the newborn's ears. If you have ever spent a day swimming and gotten water trapped in your ears, you have probably had a sense of what it's like to hear like a baby. Things sound a little muddled, with greater sensitivity to high and low pitched sounds. These limitations change quickly, however. Within a few days the baby can distinguish familiar speech from new sounds and words that they have not heard before. However, because hearing is so crucial to social development, it is important to identify infants with hearing difficulty as quickly as possible. Work by Martyn Hyde (2005) at the University of Toronto indicates that special efforts taken to identify young infants with hearing issues allows for steps to be taken to ensure that such issues have a minimal effect on development.

Vision is a baby's least developed sense (Bedinghaus, 2010; Kellman & Arterberry, 1998; Maurer & Salapatek, 1976). Newborns cannot clearly see objects much more than 20 or 25 centimetres away. Similarly, their ability to scan objects is limited. If they look at a triangle, they will focus only on one of its corners. If they look at a face, they will focus largely on the chin or hairline. And they do not develop good colour vision until they are 3 months of age. At first, these visual limitations do not have serious consequences; after all, babies do not travel very far, and they can see far enough to make eye contact with their mothers while nursing. Research by Daphne Maurer and Terri Lewis (2001) at McMaster University tells us much about the rate at which infants' visual skill develops. Interestingly, their vision improves steadily, and by the time babies start moving around, at about 7 to 8 months of age, their vision has approached adult levels.

In addition to our senses, we are also born with certain **reflexes**, programmed reactions to certain cues that do not require any conscious thought to perform. For example, babies pucker their lips and begin to suck whenever something brushes their cheeks or is put in their mouths, a response called the *rooting reflex*. Other common reflexes are listed in **Table 3-3**. Being automatic, reflexes do not tell us much about infants' current ability levels. However, reflexes do allow us to see whether the nervous system is appropriately wired and working the way it is supposed to be working (Kimmel & Ratliff-Schaub, 2007).

reflexes programmed physical reactions to certain cues that do not require any conscious thought to perform.

TABLE 3-3 Common Newborn Reflexes

Reflex	Stimulation	Response	Function
Rooting	Touch the corner of the infant's cheek	Infant turns toward the stimulation and begins to suck	Helps infant begin feeding
Grasping	Press finger against infant's palm	Infant grasps finger and holds on	Allows infant to hold onto caregiver for safety
Moro	When infant is lying flat on a blanket, slap the blanket sharply on either side of the head to startle the infant	Infant flings arms outward and then inward in a hugging motion	May help infant to hold on to caregiver when support is lost
Babinski	Stroke sole of infant's foot	Toes spread apart	Unknown (but its presence indicates the integration of the nervous system)

For this reason, checking reflexes is an important part of early infant developmental assessments.

Infancy WHAT HAPPENS IN THE BRAIN? Perhaps you have heard popular claims that most of our brain development happens before age 3. Is this claim correct? As with many questions in psychology, the answer here is not definitive. Infancy is, indeed, a time of remarkable change in the brain. Although a newborn's head is only about one-fourth the size of an adult's, there is a great deal of development and activity going on in there! As you will see throughout this book, however, the brain continues to change and develop throughout our whole lives.

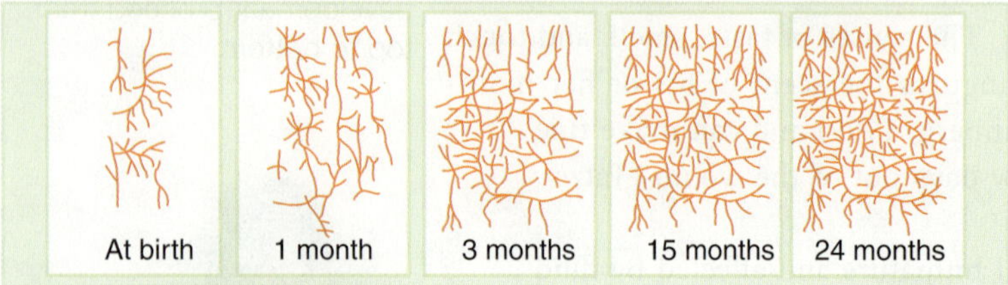

Brain growth in the first two years. This illustration shows the increases in the complexity of neurons that occur over the course of infancy.

Two key processes are responsible for the amazing growth of the brain in the earliest years of life. The first is a sheer increase in connections among *neurons*, the brain's nerve cells. As we will describe in detail in Chapter 4, information is passed from neuron to neuron at transmission points called **synapses**. Born with 100 billion neurons, the child acquires synaptic connections at a staggering rate during its first few years, expanding from 2,500 such connections per neuron at birth to around 15,000 per neuron by age 2 or 3 years (Bock, 2005; Di Pietro, 2000). Many of these connections develop as a function of normal maturation regardless of the baby's experiences and, in fact, serve as a way of helping the baby process new experiences. As babies, we actually develop far greater numbers of synapses than we will eventually need. As we grow older, two-thirds of our early synaptic connections disappear (Zelazo & Lee, 2010; Bock, 2005; Di Pietro, 2000). Our experiences help to stimulate and strengthen some of the connections, while synapses that are not used weaken and disappear. This process of reducing unnecessary connections is called **synaptic pruning** because of its similarity to pruning, or cutting away, the dead branches of a tree or bush to help the healthy, live branches flourish (Edin et al., 2007).

synapses transmission points between neurons.

synaptic pruning developmental reduction of neuronal connections, allowing stronger connections to flourish.

myelination development of fatty deposits on neurons that allow electric impulses to pass through neurons more efficiently.

The other neural process that accounts for increased brain growth is **myelination**. Myelin is a fatty white deposit that forms around and insulates portions of many neurons, helping electric impulses pass through a neuron more efficiently (we will say more about this in Chapter 4). During infancy, a great deal of myelination occurs in the spinal cord and in areas of the brain primarily associated with movement, reflexes, sensory responses, and certain low-level learning processes. For the most part, brain and body developments such as myelinization follow a proximodistal pattern, in which parts closer to the centre (that is, the spine) develop sooner than parts at the outer edges (the extremities). In this way, our most vital organs and body parts form first.

How Do We Learn to Control Our Movements? By the end of their first year, most babies are up and moving. **Motor skills**, the ability to control one's bodily movements, include achievements such as grasping objects, crawling, and eventually walking. **Table 3-4** shows the typical ages at which children in Canada and the United States reach particular motor-development milestones. As we noted earlier in the chapter, most babies acquire motor skills in roughly the same order, which suggests that there may be a maturational explanation for the way in which they unfold.

motor skills the ability to control our bodily movements.

At the same time, and as Table 3-4 also shows, there is considerable variability regarding when a child reaches a particular milestone. In addition to genetic variation, the timing of motor development can be influenced by a number of environmental factors.

Negative influences, such as abuse, neglect, or poor nutrition, can slow a child's motor development. Cultural practices that either encourage or discourage early motor development can also influence the timetable. For example, the Kipsigis people in Kenya begin working with babies shortly after birth to help them sit up, stand, and walk (Super, 1976). As a result, Kipsigis children achieve these milestones about a month before children raised

TABLE 3-4 Milestones in Motor Development

Motor Milestone	Average Age Achieved	Age Range
When prone, lifts chin up	2 months	3 weeks–4 months
Rolls over	2 months	3 weeks–5 months
Sits alone	7 months	5–9 months
Crawls	7 months	5–11 months
Stands holding furniture	8 months	5–12 months
Stands alone	11 months	9–16 months
Walks alone	11 months, 3 weeks	9–17 months
Walks up steps	17 months	12–23 months

Based on Laura E. Berk, *Infants, Children, and Adolescents, 6e* (Boston: Allyn & Bacon, 2008) Table 5.2, p. 188.

in North America. On the other hand, the Ache parents in Paraguay worry about their children moving more than a few feet away, and they actively discourage independent motor development in their children. As a result, Ache children do not walk until an average of one year later than children in North America (Kaplan & Dove, 1987). There are no indications that these differences translate into significant differences later in life. Esther Thelen and others (Thelan & Smith, 2006; Adolph & Berger, 2006; Thelan, 1989) have shown that motor development does not occur in isolation, but rather occurs as a number of complex systems blend to work synergistically. This *dynamic systems approach* is due to a number of factors coming together, including the environmental support provided for the skill.

The timetable for learning to walk provides an excellent example of the interaction of nature and nurture in our development. Although achieving a developmental milestone three months early or one year late is significant (particularly to a worried or proud parent), it is equally significant that the process keeps moving forward—that most everyone eventually hits this particular milestone.

Cognitive Development

Amazingly, in just two short years, humans proceed from speechless (but cute) babies who are completely dependent on others to little active problem solvers and social manipulators who can figure out how to get their hands on much of what catches their eye. What happens during this period of time that triggers such rapid skill development? We will talk about how we learn language in Chapter 9. Here, we discuss the important changes in thinking ability that happen during those first two years.

Piaget's Theory One of the world's most influential developmental psychologists, Jean Piaget, focused on **cognitive development**, how thinking and reasoning changes through the active manipulation and exploration of the environment (Piaget et al., 2009; Piaget, 2003, 2000, 1985). Piaget's theory began with naturalistic observations of children, particularly his own, in real life situations (Mayer, 2005). On the basis of his observations, Piaget hypothesized that young children's thinking processes might differ from those of adults. He then proceeded to test his hypotheses by making small changes in the children's situations and watching to see how they responded to those changes (Phillips, 1975; Piaget 1981). Based on the results of these tests, Piaget developed a theory of how children acquire knowledge and the abilities to use it.

cognitive development changes in thinking that occur over the course of time.

According to Piaget, all of us have mental frameworks or structures for understanding and thinking about the world. He called these frameworks **schemes**, and he believed that people acquire and continuously build their schemes through their experiences in the world. For example, children may acquire a scheme about birthday parties, based on their experiences. When they go to another birthday party, they can predict that there will be presents, some food, a cake, activities, and a treat bag to take home at the end of the party.

scheme Piaget's proposed mental structures or frameworks for understanding or thinking about the world.

assimilation one of two ways of acquiring knowledge, defined by Piaget as the inclusion of new information or experiences into pre-existing schemes.

Piaget believed that when children gain new knowledge, their schemes change. This can happen in two ways. The first, **assimilation**, was defined by Piaget as the inclusion of new information or experiences into pre-existing schemes. For example, when one of our oldest daughters was 3 years old, she visited a farm for the first time. When taken out to see the animals, she was initially terrified by the HUGE dog they had penned up. In fact the huge dog was a cow, but our city-raised daughter had *assimilated* the cow to her existing scheme for larger four-legged furry things (dogs). A brief discussion and a few bars of Old MacDonald's farm and she was fine because of changes in her thinking, involving accommodations, which we turn to next.

accommodation one of two ways of acquiring knowledge, defined by Piaget as the alteration of pre-existing mental frameworks to take in new information.

equilibrium balance in a mental framework.

Sometimes we come across new information so different from what we already know that we cannot simply add it to our old schemes. We must alter a pre-existing schema significantly to fit in new information or experiences, an adjustment Piaget called **accommodation**. With expanding experience, children like our huge-dog-fearing 3-year-old daughter can *accommodate* and expand or add to their schemes so that they can now include cows as a possible event in the world.

According to Piaget, engaging in assimilation and accommodation helps us to reach a mental balance, or **equilibrium**. When things are in balance, children are comfortable and able to assimilate new information. When things are not in balance, children experience disequilibration and are in a state of cognitive discomfort. They experience discomfort because they realize that their current schemes will not suffice and are therefore forced to modify their existing schemes to fit new information. Once they are cognitively comfortable, they move back toward equilibrium and are able to assimilate once again.

> "... [A]ssessing the impact of Piaget on developmental psychology is like assessing the impact of Shakespeare on English literature or Aristotle on philosophy—impossible. The impact is too monumental to embrace and at the same time too omnipresent to detect."
>
> —*Harry Beilin (1992), psychologist*

Piaget's theory is a stage theory. He suggested that we travel through several stages of cognitive development in life, progressing from having only reflexes as babies and being unable to even form schemes, to being able to perform complicated mental feats of logic using schemes as teenagers and adults. Piaget believed strongly that, as we move from stage to stage, *qualitative* shifts occur in our thinking. Children in one stage not only know more, but actually become different kinds of thinkers than they were at earlier stages. **Table 3-5** shows the four developmental stages and age ranges proposed by Piaget (1981). He proposed that, during infancy, we are in the earliest, or sensorimotor, stage.

Piaget named the first stage the sensorimotor stage because he thought that, early on, babies can think only about the world in terms of what they can sense directly or do with it using simple motor actions. For example, a ball, a favourite toy, or a parent is present only insofar as the baby can sense it directly or lay hold on it in some way—for infants, objects are graspable or suckable. If they lose sensory contact with an object, they cannot hold the idea of the object in their mind. For example, once that pacifier is under the couch, it's gone; out of sight is out of mind.

TABLE 3-5 Piaget's Four Stages of Cognitive Development

Stage	Age	Description
Sensorimotor	Birth to age 2	"Thinks" by using senses and motor skills; no thought beyond immediate experience
Preoperational	Age 2–7	Able to hold representations or ideas of objects in imagination; unable to consider another's point of view when it is different than their own or understand cause and effect
Concrete operational	Age 7–11	Can think about complex relationships (cause and effect, categorization); understands conservation; unable to think abstractly or hypothetically
Formal operational	Age 11 on	Able to think abstractly and hypothetically

Out of sight, out of mind. Prior to 8 months of age, babies have no recognition of object permanence. For example, here a young infant plays happily with a stuffed dog (left), but displays no awareness that the animal continues to exist after an experimenter removes it from sight (middle). In contrast, the 10-month-old on the right immediately seeks out and finds a favourite toy that has been hidden from him under a cloth.

Piaget believed that much of our early learning happens as a result of our reflexes. He observed that even though reflexes are "hardwired" into us, they are susceptible to change. As the baby engages in reflexive behaviours, he or she gets feedback about how those responses affect him or her and the surrounding world. The rooting reflex often brings food to a hungry infant, while the grasping reflex allows for basic manipulation of objects, for example. In this way, babies are acquiring knowledge that contributes to the formation of schemes. The baby may come to develop a schema relating rooting behaviour to feeding, or seeing to grasping.

Piaget believed that a major cognitive milestone of the sensorimotor stage is the development of **object permanence** at around 8 months of age (although he did not believe that infants obtained full object permanence until much later). Object permanence is the realization that objects continue to exist even when they are out of a baby's immediate sensory awareness. A child may cry when a toy rolls under the couch because he knows it still exists but is frustratingly out of reach, for example. When children eventually begin to demonstrate awareness of things out of their sensory awareness, it suggests that they are beginning to hold concepts in mind. They have developed mental schemes of those objects—they can form mental representations of objects they cannot currently see or touch. As we will see, for slightly older preschoolers, these representational skills form the basis of a new stage or way of thinking about the world and the nature of the objects it contains.

object permanence an infant's realization that objects continue to exist even when they are outside one's immediate sensory awareness.

Eventually, babies become able not only to hold objects in their minds, but also to manipulate and make predictions about those objects and how they interact with other objects. A baby may try to lift a cloth to look under it for a hidden toy, for example. By the end of the sensorimotor stage, Piaget believed that the young child's schemes have changed from needing a direct experience of the world to one in which ideas and concepts stand in for those objects.

Information Processing Views of Cognitive Development Piaget often looked at what children could not do and then used their mistakes to determine their cognitive abilities. Today, however, psychologists who adhere to the **information-processing theory**—who study how children learn, remember, organize, and use information—look to see what children *can* do, as opposed to what they cannot do. Such theorists have found that Piaget probably underestimated children's competencies in the various developmental stages (Li, 2010; Lourenç & Machado, 1996).

information-processing theory a developmental theory focusing on how children learn, remember, organize, and use information from their environment.

To see when a baby developed object permanence, for example, Piaget would hide the object and see whether the baby looked for it. Searching suggests that the baby still had the object in his or her mind. As we have noted, however, it takes some time for babies to master control over their bodies enough to move purposefully and conduct a search. If you cannot grasp a cloth that is hiding a toy, you cannot lift it and look under it. Thus, other researchers such as Quebec-born and -raised Renée Baillargeon, have suggested that a better indicator of object permanence is whether or not babies react with facial expressions of surprise when hidden objects are revealed again (Charles & Rivera, 2009; Baillargeon, 1987). After all, to be surprised, you have to have an expectation that is challenged in some way.

Such surprise implies that you have a mental representation of the situation and that your representation has been shown to be wrong. Studies focusing on facial expressions of surprise suggest that babies as young as 3 months may display some form of object permanence (Baillargeon, 2004).

Researchers also have found evidence that babies can *learn* and *remember* right after birth. Throughout life, individuals often learn to perform and repeat certain behaviours by experiencing positive consequences after they first manifest the behaviours, a process called *operant conditioning* that we will talk about in Chapter 7 (Lipsitt et al., 1966). It turns out that even very young babies learn to perform certain behaviours when they are systematically rewarded by researchers. If babies can shift their strategies to bring about positive outcomes or avoid negative ones, they must have some concepts (and, by extension, memories) of the relationships between behaviours and outcomes. Babies also display **habituation**—that is, they stop responding over time to the same stimulus if it is presented again and again—they get bored with it. If babies had no memory or no idea of external objects, they would not be able to become bored by repeated presentations. Habituation has also become a crucial research tool for measuring infant perceptions of colours, sounds, faces, and other such things. Once they get bored, you can change a feature of the thing they are looking at, like its size, shape, or colour, and if the infant dishabituates (looks at it more again) you can infer that the infant noticed the change.

habituation the process in which individuals pay less attention to a stimulus after it is presented to them over and over again.

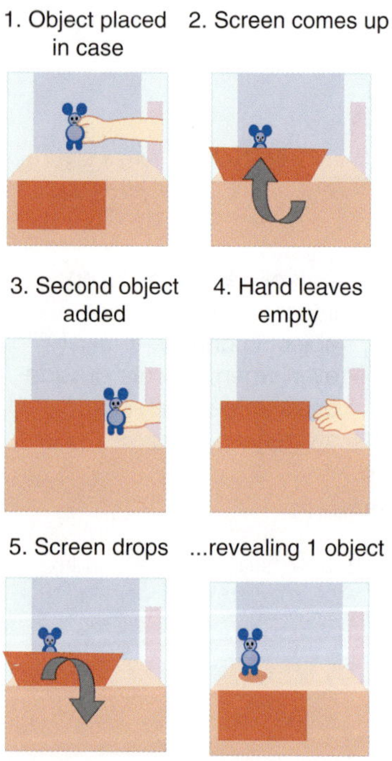

FIGURE 3-5 Baby math. To see whether 5-month-old infants have an appreciation of addition and subtraction, Karen Wynn showed them the sequence of events illustrated above. If the infants express surprise when the screen drops and they see only one object, it suggests that they understand that 1 + 1 = 2. (Adapted from Wynn, 1992)

As amazing as it may sound, infants may actually be capable of working with small numbers! As you can see in **Figure 3-5**, psychologist Karen Wynn conducted a series of studies in which she showed 5-month-old babies a sequence of events where one doll is put in a case behind a screen followed by another doll (Newman et al., 2010; McCrink & Wynn, 2004; Wynn 2002, 1992). She found that when the screen was dropped, the babies expressed surprise and looked longer if only one doll was in the case than if both dolls were present. The babies seemed to know that the case should hold two dolls. This result has been replicated with even larger numbers (five to ten dolls) in 9-month-old children!

By adjusting their approaches to focus more on the child's capacities rather than on their ability to manipulate objects or events, information-processing researchers have found that cognitive development may involve fewer qualitative shifts (and more quantitative growth) than Piaget believed. Nevertheless, Piaget's ideas remain influential. His stages still provide a general guideline for the cognitive development of children, and for that reason, we will look at his later stages in this chapter. In addition, Piaget's theory continues to encourage developmental psychologists to generate research that seeks both to support the theory and to rebut it. If nothing else, the intense research activity ignited by Piaget's ideas has helped us think about how to best study children's thought processes. Perhaps most importantly, Piaget encouraged psychologists to stop thinking of children as organisms programmed by biology or by early experiences and instead to think of them as active interpreters of their world. Piaget considered children to be little scientists constantly drawing conclusions about the world on the basis of their own personal research, conducted through their experiences in the world.

Social and Emotional Development

Parents are at the centre of an infant's social world, and many psychologists have focused on the importance of the early experiences children have with their parents. *Attachment theory* has made the best empirical case for how crucial this relationship is (Allen, 2011; Nelson & Bennett, 2008). In this section, we will talk about the principles of this theory and how parent–child relationships may influence a child's social and emotional development.

Infants are involved in the attachment process. While we tend to think of young infants as completely helpless, they actually bring a number of behavioural tendencies to their early interactions with their parents. As we noted in Chapter 1, many psychological researchers are interested in trying to determine how much of the way we think and act is influenced by our genetic inheritance, a field of study called *behavioural genetics*. Developmental psychologists are often in a position to examine the influence of genetics. One of the key areas of focus of both behavioural genetics and developmental psychology, for example, is **temperament**, often defined as a biologically-based tendency to respond to certain situations in similar ways throughout our lifetimes (Bates, Schermerhorn, & Goodnight, 2010; Henderson & Wachs, 2007; Bates, 1989). In a longitudinal study that began in the 1950s, the New York Longitudinal Study, researchers Stella Chess and Alexander Thomas (1996) suggested that, as infants, people tend to fall into one of three temperament categories:

temperament biologically-based tendencies to respond to certain situations in similar ways throughout our lifetimes.

"The first half of our lives is ruined by our parents, and the second half by our children."
—*Clarence Darrow, attorney*

- *Easy.* Babies with easy temperaments are described as cheerful, regular in routines, such as eating and sleeping, and open to novelty.
- *Difficult.* Babies with difficult temperaments tend to be irritable and are likely to have intensely negative reactions to changes or new situations.
- *Slow-to-warm-up.* Babies in this category are less active and less responsive than babies in the other two categories. In general, they tend to withdraw in the face of change, but their withdrawal is not as sharply negative as those with difficult temperaments.
- *Unique.* Babies in this category show unique blends of characteristics from the other categories. For example, a child might be cautious in new situations but have regular routines and be relatively cheerful.

Toddler temperaments. Infant and toddler temperaments can be observed in the typical behaviours they display.

Following Chess and Thomas's (1996) studies, many other researchers have also examined how our temperament relates to our later personality characteristics. In a famous line of work, psychologist Jerome Kagan (2010, 2008, 2001) conducted a longitudinal study examining the relationship between babies' levels of *behavioural inhibition*, the tendency to withdraw from new or different situations, and levels of shyness later in life. He found that children who were highly inhibited at 21 months of age were more likely than uninhibited toddlers to be shy when they were 12 to 14 years old.

Kagan's research seems to illustrate two key aspects of temperament:

1. *Temperament is inborn.* For an attribute to be temperamentally based, the behaviour that reflects that attribute must appear early (for example, shortly after birth). Considering that Kagan tested babies at such a young age, it is doubtful that they had much of an opportunity to learn to be apprehensive or fearful of new situations. Thus, many researchers believe that inhibited temperaments are biologically inherited.
2. *Temperament is stable across situations and time.* The participants in Kagan's study who were most shy temperamentally were the ones who were most inhibited at many different times and in different situations. Researchers have also established that other aspects of a person's temperament are stable over time and place (Bates et al., 2010; Henderson & Wachs, 2007). This is not to say, however, that there is no variability at all from time to time and situation to situation. Indeed, investigators have found greater stability of temperament when measuring behaviour across similar situations, such as in various family situations, than when comparing temperamental influences on children's behaviour across different situations, such as school versus home (Rothbart, Derryberry, & Hershey, 2000).

Despite the biological factors implied above, it is important to recognize that our environments also play important roles in how we behave. Kagan's studies (Kagan & Snidman, 2004) revealed, for example, that not all of the babies who were inhibited at birth later developed into shy teenagers. Similarly, being highly extroverted around new toys as a newborn did not always lead infant participants to become life-of-the-party teenagers. In fact, if genetics were destiny, we would all have a much easier time predicting how people will turn out, and this would be a much shorter chapter.

So, infants bring their temperaments to their early interactions with their parents. We now turn our attention to how those early relationships work as the infant and parents start to form the important attachment relationship.

attachment a close emotional bond to another person, such as a baby to a caregiver.

Attachment Theory Theorist John Bowlby believed that human beings are born with a drive to form an **attachment**, to become emotionally close to one particular caregiver, usually their mother. He suggested that early positive experiences with that caregiver are critical to health and well-being, and they shape how well the individual will function emotionally, socially, and even cognitively later in life (Bowlby, 1999).

Bowlby also argued that all the behaviours of infants are targeted at bringing them closer to their mothers. He believed, for example, that reflexes such as rooting or reaching out help babies build relationships with their mothers (Bowlby, 1958). To Bowlby, the presence of these reflexes provided evidence that attachment processes are inborn and crucial to the survival and well-being of babies. Bowlby also thought that children with strong attachments to their parents would actually feel safer than children who were more independent and less attached to their parents. Indeed, he suggested that appropriate, consistent responsiveness to a baby's needs is actually the best way for a mother to eventually bring about an independent and well-functioning child. Initially, the scientific community reacted negatively to this assertion (Holmes, 1993). The psychological wisdom of Bowlby's day held that parents who respond to children's needs by drawing the children in will succeed only in fostering neediness and dependence.

Mary Ainsworth was one of the first women to earn a Ph.D. in Psychology at the University of Toronto and to take up a faculty position there in 1939. She went on to work with Bowlby and conducted naturalistic observations in Uganda that supported Bowlby's ideas that mother–child attachment occurs around the world (Ainsworth, 2010,1993, 1985, 1967). Like Bowlby, Ainsworth argued that babies attach to their mothers because that is how their needs get met (Hughes, 2009; Bretherton, 1992). Ainsworth further noticed that some mothers, whom she labelled "highly sensitive," seem to form attachments that are more successful in fostering their children's independence.

Ainsworth developed a way to test the attachment between babies and their mothers in a laboratory setting. In Ainsworth's procedure, called the *Strange Situation* (see **Figure 3-6**), a baby plays in a laboratory room with mother nearby. After a time, a stranger enters the

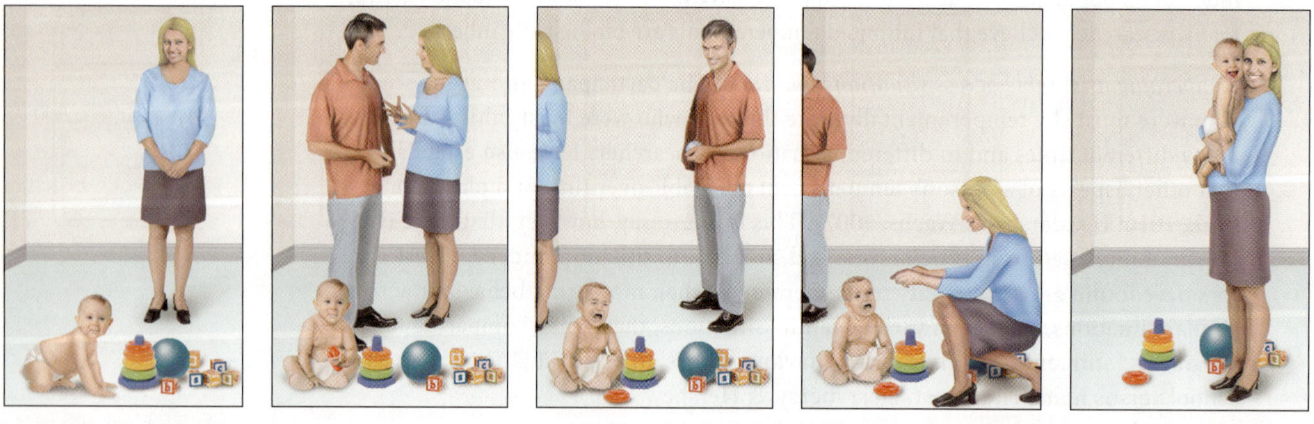

(a) (b) (c) (d) (e)

FIGURE 3-6 The Strange Situation procedure. (a) The baby plays while the mother is nearby. (b) A stranger enters the room, speaks to the mother, and approaches the child. (c) The mother leaves and the stranger stays in the room with an unhappy baby. (d) The mother returns and the stranger leaves. (e) The baby is reunited with the mother.

room, speaks with the mother, and attempts to interact with the baby. Then the mother leaves the room. The baby, left alone with the stranger, generally is in some distress. The researchers are most interested in how the baby reacts to the mother when she returns, as well as how willing the baby is to explore when the mother is present.

Based on her experimental findings, Ainsworth identified three basic attachment styles:

- *Secure attachment:* The infant uses the mother as a secure base from which to explore and as a support in time of trouble. The infant is moderately distressed when the mother leaves the room and happy when she returns.
- *Anxious/avoidant attachment:* The infant is unresponsive with the mother and is usually indifferent when she leaves the room and when she returns.
- *Anxious/ambivalent attachment:* The infant reacts strongly when the mother leaves the room. When she returns, the infant shows mixed emotions, seeking close contact and then squirming away angrily.

Later, psychologist Mary Main noted that some children fail to show any reliable way of coping with separations and reunions, exhibiting features of all three of the other styles (Main, Hesse, & Kaplan, 2005; Main & Solomon, 1990). She therefore added a fourth category to describe this pattern:

- *Disorganized/disoriented attachment:* The infant displays confused and contradictory behaviour when the mother returns. For example, the infant may ignore the mother while being held, appear flat and depressed, look dazed, cry out, and/or show a rigid posture.

The incidence of all four styles is shown in **Figure 3-7**.

Drawing on Ainsworth's work, Bowlby (1969) later suggested that early attachment experiences help people create an *internal working model* of the world, themselves, and the others with whom they form early attachment relationships. If children come to think of themselves as care-worthy, other people as supportive and responsive, and relationships as positive experiences, as a result of having sensitive mothers, Bowlby suggested that this positive model will influence their later relationships in a healthy way. In contrast, children who develop a working model that they are not care-worthy, their relationship partner is insensitive, and their early relationships are not positive may be at risk for poor adjustment or difficult relationships with other people later in their lives.

Ainsworth's work suggests that children are either securely attached or not. This categorical approach does not make it easy to talk about degrees of security or degrees of anxiousness in children's attachment patterns. An alternative approach called the *Q-sort approach* involves observers of parent–child interactions placing descriptions of various attachment behaviour into nine piles, with frequent behaviours at one end and infrequent behaviours at the other. This provides a much more fluid estimate of the child's general attachment patterns. David Pederson, Greg Moran, and Sandi Bento from the University of Western Ontario compared both the Strange Situation and the Q-sort attachment

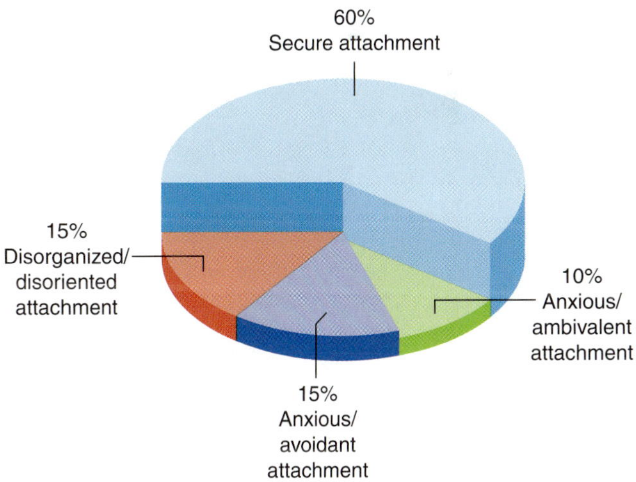

FIGURE 3-7 Styles of attachment. Ainsworth and Main identified four styles of attachment. ***Secure attachment (60 percent):*** The infant uses the mother as a secure base from which to explore and as a support in time of trouble. When the mother leaves the room, the infant is moderately distressed and happy when she returns. ***Anxious/avoidant attachment (15 percent):*** The infant is unresponsive with the mother and is usually indifferent when she leaves the room and when she returns. ***Anxious/ambivalent attachment (10 percent):*** The infant reacts strongly when the mother leaves the room. When she returns, the infant shows mixed emotions, seeking close contact and then squirming away angrily. ***Disorganized/disoriented attachment (15 percent):*** The infant displays confused and contradictory behaviour when the mother returns; for example, ignoring the mother while being held, appearing flat and depressed, looking dazed, crying out, and/or showing a rigid posture.

assessment methods (Pederson & Moran, 1996). The researchers found that there was much agreement in the ratings of security found using the Strange Situation in a lab setting and the Q-sort in the child's home setting. They also found, however, that the Q-sort technique used in the child's home was more sensitive to child ambivalence (finding it at twice the rate of the Strange Situation method). Given that ambivalence can predict later social adjustment issues, the Q-sort might be the better assessment to use if you are looking to ensure that children and families in need of support are identified and offered such support.

The vast majority of attachment research has focused on mothers, and indeed, cultural practice bears out the importance of the mother–child relationship; in almost every society, mothers do the majority of child care (Parke, 1995). Evidence also indicates, however, that fathers are capable of responding in highly sensitive ways (as defined by Ainsworth), and that highly sensitive fathers have babies that generally turn out to be securely attached (Verissimo et al., 2011; Howes, 1999; Grossmann et al., 2002).

PRACTICALLY SPEAKING Daycare in Canada: How Are We Doing?

Many Canadian families have help in caring for their children (see **Figure 3-8**; Bushnick 2006). Over 60 percent of single-parent Canadian families and over 50 percent of two-parent families use some form of non-parental care for their children (Statistics Canada, 2006). Figure 3.8 shows the different types of care arrangements used. What quality of care are Canadian children receiving? Canada recently placed 21st out of 29 countries for general child well-being in daycare (Keon, 2009; Leitch, 2007). As well, the United Nations Children's Fund found that Canada had only managed to achieve one of the ten benchmarks of quality in child care and early learning (Hertzman, 2009). Unlike Sweden, which provides universal child care from birth into the school years, Canada currently has no national child care policy.

Some provinces are starting to overcome these disadvantages. Quebec has a broad child care policy and program where many parents can obtain child care for $7 a day. The wages of Quebec child care workers have nearly doubled from where they were several years ago—on par with those of parking lot attendants. This means that more people are prepared to make daycare their career and obtain higher levels of training and experience (Hertzman, 2009). Saskatchewan and Prince Edward Island have moved responsibility for daycare into their education ministries (Beach & Bertrand, 2009). Most other provinces are implementing programs aimed at improving early childhood education with the belief that additional costs will be offset down the road by the benefits of a healthier, better educated population.

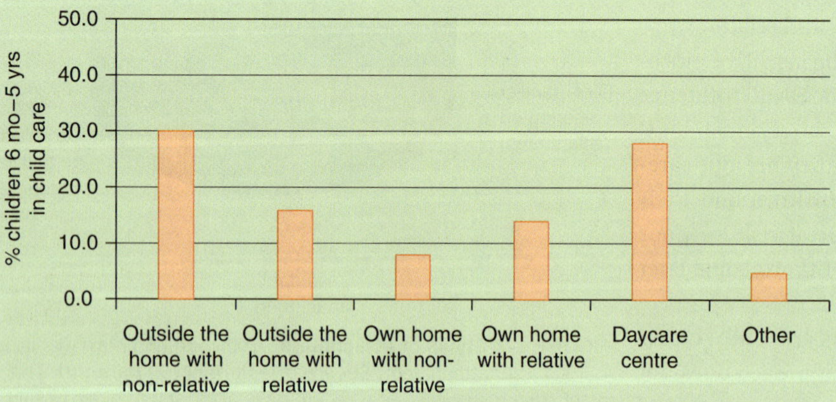

FIGURE 3-8 Distribution of children aged 6 months to 5 years by type of main non-parental care arrangement, 2002–2003.

Source: Based on Bushnick, 2006.

Parenting Styles HOW WE DIFFER

Once attachment theory gave psychologists a way of *operationalizing* (or defining in a measurable way) the relationship between parents and children, other researchers began applying those insights to understanding how parent behaviours might contribute to development. For example, Diana Baumrind, a psychologist at the University of

TABLE 3-6 Parenting Styles

Parental Style	Parental Behaviour	Associated Outcome in Children
Authoritative	Warm, sensitive to child's needs, nurturing; makes reasonable demands and encourages appropriate autonomy	High self esteem, cooperativeness, self control, social maturity
Authoritarian	Cold, rejecting; makes coercive demands; frequently critical of child	Low self esteem, anxious, unhappy, often angry and aggressive
Permissive	Warm, accepting but overindulgent and inattentive	Impulsive, disobedient, overly dependent on adults, low initiative
Uninvolved	Emotionally detached and depressed; little time or energy for child rearing	Anxious, poor communication skills, antisocial behaviour

California-Berkeley, conducted interviews and observations of primarily white, middle-class preschool children and their parents and found that two characteristics of parental behaviour seem particularly important: how many demands the parent puts on the child and how responsive the parent is to the child (Baumrind et al., 2010; Baumrind, 1991). Combining those two dimensions, Baumrind identified four parenting styles and the child outcomes associated with them, as depicted in **Table 3-6**.

A key question about Baumrind's theory has been how well it applies outside largely white, individualistic cultures. As we discussed in Chapter 1, *individualistic cultures* are those in which people are expected to be self-reliant and self-achieving, while *collectivist cultures* expect people to be focused primarily on the needs of the group. Cross-cultural research has found that parents in a variety of cultures can be classified into the same four styles. It is not clear, however, that the outcomes of the four parenting styles are the same across different cultures. Research by Xinyin Chen at the University of Western Ontario (Chen et al., 1999) suggested, for example, that in Asian cultures, the high-demand, low-responsiveness authoritarian parenting style does not necessarily lead to negative child outcomes as it often does in Canada. In fact, the authoritarian style can benefit children's academic performances during adolescence.

Another important question researchers have examined is how children's behaviours affect parenting styles, a transaction known as **reciprocal socialization**. Highly rambunctious children are, for example, more likely to evoke authoritarian control behaviours in their parents (Chan, 2010; Caspi, 1998). Most of today's research on reciprocal socialization emphasizes the transaction between the parent and the child and holds that a *good fit* between a parent and child's behavioural styles is more important than some objectively right or wrong style (Talwar, Nitz, & Lerner, 1991).

reciprocal socialization the transactional relationship between parent and child.

PSYCHOLOGY AROUND US Worth a Thousand Words

One thing most parents seem to share, regardless of parenting style, is a love for baby photos. As a result, the embarrassing baby photo is a fact of life for all of us. We all dread the first moment we bring a friend (or worse, boyfriend or girlfriend) home and a family member whips out the photo album or turns on the computer. And given the new age of social media, a whole new level of embarrassment may be about to strike the next generation.

In 2010, AVG, an Internet security firm, polled mothers with Internet access in Europe, North America, Australia, New Zealand, and Japan. Their survey found that 92 percent of newborns have some level of presence on the Internet! That includes 23 percent with uploaded ultrasound scans—that's right, their Internet presence preceded their actual birth—and 7 percent with their very own email address. Growing up is becoming a much more public and potentially embarrassing experience.

Will this new connectedness have an impact on the way in which children grow up and develop? Whom will they think of as a peer group—just their immediate friends, or 20,000 commenters on YouTube? The next time you watch a YouTube video of a baby laughing hysterically while ripping paper, perhaps spare a thought for how that child might look back on that experience a few years down the road.

What Do Fathers Have to Do with Development? A Lot!

Is the involvement of fathers important for their children's development? The quick and obvious answer is yes, of course. However, much of what we have historically seen in research on parent involvement in child development has been somewhat mother-centric. This view was based on the traditional or stereotypical family model in which parents divide family tasks, with mothers taking responsibility for child care and rearing and fathers taking responsibility for work and resource acquisition. Increasingly, however, both parents work outside the home, there are more single-parent or divorced families, and as such fathers are playing more active and direct roles in both their homes and in their child's development. It is also important to note that although mothers have traditionally been responsible for children, many fathers have, in fact, been very active in their children's development. However, developmental theory and developmental researchers have frequently neglected the important role of fathers in children's developmental experiences. What research is available that looks directly at the role of fathers in the development of young children?

Jessica Ball at the University of Victoria (Ball & Moselle, 2007) reviewed the Canadian and relevant international research on fathers' contributions to children's well-being. The Public Health Agency of Canada included Dr. Ball's review in a general initiative looking at father involvement for healthy child outcomes (PHAC, 2007). The following findings indicate that fathers today are playing a direct and active role in their children's development:

- Fathers play a direct role in ensuring that their children have access to quality early childhood education, schooling, and supportive media. These opportunities support early literacy development, which goes on to support positive health outcomes.
- Fathers' ability to generate income for their families provides stability in housing, nutrition, and leisure activities, among other areas, which in turn reduces the risk of negative heath outcomes associated with poor nutrition, obesity, and injuries.
- Youth who are close to their fathers are less likely to engage in substance use.
- When fathers are more actively involved in their children's school, the children do better academically.
- Fathers' involvement in their children's development is self-sustaining, meaning that the more involved fathers become, the more satisfaction they receive and the more skill they develop. As a result, the more likely they are to sustain their involvement with their developing children.

So given that father involvement is so good, shouldn't we find ways to encourage more fathers to play a more active role in their children's lives? That is precisely what members of the fathers' Involvement Research Alliance under the guidance of Kerry Daly from the University of Guelph are trying to do (Allen and Daly, 2007). This group consists of researchers, community agencies, and fathers, and is committed to exploring and enhancing fatherhood among seven Canadian populations including indigenous fathers, new fathers, young fathers, immigrant and refugee fathers, gay fathers, divorced fathers, and fathers of children with special needs.

Karen Benzies at the University of Calgary, along with her colleagues there and at the University Alberta (Benzies et al., 2008), have shown that a simple program (two home visits with the father and infant), designed to encourage first-time fathers to become more actively involved in their new child's development, successfully increased father commitment and involvement. So, fathers can—and many fathers do—make a difference in their young children's early development, and respond quickly and positively to being trained and encouraged to be even more actively involved. Father involvement has always been a positive force in child development. Efforts to increase it further in areas where it might not yet be optimal seems to be improving developmental outcomes for Canadian children.

Before You Go On

www.wiley.com/go/comer

What Do You Know?

8. What is the role of myelination in the development of the brain?
9. What is the Strange Situation?
10. What are the major parenting styles, and what are the major child outcomes associated with each style?

What Do You Think?

How do you think the various attachment styles correlate with Baumrind's parenting styles? Do you think there is one optimal form of parenting?

SCAN TO GET THE ANSWERS

Childhood

HOW WE DEVELOP

LEARNING OBJECTIVE 5

Summarize the major physical, cognitive, and emotional developments that take place during childhood.

Although physical growth slows somewhat during childhood, our cognitive and social lives become increasingly complex. We develop the cognitive capacity to think and talk about the world in ways that do not involve the concrete reality we experience directly. Our social and emotional lives also become more complex and expand to include peers and teachers. In this section, we will focus on how the world gets a lot bigger during childhood and how children manage to keep up.

Physical Development

Growth during early childhood, which lasts from about the ages of 2 to 6 years, and middle childhood, which lasts from about age 6 until 12, is not as dramatic as it is during infancy. Although progress is more gradual, children's brains and bodies still experience major changes. For example, both become much more efficient.

How Does the Body Grow During Childhood? The dramatic physical growth that occurs from conception through to our second year slows down during early childhood, such that we grow only about 5 to 7 centimetres a year. We master a good deal of motor

PSYCHOLOGY AROUND US "Healthy Competition?"

The reality show *Toddlers and Tiaras* explores families who participate in child beauty pageants. The show focuses mainly on children between ages 2 and 10. These children compete in categories including talent, interview, sportswear, swimwear, western wear, and evening wear.

Critics have blasted the show, saying that the competitions are more about the parents' needs than the children's. What with the pressure to win, the fancy outfits, and the often elaborate makeup and hairdos, the children are pushed into adult roles before they are ready. The official network website for the show, which includes a place where visitors can rate the child "beauty queens" on a scale from 1 to 10, seems to support this criticism.

Perhaps not surprisingly, the parents who sign up their children for these pageants see things differently. With a small undergraduate grant, Harvard college student Hilary Levey (now a sociologist) conducted research on 41 families involved in child pageants. She found that the parents hoped that their children would gain confidence, poise, and social skills from participation in the competitions. The parents with lower incomes and lower education levels wanted their children to learn skills that would help them move up in the world. Among higher-income parents, the focus was on helping children learn to manage competition. What do you think—are beauty pageants harmless introductions to competition, akin to spelling bees, Little League, and soccer? Or are they traumatic experiences that run counter to the needs of childhood?

Getting a Good Start Sometimes Means Getting a Head Start

How children do when they enter school is strongly influenced by what they do during their preschool years. Play school, preschool, and kindergarten, along with parent and community support and encouragement, means that most children are ready for the academic and social challenges of grade 1.

However, this general process does not seem to work so well for many of Canada's Aboriginal children. The school dropout rate for Canadian Aboriginal and Métis youth is three times that of the general population (25 percent versus 8 percent) (Gingras, 2002; Bushnick, 2003). In an effort to address this issue, the government of Canada provided funds for the development of Aboriginal Head Start (AHS) preschool programs in urban and northern communities across Canada. Aboriginal Head Start programs provide a half-day preschool experience for 3- to 5-year-old Aboriginal and Métis children. Parents are encouraged to participate as well, to become optimal supporters of and advocates for their children's academic and social development. In addition, the program provides support for development of Aboriginal culture and language, education, and school readiness programming, along with health promotion, nutrition, and social support (PHAC, 2011).

Early evaluation data gathered at Alberta Aboriginal Head Start sites (dela Cruz, 2010) shows that AHS participants perform at or above the averages for children their age in the general Canadian population as they enter the school system. This indicates that the AHS program is working. Now we need to follow these children through school to see if the AHS also helps to reduce Canadian Aboriginal and Métis youth school dropout rates. Hopefully the AHS graduates are already enjoying a stronger sense of academic success and are viewing themselves as competent learners.

and physical control during this period. Children develop basic control over their urination and bowel movements, and they solidify a preference for their right or left hand for most tasks. Of course, during early childhood, many aspects of development remain works-in-progress. Although our coordination improves and we can work the buttons, zippers, and shoelaces necessary to dress ourselves, that doesn't necessarily mean that we can select clothes that are appropriate for every event or occasion. While a 3-year-old's Spiderman pyjamas may be the coolest thing in the world, they are not appropriate attire for Thanksgiving dinner with all the relatives.

As children move from early into middle childhood, around age 6, there is a jump in coordination and skill. Children's motor abilities improve dramatically as they gain coordination, agility, and strength (Drummond, 2011). At the same time, the first major physical distinctions between boys and girls begin to appear. Girls experience a growth spurt in height and weight during their tenth or eleventh year, while boys have to wait a couple of years more for their spurt. On the other hand, boys develop somewhat more muscle mass, meaning they can throw and jump a little farther and run a little faster. Girls tend to be a bit more agile on average. As we will see later in the chapter, these average differences in childhood become much more pronounced as children move into adolescence.

Childhood **WHAT HAPPENS IN THE BRAIN?** Throughout early and middle childhood, the brain becomes more efficient due to a continued combination of the myelination and synaptic pruning that began in infancy. During childhood, myelination is concentrated in the brain areas known as the *association regions.* These areas of the brain coordinate the activity and operation of other regions of the brain, such as putting together sensory information so that we connect what things look like with what they sound like, feel like, or taste like (Bartzokis et al., 2010; Paus et al., 1999). The increased efficiency of the association regions as they become myelinated leads to more sophisticated planning and problem-solving abilities. Most 4-year-olds cannot play chess very effectively, for example, but many elementary school children have the strategic skills to be good chess players.

As we discussed earlier, synaptic pruning helps solidify the neural connections that are most beneficial to the child. As childhood draws to a close, pruning tails off. The numbers of synaptic connections between particular neurons and the overall electric activity in the brain both begin to stabilize.

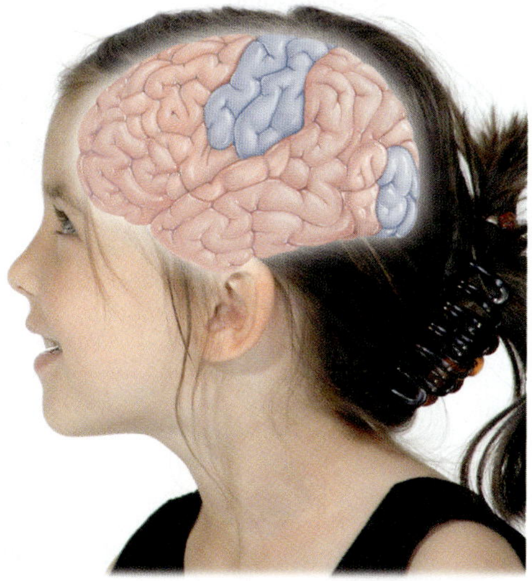

Association regions of the brain. The association regions (all areas of the cortex not coloured blue in this illustration) undergo extensive development during childhood, leading to further growth of the cognitive processes.

Cognitive Development

One of the major activities of childhood is attending school; in most countries, formal education begins around the age of 6 or 7. School entry coincides with the development of the cognitive skills that Piaget called operations, the ability to hold an idea in mind and manipulate it mentally. We talked earlier about how infants become able to hold a mental image or symbol in mind and thus allow themselves to represent or consider things that are not immediately present (e.g., a lost toy). Work by Ellen Bialystok and Fergus Craik at York University shows that what emerges as part of this period is the ability to logically (mentally) manipulate these representations (Bialystok & Craik, 2010). Piaget suggested that between the ages of about 2 and 12, children go through two stages of cognitive development: the *preoperational stage*, which lasts from age 2 through 7, followed by the *concrete operational stage*, lasting from age 7 through 12.

operations Piagetian description of a child's ability to hold an idea in his or her mind and mentally manipulate it.

preoperational stage according to Piaget, a developmental stage during which the child begins to develop ideas of objects in the external world and the ability to work with them in his or her mind.

Piaget's Preoperational Stage According to Piaget, as children move into the preoperational stage, they become able to hold memories, or representations, of objects in their imaginations and to work with them as ideas (Müller & Racine, 2010). This represents a dramatic shift from the earlier sensorimotor stage in which they were able to manipulate actual objects only. The thinking of children at this stage still shows some limitations compared to adult thinking, however.

One major limitation is what Piaget called *irreversibility*. Although they can work with symbols and concepts (representations) that stand in for real-world objects, children at the preoperational stage still think in rather simplistic ways about the relationships between those concepts and objects. For them, changes in relationships happen in one direction only. One researcher offers the following example of a 4-year-old boy who was asked about his family:

> "Do you have a brother?"
> "Yes."
> "What's his name?"
> "Jim."
> "Does Jim have a brother?"
> "No."
>
> (Phillips, 1975)

The boy is able to hold the idea of his brother Jim in his head, even though Jim is not there, indicating he has developed object permanence. At the same time, he has adopted this concept in one direction only: Jim is *my* brother. The boy is unable to think about the reverse relationship—that he is Jim's brother also.

The reason this child cannot think of himself as Jim's brother, according to Piaget, is because he cannot take Jim's point of view, an inability Piaget referred to as egocentrism (Kesselring & Müller, 2010). Piaget did not use the term *egocentrism* to mean the boy is arrogant or self-centred. His use of the term refers strictly to children's flaws in logical reasoning. This boy cannot yet realize that he, himself, is also a brother. Piaget believed that this type of *perspective-taking* skill, the ability to take another person's point of view, is not mastered until the next, concrete operational, stage.

egocentrism flaws in a child's reasoning based on his or her inability to take other perspectives.

conservation the understanding that certain properties of an object (such as volume and number) remain the same despite changes in the object's outward appearance.

Irreversibility is also related to a lack of conservation, the ability to understand that something can stay the same even though its appearance changes. Piaget used a now-famous task to demonstrate young children's problems with conservation. He gave a child two identical beakers with equal amounts of water in each and asked which of the beakers

Shapes can be misleading. In the classic test for conservation, a child is shown two identical short thick glasses, each filled with liquid. The child then watches as the liquid from one glass is poured into a tall thin glass and is asked to indicate which glass now has more liquid. Most children between 2 and 7 years incorrectly pick the tall thin glass.

held more water. Children over 2 years old were usually able to say that both beakers held the same amount. Piaget would then ask the child to pour the water into two new beakers that were shaped differently, one shallow and wide and the other tall and narrow. After the children poured the water, Piaget again asked which held more water. Children between the ages of 2 and 7—even after they themselves had poured the water into the new beakers—were more likely to say the tall, narrow beaker held more water. Piaget believed this indicated that the children could not mentally reverse the pouring of the water to imagine that the two amounts of water would once again match if both were returned to their original containers, nor could they see that, logically, it was still the same water just in a different containers, or that the new container was taller but also narrower than the previous container.

Children's lack of conservation also may be related to difficulty in making distinctions between *appearance* and *reality*. In one classic example of this confusion, researcher Rheta DeVries (1969) allowed children to play with her cat, Maynard. After a while, DeVries and her assistants hid Maynard's front half from view while they strapped a dog mask onto the cat's face. (We have no idea how she got a cat to agree to wear a dog mask.) DeVries then asked the toddlers what kind of animal Maynard was. Even though Maynard was never completely out of view, the majority of the 3-year-old participants, and a good number of 4- and 5-year-olds, thought the cat had magically become a dog. By the age of 6, when they were nearing the concrete operational stage, none of the children made this mistake. The younger children could not look past the surface appearance of the masked cat to see that in reality it was still a cat and not a dog. For these preschool children, appearances were the only reality they could conceive of.

"A child of five would understand this. Send someone to fetch a child of five."
—*Groucho Marx, comedian*

concrete operations Piagetian stage during which children are able to talk about complex relationships, such as categorization and cause and effect, but are still limited to understanding ideas in terms of real-world relationships.

Piaget's Concrete Operational Stage During the stage of concrete operations, children demonstrate the ability to think about ideas. They show that they are capable of applying simple logic to their thinking. They start to talk with confidence about complex relationships, such as cause and effect and categorization. They can take others' perspectives and reverse (mentally undo) operations or actions, as in conservation tasks. By now, they consider the notion that a cat can mysteriously become a dog ridiculous. They know dogs and cats fit into certain hard and fast categories, and they can now extend those categories to other organisms that share the same features.

Children at this stage show a mastery of real-world relationships. This mastery is limited, however, to ideas that have real-world counterparts, such as brothers and sisters and other family members, categories of plants or animals, or causes of weather conditions. That's why Piaget refers to the stage as *concrete* operations. Children in this stage have difficulty with abstract relationships between objects that do not exist in the real world, such as abstract mathematical relationships or logical questions, such as how many unique combinations can be made from four different things. They also find it difficult to think about hypothetical, alternate possibilities and have trouble speculating on questions such as "What ways can this situation play out?" A mastery of those kinds of relationships is left for the next stage of development, the formal operational stage.

Criticisms of the Preoperational and Concrete Operations Stages Many critics have challenged Piaget's belief that children in the preoperational and concrete operations stages have problems taking others' point of view. In fact, some researchers have become very interested in young children's awareness of their own minds and the minds of others, a field of research called theory of mind (Carpendale & Lewis, 2010; Mar, Tackett, & Moore, 2010).

theory of mind an awareness of one's own mental states and the mental states of others.

Theory of mind was first studied in an experiment with children between the ages of 3 and 9. Each child participant was told a story about a boy named Maxi who tries to sneak some chocolate from his mom (Wimmer & Perner, 1983). According to the story, Maxi's mother brings home some chocolate to make a cake, and while Maxi is watching, she puts the chocolate in a blue cupboard (see **Figure 3-9**). Maxi then goes out to play. While he is outside, his mother makes the cake and puts the remaining chocolate in a green cupboard. Next, Maxi comes back in, wanting some chocolate. The researchers then asked the children in the study where Maxi would look for the chocolate.

This deceptively simple task actually requires a high level of thought. Children have to not only remember where the chocolate has travelled, but also take the viewpoint of Maxi and realize that Maxi has no way of knowing that his mom moved the chocolate. Three- and 4-year-olds regularly fail such tests, suggesting this task is too complicated for them, while 6-year-olds regularly succeed. Experiments such as these support Piaget's notion that young children are egocentric or focused on their own knowledge or perspective, but also suggest that children are able to take other people's thoughts and feelings into account much sooner than Piaget had predicted—at around 4 as opposed to 6 or 7 years of age.

Another way that researchers assess theory of mind is to assess children's understandings of *false-beliefs*. False beliefs are based on a premise that is not true; the ability to understand false beliefs develops in most typically-developing children by the age of 5 years (Wellman, Cross, & Watson, 2001). Canadian researchers Alison Gopnik and Janet Astington (1988) devised the well-known Smarties task to test a young child's understanding of false beliefs. They asked children to guess what was in a Smarties box. The children confidently guessed candy, but were then shown that the box was in fact full of small pencils. After the researcher closed the box, they asked the children to guess what they thought a peer who had not yet seen the actual contents of the box would say when asked what

FIGURE 3-9 Theory of mind. Young research participants are told a story in which a child first sees his mother place chocolate in an upper cupboard, then he leaves while she makes a chocolate cake. In his absence, the mother places the leftover chocolate in a lower cupboard, and the child then returns looking for leftover chocolate. Participants with a theory of mind recognize that the child in the story will look for the leftover chocolate in the original upper cupboard, because the child is not aware of the mother's switch of locations.

was in it. Many 4-year-olds and most 5-year-olds were able to guess "Smarties," but some 4-year-olds and most 3-year-olds incorrectly guessed, "Pencils." When the children who failed the task were asked why they thought their peer would not guess Smarties, they said, "Because it *isn't* Smarties, it's pencils."

In part, Piaget's approach may have been limited by a failure to listen to his own theory. Piaget believed that thought preceded language—that our thinking develops faster than our ability to use words. Yet, his tests of his theories rested on observations of children's performances on language-based tasks, such as the question about Jim's brother. Other researchers, by focusing on non-verbal responses or by making their questions more age-appropriate or child-friendly, have found evidence that children develop certain cognitive competencies sooner; for example, pictures accompanied the story of Maxi. More recent research has linked theory of mind to general language development (Astington & Baird, 2005).

"Parents can only give good advice or put them on the right path, but the final forming of a person's character lies in their own hands."
—*Anne Frank, diarist and Holocaust victim*

Still other critics, such as Jeremy Carpendale from Simon Fraser University, have charged that Piaget's theory fails to account fully for *social* factors, the influences that other people may have on a child's cognitive development (Carpendale & Lewis, 2010; Freund & Lamb, 2010; Symons, 2004). Instead, Piaget's theory focuses on how children guide their own development through experimentation and reflection. Later in his life, Piaget himself also wondered whether his theory said enough about the role of social experiences in development (Inhelder & Piaget, 1979; Piaget, 1972). As we will see next, a contemporary of Piaget's had more to say about social influences on cognitive development.

Vygotsky and the Role of Sociocultural Theory While Piaget was focusing on how children's private experiments and reflections shape their thinking, a Russian psychologist named Lev Vygotsky was becoming increasingly interested in how social interactions with more mature members of their culture might drive the development of children. Unlike Piaget, who viewed a child's development as a process of individual achievement, Vygotsky (2004, 1991, 1978) believed that constructive interactions with parents, older children, teachers, and siblings help the child develop ways of thinking about and functioning in the world. In Vygotsky's view, an older mentor, such as a parent, helps the child by initially taking responsibility for the basic skills and capabilities the child is developing. Over time, the mentor takes less and less responsibility. Jerome Bruner (1983, 1986), a Vygotskian researcher, referred to the mentor's step-by-step assistance as **scaffolding**, while Barbara Rogoff (1990) referred to this process as an *apprenticeship in thinking*. Vygotsky labelled the gap between what children can accomplish by themselves and what they can accomplish with the help of others as the **zone of proximal development**.

scaffolding developmental adjustments that adults make to give children the help that they need, but not so much that they fail to move forward.

zone of proximal development the gap between what a child could accomplish alone and what the child can accomplish with help from others.

Because of his death at the young age of 37 and the chilly political climate between the former Soviet Union and the West, Vygotsky's ideas have only become more widely studied in North America in recent years. However, developmental psychologists have found numerous ways to apply Vygotsky's ideas (Trawick-Smith & Dziurgot, 2011). He has become one of today's most influential developmental theorists (Eun, 2010; Feldman, 2003). Indeed, ideas of scaffolding and zones of proximal development are now an important part of educational systems throughout North America (Holzman, 2009). When helping children learn to read, for example, many teachers begin by reading books to them, then gradually turn over responsibility for various reading skills. The children may first follow along with the pictures as the teacher reads the words, then point to letters. Eventually, they learn to read single words, then sentences, and finally entire books on their own, as the teacher provides less and less scaffolding and the children's zone of proximal development becomes smaller.

Whereas Piaget believed that thinking preceded language, Vygotsky believed that language is crucial to cognitive development because a great deal of mentoring relies on talking and listening (Eun, 2010). Both theorists noticed that preschool-aged children talk to themselves. Piaget noted that this talk did not seem to be serving a social purpose and so described this speech as largely *egocentric speech*—cognitive noise. Vygotsky, however, called this inner speech **private speech**. He believed that children use private speech to regulate or self-guide their behaviour and internal experiences, to plan, and to solve problems, often repeating or imitating the words of their mentors. Vygotsky believed that, eventually, this self-directive speech turns into silent, internal dialogues. Researchers have shown that children increase their use of private speech when tasks are difficult, when they have made an error, or when they are uncertain (Berk, 1994).

private speech a child's self-talk, which Vygotsky believed the child uses to regulate behaviour and internal experiences.

Because Vygotsky believed that other individuals are critical to helping children develop, he also believed that there is a great deal more variability in how children develop. He believed that each culture has its own specific challenges, and that those challenges change over the course of life, meaning that development has to meet those challenges.

> "Every function in the child's cultural development appears twice: first, between people (interpsychological) and then inside the child (intrapsychological). This applies equally to voluntary attention, to logical memory, and to the formation of ideas. All the higher functions originate as actual relationships between individuals."
> —*Lev Vygotsky, Russian psychologist*

Moral Development

Chapters 12 and 14 focus on many broad features of a child's social and emotional development. This chapter focuses on *moral* development, how children acquire an understanding of right and wrong that is necessary if they are to function autonomously and safely in a complex society.

Kohlberg's Theory of Moral Development Lawrence Kohlberg was particularly interested in Piaget's ideas on moral development. Piaget believed that, as with general logical reasoning, children learn how to reason morally by applying their emerging logical thinking to the issue of different perspectives and social wants and interactions—particularly easily seen in children's games and their understanding and application of game rules. He proposed that children's morality is based initially on obeying adults. As they get older, the basis of their moral reasoning shifts toward cooperation with peers (Piaget, 1965).

Kohlberg expanded upon Piaget's ideas and developed a method to evaluate the moral reasoning processes of children. He presented children, adolescents, and young adults with stories that include moral dilemmas, such as the story of Heinz in **Figure 3-10**, and asked them to say what the main characters in the stories should do and why.

On the basis of his studies, Kohlberg developed a stage theory of moral development, depicted in **Table 3-7** (Kohlberg, 2008, 1994, 1963). The focus of this theory is *moral reasoning*, how children come to their decisions about what is right and wrong, rather than on the particular decisions that they make. Like Piaget, Kohlberg believed that young children make moral choices that seem likely to ensure the least amount of trouble with authority figures (e.g., to avoid getting caught and punished). However, Kohlberg also looked beyond childhood to adolescence and described how older children and adults become more independent in their moral reasoning.

Heinz and the Drug

In Europe, a woman was near death from a special kind of cancer. There was one drug that the doctors thought might save her. It was a form of radium that a druggist in the same town had recently discovered. The drug was expensive to make, but the druggist was charging ten times what the drug cost him to make. He paid $400 for the radium and charged $4,000 for a small dose of the drug. The sick woman's husband, Heinz, went to everyone he knew to borrow the money and tried every legal means, but he could only get together about $2,000, which is half of what it cost. He told the druggist that his wife was dying, and asked him to sell it cheaper or let him pay later. But the druggist said, "No, I discovered the drug and I'm going to make money from it." So, having tried every legal means, Heinz gets desperate and considers breaking into the man's store to steal the drug.

Question: Should Heinz steal the drug? Why or why not?

FIGURE 3-10 Kohlberg's moral dilemma story. Paragraph excerpted from Scot Lilienfeld, Steven Lynn, Laura Namy, and Nancy Wolf, *Psychology: From Inquiry to Understanding* (2008; Boston: Pearson: Allyn & Bacon.)

TABLE 3-7 Kohlberg's Stage Theory of Moral Development

Stage	Reason to Steal Drug	Reason Not to Steal Drug
Preconventional: Morality centres on what you can get away with	He likes his wife and considers it worth the risk and bother.	He will be caught and go to jail.
Conventional: Morality centres on avoiding others' disapproval and obeying society's rules	If he doesn't steal the drug people will think he is a bad husband.	If he steals people will think he is a criminal; it's against the law.
Postconventional: Morality is determined by abstract ethical principles.	The right to life is universal and takes precedence over the right to property.	Laws are necessary to maintain order in society.

Although Kohlberg believed that moral reasoning often is correlated with other areas of development, such as cognition or intelligence, he held that it develops independently. Larry Walker (1980), at the University of British Columbia, demonstrated that children's cognitive development makes it possible for them to take up more mature understandings of the nature of others' perspectives, which in turn make it possible for them to develop higher (Kohlberian) stages of moral reasoning. To reach the highest stages of moral reasoning, Kohlberg believed, individuals must be exposed to complex social situations, such as working at jobs that involve lots of people or going to college.

Like Piaget's theory of general cognitive development, Kohlberg's (1981) theory suggests that each stage of moral development is not just a shift in complexity, but instead represents a new framework for making moral decisions. Each such stage forms a foundation for the next stage, and children must travel through the stages of moral development in sequence. A child may be delayed, or perhaps even fail to reach some of the higher stages, but he or she must go through each earlier stage to reach the next one.

Finally, Kohlberg believed that the process of moral development is universal and happens the same way in every culture. Kohlberg's original research included boys only, but he later studied girls and conducted moral dilemma interviews in villages in Mexico, Taiwan, and Turkey (Nisan & Kohlberg, 1982).

Gilligan's Theory of Moral Development One of Kohlberg's collaborators, Carol Gilligan (1993), eventually questioned some of his findings and ideas, partly because his studies initially focused on boys alone, and also because his later studies that did include girls seemed to suggest that girls are morally less developed than boys. Kohlberg believed that girls do not have as many complex social opportunities as boys and, as a result, are excessively concerned with the standards of others and often fail to achieve higher stages of moral reasoning.

Gilligan (1993) interpreted the boy–girl findings differently. She argued that the moral reasoning used by girls is indeed different from that of boys, but not inferior. She noticed that boys tend to base their decisions about moral dilemmas on abstract moral values, such as justice and fairness. Many girls look at the situations differently. Instead of the abstract values involved, they focus more on care—on the value of relationships between the principal players. A boy's answer to the Heinz dilemma might centre on the importance of property value for the druggist, for example, while a girl's answer might stress that Heinz will not be able to help his wife if he is jailed for stealing the drug (Gilligan, 1993). Gilligan argued that the reasoning of boys and girls is equally sophisticated, but the moral orientation with which they approach dilemmas may differ. Gilligan went on to conduct her own interviews with men and women and found further support for her theory that women are inclined to make moral judgments based more on caring and managing relationships than on Kohlberg's notions of justice and fairness. She found further that both males and females were capable of both justice- and care-based moral thinking, and which one they used varied depending on the circumstances in which they were asked.

Other studies have not always supported Gilligan's theory that women and men differ in their moral orientation. Nor, however, have they always supported Kohlberg's notions of moral superiority among males (Turiel, 2010; Walker, 2006). Some recent studies, for example, suggest that differences in the education levels of their research participants may have accounted for the apparent moral differences between males and females observed by these two investigators; when education level is controlled for, females and males often earn similar moral stage scores (Dawson, 2002).

Gilligan's ideas have had a broad influence on psychology, anthropology, and other social sciences. In a classic book, *In A Different Voice*, Gilligan (1993) noted that over the years, many psychological theorists have embraced male development patterns as the norm and viewed differences from that norm as inferior. Similarly, she argued that women have been underrepresented in many of psychology's most influential studies and theories. As a result of her arguments, many researchers now include more females in their studies. In addition, most of today's researchers think of differences among participants as individual variations rather than positive or negative characteristics (Jensen, 2011).

Current Directions in Moral Development Much research in moral development over the last 50 years has been influenced by Kohlberg's and Gilligan's theories. Many researchers have focused on Kohlberg's notion that the stages of moral development are the same for everyone, and indeed a review of 45 studies conducted across a wide range of cultures found that Kohlberg's claims of universality hold up pretty well for the early stages of moral development (Snarey, 1985). Such research also suggested that people from different cultures rarely skip stages or revert to previous ones.

Cross-cultural researchers have also noted cultural differences that support Gilligan's ideas. Some researchers found, for example, that respondents from *collectivist* cultures tend to score lower on the Kohlberg scales than do those from *individualistic* cultures (Gibbs et al., 2007). Close examinations indicate, however, that these score differences reflect differences in the kinds of moral problems faced by people in each of these cultures, not moral superiority or inferiority (Jensen, 2011). As described in Chapter 1, collectivistic cultures put greater emphasis on society and relationships than individualistic cultures, which tend to emphasize individual justice and fairness.

Finally, a number of moral development researchers, including Denis Krebs at Simon Fraser University, have wondered how much the expressed moral attitudes of people reflect their actual decision-making (Krebs & Denton, 2006). As we will see in our discussion of attitudes in Chapter 14, people do not always actually do what they say they will do (an experience you've probably had once or twice in your own life). Because the vast majority of research into moral reasoning has relied on Kohlberg's moral dilemma interviews, many researchers argue that we may be able to say a fair amount about people's moral *philosophies* but little about their moral *behaviour*.

Before You Go On

www.wiley.com/go/comer

What Do You Know?

11. In what areas of the brain is myelination concentrated during childhood, and how does myelination of these areas affect the child's cognitive functioning?
12. What are the crucial differences between Piaget's view of cognitive development and Vygotsky's view of cognitive development?
13. How are the ideas of scaffolding and zone of proximal development reflected in contemporary educational practices?
14. How do contemporary theories of moral reasoning differ from Piaget, Kohlberg, and Gilligan?

SCAN TO GET THE ANSWERS

What Do You Think?

Do you think that men and women reason differently about morality? If the outcome is the same in our moral choices, does the reasoning we used to achieve that outcome matter?

Adolescence

HOW WE DEVELOP

LEARNING OBJECTIVE 6

Summarize the major physical, cognitive, and emotional changes that take place during adolescence.

With the possible exception of the first couple years of life, the amount of change that occurs during adolescence rivals that of any other developmental passage. Most crucially, puberty begins. In the cognitive sphere, adolescents display features of both children and adults, and they begin to learn how to function independently. In this section, we will describe the key biological, cognitive, and social transitions that characterize this dramatic period.

Physical Development

puberty development of full sexual maturity during adolescence.

primary sex characteristics changes in body structure that occur during puberty that have to do specifically with the reproductive system, including the growth of the testes and the ovaries.

secondary sex characteristics changes that occur during puberty and that differ according to gender, but aren't directly related to sex.

Puberty refers to the physical development of primary and secondary sex characteristics (Herdt, 2010). **Primary sex characteristics** are the body structures that have to do specifically with the reproductive system, including growth of the testes and the ovaries. **Secondary sex characteristics** refer to non-reproductive body events that differ according to gender, such as the deepening of the male voice or the increase in female breast size (see **Figure 3-11**).

The onset and course of puberty is influenced largely by the *pituitary gland,* which coordinates the activities of the rest of the endocrine system (Blakemore, Burnett, & Dahl, 2010). As you will see in Chapter 4, the endocrine system includes the *adrenal glands, testes,* and *ovaries.* During adolescence, events throughout this system stimulate the growth of body hair and muscle tissue and trigger the onset of the female menstrual cycle, among other changes. One of the most important changes is a *growth spurt* triggered by the thyroid gland that, as we observed earlier, actually begins for girls in middle childhood and for boys during early adolescence (Drummond, 2011) (see **Figure 3-12**). The growth spurt happens about two years before the primary sex characteristics kick in and is not only a harbinger of those later changes, but also helps prepare the body for them (Rekers, 1992).

The changes of puberty stabilize after a couple years. In the meantime, however, many of those changes can be very disruptive to adolescents. Of course, we're all familiar with

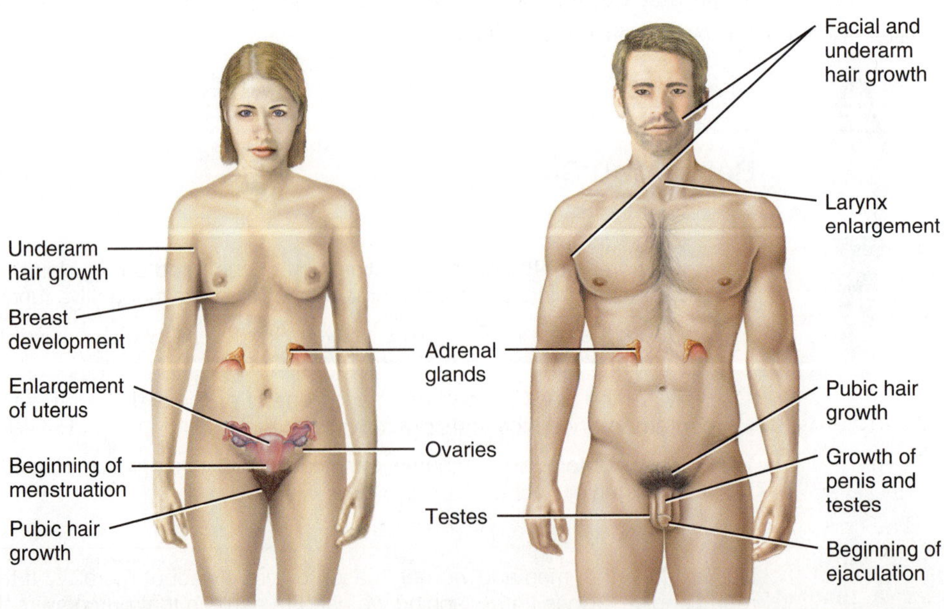

FIGURE 3-11 Primary and secondary sex characteristics. The complex changes in puberty primarily result when hormones are released from the pituitary gland, adrenal gland, and ovaries and testes.

the big ones: hair (or the lack of hair) in embarrassing places, acne, cracking voices (Drummond, 2011). For both boys and girls, variations from age norms for puberty can be upsetting; girls who mature early and boys who mature late report more problems making the transitions through adolescence than those who hit puberty "on time" (Blakemore et al., 2010; Hayatbakhsh et al., 2009).

The brain also goes through significant changes during adolescence (Roberson-Nay & Brown, 2011; Ernst & Hardin, 2010). Myelination continues to increase and synaptic connections continue to decrease as a result of synaptic pruning. As with middle childhood, many of these changes appear to be localized; they now focus on the *prefrontal cortex*, the brain area that helps coordinate brain functions and is instrumental in making sound judgments. Many psychologists point to the pruning that occurs in the prefrontal cortex as the reason teenagers often display poor judgment in their daily functioning for a while (Compas, 2004).

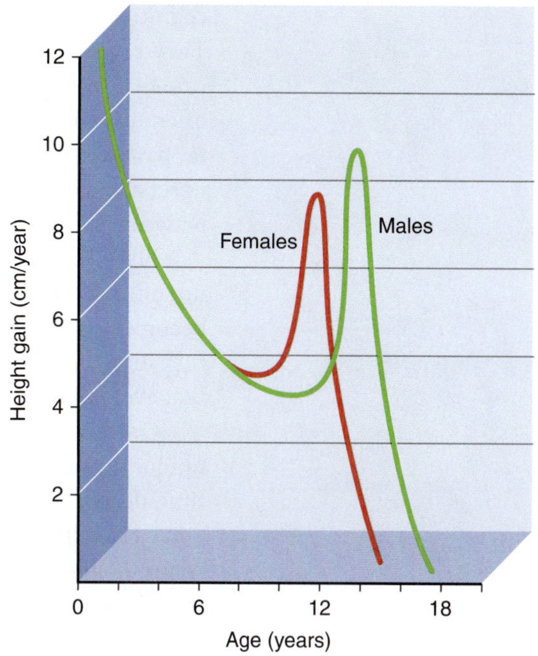

FIGURE 3-12 Adolescent growth spurt. The growth spurt of girls occurs, on average, two years before that of boys. Thus, between the ages of 10 and 14 years, the average girl is taller than most boys.

Cognitive Development

As we mentioned above, adolescent thinking has features of both child cognition and adult cognition. Teenagers show increased capacity for reasoning about abstract things, but also have deficits in their abilities to see outside of the moment or to take others' points of view. These strengths and limitations both come into play in their social and emotional growth as adolescents attempt to define themselves as persons.

PSYCHOLOGY AROUND US Road to Intelligence

Would you rather think of yourself as "smart" or as a "hard worker"? During adolescence, our ability to theorize about ourselves becomes more complex and begins to have complicated implications for how we behave. Psychologist Carol Dweck has studied teens who have "entity" theories of intelligence and those who have "malleable" theories of intelligence. Teens with entity theories believe that intelligence is a resource that you either have a lot of or a little of—and that there's little you can do to change your intelligence. Teens with malleable theories, in contrast, believe that with work, you can improve your intelligence level.

Based on Dweck's research, teens with entity theories of intelligence tend to feel better about themselves initially and tend to be oriented toward goals that let them demonstrate how smart they are. They also tend to be more afraid of failure and less confident about their overall ability. Teens with malleable theories of intelligence tend to feel a little worse about themselves initially, but also tend to persist at challenging tasks longer with the idea that they are building themselves up. By treating intelligence as a muscle that needs exercise to grow, these teens are able to improve their confidence and academic performance over the long term.

We're willing to bet that the majority of you thought "smart" when we first posed the question. What do you think now?

Piaget's Formal Operations Stage Piaget suggested that at around the age of 12, we cross over into mature adult thinking processes, a final stage known as **formal operations**. Piaget believed that the hallmark achievement of this stage is the ability to think about ideas conceptually without needing concrete referents from the real world. The successful transition to formal operations means that teens are no longer bound by the concrete realities of their world. For example, in math class they have moved beyond using real-life representations of numbers, such as counters, and now can use rules to solve problems, even algebra problems involving variables. They can conceive of other worlds and other possible realities, even ones that do not exist outside their own imaginations.

formal operations Piaget's final stage of cognitive development when the child achieves formal adult reasoning and the ability to think about things that don't have a concrete reality.

The crossover into formal operations also opens the door to higher-level moral thinking, as you saw earlier (Kohlberg, 2008, 1994, 1963). Adolescents may recognize, for example, that rules serve a societal purpose, not just a personal one. With this growth in cognitive and moral thought, adolescents begin looking at the validity of rules very closely. They realize, for example, that an 11:00 p.m. bedtime is, in many respects, an arbitrary rule that can be challenged and perhaps changed. Similarly, they become aware that adults often do things that contradict what the adults say. According to pioneering developmental psychologist David Elkind, these realizations may cause adolescents to feel angry and upset and may produce a desire to rebel (Elkind, 2007, 1978; Oda, 2007). And so the battle between adolescents and their parents (or other adults) begins.

Elkind notes that adolescents' mastery of formal operational thinking enables them not only to tune in to the flaws of other people, but also to recognize their own flaws. They become very sensitive to what other people may be thinking about them. Correspondingly, they display a psychological phenomenon called *adolescent egocentrism*, the mistaken belief that everyone else is focusing largely on them and their behaviour.

One feature of adolescent egocentrism is the *personal fable,* the belief that they are unique and invincible. Over the course of searching for a sense of identity and spending time deeply focused on their own thoughts and feelings, adolescents may become convinced that they are special—the only person to have particular thoughts and feelings (e.g., Alain thought that no one could have ever been more embarrassed than he was when he went on stage with toilet paper trailing from his shoe). This sense of being special extends to feeling invincible; bad things happen to other people, other people get pregnant, get caught drinking and driving, or become addicted to cocaine. Another feature of adolescent egocentrism is the *imaginary audience.* Teenagers feel that everyone is scrutinizing them, a notion that leads to strong feelings of inhibition and self-consciousness.

Social and Emotional Development

We're all familiar with the fact that adolescents spend a lot of time trying to figure out who they are and how they fit into the world. Because this is such a central task of adolescence, we will focus on it here, paying particular attention to the work of German psychologist Erik Erikson, an important contributor to our understanding of the social and emotional life of adolescents.

Erikson didn't restrict himself to theorizing about adolescents. Indeed, he was one of the few major developmental theorists to look at development across the *entire* lifespan (Erikson, 1985, 1984, 1959). Erikson divided the span from birth to old age into eight stages. Each of Erikson's stages is associated with a "main task," a challenge the person must meet and reconcile. An individual's achievement at each stage has a direct impact on how he or she meets the challenges of the next stage. Erikson believed that culture and relationships play strong roles in personality formation, and so he referred to his work as a stage theory of *psychosocial* development (Clark, 2010).

As **Table 3-8** shows, Erikson believed that each stage of development is associated with a potentially positive outcome versus a potentially negative outcome. For example, the conflicts and challenges associated with infancy determine whether a baby will develop a basic trust of the world (positive outcome) or mistrust (negative outcome). Babies whose parents respond attentively when they cry with hunger learn that the world is a good place and that other people can be trusted.

The key developmental task faced by adolescents is to resolve the conflict between *identity* and *role confusion.* During adolescence, teenagers start making decisions that affect their future roles, such as where they want to go to college or university or what they want to do with their lives, as well as decisions about abstract aspects of their identities, such as political or religious beliefs.

According to Erikson, if we do not reach a successful resolution of the conflict confronted at a particular stage, we may find it harder to meet the challenges of subsequent stages. Teenagers who do not effectively resolve the conflicts of their earlier psychosocial stages may enter adolescence with heightened feelings of mistrust and shame. These lingering feelings may render the teens particularly confused about which roles and beliefs truly reflect their own values and which ones reflect excessive peer and family influences. Peer relationships are extremely important to all teenagers, and Erikson believed that vulnerable teens are

TABLE 3-8 Erikson's Stages of Psychosocial Development

Stage 1 Trust versus mistrust (birth–age 1) Infants develop a basic trust in others. If their needs are not met by their caregivers, mistrust develops.
Stage 2 Autonomy versus shame and doubt (ages 1–3) Children exercise their new motor and mental skills. If caregivers are encouraging, children develop a sense of autonomy versus shame and doubt.
Stage 3 Initiative versus guilt (ages 3–6) Children enjoy initiating activities and mastering new tasks. Supportive caregivers promote feelings of power and self-confidence versus guilt.
Stage 4 Industry versus inferiority (ages 6–12) Children learn productive skills and develop the capacity to work with others; if not, they feel inferior.
Stage 5 Identity versus role confusion (ages 12–20) Adolescents seek to develop a satisfying identity and a sense of their role in society. Failure may lead to a lack of stable identity and confusion about their adult roles.
Stage 6 Intimacy versus isolation (ages 20–30) Young adults work to establish intimate relationships with others; if they cannot, they face isolation.
Stage 7 Generativity versus self-absorption (ages 30–65) Middle aged-adults seek ways to influence the welfare of the next generation. If they fail, they may become self-absorbed.
Stage 8 Integrity versus despair (ages 65+) Older people reflect on the lives they have lived. If they do not feel a sense of accomplishment and satisfaction with their lives, they live in fear of death.

particularly likely to be confused about where their own beliefs start and the wishes of others end.

A number of other theorists and researchers have also highlighted the critical role that identity formation plays while teens are seeking to successfully negotiate their way through adolescence (Phinney & Baldelomar, 2011). James Marcia, working at Simon Fraser University in Burnaby, British Columbia (Kroger, Martinussen, & Marcia, 2010; Marcia, 2010, 2007, 1994), for example, expanded Erikson's theory, suggesting that a combination of identity "crises" (also called identity explorations) and personal commitments in life help to define an individual's identity. Marcia identified four statuses of identity. He argued that identity does not necessarily remain stable throughout life, but instead changes with age *and* experience (Marcia, 2002).

> "The best way to keep children home is to make the home atmosphere pleasant—and let the air out of the tires."
> —*Dorothy Parker, author*

Other issues can make it difficult to establish a strong sense of personal identity. For minority groups, such as Canada's Aboriginal youth, identity development is made more difficult both by a sense of difficulty in fitting into mainstream cultural identity options and opportunities, as well as difficulty in finding positive, healthy images of personal and cultural history and ideals to lean on for support.

One large scale study conducted in British Columbia shows the central roles of culture and community in positive adolescent developmental outcomes. Michael Chandler at UBC and Chris Lalonde from the University of Victoria (2008; Chandler, Lalonde, Sokol, & Hallett, 2003) examined the rates of youth suicide in many of the First Nations bands across the province. But instead of looking at individual suicides and trying to figure out case-by-case causes, they examined markers of culture and community efforts to take charge of and advance their own culture and heritage. Specifically, they looked to see whether each band had taken or were taking steps toward self-government, control of the education of their children, control of their health services, control of police and fire services, and had initiated land claims, and finally whether there was a structure on their land specifically dedicated to the recognition and promotion of their culture and heritage. While there may not be any obvious connection between these things and adolescent suicide rates, the data in **Figure 3-13** clearly indicate otherwise.

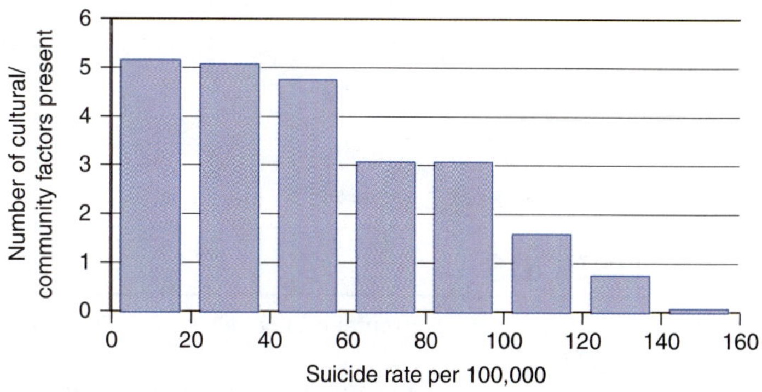

FIGURE 3-13 Aboriginal youth suicide rate by number of cultural factors present in the community. This figure shows that the more a First Nations band community does to take active control of their culture, the lower is the rate of youth suicide in that community.

Source: Based on Chandler & Lalonde, 2008.

Tying It Together: **Your Brain and Behaviour**

Growing from Infancy to Adolescence

Although all brain regions have already started to form before a baby is born, we can tell by their limited abilities and dependence on others that they still have a long way to go. The production of new nerve cells or neurons continues to occur in several brain regions, including those important for learning and memory, throughout infancy, childhood, and beyond

Somewhat surprisingly, many of the neurons and connections that formed during early development are lost during the postnatal period. Neurons that fail to make appropriate connections die and connections that are not strong enough are eliminated. The death of neurons and elimination of connections play an important role in sculpting the circuitry that develops into a fully functioning mature brain. And last but not least, the insulation of nerve fibres by a fatty sheath, produced by nonneuronal cells called glia, continues throughout childhood and into young adulthood. This process enables brain regions to send information more quickly and efficiently—its completion during young adulthood coincides with more mature cognitive abilities.

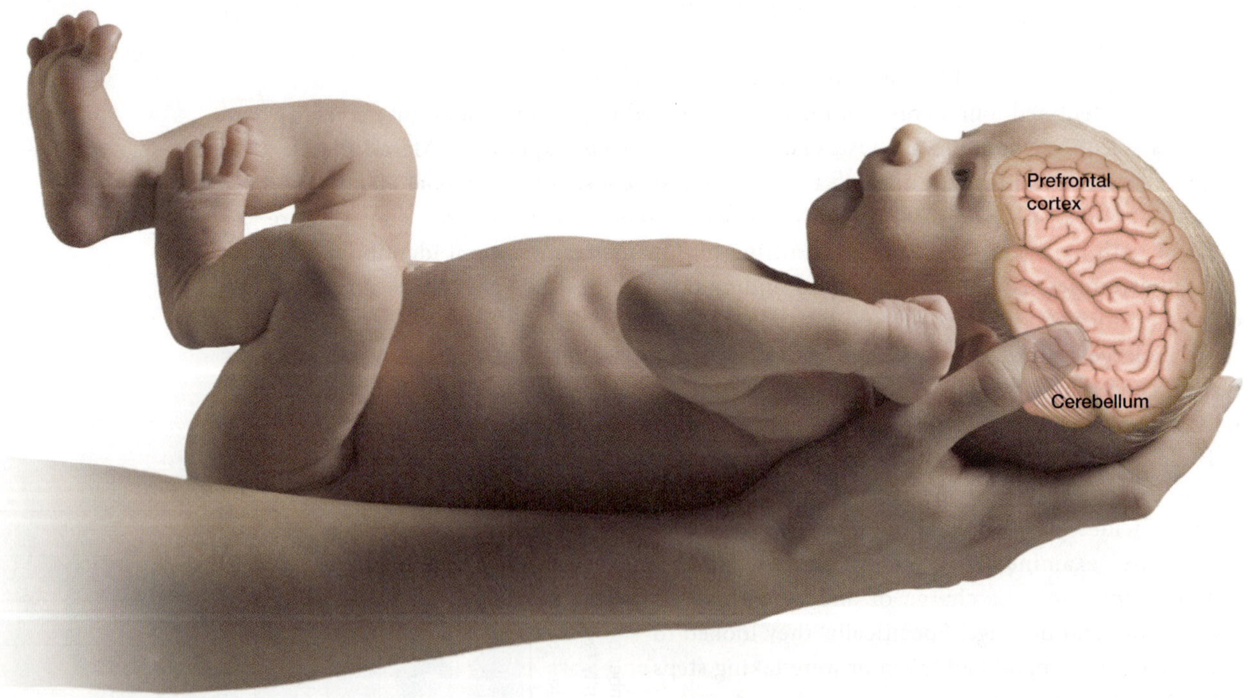

Questions

1 **How do changes in the prefrontal cortex help explain infants' enjoyment of hide and seek games?**

2 **Improvement in which skills is most directly related to the development of the cerebellum during childhood?**

3 **Explain how the sequence of brain development contributes to the finding that adolescents tend to make more impulsive decisions than adults do.**

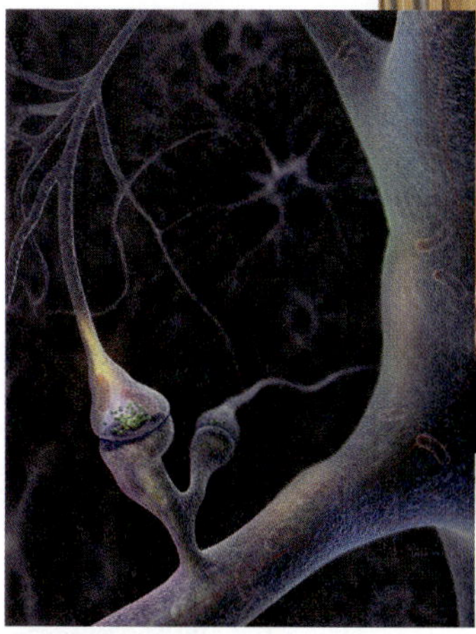

PLAYING PEEK-A-BOO

Around 9 months, synapses (shown in this image) in the prefrontal cortex are eliminated. The prefrontal cortex is a brain region that is important for cognitive processes like short-term memory. This reduction in the number of synapses seems to coincide with the ability to hold a memory of an object while it is out of sight. Around this time, babies seem to delight in playing peek-a-boo.

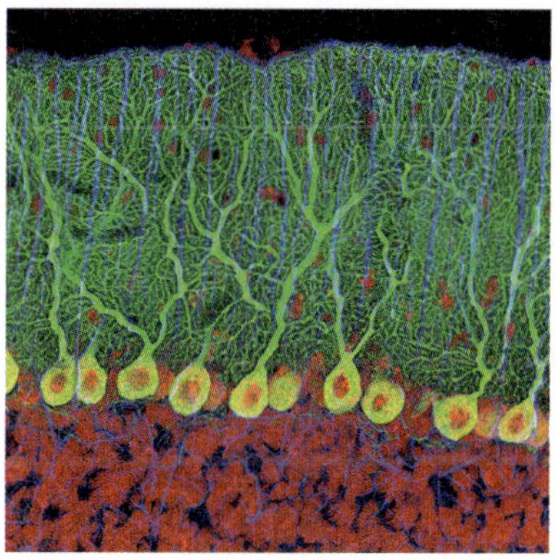

WALKING, RUNNING, KICKING

Postnatal neurogenesis occurs in the cerebellum (as shown in this image), a brain region important for coordination of movement and certain types of learning. The continual addition of new neurons to this brain region after birth and into childhood may participate in the emergence of motor skills such as walking, running, and kicking a ball.

MAKING BETTER DECISIONS

During adolescence, more myelin (shown here in red) forms in the prefrontal cortex. Myelin levels develop earlier in other brain regions, making the prefrontal cortex the latest brain region to reach maturity. The prefrontal cortex is important for moral reasoning, decision making, and planning. The late development of this brain region may explain why teenagers often seem to lack the ability to make good decisions about the future!

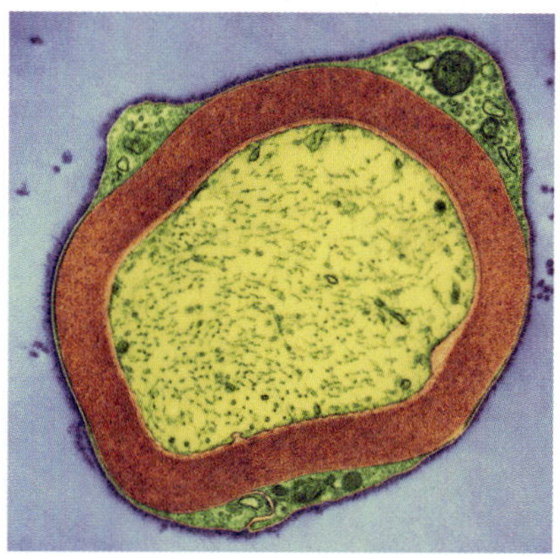

The more engaged in taking or re-taking cultural control a First Nations community is and the more they are asserting their cultural authority over aspects of self-determination, the lower is their rate of adolescent suicide—approaching zero when all six markers of community control of culture and heritage are present. When the cultural or social side of the individual/community interaction that defines identity formation is strong, youth can develop strong identities and can see clear, culturally- and community-defined and supported pathways for them to walk as they move forward into adulthood.

Jessica Ball of the University of Victoria states that the culture within the individual (2004, 2008, 2010; Ball & Simpkins, 2004) is an important determinant of healthy development. Successful identity development is an integral part of a successful transition to adulthood, and one that for Aboriginal youth can involve community as well as individual development (Kirmayer, Tait, & Simpson, 2009).

Before You Go On

www.wiley.com/go/comer

What Do You Know?

15. If a child arrives at puberty significantly earlier or later than his/her peer group, how might that affect his/her adjustment?
16. Define formal operations.
17. Describe what Erikson believed was the major dilemma and risk for adolescence.

What Do You Think?

How might Erikson explain extremely altruistic or aggressive adolescents?

SCAN TO GET THE ANSWERS

Adulthood

HOW WE DEVELOP

LEARNING OBJECTIVE 7

Describe key physical, social, and emotional changes that take place throughout adulthood.

Traditionally, developmental psychology viewed adulthood as an outcome rather than a period of time worthy of study. As we will see, however, adulthood is in fact a time of continuing change—and by change, we do not necessarily mean decline. Let's look at some of the developmental changes that happen during adulthood.

PSYCHOLOGY AROUND US Suddenly, I'm the Adult?

When does adulthood first strike? For columnist Richard Cohen, it was on a summer night in Cape Cod:

"Several years ago, [my parents and my family were eating at a restaurant]. That's when it happened. My father did not reach for the check.

"In fact, my father did nothing. Conversation continued. Finally, it dawned on me. Me! I was supposed to pick up the check. After all these years, after hundreds of restaurant meals with my parents, after a lifetime of thinking of my father as the one with the bucks, it had all changed. I reached for the check and whipped out my American Express card. My view of myself was suddenly altered. With a stroke of a pen, I was suddenly an adult....

"One day you go to your friends' weddings. One day you celebrate the birth of their kids. One day you see one of their kids driving, and one day those kids have kids of their own. One day you meet at parties and then at weddings and then at funerals....

"One day I made a good toast. One day I handled a headwaiter. One day I bought a house. One day—what a day!—I became a father, and not too long after that I picked up the check for my own. I thought then and there it was a rite of passage for me. Not until I got older did I realize that it was one for him, too." (Cohen, 1987)

Physical and Cognitive Development

With the end of adolescence comes full maturity. Nevertheless, the body continues to go through changes during adulthood. And, so does the brain.

What Happens in the Body During Adulthood? Generally, physical attributes, such as strength, reaction time, and overall body function, are at their peak during our 20s. As we move into our 30s, the body begins to decline slowly. Our metabolism slows, for example, so it takes a bit more work to keep some roundness from appearing around the waist.

During our 30s and 40s, we begin to show the first significant signs of aging. Skin begins to lose some of its tautness and grey hairs begin to sprout. Although we're significantly past our sensory peak, only in their 40s do most people begin to notice decline in that area of functioning (Drummond, 2011; Fozard et al., 1977). We become more farsighted, finding it hard to read or see small objects close to us, and we have difficulty seeing in the dark or recovering from sudden glares of light. We also become less sensitive to high-frequency noises.

Women in their 50s typically go through a major change called *menopause* (Nosek et al., 2010). **Menopause** involves a series of changes in hormonal function that eventually lead to the end of the menstrual cycle and reproductive capabilities. The early phase of menopause is often associated with a variety of physical experiences, such as hot flashes, headaches, and sudden shifts in mood.

menopause series of changes in hormonal function occurring in women during their 50s, which lead to the end of the menstrual cycle and reproductive capabilities.

As we move into late adulthood during our 60s and 70s, we may become a bit shorter and thinner due to changes in our skeletal structure and metabolism (Drummond, 2011; Bord-Hoffman & Donius, 2005). Our immune systems also begin to decline in function, leaving us at higher risk for illness. Our vision and hearing continue to decline, joined by our sense of taste. Our pupils shrink, so that less light reaches the retina, making it harder for us to see in low light.

The story is not as simple as a long, slow, inevitable decline, however. Exogenous factors, such as exercise, stress, diet, and life experience, can have a dramatic influence on the course and impact of these changes (Drummond, 2011; Larson et al., 2006; Brach et al., 2003). Although declines are common, many of the changes can be subtle and have minimal impact on how well we function in the world.

Adulthood WHAT HAPPENS IN THE BRAIN? Until recently, neuroscientists believed that our brains begin to shrink during adulthood, both in terms of volume and weight, and that much of this loss is attributable to the shrinkage and loss of active brain cells (Miller & O'Callaghan, 2005). Research over the past decade, however, has revealed that no significant loss of neurons occurs in adulthood, except in cases of brain pathology (Miller & O'Callaghan, 2005); that new neurons keep being formed in certain parts of the brain throughout life, including during adulthood (Leuner & Gould, 2010; Gould, 2007); and that such neurons may be the result of new learning, play a role in further learning, or both (Leuner, Glasper, & Gould, 2010; Leuner, Gould, & Shors, 2006). Given the stability and even addition of neurons during adulthood, it is not surprising that most of our broad intellectual capabilities remain intact throughout our lives. We're able to solve problems and process information in our adult years about as quickly as we could in our 20s (Park & Gutchess, 2006; Park et al., 2002).

Downward slide. In this computer illustration, the green-glowing proteins at the end of the chromosomes are telomeres, tiny structures that help cells to reproduce. The structures appear to grow shorter and shorter with repeated use, leading eventually to reduced cell reproduction and poor self-repair by the body.

As we move into our 40s and 50s, however, we do begin to see *some* intellectual shifts. Recovering information from long-term memory starts to take a little longer, and it takes a bit longer to learn new material. During our 60s and 70s, our memories decline, as does our confidence in our ability to remember and to solve problems (Ornstein & Light, 2010; Freedman et al., 2001).

Some declines are more serious. In *dementia,* severe memory problems combine with losses in at least one other cognitive function, such as abstract thinking or language (APA, 2000). The occurrence of dementia is strongly related to age. Around 1 to 2 percent of people 65 years of age have dementia, compared with some 50 percent of people over 85 (Apostolova & Cummings, 2008). We will discuss dementia in depth in Chapter 8.

Why Do We Age? Although scientists have offered many theories about why we age, no single explanation is widely accepted (Pierpaoli, 2005). One important theory of aging, the **cellular clock theory**, suggests that aging is built into our cells. Tiny structures on the ends of DNA strands, called *telomeres*, aid in cell reproduction but grow shorter each time they are used. Eventually they become too short, and cells can no longer reproduce themselves. As a result, the body is less able to repair itself. The various changes of aging—saggy skin and decreases in vision and memory, for example—are the direct result of those events.

cellular clock theory theory suggesting that we age because our cells have built-in limits on their ability to reproduce.

Two other theories of aging are more rooted in our experiences and the impact that life events can have on us. The *wear-and-tear* and *free-radical* theories suggest that years of use help wear out our bodies. The **wear-and-tear theory** boils down to this: the more mileage we put on our bodies through living (augmented by factors such as stress, poor diet, and exposure to environmental teratogens), the sooner we wear out (Hawkley et al., 2005). The **free-radical theory** provides a chemistry-oriented explanation (Perluigi et al., 2010; Boldyrev & Johnson, 2007). Free radicals are oxygen molecules that are negatively charged. A negative charge on a molecule can attract small particles of matter called *electrons* from other molecules. According to the free-radical theory of aging, free radicals become more prevalent in our system as we get older, increasingly destabilizing cell structures and doing progressively more damage to our bodies—resulting in the aging effects described above.

wear-and-tear theory theory suggesting we age because use of our body wears it out.

free-radical theory theory suggesting we age because special negatively charged oxygen molecules become more prevalent in our body as we get older, destabilizing cellular structures and causing the effects of aging.

Social and Emotional Development

Although the social and emotional changes that occur in adulthood are more gradual than those that characterize childhood, adults do in fact experience multiple transitions in these areas (Aldwin, Yancura, & Boeninger, 2010; Freund & Lamb, 2010; Holcomb, 2010 Roberts et al., 2002, 2006; Palkovitz et al., 2001). As you saw in Table 3-8, Erikson proposed that individuals confront important psychosocial conflicts as they travel from early adulthood to old age. A number of other theorists have made similar claims.

Social and Emotional Features of Early and Middle Adulthood According to Erikson, during early adulthood (20 to 30 years of age), people form intimate relationships and sexual unions that call for self-sacrifice and compromise. In fact, he believed that the primary goal of this period is to attain love. The ethical convictions developed in adolescence and the sense of moral obligation formed in childhood contribute to ethical strength in young adulthood. These early acquisitions are important, he believed, because a sense of morality is required for the truly loving relationships of adulthood. Erikson further believed that people who are unable to successfully meet the challenges of young adulthood tend to become isolated and may actually avoid the contacts that create and sustain intimacy. Thus, he concluded that young adulthood is dominated by a conflict between *intimacy* and *isolation*.

Erikson proposed that during middle adulthood (30 to 65 years of age), people are inclined to turn their attention to younger people. Their focus is to help create, or at least contribute to, the next generation. Erikson used the term *generativity* to describe this focus. Caring for younger people, whether through parenthood or by mentoring junior colleagues at work, is a major concern. This process enriches individuals who engage in it. Erikson believed that people who fail to develop such activities may experience stagnation and boredom. Middle adulthood, then, is dominated by a conflict between *generativity* and *stagnation*.

Several theorists have extended Erikson's work on early and middle adulthood. One particularly broad investigation of these life stages was conducted by psychologist Daniel Levinson (1996, 1986, 1984, 1977). According to Levinson's findings, the stage of *early adulthood* (which he defined as 22 to 40 years of age) is characterized simultaneously by high energy and abundance and by contradiction and stress. The aspirations of individuals in this age range tend to be youthful. They establish a niche in society, they may raise a family, and ultimately they reach a relatively "senior" position in the adult world.

For many, this period brings great satisfaction and creativity. But early adulthood can also be a period of enormous stress. The burden of becoming a parent, undertaking an occupation, incurring financial obligations, and making other critical decisions about marriage, family, work, and lifestyle often fills people with anxiety and tension.

Levinson described *middle adulthood* (30 to 65 years of age) as a stage in which biological functioning, although less than optimal, is still sufficient for an "energetic, personally satisfying and socially valuable life." During this stage, people usually become "senior members" of their particular world. They take responsibility for their own work, that of others, and the development of younger adults. This, too, can become a period of self-satisfaction and peace of mind. At the same time, growing biological problems, numerous responsibilities, and anticipation of upcoming old age may also produce considerable stress and tension.

Although the stages of early and middle adulthood may themselves be sources of stress, Levinson believed that the periods of *transition* that people must pass through as they move from one stage to another can be even more pressure-filled. During such transitional periods, people confront particularly difficult career, marital, and family issues and reflect on and adjust their dreams.

The *early adult transition*, often called "emerging adulthood," bridges adolescence and early adulthood. During this period, which lasts from approximately 17 to 22 years of age, people may go through a very unsettled time. They take steps toward individuation and modify their relationships with family, friends, and social institutions, but they may feel insecure in these efforts and, correspondingly, may experience anxiety and confusion. Indeed, in today's world, more and more individuals seem to be having difficulty completing this early adult transition.

PSYCHOLOGY AROUND US Moving Ahead?

Generally, when we think of 20-somethings, we think of young people making their initial journey into independence. But increasingly, and around the world, young adults are returning home after college or university, or never leaving in the first place. In some countries, the trend is so strong that it has inspired name-calling. In Germany, young adults who live with their parents are called *Nesthockerin*, or birds that stay too long in the nest. In Italy, they're *bamboccioni*, or overgrown babies. In the United Kingdom, they're *kippers*, or "kids in parents' pockets, eroding retirement savings."

This group has received the most negative attention in Japan, where sociologist Masahiro Yamada coined the term *parasite singles* to describe them. Parasite singles are often accused of being unwilling to take on the responsibilities of adulthood, spending their money on nights out and personal luxuries instead. In their own defence, many of these young adults point out that entry-level jobs are hard to come by, and those that are available do not pay enough. The average rent in Japan constitutes two-thirds of the average young adult's salary.

Some researchers have begun to study this widespread phenomenon and argue that a new stage of development might be emerging, much as adolescence developed initially in response to social changes that outlawed child labour and made education more widely available. But other observers consider this view to be misguided—a soft-hearted way of looking at a bunch of overgrown teenagers who need to grow up and get a job.

Even more stressful for some people, according to Levinson, is *middle life transition*, a period lasting from ages 40 to 45 that bridges early and middle adulthood. During this period, individuals experience significant changes in the character of their lives. On the positive side, they may become more compassionate, reflective, and judicious; less conflicted; and more accepting and loving of themselves and others during these years. On the negative side, however, some individuals feel overwhelmed as they increasingly recognize that they are no longer young and vibrant, that time is passing, that life's heaviest responsibilities are falling on them, that they must prepare for the future, and that some of their dreams may not be met. These persons may question their accomplishments in life and conclude that they have achieved and will continue to achieve too little. In certain cases, they may even try to deny the passage of time and to recapture their youth, a phenomenon popularly labelled the *midlife crisis*.

Social and Emotional Features of Old Age "Old age" is typically defined in our society as referring to people who are 65 years old and above. Psychologists further distinguish between the young-old, people between 65 and 74; the old-old, those between 75 and 84; and the oldest-old, individuals 85 and above. By this account, around 36 million people in the United States are old. They represent nearly 12 percent of the total North American population. By the year 2030, 20 percent of the total population is expected to be old.

Old age brings special pressures, unique upsets, and, as we saw earlier, profound biological changes. People become more prone to illness and injury as they age. They also are likely to experience the stress of loss—the loss of spouses, friends, and adult children, as well as the loss of former activities and roles (Etaugh, 2008). Some lose their sense of purpose after they retire. Even favoured pets and possessions are sometimes lost.

Despite such difficulties and despite their awareness that death eventually awaits them, elderly people do not necessarily become depressed or feel overwhelmed (Edelstein et al., 2008). Indeed, Erikson believed that, for many, old age is characterized by accumulated knowledge and understanding and by mature judgment. The goal of old age, he proposed, is to attain wisdom, a detached yet active concern with life in the face of death. Wisdom is achieved through the integration of insights gained from the past and the present regarding one's place in the stream of life. Erikson believed that those who do not effectively meet the challenges of this stage may experience an extreme fear of death or despair, show bitterness and disgust, and feel that time is too short. He therefore categorized old age as a conflict between *integrity* and *despair*.

Research indicates that many older persons do indeed use the changes that come with aging as opportunities for learning and growth. One case in point: the number of elderly—often physically limited—people who use the Internet to connect with people of similar ages and interests doubled between 2000 and 2004, doubled again between 2004 and 2007, and doubled yet again by 2011. Individuals such as these Web searchers seem likely to remain involved and active right up to the end of their lives, health permitting.

It is also worth noting that, despite the common themes of old age, the population of elderly adults is actually quite heterogeneous. That is, older adults are more *unlike* than similar to one another. Elderly people have very different life experiences, adapt to change in uniquely personal ways, and age at different rates. Thus, psychologists make a point of distinguishing between chronological age and functional age. *Chronological age*, or the number of years one has lived since birth, is regarded as little more than a "short-hand variable" because it is not a true indicator of an elderly person's functional capacities. *Functional age*, however, reflects the individual's capacity to adapt his or her behaviour to the changing environment. As you will see in Chapter 15, this aspect of aging is influenced by one's coping skills, social pursuits, emotions, motivation, and self-esteem, among other factors.

The Changing Face of Adulthood

The journeys through each of these stages correspond to many of the rites of passage associated with adulthood, including marriage, parenting, retirement, and death—events that we will be discussing further throughout the book. It is worth noting that, in many societies, the timing and form of such milestones of adulthood are now more variable than they were in earlier days. In the past, for example, the length of time a couple would spend married before having their first child was relatively short; that time has extended greatly in recent decades. Moreover, the number of couples who choose to remain childless has doubled since 1960 (Rubino, 2011; Demo et al., 2000). It has also become more acceptable in some societies for people who are not married to raise children (Weinraub et al., 2002).

Similarly, the average human lifespan continues to increase, lengthening the time that older adults remain part of the workforce, as well as part of the retired population, before dying (Elrod, 2010; Volz, 2000). Such cultural shifts have opened new areas of study for psychologists, who are seeking to understand how these shifts may affect adult development.

Before You Go On

www.wiley.com/go/comer

What Do You Know?

18. What is the difference between the wear-and-tear theory of aging and the free-radical theory of aging?
19. Describe and define Erikson's major crises of adult development.

What Do You Think?

Do you think that life experiences may actually increase adults' cognitive, or mental, abilities? Why might this be so?

SCAN TO GET THE ANSWERS

Developmental Psychopathology

WHEN THINGS GO WRONG

LEARNING OBJECTIVE 8

Understand how the developmental psychopathology approach uses a developmental perspective to look at problematic behaviours.

Throughout the textbook, we will consider the ways that different psychological attributes and faculties develop and how those attributes and faculties may go wrong. For example, Chapter 8 examines memory disorders in depth, and Chapter 16 examines autism. For now, however, we will offer just a broad understanding of how things can go wrong during development.

Psychologists in the field of **developmental psychopathology** are interested in how problematic behaviour patterns evolve, based on both genetics and early childhood experiences, and in how those early problematic patterns affect functioning as individuals move through later life stages (Cicchetti, 2010; Santostefano, 2010; Hinshaw, 2008; Hudziak & Bartels, 2008). Developmental psychopathologists also compare and contrast problematic behaviour patterns with more normal behaviour patterns, seeking to identify **risk factors**—biological and environmental factors that contribute to problematic outcomes. In addition, they seek to identify other factors that can help children avoid or recover from such negative outcomes.

One disorder of special interest is called *conduct disorder*, a diagnosis applied strictly to children and adolescents. **Conduct disorder** (and its less severe cousin, *oppositional defiant disorder*) is characterized by a number of emotional and behavioural problems, including frequent rule-breaking, trouble following the limits imposed by authority figures, bullying and fighting, and cruelty. Looking at how developmental psychopathologists approach this disorder can help us understand how they approach all psychological disorders.

Developmental psychopathologists focus first on the various behaviours shown by children with conduct disorders (Murray & Farrington, 2010; Hinshaw, 2002) to distinguish the conduct disorder from other disorders and see whether it has any relationships

developmental psychopathology the study of how problematic behaviours evolve as a function of a person's genetics and early experiences and how those early problematic issues affect the person at later life stages.

risk factors biological and environmental factors that contribute to problematic outcomes.

conduct disorder clinical disorder in children and adolescence associated with emotional and behavioural problems, such as rule-breaking, trouble with limit-setting from authority figures, bullying and fighting with other people, and cruelty.

PSYCHOLOGY AROUND US Bad Seeds?

Horror movies are often thought to be most effective when they reflect and exaggerate the fears and anxiety of their culture. Every few years, a new horror film appears exploring the evil child. Think *The Bad Seed*, *The Omen*, *Orphan*, *The Exorcist*, *The Grudge*, and *The Ring*, just to name a few. Even outside Hollywood, we see writers coping with anxiety about the violence and chaos that would erupt if children took over society—look at *Lord of the Flies*, for example, or at a particularly memorable episode of *South Park* where Cartman and the rest of the kids get their parents hauled off to prison and immediately go to war with one another.

Film theorists suggest that the evil child is an effective and recurring movie image because it can be so hard to know or understand what a child is thinking or feeling, even under ordinary circumstances. That's even more true when a child is troubled or angry, or struggling with a severe clinical disorder. In such situations, parents, teachers, and mental health care professionals often find themselves struggling, in turn, with feelings of confusion, helplessness, concern, and fear. Fortunately, there are psychologists who have dedicated their lives to figuring out how to identify, prevent, and treat clinical disorders. With their help, we can see these children not as evil supernatural beings, but instead as people who struggle and who can be saved.

Violating, hurting, and disregarding others. Many children with conduct disorder wind up in trouble with the law. Here, a teenager and two 10-year-olds are led from a courtroom after being accused of attacking a homeless day labourer.

to milder problems, such as impulsiveness and distractibility. The negative behaviours of conduct disorder, such as defying authority, breaking rules, and fighting, are categorized as *externalizing behaviours* (as opposed to *internalizing behaviours*, such as fearful responses, crying, or withdrawal).

Like other developmental psychologists, developmental psychopathologists look for patterns and changes over time. Some studies have suggested, for example, that when externalizing behaviours begin in early childhood, they are more likely to be due to biological factors, such as genetic inheritance (Taylor, Iacono, & McGue, 2000), placing children with early-onset conduct disorders at greater risk for problems later in life than those whose conduct problems begin in adolescence. Still other studies indicate that, although externalizing behaviours tend to be moderately stable over time, the specific forms of the behaviours do shift with age. For example, explicitly aggressive acts, such as picking fights, typically decrease over time, while less overt acts of aggression tend to

Bullying: A Continuing Problem

According to the Canadian Public Health Association, *bullying* is the intentional use of power by one person over another and can be seen in physical, social, verbal, and electronic forms (CPHA, 2010). A report examining the many school shootings that have occurred across Canada and the United States over the past decade found that bullying was a factor in most of them (Gonzalez, 2010; Crisp, 2001). Sometimes, the shooters had been bullies; more often, they had been the *victims* of bullying. One survey asked children aged 8 to 15 what issues in school troubled them most, and the children pointed to teasing and bullying as "big problems" that ranked even higher than racial discrimination, AIDS, and sex or alcohol peer pressures (Cukan, 2001). Overall, over one-quarter of students report being bullied frequently, and more than 70 percent report having been victimized at least once, leading in many cases to feelings of humiliation or anxiety (Smith, 2010; Jacobs, 2008; Nishina et al., 2005). In addition, our online world has broadened the ways in which children and adolescents can be bullied, and today cyberbullying—bullying by email, text-messaging, or the like—is increasing (Jacobs, 2008). Qing Li (2005) of the University of Calgary found that 25 percent of grade 7 students had experienced cyber bullying. Shaheen Shariff of McGill University describes cyberbullying as verbal and written assaults carried out by way of websites, chat rooms, cell phones, social networking sites, and email (Shariff, 2005).

In response to these alarming trends, many schools—elementary through high school—have started programs that teach students how to deal more effectively with bullies, work to change the thinking of bullies, train teachers, conduct parent discussion groups, and apply classroom prevention measures (Jacobs, 2008; Frey et al., 2005; Twemlow, 2003). Furthermore, public health campaigns try to educate the public about antibullying programs, including information and links from the Canadian Children's Rights Council at www.canadiancrc.com/Bullying_Canada_Resources_Provincial_Programs.aspx, online information from the Canadian SafeSchool Network at www.canadiansafeschools.com, and a Bullying Prevention in Schools Program from the Government of Canada (Public Safety Canada) at www.publicsafety.gc.ca/res/cp/res/bully-eng.aspx.

Although recognizing the negative—and potentially tragic—impact of bullying, some experts worry that the sheer prevalence of bullying may make it a very difficult problem to overcome. It is hard, for example, for educators and clinicians to identify which bullies or bullied children will turn violent, given that a full 70 percent of children have experienced bullying. Can we really rid our schools and communities of a problem as common as this? One observer has even argued, "Short of raising kids in isolation chambers . . . bullying behaviours can never be eliminated entirely from the sustained hazing ritual known as growing up" (Angier, 2001).

increase during early adolescence (Hinshaw, 2002). It seems that many children with conduct disorders learn as a result of the negative consequences for their bad behaviour, but they do not really change internally. They learn primarily to hide their aggressive behaviour so that they do not get into as much trouble.

Again, like other kinds of developmental psychologists, those interested in developmental psychopathology hold that behaviour can be analyzed in a variety of ways. According to this view, a full accounting of how children get off-track (or stay on-track) requires looking at how genetics, environmental influences, and the children's own psychological processes all collaborate to bring about their current pattern of behaviour and functioning.

Two concepts that developmental psychopathologists have provided to the field of psychology are *equifinality* and *multifinality* (Fanti & Henrich, 2010; Mitchell et al., 2004). The concept of **equifinality** holds that individuals can start out from all sorts of different places and yet, through their life experiences, wind up functioning (or dysfunctioning) in similar ways. **Multifinality** follows the opposite principle. It suggests that children can start from the same point and wind up in any number of different psychological places. Applying these two concepts to conduct disorders, it appears that various roads may lead to the development of a conduct disorder during adolescence (Litschge, Vaughn, & McCrea, 2010). A child with a conduct disorder may have been born with a difficult temperament, experienced poor parenting, or developed poor social skills. **Table 3-9** lists risk factors that link conduct disorders to the likelihood of committing serious and violent crimes during adolescence or adulthood. As suggested by the notion of equifinality, regardless of which set of risk factors is at play, the outcome is often similar.

equifinality the idea that different individuals can start out from different places and wind up at the same outcome.

multifinality the idea that children can start from the same spot and wind up in any numbers of other outcomes.

At the same time, multifinality assures us that not every difficult baby and not every baby with ineffective parents will wind up with a conduct disorder. Indeed, the vast majority will wind up with no pathology at all. Developmental psychopathologists are very interested in the biological, psychological, or environmental factors that help buffer against or negate the impact of risk factors—factors that help produce **resilience**, an ability to recover from or avoid the serious effects of negative circumstances (Dudley et al., 2011; Flouri et al., 2011; Hudziak & Bartels, 2008). In short, according to this viewpoint, it is just as critical to understand what goes right as it is to understand what goes wrong.

resilience the ability to recover from or avoid the serious effects of negative circumstances.

Let's return one more time to one of the adopted orphans at the start of this chapter. A developmental psychopathologist might hypothesize that the indiscriminate friendliness toward strangers shown by some Romanian adoptees could be the result of a lack of early social contact and trauma due to issues arising from abandonment. The psychologist would be equally interested in identifying those factors that may have helped contribute to many orphans' resilience, including their development of solid trust and attachment to their adoptive parents and the social success experienced by many of the adoptees as they entered Canadian preschools, kindergartens, and grade schools.

TABLE 3-9 Risk Factors that Link Conduct Disorders to the Commission of Violent Crimes During Adolescence or Adulthood

Family violence	Multiple clinical disorders
Family dysfunction/conflict	Risky behaviour
Family distress	Gun availability/risk
Childhood exposure to violence	Antisocial parent
Childhood maltreatment	Gang membership
Childhood neglect	Peer violence
Childhood adversity	Personality disorder
Substance abuse	Academic failure
Hyperactivity	Social incompetence

Sources: FAS, 2008; Weaver et al, 2008; Gonzales et al., 2007; Lahey & Waldman, 2007; Mueser et al., 2006; Panko, 2005.

Before You Go On

www.wiley.com/go/comer

What Do You Know?

20. How do externalizing behaviours differ from internalizing behaviours?
21. Why is resilience important to developmental psychopathology?
22. What is the difference between equifinality and multifinality?

What Do You Think?

Consider problems such as anxiety and depression. Do you see any advantages to looking at emotional or mental problems from a developmental perspective—as the product of a lifetime of biological and environmental experiences—rather than just examining the symptoms displayed by people with these problems? Do you see any disadvantages to this approach?

SCAN TO GET THE ANSWERS

Summary

Understanding How We Develop

LEARNING OBJECTIVE 1 Understand the key debates underlying research and theory in child development.

- Developmental psychology is the study of changes in our behaviour and mental processes over time and the various factors that influence the course of those changes.
- Key philosophical issues in the study of developmental psychology are what drives change (biological or environmental factors); what is the nature of the change (qualitative or quantitative); and the role of early experiences in shaping later development.

How Is Developmental Psychology Investigated?

LEARNING OBJECTIVE 2 Describe and discuss the advantages and disadvantages of cross-sectional and longitudinal designs for researching development.

- Two major research approaches in developmental psychology are cross-sectional (comparing different age groups to assess change) and longitudinal (studying the same group to see how responses change over time).
- The cohort-sequential research design combines elements of the cross-sectional and longitudinal approaches.

Before We Are Born

LEARNING OBJECTIVE 3 Discuss patterns of genetic inheritance and describe stages and potential problems during prenatal development.

- Our genetic inheritance comes from both parents, who each contribute half our chromosomes. Genes can combine in various ways to make up our phenotype, or observable traits.
- Genetics can influence the manifestation of both physical traits and psychological traits, including temperament, although environment also plays a role.
- Prenatal development begins with conception and is divided into three stages: germinal, embryonic, and fetal, each characterized by specific patterns of development.
- Individuals are susceptible to multiple influences by biological and environmental forces before they are even born, during the prenatal period.

Infancy

LEARNING OBJECTIVE 4 Summarize the major physical, cognitive, and emotional developments that take place during infancy.

- Infants make dramatic gains in both physical and psychological capabilities. Our brains grow during this period, preparing us to learn and encode the information that will organize those changes.

- One of the most important developmental theorists, Jean Piaget, proposed a theory of cognitive development that suggested that through learning and self-experimentation, we help our thinking to grow progressively more complex.
- Piaget believed we pass through multiple stages on the way to formal adult reasoning and that each transition is accompanied by the acquisition of a new cognitive capability. During the sensorimotor stage, in infancy, we become able to hold memories of objects in our minds.
- Information-processing researchers have suggested that babies may develop mental capacities at earlier ages than Piaget believed they did.
- Attachment theory suggests that the baby is biologically predisposed to bond and form a relationship with a key caregiver, thus ensuring that his or her needs are met. The security of the attachment relationship will have later implications for how secure the person feels in his or her emotional and social capabilities.
- Baumrind found evidence that different parenting styles can also affect the overall well-being of the child, although subsequent research suggested that outcomes might vary depending on other environmental and cultural influences.

Childhood

LEARNING OBJECTIVE 5 Summarize the major physical, cognitive, and emotional developments that take place during childhood.

- Physical growth continues at a generally slower pace in childhood than in infancy. Myelination and synaptic pruning continue to shape the brain.
- Piaget believed that children pass through the stages of preoperational and concrete operations thinking, learning to manipulate their mental schema. Other researchers have suggested children's thinking may not be as limited during these stages as Piaget thought it was.
- Theories of moral development often focus on moral reasoning (the reasons why a child would do one thing or another) rather than values. Generally, research supports the movement from morality rooted in submitting to authority to morality rooted in more autonomous decisions about right and wrong.
- Some researchers suggest that moral reasoning may vary across gender and culture. Other researchers question whether morality theories would be better served by measuring behaviour instead of expressed reasoning or attitudes.

Adolescence

LEARNING OBJECTIVE 6 Summarize the major physical, cognitive, and emotional changes that take place during adolescence.

- Adolescence is generally associated with many substantial changes, including the onset of full sexual and physical maturity, as well as reasoning capabilities that approach adult levels. However, the teenager has certain limitations that influence his or her ability to make sound judgments and avoid risky situations.
- Erikson proposed a theory of development that stretches across the lifespan and incorporates various dilemmas that need to be successfully reconciled for development to stay on track.

Adulthood

LEARNING OBJECTIVE 7 Describe key physical, social, and emotional changes that take place throughout adulthood.

- Adult physical and psychological development is often characterized by some degree of decline. However, most basic faculties remain intact across the lifespan.
- According to Erikson, the challenge of early adulthood is to resolve the conflict between intimacy and isolation; of middle adulthood, to resolve the conflict between generativity and stagnation; and of old age, to resolve the conflict between integrity and despair. Levinson pointed out that transitions from one stage to the next can also cause conflicts.
- The ages at which adults are expected to reach major social and emotional milestones, such as marriage and parenting, are more flexible now in many societies than they were in the past.

Developmental Psychopathology

LEARNING OBJECTIVE 8 Understand how the developmental psychopathology approach uses a developmental perspective to look at problematic behaviours.

- The developmental psychopathology approach studies how early problematic behaviours evolve as a function of a person's genetics and early experiences and how those behaviours affect the person in later life.
- Developmental psychopathologists are particularly interested in identifying the risk factors that contribute to problematic outcomes.
- The concept of equifinality holds that although children may start out at different places, through their life experiences they wind up functioning (or dysfunctioning) in similar ways. The concept of multifinality holds that children can start out at the same place but may wind up in a number of different psychological places.
- Developmental psychopathologists are also interested in the factors that contribute to resilience, the ability to recover from or avoid the serious effects of negative circumstances.

Key Terms

accommodation 82
allele 73
assimilation 82
attachment 86
cellular clock theory 108
cephalocaudal pattern 79
chromosomes 73
codominance 74
cognitive development 81
cohort-sequential design 72
concrete operations 94
conduct disorder 111
conservation 93
critical periods 69
cross-sectional design 71
deoxyribonucleic acid (DNA) 73
developmental psychology 66
developmental psychopathology 111
discrete trait 75
dominant trait 74
egocentrism 93
equifinality 113
equilibrium 82
formal operations 101
free-radical theory 108
genes 73
genotype 73
habituation 84
heterozygous 74
homozygous 73
information-processing theory 83
longitudinal design 72
maturation 68
menopause 107
miscarriage 76
motor skills 80
multifinality 113
myelination 80
object permanence 83
operations 93
phenotype 73
placenta 76
polygenic trait 75
prenatal period 73
preoperational stage 93
primary sex characteristics 100
private speech 97
proximodistal pattern 79
puberty 100
recessive trait 74
reciprocal socialization 89
reflexes 79
resilience 113
risk factors 111
scaffolding 96
scheme 81
secondary sex characteristics 100
stage 68
synapses 80
synaptic pruning 80
temperament 85
teratogens 77
theory of mind 95
wear-and-tear theory 108
zone of proximal development 96
zygote 76

TYING IT TOGETHER

The study of development is closely connected to all other areas of psychology. Throughout this chapter, we have stressed how this topic interfaces with psychology's other areas, including our highlighted sections on brain function, individual differences, and abnormal functioning. To remind you of how development is tied to such areas, here are some interesting points from throughout the chapter.

WHAT HAPPENS IN THE BRAIN?

- At birth we have approximately 100 billion neurons. A newborn has around 2,500 synaptic connections per neuron, while a 3-year-old has six times that many connections! But a 20-year-old has only around one-third the synaptic connections per neuron of a 3-year-old, a huge reduction due to synaptic pruning.
- *Myelination*, the formation of fatty white coverings around neurons, helps neurons transmit information more efficiently. During infancy, much of myelination occurs in brain areas tied to movement, reflexes, and sensory responses. During childhood, myelination is concentrated in brain areas that help coordinate activity, planning, and problem solving.
- Despite past beliefs, no significant loss of neurons occurs in adulthood, except in cases of brain pathology.
- New neurons keep being formed in certain parts of the brain throughout life, including during adulthood.

HOW WE DIFFER

- Only a few human traits are the product of a single gene pair. Most traits, particularly behavioural ones, are *polygenic*, helping to produce many variations in how traits are expressed from person to person.
- Babies tend to display either an *easy*, *difficult*, or *slow-to-warm-up* temperament, and their particular infant temperament often helps predict their reactions to situations throughout the lifespan.
- On average, Kipsigis in Kenya walk a month before babies in Canada and the United States, and Ache babies in Paraguay begin walking a year later than Canadian and American children—variations due to cultural differences in parenting.
- Babies may display either a *secure*, *anxious/avoidant*, *anxious/resistant*, or *disorganized attachment style*—a style that helps predict later relationship needs.
- On average, girls experience a growth spurt during their tenth or eleventh year, a couple of years prior to boys.
- Primary sex characteristics during puberty include growth of the testes for boys and growth of the ovaries for girls. Secondary sex characteristics include a deepening of the voice for boys and increase in breast size for girls.
- According to some research, the higher stages of moral development of males tend to focus on justice, fairness, and other abstract moral values, whereas those of females factor in relationship needs and responsibilities.

WHEN THINGS GO WRONG

- Environmental risks, called *teratogens*, can influence prenatal development adversely. Thus, pregnant women should avoid risks, such as smoking or ingesting alcohol, each of which has been linked to birth defects.
- Developmental psychopathologists seek to identify biological, psychological, and environmental *risk factors* that contribute to the development of behavioural problems and psychological disorders.
- Risk factors for the development of *conduct disorders* in children and adults include family violence or dysfunction, childhood maltreatment, substance abuse, peer violence, and personality disorders.
- Despite the appearance of such risk factors, many children do not develop conduct disorders—a phenomenon attributed to their *resilience*. Like risk factors, the biological, psychological, and environmental factors that help produce resilience are of enormous interest to developmental psychopathologists.

HOW WE DEVELOP

- At birth, the senses of taste, smell, and touch are highly developed, hearing is somewhat immature, and vision is extremely limited.
- Babies may have some sense of mathematics as early as 5 months of age.
- Most children do not develop a *theory of mind*, the ability to recognize that other persons have a perspective different from their own, prior to 3 years of age.
- Young children tend to make moral decisions that help ensure they will not get into trouble with parents or adults. In contrast, the moral decisions of adolescents and young adults tend to be more complex and guided by broader principles of right and wrong.
- Although less egocentric than younger children, many teenagers often display personal fables in which they are convinced that they are special—the first persons to have various thoughts and feelings—and perceive an imaginary audience in which they believe everyone is scrutinizing them.
- It is not entirely clear why we age and grow old.
- The human lifespan has continued to increase with each generation.

Psychology Around Us

School Days, "Cool" Days

Young children spending recess in their elementary schoolyard—breaking into different groups, playing various games, having all kinds of interactions. Each doing their own thing? Not really. The schoolyard conversations, physical activities, and mental processes generally follow the principles, milestones, and even rules cited in developmental stage theories. While the children recess away, your job is to identify and explain the stages of physical, cognitive, and social-emotional development reflected by their recess activities.

Fast forward to adolescence and to a teenage party. Individuals finally doing their own thing? Once again, the answer is no. And once again, your job is to detect the developmental stages and principles that their cool behaviours, talk, and posturing reflect.

View this in Action WILEY PLUS www.wileyplus.com

Video Lab Exercise

As you are working on this online exercise, consider the following questions:

- What does this lab exercise say about the nature-versus-nurture debate in developmental psychology?
- Do the behaviours and interactions on display in the lab exercise indicate that stage differences are *qualitative* or *quantitative*?
- What events and steps have helped transform the enthusiastic (but awkward) elementary school kids of one video into the cool (though still awkward) high school kids of the second video?
- Stages or no stages, the children and teenagers in the lab exercise also show many individual differences. How did that happen?

CHAPTER 4

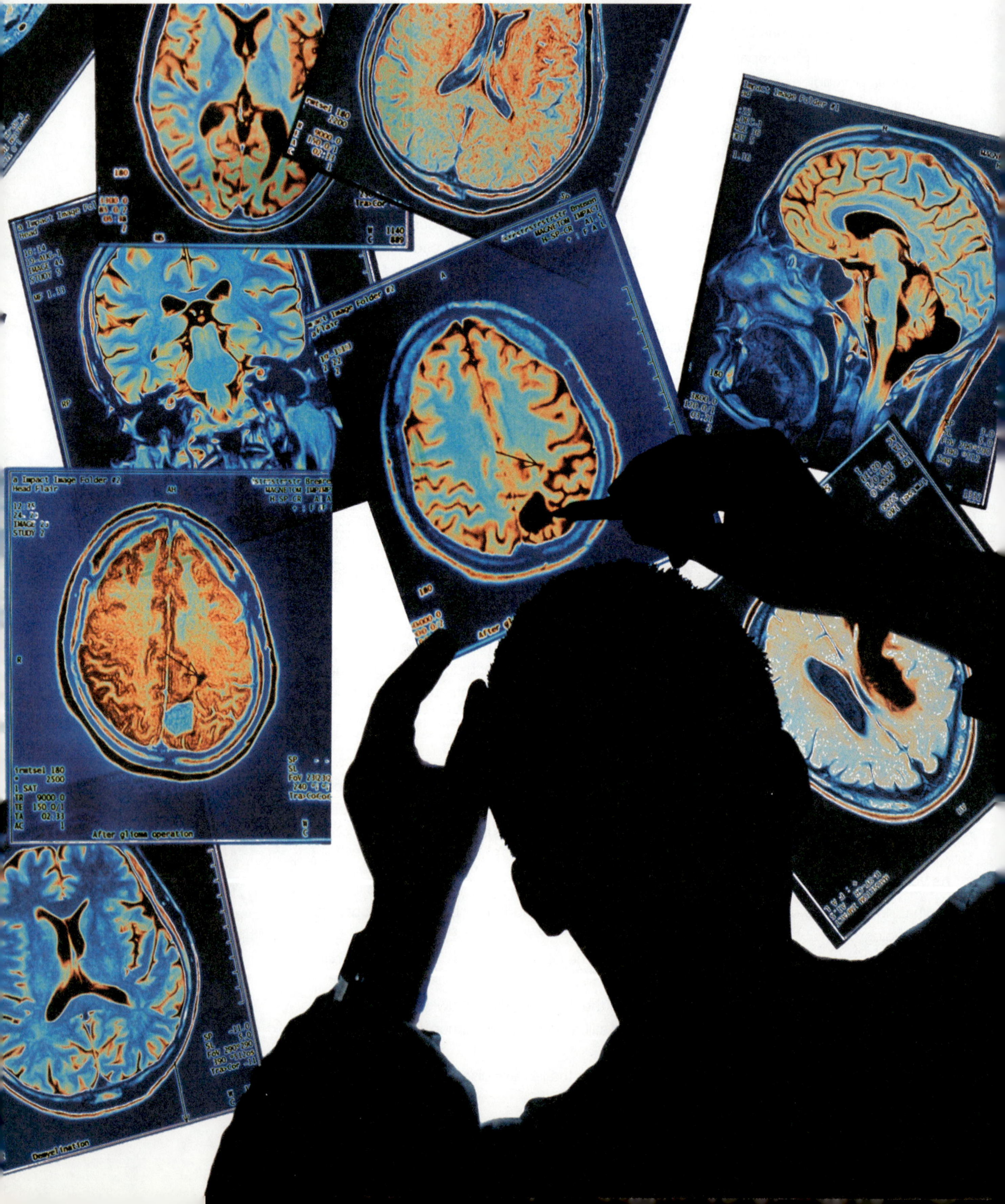
a Impact Image Folder #2
Head Flair
After glioma operation
Demyelination

Neuroscience

CHAPTER OUTLINE

- How Do Scientists Study the Nervous System?
- How Does the Nervous System Work?
- How Do Neurons Work?
- How Is the Nervous System Organized?
- Structures of the Brain
- Evolutionary Psychology
- Brain Side and Brain Size *How We Differ*
- Neurological Diseases *When Things Go Wrong*

YOUR BRAIN AND YOUR LIFE

Some people hope that once scientists figure out the human brain and nervous system, all of our experiences—our thoughts, our feelings, our plans and strategies, our ups and downs—will be explained by our understanding of the actions and interactions of the neurons in our brain and nervous system. How does that sound to you? Will we ever be able to potentially control or adjust any facet of our experience? Do you think it would be a good thing if we could? Does this sound fantastic or unlikely? Well, we are not there yet, but there are some amazing things arising out of neuroscience research. Some groups are even claiming that discoveries in this area will eventually lead to immortality (Fossel et al., 2010).

Human life spans have quadrupled in the last 300 years. Relatively recently, neuroscientists have begun to look more closely at the cellular factors associated with aging. One promising area involves telomeres. Telomeres are repetitive sequences of DNA at the end of chromosomes that are central to the process by which our bodies' cells reproduce themselves. Telomeres have been compared to the plastic tips on the ends of your shoelaces that keep the laces from fraying or unravelling. Telomeres protect genes at the ends of the chromosome by preventing these genes from degrading or recombining with other DNA in the cell nucleus. They also prevent the chromosome from fusing into a ring. Telomeres get smaller and smaller with each cell replication, until they stop replicating and eventually die. The telomere theory of aging holds that aging occurs as an increasingly large number of cells become unable to replicate (Blackburn, 1991; Cawthon et al., 2003; Waterstrat et al., 2008). Some researchers believe that if we could protect our telomeres or even rebuild them, our cells could go on replicating for years and we might be able to live longer (Fossel et al., 2010); other researchers point out that longer term replication comes with other health risks, such as increased risks for cancer and other disorders (Chan & Blackburn, 2002).

We rely on our brains and our nervous systems every day. We experience sensory input, remember things we have already learned, and learn new things. Without a nervous system, we wouldn't be able to register changes in the environment, nor would we be able to react to those changes. **Neuroscience** is the study of the nervous system. In this chapter—and in *What Happens in the Brain* sections of all the other chapters of the book—we will examine many of the discoveries in this fascinating field.

neuroscience the study of the nervous system.

We will see in this chapter that, although considerable progress has been made in understanding the organization and function of the brain, there remain large gaps in our knowledge about how the actions of the millions of microscopic cells in the brain produce complex behaviours, such as thought. ■

How Do Scientists Study the Nervous System?

LEARNING OBJECTIVE 1

Understand the key methods that scientists use to learn about brain anatomy and functioning.

In the past, researchers of psychological issues in humans often avoided analyzing the brain, mainly because of limits in our study methods and technologies. Until recently, it was difficult, if not impossible, to study what goes on in the human brain without causing damage to brain tissue (Chudler, 2011). As a result, human neuroscience relied on one of the following methods:

- *Examining autopsy tissue.* This method allows neuroscientists to see what our brains look like, but has the obvious drawback of telling them little about how these systems worked while the person was alive and using them.
- *Testing the behaviour of patients with damage to certain parts of the brain.* Scientists called *neuropsychologists* have learned a lot about the brain from studying patients with brain damage. Patients with localized brain damage often have loss of some function. The loss of function then suggests what the brain region does when it is undamaged. The obvious drawback of this approach is that it involves inferring information about the normally functioning brain from the damaged brain. Even patients with localized brain damage may have smaller undetectable abnormalities in other areas of the brain. Also, the damaged brain may undergo reorganization over time so abnormalities in behaviour may not reflect what goes on in the intact brain (Benton, 2000).
- *Recording brain activity, or brain waves, from the surface of the scalp.* Scientists have used *electroencephalograms*, or EEGs, to learn about the activity of our brains during certain states (awake and asleep), as well as during certain behavioural tasks (Niedermeyer & da Silva, 2004). The drawback of this type of analysis is that surface recordings only provide a summary of activity over a large expanse of tissue—pinpointing the location of activity using this method can only be done in a general sense.
- *Animal studies.* Studies on animal nervous systems made it possible to look closely at parts of functioning brains. Animal studies include microscopically examining specific brain regions, electrically recording from specific brain areas, or targeting specific brain areas for destruction and observing the effects on behaviour, a process called *lesioning* (Mukerjee, 1997).

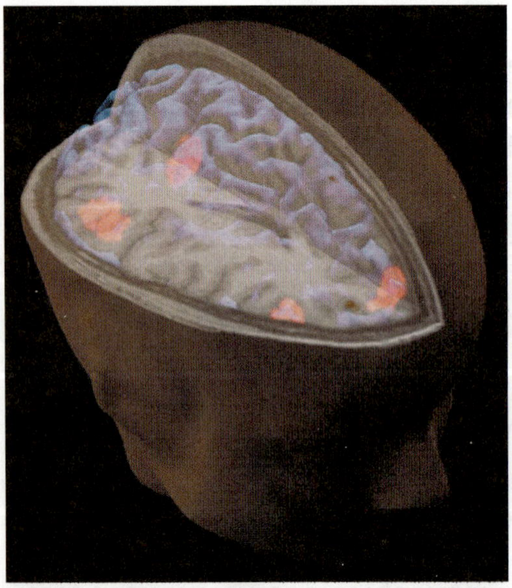

The brain at work. This 3D computer-generated image of a human brain shows areas of brain activation (coloured areas) in individuals undergoing a moral decision-making task. This study employed fMRI technology that uses changes in blood flow as a measure of changes in the neural activity.

Taken together, these approaches have provided us with a great deal of information about the brain and the nervous system in general, but they all share drawbacks: they tell us little about activity in specific regions of healthy, living, human brains.

PSYCHOLOGY AROUND US Make Up Your Mind!

PET scans and fMRI enable researchers to see what parts of the brain are active during certain tasks. Researchers have taken advantage of this ability to study a wide range of issues in psychology. One group of researchers, for example, used fMRI to locate areas of the brain that are activated in people who must make a difficult decision for which the correct answer is unclear (Botvinick et al., 1999). The subjects were monitored using fMRI so the researchers could see which areas of the brain were active under different conditions. The researchers found when a decision was particularly difficult, a part of the frontal lobe called the anterior cingulate is activated. Since the anterior cingulate is also involved in processing information about pain, it is not surprising that we often find making a choice under doubtful circumstances to be emotionally difficult!

Over the past few decades, however, several new techniques, collectively referred to as **neuroimaging**, have been developed to study brain activity. These techniques enable researchers to identify brain regions that become active under certain conditions. Among the most useful neuroimaging methods are positron emission tomography (PET) and functional magnetic resonance imaging (fMRI). PET scans enable the detection of the uptake of certain molecules so that brain areas with increased activity can be identified (Phelps, 2006). fMRI allows for the detection of changes in blood flow, a presumed indicator of changes in the activity of neurons (Ogawa et al., 1992).

neuroimaging techniques that allow for studying brain activity by obtaining visual images in awake humans.

The availability of these neuroimaging technologies has produced an explosion of research. While the results have confirmed many previously held claims about brain function, they have also raised additional questions. As a result of rapid improvements in neuroimaging, methods are becoming more and more sensitive.

Before You Go On www.wiley.com/go/comer

What Do You Know?

1. Describe how studies of people with brain damage and EEGs have contributed to our knowledge of the brain and nervous system.
2. What are the main advantages of neuroimaging methods over earlier neuroscience research methods?

What Do You Think?

Do you think it will eventually be possible to use neuroimaging techniques to determine what a person is thinking? What are the ethical implications of using this technology?

SCAN TO GET THE ANSWERS

How Does the Nervous System Work?

LEARNING OBJECTIVE 2

Describe the two major types of cells in the nervous system and describe the primary functions of each.

The **neuron**, or nerve cell, is the fundamental building block of the nervous system (Jones, 2007). Communication among neurons is necessary for normal functioning of the brain and spinal cord. The peripheral nervous system that runs throughout the rest of our bodies, outside the brain and spinal cord, is also made up of neurons.

neuron a nerve cell.

The structure and function of individual neurons, as well as the ways in which these cells work together in groups, called *networks*, has been the subject of considerable scientific inquiry for over a century (Jones, 2007). Neuroscientists have discovered that neurons have specialized structures that enable them to communicate with other neurons using both electrical and chemical signals. As we will see later, our emerging understanding of how these signals work is leading toward the development of treatments for adjusting our neurochemistry when things go wrong.

But neurons are not the only cells in the nervous system. As we will see, neuroscientists have increased their attention to *glia*, the other type of cell found in our nervous systems.

Neurons and Glia

The human brain contains about 100 billion neurons. **Figure 4-1** shows the basic structure of a neuron. Like most of our other cells, neurons have a cell body filled with cytoplasm that contains a nucleus (the residence of chromosomes that contain the genetic material). In addition, neurons contain organelles that enable the cell to make proteins and other molecules, produce energy, as well as permit the breakdown and elimination of toxic substances. Just as our own organs make it possible for our bodies to live and function, so to do organelles make it possible for our neurons to live and function (López-Muñoz, Boya, & Alamo, 2006).

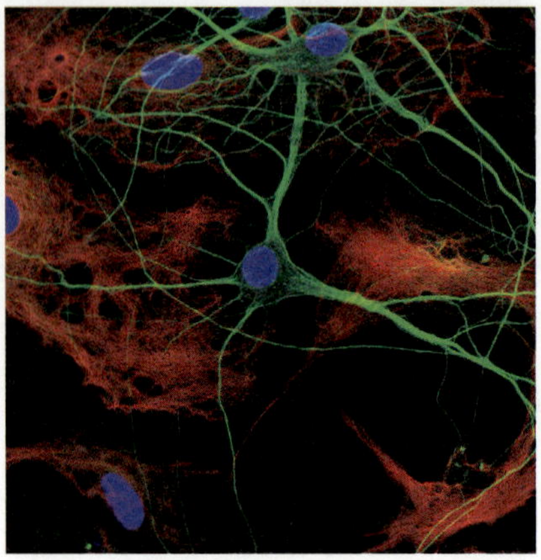

However, as Figure 4-1 shows, neurons are different from other cells, in that they have specialized structures called *dendrites* and *axons* that are important for communication with other neurons.

Dendrites extend like branches from the cell body to collect inputs from other neurons. Neurons can have many dendrites and, indeed, some have very extensive dendritic "trees" that allow a single neuron to receive more than 200,000 inputs from other neurons.

Axons also extend from the cell body. Unlike dendrites, however, axons typically function to carry information away from the cell body, toward other neurons. Axons have a specialized region at the end, called the **axon terminal**. Unlike dendrites, neurons have only one axon, which can be very long. For example, the axon you have to report pain in your big toe (when you stub it) runs from your spinal cord all the way to the end of your big toe. In addition, axons can be highly branched. These branches, or *collaterals*, greatly increase the number of neurons that the axon contacts.

dendrites the parts of neurons that collect input from other neurons.

axon the part of the neuron that carries information away from the cell body toward other neurons.

axon terminal the end of a neuron's axon, from which neurotransmitters are released.

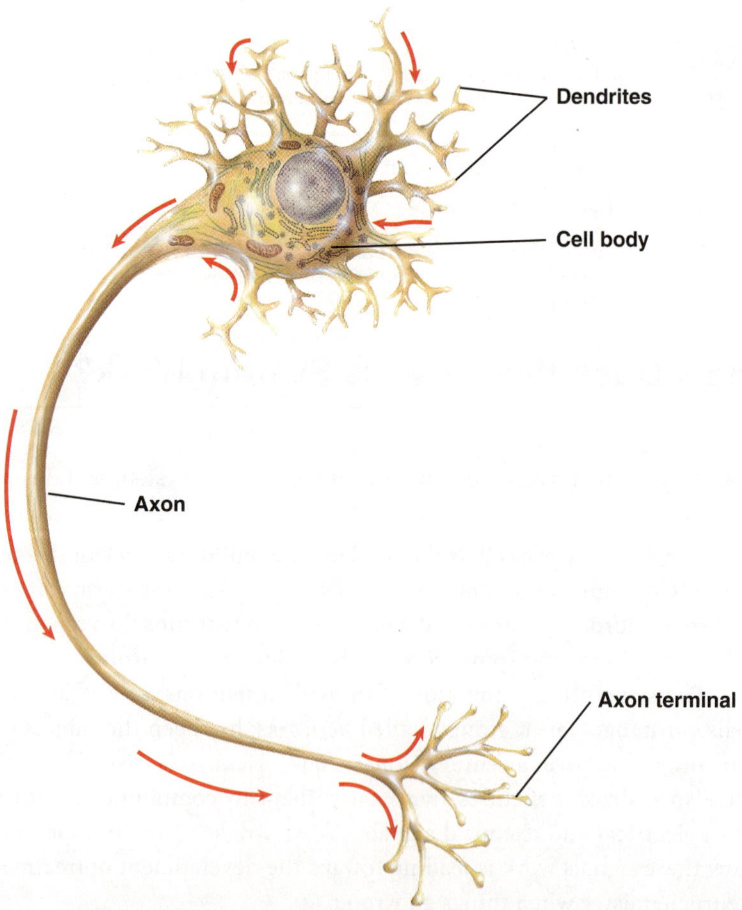

FIGURE 4-1 The neuron. The major structures of the neuron include the cell body, the axon, and the dendrites. Dendrites typically receive information from other neurons, while axons send information away from the cell body to communicate with other neurons. Arrows indicate the direction of information flow.

Some axons (but not all) are covered with a *myelin sheath* (which we describe in greater detail later in the chapter).

There are many different kinds of neurons (e.g., sensory neurons in the skin; muscles that respond to pressure, temperature, or pain; motor neurons that stimulate our many muscle cells into action; and interneurons that connect these two types of neurons). Some are large (such as the sensory neurons that keep us informed about our feet), while others are relatively small (such as many of the neurons found in the brain). Some have very elaborate dendritic trees (brain neurons), while others possess a single unbranched dendrite (some sensory neurons). Although these cells all look quite different from one another, they have two features in common: all neurons are covered by a membrane that surrounds the entire neuron, including its axon and dendrites; and all neurons are capable of communicating with other cells by producing and sending electrical signals (Martin, 2003).

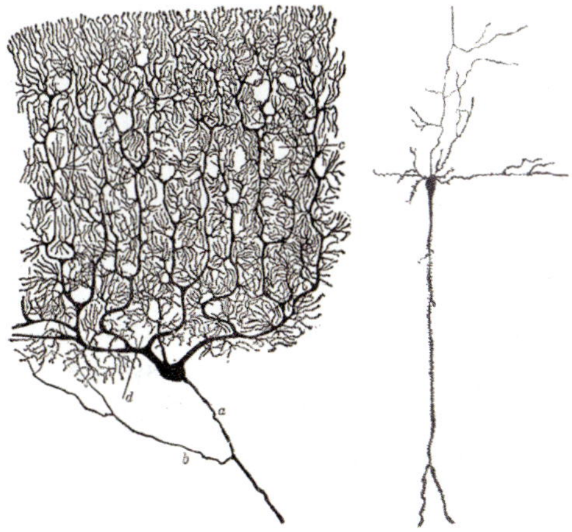

Various shapes. These drawings by the early neuroanatomist Santiago Ramon y Cajal are just two examples of the vast diversity in the shape of neurons in the brain.

In addition to neurons, the nervous system contains a large number of non-neuronal cells called glia (or *glial cells*). In fact, in some parts of the human brain, glia outnumber neurons by a factor of about 10 to 1 (Laming et al., 2011). Glia buffer the neurons from the rest of the body, control the nutrient supply to neurons, and destroy and remove diseased and dead neurons. As well, discoveries over the past two decades have confirmed that glial cells also modulate neurotransmission (Gourine et al., 2010). For additional detail on glial cells, see the "More than Just Glue" box below. We will return to glial cells periodically throughout the rest of this chapter.

glia the cells that, in addition to neurons, make up the nervous system.

More than Just Glue

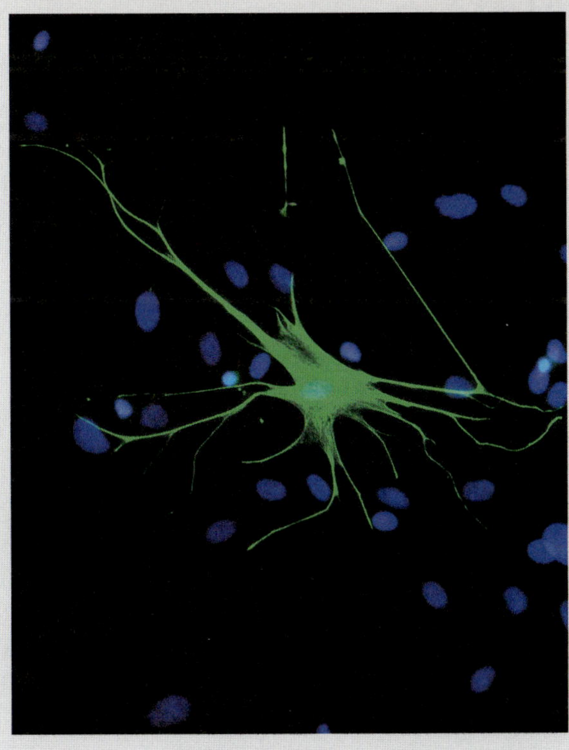

When glial cells were first discovered, they were given a Greek name that means "glue" because scientists believed their chief function was to form a physical medium to hold the brain together. Now more than 100 years later, we know that glia play many roles in the brain that are critical for normal functioning (Laming et al., 2011). There are several categories of glia: *astroglia*, *oligodendrogli* and *Shwann cells*, which are myelinating glia, as well as *ependymal cells* and *microglia*.

Astroglia are so-named because most are shaped like stars (see photo on left). This glial type is important for creating what is referred to as the blood–brain barrier, a system that tracks the passage of molecules from the blood to the brain. Astroglia regulate the flow of blood into regions with increases or decreases in neuronal activity, thus requiring more or less nutrition support or oxygenation (Iadecola & Nedergaard, 2007). Astroglia also function to absorb or clean up chemicals released by neighbouring neurons and to provide important growth-promoting molecules to neurons. Astroglia migrate to the site of brain injury, where they enlarge and multiply to form a glial scar (Fitch & Silver,

2008). In addition, astroglia also serve to communicate with neurons, influencing their electrical activity by absorbing unneeded potassium ions (Haydon et al., 2009). Another type of astroglia serves as a stem cell in the adult brain. These cells are capable of dividing and producing new cells, including new neurons (Doetsch, 2003).

The *oligodendroglia* (central nervous system) and Schwann cells (peripheral nervous system) are important for providing a protective fatty sheath, or coating, called *myelin* that insulates the axons of neurons from nearby neuronal activity (Baumann & Pham-Dinh, 2001). This protective function is particularly important in the brain and spinal cord, where neurons are very closely packed and axons are often organized into bundles. As we already have discussed, myelin also speeds up the passage of electrical signals down the axon. However, although both cell types maintain axons and produce myelin, unlike the oligodendroglia of the CNS, Schwann cells are important for digesting debris from the PNS and also act as guides for the regrowth of PNS axons (Jessen & Mirsky, 2005).

Ependymal cells are specialized neuroglial cells that line the walls of the ventricles of the brain. They create and secrete cerebrospinal fluid, and are thought to make up the blood–cerebrospinal fluid (CSF) barrier (Del Bigio, 1995; Johansson et al., 1999). Finally, *microglia*, so-named because they are very small, are important for cleaning up the debris of degenerating or dead neurons and glia so that brain regions can continue with their normal functioning. This cleaning function makes microglia an important brain defence against infection and illness (Gehrmann, 1996; Streita, 2006).

Before You Go On

www.wiley.com/go/comer

What Do You Know?

3. What are the two types of cells in the nervous system?
4. What are the three major types of glia and the functions of each type?

What Do You Think?

Why do you think the function of glia was overlooked by researchers for so long?

SCAN TO GET THE ANSWERS

How Do Neurons Work?

LEARNING OBJECTIVE 3

Describe what happens when a neuron "fires" and how neurons send messages to one another.

As we mentioned, communication among neurons is vital to the functioning of the nervous system. Neurons send messages to one another via electrochemical actions, meaning that chemicals cause an electrical signal to be generated. A sudden change in the electrical charge of a neuron's axon causes it to release a chemical (neurotransmitter) that can be received by other neurons, thereby passing an electrical signal along from one neuron to the next.

Your brain uses 20 percent of your body's energy, but it makes up only 2 percent of your body's weight.

The Action Potential

Neurons are covered by a membrane. Nerve cells are surrounded by liquid called *extracellular fluid* that contains charged particles called *ions*. Ions are molecules that contain a relative imbalance of protons or electrons and are thus either negatively or positively charged.

Ions are also found in the cytoplasm that fills the neuron. The presence of these ions gives neurons an electrical charge, even when they are resting. (When a neuron is not sending a message, it is said to be resting.) This resting charge, called the **resting potential**, is negative; this is because the fluid inside the neuron is more negatively charged than the fluid outside the cell. If you put a recording electrode into an axon, it will read a negative charge, typically around −70 millivolts, relative to outside of the cell.

resting potential the electrical charge of a neuron when it is at rest.

The neuron's membrane exhibits *selective permeability* to ions. Embedded in the membrane are specialized ion channels, or pores, that only allow the passage of certain ions into and out of the cell. These ion channels can open or close depending on information thecell receives from other neurons. Some of the key ions that are involved in determining the resting potential are the positively charged ions sodium (Na+) and potassium (K+) and the negatively charged chloride (Cl–) ion. When the neuron is at rest, positive sodium ions are higher in concentration outside of the cell. This unequal distribution of ions on each side of the cell membrane is known as a concentration gradient. This resting charge is maintained through the actions of sodium-potassium pumps that use energy to hold the resting potential at the negative charge by continuously pumping Na+ out of the axon, exchanging Na+ for K+. How does exchanging one positive ion for another maintain a negative charge? The pumps are not evenhanded; the pumps push out three sodium ions but only put in two potassium ions. This concentration gradient changes when an electrical charge increases the permeability of the membrane to Na+, allowing Na+ ions to pour into the cell.

ion channels pores in the cell membrane that open and close to allow certain ions into and out of the cell.

concentration gradient the relative concentration of sodium ions inside and outside of the neuron.

sodium potassium pump protein molecules in the membrane of cells that push out sodium ions and push in potassium ions.

This rapid reversal in voltage across axon membranes is caused by the exchange of ions across the membrane and is called an action potential. The action potential is a brief electrical charge and is also called a "spike" or an "impulse." When an action potential has been generated, the neuron is said to "fire." An action potential occurs when *excitatory* signals outweigh the number of *inhibitory* signals and reach a certain threshold (this is explained in greater detail below). The action potential is shown in **Figure 4-2**. During an action potential, ion channels that allow the passage of sodium (Na+) through the membrane open rapidly. This enables Na+, which is present in higher concentrations outside of the axon, to rush through the Na+ channels into the axon. The sudden influx of positive ions shifts the electrical charge of the axon from negative to positive. At the peak of the action potential, the membrane charge is about +50 mV. At that point the sodium channels close, but not before this action has caused neighbouring sodium channels to open and the action potential to sweep down the axon of the neuron. As the sodium channels close in an axon section, potassium channels open and potassium ions exit the cell, restoring the negative charge within that area of the cell (Siegel et al., 2006).

action potential a sudden positive change in the electrical charge of a neuron's axon. Also known as a spike or firing, action potentials rapidly transmit an excitatory charge down the axon.

threshold the point at which the relative excitatory influence of other neurons succeeds in causing a neuron to initiate an action potential.

As Figure 4-2 shows, the action potential travels down the axon, away from the cell body toward the terminal. As each portion of the axon spikes, or *fires*, the Na+ channels on the next patch of membrane open, letting the spike continue its progress toward the axon terminal. After the action potential has passed a particular segment of the axon, K+ channels open, allowing positively-charged K+ ions to exit the cell, restoring the negative charge in that area. Now in a recovering or refractory state, the membrane in that segment works to restore the original ion balance by using specialized proteins to pump K+ ions into the cell and Na+ ions out of the cell, thus returning it to its initial resting state (Siegel et al., 2006).

Action potentials are not graded—that is, there cannot be weaker or stronger action potentials. Instead, action potentials follow an *all-or-none* principle. Since action potentials are all-or-none, they don't convey a lot of specific information. If the stimulation reaching the neuron exceeds a certain threshold, it fires; otherwise, it does not. The analogy most commonly used to describe the all-or-none principle is the analogy of firing a gun. If you squeeze the trigger on a gun, the bullet fires or it doesn't fire. Regardless of how hard you squeeze the trigger, the bullet has only one velocity. So, how do we detect when one stimulus is more intense than another? Stronger stimuli cause more neurons to fire and to fire more often; thus, higher frequencies send information about more intense stimuli (Stein et al., 2005). The pattern of action potentials, whether they occur in rapid succession or at a slow pace, whether they are regular or more sporadic, can provide a neural code that is specific.

To facilitate the movement of the electric action potential down the axon, the axons of many neurons are insulated by myelin, produced by specialized glial cells. Wrapped areas of the axon are broken up at regular intervals by regions that expose the neuronal membrane to the extracellular fluid. These exposed regions are called *nodes of Ranvier*.

myelin a fatty, white substance, formed from glial cells, that insulates the axons of many neurons.

FIGURE 4-2 The action potential.

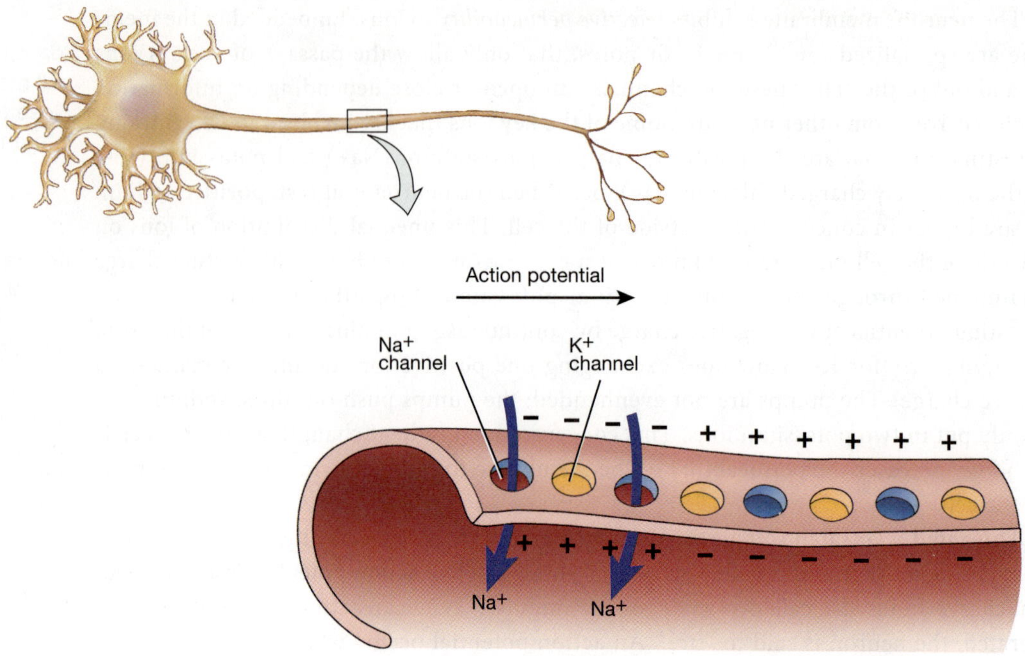

(a) This figure shows an action potential occurring along a segment of the axon membrane. During an action potential, Na+ channels in the axon membrane open and Na+ enters that area of the cell giving it a more positive charge.

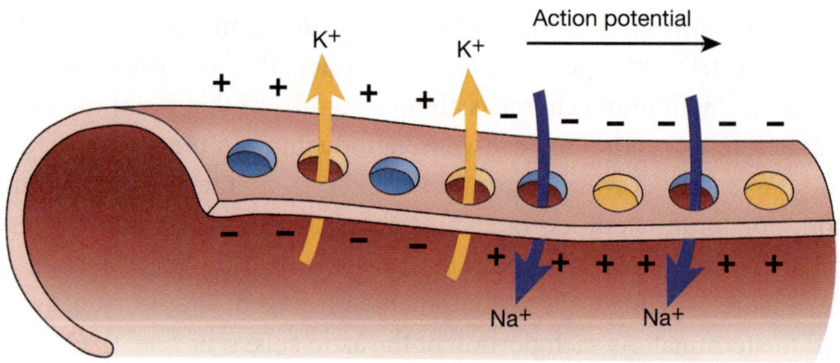

(b) As the action potential moves past a certain patch of membrane, the membrane works to restore the resting potential by closing the Na+ channels so no more Na+ enters the cell. K+ channels are opened and K+, which is more concentrated inside the cell, exits through the channels. Thus, the resting potential is restored.

absolute refractory period a short time after an action potential during which a neuron is completely unable to fire again.

relative refractory period just after the absolute refractory period during which a neuron can only fire if it receives a stimulus stronger than its usual threshold level.

synapses tiny spaces between the axon terminal of one neuron and the next neuron through which communication occurs.

neurotransmitters specialized chemicals that travel across synapses to allow communication between neurons.

As shown in **Figure 4-3**, action potentials travel very quickly down myelinated axons by jumping from node to node, a process known as *saltatory conduction*.

After it fires, the neuron cannot fire again for a short time, known as a *refractory period*. Immediately following an action potential, the axon is completely unable to fire no matter how strong the stimulus to the neuron. This time is called the absolute refractory period. During the relative refractory period, which begins a little later, the cell can fire if it is given a strong enough stimulus, but the threshold for spiking is higher than usual (Siegel et al., 2006).

Communication Across the Synapse

Once the positive charge of an action potential reaches the axon terminal, it initiates actions that enable the passage of information to other neurons. Neurons are not physically connected to one another; they are separated by small gaps. These gaps, called synapses, are tiny spaces (about 20 nm or 0.00002 mm wide) usually between the axon terminal of one cell and the dendrite of another cell by which neurons communicate. Communication across these spaces involves specialized chemicals called neurotransmitters. Neurotransmitter

FIGURE 4-3 Nodes of Ranvier. The nodes of Ranvier are the regions of bare axon that are between areas wrapped in myelin. Action potentials travel down the axon by jumping from node to node.

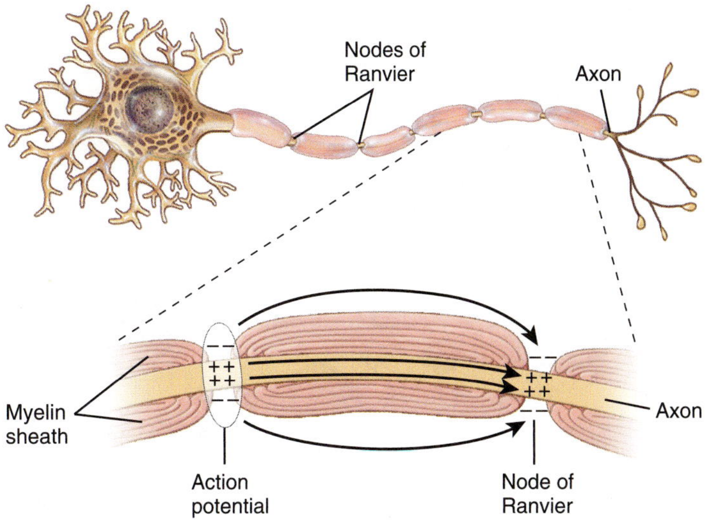

molecules are usually contained within small synaptic vesicles in the axon terminal, also known as the *presynaptic* terminal, of the neuron sending information.

synaptic vesicles membrane-bound spheres in the axon terminals of neurons where neurotransmitters are stored before their release.

When an action potential reaches the presynaptic axon terminal, it causes the release of neurotransmitter molecules into the synapse. As **Figure 4-4** shows, the neurotransmitter then diffuses across the synapse and binds to neurotransmitter receptors on the dendrite of the receiving, or *postsynaptic,* neuron. Neurotransmitter receptors are proteins in the cell membrane that recognize specific molecules. They operate in a lock and key fashion, so that receptors can only receive the specific neurotransmitter that "fits" them. There are several different neurotransmitters, including dopamine, serotonin, and

neurotransmitter receptors proteins in the membranes of neurons that bind to neurotransmitters.

Neurotransmitters and Their Functions

There are a number of different neurotransmitters, and some are associated with specific brain functions—though the relationships are far from simple. Many drugs that alter psychological functioning are designed to interfere with or enhance neurotransmitter functions. For example, the neurotransmitter *serotonin* has been implicated in a number of important functions, such as activity levels and mood regulation (Lowry et al., 2008). Several popular drugs used to treat depression and anxiety increase the action of serotonin, thereby improving mood. The table below lists some major neurotransmitters, their associated functions, and some drugs that can be used to manipulate these systems. Later in the chapter, you will see that certain neurotransmitters are also associated with specific brain regions.

Neurotransmitter	Function	Associated Drugs
Glutamate	Learning, movement	Ketamine (an anesthetic)
GABA	Learning, anxiety regulation	Valium (diazepam, used to relieve anxiety, muscle spasms) Ambien (Zolpidem, used to treat insomnia)
Acetylcholine (ACh)	Learning, attention	Nicotine
Dopamine	Movement, reward learning	Cocaine, heroin, methamphetamine
Serotonin	Mood regulation	Ecstasy (MDMA), LSD (hallucinogens); monoamine oxidase inhibitors (MAOIs), selective serotonin reuptake inhibitors (SSRIs) (antidepressants)
Norepinephrine	Attention, arousal	Adderall (a stimulant made up of dextroamphetamine and amphetamine)

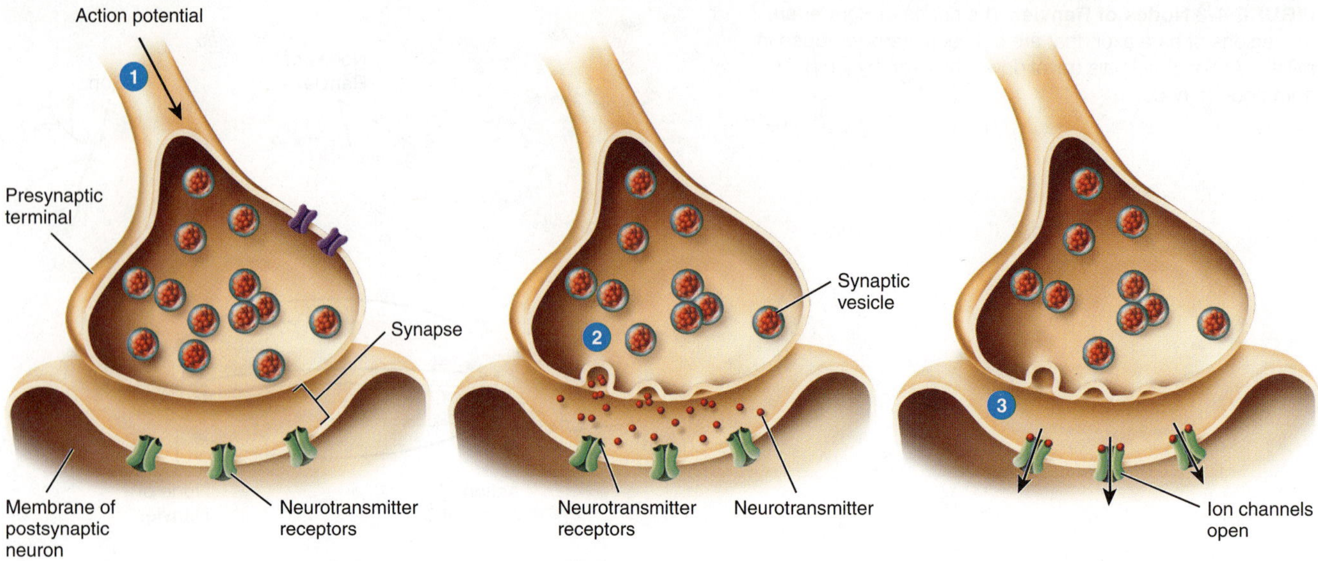

FIGURE 4-4 Communication across the synapse. (1) A positive charge reaches the end of the axon; (2) the positive charge stimulates release of neurotransmitters contained in membrane-bound vesicles into the synapse; (3) neurotransmitters bind to receptors on the postsynaptic neuron; ion channels open and electrical charge in postsynaptic neuron changes.

norepinephrine (Webster, 2001). We will discuss these chemicals in more detail throughout this chapter.

When a neurotransmitter binds to a receptor, the combination stimulates an electrical event in the postsynaptic membrane. These electrical events, called **postsynaptic potentials**, can be *excitatory* or *inhibitory*. The electrical response of the postsynaptic cell is determined by the receptor. If the receptor has an excitatory action, then the postsynaptic cell will be **depolarized**; the membrane potential will become less negative. Depolarizations that arise from inputs of a single neuron may not be great enough to trigger an action potential in the postsynaptic neuron, but they can be summed together with other depolarizations. In this way, the threshold will be reached and the neuron will fire, sending the information on to the next neuron in the chain. Alternatively, if the neurotransmitter has an inhibitory action, then the postsynaptic cell will be **hyperpolarized**: its membrane potential will become more negative. Hyperpolarization makes it less likely that the postsynaptic neuron will fire an action potential.

postsynaptic potentials electrical events in postsynaptic neurons that occur when a neurotransmitter binds to one of its receptors.

depolarized regions of postsynaptic membranes have been stimulated by excitatory neurochemicals to open their ion channels and increase the likelihood that the neuron they are part of will initiate an action potential.

hyperpolarized areas of a cell have had their negative charge increased in an inhibitory fashion, making it less likely that the cell will generate an action potential.

Repeated release of neurotransmitters into the synapse can result in long-lasting changes in neurotransmitter receptors located on the postsynaptic membrane. According to Mauro Costa-Mattioli and his colleagues at McGill University in Montreal (2009), these effects may play a role in memory consolidation. Glial cells also release chemicals, called *gliotransmitters*, that can cause long-term changes in postsynaptic membranes or that can act as excitatory or inhibitory influences for neighbouring neurons (Angulo et al., 2008). These receptor changes may make the postsynaptic response stronger or weaker, depending on the characteristics of the input.

Change in the nervous system is generally referred to as **plasticity**. In general terms, plasticity refers to the brain's ability to fix itself or to repurpose neurons (Doidge, 2007) to take up functions lost through the loss of other neurons. There is evidence that some areas of the brain, including the hippocampus and the olfactory bulb (Rakic, 2002), as well as the cerebellum (Ponti et al., 2008), can generate new brain cells to replace list cells. Plasticity at the synapse, such as the changes that occur from repeated release of neurotransmitters, is called *synaptic plasticity*. Neuroscientists have extensively studied synaptic plasticity because evidence suggests that it may explain some types of learning, as we will describe further in Chapter 7.

plasticity change in the nervous system.

Neural Networks

In the brain, neurons do not work alone or even in small numbers. Collections of neurons that communicate with one another are referred to as *neural circuits* or *neural networks*. Donald Hebb, perhaps one of the Canada's most famous psychologists, identified what he called *cell assemblies*. Hebb's (1949) discovery of cell assemblies was one of the first steps toward the current approach to the study of neural networks. Cell assemblies are networks of neurons that work as an interconnected entity, strengthening synaptic connections as certain mental processes are repeated, building units for memory and cognitive functioning. Given that the human brain contains about 100 billion neurons, each of which receives numerous synaptic inputs from a multitude of other neurons, the computational power of this organ is vast. Neuroscientists have focused attention on individual neural systems to better grasp the functioning of neural circuits related to specific behaviours (Schultz et al., 1997; Paulsen & Sejnowski, 2000).

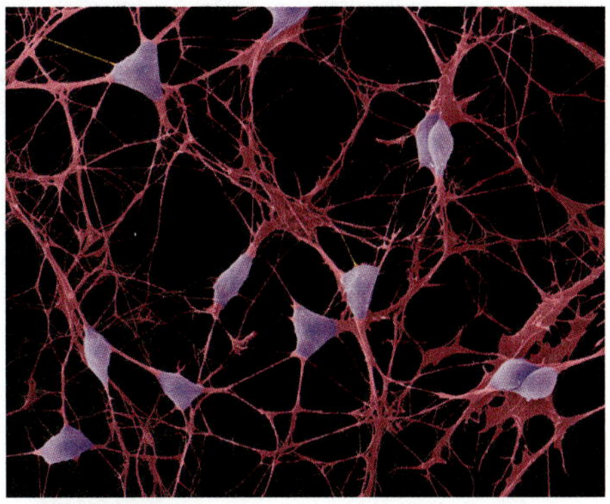

Neural network. Neurons form circuits or networks that expand the communication among different brain regions. This image shows axons and dendrites (red) extending from the neuronal cell bodies (shown in blue).

PSYCHOLOGY AROUND US Artificial Neural Networks

Some neuroscientists have tried to understand how neural networks operate by creating their own versions: artificial neural networks, or ANNs. Artificial neural networks are simplified computer models made up of units that represent neurons, together with values that represent the strength of the connections between the neuron units. The first artificial neural network, called Perceptron, was created in 1958 by psychologist Frank Rosenblatt. It was intended to model how the human brain processes visual data and learns to recognize objects. Since then, other researchers have used ANNs to study other aspects of human behaviour, especially cognitive behaviour. Experiments have demonstrated that models of this kind can learn face recognition, reading, and simple grammatical structure, among other things.

Before You Go On

www.wiley.com/go/comer

What Do You Know?

5. How do neurons work?
6. What happens in the axon of a neuron during an action potential?
7. When an action potential reaches the axon terminal, what happens?
8. How does a postsynaptic neuron receive and respond to messages from other neurons?

SCAN TO GET THE ANSWERS

What Do You Think?

Long axons are vulnerable to damage. What do you think some advantages might be of having a neuron with a very long axon (for example, one with a cell body in the spinal cord and axon terminal in the toe or finger)?

How Is the Nervous System Organized?

LEARNING OBJECTIVE 4

Name and describe the functions and subdivisions of the two major parts of the nervous system.

As shown in **Figure 4-5**, the human nervous system can be divided into two main components: the central nervous system and the peripheral nervous system. The *central nervous system* consists of the brain and spinal cord. The *peripheral nervous system* is made up of the many nerves throughout our bodies that deliver information back and forth between the periphery (for example, your arm) and the central nervous system.

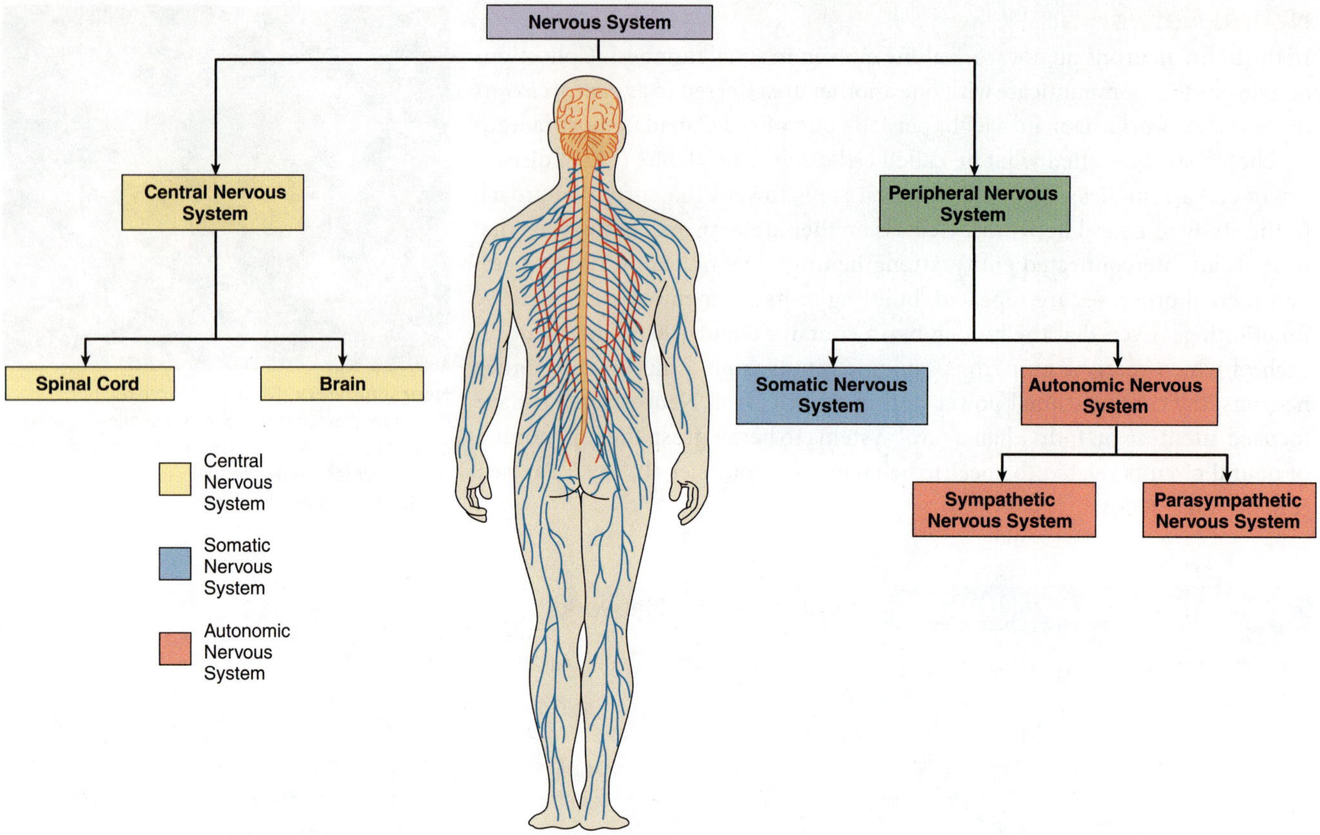

FIGURE 4-5 Organization of the nervous system. The nervous system is divided into the central nervous system (consisting of the brain and spinal cord) and the peripheral nervous system (consisting of the somatic nervous system and the autonomic nervous system). The autonomic nervous system is further subdivided into the sympathetic and parasympathetic nervous systems.

The Peripheral Nervous System

The peripheral nervous system consists of the somatic nervous system and the autonomic nervous system. The **somatic nervous system** consists of all of the nerves that gather sensory information (typically about touch and pain) from all over the body, neck, and head, and deliver it to the spinal cord and brain, as well as the nerves that send information about movement from the central nervous system to the muscles of the body, neck, and head. As we will see shortly, the somatic nervous system doesn't serve any function without the integrating capacity of the central nervous system. Even very simple reflexes require the central nervous system.

somatic nervous system all the peripheral nerves that transmit information about the senses and movement to and from the central nervous system.

By contrast, parts of the **autonomic nervous system** operate mostly without help from the central nervous system. The autonomic nervous system can be subdivided into two parts: the *sympathetic nervous system* and *parasympathetic nervous system*. Both components of the autonomic nervous system are made up of collections of nerve cells distributed throughout the body. However, they serve opposing functions. The sympathetic nervous system is activated under conditions of stress, whereas the parasympathetic nervous system is inhibited during those times, but active during more restful times.

autonomic nervous system portion of the peripheral nervous system that includes the sympathetic and parasympathetic nervous systems.

The **sympathetic nervous system** is responsible for the "fight-or-flight" reaction, the physiological response that enables us to respond to potentially life-threatening situations. The **parasympathetic nervous system**, on the other hand, is important for controlling basic functions that occur when the individual is not at immediate risk. For instance, digestion is a function under the control of the parasympathetic nervous system. Not surprisingly, when stressful situations occur and the sympathetic nervous system is activated, digestion stops. This makes good adaptive sense. Energy spent digesting food could be diverted to serve other functions (such as increasing blood flow to the leg muscles) so that the individual can escape the threatening situation (Robertson, Low, & Polinsky, 1996).

sympathetic nervous system the division of the autonomic nervous system activated under conditions of stress.

parasympathetic nervous system the division of the autonomic nervous system active during restful times.

The social kind of threat. The sympathetic nervous system doesn't distinguish between threats of physical harm or situations of social stress. It arouses the body to respond to both, with physiological reactions such as dry mouth, lack of appetite, or pounding heart.

Sometimes the sympathetic nervous system is activated when humans are not necessarily at risk of bodily harm, but under social situations where the major fear is one of embarrassment and humiliation, such as standing up to present in front of a class or to give a speech. Have you ever given a speech in front of a group of people? Many people experience a strong stress response to such situations. They develop a rapid heart rate and a dry mouth, signs that the sympathetic nervous system has kicked in. Although this reaction can be particularly disturbing, given that it often lessens the quality of your speech, it is a clear example of stress activating a physiological system.

Some aspects of the autonomic nervous system, such as the components that regulate digestion, are active without input from the central nervous system (CNS), but activation of the sympathetic nervous system definitely requires input from the brain, since recognizing and responding to an experience as stressful requires the CNS. We talk more about the role of the brain in stress in Chapter 15.

PSYCHOLOGY AROUND US If You Don't Ask, the Answer Is Already "No"

Have you ever invited a potential romantic interest out on a date? Many people experience a strong stress response in such situations, even if they have every reason to believe their invitation will be met with an enthusiastic "I'd love to." Their heart rates speed up and their mouths feel dry, signs that the sympathetic nervous system has kicked in—a clear example of how stress can activate a physiological system. This reaction can be quite disturbing, and it may negatively affect how appealing the invitation seems. Mentally reframing such experiences can lessen the negative effects of stress. For example, you might try thinking about the fact that if you don't have the nerve to ask, you won't be going out with the person at all. So even if the answer is "no," you haven't lost anything, since that's the situation you started out with!

The Central Nervous System (CNS)

As we have noted, the CNS consists of the spinal cord and the brain. The **spinal cord** extends from the base of the brain down the back. The spinal cord is very important for gathering information from the body and sending it to the brain, as well as for enabling the brain to control movement of the body.

spinal cord portion of the central nervous system that extends from the base of the brain and mediates sensory and motor information.

As described earlier, the somatic nervous system operates in concert with the CNS to integrate sensory information with motor output. In most cases, this integration involves the brain (voluntary movement, for example, requires brain involvement). However, some very basic functions, including reflexes, involve just the somatic nervous system and the spinal cord.

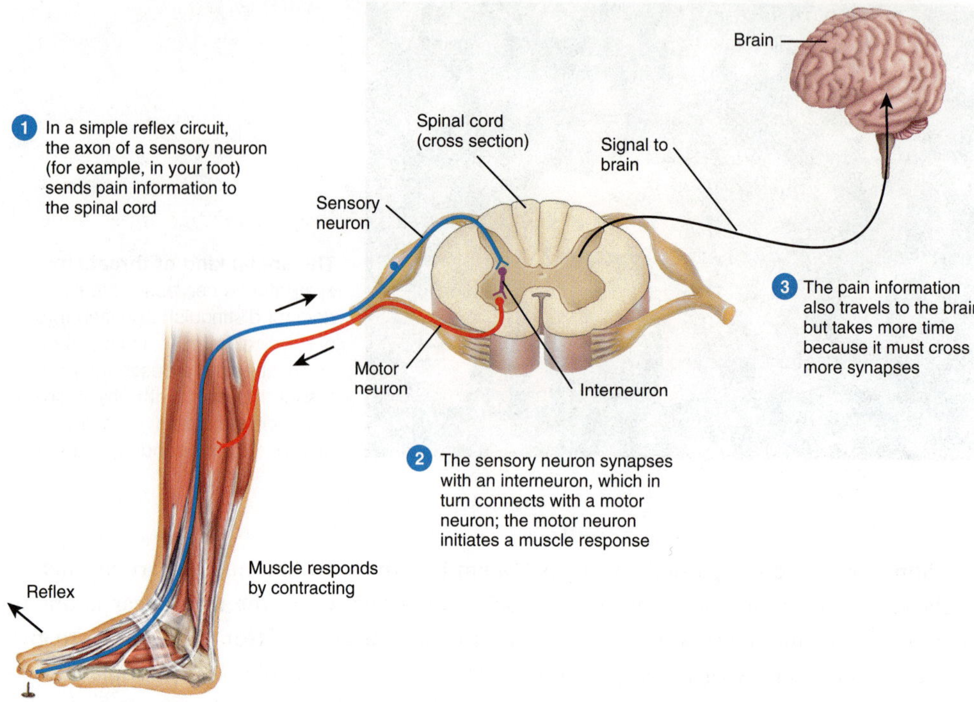

FIGURE 4-6 The reflex circuit of the spinal cord. Sensory information travels into the spinal cord where it synapses on interneurons. Interneurons send information to the motor neurons, which then send impulses back out to the periphery to induce movement.

interneuron neuron that typically has a short axon and serves as a relay between different classes of neurons. In the spinal cord, interneurons communicate with both sensory and motor neurons.

Have you ever stepped on something sharp, possibly a tack, and pulled your foot back before you even get a chance to yell "ouch"? Shortly later, you felt the pain, which may even have brought tears to your eyes. This rapid reaction is the result of activity in the pain reflex circuit of your spinal cord, as shown in **Figure 4-6**. Simple circuits consisting of three neurons—a sensory neuron whose cell body is located out in the periphery but whose axon travels into the spinal cord; a connecting neuron, called an **interneuron**; and a motor neuron whose cell body is located in the spinal cord and whose axon travels out to the body—can control pain reflexes without any communication with the brain.

Pain information also travels up to the brain and enables you to vocalize about the pain and carry out other movements, such as hobbling to a chair, sitting down, and pulling the tack out. However, these reactions are slower than the reflex because the information must travel greater distances, and more importantly, it must travel across many more synapses. Information flows more slowly across synapses because synaptic communication involves the flow of chemicals as well as receptor events, both of which take more time than it takes for action potentials to travel down the axon (Lenz et al., 2010).

Spinal Cord Injuries

WHEN THINGS GO WRONG

A neck "break" refers to when the bones (vertebrae) in the neck are broken. A spinal cord injury occurs when the nerves that make up the spinal cord itself are damaged. As such, it is possible to break your neck and not have a spinal cord injury, though the two often occur together. In addition to controlling simple reflexes, the spinal cord is very important for carrying sensory information up to the brain and motor information back out to the body. When the spinal cord is damaged such that the flow of information to and from the brain is disrupted, individuals become paralyzed, as well as incapable of noticing touch or pain sensations on the body. The higher up the spinal cord the damage occurs (the closer it occurs to the brain), the larger the proportion of the body that is afflicted. Thus, when individuals break their necks and permanently damage the spinal cord close to the brain, they lose touch and pain sensation everywhere but their heads and faces, and they become *quadriplegic*, paralyzed everywhere but the head and neck. If the damage occurs farther down the back, then they may retain sensation and usage of the upper limbs and torso, but not of the lower limbs.

Rick Hansen, a well-known Canadian with a spinal cord injury, began to raise awareness and money for spinal cord research with his Man in Motion world tour in 1985. Since then he has established the Rick Hansen Institute, which encourages and supports spinal cord research. Spinal cord damage is devastating and afflicts a large number of people; currently about 86,000 Canadians are living with some form of spinal injury (Farry & Baxter, 2010). Scientists are looking to find ways to enhance regeneration of severed axons in the spinal cord, as well as examining the potential for replenishing motor neurons destroyed by injury (Barnabé-Heider et al., 2008).

Although some progress has been made in the treatment of spinal cord injury, there is much work to be done. Freda Miller, working at the Sick Kids Hospital in Toronto along with colleagues in Toronto and British Columbia, accomplished a big step in this area in 2007 (Miller & Gauthier, 2007). Miller discovered that stem cells produced from a person's own skin are similar to neural stem cells and are capable of producing Schwann cells. This is promising because Schwann cells seem to create an environment in which injured nerve fibres can be repaired and even remyelinated. While this work is still in the experimental phase, it holds out the possibility that we may one day in the not too distant future be able to repair damaged spinal columns.

Before You Go On

www.wiley.com/go/comer

What Do You Know?

9. What are the two parts of the central nervous system?
10. What happens when the sympathetic nervous system is operating? How does that compare to the operation of the parasympathetic nervous system?
11. How do the brain and spinal cord work together?
12. What neuron types are important for simple reflexes?
13. What determines how much disability will result from a spinal cord injury?

SCAN TO GET THE ANSWERS

What Do You Think?

Describe an occasion when you have experienced the workings of the sympathetic nervous system. Have you ever been able to control your sympathetic or parasympathetic reactions? If so, how?

Structures of the Brain

LEARNING OBJECTIVE 5

List key structures of the brain and describe their relationships to our behaviour.

The brain is also divided into three regions, which serve varying functions: the hindbrain (or brain stem), the midbrain, and the forebrain. **Figure 4-7** shows the major structures of the brain.

The Hindbrain

The part of the brain closest to the spinal cord is called the **hindbrain** (brainstem). The hindbrain consists of the medulla, the reticular formation, the pons, and the cerebellum.

hindbrain the part of the brain closest to the spinal cord that consists of the medulla, the reticular formation, pons, and cerebellum.

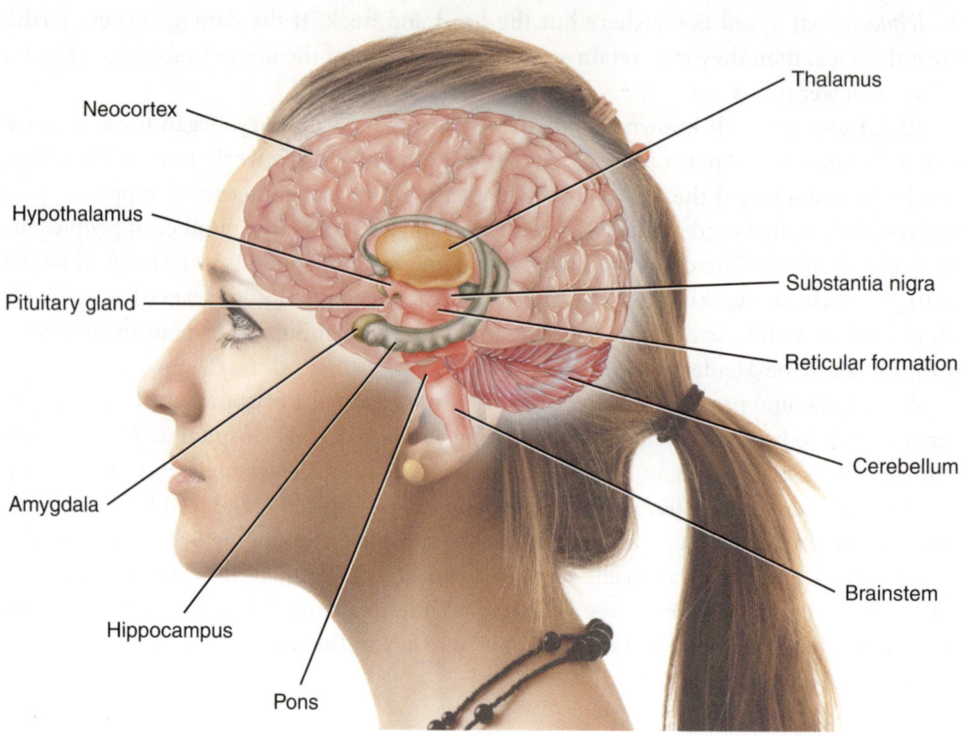

FIGURE 4-7 Major structures of the brain. The brain is subdivided into several major structures, each with specific functions.

medulla part of the brain that controls basic bodily processes and regulates reflexes.

The Medulla The **medulla** is attached to the spinal cord and is important for basic bodily functions, including respiration and heart rate regulation, as well as for regulating reflexes such as sneezing and coughing. Although most of the actions of the brainstem occur without our conscious knowledge or involvement, this part of the brain is critical for survival and normal functioning. Damage to the medulla, as a result of stroke or trauma, is often fatal (Oshima & Kondo, 1998).

reticular formation a brain structure important for sleep and wakefulness.

serotonin neurotransmitter involved in activity levels and mood regulation.

Several neuron groups, or *nuclei*, in the brainstem work together to form an area known as the **reticular formation**, which is important for sleep and wakefulness. Groups of neurons in the reticular formation are the major brain source of the neurotransmitter **serotonin** (Lowry et al., 2008). These serotonin neurons send axons throughout the brain. Brain serotonin has been implicated in a number of important functions, such as activity levels, mood, and anxiety regulation. Several popular drugs for depression and anxiety increase the action of serotonin (Williams, 1998).

pons part of the brain anterior to the brainstem that includes the locus coeruleus.

norepinephrine neurotransmitter important for arousal and attention.

The Pons Above the medulla is a region called the **pons**. The pons acts as a bridge, sending signals to and from the forebrain and cerebellum. The pons is involved in sleep, breathing, swallowing, eye movements, and facial sensation and expression. This part of the brain also contains cell groups, such as the *locus coeruleus*, that belong to the reticular formation. Neurons of the locus coeruleus have long axons projecting throughout the brain and spinal cord. These neurons use the neurotransmitter **norepinephrine** and are important for arousal and attention. It may be, for example, that under-functioning of the neurons in this area may play a role in attention deficit disorder (Viggiano et al., 2004).

cerebellum part of the brain, near the back of the head, important for motor coordination.

The Cerebellum Sitting at the back of the brain, connected to the brainstem by the pons, is the highly convoluted **cerebellum**. This part of the brain is important for motor coordination. People with cerebellar damage often have an awkward gait and have difficulty reaching for objects without trembling (Spencer et al., 2003). In addition to its role in motor coordination, the cerebellum is important for certain types of learning involving movement. For example, when you learn to tie your shoelaces or to play the piano, your cerebellum is at work. Also, if you are asked to participate in a field sobriety test, to see if you are impaired, you could be asked to walk heel to toe along a line or close your eyes and touch your nose with your finger (Rubenzer, 2008). Both of these tasks require the sort of smooth movements that the cerebellum makes possible (unless you are drunk!). Other parts of the brain participate as well, particularly in cases where the task involves paying attention to a complicated series of instructions. Once it's completely learned, the cerebellum then stores the learned motor information to be recalled automatically when needed (Barlow, 2002).

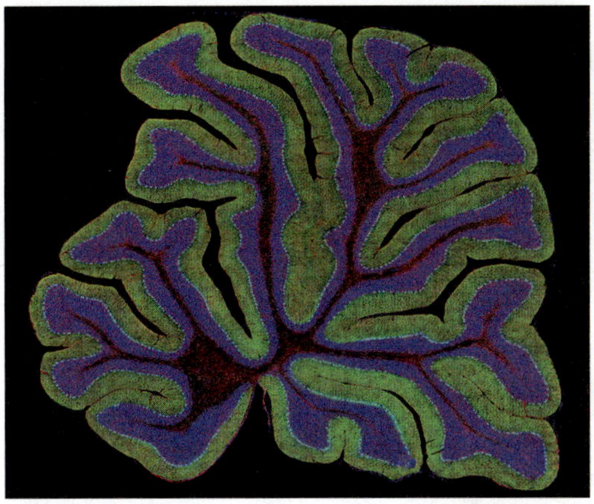

A convoluted brain region. The cerebellum has many folds on its surface, shown here in this fluorescent image of a slice through this part of the brain.

The Midbrain

Above the pons sits a collection of brain regions collectively called the *midbrain*. The midbrain contains a number of different nuclei. One of these cell groups or nuclei is called the substantia nigra. Like the cerebellum, the substantia nigra is important for movement, but this area serves different functions from those of the cerebellum. Like neurons in some other regions of the brain, neurons in the substantia nigra produce a neurotransmitter called dopamine. These particular dopamine producers communicate with other brain regions located in the forebrain. These pathways are critical for fluidity of movement as well as inhibition of movement. This brain region is the major structure damaged in a neurological disorder called *Parkinson's disease* (Cenci, 2007) that we discuss in more detail later in this chapter.

substantia nigra brain region important in fluidity of movement and inhibiting movements.

dopamine neurotransmitter plentiful in many brain areas involving movement and rewards.

The Thalamus

The thalamus is a large collection of nuclei located anterior to, or in front of, the substantia nigra. It sits between the midbrain and higher areas of the brain. Many of the thalamic nuclei serve as relay stations for incoming sensory information. In fact, all of our sensory systems, with the exception of the sense of smell, have a major pathway that synapses in the thalamus (Buck, 1996). Two major components of the thalamus are the *lateral geniculate nucleus* (LGN) and the *medial geniculate nucleus* (MGN). The LGN is important for relaying information about visual stimuli and the MGN is important for relaying information about auditory stimuli (Carlson, 2009).

thalamus an area of the brain that serves as a relay station for incoming sensory information.

The Hypothalamus

The hypothalamus is aptly named because this collection of nuclei sits beneath the thalamus (the prefix *hypo* comes from ancient Greek for below or under). Regions of the hypothalamus are important for a number of motivational processes, including eating, drinking, sex, and maternal behaviour. Damage to discrete parts of the hypothalamus can dramatically alter these basic behaviours. The hypothalamus is also critical for the control of the endocrine, or hormonal, system.

hypothalamus brain structure important for motivation and control of the endocrine system.

endocrine system the system that controls levels of hormones throughout the body.

The Pituitary Gland and the Endocrine System

The hypothalamus is connected to a structure called the pituitary gland. The pituitary works with the hypothalamus to control a particular class of chemical messengers in the body—*hormones*—that are important for growth, reproduction, metabolism, and stress reactions.

pituitary gland brain structure that plays a central role in controlling the endocrine system.

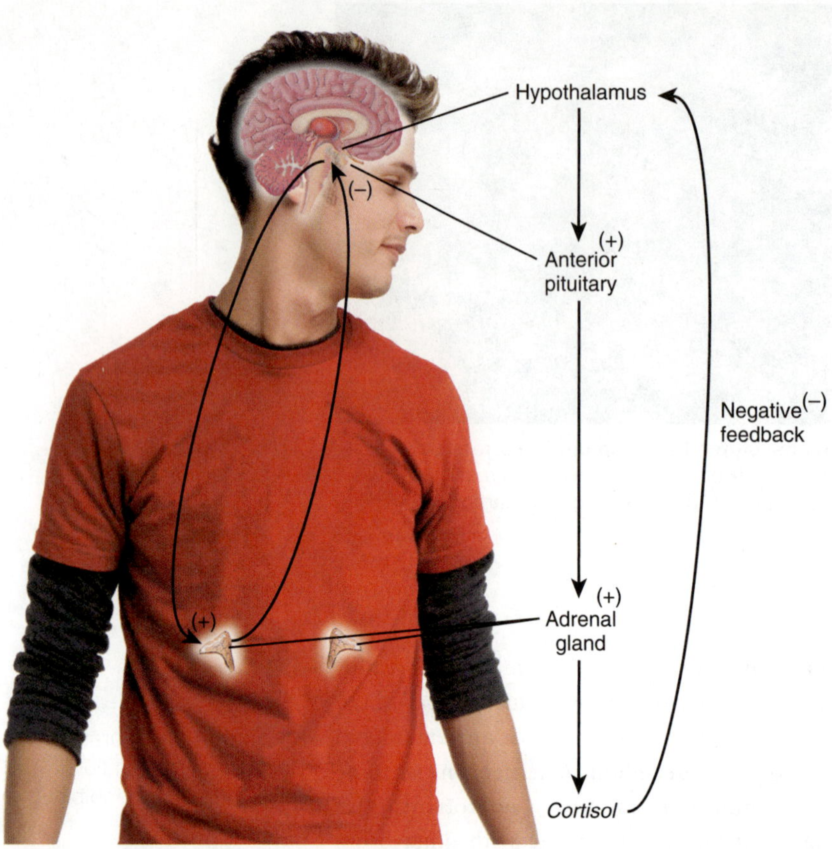

FIGURE 4-8 The hypothalamic-pituitary-adrenal (HPA) axis. In response to stress, the HPA axis is activated. The hypothalamus produces a hormone that stimulates the anterior pituitary to release another hormone into the blood stream. The adrenal gland then releases the stress hormone cortisol. Cortisol travels to the brain and shuts off the HPA axis via negative feedback.

The pituitary produces releasing factors that control endocrine glands, such as the ovaries, the testes, the thyroid, and the adrenal glands. The ovaries and testes are sex glands, or gonads. They produce our reproductive hormones: estrogen and progesterone for the ovaries, testosterone for the testes. The thyroid gland produces thyroid hormones that are important for metabolism. The *adrenal glands* produce hormones that are critical for responding to stressful situations. As shown in **Figure 4-8**, the hypothalamus, pituitary, and adrenals work together in a system called the *hypothalamic-pituitary-adrenal (HPA) axis*, which is an important component of the stress response. The HPA axis works in concert with activation of the sympathetic nervous system to maximize our chances of survival under threatening conditions. The stress response will be discussed further in Chapter 15.

The Amygdala

amygdala brain area involved in processing information about emotions, particularly fear.

The **amygdala** is located deep within the brain, in a region referred to as the temporal lobe. Like the thalamus and hypothalamus, the amygdala is not a homogeneous structure. Instead, it is a collection of nuclei that serve different functions. The amygdala is involved in recognizing, learning about, and responding to stimuli that induce fear (LeDoux, 2007). This brain region has been the focus of considerable attention by neuroscientists because it may be involved in the development of phobias, or abnormal fears (File et al., 1998). In addition, the amygdala has been implicated in processing information about more positive emotions (Hamann, Ely, Hoffman, & Kilts, 2002).

The Hippocampus

hippocampus brain region important for certain types of learning and memory.

The amygdala communicates with the **hippocampus**, a brain region important for certain types of learning and memory. Neuroscientists have extensively studied individuals with damage to the hippocampus and found that they are incapable of forming new *episodic* memories, or memories about events (Bindschaedler, Peter-Favre, Maeder, Hirsbrunner, & Clarke, 2011) (described in more detail in Chapter 8). Destruction of the hippocampus in adulthood doesn't wipe out all memories of early life or one's identity, merely those that occurred relatively close to the time of brain damage. This suggests that the hippocampus only temporarily stores information about events (Squire et al., 2004). In addition to its role in the formation and transient storage of episodic memories, the hippocampus is important for learning about one's spatial environment. Learning how to navigate around a new campus, for instance, requires the hippocampus. Animal research shows that the hippocampus has neurons called *place cells* that show changes in activity only when the animal is located in a specific location in space (Moser et al., 2008). Unlike the situation for the temporary role of the hippocampus in episodic memory, the hippocampus seems to play a more direct role in the storage of spatial navigation information for a long time, perhaps an entire lifetime.

The hippocampus doesn't consist of well-delineated collections of neurons or nuclei. Instead, it is organized in regions and layers. Because of the layered structure of the hippocampus, neuroscientists have been able to both record from and stimulate individual parts of the hippocampus, so that much of the function and connectivity of this brain region has been studied. The hippocampus is a major site of plasticity, or the ability of neurons to change, as we described earlier. Neurons in the hippocampus show both synaptic and structural plasticity, meaning that both size and shape of neurons and their connections to other neurons can change. In fact, it is a region known to produce entirely new neurons in adulthood (Gould, 2007; Cameron & McKay, 2001). The function of these new neurons remains unknown, but their presence suggests that the adult brain is capable of regenerative processes, and furthermore, the process of neuron birth, or neurogenesis (which we discuss in more detail later in this chapter), may be harnessed for purposes of brain repair. We will return to the hippocampus at length when we discuss learning and memory in Chapters 7 and 8.

The amygdala in action. The amygdala processes the stimuli that elicit fear, such when one is out alone on a dark night.

All of these areas—the thalamus, the hypothalamus, the amygdala, and the hippocampus—are together sometimes grouped into something called the limbic system. While its anatomical boundaries are somewhat unclear, the limbic system is viewed as being involved in the regulation of motivation, emotion, and memory. Its name means "edge" in Latin, which refers to the way that the limbic system connects many other brain areas (MacLean, 1954). There is some debate about whether the limbic system designation should be abandoned and is no longer useful (Ledoux, 2003). We mention it here, but have invested more energy in describing in more detail the various brain areas that are said to make up the limbic system.

The Striatum

Located more toward the midline of the brain are the **striatum** and its related structures. This brain region works with the substantia nigra to produce fluid movements, such as those needed to hit a squash or tennis ball or to skate gracefully. Damage to either of these brain regions produces a collection of debilitating motor symptoms, such as uncontrollable shaking as seen in Parkinson's disease (Schnabel, 2010). In addition to its role in movement, the striatum is important for certain types of learning and memory (Grahn et al., 2008), namely those that do not require conscious awareness. As we will see in the later chapters on learning and memory, we learn some information unintentionally and often are unaware that learning has occurred. Under some circumstances, this ability involves the striatum.

striatum a brain area that works with the substantia nigra to enable fluid movements.

The Nucleus Accumbens

Anterior to the striatum is a brain region called the **nucleus accumbens**, an area important for motivation and reward learning (Goto & Grace, 2008). It receives important projections from neurons in the midbrain that use dopamine as a neurotransmitter. Dopamine release in the nucleus accumbens has been associated with reward learning and has been implicated in drug abuse (Nestler, 2004).

nucleus accumbens a brain area important for motivation and reward.

All of the above-mentioned brain regions are collectively referred to as *subcortical* because they are located beneath the largest and most complex part of the human brain: the neocortex. We now turn to a discussion of the higher areas of the brain found in the neocortex.

The Neocortex

The human neocortex is huge, much too large to fit in the skull if it were stretched out. This is the reason why the human brain is all folded on the surface. The neocortex has many

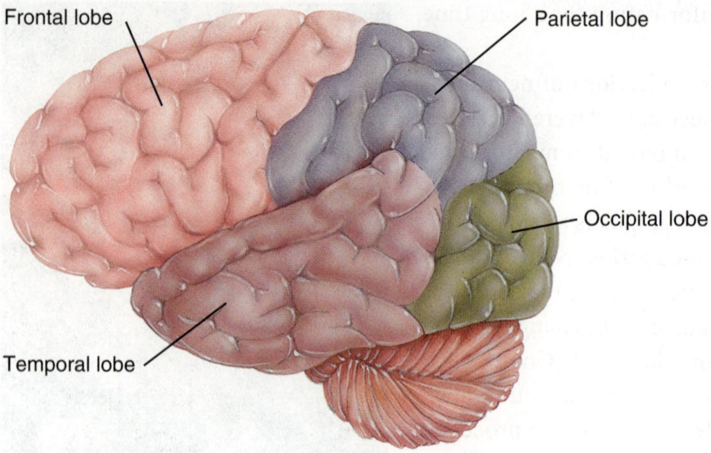

FIGURE 4-9 The lobes of the neocortex. The neocortex can be subdivided into four lobes—frontal, parietal, occipital, and temporal.

convolutions or folds that enable it to cram a large number of neurons into a head small enough to be supported by the human neck.

The neocortex is highly developed in humans and is responsible for many of our most complex behaviours, including language and thought. Although some of the functions of neocortical regions are not well understood, there is consensus among neuroscientists that within the neocortex, there is localization of function. This means that certain parts of the neocortex are important for specific behaviours or abilities (Krubitzer, 1995).

At the most macroscopic level, the neocortex can be subdivided into four different parts or *lobes*, as shown in **Figure 4-9**: occipital, temporal, parietal, and frontal. Within each of these regions, there are two major classifications:

neocortex the largest portion of the brain, responsible for complex behaviours including language and thought.

association cortex areas of the neocortex responsible for complex functions, including higher-order sensory processing, thinking, and planning.

occipital cortex lobe of the neocortex at the back of the skull, important for processing very visual information.

1. *Primary sensory and/or motor areas.* These areas are responsible for processing basic information about the senses as well as for producing signals that lead to voluntary movement. As we will see, many of the primary sensory and motor parts of the neocortex process information related to the opposite, or *contralateral*, side of the body.
2. *Association cortex.* Association cortex in each region are responsible for many complex functions, including higher-order sensory processing, integrating information from different senses (how you know that an object that looks like a violin is producing the music), thinking, planning, and other complex functions.

The Occipital Cortex The occipital cortex, the cortical area at the back of the skull, contains primary sensory regions important for processing very basic information about visual stimuli, such as orientation and lines. As shown in **Figure 4-10**, visual information arrives in the occipital cortex via partially crossed connections. The visual information from each eye that is closest to the midline between the two eyes is actually projected to the opposite side of the brain. As a result, the representation of your left visual field is on your right primary visual cortex, and vice versa (Bear, Connors, & Paradiso, 2007).

Association areas in the occipital cortex integrate information about colour, complex patterns, and motion (Braddick et al., 2001). Since vision is such an important sense for primates, the occipital cortex is very well developed in humans. Although the occipital cortex is often referred to as the visual cortex, it's important to realize that visual information is also processed in other parts of the neocortex. In fact, some estimates suggest that 50 percent of the human neocortex is devoted to some sort of visual task! Connections to other parts of the neocortex enable us to hook up visual information with information from other sensory modalities as well as with our memory stores (for example, connecting the sight of a potato chip with its smell, taste, sound when crunched, feel, and memories of having that type of food). This should remind you of our earlier statement that no brain region operates entirely alone. Brain regions and brain functions are richly interconnected. Each receives input from other areas and communicates with many other regions to produce integrated responses.

Parallel processing. Air traffic controllers must react to an array of sensory stimuli and make quick decisions. Communication among the association cortex within and between the lobes of the brain allows us to perform such complex functions simultaneously.

The Temporal Cortex The temporal cortex is located on the sides of the head covering the temporal lobe. It wraps around the hippocampus and amygdala. The temporal cortex includes areas important for processing

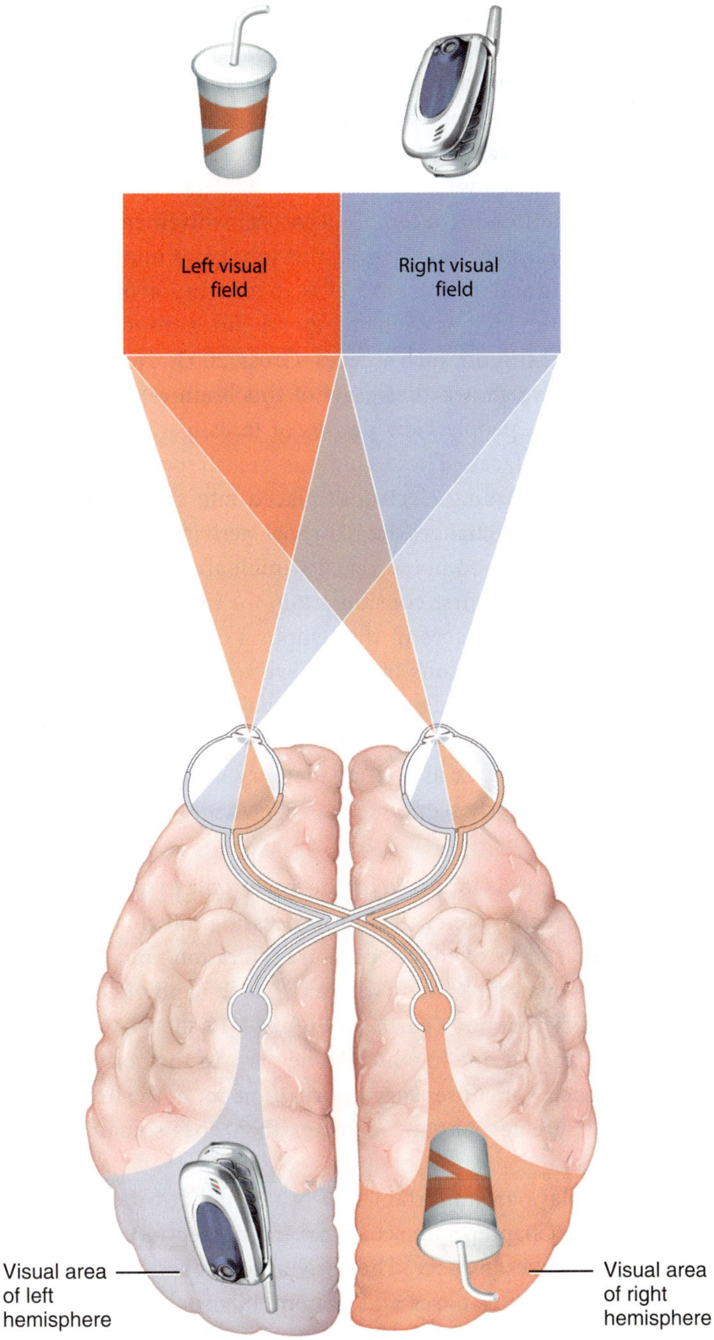

FIGURE 4-10 The visual system is a partially crossed pathway. Visual cues from the temporal (toward the side) part of the visual field are sent to the opposite side of the brain, while those of the medial (toward the nose) part of the visual field are transmitted to the same side of the brain.

information about auditory stimuli, or sounds. Abnormal electrical activity in the temporal cortex, such as what occurs with seizures or epilepsy (i.e., the uncontrolled rapid firing of neurons in an area of the brain), has been shown to result in auditory hallucinations. People who have epileptic seizures centred in this region sometimes "hear" very loud music in their minds during seizures (Engmann & Reuter, 2009). Neurosurgery to remove neurons that appear to be generating seizures is particularly dangerous in this part of the brain since there are so many critical functions that may be disrupted though the removal of problematic and neighbouring neurons (Foldvary et al., 2000).

temporal cortex part of the neocortex important in processing sounds, in speech comprehension, and in recognizing complex visual stimuli, such as faces.

For instance, the temporal cortex also contains regions important for language comprehension (Damasio et al., 2004). Shown in **Figure 4-11**, this area, called Wernicke's area, is located on the left side of the brain in the vast majority of humans (over 90 percent). (Finding Wernike's area in the left hemisphere of the brain is a good example of a phenomenon called *lateralization of function,* which means that a particular ability is localized

Wernicke's area an area of the temporal cortex important in helping us understand language.

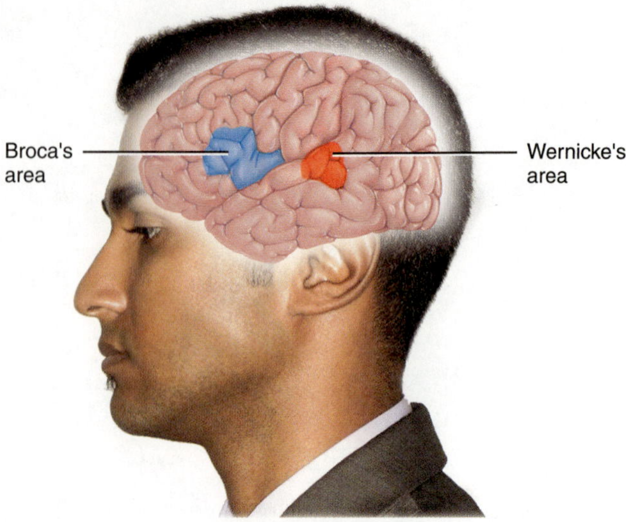

FIGURE 4-11 Major brain regions important for speech production and language comprehension. Broca's area, located in the frontal lobe, is critical for speaking; Wernicke's area, located in the temporal lobe, is critical for understanding language.

to one side of the brain. We will return to this general issue later in the chapter.) Wernicke's area communicates with other areas, including a region located in another cortical area important for the recognition of appropriate syntax (language rules) and the production of speech, called Broca's Area (more below).

In addition to the temporal cortex involvement in hearing and language comprehension, this lobe plays important roles in learning and memory as well as in recognition of objects via visual cues. Regions of the temporal cortex respond to complex visual stimuli, such as faces (Gross, 2005). Neuroimaging studies have shown that parts of this brain region are activated when people view photos of faces, particularly those of familiar faces. These findings are strengthened by the fact that recording electrodes placed into these same brain regions show changes in neuronal activity, or firing rate, when the same complex visual stimuli are presented (Seeck et al., 1993). At first consideration, the presence of neurons that respond to faces in the temporal cortex might suggest that direct projections from the eye activate a set of cells in the temporal lobe that are programmed to respond to complex visual stimuli. However, this is not the case. The "face cells" in the temporal cortex respond to faces because they receive inputs from visual areas in the occipital cortex as well as memory centres in the brain, allowing for the recognition of faces previously seen.

parietal cortex lobe of the neocortex involved in processing information related to touch and complex visual information, particularly about locations.

somatosensory strip an area of the parietal cortex that processes tactile information coming from our body parts.

The Parietal Cortex The parietal cortex is localized on the top middle of the brain. The primary sensory parts of this cortical region are critical for processing information about touch or somatosensory stimuli: our senses of touch, pressure, vibration, and pain. The parietal cortex contains a region known as the somatosensory strip, a band of cortex that processes tactile information about different body parts. As **Figure 4-12** shows, this area of the brain forms a systematic body map, but one in which some parts of the body are represented more than others. For instance, somatosensory information about the lips (which are particularly sensitive) occupies a greater amount of cortex than does somatosensory information about the elbow.

In addition, the parietal cortex plays an important role in the higher-order processing of visual stimuli. As we will see in Chapter 5 on sensation and perception, processing visual stimuli involves localizing visual cues in space. The parietal cortex contains a system known as the "where pathway" that enables us to see and respond to visual information in a spatially appropriate way. People with damage to the "where pathway" can find it impossible to pour water from a pitcher into a glass. This deficiency is not due to a motor disturbance, but rather to an inability to properly determine where the glass is located relative to the pitcher.

frontal cortex lobe of the neocortex involved in many functions, including movement and speech production.

The Frontal Cortex Located at the front of the brain (behind the forehead) is the frontal cortex. The frontal cortex is a relatively large cortical region and is proportionately larger in humans compared to less complex animals. Like the other cortical regions, however, the frontal cortex is not just one area, but a large collection of regions that serve numerous functions. The frontal cortex is important for planning and movement. The *primary motor strip*, shown in Figure 4-12, is involved in the control of voluntary (non-reflexive) movement. For a long time it has been known that stimulation of different parts of the primary motor strip invokes movement in specific groups of muscles (Fulton, 1938). However, recent research suggests that parts of motor cortex are not just involved in contracting specific muscles, but also in coordinating the use of these muscles in complex movements (Graziano, 2006).

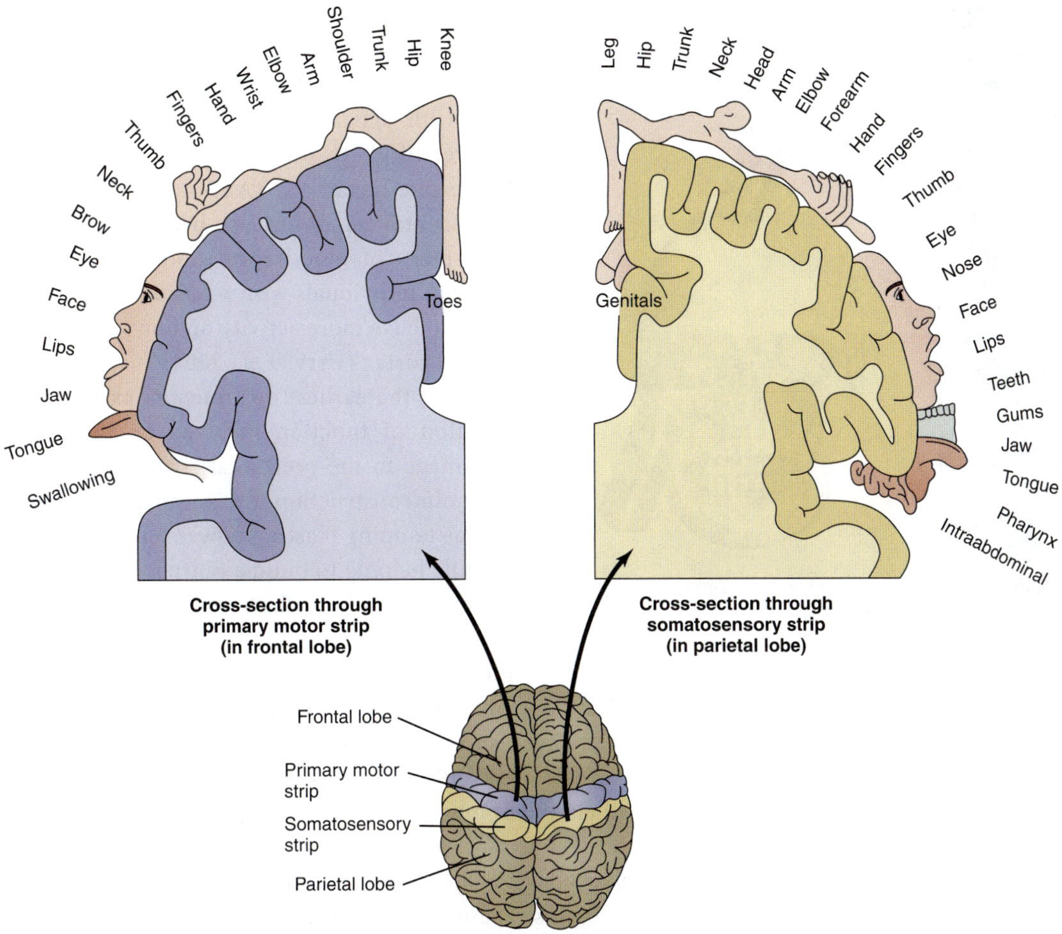

FIGURE 4-12 Motor and sensory cortices are organized according to body parts. Areas of motor cortex that control the movement of specific body parts and those of somatosensory cortex that receive tactile information are grouped according to body parts. Some regions are overrepresented, including the mouth and hands.

PSYCHOLOGY AROUND US Brain Implants

With their ever more sophisticated knowledge of brain structure and function, neuroscientists are developing new methods to treat malfunctions in the brain. For example, scientists at the University of Pittsburgh are currently testing brain implants that they hope will enable paralyzed patients to move prosthetic arms with their thoughts. In some of these experiments, electrodes implanted in the motor cortex will interpret patients' brain signals and send them to a computer, which will in turn control the movement of a prosthetic arm and hand. People who have suffered spinal cord damage, as discussed earlier in this chapter, might someday benefit from this research.

In addition to its role in controlling movement, the frontal cortex contains a region called Broca's area, which is critical for speech production and for providing grammatical structure. Individuals with damage to this region, or to the connections between Wernicke's and Broca's area, suffer speech impairment despite normal language comprehension (Code et al., 1999).

Broca's area brain region located in the frontal lobe that's important for speech production.

The part of the frontal cortex closest to the front of the head is referred to as the prefrontal cortex and is important for a large number of functions, such as short-term memory or working memory (Soto et al., 2008). When you look up a phone number and hold that number in your mind while you dial, you are using your prefrontal cortex. In addition, when you execute complex plans, such as figuring out how to fit studying around your work schedule, or planning how to get to a friend's house, you are using your prefrontal cortex.

prefrontal cortex portion of the frontal cortex involved in higher-order thinking, such as memory, moral reasoning, and planning.

FIGURE 4-13 After the accident. Phineas Gage holds the railroad spike that passed through his brain (left). A reconstruction shows how the spike likely entered Gage's head, damaging the frontal cortex (right).

Moral reasoning (discussed in Chapter 3) has also been localized, at least in part, to a component of the prefrontal cortex (Greene, 2003). People with damage to the prefrontal cortex can have difficulty understanding ethical principles despite normal IQ (Anderson et al., 1999). The prefrontal cortex has also been implicated in some aspects of mood regulation. Studies have shown that individuals with a positive outlook on life tend to have more activity on one side of their prefrontal cortex (Urry et al., 2004).

One of the earliest documented examples of localization of function involved an individual with damage to the prefrontal cortex. In 1848, a 25-year-old construction foreman named Phineas Gage was tamping blasting power into a hole in a rock while helping to build a railroad in Vermont. Unbeknownst to him, there was flint in the rock and the flint generated a spark when it was struck by the tamping rod, causing the charge to explode prematurely. As shown in **Figure 4-13**, the force of the explosion drove the rod (3 cm thick and 90 cm long) through Gage's left cheek and out the top of his head, passing through the frontal lobes of his brain (Damasio et al., 1994). Almost immediately following the accident, Gage was able, with the help of his men, to talk and to walk back to the wagon. He miraculously recovered physically, but those who knew him previously reported that his personality changed. Once a responsible, likeable, mild-mannered individual, Gage became irreverent, impatient, and impulsive, and was so unreliable that he lost his job and was never able to hold a responsible position again (Harlow, 1848; Macmillan, 2008). Gage's accident and the consequences of the accident were of particular importance because at the time of his accident, physiologists were debating whether different parts of the brain were equally effective at carrying out particular functions, or whether specific brain areas carried out specific functions. The case of Phineas Gage provided clear support for the localization of function hypothesis. Hanna Damasio and colleagues (1994) concluded that the damage to Gage's brain affected areas in both frontal lobes (medial prefrontal lobes) important for processing emotions and for making rational decisions regarding personal and social matters.

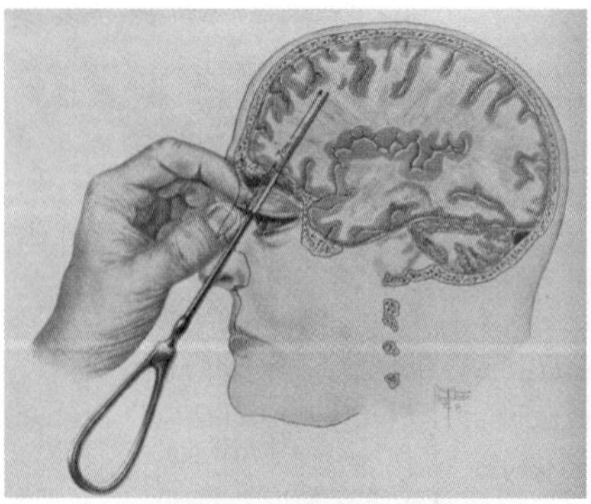

Transorbital lobotomies. In transorbital lobotomies, a patient was anesthetized and a sharp instrument was inserted through the eye socket and then moved back and forth to destroy brain tissue (Mashour et al., 2005).

Additional data supporting localization of function occurred in the 1930s when two neuroscientists, Klüver and Bucy (1939), discovered that bilateral (two sides) removal of the temporal lobes in monkeys led to significant reductions in aggression and fear. The animals displayed difficulties with visual recognition, as well as a tendency to fixate on oral stimulation and a marked increased interest in sex. Following discoveries that brain lesions alter emotional responding, clinicians began to devise surgical means of treating serious behavioural disorders in people. A procedure called a prefrontal lobotomy was used to treat individuals with problems ranging from severe mental illness to non-conformity and rebellion (Heller et al., 2006). Although reports indicated that such surgery had a calming effect on chimpanzees (Jacobson et al., 1935), in humans it was associated with apathy, dampened emotional responding, changes in personality, irresponsibility, and seizures. However, more limited destruction of the prefrontal cortex is still used for a small number of patients suffering from severe depression or other forms of mental illness who do not respond to drug therapy (Abosch & Cosgrove, 2008).

The four general regions of the neocortex can be further subdivided into many areas that serve different functions and have different neural connections. However, all parts of the neocortex share some neuroanatomical features.

The eight lobes of the neocortex consist of six layers. Although some variations exist in the composition of the layers across regions, in general the output neurons (those that project to subcortical structures) are located in the deepest layers (Northcutt & Kaas, 1995).

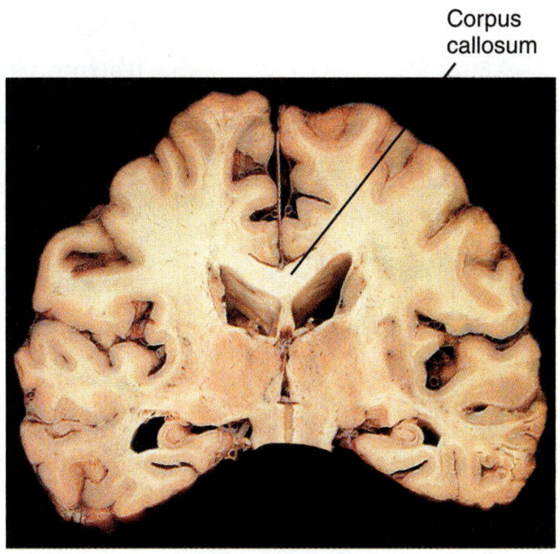

FIGURE 4-14 The corpus callosum. This cross section of the human brain shows the large bundle of axons that allows communication between the two hemispheres.

The Corpus Callosum

Communication from one side of the neocortex to the other occurs via a dense bundle of neural fibres (axons) that make up a large structure called the corpus callosum, shown in **Figure 4-14**.

The corpus callosum connects the two halves of the brain, called hemispheres. The hemispheres do not work quite the way you might expect. For instance, you might expect the right hemisphere to control things that happen on the right half of the body, and the left to control the left. Things are not that simple, however. There are many crossed connections to and from the primary cortex, leading to asymmetries, or differences in function between the hemispheres. Input from our visual, auditory, and somatosensory systems is at least partially crossed, for example. The left part of somatosensory cortex receives tactile input from the right part of the body and vice versa. Crossed connections also contribute to asymmetries in the primary motor cortex. The left part of the primary motor cortex controls movement on the right part of the body and vice versa. Furthermore, as we describe later in this chapter, not everybody's hemispheres are identical.

corpus callosum bundle of axons that allows communication from one side of neocortex to the other.

hemispheres halves of the brain.

THINGS STUDENTS WANT TO KNOW

Do we really use only 10 percent of our brains?

A popular claim about brain function is that we only use a small fraction of our brains while the rest lies dormant. Many claim that we could transcend what we commonly consider human limitations if we could only tap into the potential of this large "unused" percentage of the brain. The idea that we only use 10 percent of our brain is false and has no support at all in today's scientific literature. In fact, scientists have shown that large parts of our brains are activated at all times, both while we are awake and asleep.

The myth that we use very little of our brains was probably based, in part, on neuroscience studies done by the psychologist Karl Lashley in the early part of the twentieth century (Lashley, 1929). Lashley showed that rats could learn some mazes even after very large parts of their brains had been removed. Those who supported this myth also pointed out that in some instances, large parts of the brain can be damaged in humans with little functional deficit (remember Phineas Gage); people with major brain damage often seem "as good as new." Barry Beyerstein (1947–2007), who was a researcher in the Behaviour Brain Laboratory at Simon Fraser University in Burnaby, British Columbia (2004), suggested that the belief or hope that we have huge untapped brain potential may just be wishful thinking. Beyerstein pointed out that our brain, like all of our other features and organs, are the result of natural selection. He argued that as brains are metabolically costly to grow and operate, it does not seem likely that evolution would have permitted it to be 90 percent overbuilt. As well, losing even small amounts of brain tissue to stroke or other damage significantly negatively impacts human performance, and there is no brain area where damage is not correlated with decrements in some sort of functioning.

It's important to consider that although a brain region may not be critical for solving a maze or carrying out another task, it may be active nonetheless. Neuroimaging studies have shown that even when humans engage in relatively simple tasks, such as pressing an elevator button, visual, motor, memory, and attention areas are activated. Thus, people without brain damage actually are using large areas of the brain in these tasks (Bédard & Sanes, 2009), even though we could get along without some of those regions if we had to.

Some of us may seem at times to be using only 10 percent of our abilities, but how *well* we are putting our brains to use is a whole other question. The research is clear about the brain's activity: most of the brain is active, much of the time.

The Integrated Brain

It's important to remember that many of the above-mentioned brain areas, including the cortical regions, can be subdivided into multiple areas or nuclei, each of which is involved in different functions. However, no brain region works alone. To process information, integrate it with previous information, and then to formulate and execute a reaction requires neural circuitry undoubtedly not contained within a single brain region. For example, a person whose brain contained only a hippocampus would not be able to store information about anything because it would lack the sensory pathways necessary to provide stimuli about events or the spatial environment. Understanding how a brain region works requires sophisticated knowledge about information that flows into and out of the area, and of course, the important computations that occur within the neurons of that given brain region.

Before You Go On

www.wiley.com/go/comer

What Do You Know?

14. Which part of the brain is essential to basic functioning, such as breathing?
15. Describe the role of the brain in regulating hormones throughout the body.
16. Which part of the brain has been linked with our fear responses?
17. What behaviour is most closely linked to the hippocampus?
18. Which of our senses is linked primarily with the occipital cortex? Which with the temporal cortex? Which with the parietal cortex?
19. What are the primary functions of Broca's and Wernicke's areas, and where are they located?
20. What mental functions are associated with the frontal cortex?
21. How do the two hemispheres of the brain communicate?

SCAN TO GET THE ANSWERS

What Do You Think?

What are the potential pitfalls in making inferences about brain function from studying a single brain area?

Evolutionary Psychology

LEARNING OBJECTIVE 6

Describe the basic theory of evolution and explain how it has influenced our understanding of the human brain and behaviour.

evolutionary psychology field of study that examines how the process of evolution has shaped the body and brain via the interaction of our genes and the environment to produce our thoughts and behaviours.

As we have seen, the brain is a complex organ. But how did it develop this way? Back in Chapter 1 we briefly introduced you to the subfield of **evolutionary psychology**. In this section, we will explore the theory of evolution in more detail and how this has shaped the development of both our brain and behaviour.

The Theory of Evolution

phylogeny the development of unique species over time.

The theory of evolution proposes that all life on Earth is interrelated and derives from one common ancestor, also referred to as LUCA (last universal common ancestor). From this original common ancestor we can trace the **phylogeny**, or evolutionary history, of all life on the planet. As time progressed, those animals that survived and reproduced passed on their traits via their genetic material to their offspring; those that did not pass on their genetic material did not contribute their unique physiology and behaviour to future generations.

Fossil evidence of multicellular organisms (of which we are one) suggests that they evolved about 1.8 billion years ago. It isn't until somewhere between 600–500 million years ago (mya), however, that we see a sudden increase in the variety of plants and animals living on earth (Zimmer, 2001). Over millions of years, the process of evolution shaped the development of *chordates* (about 450 mya), which had large nerves that ran just below the surface of their backs (also called the dorsal surface), then *vertebrates* (about 425 mya), which had a boney structure protecting the dorsal nerve cords. *Amphibians* (about 400 mya) were the first creatures to move onto land because of the emergence of structures such as air breathing lungs and legs to move around on. *Reptiles* (about 300 mya) had new adaptive traits that allowed them to move even farther away from the water, such as thick skin that prevented dehydration and the ability to lay shell-covered eggs that could survive out of water. About 180 mya, *mammals* evolved from an offshoot of reptiles. Mammals are differentiated by the ability of females to keep their eggs inside their bodies and gestate their young internally, and also the ability to nurse their young with milk produced by mammary glands (hence the name *mammals*).

The missing link. For many years, one of the criticisms of evolutionary theory was the lack of fossil evidence of a transitional animal; that is, how did fins, which aren't very well suited for moving around on land, evolve into arms or legs? In 2005–2006, Neil Shubin discovered the missing link—a fish in the Canadian Arctic (dated around 375 mya) that had a primitive wrist with finger-like bones. The Nunavut Council of Elders were consulted as to what to call this species, and it was named *Tiktaalik*, an Inuit word meaning fresh water fish (Shubin, 2008).

At present all life forms, current or extinct, are classified into one of three super kingdoms—Eucharia, Archea, or Bacteria (Woese, Kandler & Wheelis, 1990). Each super kingdom is further broken down into smaller kingdoms of living things; for instance, human beings fit into the kingdom Animalia, which is part of the super kingdom Eucharia (**Figure 4-15**). The Animalia kingdom is unique

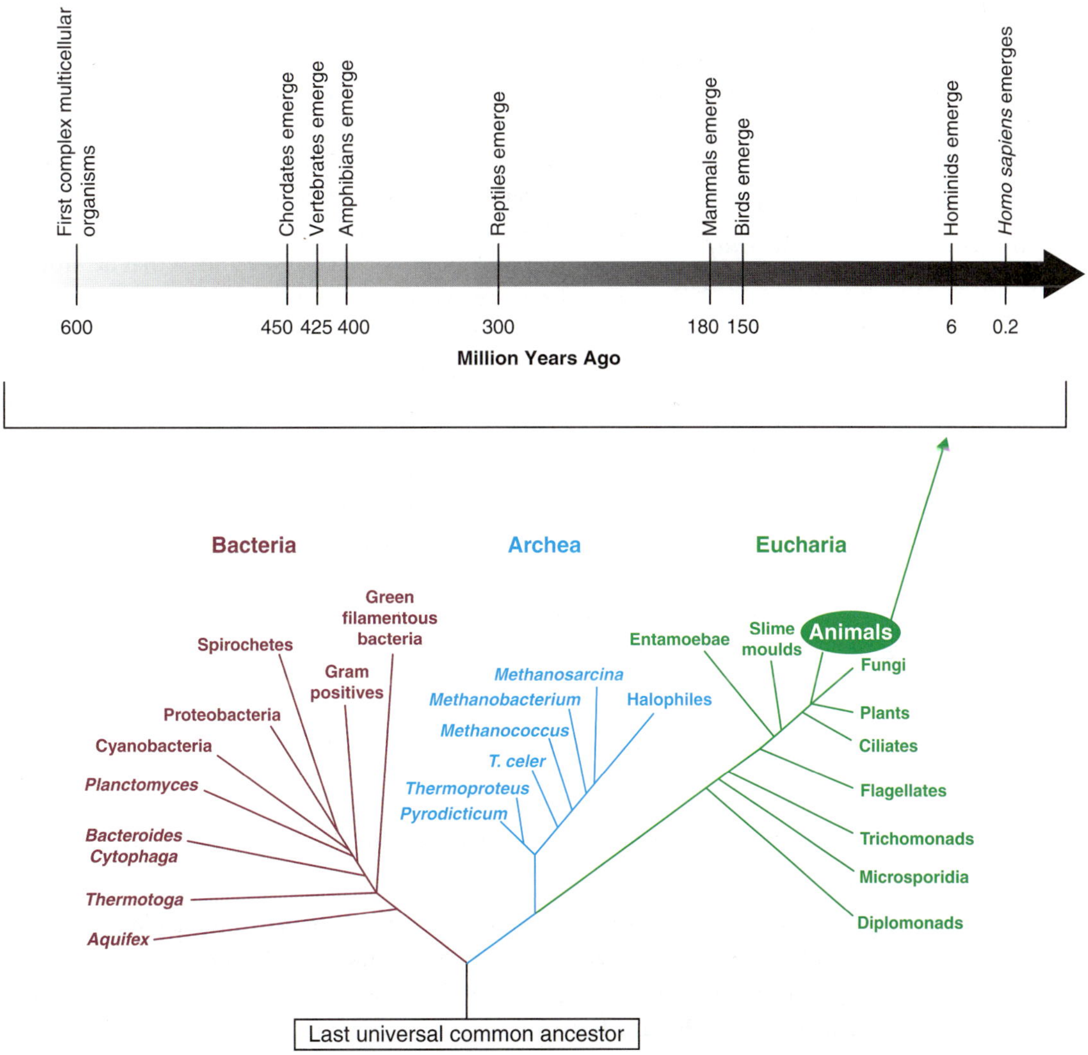

FIGURE 4-15 The universal tree of life and a timeline of evolution. This figure shows the overall relationship of the three domains to the kingdoms in which life is organized. The timeline shows the evolutionary history of animals; *Homo sapiens* come from the Hominid line and have only been in existence for a short period of time (approximately 200,000 years).

because it is the only division of life on Earth that contains organisms with nervous systems. While it may seem that plants and animals are the most prevalent life forms on Earth, there are a huge number of life forms that you can't see, such as bacteria. The reality is that plants and animals represent only a small fraction of the types and numbers of individual organisms that live on the planet.

Characteristics that are similar between species and that can be traced back to a common ancestor are referred to as *homologous*; the traits that have evolved independently in different species are called *analogous*. The way to determine if a physical adaptation or behavioural trait is homologous or analogous is to do a comparative analysis between species and to ascertain whether animals that have the same traits can be linked to a common ancestor. The process of analogous evolution leading to similar adaptations is called **convergent evolution**. For example, birds and bees both have wings, but when you trace their ancestral tree they do not have a common ancestor that had wings. Thus, the evolution of wings has happened at least twice in two different species, making it an example of an analogous process leading to similar adaptations in distinct species.

convergent evolution the development of similar physical characteristics or behaviours in different species that do not share a common ancestor; occurs because of exposure to similar environmental conditions for different species.

People have been working on and thinking about the idea of evolution for centuries, but the theory of evolution as we know it today is relatively new (Mayr, 2001). Charles Darwin's famous book *On the Origin of Species* (1859), which shifted scientific attention toward human origins, was only published about 150 years ago. For many years, however, biologists had been studying fossilized remains and noticing differences among the same species over time. In addition, many of Darwin's scientific contemporaries, specifically Arthur Wallace, were also putting together the fundamentals of the theory of evolution. What set Darwin apart was the enormous amount of work he conducted describing differences between species and how changes in the environment could influence which individuals within a species would survive and reproduce. Much of this work came from the five-year trip Darwin took on the HMS Beagle (1831–36), which sailed from England to South America, Australia, and South Africa. Darwin, who was hired as the ship's botanist at the last minute, made critical observations supported by copious notes and dozens of animal specimens that he brought back from the five-year journey (Hergenhahn, 2009).

Darwin almost lost the job as the HMS Beagle's botanist because the captain didn't like the shape of his nose. During the early 1800s, it was thought that you could determine the characteristics of a person's personality by assessing the bumps on their skull (phrenology) and from the shape of their face (physiognomy), claims that have been proven incorrect over the years.

From the specimens he gathered, Darwin began to realize that the process of change in a specific species over generations was likely due to how well a particular animal adapted to the environment it lived in. The animals with physical and behavioural attributes that were well suited to their environment were more likely to survive, reproduce, and pass on their traits to their offspring, a process he called **evolution by natural selection**, which is influenced by an individual's **fitness**, or ability to survive and reproduce in a given environment. Genetic inheritance is something many people take advantage of today by breeding specific animals to enhance the development of specific traits. For example, dog breeders will breed specific dogs to end up with offspring that are bigger, faster, meaner, or cuter than the parents.

evolution by natural selection the differential likelihood between members of a species in their ability to survive and reproduce.

fitness the ability of an individual to successfully grow to maturity and have offspring that perpetuate the existence of the species that the individual belongs to.

Darwin made four critical observations to explain the diversity of life on the planet:

1. As more and more fossil evidence became available, Darwin realized that there were subtle changes in the form of animals that were fossilized. That is, animals were changing over time.
2. Aspects of species that seem different on the surface, such as a human hand, a bat's wing, and a cat's paw, had structural similarities underneath. For all three of these animals, the number and arrangement of the bones under the skin, while different sizes, are the same (**Figure 4-16**).
3. Selective breeding of captive animals leads to changes in the appearance of the animal in question.
4. Not all animals that are born will survive to maturity and reproduce.

In addition to these four observations, Darwin also made a fundamental inference from his observations: animals of a given species that will survive and reproduce are those that can adapt and therefore survive best in their current environment. These individuals are considered to be the fittest members of their species. (Note that the phrase "survival of the fittest," which was coined by sociologist Herbert Spencer, is not completely accurate because it implies some level of perfection in an individual that is able to survive and reproduce. "Survival of the fit enough" would be a more accurate phrase.) Thus, as the environment changes, the organisms that successfully live in that environment will also change, and these changes will be passed on to their offspring. Therefore, over generations, shifts in the physical and behavioural aspects of a species will occur. Canadian researcher Bill Cade, who is currently at the University of Lethbridge, is studying aspects of this evolutionary process in *Teleogryllus oceanicus* crickets (Logue et al., 2010). The male of this species sings to attract mates, but their song also attracts parasitic flies that lay their eggs on the cricket. After the eggs of the fly hatch, the young flies use the cricket as their food source. Over generations the crickets that are quieter have preferentially survived, and now this is a species with a significant proportion of silent male crickets. The implications of the loss of song on the long-term survival of this cricket species are still unknown, but research to answer this question is underway (Tinghitella & Zuk 2009).

The father of evolution. Darwin's extensive cataloguing of various life forms he encountered during his voyage on the HMS Beagle led to his famous book, *On the Origin of Species*, and to scientific acceptance of the theory of evolution.

Darwin did not know about the underlying genetic processes that led to the inheritance of traits between generations. He did speculate about the existence of genes (which he called *gemmules*), but had no evidence for them. It wasn't until many decades later that Darwin's theory of evolution was integrated with Gregor Mendel's discovery of genetic processes. The initial integration of our knowledge of genetics and evolution occurred in the early 1920s and is now known as the *modern synthesis* (Mayr, 2001).

It is important to remember that the process of evolution never stops. All living things continue to evolve today in response to changes in the environment (a present-day example is antibiotic-resistant bacteria). There are no perfect animals, only animals that can survive and reproduce in the environment they currently live in. This is true of *all* animals, including humans. If our environment changed drastically tomorrow, say an asteroid hits the earth or there is an explosion of a super volcano, we might not have the tools or resources to survive the dramatic change in the environment. Remember, as *Homo sapiens* we have only been around for a blink of the geological eye, and there is no guarantee that we will be around for much longer from the perspective of geological time.

The Evolution of the Brain

Scientists today do not see humans as the pinnacle of life on earth, but rather as one species out of many that has adapted to fit a particular (and admittedly very broad) niche. However, the evolution of our species has led to some noticeable differences between us

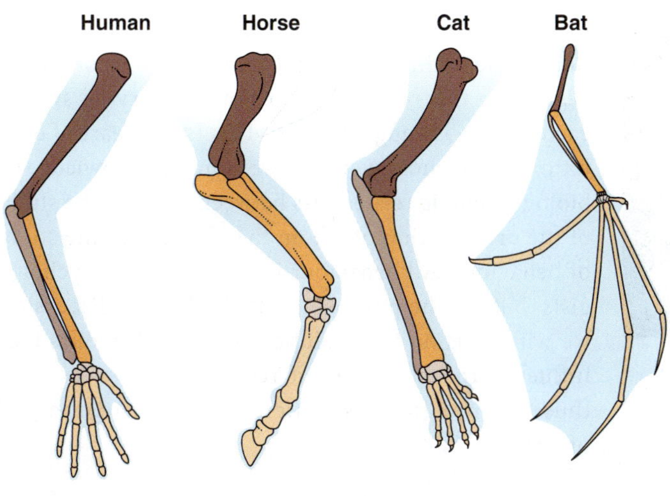

FIGURE 4-16 Comparative anatomy. Similarities among organisms demonstrate how they are related. These similarities among four vertebrate limbs illustrate that, while proportions of bones have changed in relation to each organism's way of life, the forelimbs have the same basic bone structure. Notice that the number of "fingers" on the human hand, cat paw, and bat wing are the same on all three.

and other species on Earth—most notably in the development of our nervous system, of which our brain is a part.

One way to understand how the human brain has evolved differently from that of other animals is to compare the difference in the size of our brain relative to the brain size of other organisms. Clearly we're not referring to simple volume and weight comparisons—by these measurements the brain of an elephant will beat out a human brain every time. To compare the overall size of the brain between species, it is more appropriate to discuss the ratio of brain weight to body weight for the animal in question. This ratio gives us a number that is referred to as the animal's *encephalization factor (EF)*. For example, if we compare a typical human to a typical mouse, we find that humans have an EF of 7.4–7.8 and mice have an EF of 0.5 (and in case you're wondering, the encephalization factor of an elephant is 1.13–2.36). This difference is due in part to the large neocortex that humans have. Interestingly, when you look at other species of primates (chimpanzees, monkeys, etc.) and compare their brain and body size, most primates have high encephalization factors. What specifically sets apart the brains of primates relative to other species is the size of the neocortex. For most primates it is the largest part of the brain, taking up about 50 percent of the brain. For modern humans this number is even larger, with about 80 percent of our brain consisting of the neocortex (Dunbar, Barrett, & Lycett, 2007).

It would be wonderful to actually be able to study and dissect the brains of our extinct ancestors, but unfortunately tissue doesn't fossilize well (the earliest preserved brain scientists have found to date is only a couple thousand years old). But fossilized skulls tell us that brain size has increased significantly in Hominids. To give you an example of these differences in skull size, compare the skull of an Australopithecus (which became extinct about 2 million years ago) to that of a *Homo sapiens* in **Figure 4-17**. The first major difference you can see is that the overall size of the Australopithecus skull is much smaller. Scientists estimate that the Australopithecus brain was about the size of a current chimpanzee brain (Larry, Young Owl, & Kersting, 2005), which is about one-third the size of a *Homo sapiens* brain. (That being said, the Australopithecus were quite successful as a species and existed for about 2 million years before going extinct.)

Finally, look at the shape of the skull as well as its size. The area at the front of the skull has expanded in modern *Homo sapiens*, which implies that the area underneath, presumably the frontal cortex, has expanded as well. It is this expansion of the neocortex in modern humans that has been essential to the development of many of the social and technological advancements we have made as a species. While we cannot easily go back and look at the environmental events that have shaped the development of the modern human brain, specifically the expansion of the neocortex, many theories have been proposed, including the development of complex societies (Dunbar, 2009; Dunbar & Schultz, 2007), tool use, and language development (Stout & Chaminade, 2012).

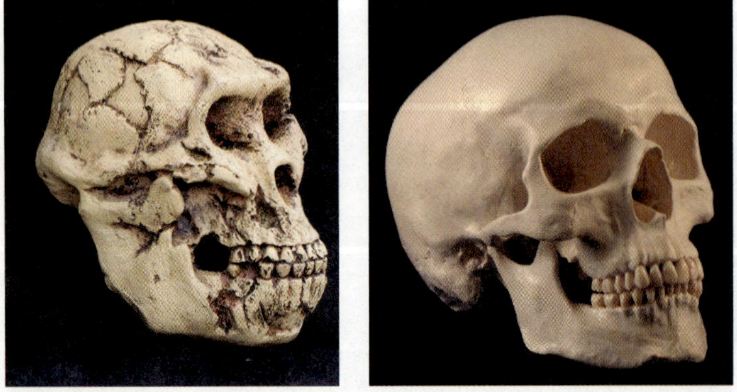

FIGURE 4-17 Skull size. The Australopithecus skull on the left is not only smaller in size than the present-day human skull on the right, but it has a much smaller frontal area, which leads to the assumption that the frontal cortex in the Australopithecus was also smaller.

The Evolution of Behaviour

Psychologists are not only interested in the evolution of the brain itself, but also in the evolution of the *behaviours* that result from the brain or nervous system each species is equipped with. This is the heart of evolutionary psychology, where we combine knowledge of biology, genetic relatedness between species, the study of the organization of life on the planet, and the study of behaviour. All behaviour is interesting to psychologists, but for the purposes of the following discussion we will focus on the evolution of two behaviours that influence the likelihood of reproductive success and thus survival: mate selection and the parenting of offspring.

Evolution at work. A peacock's elaborate tail is a consequence of evolution in action. Peahens prefer mating with peacocks that have many eyes on their tails, which has led to the large, ornate fan you see here.

Mate Choice All species need to reproduce to survive. For the majority of animal species, there are certain qualities they find desirable in a mate; quite simply, members of a species that display those qualities have a better chance of mating and reproducing. This is true for humans, too. Even if you can't fathom the thought of being a parent right now, for many of you, chances are good that at some point you will want to have children. Whether you realize it or not, the person you choose to have children with has been or will be selected based in part on your perception of his or her fitness to reproduce.

Peacocks provide an excellent example of how evolution has led to desirable qualities for mating. Female peahens prefer mates with elaborate tails—the more elaborate the better! Over time, this preference has led to a male phenotype with an elaborate tail; that is, males with elaborate tails are more frequently chosen as mates by females, and therefore the genes necessary for the production of more elaborate tails have been passed on. What females prefer about a male peacock's tail feathers is still being studied, but Canadian researchers Roslyn Dakin and Robert Montgomerie (2011) have shown that one factor that seems to matter to peahens is the absolute number of "eyes" the tail has. Their data indicate that if a peacock has only 120 to 130 eyespots on his tail, his chances of mating are low; but having more than 138 eyespots make a male a definite contender as a future mate. Thus, the peacock's tail is thought to have evolved the elaborate fan that it currently sports because of females choosing males with bigger and more elaborately designed tails.

Humans don't have elaborate tails, but clearly there are many physical differences between men and women. Think about what you would like in a potential partner. If a male reproductive partner is what you are looking for, chances are you would prefer broad shoulders and narrower hips. If you are looking for a female reproductive partner, a small waist and curvy hips is likely your preference. Scientists have determined that females prefer males with a hip to waist ratio of 0.9, and males prefer females with a hip to waist ratio of 0.7–0.8 (Singh, 1994; 1995), and these preferences are not culturally specific. Hip to waist ratio is only one example of the physical qualities that we rate as attractive—facial symmetry (Fink et al., 2006), the perceived masculinity and femininity of a face (Glassenberg et al., 2010; Johnston 2006), symmetry in movement (Brown et al., 2005), voice pitch (Apicella et al., 2007; Feinberg et al., 2006), and body odour (Gangestad & Thornhill, 1998) have also been shown to play a role in what we perceive as attractive in a potential mate.

Why have these preferences evolved? We don't know for sure, but what has been hypothesized is that these differences give us clues about the physiological and reproductive health of a potential mate. For instance, some argue that these traits tell us about an individual's development (Shackelford & Larsen, 1997), current hormonal status (Miller et al., 2007), or immune system function (Roberts et al., 2005). Ultimately it will take further scientific research to determine why these preferences have evolved. For now, what we can say is that, just like peacocks, humans have preferences for certain physical and/or behavioural traits in potential mates.

We partly choose mates based on physiology and behaviour, but we also choose based on the resources that the individual might be able to contribute to caring for our offspring. Resources are essential due to the length of time that it takes to get a human child to reproductive maturity. Beginning in the 1990s, David Buss established that across cultures, males prefer younger women who have a greater likelihood of being able to become pregnant and carry to term viable offspring. Females, in contrast, prefer males with resources—in the case of humans, the idea of "resources" often equates to money (Botwin, Buss & Shackelford, 1997; Buss, 2009). Reproductive females put a great deal of their biological resources into carrying a child to term and then caring for it after birth. Males, by contrast, can fertilize and "run." Thus, for males, physical resources in potential female mates may not be as important as physiological characteristics such as age. Ultimately, however, both males and females want to put their resources into raising children that are their own.

Parental Investment Compared to many other animals, humans spend an enormous amount of time—often decades—caring for their offspring. In contrast, Pacific coast salmon provide no parental care for their offspring. Once the eggs have been laid by the female and fertilized by the males, both parents die. Canadian geese care for their young for the first year of life, and grizzly bears care for their young for up to two years. In part, the increased need for parental investment in humans is due to the decades that it takes for the human brain to mature. In order for us to increase the likelihood of the survival and eventual reproduction of our offspring, we need to take care of our young until they can survive independently. This takes us back to mate selection—selecting a genetically strong reproductive partner that will provide some level of parental care increases the likelihood that the offspring will reach the age of reproduction.

For females, maternity is generally a certainty—a woman knows that the offspring she is carrying is her own (surrogates are an obvious exception to this). For males, however, paternity is not a certainty; it is possible that a female is carrying a child that she says has been fathered by one individual when in fact another has fathered it. When it comes to parental investment of resources, most males want to support infants that carry their genes. To test this idea in humans, Canadian researchers Daly and Wilson (1988) examined perpetrators of child murders. They speculated that step-fathers would be more likely to murder step-children than fathers would be to murder their biological children. Mercifully such events do not happen often, but the data in both Canada and the United States indicate that men are more likely to kill children they are not genetically related to than those they are genetically related to (Weekes-Shackelford & Shackelford, 2004). Not all scientists agree with these findings, however. Temrin and colleagues (2000) conducted a similar study in Sweden and did not find that child homicide rates were higher in families with a male step-parent. Thus, further research into social and cultural influences on child homicide, in addition to potential explanations from an evolutionary perspective, still need to be conducted.

Ultimately, we still have a great deal to learn when it comes to understanding how our evolutionary history has shaped behaviours such as mate choice and parental involvement. And these are not the only two behaviours that are influenced by our evolutionary past. Behaviours such as childhood play, aggression, and social networking are also areas of study by evolutionary psychologists. While the field of evolutionary psychology is still in its infancy, there are likely to be many exciting new findings in the decades to come describing how our evolutionary past has influenced the development of our nervous systems and behaviours.

Before You Go On

www.wiley.com/go/comer

What Do You Know?

22. What are Darwin's four observations and one inference, and how are they important for our understanding of how to breed domestic animals, such as cats, dogs, and dairy cows, for specific traits?
23. Describe how mate selection in humans has been influenced by our evolutionary history.

What Do You Think?

Given the information you now have on the process of evolution and its role in shaping our behaviour, what other areas of human behaviour do you think should/could be studied from an evolutionary perspective? How could this be accomplished?

SCAN TO GET THE ANSWERS

Brain Side and Brain Size

HOW WE DIFFER

LEARNING OBJECTIVE 7

Explain the neuroscience evidence about brain lateralization and the significance of brain size.

You may have heard popular theories about "left-brained" or "right-brained" types of people, or jokes about the female brain versus the male brain. Neuroscience tells us that, although the importance of such generalizations may be exaggerated in the public mind, there are, indeed, some differences among the brains of different groups of individuals. Much of the research in the area of hemispheric specialization has come from the study of *split brain patients*.

Differences in Brain Lateralization

In most people, there are specialized areas of cortex that exist only on one side of the brain. Wernicke's and Broca's areas related to speech and language, for example, are usually on the left side of most people's brains; but not everybody's. The exceptions occur most often in left-handed individuals. Some left-handers (about 18 percent, Springer & Deutsch, 1993) have these language areas located on the right side of their brains, or on both sides, suggesting that lateralization of more than one function (handedness and language) may be linked in some way.

Roger Sperry won the Nobel prize in 1981 for his work on brain lateralization. He and his colleague Michael Gazzaniga (Sperry, Gazzaniga, & Bogen, 1969) designed a number of study techniques that allowed them to examine the functioning of the hemispheres of *split-brain patients*. These are individuals who have undergone a surgical treatment used to treat severe epilepsy where the corpus callosum is severed to stop the spread of seizures from one side of the brain to the other. These patients are normal in many respects, but they lack the ability to integrate information from the two hemispheres (Gazzaniga, 2005; 2009). Studies on these patients have highlighted the fact that the two hemispheres need the corpus callosum to communicate. Although split brain patients are largely unaffected by the surgery in their day-to-day lives, the results of split brain studies clearly show the hemispheric localization of a number of perceptual and cognitive functions.

For example, a split brain patient is given a pencil in his left hand under a table where he cannot see it; a divider is placed beneath the table so that he cannot pass the pencil to his right hand. (Remember that tactile and visual information cross over from one side of the body to the opposite side of the brain, so that information gathered by touch on the left side of our body or visually from our left visual field is sent first to the right hemisphere of our brain for processing.) If a person's corpus callosum is intact, then information from either side of the body is almost immediately shared with both hemispheres. In split-brained patients this is not the case; information received by only one side of the body goes only to the opposite hemisphere in the brain. So, if we asked this patient what he was holding in his left hand, do you think he could tell us in words? If you remembered that the language production area (Broca's area) is located in the left hemisphere of the brain, you would have answered this question correctly—no, he could not verbally tell us what was in his hand. If shown a set of pictures, however, he could use his left hand to point to a picture of a pencil. He can do this because his left hand is controlled by his right hemisphere; therefore, tactile information about the pencil would go to his right hemisphere and he would then be able to use his left hand to identify the object. That is, he knows what the object is but he cannot say it. Sperry and Gazzaniga also found that split brain patients had average response time when completing a block arrangement spatial task with their left hands (right hemisphere controlled) and far below average response time when asked to only use their right hand (left hemisphere controlled) (Sperry, Gazzaniga, & Bogen, 1969).

> "Can the brain understand the brain?"
> —*David Hubel, neuroscientist and Nobel laureate in medicine*

Although split-brained patients show processing problems under very artificial laboratory conditions, they show very few problems overall. This is because in their real world interactions they are not delinking what one side of the brain gets and what the other side of the brain gets. In their day-to-day lives, both sides of the brain get almost exactly the same information.

In addition to these rather clear-cut functional and anatomical asymmetries, many people believe that more general thought processes are lateralized, such that people who think a certain way are using proportionately more of one side of their brain than they

are the other side. The right hemisphere of the brain is thought to be dominant in artists and engineers. By contrast, the left hemisphere of the brain is thought to be dominant in individuals with strong analytical and verbal skills.

What then is the scientific evidence for "right-brain" and "left-brain" dominant thinking? Certainly the work with split-brained patients shows that there is, indeed, some localization of function in one or the other of our hemispheres. However, the possibility that one side of our brain is in charge and dominates the functioning of the other side of our brain is not supported by neuroscientific research, as the corpus callosum allows for virtually instant communication from one side of the brain to the other. This means that in everything we do, both sides of the brain are involved (Hines, 1987).

> "What it comes down to is that modern society discriminates against the right hemisphere."
> —*Roger Sperry, neuroscientist and Nobel laureate in medicine*

Overall, the research shows that, aside from the language areas noted above, the two hemispheres are more similar than they are different. Indeed, even when right–left differences are detected in function, these differences are usually relative. For example, the left brain can accomplish what the right brain can accomplish, it's just less efficient at some tasks and more efficient at others.

Gender Differences

On average, the brains of women are smaller than those of men. Does this mean men are smarter than women? It does not. The overall size of the brain appears to be more closely related to the size of the body than to function. In fact, a relationship between brain size and intelligence doesn't exist (Tramo et al., 1998), except at the two ends of the spectrum; people with abnormally small or abnormally large brains are both more likely to exhibit mental deficiencies than those with brains whose size falls in the normal range.

In addition to the overall size difference, researchers have reported some differences in the size of certain brain regions in humans. For example, part of the corpus callosum, connecting the two hemispheres of the brain, has been shown to be larger in women (Johnson et al., 1994). This finding has contributed to the much-overstated suggestion that women are more likely to use both sides of their brains than men are. Most recently, Doreen Kimura at Simon Fraser University has looked closely at how the brains of males and females process information. Kimura's research shows that on some tasks, such as defining words, men use only their left hemisphere while women tend to use both hemispheres (Kimura, 2000). Even in cases where differences have been reported in the size of brain regions, the overall differences between men and women are very small, so much so that they really don't tell us much about the individual person of either gender.

Before You Go On

www.wiley.com/go/comer

What Do You Know?

24. What does research show about "right-brained" spatial thinking versus "left-brained" logical thinking?
25. On which side of the brain do most people have their language-related areas? What about left-handed people?
26. Does overall brain size matter in how well brains function?

SCAN TO GET THE ANSWERS

What Do You Think?

What are some of the ethical problems associated with searching for structural differences in the brains of different groups of people?

PRACTICALLY SPEAKING How Can You Prevent Age-Related Decline in Brain Function?

A common adage used today with regard to the aging brain is "Use it or lose it!" Stories in the media encourage aging individuals to keep their brains active by spending time on crossword puzzles, Sudoku, or other brainteasers. Some companies have even developed and marketed brain puzzles they claim are specifically designed to keep the brain agile and prevent declines in a wide range of general cognitive abilities, such as day-to-day problem solving and memory.

Unfortunately, the scientific evidence available does not support these claims. While it's true that people with a higher level of education and also those with multiple interests and socially active lives seem somewhat protected from age-related cognitive dysfunction (Perneczky et al., 2008), there is no evidence that engaging in brain puzzles is beneficial for any purpose other than making you better at solving similar brain puzzles! In other words, mastery of these tasks does not generalize to overall cognitive performance.

One type of experience, however, that does seem to make a difference in cognitive performance is physical exercise. In humans, aerobic exercise increases blood flow to the brain, improves performance on cognitive tasks, and elevates mood (Pereira et al., 2007). Studies in experimental animals have shown that physical exercise increases the birth of new neurons in the hippocampus and also stimulates the growth of neurons in general throughout brain structures that support cognitive function (Stranahan et al., 2006, 2007).

So add protection of your brain to the list of other reasons of why it's a good idea to hit the gym regularly. There's good scientific evidence to support this claim!

Neurological Diseases

WHEN THINGS GO WRONG

LEARNING OBJECTIVE 8

Describe four neurological disorders and the current directions in research for treating them.

Neurological disorders involve problems with the functioning of the nervous system, the brain, the spinal cord, and nerves in the body. These disorders involve structural, biochemical, or electrical circuit abnormalities and cause pervasive problems with moving, speaking, swallowing, breathing, learning, remembering, and so on. Janca and colleagues (2006) present data backing their claim that the global prevalence of neurological disorders has been underestimated. Further, they argue that worldwide, policy makers and health care professionals are underprepared to deal with the predicted increases in these disorders likely to occur given the rapidly aging population. We will focus here on some key neurological diseases that typically strike in adulthood.

> "All the most acute, most powerful, and most deadly diseases, and those which are most difficult to be understood by the inexperienced, fall upon the brain."
>
> —*Hippocrates, fourth-century* B.C.E. *Greek philosopher*

- Multiple sclerosis involves demyelination, or loss of myelin, on the axons of neurons. This leads to the inefficient transmission of electrical information among neurons and a range of symptoms, including vision loss, pain, and muscle weakness, depending on where the demyelination occurs. Research on multiple sclerosis has focused on finding ways to stimulate myelination (Franklin & French-Constant, 2008).
- Amyotrophic lateral sclerosis (ALS or Lou Gehrig's disease, so-named after a famous baseball player who had the illness) is another condition that affects movement. People with ALS experience degeneration of motor neurons in the spinal cord. The symptoms of this disease begin with localized muscle weakness, and ultimately

multiple sclerosis neurological disease that causes a loss of myelin on the axons of neurons.

amyotrophic lateral sclerosis (ALS or Lou Gehrig's disease) neurological disease that causes degeneration of motor neurons in the spinal cord, leading to loss of movement and eventual death.

the entire body is afflicted. People with ALS typically die when the motor neurons that control basic functions, including breathing, die.

Interestingly, some populations of motor neurons appear to be more resistant to ALS than others. Examples of the resistant populations include the cells that control eye movements (Laslo et al., 2001) and those involved in motor control of the anus and genitals (Mannen et al., 1982). Investigators are studying these neuron groups to determine whether molecular differences between vulnerable and resistant populations of cells can be used to stimulate protective mechanisms in motor neurons that degenerate in this devastating disease.

PSYCHOLOGY AROUND US The Importance of Helmets

Lou Gehrig was a legendary baseball player, a member of the New York Yankees from 1925 to 1939. He retired because of his failing health. Gehrig had developed symptoms of ALS, which was later named Lou Gehrig's disease for that reason. However, scientists now think that Lou Gehrig may not have had ALS. Instead, he may have developed symptoms that were similar to those of ALS because he was so often hit in the head with baseballs (he played before batting helmets were required). Gehrig lost consciousness on many such occasions, as well as during fights on the baseball field.

Repeated head trauma, particularly when associated with loss of consciousness, can lead to the death of motor neurons. Head trauma can kill other groups of neurons, too, and produce a different set of symptoms. More recently, we are starting to find similar issues with hockey players. Reggie Fleming played left wing for a number of teams from 1959 to 1974 and was known for fighting as well as scoring. Fleming gave permission for his brain to be closely examined after his death. When he died in 2009 at 73 years of age, researchers at the Center for the Study of Traumatic Encephalopathy (CSTE) at Boston University conducted the analysis. They found clear evidence of chronic traumatic encephalopathy, a neurodegenerative disease known to cause cognitive decline, short temper, and other behavioural abnormalities, and eventually dementia (McKee et al., 2009).

As more data become available, we will need to look more closely at the rates of repeated concussions in many of our contact sports. Many athletes, including football players, soccer players, and boxers, have been initially diagnosed with Parkinson's disease or Alzheimer's disease, but have later had these diagnoses changed when it became clear that their symptoms were due to repeated brain damage.

Parkinson's disease neurological disease that involves the death of dopaminergic neurons in the substantia nigra, leading to tremors, muscle rigidity, and other motor problems.

- **Parkinson's disease** is a neurological condition that involves the death of dopaminergic neurons—those that rely on the neurotransmitter dopamine—in the substantia nigra (Jankovic & Aguilar, 2008). Patients with this condition often have a tremor in their hands and muscle rigidity. Parkinson's disease can have many different causes and affects a relatively large percentage of the population. In most cases, however, the cause is not known.

  People with Parkinson's disease can be treated with drugs that replace the dopamine that is lost when the neurons in the substantia nigra die. However, this replacement is only temporary. As time passes, patients become resistant to the dopamine drugs and/or develop intolerable side effects to the drugs. Because drug therapy is only temporary and so many people suffer from the condition, scientists have spent considerable effort searching for novel therapies, including the transplantation of stem cells, which can be induced to produce new neurons that make dopamine. Although these treatments are promising, there is much work to be done before they can be used routinely (Isacson & Kordower, 2008).

Huntington's disease inherited neurological condition that results in the death of neurons in the striatum.

- **Huntington's disease** is an inherited condition that results in the death of neurons in the striatum. People suffering from this disease exhibit awkward movements and often show symptoms of psychosis (Paulsen, 2009). Like ALS and Parkinson's disease, Huntington's disease is progressive and as yet, there is no cure.

Transplanting Stem Cells to Treat Neurological Disorders

Medical and neuroscience researchers have not yet developed significantly effective treatments for these devastating neurological diseases, so some neuroscientists have turned their attention to the possibility of repairing damaged brain regions by transplanting new tissue into the brain.

Early work ruled out the possibility of transplanting fully differentiated brain tissue into a damaged region. In most cases, these transplants did not survive or integrate properly into the existing circuitry. Subsequent attempts to transplant fetal brain tissue into brains of adults suffering from Alzheimer's or Parkinson's disease also met with limited, if any, success. Fetal tissue may integrate into the damaged brain, but it remains foreign and often does not function normally for extended periods of time (Freed, 2000).

Parkinson's disease. Canadian Michael J. Fox was diagnosed with Parkinson's in 1991 and went public with it in 1998. He founded the Michael J. Fox foundation to support research and Parkinson's patient care, which has raised over $225 million to deal with this brain disease.

Thus, transplantation research has focused primarily on the possibility of restoring damaged circuits by transplanting stem cells. **Stem cells** were first identified by Ernest McCulloch and James Till working at the University of Toronto in 1960. Stem cells are undifferentiated cells that have the potential to grow into any cell type if given the appropriate environmental cues. The most versatile stem cells come from embryonic tissue (Srivastava et al., 2008). Researchers have obtained stem cells from embryos created as part of in vitro fertilization, a procedure sometimes used to help infertile couples have babies. Eggs are fertilized with sperm in the laboratory, and some of the resulting embryos are implanted into a woman's uterus. Remaining, or extra, embryos, at very early stages of development, can provide a source for stem cells, but are destroyed in the process of obtaining the stem cells that can then be cultured or reproduced. Researchers are now working to find other sources of stem cells, including reproducing them from adult tissue (Temple, 2001).

stem cell undifferentiated cell that can divide to replace itself and create new cells that have the potential to become all other cells of the body, including neurons.

Thus far, stem cell transplantation studies in animals have been successful in some cases, particularly in animal models of Parkinson's disease (Takahashi et al., 2009; Hovakimyan et al., 2008). The effectiveness of stem-cell treatment may depend on what kind of brain cell is damaged and where the damaged cells are located. For instance, Parkinson's disease arises predominantly from the death of dopaminergic neurons in the substantia nigra. Thus, restoring this population of neurons, providing they make appropriate connections and synthesize the correct neurotransmitter, is likely to repair the deficit. Other neurological diseases that cause more widespread damage might not respond as well to stem cell treatment. For example, patients with Alzheimer's disease (which we discuss in some detail in Chapter 8) lose neurons throughout their brains. The disease also causes the formation of abnormal clusters of non-degradable protein that interfere with neuronal function (Rafii & Aisen, 2009). Therefore, replacing only certain types of dead neurons may not be sufficient to overcome the widespread devastation characteristic of this disease.

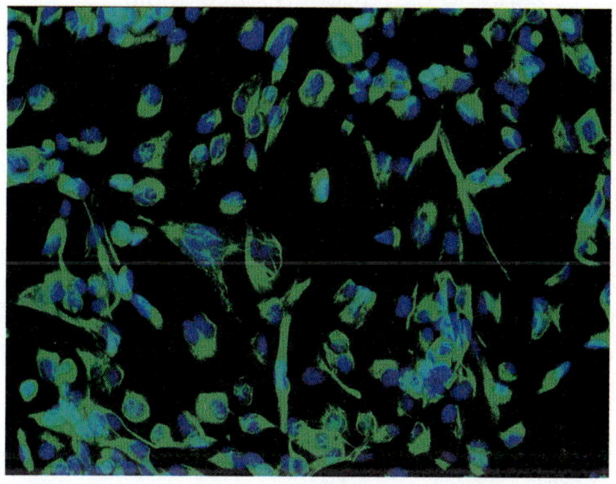

Neural stem cells. Shown in this microscopic image, neural stem cells have been used to repopulate damaged brain regions. These cells can divide and produce different types of neurons depending on their environment.

Before You Go On

www.wiley.com/go/comer

What Do You Know?

27. What goes wrong in the nervous system to cause multiple sclerosis, ALS, Parkinson's disease, and Huntington's disease?
28. What have neuroscientists learned to date about transplants of brain tissue as a way to treat neurological diseases?

What Do You Think?

What are the technical and ethical pitfalls stem cell researchers must contend with?

SCAN TO GET THE ANSWERS

Summary

How Do Scientists Study the Nervous System?

LEARNING OBJECTIVE 1 Understand the key methods that scientists use to learn about brain anatomy and functioning.

- Neuroscientists examine autopsy tissue and patients with localized brain damage to learn about brain anatomy and brain function.
- EEGs and neuroimaging, such as PET scans and fMRI, allow us to study brain function in the living brain.

How Does the Nervous System Work?

LEARNING OBJECTIVE 2 Describe the two major types of cells in the nervous system and describe the primary functions of each.

- The two major types of brain cells are neurons and glia.
- Neurons communicate with other cells by producing and sending electrochemical signals.
- Glia are involved in various functions, such as forming the blood–brain barrier, producing myelin, and clearing the brain of debris.

How Do Neurons Work?

LEARNING OBJECTIVE 3 Describe what happens when a neuron "fires" and how neurons send messages to one another.

- Communication within a neuron occurs electrically by means of the action potential, whereas communication between neurons occurs at the synapse via chemical signals called neurotransmitters.
- Neurotransmitters are released by the presynaptic neuron, diffuse across the synapse, and bind to receptors on the postsynaptic site.
- The response of a receiving neuron to a neurotransmitter is determined by the receptor on the postsynaptic, or receiving, neuron's membrane. Depending on the type of receptor, the postsynaptic neurons will fire or not.

How Is the Nervous System Organized?

LEARNING OBJECTIVE 4 Name and describe the functions and subdivisions of the two major parts of the nervous system.

- The two major divisions of the nervous system are the central nervous system, which consists of the brain and spinal cord, and the peripheral nervous system, which consists of nerves that extend throughout the body outside the central nervous system.
- The peripheral nervous system has two divisions: the somatic nervous system, which sends information about the senses and movement, and the autonomic nervous system, which controls involuntary functions and responses to stress.
- The autonomic nervous system is divided into the sympathetic nervous system, which responds to stress, and the parasympathetic nervous systems, which is responsible for digestion and other processes that occur when the body is at rest.

Structures of the Brain

LEARNING OBJECTIVE 5 List key structures of the brain and describe their relationships to our behaviour.

- The brain can be subdivided into many regions, each of which serves one or more specialized functions.
- The brainstem participates in movement and sensation of the head and neck as well as in basic bodily functions, such as respiration and heart rate.
- The midbrain includes the substantia nigra, an area important for movement.
- The hypothalamus controls basic drives (food, drink, sex) and hormones, while the thalamus serves as a relay station for sensory information on its way to the cerebral cortex.
- Many brain regions participate in different types of learning—the hippocampus is important for spatial navigation learning and learning about life's events; the amygdala is important for fear learning; the cerebellum and striatum are important for motor learning; and the nucleus accumbens is important for reward learning.
- A large part of the brain consists of the neocortex. The neocortex can be subdivided into frontal, parietal, temporal, and occipital regions. The cortex controls movement, integrates sensory information, and serves numerous cognitive functions.

Evolutionary Psychology

LEARNING OBJECTIVE 6 Describe the basic theory of evolution and explain how it has influenced our understanding of the human brain and behaviour.

- All life on Earth is interrelated and derives from one common ancestor through a process known as evolution.
- An organism's ability to survive and reproduce (thereby transferring their traits to their offspring) is referred to as the individual's *fitness*.

- The brains of modern-day humans are much larger than any other animal species or of Hominid species that have gone extinct.
- Many of our behaviours are shaped by our evolutionary past, including mate choice and parental investment.

Brain Side and Brain Size *How We Differ*

LEARNING OBJECTIVE 7 Explain the neuroscience evidence about brain lateralization and the significance of brain size.

- Research shows that the two hemispheres are more similar than different and that any differences are usually relative.
- Brain size appears to be related to overall body size and not to brain function.

Neurological Diseases *When Things Go Wrong*

LEARNING OBJECTIVE 8 Describe four neurological disorders and the current directions in research for treating them.

- Multiple sclerosis involves the loss of myelin on the axons of neurons.
- In amyotrophic lateral sclerosis, the motor neurons in the spinal cord degenerate.
- Parkinson's and Huntington's diseases are primarily the result of neuronal destruction in the substantia nigra and striatum, respectively.
- Some regeneration occurs in the brain after it is injured, but repair is typically not complete and functional impairment often remains. Researchers believe transplantation of brain tissue, particularly embryonic stem cells, may provide relief for some neurological diseases.

Key Terms

absolute refractory period 126
action potential 125
amygdala 136
amyotrophic lateral sclerosis (ALS or Lou Gehrig's disease) 153
association cortex 138
autonomic nervous system 130
axon 122
axon terminal 122
Broca's area 141
cerebellum 134
concentration gradient 125
convergent evolution 146
corpus callosum 143
dendrites 122
depolarized 128
dopamine 135
endocrine system 135
evolution by natural selection 146
evolutionary psychology 144
fitness 146
frontal cortex 140
glia 123
hemispheres 143
hindbrain 133
hippocampus 136
Huntington's disease 154
hyperpolarized 128
hypothalamus 135
interneuron 132
ion channels 125
medulla 134
multiple sclerosis 153
myelin 125
neocortex 138
neuroimaging 121
neuron 121
neuroscience 120
neurotransmitter receptors 127
neurotransmitters 126
norepinephrine 134
nucleus accumbens 137
occipital cortex 138
parasympathetic nervous system 130
parietal cortex 140
Parkinson's disease 154
phylogeny 144
pituitary gland 135
plasticity 128
pons 134
postsynaptic potentials 128
prefrontal cortex 141
relative refractory period 126
resting potential 124
reticular formation 134
serotonin 134
sodium potassium pump 125
somatic nervous system 130
somatosensory strip 140
spinal cord 131
stem cell 155
striatum 137
substantia nigra 135
sympathetic nervous system 130
synapses 126
synaptic vesicles 127
temporal cortex 138
thalamus 135
threshold 125
Wernicke's area 139

TYING IT TOGETHER

The study of neuroscience is closely connected to the study of all other areas of psychology. Throughout this chapter, we have stressed how neuroscience interfaces with psychology's various subfields, including our highlighted sections on individual differences, abnormal functioning, and development. To remind you of how neuroscience is tied to other psychology subfields and issues, we have selected some interesting points from throughout the chapter.

WHAT HAPPENS IN THE BRAIN?

- The human brain contains about 100 billion neurons. In addition, some parts of the brain contain 10 times that many non-neuronal cells, called glia.
- If you put a recording electron into a "resting" neuron, it will read a negative charge of approximately –70 millivolts. At the peak of a neuron's action potential, the membrane charge is around 150 millivolts.
- Action potentials of neurons follow an all-or-none principle. When sufficiently stimulated, a neuron fires; otherwise, it does not.
- Synaptic spaces are about 20 nanometres wide. A nanometer is 1 billionth of a metre.
- The sympathetic nervous system is responsible for the "fight-or-flight" reaction; the parasympathetic nervous system helps control the basic functions of life, such as digestion.
- The hypothalamus helps regulate eating, drinking, sex, maternal behaviour, and the endocrine system.
- Although the two halves of the brain are called hemispheres, the brain is not completely symmetrical.

HOW WE DIFFER

- Although the speech and language areas—Wernicke's and Broca's areas—are on the left side of most people's brains, these areas may be located on the right side or both sides for some people—particularly left-handed people.
- On average, the brains of women are smaller than those of men, although such size differences have no relationship to intelligence or other faculties.
- Some theorists believe that women are more likely than men to use both sides of their brain.

WHEN THINGS GO WRONG

- When the spinal cord is damaged and information to and from the brain is interrupted, individuals become paralyzed. The higher up the damage—the closer it occurs to the brain—the larger the proportion of body affliction.
- People with damage to the frontal cortex region, called *Broca's area*, cannot generate speech but can understand language.
- With some notable exceptions, psychiatric disorders (for example, clinical depression) seem tied most often to biochemical imbalances in the brain, while neurological disorders (for example, Parkinson's disease and Alzheimer's disease) seem tied to brain-structure abnormalities, including the degeneration of neurons.
- Many neuroscientists currently are trying to develop treatments for certain neurological diseases in which they restore damaged neural circuits by transplanting new tissue into those areas of the brain, particularly by transplanting stem cells—undifferentiated cells that can grow into particular cell types.

HOW WE DEVELOP

- Over the course of development, a process of programmed cell death, or cellular pruning, results in the death of over 75 percent of the neurons initially produced by the brain.
- Our environmental experiences also help determine which synapses are maintained and which are pruned during infancy and childhood.
- Myelination of the frontal cortex is not completed until after puberty.
- Contrary to past beliefs, some populations of neurons continue to be produced well into adulthood—for example, neurons in the hippocampus.
- Adult brains also continue to undergo dendrite remodelling and synaptogenesis.

Psychology Around Us

The Amazing Brain

A teenager who has had his left-brain hemisphere removed to alleviate very severe epilepsy. A young woman recovering from a car accident. A middle-aged man undergoing rehabilitation after a stroke. The cognitive and physical functioning of each of these individuals reflects various kinds of brain damage. For years, prior to the development of neuroimaging technologies, neuroscientists learned about the brain largely by observing the behaviours of brain-impaired individuals, and then working backward, figuring out what those altered behaviours seemed to say about the operation of the affected brain areas.

You have a similar task in this video lab exercise. Observe the behaviours and functioning of each of the individuals in the video and suggest which of their brain areas have been damaged, how those brain areas usually operate when they are not damaged, and how rehabilitation might help change the brain and restore the behaviours and functioning of the individuals.

Video Lab Exercise

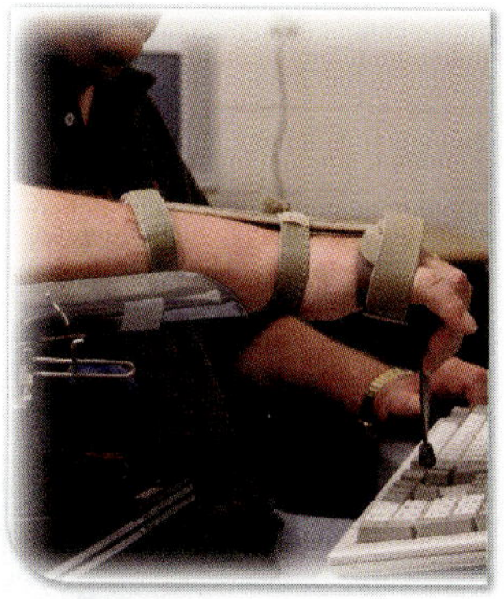

As you are working on this online exercise, consider the following questions:

- What examples of *brain lateralization* are on display for each of the individuals in the lab video?
- What do the treatment gains of each individual reveal about *brain integration* and *brain plasticity?*
- How might *stem cell* transplantations, if such techniques are successfully developed and socially approved, improve on the rehabilitation techniques applied in this lab video?

CHAPTER 5

Sensation and Perception

CHAPTER OUTLINE

- Common Features of Sensation and Perception
- The Chemical Senses: Smell and Taste
- The Tactile or Cutaneous Senses: Touch, Pressure, Pain, Vibration
- The Auditory Sense: Hearing
- The Visual Sense: Sight

ON AND OFF SENSATION

Have you ever noticed how enticing the aroma of your favourite restaurant is when you first walk through the front door? The smell of foods you enjoy coming from the kitchen makes your mouth water. Depending on how long it's been since you last ate a meal, you might develop an urgent craving to order as soon as possible!

After you order, while you wait for your meal to arrive, you may not even notice it, but your awareness of the food odours in the room is probably gradually diminishing. By the time your meal is delivered to your table, you probably do not even notice the smells that seemed so strong when you first entered the restaurant. When the server places your plate on the table, right under your nose, however, you might suddenly begin to notice the smell of food again—this time your own.

Our sense of smell contributes greatly to our enjoyment of a good meal. In fact, all of our senses become involved when we enjoy a meal. We use vision, our sense of sight, to admire the food on the plate. Hearing lets us listen to the sizzle of a particularly hot dish, or enjoy conversation with our dining companions. Obviously, our sense of taste is involved once we actually take a bite of food, but so is our sense of touch, as we discern the temperature and texture of the food. Without our sense of touch, we could not tell a rough, cool salad from a smooth, warm soup.

Psychologists generally agree that there are five senses: smell, taste, touch, sound, and sight. Beyond these five senses we can also consider our kinesthetic or proprioceptive sense (our understanding of where we and our body parts are located in space—this is the sense that stops working if we are drunk, preventing us from touching our nose with our eyes closed). We can also consider our vestibular sense or system, which provides us with information about our movement through space (which stops working if we are on a ship that is rolling and pitching on rough water). Touch is actually a complex of senses collectively referred to as the cutaneous senses or the somatosenses. These include pressure, vibration, pain, temperature, and position. Although we will discuss each of these five major senses separately in this chapter, in most of our day-to-day experiences, we actually use these sensory systems or modalities to experience the world.

We use our senses in two tightly related processes. One process is **sensation**, the act of using our sensory systems to detect stimuli present in

sensation the act of using our sensory systems to detect environmental stimuli.

perception recognition and identification of a sensory stimulus.

the environment around us. Once acquired, sensory information must be interpreted in the context of past and present sensory stimuli. This process, which also involves recognition and identification (for example, the realization that you recognize the smell in a restaurant as pizza is cooking), is broadly defined as **perception**.

Sensation and perception are both critical for our interpretation of, and interaction with, the environment. Accurate functioning of our sensory systems is critical for survival. Imagine how greatly diminished your chances of survival would be if you could not see a fire, feel its heat, hear others crying "fire," smell the smoke, or interpret any of these sensations appropriately. Aside from the clear adaptive significance of our ability to sense and perceive the world, our life experiences are greatly enriched by these processes. Let's explore them in more detail. ■

Common Features of Sensation and Perception

LEARNING OBJECTIVE 1

Describe characteristics shared by all the senses, including receptor cells, transduction, and thresholds, and differentiate between top-down and bottom-up processes of perception.

sensory receptor cells specialized cells that convert a specific form of environmental stimuli into neural impulses.

sensory transduction the process of converting a specific form of environmental stimuli into neural impulses.

absolute threshold the minimal stimulus necessary for detection by an individual.

difference threshold or **just noticeable difference** the minimal difference between two stimuli necessary for detection of a difference between the two.

Each of our sensory systems is set up to convert the physical stimuli we receive from the world outside our bodies into neural information. Sensation and perception occur differently in each of our sensory modalities, but our senses also share some common processes. Each of the senses has a set of specialized cells called sensory receptor cells that convert a specific form of environmental stimuli into neural impulses, the form of communication used in our brains and nervous systems (see **Figure 5-1**). This conversion is called sensory transduction. The different physical stimuli for each sensory system that are converted to brain activity through sensory transduction are listed in **Table 5-1**.

The Limits of the Senses: Thresholds

Our sensory receptors can be activated by very weak stimuli. A stimulus must, however, reach a certain level of intensity before we can detect it, because the conversion of physical stimuli into neural impulses only occurs when the stimuli reach this level or threshold. The minimal stimulus necessary for detection by an individual is called the absolute threshold (**Table 5-2**). Although the absolute threshold varies from person to person, in most cases it is surprisingly small. For instance, many normal humans are capable of detecting a candle flame up to 50 kilometres away on a clear pitch black night (Galanter, 1962). Researchers have also worked to determine the smallest difference that we can detect between two stimuli, called the difference threshold or just noticeable difference. If you are listening to a radio, how much do you have to turn the radio up before you notice that it is louder? This amount, or just noticeable difference, depends on how loud the radio is in the first place. When sensory systems are working optimally, the difference threshold is also remarkably small.

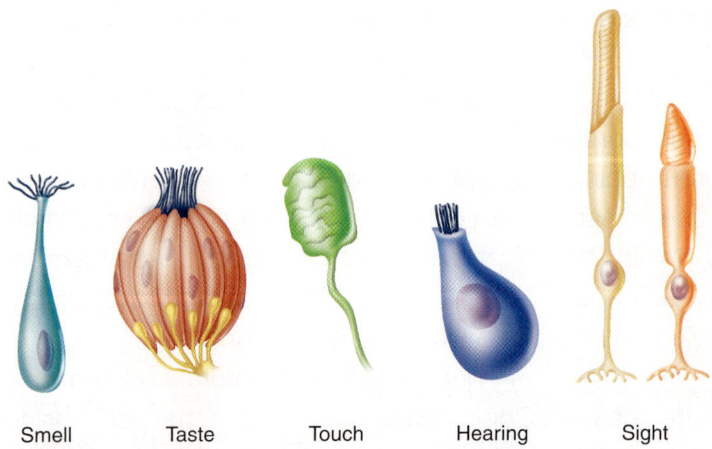

FIGURE 5-1 Sensory receptor cells. Each sensory system contains specialized cells that are activated by particular physical stimuli.

Thresholds may limit our abilities in some ways, but they are also very useful to us. Imagine if you

TABLE 5-1 Sensory Transduction Converts Environmental Stimuli into Neural Activity

Sensory System	Physical Stimuli
Olfactory (smell)	Odorants (airborne chemicals)
Somatosensory (touch, heat, pain)	Pressure or damage to the skin
Gustatory (taste)	Chemicals (typically in food)
Auditory (hearing)	Sound waves
Visual (sight)	Light (photons)

TABLE 5-2 Absolute Thresholds for Various Senses

Sense	Absolute Threshold
Smell	A drop of perfume diffused throughout a six-room apartment
Taste	5 millilitres of sugar in 9 litres of water
Touch	An insect's wing falling on your cheek from a height of about a centimetre
Hearing	The tick of a watch at 6 metres in a quiet room
Sight	A candle flame 50 kilometres away on a clear, dark night

noticed every little change in wind pattern or each individual fibre in your clothing. You probably wouldn't be very comfortable if you noticed all these small details.

Surrounded by Stimuli: Sensory Adaptation

Our senses are generally organized to detect change. This makes adaptive sense since most stimuli we are exposed to are not important enough to warrant our attention. Imagine how difficult it would be to concentrate on reading this chapter if sensory information about the odours of your breath, the taste of your mouth, the sound of the clock ticking, and the touch of your clothing were all competing with your ability to read! To combat the possibility of being unable to focus on the salient or important cues, our sensory systems respond to the continual presence of the same stimulus with a decreased response to that stimulus, a process called **sensory adaptation**. What happens is this: when some stimulus in our surroundings stays the same for a period of time, such as the pressure of our clothing on our skin, our sensory cells respond to it less and less. Sometimes, in fact, we no longer notice the stimulus at all. All of our sensory systems exhibit some form of adaptation, but the sense of smell seems especially prone to this response.

sensory adaptation the process whereby repeated stimulation of a sensory cell leads to a reduced response.

Although it's possible that the diminished sense of smell people experience as they sit in a restaurant may be due to blocked sinuses, it's much more likely that this experience occurs as a result of sensory adaptation. Our ability to detect odours gradually fades when we are in their presence for a prolonged period. Sensory adaptation can be overcome by providing a much stronger stimulus, which is what happens when your restaurant meal is delivered to your table. Now that the source of the smell is more concentrated in your vicinity, your ability to smell is renewed. Although the sense of smell is perhaps most prone to this response, all of our sensory systems exhibit some form of adaptation.

Processing Sensory Information

bottom-up processing perception that proceeds by transducing environmental stimuli into neural impulses that move onto successively more complex brain regions.

Sensation and perception almost always happen together. Researchers, however, have studied each process separately to determine how the two work together. Perception can occur through **bottom-up processing**, which begins with the physical stimuli from the environment, and proceeds through transduction of those stimuli into neural impulses. The signals

top-down processing perception processes led by cognitive processes, such as memory or expectations.

perceptual set readiness to interpret a certain stimulus in a certain way.

are passed along to successively more complex brain regions, and ultimately result in the recognition of a visual stimulus. For example, when you look at the face of your best friend, your eyes convert light energy into neural impulses, which travel into the brain to visual regions. This information forms the basis for sensing the visual stimulus and ultimately its perception. Equally important to perception, however, is **top-down processing**, which involves previously acquired knowledge. When you look at your best friend's face, for example, brain regions that store information about what faces look like, particularly those that are familiar to you, can help you to perceive and recognize the specific visual stimulus.

FIGURE 5-2 Old or young? What you see when you look at this drawing depends in part on what you expect to see.

The power of top-down processing goes far beyond just using our memories to recognize our best friend's face. Our perceptual expectations, or **perceptual sets**, actually prepare us to perceive certain things in particular ways. For example, a photo showing a fuzzy UFO will look very different to you depending on whether you believe there is such a thing as UFOs. And perceptual sets do not relate only to vision. Consider, for example, whether a dish in your favourite restaurant would taste exactly the same to you if you thought it was chicken or if you thought it was rattlesnake. Many elements—our experiences, our cultures, the contexts in which we find ourselves—affect our perceptual sets.

Perceptual sets may come into play when we are faced with *ambiguous stimuli*—stimuli that could be interpreted in different ways. A well-known visual example is presented in **Figure 5-2**. Looked at one way, the drawing shows a young woman looking over her shoulder—you can see her jawline, her ear, and a bit of her nose. Looked at another way, it shows an old woman with her chin to her chest. If someone pointed out this drawing to you by saying, "Look at this picture of an old woman with a big nose," that's most likely what you would see—because that's what you would expect to see.

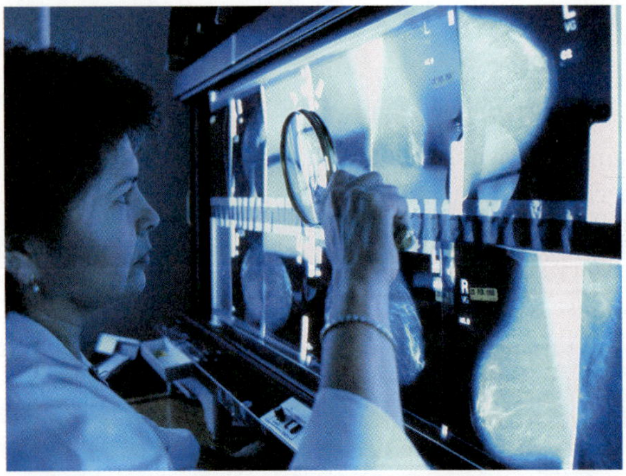

A critical difference. A radiologist carefully examines a mammogram, looking for the slightest indication of a tumour. An individual's ability to detect a difference between two visual stimuli (such as normal versus abnormal tissue) can be increased by special training, practice, and instruments, but it is still limited to some degree by sensory difference thresholds.

Typically, perception involves both bottom-up and top-down processing occurring at the same time. The combination lets us rapidly recognize familiar faces and other stimuli. Bottom-up and top-down processing are involved in sensation and perception of all sensory modalities. For example, recognizing familiar songs involves not only information carried from the ear to the brain, but also the matching of that information with previously stored information about the music. We also combine bottom-up and top-down processes to help us recognize the smell or taste of a familiar food.

Before You Go On

www.wiley.com/go/comer

What Do You Know?

1. What is sensory transduction?
2. What are absolute and difference thresholds?
3. Compare and contrast bottom-up and top-down processing.

What Do You Think?

Describe examples of sensory adaptation that you have experienced in two or more of your sensory modalities.

SCAN TO GET THE ANSWERS

The Chemical Senses: Smell and Taste

LEARNING OBJECTIVE 2

Summarize the biological changes that underlie smell and taste.

Smell and taste are usually called the *chemical senses* because they involve responses to particular chemicals. Smell, our **olfactory sense**, and taste, our **gustatory sense**, emerged early in our evolutionary history (Doty, 1986). The sense of smell, in particular, is more sensitive and of greater significance to less complex animals, who use it for social communication as well as finding food and avoiding predators (Yahr, 1977; Mech & Boitani, 2003). This is less so for humans who rely more heavily on vision. However, the contributions of both smell and taste to the safety, social communication, and overall quality of life in humans are often underestimated. The ability to detect dangerous odours, such as smoke or a gas leak, or dangerous flavours, such as tainted food or poison, can be critical to our survival. In addition, some of our greatest pleasures in life come from the ability to smell and taste—to smell a rose or, as we all know, to enjoy a good meal.

olfactory sense our sense of smell.

gustatory sense our sense of taste.

In this section, we will explore the environmental stimuli that create aromas and flavours, the organs we use to sense those stimuli, and how we transform environmental stimuli into brain signals that eventually help us perceive different smells and tastes. We will also discuss the development of these abilities, some very interesting differences among people in their ability to taste and smell things, and some problems that can occur in the olfactory and gustatory systems.

Smell and Taste: How They Work

Smells Around Us Sensation in the smell or olfactory system begins when chemicals called **odorants** enter the nose, as shown in "What Happens in the Brain When We Eat Pizza" on pages 168 and 169. Odorants are converted to neural signals at sensory receptors located in our nasal mucosa. These sensory receptors are located on the *cilia*, or hairlike structures, of **olfactory receptor neurons** (McEwen et al., 2008).

odorants airborne chemicals that are detected as odours.

olfactory receptor neurons sensory receptor cells that convert chemical signals from odorants into neural impulses that travel to the brain.

When odorants enter the nose, these chemicals bind to specific receptors located on the olfactory receptor neurons in a lock-and-key fashion. Only certain airborne chemicals bind to specific receptors (Buck, 1996). When enough odorant molecules have bound to receptors, the combination sets off an action potential in the olfactory receptor neuron. As we described in Chapter 4, the action potential or *firing* of a neuron sends a message to other neurons. The firing of olfactory receptor neurons is transmitted to the brain, as we will see next.

Continuous binding of certain odorants, such as those contained in the main ingredients of a restaurant dinner, will result in fatigue of the olfactory receptor neurons to which they bind. In other words, the cell will stop responding to the odorant unless it's given a chance to recover so it can fire again (Dalton, 2000). If you were to step outside the restaurant to make a phone call, for example, you would probably notice the food smells again when you stepped back into the restaurant, because your olfactory receptor neurons would have gotten a break from constant exposure to the food odorants. When a stimulus is continuously present, however, as when you remain sitting in the restaurant, the only way the olfactory receptor neurons will respond to the odorant would be if the stimulus is increased in magnitude. As we saw, this is the case when the food is brought directly to your table. Many more odorant molecules are now available to your nose and its olfactory receptor neurons.

Types of Tastes In humans, the sense of smell is very closely tied to the sense of taste. In fact, what we normally call *taste* is really *flavour*, which is a combination of smell and taste. Taste, the gustatory sense, is itself independent of smell. The top of the tongue, the major organ of taste, is covered with bumps, called **papillae**. As shown in **Figure 5-3**, papillae contain clumps of **taste buds**, each of which contains 60 to 100 sensory receptor cells for taste.

papillae bumps on the tongue that contain clumps of taste buds.

taste buds clusters of sensory receptor cells that convert chemical signals from food into neural impulses that travel to the brain.

PSYCHOLOGY AROUND US Starve a Cold

Have you ever noticed how food doesn't taste good when you have a bad cold? Often you can't taste much of anything at all for a few days. This effect is due, in large part, to mucous blocking the olfactory receptors located on the cilia in your nose. Air can't get to these receptors, and so the odorants that travel in the air can't get there either. A cold doesn't affect your taste buds, so the actual taste of the food remains the same. It's the *flavour* that suffers—and that's because flavour results from taste and smell working together.

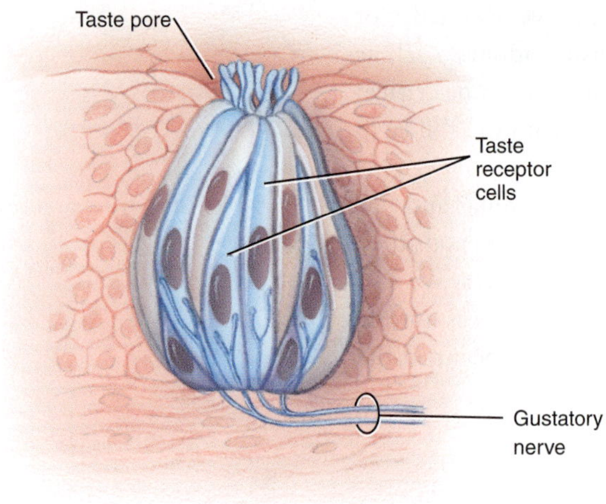

FIGURE 5-3 A taste bud. The receptor cells for taste are clustered within the taste buds found in the bumps, or papillae, covering your tongue.

Taste receptor cells have cilia that contain the actual receptors. These cilia extend through the pores of the taste receptor and are exposed to the contents of your mouth.

There are five major kinds of taste receptors. Each responds to a specific taste in our food: sweet, sour, bitter, and salty (Sugita, 2006). A fifth type of taste receptor has also been discovered—*umami.* Umami is the taste of monosodium glutamate (MSG). It is a chemical additive used in cooking some Asian food and Western fast food. Each of these five types of taste receptors uses a slightly different mechanism for transduction of the chemicals in food to neural impulses in the gustatory system. For example, salt activates its taste receptors by sending sodium ions into the channels on the taste receptor cell. Since sodium ions are positively charged, the electrical charge of the taste receptor then becomes more positive. Taste buds are not evenly distributed across the tongue, but most tastes can be recognized to a greater or lesser degree on most parts of the top of the tongue.

Eating: It's More Than Smell and Taste The overall sensations we experience when we eat food are not just the result of combined interactions between olfactory and gustatory senses. Much of the information we get about food is delivered to us through one of the touch or *tactile* senses. The consistency of a particular food is not relayed to the brain via the taste receptors, but rather by inputs from touch receptors located on the tongue. The role of food consistency in determining preference is much greater than you might imagine. Many adult humans reject certain foods, such as raw oysters or cooked okra, specifically because those foods have a "slimy" texture.

In addition, the sensation we experience when we eat a spicy meal is related to a component of the tactile system that communicates information about pain. A chemical called *capsaicin,* from chili peppers, activates pain receptors located in the tongue (Numazaki & Tominaga, 2004). These pain impulses, in conjunction with tactile information about the food texture, as well as the flavours (smell and taste) associated with the food, can combine to produce a sensation that is pleasurable to many people.

Suppose a food is hot because it just came out of the oven. We have all had the experience of burning our mouths, which can damage the taste receptors on the tongue. As the box on the opposite page points out, the sensory receptors of taste are unusual because they regenerate when this happens.

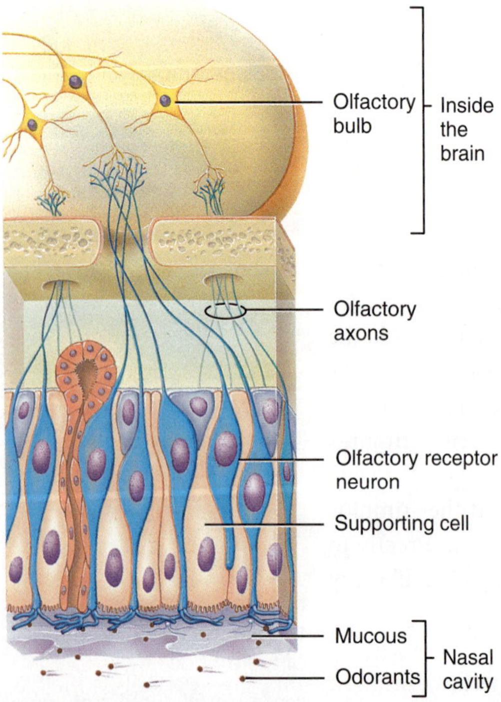

The smell route. Olfactory receptor neurons (shown here in blue) transduce information from odorant molecules that enter the nose. This information is carried by the olfactory nerve into the brain where it synapses in the olfactory bulb.

Smell and Taste — WHAT HAPPENS IN THE BRAIN?

Signals from our olfactory receptor neurons travel to the brain via the olfactory nerve. As the figure on the left shows, information carried along the olfactory nerves travels first to a structure called the **olfactory bulb**, located at the base of the front of the brain, beneath the frontal lobes. Olfactory information is then sent to regions of the cerebral cortex that are important for recognizing and discriminating among odours, including the piriform cortex (Wilson, 2001).

olfactory bulb the first region where olfactory information reaches the brain on its way from the nose.

The ability of our cortex to recognize patterns of inputs from a variety of olfactory receptors is most likely responsible for our detection of certain odours. Studies have shown that the piriform cortex is *plastic* or changeable in adulthood (Li et al., 2008). That is, the parts of piriform cortex that normally recognize specific odorants can change with experience, actually remapping this brain region. The chemical structures of some pairs of molecules are so similar that untrained humans can't discriminate between them (the two odours are usually below the just noticeable difference). However, if exposure to one of the chemicals is paired with a painful shock to the leg, humans can be taught to discriminate between the odours (Li et al., 2008). This is a remarkable example of top-down processing. Learning about associations between odours and other experiences (such as a shock) can influence our ability to perceive sensory information in the future. In parallel with the new ability to discriminate the odours of closely related molecules, the areas of the piriform cortex that are activated by each of the previously indistinguishable molecules become more distinct from each other.

The olfactory bulb also sends information to the amygdala, an area important for emotions and fear, as well as indirectly to the hippocampus, an area important for learning and memory. Many people report that certain smells are evocative of past events (Lehrer, 2007). The smell of baking might remind you of visiting your uncle the baker as a young child, the smell of school paste and old lunches might remind you of your elementary school, and so on. The ability of smells to call up memories is probably related in part to olfactory connections to the hippocampus and amygdala.

Taste receptor cells do not have axons, but instead connect with sensory neurons in the tongue to send information to our brains. Taste information is sent to the *thalamus*, and eventually, the cerebral cortex. We will see throughout this chapter that the thalamus is a relay station for incoming sensory information of many kinds; all of our sensory systems except olfaction have a main pathway through the thalamus.

Taste information is integrated with reward circuits in the brain (Norgren et al., 2006), and rewarding tastes seem to be processed separately from aversive tastes. Tastes that are considered to be rewarding, such as salty and sweet, activate overlapping areas in the taste cortex.

Regeneration in the Taste and Smell Systems

If you, like most people, have had the experience of burning your tongue on too-hot food, you've probably noticed that by the next day or so, your ability to taste has returned and your tongue is no longer painful. This is due to the remarkable regenerative characteristics of the taste buds. Taste receptor cells normally turn over—they die and are replaced—in a matter of days. The process happens even faster when they are damaged. Under normal circumstances, our olfactory receptor neurons are also constantly turning over (Farbman, 1997).

The capacity to regenerate on such a large scale and so rapidly is probably necessary because the receptor neurons for both taste and smell are exposed to the external environment. Unlike the sensory receptors of the eye, which are protected by the eyeball, or those of the ear, which are protected by the eardrum, the surface of the tongue and the mucosa of the nose are directly exposed to any number of noxious chemical molecules that may enter our mouths or noses. Because destruction of receptors is likely under such circumstances, we need to constantly regenerate receptor cells just to continue normal functioning of our smell and taste systems.

Neurobiologists study the regenerative capabilities of the taste buds and olfactory receptor neurons in hopes of understanding exactly *how* these cells are constantly rejuvenating. Scientists and medical professionals hope that understanding these mechanisms may some day enable replacement of other types of cells, ones that currently don't seem capable of repair when they are damaged.

Tying It Together: **Your Brain and Behaviour**

Eating Pizza

Is this the best pizza you have ever had or does it fall short? When you dig into a slice of pizza, several neural circuits are activated to give you the overall experience. The appearance of your food can play an important role in its enjoyment. Photoreceptors in the eye transmit this information to the brain via the optic nerve, which passes through the brainstem, followed by the thalamus, and finally the visual cortex. Taste receptor cells, as well as sensory cells that respond to touch and temperature, are activated on your tongue. These nerves carry impulses into the brain where they pass through the brainstem, thalamus, and sensory cortex (gustatory cortex and somatosensory cortex). Taste is combined with smell information to produce flavour. Olfactory receptor neurons transduce pizza odorants and send this information on to the olfactory bulb and then to the olfactory cortex (smell is the only sensory modality that bypasses the thalamus on its way to the cortex).

Information about taste, smell, texture, temperature, and appearance is integrated in various association regions of the neocortex. These circuits, together with those that store memories related to your previous pizza experiences, work together to produce your perception of this particular slice.

Questions

1 **Explain how multiple senses (vision, smell, taste, touch) are involved in our experience of eating.**

2 **Explain how the taste of food may be enhanced if we close our eyes.**

3 **Which areas of the brain are responsible for integrating information about various components of eating (e.g., taste, smell, texture)?**

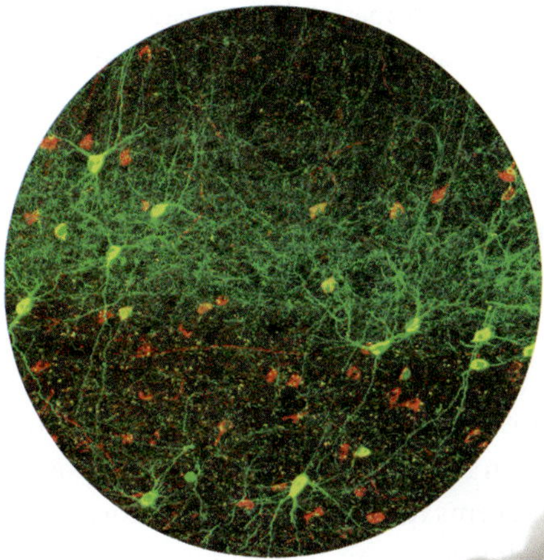

SENSING MORE THAN TASTE

A large part of somatosensory cortex (shown here with neurons genetically engineered to produce fluorescent dyes) is devoted to processing information about texture, temperature, and pain from the tongue. Somatosensory information from the tongue is critical for the enjoyment of food; many people prefer their crust crispy while others like it soft.

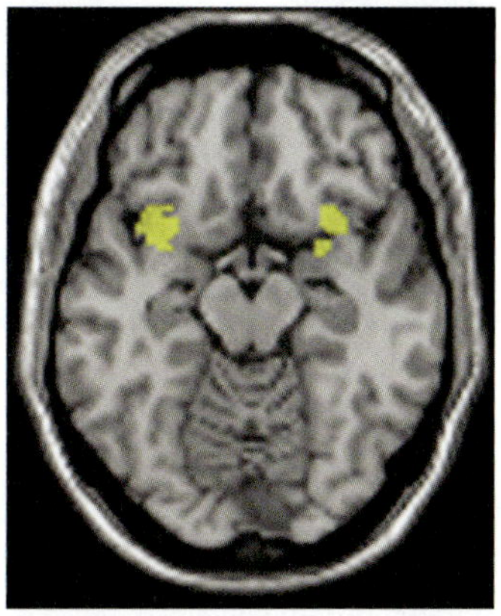

MAXIMIZING THE EXPERIENCE

When you eat something delicious and close your eyes, you may be maximizing the experience by turning up the activity in certain parts of cortex. When your eyes are open, activity in parts of cortex serving nonvisual senses is decreased. Closing your eyes increases activity in these areas, including in taste and smell cortex. This fMRI image shows such increased activation in the olfactory cortex (yellow).

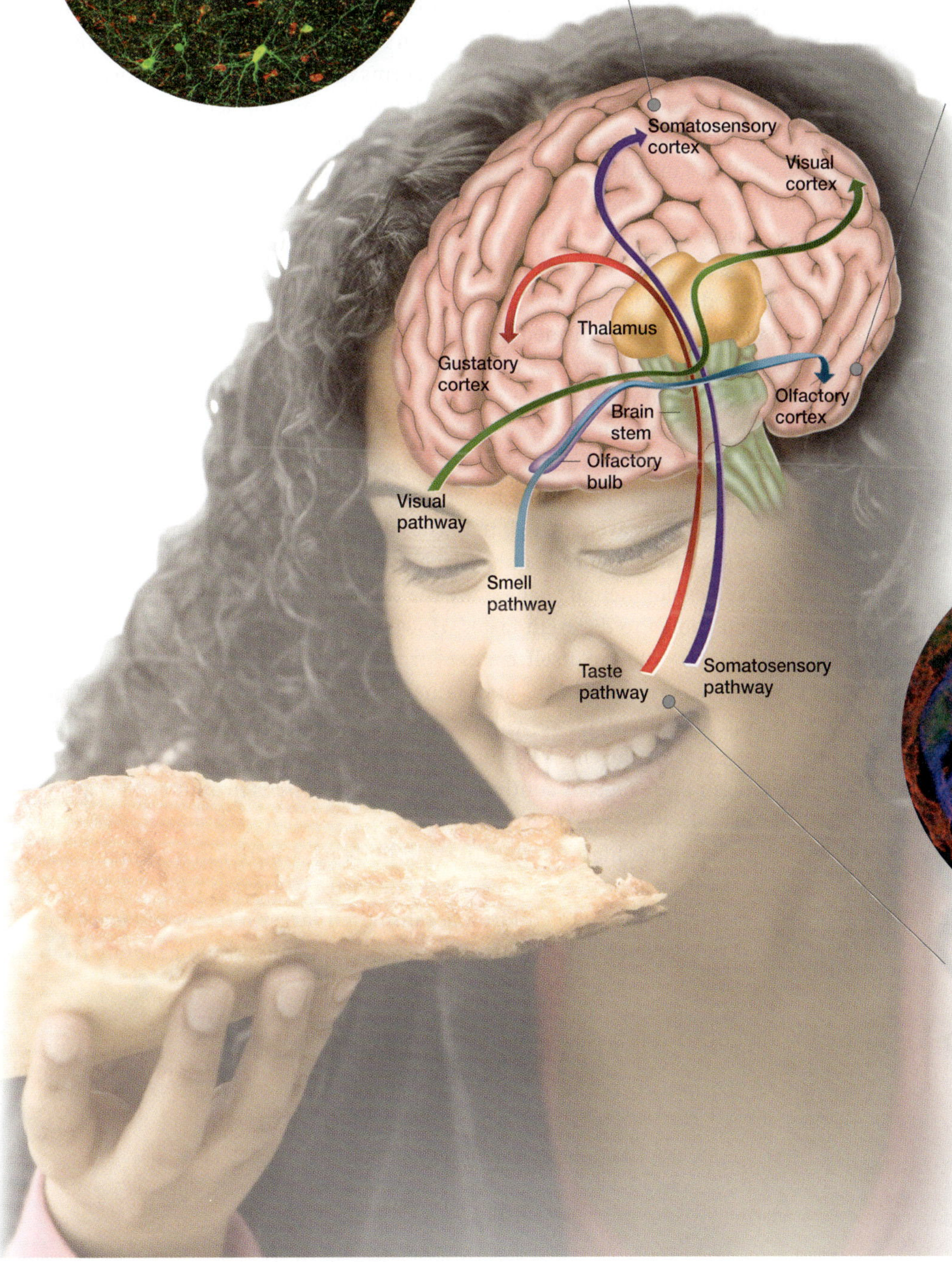

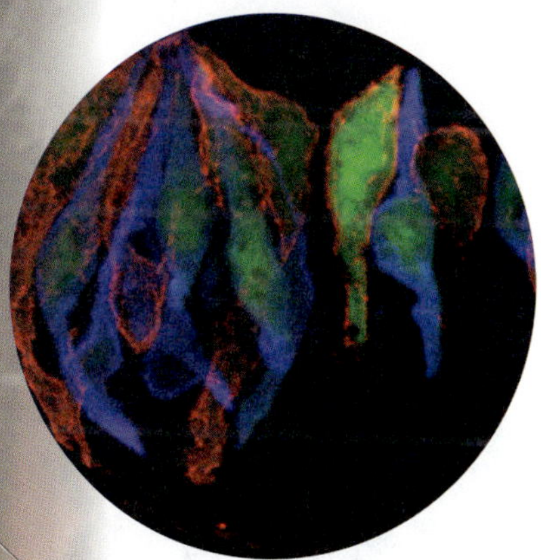

BURNING YOUR TONGUE

Taste buds contain taste receptor cells (shown here marked with fluorescent dyes) that continually regenerate. The process is hastened when tissue is damaged, such as when you burn your tongue.

Unspeakable pleasure. The ecstasy demonstrated on this woman's face as she bites into a chocolate covered strawberry serves as a vivid reminder that taste information is integrated with the reward circuits in the brain.

By contrast, tastes generally considered to be less pleasurable, such as bitter and sour, activate regions that overlap less with rewarding tastes and more with one another in the taste cortex (Accolla et al., 2007). Taste and smell information is processed through separate pathways, but there is convergence in the associated parts of neocortex, namely in the prefrontal cortex.

In addition to integrating information about taste in general, part of the cortex that receives taste information, called the *insula*, is associated with the emotion of disgust. Neuroimaging studies have shown that this brain region becomes activated not only when we smell or taste something revolting, but also when we view repulsive visual images (Calder et al., 2007; Schienle et al., 2008).

Smell and Taste — HOW WE DEVELOP

The sense of smell is relatively well developed at birth. Research suggests that, within hours of birth, newborn babies are capable of telling their own mother from another woman using only the sense of smell. In fact, olfactory functioning seems to be in place even before birth. Newborn infants show a learned preference to the odours of their mother's amniotic fluid. After birth, infants quickly learn to recognize the smell of their own mother's milk. Exposure to odours of their mother's milk has a calming effect on infants when they are experiencing a brief, minor painful stimulus, such as a needle stick in the heel (Nishitani et al., 2009). This effect doesn't appear to be as specific to the milk as it is to the mother—exposure to other odours that the baby has associated with the mother, such as vanillin, has the same calming effect as mother's milk odour (Goubet et al., 2007).

The ability to taste is also well formed in humans at birth. Newborn humans show an innate preference for sugar and aversion to bitter or sour tastes. Babies move their faces toward a sweet substance and make sucking movements with their mouths, but turn away and grimace when presented with a sour or bitter substance (Rosenstein & Oster, 1988).

Researchers have shown that by about 7 years of age, children develop a preference for sour tastes (Liem & Mennella, 2003). This may explain the popularity of candies such as Sour Patch Kids. However, the aversion to bitter tastes typically lasts until young adulthood when bitter foods, such as blue cheese and dark chocolate, start to emerge as favourites.

Many of these developmental changes are the result of learning. As children grow, they become accustomed to different tastes. However, there is some evidence to suggest that the gustatory system itself changes from infancy to adulthood. We form taste buds before we are even born, and as newborns, have higher concentrations of them on our tongues than we will as adults. Children also have taste buds on their palates, inside the cheeks, and at the back of their mouths (Nilsson, 1979). Although these regions continue to contain taste buds in adults, their numbers decline with time.

The high number of taste buds in children may explain why they are often picky eaters. The tastes of certain foods may seem too strong to children because their larger number of taste buds produce more neural impulses than adults would generate from

PSYCHOLOGY AROUND US Eat Your Vegetables!

Perhaps the phrase "Eat your vegetables" is familiar to you from your childhood. Many children dislike the tastes of fruits and vegetables that are bitter, such as Brussels sprouts, grapefruit, cabbage, kale, mustard greens, and spinach. It turns out, though, that the bitter taste in these foods comes from chemical substances that have health benefits. Although our parents' urging may have had little effect on us as children, most of us learn to make healthy choices about what we eat as we grow older. But many of us also eat more of these nutritious foods when we are older because we begin to enjoy bitter tastes.

the same food. Some researchers suggest that this developmental phenomenon might actually be adaptive in helping us survive. If young children enjoyed ingesting substances with strong or bitter tastes, they might be at higher risk of poisoning.

Children often refuse or eat very little of unfamiliar foods (Koivisto Hursti, 1999). Although neuroimaging studies on developing humans have yet to be done with regard to taste, it's tempting to speculate that as individuals grow and their tastes broaden, areas in the taste cortex represented by certain tastes are modified. It's likely that increased exposure to certain foods, especially when paired with positive social interactions and encouragement from parents, result in a remapping of previously aversive taste information on the gustatory cortex.

Smell and Taste HOW WE DIFFER

Have you ever felt a bit faint when you were closed in an elevator with someone wearing perfume, while others in the elevator seemed not to notice? Humans vary greatly in their ability to detect certain odours. Some people seem relatively insensitive to even very strong smells, while others seem very sensitive. Some of these individual differences are related to learning. Exposure to particular odours during childhood lessens the reaction to those odours in adulthood.

In addition to these learned differences, research suggests that females are generally more sensitive to smell than males are, and that this sensitivity varies with the stage of the menstrual cycle (Pause et al., 1996). Around the time of ovulation, women are more sensitive to odours than during other stages of the cycle. Women's ability to detect different odours also diminishes after menopause (Hughes et al., 2002). The exact biological mechanisms that underlie these differences are not known, but it is possible that reproductive hormones, such as estrogen, alter the excitability, or the likelihood, of firing of olfactory neurons.

There is also considerable individual variability in the ability to taste. Researchers group people into three different categories with respect to taste sensitivity: non-tasters (25 percent of people), medium tasters (50 percent), and supertasters (25 percent). These groups are distinguished based on their ability to detect and respond negatively to a specific bitter substance (Bartoshuk et al., 1996). Supertasters are repulsed by the bitter chemical. Non-tasters do not even notice the bitter taste, although they are capable of detecting other tastes. Medium tasters notice it, but do not find the taste particularly offensive. These functional differences are the result of variations in the concentration of taste buds on the tongue.

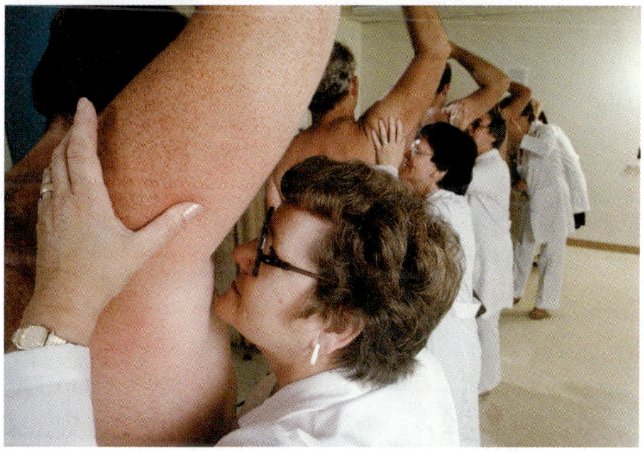

A special gift? These scent testers (or "noses") determine whether a new deodorant produces a pleasant result. People who are highly sensitive to odours often find employment that puts their special ability to use.

Women make up a higher proportion of supertasters than do men (Bartoshuk et al., 1994). This heightened sensitivity of both chemical sensory systems, smell and taste, is likely to have had adaptive significance for women. Since the chemicals in women's diets are passed along to their children when women are pregnant or nursing, the ability to detect and avoid potentially harmful odours and tastes may have contributed to survival of the species by protecting infants from toxic substances.

Finally, the number of taste buds starts to decline at about 50 years of age, and the sense of smell may decline starting at 60. A consequence of these two declines may be a gradual loss of interest in food, which can be counteracted by adding taste to food by way of spices and food choices (Mojet, Christ-Hazelhof, & Heidema, 2001).

Smell and Taste Disorders WHEN THINGS GO WRONG

True taste disorders are rare. In fact, most people who seek medical assistance complaining that they cannot taste are actually suffering from problems with their olfactory, as opposed to gustatory, systems. People with a condition called anosmia have lost the ability to smell.

anosmia inability to smell.

They can often still taste sweet, salty, sour, bitter, and umami, but they can no longer detect other flavours, since those require the additional information provided by food odorants.

ageusia inability to taste.

In some rare cases—typically as a result of head trauma or problems during oral surgery—humans lose the ability to taste itself, a condition called **ageusia**. They can often still taste sweet, salty, sour, bitter, and umami, but they can no longer detect other flavours that require the information from the odorants of food.

Head trauma is also a leading cause of anosmia (Haxel et al., 2008). Sometimes the nerves that carry olfactory information from the olfactory receptor neurons to the olfactory bulb can be sheared, cutting off the pathway by which information about smell reaches the brain. People with Alzheimer's disease also suffer from a diminished sense of smell that is probably due to a combined degeneration of olfactory receptor neurons and neurons located in olfactory brain regions (Djordjevic et al., 2008).

Although humans can certainly survive without the ability to smell, their quality of life is considerably diminished. Many people with anosmia report feelings of depression. In addition, there are safety and social issues to consider. Since we use our sense of smell to detect dangers, such as smoke or spoiled food, anosmia increases the risk of injury. Moreover, socially acceptable cultural practices of hygiene may become difficult to follow with anosmia, since humans often use olfactory cues to make decisions about bathing, washing clothes, and brushing teeth. People with anosmia can learn to cope effectively with their condition by using other sensory systems to detect danger. They might, for example, use sound cues, such as a blaring smoke detector to notice smoke, or visual cues, such as appearance and freshness dates, to detect spoiled food.

Migraines and the senses. Migraine sufferers often experience sensory distortions—for example, a strange light or unpleasant smell—just before or during their headaches. In some cases, specific odours actually trigger migraines.

Migraines, Epilepsy, and the Sensory Systems The chemical senses are also involved in the symptoms of some people with migraine headaches or epilepsy. For instance, a specific odour can initiate the onset of a migraine (Kelman, 2007). Likewise, patients with a certain form of epilepsy, called *reflex epilepsy*, will experience a seizure only after exposure to a specific odour. Although the reasons for this remain unknown, these individuals find it necessary to avoid specific intense odorants. In other patients suffering from migraines or epilepsy, stimuli from the other sensory systems, such as touch, sound, and sight, can initiate the headaches or seizures.

Some people experience hallucinations called *auras* either before or during migraine headaches or epileptic seizures. Auras can involve any of the sensory systems. People with these conditions might have touch, sound, or sight hallucinations, and some experience strong, often unpleasant, smells or tastes. The involvement of different senses indicates which brain circuits are compromised in these conditions. For example, if a person's seizure is preceded by strong olfactory hallucinations, it's likely that the olfactory pathways are initiating the seizure, or at least participating in its generation.

Before You Go On

www.wiley.com/go/comer

What Do You Know?

4. What five tastes have specific receptors?
5. Which parts of the brain are involved in sensing and perceiving odours?
6. What are supertasters?
7. How are smell and taste involved with migraines and epileptic seizures?

SCAN TO GET THE ANSWERS

What Do You Think?

This section of the chapter listed some ways for people with anosmia to compensate for their lack of smell, such as using smoke detectors. What other ways can you suggest that people with anosmia might use to replace the safety and pleasures that a sense of smell provides?

The Tactile or Cutaneous Senses: Touch, Pressure, Pain, Vibration

LEARNING OBJECTIVE 3

Describe how the different senses of touch work and what can happen when things go wrong.

Tactile, as we mentioned earlier, means "touch." As with the chemical senses, there are rewarding and aversive types of tactile stimuli. The pleasure associated with a relaxing back massage or stroking a baby's cheek stands in stark contrast to the discomfort of getting a scrape or burn. The tactile or somatosensory system is actually a complex sense. As shown in **Figure 5-4**, our skin contains a variety of sensory receptors to register different types of physical stimuli (Munger & Ide, 1988).

- **Free nerve endings** are located mostly near the surface of the skin and function to detect touch, pressure, pain, and temperature.
- **Meissner's corpuscles** transduce information about sensitive touch and are found in the hairless regions of the body, such as the fingertips, lips, and palms.
- **Merkel's discs** transduce information about light to moderate pressure on the skin.
- **Ruffini's end-organs** are located deep in the skin. They register heavy pressure and movement of the joints.
- **Pacinian corpuscles** are also buried deep in the skin and respond to vibrations and heavy pressure.

Pressure on the skin activates free nerve endings that give us the sense of being touched. As you may have noticed, your skin is not equally sensitive to tactile stimuli over your whole body. Certain parts of your body, for example, the skin on your elbow, are much less

free nerve endings sensory receptors that convert physical stimuli into touch, pressure, or pain impulses.

Meissner's corpuscles sensory receptors that convert physical stimuli about sensory touch on the fingertips, lips, and palms.

Merkel's discs sensory receptors that convert information about light to moderate pressure on the skin.

Ruffini's end-organs sensory receptors that respond to heavy pressure and joint movement.

Pacinian corpuscles sensory receptors that respond to vibrations and heavy pressure.

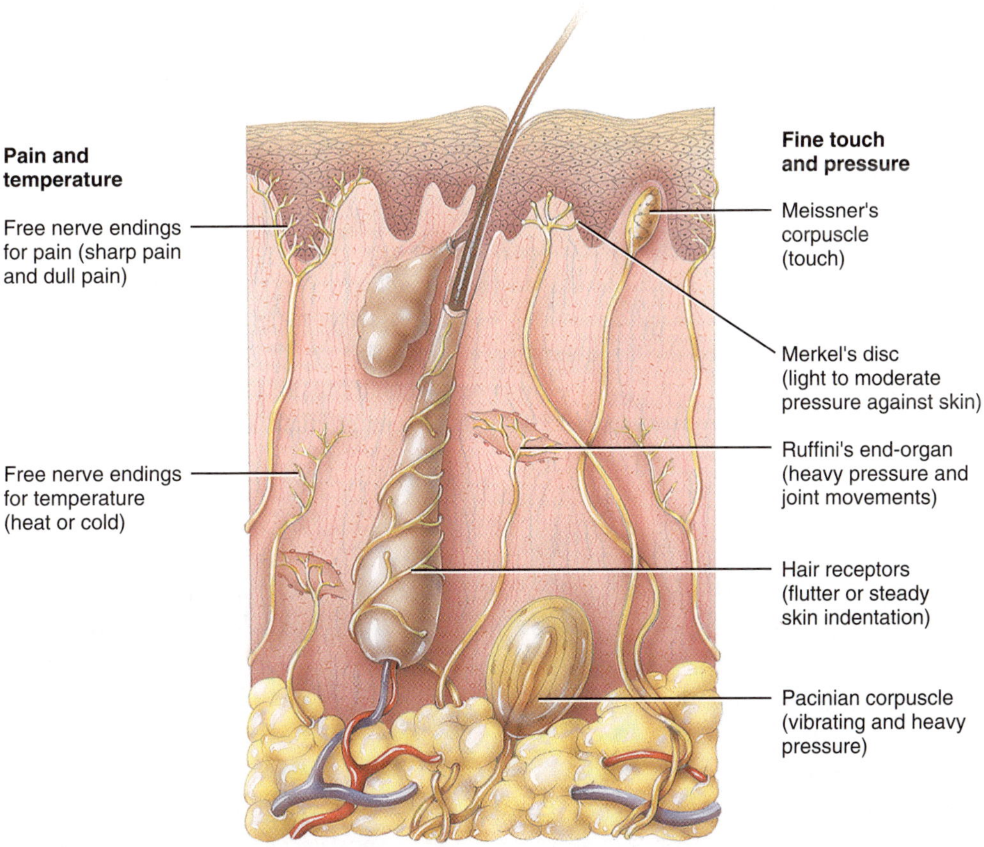

FIGURE 5-4 Sensory receptors in the skin. The tactile senses rely on a variety of receptors located in different parts of the skin.

sensitive to touch than other areas, such as your face and hands. These differences likely arise as a result of different densities of free nerve endings. Areas that are more sensitive have more free nerve endings.

We can also experience sensory adaptation, resulting in reduced tactile sensation from depression of the skin that continues for a period of time. This happens to you every day when you put on your clothing; shortly after getting dressed, you are no longer aware of the tactile stimulus your clothing provides (unless, of course, it is too tight).

Tactile Senses — WHAT HAPPENS IN THE BRAIN?

Our brains use a variety of related processes to help us perceive general information about a range of non-painful touch sensations, including pressure, temperature, and general touch. Pain perception is also an important function.

The Touching Brain When we touch something, or something touches us, our free nerve endings send tactile information into the spinal cord. The signals travel up the spinal cord to the brain, as shown in **Figure 5-5**. In the brain, touch information is first received in the thalamus, and then routed from there to the somatosensory cortex (located in the parietal lobe). Information about pressure and vibration is generally transmitted to the brain in a similar way, after being converted to neural impulses by the specialized receptors described above.

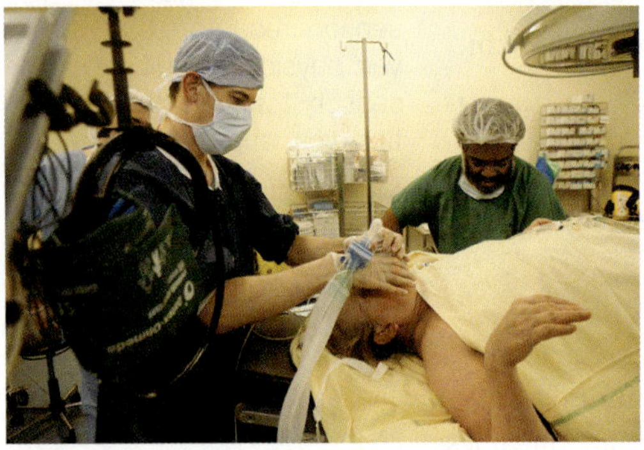

Using the brain to counteract pain. Anesthesia is a procedure that helps block pain sensations, enabling patients to undergo surgery. Drug-induced anesthetic approaches that act through the brain are general anesthesia (seen here) and sedation.

Our brain processes tactile information *contralaterally*, or on the opposite side of the brain from the side of the body where the touch occurred. So, if you touch something with your left hand, the information is eventually processed by the somatosensory cortex on the right side of your brain.

As we discussed in Chapter 4, the somatosensory cortex does not have an equal representation of all parts of the body (Kakigi et al., 2000). For example, tactile inputs from the hands take up proportionately more space in the somatosensory cortex than those from the back. This seems reasonable, given the fact that our hands are specialized for object manipulation, and we need to process information from them in great detail. As described in the Psychology Around Us box below, other animals have somatosensory systems that are adapted to provide high-resolution tactile information from the parts of their bodies that are especially important to their daily lives. Information about pressure and vibration is generally transmitted to the brain in a similar way after being converted to neural impulses by the specialized receptors described above.

Beyond these sorts of sensory reactions, we can extend our senses mechanically. The Canadian Space Agency, which developed the Canadarm used to manipulate cargo on the space shuttle, has been working with NASA on the development of virtual environment generating headgear called the Canadian Space Vision System. This technology will allow operators to "see" what the next generation of remote manipulator arms can see. Using this equipment will allow astronauts to literally "walk" the manipulators hand over hand along

PSYCHOLOGY AROUND US The Nose Knows

Just as humans have a very high concentration of tactile receptors on our hands, other mammals, particularly those without hands, have concentrated tactile receptors on different parts of their bodies. They rely on these specific body parts for fine touch information, much in the same way we rely on our hands. The star-nosed mole, for example, is named for its specialized nose, shaped like a star. This creature lives mostly underground and is almost completely blind. It navigates throughout its dark environment by using its star-shaped nose in a similar way as blind people use their hands, to accomplish such tasks as finding food and exploring its environment. Accordingly, the nose representation in the star-nosed mole's somatosensory cortex is proportionately larger than that devoted to other body parts.

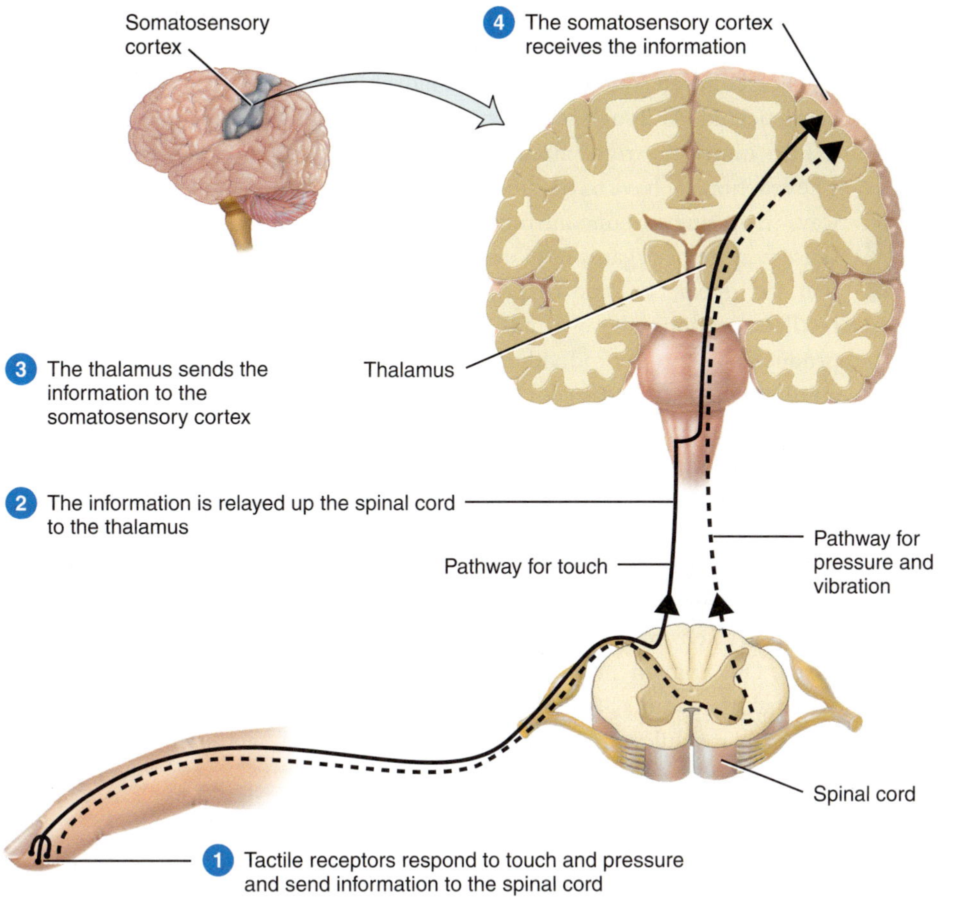

FIGURE 5-5 Somatosensory pathways in the central nervous system.

the outside of the space ship, and then perform manipulation tasks that the operator can see and control despite being safely back inside the ship (Paquet, 2000).

Pain and the Brain Like general touch information, painful sensations are also transmitted to the brain via free nerve endings. Pain information travels to the brain via two different types of pain fibres. One system, called the *fast pathway*, uses myelinated axons that, as we discussed in Chapter 4, carry signals faster than unmyelinated axons. Messages about sharp, localized pain travel along the fast pathway directly up the spinal cord to the thalamus and to areas of the somatosensory cortex. Pain information received via the fast pathway helps us to respond quickly with a withdrawal reflex, such as pulling a hand away after touching a hot stove. The slower pain pathway uses more unmyelinated axons—these inputs communicate with brain regions involved in processing emotions. Pain we perceive via the slow pathway is more often burning pain than sharp pain.

Like all other sensory systems we have discussed so far, the pain system shows evidence of sensory adaptation. A common example of this can be experienced when eating a spicy meal. Recall that the sensation of eating chili peppers is mostly due to the activation of pain fibres located on the tongue. Oftentimes, when a very spicy food is first ingested, the pain response seems great. However, as the meal progresses, the response diminishes and we are less likely to experience discomfort. This is due to adaptation of the pain fibres and a subsequent decrease in their activity. However, when pain is associated with actual tissue damage or an abnormality in the pain system, as discussed below, pain can be persistent and debilitating.

Tactile Senses HOW WE DEVELOP

Like smell and taste, the tactile senses are generally in place at birth. In fact, studies have shown that fetuses can respond to the touch of a hair at a relatively early stage in prenatal development (Lagercrantz & Changeux, 2009). However, the ability to recognize and

respond to different somatosensory stimuli occurs only after birth and involves further brain development as well as learning.

For children, one of the most enjoyable types of somatosensory input is being tickled. Although rough or prolonged tickling can become abusive, when tickled under the right circumstances, children often explode with laughter. The reaction we have to tickling is a result of activation of somatosensory pathways in an uneven, uncontrollable, and unexpected manner. Not only are our sensory systems organized to detect change, but they are most-tuned to stimuli that are unexpected and surprising. When you move your body and produce tactile sensations, these stimuli are less noticeable to you than are sensations produced by another individual. The sensations of your own legs touching one another when you cross your legs, for example, is generally less noticeable than a similar touch on your leg would be if someone sitting next to you brushed their leg against yours.

Likewise, your reaction to your cat jumping onto your lap is likely to be much greater if you have your eyes closed when it happens. This differential response to surprising tactile stimuli appears to be a defense mechanism that has adaptive significance. It is probably also the reason why being tickled by someone else is more effective at producing an emotional reaction than trying to tickle yourself. Our enjoyment of being tickled generally diminishes as we age. This is likely due to the fact that adults are better at anticipating stimuli, and hence are more difficult to surprise, than are children. It may also reflect a change in tactile thresholds (becoming less sensitive to touch) with age.

Tactile Senses HOW WE DIFFER

Humans differ greatly in their ability to detect physical stimuli on the skin. In addition, they differ in the degree to which they find certain tactile stimulation pleasurable or aversive. For example, some people enjoy an intense back massage while others do not. Of all the somatosensory experiences, the one that has received the most research attention is that of pain. Pain management for surgical procedures and other medical conditions is a critical part of patient care. There are dramatic differences in both the threshold to detect pain and the degree to which pain causes emotional suffering. Some of these differences can be attributed to ethnicity. For example, studies have shown that Japanese people have a lower pain threshold than Caucasians. These differences extend to reports of the detection of non-painful stimuli as well (Komiyama et al., 2009).

Although learning plays some role, groups of people also differ in the actual sensation and perception of pain as a result of physical differences in their sensory systems. Studies have shown, for example, that women have a lower threshold for detecting pain than do men. They report greater pain intensity than men in response to the same stimulus (Garcia et al., 2007). One interpretation of this sex difference is that women are just less able to cope psychologically with painful stimuli since they haven't been "toughened up." In fact, research suggests that women may have about twice as many pain receptors in their facial skin than men. This suggests a physical cause for at least some of the differences in pain sensitivity. It is not yet known whether this difference exists throughout the body, or whether it is specific to the face.

Neuroimaging studies show that people's brains react differently depending on their sensitivity to pain (Dubé et al., 2009). People exposed to a high temperature stimulus in one study exhibited varied responses, for example. Those who reported feeling pain showed changes in activity in their thalamus, somatosensory cortex, and cingulate cortex areas. Those who did not report feeling pain showed similar activity in the thalamus, but no changes in the cortical regions. Although there may be differences in the two groups' sensory receptors in their skin, these findings suggest that differences in activation of brain circuitry may also underlie varied responses to painful stimuli.

One theory, the **gate control theory of pain**, attempts to explain the relationship of brain activity to pain by suggesting that some patterns of neural activity can actually create a "gate" that prevents messages from reaching parts of the brain where they are perceived as pain (Melzack, 1999).

Early versions of this theory hypothesized that pain signals were blocked in the spinal cord, but later research has focused on neurochemicals or patterns of activity in the brain itself. Individual differences in gating mechanisms may result in the wide range of pain sensitivity across people (Romanelli & Esposito, 2004).

gate control theory of pain theory that certain patterns of neural activity can close a "gate" to keep pain information from travelling to parts of the brain where it is perceived.

Tactile Senses WHEN THINGS GO WRONG

As we have seen, sensing and perceiving pain are normal, and important, functions of our tactile senses. Some people, however, experience either too much pain or too little. Sometimes, people even feel pain and other sensations in limbs or other body parts that have actually been removed.

High pain threshold. This performer lifts concrete blocks and other heavy objects with a chain attached to his pierced tongue—an act that is unbearable for most people to even watch. Although hours of practice and conditioning and certain tricks of the trade each play a role in this behaviour, a high pain threshold is certainly a prerequisite.

Chronic Pain The most common abnormality associated with the somatosensory system is that of chronic pain, pain that lasts longer than three months. In the United States, a relatively large percentage of the population, about one in six people, suffers from chronic pain. There are multiple causes of chronic pain, although in some cases the cause cannot be identified. In all cases, however, pain management is a critical issue, since prolonged pain sensations can interfere with daily functioning, and may lead to depression or even suicide.

Researchers have identified two groups of chemicals naturally produced by our nervous systems that have pain-relieving properties: **endorphins** and **enkephalins**. Endorphins and enkephalins belong to a class of molecules called *opiates*. As we will see in Chapter 6, this class of chemicals also includes pain-killing drugs, such as morphine, heroin, and OxyContin. When opiates are naturally present in the nervous system, they are referred to as *endogenous opiates*. These molecules are released by neurons after intense physical exercise, stress, and sexual experience. They are thought to be responsible for the so-called *runner's high* as well as for the ability of some people to perform heroic physical actions under extreme duress (Boecker et al., 2008).

Medical practitioners use opiate drugs that mimic or stimulate the endogenous opiate system for pain relief. However, this approach has been problematic because people easily become addicted to opiate drugs. Opiate drugs are not only addictive when they are abused illegally, such as heroin, but when they are prescribed medically, as happens with morphine, and more recently, OxyContin. A study by Edward Adlaf and Angela Paglia-Boak at the University of Toronto (2007) shows that OxyContin is among the most abused drugs by Ontario high school and university students. Repeated use of these drugs to treat chronic pain can produce a physiological dependence that is very difficult to overcome. In addition, these drugs become less effective with continual use, so higher and higher doses are needed to achieve pain relief. Opiates suppress breathing, however, so they can be very dangerous at high doses. Eventually, people with chronic pain can reach a point where the dose of medicine needed to reduce their pain would be enough to stop their breathing and kill them, but lower doses do not provide them with pain relief. Scientists continue to explore new avenues for pain relief that do not produce addictions or unwanted side effects.

endorphins naturally-occurring pain-killing chemicals in the brain.

enkephalins naturally-occurring pain-killing chemicals in the brain.

In extreme debilitating cases of chronic pain, physicians have turned to neurosurgery. Destroying the pathways that carry information about pain stimuli to the brain can be effective for some people. An extreme form of neurosurgery to relieve intractable chronic pain is a *cingulotomy*, destruction of the cingulate cortex (Cetas et al., 2008). With all this understandable focus on pain and pain management, it is easy to assume that too much pain is the only issue to consider. However, it is worth considering the important role that pain plays in helping us to notice and respond to physiological issues in a timely manner.

PRACTICALLY SPEAKING Quick Ways to Reduce Acute Pain

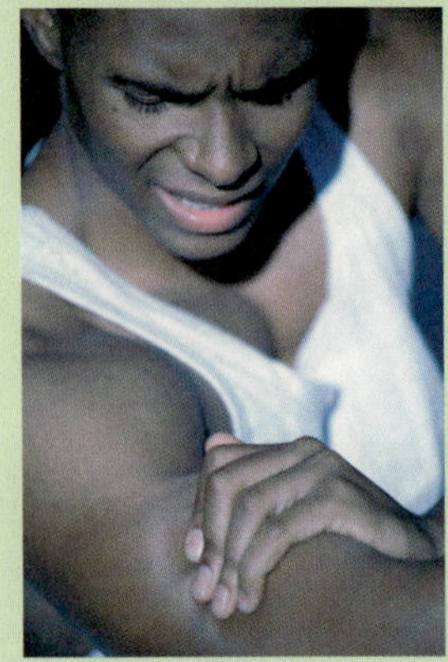

As we discuss in this chapter, medical practitioners are constantly seeking ways to provide relief to patients in chronic, or continuing, pain. But what about acute pain, the short-term pain you feel when you bump your leg on a table, for example?

Gate control theory suggests that touch sensations, which frequently travel along fast fibres, can help prevent some pain sensations travelling on the slow pathways from reaching areas of your brain where they are perceived. According to this theory, the brain only processes so much input, so touch can help to set up a "gate" that stops pain. This explains why we have a tendency to rub the skin of areas of our body that have been injured. For example, if you walk into a piece of furniture, you might rub your leg to dampen the pain.

Focusing on your breathing may also help. We often tend to gasp and then hold our breath when we injure ourselves, such as bumping a leg. Formal methods of pain control, such as the Lamaze method for childbirth, work in part by altering this natural tendency by teaching people to breathe in short, panting gasps (Leventhal et al., 1989).

Distraction can also help (and distraction may actually be why focusing on your breathing helps), whereas anxiously focusing on pain can make it worse (al Absi & Rokke, 1991). Some studies suggest that simply looking at a pleasant view can affect pain tolerance (Ulrich, 1984). Other evidence suggests that for a distraction to be effective, the experience must be active. Studies have shown that playing an interesting videogame can dampen pain detection, whereas passive watching of a TV show has little effect. Stress and sexual experience also decrease the perception of pain. So, if you bump your leg on the way into a big job interview or on a date, perhaps you would not notice the pain as much as you would under other circumstances!

No Pain Some people are incapable of detecting painful stimuli. While the idea of feeling no pain may sound appealing at first, the fact is that our ability to recognize and respond to discomfort is critical for preventing physical damage to the body. Consider how often you shift position in your chair when you are studying or sitting in a lecture. If you were unable to receive signals of discomfort from your body, you would not move to relieve pressure on your skin. The parts of your skin under continuous pressure would develop sores or bruises. Since many everyday experiences would be damaging to our bodies if we were not able to detect discomfort, a lack of ability to detect pain can be very dangerous.

She feels no pain. The child on the right looks like any other 3-year-old welcoming her big sister home from school, except for the goggles she is wearing. The child, who suffers from a severe case of familial dysautonomia, cannot detect any pain to her body and must wear goggles to protect her eyes from excessive rubbing and scratching and the effects of various injuries. She has lost one eye, damaged the other, and inadvertently chewed apart portions of her tongue and mouth.

Some people are born unable to feel pain. A rare genetic condition called *familial dysautonomia* is associated with an inability to detect pain or temperature (Axelrod, 2004). Children with this disorder are at grave risk of life-threatening injuries and must be monitored very carefully. Loss of pain sensation can also be acquired later in life. Some medical conditions, including diabetes, can cause *neuropathies*, or nerve dysfunction, that block pain sensations arising from the person's extremities. People with such neuropathies may not notice if they sustain an injury in an affected area, such as a toe. Sometimes tissue can get so damaged that it must be amputated.

Phantom Limb Sensations Many individuals with amputated limbs report tactile hallucinations or *phantom* sensations of touch, pressure, vibration, pins and needles, hot, cold, and pain in the body part that no longer exists. Some people even feel the sensation of a ring on the finger or a watch on the wrist of an amputated arm. Others report feeling as if their phantom limb is tightly curled up and very painful. Similar phantom experiences have been reported in women who have undergone a mastectomy for the treatment of breast cancer (Björkman et al., 2008).

Researchers believe that such phantom sensations are the result of abnormal activity in the somatosensory cortex of the brain. When a body part is removed, the part of somatosensory cortex that previously received its input does not become inactive. Instead, somatosensory inputs from intact body parts expand to occupy those regions of the cortex (Ramachandran, 2005). Since information from the face is represented in an area of the somatosensory cortex located near that of the arm and hand, a person whose arm was amputated is likely to experience an expansion of the somatosensory inputs from her face into the arm and hand regions of cortex.

Although researchers do not fully understand how reorganization of the somatosensory cortex produces phantom sensations, there is clearly a memory component to the phenomenon. People are more likely to experience phantom sensations that they actually felt previously, as opposed to random sensations. For example, someone who previously wore a ring or a watch is more likely to have the sense of wearing one after an amputation than is a person who didn't wear a watch or ring. Similarly, people who previously experienced considerable pain in their now-missing body part are much more likely to feel phantom pain. There are some amazing case studies involving phantom body parts. For example, a woman born with only stumps of arms can still sense her "hands" and reports gesturing with them when she talks. Children who have lost a hand say they still use their missing "fingers" to help them with counting (Gawande, 2008).

Vilayanor Ramachandran developed "mirror box" therapy for amputees experiencing pain in a missing limb. The mirror box, as its name suggests, involves placing mirrors around the individual on the same side as their missing arm. To the participant it looks like their missing arm is back, though it is only the reflection of their remaining arm. Moving their intact limb creates the sensation of movement in their missing limb and, over time, can recede the pain in the missing or phantom limb (Ramachandran & Rogers-Ramachandran, 1996; Chan et al., 2007).

Before You Go On

www.wiley.com/go/comer

What Do You Know?

8. List the different types of tactile receptors in the skin and the primary functions of each.
9. Compare and contrast slow and fast pain pathways.
10. Why do children so often enjoy getting tickled?
11. What are some possible explanations for individual differences in pain sensitivity?

What Do You Think?

Have you experienced an occasion when your senses have worked together to either enhance or diminish pain or another touch sense? For example, did certain sights or sounds make pain better or worse?

SCAN TO GET THE ANSWERS

The Auditory Sense: Hearing

LEARNING OBJECTIVE 4

Summarize what happens when we hear.

Hearing, the auditory sense, plays a very important role in social communication, as well as in our ability to detect danger. In addition to these clearly adaptive roles, the ability to hear enriches our lives through music and other pleasurable sounds.

From Sound Waves to Sounds

The auditory system is designed to convert sound waves, vibrations of the air, into neural impulses. **Sound waves** have two major qualities that produce our perceptions of different sounds:

sound waves vibrations of the air in the frequency of hearing.

- *Frequency*. The *frequency* of a sound wave refers to the number of cycles the wave completes in a certain amount of time. Frequency of a sound wave is measured in units called *Hertz* (Hz), which represent cycles per second. The frequency of a sound wave is responsible for producing the *pitch* of a sound. The voice of Mickey Mouse is a high-frequency sound wave that produces a high-pitched sound. Although the range of human hearing is quite large, we hear sounds best within the range of 2,000–5,000 Hz, which encompasses the frequencies of most sounds that humans actually make, such as babies crying and people talking.

- *Amplitude.* The *amplitude* of a sound wave refers to the strength of a given cycle. Waves with higher peaks and lower bottoms are of higher amplitude than those that do not reach such extremes. The amplitude of a sound wave is responsible for our detection of *loudness.* Waves with high amplitudes produce loud sounds, while those with low amplitudes sound soft. Loudness is measured in units called *decibels* (dB).

Our detection of sound begins, of course, in the ear. Sound waves are converted to neural impulses in the ear through several steps, as shown in **Figure 5-6**.

tympanic membrane the ear drum.

ossicles tiny bones in the ear called the maleus *(hammer)*, incus *(anvil)*, and stapes *(stirrup)*.

oval window a membrane separating the ossicles and the inner ear, deflection of which causes a wave to form in the cochlea.

cochlea fluid-filled structure in the inner ear; contains the hair cells.

basilar membrane structure in the cochlea where the hair cells are located.

hair cells sensory receptors that convert sound waves into neural impulses.

1. First, sound waves enter the outer ear and at its deepest part, deflect the ear drum or tympanic membrane.
2. Vibrations of the tympanic membrane set in motion a series of three tiny bones or ossicles, called the maleus *(hammer)*, incus *(anvil)*, and stapes *(stirrup)*. The stapes, which is the last bone in the chain, hits the oval window, a membrane separating the ossicles and the inner ear.
3. Deflection of the oval window causes a wave to form in the fluid-filled cochlea of the inner ear. When fluid moves in the cochlea, it deflects the basilar membrane that runs down the middle of the cochlea. The basilar membrane is covered with rows of hair cells, the auditory sensory receptors. Movement of the basilar membrane bends the hair cells that transduce the "fluid sound wave" into electrical activity.
4. The hair cells communicate with nerves in the cochlea that, in turn, send the neural impulses to the brain.

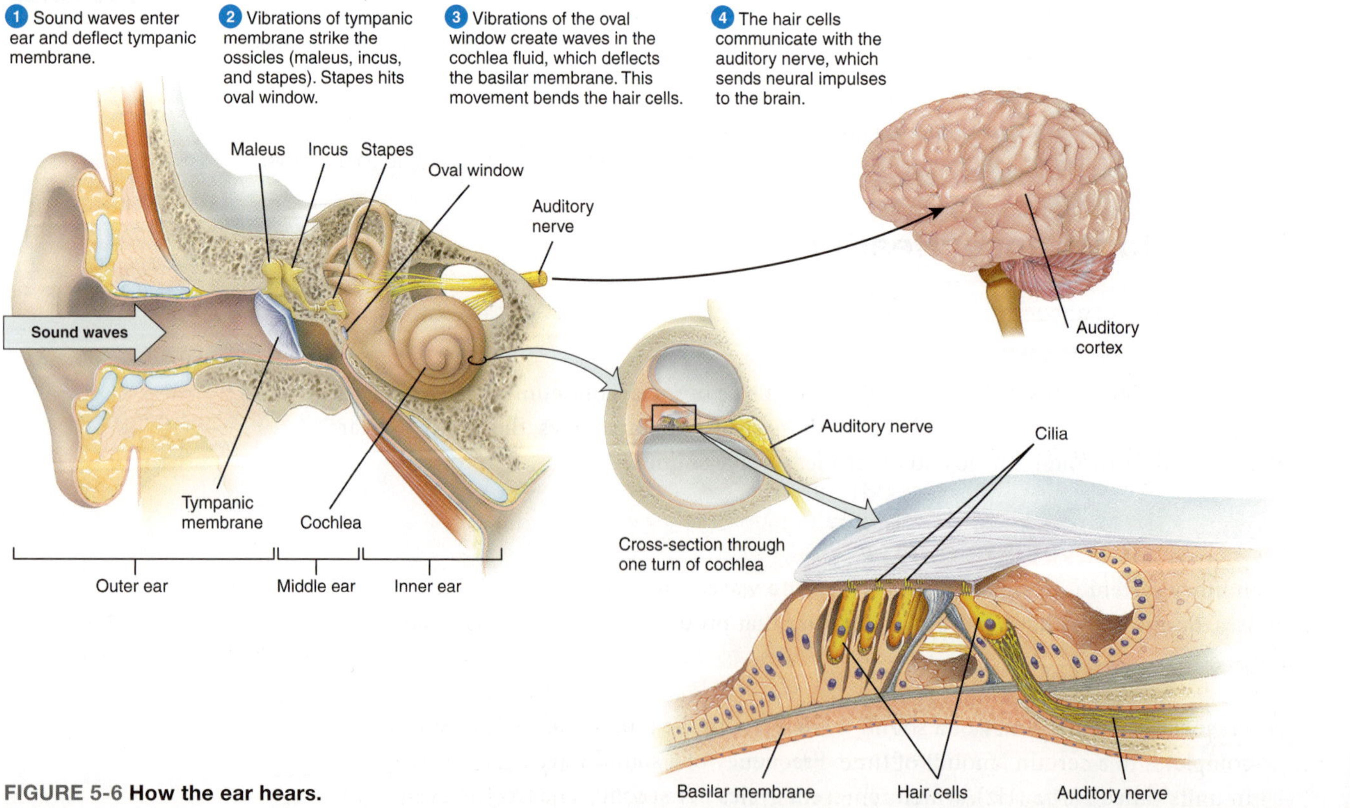

FIGURE 5-6 How the ear hears.

There are two major theories about how the auditory system converts sound waves into all the various sounds we can perceive. The first, called *frequency theory*, suggests that different sound frequencies are converted into different rates of action potentials or firing in our auditory nerves. According to this theory, high-frequency sounds produce a more rapid firing than do low-frequency sounds. Although there may be some truth to frequency theory—different firing rates contribute to sound perception of low tones—researchers agree that this theory cannot fully explain sound perception.

The second theory, called *place theory*, seems to account for a greater degree of auditory perception. Place theory holds that differences in sound frequency activate different regions on the basilar membrane. Regions along the basilar membrane send inputs to the brain that are encoded according to the place along the membrane where the inputs originated. It may be that aspects of both theories are actually at work in processing frequency information.

Based on the above description of the auditory system, you might be able to predict the two major causes of deafness. One, called *conduction deafness*, occurs when there is some sort of occlusion or break in the various processes by which sound is transmitted through the inner ear. Wax buildup, infection, ear drum damage, or water in the ear can cause temporary or permanent deafness. *Nerve deafness* results from damage or malformations of the auditory or hearing nerve in the brain. All congenital (from birth) incidents of deafness are of this second type.

PSYCHOLOGY AROUND US What Did You Say?

Have you ever left a loud concert with a ringing in your ears? It may have been a great show, but you have probably done irreparable damage to your hearing. In fact, hearing loss among young people in North America is on the rise. About one in five U.S. teens has some hearing loss, according a recent study—an increase of about 30 percent over the past 20 years or so (Shargorodsky et al., 2010). And frequent exposure to loud music—whether live or through earphones—gets a lot of the blame. While this study was conducted with American teens, there is no difference in the listening patterns of Canadian and American teens. Work by Robert Harrison at Toronto's Hospital for Sick Children indicates that Canadian teens also listen to music that is dangerously loud (Harrison, 2008). So if you want to continue to enjoy concert performances in the future, you would do well to protect your hearing with ear plugs—if the music is that loud, chances are you will still be able to hear the band, even with ear protection.

Drowning Out the Noise

As with the other sensory systems we have discussed, adaptation also occurs in the auditory system when we are continuously exposed to sounds. We can adapt to sounds in several ways. First, our ears respond to very loud sounds by contracting muscles around the ear's opening so that less of the sound wave can enter the ear. This also happens when we talk, so that the sound of our own voice, which is so close to our ear, is not deafening.

Second, the hair cells of the ear also become less sensitive to continuous noises. Unfortunately, if the noise is loud enough, it can actually damage the hair cells (Petrescu, 2008). Unlike receptors for the chemical senses, our sensory receptors in the ear are not readily replaced, so such damage to the hair cells makes the ear permanently less sensitive. To protect your own hair cells from such permanent damage, which is associated with hearing loss, avoid prolonged exposure to loud noises—including the music coming through your iPod!

Finally, the brain can filter out many sounds that are not important, even if they are relatively loud. This ability enables you to carry on a conversation with your friends at a noisy party. This phenomenon, often referred to as the *cocktail party effect*, is another example of top-down processing. The brain is able to attend to, and pick up on, relevant sounds, even in a very noisy environment. These relevant sounds, such as your name or the names of people who interest you, grab your attention and focus your auditory perception because you have previously learned their importance. So background noise, even if it's

What television? This father, who has set up shop in his family room, seems oblivious to the loud sounds coming from the television that his son is watching. He is concentrating on his phone conversation and professional work while filtering out the irrelevant TV noise.

also the sounds of people talking, interferes minimally with hearing a conversation, as long as the conversation is of interest to us.

Sounds in Space

To determine the importance of a particular sound, it's necessary to localize it in space, to figure out where it is coming from. For example, if you're driving in a car and you hear the sound of an ambulance siren, you need to determine whether the ambulance is far away or close up so you can decide whether or not to pull over to the side of the road to let the ambulance pass. You also need to determine from which direction the sound is approaching. The auditory system uses several cues to help localize sound:

- *General loudness* We learn from many early experiences that loud sounds are usually closer to us than are quiet sounds, so that eventually we automatically use the loudness of a sound to assess the distance between ourselves and the source of the sound.
- *Loudness in each ear* Because of the distance between our ears and the presence of the head between our ears, there are slight differences between each ear in the loudness of the same sound wave. The ear closer to the sound hears a louder noise than the ear farther from the sound. This difference is particularly useful in detecting the location of high-frequency sounds.
- *Timing* Another cue used to localize sound is differences in the time at which sound waves hit each ear. Sound waves will reach the ear closer to the source of the sound before they reach the ear farther away. Since the ears are separated in space, a sound wave will also hit each ear at a slightly different part of its wave cycle, creating a phase difference. This cue is particularly useful to us in localizing sounds with low frequencies.

We also adjust our heads and bodies to assess the location of sounds. These movements allow us to hear how the sound changes while we're in different positions and to use those changes to help make a reasonable approximation of its location. Finally, the use of other sensory systems, such as vision, may come into play. For instance, you might confirm the location of the ambulance when you look into your rearview mirror and see it approaching.

Hearing WHAT HAPPENS IN THE BRAIN?

After auditory information is transduced from sound waves by the hair cells in the basilar membrane of the cochlea, it travels as signals from nerves in the cochlea to the brainstem, the thalamus, and then the auditory cortex, which is located in the temporal lobe. Part of the primary auditory cortex is organized in a **tonotopic map**. That is, information transmitted from different parts of the cochlea (sound waves of different frequency and, hence, sounds of different pitch) is projected to specific parts of the auditory cortex, so that our cortex maps the different pitches of sounds we hear. Auditory information from one ear is sent to the auditory cortex areas on both sides of the brain. This enables us to integrate auditory information from both sides of the head and helps us to locate the sources of sounds.

tonotopic map representation in the auditory cortex of different sound frequencies.

From the primary auditory cortex, auditory information moves on to the auditory *association areas* in the cortex. As we described in Chapter 4, association areas of the brain's cortex are involved in higher-order mental processes. Association areas help to link the sounds we hear with parts of the brain involved in language comprehension.

Association areas also integrate or coordinate auditory information with signals from other sensory modalities. Have you ever noticed how distracting it is to watch a movie that has an audio slightly out of synchrony with the video image? This is because the brain is set up to integrate information from multiple sensory systems. Over time, we learn to have expectations about the coincidence of certain visual stimuli with specific sounds. When the sounds in a movie do not match the visual images the way they would in real life, our expectations are violated and our attention is drawn to this discrepancy from the norm.

In some people, the integration of sensory systems in the brain can sometimes lead to abnormal crossover of different modalities. As described in the box below, people who experience a condition known as *synesthesia* perceive sensations in a different modality from that of the original stimulus. Synesthesia is not a debilitating abnormality; in fact, it has sometimes been described as enriching, particularly when it occurs in artistic or musical individuals.

Digitized music not perfect (yet). M.I.T. professor Neil Gershenfield and a graduate student work on project Digital Stradivarius, an attempt to build a digital model that can match the sound of the great violins of Stradivarius. When digital-produced and instrument-produced sound waves are each converted into neural impulses in the brains of musical experts, the experts can detect a difference. The instrument remains the champ.

Specialized Somatosensory Systems: Synesthesia

"The best kaleidoscope ever." Performer and songwriter Tori Amos has said that she often experiences the notes and chords in her music as colours and light filaments. She says, "Try to imagine the best kaleidoscope ever."

Can you see noise or taste words? Some people can. This condition is called *synesthesia*. The name comes from two Greek words: *syn*, meaning together, and *aesthesis*, meaning perception, and therefore refers to "joined perception." People who have synesthesia experience a stimulus that normally would be perceived by one sense in a different sensory modality. They may actually see colours or images when they hear music.

The most common form of synesthesia is called *coloured letters or numbers*. A person who has this form always sees a colour in response to a specific letter or number. There are also synesthetes who smell particular odours in response to touch, who hear noises in response to smell, or who feel a tactile stimulus in response to sight. There are even some individuals who possess synesthesia involving three or more senses, but this is especially unusual.

People who experience synesthesia are not simply imagining their unusual sensations. Neuroimaging studies have shown that sensory areas normally not affected by particular stimuli are activated if that sense is involved in the synesthetic experience (Nunn el al., 2002). For example, the auditory cortex of sight–sound synesthetes, as well as the visual cortex, becomes active in response to particular visual stimuli that cause synesthesia. The brain of a person who can hear a picture or colour really does respond as though the stimulus were producing sound waves, as well as reflecting light waves.

Hearing — HOW WE DEVELOP

Our ears are formed and capable of transducing sound waves before we are even born. In fact, human fetuses have been shown to respond to noises long before birth. Research has shown that fetuses respond to loud noises with a startle reflex, and that after birth, they are capable of recognizing some sounds they heard while in utero. However, the ability

A bit too early. A pregnant woman tries to introduce music to her fetus by positioning headphones on her stomach. Although fetuses do indeed respond to loud noises and can detect certain sounds, the acquisition of musical skills cannot take place until sensitive periods unfold during the preschool years.

to recognize and respond appropriately to a wide variety of sound stimuli is acquired over many years of postnatal life. Sounds associated with language, for example, become recognizable over postnatal development, as do those associated with music. We describe language development in more detail in Chapter 9.

Sensitive periods exist for the development of both language and music learning (Knudson, 2004). As we described in Chapter 3, we acquire certain abilities during sensitive periods of development much more easily that we do after the sensitive period has ended. The tonotopic map in the primary auditory cortex of the brain is organized during such a sensitive period of development (deVillers-Sidani et al., 2007). Studies in experimental animals have shown that exposing animals to pure tones during a certain time in development leads to a larger representation of those sounds in the auditory cortex. The same exposure after the sensitive period in development is over has no such effect. If a sound is made important to the animal, however, by pairing it either with a reward, such as water, or a punishment, such as an electric shock, the primary auditory cortex can be reorganized so that more of it responds to the relevant tone (Bakin et al., 1996). Such top-down processing of tones indicates that this region of the brain still shows plasticity after the sensitive period is over. However, it is not as easy to remap the brain after a sensitive period as it is during one. The stimuli needed to produce changes in older animals must be very strong and important compared to those needed for younger animals (Kuboshima & Sawaguchi, 2007). In humans, the auditory brain is set up to acquire information about speaking and music most readily relatively early in life, during the preschool years. It is more difficult, but by no means impossible, for us to learn additional languages or certain music skills after we mature.

absolute pitch the ability to recognize or produce any note on a musical scale.

Identifying Pitch — HOW WE DIFFER

We differ greatly in our ability to detect specific sounds. People show particular differences in their ability to identify certain notes in a scale. **Absolute pitch** refers to the ability to recognize an individual note in isolation. This is very difficult for most people. Only about one in 10,000 people in Western countries has absolute pitch. This ability seems to originate in childhood between the ages of 3 and 6 years, through musical training. It is associated with differences in brain anatomy (Zatorre, 2003). Research has shown that portions of the cortex are actually thinner in individuals with absolute pitch (Bermudez et al., 2009). Although it's not clear whether people with absolute pitch start out with a thinner cortex or whether they develop it through training, it's possible that synaptic pruning contributes to this structural difference.

Breaking the bad news. Simon Cowell, a judge on *American Idol* for eight years and now a judge on his new series *The X Factor*, is famous for calling contestants "tone deaf." Both the *Idol* and *X Factor* series include performers whose musical abilities vary from absolute pitch to tone deafness.

Studies have shown, however, that people who speak tonal languages, or languages in which differences in tone convey meaning, such as Vietnamese and Mandarin Chinese, are more likely to develop absolute pitch than those speaking Western languages. This again suggests the possibility that early learning of auditory information related to tones can have a permanent effect on the functioning of this sensory system (Liu, Xu, & Larson, 2009).

Just as some people exhibit absolute pitch, others are tone deaf, or unable to discern differences in pitch. Although tone deafness or *amusia* is sometimes the result of damage to the auditory system, it can be present from birth, and researchers believe it may be related to genetics (Peretz et al., 2007). Tone deafness affects up to 4 percent of the population and mostly results in a diminished appreciation for music. Although music appreciation is an important enriching ability, people with tone deafness are able to enjoy all other aspects of life. This condition only presents serious social problems when it occurs in cultures where the language is tonal.

Hearing WHEN THINGS GO WRONG

There are many conditions that lead to abnormalities in the auditory system. Some cause either partial or total **deafness**, the loss of hearing. Abnormalities in the auditory system can also add unwanted auditory perceptions.

deafness loss or lack of hearing.

Deafness Deafness has a variety of causes. It can be genetic or caused by infection, physical trauma, or exposure to toxins, including overdose of common medications such as aspirin.

Since speech is an important mode of communication for humans, deafness can have dramatic consequences for socialization. This is particularly a concern for children, because young children need auditory stimulation to develop normal spoken language skills. For this reason, physicians try to identify auditory deficits at an early life stage. Parents can then make choices among different options to help their children with deafness. Some deaf individuals learn to use sign language and other methods of communication that rely on the senses other than hearing. Research over the past years has made progress in the construction of cochlear implants that help individuals with deafness to hear sounds (Sharma et al., 2009). Although this work is developing at a rapid pace, there remain many deaf people who are not helped by cochlear implants (Battmer et al., 2009). This is one reason why many individuals and families choose to avoid them. Some in the deaf community also believe that hearing is not necessary to lead a productive and fulfilling life. For them, the potential benefits of implants may not outweigh the potential risks of surgery required to place them in the cochlea (Hyde & Power, 2006).

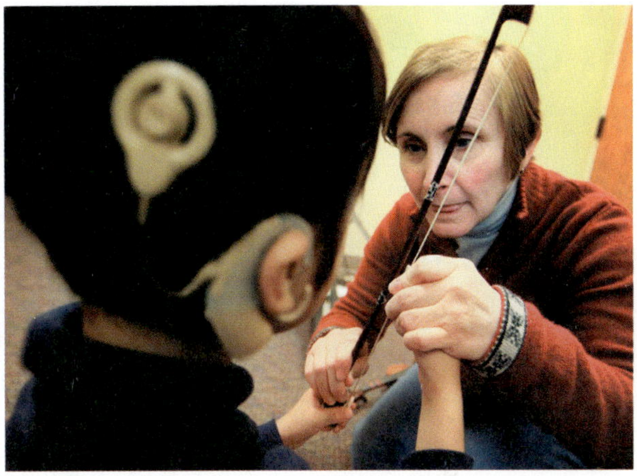

A world of new possibilities. After undergoing successful cochlear implant surgery, this 4-year-old child practises the violin under the instruction of his music teacher at the Memphis Oral School for the Deaf.

Hearing Unwanted Sounds About one of every 200 people is affected by *tinnitus*, or ringing in the ear. Tinnitus has multiple causes, some of which are related to abnormalities in the ear itself (Lanting et al., 2009). Most people are able to cope with the noise, but some find it too loud and distracting to ignore.

Patients with epilepsy in the temporal cortex have reported the perception of hearing complex auditory stimuli, such as a musical tune (Wieser, 2003). This symptom, which can be completely distracting and disturbing to the patient, is the result of abnormal electrical activity in brain circuits that store complex auditory memories. Treatment for epilepsy sometimes involves neurosurgery to remove the part of the brain that is responsible for starting the seizures. Brain surgery in the temporal lobes, where auditory information is processed, is particularly dangerous, however, because the temporal lobe also houses Wernicke's area, which is critical for language comprehension.

> "I have unwittingly helped to invent and refine a type of music that makes its principal exponents deaf. Hearing loss is a terrible thing because it cannot be repaired."
>
> —*Pete Townshend, rock musician of the band The Who*

Before You Go On

www.wiley.com/go/comer

What Do You Know?

12. What happens in the ear to transduce sound waves into neural signals?
13. What is a tonotopic map?
14. What are sensitive periods and how are they important for hearing?
15. What is tinnitus?

What Do You Think?

What would you suggest including in an ideal early school curriculum to develop children's auditory systems to their maximum capabilities?

SCAN TO GET THE ANSWERS

The Visual Sense: Sight

LEARNING OBJECTIVE 5

Describe key processes in visual sensation and perception.

The ability to see and make sense of the visual world around us plays a very important role in human life. We use vision in virtually all of our activities. Vision is especially important for non-verbal communication, facial expressions and body language used to convey information that is often lost in spoken language alone. Have you ever experienced a misunderstanding over text or email because, without non-verbal facial and body cues accompanying your message, the receiver misunderstood what you were trying to say? No doubt related to its importance to us, the visual sense is particularly well-developed in humans. Some estimates suggest that about half of the cerebral cortex of our brains is devoted to processing some type of visual stimuli (Grady, 1993).

As we have seen, each sensory system is most receptive to some form of physical energy. Taste and smell respond to chemical stimuli, touch to changes in temperature or pressure, and hearing to vibrating air molecules (sound waves). The stimulus for vision is electromagnetic radiation, which produces light. Light is made up of particles called *photons*. The light that we can see is part of the electromagnetic spectrum of energy that also includes many forms we cannot see, such as X-rays and radio waves. Like sound, light travels in waves. The visible spectrum of light ranges from about 400 to 700 nanometres in wavelength (a nanometre is a billionth of a metre). As shown in **Figure 5-7**, different wavelengths within our visible spectrum appear to us as different colours. Objects in the world absorb and reflect light in varying levels and patterns—those that reflect more light are perceived as brighter.

Seeing the Lights

Vision begins when light enters the eye, as shown in **Figure 5-8**. Muscles in the iris—the coloured part of the eye—adjust the size of our pupils to let in more or less of the light reflected from objects around us. Muscles also adjust the shape of the lens, enabling it to bring both near and far objects into focus. The lens therefore serves to focus the light that enters the eye onto a specialized multi-layered sheet of nerve cells in the back of the eye, called the **retina**. If the lens of the eye cannot quite manage the task of focusing light, it can be assisted by glasses or contact lenses, or it can sometimes be reshaped by laser surgery so that it can do its job of focusing light onto the retina. The retina is an extension of the brain and is where light produces chemical changes that in turn produce a neural signal.

retina a specialized sheet of nerve cells in the back of the eye containing the sensory receptors for vision.

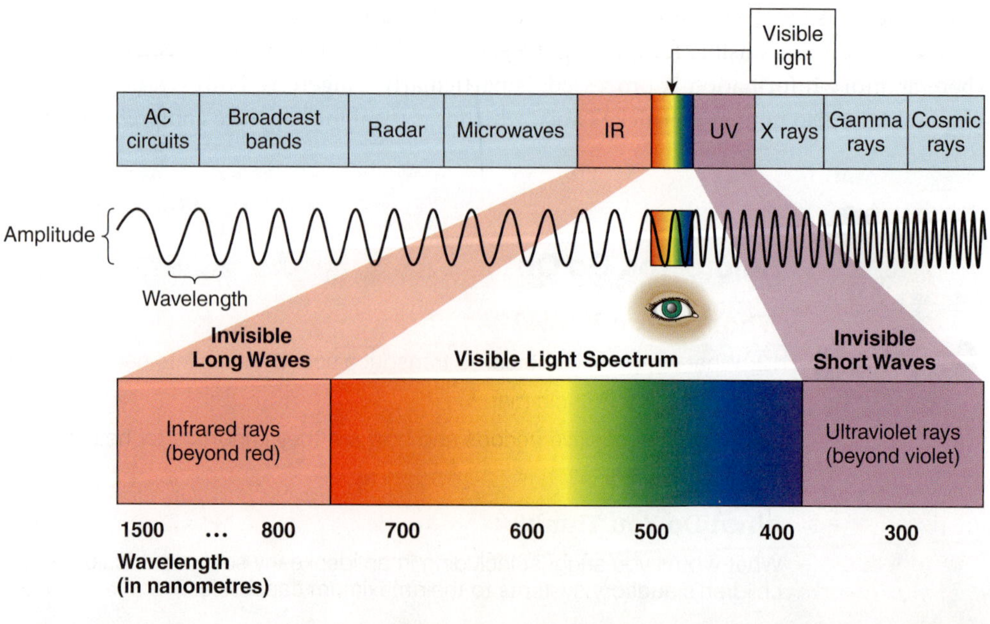

FIGURE 5-7 Visible light and the electromagnetic spectrum. The part of the electromagnetic spectrum that our visual receptors can detect is restricted to a narrow range.

FIGURE 5-8 How the eye sees.

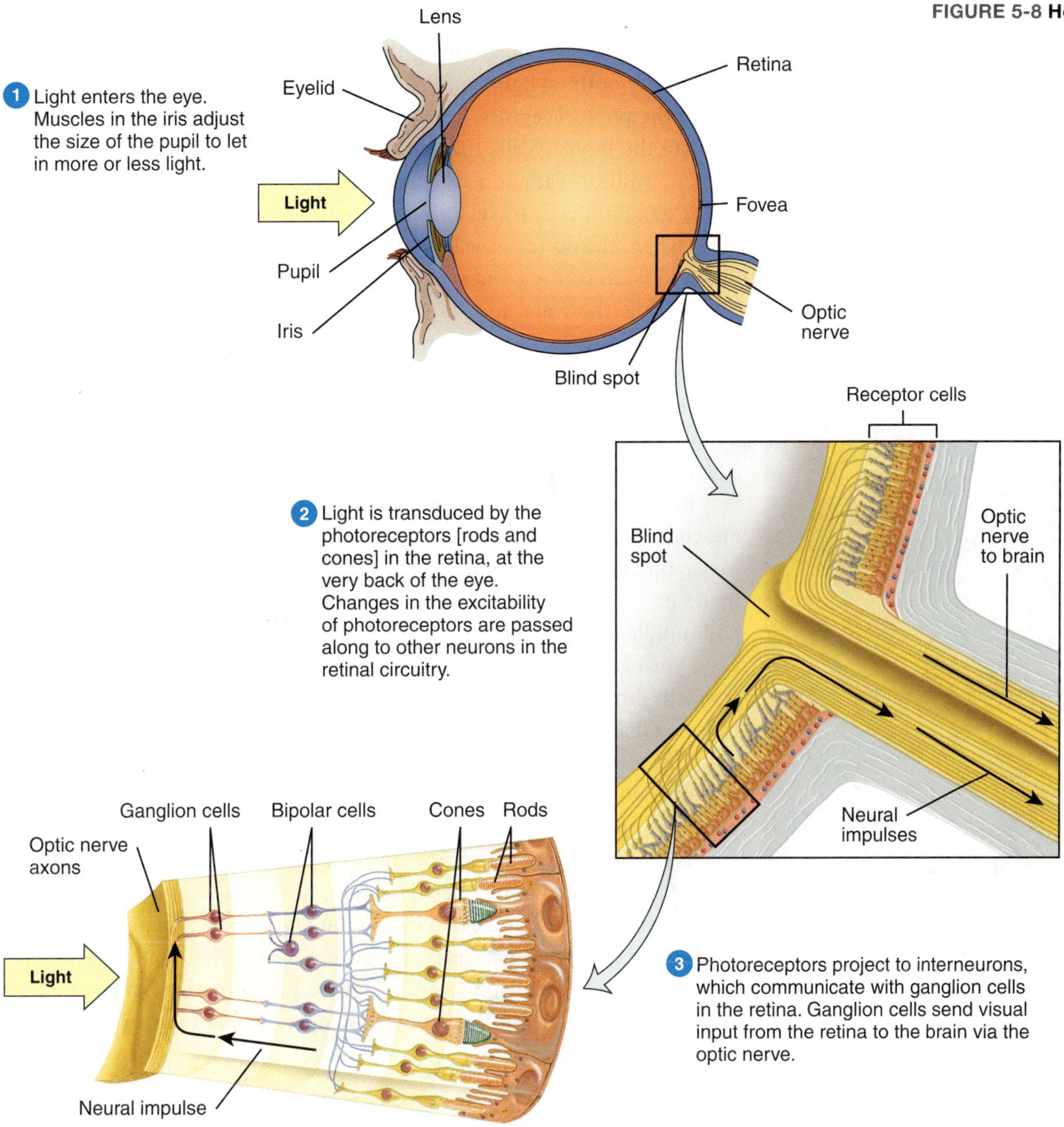

Find your blind spot

The blind spot is not normally noticeable. To find yours, hold this book about a foot away, close your right eye, and stare at the X with your left eye. Very slowly, bring the book closer to you. The worm should disappear and the apple become whole.

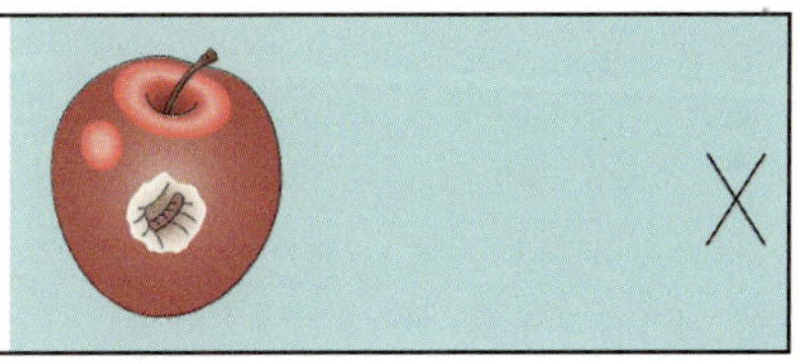

This process of converting light waves into neural impulses that the brain can process is known as **transduction**.

Two major classes of visual receptors or **photoreceptors** exist in the retina, the **rods** and the **cones**. The rods predominate. There are over 100 million rods in the human retina. Rods are important for detecting light; they are highly sensitive to small amounts of light and are critical for functioning in dim light or at night. Rods give the perceiver no colour sensation. Cones, on the other hand, are colour receptors because they respond to light of different wavelengths. The cones are much fewer in number, with only about 4.5 to 6 million per human retina (Curcio et al., 1990). People have to function both during the day and the night, and so have both rods and cones. Animals that primarily function in only the day or the night have either one set of receptors or the other. For example, nocturnal birds and animals such as owls have retinas composed entirely of rods, allowing them to survive

transduction converting stimulus energy into neural impulses that can be interpreted by the brain.

photoreceptors the sensory receptor cells for vision, located in the retina.

rods photoreceptors most responsive to levels of light and dark.

cones photoreceptors responsive to colours.

in very low light conditions. Conversely, diurnal birds and animals such as the pigeon or chipmunk have only cones in the retina, allowing them to function effectively in a richly coloured environment under optimal light conditions (Dossenbach & Dossenbach, 1998).

When light reaches the photoreceptors, a series of chemical reactions take place. The rods and cones stimulate the bipolar cells that, in turn, cause ganglion cells to then fire. The axons of almost one million ganglion cells are bundled together to form the **optic nerve.** Signals from the ganglion cells travel along the optic nerve out of the eye and into the brain. The location where the optic nerve leaves the retina is therefore completely lacking in rods and cones and is called the *blind spot*, or *optic disc*. This means that when light strikes that area of the retina, there are no visual receptor cells to respond to it. Although there are no receptor cells in this area, you do not experience a "hole" in the visual field because the brain fills in the incomplete image. Also, the blind spot in each eye is offset, so that missing information from one eye is replaced by the other. With some manipulation of the visual input shown in Figure 5-8, however, you can identify your blind spot.

optic nerve the bundle of axons of ganglion cells that carries visual information from the eye to the brain.

fovea centre of the retina, containing only cones, where vision is most clear.

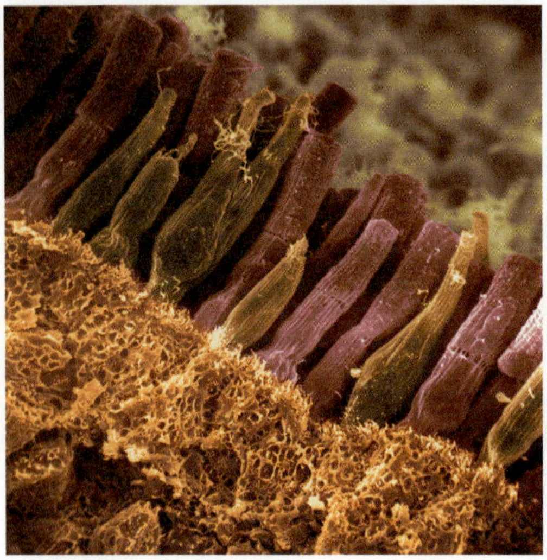

The photoreceptors. This colourized scanning electron micrograph shows the retina's photoreceptors—the rods and cones—which help pass visual signals through the optic nerve to the brain. Rods (*pink*) are the photoreceptors that detect light. Cones (*olive*) are photoreceptors that detect wavelength, creating the perception of colour.

Rods and cones are not evenly distributed throughout the retina. Cones are concentrated more in the centre than the periphery of the retina. The **fovea**, the region of the retina where our vision is at its sharpest, is entirely made up of cones. Rods are distributed throughout the rest of the retina and, unlike cones, are concentrated at the peripheral edges of the retina. Have you ever noticed that your peripheral vision is not particularly acute? It mostly enables you to detect movement, but not necessarily details. This is due to that fact that rods dominate the peripheral parts of the retina.

Like the other sensory systems we previously discussed, the visual system also undergoes sensory adaptation. Dilation and constriction of the pupil, the opening in the centre of the iris, is one way that the visual system adapts to light. When you go from inside your home to outside on a bright, sunny day, you may immediately feel the need to squint and shade your eyes. Your eyes quickly adapt to the brighter light, however, in part by constriction of the pupil that decreases the amount of light entering the eye. Conversely, to allow vision to occur in dark places, such as when you first enter a dark movie theatre, the pupil will open further to let in more light.

PSYCHOLOGY AROUND US Artificial Pupil Dilation

Have you ever had your eyes dilated by an eye doctor? Eye doctors use special eye drops to make your pupils dilate, or get bigger, so they can see inside your eyes. Normally, your pupils adjust automatically to the amount of light available. When you step outside into daylight, your pupils therefore become smaller. When your eyes are dilated artificially, however, your pupils cannot adjust themselves for a period of time. Patients with dilated eyes are especially sensitive to light and need to wear sunglasses until the effect of the drops wears off—usually in three to four hours. Interestingly, the effect wears off faster in dark-eyed people than in people with lighter-coloured eyes.

Seeing in Colour

As we noted earlier, cones enable us to see colour. In fact, colour exists only in the brain. An object reflects a particular wavelength, which is then detected by the cones, creating chemical changes that in turn generate a neural signal. This signal is processed by the brain, giving rise to the sensation of colour. How does the brain experience so many colours? The experience of colour can be described along three dimensions: hue, saturation, and brightness. The variety of colours we can perceive is related to the different combinations of these three characteristics. In fact, using these three dimensions it has been estimated that humans can detect about seven million different colours (Geldard, 1972). Not surprisingly, people can only name a small subset of these colours!

- *Hue* refers to the experience of colour based on the wavelength of light that the visual stimulus emits or reflects. This is the most basic aspect of colour, whether the stimulus is perceived as red, green, orange, blue, yellow, or some other colour.
- *Saturation* refers to the purity of a colour; that is, how bright or vivid the colour appears. If a colour is desaturated, it has white or grey mixed into it. For example, a pure red would be saturated, pink would be more desaturated, and grey would be completely desaturated (i.e., zero saturation).
- *Brightness* of a colour refers to how much light emanates or is reflected from the visual stimulus (light intensity). White is considered to be the brightest colour and black the least bright.

Theories of Colour Perception No single theory yet entirely explains how we perceive colour. Two theories of colour vision in combination help to explain a good deal, however. One theory, first hypothesized in the nineteenth century, is the *Young-Helmholtz trichromatic theory* of colour vision. This theory maintains that there are three different receptors for colour and that each type of receptor responds to a different range of wavelengths of light (Balaraman, 1962). This theory is largely correct, in that people with normal colour vision have three receptor types (cones), each maximally sensitive to a particular wavelength (colour). One receptor type responds to yellowish-red wavelengths, another to green wavelengths, and the third to bluish-purple wavelengths. Why is it that we can see more than three colours if we only have three receptor types? Typically, at least two cone types will respond to a certain wavelength of visible light, but in varying increments. The combination of the signals produced by cones is what enables the brain to respond to such a multitude of colours.

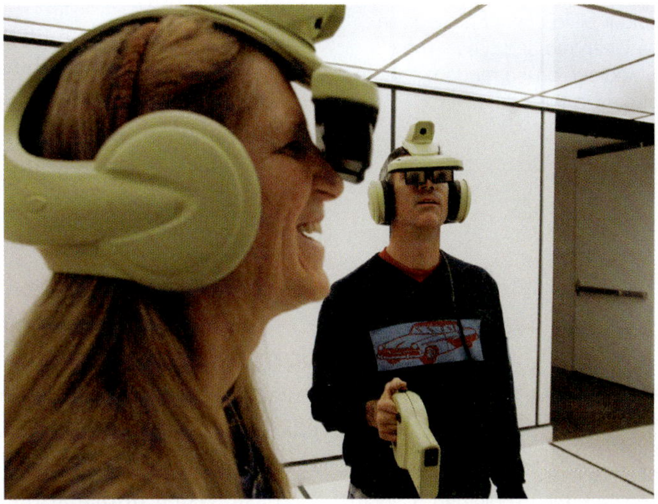

Changing one's view. These two people at the Sensorium museum exhibit at M.I.T. wear wireless head gear that causes each of them to view the world from the visual perspective of the other. This visual manipulation is eventually adjusted to, but, for a while, it interferes with many aspects of visual functioning, including shape, light, and colour perceptions; activity in visual regions of the brain; depth perception; and perceptual constancies.

Another nineteenth century theorist, Hering, proposed an alternative theory about colour vision called *opponent process theory* (Buchsbaum & Gottschalk, 1983). Opponent process theory maintains that colour pairs work to inhibit one another in the perception of colour. In the retinal ganglion cells, as well as the thalamus and visual cortex, colour information is analyzed in terms of antagonistic opponent colour pairs: red-green, yellow–blue, and black–white. The hypothesis of antagonistic colour-pairings is supported by the observation that we cannot mix certain combinations of colours. For example, we cannot see reddish green or bluish yellow, but we can see greenish yellow or bluish red. Opponent processing is the result of activity in a region of the thalamus that receives visual information, called the *lateral geniculate nucleus*. Inputs to this nucleus from one colour of an opposing pair inhibit those from the other colour in the pair. For example, some neurons here are turned on (excited) by red and off for green (inhibited). Other neurons are turned off by red and on for green, and so on for the other opponent pairs (DeValois & DeValois, 1975).

FIGURE 5-9 **The negative afterimage effect.** Afterimages occur because one colour in an opponent pair is fatigued when it is viewed for a sustained period of time. When you look away from the first colour, the previously inhibited colour is activated. To see opponent processing in action, stare at the black dot in the centre of the leaf for about 30 seconds, then look away at a white sheet of paper.

You can observe opponent processing at work by staring at the black dot in the middle of the green and black flag in **Figure 5-9**. After about 30 seconds, stare at a white sheet of paper. You will see a negative *afterimage* that is red and white.

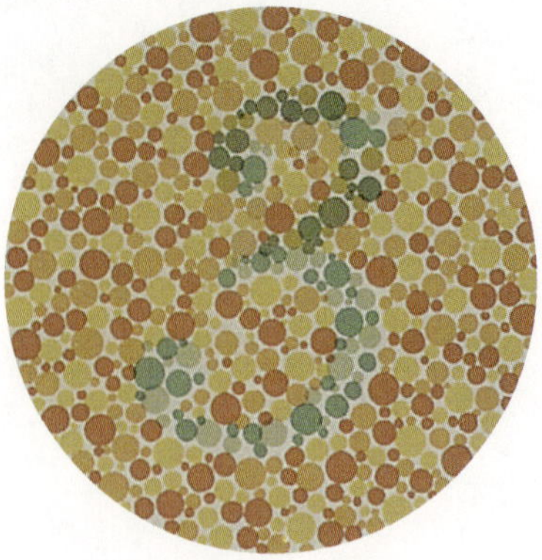

FIGURE 5-10 **Colour blindness.** Most people who are colour blind cannot distinguish between red and green; they would see only a random pattern of dots in this figure.

The term "negative" is used to acknowledge that the afterimage is the opposite colour of the original image. This also works with other colours in the opponent pairs. A white-on-black image will produce a black-on-white afterimage, and a yellow image will produce a blue afterimage. Afterimages happen when one colour in an opponent pair inhibits the other. When we release this inhibition by looking away from the first colour, the previously inhibited colour overcompensates and creates an image in the opponent colour.

Very few people are actually unable to see any colours at all. Most people who have what is called *colour blindness* are really just unable to distinguish certain colours (more accurately called colour-deficient). Most common is red–green colour blindness, which is tested with images, such as the one shown in **Figure 5-10**. Studies suggest that people with this problem have a shortage of cones that respond to either the greenish or reddish wavelengths. Therefore, the lateral geniculate nucleus of their thalamus does not receive sufficient inputs that enable it to inhibit either red or green colours, making people unable to distinguish between the two colours (Weale, 1983; Wertenbaker, 1981).

In sum, trichromacy theory and opponent process theory are not in conflict and can be used together to create a successive physiological two-stage model of colour vision. In stage one, the cones in the retina respond to three primary wavelengths and send signals to the visual cortex. Along the way, in stage two, the signal is processed by opponent process cells. The result? Colour.

Sight WHAT HAPPENS IN THE BRAIN?

Visual information leaving the retina travels via the optic nerve to neurons in the *superior colliculus*, and then communicates with the thalamus. From the thalamus, visual input travels to the primary visual cortex, located in the occipital lobe.

Basic visual information is transmitted throughout the brain via a partially-crossed set of axons (**Figure 5-11**). Visual information from the middle part of your visual field, closest to your nose, is sent, via axons that cross to the other side of your brain, to the opposite side of your visual cortex. Visual information from the lateral part of your visual field, closest to your temples, travels to the same side of the visual cortex.

FIGURE 5-11 **The crossed visual pathway.** Before entering the brain, the optic nerves partially cross. Visual information from the middle part of your visual field travels to opposite sides of your visual cortex, while information from the lateral part of the field (closest to your temples) travels to the same side of the visual cortex.

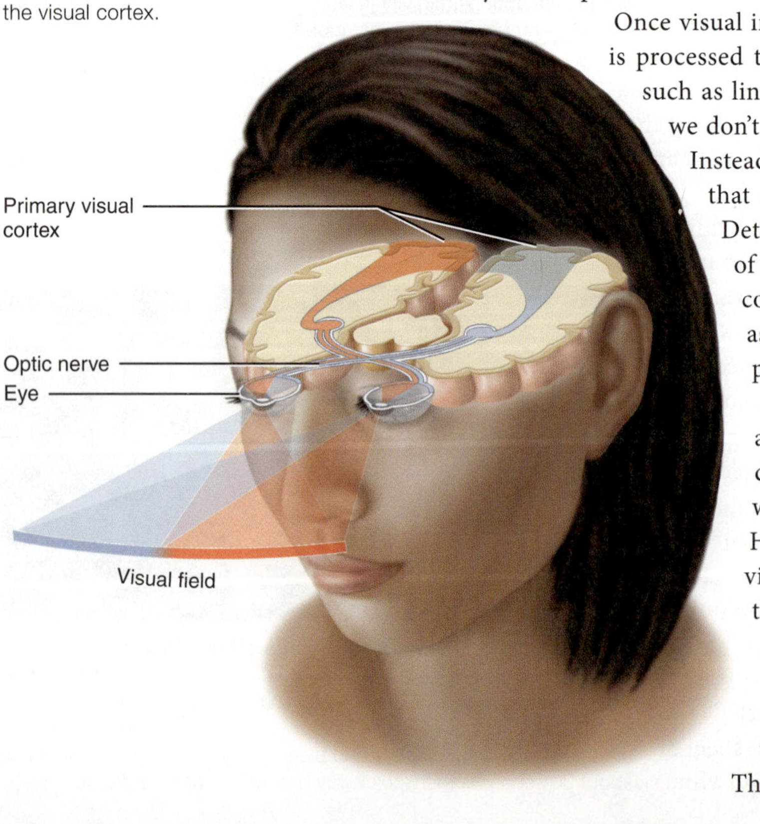

Once visual information reaches the primary visual cortex, it is processed to enable the detection of very simple features, such as lines and edges (Hubel & Wiesel, 1959). However, we don't see the world as a collection of lines and edges. Instead, we see a rich set of complex visual stimuli that change as we and the world around us move. Detection of complex visual stimuli occurs as a result of circuitry that involves association areas of visual cortex. Recall from our discussion of hearing that association areas are involved with higher-order processes of perception: thinking and memory.

The pathways that process information about complex visual stimuli can be roughly divided into the "*what*" and the "*where*" pathways, as shown in **Figure 5-12** (Ungerleider & Haxby, 1994). That is, the regions that process visual information to help us determine *what* is the identity of an object (is it an apple, a car, or a house) are different from those where we process the visual information to figure out *where* in space the object is located (is the apple on the table, under the table, or behind the table). The "what" pathway involves axons that travel from the occipital cortex to the temporal cortex. The "where" pathway involves axons that travel from the occipital cortex to the parietal cortex.

How do researchers know about the brain regions that serve these complex functions? Recall from Chapter 4 that one way scientists have determined the function of certain brain regions is by examining the deficits displayed by people who have sustained damage in particular areas of their brains, usually as a result of stroke, disease, or head trauma. Patients with damage to the parts of the temporal cortex, which houses the "what" pathway, exhibit a condition called *visual agnosia*. Although their vision remains intact, they cannot recognize objects visually. When shown a rose, they can describe it, but they cannot name it. If they are allowed to touch or smell the rose, however, they can immediately identify it as a rose. A more specified form of visual agnosia that happens to people with damage to a certain part of the "what" pathway is called *prosopagnosia*. Individuals with prosopagnosia cannot recognize faces (Farah et al., 1995). Sometimes these patients can recognize familiar individuals by concentrating on some visual characteristic that is not directly related to facial features, such as the person's hairstyle or eyeglasses, but their ability to recognize the face itself is lost (Sacks, 1985).

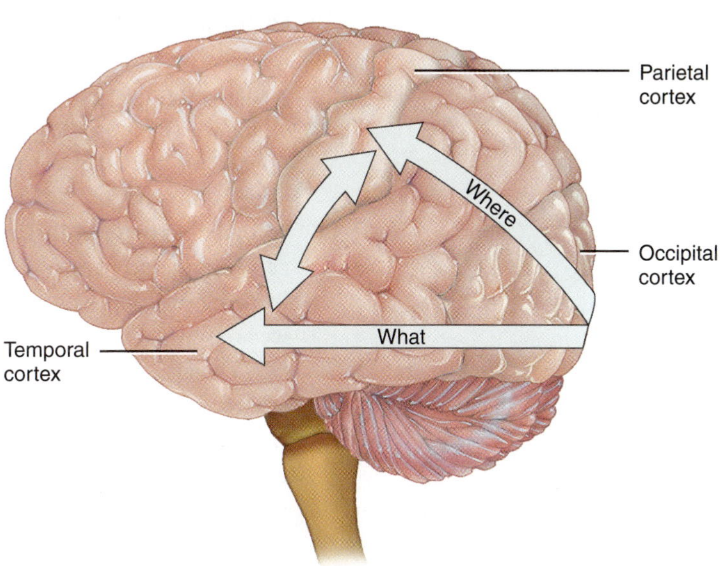

FIGURE 5-12 The "what" and "where" pathways. The "what" pathway of the brain processes information that helps us identify an object, while the "where" pathway helps us identify its location in space. Communication between the two pathways allows us to integrate complex visual stimuli.

Patients with damage to the "where" pathway also have normal vision, but they have lost the ability to locate objects in space. For example, when given the task of pouring water from a pitcher into a glass, they will invariably miss and pour the water onto the table or floor. A very peculiar form of damage to the "where" pathway results in a condition called *hemi-neglect* (Mesulam, 1981). Patients with hemi-neglect often completely ignore one side of their visual field. Hemi-neglect is most apparent and long-lasting after damage to the right hemisphere. People with damage to the right side of their "where" pathways neglect the left side of their visual field. For example, when asked to copy a drawing, people with hemi-neglect will leave out one half of it (**Figure 5-13**). People with this condition have been known to apply makeup to only one side of their face, to shave only one side of their face, and to eat food on only one side of their plate (Corbetta et al., 2005; Corbetta & Shulman, 2002).

Prosopagnosia. People with prosopagnosia would see others like this and would need to recognize their friends by features other than their face—like their hat or hair, perhaps.

In addition to the information researchers have gained from studying patients with brain damage, neuroimaging studies of people without brain damage have confirmed the presence of the "what" and "where" pathways. Indeed, these types of studies have shown that brain activity changes in specific parts of the "what" pathways when the participants are viewing objects (Reddy & Kanwisher, 2006).

Visual Perception from the Top Down

So far we have discussed vision from a bottom-up perspective. Light comes in through the eye and the neural impulses generated are passed to successively more complex brain regions that ultimately result in the perception of a visual stimulus. Equally important to visual perception, however, is top-down processing, which involves previously acquired knowledge. Like perception involving the other sensory systems, visual perception involves both bottom-up and top-down processing occurring at the same time. Brain regions that store information about what objects look like can help us to perceive visual stimuli that are partially hidden or of a different size from when we originally encountered them.

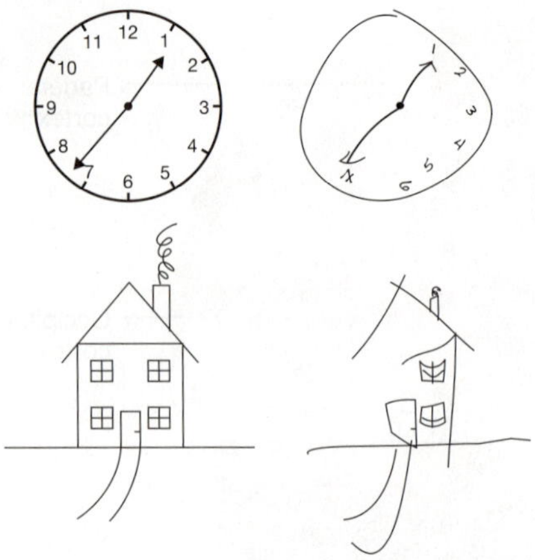

FIGURE 5-13 Seeing only half the picture. When asked to copy a drawing of a clock, a house, and a cat, a patient with hemi-neglect copies only the right side of each image. She ignores the left side of her visual field.

Putting Together the Parts: Gestalt Principles We don't see images as a series of small patches of colour or a series of simple features. Instead, our visual system assembles this information into coherent objects and scenes. Even when we see a small part of an object or scene partially obscured by another object, we are able to perceive it as a whole, given limited visual information. Our brains are organized to fill in the missing parts so that we perceive and recognize meaningful stimuli. As we described earlier, part of our ability to perceive images comes from our use of cognitive processes, such as memory and learning, to help us recall from prior experience images that match the stimuli we are sensing.

The area of study focused on understanding principles by which we perceive and recognize visual stimuli in their entirety despite limited information is called *Gestalt* psychology. As mentioned in Chapter 1, Gestalt psychologists believe that perception helps us to add meaning to visual information, so that the whole is more than the sum of its parts. As Kurt Koffka pointed out, though, "*It is more correct to say that the whole is something else than the sum of its parts*, because summing up is a meaningless procedure, whereas the whole-part relationship is meaningful" (Koffka, 1935, p. 176). Gestalt psychologists have identified several laws by which visual information is organized into coherent images:

- *Proximity* The law of proximity indicates that visual stimuli near to one another tend to be grouped together. For example, AA AA AA is seen as three groups, while AAA AAA is seen as two groups, despite the fact that each set has six *A*s.
- *Similarity* The law of similarity indicates that stimuli resembling one another tend to be grouped together. So AAaa is viewed as two groups because of the dissimilar appearance of upper and lowercase letters.
- *Continuity* The law of continuity indicates that stimuli falling along the same plane tend to be grouped together. $_{\text{AAA}}$ ^{AAA} would be organized into two perceptual groups because they are not on the same line.
- *Good form* The law of good form indicates that stimuli forming a shape tend to be grouped together, while those that do not remain ungrouped. Compare ☺ to :). The former is perceived as a smiley face, while the latter is perceived as two separate symbols.
- *Closure* The law of closure indicates that we tend to fill in small gaps in objects so that they are still perceived as whole objects.

FIGURE 5-14 Impossible figure. The brain is organized to perceive meaningful images; with impossible figures such as this, the brain tries but cannot form a stable perception. (M.C. Escher's "Convex and Concave" ©2009 The M.C. Escher Company-Holland. All rights reserved. www.mcescher.com)

These laws of visual organization put together all the "pieces" of visual stimuli to complete a "puzzle" to build meaningful information from everything we see when we look at something. Sometimes, however, the fact that our brain tends to create order among the things we are seeing can lead us to perceive sights that are illusions, such as those shown in **Figure 5-14**. If you look closely, you can see that the drawings depict situations that are simply physically impossible.

Getting in Deep: Binocular and Monocular Cues When you look at the items on the table in a restaurant, how do you know which items are closer to you and which are farther away? We use a number of methods for depth perception, determining the distance of objects away from us and in relation to one another.

retinal disparity the slight difference in images processed by the retinas of each eye.

Because our eyes are set a slight distance apart, we do not see exactly the same thing with each eye. This **retinal disparity**, the slightly different stimuli recorded by the retina of each eye, provide us with a *binocular* cue of depth. Our brains use the discrepancies between the visual information received from our two eyes to help us judge the distance of objects from us. You can observe your own retinal disparity by holding up a finger at arm's length away from your face. Close first one eye, then the other, and note how the position of your finger seems to change relative to objects in the background beyond the finger.

Another binocular cue to depth is actually tactile. We feel the changes in the muscles around our eyes as we shift them to look at objects at various distances. Closer objects require more convergence, turning our eyes inward toward our noses. Use your finger again to demonstrate **convergence**. Start with the finger at arm's length from you and watch it as you bring it closer and closer to your face. Note the sensations you feel as you do so.

convergence inward movement of the eyes to view objects close to oneself.

We also use a number of other cues to determine depth. The following are sometimes called **monocular cues**, because, if needed, they can help us judge depth based on information from only one eye. You can see them all in the photo in **Figure 5-15**.

monocular cues visual clues about depth and distance that can be perceived using information from only one eye.

- *Interposition* When one object blocks part of another from our view, we see the blocked object as farther away.
- *Elevation* We see objects that are higher in our visual plane as farther away than those that are lower.
- *Texture gradient* We can see more details of textured surfaces, such as the wood grain on a restaurant table, that are closer to us.
- *Linear perspective* Parallel lines seem to converge in the distance.
- *Shading* We are accustomed to light, such as sunlight, coming from above us. We use differences in the shading of light from the top to the bottom of our field of view to judge size and distance of objects.
- *Clarity or arial perspective* We tend to see closer objects with more clarity than objects that are further away. Realizing that this is sometimes referred to as a fog or smog effect will *clarify* what we mean by it.
- *Familiar size* Once we have learned the sizes of objects, such as people or restaurant plates, we assume that they stay the same size, so objects that look smaller than usual must be farther away than usual.
- *Relative size* When we look at two objects we know are about the same size, if one seems smaller than the other, we see it as farther away than the other.
- *Motion parallax* If we look out the side window of a moving car or train, objects that are closer to us appear to move past us more quickly than do objects that are further away (and very distant objects, like mountains, sometimes do not appear to move at all).

FIGURE 5-15 Monocular depth cues. How many monocular depth cues can you identify in this photograph of the Taj Mahal in India?

Pavement Patty. Would seeing this on the road ahead slow you down? The BCAA Traffic Safety Foundation and West Vancouver District had an artist design a decal that when applied flat on the road creates a three-dimensional image of what appears to be a child on the road. The image of "Pavement Patty," which plays with our two-dimensional depth cues, really made drivers slow down during its week on the road.

(a) (b)

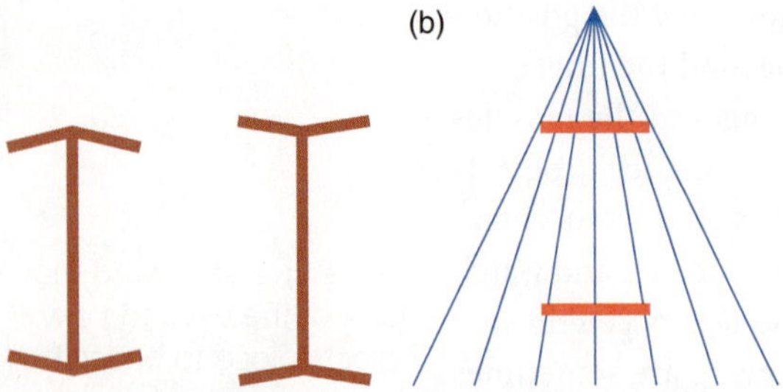

FIGURE 5-16 Perceptual illusions. (a) The Müller-Lyer illusion: The line on the right appears longer, but both lines are the same length. (b) The Ponzo illusion: The converging lines make the upper bar seem larger, but both bars are identical in length.

Although some studies show that we can perceive depth at very early ages, and may even be born with some depth perception abilities, top-down processing also plays a part in depth processing (Banks & Salapatek, 1983). We use our memories of the sizes of objects around us, for example, to help judge depth.

Artists use monocular depth cues to help us "see" depth in their two-dimensional representations. In essence, they create an illusion of depth. Because visual perception happens nearly automatically, we are quite susceptible to such visual illusions. For example, people from cultures that have a lot of architecture and structures featuring straight edges, such as the United States and Canada, are easily fooled by the Ponzo illusion and Müller-Lyer illusion, shown in **Figure 5-16**, which both take advantage of our tendency to use linear perspective to judge distance (Berry, 1992; Brislin & Keating, 1976).

perceptual constancies our top-down tendency to view objects as unchanging, despite shifts in the environmental stimuli we receive.

Seeing What We Expect to See: Perceptual Constancies Top-down processing also contributes to **perceptual constancies**, our tendency to view objects as unchanging in some ways, even though the actual visual sensations we receive are constantly shifting. We tend to see the food on our plate as the same colours, for example, even when a restaurant owner dims the lights for the evening and the actual light waves we are receiving change in intensity, a phenomenon known as colour *constancy* (Schiffman, 1996).

Another consistency, *size consistency*, helps us in depth perception, as noted above. Once we have learned the size of an object, we expect it to stay the same. Top-down processing, based on our memory of the object's size, leads us to assume that if it looks smaller than usual, it is probably far away, instead of thinking that the object has somehow shrunk. As with our other perceptual processes, perceptual constancies, while usually very useful in helping us understand the world, can sometimes lead us to "see" illusions. A common size illusion, for example, is the moon illusion. The moon stays the same size all the time, but when we view it close to a horizon it appears much bigger than when we see it farther from the horizon; the landscapes and objects we are viewing the moon through strip away some of the size constancy effect and we see the moon as larger (see **Figure 5-17**) (Kaufman & Rock, 1989).

FIGURE 5-17 The moon illusion. The moon is the same size all the time, but it appears larger near the horizon than higher in the sky, partly because no depth cues exist in space.

Once we have formed expectations about the shape of an object, we also experience *shape constancy* (Gazzaniga, 1995). We may get visual input of only the edge of a plate as our server carries it toward us, for example, but we perceive the plate as a round disk. A famous illusion based on both shape and size constancy involves the Ames room, shown in **Figure 5-18**. The person on the right-hand side looks huge compared with the one on the left. Why? First, we expect the room to be square, but it actually is irregularly shaped. Second, because we think the room is square, we believe that both people are the same distance from us, leading us to perceive one as much larger than the other. You may notice that even when you know how this illusion works, the people's respective sizes don't look right—indicating how strongly our expectations affect our perception.

Sight — HOW WE DEVELOP

Newborn infants are capable of seeing, but their visual acuity is much less than it will be after a few months. For a short time after birth, human babies focus mostly on contrasts. For example, babies will stare at the hairline of their caregiver instead of the face.

By the time babies are about 2 months old, visual acuity has improved and infants seem to focus intently on faces. Their focal range is limited, though. They see objects best that are within a foot away. Perhaps not coincidentally, this is about the distance people tend to place their faces when interacting with babies. Over the next several months, our visual acuity improves so that by the end of the eighth month, vision in babies is quite similar to that of normal adults. These early life changes in vision are due to the postnatal development of the visual nervous system. As we will see next, proper development of the visual system requires visual experience during a specific part of early life.

FIGURE 5-18 The Ames room. This specially constructed room is trapezoidal in shape, with sloping floors and ceilings. An observer can see inside only through a peephole, using one eye, so that the room appears normal. Because the observer assumes both people in the room are the same distance from him, he "sees" the people as being very different in size.

Sight WHEN THINGS GO WRONG

Today, many common vision problems can be corrected. Increasingly common laser surgeries or the lenses in glasses or contacts can help people cope with nearsightedness, or difficulty seeing things clearly far away, and farsightedness, problems seeing near objects clearly, for example. Eye-care practitioners help with a variety of other problems as well. Sometimes, however, there is no treatment available, or treatment is begun too late to prevent people from losing vision in one or both eyes.

Amblyopia To see the world as a whole, both eyes must work together to produce not two separate images, but one comprehensive image. To do this, motor control of both eyes is important. Newborn infants often do not move their eyes in tandem. It is not uncommon for parents to report concern that their young infants sometimes appear to have crossed eyes. This is a normal characteristic that typically resolves itself within a few months after birth as the eye muscles and the motor system that controls them mature.

Some people, however, do not naturally develop coordinated movement of both eyes. This condition is called *strabismus* and affects about 2 percent of the population. To avoid seeing double images, children with strabismus will rely on the visual information from one eye while ignoring information from other. Strabismus is commonly treated by surgery or by having the child wear a patch over the stronger eye, thus forcing the child to use the weaker one. If children are treated during early life, their normal binocular vision can be preserved.

Sometimes what we expect is not what we get. Magnetic Hill near Moncton, New Brunswick, creates an odd impression. Which way would you expect this car to roll if it is placed in neutral and its brakes released? It looks like it should roll away from the camera, but in fact it would roll back toward the camera. The explanation has nothing to do with magnetism, but is rather an optical illusion created by the landscape suggesting that the hill runs the opposite of the way it is actually sloped. See a video version here: www.youtube.com/watch?v=F3jDOFelogg&feature=related.

If strabismus remains uncorrected past the age of about 6 years of age, however, it will eventually lead to a loss of visual abilities in the weaker eye, or *amblyopia*. Amblyopia can be a permanent condition that results from abnormal development of the brain's visual cortex. As we discussed in Chapter 3, many development psychologists suggest that there are not only sensitive periods when we can develop certain skills with greater ease than at other times in our lives, but also "critical periods," which are the *only* times during which certain development can take place. Amblyopia develops if we do not receive visual stimulation from both eyes during the critical period of development for the normal maturation of the visual brain. After about the age of 6 years, the brains of children with strabismus seem to lose the ability to use information from both eyes and instead process inputs only from one eye.

Blindness About 278,000 people in Canada suffer from visual impairments. Of them, 108,000 have impairments

A life of accomplishment. Braille, devised in 1821 by blind Frenchman Louis Braille, has greatly improved the level of accomplishment and quality of life of people who are sightless. Here a blind computer developer reads Braille at his workstation.

that are total or so severe that they are legally blind (National Coalition for Visual Health, 2008). There are many potential causes of blindness. Some are congenital, or present at birth, while others are acquired later in life. Diseases that can produce blindness include diabetes, glaucoma, and macular degeneration.

Since humans rely so heavily on visual information, living without adequate visual input is very challenging. A number of devices have been created to help blind people live independently. Braille, a system of reading that involves touch, has significantly improved quality of life for the blind. Braille uses various combinations of raised dots to replace traditional printed letters and numbers. Visually impaired individuals can become so proficient at reading Braille that they can actually read faster than people with normal vision typically read printed material. Researchers have found that blind individuals who become experts at reading Braille are actually using parts of their "visual" brain to process the sophisticated tactile information. Neuroimaging studies have shown that parts of the occipital and temporal cortices that normally process visual information are activated in blind individuals while they read Braille. It is also noteworthy that the individuals with congenital blindness use more of their visual brains to read Braille than do those who become blind later in life. This may be another example of a critical period at work.

The acquisition of Braille reading skills as a child may allow for the reorganization of the visual system to serve some new function. Learning Braille later in life may lead to less dramatic reorganization because those parts of the visual brain have already become "hard-wired," or less plastic and open to change (Amedi et al., 2005). It also seems to be the case that many blind individuals are able to purpose some of their visual system neural wiring to assist them in processing speech. Some blind people are able to turn up the speed of the devices that play them audio books to such a rate that they can get though three books in the time it takes a sighted person to read just one (Dietrich et al., 2010; Hertrich et al., 2009). This is another example of neural plasticity, or the brain's ability to adapt to new ways of interacting with the world.

The Other Senses: Vestibular and Kinesthetic Senses

How do you know when you are moving if your eyes are closed? As you wake up and before you open your eyes, how can you tell if you are lying flat on your bed or are propped up on a bunch of pillows? Why is it that many spinning carnival rides, some movie scenes, and some boat trips make some people throw up? The answers to all of these questions involve your kinesthetic and vestibular systems. Receptor cells in your muscles respond if they are squeezed and their shape is changed by movement, thus they tell us when our muscles are moving; other cells respond when stretched and tell us that our muscles are working hard. This information tells us whether we are still or moving in a particular direction without having to look—this is our *kinesthetic sense* (Schmukler, 1995).

Our *vestibular sense* is located in the semicircular canals of our inner ear where the fluid the canals contain shifts as we move in space—standing up, lying down, or swaying from side to side. The movement of the fluid is detected by hair cells embedded in a gelatinous substance that gets shifted around when our inner ear fluid moves and provides special information about our body position. Most of the time our vestibular system provides us with body movement and location information that matches the visual information provided by our eyes. However, when we are on a rolling boat, our visual and vestibular information do not match up well and we can start to feel quite ill. Ride-related illness may be partially due to a similar phenomenon, but is also likely due to our inner ear's vestibular reporting functions being overwhelmed by spinning and sudden jerky motions. If you start to feel sick at the carnival or in a boat, look into the far (and stable) distance and that may calm your inner ear. If not, try closing your eyes and taking a nap, or try chewing gum; both work to calm the inner ear (Gahlinger, 2000).

Before You Go On

www.wiley.com/go/comer

SCAN TO GET THE ANSWERS

What Do You Know?

16. What are rods and cones?
17. What are the two theories of colour vision and how do they work together?
18. What do the "what" and "where" pathways in the brain do?
19. What are the two major types of depth perception cues and what is the difference between them?
20. What is strabismus, how is it treated, and what can happen if it is not treated promptly?
21. Where is our vestibular sense located and how does it work?

What Do You Think?

Is the cliché, "Seeing is believing," really true? Why or why not?

Summary

- Sensation is the process of converting physical stimuli from our environment into neural impulses that the brain can process. Perception is the process of interpreting the neural signals to understand the information we receive.

Common Features of Sensation and Perception

LEARNING OBJECTIVE 1 Describe characteristics shared by all the senses, including receptor cells, transduction, and thresholds, and differentiate between top-down and bottom-up processes of perception.

- Our sensory systems convert physical stimuli into neural information with specialized cells called sensory receptor cells that convert a specific form of environmental stimuli into neural impulses by a process called sensory transduction.
- The conversion of physical stimuli into neural impulses only occurs when the stimuli reach a certain level, or threshold. The absolute threshold is the minimum level of a stimulus we can detect. The difference threshold is the smallest difference we can detect between two similar stimuli.
- Our sensory systems are set up to detect change. With continuous exposure to a stimulus, adaptation occurs.

The Chemical Senses: Smell and Taste

LEARNING OBJECTIVE 2 Summarize the biological changes that underlie smell and taste.

- Smell, our olfactory sense, converts chemical odorants into neural signals that the brain can use. Taste, our gustatory sense, is closely intertwined with smell. Most flavours are a combination of scents with the five basic tastes we can discern: sweet, salty, sour, bitter, and umami.
- Taste buds in papillae on the tongue convert chemicals in our food to neural signals the brain can use. Taste receptors and smell receptors are routinely replaced, since they are more vulnerable to damage than other sensory receptors.
- Information about smell goes directly from the olfactory bulb to the olfactory cortex. Areas of the brain that process smells and tastes are plastic, or changeable. Processing of smells also sometimes overlaps with emotions and memories.
- Our preferred tastes change as we mature from childhood to adulthood, probably from a combination of learning and physical changes in the mouth.
- True disorders of taste are rare; people more frequently lose part or all of their sense of smell. Anosmia can present safety risks and diminish pleasure in life.

The Tactile or Cutaneous Senses: Touch, Pressure, Pain, Vibration

LEARNING OBJECTIVE 3 Describe how the different senses of touch work and what can happen when things go wrong.

- A variety of sensory receptors throughout our bodies convert touch, pressure, or temperature stimuli into neural impulses that our brains can perceive.
- The sensory cortex of the brain maps touch sensations. Especially sensitive or important body parts receive disproportionately large representation in the cortex.
- Pain travels to the brain via both a fast pathway and a slow pathway.
- The gate control theory of pain suggests that certain patterns of neural activity can close a "gate" so that pain information does not reach parts of the brain where it is perceived.
- Medical professionals continue to search for ways to relieve people's chronic pain. Opiate drugs that simulate natural pain-killing endorphins or enkephalins are

addictive. Sometimes practitioners resort to neurosurgery, which stops a patient from receiving all touch signals.

- People who have lost body parts surgically or through accidents often feel phantom sensations in the missing body part. These may be related to reorganization of the somatosensory cortex after an amputation.

The Auditory Sense: Hearing

LEARNING OBJECTIVE 4 Summarize what happens when we hear.

- The frequency and amplitude of sound waves produce our perceptions of pitch and loudness of sounds.
- When sounds enter the ear, they move the ear drum, which sets in motion the ossicles. The last of these, the stirrup, vibrates the oval window, setting into motion fluid in the cochlea. Hair cells on the basilar membrane in the cochlea transduce movements along the basilar membrane into neural signals the brain can interpret.
- Frequency theory suggests that patterns in the firing rates of the neurons are perceived as different sounds. Place theory suggests that information from different locations along the basilar membrane is related to different qualities of sound.
- Top-down processing lets us use the general loudness of sounds, as well as differences in the signals received from each ear, to determine location of a sound.
- Different pitches are represented in a tonotopic map in the auditory cortex of the brain. Association areas of the cortex help us recognize familiar sounds, including speech.
- The brain integrates information from multiple sensory systems to enable the appropriate recognition and response to stimuli. Some people experience an overlap of sensory systems, known as synesthesia.
- As young children, we experience a sensitive period during which it is especially easy for us to learn auditory information, including language and music. Some people, particularly those exposed to pure tones during this sensitive period, develop absolute pitch.
- Common hearing problems include hearing loss and deafness, as well as hearing unwanted sounds, such as tinnitus.

The Visual Sense: Sight

LEARNING OBJECTIVE 5 Describe key processes in visual sensation and perception.

- Rods and cones in the retina at the back of the eye change light into neural impulses. Cones provide detailed vision and help us perceive colour, while rods provide information about intensity of light.
- Two different theories in combination—trichomatic theory and opponent process theory—explain a good deal of how we perceive colour.
- The fovea at the centre of the retina contains only cones and provides our sharpest vision. We have a blind spot where the optic nerve leaves the retina to carry information to the brain.
- Damage to the brain can produce deficits in sensation, as well as abnormal sensory experiences.
- Top-down processing is involved in much visual perception. Gestalt theorists have identified several principles by which we recognize stimuli even when visual inputs are limited. We use binocular and monocular cues for depth perception. Perceptual constancies, based on learning from previous experiences, help us to see things as stable despite constant shifts in our visual inputs. These top-down processes can be "fooled" by visual illusions.
- Without adequate visual stimulation through both eyes during a critical period of life, we may not develop binocular vision, a condition known as amblyopia.
- Blind individuals can use other sensory modalities to compensate for the loss of visual information. Learning Braille with touch involves the use of brain areas normally used for vision.

Key Terms

TYING IT TOGETHER

The study of sensation and perception is closely connected to the study of all other areas of psychology. Throughout this chapter, we have stressed how sensation and perception interface with psychology's various subfields, including our highlighted sections on brain function, individual differences, abnormal functioning, and development. To remind you of how sensation and perception are tied to other psychology subfields and issues, we have selected some interesting points from throughout the chapter.

WHAT HAPPENS IN THE BRAIN?

- The brain normally integrates information from multiple sensory systems. In people who experience synesthesia, brain areas for one sense are activated by stimuli related to different senses, so that they might, for example, hear colours.
- Different parts of our brains are active in figuring out what we see from those that help us figure out where things are when we see them.
- Blind people who learn to read Braille at early ages actually use parts of their visual cortex to do so, in addition to areas normally associated with touch.

HOW WE DIFFER

- About one-quarter of all people are supertasters, able to discern bitter tastes that others do not even notice.
- On average, women have more sensory receptors for pain in their faces than men do.
- Only about one person in 10,000 in Western countries develops absolute pitch, the ability to identify tones heard in isolation. More people who speak tonal languages have absolute pitch.
- About four people in 100 in North America are tone deaf.

WHEN THINGS GO WRONG

- People rarely lose their sense of taste. Most problems with taste are related to loss of sense of smell.
- When we damage taste buds or odour receptors in the nose, they are replaced, but damage to other sensory receptors, such as photoreceptors and hair cells, is permanent. They are not replaced.
- People who experience phantom sensations in missing body parts usually feel things they actually felt before losing the body part.

HOW WE DEVELOP

- All of our sensory systems begin to develop during fetal life. We can hear, feel, smell, and taste before we are born.
- Sight is our least developed sense at birth.
- Children have more taste buds in more locations in their mouths than adults, which may explain in part why they dislike many new foods.

Psychology Around Us

The Ups and Downs of Visual Perception

"Seeing Is Not Always Believing"

View this in Action
WILEY PLUS
www.wileyplus.com

Video Lab Exercise

Whether driving through the streets of a city, looking out a train window at the passing landscape, or viewing events on the ground from a plane above, you are relying on your visual senses. Come along for a video ride in which nothing can be taken for granted and during which you will be asked to not only enjoy the view, but to explain it, ignore it, adjust to it, or change it.

As you are working on this on-line exercise, consider the following questions:

- What does this lab exercise say about both the power and the limits of visual perception?
- What's going on in your brain as you correctly observe objects, adapt to visual events, or are fooled by visual illusions?
- What role does attention play in visual perception?
- How might your auditory sense affect what you see?

CHAPTER 6

Consciousness

CHAPTER OUTLINE

- When We Are Awake: Conscious Awareness
- Preconscious and Unconscious States
- When We Are Asleep
- Hypnosis
- Meditation
- Psychoactive Drugs *What Happens in the Brain*

AWARENESS AND DRIVER PERFORMANCE

If you have your driver's licence, think back to what it was like when you first started to drive. Fasten your seatbelt, adjust your seat, check your mirrors, start the car, check your front end clearance, check your mirrors, shoulder check, and pull out when safe to do so, look far ahead down the road, look for hazards, watch cross streets and between parked cars for vehicles and pedestrians, watch oncoming vehicles, watch the vehicle following you, prepare to stop when approaching a light, decelerate smoothly, check your mirrors to ensure those behind you are stopping, and ease up on the brake so that the front end of your vehicle does not bounce up as you come to a complete stop. You have made it a whole block, and you had to pay conscious attention to each and every one of the things mentioned above. Who thought driving would be so hard! Good thing there was only one other person (a licensed adult driver) in the car with you, and good thing your cell phone was turned off and the radio was not on! Two months later you have practised driving a lot and have gained experience; now you do most of those driving behaviours automatically (unconsciously). You can listen to the radio while driving and think about your plans for the day or evening, and yet still scan for hazards, anticipate potential problems, remain aware of the location of other vehicles around you, and stop smoothly without really thinking consciously about any of it—perhaps with the exception of your driving instructor's suggestion that you remember to shoulder check your blind spots before changing lanes or turning. Our consciousness and awareness is an amazingly flexible thing. With experience and a commitment to maintaining a sufficient level of attention on our driving, we can drive quite comfortably most of the time.

Consciousness is often defined as our immediate awareness of our internal and external states. But how aware is "aware"? Sometimes we are keenly aware of something, and other times only dimly so. In addition, sometimes we do not seem to be paying much attention to complex stimuli, yet we wind up recalling information about them later. Consciousness is one of the most intriguing—as well as one of the most mysterious—things that psychologists study.

The study of consciousness has undergone many historical shifts. As you may recall from Chapter 1, early psychologists defined psychology entirely as the study of consciousness. The influential American psychologist William James, for example, noted that our conscious awareness continually shifts based on what we're paying attention to and how intensely we are attending (Schooler, 2011; Singer, 2003).

At the same time, we feel continuity from moment to moment. As the opening story

consciousness our immediate awareness of our internal and external states.

describes, many things we do, like driving, require little or none of our conscious awareness. Yet if that changes while we are driving, we are able to turn more of our attention to the new situation and respond in a safe and appropriate manner. James coined the term "stream of consciousness" to signify how we experience our conscious life, because consciousness, like a running stream, keeps moving, yet seems to be the same.

Heightened awareness. Navigating an automobile requires full concentration for new drivers such as this individual. This is not the case, however, for people who have been at it for years, many of whom are barely conscious of the driving-related tasks they are performing.

You may also recall from Chapter 1 that one of psychology's most influential theories of consciousness has been Sigmund Freud's psychoanalytic theory. Freud introduced the idea that we can have unconscious thoughts and feelings of which we are not even aware. Right up to his death in 1939, Freud kept defining and revising his ideas about states of consciousness, and we will discuss these in some detail later in this chapter (Elisha, 2011).

Partly in response to the difficulties of conducting research on elusive concepts, such as the unconscious mind, many researchers during the first half of the twentieth

Going Toward the Light: Near-Death Experiences

A man lies dying. He hears himself pronounced dead by his doctor. He feels himself rushing through a long, dark tunnel and suddenly finds himself outside his body, observing it from a distance as the doctor tries to revive him. Soon, a loving, warm spirit—a being of light—comes to meet him and directs him through a panoramic review of the major events of his life. He feels himself approaching a barrier—a sort of border between earthly existence and some other state. He is overwhelmed by joy but must return to his body, for the time has not come for him to die. Later, he has trouble describing this experience, but it profoundly affects his life and his feelings about death.

Thus does Dr. Raymond Moody describe a typical near-death experience (NDE) in his best-selling 1975 book, *Life after Life*, which introduced NDEs into the popular culture. Typically these experiences include some or all of the features just described—the tunnel, the out-of-body experience, the bright light, and so forth. Over the past several decades, many people have reported having such experiences (Carter, 2010; Carey, 2009). The question is, what causes them?

Some observers offer a religious or supernatural explanation, saying that the soul leaves the body during an NDE and encounters a "spirit of light" (Sheikh et al., 2007). Moody himself has adopted this view.

But many researchers disagree and look instead to more scientific explanations (Nelson et al., 2006). Some point out, for example, that certain drugs produce the same effects as NDEs. Perhaps the brain, under great stress, releases chemicals that, like these drugs, induce hallucinations (Augustine, 2007). Others attribute NDEs to the brain's constant efforts to process our sensory experiences and maintain a stable sense of reality. As a person nears death, the senses shut down, sending faulty information that the brain tries to interpret as best it can. This effort may lead to misinterpretations about where the body is in space, or produce the sensation of being in a dark tunnel with bright light at the end. These and other scientific explanations share the notion that NDEs often reflect an altered state of consciousness that is brought about by sensory arousal, a heightened state of awareness, and the brain's ongoing efforts to determine what we experience as real.

century, especially those in North America, shifted their interest from consciousness to observable behaviour and, as you read in Chapter 1, equated psychology with behaviourism (Moore, 2010; Baars, 2003). Theorists and researchers in Europe, however, continued to pay significant attention to consciousness, and even unconsciousness.

Test your own powers of attention. Before finishing this introduction, take a break and watch the video at http://viscog.beckman.illinois.edu/flashmovie/15.php. Count how many times the players in white shirts complete a pass of the basketball.

During the latter part of the twentieth century, with important developments in neuroscience and computer technology, consciousness reemerged as a topic of major interest in psychology (Frith, 2003). With the help of neuroimaging techniques, investigators have been able to meaningfully explore the relationship between brain activity and various states of consciousness (Baars & Gage, 2010). Indeed, a considerable body of research is now directed at the study of conscious, less conscious, and non-conscious states (Revonsuo, 2010). ■

When We Are Awake: Conscious Awareness

LEARNING OBJECTIVE 1

Define different levels of conscious awareness and describe key brain structures and functions associated with those levels.

As the opening vignette illustrates, *attention* is a key part of our conscious awareness. Psychiatric researcher John Ratey (2001) has pointed out that "Before we can be conscious of something... we have to pay attention to it." At the same time, attention does not equal consciousness; we need something more. To be fully conscious of something, we must be *aware* that we are attending to it (Lewis, 2010).

Conscious awareness of ourselves, our needs, and how to satisfy them has directly helped us in survival, contributing mightily to our evolutionary progress. To be conscious of our thirst, for example, is to understand that water is necessary to quench it, and to know that we may need to plan to get or have water even before we are thirsty. Clearly, conscious awareness involves elements beyond attention (Sewards & Sewards 2000), and in fact, a number of such elements have been suggested by theorists. Three of the most prominent are *monitoring*, *remembering*, and *planning*.

- We *monitor* ourselves and our environment as we decide (implicitly) what items to be aware of (Kannape et al., 2010; Glaser & Kihlstrom, 2005). A car that is weaving as it approaches us might catch our awareness, for example.
- To be aware of a current event, we often must bring forth *memories* of past experiences and previously acquired knowledge and skills (Johannsdottir & Herdman, 2010; Baars, 2003). Such memories establish a context for our current situation, provide us with the motivation and ability to focus on it, and may even become part of the present situation. We might remember that on previous times when it was snowing the road by the stop sign at the end of the block was slippery, and add that data into our conscious calculations about speed and stopping distance as we drive in that direction.

No room for error. As we interact with our environment, we constantly monitor both ourselves and the situations at hand to help ensure that we attend to key features of the interactions. When performing a dangerous task, such as climbing a mountain, careful monitoring can take on life-and-death importance.

- *Control* and *planning* are also often at work. In fact, to help us plan for the future—from which route to travel on our way to college or university, to what we will major in—we often bring into conscious awareness images, events, and scenarios that have never occurred. In such cases, conscious awareness may help us to initiate more effective behaviours or make wiser decisions.

PSYCHOLOGY AROUND US A Different Kind of Thoughtlessness

Human beings have a remarkable ability to multi-task—to keep whole sets of complicated tasks and ideas in mind while still managing to engage in the basic activities of living. On the other hand, consciousness sometimes has "blind spots"—episodes in which conscious behaviours and intentions seem to break down.

Dr. Baba Shiv, a marketing professor, conducted a study with undergraduates at the University of Iowa (Ferraro, Shiv, & Bettman, 2005). He asked students to memorize a number that was either two digits long or seven digits long. After the memorization task, the students were asked to go down a hall to another room where they were to be tested on their recollections. On the way down the hall, however, a stranger (actually a confederate of Shiv's) stopped them and offered them a snack—either a nutritious, healthy fruit salad, or a decadent, tempting chocolate cake.

Shiv found something interesting—people who had been required to hold a seven-digit number in mind chose the chocolate cake twice as often as the people who were holding on to only a two-digit number. Shiv believed that this happened because the cognitive processes of people holding seven digit numbers in mind were too overloaded to have the conversations we usually have with ourselves when we are offered chocolate cake. That is, their minds were too overloaded to consider notions such as "Chocolate cake is just too fattening" or "I don't want my teeth to get all chocolatey." Shiv also believed that this is the kind of thing that happens to our cognitive processing whenever we get stressed or overloaded in life.

Something to think about the next time you reach for the cookie dough ice cream when you're studying for an exam or fighting with a girlfriend or boyfriend.

When We Are Awake WHAT HAPPENS IN THE BRAIN?

Brian Kolb and Ian Wishaw, working at the University of Lethbridge, are two respected Canadian neuroscientists. They argue that multiple brain processes and structures must be operating simultaneously for us to be conscious of our world or ourselves (Kolb & Whishaw, 2009). In fact, research has shown that when we are awake, most if not all of the neurons in our brains are constantly active. Of course, certain neurons become especially active when an individual is stimulated by particular objects or events, but even in the absence of such stimulation, neurons are still active at a steady, low level and are communicating with other neurons (Hopkin, 2010; Llinas & Ribary, 2001).

Recall from Chapter 4 that neurons tend to work together in groups, or *networks*, and those networks become more and more efficient with repeated use (Jones, 2007). For us to experience conscious awareness of something, such as a thought or pedestrian about to run out into the road in front of us, many of these networks must become particularly active at once. While one set of networks is enabling us to pay attention to the stimulus, other biological events must also be at work, enabling us to be aware and recognize that we are attending. Still others are allowing us to monitor, remember, and control.

Researchers have not yet pinpointed all of the brain areas and events that are responsible for such complex processing, but research has suggested that two areas of great importance to consciousness are the *cerebral cortex*, the brain's outer covering of cells, and the *thalamus*, the brain structure that often relays sensory information from various parts of the brain to the cerebral cortex (Haber, 2003).

Think back to the basketball video. Did you immediately notice the gorilla among the players, or did you miss it? What do you think that implies about your consciousness?

The work of Ronald Resnick (Resnick, 2000; Resnick, O'Regan, & Clark, 1997) at the University of British Columbia shows that unless you pay attention to the appropriate aspects of a scene, you can miss even the most conspicuous events around you (like a gorilla walking through a video you are watching). If you go to Resnick's website, you can download several short videos containing examples of inattentional blindness, which is basically our failure to notice things around us to which we are not paying attention (http://psyclab1.psych.ubc.ca/~viscoglab/demonstrations/).

The Cerebral Cortex Evidence has accumulated that some areas of the brain are responsible for attention, while other areas—particularly ones in the cerebral cortex—are in charge of one's awareness of that attention. Investigations by Lawrence Weiskrantz (2002, 2000, 2009; Sahraie et al., 2010) on *blindsight* illustrate how this works in the visual realm.

Weiskrantz studied people whose visual areas in the cerebral cortex had been destroyed, leaving them blind, so far as they were aware. When Weiskrantz presented such people with a spot of light on a screen and asked them to point to it, the individuals were totally unaware of the light and could not fulfill the request. Yet, when he told the same individuals to "just point anywhere," they typically pointed in the direction of the light. Similarly, these individuals could generally avoid chairs, tables, and other objects as they walked through a room, denying all the while that they were seeing anything at all. In short, the patients in Weiskrantz's studies could and did readily attend to visual objects, yet because the visual areas in their cerebral cortex had been destroyed, they were unaware of those objects. Weiskrantz and others have concluded that the areas of the brain that help us *attend* to visual stimuli are different from the visual areas in the cerebral cortex that help us to be *aware* that we are attending to such stimuli.

Remarkable studies of "split-brain" patients, conducted by investigators Roger Sperry and Michael Gazzaniga, also point to the cerebral cortex as a centre of conscious awareness (Gazzaniga, 2010, 2005; Colvin & Gazzaniga, 2007; Sperry, 1998, 1982). As you will recall from Chapter 4, people with severe seizure disorders can sometimes be helped by cutting the nerve fibres of their *corpus callosum*, the brain structure that connects the two hemispheres of the brain, to keep abnormal activity from travelling from one side of the brain to the other. By carefully studying such split-brain patients, Sperry and Gazzaniga learned that the left and right sides of the cerebral cortex may play different roles in conscious awareness.

As shown in **Figure 6-1**, in the split-brain patients, the objects presented briefly in the left visual field (so that the viewer could not shift to their right visual field by moving their head or eyes) project only to the visual area in the right hemisphere (Thompson, 2000). Similarly, visual information presented to the right visual field projects only to the visual area in the left cortex.

Using this information, the investigators found that when they showed a word to a patient's left hemisphere, the individual was readily able to say and write the word. When a word was flashed to the right hemisphere, however, the individual could *not* name or write it. Apparently, the left cerebral cortex is responsible for verbal awareness.

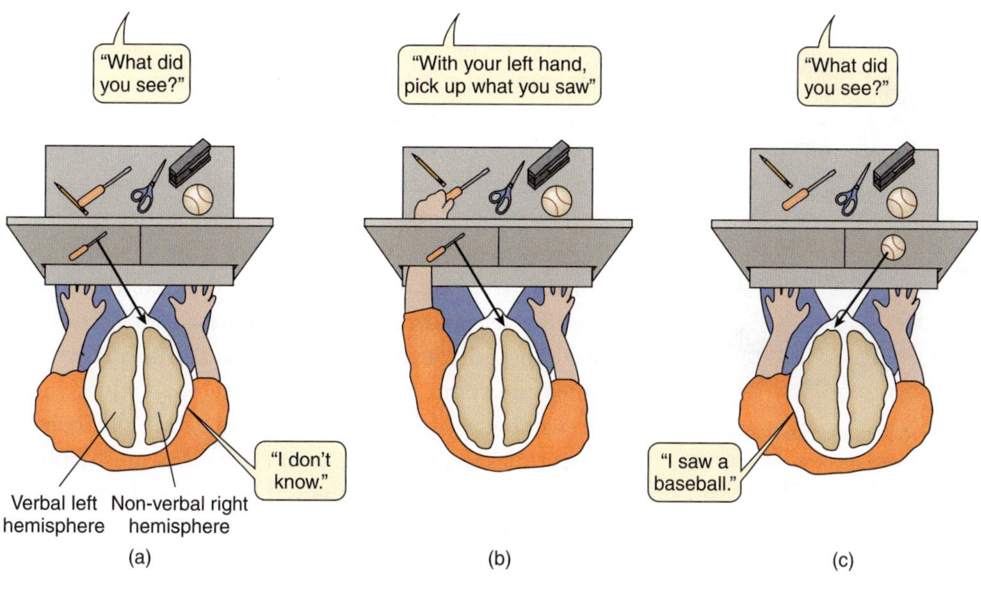

FIGURE 6-1 Split-brain research. (a) When a picture of a screwdriver is flashed to a split-brain patient's left visual field, the information goes to his non-verbal right hemisphere and he cannot name the object. (b) When instructed to feel behind a screen among a variety of objects and select the one that matches the picture just seen using his left hand (controlled by his right hemisphere), the patient correctly selects the screwdriver. (c) When a picture of a baseball is flashed to the patient's right visual field, he easily names it.

In contrast, the right cerebral cortex seems to be responsible for non-verbal forms of conscious awareness. In one study, for example, the experimenters flashed a picture of a screwdriver to the patient's right hemisphere. The individuals were then instructed to feel a variety of real objects with their left hand, from behind a screen, including a real screwdriver, and on the basis of touch, to select the object that matched the picture they had just seen; all correctly selected a screwdriver. This suggests that the right cerebral cortex can produce tactile awareness, and perhaps other kinds of non-verbal awareness as well, but not verbal awareness. Of course, for most of us, our two hemispheres are connected, and these various kinds of awareness occur simultaneously, helping to produce a broad and complete sense of conscious awareness.

The Thalamus We might think of the networks of neurons in the brain as similar to the different train lines in a complicated subway system, like that of London, England. For trains to get from place to place on schedule without collision, a train conductor or a system manager (or even a whole group of them) must oversee the process. Researchers have nominated several brain areas as potential conductors, involved in routing messages along the proper neural network "subway lines" of our brains. Two of the most prominent candidates are the *intralaminar nuclei* and *midline nuclei* of the *thalamus* (Benarroch, 2011, 2008; Van der Werf et al., 2003; 2002). Research indicates that the intralaminar and midline nuclei receive and project long axons to neurons throughout the cerebral cortex, including areas that, as we have seen, are involved in conscious awareness (Ratey, 2001).

Consistent with this theory, investigators have observed that people actually lose all consciousness and enter a deep coma if their intralaminar and midline nuclei are broadly damaged. If, however, the damage to the nuclei occurs in only one hemisphere, individuals lose awareness of only half of their bodies. They become unaware of all events that occur on one side of their visual field, for example, or unaware of all objects that touch one side of their body (Van der Werf, Witter, & Groenewegen, 2002). In short, the intralaminar and midline nuclei seem to play an important role in conscious awareness.

Alert Consciousness

HOW WE DEVELOP

There have been a number of attempts to identity consciousness in infants. As we saw in Chapter 3, there is evidence that even babies can direct their attention, hold concepts in mind, and engage in planned or intentional behaviours—the component skills of consciousness. Because babies are not yet able to talk very well, however, it's difficult to determine how aware they are that their experiences are things happening to them, or even whether they are fully aware of themselves as separate beings from others, a concept known as *sense of self*.

Hello there. Does this baby know he is looking at himself in the mirror? We can test this by secretly putting red makeup on his nose and then watching how he reacts in front of the mirror. When babies look into a mirror and then touch their own nose because it is red, they show us that they are aware of themselves as separate beings from others.

Researchers have developed some ingenious ways to try to determine when babies first experience a conscious sense of self. In one test, called the Rouge test, experimenters secretly dabbed red makeup on babies' noses while pretending to wipe them. Then they placed the babies in front of a mirror. The researchers reasoned that babies who had developed a sense or conscious awareness of self would see the makeup and touch their own noses, while those who did not understand they were looking themselves in the mirror would try to touch the makeup on the baby in the mirror. Based on such tests, it seems that most children develop a stable concept of the self by around 18 months of age (Lewis, 2010; Amsterdam, 1972; Gallup, 1970; Lewis & Brooks-Gunn, 1979).

Some researchers suggest that the early cognitive development we discussed in Chapter 3 and the development of consciousness contribute to one another. That is, if infants demonstrate the ability to develop concepts and to think through their behaviours if they cannot express such thinking, they should be viewed as having a rudimentary sense of self-consciousness. Without this rudimentary sense of consciousness, babies would not be able to develop any concepts at all (Lewis, 2010; Mandler, 2004).

Other theorists suggest that consciousness itself is rooted in language and representation. Because babies do not have language—the ability to let words represent events and experiences—they cannot reflect on their thoughts and behaviours and do not have full consciousness yet (Neuman & Nave, 2010; Zelazo, 2004). These theorists suggest that a shift happens at around 22 months of age (about the time they start to recognize themselves in the mirror on the Rouge test), when babies show the abilities to reason inductively and to name and categorize concepts, which in turn enable them to represent concepts in a richer and deeper way.

Thus, describing how consciousness develops during awake states remains both a philosophical and empirical question, influenced in large part by how we define consciousness. The matter is further complicated by the question we asked at the beginning of this chapter: Just how aware is "aware"? We'll see next that there may be levels of alert consciousness at which we are not fully aware of all our thoughts.

Before You Go On

www.wiley.com/go/comer

What Do You Know?

1. List the core cognitive processes of consciousness.
2. What is blindsight?

What Do You Think?

What characteristics do you believe are essential to define alert consciousness?

SCAN TO GET THE ANSWERS

Preconscious and Unconscious States

LEARNING OBJECTIVE 2

Summarize the ideas of preconscious and unconscious states, including Freud's thinking on the unconscious.

Theorists often talk about different "levels of consciousness" or "degrees of consciousness," and some believe that consciousness should be distinguished from two alternative states, *preconsciousness* and *unconsciousness*.

preconsciousness level of awareness in which information can become readily available to consciousness if necessary.

Preconsciousness is a level of awareness in which information can become readily available to consciousness if necessary. Have you ever tried to remember something that you're certain you know, but just cannot recall at the moment? When something is on the tip of your tongue (a phenomenon we'll talk about again in Chapter 8), it is in your preconsciousness. When (or if) you finally do remember it, the memory has reached consciousness.

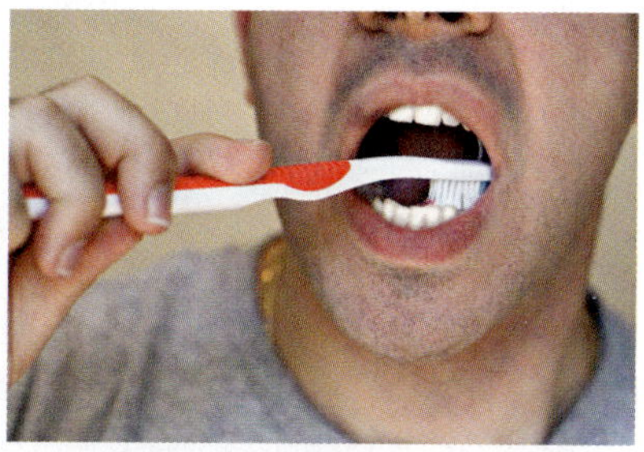

Automatic behaviours. Do you remember the details of every time you brushed your teeth in the past week?

Many of our most familiar behaviours occur during preconsciousness. Take a second—can you remember exactly what your morning ritual was this morning? What song was playing when you woke up? Did you count every tooth as you brushed it? Can you recall the details of every kilometre of your drive or ride into the college or university today? For many morning activities, you probably do things in the same order, but you do not necessarily need to plan all the steps or think about what you're doing as you move through your ritual. Preconscious behaviours of this kind are sometimes called *automatic behaviours*. As we saw at the beginning of the chapter, driving can involve automatic behaviours.

unconscious state state in which information is not easily accessible to conscious awareness.

An **unconscious state** is one in which information is not easily accessible to conscious awareness. Perhaps you cannot remember the name of someone you saw from a distance, despite being sure you know them. Or you cannot call up the name of someone who bullied you in school when you saw a stranger who reminded you of him or her. Unexpectedly, minutes or days later the name of the person or the song you could not recover earlier jumps right out of your memory. Psychoanalytic theorists, influenced by the ideas of Sigmund Freud, would suggest that something triggered the release of the appropriate memory.

Cognitive Views of the Unconscious

Throughout much of the twentieth century, scientists paid little, if any, attention to the unconscious. Rejecting Freud's psychoanalytic ideas (discussed a bit later below), they also rejected the notion that people's behaviours, thoughts, and feelings may be influenced by mental forces of which they are totally unaware. This dismissal of the unconscious has shifted dramatically in recent decades. Today, most psychologists believe that unconscious functioning does occur and a number of explanations—particularly cognitive explanations—have been proposed.

implicit memory knowledge that we have stored in memory that we are not typically aware of or able to recall at will.

Perhaps the most prominent cognitive explanation for unconscious processing points to the concept of **implicit memory** (Manelis, Hanson, & Hanson 2011; Kihlstrom et al., 2007, 2000). As we shall observe more closely in Chapter 8, cognitive theorists distinguish between two basic kinds of memory: *explicit memory* and *implicit memory.* Explicit memories involve pieces of knowledge that we are fully aware of. Explicit memory is the conscious, intentional recovery of a memory. Knowing the date of your birth is an explicit memory. Implicit memories refer to knowledge that we are not typically aware of—information that we cannot recall at will, but that we use in the performance of various tasks in life.

Implicit memory is usually on display in the *skills* we acquire, such as reading, playing an instrument, driving a car, or speaking a second language. Our performance of such skills improves as we gain more and more of the knowledge, motor behaviours, and perceptual information required for the skills. These gains—that is, these implicit memories—are usually revealed to us indirectly by our improved performances, not by our consciously recalling the acquired information and experiences that led to the improvements. Shortly after learning to drive, you may realize one day that you are able to drive and talk to a passenger at the same time, for example, but not recall the exact moment that you learned how to control the wheel and pedals well enough to add the additional activity of carrying on a conversation.

PSYCHOLOGY AROUND US Snap Decisions

Freud once said: "When making a decision of minor importance, I have always found it advantageous to consider all the pros and cons. In vital matters, however, such as the choice of a mate or a profession, the decision should come from the unconscious, from somewhere within ourselves."

Many psychologists have begun to look at the benefits of "unconscious" decision-making—quick, intuitive judgments. Psychologist Gary Klein, for example, has examined decision-making in firefighters. Klein had expected that, given the huge stakes involved in fighting fires, fire chiefs typically must consider a range of scenarios and carefully weigh the pros and cons before acting. What he found instead was that when fighting fires, fire chiefs typically identify one decision immediately, run the scenario in their head, and if it doesn't have any glaring errors, they go with it. Basically, the fire chiefs let their experience automatically generate a solution (Klein, 2004).

In contrast, neuroscientist Antonio Damasio (2010) has worked extensively with patients who have suffered damage to certain parts of their prefrontal cortex. Damasio found that these perfectly intelligent individuals are only able to make "deliberate" decisions; they can only make decisions in which they have time to systematically weigh options and arrive at a clearly advantageous course of action. If they are required to make a quick choice, like when to schedule an appointment or where to go for dinner, they become paralyzed and simply can't decide. Damasio argues that intuition and unconscious decision-making allow us to operate effectively under situations of uncertainty, and that most of life's decisions, even the big ones, involve a lot of uncertainty.

Implicit memory may also involve factual information. When we vote for a particular candidate on election day, a wealth of past experiences and information may be at the root of that behaviour—childhood discussions with our parents about political parties, websites we have seen, articles we have read, political science classes we have taken, interviews or news stories we have read or heard, and more. As we mark an X on our ballot, however, we typically are not aware of all these past experiences or pieces of information.

Cognitive and cognitive neuroscience theorists see implicit memories as a part of everyday functioning, rather than as a way to keep unpleasant information from reaching our awareness (Czigler & Winkler, 2010; Kihlstrom et al., 2007, 2000). They have discovered research methods to test our unconscious—implicit—memories and have gathered evidence that explicit and implicit memories are stored in different pathways in the brain (Sheldon & Moscovitch, 2010).

Ideas about the nature of consciousness were around long before cognitive psychology started to study them. Freud developed an interesting historical perspective on consciousness. While little data has been found that support his particular view, you can see that he was quite successful in getting us to think about the possibility that there is a LOT going on in our minds to which we do not have easy or simple access.

Freud's Views of the Unconscious

Although there are many current views about the unconscious, most have some relationship to the historic (not scientific) explanation advanced by Sigmund Freud (Gödde, 2010). As we discussed in Chapter 1, Freud believed that the vast majority of our personal knowledge is located in our unconsciousness, and thus is not readily accessible (see **Figure 6-2**). According to him, one of the key functions of the unconsciousness is to house thoughts and memories too painful or disturbing for consciousness (Wilson, 2010). Indeed, Freud maintained that at some level, we may *repress* such thoughts and memories (of bullies we have known, for example), pushing them into our unconscious and preventing them from entering our conscious experience.

Freud also suggested that, although it is typically inaccessible, unconscious material can enter conscious awareness (Johnson, 2011). Have you ever meant to say one thing, but something very different comes out, often to your embarrassment? Freud identified this slip of the tongue (called a *Freudian slip*) as a moment when the mind inadvertently allows a repressed idea into consciousness. Let's say that you do not enjoy your job but you're not sure why. One day you arrive at work 15 minutes late and your boss is waiting for you. Whereas you intend to say, "I'm sorry I'm late, boss," you say instead, "I'm sorry I hate boss." Suddenly you—and your boss—are well aware of why you don't like your job!

Freud also believed that our unconscious can work against us and that people who store too many emotionally-charged memories and needs in their unconscious may eventually develop psychological disorders (as we will discuss in further detail in Chapters 13 and 16). His theory suggests that the knowledge and memories stored in the unconscious maintain their ability to influence how we think, feel, and relate to others. If we repress too much, we may experience distortions in how we feel or relate to others, and, at the same time, we may feel helpless to change. Based on this part of Freud's theory, psychoanalytic psychotherapy attempts to bring patients' unconscious material into their conscious awareness.

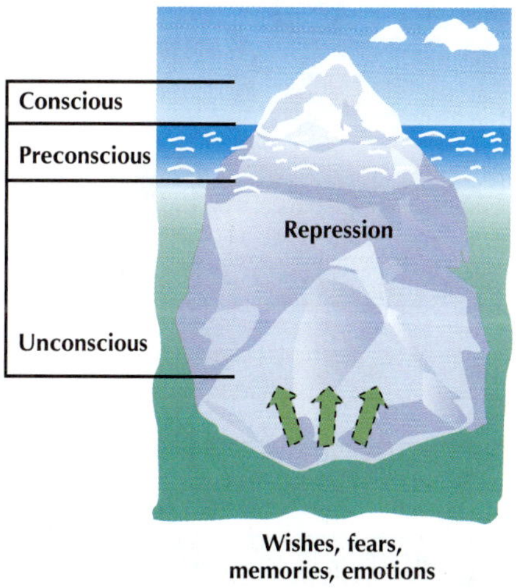

FIGURE 6-2 Freud's view of the unconscious. According to Freud, material that is relegated to the unconscious, such as repressed material, enters preconscious awareness or conscious awareness only accidentally or indirectly.

Freud's ideas about unconsciousness can be quite compelling. His ideas have been drawn into aspects of popular culture so that we often wonder what our motive is for not being able to remember something. The problem is that there is really no research data supporting most of Freud's views of the unconscious (Holmes, 1990). This does not mean that all of our mental processes are conscious. Rather, it just means that the actual nature of unconscious processing is more complex than Freud envisioned (Westen, 2002).

Before You Go On

www.wiley.com/go/comer

What Do You Know?

3. What is the difference between preconscious and unconscious states?
4. What is the importance of implicit memory in terms of the notion of the unconscious?

What Do You Think?

Do you think there are unconscious forces driving people's behaviours? If not, is it all conscious choice, or do you believe there are other explanations?

SCAN TO GET THE ANSWERS

When We Are Asleep

LEARNING OBJECTIVE 3

Describe what happens when people sleep, key theories of why we sleep and dream, and problems with sleep and how they affect functioning.

"Everyone needs to sleep." These two bees take time out from their busy agenda to sleep in a comfortable flower.

To Benjamin Franklin's famous acknowledgment that the only sure things in life are death and taxes could be added a third: that sooner or later we must—absolutely must—fall and stay asleep. Sleep is so central to our lives—indeed, most people spend 25 years of their lives asleep—that we first need to ask, what important purpose does it serve?

Why Do We Sleep?

Interestingly, despite considerable research into the matter, no consensus exists about why people need to sleep (Thakkar & Datta, 2010). After all, as we shall see, the brain does not rest when we are sleeping, nor, on the surface, does sleep offer the body much more rest than it would get by sitting down and relaxing for a while. Yet all animals, including we humans, sleep (though in different amounts) (see **Figure 6-3**), and would, in fact, die if deprived of sleep for too long.

One theory, the adaptive theory of sleep, suggests that sleep is the evolutionary outcome of self-preservation (Worthman, 2011; Rial et al., 2010). Proponents of this view suggest that organisms sleep to keep themselves away from predators that are more active at night when our visual system, which is adapted for optimal use in daylight, does not provide us with much protection (Siegel, 2009). Our ancestors, for example, tucked themselves away in safe places to keep from being eaten by nocturnal animals on the prowl. Animals that need to graze and so have less chance of hiding from predators tend to sleep less. A giraffe, for example, sleeps only two hours, whereas a bat sleeps around 20 hours (Siegel, 2005). This evolutionary argument, however, seems to account more for why we sleep at night than for why we sleep in the first place.

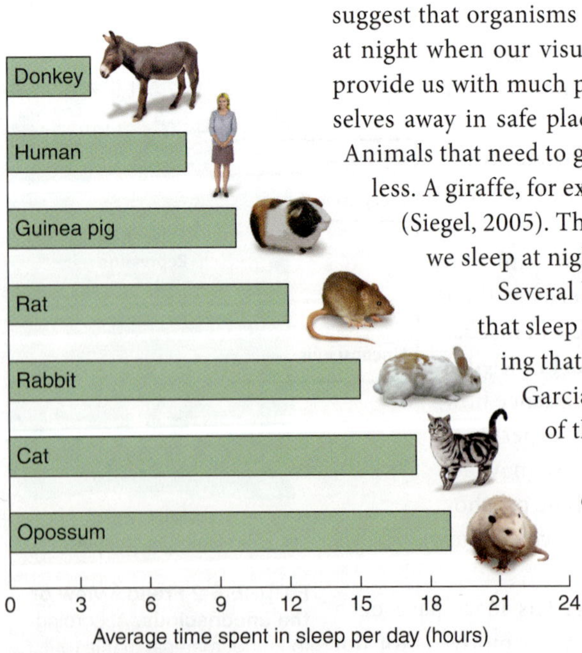

FIGURE 6-3 Sleep needs of various animals. Animals vary greatly in how much sleep they need each day. Their sleep needs are related in part to how much awake time is needed to obtain food and protect themselves from predators (Siegel, 2005).

Several biological theories of sleep have also been proposed. One suggests that sleep plays a role in the growth process, a notion consistent with the finding that the *pituitary gland* releases growth hormones during sleep (Garcia-Garcia et al., 2011; Gais et al., 2006). In fact, as we age, we release fewer of these hormones, grow less, and sleep less.

Researchers have also observed changes in neuron activity in other areas of the brain during sleep, including the *reticular formation* and the *pons*, as well as the *forebrain region*. As we described in Chapter 4, these regions are important in alertness and arousal. Researchers have not established, however, that changes in the activity of these areas *cause* us to sleep.

Another biological theory, the restorative theory of sleep, suggests that sleep allows the brain and body to restore certain depleted chemical resources, while eliminating chemical wastes that have accumulated during the waking day (Dworak et al., 2010; Irwin, 2001). There is some evidence that supports this theory. Burns on rats take longer to heal if they are sleep-deprived (Gumustekin et al., 2004). Sleep deprivation also reduces the functioning of the immune system (Zager et al., 2007). As well, growth hormone production increases during sleep in adults, a process that would also promote restoration of body tissues and structures (Van Cauter, Leproult, & Plat, 2000).

While we may not yet know exactly what causes sleep, we do know that sleep occurs in regular patterns, or *rhythms*, and that these rhythms reflect changes in the body's chemistry (Moorcroft, 2003).

adaptive theory of sleep theory that organisms sleep for the purposes of self-preservation, to keep away from predators that are more active at night.

restorative theory of sleep theory that we sleep to allow the brain and body to restore certain depleted chemical resources and eliminate chemical wastes that have accumulated during the waking day.

Rhythms of Sleep

Human beings' basic pattern is called the **circadian rhythm** (see **Figure 6-4**). Within each 24-hour cycle, we experience a sustained period of wakefulness that gives way to a period of sleep. Although we tend to be awake during the day and to sleep at night, our circadian rhythms are not fully dependent on the cycles of daylight (Cartwright, 2010; Thompson, 2000).

circadian rhythm pattern of sleep–wake cycles that in human beings roughly corresponds to periods of daylight and night.

During the circadian cycle, we also experience other, more subtle patterns of biochemical activity. As morning nears, for example, our temperature rises and continues to rise until it peaks at midday. Then it dips and we feel fatigued. Many people around the world take naps during this early afternoon lull. Later in the afternoon, body temperature rises once more, only to drop again as we approach our full evening sleep (Danovi, 2010; Johnson et al., 2004). It seems that, on average, we are most alert during the late morning peak in the circadian rhythm. This "rule," however, varies with age. Younger people tend to peak later in the day, while older people peak earlier (Yoon et al., 2003).

Along with shifts in body temperature, we also experience changes throughout the 24-hour period in blood pressure, the secretion of hormones, and sensitivity to pain. As we have discussed, for example, the release of growth hormones tends to occur during periods of sleep (Benloucif et al., 2005).

The circadian rhythm has been called our *biological clock* because the pattern repeats itself from one 24-hour period to the next. This clock, however, can be made to go haywire by certain events (Cartwright, 2010; Waterhouse & DeCoursey, 2004). For example, the clock can be disrupted by long-distance airplane flights when we are awake at times that we should be sleeping—a problem compounded by crossing time zones. The result: jet lag. Similarly, people who work nightshifts, particularly those who keep irregular schedules of dayshifts and nightshifts, may experience sleep disorders and, in some instances, develop problems such as depression or health difficulties (Drake et al., 2004). People with a pattern called *circadian rhythm sleep disorder* experience excessive sleepiness or insomnia as a result of a mismatch between their own sleep–wake pattern and the sleep–wake schedule of most other people in their environment (Ivanenko & Johnson, 2010; Lack & Bootzin, 2003).

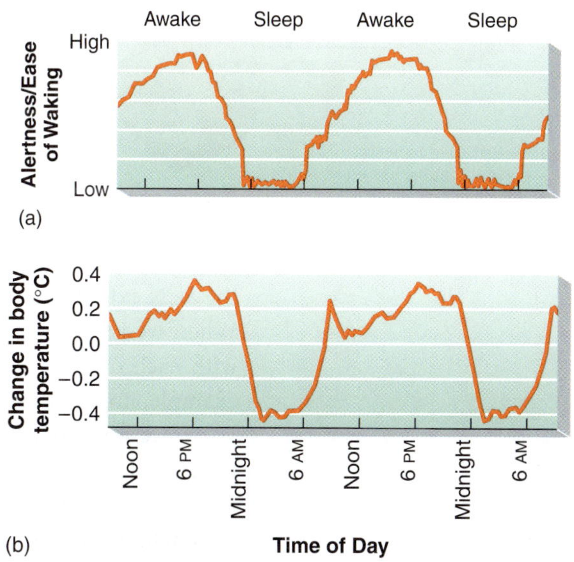

FIGURE 6-4 Circadian rhythms. Two prime examples of circadian rhythms are our cycles of alertness and shifts in body temperature.

"Owls" and "Larks" — HOW WE DIFFER

Do you get up at the crack of dawn, head to the gym, and complete all of your class assignments before noon? Then you are probably a morning person (a "lark"). Or do you have trouble getting up before noon and can't really concentrate on your work until much later in the day? If so, you are likely an evening person (an "owl").

Most people have no preference for the time of day when they are most alert and active; they may shift their sleep–wake rhythms two hours earlier or later than normal with no adverse effects on their alertness or activity level (Sack et al., 2007). But for some, there is a strong preference for either earlier or later in the day.

Researchers now believe that genetics plays an important role in determining these variations in sleep–wake rhythms, and that age, ethnicity, gender, and socioeconomic factors have almost no influence (Hellman et al., 2010; Paine, Gander, & Travier, 2006). Every cell in your body has its own internal clock, and scientists are able to measure your unique body clock at the cellular level (Cuninkova & Brown, 2008). As we shall see, the master control centre for your body's internal clock and your own sleep–wake rhythm may be found in the brain area known as the *suprachiasmatic nucleus*.

When We Sleep — WHAT HAPPENS IN THE BRAIN?

Research has uncovered what happens in our brains to control the circadian rhythms of when we wake and sleep, as well as what happens in the brain while we sleep.

suprachiasmatic nucleus (SCN) a small group of neurons in the hypothalamus responsible for coordinating the many rhythms of the body.

Controlling the Clock The **suprachiasmatic nucleus (SCN)**, a small group of neurons in the *hypothalamus*, is ultimately responsible for coordinating the many rhythms of the body (Danovi, 2010; Kalsbeek et al., 2010). As daylight fades into night, the SCN "notices" the change and directs the *pineal gland* to secrete the hormone *melatonin*. Increased quantities of melatonin, travelling through the blood to various organs, cause sleepiness. Melatonin production peaks between 1:00 and 3:00 A.M. As dawn approaches, this production decreases and sleepers soon awaken. There is increasing evidence (Petrie et al., 1989; Herxheimer & Petrie, 2002) that melatonin taken in pill form after long-haul flights reduces the severity of jet lag, likely by resetting the circadian clock.

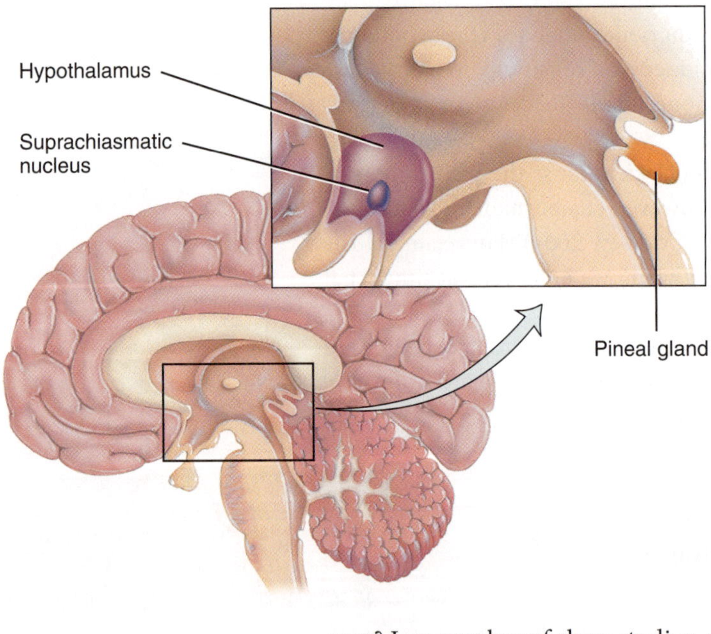

During the day, photoreceptors in the retina of the eye communicate the presence of sunlight to the SCN and melatonin secretions remain low (Berson, 2003). Photoreceptors are also sensitive to artificial light. In fact, the invention of the light bulb just over a hundred years ago has disturbed the human experience of the circadian rhythm by increasing the number of hours of light people are exposed to in a given day. This may be one reason why many people today sleep much less than our forbearers.

What happens if a person is entirely deprived of access to environmental shifts in sunlight and darkness? In a number of sleep studies, participants have been placed in special settings where they are totally deprived of natural light and have no way to measure time. In such settings, the SCN extends the body's "day" by as much as an hour, to about 25 hours (Lavie, 2001). When we are deprived of light, the various circadian rhythms also become out of synch with each other. The normal cycles of body temperature and melatonin production, for example, no longer coordinate with one another (Lavie, 2001).

If we speak of a biological clock, we should also be able to speak of *setting*, or *resetting*, the clock (Waterhouse & DeCoursey, 2004). In fact, when a person who has been kept in an environment without sunlight is returned to normal living conditions, the usual 24-hour circadian rhythm is quickly restored.

Patterns of Sleep Every 90 to 100 minutes while we sleep, we pass through a sleep cycle that consists of five different stages (Fedotchev, 2011; Lavie, 2001). Researchers have identified these stages by examining people's brain-wave patterns while they sleep, using a device called an *electroencephalograph* (*EEG*). EEG readings indicate that each stage of sleep is characterized by a different brain-wave pattern, as shown in **Figure 6-5**.

Studying circadian rhythms. Maurizio Montalbini spent months living in a cavern, with no external light or means of telling the time, to study the circadian rhythms free of external or artificial influences.

When we first go to bed and, still awake, begin to relax, EEG readings show that we experience what are called *alpha waves*. As we settle into this drowsy pre-sleep period, called the **hypnagogic state**, we sometimes experience strange sensations. We may feel that we are falling or floating in space, or "hear" our name called out, or we may hear a loud crash. All of these sensations seem very real, but none actually has happened. Such sensory phenomena are called *hypnagogic hallucinations* (Jones et al., 2010). Also common during this pre-sleep stage is a *myoclonic jerk*, a sharp muscular spasm that generally accompanies the hypnagogic hallucination of falling.

When we finally doze off, EEG readings show that our brain waves become smaller and irregular, signalling that we have entered *Stage 1 sleep*. Alpha-wave patterns are replaced by slower waves, called *theta waves*. This first stage of sleep actually represents a bridge between wakefulness and sleep; it lasts only a few minutes. Our conscious awareness of street noises or the hum of an air conditioner fades. If we are roused from this stage, we might recall having just had ideas that seem nonsensical.

Falling deeper into sleep, we next pass into *Stage 2 sleep*. A still further slowing of brain-wave activity occurs during this stage, although we may also exhibit **sleep spindles**—bursts of brain activity that last a second or two. During Stage 2, breathing becomes steadily rhythmic. Occasionally the body twitches, although generally our muscle tension relaxes. During this stage, which lasts 15 to 20 minutes, we can still be awakened fairly easily. Toward the end of Stage 2 sleep, our brain waves slow even further and *delta waves* start to appear in addition to the theta waves. Delta waves indicate *delta sleep,* or deep sleep.

hypnagogic state a pre-sleep period often characterized by vivid sensory phenomena.

sleep spindles bursts of brain activity lasting a second or two; occur during Stage 2 sleep.

The next two stages of sleep, *Stage 3* and *Stage 4*, are characterized by very deep sleep. In Stage 3, between 20 and 50 percent of our EEG waves are delta waves. During Stage 4, the percentage of delta waves increases to more than 50 percent (Giedd, 2009; Bertini et al., 2007). During Stage 4, heart rate, blood pressure, and breathing rates all drop to their lowest levels, and the sleeper seems cut off from the world. Interestingly, although our muscles are most relaxed during this deepest phase of sleep, this is also the time when people are prone to sleepwalking. Similarly, children who wet their beds tend to do so during this stage.

Passing through all of the first four stages takes a little more than an hour of each 90-to 100-minute sleep cycle. After that, we experience the most interesting stage of sleep,

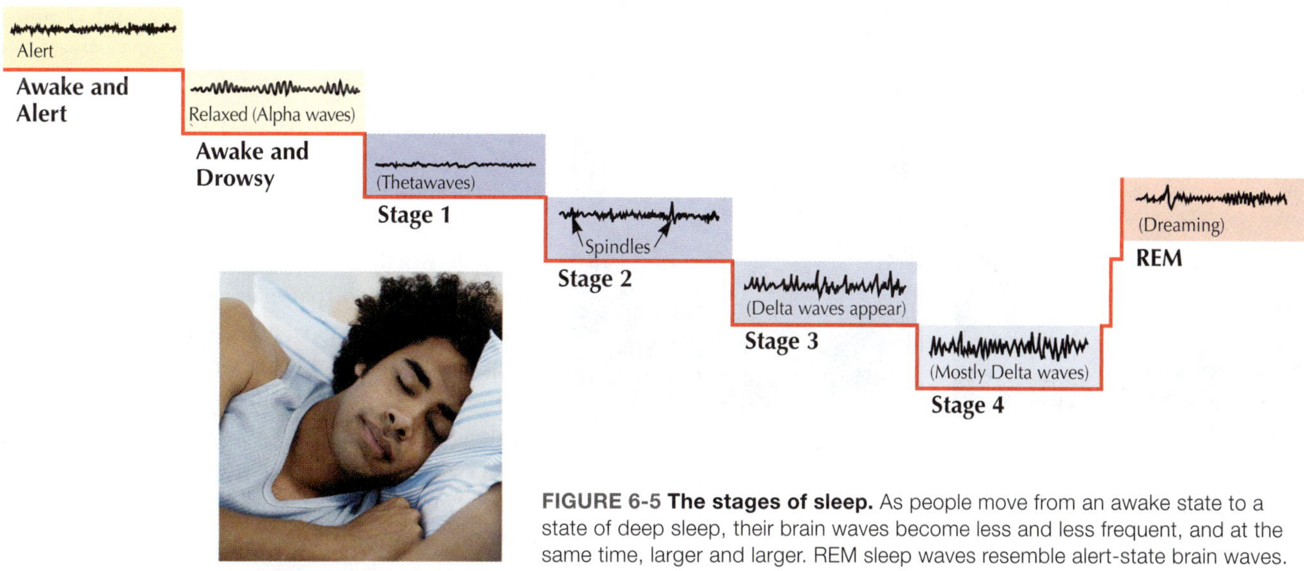

FIGURE 6-5 The stages of sleep. As people move from an awake state to a state of deep sleep, their brain waves become less and less frequent, and at the same time, larger and larger. REM sleep waves resemble alert-state brain waves.

rapid eye movement sleep (REM) stage of sleep associated with rapid and jagged brainwave patterns, increased heart rate, rapid and irregular breathing, rapid eye movements, and dreaming.

non-REM sleep (NREM) Stages 1 through 4 of normal sleep pattern.

rapid eye movement, or **REM, sleep**. In fact, all the preceding stages (Stages 1–4) are collectively called **non-REM sleep**, or **NREM**. During REM sleep, we experience rapid and jagged brain-wave patterns, in contrast to the slow waves of NREM sleep. REM sleep has been called *paradoxical sleep* because, even though the body remains deeply relaxed on the surface—almost paralyzed—we experience considerable activity internally (Thakkar & Datta, 2010; Wickwire et al., 2008). The rapid brain-wave pattern of REM sleep is accompanied by increased heart rate and rapid and irregular breathing, for example. Moreover, every 30 seconds or so, our eyes dart around rapidly behind our closed eyelids. Perhaps most interesting, during REM sleep people's brains behave just as they do when they are awake and active (Ratey, 2001).

Along with this brain activity, the genitals become aroused during REM sleep. Indeed, except during nightmares, men usually experience erections and women vaginal lubrication and clitoral engorgement during REM sleep, even if the content of the dream is not sexual (Andersen et al., 2010; Solms, 2007). Men often retain their erections beyond the REM stage, explaining the occurrence of morning erections.

As we will discuss shortly, dreams usually occur throughout REM sleep. If people are awakened during this stage, they almost always report that they have been dreaming. Unlike the hypnagogic hallucinations of pre-sleep, which are often fleeting and isolated images, dreams tend to be emotional and are experienced in a story-like form. Dreams are less common during NREM sleep, and when they do happen, they are less vivid or fantastic than REM dreams.

Many researchers believe that REM sleep serves a particularly important function—the consolidation of memories of newly learned material, a process that we will be talking about more in the coming chapters on learning and memory (Diekelmann & Born, 2010; Legault et al., 2010). In fact, REM sleep tends to extend longer than usual in both animals and humans if the organisms go to sleep after just having learned a new task (Smith, 2006, 1996). In one study, a group of volunteers were trained on a perceptual task just before going to sleep (Karni et al., 1994). Half of the sleepers were awakened during REM sleep, while the other half were awakened later, during the next cycle of NREM sleep. The next day, those who had been awakened during REM sleep performed more poorly on the perceptual task than those who had been awakened during the later NREM phases. Presumably, the REM-awakened volunteers had not yet had the opportunity to fully consolidate their memories of the newly learned task. (See "What Happens in the Brain When We Sleep" for more information.)

This memory consolidation theory has, however, been challenged by some studies showing that when animals are administered antidepressant drugs, which typically disrupt REM sleep, they nevertheless continue to learn and remember quite well (Vertes & Eastman, 2003). Research also finds that people with lesions to the *pons* portion of the brain, which may contribute to REM sleep, learn, remember, and function quite normally despite the disruption to the functioning of the pons.

It is worth noting that every kind of mammal whose sleep patterns have been studied, including birds, experience both NREM and REM sleep. Thus, many theorists believe that animals also dream. Of course, this comes as no surprise to dog owners who have, no doubt, frequently observed their pets twitch their paws in a regular rhythm during REM sleep, as if running in a dream (Thompson, 2000).

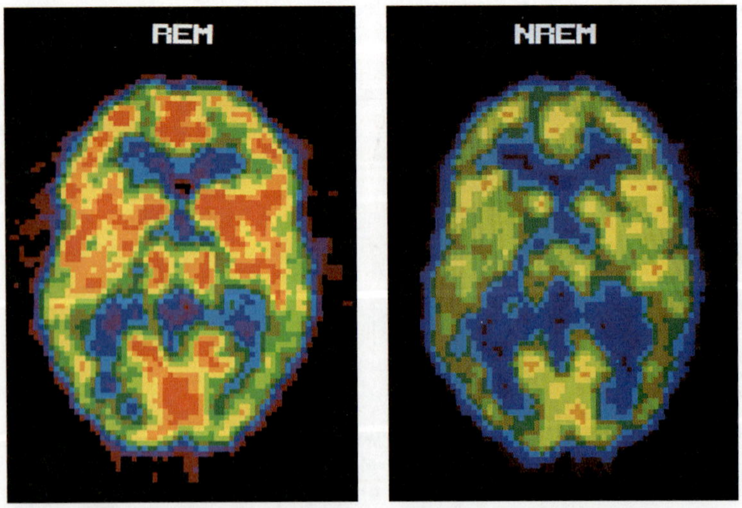

Almost like being awake. When we are in REM sleep, our brains behave much like they do when we are awake and active, and indeed it is during this stage of sleep that we dream. The PET scan of a brain during REM sleep (left) reveals much more activity (indicated by the colours "red" and "orange") than does the scan of a brain during non-REM sleep (right).

Dreams

Dreams—emotional, story-like sensory experiences that usually occur during REM sleep—have proven to be endlessly fascinating to scientists, clinicians, philosophers, artists, and laypeople, probably because of how vivid and mysterious they are. A woman dreams of being punched in the stomach and doubling over in pain. In thinking about the dream the next day, she notices that she feels very vulnerable. She also recalls that earlier on the day of the dream, she had learned about a poor midterm mark and about an increase in the entrance GPA to a program she had planned to enter, and she remembers having felt vulnerable because her planned major is in jeopardy. Could the dream and the poor midterm grade be related? Some psychologists would say yes, while others would be skeptical (Duesbury, 2011). In this section we shall examine ways in which different theorists and researchers have come to understand dreams (Cartwright, 2010; Moorcroft, 2003).

Research suggests that actions in dreams run in real time—that is, it takes you as long to accomplish something in the dream as it would if you were performing the action while you were awake.

Information-Processing Theory Information-processing theory offers a cognitive view of dreaming. According to this view, dreams are the mind's attempt to sort out and organize the day's experiences and to fix them in memory. Consistent with this perspective, studies have revealed that interrupting REM sleep—and so interrupting dreams—impedes a person's ability to remember material that he or she learned just before going to sleep (Empson, 2002). Also, in support of this view, researchers have found that periods of REM sleep (during which we dream) tend to extend longer when people's days have been filled with multiple stressful events or marked by extensive learning experiences (Fogel et al., 2011; Palumbo, 1978). Thus, according to an information-processing perspective, the student who dreamed of being punched may simply have been attempting to process and give order to the stressful academic challenges that she had experienced earlier in the day.

information-processing theory hypothesis that dreams are the mind's attempt to sort out and organize the day's experiences and to fix them in memory.

Activation-Synthesis Hypothesis Researchers J. Allan Hobson and Robert McCarley have proposed a more biological hypothesis about dreaming, the activation-synthesis model (Hobson, 2009; 2005; Hobson & McCarley, 1977) (see **Figure 6-6**). They argue that as people sleep, their brains activate all kinds of signals. In particular, when dreams occur, neurons in the *brainstem* are activated. These, in turn, activate neurons in the *cerebral cortex* to produce visual and auditory signals. Also aroused are the emotion centres of the brain, including the *cingulate cortex, amygdala*, and *hippocampus*. Neuroimaging scans of people who are experiencing REM sleep confirm heightened activity and neuron communication in each of these brain regions.

activation-synthesis model theory that dreams result from the brain's attempts to synthesize or organize random internally generated signals and give them meaning.

Hobson and McCarley suggest that the activated brain combines—or *synthesizes*—these internally generated signals and tries to give them meaning. Each person organizes and synthesizes this random collection of images, feelings, memories, and thoughts in his or her own personal way—in the form of a particular dream story (Hobson et al., 2011, 2003,1998). Someone who dreams of being punched in the stomach might be trying to synthesize activation in brain areas that normally receive signals from the muscles of the stomach with signals from areas of the brain that process emotions, for example.

What remains unclear in this model is why different people synthesize their onslaught of brain signals in different ways. Freud, of course, might suggest that each person's particular synthesis is influenced by his or her unfulfilled needs and unresolved conflicts.

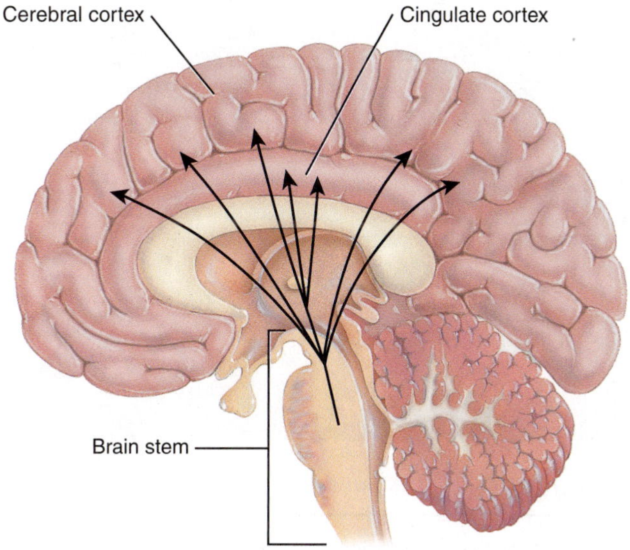

FIGURE 6-6 Activation-synthesis. According to the activation-synthesis theory of dreaming, neurons in the brainstem activate neurons in other areas throughout the brain. The brain combines these various signals into a story, or dream.

Tying It Together: **Your Brain and Behaviour**

Getting a Good Night's Sleep

If you're like most people, you fall asleep when you are tired and need to rest. After an uninterrupted night's sleep or nap, you probably feel refreshed and better able to face life's challenges. Given how rested you feel after sleeping, it may surprise you to hear that while you sleep, your brain is incredibly active—it's not resting at all, or at least it is certainly not inactive! Each stage of sleep is characterized by a different pattern of brain activity.

During REM sleep, a time of active dreaming, signals in the brain shut down the system that controls movement. Preventing movement probably saves us from potentially dangerous actions we could take if we acted out our dreams.

During slow-wave sleep, studies have shown that many circuits in the brain replay patterns of activity that work to strengthen new memories. That may be why being deprived of sleep, a common occurrence for college or university students, is associated with problems remembering facts over the long term. Scientists don't fully understand why we sleep, but they all agree that the brain doesn't function optimally without it.

Questions

1. **What is the physiological explanation for why people typically do not act out their dreams?**
2. **Inadequate sleep seems to disrupt neuron formation in which region of the brain?**
3. **Explain the relationship between sleep, hunger, and weight.**

IMPROVING COGNITION

Sleep allows for neuronal growth in the brain. Sleep deprivation prevents the addition of new neurons to the hippocampus, a brain region important for cognition and anxiety regulation. This may be one reason sleep deprivation weakens our ability to learn and increases the likelihood of mood disturbances.

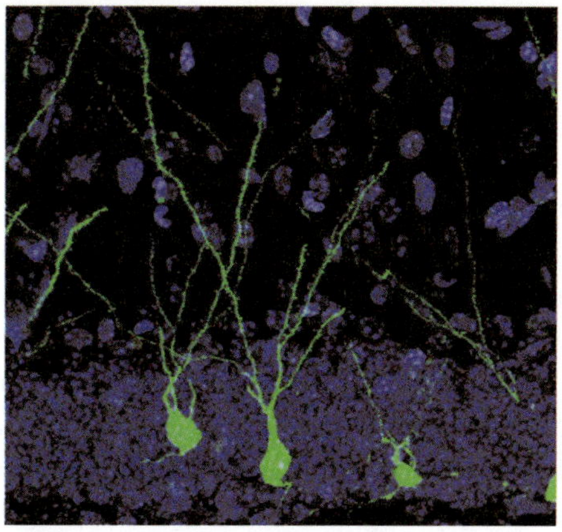

IMPROVING METABOLISM

Sleep helps the brain to regulate metabolism. Sleep deprivation increases the peptide ghrelin and decreases the peptide leptin. Changes in the levels of these chemicals both work on neurons of the hypothalamus, shown here as green-stained neurons, to stimulate hunger—this may be one reason why sleep-deprived people are more likely to gain weight.

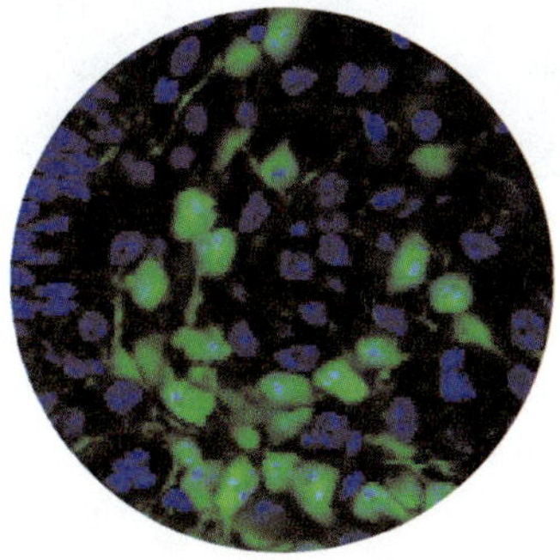

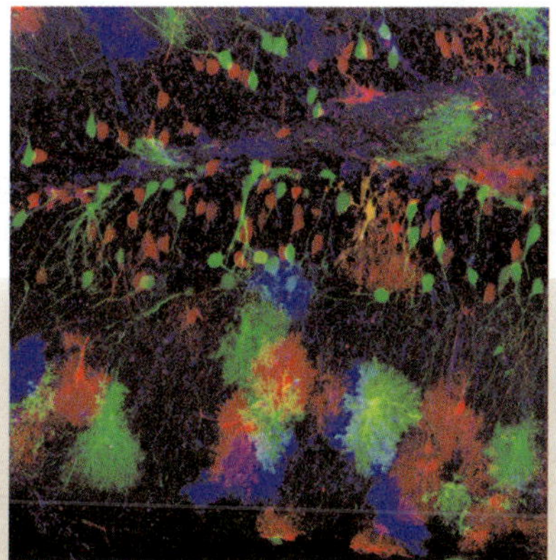

LOCKING IN MEMORIES

During slow-wave sleep, patterns of activity that result from learning are replayed multiple times in the neurons of the hippocampus, a brain region shown here stained with fluorescent dyes. This replaying serves to strengthen connections and consolidate memories.

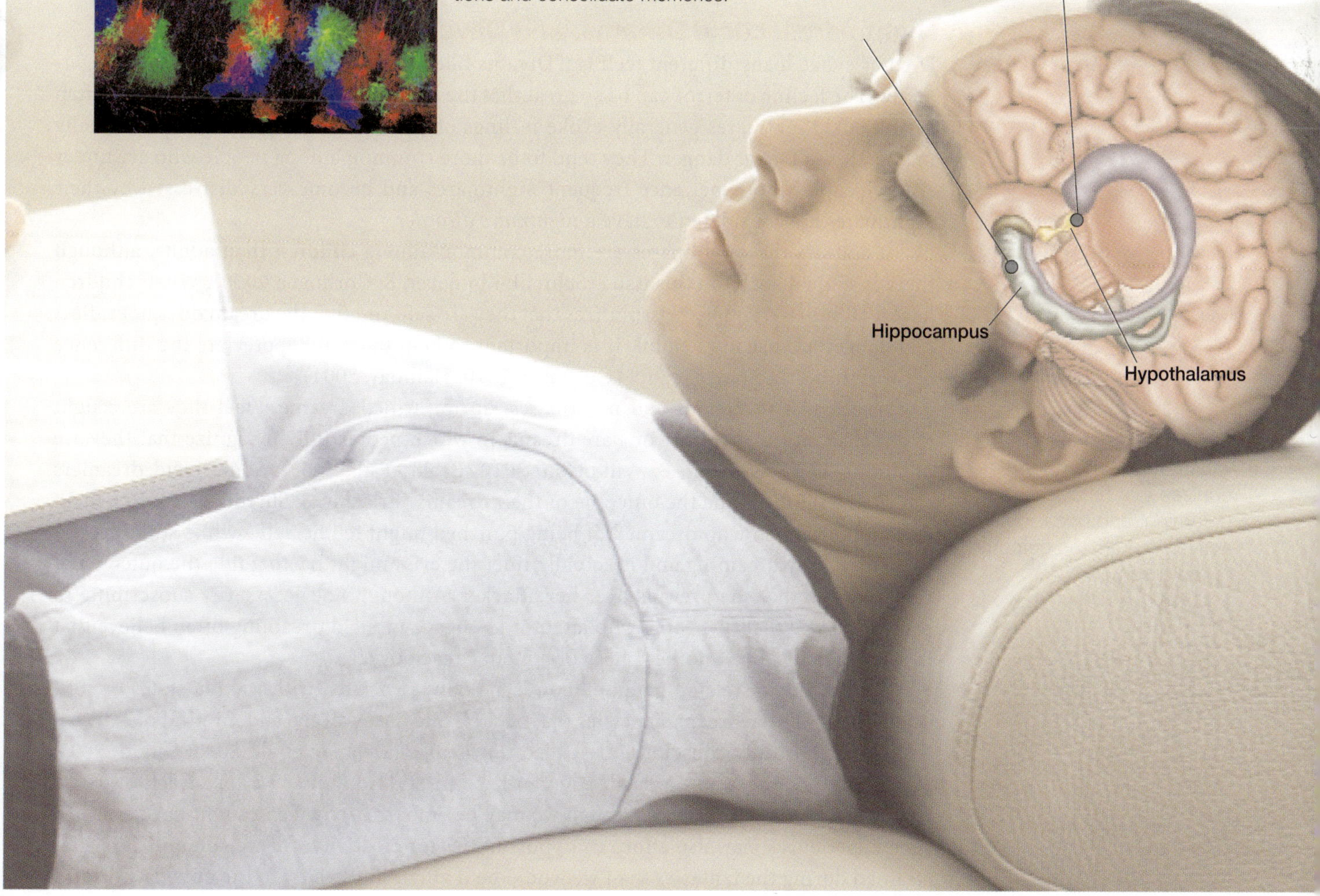

Dream stories. People often experience similar dream stories. For example, 80 percent of all people have had repeated dreams of running toward or away from something.

Freudian Dream Theory Sigmund Freud argued that dreams represent the expression of unconscious wishes or desires. He believed that dreams allow us to discharge internal energy associated with unacceptable feelings (Freud, 1900). Freud suggested that *dream interpretation,* in which a psychoanalytic therapist facilitates insight into the possible meaning behind a dream, may help clients appreciate their underlying needs and conflicts with the goal of being less constrained by them during waking life. For example, if a lonely and morally upstanding young man is sexually attracted to his brother's wife but is not consciously aware of this desire, he might have a dream in which he goes swimming in a private pool that is marked "No Trespassing." His therapist might help the man arrive at the conclusion that the dream about swimming in an off-limits pool symbolizes his wish to be with his sister-in-law. Such an insight eventually might help the man to overcome inhibitions he feels about finding a suitable partner for himself.

Freud called the dream images that people are able to recall the *manifest content* of the dream. The unconscious elements of dreams are called the *latent content.* In our example, the young man's desire for his sister-in-law (latent content)—a scandalous idea that he would never allow himself to have—is symbolized in the dream by a swim in the pool (manifest content). His dream of a happy swim in forbidden territory is his mind's solution to a problem that he could not work out consciously.

Many of today's theorists, including a number of psychoanalytic ones, criticize Freud's theory. For example, *object-relations theorists,* psychoanalytic theorists who place greater emphasis on the role of relationships in development, focus more on relationship issues when interpreting dream material (Wolman, 1979). Regarding the earlier dream in which a student gets punched, an object-relations therapist might be inclined to help the patient explore her feelings of vulnerability in various parts of her life, rather than her educational fears.

Nightmares, Lucid Dreams, and Daydreams

Dreams evoke many different feelings. Dreams filled with intense anxiety are called *nightmares.* The feeling of terror can be so great that the dreamer awakens from the dream, often crying out. Nightmares generally evoke feelings of helplessness or powerlessness, usually in situations of great danger. They tend to be more common among people who are under stress. People who experience frequent nightmares and become very distressed by their nightmares are considered to have a *nightmare disorder.*

It appears that nightmares are more common among children than adults, although there is some dispute on this issue (Schredl, Blomeyer, & Gorlinger, 2000). When children have a nightmare, simple reassurances that they are safe and that the dream does not reflect real danger are usually helpful. It is important to help the child appreciate the difference between inner and outer reality (Gonzalez, 2010; Halliday, 2004).

lucid dreams dreams in which the sleeper fully recognizes that he or she is dreaming, and occasionally actively guides the outcome of the dream.

In contrast to dreams and nightmares, during which dreamers feel they are caught in a real situation, **lucid dreams** are dreams in which people fully recognize that they are dreaming (Blagrove, Bell, & Wilkinson, 2010; Baars et al., 2003). Some lucid dreamers can even willfully guide the outcome of their dreams (Erlacher & Shredl, 2010). In a lucid dream, the woman who dreamed of being punched might tell herself—while still asleep—that she is only dreaming and is actually fine; she even might try to guide the outcome of the dream so that she prevails over her attacker. Although not necessarily subscribing to psychoanalytic theory, people who attempt to engage in lucid dreaming often believe that it is a way to open up another phase of human consciousness.

A third dream-related phenomenon is actually associated with waking states of consciousness—the daydream. Fantasies that occur while one is awake and mindful of external reality, but not fully conscious, are called *daydreams* (Delaney et al., 2010; Schon, 2003; Singer, 2003). Sometimes a daydream can become so strong that we lose track of external reality for a brief while. Although we may be embarrassed when caught daydreaming, such experiences may also afford us opportunities for creativity; we are, after all, less constrained during the fantasies than we would be if attending strictly to the outside world.

Sleep HOW WE DEVELOP

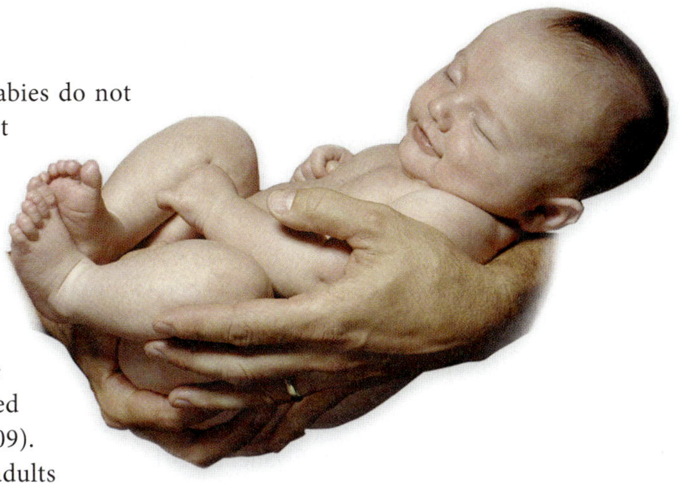

Parents or older siblings know all too well that young babies do not sleep quite like older children or adults. Through the first four months of life, babies sleep between 14 and 17 hours each day. The amount of time that they spend sleeping declines steadily as they get older (Blumberg & Seelke, 2010; Sadeh et al., 2009). Although babies spend a lot of time asleep overall, the lengths of their sleep periods can last anywhere from minutes to hours before they are awake and crying out for attention. For parents, the good news is that sleep tends to become more structured at around six months of age (McLaughlin & Williams, 2009).

Babies appear to spend a great deal more time than adults in REM sleep—around eight hours per day for infants, compared with two hours for adults (Sankupellay et al., 2011; Siegel, 2005). The size of this difference has led theorists to suspect that infant sleep patterns are crucial to development in various ways. Several have speculated, for example, that REM sleep aids in the development of the central nervous system by facilitating synaptic pruning and preventing the formation of unnecessary connections, although research has not yet confirmed this belief (Krippner, 1990). Also, by slowing body activity, the extended REM sleep of babies may help to regulate the temperature of their developing brains. REM sleep tends to decrease to adult levels somewhere between the ages of 2 and 6 years (El-Sheikh, 2011; Curzi-Dascalova & Challamel, 2000).

By early childhood, an individual's total daily sleep requirement also decreases significantly (see **Figure 6-7**). Most children sleep around nine hours each day, although pediatricians recommend between 12 and 15 hours of sleep for anyone between 2 and 5 years of age. Teenagers average around seven hours of daily sleep, although pediatricians recommend at least eight hours for them (Crisp, 2010; Acebo et al., 2005). As adults, our sleep patterns continue to change. As we age, we spend less and less time in deep sleep and REM sleep, our sleep is more readily interrupted, and we take longer to get back to sleep when awakened (Bliwise, 2010; Garcia-Rill et al., 2008).

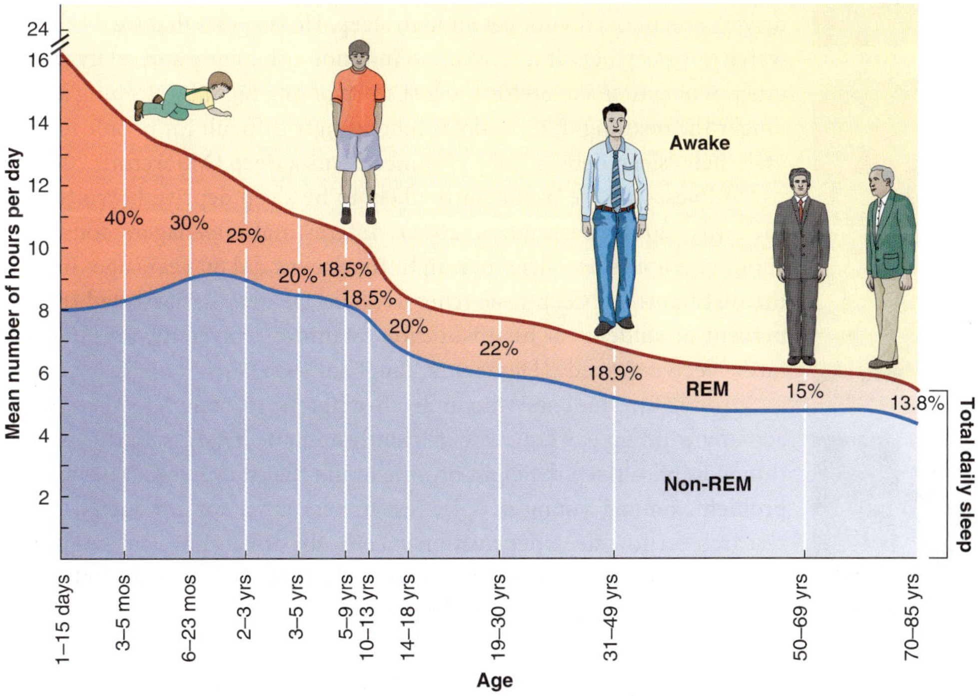

FIGURE 6-7 The effects of aging on the sleep cycle. As we get older, our total daily sleep and our REM sleep decrease. The largest shifts occur during our first three years of life.

As discussed earlier, our sleep–awake cycle is tied to our body's circadian rhythms. These biological clocks are also affected by environmental demands and expectations (Worthman, 2011). Studies have, for example, contrasted parenting practices in North America with those in the Kipsigis tribe (you may remember them from Chapter 3). Many Western parents structure their babies' sleep by putting them down at designated times and not responding to their cries. In contrast, Kipsigis mothers keep their babies with them constantly. As a result, Kipsigis babies sleep for much shorter periods of time later into infancy than do American babies; in many cases, they do not sleep for long stretches even as adults (Super & Harkness, 2002, 1972). The body clocks of teenagers also seem to be compromised by the increased social and academic pressures that they encounter (El-Sheikh, 2011; Crowley, Acebo, & Carskadon, 2007). Many adolescents, for example, stay up late largely because that's what it takes for them to finish their homework or to keep up with their friends.

A graduate student in physiology, Eugene Aserinsky, discovered REM sleep when he attached electronic leads to his 8-year-old son's head and eyelids to monitor his sleep and waking brain waves. He found unexpected brain-wave activity, suggesting his son "had woken up even though he hadn't" (Aserinsky, 1996).

Sleep Deprivation and Sleep Disorders

WHEN THINGS GO WRONG

How much sleep a person needs varies, depending on factors such as age, lifestyle, and genetic disposition. The amount of sleep a person actually gets may also be different from how much they need. Lifestyle deprives many people of sleep, and sleep disorders may also make it impossible to sleep properly.

Sleep wins. Whether it's a bassist collapsing in mid-play on a couch or a gardener dozing on a bench, the need to drift off eventually catches up with those who are sleep deprived.

Sleep Deprivation

Left unhindered, most people would sleep for nine or ten hours a day in order to awaken alert and refreshed. However, we've all had the opposite experience—that of not getting enough sleep. We become generally sleepy and maybe a little cranky. After a while, we may yearn for sleep.

Researchers have found that without enough sleep, people also experience a general depressed state (Orzel-Gryglewska, 2010). They display lower productivity and are more apt to make mistakes (Gunzelmann et al., 2011). Stan Coren, a researcher at the University of British Columbia, has shown that accidents and deaths sometimes occur when drivers and pilots do not get enough sleep. He suggests that we all should watch our sleep deficit if we want to function coherently and safely. While it is possible to make up for the lost sleep of one night by sleeping a little longer the next night, it becomes increasingly difficult for people to "pay off" their "sleep debt" if they chronically miss sleep (Moorcroft, 2003).

Adolescents are particularly likely to be sleep deprived (Wolfson & Richards, 2011; Carskadon, 2002). Interestingly, teenagers today get about two hours less sleep per night than teens did 80 years ago. In fact, the distinguished sleep researcher William Dement has asserted that 80 percent of students at his institution, Stanford University, are "dangerously sleep deprived" (Dement & Vaughan, 1999).

Ironically, students who pull all-nighters to complete their work actually wind up working less efficiently and effectively than they would if they were to sleep the eight or nine hours that they need. Despite such problems among young people, researchers have not conducted much research on how sleep deprivation specifically affects physical, cognitive, and emotional development (Kopasz et al., 2010; Loessl et al., 2008).

Sleep researchers used to spend most of their time examining the impact of lost sleep on simple or monotonous tasks. Today's researchers, however, often look at the impact of sleep deprivation on more complex

PSYCHOLOGY AROUND US "Give me 5 more minutes!"

Sylvio woke up exhausted . . . yet again. Personally, he blamed getting home late from soccer practice and excessive homework for his tiredness. But he knew his parents would blame Facebook or his chatting with his friends. Since Sylvio certainly wasn't ready to give up those activities, he splashed water in his face and tried to look as awake as possible when he first saw his parents.

Like most other teenagers, Sylvio runs on at least some level of chronic sleep deprivation. Much of today's research on teenage sleep deprivation seeks to identify environmental factors for this problem. For example, teens and college and university students tend to be overscheduled and overworked for a variety of reasons. And such patterns clearly have an impact on sleep. However, scientists have also found evidence for a phase shift associated with puberty. This means that Sylvio's body clock makes him want to go to bed a couple of hours later than he did when he was younger. The problem is that he still needs the same amount of sleep he did in the past. And school tends to open at the same early hours as in the past.

Basically, in all conflicts between a young person's biological needs and the demands of the environment, sleep deprivation is the only possible outcome. This losing battle has led some major pediatricians to suggest that a later start time for high school might be an appropriate intervention (Carskadon, Acebo, & Jenni, 2004). It is also worth thinking about scheduling some nap time in the afternoon so that you do not build up such a sleep deficit that your ability to perform cognitively (and academically) is impaired.

activities (Andersen & Platten, 2011; Moorcroft, 2003; Harrison & Horne, 2000) or as Frank Wimmer at Carleton University has done, at the effects of sleep deprivation on creativity and attention management (Wimmer et al., 1992). Studies suggest, on the one hand, that sleep deprivation does *not* necessarily lower one's performance on complex logical tasks. Sleep-deprived participants in such tasks often are able to avoid poor performances by being highly interested in the complex tasks at hand. Many sleep-deprived college students, for example, seem able to conduct research or write papers, particularly if those works interest them a lot.

Problems arise, on the other hand, when a sleep-deprived person faces unexpected turns of events, distractions, or innovations while working on a complex task, or needs to revise the task. If, for example, someone turns on the television while you're studying in a sleep-deprived state, your learning is likely to suffer considerably.

In an important set of findings, researchers have also learned that sleep loss can lower the effectiveness of people's immune systems (Bollinger et al., 2010; Dement & Vaughan, 1999). Sleep-deprived people apparently have a more difficult time fighting off viral infections and cancer, for example. Thus, it may not be surprising that people who average at least eight hours of sleep a night tend to outlive those who get less sleep (Dement & Vaughn, 1999).

Sleep Disorders Sleep disorders occur when normal sleep patterns are disturbed, causing impaired daytime functioning and feelings of distress (Ivanenko & Johnson, 2010; Espie, 2002; APA, 2000). Almost everyone suffers from some kind of sleep disorder at one time or another in their lives. The sleep disorder may be part of a larger problem, such as life stress, a medical condition, or substance misuse, or it may be a *primary* sleep disorder, in which sleep difficulties are the central problem. Primary sleep disorders typically arise from abnormalities in the people's circadian rhythms and sleep–wake mechanisms.

People who suffer from **insomnia**, the most common sleep disorder, regularly cannot fall asleep or stay asleep (Bastien, 2011; Horne, 2010). More than 20 percent of the entire population experience significant extended episodes of insomnia each year (APA, 2000). The National Sleep Foundation claims that 43 percent of adults experience at least one symptom of insomnia a few nights or more each week.

insomnia sleep disorder characterized by a regular inability to fall asleep or stay asleep.

As you might expect, many cases of insomnia are triggered by day-to-day stressors. In particular, job or school pressures, troubled relationships, and financial problems have been implicated. For many people, a subtle additional stress is worrying about not getting enough sleep while trying to fall asleep. This vicious cycle can further intensify anxiety and make sleep all the more elusive (Jansson-Frojmark et al., 2011).

Insomnia is more common among older people than younger ones (Jaussent et al., 2011). Elderly individuals are particularly prone to this problem because so many of them have medical ailments, experience pain, take medications, or grapple with depression and anxiety—each a known contributor to insomnia (Taylor et al., 2008). In addition, some of the normal age-related sleep changes we described earlier may heighten the chances of insomnia among elderly people. As individuals age, for example, they naturally spend less time in deep sleep and their sleep is more readily interrupted (Bliwise, 2010; Edelstein et al., 2008). *Sleepwalking* most often takes place during the first three hours of sleep (Dogu & Pressman, 2011; Wickwire et al., 2008). Sleepwalkers will often sit up, get out of bed, and walk around. They usually avoid obstacles, climb stairs, and perform complex activities. Accidents do happen, however: tripping, bumping into furniture, and even falling out of windows have all been reported. People who are awakened while sleepwalking are confused for several moments. If allowed to continue sleepwalking, they eventually return to bed. The disorder appears to be inherited (Hublin et al., 2001). Up to 5 percent of children experience this disorder for a period of time, and up to 17 percent have at least one episode (Wickwire et al., 2008).

Night terrors are related to sleepwalking. Individuals who suffer from this pattern awaken suddenly, sit up in bed, scream in extreme fear and agitation, and experience heightened heart and breathing rates. They appear to be in a state of panic and are often incoherent. Usually people suffering from night terrors do not remember the episodes the next morning. Night terror disorder is not the same thing as a *nightmare disorder*, discussed earlier in the chapter, in which sufferers experience frequent nightmares. Sleepwalking and night terrors are more common among children than among adolescents or adults. They tend to occur during Stages 3 and 4, the deepest stages of NREM sleep (Hublin et al., 1999). Because night terrors typically stop after childhood, we do not treat them as sleep disorders but rather as developmental issues (Mindell & Owens, 2003).

THINGS STUDENTS WANT TO KNOW

Do people who are sleepwalking know what they're doing?

The answer is likely no, sleepwalkers are not aware of what they are doing. While most sleepwalkers just sit up or wander around the house, some engage in more complex behaviours such as cooking meals, climbing out of windows, or even driving cars.

Sleepwalking typically occurs in deep Stage 3 to Stage 4 sleep with little or no dreaming. If you awaken a sleepwalker loudly or suddenly, it may startle or frighten them and being frightened might cause them to react defensively. Mainly they will be confused and disoriented. If possible, it is best just to speak softly to them and lead them back to bed. It is most likely that they will have no memory of their late-night stroll when they get up in the morning (Boyd, 2004).

As an extreme example, consider the case of Ken Parks who lived in Pickering, Ontario. One night Ken fell asleep on the couch, arose in the middle of the night, drove across town, entered the home of his parents-in-law and, using a tire iron and knife, killed his mother-in-law and nearly killed his father-in-law. He drove himself to a police station and turned himself in saying, in a confused state, he thought he had killed someone. At trial, Ken's lawyer argued he was sleepwalking (actually, that he was in a state of non-insane automatism, or that he was not acting voluntarily) and therefore should not be held accountable for his actions. The jury agreed and acquitted him of murder. The Supreme Court of Canada upheld the acquittal. Others have tried to use this defence and been found guilty. There is currently much debate in legal, medical, and psychological circles as to whether sleepwalking ought to be considered a legitimate defense (Horn, 2005).

sleep apnea sleep disorder characterized by repeatedly ceasing to breathe during the night, depriving the brain of oxygen and leading to frequent awakenings.

Fifty-four percent of married Canadians say their partners snore while sleeping. Of those, 63 percent say their partner's snoring keeps them awake at night and adds to their own fatigue (Nutravite, 2006). It is likely that many of these serious snorers suffer from **sleep apnea**, the second most common sleep disorder. People with this condition repeatedly stop breathing during the night, depriving the brain of oxygen and leading to frequent awakenings. Sleep apnea can result when the brain fails to send a "breathe signal" to the diaphragm and other breathing muscles, or when muscles at the top of the throat become too relaxed, allowing the windpipe to partially close. Sufferers stop breathing for up to 30 seconds or more as they sleep. Hundreds of episodes may occur each night. Often the individual will not remember any of them, but will feel sleepy the next day. The biggest concern with sleep apnea is that the repeated episodes of breathing cessation stress the heart and can eventually lead to cardiac arrest. As well, people with sleep apnea are not getting sufficient rest and are at increased risk for fatigue-related problems while driving or working (Shah, 2007). Sleep apnea can usually be stopped completely by using a positive flow ventilator that keeps throat tissue open and stops snoring and the breathing interruptions associated with this issue.

narcolepsy sleep disorder marked by uncontrollable urge to fall asleep.

Narcolepsy, marked by an uncontrollable urge to fall asleep, is diagnosed in 24,000 people in the Canada; almost as many people (18,000) may not be diagnosed but still have the disorder (U.S. Census Bureau, 2004; NINDS, 2006). People with this disorder may suddenly fall into REM sleep in the midst of an argument or during an exciting football game. When they wake, they feel refreshed. The narcoleptic episode is experienced as a loss of consciousness that can last up to 15 minutes. This disorder can obviously have serious consequences for people driving cars, operating tools, or performing highly precise work. Its cause is not fully known. Narcolepsy seems to run in families, and some studies have linked the disorder to a specific gene or combination of genes (Quinnell et al., 2007). Recent work by Maan Lee and his colleagues at the Montreal Neurological Institute has helped to identify orexin or hypocretin receptors in the hypothalamus and their potential role in narcolepsy. When these receptors under-function, narcolepsy results (Lee, Hassani, & Jones, 2005). This sort of finding could eventually lead to a treatment for narcolepsy.

Studying narcolepsy. Some people with narcolepsy, a sleep disorder marked by uncontrollable urges to fall asleep, further experience sudden losses of muscle tone during their narcoleptic episodes. To learn more about this abnormal pattern, famous sleep researcher William Dement studies dogs such as Tucker, seen here before and during a sudden narcoleptic episode.

Before You Go On

www.wiley.com/go/comer

What Do You Know?

5. What are the major theories of why people sleep?
6. What is the difference between the manifest content of a dream and its latent content?
7. What is the role of the suprachiasmatic nucleus in human consciousness?
8. What is the difference between a nightmare and a night terror?

SCAN TO GET THE ANSWERS

What Do You Think?

Which of the theories of dreams described in this section is closest to your own theory of dreams (before you read this section and found out about the science in this area)? Are there other studies we should do to better understand dreaming?

Hypnosis

LEARNING OBJECTIVE 4

Discuss theories and evidence about what hypnosis is, how it works, and how it can be used.

In movie and cartoon portrayals of hypnosis, a creepy guy dressed in black tells an unsuspecting person to stare at a swinging pocket watch and says, "Follow the watch... You are getting sleepy, sleeeeepy, sleeeeepy." Soon, the person is completely under the power of the hypnotist, who often makes him or her do something completely out of character or, in more sinister films, illegal and dangerous. As you might expect, this portrayal is exaggerated and distorted.

hypnosis a seemingly altered state of consciousness during which individuals can be directed to act or experience the world in unusual ways.

The idea that hypnosis produces an altered state of consciousness or a trance-like state is only one explanation for **hypnosis** offered by psychologists (Lynn, Rhue, & Kirsch, 2010; Kihlstrom, 2007). During hypnosis, people can be directed to act in unusual ways, experience unusual sensations, remember forgotten events, or forget remembered events. An alternative explanation for these behaviours was developed by Nick Spanos working at Carleton University (Spanos et al., 1995). Spanos argued that hypnosis subjects are actually role-playing—acting as they believe hypnotized people should act. We will look at these two explanations for hypnosis in more detail.

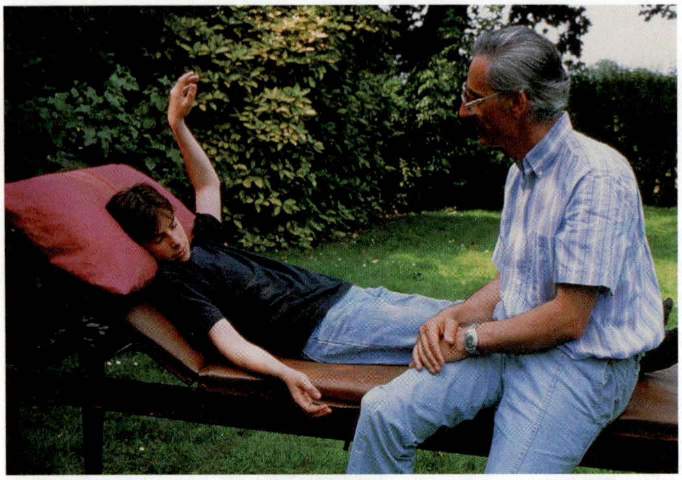

The power of suggestion. People can be directed to experience unusual sensations and act in unusual ways when in a hypnotic state—a trance-like altered state of consciousness marked by extreme suggestibility. Here, a hypnotized young man believes that a balloon is tied to his left hand and that his right hand is extremely heavy.

People typically are guided into this suggestible state by a trained hypnotist or hypnotherapist. The process involves their willing relinquishment of control over certain behaviours and their acceptance of distortions of reality. For hypnosis to work, individuals must be open and responsive to suggestions made by the hypnotist.

Some people are more open to a hypnotist's suggestions than others, a quality that often runs in families (Barnier & Council, 2010; Gfeller & Gorassini, 2010). Approximately 15 percent of adults are very susceptible to hypnosis, while 10 percent are not at all hypnotizable. Most adults fall somewhere in between (Hilgard, 1991, 1982). People who are especially suggestible are also more likely to do what other people tell them to do even when they are not hypnotized, a finding that supports Spanos' view of hypnosis as role-playing (Braffman & Kirsch, 2001). Perhaps not surprisingly, therefore, children tend to be particularly suggestible (Olness & Kohen, 2010). There are big differences between the scientific study of hypnosis and the stage shows put on by hypnotists.

PSYCHOLOGY AROUND US Not for Humans Only

Maybe you have seen it on a TV show. Maybe you have seen it in a movie. Maybe you have even seen it happen live. But at some point, you have probably seen or heard of a hypnotist getting a person to act like a chicken or some other animal. But have you ever heard of a person hypnotizing an animal? Turns out, it happens a lot.

Any interest in hypnotizing a shark, for example? Flip it on its back or massage its nose. The shark will fall into a trance-like state that makes it so unaware of pain that scientists can tag it with electronics that allow them to track the shark. Scientists have even been able to conduct minor surgery on a hypnotized shark. Want to hypnotize a lobster instead? Flip it upside down, with the tail in the air, and stroke along its back. The lobster's tail will curl and it will freeze in place. Don't care so much about sea creatures? Find yourself a chicken, tuck its head under its wing, and rock it back and forth. Soon you may find yourself in possession of one hypnotized chicken (Fowler, 2008).

Hypnotic Procedures and Effects

Hypnotists use various methods to induce the hypnotic state (Gibbons & Lynne, 2010). Sometimes—in a much tamer version than the movie portrayals—a person is asked to relax while concentrating on a single small target, such as a watch or an item in a painting on the wall. At other times, the hypnotist induces a *hyperalert* hypnotic trance that actually guides the individual to heightened tension and awareness. In either case, the hypnotist delivers "suggestions" to the subject, not the authoritarian commands on display in the movies.

One area of functioning that can be readily influenced by hypnotists is motor control. If the hypnotist suggests that a person's hand is being drawn like a magnet to a nearby stapler, the individual's hand will soon move to the stapler, as if propelled by an external force.

In some cases, people can be directed to respond *after* being roused from the hypnotic trance. A predetermined signal prompts such *posthypnotic responses.* A posthypnotic response is a behaviour that was suggested while the person involved was hypnotized, but which is engaged in later when a specified sign is observed (Spiegel & Spiegel, 2004). During hypnosis, the hypnotist may suggest, for example, that the person will later stand up whenever the hypnotist touches a desktop. After being roused, and with no understanding of why, the person will in fact stand when the hypnotist touches the desk.

Related to posthypnotic responses is the phenomenon of *posthypnotic amnesia*, in which the hypnotist directs the person to later forget information learned during hypnosis. Once again, after being roused from the hypnotic trance, the person does not remember the learned material until the hypnotist provides a predetermined signal to remember (Spiegel & Spiegel, 2004). The degree to which the earlier information is forgotten varies. Some people will not remember any of the learned material, while others will remember quite a bit.

Hypnosis can also induce *hallucinations*, mental perceptions that do not match the physical stimulations coming from the world around us. Researchers have distinguished between two kinds of *hypnotic hallucinations:* positive and negative. Positive hallucinations are those in which people under hypnosis are guided to see objects or hear sounds that are not present. Negative hallucinations are those in which hypnotized people fail to see or hear stimuli that are present. Negative hallucinations are often used to control pain. The hypnotized person is directed to ignore—basically, to simply not perceive—pain. The hallucination may result in a total or partial reduction of pain (Jensen, 2010; Patterson, 2010). Some practitioners have even applied hypnosis to help control pain during dental and other forms of surgery (Auld, 2007). Although only some people are able to undergo surgery while anesthetized by hypnosis alone, combining hypnosis with chemical forms of anesthesia apparently helps many individuals (Hammond, 2008; Fredericks, 2001). Beyond its use in the control of pain, hypnosis has been used successfully to help treat problems, such as anxiety, skin diseases, asthma, insomnia, stuttering, high blood pressure, warts, and other forms of infection (Covino & Pinnell, 2010; Mellinger, 2010).

Many people also turn to hypnosis to help break bad habits, such as smoking, nail biting, and overeating. Does hypnosis help? Research has shown that hypnosis does indeed help some people to quit smoking (Green, 2010). It also helps many people to better control their eating and lose weight, particularly if hypnosis is paired with cognitive treatments, interventions that help people change their conscious ways of thinking (Ginandes, 2006; Lynn & Kirsch, 2006).

Why Does Hypnosis Work?

There are various theories about why hypnosis works (Lynn et al., 2010; Kallio & Revonsuo, 2003). One views hypnosis as a state of *divided consciousness* (Sadler & Woody, 2010; Hilgard, 1992). Another theory suggested by Canadian Nick Spanos (Spanos et al., 1995), who worked at Carleton University (prior to his death in 1994), sees it as an implementation of *common social and cognitive processes* or role-playing (see **Figure 6-8**).

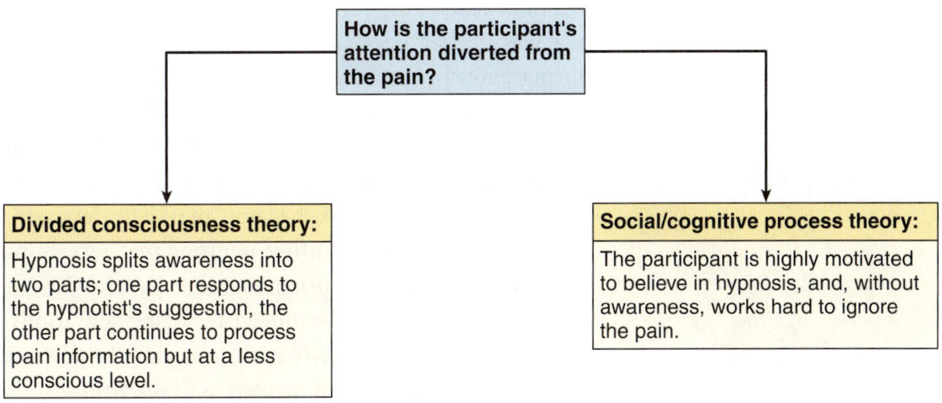

FIGURE 6-8 Explaining hypnosis. Two theories explain how a hypnotized individual is able to ignore pain.

Ernest Hilgard demonstrated that people hypnotized and instructed that they could "not hear" loud noises can indicate, by raising a finger or other behavioural response, that "some part" of the them could still hear noise (Hilgard, 1992). From this result, Hilgard concluded that consciousness splits into two parts and that both act at once during hypnosis, an experience called **dissociation** (Sadler & Woody, 2010; Hilgard, 1992). One part of our consciousness becomes fully tuned into and responsive to the hypnotist's suggestions. The second part, which Hilgard called the *hidden observer*, operates at a subtler, less conscious level, continuing to process information that is seemingly unavailable to the hypnotized person. According to Hilgard, the hidden observer was the part of the student's mind that was still able to hear while hypnotized.

dissociation a splitting of consciousness into two dimensions.

In direct opposition to Hilgard, Nick Spanos developed an alternative theory of hypnosis, which held that hypnosis is not an altered state of consciousness. Spanos' theory is that, instead of resulting from a divided consciousness, hypnotic phenomena consist simply of highly motivated people performing tasks, being extra attentive, and enacting roles that are asked of them—that is, they are playing a part in a social interaction between themselves, the "hypnotist," and the audience. Because of their strong beliefs in hypnosis, the people fail to recognize or ignore their own active contributions to the process (Dienes et al., 2010; Spanos et al., 1995). In a similar manner, people who are hypnotized and regressed to an earlier age will often be able to describe their sixth birthday in great detail, suggesting that hypnosis has greatly enhanced their memory abilities. Typically, however, audiences at hypnosis shows do not check the details of those hypnosis-assisted memories. Martin Orne (1951), in a classic study, did check the accounts of early life events told by hypnotically regressed people (by talking to their parents); he found that their vivid accounts of early birthdays and other life events were largely made up. These data better supports Spanos' view than Hilgard's.

Hypnosis WHAT HAPPENS IN THE BRAIN?

When people are hypnotized, they are usually first guided into a state of *mental relaxation*. Studies have found that during this state, neural activity in key areas of the cerebral cortex and thalamus—brain regions that, as we noted earlier, are implicated in conscious awareness—slows down significantly (Rainville et al., 2002). Hypnotized individuals are next guided into a state of *mental absorption,* during which they focus carefully on the hypnotist's voice and instructions and actively block out other sources of stimulation, both internal and environmental. In fact, mental absorption has often been described as a state of *total focus*. During this state, cerebral blood flow and neural activity actually pick back up in key areas of the cerebral cortex, thalamus, and other parts of the brain's attention and conscious awareness systems (Naish, 2010; Oakley & Halligan, 2010; Rainville et al., 2002).

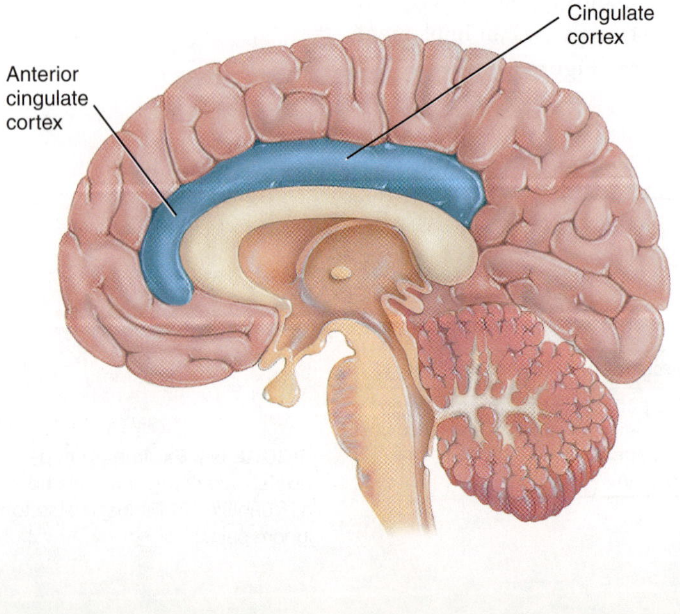

Neuroimaging research suggests that one part of the brain's cerebral cortex, the *anterior cingulate cortex,* may be particularly involved when hypnosis is used to anesthetize or reduce pain. This region has been implicated both in general awareness and in the unpleasantness we feel during pain. In one study, participants were hypnotically induced to ignore their pain while placing their hands in painfully hot water (Rainville et al., 1997). While the individuals were in a hypnotic pain-free state, neurons in their anterior cingulate cortex became markedly less active. Although the activity of other neurons that receive pain messages continued as usual in these people's brains—suggesting that they were indeed receiving sensations of pain—the decreased activity in the anterior cingulate cortex seemed to reduce their *awareness* of the pain.

Before You Go On

www.wiley.com/go/comer

What Do You Know?

9. What are hypnotic hallucinations and how might they be useful?
10. How does Hilgard use the idea of a divided consciousness to explain hypnosis?

What Do You Think?

What are the ethical implications of using hypnosis to control behaviour?

SCAN TO GET THE ANSWERS

Meditation

LEARNING OBJECTIVE 5

Describe the techniques and effects of meditation.

PSYCHOLOGY AROUND US Inhale...Exhale...

Reyna was worried. She was trying to study for her organic chemistry midterm, but she couldn't get past her fight with Lisa. And Lisa wasn't responding to her texts. Reyna's anxiety continued to climb about both the exam and the fight. She just couldn't find her focus. She certainly couldn't study.

Reyna finally decided to try one of the techniques she had learned in her meditation and yoga class. She sat cross-legged on the floor and closed her eyes. She noticed her breathing coming in from her nose and down into her chest. She decided to shift her breathing to take in deeper breaths through her mouth and down into her diaphragm. She began to count. Inhale one. Exhale two.

Some thoughts of organic chem and of the nasty things that Lisa had said still came to Reyna's mind, but now she was able to just let the thoughts drift away. And she kept pulling her focus back to her breathing. Inhale 51. Exhale 52. Reyna noticed a tingling relaxation in her hands and her back—it was a little weird, but not uncomfortable. Inhale 85. Exhale 86.

When Reyna reached 100, she let her consciousness shift away from her breathing and onto her body instead. She then opened her eyes to look around the room. She took one more quick, wistful look at her cell phone, and then returned to her desk to give studying another shot.

In this example, Reyna employed meditation to help her focus. **Meditation** is a technique designed to turn one's consciousness away from the outer world, toward inner cues and awareness, ignoring all stressors (Butler, 2011; Fontana, 2007). The technique typically involves going to a quiet place, assuming either a specific body position or simply a comfortable position, controlling one's breathing, limiting one's outward attention, and forming internal images. The result of such efforts is an altered state of consciousness, accompanied by deeply relaxing and pleasant feelings.

meditation technique designed to turn one's consciousness away from the outer world toward one's inner cues and awareness.

Meditation is an ancient practice that can be traced through the history of all the world's major religions. Perhaps the best known practices derive from the yoga traditions of the Hindu religion and from the Zen traditions of Buddhism. *Yoga* is a form of meditation that involves adjusting the body into different positions, or *poses*, in an attempt to also regulate blood flow, heart rate, and digestive processes.

Two major techniques to meditation seem to use opposite approaches. In *opening-up* approaches, meditators seek to clear their mind to receive new experiences. One opening-up technique is to imagine oneself as another person; a related opening-up technique involves the performance of a common task in a slightly different way, to call better attention to one's daily routine. In the other kind of meditation approach, *concentrative meditation*, people actively concentrate on an object, word, or idea, called a *mantra*. In some versions of this approach, people concentrate instead on a riddle, called a *koan*. A well-known koan involves answering the question, "What is the sound of one hand clapping?"

One of meditation's greatest appeals is that it can help people relax (Brown et al., 2010). In fact, studies have shown that people in meditative states experience increases in the same brain waves that are associated with the relaxation phase individuals experience just prior to falling sleep (Aftanas & Golasheiken, 2003). Research has found that meditation also can lower respiration, heart rate, blood pressure, and muscle tension. Because of its positive impact on physical functioning, it has been used to help treat pain, asthma, high blood pressure, heart problems, skin disorders, diabetes, and viral infections (Gregoski et al., 2011; Wootton, 2008). One form of meditation that has been applied in particular to patients suffering from severe pain is *mindfulness meditation* (Labbe, 2011; Kabat-Zinn, 2005). Here, meditators pay attention to the feelings, thoughts, and sensations that are flowing through their minds during meditation, but they do so with detachment and without judgment. By just being mindful but not judgmental of their feelings and thoughts, including feelings of pain, the individuals are less inclined to label or fixate on them and, in turn, less likely to react negatively to them. Being mindful or being in the moment can help us look past distracters and focus on the tasks immediately at hand. For example, a group of people who were asked to take a brief course in Zen meditation had their driving performance assessed before and after they completed the meditation course. Overall driving performance scores increased following the meditation course (Berger, 1988), suggesting that being in the moment is a good thing when you are driving!

Before You Go On

www.wiley.com/go/comer

What Do You Know?

11. What are the physical effects of meditation?
12. What are the main benefits of altering consciousness through meditation?

What Do You Think?

Which approach to meditation appeals more to you, opening-up meditation or concentrative meditation? Why?

SCAN TO GET THE ANSWERS

Psychoactive Drugs

WHAT HAPPENS IN THE BRAIN?

LEARNING OBJECTIVE 6

List and describe common depressant, stimulant, and hallucinogenic psychoactive drugs and their effects.

What is one of the first things you do every day? For millions of people, the answer is to have a cup of coffee (maybe more than one). Why do so many people do this? For most, it is to give themselves a bit of a jolt and get the day going. Similarly, people often use other substances to help improve, or at least change, how they feel or function. Many people smoke cigarettes to feel more alert, less anxious, or both. Others may have a glass of wine or beer in the evening to wind down from a hectic day.

These substances—coffee, cigarettes, and alcohol—along with many others, alter our state of consciousness and influence our moods and behaviours. Collectively, they are examples of **psychoactive drugs**, chemicals that affect awareness, behaviour, sensation, perception, or mood. Some such drugs are illegal chemicals (heroin, ecstasy, marijuana), while others are common and legal. **Table 6-1** shows the three broad categories of drugs and lists examples of specific drugs that fall within those categories.

psychoactive drugs chemicals that affect awareness, behaviour, sensation, perception, or mood.

addiction psychological or physical compulsion to take a drug, resulting from regular ingestion and leading to maladaptive patterns of behaviour and changes in physical response.

Some of the changes brought about by psychoactive drugs are temporary, lasting only as long as the chemicals remain in the brain and body. But certain psychoactive drugs can also bring about long-term changes and problems. People who regularly ingest them may develop maladaptive patterns of behaviour and changes in their body's physical responses, a pattern commonly called **addiction**. We will also be discussing addiction in Chapter 11

TABLE 6-1 Psychoactive Drugs and Their Effects

Drug Class	Action in the Brain	Effects
Depressants		**Depress activity of central nervous system**
Alcohol	Influences the neurochemical GABA	Slows down brain areas that control judgment, inhibition, behaviour (speech, motor functioning, emotional expression)
Sedative-hypnotics (benzodiazepines)	Influences the neurochemical GABA in calming neural activity	Produces relaxation and drowsiness, relieves anxiety
Opioids (opium heroin, morphine, codeine, methadone)	Activates the opiod receptors in the brain, providing their anagesic effect and their related high	Reduces pain and emotional tension, produces pleasurable and calming feelings
Stimulants		**Increase activity of central nervous system**
Caffeine	Blocks access to adenosine receptors, which produce sensations of drowsiness when stimulated	Increases alertness
Nicotine	Influences dopamine and acetocholene	Increases alertness, reduces stress
Cocaine	Blocks re-uptake of dopamine, norepinephrine, and serotonin	Increases energy and alertness, produces euphoric feelings of well-being and confidence
Amphetamines	Increase release of dopamine and norepinephrine	Increases energy and alertness, reduces appetite, produces euphoric feelings
Hallucinogens		**Enhance normal perceptions**
LSD	Stimulates dopanine and serotonin receptors	Dramatically strengthens visual perceptions (including illusions and hallucinations) along with profound psychological and physical changes
Cannabis (marijuana, THC)	Encourages release of endorphins and dopamine	Produces a mixture of hallucinogenic, depressant, and stimulant effects
MDMA (Ecstasy)	Causes a "dump" of serotonin stores	Enhances sensory perceptions, increases energy and alertness, produces feelings of empathy and emotional well-being

PRACTICALLY SPEAKING Addictions: Living out of Control

Reducing harm. Vancouver's Coastal Health Service opened a safe injection site near Vancouver's Downtown Eastside in 2003. It offers clean needle and supervision of injections by heroin users, as well as support and referrals for treatment.

Many people struggle with addiction problems. According to some clinical theorists, addictions are not only about alcohol and substance abuse; they may also cover dependencies such as food, the Internet, gambling, caffeine, shopping, sex, and exercise, to name a few (Page & Brewster, 2009; Stein, 2008). Addictive patterns do not suddenly appear; they are usually long-standing and may be rooted in various psychological problems. Whereas it takes time for individuals to lose control of their life to a dependency, it also takes time, motivation, commitment, discipline, and often the help of a professional treatment program to regain control and recover from an addiction. There are no quick fixes for recovery.

How do you know whether you or someone close to you is experiencing an addiction? This is a complex issue that typically requires careful clinical assessment for a definitive answer. Nevertheless, there are some straightforward questions that you can use to determine whether professional attention is in order. For example, is the person unable to meet responsibilities at home, school, or the office? Has the person tried to stop the repeated behaviour but cannot, and continues to engage in it despite the apparent dangers?

Although most clinicians agree that there is no substitute for careful clinical assessment and treatment of addictions, some have developed basic detection devices that can help get the ball rolling. For example, a brief tool to detect alcohol addiction is known as the CAGE questionnaire. It asks these questions: (1) Has the person ever felt that he or she should CUT DOWN on the drinking? (2) Has the person ever been ANNOYED by people criticizing the drinking?

(3) Has the person ever expressed remorse or GUILT about drinking? (4) Has the person ever started to drink in the morning as an EYE-OPENER to start the day or get rid of a hangover? A "yes" answer to at least two of these questions may indicate a problem with alcohol addiction and a corresponding need for professional assessment and treatment. More than a quarter century after the CAGE questionnaire was first developed, it has been validated in many studies as an effective, quick indicator of the need for help (O'Brien, 2008).

when we examine the motives and drives that direct behaviour, including chronic drug-taking behaviour.

Those addicted to a drug feel psychologically and physically compelled to keep taking it. They rely on the drug excessively and chronically, and may damage their family and social relationships, function poorly at work, or put themselves and others in danger. Addicted individuals may also acquire a physical dependence on the drug. They may develop a **tolerance** for the drug, meaning they need larger and larger doses to keep feeling its desired effect. And, if they try to stop taking or cut back on the drug, they may experience unpleasant and even dangerous **withdrawal symptoms**, such as nausea, cramps, sweating, or anxiety. People in withdrawal may also *crave* the drug that they had been taking regularly. Even if they want to quit taking it, the knowledge that they can quickly eliminate the unpleasant withdrawal symptoms by simply ingesting the drug makes it difficult for many users to persevere through the withdrawal period (Verster et al., 2011). In any given year, 2 percent of all teens and adults Canada, around 600,000 people, use cocaine, ecstasy, or hallucinogens, and 194,000 Canadians (0.8 percent) are dependent on illicit drugs (Statistics Canada, 2004).

tolerance mark of physical dependence on a drug, in which the person is required to take incrementally larger doses of the drug to achieve the same effect.

withdrawal symptoms unpleasant and sometimes dangerous side effects of reducing intake of a drug after a person has become addicted.

Depressants

Psychoactive drugs that slow down the central nervous system are called **depressants**. They reduce tension and inhibitions and may interfere with a person's judgment, motor activity, and concentration. The three most widely used groups of depressants are *alcohol, sedative-hypnotic drugs*, and *opioids*.

depressants class of drugs that slow the activity of the central nervous system.

Alcohol *Alcohol,* a depressant that is taken in liquid form, is one of the most commonly used psychoactive drugs. More than three-quarters of the people in Canada drink beverages that contain alcohol, at least from time to time (Statistics Canada, 2004). Nearly 35 percent of Canadians over age 15 engage in heavy drinking (five or more drinks) at least once a year, and nearly half of those (48 percent) do so at least once a month. Among heavy drinkers, males outnumber females by more than two to one, around 8 percent to 4 percent (Statistics Canada, 2004).

Cultural endorsement? Five men and hundreds of others around them celebrate at Oktoberfest, Germany's annual 16-day festival, marked by eating, special events, and perhaps most prominently, drinking. Almost 7 million litres of beer are served to thousands of revellers at each year's festival, an excessiveness that many believe contributes to binge drinking and alcoholism.

All alcoholic beverages contain *ethyl alcohol*, a chemical that is quickly absorbed into the blood through the lining of the stomach and the intestine. The ethyl alcohol immediately begins to take effect as it is carried in the bloodstream to the central nervous system (the brain and spinal cord). There, it acts to slow functioning by binding to various neurons, particularly those that normally receive a neurotransmitter called *gamma aminobutyric acid*, or *GABA*, and reduces the influence of GABA in causing neurons to fire.

At first, ethyl alcohol slows down the brain areas that control judgment and inhibition; people become looser and more talkative, relaxed, and happy. When more alcohol is absorbed, it slows down additional areas in the central nervous system, causing the drinkers to make poorer judgments,

Binge Drinking and Post-Secondary Students

Binge drinking—the consumption of five or more drinks in a row—is a major problem in many settings, not the least of which are college and university campuses (NSDUH, 2008; Read et al., 2008). According to research, 60 percent of college- and university-aged students binge drink at least once each year, many of them at least monthly (Statistics Canada, 2004). These are higher rates than those among similar-aged individuals who do not attend college or university (Ksir et al., 2008). On many campuses, alcohol use often is an accepted part of life. Thirty-two percent of Canadian undergraduates report engaging in hazardous or harmful patterns of drinking, with the percentage being higher (43 percent) for those living in residence. Happy hours and other promotions at campus bars are seen to be part of the problem (Centre for Addiction and Mental Health, 2004).

Alcohol poisoning can lead to death; a level of blood alcohol of five times the legal limit or 0.40 percent will kill about half of those affected. As well, a high blood alcohol level reduces gap reflexes and can cause people to vomit and then choke on the vomit, also potentially leading to death (Mittal, Desai, & Khade, 1991).

Efforts to reduce college/university binge drinking have begun to make a difference. Some universities, for example, now provide substance-free dorms (Wechsler et al., 2002). The implications are clear: college/university drinking, including binge drinking, is more common and harmful than previously believed. And most experts agree that the time has come to attack this enormous problem head on.

become careless, and remember less well. Many people become highly emotional, and some become loud and aggressive.

As drinking continues, the motor responses of individuals decline and their reaction times slow. They may be unsteady when they stand or walk, for example. Their vision becomes blurred, and they may misjudge distances. They can also have trouble hearing. As a result, people who have drunk too much alcohol may have enormous difficulty driving or solving simple problems.

As summarized in **Table 6-2**, the *concentration*, or proportion, of ethyl alcohol in the blood determines how much it will affect a person (Ksir et al., 2008). When the alcohol concentration reaches 0.06 percent of the blood volume, a person usually feels relaxed and comfortable. By the time it reaches 0.09 percent, the drinker crosses the line into *intoxication*. If the level goes as high as 0.55 percent, death will probably result. Most people, however, lose consciousness before they can drink enough to reach this level. The effects of alcohol subside only when the alcohol concentration in the blood falls.

Though legal, alcohol is actually one of society's most dangerous drugs, and its risks extend to all age groups. In fact, 10 percent of Canadian elementary school students admit to some alcohol use, and nearly 45 percent of 15- to 19-year-olds reported at least one episode of heavy drink over a year, with about half of those doing so at least

TABLE 6-2 Alcohol's Effects on the Body and Behaviour

Number of Drinks[a] in Two Hours	Blood Alcohol Content (%)[b]	Effect
(2)	0.06	Relaxed state; increased sociability
(3)	0.09	Everyday stress lessened
(4)	0.10	Movements and speech become clumsy
(7)	0.20	Very drunk; loud and difficult to understand; emotions unstable
(12)	0.40	Difficult to wake up; incapable of voluntary action
(15)	0.55	Coma and/or death

[a]A drink refers to one 12-ounce beer, a 4-ounce glass of wine, or a 1.25-ounce shot of hard liquor.
[b]In Canada, the legal blood alcohol level for "drunk driving" varies from 0.05 to 0.08.

monthly (Statistics Canada, 2004). Surveys indicate that over a one-year period, 6.6 percent of all adults in the world fall into a long-term pattern of alcohol addiction, known as **alcoholism** (Somers et al., 2004). More than 13 percent of adults experience the pattern at some time in their lives, with men outnumbering women by at least two to one (Kessler et al., 2005).

alcoholism long-term pattern of alcohol addiction.

According to work by Deborah Chansonneuve of the Aboriginal Healing Society in Ottawa, 75 percent of Aboriginal Canadians say they have a problem with alcohol in their community, 33 percent say it is a problem in their household, and 25 percent say they have a personal problem with alcohol (Chansonneuve, 2007). Generally, Asians in North America have lower rates of alcoholism than do people from other cultures. As many as one-half of Asians have a deficiency of *alcohol dehydrogenase*, a chemical responsible for breaking down and eliminating alcohol from the body, so they react very negatively to even a small intake of alcohol. Such extreme reactions help prevent heavy use (Wall et al., 2001; APA, 2000).

People who abuse alcohol drink large amounts regularly and rely on it to help them to do things that would otherwise make them nervous. Eventually the drinking disrupts their social behaviour and their ability to think clearly and work effectively. Many build up a tolerance for alcohol, and they need to drink greater and greater amounts to feel its effects. They also experience withdrawal when they stop drinking. Within hours, for example, their hands and eyelids begin to shake, they feel weak, they sweat heavily, their heart beats rapidly, and their blood pressure rises (APA, 2000).

Alcoholism can wreak havoc on an individual's family, social, and occupational life (Murphy et al., 2005). Medical treatment, lost productivity, and losses due to death from alcoholism cost society many billions of dollars each year. The disorder also has been implicated in more than one-third of all suicides, homicides, assaults, rapes, and accidental deaths (Ksir et al., 2008). A total of 34 percent of all fatal automobile accidents in Canada involved alcohol use (Mayhew, Brown, & Simpson, 2002). Children whose parents have alcoholism are also severely affected by this disorder. The home life of these children often features much conflict and, in some cases, sexual or other forms of abuse. The children themselves have elevated rates of psychological problems and substance-related disorders over the course of their lives (Hall & Webster, 2002). Many display low self-esteem, weak communication skills, poor sociability, and marital problems compared to general averages (Watt, 2002; Lewis-Harter, 2000).

Spreading the word. Perhaps the most successful public effort to reduce drunk driving fatalities has been undertaken by Mothers Against Drunk Driving (MADD). Raising public awareness through ads, campaigns, and lobbying efforts, this organization has helped reduce the number of alcohol-related automobile deaths by 47 percent since it was formed in 1980.

Long-term excessive drinking can also cause severe damage to one's physical health (Myrick & Wright, 2008). It so overworks the liver—the body organ that breaks down alcohol—that people may develop an irreversible condition called *cirrhosis*, in which the liver becomes scarred and dysfunctional (CDC, 2008). Alcohol abuse may also damage the heart and lower the immune system's ability to fight off infections and cancer and to resist the onset of AIDS after infection.

Finally, women who drink during pregnancy place their fetuses at risk (Finnegan & Kandall, 2008). Heavy drinking early in pregnancy often leads to a miscarriage. Excessive alcohol use during pregnancy may also cause a baby to be born with *fetal alcohol syndrome (FAS)* or *fetal alcohol effects (FAE)*, a pattern that can include intellectual disability, hyperactivity, head and face deformities, heart defects, and slow growth. It has been estimated that in the overall population, approximately 1 to 3 of every 1,000 babies is born with FAS, and 30 in every 1,000 babies is born with FAE (Health Canada, 2005).

sedative-hypnotic drugs class of drugs, the members of which produce feelings of relaxation and drowsiness.

Sedative-Hypnotic Drugs At low dosages, **sedative-hypnotic drugs** produce feelings of relaxation and drowsiness. At higher dosages, they are sleep inducers, or hypnotics.

Benzodiazepines, antianxiety drugs developed in the 1950s, are the most popular sedative-hypnotic drugs available today. More than 100 million prescriptions are written each year for this group of chemical compounds (Bisaga, 2008). Xanax®, Ativan®, and Valium® are three of the benzodiazepines in wide clinical use.

This group of drugs reduces anxiety without making people as overly drowsy as alcohol or other depressant substances. Nevertheless, in high enough doses, benzodiazepines can cause intoxication and lead to addiction (Dupont & Dupont, 2005). As many as 2 percent of adults in North America become addicted to these drugs at some point in their lives (Kassam & Scott, 2006).

Opioids The term opioids refers to *opium* and drugs derived from it, including *heroin, morphine, codeine,* and *OxyContin.* Opium, a substance taken from the sap of the opium poppy, has been used for thousands of years. In the past, it was used widely in the treatment of medical disorders because of its ability to reduce both physical pain and emotional distress. Physicians eventually discovered, however, that the drug was addictive. Morphine and heroin, each of which was later derived from opium for use as a safer painkiller, also proved to be highly addictive. In fact, heroin is even more addictive than the other opioids.

opioids class of drugs derived from the sap of the opium poppy.

Additional drugs have been derived from opium, and several synthetic (laboratory-blended) opioids such as *methadone* have also been developed. Each of these various drugs has a different strength, speed of action, and tolerance level. Today, morphine and codeine are used as medical opioids, usually prescribed to relieve pain. Heroin is illegal in Canada under all circumstances.

Outside of medical settings, opioids are smoked, inhaled, snorted (inhaled through the nose), injected by needle just beneath the skin ("skin popped"), or injected directly into the blood stream ("mainlined"). An injection quickly produces a *rush*—a spasm of warmth and joy that is sometimes compared with an orgasm. The brief spasm is followed by several hours of a pleasant feeling and shift in consciousness called a *high* or *nod.* During a high, the opioid user feels very relaxed and happy and is unconcerned about food or other bodily needs.

Opioids depress the central nervous system, particularly the brain areas that control emotion. The drugs attach to brain receptors that ordinarily receive endorphins, neurotransmitters discussed in the previous chapter, that help reduce pain and emotional tension (Hart et al., 2010). When neurons receive opioids at these receptors, the opioids produce the same kinds of pleasant and relaxing feelings that endorphins would produce.

The most direct danger of heroin use is an overdose, which shuts down the respiratory centre in the brain, almost paralyzing breathing, and in many cases, causing death. Death is particularly likely during sleep, when individuals cannot fight the respiratory effects by consciously working at breathing. Each year, 2 percent of those addicted to heroin and other opioids are killed by the drugs, usually from an overdose (Theodorou & Haber, 2005; APA, 2000).

Stimulants

Psychoactive drugs that speed up the central nervous system are called stimulants. They produce increases in blood pressure, heart rate, alertness, thinking, and behaviour. Among the most problematic stimulants are *caffeine, nicotine, cocaine,* and *amphetamines.*

stimulants substances that increase the activity of the central nervous system.

Caffeine *Caffeine,* a mild (and legal) stimulant, is the world's most widely used stimulant. It is found in coffee, tea, chocolate, cola, and so-called *energy drinks.* Worldwide, 80 percent of all people consume caffeine in one form or another every day (Rogers, 2005). Like many other psychoactive drugs, caffeine is addictive, although this addiction does not cause the significant social problems associated with substances such as alcohol, heroin, and cocaine (Paton & Beer, 2001; Silverman et al., 1992). Still, quitting caffeine can cause unpleasant withdrawal symptoms for chronic users, including lethargy, sleepiness, anxiety, irritability, depression, constipation, and headaches. Withdrawal symptoms can start only a few hours after the individual's last consumption of caffeine.

Energy drinks are a relatively new way in which people are getting caffeine. Energy drinks contain very large amounts of caffeine and if not taken in moderation, can result in caffeine intoxication (Red Bull cans have a label saying not to drink more than two). Caffeine intoxication can involve restlessness, fidgetiness, nervousness, excitement, euphoria, insomnia, flushing of the face, increased urination, gastrointestinal disturbance, muscle twitching, a rambling flow of thought and speech, irritability, irregular or rapid heartbeat, and psychomotor agitation (Reissig, Strain, & Griffiths, 2009). If you notice any of these symptoms, check the amount of caffeine in the things you are drinking (remember cola beverages have caffeine in them, too) and pace yourself a bit more carefully.

Nicotine Although legal, *nicotine* is one of the most highly addictive substances known (Hart et al., 2010). Most commonly, it is taken into the body by smoking tobacco. Nicotine is then absorbed through the respiratory tract, the mucous membranes of the nasal area, and the gastrointestinal tract. The drug proceeds to activate nicotine receptors located throughout the brain and body. Inhaling a puff of cigarette smoke delivers a dose of nicotine to the brain faster than it could be delivered by injection into the blood stream.

Regular smokers develop a tolerance for nicotine and must smoke more and more to achieve the same results (Hymowitz, 2005). When they try to stop smoking, they experience withdrawal symptoms such as irritability, increased appetite, sleep disturbances, and a powerful desire to smoke (Dodgen, 2005; APA, 2000).

Almost one-fifth of all individuals over the age of 14 in Canada regularly smoke tobacco. Surveys also find that nearly 15 percent of all high school students smoke (Health Canada, 2008). All of this smoking eventually takes a heavy toll: 37,000 people in Canada die each year as a result of smoking. Chronic smoking is directly tied to lung disease, high blood pressure, coronary heart disease, cancer, stroke, and other fatal medical problems (Health Canada, 2008). Moreover, pregnant women who smoke are much more likely than non-smokers to deliver premature and underweight babies (NSDUH, 2008).

Cocaine *Cocaine,* the key active ingredient of South America's coca plant, is the most powerful natural stimulant currently known. The drug was first separated from the plant in 1865. For many centuries, however, native people have chewed the leaves of the plant to raise their energy and increase their alertness.

Processed cocaine—a white, fluffy powder—is snorted and absorbed through the mucous membrane of the nose. Some users, however, prefer the more powerful effects of injecting cocaine intravenously or smoking it in a pipe or cigarette. Around 311,000 Canadians over 14 years of age used cocaine in 2008 (Health Canada, 2009).

Cocaine brings on a rush of euphoria and well-being—an orgasmic-like reaction if the dose is high enough. Initially, cocaine stimulates the higher centres of the central nervous system, shifting users' levels of awareness and making them excited, energetic, and talkative. As more cocaine is taken, it stimulates additional areas of the central nervous system, resulting in increases in heart rate, blood pressure, breathing, arousal, and wakefulness. Cocaine apparently produces these effects largely by increasing activity of the neurotransmitter *dopamine* at key neurons throughout the brain (Haney, 2008). As the stimulating effects of cocaine subside, the user experiences a depression-like letdown, popularly called *crashing* (Doweiko, 2006).

Regular use of cocaine may lead to a pattern of addiction. Tolerance to the drug may develop, and suddenly withdrawing from it results in depression, fatigue, sleep problems, anxiety, and irritability (Hart et al., 2010). Today, almost 1 out of every 100 people over the age of 12 in the United States is addicted to cocaine (NSDUH, 2008).

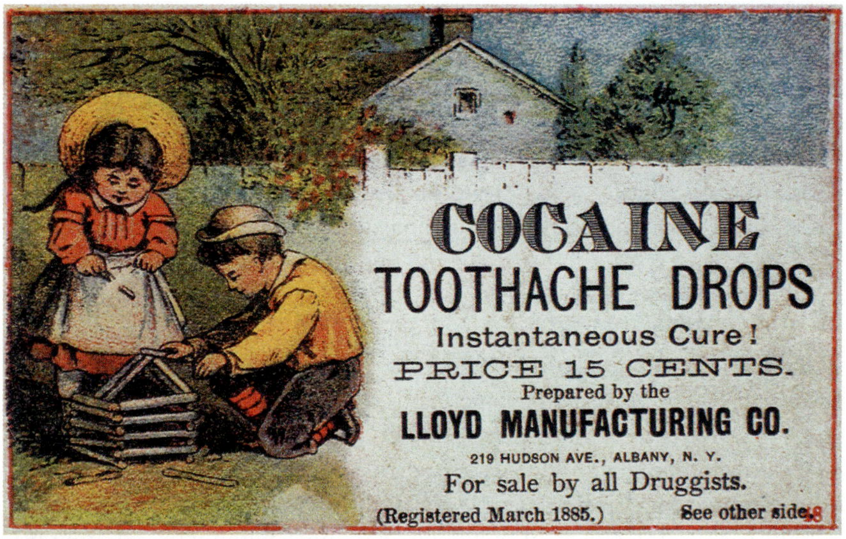

The early days. In the early twentieth century, cocaine was an ingredient in such products as Cocaine Toothache Drops and Coca-Cola soft drinks.

Cocaine also poses serious physical dangers (Kosten et al., 2008). Use of the drug in powerful, smokable forms, known as *freebasing* and *crack,* are the major contributors to the annual number of cocaine-related overdoses (SAMHSA, 2008). In addition, cocaine use has been linked to as many as 20 percent of all suicides among people under 61 years of age (Garlow, 2002). The greatest danger of cocaine use is an overdose, which may impair breathing, produce major—even fatal—heart irregularities, or cause brain seizures (Doweiko, 2006).

Amphetamines *Amphetamines* are manufactured in the laboratory. These stimulants are most often taken in pill or capsule form, although some individuals inject the drugs intravenously or smoke them for a quicker and more powerful effect. Like cocaine, amphetamines increase energy and alertness and lower appetite in small doses, produce intoxication and psychosis in higher doses, and cause an emotional letdown when they leave the body. Also like cocaine, these drugs produce such effects by increasing the activity of the neurotransmitter *dopamine* (Haney, 2008).

Tolerance to amphetamines builds very rapidly, thus increasing the chances of users becoming addicted (Acosta, Haller, & Schnoll, 2005). People who start using the drug to help reduce their appetite, for example, may soon find they are as hungry as ever and increase their dose in response. Athletes who use amphetamines to increase their energy may also soon find that they need increasing amounts of the drug. When people who are addicted to the drug stop taking it, they fall into a pattern of deep depression and extended sleep identical to the withdrawal from cocaine. Around 0.1 percent of the Canadian population uses amphetamines (Health Canada, 2009).

"Drugs are a bet with your mind."
—Jim Morrison, singer, The Doors. Died of suspected overdose in 1971.

One powerful kind of amphetamine, *methamphetamine* (nicknamed *crank* in one impure form or crystal meth in a more pure form), currently is experiencing a major surge in popularity. Over 6 percent of all people over the age of 15 in the Canada have now used a form of this stimulant at least once (Department of Justice, 2007). It is available in the form of crystals (known as *ice* or *crystal meth*), which users smoke.

Most of the non-medical methamphetamine is made in small, illegal "stovetop laboratories," which typically operate for a few days and then move on to a new location (Hart et al., 2010). Although such laboratories have been around since the 1960s, they have increased eightfold over the past decade. A major health concern is that the secret laboratories produce dangerous fumes and residue (Burgess, 2001).

Around 60 percent of current methamphetamine users are men (NSDUH, 2008). The drug is particularly popular among biker gangs, in rural areas, and urban gay communities, and has gained wide use as a "club drug," the term for drugs of choice at all-night dance parties, or "raves" (Ksir et al., 2008).

Like other kinds of amphetamines, methamphetamine increases activity of the neurotransmitter dopamine, producing increased arousal, attention, and related effects. This particular drug also may damage nerve endings, a *neurotoxicity* that is compounded by the drug's tendency to remain in the brain and body for a long time—more than six hours (Rawson & Ling, 2008). But, among users, such dangers are less important than methamphetamine's immediate positive impact, including perceptions by many that it makes them feel hypersexual and uninhibited (Jefferson, 2005). All of this has contributed to major public health problems. For example, one-third of all men who tested positive for HIV in Los Angeles in 2004 reported having used this drug (Jefferson, 2005). Similarly, according to surveys, a growing number of domestic-violence incidents, assaults, and robberies have been tied to the use of methamphetamine (Jefferson, 2005). A likely explanation for these findings links back to the effects of methamphetamine, where increased arousal leads to increased sexual activity and/or violence (Hirshfiled et al., 2004).

Methylenedioxymethamphetamine, or MDMD (better known as ecstasy), is another "club drug" form of methamphetamine often found at raves. Ecstasy produces its effects by causing a dump of the serotonin neurotransmitter substance stored in neurons in the mood regulation centre of the brain. The result is a sense of euphoria, reduced anxiety, and increased social intimacy lasting for two to four hours. The complete dump of serotonin initiated by the ecstasy means that if one takes more of the drug when the effects of the initial dose wear off, there is no additional effect. Short-term issues can include dehydration, difficulty concentrating, lack of appetite, and dry mouth. Longer-term negative effects can include depression, anxiety, paranoia, and irritability (Verheyden, Henry, & Curran, 2003; Verheyden, Maidment, & Curran, 2003).

Hallucinogens

hallucinogens substances that dramatically change one's state of awareness, causing powerful changes in sensory perception.

Hallucinogens, or *psychedelic drugs*, are substances that dramatically change one's state of awareness by causing powerful changes in sensory perception, such as enhancing a person's normal perceptions and producing illusions and hallucinations. The substance-induced sensory changes are sometimes called "trips," and these trips may be exciting or frightening, depending on how a person's mind reacts to the drugs. Many hallucinogens come from plants or animals; others are laboratory-produced.

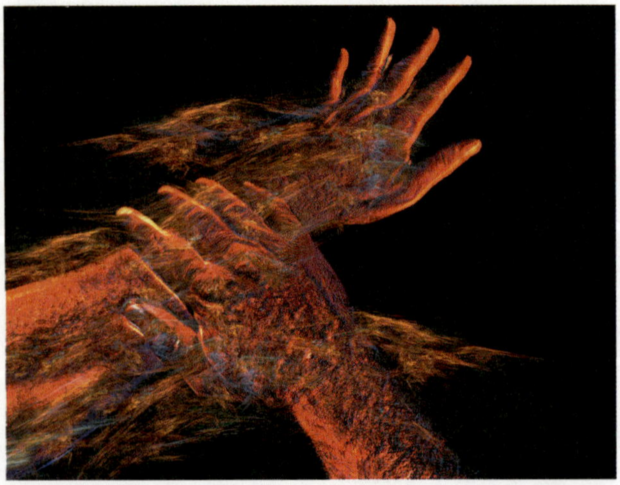

Bad trip. Ingesting LSD brings on hallucinosis, a state of sensory and perceptual distortions. Sometimes this state can be very frightening and disorienting, as captured in this photo illustration of a hallucination of hands and arms burning.

LSD *Lysergic acid diethylamide*, or *LSD*, is a very powerful hallucinogen that was derived by the Swiss chemist Albert Hoffman in 1938 from a group of naturally occurring substances. During the 1960s, a period of rebellion and experimentation, millions of users turned to the drug in an effort to raise their consciousness and expand their experiences. Within two hours of being swallowed, LSD brings on *hallucinosis*, a state marked by a strengthening of visual perceptions and profound psychological and physical changes. People may focus on small details—each hair on the skin, for example. Colours may seem brighter or take on a shade of purple. Users often experience illusions in which objects seem distorted and seem to move, breathe, or change shape. LSD can also produce strong emotions, from joy to anxiety or depression. Past thoughts and feelings may return. All these effects take place while the user is fully alert, and wear off in about six hours. Scientists believe that LSD produces these effects primarily by binding to many of the neurons that normally receive the neurotransmitter *serotonin*, changing the neurotransmitter's activity at those sites (Julien, 2008).

Just under 1 percent of all people in Canada have used LSD or another hallucinogen over the past year (Health Canada, 2009). A key problem is that LSD is so powerful that any dose, no matter how small, is likely to produce very strong reactions. Sometimes the reactions are quite unpleasant, an experience called a "bad trip." In addition, some LSD users have **flashbacks**, recurrences of the sensory and emotional changes even after the LSD has left the body (Doweiko, 2006).

flashbacks recurrence of the sensory and emotional changes after the LSD has left the body.

Cannabis The hemp plant *Cannabis sativa* grows in warm climates. Collectively, the drugs produced from varieties of hemp are called *cannabis*. The most powerful of them is *hashish*; the weaker ones include the best-known form of cannabis, *marijuana*, a mixture derived from the buds, crushed leaves, and flowering tops of hemp plants.

Although there are several hundred active chemicals in cannabis, *tetrahydrocannabinol* (*THC*) is the one most responsible for its effects. The greater the THC content, the more powerful the cannabis. Due to changes in growing patterns, today's marijuana is at least four times higher in THC content than was the marijuana of the early 1970s (Doweiko, 2006; APA, 2000).

When smoked, cannabis changes one's conscious experiences by producing a mixture of hallucinogenic, depressant, and stimulant effects. At low doses, the smoker typically has feelings of happiness and relaxation, although some smokers become anxious or irritated, especially if they have been in a bad mood. Many smokers have sharpened perceptions and become fascinated with the intensified sounds and sights that they are experiencing. Time seems to slow down, and distances and sizes become greater. This overall reaction is often called getting "high." In strong doses, cannabis produces particularly unusual visual experiences, changes in body image, and even hallucinations (Mathew et al., 1993). Most of the drug's effects last two to six hours.

Because marijuana can interfere with complex sensorimotor tasks and cognitive functioning, it has been tied to many automobile accidents (Kauert & Iwersen-Bergmann, 2004). In addition, many people on a marijuana high fail to remember information, especially recently learned material; thus, heavy marijuana smokers may function poorly at school or work (Lundqvist, 2005). Some research also suggests that regular marijuana smoking may contribute to long-term medical problems, including lung disease (Ksir et al., 2008; NIDA, 2010), lower sperm counts in men, and abnormal ovulation in women (Schuel et al., 2002).

THINGS STUDENTS WANT TO KNOW

What is salvia?

In 2010, pictures of tween pop star Miley Cyrus smoking from a bong appeared on the Internet gossip site TMZ. Miley defended herself, claiming that she was simply using the legal psychoactive drug "salvia." Salvia is a substance derived from a psychoactive plant called salvia divinorum. It is a form a sage from the mint family. It is currently illegal to sell salvia in Canada under Health Canada regulations regarding "natural health products." It is, however, still being sold. Advocates and critics have gone to war over this substance, whose risks are not yet fully understood.

Salvia is reputed to induce short, minutes-long hallucinations and feelings of disconnection from one's body. In North America, this substance is best known as the subject of over 5,000 YouTube videos in which people take the drug and become violently ill or start acting without any inhibitions. Because of how short and unpleasant the effects are, proponents claim that salvia does not have much potential for abuse or addiction.

Today's lawmakers often show the YouTube videos to demonstrate the need to make salvia illegal. They compare it to illegal drugs like LSD or marijuana, although it bears little resemblance to either of these substances in either chemical makeup or effects. Currently there is no clear evidence that salvia is toxic (Mowry, Mosher, & Briner, 2003).

Because of the higher THC content in marijuana grown today, many people, including 5 percent of high school seniors, are now caught in a pattern of heavy and regular use, getting high on marijuana daily, although it is not clear whether such use represents a true addiction or a strong habit (Johnston et al., 2007). Either way, a number of these users do indeed find their social, occupational, or academic lives greatly affected. Around 10 percent of people in Canada have used marijuana in the past year; just over 40 percent have use it at some point in their lives (Health Canada, 2009).

Marijuana as Medicine

An uncommon medicine. A man suffering from chronic arthritis smokes marijuana at a protest rally, calling on the government to implement a medical marijuana program.

Movies, such as *Your Highness*, *Pineapple Express*, and *Hottub Time Machine*—so-called "stoner films"—have helped to popularize the image of a marijuana user as a mellow hippie trying to avoid the wrath of inept authority figures (Meltzer, 2007). In fact, however, the many millions of individuals who have tried marijuana come in all sizes, shapes, and personalities (Earleywine, 2007). Indeed, tens of thousands of them use marijuana for a very serious purpose—as medicine.

Common medicinal uses of marijuana, or cannabis, include treatment of chronic pain, nausea associated with chemotherapy, glaucoma, and disease-related anorexia (Okie, 2005). It is not clear just what it is about cannabis that seems to help, as it contains at least 300 substances (Grotenhermen, 2002). In Canada, the use of marijuana for medicinal purposes is legal and regulated by Health Canada. For those who qualify, Health Canada provides dried marijuana from Prairie Plant Systems Inc., which has been contracted to grow it for Health Canada, and does so in an old cold war nuclear attack bunker built in Flin Flon, Manitoba, during the Diefenbaker years. Alternatively, patients can apply for seeds to grow their own.

With the help of their doctors, Canadians can apply for medical marijuana if they suffer from multiple sclerosis, spinal cord injury or disease, cancer, AIDS or HIV, severe arthritis, or epilepsy, or as part of end-of-life care. As well, doctors have the discretion to recommend medical marijuana for patients with other conditions if the doctor believes it to be appropriate.

The differences in the Canadian and American legal positions on marijuana have created a number of issues. Marc Emery, a Canadian cannabis policy reform advocate, was extradited to the United States to face charges for selling marijuana seeds to Americans as part of a mail-order business out of Vancouver. In September 2010, Emery was sentenced to five years in prison in the United States. Emery's case remains a rallying point for people on both sides of the border wishing to loosen marijuana laws.

Psychoactive Drugs — WHAT HAPPENS IN THE BRAIN?

As you have seen, an ingested drug increases the activity of certain neurotransmitters in the brain—chemicals whose normal purpose is to reduce pain, calm us, lift our mood, or increase our alertness—and these neurotransmitters, in turn, help produce the particular effects of the drug. Alcohol, for example, heightens activity of the neurotransmitter *GABA;* opioids raise *endorphin* activity; and cocaine and amphetamines increase *dopamine* activity. Similarly, researchers have identified a neurotransmitter called *anandamide* (from the Sanskrit word for "bliss") that operates much like THC (Hitti, 2004).

reward learning pathway brain circuitry that is important for learning about rewarding stimuli.

It used to be thought that each drug, along with its corresponding neurotransmitters, sets in motion a unique set of brain reactions. However, recent brain-imaging studies suggest that while each drug has its own starting point in the brain, most (perhaps all) of them eventually activate a single **reward learning pathway**, or "pleasure pathway," in the

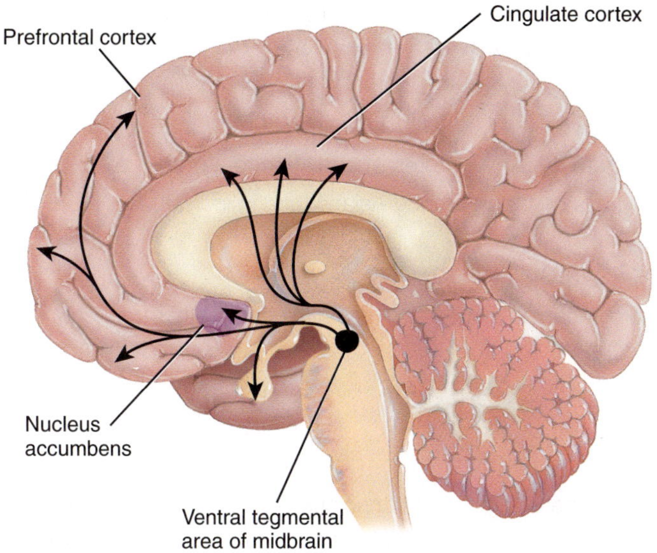

Reward learning pathway. The brain's reward learning pathway, or "pleasure pathway," extends from an area in the midbrain called the ventral tegmental area to the nucleus accumbens, as well as to the prefrontal cortex.

brain (Haney, 2008; Koob & LeMoal, 2008). The reward leaning pathway is activated by pleasurable stimuli or events and comes to anticipate (and thus motivate action toward) the arrival of desirable food, sexual experiences, or other pleasurable or rewarding experiences (Arias-Carrión & Pöppel, 2007). This brain reward learning pathway apparently extends from the midbrain to the nucleus accumbens and on to the frontal cortex (see Chapter 4).

The key neurotransmitter in this pathway appears to be *dopamine*. When dopamine is activated there, a person wants—at times, even craves—pleasureable rewards, such as music, a hug, or, for some people, a drug (Higgins & George, 2007; Higgins et al., 2004).

Certain drugs apparently stimulate the reward learning pathway directly. You will recall that cocaine and amphetamines directly increase dopamine activity. Other drugs seem to stimulate it in roundabout ways. The biochemical reactions triggered by alcohol and opioids each set in motion a series of chemical events that eventually lead to increased dopamine activity in the reward learning pathway.

Research also suggests that people prone to abuse drugs may suffer from a reward-deficiency syndrome—their reward learning pathway is not activated readily by the events in their lives (Blum et al., 2000; Nash, 1997)—so they are more inclined than other people to turn to drugs to keep their pathway stimulated. Abnormal genes have been pointed to as a possible cause of this syndrome (Finckh, 2001; Lawford et al., 1997).

reward-deficiency syndrome theory that people might abuse drugs because their reward centre is not readily activated by usual life events.

But how might people become ensnared in a broad pattern of addiction, marked by tolerance and withdrawal effects? According to one explanation, when a person takes a particular drug chronically, the brain eventually makes an adjustment and reduces its own production of the neurotransmitter whose activity is being increased by the ingested drug (Kleber & Galanter, 2008; Kosten, George, & Kleber, 2005). That is, because the drug is increasing neurotransmitter activity, natural release of the neurotransmitter by the brain is less necessary. As drug intake increases, the body's production of the neurotransmitter continues to decrease, and the person needs to take more and more of the drug to feel its positive effects. In short, drug takers are building tolerance for a drug, becoming more and more dependent on it, rather than on their own biological processes to feel comfortable or alert. In addition, if they suddenly stop taking the drug, their supply of neurotransmitters will be low for a time, producing symptoms of withdrawal that will continue until the brain resumes its normal production of the necessary neurotransmitters.

Before You Go On

www.wiley.com/go/comer

What Do You Know?

13. What are the major drug categories and the characteristics of each category?
14. What is addiction, and what are two key features of addiction to a drug?
15. Why is alcoholism relatively less common among Asians than in individuals of other ethnic groups?

What Do You Think?

Why do you think alcohol is more acceptable culturally than some of the other drugs we are discussing here?

SCAN TO GET THE ANSWERS

Summary

- Consciousness is defined as our immediate awareness of our internal and external states.
- The study of consciousness has proven difficult for researchers because of the difficulty measuring its associated phenomena, such as dreams and awareness. In part, the rise of behaviourism in the United States during the 1950s was a reaction to these difficulties, focusing more on objective behaviours that could be easily measured.
- Recent developments in neuroimaging have allowed researchers to look at brain activity during various states of consciousness.

When We Are Awake: Conscious Awareness

LEARNING OBJECTIVE 1 Define different levels of conscious awareness and describe key brain structures and functions associated with those levels.

- Attention is one of the key aspects of conscious awareness. Other key cognitive activities underlying cognitive awareness include monitoring (our implicit decisions about what to attend to), memory, and planning.
- Most biological investigators believe that consciousness results from a combination of brain activities in several brain regions. Two key brain structures appear to be the cerebral cortex, which helps regulate our awareness of attentional processes, and the thalamus, which relays sensory information from various parts of the brain to the cerebral cortex for processing.

Preconscious and Unconscious States

LEARNING OBJECTIVE 2 Summarize the ideas of preconscious and unconscious states, including Freud's thinking on the unconscious.

- In addition to our conscious level of awareness, many psychologists believe there are other levels or degrees of consciousness, and distinguish conscious awareness from two other states—unconsciousness and preconsciousness.
- Cognitive psychologists have demonstrated the existence of implicit memory; that is, memory that we do not consciously reflect upon but which, nevertheless, influences our behaviour.
- Preconsciousness is a level of awareness in which information can become readily available to consciousness if necessary.
- Unconsciousness is a state in which information is not easily accessible to conscious awareness.
- Freud viewed the human unconscious as an important storehouse for knowledge and experience, which although not directly accessible to our conscious awareness, still influences our behaviour.
- Although Freud's ideas fell into disfavour for several years, in recent years, scientists have begun to reexamine the unconscious from different points of view. For example, implicit memory describes knowledge that we have and are able to apply to various tasks, without being able to recall it at will.

When We Are Asleep

LEARNING OBJECTIVE 3 Describe what happens when people sleep, key theories of why we sleep and dream, and problems with sleep and how they affect functioning.

- Every 90 to 100 minutes when we sleep, we pass through a sleep cycle consisting of five different stages. The fifth stage of sleep, rapid eye movement, or REM sleep, is characterized by rapid and jagged brain-wave patterns and eye movements and irregularities in heart rate and breathing. Dreaming usually occurs during this phase of sleep.
- Scientists have identified brain activities that maintain the regular rhythms of life. Our move from a sustained period of wakefulness into a period of sleep during each 24-hour period is known as a *circadian rhythm*.

- Scientists have not reached a definitive conclusion about why people sleep, although some scientists have suggested sleep serves an evolutionarily adaptive function, keeping our ancestors away from predators that hunted at night. Others have suggested that sleep might play a role in growth, or allow us time to restore depleted chemical resources in the brain and body and eliminate chemical wastes that have accumulated throughout the day.
- We also do not understand why people dream. Recent theories about dreams emphasize cognitive approaches. The information-processing theory of dreams suggests that dreams are the mind's attempt to sort out and organize the day's experiences and fix them in memory. The attention-synthesis hypothesis suggests that dreams are the mind's attempts to give meaning to internally generated signals firing throughout the brain during deep sleep. Freud believed that dreams represent expressions of the internal desires and wishes that have been repressed and stored in the unconscious.
- Sleep deprivation can lead to feelings of fatigue, irritability, and malaise, resulting in lower productivity and a tendency to make mistakes. Loss of sleep can also affect the functioning of the immune system. The regular inability to fall asleep or stay asleep is called insomnia. Other sleep disorders include sleep apnea, narcolepsy, sleepwalking, and night terrors.

Hypnosis

LEARNING OBJECTIVE 4 Discuss theories and evidence about what hypnosis is, how it works, and how it can be used.

- Hypnosis is a suggestible state during which people can be directed to act in unusual ways, experience unusual sensations, remember forgotten events, or forget remembered events.
- Ernest Hilgard's theory suggests that hypnosis divides consciousness into two parts: one focused on the suggestions of the hypnotist, and the other a hidden observer. Other theorists suggest that motivated role-playing is at work in hypnosis.
- Hypnosis has been used to successfully help control pain, as well as treat anxiety, skin diseases, asthma, insomnia, stuttering, high blood pressure, warts, and other forms of infection.

Meditation

LEARNING OBJECTIVE 5 Describe the techniques and effects of meditation.

- Meditation is designed to help turn one's consciousness away from the outer world toward inner cues and awareness, and to ignore all stressors.
- Like hypnosis, meditation has been suggested to have numerous positive benefits, including successfully treating many of the same illnesses, and helping people to relax.

Psychoactive Drugs

LEARNING OBJECTIVE 6 List and describe common depressant, stimulant, and hallucinogenic psychoactive drugs and their effects.

- The three main classes of psychoactive drugs are depressants (substances that slow down brain activity), stimulants (substances that excite brain activity), and psychedelic or hallucinogenic drugs (substances that distort sensory perceptions).
- Regular ingestion of some drugs can lead to maladaptive changes in a person's behaviour patterns and physical responses, a pattern known as *addiction*. Signs of addiction can include increased tolerance, the need for larger and larger doses of a substance to get the desired effect, and symptoms of withdrawal when one discontinues the drug.
- Review the list of drugs and their effects in Table 6.1.

Key Terms

TYING IT TOGETHER

The study of consciousness is closely connected to the study of all other areas of psychology. Throughout this chapter, we have stressed how consciousness interfaces with psychology's various subfields, including our highlighted sections on brain function, individual differences, abnormal functioning, and development. To remind you of how consciousness is tied to other psychology subfields and issues, we have selected some interesting points from throughout the chapter.

WHAT HAPPENS IN THE BRAIN?

- People who are blind because of damage to visual areas in the cerebral cortex are still able to point in the direction of light projected onto a screen, even though they are not aware of attending to the light. That's because the areas in the cerebral cortex that are in charge of awareness of attention are not the same as the areas responsible for attention itself.
- Similarly, hypnosis used to anesthetize or reduce pain doesn't keep sensations of pain from reaching neurons. Instead, it reduces awareness of the pain by decreasing activity in a particular part of the cerebral cortex.
- Humans are probably not the only animals that dream. Dreaming takes place during rapid eye movement (REM) sleep, the final stage of the brain's five-stage sleep cycle, and every kind of mammal that has been tested experiences these sleep stages.
- There are various theories to explain dreaming. Some researchers, for instance, believe that we dream because while we sleep, the brain produces a variety of visual and auditory signals and then tries to combine these self-produced signals in a way that makes sense.
- Most, or perhaps all, psychoactive drugs eventually work by activating a single reward learning pathway in the brain. The key neurotransmitter in this reward learning pathway is dopamine.

HOW WE DIFFER

- Athough most of us don't have a strong preference, some of us are "morning people" who like to get everything done early in the day, while others are "night people" who prefer to sleep late and do our work in the evening.
- Such preferences depend on our internal clocks, and the settings of those clocks are thought to be determined primarily by genetic factors.
- At least twice as many men as women display alcoholism.
- Aboriginal Canadians, particularly men, display a higher rate of alcoholism than other racial minority groups or white Canadians.

WHEN THINGS GO WRONG

- Adolescents are especially likely to suffer from sleep deprivation. In fact, teenagers today get about two hours less sleep per night than teens 80 years ago.
- Over time, going without sleep causes a variety of problems: general malaise, lower productivity, an increased tendency to make mistakes, and even lower immune system functioning.
- The most common sleep disorder is insomnia. Insomnia sufferers, who are generally older people, regularly have trouble falling asleep or staying asleep. Less common is narcolepsy, which involves suddenly falling asleep for short periods of time—sometimes even in the midst of an argument or during an exciting football game.
- In any given year, more than 9 percent of all teens and adults in the United States display drug or alcohol addiction.
- Intoxicated drivers cause 12,000 deaths each year.

HOW WE DEVELOP

- The question of when babies develop alert consciousness is a matter of debate. On the one hand, some researchers argue that early cognitive development, such as that discussed in Chapter 3, shows that babies do have a rudimentary sense of consciousness. Others argue that consciousness comes later, with the development of language.
- During the first four months of life, babies sleep between 14 and 17 hours a day, but the time spent sleeping declines steadily as they get older.
- Environmental demands and expectations affect babies' sleep-awake cycles. In the Kipsigis tribe, for example, babies sleep for much shorter stretches longer into infancy than American babies. That's because Kipsigis mothers keep their babies with them constantly, while American parents structure their babies' sleep by putting them to bed at regular times.

Psychology Around Us

Sleep's Impact on Daily Functioning

"It's Not Nice to Fool Mother Nature"

View this in Action
WILEY PLUS
www.wileyplus.com

Video Lab Exercise

Try though we might, we cannot exercise a lot of control over sleep. Whether we like it or not, we are at the mercy of our circadian rhythms; once we are asleep, we are along for a ride through our sleep cycle; and if we deprive ourselves of too much sleep, we function poorly while we are awake.

In this video lab exercise, your job is to perform video tasks and react to various scenes at various times throughout the day and under various states of sleep deprivation. You may think you are on top of your game most of the time, but as you will see, sleep–awake rhythms and sleep deprivation strongly affect how you think, how you learn, and how you feel about various people, objects, and situations.

As you are working on this online exercise, consider the following questions:

- What does this lab exercise say about our sleep needs and the impact of sleep on our daily lives?
- Do we become "morning people" or "night owls" based on our experiences or on our biological predispositions?
- How might dreams fit into the equation?
- Are there any ways to get around sleep rhythms and sleep needs?

CHAPTER 7

Learning

CHAPTER OUTLINE

- What Is Learning?
- Classical Conditioning
- Operant Conditioning
- Observational Learning
- Learning and Cognition
- Factors that Facilitate Learning
- Prenatal and Postnatal Learning
- Learning Disabilities

PERFUME AND GARAGES AND CANDY! OH, MY!

You and your sister often shop together. On these expeditions, a few things commonly occur. First, your sister wears very strong smelling perfume. When you first get into the car, you find the scent quite overpowering. However, by the time you reach the shopping centre you barely notice it.

Second, your sister, who usually drives, insists on parking in the underground parking garage. You are quite anxious at the thought of parking underground and insist on being dropped outside. You can't explain why, but you find yourself distressed at being in such an enclosed space. You know this fear is irrational and you always promise yourself that you will not get out of the car before your sister parks. But each time you end up insisting on exiting the car above ground. Why? Why can't you go into the garage when you know that your fear is irrational?

Third, your sister frequently brings along her 4-year-old daughter. While shopping, your niece often asks her mother to buy her candy. Your sister is strict about candy because she does not want her daughter to have sugar, but, like most children, your niece loves sweets. So, when her mother tells her "no," your niece begins to whine and fuss, begging her mother for the candy. Especially when she is tired, your sister will give in to the whining, telling her daughter, "Alright, if you stop being so obnoxious I will let you have candy, just this once." Most times, however, your sister does not give into the demands of her daughter. In fact, usually your sister becomes completely exasperated by her daughter's begging and snaps at her, making your niece cry. At these times your sister often says to you, "Why does she keep doing this? She never listens to me." Why does this happen? Why doesn't your niece listen when her mother tells her no? After all, most of the time when your sister says "no" she means "no"; as well, your niece is clearly upset by her mother's anger. So why doesn't your niece stop asking? And why is it so difficult for your sister to make her daughter stop whining?

Finally, recently your 2-year-old niece has also begun to accompany her mother and sister and you on these shopping expeditions. She too is beginning to whine and beg for candy—this in spite of the fact that she has never even had candy. Why? As we will see, there are many forms of learning, and all are governed by particular processes that explain the regulation of behaviour.

A lot of learning has gone on in these examples of behaviour that occur during your regular shopping trips; it is worth reflecting on some of the differences and similarities in these examples. How is it that we can stop noticing things like strong perfume with exposure to it over time? How do we learn to be anxious about being in a confined space like an underground garage? Why do some children whine and fuss to get what they want, while others don't? If a parent only gives in to a whining, fussing child once in a while, what effect does that have on the child's future begging behaviour? Why is it that the word "no" seems to work for some parents but not others? And finally, how might younger siblings learn a familiar pattern of whining and fussing to get what they want?

As we will see in this chapter, learning situations are influenced by many variables, including how difficult the learning task is, how much attention the learner is paying, what sorts and levels of emotions are involved, and whether any required biological precursors to learning are in place—to name a few. The study of each will come up later in this chapter, and you will also find out what learning theory has to say about each of the learning situations described above. The overall picture underscores how learning is complex and multidimensional. ■

What Is Learning?

LEARNING OBJECTIVE 1

Define learning and distinguish between associative and non-associative learning.

learning a lasting change caused by experience.

associative learning learning that involves forming associations between stimuli.

non-associative learning learning that does not involve forming associations between stimuli.

Learning is defined as a lasting change caused by experience. In the laboratory, scientists study learning by measuring changes in behavioural responses. This is particularly true for studies of animals, where it's impossible to assess the degree to which the subject has learned. However, it's also clear that considerable learning occurs in the absence of overt behavioural change.

It may seem strange to separate a discussion about learning from a closely related subject, memory, which is covered in the next chapter. Although learning and memory are indeed interrelated and many of the biological mechanisms (and brain regions) that underlie learning are also critical for memory, the study of these topics has diverged in the laboratory. Traditionally, animals (dogs, monkeys, rats, and mice) were the focus of studies on learning, whereas humans were the predominant focus of studies on memory. With the advent of neuroimaging technology and a greater public concern for understanding learning disabilities, more research on learning is focused on humans as well (Katzir & Pare-Blagoev, 2006; Guttorm et al., 2005). Throughout this chapter, we will discuss how information that scientists have gained from animal experimentation can be applied to questions of human learning.

In general, learning can be divided into two major categories: *associative* and *non-associative* learning. **Associative learning** is a change that occurs as the result of experiences that lead us to link two or more stimuli together. An example of associative learning would be flinching at the whine of a dental drill because you associate the sound with the pain the drill has caused you in the past. **Non-associative learning** also involves change based on experience, but happens when a person realizes that two disparate events may be unrelated; that is, the person fails to create a connection between two or more different pieces of information. For example, the first time you sleep in a new apartment you may find yourself awakened a number of times by sounds in the apartment (the fridge) or in the neighbourhood (buses, trains, or trucks going by). However, after a few nights you find you are able to ignore these regular sounds and are able to sleep without interruption. You have learned not to associate those sounds with anything of meaning.

Non-associative Learning

Non-associative learning is by far the simpler of the two types of learning. The most basic forms of learning are non-associative. As we just illustrated, this means that a connection between two or more stimuli is not made. Rather, non-associative learning refers to a change that occurs as a result of our experiences with a single sensory cue. There are two major types of non-associative learning, *habituation* and *sensitization*.

Habituation Habituation happens when our senses begin to respond less strongly to repeated presentations of the same sensory cue (such as the smell of your sister's strongly scented perfume). Although habituation can occur in any sensory system, consider another example using the sense of smell. A smell, such as baking cookies, might be a very welcome and noticeable aroma as you first walk into your house, but after a while you may barely notice it. Even though the baking cookies continue to smell as wonderful after you have been home for a while as they did when you first walked in the door, you are no longer aware of the delicious smell—you have become habituated. Your olfactory sense responds less and less strongly, though the same stimulus repeatedly reaches the sensory receptors in your nose. As happened here, in most cases, sensory habituation occurs without our awareness; it does not require attention to the stimulus for learning to occur. However, if the cookies were to burn, we would experience dishabituation, and we would once again be alert to olfactory sensory cues from the cookies.

When we use the term habituation to talk about learning, it also refers to a decrement in response after repeated stimulus presentation. Thus a habituation response has clear adaptive value because it allows organisms to ignore stimuli that do not convey information of biological significance. Habituation, however, is not the exclusive result of sensory adaptation or fatigue of neurons in the sensory receptors. Learning theorists also study habituation by examining changes in patterns of neuronal activation in various regions of cortex (Nakano et al., 2006; 2009). For example, Nakano and colleagues (2009) demonstrated that when young infants become habituated to a particular sound (as the syllable "ba" is repeated over and over), there is activation observed in the temporal region of cortex but no activation in the prefrontal cortex. However, this neural activation pattern changes when the infant responds to a novel sound (e.g., the syllable "pa"). Although activation continues in the temporal regions of cortex, the prefrontal cortex also activates. As shown in the photos, infants can habituate/dishabituate to stimuli in other sensory systems as well.

dishabituation a form of non-associative learning whereby there is a recovery of attention to a novel stimulus following habitation.

habituation a form of non-associative learning whereby repeated presentation of a stimulus leads to a reduction in response.

sensitization a form of non-associative learning whereby a strong stimulus results in an exaggerated response to the subsequent presentation of weaker stimuli.

Sensitization Sensitization is another form of non-associative learning that involves an altered response after the presentation of a single sensory cue. Unlike habituation, sensitization involves an increase, as opposed to a decrease, in response with learning. Imagine you are home alone at night reading quietly. Without any warning, your pet cat knocks over a lamp, startling you. You may jump or even shout out in fear before realizing what has happened. And, for some time after you calm down, you are likely to startle again in response to normal auditory stimuli, such as the ring from your cell phone. Your enhanced response to this typical stimulus may reflect the fact that sensitization has occurred. As in the case of habituation, sensitization makes good adaptive sense. An unexpected stimulus may signal danger, so a greater than usual response to stimuli that follow may be helpful for survival.

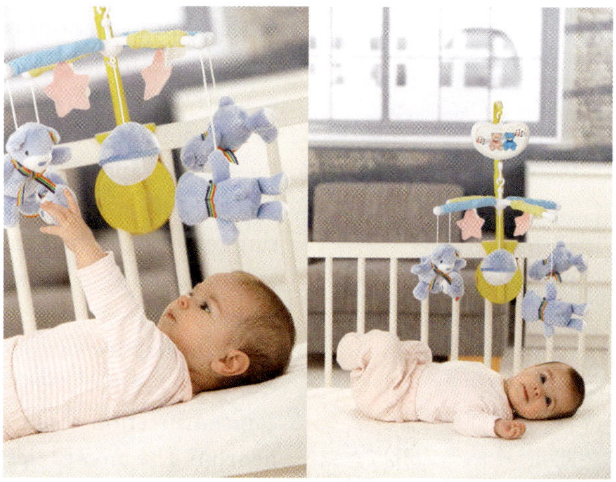

Habituation in action. When this infant was first presented with the patterned image, she was interested in it and stared at it intently. After a minute or two, however, she stops looking at it and appears to be looking for something less boring to look at.

PSYCHOLOGY AROUND US Yikes!

You're at the movies and the situation on the screen has become pretty intense. The lead female actor is creeping slowly through the dark woods. Where is the homicidal maniac? She knows he's looking for her. He may be behind that tree, or that big rock.... Waiting nervously for the inevitable attack, you don't notice that your companion is about to lay his hand on your shoulder until you feel his touch. Startled, you gasp out loud, and some of the people sitting around you gasp in response.

As this example shows, scary movies manipulate our sensitization response. Have you ever noticed that after watching a scary movie on television, you are easily startled by noises in the house, like a door opening or the wind blowing outside, that you usually wouldn't notice? You have become temporarily sensitized to these stimuli.

Non-associative Learning WHAT HAPPENS IN THE BRAIN? Habituation and sensitization are very basic forms of learning; therefore, both forms of learning can occur in animals with very simple nervous systems. Neuroscientists have taken advantage of this basic learning in simple animals and have used one of the simplest—the nervous system of a sea slug—to study the biological basis of non-associative learning (Kandel, 2001).

Learning from the slug. By studying sea slugs, scientists have gained insights into how the nervous system changes in response to learning.

Sea slugs do not have brains or spinal cords, but they have neurons that can actually be seen with the naked eye. This makes it easy for researchers to record from the neurons using electrodes, a process described in Chapter 4. Researchers use electrode recordings from sea slugs to enhance their understanding of how simple nervous systems change in response to learning.

If you lightly touch a sea slug once, it will withdraw two vulnerable parts of its body, the gill and the siphon. If you touch it lightly multiple times, this withdrawal response will eventually diminish as habituation sets in. Recordings from the sea slug's neurons have shown that in habituation, the amount of neural activity in the motor neurons (the neurons that control the gill and siphon muscles) decreases as the animal is repeatedly touched (Gingrich & Byrne, 1985). This decrease in activity is largely due to the fact that the neurotransmitter in the synapse between the sea slug's sensory neuron and the motor neuron gets depleted with repeated presentations of the tactile stimulus. Eventually, the same level of sensory stimulus becomes ineffective at causing the gill and siphon withdrawal response—the amount of neurotransmitter has diminished to the point that the synapse can no longer be activated. At this point, the same level of sensory stimulus no longer causes the sea slug to withdraw the gill and siphon (**Figure 7-1**).

To study sensitization, scientists apply an electric shock to the tail of the sea slug. The slug responds with a strong gill and siphon withdrawal reflex. Then they apply a very mild tactile stimulus to the slug's body. It still strongly withdraws its gill and siphon because it is sensitized.

Sensitization can occur even when a slug has undergone trials of habituation (Hawkins, Cohen, & Kandel, 2006). If habitation occurs as a result of neurotransmitter depletion, how can sensitization result in an almost immediate restoration of activity in the same motor neuron? The answer lies in the fact that the tail shock recruits another population of neurons, called *interneurons*, into the circuitry. Interneurons release excitatory neurochemicals that work to enhance the weakened sensory neuron input to the synapse of the sensory and motor nerves. The combined action stimulates the motor neurons enough to produce the augmented withdrawal response.

You may be wondering what all of these experiments on sea slugs tell us about learning in more complex animals, including humans. Although there are many important differences between sea slugs and humans, it's likely that these basic mechanisms, or something

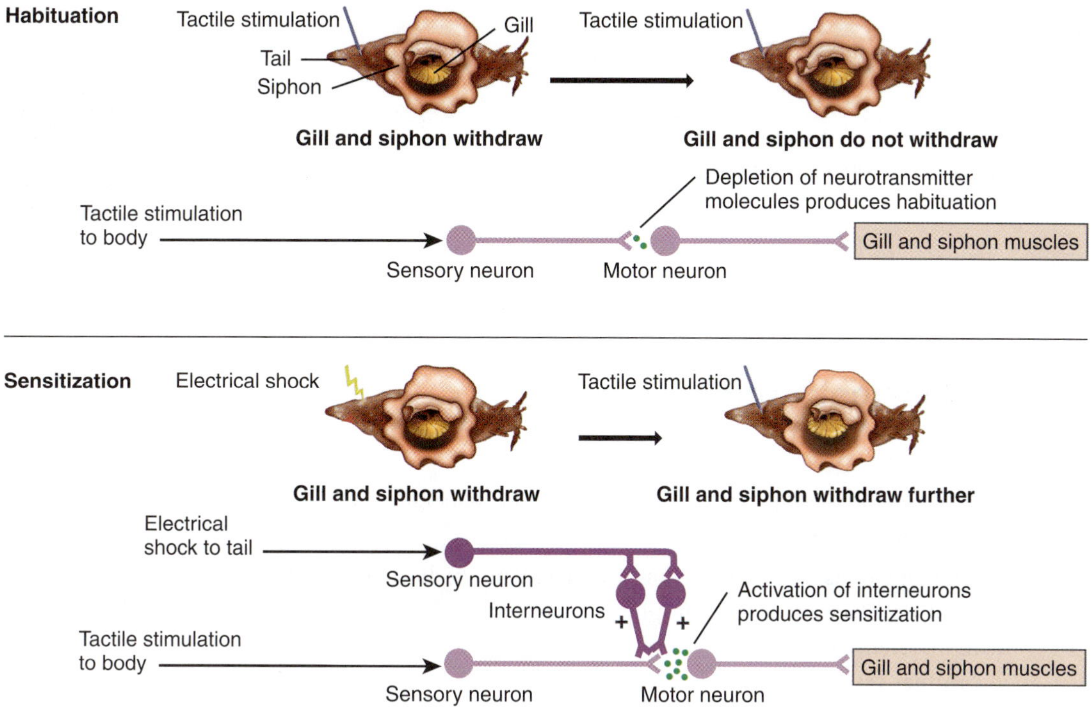

FIGURE 7-1 Habituation and sensitization in the sea slug. (Above) The sea slug gill and siphon withdrawal reflex becomes habituated to a repeated tactile stimulus when the neurotransmitter needed to activate its motor neurons has been depleted. (Below) The sea slug experiences sensitization to mild tactile stimulation if it is first exposed to a noxious stimulus like electric shock—a stimulus that activates a group of neurons called interneurons. These latter neurons stimulate the animal's motor neurons, which in turn produce responses to mild tactile stimuli.

very close to them, also operate in more complex nervous systems, such as our own. We, too, may experience habituation because of depleted neurotransmitters, and sensitization because of the added recruitment of interneurons.

Associative Learning

Non-associative learning does not account for the majority of learning; the majority of learning is considered to be associative. It involves making connections between two or more stimuli. Most of the learning you engage in as a student is highly associative. Course material involves connecting numerous concepts and facts to produce an overall picture of a certain subject. Learning people's names or learning how to please or manipulate a parent involves forming associations. Animals also engage in associative learning. For example, when a dog barks at the mail carrier and the mail carrier leaves, the dog learns that its actions have particular consequences.

Associative learning. Dogs associate their barking with the retreat of the mail carrier, indicating that not all associations are necessarily accurate reflections of reality.

Two major types of associative learning are *classical conditioning* and *operant*, or *instrumental*, *conditioning*. In classical conditioning, as we will see next, we come to associate two stimuli, eventually responding the same way to both. In operant conditioning, which we will examine after classical conditioning, we come to associate stimuli with our behaviours. It is important to note that many situations involve both classical and operant conditioning. However, we will discuss each type of conditioning separately, and then come back to this notion following the discussion of both types of conditioning.

Before You Go On

www.wiley.com/go/comer

What Do You Know?

1. What is learning?
2. What happens in synapses during habituation? What happens during sensitization?

What Do You Think?

Give an example from your own life of a time when you experienced non-associative learning.

SCAN TO GET THE ANSWERS

Classical Conditioning

LEARNING OBJECTIVE 2

Describe the basic processes of classical conditioning and explain how classical conditioning is relevant to learning.

One type of associative learning was accidentally discovered, around the turn of the nineteenth century, by a Russian physiologist named Ivan Pavlov. His discoveries led the way to a systematic investigation of associative learning in the laboratory, and versions of his original research methods are still being studied in psychology laboratories today (for examples see Dijksterhuis, 2004; Fanselow & Poulos, 2005).

Pavlov was interested in understanding the role of the salivary reflex during digestion. Many animals experience reflexive salivation—mouthwatering—at the sight or sound or thought of food. For this reason, Pavlov conducted his research on the salivary reflex with dogs, giving hungry dogs food and measuring salivary output. His laboratory apparatus and method are shown in **Figure 7-2**. As time progressed in his studies, Pavlov noticed that his dogs were salivating even when food wasn't present. They salivated when the lab assistants arrived or when they heard noises that signalled the arrival of the assistants. Pavlov recognized this as evidence that the dogs had learned to associate the appearance of a lab assistant with getting food. Thus, the dogs were experiencing a behavioural response (salivation) in *anticipation* of getting food. Pavlov realized that the dog's responses indicated that they were experiencing a type of learning. He therefore began to study this type of learning in greater detail, eventually systematizing this basic form of associative learning into what is now called Pavlovian or classical conditioning (Windholz, 1987).

Pavlovian or **classical conditioning** a form of associative learning whereby a neutral stimulus is paired with a salient stimulus so that eventually the neutral stimulus predicts the salient stimulus.

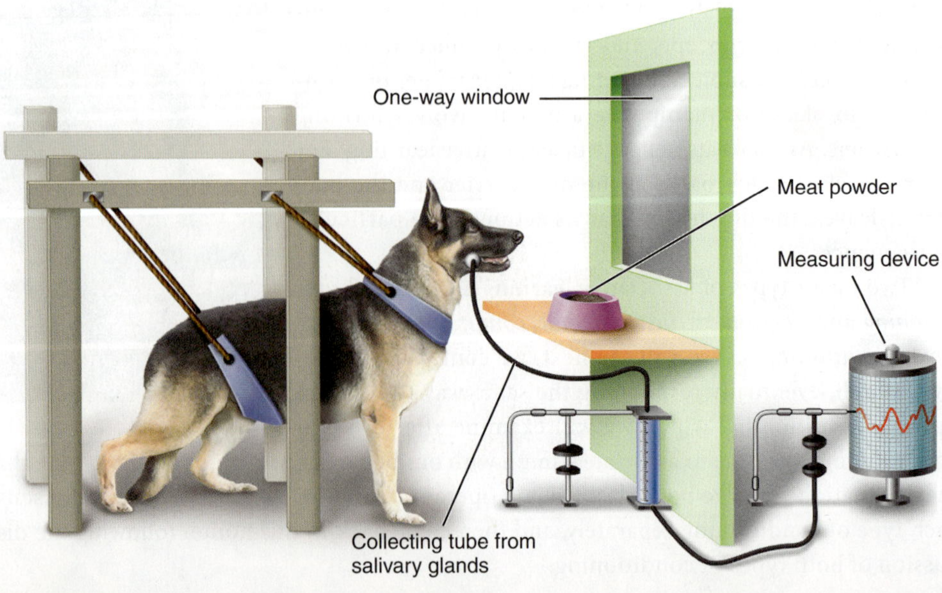

FIGURE 7-2 Pavlov's setup for collecting and measuring salivation in dogs. The dog is placed in a harness and given a bowl of meat powder. A tube from the salivary gland collects the saliva, which is measured and recorded.

How Does Classical Conditioning Work?

In classical conditioning, a person or animal learns to associate a previously neutral stimulus with an **unconditioned stimulus (US)**, one that normally elicits a physiological response. Because the response doesn't have to be learned, it is called the **unconditioned response (UR)**. With repeated pairings, the neutral stimulus alone elicits the physiological response. After that happens, the stimulus is no longer neutral. It is now called the **conditioned stimulus (CS)**, and the physiological response it elicits is called the **conditioned response (CR)**.

unconditioned stimulus (US) a stimulus that on its own elicits a response.

unconditioned response (UR) a physical response elicited by an unconditioned stimulus; it does not need to be learned.

conditioned stimulus (CS) a neutral stimulus that eventually elicits the same response as an unconditioned stimulus with which it has been paired.

conditioned response (CR) a physical response elicited by a conditioned stimulus; it is usually the same as the unconditioned response.

Let's apply these newly introduced terms to Pavlov's experiment. For Pavlov's dogs, the unconditioned stimulus was food. The dogs' unconditioned response was to salivate. So, for the dogs, without any learning, the unconditioned stimulus (meat powder: US) elicited an unconditioned response (salivation: UR). The arrival of a lab assistant was, originally, a neutral stimulus to the dogs. However, repeated pairings of the lab assistant with meat powder meant that over time, the assistant's arrival became a conditioned stimulus. Thus the unconditioned stimulus (the meat powder: US) became paired with the conditioned stimulus (the arrival of the lab assistant: CS). The dog had learned the association between the arrival of the lab assistant and the presentation of the meat powder. Eventually the dog responded to the conditioned stimulus (the arrival of the lab assistant) by salivating. Thus, the conditioned stimulus elicited the conditioned response (salivation: CR). The dogs' salivation, once an unconditioned response to the food, was now a conditioned response to the assistant. This process is summarized in **Figure 7-3**.

A classic moment. In this famous image, Ivan Pavlov (centre, with beard) stands with his assistants and students prior to demonstrating his classical conditioning experiment on a dog.

Classical conditioning is not just for dogs, however. It happens to people, too. Suppose that you unknowingly eat bad clams (US) and they make you very ill (UR). Following this experience, even the sight of clams (CS) makes you feel sick (CR), even though your first sight of clams elicited no real reaction from you at all.

Pavlov identified a number of important processes related to classical conditioning. The first of these processes is related to the acquisition of the association between the conditioned stimulus and the unconditioned stimulus. Not surprisingly, learning is more robust when the number of CS–US pairings is high. That is, the more times that the CS and US are paired, the more likely it is that the association will be learned. For example, if every time you open a drawer

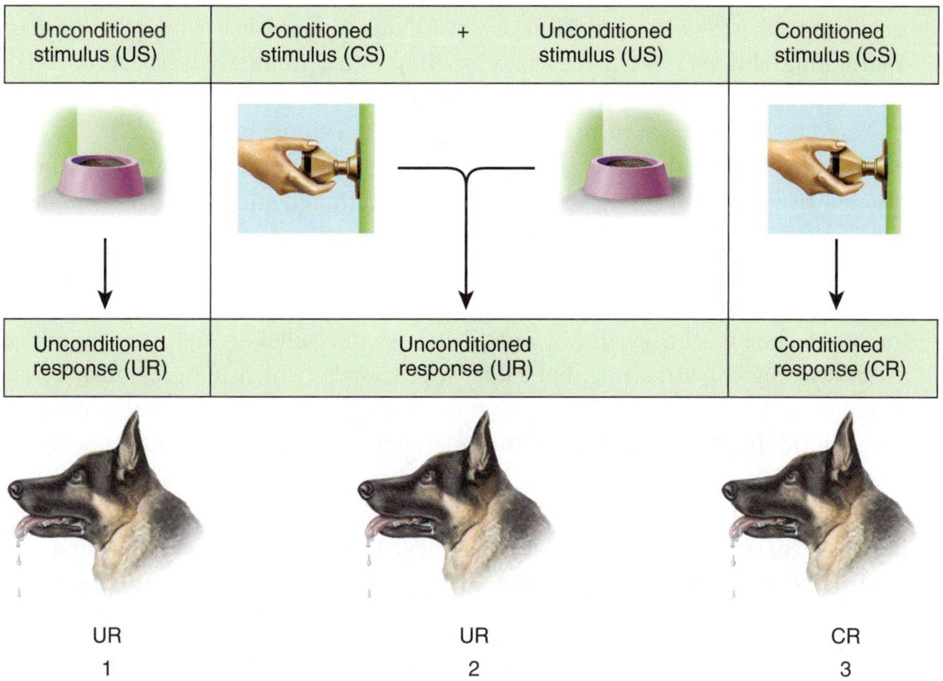

FIGURE 7-3 Classical conditioning. The sequence of classical conditioning is shown here, from left to right. (1) The US (meat powder) produces the UR (salivation). (2) During conditioning, the US is paired with a CS, a neutral or conditioned stimulus (a sound such as a doorknob being turned). (3) After conditioning, the CS alone produces the conditioned (learned) response of salivation.

it makes an unpleasant squealing sound, you will tense up prior to opening the drawer after only a few attempts. If the drawer only catches once in a while, it will take you longer to acquire an uneasy response in anticipation of the sound.

However, timing also plays an important role in the formation of learned associations. The most effective presentation schedule would be to pair the US and the CS together, with the CS occurring slightly before the US, so that the CS has predictive value. How much is slightly before? For most species, the optimal delay—that is, the most rapid acquisition followed by the strongest response—is a half a minute delay. Why? Imagine that each time you see a particular friend in the hall at school he shouts your name (CS) and then rushes over and clouts you on the back (US), causing you to cringe (UR). After several instances of being clouted on the back in the hall, you begin to cringe (CR) as soon as your friend calls your name (CS). Now imagine a scenario where you see your friend at school in the morning in a crowded hallway; he calls your name and waves, but does not clout you on the back until he sees you later that evening. Even if your friend called and waved and then later clouted you on the back several times that week, you would be much less likely to cringe simply hearing your friend call your name.

> "While you are experimenting, do not remain content with the surface of things. Don't become a mere recorder of facts, but try to penetrate the mystery of their origin."
> —*Ivan Pavlov, Russian physiologist*

stimulus discrimination what occurs when an organism learns to emit a specific behaviour in the presence of a stimulus, but not in the presence of stimuli similar to the original stimulus.

Stimulus discrimination occurs when an organism learns to discriminate between similar conditioned stimuli. For example, a rat is conditioned to expect a shock (US) when it hears a tone (CS). Following the acquisition of this response, the rat can then be taught to discriminate between different tones. If shock only follows a high tone, the rat can learn to distinguish the tone paired with the unconditioned stimulus (shock) from the other lower tones (no shock). Similarly, at home your dog may be able to discriminate between the sound of a particular kitchen cupboard opening—the one containing his treats—and the sound of any other kitchen cupboard being opened.

Consider Pavlov's dog for a moment. As you now know, a dog was conditioned to salivate to the arrival of the lab assistant. Following the acquisition of the learned association between the lab assistant (CS) and the meat powder (US), let's say that a red light becomes paired with the arrival of the lab assistant. Even though the red light has never been paired with the meat powder, the dog begins to salivate at the sight of the red light. This occurs because the red light (CS2) has become paired with the arrival of the lab assistant (CS). In this case the original conditioned stimulus (the lab assistant) is functioning as if it were an unconditioned stimulus. This phenomenon is known as **higher order conditioning**. Evidence of higher order conditioning is often observed in advertising. Advertisers often pair their products (CS) with sexual imagery (US); this type of advertising relies on classical conditioning. However, when a celebrity is paired with a product, advertisers are relying on higher order conditioning. The celebrity (CS) has become associated with sexual imagery (US), and the celebrity, in turn, becomes associated with the product (CS2).

higher order conditioning what occurs when a previously conditioned stimulus functions as if it were an unconditioned stimulus for further conditioning.

Pavlov also showed that a learned response could be eliminated by presenting the conditioned stimulus repeatedly, without the unconditioned stimulus. For example, the lab assistant could come to the lab many times without offering any food to the dogs, or your friend may well resort to friendly waves after calling your name. In time, the dog no longer associates food with the lab assistant and you stop cringing when your friend calls out your name in a busy hallway. This phenomenon, called **extinction**, does not represent "unlearning" or forgetting, but rather a process by which the previously learned CR is actively inhibited (Quirk, 2006). That is, we don't forget responses that have been conditioned; we simply see a reduction in the strength of the conditioned response (CR). Therefore, a child who associates a parent with pain/fear does not forget the association even though she may no longer cower when the parent is present. For the conditioned response to be permanently removed it would have to be completely extinguished.

extinction reduction of a conditioned response after repeated presentations of the conditioned stimulus alone.

Evidence that the information about the previous CS–US pairing still exists after extinction training can be observed by allowing time to pass with no training after extinction has occurred. In this case, the CR will often re-emerge at a later date, at up to half the intensity of its original conditioned level, a phenomenon called spontaneous recovery (**Figure 7-4**). For example, if the assistant hasn't brought food for several visits and the dogs' salivation response has been inhibited by extinction, the dogs might still salivate a week after extinction when the assistant arrives, indicating that the response was not "unlearned." For this reason, a parent who has not engaged in abusive behaviour for some time may continue to elicit a fear response from a child. It is therefore obvious that the previously learned information has not been lost or forgotten, because it can be spontaneously recovered without any further learning.

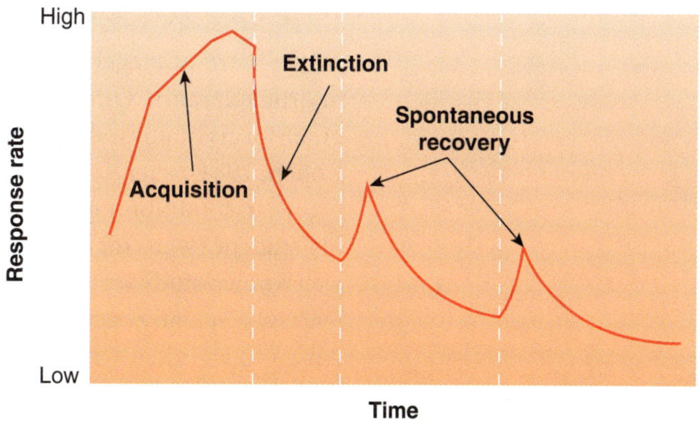

FIGURE 7-4 Acquisition, extinction, and spontaneous recovery. Acquisition occurs as the US and CS are repeatedly paired. When the CS is presented repeatedly without the US, the individual's learned response gradually decreases until extinction occurs. But the information about the previous CS–US pairing is not lost, and the extinguished response spontaneously reappears.

Classical Conditioning WHAT HAPPENS IN THE BRAIN?

The research of Shepard Siegel and his colleagues at McMaster University has focused on the role of classical conditioning in drug dependency. Drug use begins when an individual experiences the effects of a drug as pleasurable. Drug dependency involves the psychological and physiological experiences that occur as the individual continues to use the drug; the body adapts to the presence of the drug and the individual experiences withdrawal if the drug is reduced or stopped. Withdrawal occurs as the brain requires more and more of the drug to return to its "normal" state.

Siegel has studied the role that classical conditioning plays in both the physiological and psychological tolerance that builds up within addicts who regularly inject heroin (Siegel, 2005; McDonald & Siegel, 2004). *Tolerance* develops in drug users and abusers as they require increasingly larger doses of the drug to obtain the same intensity of effect initially obtained by a smaller dose. Tolerance involves a number of factors, including possible changes at the cellular level in response to the drug (Koch & Höllt, 2008).

spontaneous recovery re-emergence of a conditioned response some time after extinction has occurred.

Deaths among addicts due to overdoses of heroin were initially thought to be accounted for by unexpected jumps in the purity or strength of the heroin being injected. However, Siegel and his colleagues (Siegel, 2005; McDonald & Siegel, 2004) argue that a learned compensatory response (US) can trigger drug tolerance (UR) and may be involved in some drug overdoses. They argue that the body seeks to compensate for the effects of a drug by initiating a compensatory response (for example, lowering body temperature in anticipation of a rise in temperature caused by heroin injection) when there are environmental cues that the drug is on its way. The greater the compensatory response, the larger the dose required to offset it.

Compensatory responses. The environmental context in which heroin addicts inject themselves becomes associated with their body's compensatory response to the heroin. As a result, if they inject themselves in a novel location their body's compensatory response may not be sufficient to counter the effects of the heroin, resulting in an overdose.

Siegel and his colleagues further argue that the physiologic counter reaction to heroin becomes classically conditioned over time to the process of self-injection and to the location in which the injection is administered (CS). This means that the nervous system, due to classical conditioning, anticipates the arrival of the heroin based simply on external environmental cues (called extroceptive cues) provided by the location (e.g., the room, drug paraphernalia, or other characteristic sights and sounds) in which the addict shoots up. When the addict injects in a new environment without the familiar environmental cues, the body's anticipatory response is absent; without these counterbalancing effects, the addict's system may become overwhelmed by the usual dose of heroin, suppressing respiration and killing the individual. The work of McDonald and Siegal (2004) also explains why addicts experience cravings when attempting to quit drugs. Exposure to external drug-related cues (CS) causes withdrawal symptoms caused by a compensatory response (CR) in the absence of the drug (US), causing cravings that can lead to relapse.

Classical Conditioning and Fears

As the work of Siegel and his colleagues demonstrates, classical conditioning is involved in drug tolerance. Other research has shown that classical conditioning also plays a role in other forms of physiological responding, including immune response (Ader, 2003; Ader & Cohen, 1984), allergic reactions (MacQueen et al., 1989), and fear conditioning.

Fear conditioning was first studied by the American psychologist, John Watson and his student (who, incidentally, later became his wife) Rosalie Rayner (1920). Their most well-known study was the classical conditioning of an 11-month-old baby named Albert B, who subsequently became well known as "Little Albert." In the study, Watson exposed baby Albert to an initially neutral stimulus, a white rat. As Albert reached forward to touch the rat, Watson used a hammer to strike a steel bar just behind Albert's head. This loud sound frightened Albert so much that he burst into tears. Seven pairings of the white rat (CS) with the loud noise (US) made Albert cry and avoid the rat (CR).

> "Give me a dozen healthy infants, well-formed, and my own specified world to bring them up in and I'll guarantee to take any one at random and train him to become any type of specialist I might select—doctor, lawyer, artist, merchant-chief, and, yes, even beggar-man and thief, regardless of his talents, penchants, tendencies, abilities, vocations, and race of his ancestors."
>
> – *John B. Watson*

There are serious ethical problems associated with Watson's research with Little Albert, and this study would be considered unethical under current Canadian Psychological Association guidelines. For example, Albert's mother was never informed of Albert's participation in the study, and the study was carried out without regard for the suffering caused to Albert or for the possibility that there would be lasting harmful effects on Albert's emotional state (Field & Nightingale, 2009). Further, there are clear suggestions that Watson overstated his results, as several other researchers have failed to replicate his findings (Samelson, 1980).

stimulus generalization what occurs when similar stimuli elicit the same response as a conditioned stimulus after classical conditioning has occurred.

Watson's studies also looked at **stimulus generalization**, which refers to the fact that similar, but not identical, stimuli can take the place of a CS. Watson claimed that Albert, for example, came to fear not only the white rat, but also other stimuli, including a rabbit, a dog, and a sealskin coat.

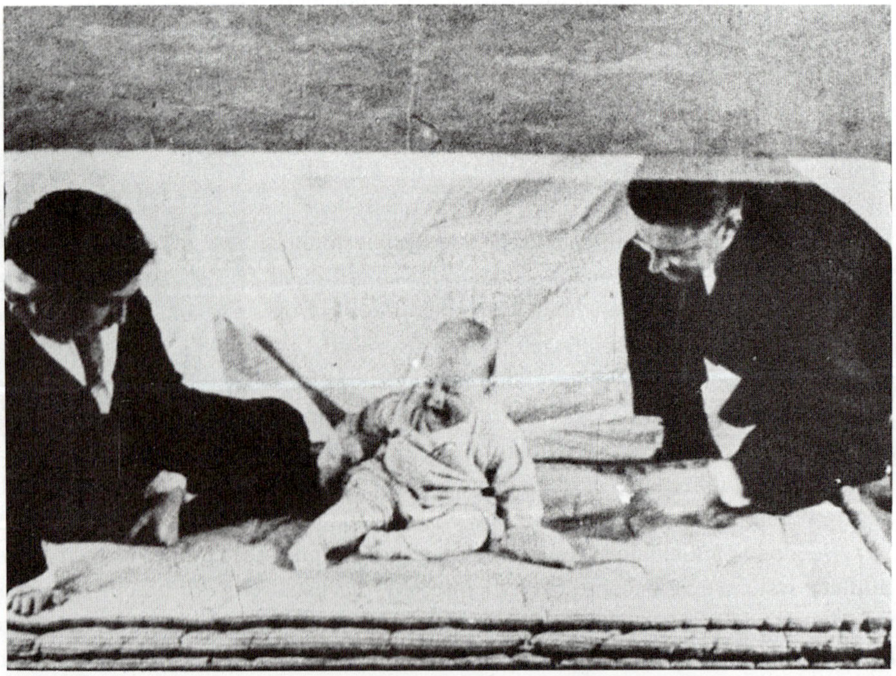

Teaching a child to fear. In an ethically-questionable study by today's standards, John Watson and his colleague Rosalie Rayner used classical conditioning principles to teach 11-month-old "Little Albert" to fear white rats.

Subsequent laboratory studies with animals show that fears are very easily learned. Fear conditioning of laboratory rodents involves training them to associate a neutral cue (usually a tone) with a painful unconditioned stimulus, usually an electric shock to the feet (**Figure 7-5**). Naïve rodents will respond to foot shock by adopting a characteristic posture of immobilization, or "freezing." This response probably reflects adaptive behaviour small mammals engage in when confronted with a predator and have no way to escape; they minimize movement to escape detection. Typically just a few pairings of a tone with foot shock are needed to lead to a lasting CS–US association, causing the rat to freeze to the CS tone alone (LeDoux, 2000, 2003).

Animal fear-conditioning studies such as these also provide examples of how emotion can facilitate the learning process. Since shock is painful, and thus fear-inducing, its presence in a learning situation can speed up the formation of an association between the CS and US.

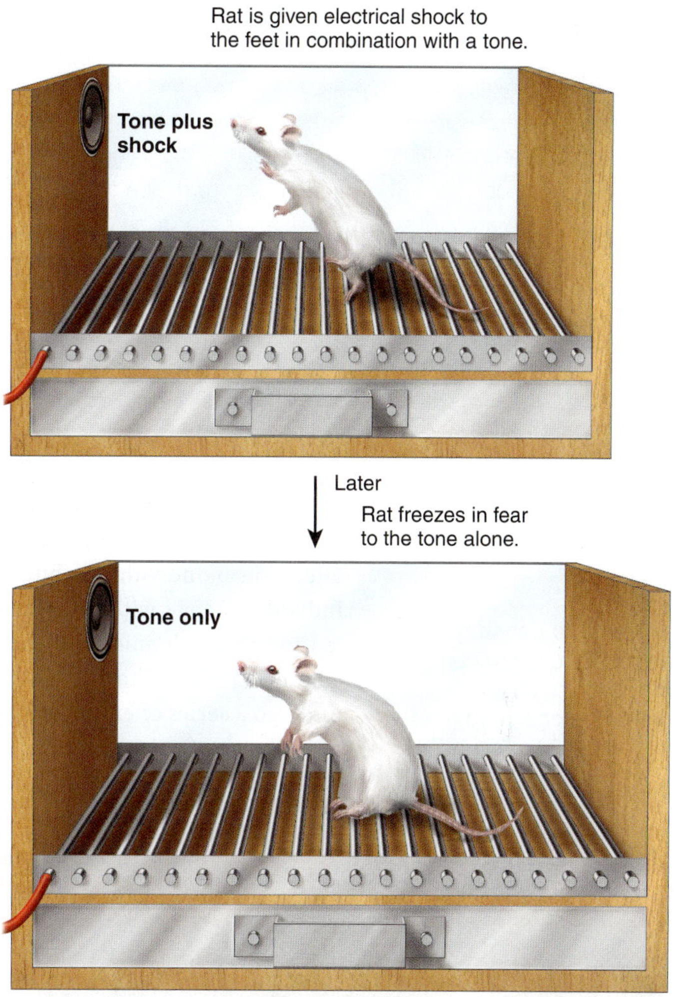

FIGURE 7-5 Fear conditioning in rats. In fear conditioning, a laboratory rat is given an electrical shock (US) to the feet just after exposure to a neutral stimulus (CS), such as a tone. Only a few pairings of the US and CS are needed for the rat to freeze in fear at the tone alone.

Phobias WHEN THINGS GO WRONG Some scientists believe fear conditioning is the basis of the development of a category of anxiety disorders called *phobias* (LeDoux, 1998; Morgan, Romanski, & LeDoux, 1993). **Phobias** are exaggerated fears of stimuli, many of which have little or no inherent danger. People who suffer from phobias are believed to have learned an association between neutral (CS) and dangerous (US) stimuli, thus being conditioned to fear a relatively harmless cue (i.e., the CS). For example, take a case where an adult has acquired a fear (CR) of all dogs (CS) due to being injured/frightened (UR) as a small child when knocked to the ground by an over-exuberant Labrador retriever (US). Due to the generalized association of fear (CR) to all dogs (CS), this person now refuses to go outside if he sees a dog, big or small. In this way, people become conditioned to fear specific objects or situations. Any neutral stimulus can become associated with a dangerous stimulus. See **Table 7-1** for a short list of specific phobias.

phobia persistent, irrational, or obsessive fear of a specific object or situation that may arise as a result of fear conditioning.

TABLE 7-1 Common and Uncommon Phobias

Acrophobia	Fear of heights	Hemophobia	Fear of blood
Agoraphobia	Fear of open spaces or crowds	Hydrophobia	Fear of water
Anthrophobia	Fear of flowers	Hylophobia	Fear of forests
Apiphobia	Fear of bees	Mysophobia	Fear of dirt and germs
Arachnophobia	Fear of spiders	Necrophobia	Fear of death, dead things
Astraphobia	Fear of thunder and lightning	Ophidiophobia	Fear of snakes
Claustrophobia	Fear of confined spaces	Papyrophobia	Fear of paper
Coulrophobia	Fear of clowns	Podophobia	Fear of feet
Cynophobia	Fear of dogs	Pteromerhanophobia	Fear of flying
Dentophobia	Fear of dentists	Selachophobia	Fear of sharks
Ergophobia	Fear of work	Sociophobia	Fear of social evaluation
Emetophobia	Fear of vomit	Trypanophobia	Fear of injections
Gamophobia	Fear of marriage	Xenophobia	Fear of strangers or foreigners

PSYCHOLOGY AROUND US No—Not Santa Claus!

Phobias often interfere with individuals' ability to pleasurably experience some enjoyable experiences in life. Although there is some question of whether Little Albert actually formed a generalized phobia to fur (Harris, 1979), imagine for a moment the long-term impact of such a childhood association on Little Albert if it did exist. At first, it may seem like his fear of white fur would not have had a significant impact on his life. After all, outside Watson's laboratory, how often would he have been likely to come across white rats? But remember that Little Albert's fear of white fur was said to be generalized, so that he might also fear a man with a white beard. Also, as white hair is not uncommon among older people, Little Albert might often have found himself in situations that aroused his fear. Furthermore, if his phobia continued into adulthood, it could have significantly affected his ability to interact with others, and might have ultimately caused him to fear his own reflection in his own old age! We are of course being facetious, but this gives you the idea of how generalization can lead to the development of a phobia.

In fact, phobias can be very debilitating (for example, preventing a person from being able to enter an underground parking structure and worse), and can have detrimental effects on an individual's ability to live normally. Therefore, therapies are important to help individuals cope with phobias. The theory that phobias arise from fear conditioning has led to the development of therapies that are also based on classical conditioning. In one common process, known as **systematic desensitization**, people who suffer from phobias undergo a series of extinction trials—repeated exposure to the feared object or situation in the absence of pairing with a US.

systematic desensitization a process used to condition extinction of phobias through gradual exposure to the feared object or situation.

Learning to Love Pain?

Tough love. This peaceful domestic scene belies the fact that female rats are often very rough with their young pups—perhaps explaining why many rat pups are attracted to, instead of repelled by, stimuli associated with pain.

Some researchers made an interesting discovery when attempting to use olfactory cues to fear condition very young rat pups. Adult rats will avoid stimuli that are associated with punishment. If an odour is paired with a shock, rats will learn to distinguish that odour and avoid it in the future. This response to olfactory learning, however, is not present during the first week of life for rats. Instead, rat pups will display the opposite effect of such conditioning. Odour pairings with shock produce an approach response in the pups (Moriceau & Sullivan, 2006). An approach response means that the rat pups are attracted to the odour and move toward it, even though they are shocked whenever the odour was present. Why would rat pups learn to move toward, instead of away from, an odour that predicts pain?

The answer may lie in rats' normal lifestyles. Rat pups live in the nest, staying close to their mothers for the first two weeks of life, until they start weaning. During this early time in the nest, the mother is likely to do many things to the pups that elicit pain. Mothers retrieve pups by picking them up by their teeth, they lick them vigorously, and they routinely step on their babies. Despite these painful events, it is essential that rat pups become attached to their mother if they are to survive, and odour is the primary means by which they keep track of her. Thus, a tendency to form avoidant reactions to odours associated with pain would be detrimental to the survival of a very young rat (Sullivan, Landers, Yeaman, & Wilson, 2000).

As time passes, however, and the pup becomes less dependent on the mother and more capable of avoiding her sharp teeth and heavy foot, the pup develops a healthy aversion to painful stimuli. Around this time, avoidance becomes the natural response to odour pairings with noxious stimuli; rats at this age learn, for example, to avoid smells associated with electric shock.

Some investigators have speculated that a similar conditioning process may contribute to the development of *attachment disorder* in humans. This condition is characterized by an inability to form healthy emotional relationships with others. People with attachment disorder do not respond positively to nurturing behaviour, and they often seek out situations that are likely to result in physical and emotional pain. Since a principal cause of this condition is early childhood abuse and neglect, it is possible that excessive strengthening of associations between painful stimuli and one's caregiver during development lead to persistent maladaptive responses to social interactions (Chaffin, Hanson, Saunders, et al., 2006).

Systematic desensitization is a treatment approach that sometimes helps people with phobias to overcome their anxiety and function normally in the presence of the fear-inducing cue. In systematic desensitization, individuals with phobias are taught to remain relaxed in the presence of progressively more threatening aspects of the phobia. The affected individual and the therapist create a hierarchy of the feared stimuli, moving from stimuli the phobic person finds least threatening and gradually moving toward stimuli the person finds very threatening. This "exposure" often occurs in the person's imagination. For example, a woman with a dog phobia might gradually work from looking at pictures of puppies to imagining that she is in the presence of a snarling dog. Depending on what a given individual finds frightening, this step might precede actual contact with a dog. Remember, however, that extinction trials do not produce "unlearning," but instead involve active inhibition of the previously learned association (Quirk, 2006). This means that the previously learned fear may reappear at some point following extinction.

Neuroimaging studies suggest that phobias involve abnormal activity in the amygdala, a part of the brain that is active when we experience emotions, including fear (Ledoux, 2003). People with phobias show rapid activation of this brain region when exposed to the stimuli they fear most. Extinction training, by contrast, is known to activate part of the prefrontal cortex as phobias diminish (Quirk, Garcia, & González-Lima, 2006). Recall from Chapter 4 that our prefrontal cortex can help us inhibit emotional impulses. Thus, phobias that have been desensitized still exist. As a result, they are prone to spontaneous recovery, similar to other classically-conditioned behaviours.

conditioned taste aversion a form of classical conditioning whereby a previously neutral stimulus (often an odour or taste) elicits an aversive reaction after it's paired with illness (nausea).

Classical Conditioning and Taste Aversions

Another type of classical conditioning that has been studied in the laboratory has relevance to human learning. **Conditioned taste aversion** involves learning an association between

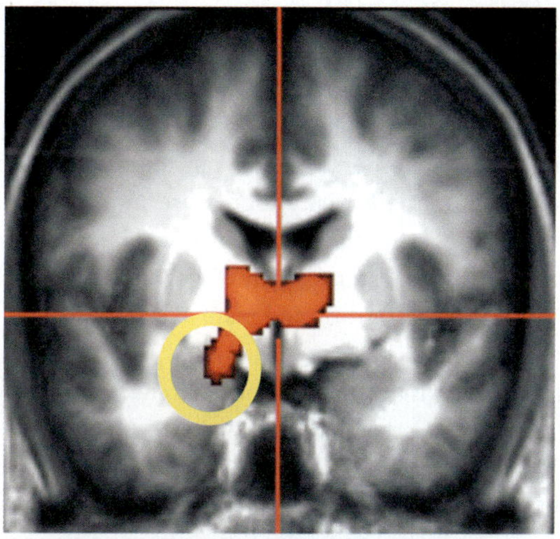

Phobias and the brain. This coloured brain scan of a cross section of the brain reveals increased activity in a phobic individual's amygdala (region circled in yellow) while the person is looking at a feared object.

Arachnophobia. An extreme fear of spiders is one of the most common of all phobias. Around half of all women and 10 percent of all men have at least a mild fear of spiders.

Producing a taste aversion. In pioneering work, researcher John Garcia and his colleagues used classical conditioning to induce conditioned taste aversions in laboratory animals by giving them specific foods to eat or drink and then inducing nausea through injection or radiation (Garcia & Koelling, 1971). Such conditioned taste aversions, often referred to as the *Garcia effect*, have been used in Alberta to protect livestock from wolves, in Saskatchewan to protect cows and sheep from coyotes, and in British Columbia to keep black bears from eating human food (Homstol, 2011).

a particular food and a subsequent stomach illness (Garcia et al., 1985). Many of us have had this type of experience. You eat a certain type of food and a short time later, you are stricken with nausea and vomiting. Whether or not the symptoms are related to the food, you will probably have an aversion to that particular dish for some time afterwards. In this case, the US is whatever agent actually made you nauseous, be it bacterial, viral, or chemical. The food is the CS. The unconditioned physiological response (UR), which becomes the CR, is nausea itself. Nausea will be elicited by exposure to the food in the future.

Some people are especially vulnerable to conditioned taste aversions. Pregnant women with severe morning sickness may develop intense aversions to foods that are followed by nausea. Similarly, research done by Gary Challis and Hank Stam at the University of Calgary shows that people undergoing chemotherapy for cancer treatment can develop aversions to foods they ingest right before a chemotherapy session, due to the nausea occurring as a side effect of the drug (Challis & Stam, 1992).

Conditioned taste aversions happen very quickly. Laboratory research has shown that a single pairing of food and nausea is frequently all that is necessary for a conditioned taste aversion to be formed (Garcia et al., 1985; Garcia & Koelling, 1971). Perhaps you once ate dill pickle chips at a movie and upon arriving home several hours later were violently ill with the flu. To this day you cannot even think about dill pickle chips without feeling queasy, in spite of the fact that it was the flu that actually made you ill. Not only did you develop this aversion from a single experience, but this aversion to dill pickle chips is also particularly impressive given the length of time that intervened between your exposure to the CS (chips) and your illness. In fact, research shows that the taste of a specific food or drink can be associated with illness up to 12 hours after its ingestion (Cowan et al., 2000). Forming an association with such a long delay between the CS and US is quite remarkable; recall that we said earlier that a delay of more than 30 seconds between a CS and a US often makes it difficult to establish a relationship between two stimuli. Separation of a tone from a shock by several hours would make it very difficult, if not impossible, to produce fear conditioning, and yet conditioned taste aversions develop even when the US does not immediately follow the CS.

Scientists suggest that we have a biological readiness to learn certain associations due to their survival value (Gaston, 1978). This biological readiness may be rooted in our evolutionary history. The ability to associate potentially tainted food with a subsequent illness was most likely highly adaptive during human evolution. Those who could not do this were more likely to be poisoned and to risk poisoning members of their families. Those who readily formed such associations and avoided potentially risky food were more likely to survive and successfully reproduce. We would expect that those who survived because they could make this association would have passed this trait on to their offspring. As a result, over time most people in the population would form conditioned taste aversions—which, indeed, is what we see today.

Biological preparedness also may help explain why taste aversions are easy to learn for animals that use odour and taste for food detection (e.g., mice, rats, wolves). In these same animals, it is difficult to form an association between a visual or auditory cue and nausea. However, in animals such as birds, who select their food using visual cues, conditioned aversions to flavours or odours are difficult to produce. Birds can be more readily conditioned to avoid visual cues (such as a certain coloured bead) when those cues have been paired with stomach illness (Werner, Kimball, & Provenza, 2008). Since birds often search out food using vision (consider the bird searching for a wiggly worm), it's more natural for them to associate a visual cue, than a gustatory or olfactory one, with a subsequent stomach illness.

Before You Go On

www.wiley.com/go/comer

What Do You Know?

3. You take your dog in the car when going to the veterinarian. After several visits, your dog cowers and whimpers whenever he sees the car. Identify the US, UR, CS, and CR in this example of conditioned fear.
4. What is conditioned taste aversion? How does it happen?

What Do You Think?

How might the principles of classical conditioning be used to keep chemotherapy patients from forming taste aversions to foods they enjoy?

SCAN TO GET THE ANSWERS

Operant Conditioning

LEARNING OBJECTIVE 3

Describe the basic processes of operant conditioning and explain how shaping can be used to teach new behaviours.

Classical conditioning does not account for the vast majority of learning by complex organisms. Classical conditioning is a passive form of learning that does not involve the active participation of the learner. In fact, most forms of classical conditioning occur without awareness that the association is being formed. The learner has very little control over the stimuli being associated. For example, a light flashes and a shock follows. The animal or person learns to make the association between the two stimuli, but the learning is involuntary and, importantly, precedes the response. That is, the person or animal does not actively choose to make (or not make) the association.

operant or **instrumental conditioning** a form of associative learning whereby behaviour is modified depending on its consequences.

In everyday life, however, the majority of our learning is active. Most of us are not passive participants in the environment. Instead, we respond to our environment and modify our behaviour according to the consequences that follow our initial response. For example, if you are only a few minutes late for work but your boss docks you an hour's pay, you can alter your behaviour the following day to increase your chances of being on time. Or, if a parent praises a child for treating a younger sibling with kindness, the older child will more likely be kind to their sibling in future encounters. Psychologists use the terms **operant** or **instrumental conditioning** to describe another type of associative learning that is voluntary (rather than reflexive) and that acts on the environment to produce specific outcomes. Organisms associate their behaviour with specific consequences as they attempt to receive rewards and avoid punishment.

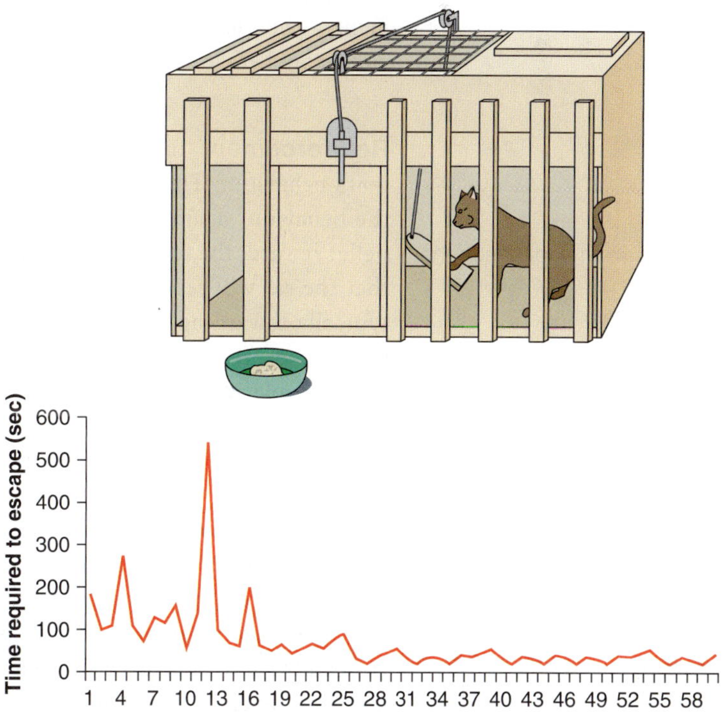

FIGURE 7-6 Thorndike's puzzle box. Edward Thorndike used a puzzle box to study operant conditioning in cats. When the cat accidentally stepped on a pedal that pulled a string, the cat escaped from the box and received a fish reward. Once the cat had done this, it performed the action more quickly when it was put back into the box, until eventually it stepped on the pedal immediately each time.

For some of the earliest laboratory studies of operant conditioning, psychologist Edward Thorndike created a contraption called a "puzzle box." This was a cage, into which Thorndike placed a hungry cat. As shown in **Figure 7-6**, the animal could escape from the box by pressing a pedal that pulled a string. Thorndike measured the amount of time that it took the cat to free itself. Escape from the box led to a food reward. The first escape from the box probably occurred through the random actions of the experimental animal. In moving about, pawing at the door, floor, and walls, the cat would accidentally step on the pedal and thus receive temporary freedom and a food reward. Each time Thorndike put the cat back in the box, the cat began to more quickly engage in the same behaviour (pressing the pedal) that helped it to escape the box and obtain the food. Eventually, the cat would immediately step on the pedal when placed into the puzzle box. This work led Thorndike to develop a theory known as the **law of effect** (Thorndike, 1933), which suggests that behaviours are selected by their consequences: behaviours leading to success or to rewards are more likely to occur again, and behaviours producing unsuccessful or unpleasant outcomes are less likely to occur again. He proposed that the law of effect applied not only to other animals, but also to humans. He called this type of learning *instrumental conditioning* because the response (stepping on the pedal) was essential (instrumental) to receiving the reward (escape and food).

law of effect law stating that behaviours leading to rewards are more likely to occur again, while behaviours producing unpleasantness are less likely to occur again.

How Does Operant Conditioning Work?

Thorndike's ideas about instrumental conditioning became highly influential. For several decades of the twentieth century, the dominant school of thought in psychology was **behaviourism**, the systematic study of observable behaviour (Gantt, 1980). Behaviourists believed that behaviour could be objectively studied and measured, as opposed to internal events such as thoughts or emotion. Further, they believed that all behaviour could be learned through stimulus–response associations via either classical or operant conditioning. Many researchers, such as leading behaviourist B. F. Skinner, conducted learning research with laboratory animals such as rats and pigeons to understand the principles of instrumental, or operant, conditioning. Skinner believed that organisms didn't simply respond to the environment, they exerted influence (or "operated") on the environment, so he called this form of learning *operant conditioning*.

behaviourism the systematic study and manipulation of observable behaviour.

Skinner's work expanded on Thorndike's law of effect. Skinner developed behavioural principles based on the fact that *behaviours that are followed by favourable consequences will likely be repeated*. Using these principles, birds and animals have been taught a variety of behaviours: cockatoos playing the piano or dunking a basketball, rats hoisting flags, pigeons bowling, or whales waving. A great deal of human behaviour is also influenced by reinforcement: a child learning to say please, taking medicine for a headache, stopping at red lights, and so on. Let's look at some of the key concepts associated with operant conditioning.

Reinforcement In typical experiments, stimuli are provided in response to the animal's behaviour. These stimuli make it more or less likely that the animal will engage in the behaviour again. For example, if a laboratory rat presses a lever and receives a food pellet reward, the food works as a **reinforcer**, a consequence that *increases* the likelihood that the rat will repeat the behaviour or press the lever again. Reinforcers are therefore typically rewarding. However, what is reinforcing for one person may not be rewarding for another; the power of reinforcers varies across individuals and cultures. For example, most people work for a paycheque, but volunteers work for the satisfaction of helping others; a trip to an exotic locale would be reinforcing to some, but anxiety-producing for others; additional income is reinforcing to some people, whereas additional time off is reinforcing to others; and so on. In some cultures money and achievement are valued above most other reinforcers, whereas in others the approval and respect of other members of the group is most reinforcing.

reinforcer an experience that produces an increase in a certain behaviour.

There are two kinds of reinforcement: **positive reinforcement** and **negative reinforcement**. In this instance the terms positive and negative do not mean "good" and "bad." Instead the terms are used in a manner similar to the way they are used in medical terminology. The term "positive" here means that something is present or has been added. For example, if you test positive for a sexually transmitted infection (STI), then an STI is present. On the other hand, a "negative" result would mean that there is no infection; in this case, negative means that something is absent.

positive reinforcement presentation of a pleasant consequence following a behaviour to increase the probability that the behaviour will reoccur.

negative reinforcement removal of an unpleasant stimulus after a response to increase the probability that the behaviour will reoccur.

Therefore, a positive reinforcer *presents* (or adds) something to *increase* the likelihood of a response: if your dog sits when you ask her to, you give her a treat; if a child says please, he gets a piece of candy; or if an adult works extra hours, she is given a raise in pay. In every instance, the animal or person is likely to repeat the behaviour because they have been given something desirable for their initial response. They have all been positively reinforced.

Negative reinforcement is less intuitive than positive reinforcement. To help this concept make sense to you it is important to remember that reinforcement *always* increases the likelihood that a specific behaviour will be repeated. Positive reinforcement increases the probability that a particular behaviour will occur by adding a pleasant stimulus. Negative reinforcement, on the other hand, increases a specific behaviour by *removing* an *unpleasant* stimulus. For instance, when you have a headache, you take a pain reliever. The pain reliever *takes away* your headache, thereby *increasing* the chances that next time you have a headache you will take a pain reliever. Similarly, say that you normally leave your house for school mid-morning, but in so doing you are consistently stuck in heavy traffic. One day you leave earlier and are pleasantly surprised to see that there is virtually no traffic. You start leaving for school earlier. In this case you *avoid* the heavy traffic (that is, you *take away* the heavy traffic) by increasing your behaviour of leaving home early.

Negative reinforcement is an important consideration in the behaviour of drug addicts. Addicts escape the cravings and other symptoms of withdrawal by taking a drug, thereby increasing the chances that they will take the drug again as soon as they begin to experience the symptoms of withdrawal on another occasion (Baker et al., 2006). Negative reinforcement also plays an important role in the maintenance of phobias. As already discussed, a phobia is acquired through classical conditioning. However, once the association between the US and CS has been formed, the phobia is maintained as the individual *escapes* anxiety by avoiding the feared object. For example, consider our example of the woman who is afraid of dogs. She is invited to a friend's house for tea, but to get there she has to walk by a house with a barking dog in the yard. The woman will feel anxious at the thought of going outside and encountering the dog. As her anxiety increases, she decides to stay at home and therefore her anxiety drops. She has escaped unpleasant anxiety by avoiding the feared object (the dog), and is therefore likely to resort to avoiding the feared object the next time she is anxious.

punishment an experience that produces a decrease in a certain behaviour.

positive punishment presentation of an unpleasant consequence following a behaviour to decrease the probability of the behaviour being repeated.

negative punishment removal of a pleasant stimulus as a consequence of a behaviour to decrease the probability of the behaviour being repeated.

Punishment *decreases* the likelihood a response will reoccur, weakening the tendency to make the same response. As there is with reinforcement, there are two kinds of punishment: **positive punishment** and **negative punishment**. Students often ask how punishment can be good. It can't. Positive punishment means that something aversive has been *presented* (added) to *weaken* a response. A child is rude to his grandmother, and his mother scolds him; a young woman is texting while driving to work, and drives her car into the car in front of her; a man is not watching carefully as he slices a loaf of bread, and cuts his hand; or, you decide to try a new restaurant, and the food is awful. In every instance, an undesirable consequence was *presented* following each person's actions, thereby reducing the probability that they will repeat the initial behaviour. They have been positively punished.

Negative punishment involves *taking away* a pleasant stimulus to *weaken* a response. An adolescent is late for his curfew and so his parents say that he cannot use the family car the following weekend; a child spits food at her sister during dinner and is therefore not allowed to have dessert; a preschooler hits another child at daycare and is put into the time out corner (without toys and away from the other children). In each situation, a positive stimulus had been removed, thereby decreasing the probability that the behaviour will be repeated.

Let's review by taking the case of a lever-pressing rat, in four different possible experiments, as shown in **Figure 7-7**. Positive reinforcement would provide a food reward each time the rat pressed the lever; negative reinforcement would turn off an electric shock each time the rat pressed the lever. In both cases, the rat's rate of lever pressing would increase. Positive punishment would provide an electric shock each time the rat pressed the lever, and negative punishment would remove food each time the rat pressed the lever. In these instances, the rate of lever pressing would go down.

Types of Reinforcers Most reinforcers have survival value for organisms and include food, water, mates, or the ability to terminate pain. These types of reinforcers are called

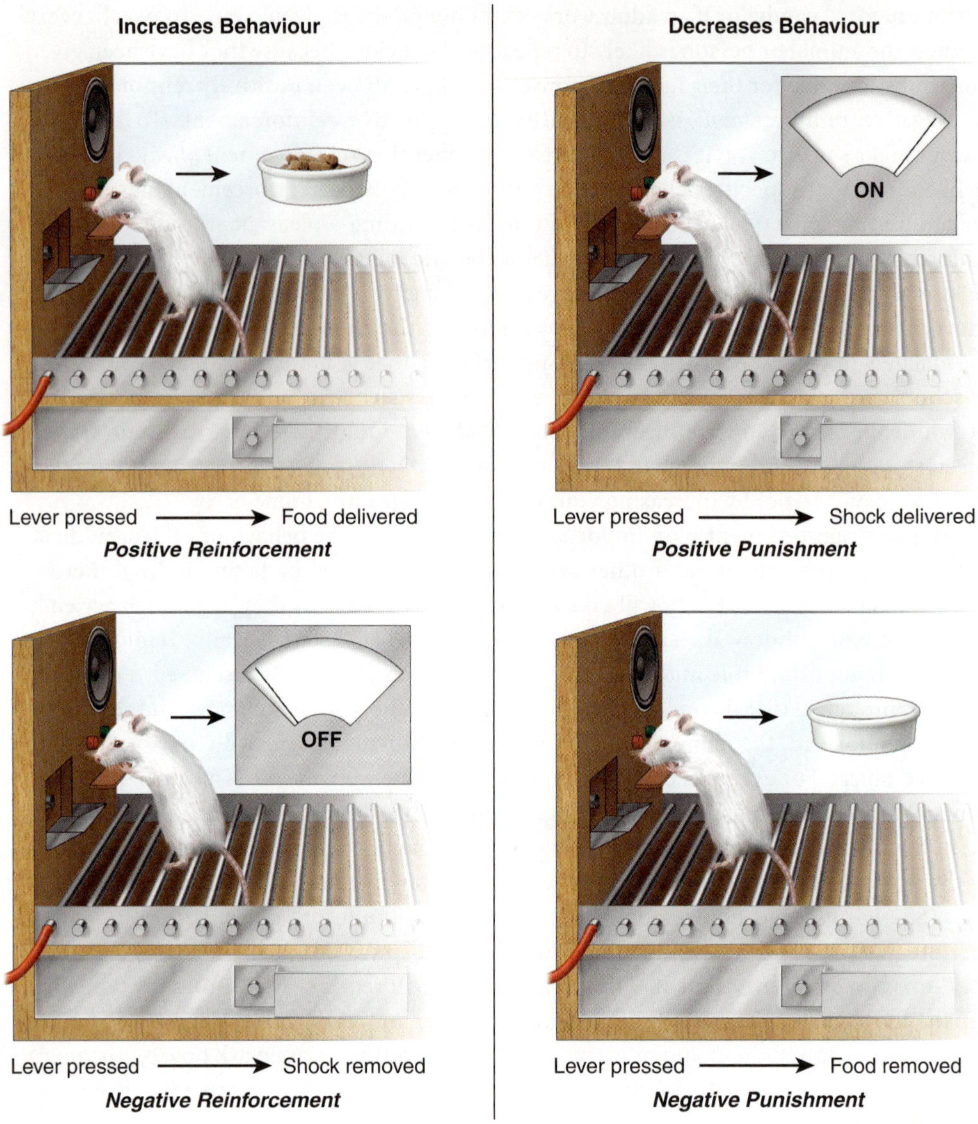

FIGURE 7-7 Reinforcement and punishment. The apparatus shown here is called a Skinner box. The rat can press a lever to receive a food pellet. The floor of the box is wired to give an electric shock. The box is used to test the effects of positive and/or negative reinforcement and/or punishment on behaviour.

primary reinforcer a stimulus that has survival value and is therefore intrinsically rewarding.

secondary reinforcer a neutral stimulus that becomes rewarding when associated with a primary reinforcer.

primary reinforcers because they satisfy biological needs and are therefore intrinsically pleasurable; that is, they are rewarding by their very nature. However, not all reinforcers satisfy physiological needs. For example, many people work for money or for grades rather than for food or for water. Some reinforcers become associated with primary reinforcers and become *conditioned* (i.e., learned) reinforcers because of this association. We call this type of reinforcer a **secondary reinforcer**. Since secondary reinforcers are learned, they vary from one species to another and from one culture to another. Common secondary reinforcers for human beings include money, grades, praise, approval, acceptance, and so on. Animals will respond to secondary reinforcers such as attention, praise, touch, toys, opportunities to engage in physical play (e.g, a walk), and so on.

primary punisher a stimulus that is naturally aversive to an organism.

secondary punisher a stimulus that becomes aversive when associated with a primary punisher.

Types of Punishers Punishers can also be distinguished by whether or not they are naturally aversive or whether they are learned. A **primary punisher** is a stimulus that is naturally aversive to an organism. As such, primary punishers are usually associated with pain or discomfort. Primary punishers include stimuli such as slapping or hitting, shock, uncomfortably loud or high-pitched sounds, exposure to extreme temperature, and so on. **Secondary punishers** are neutral stimuli that take on punishing qualities due to their association with a primary punisher. Like secondary reinforcers, secondary punishers are learned and are consequently also both species and culture bound. For humans, secondary punishers include disapproval, indifference, a verbal "no," criticism, bad grades, demerits,

PRACTICALLY SPEAKING Using Punishments and Rewards to Teach Children

Although both reinforcement and punishment are effective ways of altering behaviour in laboratory learning studies, evidence from real-life situations suggests these two approaches may not be equally effective. In general, positive reinforcement is more effective than punishment. Punishment tells an organism what not to do by suppressing immediate behaviour, but doesn't show them what they should do instead. Reinforcement is effective at establishing new and more appropriate behaviours. For example, if a child puts himself in immediate danger by running in front of a car, a harsh scolding might be effective at stopping the immediate behaviour. However, positive reinforcement (e.g., praise) for holding a parent's hand or for remaining on the sidewalk instead of chasing a ball will teach the child what to do in future situations, rather than simply what *not* to do in the current situation. Skinner argued that what people really learn about punishment is only how to avoid it. Consequently, if we want to *change* behaviour, we have to use reinforcement.

Positive punishment, especially physical punishment, also has a number of alarming ethical implications. Joan Grusec at the University of Toronto has reported that children who experience physical aggression are more aggressive to others (Grusec & Ungerer, 2003; Grusec et al., 2000). And, in a meta-analysis of 88 studies, Gershoff (2002) concluded that physical punishment is associated with a number of long-term problems, including low self-esteem, poor self-concept, and lack of interpersonal skills, as well as delinquency, criminal behaviour, child abuse, and mental health issues. Her findings have been replicated by other researchers (Lynch et al., 2006; Marshall, 2002; Mulvany & Mebert, 2007). These findings regarding the adverse effects of positive punishment are of particular concern because researchers in Quebec presented data showing that approximately 40 percent of parents in their study reported slapping or spanking their children (Clément & Chamberland, 2007). And of greater concern, parents who use physical punishment are backed by the Supreme Court of Canada, which, when challenged, upheld a ruling of the Criminal Code of Canada allowing parents and teachers to use "reasonable corrective force" to discipline children between the ages of 2 and 12.

Another problem with physical punishment is that children not only learn to associate fear with the unwanted behaviour, but with the punisher as well. Although earlier we discussed discriminating classical and operant conditioning by noting that classical conditioning relies on reflexive, involuntary responses whereas operant conditioning relies largely upon voluntary responses, this distinction is not absolute. In some ways, the two types of conditioning may work together to manage various aspects of behaviour. For example, using spanking to punish a child to decrease unwanted behaviour is considered to be operant conditioning. However, if a parent regularly spanks a child, the child will form a classically conditioned association between the parent and pain/fear. The two types of learning are therefore related and may in fact simply be two aspects of a single learning experience (Allan, 1998), and both contribute to a child learning to fear a punisher and to emulate the punisher's behaviour.

Negative punishment is generally considered to be less ethically problematic than positive punishment (Kazdin & Benjet, 2003), but may still fail in some circumstances. Many parents and preschool teachers use a negative punishment technique called "time out" as a consequence for unwanted behaviour. This method involves removing a child from her surroundings, generally by putting her in a separate location in the classroom or home. The child has thus had a pleasurable stimulus (access to playthings and classmates) removed. Time out also removes the child from the environment that may have contributed to the bad behaviour and allows quiet time to think about the situation. The effectiveness of time out depends on the specific circumstances motivating the individual. If the child was acting out to gain attention, then intervening with a positive punishment may not effectively eliminate the behaviour. Also, removal from a certain environment, such as the classroom or the dinner table, may not be sufficiently aversive to alter the offensive behaviour. Removing a child to his bedroom might also be counterproductive, as this might be rewarding to some children, especially if they have television and/or games in their rooms.

In spite of the greater efficacy of reinforcement (van Duijvenvoorde et al., 2008), there are situations where punishment is deemed necessary. Research suggests the following guidelines for using punishment effectively to promote learning:

- Positive punishment is most effective when it occurs immediately after the incorrect behaviour (Abramowitz & O'Leary, 1990).

- Negative punishment is generally more effective than positive punishment (Kazdin & Benjet, 2003).
- Punishment is most effective when it is consistent. If behaviour warrants punishment once, the behaviour needs to be punished each time it occurs (Parke & Deur, 1972; Rudy & Grusec, 2001).
- Punishment is effective only when it is clear that the punishment is a consequence of a specific behaviour, rather than, say, a result of the teacher or caregiver's bad mood or general dislike for the child.
- Punishment should be combined with an explanation for the punishment as well as suggested alternative behaviours.

and so on. For animals, secondary punishers include isolation, verbal rebuke, sounds (e.g., clickers or rattling objects), and so on.

continuous reinforcement what occurs when behaviour is reinforced every time it occurs.

intermittent or **partial reinforcement** a schedule of reinforcement where the behaviour is only followed by reinforcement some of the time.

fixed ratio schedule a schedule of reinforcement that occurs after a specific number of responses.

variable ratio schedule a schedule of reinforcement that occurs when the number of responses required for reinforcement is unpredictable.

fixed interval schedule a schedule of reinforcement that occurs every time a specific time period has elapsed.

variable interval schedule a schedule of reinforcement that occurs after varying amounts of time.

Schedules of Reinforcement In real-life situations, we are not usually reinforced or punished every single time we perform a behaviour. You may, for example, hold the door open many times a day for the person who walks in behind you, but only receive a pleasant "thank you" once or twice. Researchers have studied the effects of different schedules of reinforcement on behaviour (Skinner, 1958; Skinner & Morse, 1958). When a behaviour is reinforced every single time it occurs, reinforcement is said to be continuous. Continuous reinforcement results in rapid learning, but can be easily extinguished. In contrast, intermittent or partial reinforcement, by which the behaviour is only sometimes reinforced, is more slowly acquired, but is difficult to extinguish. Recall your niece's constant whining for candy. Since your sister occasionally gives in to her daughter when she is demanding candy, the little girl is learning to persist, because sometimes her whining pays off and she gets what she wants. There are several possible schedules of intermittent or partial reinforcement. The most common types of intermittent reinforcement schedules are described in **Table 7-2**.

In a *ratio schedule*, reinforcement is based on the *number* of behavioural responses. In a fixed ratio schedule, a person or animal is rewarded every time they make a predetermined number of responses. The "frequent drinker" card at your local coffee shop may offer you a free cup of coffee after you pay for a dozen other cups, for example. In a variable ratio schedule, reinforcement occurs for a predetermined average number of responses. Slot machines or VLTs (video lottery terminals), if they are legally regulated, have a set variable ratio payout schedule. Depending on the local laws, VLTs pay back 80 to 95 percent of the money entered into them, but on a randomly assigned schedule.

In an *interval schedule*, reinforcement is based on elapsed *time*, rather than on the number of behavioural responses. In a fixed interval schedule, such as occurs with a weekly salaried paycheque, you are reinforced every time a certain period of time passes. Like a variable ratio schedule, a variable interval schedule provides random reinforcement, giving a predetermined number of reinforcements over time. For example, imagine a teacher

TABLE 7-2 Intermittent Reinforcement Schedules

	Definition	Response Rate	Example
Schedules Based on Number of Responses			
Fixed ratio	Reinforcement occurs after a predetermined number of responses	High, with pauses after reinforcement	A rat is reinforced for every tenth bar press
Variable ratio	Reinforcement occurs after an average number of responses	High, regular rate of response	A slot machine pays out after an average of 20 tries, but the payout intervals are unpredictable
Schedules Based on Time Intervals			
Fixed interval	Reinforcement occurs after a fixed period of time	Low, with increases as time for reinforcement approaches	A worker receives a paycheque every week
Variable interval	Reinforcement occurs after varying lengths of time	Low, as reinforcement is tied to time rather than to output	Work breaks occur at unpredictable intervals, such as 60 minutes, 72 minutes, and 54 minutes

who wants to reward a student for remaining on task. The teacher will arrange for a bell to ring six times over the hour and will give the child a reinforcer (for example, a piece of candy or a token to trade for a privilege) if the child is on task when the bell rings. Rather than having the bell ring every ten minutes, the bell will ring after a random period of time has passed, but will ring six times over the hour.

Intermittent or partial reinforcement schedules take longer to train but are more effective than continuous reinforcement at maintaining behaviour. With continuous reinforcement, the behaviour is always paired with the reward. If reinforcement stops, the elimination signals a major change in the association between stimulus and response. By contrast, with intermittent reinforcement, the behaviour is only followed by reinforcement some of the time. When a response occurs but is not reinforced, it's not readily apparent whether or not the reward has stopped altogether. Continuing to engage in the behaviour makes sense in case a reward might happen. Thus, behaviours that are acquired through partial reinforcement are harder to extinguish than behaviours that are acquired through continuous reinforcement.

The house always wins. Slot machines are a good example of a variable ratio schedule reinforcement strategy. The big payout will come eventually, but you don't know when!

Using Operant Conditioning to Teach New Behaviours

Until now, we have described how operant conditioning can lead people and animals to increase or decrease behaviours that they already display at least some of the time. Thorndike's cats, for example, learned to press the pedal in the puzzle box more often than they would have by chance, but they already pressed the pedal at least once in a trial and error fashion before learning the association. Operant conditioning can also be used to teach people and animals entirely new complex behaviours.

A method, called **shaping**, rewards actions that are increasingly closer to a desired final behaviour, rather than waiting for the exact behaviour to happen before providing reinforcement. Consider training a dog to roll over. First you might provide a treat if the animal lies down on its stomach. Eventually, you would require the dog to perform something closer to rolling over in order to get the same reward; for example, you might offer a treat only when the dog lies down and turns a bit to the side. You carry on in this way, rewarding *successive approximations* of the desired behaviour until the complete behavioural sequence emerges. Shaping is highly effective in modifying the behaviour of animals and can be used to teach people, too. Humans regularly learn behaviour through shaping.

shaping introducing new behaviour by reinforcing close approximations of the desired behaviour.

behaviour modification a systematic approach to change behaviour using principles of operant conditioning.

A process called **behaviour modification** is frequently employed to shape the behaviour of people. The behaviour of individuals can be shaped to teach them new academic or athletic skills or to modify behaviours that are undesirable. For example, imagine a child who is disruptive in a classroom. The child's teacher wants him to sit quietly in his desk. So, the teacher systematically begins to shape the child's behaviour toward the outcome he (the teacher) desires. The teacher has determined that playing video games is rewarding to the child. So the teacher gives the child a sticker whenever he is quiet (even if he is out of his desk). After the child gets a particular number of stickers (say seven), he is allowed to play a video game for ten minutes. Eventually the child is only rewarded for standing quietly near his desk, then for sitting at his desk talking quietly, and so on. In this way the child's behaviour is shaped toward the desirable outcome.

A natural surfer? No. This boogie-boarding terrier underwent many learning trials and received rewards for many successive approximations of this behaviour before it became a skilled wave rider.

THINGS STUDENTS WANT TO KNOW

Are Rewards and Punishments the Same for Everyone?
Students have asked us if rewards are the same for everyone. They notice that the value of rewards can vary from person to person. It may well be that there are some significant individual differences in how people respond to rewards and punishments. The Reinforcement Sensitivity Theory (RST) developed by Jeffery Gray (1970; Gray and McNaughton, 2000) was developed to specifically address this question. The dimension of introversion and extroversion is a common one among many theories of personality (you will learn more about this dimension of personality later in this text in Chapter 13). Extroverts are outgoing, driven to find and engage in social contacts, and are typically described as sociable, while introverts are less outgoing. Gray noted that introverts are more sensitive to punishment, while extroverts are more sensitive to rewards. Gray suggests that extroverts are more driven by rewards, seeking out reward opportunities in the form of novelty and exciting possibilities in any social or work situation. Introverts, on the other hand, are more driven to avoid punishment, focusing less on rewards and more on leaving or avoiding situations where punishment (unpleasant experiences) is possible. Awareness of these differences has helped workplace managers understand how they might adapt their efforts to support and motivate employees by taking this aspect of their employees' personalities into account (Diefendorff & Metha, 2007).

PSYCHOLOGY AROUND US A Whale of a Story

The entertainment establishment SeaWorld has long used shaping methods to train dolphins and killer whales, or orcas, to perform impressive tricks, including doing midair flips, clapping their fins, and coming out of the water onto the side of the pool on command. Animal trainers begin by giving food rewards in response to minor movements in the direction of the desired behaviour. As the animal masters that component of the task, trainers make the food reward dependent on the animal completing more of the task. The result is impressive shows featuring marine mammals that appear to be having fun performing tasks that are unnatural to their species but of interest to ours. Despite the fact that these animals are smart enough to be shaped to perform tricks, some unfortunate incidents have highlighted the difficulty in using very large and powerful animals with a natural instinct to kill for entertainment purposes. In 2010, a killer whale at SeaWorld aggressively drowned his trainer. Over the many years of his captivity, this same animal had been responsible for two other human deaths. These events underscore the fact that although shaping can profoundly modify behaviour, the underlying instinctual responses remain.

As with classical conditioning, we should note that biology plays a role in determining how easy or difficult a particular learning task will be for a certain species. Although some trainers appear to be quite capable of teaching animals to engage in a wide range of unnatural behaviours (like skating bears), it turns out there are, of course, limits to what specific animals are able to master.

Some researchers tried to train raccoons to put coins in a piggy bank, by were stymied by biological constraints. Through shaping techniques, raccoons can be trained to pick up a single coin and place it in a piggy bank. However, raccoons are known for their natural tendency to wash food before eating it. If they are given more than one coin at a time, their natural tendency to wash objects seems to interfere with the shaping techniques. Instead of putting the coins into the bank, they become distracted, incessantly rubbing the coins together instead of completing the task of putting them in the piggy bank (Breland & Breland, 1961).

Teaching unnatural behaviours. Animal trainers have taught animals to do some very bizarre things (often to accusations of animal cruelty) by using shaping, such as teaching a bear to skate.

One of the most prominent examples of biological constraints on learning concerns language learning. Other than humans, only certain species of birds such as African grey parrots, dolphins, sea lions, and primates such as gorillas and chimps have learned to use forms of language. No matter how much reinforcement or punishment is provided, biological factors make speech impossible for most animals (Chomsky, 1959). (We will return to this topic in Chapter 9.)

Learned Helplessness

WHEN THINGS GO WRONG

Sometimes our prior learning experiences can cause problems with later learning situations. One problem that can arise as the result of operant conditioning is a phenomenon known as **learned helplessness**, in which prior experiences with inescapable punishment condition people or animals to accept punishing consequences in later situations when they could actually avoid them (Seligman et al., 1980). For instance, research with rats has found that, after repeated inescapable shocks to the tail, if rats are given the option of escaping a foot shock by moving to a different area in the testing cage, many of them fail to do so (Weiss & Glazer, 1975). The rats that could not escape the tail shocks initially failed later to learn how to stop a shock to the foot. Instead, they stayed put and took the punishment. Learned helplessness occurs when organisms are exposed to conditions over which they have no control. Since there is no association between their behaviour and the consequences of their behaviour, they learn to stop trying, even in situations where their behaviour could make a difference.

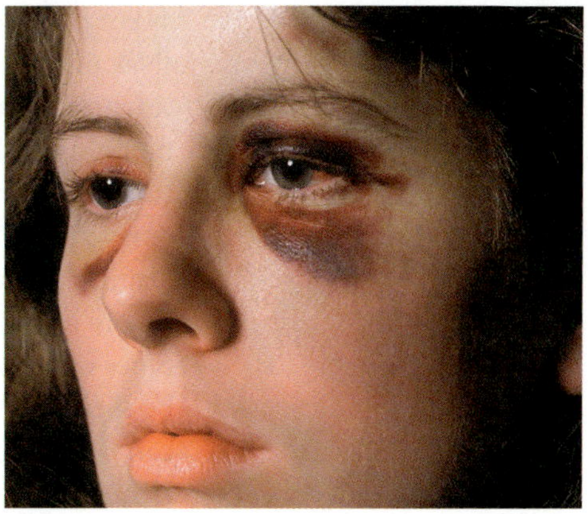

Why do they stay? Spousal abuse occurred in at least 6 percent of Canadian homes over the past five years (Statistics Canada, 2011). Psychologists believe that many victims develop feelings of helplessness and become convinced that they are incapable of changing the situation. (We want to emphasize that for some victims this perception might be accurate.)

Learned helplessness is thought by some researchers to be an animal model of depression (Porsolt, 2000). Humans with depression are often unmotivated to act on the stimuli they receive from their environments, and some theorists suggest that these people have learned this pattern of inaction from earlier, perhaps unrelated, experiences in which they were unable to make the changes they wanted. Some researchers have claimed that learned helplessness may also partially explain some of the characteristics of battered spouse syndrome (Clements & Sawhney, 2000). Repeated, inescapable abuse may cause learned helplessness. The victim can become withdrawn and unable to respond in an adaptive way, even if there is an option to escape an abusive situation. It is important to note, however, that some victims may not feel that they have a viable means of escape, and that learned helplessness cannot therefore account for all cases of battered spouses remaining in dangerous situations.

learned helplessness a situation in which repeated exposure to inescapable punishment eventually produces a failure to make escape attempts.

Before You Go On

www.wiley.com/go/comer

What Do You Know?

5. What are positive reinforcement and negative reinforcement? What are the effects of each on behaviour?
6. How does personality (extroversion/introversion) influence how people approach learning situations?
7. What is learned helplessness?

SCAN TO GET THE ANSWERS

What Do You Think?

How could you use operant conditioning principles to get a roommate or child to regularly hang up her coat instead of throwing it on the floor?

Observational Learning

LEARNING OBJECTIVE 4

Define observational learning and summarize concerns about observational learning from the media.

Studies of animal behaviour in natural habitats have shown that members of certain species learn tasks by watching each other. A good example of this can be seen by studying a troupe of Japanese macaques. This troupe of monkeys routinely washes sweet potatoes before eating them. This washing behaviour is not innate; that is, it is not practised by macaques all over the world. Instead, it began with one creative monkey who first started washing sweet potatoes after the potatoes were introduced to the macaques by researchers. After observing this behaviour, other members of the group started to wash their own

observational learning/ social learning learning that occurs without overt training in response to watching the behaviour of others, called models.

modelling what occurs when an observer learns from the behaviour of another.

sweet potatoes—similar behaviour has now been observed in the troupe with other foods (Nakamichi et al., 1998). Other studies have reported that **observational learning**, or **social learning**—learning from watching the behaviour of others—led to the use of novel tools by dolphins and certain primate and bird species (Krüetzen et al., 2005). Through observational learning, animals can culturally transmit behaviours across generations. That is, parents or older members of a group engage in behaviour that the young observe. Observation leads to imitation, or **modelling**, which is considered evidence that learning has occurred.

In addition to contributing to learning through imitation, observation can affect other types of behaviour that indirectly signal learning has occurred. A good example of this can be seen with reward studies in capuchin monkeys (Brosnan & De Waal, 2003). This species can be rather easily trained to perform a task for a food reward, such as a cucumber slice. If, however, the trained monkey observes another monkey receiving a more desirable reward (for example, a grape) for performing the same task, the monkey will respond by refusing to carry out the task again unless the reward is a grape. This suggests not only that capuchin monkeys have an internal concept of fairness, but also that they have used the experience of observing the consequences of another monkey's behaviour to modify their own.

There are many other examples of animals and birds learning through observation. For example, in a documentary, Jacques Cousteau (Cousteau & Diole, 1973), the well-known filmmaker and oceanographer, showed an octopus learning to open a jar through observation. He gave a hungry octopus a sealed jar with a crayfish inside. The octopus tried to break the jar by exerting pressure on it. Next, while the octopus watched, the researchers took the jar and unscrewed the lid. They then gave the octopus a second jar with a crayfish inside. The octopus immediately opened the jar.

Imitating Imo. A Japanese macaque washes its sweet potatoes in ocean water. This behaviour is displayed only by members of the monkey's particular troupe. Apparently, they learned it by imitating the innovative behaviour of a young monkey named Imo.

Bennet Galef and his students and colleagues working at McMaster University have shown that social learning plays a role in shaping behaviours of many animal species. For example, rats fed bad tasting food or food that tastes like food that has made them ill in the past will watch other rats make food selections and then make the same selection for themselves (Galef, Dudley, & Whiskin, 2008). In another area, female Japanese quail will show a clear mating preference for males they have observed mating successfully with other female quails, essentially copying the other quails' mate selections (Galef & Laland, 2005).

Further, Joshua Klein (2011) has had success training crows to use a vending machine. Klein was inspired by reports of crows in a particular Japanese city devising an ingenious method for cracking nuts. Crows there enjoyed a particular type of nut but could not shell them to eat. Eventually some crows discovered that if they dropped nuts on the road, cars would run over them, opening them for the crows to eat. Unfortunately, this solution produced another problem for the crows; it was very hazardous to stand in the middle of the road to eat the nuts once they were opened. Over time, one crow apparently learned that if he dropped the nuts into city crosswalks, allowing cars to crush the nuts, but then waited for the "walk signal" before retrieving the prize, it was much safer to fly down and eat. Over time, the other crows learned how to crack nuts as well, simply through observation. Now many crows in this Japanese city eat nuts using this method. Based on his knowledge of this situation, Klein designed a vending machine that produced peanuts when coins were dropped into a large slot. He started by laying peanuts and coins around on the machine. Once crows had eaten all the available peanuts, they started sweeping coins around with their beaks looking for more peanuts. When a coin happened to fall into the slot, a peanut appeared. Over time, the crows figured out how the vending machine worked, and started picking up coins lying around on the ground and dropping them into the machine to obtain more peanuts. Again, like the Japanese crows, it was not long before more crows learned how to "buy" peanuts by watching other crows. (To see Klein's crow vending machine go here: www.ted.com/index.php/talks/joshua_klein_on_the_intelligence_of_crows.html.)

Similar examples abound in the lives of humans. We also learn through observation, using others as role models and, sometimes, modifying our own behaviour in new ways to accommodate new information. Suppose a classmate is warmly rewarded with praise for asking a question in a lecture. You now have information that the instructor welcomes questions. As a consequence of observing your classmate's rewarding experience, in the future you may be more likely to ask a question of your own.

It is important to note that imitation and observational learning are not the same thing. When an animal or person imitates the behaviour of a model, they mimic or copy the behaviour of the model. However, when observational learning occurs, the behaviour observed is not necessarily repeated. Imagine if the scenario described above ended with the instructor humiliating your classmate for asking a question ("*If you had read the assigned readings you would not have to ask such a moronic question*"). You would learn *not* to ask questions, thereby learning not to repeat your classmate's behaviour; that is, you have learned not to imitate.

Observational Learning and Violence

Some of the most famous experiments of observational learning in children were carried out by psychologist Albert Bandura (born in Mundare, Alberta). Bandura was interested in whether children learned violent behavioural responses by observing aggression. He showed children a movie of a woman beating up an inflatable clown punching bag, called a Bobo doll (see **Figure 7-8**) (Bandura, Ross, & Ross, 1961). After the movie, the children were allowed to play in a room full of toys, including a Bobo doll. Those who had previously watched the Bobo video were twice as likely as those who did not watch it to display violent behaviour toward the doll.

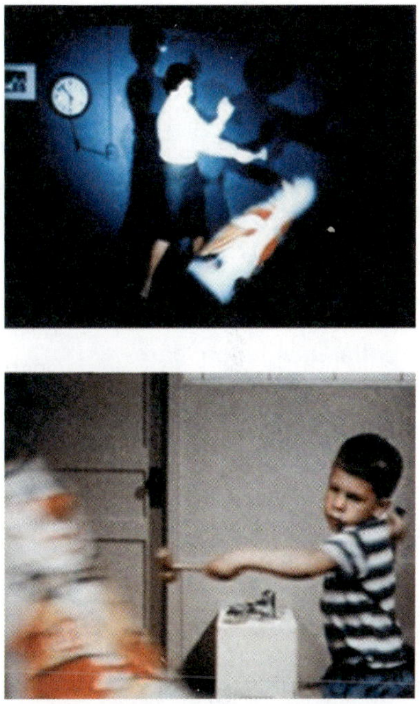

FIGURE 7-8 Aggressive modelling. Bandura found that children learned to abuse an inflatable clown doll by observing an adult model hit the doll.

The researchers further investigated whether observational learning would be influenced by information about reward and punishment. Indeed, they found such a relationship. The children who saw a video in which beating up the Bobo doll led to rewards, such as candy and praise, were more likely to act aggressively toward the doll than those who observed the woman being punished for beating up Bobo (Bandura, Ross, & Ross, 1963). This type of learning is called **vicarious learning** because an individual acquires knowledge by observing what happens to the model. For example, your 2-year-old niece has learned from watching her older sister that crying and whining gets attention from her mother.

Bandura's studies, and a great deal of research that followed, raised concerns that violence on television, in movies, and in videogames promotes aggressive behaviour among viewers, especially children (Bandura, 1978). Some studies have demonstrated a convincing link between excessive television watching and aggressive behaviour in children (Johnson et al., 2002). The number of violent acts in a short stretch of children's programming can be disturbingly high. Further, the number of such violent acts is typically highest in cartoons where there are no real consequences for violent behaviour; one study reported 18 violent acts per hour in children's Saturday morning programs (Gerbner et al., 1994). In fact, cartoon characters seem to have many lives, often returning unscathed after experiencing what would be horribly damaging events in reality.

vicarious learning learning that occurs when an individual observes the consequences to another's actions and then chooses to duplicate the behaviour or refrain from doing so.

Before You Go On

www.wiley.com/go/comer

What Do You Know?

8. What is observational learning and what does it demonstrate when it happens?
9. What has research shown about media violence and aggressive behaviour in child viewers?
10. What is spatial navigation learning and why is it difficult to explain using operant conditioning?

What Do You Think?

How might the media be used to get children—or adults—to mimic positive social behaviours?

SCAN TO GET THE ANSWERS

Learning and Cognition

LEARNING OBJECTIVE 5

Define spatial navigation learning, implicit and latent learning, and insight learning.

Strict behavioural psychologists have argued that all types of learning are forms of conditioning. During the twentieth century, some prominent behaviourist psychologists argued that everything we do comes about as a result of either classical or operant conditioning. Many also suggested that only observable changes in behaviour should be taken as evidence of learning (Mills, 1998). This interpretation of learning as strictly based on behavioural conditioning, however, seems overly simplistic when you consider the wealth of knowledge you have amassed without any overt reinforcement. Indeed, research has shown that learning does seem to happen without any obvious reinforcement. This learning that occurs without awareness is referred to as **implicit learning**. There are many examples of implicit learning; for example, you learned your native language and you learned how to walk without any instruction. We will address this topic in greater detail in Chapter 9.

implicit learning the acquisition of information without awareness.

Spatial Navigation Learning

One good example of learning without reinforcement arose from laboratory studies designed to assess the ability of reinforcement to train rats to learn information about spatial navigation. Perhaps not surprisingly, laboratory rodents can be trained to navigate through a maze by providing them with reinforcement along the way. This approach is called **spatial navigation learning** (which is a form of shaping), and it involves the presentation of food rewards as rats move in the correct direction.

spatial navigation learning learning that involves forming associations among stimuli relevant to navigating in space.

What Happens in the Brain in Spatial Learning: Taxicab Drivers

Taxicab drivers in London (England) must learn and remember a large amount of spatial navigation information to perform their jobs efficiently. Specifically, they must be able to instantly plan a route to a provided address that is direct and yet takes into account current traffic volumes. To become a taxi driver allowed to drive one of those iconic black London cabs, new drivers train for an average of 34 months, and must pass a formal test that was originally developed in 1864 called the Knowledge of London Examination System. Due to its level of difficulty, most drivers must take the test at least 12 times before passing it. Would it seem possible that this detailed learning could have a physical effect on the new cab drivers' brains?

Not surprisingly, this job has been linked to differences in brain regions that are important for spatial navigation learning. MRI studies of the brains of London taxi drivers showed that they have a slightly larger hippocampus than people of the same age who do not have taxicab training (Maguire et al., 2000).

Whether this finding reflects cause or effect remains unknown. It may be that individuals with larger hippocampi gravitate toward jobs that make use of their spatial navigation skills. Alternatively, exposure to a significant amount of spatial information may enlarge the hippocampus through training. Some studies in experimental animals suggest that the second explanation is likely: the hippocampus may grow in response to experience. Living in a complex environment, learning, and physical activity all increase the size and number of neurons in the hippocampus in lab animals (Shors, 2009; Leuner, Gould, & Shors, 2006; Mirescu & Gould, 2006). Something similar many occur in humans as well.

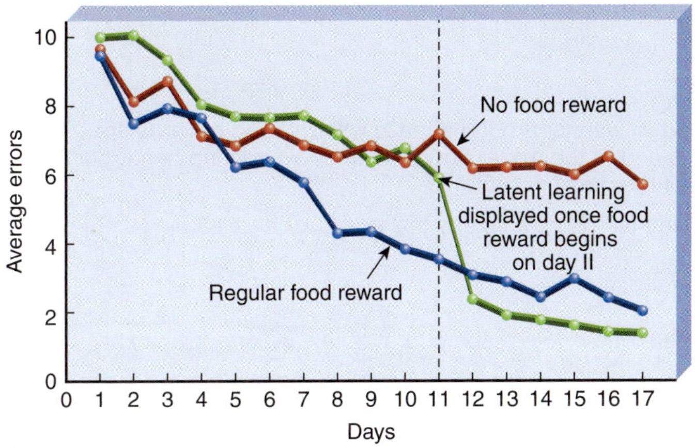

FIGURE 7-9 Latent learning in rats. Rats are motivated to explore a maze, but when given a food reward, they make fewer errors in finding the quickest route to the end of the maze and the reward. When the reward is introduced after the rats explore the maze, the error rate drops sharply, indicating that learning occurred all along.

In the absence of reinforcers, rats typically explore a maze, but are not motivated to find the quickest route from start to finish. However, when rats are allowed to first explore the maze and are then provided with reinforcement, they learn the task much faster than naïve rats. Studies of this type show that the rats were learning information about the spatial environment while they were randomly exploring the maze—even though they were not receiving any reinforcement for learning. The fact that they were able to navigate the maze much faster than rats that had not explored it earlier showed that they had learned and retained information about the layout of the maze as they explored it without reinforcement. When reinforcement was introduced, the rats demonstrated their previous, *latent*, learning (**Figure 7-9**) (Tolman & Gleitman, 1949).

You can probably imagine yourself in a similar situation. Say, for instance, you have a job interview in a particular part of town. You will find the office where your interview is to take place much more easily if you have already explored the general neighbourhood while riding your bicycle or driving than if you have never been to that area before.

This particular example of spatial navigation learning probably represents another form of biological readiness for certain types of learning. Rodents, and probably humans, seem predisposed to form spatial maps of their environments through learning (O'Keefe, 1990). Learning spatial information about their environments would have had adaptive value to our ancestors—and it still does for modern-day rats—in terms of finding food, shelter, and escape routes. Spatial navigation learning requires an intact hippocampus, a brain region that is also important for learning about other non-spatial events (Morris, 1990).

"Ah-hah." During the 1920s, psychologist Wolfgang Kohler conducted pioneering studies on insight learning. Here, one of Kohler's chimpanzees piles three crates on top of each other to reach a banana that had been placed out of its reach. When first confronted with this complex task, the chimp sat and contemplated the situation; then, in an apparent flash of insight, it stacked and climbed up the crates.

Insight Learning

In addition to spatial navigation learning, there are other types of learning that cannot be readily explained in behaviourist terms. One example of this type of learning is **insight learning**. Most of us have had experience with insight learning. When faced with a difficult problem, we may puzzle and struggle over it, unsure how to find a solution. Then, later—perhaps while we are not even working on the problem—we may have an "ah-ha!" or "eureka" moment, when the solution suddenly pops into our mind. Some individuals even report solving problems in their dreams (Wagner et al., 2004). The Nobel laureate Otto Loewi, the discoverer of the actions of neurotransmitter chemicals, claims to have come up with his definitive study while sleeping, after pondering the question over and over while awake (Loewi, 1957). Although finding the solutions to our problems in our dreams is fairly rare, insight learning is widespread and is another type of learning that doesn't involve any obvious reinforcement.

insight learning a sudden realization of a solution to a problem or leap in understanding new concepts.

Before You Go On

www.wiley.com/go/comer

What Do You Know?

11. When rats who have been allowed to wander around a maze without food rewards are provided with food rewards at the end of the maze, how does their wandering behaviour affect their learning and running of the maze?
12. Describe the difference between learning something by trial and error and learning it through insight learning.

What Do You Think?

Does it make sense to argue that all learning involves some form of reward or punishment?

SCAN TO GET THE ANSWERS

Factors that Facilitate Learning

LEARNING OBJECTIVE 6

Define massed and spaced practice and tell what conditions are best for learning semantic material, such as facts in your classes.

It's clear that we can learn in a variety of ways: through simple habituation and sensitization, by linking stimuli in classical conditioning, by associating our behaviour to its consequences through operant conditioning, or by using our observations of the consequences of another's behaviours as a model for our own. We also know that several factors can affect how well each of these learning methods works. Timing, as we have seen, is crucial in classical conditioning. It can also affect other types of learning. The amount of attention we pay when trying to learn is another factor that can facilitate, or alternatively, impede our learning, depending on the type of learning.

Timing

You have probably noticed that you learn more information when you study for an exam over an extended period of time, as opposed to cramming for the test by pulling an "all-nighter." Why is this?

Oh, those all-nighters! Cramming for a test the night before an exam leads to the acquisition of less information than studying for the test over an extended period of time.

Much of the learning that you, as a student, undertake on a daily basis involves acquiring information about facts. Psychologists distinguish between this type of learning, called *semantic learning*, and *episodic learning*, which is learning about events in our own lives. We will return to the distinction between episodic and semantic learning in the next chapter dealing with memory, but we can offer some advice now about how to improve your learning of semantic material.

Most importantly, repetition helps. Semantic learning is facilitated by multiple exposures to the same material, such as reading the textbook, then listening carefully in class, and then reviewing your notes and textbook. Multiple exposures make it more likely that learning will occur, compared to a single exposure, such as just reading the book or just going to class.

Your learning will also be facilitated by having time intervals between these exposures. When learning trials occur close together, as they do when you try to cram reading the book and reviewing all into the night before a big test, they are referred to as *massed*. When they are separated in time, they are referred to as *spaced*. The difference in efficiency between massed and spaced trials for learning has been demonstrated not only in the laboratory, but also in real life (Healy, Kosslyn, and Shiffrin, 1992). Massed studying, or cramming, is ineffective for two reasons. First, it does not allow enough time between learning trials to maximize learning, and second, it leads to sleep deprivation.

Context

Psychologists have long recognized that context plays an important role in learning and remembering. For example, if you take a test in the same location in which you learned the material, you are more likely to do your best. If you want the information to stick with you beyond the end of the semester, however, you may want to move to different locations during your study periods. This may be the opposite of what your parents or high school teachers advised: the longstanding recommendation has been to find a quiet place with good lighting in which to do your nightly homework. More recent studies, however, have shown that studying in several different locations increases the likelihood that you will form strong memories about the information. This phenomenon relates to the *context effect*—if you learn information in only one context (for example, in the classroom) you may be less likely to recall it when you are in a different location (at a job interview or while taking a standardized test for graduate or professional school). If you learn the information in multiple locations, then that knowledge may be less tied to the place in which it was acquired, and it may be more readily recalled later on (Smith, 1984).

Awareness and Attention

It's clear that much learning occurs without our awareness. Non-associative learning and some forms of associative learning—including some forms of classical conditioning and procedural, or motor-skill, learning—often occur without the individual realizing that information has been acquired. Another good example of this is learning the lyrics and tune to a new song, which often occurs without the intention to memorize. Observational learning also often occurs without awareness, as in the case of children modelling aggressive behaviour observed on television. In some instances, awareness and excessive attention can actually interfere with learning. Gymnasts, for example, sometimes find that explicit mental rehearsal breaks their concentration and interferes with their performance when they are trying to learn a new move.

In most instances, however, awareness and attention enhance learning. Many forms of associative learning, including semantic and episodic learning, require awareness and are greatly enhanced by attentional processes. You have probably experienced this firsthand on days when you are feeling out of sorts and have difficulty concentrating on your coursework. The information you read or hear in lectures at such times is much less likely to be learned than material presented at a time when you are more attentive.

Because attention is so important to learning, it is worth considering an important question: how does attention work? Scientists have found that the answer to this question depends on the circumstances. Some attentional processes are automatic and occur when a particular stimulus is very different from those that surround it. Psychologist Anne Treisman, while working at the University of British Columbia, studied attention to visual stimuli and showed that in the case of a simple scene, if one stimulus differs considerably

PSYCHOLOGY AROUND US Too Much Social Networking?

According to a recent report, students who use Facebook while they study get lower grades than those who don't (Kirschner & Karpinski, 2010). Specifically, the research found that college students who had Facebook running while they studied—even if it was simply running in the background—tended to have lower grade point averages and fewer study hours than students who were not similarly distracted. Unfortunately, the students themselves don't seem to be aware of the problem. About three-quarters of the Facebook users said they didn't think the practice had any negative effects on their studying. Although one reasonable interpretation of these results is that Facebook is so distracting that it prevents the focused attention necessary for effective studying, it is also possible that students who use Facebook while studying are weaker students with poorer study habits in general to begin with. And it's not clear which would have a worse impact on learning: having Facebook running while studying or rushing through studying in an effort to get back to your electronic social scene!

from others, it will immediately grab our attention, a phenomenon referred to as "*pop-out*." In order for pop-out to work, the stimulus must be singularly different from the surroundings (Treisman & Kanwisher, 1998). As scenes get more and more complicated, pop-out is less likely to help in guiding attentional processes. Instead, we must rely on an active searching method, where we examine material in search of the most relevant stimuli. Anyone who has enjoyed children's books such as "Where's Waldo" or "I Spy," where a relevant stimulus is buried in a complex visual scene, has engaged an *active searching* attentional process. Recall from Chapter 5 the distinction between bottom-up and top-down processing. Pop-out, because of its simplicity and speed, employs bottom-up processing; active searching, because of the need to draw on cognitive processes and memory, uses top-down processing.

Sleep deprivation, attention, and learning. Sleep deprivation makes it difficult to pay attention, thus impairing our ability to learn. In addition, sleep deprivation after learning reduces our ability to retain newly-learned material.

Sometimes attentional processes can get in the way—if information is inherently contradictory, for example, attending to one stimulus can block our ability to attend to the relevant one. A good example of this is the *Stroop Effect*, a psychological test that involves presenting a list of words printed in different colours. Each of the words is a colour word (green, red, black, blue), but each is printed in a colour that differs from that of the word (green, red, black, blue). Participants are asked to list the colours of the ink, thus ignoring the word colour—this is very difficult to do quickly because bottom-up attentional processing interferes with the ability to focus on just one contradictory stimulus (Herd et al., 2006).

What can we do then to maximize our attention to relevant information while trying to learn? First, it's a good idea to identify relevant information and focus on it throughout your reading. If your professor mentions topics repeatedly in class, you might use an active searching method to find additional similar material in your readings. Second, avoid dividing your attention. Our attentional processes are generally at their best when they are focused on one task. Performing other behaviours, such as answering text messages or watching TV, while trying to study usually interferes with our ability to attend to relevant material. In fact, a recent study showed that people who engage in a high degree of "multi-tasking" are less likely to perform well overall (Ophira et al., 2009).

Sleep

Your mother was right—it's important to get a good night's sleep! Studies have shown that sleep is important for learning and memory. Sleep deprivation impairs our ability to pay attention and learn. In addition, sleep deprivation can prevent learned information from moving into more permanent long-term memory storage. Studies in experimental animals have confirmed that sleep deprivation interferes with learning and memory (Rauchs et al., 2005; Saxvig et al., 2007). These findings suggest that the brain replays information learned while awake, presumably to strengthen those connections and form longer-lasting memory traces. (As you will see in Chapter 8, memories are thought to leave physical traces in the brain—so-called *memory traces*—when they are acquired.) So while staying up late to study may be inevitable, make sure you get a decent amount of sleep so that you don't forget what you are learning. Getting enough sleep will also help you to process information you encounter for the first time the next day.

Before You Go On

www.wiley.com/go/comer

What Do You Know?

13. Which would be better for helping you learn psychology facts: massed or spaced practice? Why?
14. What kinds of learning benefit from focused attention?

What Do You Think?

How could you modify your own schedule or study habits to allow for spaced practice of your material or to take advantage of your most alert and attentive times of day?

SCAN TO GET THE ANSWERS

Prenatal and Postnatal Learning

HOW WE DEVELOP

LEARNING OBJECTIVE 7

Summarize the types of learning that occur before we are born and during early postnatal life.

Several studies suggest that non-associative learning can occur before we are even born. Fetuses show habituation and sensitization to smells and other sensory stimuli (Faas et al., 2000). In one set of studies, for example, infants who had been prenatally exposed to garlic—through their mothers' digestion—showed evidence, after they were born, of recognizing the garlic odour. They did not try to avoid the smell, as babies new to garlic typically do (Mennella, Johnson, & Beauchamp, 1995). Habituation studies of newborns also show that they can distinguish between new and familiar sights and sounds. Even very soon after birth, babies typically stop moving for a brief time when they are exposed to a new visual or auditory stimulus. This response suggests that they have already become accustomed, or habituated, to "old" sights and sounds (Slater & Morrison, 1991). They have learned to recognize them.

Early olfactory learning. In this study, infants are exposed to bottles containing smells of their mothers, their fathers, and other people. In such research undertakings, babies consistently show highest preference for the smell of their mothers and second highest for that of their fathers.

We are also capable of basic associative learning before birth. One team of researchers reported classical conditioning of human fetuses. Recall from Chapter 5 that hearing is partially developed before birth. These researchers paired specific music (initially a neutral stimulus) with relaxation exercises done by the mother. The maternal relaxation exercises served as an unconditioned stimulus, often leading to a slowing of fetal physical activity (an unconditioned response). After enough pairings of the music and the relaxation, the music became a conditioned stimulus, leading directly to a decrease in fetal movement (CR), with or without the relaxation exercises (see Chelli & Chanoufi, 2008 for review).

PSYCHOLOGY AROUND US Cat in the Hat

A classic study revealed that infants not only hear their mother's speech in the womb, but also pay attention to what they're hearing and remember it (DeCasper & Spence, 1986). The researchers had pregnant women read aloud the Dr. Seuss book *The Cat in the Hat* each day during the last several weeks of pregnancy. Soon after the babies were born, they were taught that if they sucked on a specially wired soother more rapidly than they usually do, a voice recording would be turned on for them to listen to. Babies sucked harder longer to hear their mothers' voices than the voices of others—and they sucked harder longest to hear their mothers read *The Cat in the Hat*.

Tying It Together: **Your Brain and Behaviour**

Learning to Play a Video Game

You need to find that key, but watch out for those obstacles!

How do we learn to navigate through virtual reality, avoiding dangers that prevent us from moving through the game to mastery? What parts of the brain enable us to learn the rules of the game and respond to changes in the electronic world as we play?

When we learn a new video game that involves spatial navigation through a virtual three-dimensional space, trying to avoid punishments and obtain rewards all along the way, we are engaging a number of neural circuits throughout the brain. First, spatial navigation learning requires inputs from the visual cortex to the hippocampus and temporal lobe. Second, learning about rewards involves dopamine projections extending from the ventral tegmental area to the nucleus accumbens and prefrontal cortex. And third, integration and long-term storage of the information from these systems involves other cortical regions, including the parietal and temporal cortex. These changes in the brain take place as you learn the game—as your skilled movements become more automatic, brain activity shifts to the corpus striatum (basal ganglia). Will you make it to the next level?

Questions

1. **How do brain activation patterns differ when one is using a 3D versus a landmark strategy for navigation?**
2. **Which brain region creates new neurons as we develop spatial navigation skills?**
3. **Which neurotransmitter is affected by our learning about rewards, such as those received during video game play?**

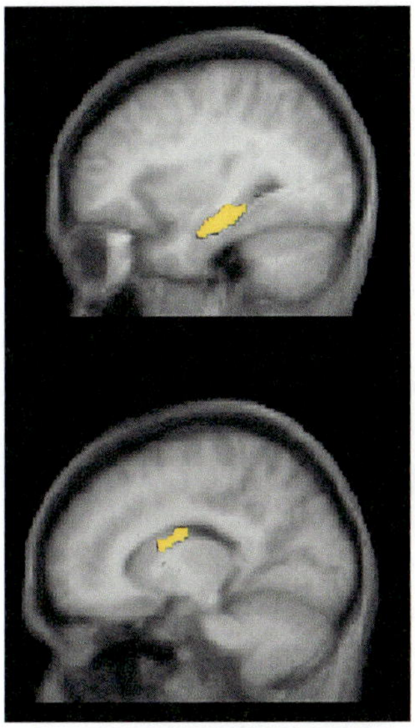

PICKING A STRATEGY

People use different strategies to solve tasks that involve navigating in space. Some people use a 3D strategy, using their position relative to the environment to find their way. Others use landmarks and numbering strategies (for example, enter the second door on your right). The different strategies engage different neural systems, shown on these fMRI images. Spatial 3D strategies activate the hippocampus (top, yellow) while landmark strategies activate the basal ganglia (bottom, yellow).

STRENGTHENING YOUR SYNAPSES

When you learn a task that involves spatial navigation and reward, synapses in a number of brain regions, including the hippocampus and nucleus accumbens, likely undergo long-term potentiation (LTP), a form of synapse strengthening. Most postsynaptic sites that undergo synapse strengthening are located on small extensions off of dendrites, called dendritic spines (shown here labelled with a green fluorescent tracer).

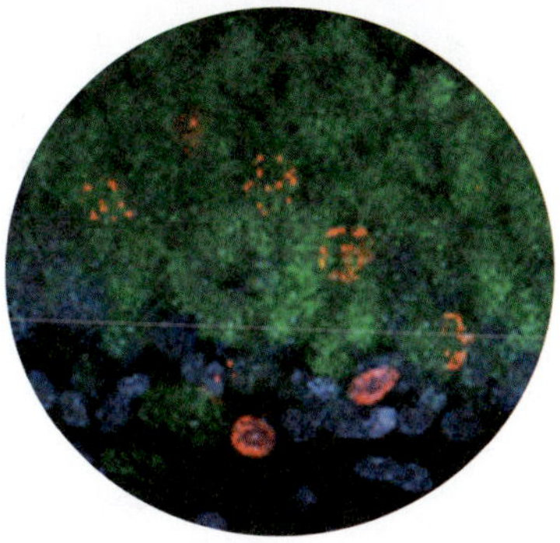

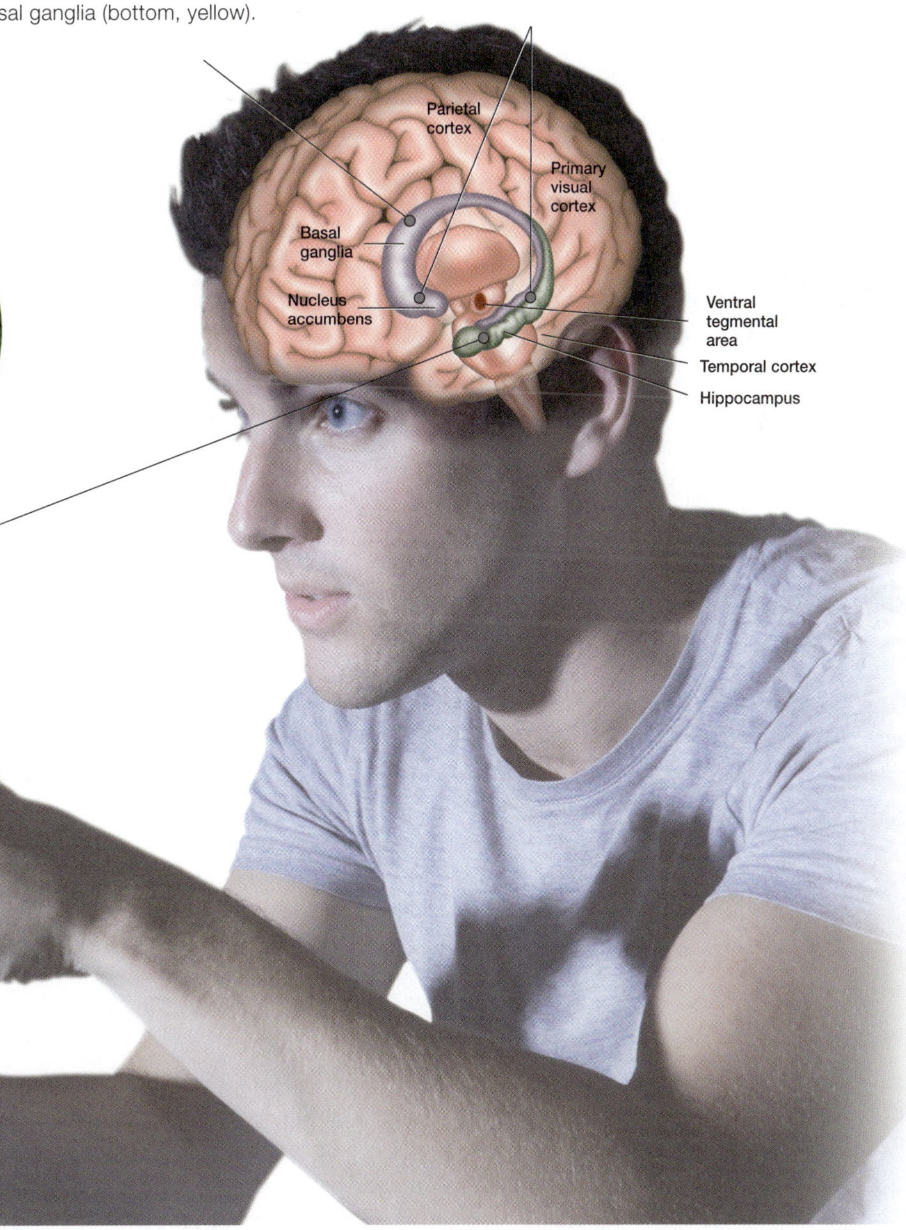

LEARNING ABOUT SPACE

Spatial navigation learning leads to an increase in the number of new neurons in the hippocampus, shown here stained with fluorescent dyes (red). Engaging the hippocampus in this way prevents newly born neurons from dying.

Newborn humans also demonstrate olfactory learning by showing an almost immediate preference for their own mothers' odour, by turning their heads in the direction of their mothers' odour much more often than toward odours of strangers. The preference for maternal odour has clear adaptive consequences in helping babies to identify the person who, throughout our evolutionary history, has been their primary source of food and care. The ability of infants to identify that source by smell is obviously to their benefit (Polan & Hoffer, 1998; Franks & Isaacson, 2005).

As we develop from infancy onward, it's clear that biological factors, such as brain development, guide the development of learning. Psychologists and pediatricians often refer to *developmental milestones*, many that require learning. The fact that these abilities, such as crawling, walking, language comprehension, and speech, typically emerge during specific time windows suggests that biological changes occurring at certain times affect when specific types of learning can take place during development (Taanila et al., 2005).

The types of learning that occur during the prenatal and early postnatal periods are simple forms that don't critically involve late-developing brain regions. More complex forms of learning, such as episodic and semantic learning, are not efficient until forebrain regions, such as the hippocampus and neocortex, have developed to a greater extent. This is one reason why young children have a difficult time learning about facts and events in an organized and accurate way. Most of us don't have clear memories about our lives before the time we were around 3 to 4 years of age (Usher & Neisser, 1993). This phenomenon, called *infantile amnesia*, is tied to learning episodic information and the development of the hippocampus and neocortex.

Before You Go On

www.wiley.com/go/comer

What Do You Know?

15. What kinds of learning can happen before we are born?

What Do You Think?

What are the advantages and disadvantages of having only very simple forms of learning intact during fetal life? What consequences would arise if we possessed intact learning about events before birth?

SCAN TO GET THE ANSWERS

Learning Disabilities — WHEN THINGS GO WRONG

LEARNING OBJECTIVE 8

Describe dyslexia, dyscalculia, and attention disorders.

learning disability a specific deficiency in one aspect of cognitive function while other aspects function normally.

A **learning disability** is a specific deficiency in one aspect of cognitive functioning, while other aspects function normally. Learning disabilities are different from mental retardation, which is a more global deficit in intellectual abilities. Individuals with learning disabilities can even have very high IQs with impairment only in one type of learning. Here, we discuss the most common learning disability, *dyslexia*, as well as a somewhat less common one, *dyscalculia*. We also look at attention deficit disorders, which are not learning disabilities but are often associated with them.

Dyslexia

dyslexia a learning disability that involves deficits in learning to read and write.

The most common form of learning disability is **dyslexia**, a deficiency in learning to read. Some estimates suggest that between 5 and 10 percent of school age children have dyslexia (Raskind, 2001).

Contrary to popular belief, dyslexia doesn't primarily manifest itself as a reversal of letters of words; instead, it is a general problem affecting the ability to read, write, or spell.

Reversal of letters or words is a problem for those diagnosed with dyslexia, but it is not their only problem. Letter reversals are common in young children as they are learning to read. However, most children outgrow this problem as they acquire reading skills. However, people with dyslexia display this characteristic until they are much older. These individuals continue to experience difficulty with reversals because they are not as far along on the reading learning curve, but also because the inability to process graphic symbols is a symptom of their larger problems in reading fluency (Hudson, High, & Al Otaiba, 2007).

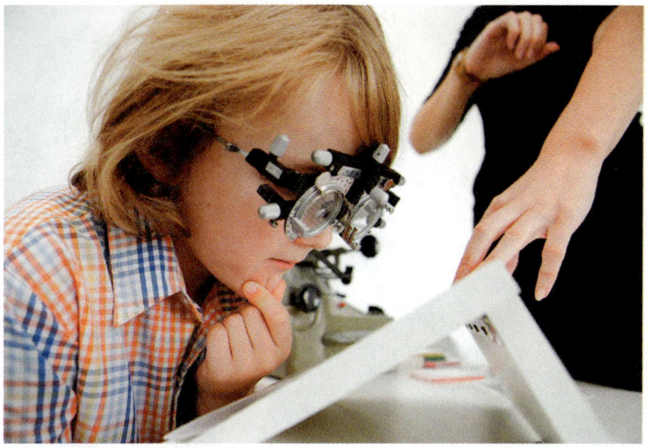

Studying dyslexia. A range of factors have been proposed to explain dyslexia, a deficiency in the ability to read, including deficits in visual processing, speech skills, auditory processing, and object or letter identification. Here a young boy with the disorder undergoes a reading test with prism glasses.

There is some evidence that the same people with dyslexia have visual processing deficits that may produce perceptual problems, which in turn contribute to their difficulty in recognizing written words. Neuroimaging studies comparing children with dyslexia to those without the disability have shown that some children with dyslexia have reduced blood flow in brain regions associated with acquisition of reading skills, such as the left parietal and temporal cortex (Hoeft et al., 2006). Most people with dyslexia can overcome their difficulties in learning to read with the help of extensive tutoring and specific educational programs.

Dyslexia and Creativity According to the Yale Center for Dyslexia and Creativity, "Many of today's leading innovators from a variety of fields—business, medicine, film, design, and even writing—are dyslexic." Observers have claimed that a number of famous innovators of the past, from Leonardo da Vinci to Walt Disney, were dyslexic, but it's hard to prove or disprove such claims. It is true, however, that a number of famous and creative people alive today have talked about their experiences with dyslexia. Many of them are in the entertainment industry—Cher, Whoopi Goldberg, and Tom Cruise, to name a few. Others include Charles Schwab, founder and director of the investment firm that bears his name, and Carol Greider, a Nobel-prize-winning scientist. Although these are interesting facts, very little research exists to establish the basis for a link between creativity and dyslexia. Perhaps this area will receive more attention from researchers as time goes by (Yale Center for Dyslexia, 2008).

Dyscalculia

A slightly less prevalent learning disability, which may exist with or without dyslexia, is a condition known as dyscalculia. This refers to an inability to readily acquire information about mathematics.

dyscalculia an inability to readily acquire information about mathematics.

Dyscalculia can occur in individuals with normal, or even higher than average, reading abilities, suggesting a deficit in specific brain circuitry associated with acquisition of mathematical skills. Less information is available about dyscalculia than about dyslexia, but some evidence suggests that parts of the left parietal and frontal cortex of the brain are less active in individuals with dyscalculia (Price et al., 2007). As with dyslexia, intensive tutoring and specific educational programs can help students with dyscalculia learn mathematical information (Butterworth, 2010; Butterworth, Varma, & Laurillard, 2011).

attention deficit disorder (ADD) a disorder characterized by an inability to pay attention.

attention deficit hyperactivity disorder (ADHD) a disorder characterized by an inability to pay attention, accompanied by excessive activity.

Attention Deficit Disorders

As we have noted, attention greatly aids some types of learning, especially the semantic learning required in school. Although not specifically designated as learning disabilities, two attention disorders often contribute to difficulties in learning. Attention deficit disorder (ADD) is characterized primarily by an inability to concentrate. Attention deficit

Learning to "play" attention. Various techniques have been used to help explain and treat ADHD, including a computer program called Play Attention. Here a child wears a helmet that measures brain waves while he performs computer tasks requiring various degrees of attention.

hyperactivity disorder (ADHD) is a similar disorder in which concentration problems are accompanied by problematically high activity levels. These attention disorders are sometimes associated with dyslexia and dyscalculia.

Neuroimaging studies have identified some brain regions that appear to be different in children with ADD or ADHD, compared to children without these disorders. Some evidence suggests that ADHD is associated with structural abnormalities in the cerebral cortex (Qiu et al., 2009; Wolosin et al., 2009; Shaw et al., 2007). Studies have also shown decreased blood flow in the basal ganglia (Bush, Valera, & Seidman, 2005) and also a portion of the prefrontal cortex called the *anterior cingulate* (Smith et al., 2008). Some studies have even shown an overall decrease in the size of these brain regions in people with ADHD (Hill et al., 2003).

ADD and ADHD can be successfully treated with stimulant drugs, including methylphenidate, widely known by the trade name Ritalin®, and dextroamphetamine, which has the trade name Adderall®. Both drugs enhance attention and, even though they are stimulants, paradoxically diminish hyperactivity. The extent to which these drugs correct abnormalities in the cerebral cortex of people with ADD and ADHD remains undetermined (Solanto & Arnsten, 2001).

Issues in Treatment The identification and study of learning disabilities and attention deficit disorder raise important ethical considerations. First, it is paramount that diagnoses be made early, so that intervention can occur before significant developmental delays occur. Second, it is equally important that diagnoses are accurate, so that children with other behavioural problems are not incorrectly medicated.

A third issue concerns misuse of the stimulant drugs often prescribed for attention disorders. For one thing, there has been some concern that attention deficit disorders may have been overdiagnosed. If so, it is likely that some children who take prescription medications do not have attention disorders, even though they have been diagnosed as having them. Needless to say, taking unneeded medications can lead to problems. In the case of the stimulant drugs prescribed for attention disorders, these problems include the drugs' possible side effects.

In addition, some recent studies have estimated that a significant percentage of college students have used Ritalin and similar drugs without a prescription. Most students surveyed report that they use the drugs to help them study. Since attention-disorder drugs enhance attention and thus learning in normal individuals, this practice raises ethical questions (Greely et al., 2008, Hall & Lucke, 2010; Farah, 2011). Do stimulants provide an unfair advantage to students who take them in settings—such as college—where success is determined by cognitive function? Is stimulant use among people without attention disorders comparable, for example, to athletes using performance-enhancing drugs to improve their competitive standing?

Before You Go On

www.wiley.com/go/comer

What Do You Know?

16. What are dyslexia and dyscalculia?

What Do You Think?

What, in your opinion, are the ethical pros and cons of taking attention-enhancing drugs when they are not needed to treat a disorder?

SCAN TO GET THE ANSWERS

Summary

What Is Learning?

LEARNING OBJECTIVE 1 Define learning and distinguish between associative and non-associative learning.

- Learning is a lasting change in the brain caused by experience.
- Non-associative learning is a lasting change that happens as a result of experience with a single cue. Types of non-associative learning include habituation, in which we display decreased responses to familiar stimuli, and sensitization, in which we display increased responses to stimuli of normal strength after being exposed to an unusually strong stimulus.
- Associative learning is a lasting change that happens as a result of associating two or more stimuli. Types of associative learning include classical and operant conditioning.

Classical Conditioning

LEARNING OBJECTIVE 2 Describe the basic processes of classical conditioning and explain how classical conditioning is relevant to learning.

- As a result of classical conditioning, a previously neutral stimulus comes to elicit a response by being paired with an unconditioned stimulus (US) that already generates the response, known as an unconditioned response (UR). The neutral stimulus becomes a conditioned stimulus (CS) when it elicits the same response as the US. The response to the CS is known as a conditioned response (CR).
- Repeated presentation of the CS without the US can lead to extinction, or suppression of the CR. Extinction does not mean we forget the CS–US association, however. The CR can be spontaneously recovered.
- Phobias and conditioned taste aversions can result from classical conditioning. Systematic desensitization uses classical conditioning to extinguish phobia responses. Conditioned taste aversions suggest that we are biologically prepared to quickly learn responses important to our survival.

Operant Conditioning

LEARNING OBJECTIVE 3 Describe the basic processes of operant conditioning and explain how shaping can be used to teach new behaviours.

- Operant conditioning is a learned association between stimuli in the environment and our own behaviour. The law of effect states that we learn to repeat behaviours that will increase our rewards and help us avoid punishment.
- Reinforcers are rewarding stimuli from the environment. Positive reinforcement provides a desired stimulus; negative reinforcement takes away an unpleasant stimulus. Both increase the chance a behaviour will be repeated. Primary reinforcers are reinforcing in and of themselves. Secondary reinforcers become reinforcing because of their association with primary reinforcers.
- Positive punishment provides an unpleasant stimulus; negative punishment takes away a rewarding one. Both types lower the chances that a behaviour will be repeated.
- Research indicates that extroverts are more focused on rewards and more driven to work toward them than introverts, who are more focused on potential punishments and more driven to avoid them.
- Schedules of intermittent reinforcement provide reinforcements after either fixed or variable intervals of time or numbers of responses. Any intermittent reinforcement modifies behaviour more effectively than continuous reinforcement.
- Shaping, or rewarding successive approximations of a behaviour, uses operant conditioning principles to teach new behaviours. People and animals are limited in the behaviours they can learn, however, by their biological endowments.
- Learned helplessness occurs when previous learning that punishment is inescapable interferes with the later ability to learn how to avoid escapable punishment. It may be related to depression or the behaviour of abuse victims.

Observational Learning

LEARNING OBJECTIVE 4 Define observational learning and summarize concerns about observational learning from the media.

- Observational learning is learning by watching the behaviour of others. We are likely to model, or imitate, others' behaviour that we see rewarded.
- Many people are concerned that high levels of violence in the media encourage viewers to model such aggression. Studies about the causal nature of media encouraging violence have been inconclusive.

Learning and Cognition

LEARNING OBJECTIVE 5 Define spatial navigation learning, implicit and latent learning, and insight learning.

- Learning that occurs without awareness is referred to as implicit learning.
- Insight learning and spatial navigation learning seem to take place in the absence of any obvious reinforcement.

Factors that Facilitate Learning

LEARNING OBJECTIVE 6 Define massed and spaced practice and tell what conditions are best for learning semantic material, such as facts in your classes.

- Repeated, spaced practice aids learning of semantic material, such as classroom information.
- According to the *context effect*, if you learn information in only one context, or location, you may be less likely to recall it when you are in a different context.
- We can learn without paying attention and some tasks are easier to learn that way, but focused attention aids semantic learning.
- Sleep deprivation impairs our abilities to pay attention and to learn.

Prenatal and Postnatal Learning

LEARNING OBJECTIVE 7 Summarize the types of learning that occur before we are born and during early postnatal life.

- We are capable of non-associative learning, both habituation and sensitization, before birth, as well as basic associative learning, such as classical conditioning.
- We become capable of increasingly complex forms of learning as relevant areas of our brains mature after we are born.

Learning Disabilities

LEARNING OBJECTIVE 8 Describe dyslexia, dyscalculia, and attention disorders.

- A learning disability is a specific deficiency in one area of learning, while learning in other areas takes place normally. Dyslexia is a common disability in learning to read. Dyscalculia is a disability in learning mathematics.
- Attention deficit disorder (ADD) and attention deficit hyperactivity disorder (ADHD) affect concentration and can impair learning. Both are commonly treated with stimulant drugs. The use and misuse of these drugs raises many ethical concerns.

Key Terms

TYING IT TOGETHER

The study of learning is closely connected to the study of all other areas of psychology. Throughout this chapter, we have stressed how learning interfaces with psychology's various subfields, including our highlighted sections on brain functioning, individual differences, abnormal functioning, and development. To remind you of how learning is tied to other psychology subfields and issues, here are some interesting points from throughout the chapter.

WHAT HAPPENS IN THE BRAIN?

- All types of learning actually involve changes in our brains, although different types of learning involve different brain regions.
- London taxicab drivers, who have intricate spatial knowledge of their cities, tend to have a larger hippocampus than people without similar geographical knowledge.
- Some research suggests that our brains might rehearse new information in our sleep, which could explain why sleep deprivation makes learning more difficult.

HOW WE DIFFER

- People who watch a lot of violent media or play violent videogames may be more likely to behave aggressively than those who watch less, but no definitive studies have shown this.
- Introverts are more focused on the potential for punishment than are extroverts, who focus more on the possibility of reward in social or workplace situations.

WHEN THINGS GO WRONG

- Phobias might result from classical conditioning, in which we learn to respond with fear to something that isn't necessarily threatening. We can learn to extinguish phobic behaviour, but can't "unlearn" the phobia.
- We can learn a long-lasting aversion to a food if it makes us sick only once, even several hours after we eat it.
- Learned helplessness might play a role in depression. If people have previously been unable to escape punishment, they may fail to act to escape unpleasant situations, even when it becomes possible.

HOW WE DEVELOP

- We can learn simple associations before we are even born.
- Very early in life, we fail to display efficient complex learning, such as episodic or semantic learning. These forms of learning depend on further development of the hippocampus and neocortex.
- Reinforcement is generally more effective and ethical than punishment for teaching children.

Psychology Around Us

Bringing Learning and Conditioning Principles to Life

You Can So Teach an Old Dog New Tricks

View this in Action WILEY PLUS www.wileyplus.com

Video Lab Exercise

We're constantly learning in life—learning new behaviours, new reactions, new lessons, new skills, and new ideas. Sometimes we are aware of it, sometimes not. We learn some things faster than others. And we learn better in some contexts than others. But we do indeed keep learning.

At the same time, we don't take advantage of every learning opportunity. Moreover, when we do learn something, it may not stay learned indefinitely. And, as we know all too well, we learn a lot of things (certain fears, for example) that we wish we hadn't learned.

This video lab exercise will bring learning principles to life by teaching you some new behaviours and skills—sometimes with your cooperation and sometimes in spite of yourself. And, by the way, while you're learning, you will also be required to identify the conditioning principles and variables at play—just to show that you learned some new material while reading this chapter.

As you are working on this online exercise, consider the following questions:

- How readily does classical, operant, and observational learning occur?
- How easy is it to resist conditioning or, at the other end, to extinguish a newly-learned behaviour or skill?
- How do attention, timing, and insight come into play?
- How can learning be enhanced?

CHAPTER 8

Memory

CHAPTER OUTLINE

- What Is Memory?
- How Do We Encode Information into Memory?
- How Do We Store Memories?
- How Do We Retrieve Memories?
- Why Do We Forget and Misremember?
- Memory *What Happens in the Brain?*
- Memories in the Young and Old *How We Develop*
- Disorders of Memory *When Things Go Wrong*

A MAN WITH NO PAST

Now a cult classic, the 2000 film *Memento* fascinated viewers with a series of harrowing situations that confronted the main character, Leonard. In the movie, Leonard is looking for the person or people who attacked him and brutally murdered his wife. His search is hard and frightening, however, because the attack left Leonard unable to form new memories. To cope with this problem, Leonard takes Polaroid instant pictures and makes notes on them as he acquires information. He also tattoos facts on his body to help him put the puzzle together. Despite these efforts, however, scenes in the movie frequently open with Leonard being attacked by people he does not know or being chased for reasons he cannot explain until he can piece the information together.

At the same time, Leonard finds himself confronted with other characters who may—or may not—have his best interests at heart as they try to "help" him along his way. On top of everything, Leonard has doubts. Given his own memory loss, how can he be sure that he didn't kill his wife and then somehow cause his own memory loss to protect himself from his guilt?

Consider everything that memory lets you do. Obviously there are the everyday tasks, such as passing tests, turning in a paper on time, or remembering a friend's birthday. But go deeper: think of the things memory lets you do that you take for granted. Because of memory, you can have favourite foods, favourite musicians, favourite movies, and favourite TV shows. Not only can you remember friends' birthdays, you can also remember their typical behaviours and their preferences, and then predict what they might want for their birthday.

You can go deeper still. If you did not somehow encode events and people in your mind, you would not know about anything that you were not directly sensing at that moment. You would only know what was in your line of sight and have no idea how the things that you were seeing connected to you or had any significance or meaning. Without memory, you would, like Leonard, be a stranger to yourself, unable to form the identity, or sense of self, that comes from linking one's present to one's past and using this information to make decisions about the future (Kihlstrom, Beer, & Klein, 2003). By keeping a record of our past, our memory takes us out of an infinite present. ■

What Is Memory?

LEARNING OBJECTIVE 1

Define the basic activities of memory and describe two major models of memory.

memory the faculty for recalling past events and past learning.

Simply put, **memory** is the faculty for recalling past events and past learning. This definition is perhaps the only thing about memory that is simple. Although psychologists often differ in their ideas about memory, they generally agree that it involves three basic activities:

encoding a basic activity of memory, involving the recording of information in our brain.

storage a basic activity of memory, involving retention of information for later use.

retrieval a basic activity of memory, involving recovery of information when we need it later.

- *Encoding*—Getting information into memory in the first place
- *Storage*—Retaining memories for future use
- *Retrieval*—Recapturing memories when we need them

When, for example, you attend a musical concert, you may transform the sights and sounds produced by the performing band into a kind of memory code and record them in your brain (encoding). This information then remains stored in the brain until you retrieve it at later times—when, for example, you see photos of the band online, watch their music videos, or decide which of the band's songs to download. At such times of retrieval, the original concert event, including the feelings of exhilaration and joy that you experienced at the concert, may come rushing back.

How do we manage to encode, store, and retrieve information? Psychologists have developed a number of models of explanation, including the *information-processing model* and the *parallel distributed-processing model,* or *connectionist model.*

information-processing model view of memory suggesting that information moves among three memory stores during encoding, storage, and retrieval.

The **information-processing model** of memory has its roots back in early computer science (Atkinson & Shiffrin, 1968) and was intended to chart the ways that, like computers, humans process information from their senses into memory. The information-processing model of memory holds that information must pass through three stages, or systems, of mental functioning to become a firmly implanted memory—sensory memory, working memory, and long-term memory (see **Figure 8-1**) (Dudai, 2011; Nee et al., 2008).

When we first confront a stimulus, our brain retains a sensory image—or *sensory memory*—of it for less than a second. Sensory memories help us to keep items that we have experienced briefly alive a bit longer, so that we can, in a sense, decide whether to pay further attention to them. Sensory memories are basically copies of the sensory data we have

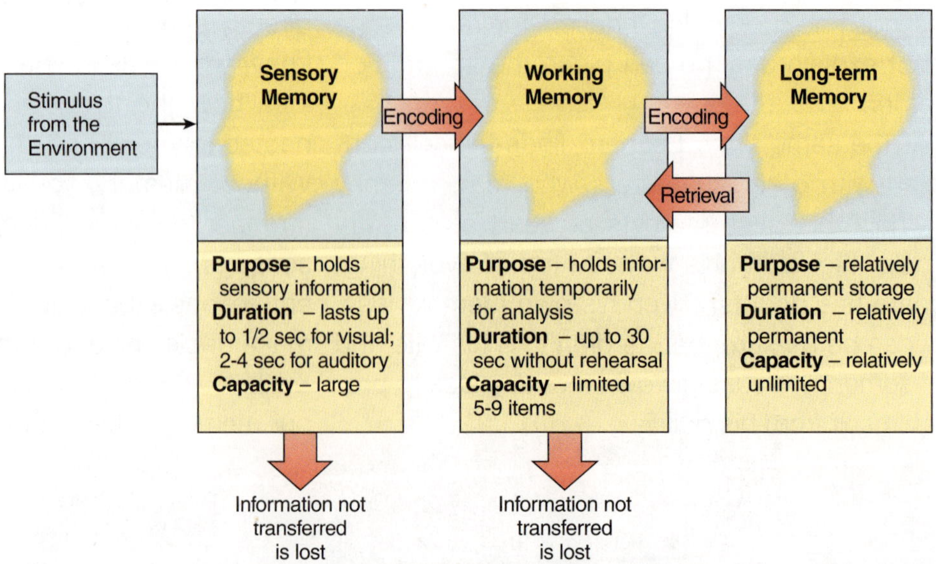

FIGURE 8-1 The three-stage memory model. This model is a useful framework for thinking about the three basic memory stages. Each stage differs in purpose, duration, and capacity.

just received. For example, visual sensory memory is also called *iconic memory*, meaning it is like a small copy of the visual event we have just encountered, just as a computer icon is a small visually descriptive representation of the program or file it represents (Dick, 1974). It is hard to know how to describe the capacity of sensory memory, but given that it can contain a complete copy of a sensory input, let's say it has a large capacity. If, for example, we look up a person's email address, our sensory memory records the address and quickly passes it on to our *short-term memory*. We can help retain the new address in working memory by concentrating hard and repeating it over and over as we address an email or type it into our computer's address book. But working memory itself can hold only so many pieces of information at a time (five to nine). Eventually the information will drop out of working memory and will disappear unless it is further passed on to our *long-term memory* system—the system that can retain a seemingly unlimited number of pieces of information for an indefinite period of time.

Short-term memory has been further divided into two related processes: *working memory,* which consists of the things we are thinking of and working with consciously (Baddeley & Hitch, 1974), and the stores or places where we can put information we need to have nearby. Baddeley and Hitch identified two of these sorts of memory stores, one called the *phonological loop* (that little voice that keeps repeating what we want to remember to keep it active in memory) and another called a *visuospatial sketchpad*, where we can temporarily store images and spatial locations we are working with (Baddeley & Hitch 1974; Baddeley, 2007). Together these components explain how we process information into and out of memory.

The three systems of memory proposed by the information-processing model are comparable to the operation of a computer (see **Figure 8-2**). The small icons on our desktop are essentially small images that represent much more complex programs. *Sensory memory* works in a similar way, giving us a quick copy of the information in our environment. In addition, information saved to *working memory* is roughly equivalent to the information that a computer retains for as long as a document or website is open, but which disappears if you do not save it. And the final memory system, *long-term memory*, is the equivalent of the computer hard drive, storing information until something causes disruption or loss of the memory. These three systems are sometimes referred to as *memory stores*. The information-processing model has generated a great deal of research that we will explore further in the sections of this chapter that focus on encoding, storage, retrieval, and forgetting.

"Memory isn't like reading a book; it's more like writing a book from fragmentary notes."
—*John Kihlström, psychologist*

Although the information-processing model suggests that sensory memory, working memory, and long-term memory correspond roughly to computer memory structures, we

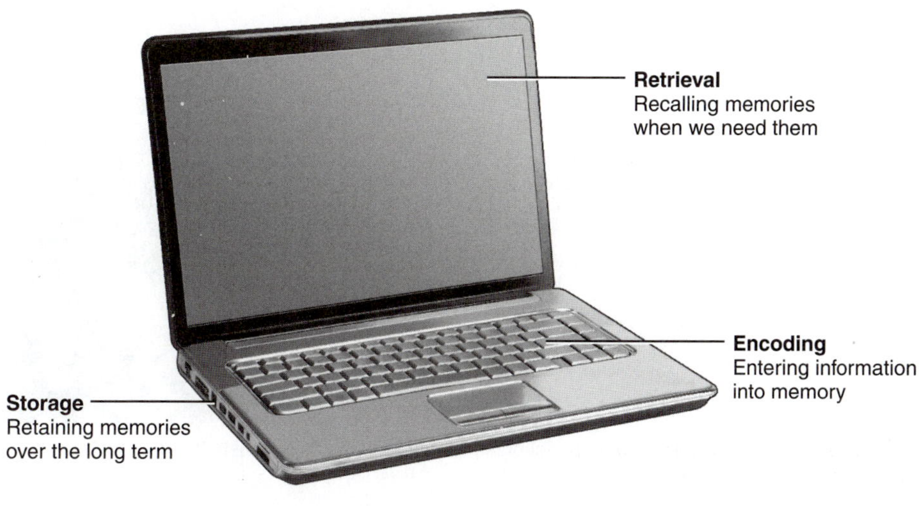

FIGURE 8-2 Memory as a computer. In the information-processing model of memory, the basic memory stages are analogous to a computer: encoding allows us to enter information into our brain; storage allows us to retain the information over the long term; and retrieval enables us to call up the information as we need it.

need to be clear that this is just a metaphor. If you break open a computer, you can find the dedicated modules where the various forms of memory are in operation. When we look at the human brain, however, there are no equivalent dedicated structures where short-term memory and long-term memory exist.

parallel distributed-processing (PDP) (or connectionist) model theory of memory suggesting that information is represented in the brain as a pattern of activation across entire neural networks.

Unlike the information-processing model, which suggests that information is stored and retrieved piece by piece, an alternative model of memory, the **parallel distributed-processing model (PDP) (or connectionist) model**, holds that newly encountered pieces of information immediately join with other, previously encountered pieces of relevant information to help form and grow networks of information (McClelland, 2011). Baddeley and Hitch use their working memory model to provide examples of parallel processing. They asked people to complete two tasks at once—one of the tasks was visual (using the visuospatial sketchpad watching for a visual target) and the other was sound based (listening for a particular sound). They found that as long as the tasks were different (one visual and one auditory), people did about as well on each task as they did when they only did one of the tasks; they were able to do two things at once. However, when the tasks were the same (both visual or both auditory), people's performance suffered when they tried to do them together (Conrad & Hull, 1964; Baddeley, 1966).

These networks of information result in sophisticated memories, broad knowledge, and the ability to make better decisions and plans in life. Look, for example, at **Figure 8-3**. When the person in the figure sees an apple, connections to information involving things that are round, the colour red, or possibly grandma (because of the apple tree in her backyard) are all activated, while other, less relevant connections are inhibited. These connections are all part of the network of information related to apples that this person has stored.

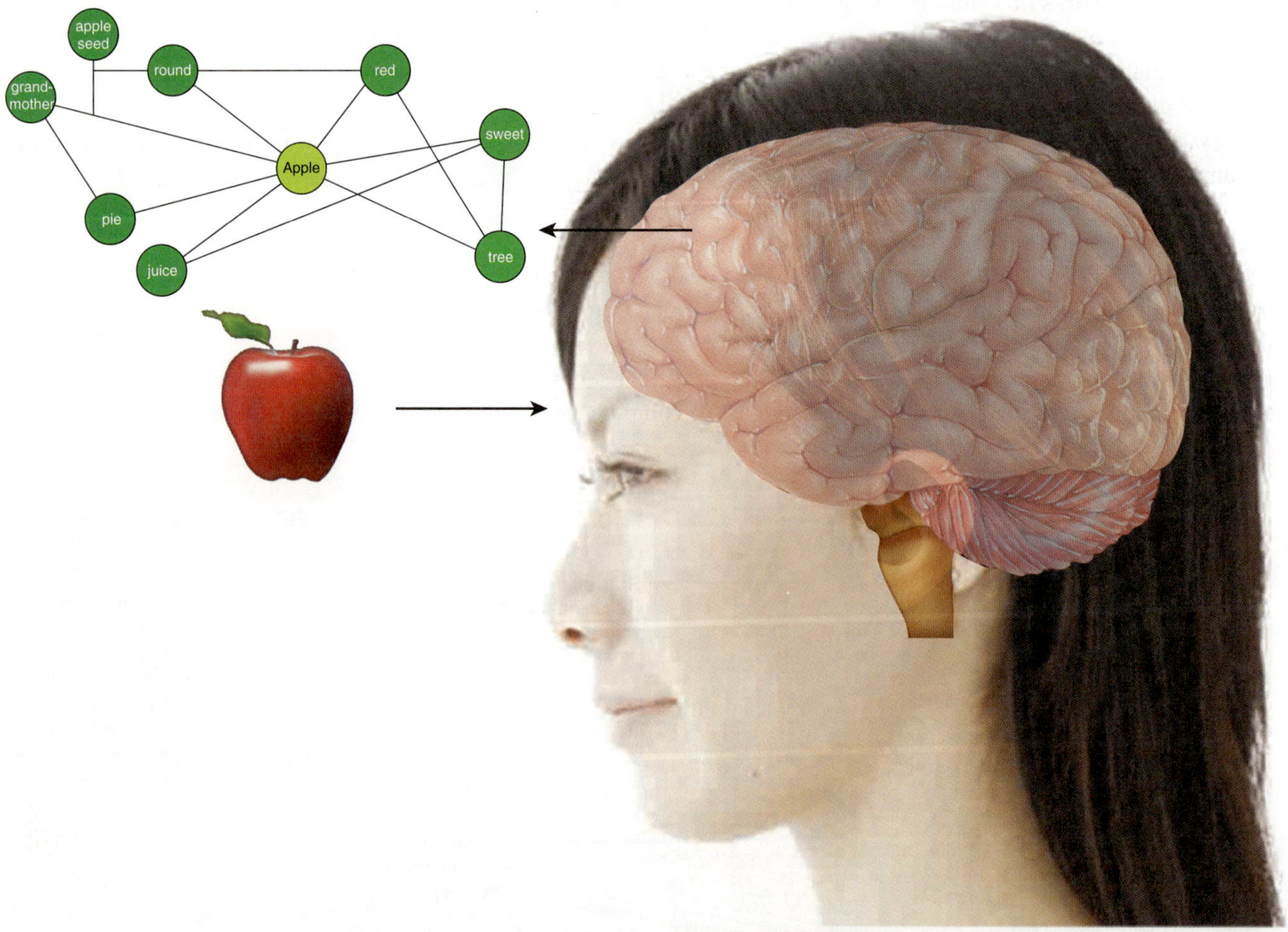

FIGURE 8-3 The PDP model of memory. The PDP, or connectionist, model of memory suggests that memories are stored in a network of associations throughout our brains.

When one part of the "apple" network is activated, related neurons throughout the brain also become active and richer memories spring forth. The PDP model of memory has gained many proponents, largely because its principles fit well with the field's growing recognition that neurons throughout our brains form networks of association as we respond to repeated learning experiences and events in life.

Before You Go On

www.wiley.com/go/comer

What Do You Know?

1. What are encoding, storage, and retrieval?
2. What are the three memory stores suggested by the information-processing model of memory?

What Do You Think?

Judging from your own experiences, do you think memory works more like a computer, with different memory stores, or more in a connectionist fashion? Could the two ideas both be useful in explaining some of your experiences?

SCAN TO GET THE ANSWERS

How Do We Encode Information into Memory?

LEARNING OBJECTIVE 2

Describe how information is encoded and transferred among different memory stores and what we can do to enhance encoding.

How many steps are there from the front door of your building to your room? Can't remember? How about an easier question: what was the first word you said yesterday morning? Most of us probably cannot recall an answer to either of these questions.

Your lack of recall may be because the information was never *encoded,* or entered into your memory. Because we fail to encode many pieces of information that we come across in

THINGS STUDENTS WANT TO KNOW

Do people who win memory competitions have great memories, or do they have a number of tricks that they use?

Contestants in the World Memory Championship are asked to memorize thousands of numbers and words, pages of faces and names, lengthy poems, and decks of cards (Schacter, 2001). Would it surprise you to learn that a recent competitor considers herself dangerously forgetful? That's right. "I'm incredibly absent-minded," winner Tatiana Cooley told a reporter. Fearful that she will forget to carry out everyday tasks, Cooley depends on to-do lists and notes scribbled on sticky pads. "I live by Post-Its," she admitted ruefully.

The image of a World Memory Championship competitor dependent on Post-Its in her everyday life has a paradoxical, even surreal, quality. Why does someone with a capacity for prodigious recall need to write down anything at all? Can't she call on the same memory abilities and strategies that she uses to memorize hundreds of words or thousands of numbers to help remember that she needs to pick up a jug of milk at the store? Apparently not.

The kinds of everyday memory failures that Cooley seeks to remedy with Post-It notes—errands to run, appointments to keep, and the like—reflect *absent-mindedness*: lapses of memory caused by inattentiveness, improper encoding, or carelessly overlooking available memories at the time of information retrieval.

life, we do not actually remember most of the things that we experience. Encoding requires *attention*—that is, we need to focus on or notice the information in the first place. We can encode only what we attend to (Eysenck et al., 2010).

Using Automatic and Effortful Processing to Encode

We are not always aware that we are attending to things in our environment. Sometimes we attend to information—particularly, information about *time*, *space*, or *frequency*—without much conscious awareness, and indeed with little or no effort. Even though you might not know how many steps there are from the front door of your building to the door of your room, you probably do not get lost very often along the way and you probably did not need to practise the route to figure out how to get to your room. The encoding process that allowed you to learn this basic route is called **automatic processing** (Hassin, 2005).

automatic processing encoding of information with little conscious awareness or effort.

Although we use automatic processing to encode many kinds of information, the encoding of other information requires that we make conscious efforts and pay very close attention (Gilchrist & Cowan, 2010). This is the type of processing you are engaging in right now as you read this chapter, whether you are preparing for tomorrow's class or studying for a test. As you read through the material, you are trying to find ways to bring this new information into your memory, because the facts won't settle there without your careful attention. This kind of encoding—which is typically needed when a person learns new information, such as new names, songs, or tasks—is called **effortful processing** (Hassin, 2005).

"The true art of memory is the art of attention."
—*Samuel Johnson, writer*

effortful processing encoding of information through careful attention and conscious effort.

Keep in mind that whether you are encoding information through automatic or effortful processing, you must be paying attention. Your attention might be less apparent in automatic processing, but if you do not attend sufficiently to information, in one way or another, you will simply not be able to encode it.

There are key differences between these two kinds of processing. First, the encoding of information by effortful processing tends to be disrupted when a person is forced to perform other tasks or to attend to other information while trying to encode the information at hand. You probably would not do very well on an intense video game if you tried to play it while carrying on a lively phone conversation, for example. In contrast, automatic processing, being so effortless, is disrupted only slightly by the performance of other tasks. For example, you would not likely spill coffee or tea if you were pouring it into your cup while talking on the phone because practice has made pouring an automatic processing task.

Memory buster. This student's upcoming test performance is clearly at risk. *Effortful processing*, such as acquiring new information from a textbook, is easily disrupted when one also attends to other tasks during the encoding process.

Second, as the name might suggest, putting extra effort into effortful processing makes it more effective. Automatic processing is not significantly enhanced by a person's extra efforts to attend and encode. You could rehearse the path from your front door to your room and count the steps, but it's unlikely that you'll know any more about the route than you knew this morning. In contrast, extra efforts can make an enormous difference in effortful processing. Reading over the material in this chapter again and again will considerably affect your ability to recall it on a test.

Encoding Information into Working Memory: Transferring from Sensory Memory into Working Memory

As we observed earlier, when we first confront a stimulus, our brains retain a very brief sensory image of it—an image called a **sensory memory**. If, for example, we are shown a photograph for just a moment, we retain a detailed image of all the shapes and items in the photograph for a few hundred milliseconds (in an iconic store). Studies by researcher

sensory memory memory involving detailed, brief sensory image or sound retained for a brief period of time.

George Sperling in the late 1950s and early 1960s provided psychologists with important insights about how sensory memories operate (Sperling, 1960).

Sperling wanted to demonstrate the presence of a brief visual storehouse—equivalent to the buffer memory of a computer—that would hold a picture of our environment for a very brief period of time. He also wanted to measure how long this buffer would last. To do so, he exposed participants to three rows of four random letters, similar to what you might see on an eye chart (although always the same size; **Figure 8-4**). He presented those letters for less than a second and found that, generally speaking, participants did a pretty good job reporting the letters, remembering about half most of the time if asked to do so right away. In a second condition of the study, Sperling displayed the grid of letters for less than a second and when the letters disappeared he played a tone that was either a low, medium, or high note. Participants only had to report the line of letters corresponding to the tone they heard, with the low note indicating the bottom row and the high note indicating the top row. If the tone sounded within about a half second of the grid disappearing, participants could usually report all the letters in the indicated row—it was like they just had to read them off their sensory or iconic store. If there was a delay of more than half a second between the visual list of letters and the tone sounding, people's recollection of row letters started to fall off as they could no longer use their sensory memory. The longer Sperling waited to play the tone after showing the letters, the more performance declined.

K	Z	R	A
Q	B	T	P
S	G	N	Y

FIGURE 8-4 Test of sensory memory. In his study of the duration of sensory memory, George Sperling flashed a chart of letters, similar to this one, for 1/20 of a second. He found that participants could recall almost all the letters in a particular row if asked to do so immediately, but half a second later, their performance declined.

If we do not focus our attention on our sensory memories, as is usually the case, they will disappear forever. Those that are attended to, however, may enter the **working memory**, the second system of memory. Working memory serves several important functions in our day-to-day lives (Hofmann et al., 2011). One of the most important is that of enabling us to hold on to information—such as a phone number—that we need for short periods. We use working memory in this way much of the time. Whenever we read, for example, our working memory enables us to keep the beginning of a sentence in mind while we are reading the last part of the sentence, so that the whole phrase will make sense to us (Just & Carpenter, 2002). It also enables us to relate new sentences, such as this one, to previous sentences we have just read. Similarly, in a conversation, working memory helps us link new comments to previous ones so that we can follow what we are hearing.

working memory a short-term memory store that can hold five to nine items at once.

One way of helping to make sure that information is encoded into working memory is **rehearsal**, consciously repeating the information. As far back as 400 B.C.E., the ancient Greek philosophers recognized the value of rehearsal in memory. They advised students to repeat whatever they heard, on the assumption that hearing and saying the same things would transfer new information into memory (Turkington & Harris, 2009, 2001). We are rehearsing when we keep repeating a phone number we've just heard until we can call it or add it to our phone's contact list. Such rehearsal increases the likelihood that the information will indeed enter our working memory and be available to us as we enter in the phone number.

rehearsal conscious repetition of information in an attempt to make sure the information is encoded.

Encoding Information into Long-Term Memory: Transferring Working Memory into Long-Term Memory

Although concentrated efforts, such as rehearsal, can lengthen the availability of information in working memory, eventually that information is either passed on to the long-term memory system or lost (Jonides et al., 2008, 2003). It is in **long-term memory** that we hold all of the information we have gathered, available for use—often at a moment's notice—in a new situation or task. When we remember past events, previously-gathered information, people we once met, past feelings, or acquired skills, we are using our long-term memory system.

long-term memory the memory system in which we hold all of the information we have previously gathered, available for retrieval and use in a new situation or task.

Just as rehearsal can help move information from the sensory memory system to the working memory system, it can help us move short-term, working memories into the long-term memory system (Neuschatz et al., 2005). Most of us rehearse information from a course's textbook and lectures, for example, when we are studying for an examination. Information is more likely to pass into long-term memory when our rehearsal sessions are spread out over a period of time, rather than attempting to take in a great deal of information all at once. As we observed in Chapter 7, this phenomenon is known as the spacing effect. Thus, *distributed practice*, such as studying material weekly, followed by reviews closer to the time of an exam, is usually more profitable than *massed practice*, such as studying in one "cram" session just before the exam.

spacing effect facilitated encoding of material through rehearsal situations spread out over time.

As we also saw in Chapter 7, sleep can help or hurt rehearsal. Information acquired in the hours before falling asleep tends to be encoded into long-term memory, as long as we have time to process it before sleep sets in (Backhaus et al., 2008; Stickgold, 2011). Information learned just as sleep is approaching is rarely retained, however, partly because we fall asleep before we can rehearse it. Furthermore, information that comes to us during sleep—a language tape, for example—does not typically enter our memories at all.

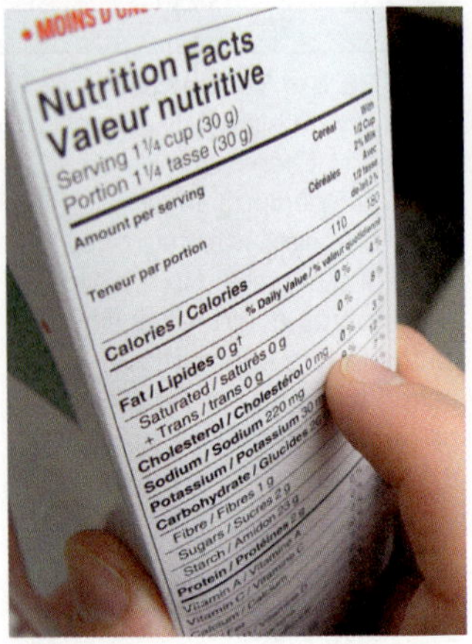

Putting working memory to good use. If you are trying to decide which cereal provides the best nutritional value, you need to keep a lot of information from the cereal boxes in mind as you decide which to buy.

In What Form Is Information Encoded?

We must use some kind of code or representation to encode information. Different codes are available to us (Martin, 2009). When encoding information into working memory—for example, trying to keep a phone number in memory long enough to dial it—we can use a *phonological code*, repeating the sounds of the numbers again and again, or we can employ a *visual code*, holding an image of how the digits would look if written down. Research suggests that people tend to favour phonological codes (as if they were spoken) when recording verbal information, such as numbers, letters, and words. We rely more on visual codes for non-verbal information, such as a person's face or a speeding car (Just & Carpenter, 2002).

Although adequate for most purposes, the phonological or visual codes that people use to record information in their working memory tend to be flawed. For example, we sometimes confuse words or other items that sound or look similar to the items we are trying to hold in working memory. Some people, however, produce visual images with extraordinary detail and near-perfect accuracy. Although recalling an object or scene that they have just witnessed, these people behave as if they are recalling items while looking at a photograph. Thus their detailed images are called *eidetic memories*, or photographic memories. Eidetic memories are unusual, but when they occur they usually occur among children: as many as 5 percent of children encode images with this level of detail. The eidetic images can last for several minutes (Hochman, 2010, 2001).

What subway? Because people tend to use semantic codes (codes based on meaning) to record important events into long-term memory, people viewing this couple's wedding pictures might wonder why they went to a subway station for a photo. For the couple themselves, a stop at the subway station where they first met was a necessary and meaningful event!

What would it be like to remember *everything*? A women identified by her initials AJ has this ability or problem (Parker, Cahill, & McGaugh, 2006). AJ can remember everything that has happened to her since she was about 3 years old. If you tell her a date in her life, she can tell you, in detail, what she did that day and what happened in the world that day. What would it be like to never forget? Depending on your point of view, this could both a blessing and a curse. Of course it would be good to be able to remember all the positive things that had happened to you, but imagine not being able to forget every slight, every insult, and every negative or distasteful event. Imagine that every new event brought forward a flood of recollections of every similar event you have ever experienced. Sometimes forgetting is a good thing.

When we encode *non-verbal information* into long-term memory, we once again tend to use phonological or visual codes (though other codes for things like smell are also likely at play). Long after a concert, for example, audience members may remember its intensity by visualizing images of the stage and the lighting effects, re-experiencing the smells of the arena and the crowd, and calling to mind the sounds of the musical instruments, the performers' voices, and the crowd's cheers.

In contrast, to encode *verbal information* into long-term memory, we tend to use semantic codes, representations based on the *meaning* of information. This means that we link the new things we learn to the things we have already memorized based on shared meaning. Hearing that a friend of yours was seen out with someone other than their boyfriend or girlfriend gets linked to existing thoughts we might have had about their fidelity.

semantic code cognitive representation of information or an event based on the meaning of the information.

Because we often rely on the meaning of information when transferring items into long-term memory, our later recall of events may be flawed to some degree. If you are listening carefully to a lecture focusing on a particularly difficult concept, you may not be able to say much later on about the facial expression or the tone of voice of the lecturer, as those bits of information are not stored semantically.

It is worth noting that the various codes may operate simultaneously when information is being encoded (Kessels & Postma, 2002). One of these codes—semantic, phonological, or visual—may be used more actively than the others in particular instances, but when we use multiple codes, the combined impact of the these codes increases the likelihood and strength of the memory.

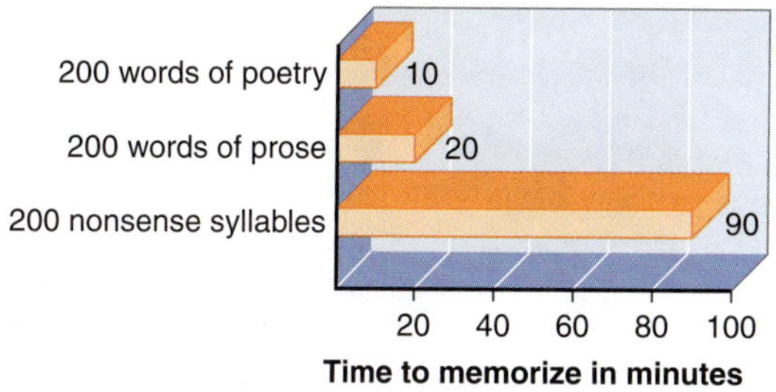

FIGURE 8-5 Meaning matters in memory. Meaning helped people memorize poetry and prose much faster than nonsense syllables. (*Based on* Turkington & Harris, 2009, 2001)

Meaning and Encoding Inasmuch as meaning often plays a key role in long-term memory, we should not be surprised that the more meaningful information is, the more readily it is encoded and later remembered. In one study, for example, people were asked to memorize 200 words of poetry, 200 nonsense syllables, and a 200-word prose passage (see **Figure 8-5**). The poetry took 10 minutes to learn and the prose less than 20 minutes, but the nonsense syllables took an hour and a half!

Similarly, the more meaningful a personal event, the more readily it is encoded and later remembered. Grandpa having to go to the hospital was recognized by everyone in the family as a significant point in the family's life. Thus, Grandpa's relatives all remembered the day of his trip to the hospital with a possible heart attack. A lesser event, such as a day at the circus or a trip to a department store, might not be encoded as readily.

People can help ensure that less meaningful information proceeds into long-term memory by artificially *adding* meaning to it (Ceci et al., 2003) or by elaborating on the meaning of the information. Such efforts are known as **mnemonic devices**, which are cognitive techniques that impose additional or intensified meaning on various pieces of information (Cavallini et al., 2003). Throughout this book, we include relevant examples that we hope will make the information more applicable and more relevant and, in turn, make your memories more available.

mnemonic devices techniques used to enhance the meaningfulness of information as a way of making them more memorable.

PSYCHOLOGY AROUND US Tricks of the Trade

Many new music students, for example, have come to appreciate that the five lines of printed music of the treble clef are called *E-G-B-D-F* by first tying those letters to the sentence "*Every Good Boy Does Fine.*" The first letter of each word in the sentence is the same as one of the lines of printed music. By giving more meaning to the musical language, the sentence helps the students to encode the information into their long-term memory.

One of the best ways to elaborate is by making the target information personally meaningful. For example, if you want to remember the difference between the spelling of the words dessert (a treat that follows a meal) and desert (a dry, hot, arid place), you might say to yourself, "I like something super sweet after dinner," to remind you that the food item is spelled with a double "s."

Organization and Encoding Another important variable that can enhance the encoding of information into long-term memory is *organization*. Actually, when we add to or elaborate on the meaning of certain pieces of information or events, we are organizing them. That is, we are giving the information a structure that is more familiar and available to us. As such, we are making it easier to encode into long-term memory. Typically, we do this intuitively. If we asked you to memorize a list of words that included FOX, BEAR, ITALY, ENGLAND, RABBIT, SPAIN, and MOUSE, you might naturally sort the words into rough categories of "Animals" and "European Countries."

PRACTICALLY SPEAKING Organizing Your Memories

As you know by now, organizing information is necessary for the proper storage and retrieval of memories. *Chunking* is one way of organizing information to help enhance memory. If you watch a lot of hockey, you might chunk or organize strings of single digit numbers into times for goals in a game—1, 3, 4, 5, 2 might become a goal at 13:45 of the second period. Another organizational technique—organizing a list of unrelated words into a story—has also been shown to be very successful. In one study, participants who used this approach were able to recall, on average, over 90 percent of the words presented to them from 12 lists, compared to only 10 percent recalled by participants who did not use this approach.

A third way to organize new material is to create a *hierarchy* of the information, separating it into sections and subsections, much like the chapter of a textbook. For example, if you need to memorize the names of all the muscles of the body for an anatomy class, you might group them according to their locations or by their actions.

One very useful study technique for helping readers—such as yourself—to learn and remember textbook information is, once again, based on the principle of organization (West et al., 2008). The PQRST method is named for its five steps, which are to be undertaken in order.

- *Preview* Skim the entire section you are required to learn. Look for the basic themes and try to get a rough idea of the information you will have to process when reading the section in more detail. If you were reading a section of a textbook about the assassination of U.S. President John F. Kennedy, your preview might focus on figuring out the principal events and people involved in the assassination.
- *Question* Examine the organization of the section and turn each subsection into a question that you want to answer over the course of your reading. If one of the subheads was, "The Assassination of an Assassin," ask yourself, "How did the assassin of President Kennedy come to be killed himself?"
- *Read* Read the section with the goal of finding the answers to your questions.
- *Self-Recitation* Ask yourself and answer aloud a set of questions that arose from the reading material, such as: "Who shot John Kennedy?" and "From what location was he shot?" Work by Colin MacLeod at the University of Waterloo has shown that saying things out loud seems to increase their distinctiveness and make it more likely that they will be remembered later (MacLeod, 2010).
- *Test* Test yourself by trying to recall as much of the learned information as you can.

By organizing your reading in this way—by asking yourself questions about the information at hand before, during, and after reading—you stand a better chance of retaining the information than if you were to spend your time simply reading through the section several times.

schemas knowledge bases that we develop based on prior exposure to similar experiences or other knowledge bases.

Organization by categories can be particularly useful in helping us to encode complicated situations. Cognitive psychologists have identified structures called **schemas**, knowledge bases that we develop based on prior exposure to similar experiences or other knowledge bases. Schemas can be helpful in allowing us to attend to and encode a lot of information in a hurry. Think about the first time you walked into a government office such as the passport office. Did it feel awkward or strange because you weren't sure of where to go or who to see? If you had visited other government offices before that one, the schemas you developed during your experiences at those offices probably helped you know what to do in the passport office with less effort than you would have needed if you had never been in a government office at all.

In need of a schema. This young patron seems confused about how things work at Round House Restaurant in Brno, Czech Republic. His previous restaurant schemas simply have not prepared him for the Round House's unusual use of a model train to deliver food and drinks to its customers.

Before You Go On www.wiley.com/go/comer

What Do You Know?

3. How does increased attention affect automatic and effortful processing?
4. Why is it more effective to study all term long, rather than in one massive session right before a final exam?
5. Which type of coding would most people use to remember someone's face? Which type would most people use to remember a person's name?

SCAN TO GET THE ANSWERS

What Do You Think?

As we noted earlier in the chapter, the author Samuel Johnson wrote, "The true art of memory is the art of attention." Can you think of experiences from your own or others' lives that bring this statement to life?

How Do We Store Memories?

LEARNING OBJECTIVE 3

Describe how we organize and store information in working and long-term memory and how we can enhance our long-term memories.

As you have seen, after entering the working memory system, information remains there for only a short period of time, usually no more that 20 to 30 seconds unless we repeat or rehearse the information (Oberauer & Kliegl, 2006). In contrast, when information moves on to the long-term memory system, it can remain there for hours or a lifetime. The retention of information—whether brief or long—in either of these memory systems is called storage.

Storage in Working Memory

Information may enter working memory from two major sources. New information, as we have seen, can be encoded after a short trip through the sensory memory system. In addition, we can bring system information that previously has been encoded in the long-term memory system back into the working memory for use in a current situation or task.

During the time that information from either of these sources is residing in the working memory system, it can, as we have seen, serve many important functions in our daily lives, from enabling us to read or carry on conversations to helping us solve current problems (Hofmann et al., 2011). The information stored in working memory also helps us do mental computations, such as mathematical problems (Maybery & Do, 2003). We could not, for example, add together the numbers 12 plus 13 if our working memory were not reminding us that we are computing those particular numbers, that addition is the task at hand, and that 3 plus 2 equals 5 and 10 plus 10 equals 20. In fact, because working memory helps us do mental computations, it is often characterized as a "temporary scratchpad" that briefly retains intermediate information while we think and solve larger problems.

Research suggests that memory and related cognitive functions peak at approximately age 25 (McGaugh, 2003, 1999).

The Storage Limits of Working Memory Once information enters working memory, it can be stored for just a limited period of time (Cowan, 2009). Concentrated efforts, such as rehearsal, can lengthen the availability of information in working memory, but eventually it is either passed on to the long-term memory system or lost (Jonides et al., 2008, 2003).

Just as striking as the limited *duration* of working memory is its limited *capacity* (Hofmann et al., 2011). On average, only five to nine items can be stored there at a given moment. This number was first uncovered back in 1885 by the German researcher Hermann Ebbinghaus (1850–1909) who pioneered memory research by studying his own memory, and it was confirmed over 70 years later by psychologist George Miller (1956).

In a typical study of this phenomenon, researchers present people with a sequence of unrelated digits, letters, or words, and then ask them to restate the items in the correct order. Because the items are unrelated and presented rapidly, it is likely that this procedure is tapping into the storage capacity of working memory only, not into some related information that has been stored in long-term memory. In study after study, almost every adult can recall sequences that consist of five items, but very few can recall lists consisting of more than nine items. Each individual displays his or her own **memory span**—the maximum number of items that can be recalled in the correct order—but no memory span strays very far from seven. Because research shows that almost everyone has a working memory capacity in this range, Miller described it as the "magical number seven, plus or minus two."

memory span maximum number of items that can be recalled in correct order.

Enhancing Working Memory Actually, the storage capacity of working memory is not quite as limited as it may seem from the Ebbinghaus and Miller studies. Each of the seven or so items that working memory holds can consist of more than a single digit, letter, or word. An item can consist of a "chunk" of information. **Chunking** pieces of information together into larger units enables us to encode more information in our working memory system, and it also enables our working memory to store more information at a given moment.

chunking grouping bits of information together to enhance ability to hold that information in working memory.

Say we are presented with a string of 23 letters, *o-u-t-l-a-s-t-d-r-i-v-i-n-g-n-i-g-h-t-w-a-s-i*. Because our capacity in working memory is only 7 ± 2 items, we would, on the face of it, be unable to store this entire sequence of items. Assuming word order is not important, we might recognized that these letters can be chunked into words—"out," "last," "driving," "night," "was," and "I"—now our task changes. We now need to store only six items (that is, six words) in working memory, rather than 23, and the task becomes manageable. In fact, these words can be re-ordered and then further chunked into one item: the sentence "Last night I was out driving." If we store the information in this way, we still have room in our working memory for several other items. Similarly, without realizing it, we may be taking advantage of chunking when we first try to master a song's lyrics. Rather than learn the song letter by letter or word by word, we may hold on to seven new lines at a time, repeating the lines again and again until we have them solidly memorized.

Our ability to chunk actually comes from our long-term memory system (Cowan & Chen, 2009). Recall that information may enter working memory as either new information arriving from sensory memory or through retrieval from long-term memory. In chunking, we use our stored, long-term knowledge that certain letters spell certain words or that words can be organized to form sentences to guide us in chunking new information.

Storage in Long-Term Memory

Whereas the sensory memory and working memory systems deal only with a limited number of short-term memories, our long-term memory system retains a seemingly unlimited number of pieces of information for an indefinite period of time, extending from minutes to a lifetime (Voss, 2009). Indeed, memory researcher Elizabeth Loftus estimates that our long-term memory system may hold as many as one quadrillion (one thousand million million) separate pieces of information (Loftus & Loftus, 1980). This expansive capacity and duration is critical to our functioning, for it is in this vast memory store that we hold—ready for use—all of the information that we have ever gathered. When we remember previously-gathered knowledge, past events and people, or acquired skills, we are using our long-term memory system.

Surveys indicate that 16 percent of adults have forgotten their wedding anniversaries (22 percent of men and 11 percent of women). People married only a few years are as likely to forget as those married for many years (Kanner, 1995).

Several factors influence whether particular events are stored in long-term memory. As we have observed, new information must first be attended to in order to have any chance of eventually winding up in this memory system. Furthermore, items that are attended to must be encoded and briefly stored in working memory, and then encoded into long-term memory, before they can be stored in this memory system (Ceci et al., 2003). Any shortcomings in these attention and encoding activities may prevent the information from being stored in the long-term system (McGaugh, 2003). Moreover, even after information is successfully stored in long-term memory, some of it may become inaccessible (Loftus & Loftus, 1980). That is, some of the information that we have previously acquired cannot be *retrieved* from long-term memory. Most of the research on long-term memory storage, including the loss of stored information, has been conducted in the biological realm, as we shall soon see.

We have observed that the number of items that can be stored in working memory is rather similar from person to person (7 ± 2). The capacity for long-term memory storage, while enormous for most of us, does, however, vary greatly among people. The differences from person to person may be due to factors such as attention and the ability to move information from working memory to long-term memory.

What Types of Memories Do We Store in Long-Term Memory? Various kinds of information are stored in long-term memory, as shown in **Figure 8-6**. We will describe many of them here and a few more in later parts of this chapter (in the section on Priming, for example). It is possible that different types of memory have evolved over time as different ways of specializing our memory function to optimize survival (Sherry & Schacter, 1987). Similarly, some species, like dogs, have a better memory for smell and others for sound as part of their adaptation to their particular living environments.

Explicit memories consist of the types of memories that you can consciously bring to mind, such as your mother's birthday or the movie discussed at the beginning of this chapter. But there are other types of memories that we are not consciously aware of, such as learned motor behaviours and perceptual information that help us to develop various skills and habits. These implicit memories might include reacting with disgust when you are given a plate of food that made you sick sometime in the past—you might not recall the initial bad meal, but you remember to avoid the food.

explicit memory memory that a person can consciously bring to mind, such as one's date of birth.

implicit memory memory that a person is not consciously aware of, such as learned motor behaviours, skills, and habits.

Neuroimaging studies of patients with brain damage suggest that these two kinds of information are stored in different brain regions (Mecklinger, Brunnemann, & Kipp, 2011;

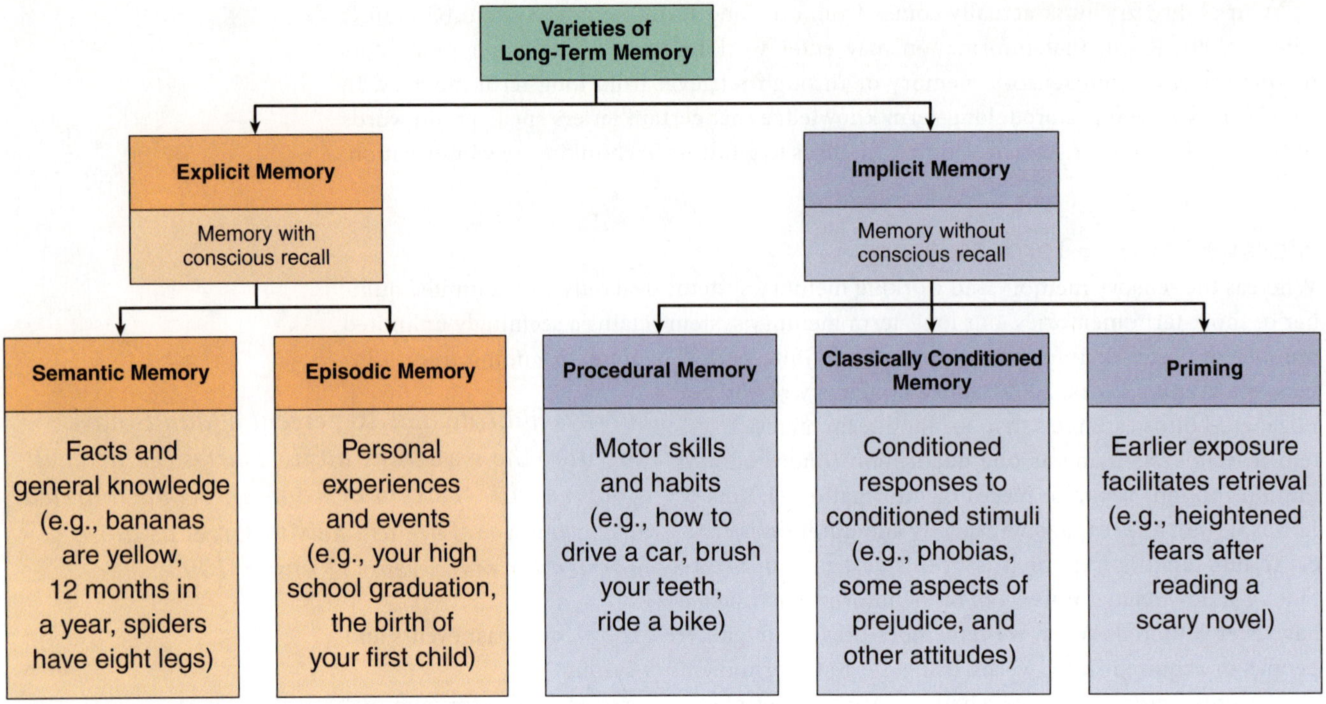

FIGURE 8-6 The long-term memories we store. Our long-term memories are of two main types, with various subdivisions within each.

PSYCHOLOGY AROUND US Remembering to Be Disgusted

In a series of studies, researchers Andrea Morales and Gavan Fitzsimons (2007) found not only that some products—trash bags, diapers, kitty litter, tampons—evoke a subconscious feeling of disgust, but they can also transfer their general ickiness to anything they come in contact with.

Where do feelings of disgust for certain products come from? In part from early life experiences with the products and perhaps, say the researchers, through evolution, from the negative experiences of our ancestors. Either way, the idea that negative qualities can be passed by a touch has become hardwired, says Fitzsimons. He and Morales set out to see whether toilet paper and other products could psychologically contaminate food in a shopping basket. They used real shopping baskets and told shoppers that the study had to do only with product preference.

Strong preferences were just what the shoppers exhibited. Any food that touched something perceived to be disgusting became immediately less desirable itself, though all of the products were in their original wrapping. The appeal of the food fell even if the two products were merely close together; an inch seemed to be the critical distance. "It makes no sense if you think about it," says Fitzsimons. "We'd take cookies out of the basket and offer them to the subjects," says Fitzsimons, "and we had some really tempting looking cookies." No takers. Moreover, he says, "everything we did suggested that these feelings were below the level of awareness. If we told someone, 'You didn't take the cookie because it touched the kitty litter,' they would say, 'That's ridiculous'" (Lemonick, 2007).

Squire & Schacter, 2002). Explicit memories are converted into long-term memories in the hippocampus and then are stored permanently in various areas of the neocortex. In a sense, the hippocampus serves as a temporary storage site within the long-term explicit memory system (Yoon, Okada, Jung, & Kim 2008). In contrast, the striatum, the region located toward the midline in the brain, plays a key role in the storage of implicit memories (Rovee-Collier, Hayne, & Colombo, 2001). As we observed in Chapters 4 and 7, when people need to call upon implicit memories to help them carry out various skills and habits, their striatum and its related structures become particularly active. In fact, an individual whose striatum is damaged by injury or disease may have enormous difficulty performing longtime skills and habits such as driving, yet retain most of his or her explicit memories.

Explicit versus implicit memories. (Left) The many details of their attendance at and viewing of Star Trek movies that this onlooker and other Trekkies love to recall are *explicit* memories. (Right) In contrast, the learned motor behaviours and perceptual information that enable this snowboarder to artfully do her thing are *implicit* memories.

To make things even more complicated, there are two types of explicit memories. Endel Tulving, a very well-known Canadian psychologist from the University of Toronto, first distinguished between semantic and episodic memory (Tulving, 1972). **Semantic memories** include our general knowledge of such facts as 2 plus 3 equals 5. **Episodic memories** are the knowledge of personal episodes from your own life, such as when you first learned to swim or ride a bike or when a good friend moved away. Some studies further hint that these two subgroups of explicit memories may, themselves, be stored in different ways from one another, but this possibility is far from certain (Christman & Propper, 2010; Markowitsch, Welzer, & Emmans, 2010).

semantic memory a person's memory of general knowledge of the world.

episodic memory a person's memory of personal events or episodes from his or her life.

How Are Our Long-Term Memories Organized? How does the long-term memory system organize the many pieces of information that are stored there? Is it set up like a bookstore in which the various items are organized first by broad categories, such as fiction and non-fiction, then by subcategories (in the case of non-fiction, for example, "art," "health," "nature," "science," or "travel"), and finally by sub-subcategories (for example, art books whose authors' names begin with *A*, *B*, and so on)? Despite years of study, we do not fully understand how pieces of information are organized when stored in long-term memory.

At the same time, psychologists do now know that, regardless of their precise organization, the pieces of information stored in long-term memory are linked to each other, forming a *network of interwoven associations*. Thus, when we retrieve one piece of information from long-term memory, a related one will often spring forth, and that piece of information may, in turn, trigger another one. This web of associations enables us to travel rapidly through our long-term memory to retrieve much of the information we need for a current situation or task. As we saw earlier, the PDP, or connectionist, model of memory helps explain such networks by suggesting that our neurons also are activated in networks.

There are other quite different ways to think about memory. One such alternative is Canadian researchers Fergus Craik and Robert Lockhart's (1972) Levels of Processing model. This model suggests that rather than passing information through distinct types of memory (short- versus long-term), we process information to shallow or deeper depths.

Information can be superficially processed, such as the colour of the words on a sign, or processed to greater depth, such as the meaning of the words, or even further in terms of their symbolic significance, such as in poetry. Information processed to greater depth is more likely to be recalled later. This theory supports standard advice to students that when studying, they should read for understanding and for depth of understanding as this will ensure better recall of material on exams.

Before You Go On www.wiley.com/go/comer

What Do You Know?

6. What is chunking, and why would you want to use it?
7. What kind of information is stored in semantic memory and episodic memory? Are semantic and episodic memories implicit or explicit memories?

What Do You Think?

What are some examples of elaboration and organizational strategies that have helped you in school or other areas of your life? What new ones are you going to try after reading this chapter?

SCAN TO GET THE ANSWERS

How Do We Retrieve Memories?

LEARNING OBJECTIVE 4

Describe how we retrieve information from memory and how retrieval cues, priming, context, and emotion can affect retrieval.

As we have noted, when information is successfully encoded from working memory into long-term memory, it is not only stored there, but is available for retrieval later. When we retrieve information from our long-term memory, it moves to the front and centre of our thinking and becomes available once again for use in our working memory system. Upon its return to working memory, the retrieved information may be used to help clarify current issues, solve new problems, or simply re-experience past events (Baddeley, 2010; Hambrick & Engle, 2003). Retrieved memories of past NHL hockey games may, for example, help us to pick teams in a playoff hockey pool. Similarly, retrieved memories of learned math tables help us calculate new mathematical problems, and retrieved memories of how to manoeuvre our car can guide when parking in a tight space. The kind or amount of information stored in long-term memory would mean little if we were unable to retrieve it. Like a library or the Internet, the information in long-term memory must be navigated efficiently and accurately to produce needed information.

The *serial position effect* demonstrates two basic retrieval effects. To demonstrate the components of the effect, read a list of 12 words to a group of people. When you get to the end of the list, have half of the group immediately write down as many of the words as they can recall, while at the same time have the other half of the group count backwards from 1,000 by threes. After 30 to 40 seconds, allow the counting half of the group to stop counting and write down as many of the words as they can remember. When you check the recall patterns of all participants (which words did they remember?), you should notice two types of serial position effect. People in both groups will remember more of the words from the top third of the list. This is called the *primacy effect*, and it reflects the fact that as they were listening to the words being read, participants were able to do more working memory work (e.g., repeating the words over and over) on the words at the top of the list before other words came along and replaced them in short-term memory. Because of this, those words were more likely transferred to long-term memory and were better recalled by all participants. A difference between the two groups is that those who got to recall words immediately will likely recall more of the words in the bottom third of the list than will those people who had to count backwards for a time following the end of the word list. The non-counters do better because the words from the bottom of the list are still in short-term memory when the reading ends. Consequently they can, and usually do, write those words down right away, sensing that they might forget them if they wait. The counting group recalls fewer of the last words on the list as they had their working memory engaged in the counting task. By the time they got to start writing down words, the ones from the end of the list were not processed into long-term memory, had faded from short-term memory, and were no longer available for recall (Ebbinghaus, 1913).

Just as researchers do not fully understand how information is organized when stored in long-term memory, they also do not know for sure how retrieval is carried out. Some theorists propose that it is a kind of "search" process (Raaijmakers & Shiffrin, 2002, 1992). In other words, the person focuses on a specific question and scans his or her memory for the specific answer to that question. Other theorists believe that retrieval is more like an "activation" process in which the questions people pose to themselves activate relevant pieces of information that have been stored in long-term memory, after which this activation then spreads *simultaneously* to every other associated piece of information. The difference between these two operations is akin to the difference between the specific results you get to a specific question on a Wikipedia search versus the hundreds of sometimes quite diverse results you get from a Google search.

Recalling the past. Looking at old family photos with a grandparent is a good way to hear about family events from previous generations. The photos can act as aids to recall past events.

If we fail to locate a particular book in a library or bookstore, it can mean either that the book is not there or that we are looking for it in the wrong section. Similarly, our failure to locate a piece of information in our long-term memory may mean that it is not stored there (encoding failure or storage loss) or that we have committed a *retrieval failure* of some kind.

We experience many retrieval failures in our daily lives. Often we find ourselves unable to recall a face, an event, or a scheduled appointment, yet it comes to mind later. Obviously the information was available in our memory all along, or we would not recall it later. Similarly, all of us have experienced the frustration of being unable to recall the answer to an exam question, only to remember it soon after the test. And in some instances we may become particularly frustrated when a piece of information feels like it is right at the edge of our consciousness, an experience called the *tip-of-the-tongue* phenomenon. We feel like the information, the memory, we need is so close we can almost taste it. Whether the recall of the information we need is blocked by other information or was not originally learned quite as well as we might have wanted, we can often recover the information if we back up and think a bit about the context of the memory. In an exam setting, think of the chapter, section, or lecture the information comes from, and then relax—that is often enough to get past the tip-of-the-tongue problem (Brown, 1991).

The retrieval of information from memory is facilitated by **retrieval cues**—words, sights, or other stimuli that remind us of the information we need (what it related to or where we learned it originally, for example). Essentially, when we come across a retrieval cue, we enter our long-term memory system and activate a relevant piece of information. Because the pieces of information in this memory system are linked to each other in a network of associations, the activation of the first piece of information will trigger the activation of related pieces until a complete memory emerges.

retrieval cues words, sights, or other stimuli that remind us of the information we need to retrieve from our memory.

Priming and Retrieval

If the pieces of information stored in long-term memory are indeed linked together in a network of associations, then the key to retrieving a specific memory is to locate one piece of information and follow associated pieces until arriving at the memory. This activation of one piece of information, which then triggers the activation of other pieces and leads to the retrieval of a specific memory, is called **priming** (Was, 2010; Ramponi et al., 2007). Sometimes we consciously try to prime a memory. If, for example, we are having trouble remembering the name of a woman who we met last week, we may bring the letter *M* to mind, recalling vaguely that her name began with that letter and hoping that the *M* sound will lead to her name. Or we may try to recall our conversation with the nameless acquaintance, hoping that this recollection will eventually lead us back to her name.

priming activation of one piece of information, which in turns leads to activation of another piece, and ultimately to the retrieval of a specific memory.

"Oh, yes, I remember them well." If asked to name several members of the Canadian Men's 2010 Olympic Hockey team (a *recall task*), even ardent hockey fans will have some difficulty. If, however, they were shown this team photo (a *recognition task*), many fans would readily come up with such names as Sidney Crosby, Jarome Iginla, Roberto Luongo, and Johnathan Toews.

Priming may also take place without our conscious awareness. Say you are in a store and you vaguely notice the Celine Dion classic song "My Heart Will Go On" (from the movie *Titanic*) playing on the store's sound system. If you were to walk out of the store and a friend were to ask you what song had just been playing on the store's speaker, you might not be able to recall it. However, if a short while later, in an unlikely turn of events, you find yourself in the *Cash Cab* (a TV show set in a real Toronto cab where the driver asks you questions and you can win money on your way to your destination), and were asked to name three classic Canadian hit songs for $500, research suggests that you would be particularly likely to include "My Heart Will Go On" in your answer. Although you had no choice in the matter and were not even aware that it was happening—and even if you dislike Celine Dion's music and were trying to ignore the song while in the store—it would have served as a retrieval cue and primed you to recall "My Heart Will Go On" when later quizzed about classic Canadian hits.

Given the operation of priming, we should not be surprised that the more retrieval cues we encounter, or the more informative they are, the better our retrieval of memory. This is why people perform better on **recognition tasks**, ones in which they must report whether or not they have seen a particular item before, than on **recall tasks**, those in which they are forced to produce memories using no or few retrieval cues (**Figure 8-7**) (Wixted & Squire, 2010; Tulving, 1974).

recognition tasks memory tasks in which people are asked to identify whether or not they have seen a particular item before.

recall tasks memory tasks in which people are asked to produce information using no or few retrieval cues.

Context and Retrieval

It is often easier to retrieve particular information when we return to the setting or situation in which we first encoded it. Most of us have had personal experiences that attest to this. Upon returning to our old home or school, for example, we may find ourselves almost overrun by memories of events that we have not thought about for years. Similarly, a return to the scene of an argument or romantic encounter may evoke detailed memories of the original event. Not surprisingly, then, some educators believe that people perform best on exams when the exams are administered in the same rooms where the material was taught (Postle, 2003).

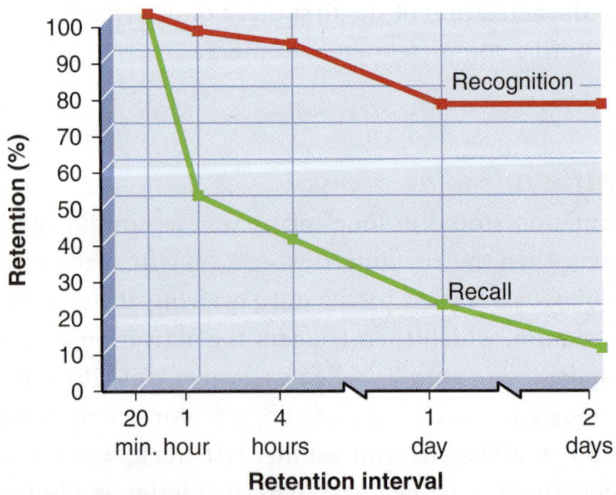

FIGURE 8-7 Recognition versus recall. In one study of retrieval, participants were tested for either recognition or recall of nonsense syllables over the course of two days. Retrieval on the recognition test was far superior than on the recall test. (*Data from*: Schwanenflugel et al., 1992; Luh, 1922)

PSYCHOLOGY AROUND US Memory Friendly

If you are asked to name everyone who was enrolled in your grade 10 history class—a recall task—you will probably be able to remember some of the individuals, but far from all of them. If, on the other hand, you are shown pictures one-by-one from your high school yearbook and asked to point to, identify, and name those individuals who were in your history class—a recognition task—you probably will perform better. The reason? The latter task offers more retrieval cues. Not surprisingly, students usually perform better on multiple-choice exams, which are recognition tasks, than on essay or short-answer exams, which are recall tasks.

Clearly, returning to or duplicating the context in which information was learned may help us to retrieve it (Postle, 2003). Why? Once again, the answer appears to be retrieval cues. Classic research by Canadian Endel Tulving provided evidence of these sorts of encoding (context) specificity principles (Tulving & Thomson, 1973). The original context, the location or situation in which we learn material, is loaded with retrieval cues, each of which activates a piece of information, setting off the activation of associated pieces and leading to memories of the original event. The likely impact of these many retrieval cues is an increase in the number, intensity, and accuracy of relevant memories.

It is not always possible to return to the original site of our learning. In such cases, one can mentally revisit the context. If, in an exam, you are unable to remember something you learned in a class, perhaps you should imagine the classroom and try to hear in your mind the instructor's voice telling you the information.

context the original location where you first learned a concept or idea, rich with retrieval cues that will make it more likely you will be able to recall that information later if you are in that same location or context.

Emotion: A Special Retrieval Cue

Just as a letter, word, song, or setting may serve as a retrieval cue and lead to specific memories, so may an emotional state or mood. If people learn something while in a particular state of mind, they may recall it more readily when they are in that state again. Gordon Bower was one of the first psychologists to recognize this phenomenon, called state-dependent memory (Bower, 2008, 1981; Forgas, 2008). In one study, he had people learn a list of words while they were in a hypnotically-induced happy state of mind. He found that they remembered the words better if they were tested later when in a happy mood rather than if they were in a sad mood. Conversely, those who learned the words when in a sad mood recalled them better if they were tested later while sad, rather than if they were happy. Apparently, a feeling can serve as a cue for retrieving information that was encoded while experiencing that feeling.

state-dependent memory memory retrieval facilitated by being in the same state of mind in which you encoded the memory in the first place.

Some theorists further believe that a person's emotions may be more than just another retrieval cue (McGaugh, 2003). As we shall see in the following sections, they suggest that strong emotions may enhance memories by leading to increased *rehearsal, elaboration,* and *organization* of a particular event, or that intense emotions may trigger a *special memory mechanism*, producing emotional memories.

Emotional Memory: Rehearsal, Elaboration, and Organization

If an event makes us particularly happy, or for that matter, distinctly upset, we will probably think about it again and again. We are likely to talk about highly emotional events with friends and relatives, perhaps write about them in a personal journal, or even try to revisit the scene or recreate the context of the event. Such behaviours are commonly displayed by people who have achieved a special personal accomplishment, observers of exciting sporting events, or victims of accidents, hurricanes, or other catastrophes. Together, responses of this kind amount to repeated rehearsals, elaborations, and organization of the emotionally-charged events. Think back to Grandpa's trip to the hospital with chest pain. Talking about the day with relatives not only helped them recall the event, but probably also helped them link it to other important events in the family and to organize their recall of the event, perhaps chronologically from the moment the family gathering started to the point where an ambulance had to be called for Grandpa. We have seen already that rehearsal, elaboration, and organization all are ways to improve the encoding and storage of memories; thus, we should not be surprised that exciting or upsetting events tend to be retrieved more readily than ordinary ones (McGaugh, 2006, 2003).

Special Emotional Memory Mechanisms: Flashbulb Memories If we were asked where we were at 9:00 A.M. on Tuesday, May 2, 2006, what we were doing, and who we were talking to, few of us would be able to answer off the top of our heads. Yet, if we were asked the same questions about our whereabouts on Tuesday, September 11, 2001, at 9:00 A.M., the fateful hour when planes crashed into and brought down the twin towers of the World Trade Center (and part of the Pentagon), many of us could state with apparent accuracy and remarkable confidence these and other details (Denver, Lane, & Cherry, 2010). Such detailed and powerful memories of emotionally significant events, or of the circumstances surrounding our learning of the events, are called **flashbulb memories**. Beyond widely-shared events, such as the 9/11 attacks, people also have flashbulb memories of emotional events that have more personal significance, such as the birth or death of a loved one.

flashbulb memory detailed and near-permanent memories of an emotionally significant event, or of the circumstances surrounding the moment we learned about the event.

The kinds of details retained in flashbulb memories seem unavailable to us in our memories of other events (Edery-Halpern & Nachson, 2004). What is it about these special events that enables us to retrieve such details? According to some theorists, it is the extraordinary level of emotionality that we experience during the event. Specifically, our intense emotions may help trigger a special memory mechanism—a mechanism above and beyond the usual memory processes—that produces a near-permanent record and more likely retrieval of nearly everything we encountered during the event (McGaugh, 2006, 2003).

The ultimate flashbulb memory. Many people have detailed memories of who they were with when they watched Sidney Crosby score the winning goal in the gold medal match at the 2010 Winter Olympics in Vancouver. Flashbulb memories of this kind are helped along by the extraordinary level of emotionality that people experience during the event.

This proposed memory mechanism has yet to be fully identified, but certain studies do support the notion that emotionally-charged memories involve mechanisms beyond those operating for more neutral memories (LeDoux & Doyère, 2011; Kensinger & Corkin, 2003). In one study, for example, some participants were given a tranquilizer drug while hearing an emotional story about a boy who received emergency surgery, whereas other participants were given a placebo drug during the same story (Cahill et al., 1994). One week later, the participants who had been tranquilized—and due to the tranquilizer, had experienced little emotionality during the intense story—remembered less about the story than did the placebo participants, whose emotions had been allowed to rise during the story. In contrast, when the study's participants were asked to recall a more neutral story, participants from both groups showed equal accuracy in their later recollections (**Figure 8-8**).

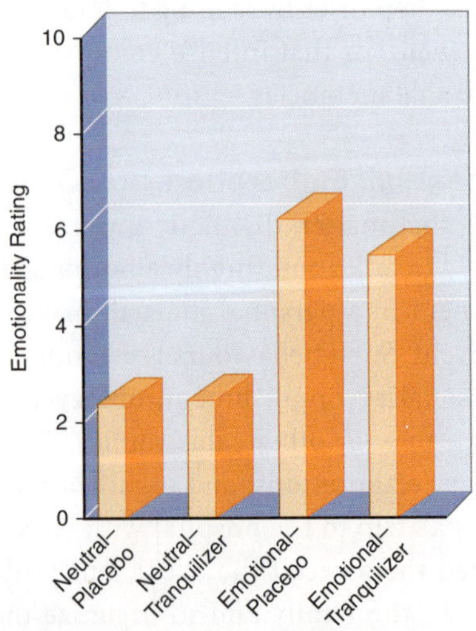

FIGURE 8-8 Emotional arousal and memory. In Cahill's study of emotion's role in memory, participants heard either an emotional or neutral story. Those given a tranquilizer while hearing the emotional story recalled less about the emotional story than those given the placebo. However, both groups recalled the same for the neutral story.

On the other hand, some recent research has called into question whether flashbulb memories are, in fact, as highly accurate as they have been purported to be (Marsh, 2007). One study, for example, compared undergraduates' memories of the 9/11 attacks with their memories of everyday events (Talarico & Rubin, 2009, 2007, 2003). Although the participants in the study reported a high level of confidence in the accuracy of their 9/11 memories, the data indicated that, in fact, such memories were no more accurate than those of more neutral events. For example, their recollection of who they were with when they learned of the 9/11 events as compared to when they experienced an everyday event were equally accurate, even though the participants themselves believed their memories of 9/11 were more vivid.

Sometimes we might wish we could forget dramatic events because they cause us too much pain. Some exciting work by Karim Nader at McGill University suggests that this might be possible. In the past we have assumed that our long-term memories are consolidated and thus hard to forget. Nader's work suggests that by recalling and speaking about a traumatic event, we may actually reactivate the memory storage process and must reconsolidate the memory to re-store it. Working with mice, Nader has found that an injection with a protein synthesis inhibiter can actually remove the memory (Nader 2003; Debiec, LeDoux, & Nader, 2002).

Before You Go On

www.wiley.com/go/comer

What Do You Know?

8. If researchers show people several pictures of small rodents, then find that a lot of people include hamsters and mice when asked to name animals that make good pets, what has happened? Why did it happen?
9. Why do many educators believe it is helpful to take an exam in the same room where you learned the material?
10. How do strong emotions affect our memory processes?

SCAN TO GET THE ANSWERS

What Do You Think?

Have you experienced flashbulb memories or state-dependent memory? If so, when?

Why Do We Forget and Misremember?

LEARNING OBJECTIVE 5

Summarize key theories of why we forget information and sometimes distort or manufacture memories.

Throughout most of this chapter, we have considered which variables help us to accurately remember events and information. But as you well know, people do not always remember things as well as they would like (Tsukiura et al., 2011). The elusive name, the missed meeting, and the overlooked birthday of a friend or relative are all instances of **forgetting**—the inability to recall information that was previously encoded. Sometimes we not only forget information, we distort or manufacture memories. We recall events differently from the way in which they occurred, or we remember things that never occurred at all.

forgetting the inability to recall information that was previously encoded into memory.

Theories of Forgetting

As we have observed, some apparent losses of memory are not really instances of forgetting at all, but rather are failures of attention. If our mind is elsewhere when we are putting down a set of keys or a treasured remote control, we simply cannot encode such acts. Correspondingly, the location of such items will not be stored in memory and available

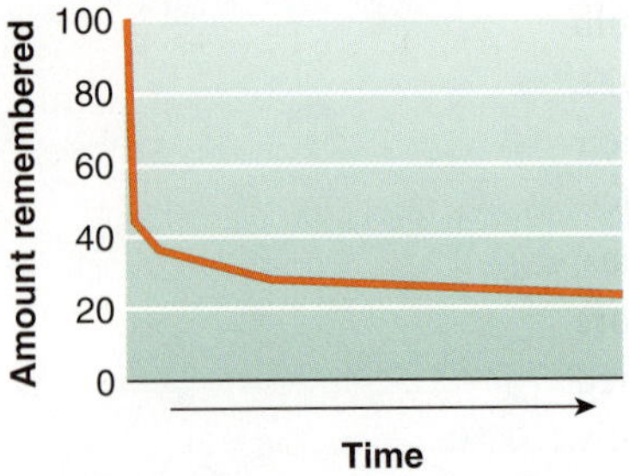

FIGURE 8-9 The forgetting curve. We forget a great deal very rapidly, but the forgetting levels off and the amount of information we retain stabilizes.

for later retrieval. At the other end of the spectrum, some material is indeed stored and available, but has weak or few retrieval cues attached to it, making it difficult for people to activate—or prime—the relevant memories from storage.

Beyond these common causes of forgetting, theorists have uncovered a number of variables that may actively interfere with memory and, in turn, produce forgetting (Macleod, Saunders, & Chalmers, 2010; Wixted, 2010, 2004). Each of today's leading explanations of forgetting has received some research support, but as you will see, each also has key limitations and raises significant questions.

Decay As we observed earlier, German researcher Herman Ebbinghaus pioneered the study of forgetting over a century ago by systematically testing his own memory of lists of nonsense syllables (for example, *lin*, *wek*, *sul*). After rehearsing and mastering a particular list, Ebbinghaus would measure how well he had retained the syllables after various intervals of time: 20 minutes, two days, a month, and so on. He found that there was a huge drop in his retention of a list soon after learning it. However, the amount that he forgot eventually levelled off; in fact, most of the information that had been retained 10 hours after first memorizing a list remained in his memory three weeks later. Known as the *forgetting curve* (see **Figure 8-9**), this pattern of rapid memory loss followed by a stable retention of the remaining information has been supported again and again by research (Erdelyi, 2010).

decay theory theory of forgetting, suggesting that memories fade over time due to neglect or failure to access over long period of time.

Many theorists explain patterns of forgetting, such as that observed by Ebbinghaus, by pointing to *decay*. According to the decay theory, memories often fade away on their own simply because they are neglected or not used for a long period of time (Wixted, 2010, 2004; McGaugh, 2006, 2003). This theory is built on the notion that memories leave a physical trace in the brain—a so-called *memory trace*—when they are acquired. Theoretically, these traces fade away over time if the person does not use them.

Decay theory is not as popular an explanation for forgetting as it once was. It cannot account for the repeated finding that people learn seemingly forgotten information or skills much more rapidly the second time around than the first time. In other words, *relearning* is faster than initial learning. If forgotten information has, in fact, eroded because of disuse—that is, if memory traces have been lost—relearning should be occurring from scratch, and it should take just as long as the initial learning did (Stone, Hunkin, & Hornby 2001).

interference theory theory that forgetting is influenced by what happens to people before or after they take information in.

Interference According to the interference theory, forgetting is affected primarily by what happens to people before or after they learn information. This theory holds that information will be retained in memory as long as competing, similar information does not interfere with it (Tillman, Peretz, & Samson, 2011; Wixted, 2010, 2004). Suppose your friend changes cell phone service providers and receives a new telephone number in which the first three digits are the same as the old number. Perhaps when dialling the new number, you find yourself mistakenly dialling her old number. According to the interference theory, the new phone number was forgotten because competing information—the old number—interfered with its retrieval.

proactive interference competing information that is learned before the forgotten material, preventing its subsequent recall.

retroactive interference learning of new information that disrupts access to previously recalled information.

When the competing information that prevents recall has been learned *before* the forgotten item, as in the case of the forgotten phone number, the process is called proactive interference. Alternatively, retroactive interference occurs when new information disrupts the retrieval of previously learned information (see **Figure 8-10**). Suppose, for example, you wish to call your friend's old number—perhaps to reach her mother who is still living at the old location—but you mistakenly dial the new number. In this scenario, you forgot the old number because competing information—the new number—interfered with its retrieval.

We should keep in mind that old information does not always interfere with the learning or remembering of new information. Sometimes it can even help us learn and retain new information. People who know how to roller skate often pick up ice skating faster than other people. Speakers of French may have an easier time learning to speak Spanish given

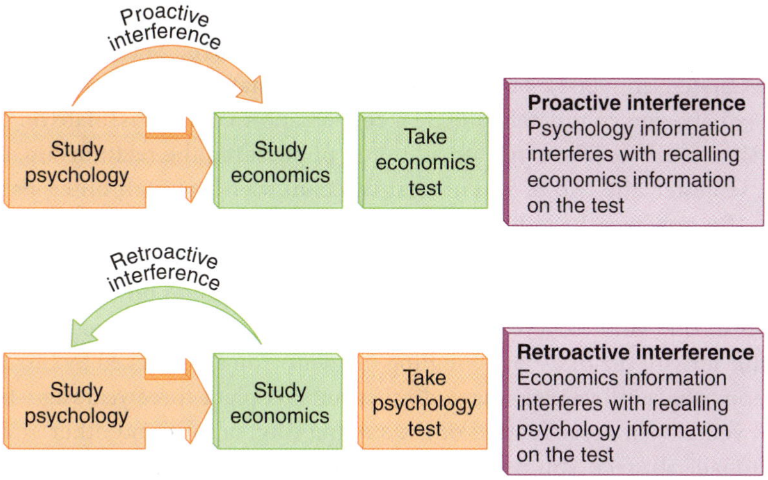

FIGURE 8-10 Proactive and retroactive interference. Forgetting is affected by interference from other information. Proactive interference occurs when information already learned interferes with learning new information; retroactive interference occurs when new information disrupts recalling previously learned information.

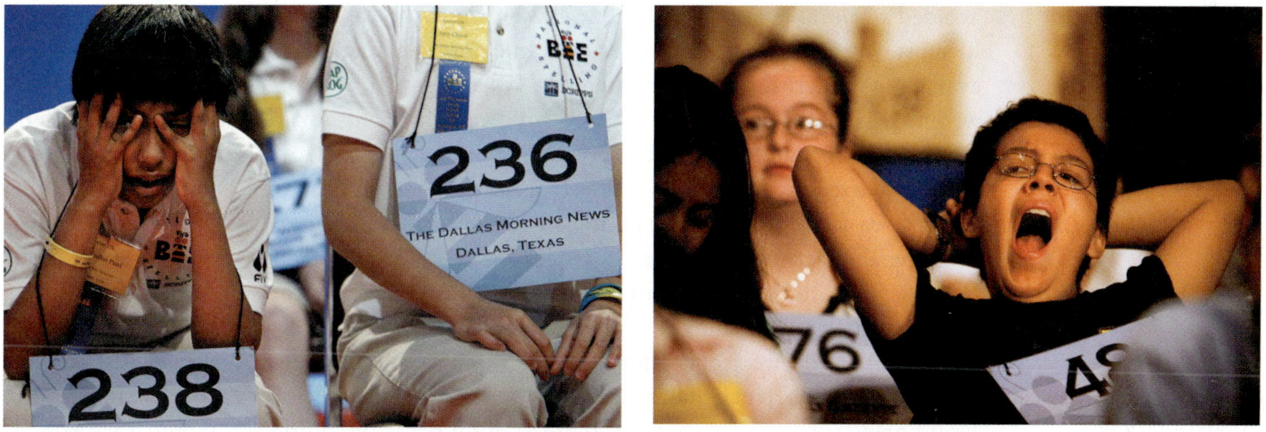

Can you spell "anxiety"? Two children await their turn at the annual Scripps National Spelling Bee. Both are fully prepared, but their emotional states are another story. Who is likely to perform better?

their similar verb structures. Interference occurs only when old and new information conflict with one another.

We have observed how emotions—both positive and negative—often enhance memory by providing powerful retrieval cues, setting up additional rounds of rehearsal, or triggering special memory mechanisms. At the same time, all of us have had experiences in which negative emotions, such as anxiety, actually interfere with memory and cause us to forget (Hawley, Grissom, & Dohanich, 2011; Eysenck et al., 2010, McGaugh, 2006, 2003).

PSYCHOLOGY AROUND US Messing with Memory

Some students experience severe test anxiety. They may prepare fully for an examination, retain all of the necessary information, and score high on practice tests. Yet, on the day of the examination, they experience feelings of anxiety that grow from butterflies in their stomach to a consuming fear that they will "not do well on the exam ... not pass the course ... perhaps not even complete university." Their anxiety grows so out of control as the test sits in front of them that they are unable to retrieve many of the answers that had been so available to them during practice tests the evening before. Many counsellors who work with such individuals suggest that the negative thoughts accompanying their anxiety (for example, "I will not pass this course") interfere with the retrieval of memories and cause the students to forget (Hambree, 1988).

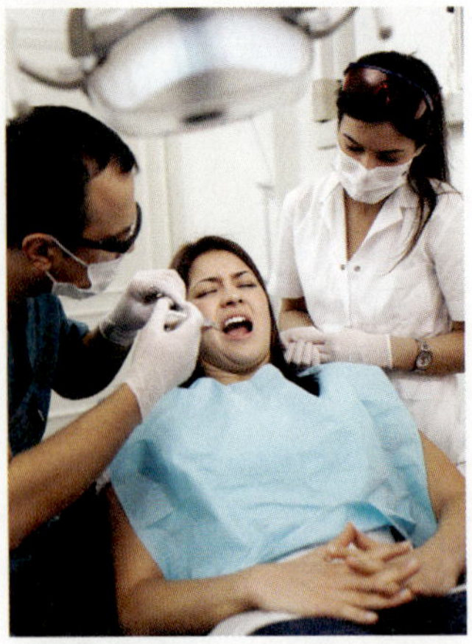

Motivated forgetting. It does not take a lot of thought to figure out why people sometimes forget their dental appointments.

Motivated Forgetting Sometimes we seem to almost purposely forget information that is unpleasant, embarrassing, or painful (Erdelyi, 2010; Mather, 2009; Kennedy, Mather, & Carstensen, 2004). Suppose, for example, that during your first year at college or university, you completely bungle a conversation with a classmate on whom you have a crush. Humiliated, you give up all hopes of pursuing the relationship, and by the end of the semester, the two of you are hardly acknowledging each other. Fast-forward three years. By now, you have become much more suave, and, as it turns out, you and your former crush meet again at a graduation party. As the two of you laugh together, talk comfortably, and discover shared values, you wonder aloud how it is that you never got together during your four years at college. Taken aback by your comment, your new friend recalls for you the first-year bungling incident. You are shocked by this revelation. On reflection, you recall vaguely that a discussion took place three years ago, but, for the life of you, you have no recollection of the stammering, falling, and other embarrassing moves you made. In fact, you do not even recall having been all that interested in this person in the first place.

Clearly, you have forgotten an incident and related information that was unpleasant. But why? One possibility is that because the event was so painful, you actively worked to forget it. You avoided opportunities for rehearsal, such as sharing the terrible experience with friends or relatives or writing about it in your personal journal. You may have even avoided retrieval cues, such as the walkway where the catastrophic interaction occurred. In short, you avoided rehearsing, elaborating, or organizing the information, making it less available for later retrieval from memory. We also sometimes forget upcoming events that we find distasteful. Many people forget dental appointments (Skaret, Raadal, Kvale, & Berg, 2000). Why do you think that might be?

Of course, anyone who has *actively* tried to forget an upsetting event knows that this is not so easy to do. Even if we do not share the event with others, we often find ourselves thinking about it (that is, privately rehearsing it) again and again. Moreover, like a flashbulb memory, the special emotional component of such an event often increases, rather than decreases, the likelihood of our remembering it.

repression process in which we unconsciously prevent some traumatic events from entering our awareness, so that we do not have to experience the anxiety or blows to our self-concept that the memories would bring.

Why then do we seem to forget certain unpleasant events or information? The leading explanation of such motivated forgetting is Sigmund Freud's theory of **repression**. Freud held that all people employ repression on occasion, a process in which we unconsciously prevent some traumatic events from entering our awareness, so that we do not have to experience the anxiety or blows to our self-concept that the memories would bring. According to Freud, the repressed material is not lost, but rather *hidden* from consciousness. He believed that our experiences, especially childhood experiences, are too rich and powerful to slip away altogether. In fact, the hidden material may influence later decisions or interpretations of events, although we are not aware of its impact in such cases. In short, the repressed information takes on the form of an implicit memory.

According to Freud, repressed memories may be jogged and brought forth under certain circumstances. Indeed, as we saw in Chapter 1, a key feature of psychoanalytic therapy, the treatment approach first developed by Freud, is to help clients rediscover their repressed memories of past traumas and, in turn, open the door to more effective functioning. Despite the wide influence of this theory and of psychoanalytic therapy, it is important to recognize that research has failed to demonstrate consistently that people repress unpleasant events (Erdelyi, 2010; Kihlström, 2006).

Distorted or Manufactured Memories

Our memories can be subject to distortions. In large part, this is because, as we observed earlier, we tend to rely on semantic codes when we encode information into long-term memory. That is, we encode the *meaning* of an event, rather than its specific words or images. In turn, when we later retrieve the memory, we have to *reconstruct* it. We must fill in details from our earlier recollection. Thus, when five persons later try to remember

TABLE 8-1 Common Reasons Why We Distort or Manufacture Memories

Source misattribution	We often fail to record where the information came from when we encode and store the information in long-term memory
Exposure to misinformation	New information that is inaccurate or misleading can distort our recall or lead us to manufacture new memories
Effects of imagination	Our own imagination can lead us to recall events that never took place

the same event—for example, when several family members recall Grandpa being taken to hospital with chest pain at a family gathering—they may each recall the details of the event quite differently.

A number of factors may contribute to faulty reconstructions of memory—that is, to the distortion or manufacture of memories. Three of the most common are *source misattributions,* exposure to *misinformation*, and the effects of *imagination* (**Table 8-1**).

PSYCHOLOGY AROUND US Dubious Source

Years ago, each evening millions of viewers watched a popular television game show named *To Tell the Truth.* On this show, three persons would claim to be an individual who was famous for a particular skill or accomplishment, for example, a famous dog trainer. Only one of the three was, in fact, the real expert; the other two were imposters. A celebrity panel would fire questions at the three individuals. They might ask questions about dogs, dog instincts, effective training techniques, and the like. Then, on the basis of the answers, they would try to decide who the real expert was. Finally, the expert would stand up and identify himself or herself.

During the questioning period, television viewers were exposed to a good deal of information. In the case of a famous dog trainer, for example, viewers would hear answers about which breeds are easier to train, which training techniques are most effective, how long training typically takes, and so on. The problem was that only one-third of this information was necessarily accurate. Only the actual trainer was "sworn to tell the truth." The two impostors were making up answers. Later, it was often impossible for viewers to remember whether a particular piece of information came from the expert (and was therefore accurate) or from one of the impostors (and was inaccurate). Unable to remember that the information came from a dubious source, many viewers carried away from each program false information, which they continued to believe for months or years.

Confident eyewitnesses are just as likely to be wrong as less-confident eyewitnesses (Gruneberg & Sykes, 1993).

Source Misattributions When we encode and store information in long-term memory, we often fail to record where it came from originally. In a similar manner, we often forget or are confused about where we have gathered information that is now stored in our long-term memory system. Such **source misattributions** can render our memories of certain events distorted, or in some cases, manufactured (Lindsay et al., 2004). Is our detailed recollection of getting lost at the mall when we were 6 years old a direct memory of that event? Or, are we actually remembering our parents' many stories about the event? Or are we confusing our own life with that of a cousin or a family friend whose young mall adventure was often discussed in your family? We may have supreme confidence in our memory of the event and even "remember" vivid details about it, yet the memory may be inaccurate or even entirely false. We are remembering something, but it may not be the event itself.

source misattribution remembering information, but not the source it came from; can lead to remembering information from unreliable sources as true.

Exposure to Misinformation Earlier we noted that retroactive interference often causes us to forget something when we are later exposed to new competing information. For example, an old phone number may be lost from memory when a fairly similar, new phone number is mastered. Similarly, exposure to new information, particularly

A terrible error. A woman talks to the man whom she had previously identified as her rapist. Her memory was eventually proved wrong by DNA evidence—after he had served 11 years of a life sentence in prison! Mistaken eyewitness memories and testimony are responsible for most wrongful convictions.

misinformation, can lead to the distortion or the manufacture of memories (Wixted, 2010, 2004).

Consider a situation in which a man witnesses a robbery. If a week later the eyewitness is asked, "Could you please describe the robber," he is being called upon to rely exclusively on his memory for a description. If, however, the eyewitness is told in passing, as part of the questioning process, "We've had a number of similar robberies lately, involving a heavy, blond-haired guy with a beard," this new information may greatly influence the witness's recall of the robber and the robbery. Such exposures to new information—often misinformation—are of great concern in police cases. Many a defendant has been accused or even convicted of a crime based on testimony from witnesses whose memories were unintentionally distorted or manufactured (Devenport et al., 2009; Wells & Loftus, 2003). (See "What Happens in the Brain When We Give Eyewitness Testimony" at the end of this section for more information.)

The impact of misinformation on memory has received considerable study in psychology laboratories. How do researchers "plant" misinformation in memory studies? A clever investigation by psychologist Elizabeth Loftus and her colleagues (1978) illustrates how this is done. Participants in her study observed a film of a traffic accident and were then asked to remember certain details of the accident. One group of subjects was asked, "How fast were the cars going when they *smashed* into each other?" A second group was asked, "How fast were the cars going when they *hit* each other?" The experimenter's use of the word *smash* implies as very severe accident, whereas the word *hit* implies a milder accident. Not surprisingly, people who heard *smash* remembered the cars going at a faster speed than did those who heard *hit*. The researchers also asked, "Did you see any broken glass?" Those who heard *smash* were much more likely to say yes than those who heard *hit*. In fact, there was no broken glass in the film.

Mistaken eyewitness testimony is the primary cause of the conviction of innocent people (Wells et al., 1998).

Study after study has demonstrated the distorting effects of misinformation on memory. In each, participants first observe an event and later receive new, misleading information about the event from researchers (Zhu et al., 2010; Loftus, 2005). A short while after observing an uneventful interaction between two spouses, for example, participants in a study may be told, in passing, that one of the spouses is a rather hostile person, or amorous, or devious. Sure enough, in their later recollections of the observed interaction, many participants "remember" hostile, amorous, or devious acts by the spouse in question. Similarly, people have been induced, by subsequent exposures to misinformation, to "remember" objects—glasses, paintings, revolvers—that were not actually present in an observed event.

A particularly powerful way of being exposed to misinformation is through *hypnosis*. As we first saw in Chapter 6, people who are hypnotized enter a sleeplike state in which they become very suggestible. While in this state, they can be led to behave, perceive, and think in ways that would ordinarily seem impossible. They may, for example, become temporarily blind, deaf, or insensitive to pain. Hypnosis can also help people remember events that occurred and were forgotten years ago, a capability used by many psychotherapists. On the other hand, in recent years, it has come to the attention of researchers that hypnosis can also make people forget, distort, or manufacture memories by supplying misinformation (Erdelyi, 2010; Mazzoni, Heap, & Scoboria, 2010; Barnier et al., 2004). Witnesses who are hypnotized to help them remember an observed crime are, in fact, likely to remember details offered or implied by the hypnotist. These details, such as the time of the crime, the clothes worn by the perpetrator, or the presence of a weapon, may be inconsistent with their actual observations. For this reason, police hypnotists must be extraordinarily careful when questioning witnesses. Even so, courts across Canada no longer admit as evidence eyewitness recollections that have been gathered initially under hypnosis.

The Effect of Imagination It turns out that our memories can be distorted not only by misinformation supplied by others, but also by false information that comes from within, from our imaginations. Researchers have found repeatedly that when people are instructed to imagine the occurrence of certain events, many come to believe that they have in fact experienced the events (Richardson, 2011; Thomas et al., 2007).

Hypnosis and memory. A police hypnotist uses the procedure to help a woman remember details of a crime that she witnessed. In fact, hypnosis often causes people to distort or manufacture memories, rather than rediscover them.

In one study, a team of researchers asked the parents of university students to list events that had, in fact, occurred during the students' childhoods (Hyman & Kleinknecht, 1999). In later interviews, the students themselves were instructed to recall those real events, along with another event that had not actually occurred according to the parents' reports. The students were not told that this event was false. A student might, for example, be instructed to recall the false event of accidentally knocking over a table at a wedding, as well as a number of events that actually had occurred. When interviewed some days later, about one-fourth of the students fully believed that the false events had occurred during their childhood, and, in fact, they could "remember" many details of the unfortunate experiences. Clearly, misinformation from others or from our own imaginations, or from a combination of the two, can greatly influence our recollections, leading at times to forgetting, distortions, or even the manufacture of memories.

Before You Go On

www.wiley.com/go/comer

SCAN TO GET THE ANSWERS

What Do You Know?

11. How does the decay theory explain forgetting?
12. What is repression?
13. A late night TV comedy show host suggests that supporters of one political party have happier lives than members of the others. Although this person is obviously unqualified to know, your friends have started to tell you it's proven that members of this party have more fun, so they're thinking of switching parties. What might be happening to your friends' memories?
14. The saying, "Elementary, my dear Watson," did not appear in any of the writings of Sir Arthur Conan Doyle, the author of the Sherlock Holmes series, yet millions of fans vividly remember reading these words. What processes can explain this manufactured memory?

What Do You Think?

What examples of proactive and retroactive interference or memory distortions have you experienced in your own life?

Memory WHAT HAPPENS IN THE BRAIN?

LEARNING OBJECTIVE 6

Describe how the brain is involved in memory.

Much of what we know about the biology of memory has come from studies of people who have suffered injuries to specific locations of the brain (Alessio et al., 2006, 2004). Important information has also been gained through experiments in which researchers surgically or chemically change the brains of animals and then observe the effects on old memories and new learning (Schwarting, 2003). In addition, over the past decade, studies using brain scans have enabled investigators to observe brain activity and structure at the very moment that people are thinking and remembering. Finally, molecular biology studies have shed light on specific changes that may occur in our brain cells as memories form (Sweatt, 2010).

Tying It Together: **Your Brain and Behaviour**

Giving Eyewitness Testimony

Imagine you have witnessed a car accident where someone was injured. You dialled 911 and stayed at the scene to tell the police officer what happened. A few months later, you were called to testify as an eyewitness at the trial. How accurate do you think your memory would be?

When people give eyewitness testimony, many regions of their brains are involved, including the hippocampus, amygdala, prefrontal cortex, visual cortex, thalamus, and mammillary bodies, among others. Let's see how several of these regioqns are involved in such eyewitness testimony.

DISTORTING THE MEMORY

Memories are often susceptible to distortions when they are recalled. Wrong information can be incorporated into an eyewitness's memory if leading questions are asked or if circumstances surrounding the inquiry are particularly frightening.

Questions

1. **Imagine a person who has witnessed a bank robbery. Provide an example of a leading question that might alter this person's memory and a non-leading question that is more likely to preserve the original memory.**
2. **Explain how the visual cortex is activated differently when a person is remembering a witnessed event accurately versus inaccurately.**
3. **Discuss the role of the prefrontal cortex and the hippocampus in the storage and recall of eyewitness memory.**

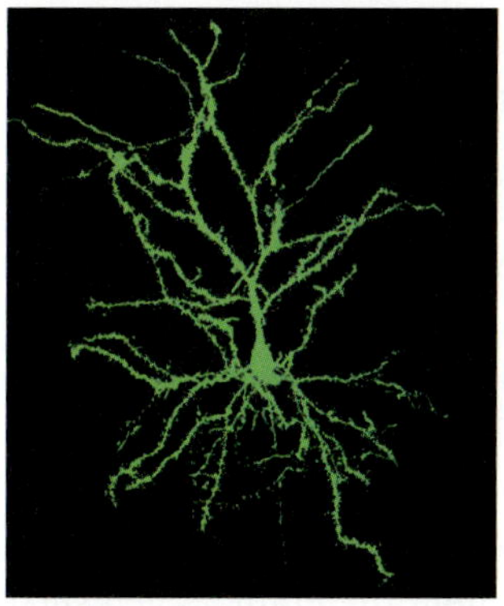

RECALLING THE EVENT

Eyewitness retrieval and recall of the observed event depends largely on neuron activity in the cerebral cortex, shown here in this image of a fluorescent pyramidal neuron. In addition, protein synthesis in the pyramidal neurons of the prefrontal cortex enables memories to be stored again after they have been used.

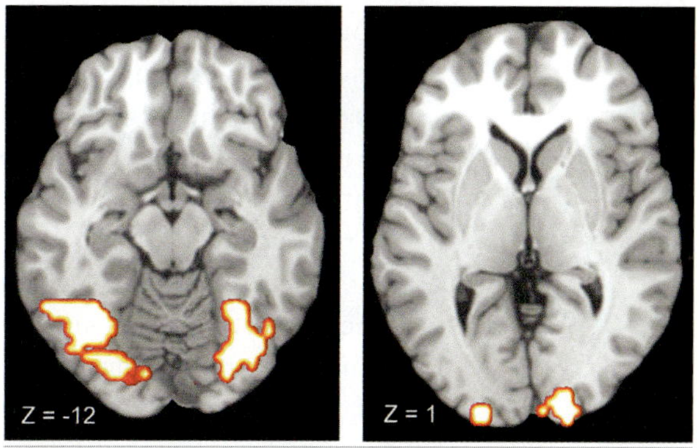

RETRIEVING AN INCORRECT MEMORY

Different parts of the visual cortex are activated when eyewitnesses accurately remember an observed event versus when they remember it inaccurately. Association parts of the visual cortex are at work in both true and false memories (orange areas on the left brain scan), whereas only true memories activate the primary visual cortex (orange areas on the right).

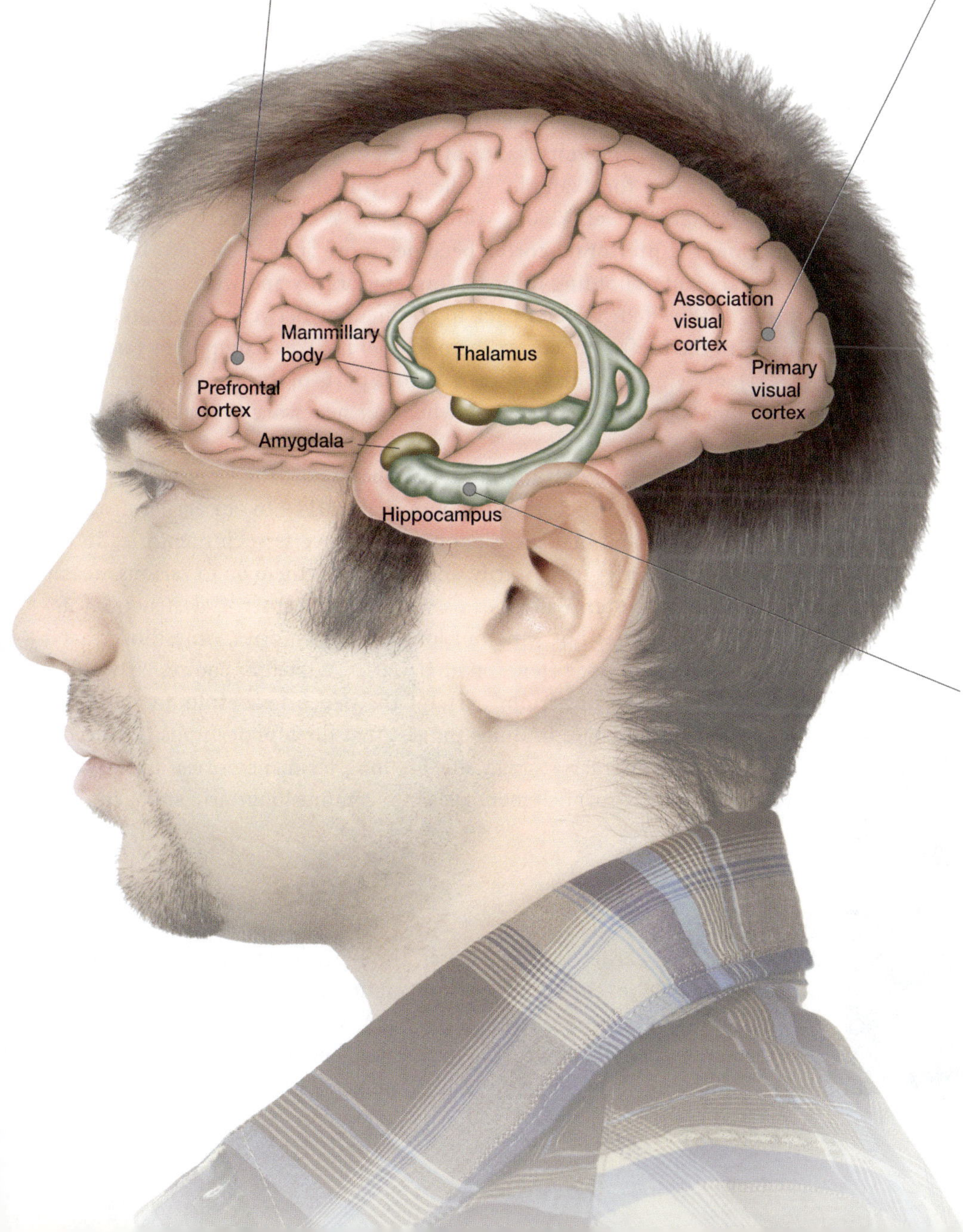

STORING THE MEMORY

A major role in the formation and storage of memories about the observed event is played by the hippocampus, shown here in this image of neurons genetically engineered to make fluorescent dyes. The synapses in this brain region are changed by experience and are activated when we remember.

What Is the Anatomy of Memory?

Memories are difficult to locate. Recall from Chapter 4 that back in the 1920s, neurological researcher Karl Lashley undertook a series of experiments with rats, in search of the specific places in the brain where memories are stored (Lashley, 1948). He trained a group of rats to run through a maze, then cut out a different section of each rat's brain tissue and, following surgical recovery, set the rats loose in the maze again, checking to see whether they still remembered how to navigate through the maze. Lashley operated on many of the rats, cutting out different sections of brain tissue for each one. He found that all rats retained at least some memory of the maze, no matter what part of the brain he removed.

Based on studies such as this, researchers have concluded that there is no specific place—no storehouse—in the brain where memories reside (Dudai, 2011), that information in the brain is encoded across various neurons throughout the brain. As we have seen, for example, connectionist theorists see memory as a *process* rather than a place, an activity that involves changes in networks of multiple neurons throughout the brain. When such networking is activated, a memory is triggered and comes forth. This conclusion that there is no single place in the brain where memories reside is similar to the Chapter 7 conclusion that a single learning centre in the brain does not exist. Indeed, because memory and learning go hand in hand, you'll see that several of the brain structures and activities discussed in Chapter 7 to account for learning are also involved here as we examine the neuroscience of memory.

Although today's theorists believe that networks of neurons located throughout the brain are involved in memory, research has clarified that some brain areas are particularly important in the formation and retrieval of memories. Among the most important structures in working memory, for example, is the **prefrontal cortex**, a key structure within the neocortex (Öztekin et al., 2009; Wang, 2005). When animals or humans acquire new information, the prefrontal cortex becomes more active (Chein, Moore, & Conway, 2011; Lian et al., 2002), holding information temporarily and working with the information as long as it is needed. To refer back to our analogy between the brain and a computer, the neurons in the prefrontal cortex seem to operate like a computer's random access memory (RAM), drawing information from various parts of the brain and holding it temporarily for use in a task, yet able to switch whenever necessary to other information and tasks.

prefrontal cortex important brain structure located just behind the forehead and implicated in working memory.

Among the most important structures in long-term memory are the *hippocampus* (see **Figure 8-11**) and other parts of the neocortex (Tsukiura et al., 2011). In our earlier discussion of explicit memories, we noted that the hippocampus converts such memories into long-term status, stores the memories temporarily, and then sends them on to various areas of the neocortex for genuine long-term storage. As we saw in Chapter 4, destruction of the hippocampus in adulthood does not wipe out long-term memories, only those that occurred just prior to the brain damage (Jeneson et al., 2010; Wixted & Squire, 2010). In contrast, destruction of certain parts of the neocortex results in the loss of older memories. These findings suggest that the hippocampus is indeed an important temporary storage site for long-term memories and a key player in the transfer of such memories into genuine long-term status in the neocortex.

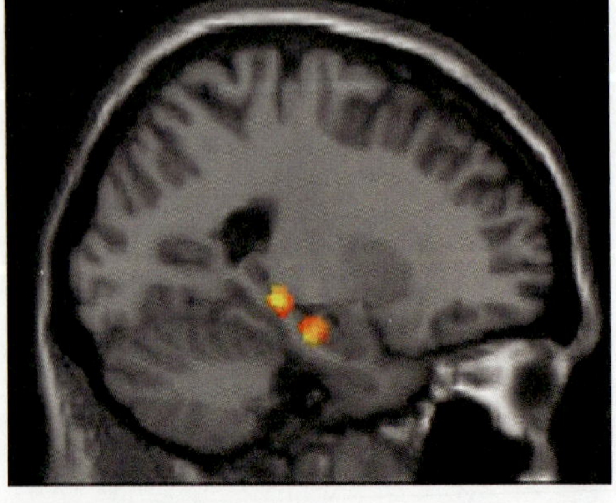

FIGURE 8-11 A key to memory. The hippocampus is a crucial structure for memory. It is activated when people recall information about facts and events (shown on this fMRI scan in yellow).

What Is the Biochemistry of Memory?

As we discussed earlier in this chapter, the PDP, or connectionist, model of memory describes the storage of information in long-term memory as a *network* of associations (McClelland, 2011). When we activate one piece of information, related ones spring into action, enabling us to travel rapidly through our long-term memory system and retrieve particular memories.

But how, in fact, does the brain manage to link such pieces of information to each other? Research increasingly points to biochemical and electrical changes in certain neurons, particularly those neurons located in the key brain regions that we have just noted.

Neural Circuits As we observed in Chapter 4, communication throughout the brain proceeds from neuron to neuron in a particular way. A given message arrives at a neuron as an impulse, travels down the axon of the neuron, and is then carried by a chemical—a *neurotransmitter*—across the synaptic space to another neuron. The next neuron is then triggered and, like the preceding neuron, passes along a message to yet another neuron, and so on. When we talk about certain pieces of information being closely linked to other pieces of information in the long-term memory system, we are really saying that certain neurons in the brain become predisposed to trigger other neurons.

The question for memory researchers is how such neural circuits form (Changeux, 2011). How is it that some neurons become predisposed to trigger other neurons, enabling us to retrieve a given memory? It appears that the repeated stimulation of certain neurons greatly increases the likelihood that these neurons will respond to future stimulation of the same kind, a phenomenon called **long-term potentiation (LTP)** (Wixted, 2004). LTP affects not just single neurons, but the networks of neurons that make up neural circuits. The effects of LTP can last quite a long time (hence the name *long-term* potentiation), long enough to be a key factor in the formation and retrieval of memories. Think of many sleds ridden one after another down a snowy slope, creating a groove that later sledders can easily find. LTP seems to create a kind of pattern that helps memories form, so a person can more easily retrieve a memory later by following the well-worn path.

long-term potentiation (LTP) repeated stimulation of certain nerve cells in the brain greatly increases the likelihood that the cells will respond strongly to future stimulation.

Researchers have gathered considerable evidence that LTP also plays a role in long-term memory. If experimental animals are given substances known to block the development of LTP, they have difficulty transferring information from their working memory into their long-term memory (Glaser et al., 2010; Sanberg et al., 2006; Lynch et al., 1991). Conversely, drugs that enhance the development of LTP seem to improve the acquisition of long-term memories. In one study, for example, rats that were given an LTP-enhancing drug learned and remembered a maze better than rats that were not administered the drug.

Many of the neurons and neural circuits that use *glutamate* as their neurotransmitter are particularly likely to exhibit LTP. This is not surprising because glutamate is a very common neurotransmitter, present in about 90 percent of all excitatory synapses. Glutamate is also a key neurotransmitter in the formation of memories, as you shall soon see. Moreover, neurons that exhibit LTP are commonly located in the hippocampus and neocortex, brain regions that play such important roles in the formation of long-term memories, as we have just observed (Glaser et al., 2010; Thompson, 2000).

Proteins Other memory researchers have tried to identify biochemical changes that occur within neurons as memories are forming (Matthews, 2011; Sweatt, 2010; Rosenzweig, 1996). When neurons receive neurotransmitters at their receptor sites, chemical changes immediately begin to occur within the neurons, including the manufacture of proteins (Fioravante & Byrne, 2011). Proteins are believed to help memories form. Although researchers have yet to identify all of the proteins involved in memory formation, they have found that disruptions in the production of proteins often interfere with the proper encoding, storage, or retrieval of memories (Chen et al., 2010).

All of these findings suggest that memory occurs as a result of changes both within and among neurons. Clearly, although no one has yet discovered all of the biological changes that account for memory, researchers are shedding more and more light on how the brain manages to provide this critical faculty.

Before You Go On

www.wiley.com/go/comer

What Do You Know?

15. Which parts of the brain are most active in memory? How are these parts related to neurotransmitters involved in memory?
16. What is a neural network and how might long-term potentiation contribute to its formation?

What Do You Think?

What side effects might occur if drugs were taken that could manipulate memory-related neurotransmitters and proteins? Should such drugs be legally available to anyone who wants them?

SCAN TO GET THE ANSWERS

Memories in the Young and Old

HOW WE DEVELOP

LEARNING OBJECTIVE 7

Describe the kinds of memories and memory changes that characterize early life and later life.

As you have seen in previous chapters, the brains of infants and young children seem to soak up information like sponges. Indeed, from the word go, the very young begin acquiring information, learning vocabularies and motor skills, and so on. Such learning tasks all require the use of memory of one kind or another.

Young babies can remember what certain objects look like (even if they don't know what they are), and can discriminate between a new object and a familiar one. Researchers assess this type of memory by measuring the amount of time a baby spends looking at an object. Babies prefer to look at, and so focus longer on, objects that they haven't seen before. This task, called *preferential looking*, is a useful way to study memory in babies who are too young to speak or to perform complex motor tasks that might otherwise reveal what they remember. Based on such research, we now know that the ability to remember objects increases from several minutes in very young infants to several days in toddlers.

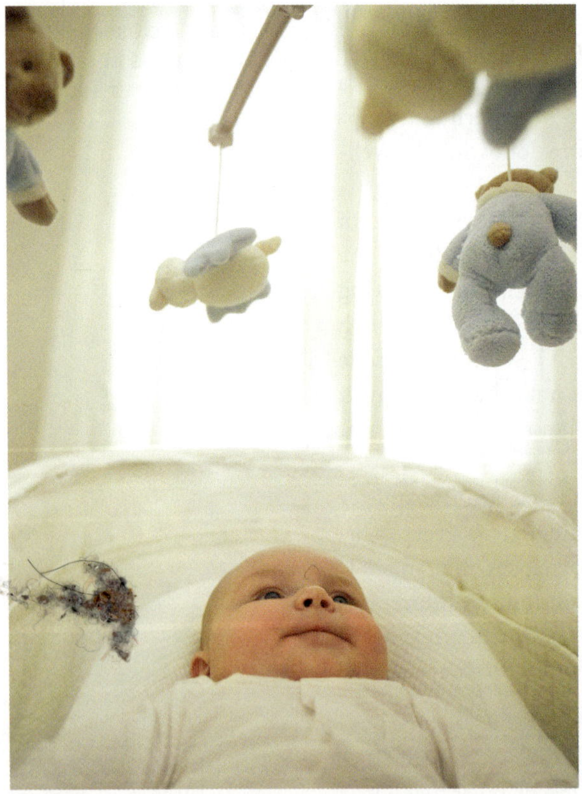

"Hey, what's that furry thing?" After being placed in his crib, this baby immediately stares at (and continues staring at) the mobile above him. Why? It has been newly added to his stimulating environment—the only object he has never seen before. Such "preferential looking" indicates that the baby, in fact, remembers all the other nearby objects.

As babies gain control over their movements, they become able to learn new skills—skills that also require memory, although a different kind of memory. Memories of skills form during the first year of life as well. For example, 1-year-olds can remember how to stack blocks or to successfully play with toys that require specific movements, such as winding a crank handle to get the jack in the box to pop up. Once learned—even in very early life—this type of procedural knowledge is rarely forgotten. That is why you will never forget how to tie your shoelaces, even if you go for years wearing only flip flops. Procedural knowledge is stored, among other places, in the brain region called the *striatum*. The early ability to store procedural information for the long term suggests that the striatum matures quickly.

In short, babies and toddlers demonstrate lots of memories—from memories of faces, places, and objects, to memories of skills and procedures. As a result, they can recognize a particular face as dad, a particular house as grandma's, and a particular animal as a giraffe. Similarly, once they get going, they can remember how to walk and get from here to there, how to use a fork, and, often, how to get their way. On the other hand, their specific memories of the *events* that occur in their lives are not very impressive.

Prior to the age of 4 years, children do not hold onto memories of life events for very long. Correspondingly, most adults do not have any recollections of the events that occurred during their first 3½ to 4 years of life. Small wonder that the early years of life are often referred to as a period of "infantile amnesia."

Why is it that young children can remember factual information, like the names of animals, from one day to the next, and remember how to play games and perform often complex motor skills, but they cannot form a permanent memory of life events? The answer to this question is that brain regions holding different types of memories do not develop at the same rate. That is, the brain circuits responsible for storing memories of events seem to develop more slowly than the brain regions responsible for storing information about language, motor skills, and simple associations.

As you learned in the previous section, in adults, memories about life events, often called *episodic memories*, are initially stored in the hippocampus. Only after temporary storage in the hippocampus is that information then distributed more widely throughout neocortical regions for long-term storage. We know that the hippocampus is a late developing brain structure, and this late development might contribute to the inability to form episodic memories early on. Alternatively, it may not be a late-maturing hippocampus that is responsible for infantile amnesia, but rather the brain's early inability to transfer information out of the hippocampus to other locations in the neocortex.

Of course, if you spend any time with talkative 2-year-olds, you will notice they have a lot to say about what has been happening in their lives. They may tell you what a friend said at nursery school, that a sibling took their toy, or that they are expecting their mom to come home from work later in the day. This shows that young children are in fact *forming* memories of life events, but that the information is not being stored permanently. If you ask those same 2-year-olds a few months later about the same life events, unless the events have been repeated over and over, the children will not recall them.

Think back to your earliest memory of a childhood event. If the memory is accurate (and not a manufactured one), it probably has an emotional component. The emotionally-charged event that you remember may be positive, such as receiving a special birthday present, going on an exciting vacation, or experiencing the arrival of your younger brother or sister. Or the remembered event may be negative, such as travelling to the emergency room after a fall off a scooter, being the victim of bullying in a preschool class, or experiencing the arrival of your younger brother or sister (depending on how you viewed this event initially!). It is unlikely that the earliest event you remember is a neutral one, particularly if it occurred before the age of 4 years. The fact that most early life memories are emotional suggests that the episodic memory system is helped along at early stages by brain regions that process emotional information, particularly the amygdala (LeDoux & Doyère, 2011).

PSYCHOLOGY AROUND US Too Scary to Forget

"One of my first, scariest memories I can recall, was when I got stuck in my dress. It was super scary—I was playing with my gigantic doll who had a very nice dress on that used to belong to me at some point in time—I remembered that I used to wear it and thought that it would be a great idea to put it on—I didn't realize that I was way too big for that dress and kept squeezing it on until I got stuck—I could not take it off or put it on—my hands were stretched up and my elbows were somewhere by my ears—I felt very uncomfortable and it was dark, since the material of the dress was covering my head. I thought I would have to stay in that position forever— that was scary!! My mother rescued me."

Having looked at memory during the earliest years of life, let's take a look at memory during the later years. As we travel through middle adulthood and old age, we become more susceptible to forgetting, distortions, and misremembering. Studies suggest that in the normal course of aging, elderly people are likely to experience declines in their working memories, their ability to encode new memories, their episodic memories (recollections of past events), certain types of short-term memory, and the sources of information that they remember (Berry et al., 2010; Hedden & Gabrieli, 2004; Nillson, 2003). Researchers also have found that older adults tend to remember positive information while ignoring the negative (Park & Reuter-Lorenz, 2009; Jacoby et al., 2005). Perhaps for these reasons, some older individuals fall prey to scams. On the other hand, the implicit (procedural) memories of aging people show little decline, several types of short-term memory remain strong throughout aging, and the semantic memories (general knowledge) of older people may actually improve (Backman & Nyberg, 2010; Fleischman et al., 2004: Verhaeghen, 2003).

Brain fitness. A growing number of cognitive fitness centres are now being developed, where elderly people work on computer tasks designed to help improve their memories and cognitive functioning. However, research has not yet clarified that brain exercises prevent cognitive decline.

An area of memory decline that is particularly upsetting to many aging people is in the operation of their *prospective* memories. A prospective memory involves remembering to perform a future intended action, as opposed to a retrospective memory, which involves the recall of past actions, events, or knowledge. Prospective memories help us to carry out our plans and effectively move through the day. They include, for example, remembering to pick up clothing at the cleaners, to call a family member, to send a birthday card, to take a prescribed medication at the right time, or to share a "juicy" piece of information with a friend. Studies find that older people perform more poorly on prospective memory tasks than do younger adults, especially when the tasks become more demanding, distracting, or complex (Einstein & McDaniel, 2010, 2005, 1990). Declines in prospective memory can often be worked around by using strategies such as to-do lists. However, the frustration that often accompanies a growing sense of absentmindedness is harder for aging people to address.

Although the age-related changes in the way our memory functions are gradual, they actually begin in our twenties (Park & Reuter-Lorenz, 2009). Certain parts of the brain, such as the hippocampus, begin to shrink. A study of the brains of elderly individuals found that the hippocampus was about 20 percent larger in those with excellent memories than those suffering from Alzheimer's disease (Winningham, 2010; Erten-Lyons et al., 2009), a finding that also may have implications for the memory losses that accompany normal aging.

As the elderly population continues to grow, an increasing amount of research is focusing on how to improve memory and prevent, or at the very least, lessen the impairments mentioned above. Fergus Craik, another very well-known Canadian researcher, now an emeritus professor at the Rotman Research Institute in Toronto, has shown that procedural and perceptual memory is not particularly effected by aging, while working memory and episodic memory decline substantially in the course of normal aging (Luo and Craik, 2008). Brain fitness approaches—using computer exercises and various mental games to keep the mind "in shape"—have become very popular and are often recommended to elderly patients by health-care professionals. Although this approach has received support in a few studies (Basak et al., 2008), many of today's researchers remain skeptical about whether brain puzzles and the like can in fact prevent memory decline. On the other hand, as we observed in Chapter 4, research has demonstrated repeatedly that *physical* exercise does indeed help to prevent or slow down deficiencies and impairments of memory and other forms of cognitive functioning (Hoveida et al., 2011; Smith et al., 2011).

Before You Go On

www.wiley.com/go/comer

What Do You Know?

17. Why are toddlers able to effectively remember faces, places, objects, and certain skills, but are not able to remember the events of their lives very well?
18. Why do the memories of elderly people tend to decline and what techniques seem to help prevent or slow down memory problems?

SCAN TO GET THE ANSWERS

What Do You Think?

Think of three of your earliest memories in life. Did the remembered events share certain characteristics, such as the arousal of great emotion or your age at the time?

Disorders of Memory

WHEN THINGS GO WRONG

LEARNING OBJECTIVE 8

Describe physical and psychological disorders that disrupt memory.

At times, each of us has been inconvenienced by imperfect memories or by outright forgetting. When our memories fail to operate as we would like, we may experience dismay, frustration, or embarrassment. Imagine how upsetting and confusing life would be if memory failure were the rule rather than the exception, as it became for Leonard, the character in the movie *Memento*. This is the experience of people who have memory disorders (McGaugh, 2003).

As you will see in Chapter 16, there are two basic groups of memory disorders: *organic memory disorders*, in which physical causes of memory impairment can be identified, and *dissociative disorders*, in which the disruptions in memory lack a clear physical cause. The latter disorders are much less common than the former.

Organic Memory Disorders

Some changes in memory have clear organic causes, such as brain injuries or medical conditions. These injuries or conditions damage one or more of the brain regions or brain chemicals that are important in the formation, storage, or retrieval of memories (Matthews, 2011). The most common kinds of organic memory disorders are *amnestic disorders*, which primarily affect memory, and *dementias*, which affect both memory and other cognitive functions.

Amnestic Disorders People with amnestic disorders, organic disorders in which memory loss is the primary symptom, experience retrograde amnesia, anterograde amnesia, or both (**Figure 8-12**). Retrograde amnesia is an inability to remember things that occurred before the organic disorder or event that triggered amnesia. Anterograde amnesia is an ongoing inability to form new memories after the onset of the disorder or event. Not surprisingly, the anterograde amnesia observed in amnestic disorders is often the result of damage to the brain's *temporal lobes* or *mammillary bodies*, areas that play a role in transferring information from working memory into long-term memory.

In severe forms of anterograde amnesia, such as that suffered by Leonard, the main character in the film *Memento*, new acquaintances are forgotten almost immediately and problems solved one day must be tackled again the next. The person may not remember anything that has happened since the physical problem first occurred. A middle-aged patient who suffered a physical trauma more than 30 years ago, for example, may still believe that Pierre Trudeau is the Canadian Prime Minister.

amnestic disorders organic disorders in which memory loss is the primary symptom.

retrograde amnesia inability to remember things that occurred before an organic event.

anterograde amnesia ongoing inability to form new memories after an amnesia-inducing event.

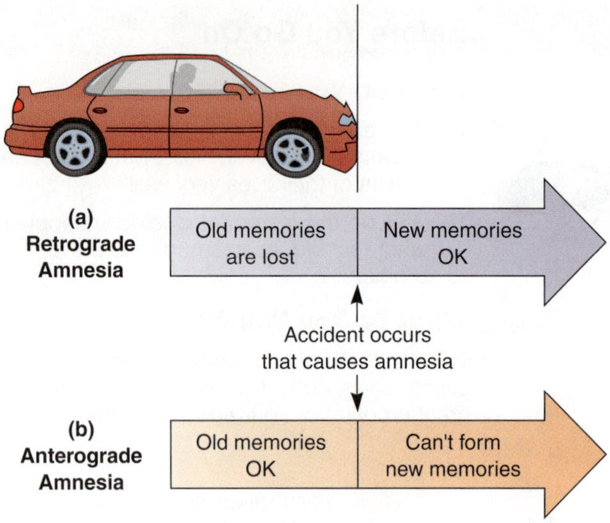

FIGURE 8-12 Two types of amnesia. An organic event can lead to two types of inability to remember. In retrograde amnesia, the individual loses memories of things that occurred before the event. In anterograde amnesia, the individual can recall the past but cannot form new memories.

Head injuries are a common cause of amnestic disorders. Although *mild* head injuries—for example, a mild concussion—rarely cause much memory loss, almost half of all *severe* head injuries do cause some permanent learning and memory problems (Sadock & Sadock, 2007). Brain surgery can also cause amnestic disorders. The most famous case of memory loss as a result of brain surgery is that of H.M., a man whose identity was protected for decades until his death in 2008 (Kensinger et al., 2001; Corkin, 1984). H.M. suffered from severe epilepsy, a disorder that produced seizures in his temporal lobes. To reduce his symptoms, doctors performed surgery in 1953 that removed parts of both his temporal lobes, the amygdala, and the hippocampus. At that time, the role of these brain areas in the formation of memories was not known. (Today temporal lobe surgery is usually done on only the right or left side of the brain.) Brenda Milner, one of Canada's best-known neuroscientists, spent many years studying the effects of the surgery on H.M.'s memory. H.M. experienced severe anterograde amnesia from the time of his surgery until his death, though his procedural memory remained intact (Milner et al., 1968; Scott & Milner, 1957). He kept failing to recognize anyone he met after the operation.

Part of the sport? Hard hits to the head are common in boxing, football, and hockey, leading, in many cases, to brain injuries that produce permanent memory and learning problems. As many as 350,000 athletes endure consciousness-losing injuries each year (Gioia, 2007).

Dementias In **dementia**, severe memory problems combine with losses in at least one other cognitive function, such as abstract thinking or language (APA, 2000). As you have seen in this chapter, forgetfulness is quite normal. In fact, as people move through middle age, memory difficulties, lapses of attention, and related cognitive difficulties increase and may occur with some regularity by the age of 60 or 70. Sometimes, however, people experience memory and other cognitive changes that are far more extensive; they may be victims of dementia.

dementia severe memory problems combine with losses in at least one other cognitive function, such as abstract thinking or language.

Between 3 and 9 percent of the world's adult population suffer from some form of dementia (Berr et al., 2005). Its occurrence is closely related to age. Among people 65 years of age, the prevalence of dementia is around 1 to 2 percent, increasing to as much as 50 percent of those over the age of 85 (Apostolova & Cummings, 2008). Current estimates suggest that there are over 60,000 new cases of dementia in Canada every year (Canadian Study of Health and Aging Working Group, 2000). More than 70 forms have been identified. Some result from metabolic, nutritional, or other problems that can be corrected. Most forms of dementia, however, are caused by neurological problems, which are currently difficult or impossible to correct.

Alzheimer's disease most common form of dementia, usually beginning with mild memory problems, lapses of attention, and problems in language, and progressing to difficulty with even simple tasks and recall of long-held memories.

Alzheimer's disease, named after Alois Alzheimer, the German physician who first identified it in 1907, is the most common form of dementia, accounting for as many as two-thirds of all cases (Brookmeyer, Johnson, Ziegler-Graham, & Arrighi, 2007). This gradually progressive disease sometimes appears in middle age, but most often it occurs after the age of 65. The disease usually begins with mild memory problems, lapses of attention, and difficulties in language and communication. As symptoms worsen over the years, the person has trouble completing complicated tasks or remembering important appointments. Eventually patients also have difficulty with simple tasks, distant memories are forgotten, and changes in personality often become very noticeable. They may withdraw from others, become more confused about time and place, wander, and show very poor judgment. They may lose almost all knowledge of the past and fail to recognize the faces of even close relatives (Förstl & Kurz, 1999).

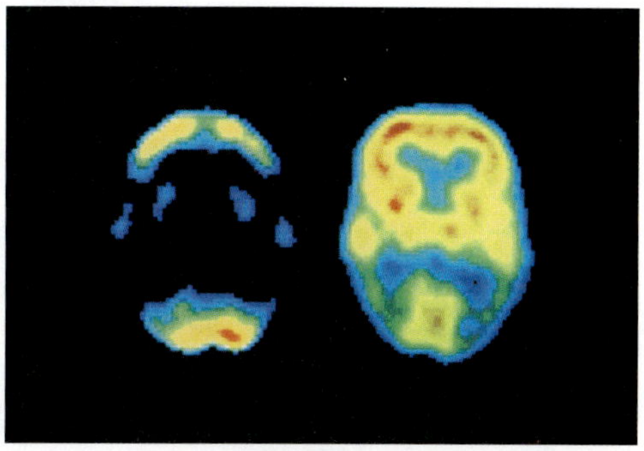

Scans tell the story. PET scans of the brains of a person with Alzheimer's disease (left) and a person without the disease (right), taken while the two individuals were trying to perform the same task, reveal how much less brain activity occurs in the Alzheimer's patient. Red and yellow colours on PET scans indicate areas of high brain activity.

Alzheimer's disease can usually be diagnosed with certainty only after death, when structural changes in the person's brain can be fully identified in autopsy (Julien et al., 2008; APA, 2000). People with Alzheimer's disease, for example, form far more than ordinary numbers of *neurofibrillary tangles* and *senile plaques*, brain changes that are normal features of aging up to a point (Selkoe, 2002, 2000, 1991). **Neurofibrillary tangles** are twisted protein fibres found within the cells of the hippocampus and several other brain areas. **Senile plaques** are sphere-shaped deposits of a protein known as *beta-amyloid protein* that form in the spaces between cells in the hippocampus, cerebral cortex, and several other brain regions, as well as in some nearby blood vessels. The presence of so many tangles and plaques indicates that enormously destructive processes take place in the brains of Alzheimer victims (Meyer-Luehmann et al., 2008; O'Connor et al., 2008). Researchers do not yet fully understand what those processes are, but they have begun to zero in on several possibilities.

neurofibrillary tangles twisted protein fibres found within the cells of the hippocampus and certain other brain areas.

senile plaques sphere-shaped deposits of a protein known as beta-amyloid that form in the spaces between cells in the hippocampus, cerebral cortex, and certain other brain regions, as well as in some nearby blood vessels.

One line of research suggests that two proteins involved in memory formation—*beta-amyloid protein* and *tau protein*—take an abnormal form and essentially behave strangely in people with Alzheimer's disease (Ramirez et al., 2011; Apostolova & Cummings, 2008). Abnormal changes in the structure of the beta-amyloid protein seem to be involved in the formation of plaques in the hippocampus and other brain areas. Similarly, abnormal changes in the structure of the tau protein lead to the formation of tangles in those brain areas. Related studies suggest that Alzheimer patients may display an imbalance in the metabolism of calcium, which, as we have seen, is used in making proteins related to memory. Still other research has linked particular genes to abnormal protein production, leading some researchers to identify certain families that carry an increased likelihood of plaque formation and of Alzheimer's disease (Turkington & Harris, 2009, 2001; Drachman, 2006).

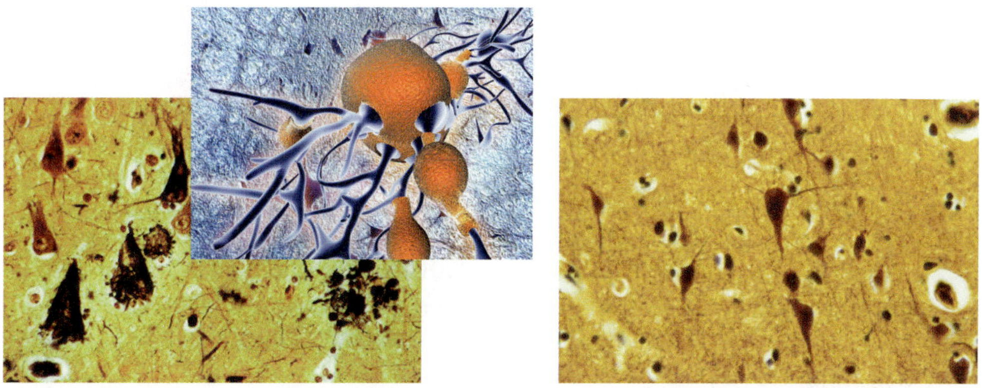

Alzheimer's disease. Both senile plaques (protein fragments that accumulate between neurons) and neurofibrillary tangles (insoluble fibres that twist together) are thought to damage neurons in the brains of Alzheimer's patients (both shown on the left). Plaques and tangles are absent in the healthy brain (right).

Yet another line of research points to reduced activity of neurotransmitters that are typically related to memory. Many studies have found, for example, that acetylcholine and glutamate are in low supply in the brains of people with Alzheimer's disease (Chin et al., 2007; Bissette et al., 1996). This decrease is probably related to the death of neurons by plaque and tangle formations.

Gender and Dementia HOW WE DIFFER Depending on whether you are a male or a female, you may be susceptible to different risk factors for dementia and Alzheimer's disease. Older women are more likely to develop dementia than men. Although this may be because women tend to live longer, natural age-related declines in estrogen, which is known to have a protective effect in the brain, could also be a factor (Sun, 2007).

As we age, certain conditions in men and women may increase the likelihood of developing dementia. A study of adults with mild cognitive impairment showed that stroke in men and depression in women increase the risk for dementia (Artero et al., 2008). In addition to risk factors, Alzheimer's disease also may "look" different in men and women. The brains of women with the disease, for example, typically have many more neurofibrillary tangles than do those of men (Barnes et al., 2005). Also, men with Alzheimer's disease tend to be more aggressive, while women are more likely to become depressed (Lovheim et al., 2009).

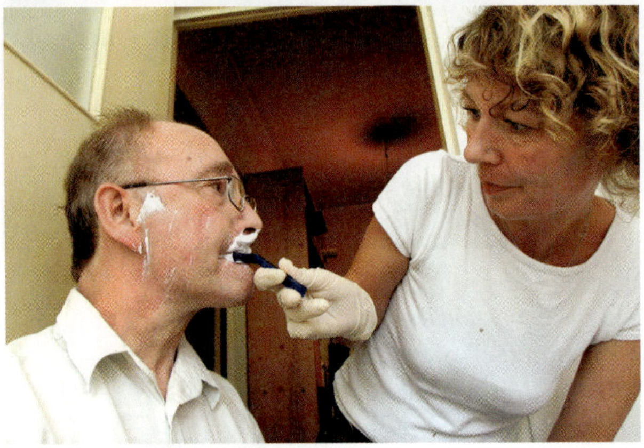

Progressive deterioration. A staff member at a special residential facility helps a man with Alzheimer's disease shave. As memory deficits and other features of the disease worsen over the years, victims have trouble performing even simple tasks.

Dissociative Disorders

People with **dissociative disorders** experience major losses of memory without any clear physical causes. Many memorable books and movies have portrayed such disorders (Vidal, 2011). Some clinicians, however, believe that they are quite rare or even doubt their very existence. A survey of Canadian psychiatrists found that only 1 in 7 believed that the validity of dissociative disorders is supported by strong scientific evidence (Lalonde, Hudson, Gigante, & Pope, 2001). There are several different kinds of dissociative disorders, including *dissociative amnesia, dissociative fugue*, and *dissociative identity disorder (multiple personality disorder).*

dissociative disorders psychological disorder characterized by major loss of memory without a clear physical cause.

dissociative amnesia psychological disorder characterized by inability to recall important information, usually of an upsetting nature, about one's life.

dissociative fugue psychological disorder characterized by loss of memory of personal identities and details of one's past life and flight to an entirely different location.

- *Dissociative amnesia* People with **dissociative amnesia** are unable to recall important information about their lives (APA, 2000). The loss of memory is much more extensive than instances of normal forgetting and is often triggered directly by a traumatic event—typically a serious threat to health and safety—as in wartime and natural disasters (Hunt, 2010; Cardena & Gleaves, 2007). Dissociative amnesia interferes mostly with memories of personal material; that is, memories of general knowledge (such as what is the capital city of Saskatchewan?) usually remain. Similarly, people with this disorder typically retain their *implicit* memories, recollections of how to write, read, drive, and other skills.

- *Dissociative fugue* In addition to forgetting their personal identities and details of their past lives, people with **dissociative fugue** flee to an entirely different location. Although some individuals travel only a short distance and make few social contacts in the new setting, others travel far from home, take new names and establish new identities, develop new relationships, and even seek new lines of work (APA, 2000; Kihlström, 2001).

- *Dissociative identity disorder* People with **dissociative identity disorder**, formerly known as *multiple personality disorder*, develop two or more distinct personalities—called **subpersonalities**—each having a unique set of memories, behaviours, thoughts, and emotions. Often one of the subpersonalities has little or no recall of the experiences, thoughts, feelings, or behaviours of the others. During activities and interactions, one of the subpersonalities takes centre stage and dominates the person's functioning.

dissociative identity disorder psychological disorder characterized by the development of two or more distinct personalities.

subpersonalities alternate personalities developed in dissociative identity disorder, each with a unique set of memories, behaviours, thoughts, and emotions.

Most cases of dissociative identity disorder are first diagnosed in late adolescence or early adulthood, but the symptoms usually begin in early childhood, often after episodes of traumatizing abuse, perhaps even before the age of 5 (Maldonado & Spiegel, 2007). Women receive this diagnosis at least three times as often as men (APA, 2000).

PSYCHOLOGY AROUND US Divided Memories

In the famous case of Eve White, depicted in the book and movie *The Three Faces of Eve*, a woman had three subpersonalities—Eve White, Eve Black, and Jane (Thigpen & Cleckley, 1957). Eve White, the primary personality, was quiet and serious; Eve Black was carefree and mischievous; and Jane was mature and intelligent. According to the book, these three subpersonalities eventually merged into a single, integrated personality named Evelyn. However, in an autobiography decades later, this woman revealed that altogether 22 subpersonalities had come forth during her life, including nine subpersonalities after Evelyn (Sizemore, 1991).

A variety of theories have been proposed to explain dissociative disorders, but none of them has received much research support. Some psychologists in fact suggest that the symptoms of dissociative disorders may originate not from within the individual, but in a therapist's office. We have seen how easy it is for people to distort or manufacture memories based on even casual suggestions. Perhaps therapists unintentionally create dissociative disorders, particularly dissociative identity disorders, by subtly suggesting to their clients over the course of treatment that they may have other personalities, or by asking the clients to produce different personalities while in a hypnotic state (Loewenstein, 2007; Piper & Merskey, 2004).

Before You Go On

www.wiley.com/go/comer

What Do You Know?

19. Compare and contrast retrograde and anterograde amnesia. What are the likely causes of both?
20. What changes happen in the brains of people with Alzheimer's disease?
21. How do dissociative disorders differ from organic memory disorders?

What Do You Think?

Do you think that media portrayals of amnesia and dissociative disorders have actually influenced psychotherapists and members of the public to increase the number of diagnoses of these conditions? What other reasons might explain increased diagnoses?

SCAN TO GET THE ANSWERS

Summary

What Is Memory?

LEARNING OBJECTIVE 1 Define the basic activities of memory and describe two major models of memory.

- Memory is our faculty for holding on to past events and past learning. It involves three basic activities: encoding, storage, and retrieval.
- Researchers typically take an information-processing approach to memory, talking about different memory stores that work together in a similar way to parts of a computer, each serving particular functions and holding information for varying lengths of time.
- PDP or connectionist models of memory suggest that information is stored not in a particular neuron or location in the brain, but instead across a network of connections.

How Do We Encode Information Into Memory?

LEARNING OBJECTIVE 2 Describe how information is encoded and transferred among different memory stores and what we can do to enhance encoding.

- Encoding refers to taking information in and putting it into memory.
- Encoding can happen either automatically or through effortful processing. Either way, however, a person must attend to something to put it into memory.
- One of the most common means of effortful processing is rehearsal of material.
- Encoding takes place in the form of phonological, sound, or visual codes.

How Do We Store Memories?

LEARNING OBJECTIVE 3 Describe how we organize and store information in working and long-term memory and how we can enhance our long-term memories.

- The retention of information in memory is known as storage. Information can be stored in memory for anywhere from fractions of a second to a lifetime.
- Sensory memory is the equivalent of the small buffer on your computer, holding a very brief visual or auditory copy of information so you can decide whether or not to encode it into working or long-term memory. Sensory memory may also help maintain the continuity of your sensory input.
- Working memory is a short-term store of slightly more information that allows us to conduct simple calculations, such as memorizing a phone number so we can dial it immediately, or remembering the beginning of a sentence as we come to the end of the sentence.
- It appears that, without rehearsal, we can hold 7 ± 2 pieces of information in working memory, although we can expand that capacity through techniques, such as chunking.
- Long-term memory appears to be both infinite in capacity and storage time.
- Information taken from working memory into long-term memory appears to be organized according to its meaningfulness and relation to other concepts in long-term storage.
- Information in long-term memory may be stored in the form of explicit memories of facts or in implicit memories, knowledge about how to do something. A person cannot always articulate implicit knowledge.

How Do We Retrieve Memories?

LEARNING OBJECTIVE 4 Describe how we retrieve information from memory and how retrieval cues, priming, context, and emotion can affect retrieval.

- The access of information from memory is known as retrieval. Retrieval can be facilitated by retrieval cues that make memories easier to access.
- Retrieval cues can include priming, context, and enhancing meaningfulness of the memory by making them more personally or emotionally relevant.

Why Do We Forget and Misremember?

LEARNING OBJECTIVE 5 Summarize key theories of why we forget information and sometimes distort or manufacture memories.

- Forgetting is the inability to recall information that has previously been encoded.
- Initially, researchers believed that failure to access information regularly led to its loss from awareness, a theory known as decay theory. This theory is less popular now, and researchers instead emphasize other problems with remembering.
- Interference theory suggests that information gets in the way of proper encoding of information, preventing it from being remembered later. Retroactive interference comes from new information that interferes with previous memories. Proactive interference comes from earlier memories that interfere with new ones.
- Motivated forgetting hypothesizes that we try to purposely forget information that is unpleasant, embarrassing, or painful.

- In addition to being forgotten, memories can also be distorted or manufactured. We can make source misattributions, where we forget where information came from. We can also be exposed to new information that distorts previous information (as described in interference theory). Also, our own imaginations can play a role in distorting how our memories play out.

Memory *What Happens in The Brain*

LEARNING OBJECTIVE 6 Describe how the brain is involved in memory.

- Because scientists have not been able to pinpoint the place where memories are stored in the brain, they have concluded that there is no single storehouse. Instead, memory appears to be a process, resulting from activation patterns throughout the brain.
- However, structures like the prefrontal cortex are extremely important in helping people hold information in working memory and to work with it as long as it is needed. Also, the hippocampus and other parts of the neocortex appear to be important in the transfer of memories into long-term memory.
- Memory itself appears to be a neural circuit, a network of neurons predisposed to trigger one another whenever one is activated. Through a phenomenon called long-term potentiation, repeated stimulation of certain nerve cells increases the likelihood that the neurons will respond strongly whenever stimulated.

Memories in the Young and Old *How We Develop*

LEARNING OBJECTIVE 7 Describe the kinds of memories and memory changes that characterize early life and later life.

- Babies and toddlers display many memories—from memories of faces, places, and objects, to memories of skills and procedures. But they do not retain memories of life events for very long.
- The slow development of the hippocampus may be responsible for the slow development of life event memories.
- Physical exercise seems to help prevent or slow down memory decline more than cognitive exercise does.

Disorders of Memory *When Things Go Wrong*

LEARNING OBJECTIVE 8 Describe physical and psychological disorders that disrupt memory.

- Disorders of memory can come about through aging, brain trauma, or the experience of traumatic events. Organic memory disorders, involving physical causes, include disorders such as amnesia and dementia. Major losses of memory without a clear physical cause are known as *dissociative disorders.*
- Amnesia refers to the inability to remember things before (retrograde) or after (anterograde) an organic event, such as a head injury or brain surgery.
- The other major class of organic memory disorders is dementia, characterized by severe memory problems combined with losses in at least one other cognitive function, such as abstract thinking or language.
- The most common form of dementia is Alzheimer's disease, a severe progressive form of dementia that accounts for at least half of all dementia cases.
- The brains of people with Alzheimer's disease have an extraordinarily high number of neurofibrillary tangles and senile plaques. The disease may stem from malfunctions of certain proteins or neurotransmitters involved in the normal formation of memories. A tendency toward developing these biochemical problems may be genetically inherited.
- Most of the time, dissociative disorders are triggered by a serious trauma or upsetting event, and the memory loss is specifically related to that trauma.
- Dissociative amnesia refers to the inability to remember important, upsetting information about one's life.
- Dissociative fugue involves the complete loss of one's identity, combined with a flight to another location.
- Dissociative identity disorder describes a disorder in which a person develops two or more distinct personalities, each with a unique set of memories, behaviours, thoughts, and emotions.
- Dissociative disorders may be a form of extreme state-dependent memory or an example of self-hypnosis, although some theorists suspect that dissociative identity disorder can also be inadvertently triggered by therapy discussions or events.

Key Terms

Alzheimer's disease 321
amnestic disorders 319
anterograde amnesia 319
automatic processing 290
chunking 296
context 303
decay theory 306
dementia 320
dissociative amnesia 322
dissociative disorders 322
dissociative fugue 322
dissociative identity disorder 323
effortful processing 290
encoding 286
episodic memory 299
explicit memory 297
flashbulb memory 304
forgetting 305
implicit memory 297
information-processing model 286
interference theory 306
long-term memory 291
long-term potentiation (LTP) 315

memory 286
memory span 296
mnemonic devices 293
neurofibrillary tangles 321
parallel distributed-processing (PDP) (or connectionist) model 288
prefrontal cortex 314
priming 301
proactive interference 306
recall tasks 302
recognition tasks 302
rehearsal 291
repression 308
retrieval 286
retrieval cues 301
retroactive interference 306
retrograde amnesia 319
schemas 294
semantic code 292
semantic memory 299
senile plaques 321
sensory memory 290
source misattribution 309
spacing effect 292
state-dependent memory 303
storage 286
subpersonalities 323
working memory 291

TYING IT TOGETHER

The study of memory is closely connected to the study of all other areas of psychology. Throughout this chapter, we have stressed how memory interfaces with psychology's various subfields, including our highlighted sections on brain function, individual differences, abnormal functioning, and development. To remind you of how memory is tied to other psychology subfields and issues, we've selected some interesting points from throughout the chapter.

WHAT HAPPENS IN THE BRAIN?

- In his pioneering neurosurgical studies, Karl Lashley found that rats retained at least some memory of their mazes, even when he removed large parts of their brains.
- Memory is not confined to any single area of the brain, although the prefrontal cortex is especially active in working memory and the hippocampus and other parts of the neocortex are heavily involved in long-term memory.
- If experimental animals are given substances that block the development of long-term potentiation (LTP) in their neurons, they have difficulty transferring information from working memory into long-term memory.
- The brains of people with Alzheimer's disease form an unusually large number of plaques, although these deposits may not be the actual cause of the disease.

HOW WE DIFFER

- The storage capacity of everyone's working memory seems to be about the same, but storage capacity in long-term memory varies greatly from person to person.
- Everyone uses phonological, visual, and semantic codes to encode information, but individuals may differ in how much they use each of these codes.
- The hippocampus size of elderly adults with excellent memories is, on average, 20 percent larger than that of people with Alzheimer's disease.
- Women are somewhat more likely than men to develop dementia.

WHEN THINGS GO WRONG

- Head injuries are a common cause of amnestic disorders, organic disorders in which memory loss is the key symptom.
- From the moment that he had both of his temporal lobes surgically removed, the famous patient H.M. was never again able to form and hold new long-term memories.
- Only 1 to 2 percent of 65-year-olds experience Alzheimer's disease and other forms of dementia, compared to as many as 50 percent of those over the age of 85.
- The symptoms of dissociative identity disorder, formerly known as multiple personality disorder, usually begin in early chilhood, often after episodes of abuse.

HOW WE DEVELOP

- Children are more likely than adults to have eidetic, or photographic, memories.
- An adult's recall of a childhood event can be influenced by emotions tied to the event, other events that have occurred since the initial one, motivated forgetting, exposure to misinformation, and the effects of imagination.
- As we age, we become more susceptible to forgetting, distortions, and misremembering.
- Although changes in the functioning of our memories unfold gradually throughout adulthood, specific declines in memory may actually begin in our twenties.
- Although forgetfulness becomes increasingly common as we age, dementia is not a normal part of aging.

Psychology Around Us

Memory Manufacturing and Eyewitness Testimony

"This Is a Stick-up!"

View this in Action WILEY PLUS www.wileyplus.com

Video Lab Exercise

Memory plays a big role in our lives and in psychology. Generally, most people believe that they can remember things pretty well. Indeed, retrieving past memories, including "buried" memories, is a major part of daily functioning. Similarly, in the criminal justice system, the memories of eyewitnesses are heavily relied upon and lead to many convictions. BUT are our memories as accurate as we like to believe? Should we have great confidence in our recollections of recent everyday events, let alone our adult memories of childhood events, the recollections of eyewitnesses, and the like?

As you are working on this online exercise, consider the following questions...

- What do you think this lab exercise says about the accuracy of our memories?
- What implications might this lab exercise hold for the field of psychology's assumptions, techniques, and interpretations?
- How might this contrived situation differ from a real-life event? Does this contrivance help account for the accuracy or inaccuracy of your memories? Pro or con?

CHAPTER 9

Language and Thought

CHAPTER OUTLINE

- Language
- The Relationship Between Language and Thought
- Thought

GT 404 W GPS (GOT LOST WITH GPS!)

If you are like the vast majority of the college students who responded to one recent survey (Elliot, 2007), you own and use a cell phone. In fact, you probably use it a lot. In June of 2010 alone, Canadians sent 4.6 billion peer-to-peer text messages. People in the traditional college age group, 18 to 24 years old, send an average of nearly 1,400 text messages per person every month, averaging more text messages than phone calls. Thirteen-to 17-year-old females send over 4,000 texts per month, while males send over 2,500 (Canadian Wireless and Telecommunications Association, 2010; Keane, 2008). As you are well aware, cell phones have an amazing number of capabilities, but they can sometimes even save lives. News reports often tell stories of lost hikers or others who were saved after calling for help from their cell phones, or when rescuers tracked them using the automatic global-positioning (GPS) information generated by their phones. But are we becoming too reliant on technology?

For example, passing the navigation of your car over to a GPS system can sometimes have negative consequences. Medical student Stephanie Parent set out from her family home in Sherbrooke, Quebec, in late February 2011 to drive to a hospital internship in Bathurst, New Brunswick. She was almost there when her GPS directed her down a remote logging road. Low on gas and with no cell phone reception, she eventually became stuck in the snow. She tried walking out at one point, but then thought it through and decided she would be better off in her car with the cooler of food her mother had packed for her. After being stranded for 72 hours, she was found by recreational snowmobilers and taken to safety. While on one hand Stephanie left the thinking of navigation up to her GPS, with unfortunate results, she did continue to think about consequences once she was in trouble, and made a good decision by staying with her car until help arrived.

Using your cell phone and GPS requires language skills. You need to speak and understand the speech of your callers. When you text or scroll through the menus, you need to read, and if you want to respond, you have to write. Not only are you using language skills when you use your cell phone, you are also using a variety of different thinking skills. For example, you may mentally envision the person you are calling or texting. You may use what you know about their habits to try to determine when would be the best time to reach them (or you may plan to leave a voice mail at a time you know they are busy if you don't actually *want* to reach them). In addition, the process of acquiring the cell phone and learning to operate it in the first place also involves some key thinking skills. You have to make several key decisions and likely solve some problems, such as how to make sure that you can transfer all of your contacts from your old phone to your new one. The necessity to plan is true of GPS systems as well. For example, it is good to find out how to turn off the "use unpaved roads" setting on your GPS before letting it lead you around in Canada (especially in winter).

Language and thought are characteristics that distinguish humans from other creatures. Language enables us to communicate in a precise and often creative way. We use language, for example, to specify to a phone salesperson exactly which model of phone, in which colour, and with which accessories, we would like to buy. We also use language to tell stories or jokes in exciting ways that make our friends gasp or laugh with us. Language has allowed us, as a species, to learn from past generations, originally by oral storytelling and then by written language. Language is a critical component of human behaviour because it greatly facilitates progressive social interactions. Consider the difficulty involved in organizing a large group of people to build a city. Such a feat would be nearly impossible without the use of language.

Although language is communicative, sometimes we use language only in our own heads. We often think using words, but many of our thoughts are not shared. Some people write extensively but only for themselves, never intending or wanting others to read their written words. Although the processes of language and thought overlap, a clear difference exists between them. In general, psychologists study these processes separately.

Human thought is highly complex, varies from individual to individual, and takes on many different forms. While much thought involves the use of words, some does not, instead relying on visual imagery or sounds. Consider, for example, what happens when a particular tune is stuck in your head. Even if you can't remember the lyrics, you can often imagine the music.

cognition mental processes of thinking and knowing.

The study of thought is a major component of cognitive psychology. As we saw in Chapter 1, the word **cognition** refers to a variety of mental processes that contribute to thinking and knowing. Cognition is involved in learning and memory, as well as thinking. In this chapter, we will discuss a number of different types of thinking, which can involve accumulating knowledge, solving problems, making decisions, and even thinking about thinking! ■

Language

LEARNING OBJECTIVE 1

Define language, describe how we learn languages, describe parts of the brain that are involved in language, and discuss differences and problems that can affect people's language skills.

language a set of symbols used to communicate.

language production the structured and conventional expression of thoughts through words.

speech the expression of language through sounds.

What Is Language?

Language, whether spoken, signed, or written, is a set of symbols used to communicate. We use symbols, mainly words, to convey our thoughts and desires to others who share an understanding of the symbols. Language can be divided into two main components: language production and language comprehension. **Language production** occurs when we generate thought through words. **Speech** involves the expression of language through sounds. Human language production is *generative* or creative; we make new sentences whenever we speak, rather than just restating old ones. In fact, humans have a remarkable capacity for producing new sentences, and we rarely repeat previously-heard sentences exactly. The ability to produce new sentences spontaneously and creatively is an important feature of human communication. We know that many other species communicate with sounds, but the vocalizations uttered by most species are inborn and do not change. A lion does not need to learn how to roar, for example, and it does not phrase its roar differently every time.

Language? . . . not. These canaries may appear to be admiring and discussing how beautiful a day it is or how well their offspring fly. However, although the word-like sounds that exit their mouths involve communication (that is, the sharing of information), it does not amount to language.

Very few species other than humans can learn new vocalizations, sounds produced in an effort to communicate (Pinker & Jackendoff, 2005). Vocal learning occurs in some species of songbirds (canaries, zebra finches), bats, aquatic mammals (whales and dolphins), and humans. It may come as a surprise to you that no primates other than humans learn language naturally, although monkeys and apes have an extensive repertoire of species-specific vocalizations. Those that have learned some vocalizations are not capable of the complexities that characterize human language. Despite years of training in the laboratory, for example, no ape has ever learned to speak, as they lack the vocal apparatus that humans evolved over many years. Gorillas have been able to use a range of signs to communicate. For example, Koko has learned over 1,000 American Sign Language based signs (Patterson & Matevia, 2001). See if you can understand Koko's signs here: www.pbs.org/wnet/nature/fun/game_flash.html. Alternatively, follow Sean Senechal's approach to teaching your dog some basic signs—using K9Sign (Senechal, 2009).

Humans are also endowed with an impressive capacity for **language comprehension**, the ability to understand communicative vocalizations or gestures. We can generally comprehend fragments of sentences or words that are mispronounced. We can understand people who speak with accents, people with speech impediments, such as lisps or stutters, as well as immature speech, such as the speech of toddlers. Our ability to understand speech that is incomplete or unclear is related to the fact that much of language comprehension is automatic. Typically we understand spoken language without concentrating, which is the reason we are able to carry on a conversation with limited pauses before responding.

language comprehension the process of understanding spoken, written, or signed language.

Language Structure

The study of speech can be divided into four general areas: *phonology*, *semantics*, *syntax*, and *pragmatics*. The building blocks of language are shown in **Figure 9-1**. The smallest units of sound in any language are called **phonemes**, and the study of how sounds are put together to form words is called **phonology**. The word *tip* has three phonemes—*t*, *i*, and *p*. The number of phonemes differs from language to language (Halle, 1990). The English language has about 40 phonemes (give or take a few depending on the dialect). At the two ends of the spectrum are the language Pirahã (an indigenous language of Brazilian people living in the Amazon), which has only 10 phonemes, and the Taa language (also known as !Xóõ), a language of indigenous people of Botswana and Namibia, which has 141 phonemes.

phoneme the smallest unit of sound in a language, an individual sound.

phonology the study of how individual sounds or phonemes are used to produce language.

Janet Werker at the University of British Columbia has demonstrated that speakers of one language often cannot distinguish sounds of other languages if their own language does not include the phoneme (Dietrich, Swingley, & Werker, 2007). For example, French does not include the h sound at the beginning of words. French speakers would say, "'Ave you 'eard about 'arry?" When learning English, French speakers will often overcompensate by voicing the h sounds in words where English speakers largely omit them, such as hour or honour. We discuss later in this chapter how it is much easier for us to learn languages during an early stage of life.

While phonemes are sounds, **morphemes** are the smallest units of language that convey *meaning* or *function* (Miller, 1978). For example, the word *jumped* has two morphemes. One is *jump* and the other is *ed* (the *ed* morpheme changes meaning, indicating that the

morpheme the smallest units of a language that convey meaning.

FIGURE 9-1 The building blocks of language.

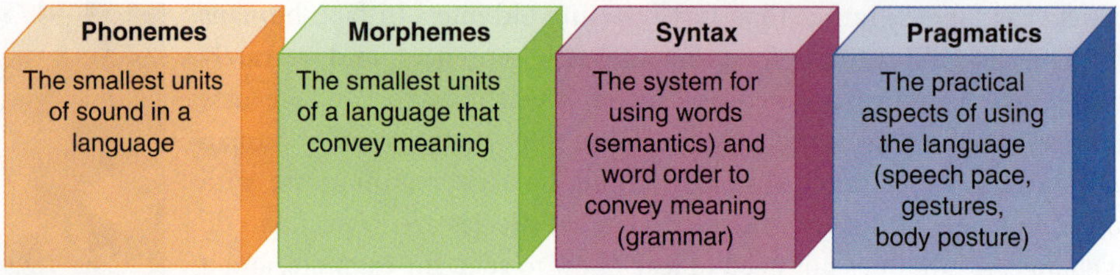

jumping has already taken place). Therefore, words can contain more than one morpheme, but each morpheme is not necessarily a word (that is, *ed* cannot *stand* alone and convey meaning). The study of the meaning of words is referred to as **semantics**. For example, if we say that it is "raining cats and dogs," you do not look outside and expect to see animals falling from the sky. Instead, you know that this expression means that it is raining very heavily. The dictionary meaning of a word is referred to as its **lexical meaning**. Lexical meaning changes over time. Consider the word *awful*; it used to mean "full of awe," but now means that something is extremely bad or unpleasant.

semantics the study of how meaning in language is constructed of individual words and sentences.

lexical meaning dictionary meaning of a word.

Knowing the meaning of individual words is important, but a word's meaning is often communicated through the position of the word in a sentence. For example, if you say that Joe kissed Kelly, then your listener knows that Joe was the giver of the kiss and that Kelly was the receiver. If, however, you say that Kelly kissed Joe, then the listener knows that Kelly was the giver of the kiss and that Joe was the receiver. As well, one word can mean two things; for example, the word *blue* can mean a colour or a depressed emotional state. When heard alone, it's impossible to tell the intended meaning, but when we hear *blue* in the context of a particular sentence, such as, "She wore a beautiful blue dress," or, "He's feeling blue today," the distinction becomes instantly clear. The way in which words are constructed into sentences is referred to as **syntax**.

syntax the system for using words (semantics) and word order to convey meaning (grammar).

Phonology, semantics, and syntax bring us to the point where we have sounds, words, and sentences. Communication also requires adhering to social norms, such as speed of speech, responding at appropriate intervals, making eye contact, and using acceptable body language. These aspects of communication are called **pragmatics**, because they refer to the practical use of language.

pragmatics the practical aspects of language usage, including speech pace, gesturing, and body language.

One aspect of pragmatics is our use of body language, or **non-verbal communication**. The way we move our hands, bodies, and faces can change the connotations of our speech. Suppose your instructor said, "I would like to meet with you after class." If this statement was delivered with one raised eyebrow, a sneer, and arms folded across the chest, you would likely interpret it differently than if the instructor said the sentence with a warm smile, while leaning forward with hands on a desk. Some people are not aware of the body language they are using and unwittingly send the wrong messages when they attempt to communicate. An employee may believe, for example, that a boss is making inappropriate advances, because the boss is unaware of the message he or she sends by standing close and touching the worker's arm while talking.

non-verbal communication body language.

Getting her message across. The facial expression, body posture, and other non-verbal cues of former Governor General Michaëlle Jean as she interacts with local children while visiting her childhood city of Jacmel, Haiti, after its earthquake, help communicate her feelings of support and happiness.

Non-verbal communication seems to be acquired automatically, often by observing the actions of others. Non-verbal communication is related to, but not identical to, gesturing, which refers to communicative movements of the arms and hands. Gesturing facilitates speech production. While the ancient Greeks provided orators with explicit lessons in gesturing to enhance their speeches, studies have shown that gesturing appears to be innate (Acredolo & Goodwyn, 1988). For example, people blind from birth, who have not had the chance to learn gestures by watching others, nevertheless use gestures. Gesturing is often difficult to inhibit; blind people will gesture even when they are talking to another blind person (Goldin-Meadow, 1999), or you may find yourself gesturing while talking on the phone.

Language HOW WE DEVELOP

You were probably too young at the time you started to speak your native language to remember learning it. Your parents may have proudly kept a record of your first words. If they did, they probably abandoned the list pretty quickly, as it became too long very fast. Within just a few years, almost every human baby goes from being incapable of speaking or understanding language to having an extensive vocabulary. In over 4,000 languages, the general sequence of language learning is the same for most people:

- *Prevocal learning* Between 2 and 4 months of age, babies are capable of perceiving the phonemes of every language, including those that are not needed for the language(s) they will ultimately learn (Aslin, Jusczyk, & Pisoni, 2000). During this time, babies have a remarkable ability to distinguish among these sounds. Researchers investigated babies' abilities to distinguish among different phonemes by training the babies to turn their heads toward an interesting visual reward when they hear a change in speech sounds. Results of studies by UBC's Janet Werker and others using this type of training (which is a form of operant or instrumental conditioning, as described in Chapter 7) suggest that young babies can discern a much wider range of phonemes than older children or adults can (Werker, 1989). This ability declines, however, as babies begin to learn their native languages (Eimas et al., 1971). With practice in only the phonemes of our native languages, we lose the ability to distinguish among sounds that are only heard in other languages (Eimas, 1975). This pruning of phoneme processing happens without specific training, and clearly suggests that infants arrive ready to notice, tune into, and acquire the language(s) being spoken around them.
- *Cooing* By about 2 months of age, babies begin to make a non-crying vocalization that consists largely of vowel-like sounds (e.g., o-o-o-o-u-u-u). Infants may also produce brief consonant-like sounds that sound somewhat like a *k* or *g*. Although infants occasionally produce these sounds when alone, they largely appear when the infant is interacting with someone else (Hulit & Howard, 1997).
- *Babbling* By about 6 months, babies start to babble (Sachs, 2009). **Babbling** refers to the production of meaningless speech sounds either repetitively (e.g., da-da-da-da-da) or in a more mixed manner (e.g., pa-da-ca-ca-mi-den-bo). These vocalizations do not work as communication, but they do enable the infant to experiment with vocalizations in a way that gradually approaches their soon-to-be-acquired native language. All babies babble, including those who are deaf (Wallace, Menn, & Yoshinaga-Itano, 1999).

babbling babies' production of meaningless sounds.

- *First words* By about 1 year, speaking begins, typically in the form of very simple words, such as *mama*, *dada*, or *hi* (Ingram, 1986). At this early stage, our ability to comprehend is much greater than the ability to speak (see **Figure 9-2**). At about 1 year of age, the average baby can understand approximately 50 words, but he will not be able to speak that many words until about six months later (Fenson et al., 1994). One-year-olds can often follow commands, such as, "Get the ball and bring it to mommy," even though their spoken vocabulary may only include *ball* and *mama*.

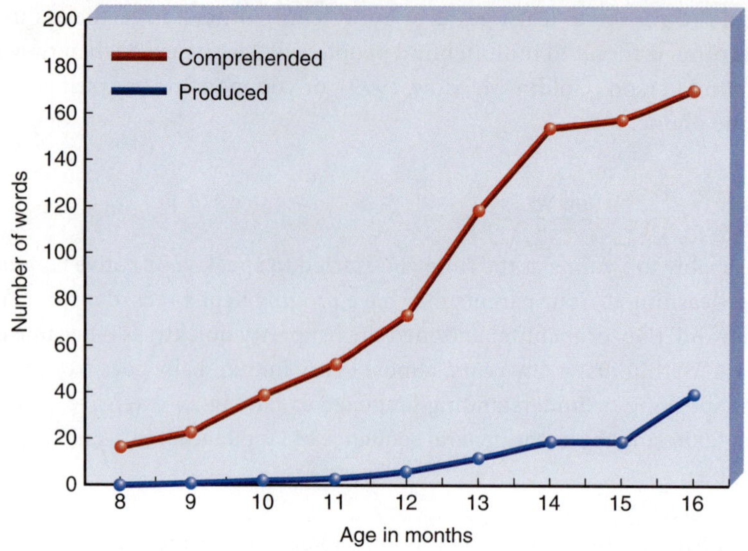

FIGURE 9-2 Babies' comprehension of words. Babies can comprehend more words than they can speak. One-year-old babies understand about 50 words, but will not be able to speak them until about six months later. (Adapted from Fenson et al., 1994.)

telegraphic speech speech that consists of minimalistic sentences. This form of speech characterizes early toddlerhood and is the first evidence of sentence formation.

- *Telegraphic speech* By age 2, toddlers in most language communities speak in very short (typically two-word) sentences (Bloom, 1970). This is called **telegraphic speech** because, as in old-fashioned telegraph messages (for which senders were charged by the word), all but the essential words are omitted. Instead of saying, "I want a cookie," a 2-year-old is more likely to simply say, "Want cookie." The dropped words are called grammatical morphemes and they are only dropped in languages where they are not necessary to determine the meaning of the spoken phrase (Slobin, 1986).
- *Pragmatics* By 3 years of age, the average toddler has naturally acquired some practical information about language use, including the need to pause between sentences and the knowledge that certain sentences are statements, whereas others are requests (Garvey, 1974). The average English-speaking 3-year-old vocabulary typically includes about 1,000 words (Huttenlocher et al., 1991).
- *Grammar* By age 4, children have automatically absorbed many of the rules of grammar, even though they have received no formal education about the grammar of their native languages (Tager-Flusberg, 2001). As discussed below, some of the early stages of reading often emerge around this time when children are exposed to written words at home or preschool. By age 6, the average child uses almost 3,000 words and likely understands a great many more, about 14,000 words (depending on the amount of language they were previously exposed to—see Poverty and Language Development on the next page). By age 9, practical aspects of language, such as inferring meaning of obscure language, interpreting metaphors, and understanding sophisticated humour, emerge (Wellman & Hickling, 1994).

Even though the majority of language learning occurs relatively early in life, vocabulary and its usage can continue to increase in size and sophistication for decades to come. In studying for the Graduate Record Exam (a part of application to many graduate programs, including those in psychology) or other college-admission exams, many teenagers find themselves learning words they haven't used before. Vocabulary can increase throughout adulthood, and seems to be one type of memory that is not adversely affected by the normal aging process. Elderly people with slowed reaction times and impaired memory for events in their own lives often score as high, if not higher, than young adults on vocabulary tests.

Theories of Language Development Recall recent experiences you have had building your vocabulary, perhaps to take exams in your school classes or as part of an English course. You may also have had experience learning a second or third language later in your

Poverty and Language Development

Children from socioeconomically disadvantaged backgrounds often struggle in academic settings. In fact, several studies suggest that poor children have deficient vocabularies when they first enter elementary school, and that these differences often get exaggerated as the years pass because vocabulary builds on itself (Lareau, 2003; Hart & Risley, 1995).

Research has shown that the initial language deficits of poor children are due to environmental differences. On average, as infants, toddlers, and young children, students from lower socioeconomic status (SES) households are exposed to fewer words than are students from households with higher socioeconomic status. As shown in the table, one study found that, in any given hour, children in poor homes heard less than half the number of words than children in high SES homes did (Hart & Risley, 1995). In addition, much more of the speech to which poor children were exposed was prohibitive, for example when a parent says, "Stop it!" or "Don't touch that."

The exact reasons why poor parents communicate less, as well as less positively, with their children remain unknown. The stress of poverty and the potential lack of suitable role models for parents (parenting skills are largely acquired through one's own upbringing) are two likely causes. Work by Monique Senechal and Jo-Anne LeFevre (2002) at Carleton University highlights the good news that the problem of reduced vocabularies in lower SES children can be prevented by preschool intervention that includes educating parents about the benefits of talking and reading to children in the home.

Research in this area also highlights one of the key challenges with human research: we are a lot better at carefully observing human behaviour (the *whats*, as in *what is going on?*) than we are at understanding the reasons for observed behaviour (the *whys*), which are a lot harder to figure out. So, we can *see* that there appear to be SES differences in parent–child communication, but at the same time we are not really clear on *why* those observed differences exist. Researchers are still working on identifying the underpinnings for many of the behavioural relationships observed in human interactions.

Socioeconomic status	Words per hour	Affirmations	Prohibitions
Low SES	176	5	11
Mid SES	251	12	7
High SES	487	32	5

education, perhaps starting in late elementary school or even in high school. In either situation, whether expanding your vocabulary in your first language or adding an entirely new language, you probably experienced a much slower learning rate than you did when you learned your first language as a very young child. Language-related learning later in life probably also required concentrated attention to your studies; it most likely did not occur automatically.

"Language is a process of free creation."
—*Noam Chomsky, American linguist*

The ease with which language is acquired by human infants has led many researchers to speculate that language has a biological basis. The linguist Noam Chomsky was among the first to suggest that language learning is built into our brains (Chomsky, 1964). The brain does appear to be set up to understand and communicate using language. As we have noted, the ability to detect all phonemes used in any human language exists in all human babies (as long as their hearing is intact). Other studies have also shown that the very young brain is wired to acquire language rapidly and automatically, because it is in a highly plastic, or changeable, state, ready to absorb new information about language. As humans grow and reach adulthood, the brain maintains the ability to change, but that ability has diminished (Johnson & Newport, 1989)—language learning becomes much slower and requires more effort.

Chomsky described our early capacity for language learning as working *as if* we had a sort of *language acquisition device* built in to our brains. As we have seen, the influence of this theoretic "device" may fade as we age and become more cognitively aware of our learning processes. Psychologists often refer to the childhood years before age 13 as an especially important period for language acquisition. Some debate exists as to whether language systems have a critical or a sensitive period (Kyle, 1980). Recall from Chapter 3 that a *critical period* refers to a window of time during which certain influences are *necessary* for appropriate formation of the brain. After the **critical period**, these influences are no longer capable of having as profound an impact on the brain. A *sensitive period* refers to a developmental time during which the brain is more *susceptible* to influences. After the **sensitive period**, change can still occur, but it doesn't happen as readily.

critical period a time during development after which we cannot develop certain capabilities.

sensitive period a time during development after which it becomes more difficult to develop certain capabilities.

As we have seen, we can still expand our vocabularies or learn new languages later in life, suggesting that, in normal cases, we go through more of a sensitive period than a critical period for language learning. Some evidence, however, such as from the sad case of Genie described in the box on the next page, suggests that there is a critical period during which we must have *some* language input or we do not acquire normal fluency with speech and, in fact, may miss out on the opportunity to develop a working understanding of the underlying syntactic features of language. The result is an inability to use the infinite variety of spoken language shown by children who acquire it early.

Baby sign. This mother is using child-directed speech to communicate with her toddler, including special intonations in her voice and a modified form of sign language. In turn, the child's responses include a form of sign language sometimes called "baby sign."

It's clear that our brains have a biological propensity to help us acquire at least one language, but the process of language learning is not exclusively hardwired into us. Much evidence suggests that the environment plays a critical role, too. Early behaviourists, including B. F. Skinner (1957), suggested that language is acquired as a result of instrumental conditioning. Toddlers are rewarded with praise for producing appropriate speech, and ignored or scolded for failure to do so. As you may have noticed, however, parents, caregivers, and other older people do not usually systematically reward toddlers for correct speech. The 2-year-old who says, "Want cookie," is just as likely to get one as another child who can ask, "Please, may I have a cookie?" Conditioning alone, therefore, cannot explain language learning.

Interactive theories suggest that experience works along with biological developmental periods to enhance and guide language learning (Goldberg, 2008). As we have described, for instance, if a baby isn't exposed to certain phonemes, her capacity to distinguish among these sounds diminishes.

The social environments of most babies and young children also typically offer a high degree of very interactive speech. Most adults in most cultures talk to babies with a special intonation in their voices; a high-pitched and sometimes exaggerated speech that is spoken directly to an infant or child is called **child-directed speech** (Fernald et al., 1989). Child-directed speech may help babies learn words by keeping them interested in the stimulus generating them. The patterns of child-directed speech are often rich in emotions, which may have the added benefit of fostering a close emotional relationship between caregiver and child, thus enhancing the quality and quantity of communication.

child-directed speech speech characterized by exaggerated emotional responses and a slower pace that is common among caregivers communicating with babies and young children.

Child-directed speech is also observed when parents use sign language to communicate with babies. Whether the adult, child, or both are deaf, the use of sign language during the learning phase naturally takes the form of child-directed speech—slower in the formation of the hand signs, with longer pauses in between signs and exaggeration of facial expressions of emotions (Masataka, 1998). Child-directed speech arises naturally; people adopt it without any formal instruction, suggesting that humans seem to have a biological predisposition to teach effective communication to the very young (Cooper & Aslin, 1994; Bornstein et al., 1992).

The development of syntax, or grammatical rules, also suggests an interaction of biology and environment. Even in children with hearing loss who are not formally trained in sign language but have instead developed their own form of signing, there is evidence of a grammatical structure. These findings suggest that the brain is predisposed to create a set of rules by which language will be used. Grammar rules differ from language to language, but within a given language, they remain the same and are followed fairly consistently by speakers of the language (Tomasello, 1999).

Even with such a strong biological basis, however, grammar is still affected by environment. We can see the effects of environment when children begin formal education. Children typically acquire a large vocabulary and the ability to form grammatically correct sentences by about age 4, generally before they receive formal training in grammar (Tager-Flusberg, 2001). Once grammatical rules are consciously learned, however, children become more prone to errors. For example, once children learn that the suffix *-ed* refers to the past tense, they apply *-ed* to verbs that are irregular. A child who previously used the past tense of "*think*" correctly as "*thought*," may begin to say "*thinked*." Such mistakes are referred to as **overregularization** (Maratsos, 2000). They provide evidence that, while the tendency to readily pick up syntax exists in the very young, some aspects of grammar are learned. At the very least, there are two systems for language acquisition: one that is automatic and the other that requires conscious attention and can be learned explicitly. Overregularization is an example of how the conscious learning system can interfere with—and actually, temporarily, do a worse job than—the unconscious system of language acquisition.

overregularization the process by which elementary school children apply learned grammatical rules to improperly "correct" an irregular part of speech, such as a verb.

Critical Period for Language Learning? The Case of Genie

In 1970, an adolescent girl and her blind mother were delivered to a welfare office in California (Rymer, 1994). At the hands of her sadistic father, the girl, named Genie, had spent her entire life in isolation chained to a potty chair. She was rarely spoken to except in a punitive way ("stop it"). Her father communicated with her mostly by grunting and barking. At age 13, when her mother finally left the father, Genie had been exposed to almost no speech and appeared to be nearly mute. Her vocabulary consisted of about 20 words.

Age 13 is the time at which most researchers had assumed that the critical period for language acquisition is over. This assumption is based on the fact that after this age, people learn new languages with greater difficulty and typically speak their second languages with accents. Because Genie was 13 years old at the time when she was rescued, she was a tragic test case of whether a critical period for language exists.

Genie's experiences tended to provide support for the theory that a sensitive period for language learning does exist. During the years that followed her rescue, Genie received extensive, interactive language training. Although she did initially show progress in expanding her vocabulary, it was always limited and didn't include the acquisition of grammatical rules. Unfortunately, Genie's vocabulary regressed even further when she was under stress.

Although the case of Genie seems to support the language critical period theory, it's important to keep in mind that Genie was not only deprived of language, but also subjected to extreme physical and emotional abuse that may have contributed significantly to her inability to learn (Kyle, 1980). It has also been suggested that she may have been mildly intellectually disabled at birth, a factor which could partially limit the critical period theory (Jones, 1995). Regardless, however, it is clear that early experiences are important in first language acquisition.

Learning to Read In western cultures, most children begin formal education and start learning to read at around the ages of 5 or 6. Reading is a complicated behaviour that emerges considerably after the foundations of language production and comprehension have been laid down.

Identical genes, different reading skills. These 5-year-old identical twins are reading as part of a study in Australia investigating how much of one's reading and spelling abilities are related to genes and how much are related to upbringing and schooling.

Carleton University researchers Monique Sénéchal and Jo-Anne LeFevre (2001) have shown that children typically begin the process of learning to read by telling stories from looking at pictures in a book and attempting to recognize a few simple words (Sénéchal & LeFevre, 2001). In schools in North America, reading and writing are usually a main focus of grade 1 and grade 2. By the end of grade 2 (around age 8), reading becomes much less laborious for most children, as it transitions to an automatic process, one that requires little or no conscious thought (Ely, 1997). At this same point, parents usually start to notice their children excitedly pointing out letters and words they recognize on signs and billboards. Reading becomes challenging and fun as children begin to acquire the basic skills.

Once reading becomes automatic, most people become very proficient at it. Just as we are capable of understanding spoken fragments of sentences or words spoken in foreign accents, we can understand written abbreviations with ease. Consider the abbreviated writing of the text message: U R L8. It's very easy to determine that this means, "You are late," because the phonemes are identical to those that are used to correctly spell out these words. More complicated and non-phonetic written messages require explicit learning. Consider the abbreviated writing of the text message: I ctn I g2g il ttyl. Without prior knowledge of the acronyms *ctn, g2g*, and *ttyl*, the message, "I can't talk now, I've got to go, I'll talk to you later" would remain a mystery.

Language — WHAT HAPPENS IN THE BRAIN?

In most people, language production and comprehension centres are located in the left hemisphere of the brain. In a small percentage of people (about 5 percent), the language centres are lateralized to the right hemisphere of the brain. In some cases, language involves both hemispheres (Taylor & Taylor, 1990). One area of the left hemisphere of the brain, known as Broca's area, is important for our ability to speak, while another area, called Wernicke's area, is important in language comprehension. In a typical conversation, both areas would be active at once, along with other parts of the brain.

Broca's area a region in the frontal lobes near the motor cortex that is important for speech production.

Broca's aphasia a neurological condition arising from damage to Broca's area where the patient is unable to produce coherent speech.

Broca's Area Broca's area is located in the frontal lobe in what is technically the motor association cortex (Damasio & Geschwind, 1984). This area was named after the neurologist who first described patients with damage to this region. People who suffer damage in or near Broca's area develop a set of symptoms called Broca's aphasia. The term *aphasia* can refer to an inability either in language production or in language comprehension. In Broca's aphasia, the problem is with production; people have great difficulty speaking. They speak unusually slowly and have trouble with pronunciations (Mohr et al., 1978).

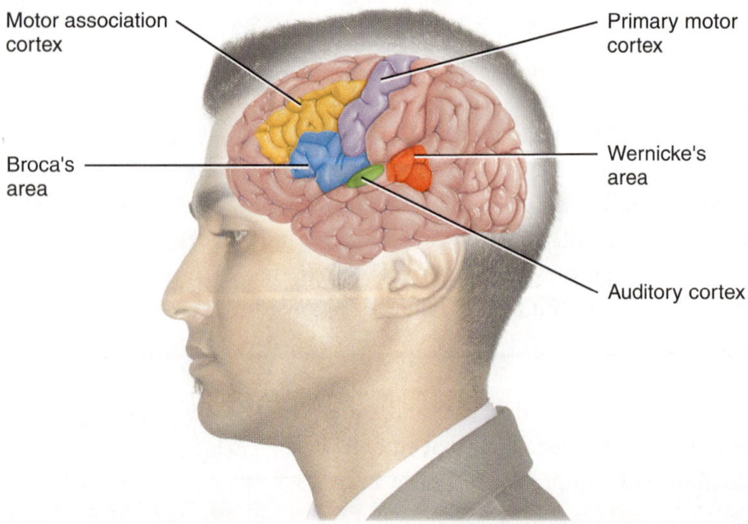

Because Broca's area is located in the motor association cortex, many researchers believe that the difficulty in speaking that characterizes Broca's aphasia is caused by difficulties in making the necessary movements. Speaking requires a complex set of movements of the lips, tongue, and larynx, and movements are largely controlled by the primary motor cortex in the brain. The content of patients' speech supports the theory that difficulties in movement, rather than in thinking, are the major problems when Broca's area is damaged. Although difficult to follow, the speech of most people with Broca's aphasia makes sense. They have clear thoughts to communicate, but they have great difficulty getting them out (Broca, 1861; Denes & Pizzaliglio, 1999).

Damage to Broca's area can, however, also produce an inability to speak with proper grammar, a condition referred to as agrammatism. This deficit suggests that our ability to use grammar is stored close to or within the same neural tissue that is responsible for speech production (Kean, 1977). This close neuroanatomical relationship probably explains how grammar is automatic once it is learned. When we speak, we don't need to carefully construct grammatically correct sentences.

agrammatism a neurological condition arising from damage to a brain region just anterior to Broca's area, where the patient is incapable of using words in grammatical sequence.

The agrammatism suffered by people with Broca's aphasia also tends to be linked to mild impairments in language comprehension (Schwartz, Saffran, & Marin, 1980). Individuals affected with this form of aphasia can produce some connected speech, but their speech is missing all of the required grammatical words (such as "the," "is," "and," "ing," "ed," or "s"). So, instead of saying, "She is going," the person with agrammatism might say, "She go." In research, people with Broca's aphasia who were asked to point to the correct picture that illustrated a phrase such as "the cat ate the food" could do so. If researchers asked these people to point to a nonsense picture illustrating the phrase "the cow was on the car," however, they were almost as likely to choose a picture of a car on a cow as to choose the correct one. The researchers concluded that people with Broca's aphasia were not able to use clues such as grammar and word order to determine the meaning of a sentence that was not obvious from its individual words.

Canadian Sign. Deaf Canadians communicate using either a version of American Sign Language (ASL) or langue des signes québécoise (LSQ). The sign above is not found in ASL but is used by Canadian signers to say "Canada." The fist is used to tap the chest, as if you were grabbing the shirt. A mnemonic for remembering this sign is the phrase "The Mounties always get their man" (even if they don't actually grab him by the shirt).

Neuroimaging studies of people without brain damage have confirmed much of what neurologists and neuropsychologists have discovered from studying the behaviour of people with Broca's aphasia (Gernsbacher & Kaschak, 2003). Broca's area itself is active during speaking, and a closely located area just in front of Broca's area becomes active when we try to comprehend sentences with complicated grammar.

Sign language uses brain areas similar to those important in spoken language. Neuroimaging studies show that, in people with intact brains, Broca's area and Wernicke's area are activated during signing (Braun, Guillemin, Hosey, & Varga, 2001). Since producing sign language does not require actual speech production, it does not involve as much activation of Broca's area. However, because sign language does involve use of grammar to construct meaningful sentences, using sign language activates the same neural tissue near Broca's area involved in the use of grammar when speaking. Deaf people with brain damage around Broca's area can experience deficits in grammar use with signing (Corina, 1998).

Wernicke's Area Although the tissue near Broca's area seems to contribute to the comprehension of grammar in language, other parts of the brain are even more important for language comprehension. Because, for most people, speech comprehension begins when we hear, it is not surprising that the brain regions most important for understanding speech are located near the auditory cortex in the upper part of the left temporal lobe. Wernicke's area was first identified by a neurologist named Wernicke, who studied patients with brain damage in this area of the temporal cortex. People who suffer destruction to this part of the brain have Wernicke's aphasia. These individuals have impairment in auditory comprehension; they cannot understand speech and therefore produce fluent but disordered speech. In other words, patients with Wernicke's aphasia are fully capable of talking, but their speech makes no sense. For example, in response to being asked, "Are there flowers on the bush?," a patient might answer something like this, "Yes. I

Wernicke's area a brain region located in the temporal lobe that is important for language comprehension.

Wernicke's aphasia a neurological condition associated with damage to Wernicke's area where a person cannot understand language.

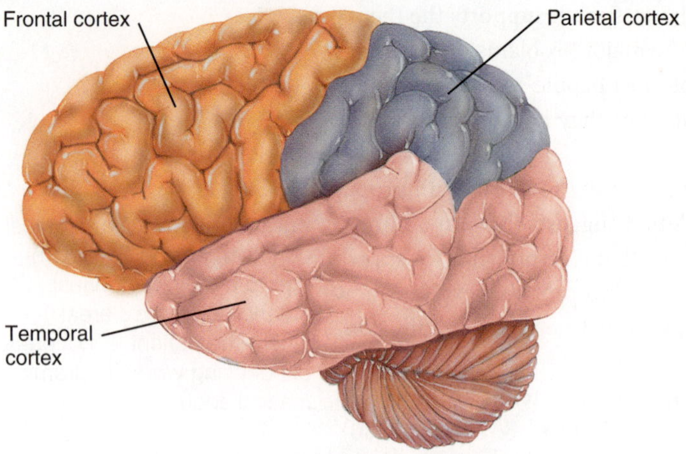

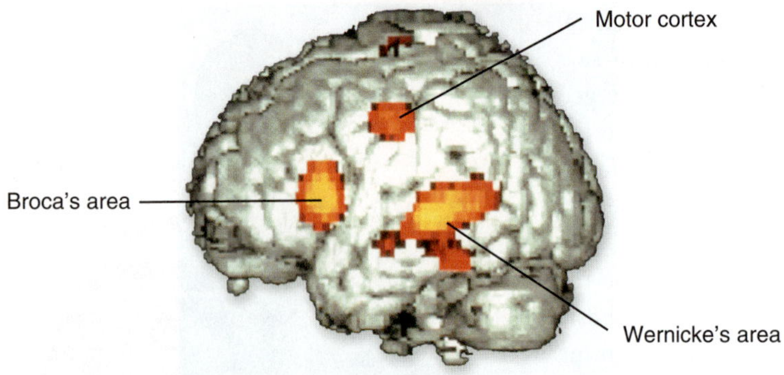

Scanning for language comprehension. This PET scan displays the brain activity of a person who is repeating the words of another individual. Such vocal repetitions activate (*red and orange*) his Broca's area for speech production, Wernicke's area for language comprehension, and a motor region tied to vocalizations.

can eat and listen and walking and talking for this now you."

Other Brain Regions In addition to Broca's and Wernicke's areas, other brain regions have important functions in specific aspects of language. For instance, the box on cursing accompanying this section describes how the amygdala, a brain region important for fear and aggression, appears to be involved in the use of profanity (Jay, 1999).

Most people also typically use regions in the right hemisphere to understand figurative language, such as metaphors. In figurative language, the meaning of a phrase is different from the literal meaning of the words used in the phrase. Damage to the right hemisphere can lead to taking figurative language literally (Schmidt, DeBuse, & Seger, 2007). For instance, a person might think the phrase "hold your horses" means to grab hold of an actual horse. Metaphors are figures of speech that compare unlike things. Damage to the right hemisphere might lead a person to think that you live with an actual farm animal when you say, "My roommate is a total pig." Perhaps because understanding humour requires a grasp of abstract language—humour often involves the use of puns and metaphors—right hemisphere damage can also disrupt the ability to understand a joke.

A role for the right hemisphere in processing information about metaphors has been demonstrated using a relatively new technique in brain science called *transcranial magnetic stimulation* or *TMS*. Researchers can aim TMS, which delivers a strong magnetic signal, into a participant's head to temporarily inactivate a specific brain region. One such study found that TMS of the right hemisphere temporarily impaired the ability of humans to understand metaphors, and that this impairment was greatest when the metaphors were unfamiliar to the participants (Pobric et al., 2008).

If a person learns two or more languages simultaneously as a child, Broca's and Wernicke's areas are involved in the use of all languages. Interestingly, however, if we do not learn a second language (or third or fourth) until adulthood, the brain does not rely as heavily on Broca's and Wernicke's areas (Perani et al., 1998). Instead, it recruits other circuits to aid in the learning process. Among these are parts of the prefrontal cortex, important for working memory, and the temporal lobe, which is active in the acquisition of semantic information. The recruitment of additional brain regions not involved in language learning early in life may contribute to the greater difficulty of learning a language later in life.

Reading also involves a wide range of brain regions. The physical actions required to read activate areas of the brain that aid in visual processing and motor functions. Since reading involves eye movements, for example, it recruits a brain region in the frontal lobe called the *frontal eye fields*. The content of what we read also affects which brain areas become more active during reading. Words of particular emotional importance, such as obscenities or disgust words, activate the amygdala. When we read words that evoke odours, such as *garlic* or *cinnamon*, the primary olfactory, or smell-related, regions of the brain become activated (González et al., 2006).

What the @#?!—Why Curse?

All languages have taboo words, those that are controversial and not considered to be part of neutral conversation. Across cultures, taboo or curse words seem to fall into one of three general categories: religious references, sexual references, and excrement references. The relative weight of each of these categories of curse words differs according to cultural beliefs. Religious profanity (such as *OMG*) is considered to be much milder in English Canada than in French Canada, where religious beliefs have played a more central cultural role.

People swear for a variety of reasons, including for intimidation, to show off, to emphasize a point, and to express negative emotions in response to a mishap. Expletives are often used to get attention and intimidate. They are commonly associated with anger. It is not surprising that the brain regions activated by swearing or hearing swear words are those that are involved in aggression and fear. Use of profanity involves activation of the amygdala, a primitive brain region that is important for emotions, including fear and rage.

It appears that the same neural circuitry that humans use for swearing is also important to other animals for responding to basic emotions, even though the manner of expressing these emotions is different. The amygdala is involved in expressions of fear and aggression in nonhumans, including monkeys, cats, and rats. While these animals are known to vocalize loudly under threatening circumstances, they can't speak (Jay, 1999). We can only imagine what they might say if they could.

Language HOW WE DIFFER

There is considerable variability among the normal population in the rate at which language is acquired and the size of vocabulary and overall verbal skills. Some evidence suggests that males and females may differ in language skills. There are even differences in the number of languages that we acquire. Although all normal people become proficient in at least one language, some people are multilingual and can become fluent in many different languages.

Language diversity. Many Canadians speak a second language, while many acquire three or more. Canadian children may acquire English, French, Inuit or any one of the many languages spoken in Canada.

Differences Among Individuals Some of the variability in the rate of language acquisition is due to our environments. Our vocabulary size, for example, is affected by our environment, particularly early in life. For example, as described in the box earlier in the chapter, children in low-income households often hear fewer words and have smaller vocabularies when they start school than those from more affluent families.

There is also a great degree of variability in the normal population with regard to reading and writing skills. For instance, people differ substantially in the speed with which they can read. This skill seems to be tied to eye movements. In English, words are written on the page from left to right, and reading speed is greatest for individuals whose eyes move in the same left-to-right direction as the printed words, with no backtracking. Slower readers tend to not only pause for longer periods of time over individual words, but also to backtrack, moving their eyes back to words already passed (Lahey et al., 1982). It's not clear whether the less fluid eye movements occur because reading is more difficult, or whether the backtracking eye movements are a distraction that interferes with rapid reading.

Gender Differences in Language One difference in verbal learning and overall skills that may be related, at least in part, to genetics is a notable gender difference in early language learning. Girls tend to learn to talk earlier, and on average, girls acquire speech

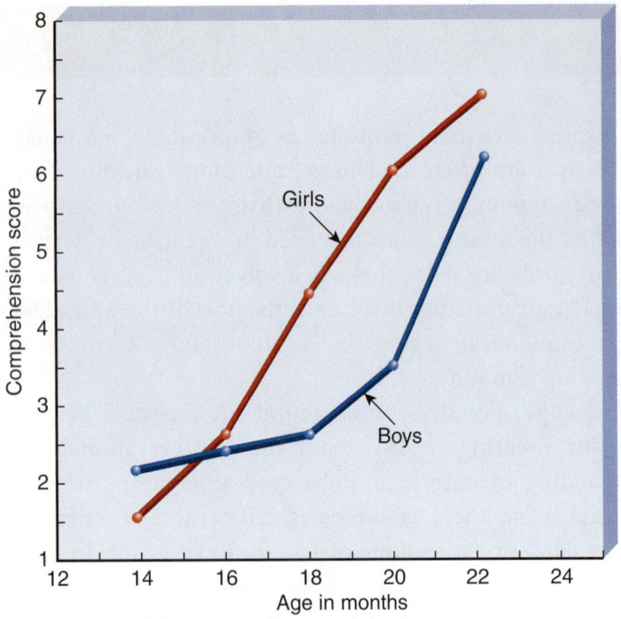

FIGURE 9-3 Gender differences in speech comprehension. Early on, there is a notable difference in language comprehension between girls and boys. Girls comprehend language at a faster rate, but this gender gap disappears by about age 2 (Reznick & Goldfield, 1992).

and language comprehension at a faster rate than boys (**Figure 9-3**) (Reznick & Goldfield, 1992). These early differences often diminish by about age 2, however, when those boys slower to acquire language catch up.

Although boys may catch up in speaking skills, girls still seem to outpace boys in the language skills used in elementary school. As a group, girls score higher on tests of English ability, according to well-known Canadian researcher Doreen Kimura (2000), retired but currently working at Simon Fraser University in Burnaby, British Columbia. It's not clear, however, whether this difference is related to a real gender difference in language ability, or to a gender difference in some of the skills necessary to be a good student, such as paying attention, taking legible notes, and studying. By young adulthood, these differences are gone. There are no substantial male–female differences in overall critical reading or writing scores.

As discussed in Chapter 7, when considering gender differences, remember to keep in mind that, even though statistical differences may exist between average scores of boys and girls or men and women, these differences do not tell us anything about individuals. Many boys acquire language skills very rapidly and become talented writers and speakers as adults.

Gender differences. Girls tend to outpace boys in language skills during elementary school.

Another important point to consider is that the gender difference in language acquisition may have an experiential component. Because boys tend to be more active than girls, and girls tend to be more social than boys, it's possible that girls are exposed to a higher degree of interactive language than boys. If young boys are constantly on the move, exploring the environment may occupy more time than language learning.

Despite the fact that there do not appear to be significant differences in overall verbal ability between adult men and women, some evidence suggests a difference in the way that women and men process language information. Neuroimaging studies have shown that, on average, women are more likely to use both hemispheres of the brain to process language information, whereas language processing in men tends to be more lateralized (Clements et al., 2006). The extent to which these differences in recruitment of neural circuitry during language processing between men and women have any functional consequence remains to be determined.

Learning More Than One Language Many children grow up in multilingual homes, where two or more languages are spoken. Such children tend to learn to speak and understand language at slightly later ages than children who only need to learn a single language (Genesee et al., 1978). The greater amount of information and decoding necessary to learn two or more languages simultaneously may explain the very slight lag.

Like first languages, multiple languages are also most readily acquired by the very young. In adulthood, the language learning process is labour intensive and often remains incomplete. By the age of 13, our language learning ability has declined substantially (**Figure 9-4**) (Johnson & Newport, 1989). The difference can be seen with accents. People who learn to speak English as a second language as children speak it without an accent, whereas those who learn it as teens or adults speak English less fluidly and typically with the accent of their native tongue. A similar phenomenon exists for deaf children learning sign language. After about age 13, it becomes more difficult to learn this skill (Johnson & Newport, 1989). Knowing this, many of us wish we had been exposed to multiple languages

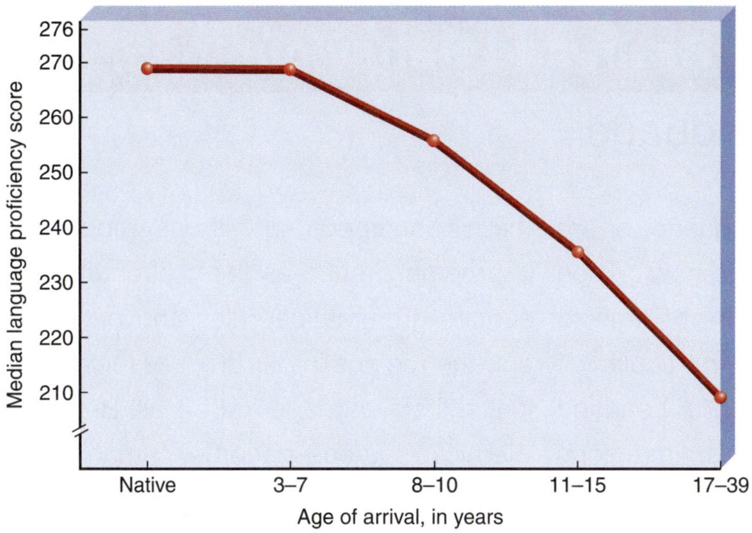

FIGURE 9-4 The earlier we learn a new language, the more proficient we become. Immigrants' mastery of English depends on when they begin the learning process. The proficiency of those adults who started learning their new language before age 7 is comparable to that of native speakers. However, the proficiency of those who started acquiring the language in young adulthood is much poorer (Johnson & Newport, 1989).

as youngsters. Those fortunate enough to have this experience can become fluent in several languages without any formal study. See "Your Brain and Behaviour: Learning a Second Language" on the following pages.

Before You Go On

www.wiley.com/go/comer

What Do You Know?

1. What is language and how does language production differ from language comprehension?
2. What are phonology, morphology, syntax, and pragmatics?
3. What is the typical sequence of language acquisition for most babies?
4. Where are Broca's and Wernicke's areas located in the brain? What is the primary function of each of these areas?

SCAN TO GET THE ANSWERS

What Do You Think?

Should preschools and early grades of elementary schools in Canada be required to teach children multiple languages? What might be the advantages and drawbacks for children of such schooling?

The Relationship Between Language and Thought

LEARNING OBJECTIVE 2

Describe how thought and language are related and summarize the linguistic relativity hypothesis.

Many of us consider our thoughts to be primarily related to language. Since we often have no trouble responding automatically with words in a conversation, it can seem that language is the natural driving force of thought. One influential psychological theory suggests that our language controls and limits our thoughts. In many cases, however, complex thoughts occur in the absence of language. So what is the relationship between thought and language? Is language simply a tool for expressing our thoughts? Or are our thoughts a consequence of the language we learn and the things we are told about the world using our native language? We will consider a few of the areas of investigation related to this question of the relationship between thought and language. You will see that the answers are not simple and not yet complete.

Tying It Together: **Your Brain and Behaviour**

Learning a Second Language

Do you speak more than one language, or are you learning a second language now? Then you probably know that it takes a lot of time to become fluent in a second language, particularly if you didn't start to learn as a young child. Learning a second language not only engages brain regions that are involved in language production and comprehension, it also activates areas important for learning semantic information, such as the hippocampus, and those important for working memory, such as the prefrontal cortex. As we acquire grammatical rules and become more fluent, the regions in our brain associated with learning a first language—such as Broca's area and Wernicke's area—become primarily involved. As we activate these language production and comprehension areas more and more, we rely less and less on semantic and working memory regions.

Questions

1. **How do patterns of brain activity change as we become more fluent in a second language?**
2. **Which part of the brain is most active when we switch from using our first language to using a second language?**
3. **Is a person who achieves fluency in a second language likely to show the exact same patterns of brain activation while using his or her first language versus the second language? Explain.**

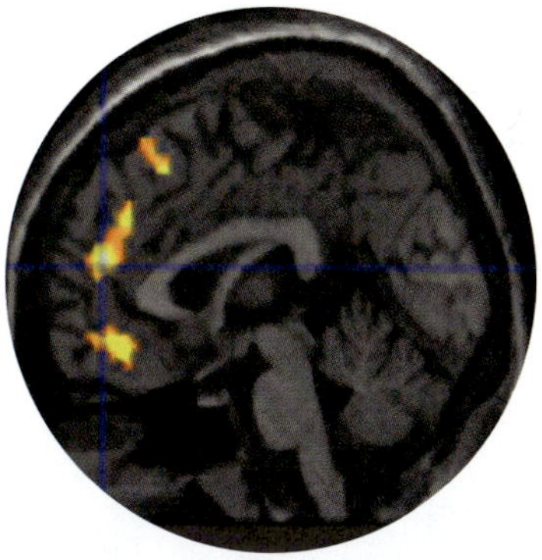

BECOMING FLUENT

As we become fluent in a second language, the brain becomes less active, as shown on these brain scans of someone new to a second language (intense red areas, top) versus someone with years of second language experience (lighter red areas, bottom). So, better performance means less brain activity.

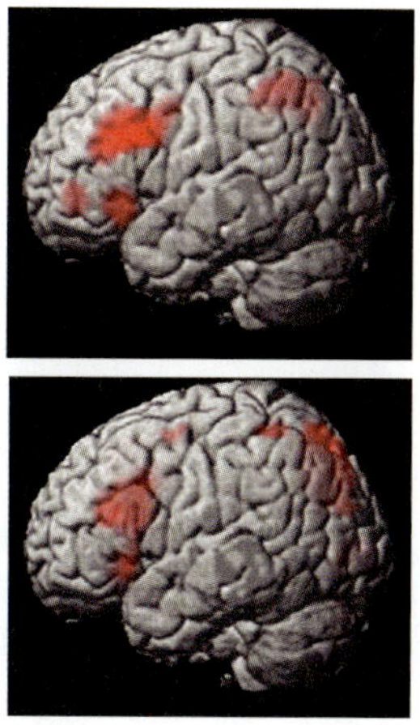

SWITCHING FROM ONE LANGUAGE TO THE OTHER

Once you have learned a second language, switching from your first language to the second one involves the prefrontal cortex, as shown here in this fMRI image (yellow areas). Switching from your second language back to your native tongue doesn't require the use of these brain areas, probably because it takes less effort.

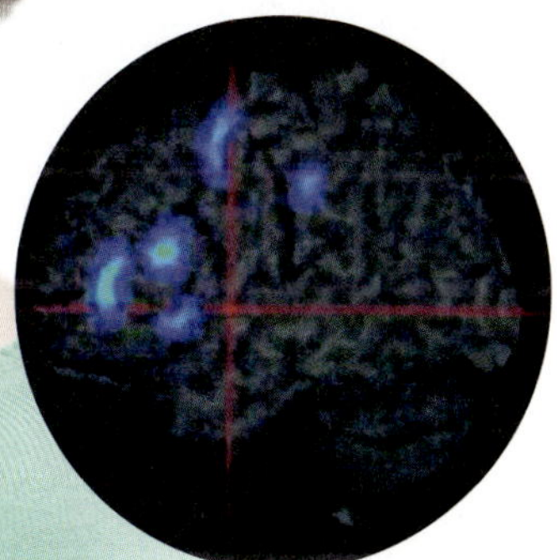

BEING BILINGUAL

But even when we reach the same level of proficiency in a second language as with a first language, the second language requires more brain activation, shown here (blue areas) in this fMRI image.

Thinking Without Words: Mental Imagery and Spatial Navigation

mental imagery picturing things in your mind.

During the weeks before spring break, you may enjoy picturing yourself lying in a hammock sipping a cool drink while overlooking the coast of Cuba, or skiing down the slopes of the Rocky Mountains in Banff National Park. **Mental imagery** refers to thoughts that involve conjuring internal visual representations of stored sensory input. Most of our mental imagery does not involve language (Finke, 1989).

Another good example where language doesn't play a major role in thinking can be observed with spatial navigation thinking. Although some people use narrative to remember directions, such as, "Turn right at the second light on Main Street," in many cases, spatial thinking occurs in the form of visual imagery. You may remember the appearance of certain street corners and automatically turn right when you are triggered to do so by your visual system. Some people use dead reckoning or a "sense of direction" to navigate. This kind of directional skill—knowing that a certain direction is north, for example—is not language driven.

PSYCHOLOGY AROUND US Driving on Autopilot

For most people, spatial navigation becomes almost automatic, especially when this navigation is part of their routine. Consider as an example a daily commute to work or school. You may climb into the car, turn on the engine, and later find yourself at your destination without recalling the details of the drive. In fact, some people become so lost in their thoughts while driving that they forget if they planned to go somewhere special or unusual at the end of the day. You may arrive at your house before even realizing that you had intended to go to the store on your way home, for example.

Our ability to use imagery to solve problems is often based closely on our spatial memories. Studies have shown that we appear to search our actual relevant memories to solve tasks requiring mental imagery. For example, if researchers give participants photos of rooms that are long and narrow, with regularly spaced objects in them, and later ask the participants to describe the objects located in those rooms, the participants do so with a greater lag time between objects than if asked to carry out a similar task after looking at a photo of a smaller room (Kosslyn & Shin, 1991).

> "Most events are inexpressible, taking place in a realm which no word has ever entered."
> —*Rainer Maria Rilke, German poet*

Interestingly, using mental imagery activates many of the same brain regions as are used for the sensory experience itself. Neuroimaging technology has allowed us to observe which regions of the brain become most active when people think. This type of research suggests that thinking about something can actually activate the same brain regions as sensing or doing it (Goldberg, Perfetti, & Schneider, 2006). There are many examples:

- When you visualize or picture in your mind an event or scene, your brain activates the visual areas that would be active if you were actually gazing at the event or scene (O'Craven & Kanwisher, 2000).
- Thinking about tastes and odours activates many of the same gustatory and olfactory brain regions involved when you really do taste or smell something (Bensafi, Sobel, & Khan, 2007).
- Thinking about fearful and anxiety-provoking subjects activates the amygdala, an area involved in anger, fear, and stress (Shin et al., 2004).

And when we do have thoughts that involve language, they activate the frontal and temporal lobes, the same areas used when we comprehend or produce spoken language.

Although some of our thinking involves mental imagery, it is obviously not sufficient for all of the complicated thoughts humans have. There are many concepts that do not have an adequate mental image. Consider thinking about love. Some symbols of love, such as a heart or Cupid with his arrow, are associated with love, but they hardly tell the whole story. Even conjuring mental images of our loved ones doesn't adequately express our thoughts about love in general. As we will discuss in the rest of the chapter, much of our thinking involves the use of words, often in combination with imagery.

The Influence of Language on Thought

Many psychologists believe that language influences our thinking a great deal. This older theory about the relationship between thought and language is called the **linguistic relativity hypothesis**. The linguistic relativity hypothesis was advanced by Edward Sapir and Benjamin Lee Whorf (Sapir, 1921; Whorf, 1940, 1956) and suggests that the more words we have available to us related to a single concept, the more complex and detailed our thoughts are about that object or idea.

linguistic relativity hypothesis hypothesis suggesting that the vocabulary available for objects or concepts in a language influences how speakers of that language think about them.

Evidence in support of the linguistic relativity hypothesis comes from cross-cultural studies that reveal large discrepancies in the number of words various languages dedicate to certain characteristics or objects. Studies have shown that extensive vocabularies for certain characteristics can lead to an ability to make finer distinctions along that dimension (Davies & Corbett, 1997). The English language, for example, has many words used to distinguish different colours. We can describe nuances of difference in shades of the colour blue, for example, by using words such as *azure, cobalt, cyan, indigo, turquoise, aquamarine,* and more. By contrast, members of the Dani tribe of Papua New Guinea have in their entire language only two words to distinguish colour, one word for light and the other for dark. These people are not colour-blind. They can perceive differences in colour, but they do not have words to describe them (Heider, 1972). The linguistic relativity hypothesis suggests that because English-speaking people have words for subtle concepts or distinctions regarding colour, we are encouraged to think more about them than we would if, like the Dani, our vocabulary did not include those words. So the strong version of the linguistic relativity hypothesis is not supported—but are there ways in which language shapes thought? More recent research suggests that there are.

Far from colour-blind. The colourful and carefully-blended war decorations of Dani tribesmen show that these individuals from Papua New Guinea are not colour-blind, despite their limited vocabulary for colours.

We learn about the world partly through our personal experiences. We also learn about the world by being told about it. Many of the concepts we learn as we develop have been put together and managed within the particular sociocultural perspective of the community in which we live. If our cultural community maps a particular concept in a particular way, then that is how we will learn that concept. Therefore the difficulty children experience when acquiring concepts depends on the way the concept is structured in the local cultural community. Think about the concept of *living things*. What sorts of things are living things? In English we make several distinctions within the concept of living things (see **Figure 9-5**). English speakers first distinguish between plants and animals, but then sometimes further divide animals into human and non-human animals. The rules about when it is appropriate or insulting to refer to another person as an animal are hard to learn. For example, English-speaking children need to learn which of the following is insulting: "You are such a pig," versus "You sing like a bird." In contrast, in Indonesia living things are conceptually divided into three categories: humans, animals, and plants. With no guesswork, this structure is easier to manage and therefore Indonesian children can properly understand and master the concept of living things at an earlier age than children speaking English can (Waxman & Medin, 2006). The simpler language structure for the concepts makes it easier to acquire developmentally.

Another example of the way that language can shape thought starts with what the comedian Steve Martin once said, "Boy, those French have a different word for everything!"

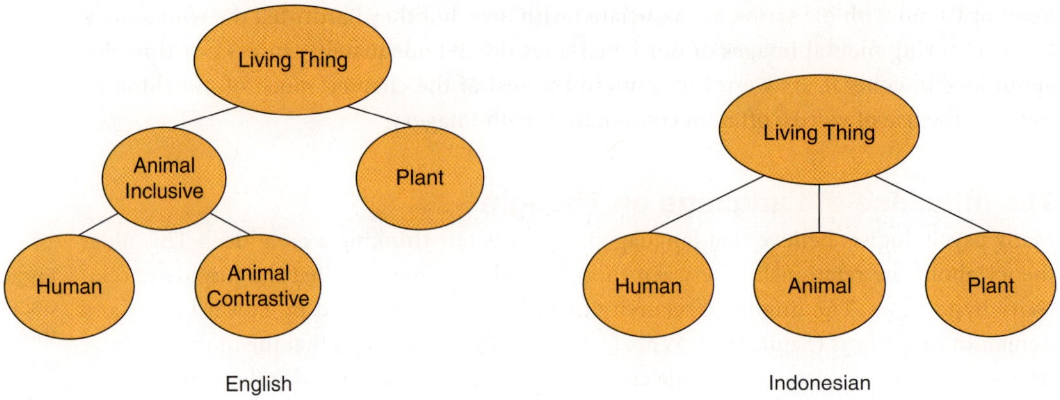

FIGURE 9-5 Cultural conceptions of living things. In English we make a subordinate distinction beneath our concept of animals to distinguish humans from animals, whereas in Indonesia the distinction is simple, handled at the first basic level.

While of course that is true, as we have just seen, the linguistic relativism theory suggested that our words actually map out the world differently. The relationship between thought and language, however, goes both ways. Even if a culture has many words for snow (the linguistic relativity hypothesis), it is possible to explain the differences so that those without specific words for different types of snow can still understand the differences.

On the other hand, having a very specific word for a complex social situation suggests a clearer understanding of the situation. Howard Rheingold (2000) set out to collect words from various languages that concisely capture specific social situations. For example, the Mayan term "bol" means something like "stupid in-laws" in English, whereas the German term "treppenwitz" means something like "clever remark that comes to mind when it is too late to use it," and the Japanese term "kyoikumama" means something like "mother who pushes her child to academic achievement," and, last, our favourite, "Korinthenkacker" is a German word that literally translates to "raisin-sh%#@er" and refers to "a person overly concerned with trivial details."

So the ways that our socio-cultural communities divide up the world and our experiences lead to the emergence of new concepts, words, or phrases that are used in language to communicate our shared observations. Through those communications, we not only acquire a language, but also a way of thinking about the world.

Before You Go On

www.wiley.com/go/comer

What Do You Know?

5. What is mental imagery? What parts of the brain does mental imagery involve?
6. What research evidence suggests that we use mental imagery to solve problems involving our spatial memories?
7. What does the linguistic relativity hypothesis suggest about the influence of our language on our thinking and what research has been done? What are some more recent examples of this type of influence?

SCAN TO GET THE ANSWERS

What Do You Think?

In what ways do you believe your language influences your thoughts?

Thought

LEARNING OBJECTIVE 3

Describe and summarize research on thinking processes, including problem solving, decision making, and metacognition.

We can think in many different ways. The study of cognition includes, for example, mental imagery and spatial navigation, as we have seen. Cognitive scientists also study the development of our thinking abilities, how we solve problems, how we make decisions, and even how we think about our own thoughts. We will take a look at some of their major findings in the remainder of this chapter. Our thinking abilities are truly impressive, but the variety and complexity of thought also means we are sometimes vulnerable to problems in our thinking. We'll also discuss two psychological disorders that are characterized primarily by disruptions in thought processes.

Different forms of thinking develop at different rates. Thoughts that involve language emerge around the time that language capabilities are forming, whereas those that involve reasoning emerge later. Michael Chandler at UBC and Jeremy Carpendale at Simon Fraser University (1998) argue that skills requiring self-awareness, such as formulating or changing long-term plans and carrying them out, require a type of thought that develops relatively late in children—not until around the time of school entrance. Changes in our thinking continue to occur throughout life. Teenagers and young adults become increasingly capable of making and carrying out long-term plans for their futures.

Thinking and Effort: Controlled and Automatic Processing

The distinction between controlled and automatic thinking is an important concept in cognitive psychology. As we discussed in Chapter 8 on memory, *controlled processing* is effortful and relies on a limited-capacity system, while *automatic processing* seems effortless. Automatic processing is not usually disrupted very much if we are distracted by other tasks. Experienced drivers can carry on a conversation while driving a car, for example. However, automatic processing, such as driving, can be severely disrupted by simultaneously engaging in a task that requires more attention than speaking, such as reading or sending a text message. Controlled processing requires more attention. Most of us cannot carry on a conversation while conducting multi-digit mental arithmetic; we must direct our thoughts toward the math problem.

Cognitive control refers to the ability to direct thought and action in accord with one's intentions (Carter, Botvinick, & Cohen, 1999). Some examples of this include:

cognitive control the ability to direct thought in accord with one's intentions.

- the ability to direct attention to a specific stimulus within other competing, and perhaps stronger, stimuli, such as finding the face you are looking for within a crowd
- maintaining a new piece of information in mind against distraction, such as remembering a telephone number until you dial while on your cell phone in a crowded mall
- overcoming a compelling behaviour, such as not scratching a very itchy mosquito bite
- pursuing a complex but unfamiliar behaviour, such as learning the moves of a new sport or how to work the controls of a new videogame
- responding flexibly and productively in new situations, such as playing a complex videogame that requires anticipating future consequences

The brain's ability of exert control over mental processing is referred to as executive function. People with damage to the frontal lobes often display a condition called dysexecutive syndrome, characterized by impairments in cognitive functions that depend on control, such as planning or the ability to flexibly respond in new situations. This deficit was dramatically documented in the classic case of Phineas Gage. As we discussed in Chapter 4, Gage was a railroad foreman who suffered damage to his prefrontal cortex when a metal spike was driven through his head in a construction accident. Before the accident, acquaintances described him as thoughtful, responsible, and of sound judgment, but following his injury, he was considered to be "capricious . . . and unable to settle on any of the plans he devised for future action (Harlow, 1868)." Changes such as these have been observed repeatedly in patients with damage to the frontal cortex.

executive function the brain's ability to control and manage the mental processing of information.

dysexecutive syndrome impairments in the ability to control and direct mental activities.

As we age, we also develop more capacity for cognitive control. Very young children, for example, often make decisions based on impulse; if they want the cookie and it's in view, they will grab it. For this reason, problems arise with social interactions. Preschool-aged children

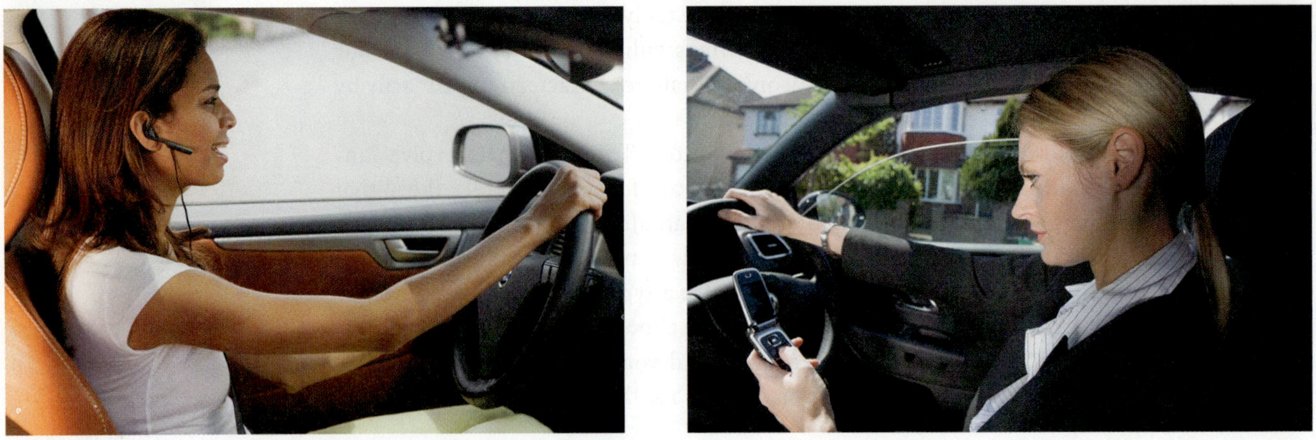

Automatic processing has its limits. Even automatic processing, such as that used when driving a car, can be severely interrupted by tasks that require significant attention, such as texting. Thus, to prevent car accidents, provincial laws typically allow people to converse (a relatively non-distracting activity) on a hands-free phone while driving, but forbid them to use a hand-held cell phone.

Enough for everyone. By the age of 6 to 8 years old, children have learned to better control their thoughts and actions in accord with their various intentions. Sharing everything from ice cream to toys becomes a more common occurrence.

will often fight over toys because they don't understand the concepts of waiting and fairness. As children grow, however, their decision-making process becomes more sophisticated. Usually by the time they are 6 to 8 years old, children are able to manage their impulses for the good of their interaction with their peers. During snacktime, William may save a cookie for Lydia, who is out of the room, rather than eat it himself. At an even later stage, between the ages of 9 and 12 years, children become able to make decisions with the long-term future in mind. They are more willing to make sacrifices in the immediate future to get a larger pay off later on. If given the option of getting one square of chocolate after completing a single math problem or an entire chocolate bar after a 24-hour waiting period, older children will often decide to hold out for the whole bar (Mischel, Shoda, & Rodriquez, 1989).

Thinking to Solve Problems

problem solving determining how to reach a goal.

One aspect of thinking that has received considerable attention from psychologists is that of *problem solving*. **Problem solving** is triggered by our desire to reach a goal. We must figure out how to get from our current state of affairs, which is in some way unsatisfactory, to our desired end state (Bourne, Dominowski, & Loftus, 1979). We use problem-solving skills in many avenues of life, from the formal mathematics problems we have all solved in school, to the informal day-to-day problems, such as how to get along with a roommate.

Defining Our Problems The first step in solving a problem is to figure out exactly what your problem is—to develop a representation of the problem.

On one end of the spectrum, we use formal problem-solving skills to solve math problems. Our goal in arithmetic is usually straightforward, to move from not knowing the correct answer to knowing it. Researchers refer to problems with easy-to-discern beginning and end states, such as arithmetic, as *well-defined problems*. We often find it fairly easy to find a strategy for solving well-defined problems because we can easily define what outcome we want from the start.

> "We only think when we are confronted with problems."
> —*John Dewey, American psychologist*

On the other end of the problem-solving spectrum are *ill-defined problems*, such as how to deal with a messy roommate. Our goal in this case might be difficult to define in precise terms. We may want to stop doing what we feel is an unfair share of housecleaning, but how will we know when we have reached that goal? As you might imagine, it's often more difficult to find solution strategies for ill-defined problems than it is for well-defined ones, because it is hard to define the desired outcome.

To define a problem, you must figure out your current state and your goal, and identify the differences between them. Consider the following problem. When driving home on a particular road, you need to make a left onto Main Street at a traffic light that is always very backed up at the time of day you travel. Your current state is frustration with the long wait at the light.

Your goal might be to find a faster way to make the turn. With this goal in mind, you could consider several ways to speed up the turn, such as altering the time of day you travel, driving faster to arrive at the intersection earlier, or merging into the line of waiting cars closer to the intersection. None of these solutions is ideal. If the problem is represented in a different way, however, a new solution may come to mind. You might, for example, change your question from, "How do I make a left onto Main Street?" to, "How can I get onto Main Street faster?"

Adopting a new goal such as this may cause you to notice that you could turn right into the parking lot of a shopping centre at the corner, then exit the lot quickly and legally onto Main Street in the direction you want to go—avoiding the left-hand turn entirely. Changing the representation of a problem doesn't guarantee you will find a solution, but it increases your chances of finding one if your new representation triggers you to consider new alternatives.

Strategies for Problem Solving After you have represented the problem, you must choose a strategy for finding a solution. Two major types of strategies—algorithms and heuristics—are used. An **algorithm** is a strategy that, if followed methodically, will always lead to a solution. For example, an algorithm strategy could be used to solve an arithmetic problem that includes adding up a series of 10 single-digit numbers by adding each number to the overall sum. Following this algorithm will produce a correct answer, but it can be time consuming. If you had to add up the total of 50 or 100 different numbers, you might begin to look for faster ways to solve the problem.

algorithm a strategy that always leads to a solution.

To save time and effort when solving problems, we often use a set of **heuristics**, or shortcut strategies. Instead of taking the time to add together a long list of numbers, you might just estimate the total. Heuristics often help us reach a satisfactory solution, but they do not guarantee a correct answer to a problem.

heuristic a shortcut thinking strategy.

You can use algorithm and heuristic strategies to solve problems in everyday life. Consider the steps you would take to find out whether or not a particular professor will be a good teacher for you before enrolling in his course. Using an algorithm method, you might question every student enrolled in the class the previous term. This method would give you the maximum amount of information and the greatest chance of reaching the correct answer. Using a heuristic strategy, you might ask a few students you know who took the course or examine the drop rate in the class for evidence of how many students decide against the course once enrolled. Heuristic methods save time and effort, but they are also riskier. Your few acquaintances might not learn as well from a teaching style that you like, for example.

Two heads are better than one. For many problems, better solutions are reached when multiple persons think the problem through together. Such collaborations may increase the likelihood of gathering sufficient information and reduce the chance of falling into common problem-solving traps.

Some helpful heuristic strategies in problem solving include working backward, forming subgoals, and searching for analogies.

- *Working backward* is helpful for problems with well-defined goals. Starting from your goal, you think backward, imagining a series of steps it would take you to move backward from your goal to your current state. Once you have determined the steps between your current state and the goal, you can actually follow them in a forward order. A working backwards example is the water lily problem. Imagine that you have planted a water lily on a pond. The number of leaves the lily produces on the water's surface doubles every day. On the 30th day, the number of leaves will cover the pond and kill off all the living things in the pond. You decide to cut out the lily when it has covered half the pond. What do you need to know to work out when to cut the lily (e.g., size of the pond, size of the lily leaves, etc.)? The answer? You need to know nothing if you work backwards, as you will cut the lily on the 29th day (before its coverage doubles one more time and covers the whole pond).

- *Forming subgoals* involves dividing a larger problem into smaller ones (Catrambone, 1998). If your ultimate goal is to find out if a professor will be a good teacher for you, you may form subgoals, such as asking three former students about the professor and arranging to sit in on one lecture. Another example that is a bit more specific is called the tower of Hanoi problem. Four disks of different diameters are stacked from largest up to smallest on the leftmost of three pegs. Your task is to shift the whole stack to the peg on the far right, but only by moving one disk at a time and by never having a larger disk set on top of a smaller disk. You can see an animated solution to this problem here: http://en.wikipedia.org/wiki/Tower_of_Hanoi. Note that the solution involves accomplishing a series of subgoals.

- *Searching for analogies* involves recalling similar problems that you have encountered (Holyoak & Morrison, 2005). Imagine you are driving a car borrowed from a friend and it breaks down. You may not have much experience figuring out what is wrong with cars but, if you have worked on motorcycles in the past, there may be some experiences that you can draw on analogously to try and figure out what is wrong with the car. Alternatively, you might remember calling your university's information technologies help desk to get help solving a computer problem, and come up with the idea of calling a relative or friend who has expertise with car repair.

We are not always aware of using a method to solve a problem. Sometimes we seem to solve a problem quickly, without intensive effort or concentration, through a phenomenon known as *insight*. In fact, several groundbreaking scientific discoveries have been described as "eureka" moments of insight. George de Mestral took his dog for a walk in the woods and when he returned home, George noticed his pants were covered in burrs that were hard to remove. Curious, he looked at one under a microscope and saw the small hooks at the ends of the burr spines. He thought about it and, eureka, Velcro was invented. Sometimes sudden solutions occur after an *incubation period* during which we have mentally "set aside" a problem that we've been working on. When we return to the problem after a period of time, the solution comes to mind without further conscious strategizing. Some studies suggest that type of problem solving is automatic (Novick & Bassock, 2005).

Problems in Problem Solving Sometimes we fall into patterns of thinking that make it difficult to solve problems to which those patterns don't apply. One common difficulty can happen early in representing the problem. We must define the problem using relevant information and ignore any irrelevant information. When deciding what movie to go and see, you might make your decision based on the number of times you have seen trailers of a movie, rather than looking at reviews or asking friends who may have seen it already. In fact, the number of trailers released may be a function of studio concerns about the quality of the movie.

> "If the only tool you have is a hammer, it is tempting to treat everything as if it were a nail."
> —*Abraham Maslow, American psychologist*

Other difficulties can occur when we get to the point of actually solving problems. Some of these are the result of heuristics. When we use the heuristic of looking for analogies, for example, we risk falling into a mental set, a tendency to use problem-solving strategies that have always worked in the past. If you have a certain solution in mind, you may see the problem as fitting that solution, when it does not. If you view getting onto Main Street with a mental set that sees the problem as how to make a left turn, you miss possible solutions that do not involve left turns (like making three right turns). The water jar problem shown in **Figure 9-6** and the nine-dot problem shown in **Figure 9-7** are good ways to practise overcoming mental sets.

	A	B	C	Goal
1	21	127	3	100
2	36	151	9	97
3	11	76	5	55
4	2	16	2	10
5	15	39	3	18

FIGURE 9-6 The water jar problem. Start at the top row (line number 1). Imagine that you have three containers (A, B, and C) that hold the number of units of water indicated across row #1. Using only those containers and no other measuring device, figure out how to end up with the goal amount of water listed in the last column of the table for that row. When you have a solution, move down to the next row and solve that problem as well. Keep moving down until you have solved all rows. Now show this problem to a friend, but have her begin with the bottom row and move up to the top row. Notice any differences? Turn the page to see what the original study found by following this same procedure.

One particular version of a mental set is referred to as functional fixedness, the tendency to view objects as having only one use or function. If you have ever used a coin to turn the head of a screw when you didn't have a screwdriver handy, you have overcome functional fixedness. The string problem, shown in **Figure 9-8** on the next page, is one test that psychologists have used to reveal when people are experiencing functional fixedness.

We can also hamper our ability to solve problems by adopting a confirmation bias, a tendency to look for information that meets our expectations when solving problems. If you have heard that all of the professors in the department in which you are thinking of taking a class are good teachers, you may only seek out opinions from students who completed the class taught by the professor whose class you are thinking of taking, rather than undertaking the more difficult task of finding people who have dropped the course. The problem with this approach is that students who stayed through the whole course would be more likely to confirm what you expect to hear, that the teacher is good, than to give you a negative, but potentially helpful, evaluation.

mental set tendency to use problem-solving strategies that have worked in the past.

functional fixedness tendency to view objects as having only one function.

confirmation bias tendency to look for information that meets our expectations.

decision making evaluating and choosing from among options.

In one classic study, researchers revealed confirmation bias by giving participants a series of numbers: 2, 4, and 6 (Wason, 1960). They asked the participants to figure out the rule for that set by generating their own sets of numbers. Each time the participants offered a series, the experimenters told them only whether their set did or did not follow the same rule as the original set. Many participants became convinced that the rule was to increase each number by 2. They offered repeated sets of numbers, such as 8, 10, 12 or 24, 22, 20. The researchers told them that their sets conformed to the original rule, but when asked to state the original rule, these participants got it wrong. The original rule was simply that each number had to have a numerical value larger than the one before it. The numbers the participants generated themselves conformed to the rules they created, but it didn't occur to them that other rules were possible.

The way to overcome confirmation bias is to purposely look for information that disconfirms your ideas. Participants who generated random series of numbers, such as 54, 3, 12, would have been more likely to correctly figure out the rule.

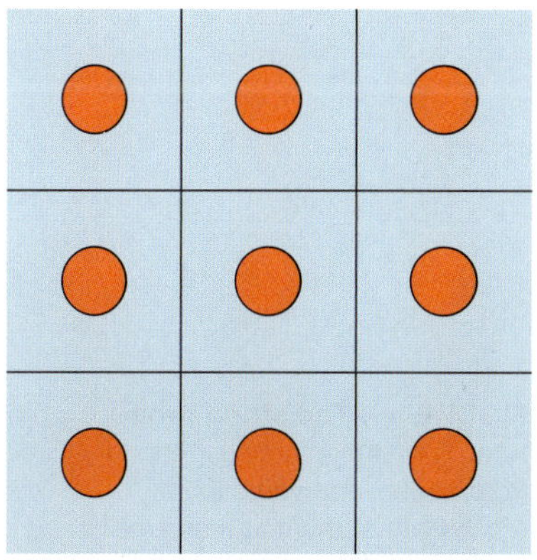

FIGURE 9-7 The nine-dot problem. Without lifting your pencil, draw no more than four straight lines to connect all the dots. (The solution is on page 354.)

Thinking to Make Decisions

Decision making involves evaluating and choosing from among the alternatives available to us. Many of your everyday thoughts involve weighing options and making choices. First you must decide what time to wake up. A series of decisions follow, including choices about what to wear, what to eat for breakfast, with whom to spend your time, and what to do. Even when we're on a regular schedule, we don't behave like robots. We often have options to deviate from our regular course of action, and we must decide whether or not to take them.

Information for Decision Making To make decisions, we need to gather or recall information relevant to each alternative. Suppose you're trying to decide which of two movies to go see. You would probably like a little information about each film

Findings on the Water Jar Problem Did your friend find the simpler solution to the 5th row problem that you missed (Jar A plus Jar C, instead of Jar B minus Jar A minus Jar C twice)? This classic experiment by Abraham Luchins (1942) demonstrates mental set. Most people who start at the top of the list figure out a solution and then apply it to all the problems. This creates a mental set that leads them to miss the simpler two-jar solution to the last row. Those starting at the bottom of the list are much more likely to see and use the simpler solution. How did you do?

representativeness heuristic the assumption that individuals share characteristics of the category of which they are a member.

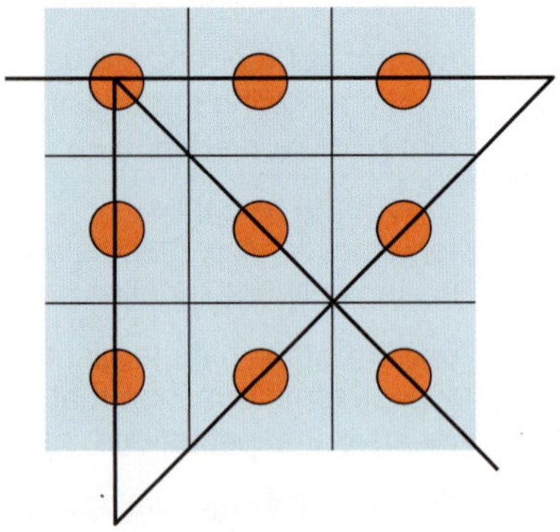

Solution to the nine-dot problem. Most people have difficulty with this problem because they see the arrangement of dots as a square and try to keep within the boundaries of the dots. This mental set limits their ability to solve the problem.

to help you make your choice. You can gather information from sources outside yourself, such as movie reviews and the comments of your friends. You can also recall relevant information that you already have. You may, for example, recognize the names of some of the actors or one of the directors.

When we draw from our memories to get information, we often use heuristic shortcuts. The use of heuristics is sometimes successful, but often leads to reaching the incorrect decision, as shown in the work of Nobel prize-winning psychologist Danny Kahneman, who developed many of his studies while working at the University of British Columbia (Stanovich, 2008; Tversky & Kahneman, 1993, 1974). Two heuristics that have been described by these researchers are the representativeness heuristic and the availability heuristic.

The **representativeness heuristic** makes the assumption that individual objects or people are members of a category if they share similar characteristics. When we use this heuristic, we draw conclusions about an object, event, or person based on a small set of specific data, often ignoring other relevant information. Suppose, for example, that one of the movies you are thinking of seeing has several characteristics that seem to identify it as a romantic comedy. You may not bother to read reviews or get other information about the movie because, based only on its presumed identity as a romantic comedy, you have a set of expectations about what the movie will be like.

Amos Tversky and Danny Kahneman (1974) nicely demonstrated people's use of the representativeness heuristic by asking research participants to read a description of an individual that included personal attributes such as, "shows no interest in political and social issues," and, "spends most of his free time on . . . mathematical puzzles." After they read this paragraph, participants were also told that the individual was randomly selected from a pool that contained 70 percent lawyers and 30 percent engineers. Ignoring the strong statistical probability that the individual

FIGURE 9-8 The string problem. Two strings are suspended from above, and you cannot reach both of them at the same time. How can you tie them together? (The solution is on page 357.)

was more likely to be a lawyer than an engineer, most of the participants used the personal characteristics of the individual to identify him as an engineer based on a few personal characteristics.

Another approximation used to make decisions is known as the availability heuristic. Answer this question: are there more words in the English language that start with the letter K or that have the letter K in the third position? We will come back to this shortly. The availability heuristic refers to the likelihood that we will judge an event as more common if it is easier to think about it (Keller, Siegrist, & Gutcher, 2006; Oppenheimer, 2004; McKelvie & Drumheller, 2001). You may easily remember the one really great film made by an actor in one of the movies you are thinking about attending, but not be able to recall much about the actor's so-so work in several other films. The availability heuristic also explains why we tend to think that infrequent but highly salient and memorable events, such as plane crashes or tsunamis, are more common than they actually are. Because such events are easy to call to mind, we assume they commonly occur when, in fact, they are very rare (Foster, 2009). So what about the K question? There are actually more words in English with the letter K in the third position. However, words starting with the letter K are much more available when we try to think of them, so people usually say there are more words that start with K than which have K in the third position (Tversky & Kahneman, 1974).

Unforgettable. Because horrific scenes of airplane crashes stay in our memories, we tend to think that such crashes are more common than they actually are.

availability heuristic judging easily-recalled events as more common.

Another aspect of the availability heuristic that affects decision making is the fact that we tend to rely on more recently stored memories to make judgments about events. For example, patients who underwent painful medical colonoscopy procedures are more likely to remember the event as excruciatingly painful if it is over quickly and ends at a time of maximal pain, than if the procedure is extended for a longer period of time with some time at the end of diminished pain (Redelmeier, Katz, & Kahneman, 2003). Because it's easier to call more recent information to mind, we assume that it is more indicative of the overall experience.

Rational Decision Making After we have gathered or brought to mind information about the alternatives, how do we evaluate each one and go about picking one of them? For thousands of years, since the time of the ancient Greek philosopher Plato, philosophers have argued that it is better to rely on logical reasoning than on emotions or instinct when making decisions. And, until relatively recently, many of the theorists and researchers who studied decision making assumed that people's decisions—particularly financial decisions about what products to buy, whether to save or spend, and how to invest—were based on purely logical reasoning.

Many models of such rational decision-making processes exist. Many assume that we choose a set of criteria and rank each alternative on its *utility*, or its ability to satisfy each criterion (Edwards & Newman, 1986; Edwards, 1977). If you are looking for a new phone, for instance, you might evaluate its size, cost, and the number of apps that are available. Some models of rational decision making suggest that we may go even farther and give more importance or "weight" to certain criteria. If, for example, it is very important to have certain apps available on a new phone, you may weigh that criterion more highly than the phone's size and cost. According to these models, after gathering and evaluating information on each phone, we could mathematically calculate which phone is the best for us. **Table 9-1** shows a model of such a calculation. According to this model, you would choose Phone C.

"Buy one now, before they're all gone." Recognizing that emotions can interfere with careful decision making, automobile dealers typically try to create a sense of urgency and excitement when selling their products.

For some decisions, rational models of decision making suggest that we might also take into account the *probability* that we can attain our choices. If, for example, you are choosing classes for next term, the course that ranks as your top choice may be so popular on campus that you rate your chance of getting into the class as low. In this case, you may decide to sign up for another course, instead of your top choice, as part of your rational decision-making process.

Reason-based decision-making methods such as these can help us when we have fairly few choices and evaluate them using fairly few attributes (Payne & Bettman, 2004). Sometimes we cannot use such a model until we narrow down the choices (Slovic, 1990; Tversky, 1972). You may, for example, have eliminated 15 other phones that were entirely beyond your budget before choosing only three to consider further. Sometimes the method of eliminating alternatives is the only one we need. If every phone but one is beyond your budget, you don't need to perform a complicated analysis before deciding which phone you can get.

Rational decision-making models tend to be based on assumptions that we have information available to us about all our alternatives and that we have time to ponder this information. As you may have experienced, a lot of decisions in real life don't fit these criteria (Gigerenzer & Goldstein, 1996). After you buy your phone, for example, you may want to stop in the food court at the mall for a snack. With only a few minutes to decide, you may focus on only a few of the available options—maybe the first couple of restaurants you walk by—or a few attributes of the choices—such as whether they offer a vegetarian dish. You may still think rationally about your choice, but you are using a model known as **bounded rationality** that limits the cognitive effort you need to invest (Simon, 1957). The theory of bounded rationality suggests that our ability to make decisions in a rational, logical manner is limited by incomplete information, time limits of decision making, and our own emotional feelings about one or more of the available options. All of these factors limit or "bound" our ability to behave purely rationally. Research suggests that we *successfully* use bounded rationality to make many of our decisions by doing the best we can with the cognitive resources and information that we have available at a given moment (Gigerenzer, 2004; Simon, 1990).

bounded rationality the fact that in many situations, our ability to make clear rational decisions is limited or "bounded" by things like a lack of information, time constraints, or emotions attached to aspects of the problem we are trying to solve.

Emotions and Decision Making Suppose you are perusing the food court for your snack and you get a craving for some French fries. You might just buy some and eat them, without putting much, if any, rational thought into your decision. For a long time, decisions such as this troubled rational decision-making theorists, because such choices are not based on logical reasons. Because of the work of Danny Kahneman, however, we now

TABLE 9-1 Model of Rational Decision Making: Considering Both Rank and Weight (Importance)

Criterion	Weight of Criteria	Phone A		Phone B		Phone C	
		Rank	Rank × weight	Rank	Rank × weight	Rank	Rank × weight
Size	+3	8	24	5	15	5	15
Cost	+6	8	48	6	36	4	24
Apps	+10	0	0	5	50	8	80
Total of rank × weight		**Phone A: 72**		**Phone B: 101**		**Phone C: 119**	

know that decision making often involves irrational processes that can be driven by our emotions. In fact, people *often* rely heavily on their emotions, or "gut instinct," rather than pure reason to make decisions.

The involvement of emotions in decision making makes predicting human behaviour very difficult. There are individual differences in emotional reactions, and many of these are driven by developmental experience and temperament. Even our moods can affect our decision making. Research suggests, for example, that when we are in a positive mood, we tend to make more efficient decisions with less rational consideration of the alternatives. We also tend to be content with those choices (Schwartz et al., 2002).

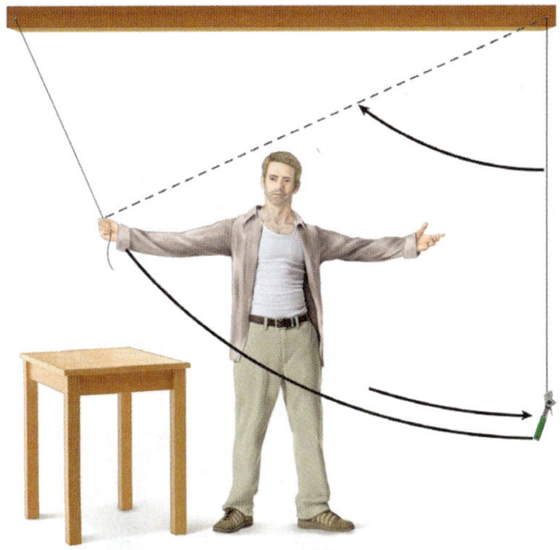

Solution to the string problem. Tie the pliers to one string and use it as a weight to swing the string closer to you. Functional fixedness can limit your ability to recognize this use for the pliers.

Researchers have discovered a few situations in which our emotions are likely to influence decisions somewhat predictably. One of these is when we try to estimate risks in anticipating the consequences of our decisions. For example, if you buy the wrong new phone, you risk being unhappy with it or needing to take it in for lots of repairs. Research suggests that we base our decisions, at least in part, on our anticipation of how we will feel if we make a bad choice (Mellers, Schwartz, & Cooke, 1998; Mellers et al., 1997; Kahneman & Tversky, 1979), and that, in general, we try hard to avoid making decisions we will regret later (Connolly & Zeelenberg, 2002). For many of us, "bad" outweighs "good" in our anticipation, so we might make less than optimal choices just to avoid the risk of feeling bad later. Given the option to receive 10 cents of a shared (with one other person) dollar, for example, most people will opt out altogether, taking nothing instead of the 10 cents, because they would feel they had been treated unfairly by having to share the dollar. This is irrational behaviour since clearly, 10 cents is better than nothing at all.

Understanding how emotions can shift the likelihood of a purchase is of particular interest to advertisers. If the context that produces positive emotion can be identified in all situations, it can be used effectively to persuade consumers to buy. In many cases, language can play a role in producing this context by framing choices in positive or negative ways. We are more likely to buy a food that is labelled "75 percent fat-free" than one that is described as "25 percent fat," for example (Sanford et al., 2002). The first statement frames the product in terms of "fat-free," and as such is preferred to the second statement, even though the product is exactly the same in both cases.

Framing is especially effective in arousing emotions when we are estimating risks. Most college students would feel safer using condoms that prevent the transmission of HIV 95 percent of the time than the same condoms when they are described as failing to prevent HIV transmission 5 percent of the time (Linville, Fischer, & Fischhoff, 1993). Tversky and Kahneman (1981) provided another classic example of framing. They asked students to imagine that they were helping Health Canada select a treatment scenario for an outbreak of an expected deadly disease. Imagine that you are one of the students in their experiment. You are told that it is estimated that 600 people will contract the disease and die without treatment. You are told that Treatment Option A will save 200 of those affected, while Treatment Option B has a 1/3 probability of saving all 600 people and a 2/3 probability that none will be saved. Which option would you pick? Now what if, instead, you were offered the following two options. Treatment Option C would result in the deaths of 400 people, while with Treatment Option D there is a 1/3 probability no one will die and a 2/3 probability that all 600 will die. Which of these options would you pick? In Kahneman and Tversky's study, most people preferred Options A and D, even though options A and C are identical, as are Options B and D. The researchers explained their finding as due to differences in framing the options in terms of life or death.

The interference of emotions in making decisions is not all negative. Although it's true that being upset or anxious or feeling cheated or irrationally hopeful may impair our judgment and increase the chance that we will make an impulsive and unnecessary purchase, it is sometimes the case that emotions help us make better decisions. Research has shown that individuals often make better decisions in games with a chance element when they claim to be operating on a "hunch." Intuition is not well understood, but it is an irrational characteristic that sometimes improves decision-making capabilities. The Practically Speaking feature gives you some tips about when it can be helpful to "go with your gut."

PRACTICALLY SPEAKING When Is It Best to Rely on Emotions for Decision Making?

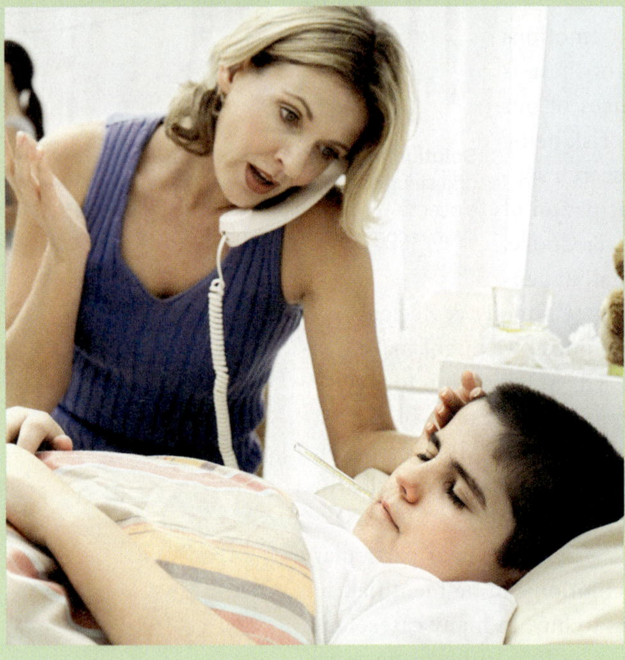

Intuition, hunches, inner voice, gut, instinct—emotional decision making goes by many names, and its importance is often downplayed compared to rational thought.

Paul Thagard at the University of Waterloo (2001) suggests that emotions can play a key role in decision making. He points out that emotional or intuitive decision making has some up-front advantages. It is fast; with no time needed to weigh options, the decision is immediate. It leads to decisions based on things you really care about (my family and friends are important to me so maybe going away to school is not a great idea). And finally, this approach to decision making leads directly to action.

Listing the plusses and minuses of decision options is a rational approach to decision making; however, some people find it to be a bit robot-like. Thagard offers a compromise that he calls using *informed intuition* to make decisions. This intuitive approach involves the following four steps:

1. Construct the decision problem with care. Identify the goals that will follow from your decision and the actions that will accomplish them.
2. Look at each goal and estimate its importance. This is a more intuitive or emotional process, but it will help you clearly see what you care about in the decision. Tag those goals whose importance you may have exaggerated (be honest!) or that you are emotionally over-focused upon and adjust them a bit.
3. Review how likely it is that the potential actions being considered will accomplish the goals you have in mind. How much evidence do you have for these assessments about whether the actions will accomplish the goals? If you do not have enough evidence, you probably need to change the possible actions.
4. Make your intuitive/emotional judgment about the best action to perform, while at the same time checking your emotional reaction to different options. Finally, run your decision past other people to see if it seems reasonable to them.

Let's try an example. Imagine you are trying to decide what sort of vehicle to buy to get around on for your summer job as a courier and through the term at school.

Step 1. The vehicle needs to be affordable and reliable, and so a well-researched small four-door car might be best. But you have also been thinking that a motorcycle would be a LOT of fun.

Step 2. How important is it that your transportation be reliable, affordable, and fun? Is the fun goal maybe a bit exaggerated? Maybe it needs to be downscaled a bit.

Step 3. Would a motorcycle get you around as a courier in the summer? How about getting around town while at school in the winter? What about the car? Would a car (with a good heater) be more fun to have in the winter? What, if any, additional data would help?

Step 4. Decide to buy a car, but think about the emotional impact of making that decision. Talk to other people who have perhaps tried to keep a motorcycle running in the winter. Ask others what they think of your decision.

So, the bottom line is that decision making can (and Paul Thagard suggests should) involve an emotional or intuitive component, but one that we are aware of and use to make informed decisions.

Metacognition

One of the most complicated forms of thought is **metacognition**, thinking about thinking. When we consider our own memories, for example, we engage in a form of metacognition. We may mull over specific facts we remember, thinking about their sources and when we learned them. We may also think about how information we have learned in the past is influencing our current interpretations of events. Metacognition involving thinking about the source of memories involves activation of the frontal cortex of the brain, as well as the hippocampus, a region important for storage of information. Damage to the hippocampus can result in source amnesia, a condition that prevents accurate thinking about one's own memories (Lakhan, 2007).

metacognition thinking about one's own thoughts.

Self-reflection is another form of metacognition. It involves thinking about our own identities, how we influence other people, and our relative self-worth. Self-reflection is an important human behaviour because it enables us to evaluate and modify our responses based on our past experience. We may reflect on our behaviour at a recent party, for example, and decide that we would feel better about ourselves if we were more, or perhaps less, outgoing. Then we might take steps either to overcome shyness or tone down our party persona. Self-reflection can sometimes have negative consequences if it leads to repetitive thoughts of worthlessness and anxiety. For people with specific biological tendencies, excessive self-reflection can lead to psychological disorders, such as depression and anxiety disorders (Takano & Tanno, 2009).

Assessing metacognition in animals. Because chimps and gorillas cannot vocalize as humans do, researchers can assess their capacity for metacognition only with special strategies, such as by having them point to symbols on a keyboard or by observing their behaviour in certain learning tasks.

Another type of metacognition occurs when we infer what someone else is thinking by watching or hearing about that person's actions. This phenomenon, called *theory of mind*, is an important aspect of human thought. However, as the box, "Things Students Want to Know: Theory of Mind" discusses, it may also exist in a few other species. As we discussed in Chapter 3, theory of mind is an adaptive trait because it facilitates communication and peaceful living with other people. If we did not have theory of mind and instead needed explicit verbal information about the feelings and intentions of another person, social communication would be stilted.

Once we acquire this ability during development, it becomes automatic. You probably exercise your theory of mind many times a day, while assessing your roommate's mood on the basis of his actions, gauging a professor's expectations based on her demeanor, or trying to figure out what type of a person your date is from the cues you receive on the first date.

Metacognition HOW WE DEVELOP Children gradually develop a theory of other peoples' minds, starting during the toddler years. Young children, ages 2 to 3 years, demonstrate that they lack the ability to infer the thinking of the person who is searching for them when trying to play hide-and-seek. Children this age will often "hide" by covering their eyes while remaining in a location that is not out of view. Rather than take the point of view of the searcher, they rely on their own experience, "If I can't see because my eyes are covered, no one else can see me." This lack of theory of mind disappears by about age 4 (Sabbagh et al., 2009; Aschersleben, Hofer, & Jovanovic, 2008).

Hiding in plain sight. Young children lack the ability to infer what another person is thinking and will often "hide" by covering their eyes . . . "If I can't see you, you can't see me!"

Young children's developing theory of mind may contribute to jealousy and an inability to share when it enables a child to

THINGS STUDENTS WANT TO KNOW

Theory of mind: Does your pet know what you are thinking?

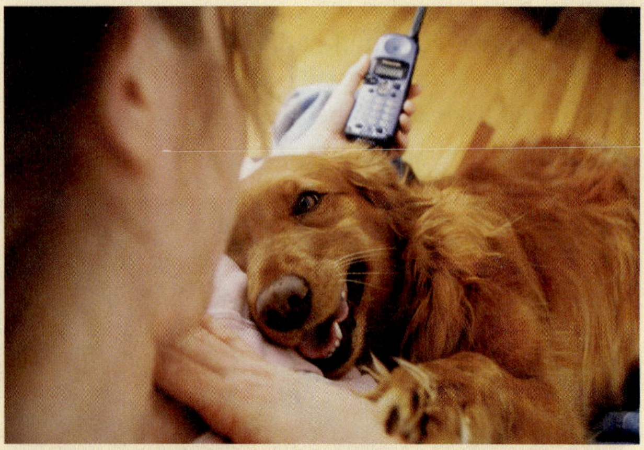

Pet owners have long noted that their dogs seem to watch their faces and respond as if they are inferring the owner's thoughts. A dog that sees the owner smiling might eagerly approach with tail wagging, looking for a food treat, while one who sees the owner scowling might retreat, whimpering. It's impossible to determine, however, whether the dog is just responding to stimulus cues as a result of operant conditioning or learning based on past experiences. The question, "Do animals think about what we are thinking?" is better characterized as, "Do animals have a theory of mind?"

Increasing evidence suggests that many animals are, indeed, capable of complicated thought and seem to possess a theory of mind (Hirata, 2009; Reid, 2009). Researchers have devised methods to study theory of mind in experimental animals, including non-human primates and birds. Chimpanzees and capuchin monkeys can be trained to trade certain less palatable food items for rewards the monkeys prefer. These animals seem to infer a negative reaction on the part of an experimenter to a partially eaten piece of food and attempt to hide the evidence by passing off an apple with the bite mark hidden from view.

Outside the lab, some species of birds seem to infer the intentions of other birds. Western scrub jays, for example, will re-hide stored food if they notice they were being watched when the food was hidden. This evidence strongly suggests that the scrub jay has a theory of mind. The scrub jay seems to infer that the intention of a watching bird is to steal hidden food. In response to this inference, the scrub jay moves the food to a new secret location after the watcher stops looking (Dally, Emery, & Clayton, 2006).

think of another child as a rival, with intentions to take away the child's toys. Another behaviour that is tied to thinking about what's going on in another person's head is lying. In general, people lie for two main reasons: to prevent themselves from being punished or to make someone else feel good (Feldman, 2009; Feldman, Forrest, & Happ, 2002). Children learn very early to lie in order to avoid punishment. This behaviour seems to emerge around age 3 for most children, and by age 5 it is a fairly universal phenomenon (Talwar & Lee, 2008). If "backed into a corner" so that a child believes it's likely he will be punished, almost all 5-year-olds will lie. Theory of mind allows people to lie in hopes of preventing punishment, even if they have not explicitly been warned about the punishment (Talwar, Gordon, & Lee, 2007). Because the child is able to imagine that an adult believes the child's behaviour is wrong, she can then infer that the adult intends to punish the child for the wrong behaviour.

Lying to make another person feel better, such as giving false compliments or reassurances, is another behaviour that arises during the preschool years. Unlike lying to avoid punishment, however, this type of lying seems to increase in frequency as we get older (Lind & Bowler, 2009). Have you ever complimented a friend on a new haircut or new outfit that you actually felt was less than flattering? The chances are you did not feel particularly guilty afterward, because your thoughts about how your friend feels are stronger than your desire to always tell the truth.

Although theory of mind seems to be present in very young children, other forms of metacognition are not evident until much later in development. For example, thinking about one's memories and evaluating current information in the context of the past is not a common thought process of young children. Young children often suffer from source amnesia (not remembering where they heard about certain information), which not only makes them prone to develop false memories, but also interferes with their ability to think about their memories in a meaningful way (Zola, 1998).

Theory of Mind — WHAT HAPPENS IN THE BRAIN?

Neuroscientists believe that the ability to think about another person's intentions is directly linked to a set of cells in the brain called mirror neurons (Rizzolatti & Fabbri-Destro, 2008). Mirror neurons are located in the frontal and parietal cortex. These cells are activated not only when an individual engages in a particular task, but also when he watches another person engage in this task. Activation of the same set of neurons, whether it is you or another person who acts, produces overlap in the neural circuitry that probably leads to predictions about the other person's behaviour.

mirror neurons neurons located in the frontal and parietal cortex, which respond similarly when the individual engages in an activity and when the individual watches someone else engage in the activity.

Consider, for instance, what might happen in your brain when you reach into a cookie jar. Usually when you reach into a cookie jar, you are hungry and looking for something good to eat. This might activate several neurons in your frontal cortex, including those involved in movement, as well as those important for anticipation and for reward. For the sake of this discussion, let's refer to these neurons as A, B, and C. Reaching into the jar activates neuron A, which in turn activates B and C. If neuron A is a mirror neuron, your neuron A can also be activated in your brain when you watch somebody else reach into a cookie jar. Activating your neuron A will, in turn, activate your neurons B and C, which carry information about intention. They tell you that the anticipated reward of reaching in the cookie jar is finding the cookie. Based on this activation in your brain, you may infer that the other person is reaching into the jar because she hopes to find a cookie in there.

"Mental illness affects one in six Quebecois." A poster from the Mental Illness Foundation asks us to think about the impact mental illness has on those who suffer with it.

Thought — WHEN THINGS GO WRONG

Many disorders include problems with thinking. In many cases, however, these conditions are primarily associated with deficits in other psychological processes; impairments in the person's thinking are not the main difficulty. Individuals with Alzheimer disease are often in a confused state, for example, but the reason they are not thinking clearly is because their memories are disrupted. In other cases, problems with thinking are tied to aberrant emotional states. Depression is often accompanied by repetitive thoughts about worthlessness and hopelessness, and cognitive therapy that targets these thoughts can often be a successful form of treatment (Rupke, Blecke, & Renfrow, 2006). Although the thought components of dementia and mood disorders are real and significant symptoms, we discuss them in other chapters because these conditions are primarily associated with other psychological processes. Another two disorders, obsessive-compulsive disorder and schizophrenia, are characterized primarily by difficulties in controlling one's thoughts, so we will describe them briefly here. They will, however, be discussed in greater detail in Chapter 16.

Obsessive-compulsive disorder (OCD) is defined as having uncontrollable, anxiety-provoking thoughts called *obsessions*. Many people with this disorder feel *compulsions*, or irresistible urges, to perform mental or physical ritual actions to help reduce their anxiety around their obsession (APA, 2000). People with OCD know that their obsessions are out of contact with reality, but they often find the thoughts impossible to inhibit and ignore. For example, someone might have obsessive thoughts about germs and anxiety and this could lead to compulsive hand washing, or someone may have obsessive

obsessive-compulsive disorder (OCD) a mental disorder associated with abnormal anxiety-provoking thoughts that can lead to ritualistic behaviours.

thoughts about his children being harmed and this could lead to compulsively checking that the stove is not on. The impulse to engage in compulsive behaviour, such as washing one's hands over and over or repeatedly checking whether a stove has been turned off, is so strong that anxiety builds with each passing moment that the behaviour is inhibited (Magee & Teachman, 2007). OCD can range from relatively mild to extremes that render people unable to participate in normal life activities. Estimates of the prevalence of OCD are uncertain because many people with mild OCD do not receive a formal diagnosis. Conservative estimates suggest that OCD affects about 1 percent of the population (Kessler et al., 2005).

The rise of anxiety-provoking thoughts associated with OCD is a good example of the complexity of human thinking. The relationship between our thoughts and our reality is actually something that can be stretched or even broken with disorders like OCD. As we come to understand the factors underlying OCD, we may also come to understand some of the key control factors involved in non-disordered human thinking. We will examine this topic in greater detail in Chapters 16 and 17.

schizophrenia a mental disorder characterized by disorganized thoughts, lack of contact with reality, and sometimes auditory hallucinations.

Schizophrenia is another disorder that involves some of the most basic and most important aspects of the human thinking process. Schizophrenia is a relatively common psychotic disorder, characterized by extreme disorganization of thinking. About 1.1 percent of people in Canada have been diagnosed with some form of schizophrenia (IMHRO, 2009). Although schizophrenia can exist in multiple forms, a common theme in the disease is a break from reality in thoughts and actions. Some people with schizophrenia experience distortions of reality, distortions in the form of *hallucinations* (usually auditory), and *delusions*, beliefs that are not based in reality (APA, 2000). They also exhibit a devastating inability to plan and control their own thoughts (Berenbaum & Barch, 1995). Furthermore, many people with this disorder suffer impaired working memory and find it impossible to keep track of information necessary to execute a simple series of actions (Piskulic et al., 2007).

Schizophrenia often also includes a language component. Sometimes a person's speech and writing become entirely disorganized and out of touch with reality (Covington et al., 2005). However, in spite of the nonsensical content, many people diagnosed with schizophrenia are able to retain intact semantics and syntax in sentence construction (Covington et al., 2005). Essentially, schizophrenia attacks the parts of our thinking processes that make us rational. Understanding the effects of schizophrenia on the brain will also provide us with an understanding of higher level human thinking. Potential causes and treatments of schizophrenia will be discussed in Chapters 16 and 17.

Before You Go On

www.wiley.com/go/comer

What Do You Know?

8. Compare and contrast controlled and automatic cognitive processing.
9. What are the two main types of strategies for solving problems? How do these two strategies differ? Give at least one example of each type.
10. What are the representativeness and availability heuristics and how do they affect decision making?
11. How can emotions affect our decision making?
12. What is metacognition? What is a theory of mind?
13. How is thinking disturbed in OCD? How are thinking and language disturbed in schizophrenia?

SCAN TO GET THE ANSWERS

What Do You Think?

Which of the barriers to problem solving described in this chapter most often seem to affect you? Which problem-solving strategies seem to work best for you?

Summary

Language

LEARNING OBJECTIVE 1 Define language, describe how we learn languages, describe parts of the brain that are involved in language, and discuss differences and problems that can affect people's language skills.

- Language is a set of symbols used to communicate. Language comprehension understands verbal messages, and language production is creating them.
- The study of language can be broken into phonology (sounds), semantics (meaning), syntax (grammar), and pragmatics (practical usage).
- Most people follow a typical sequence of language acquisition that includes the ability to distinguish, but not produce, all possible phonemes at about 2 to 4 months of age, babbling at about 6 months, and speaking first words at around 1 year of age.
- The standard way we learn language suggests that we have an inborn capacity for language learning, although environment contributes as well. There appears be a sensitive or critical period before about 13 years old when it is easiest to acquire language.
- In most people, the language centres in the brain are in the left hemisphere. The main brain region important for speech production is Broca's area. The main region for language comprehension is called Wernicke's area. Several other areas of the brain are also active in language, including the frontal eye fields when we read.
- There are small average gender differences in early language learning, with girls initially learning faster. These differences disappear with time.

The Relationship Between Language and Thought

LEARNING OBJECTIVE 2 Describe how thought and language are related and summarize the linguistic relativity hypothesis.

- Some thoughts, including mental imagery and spatial navigation, require no words.
- The linguistic relativity hypothesis suggests that the amount of vocabulary we have available in our language for objects or concepts influences the way we think about those objects or concepts.

Thought

LEARNING OBJECTIVE 3 Describe and summarize research on thinking processes, including problem solving, decision making, and metacognition.

- We are capable of several different kinds of thought, and different types of thinking involve different brain regions, often including those related to the specific thoughts. We develop various thinking abilities gradually with age.
- Controlled processing relies on the executive function of the brain. We become increasingly able to exert cognitive control as we age.
- Problem solving is finding a way to reach a goal. Algorithms, problem-solving strategies that guarantee a solution if followed methodically, work best for well-defined problems. Short-cut strategies called heuristics may help with ill-defined problems.
- Common problem-solving heuristics include working backwards, finding analogies to other problems, and forming subgoals. Heuristics can lead to difficulties in problem solving, including mental sets, functional fixedness, and confirmation bias.
- Decision-making involves evaluating and choosing from among the options available to us. We often use heuristics to recall information to make decisions, but some, including the representativeness and availability heuristics, can bias our evaluations.
- Rational models of problem solving suggest that we make elimination options and/or make weighted evaluations of the utility and probability of options. We often lack time, information, or cognitive resources for rational decision making, however, so we use a strategy of limited or bounded rationality.
- Emotions often play a role in decision making, sometimes interfering with our ability to make rational decisions, but other times helping us to make efficient choices.
- Metacognition is thinking about our own thoughts. It includes reviewing and evaluating our own memories, self-reflection, and theory of mind—inferring the intentions of other people. Mirror neurons in the brain contribute to theory of mind.
- Obsessive-compulsive disorder (OCD) and schizophrenia are two mental disorders that include a major thought disruption.

Key Terms

agrammatism 339
algorithm 351
availability heuristic 355
babbling 333
bounded rationality 356
Broca's aphasia 338
Broca's area 338
child-directed speech 336
cognition 330
cognitive control 349
confirmation bias 353
critical period 336

TYING IT TOGETHER

The study of language and thought is closely connected to the study of all other areas of psychology. Throughout this chapter, we have stressed how language and thought interface with psychology's various subfields, including our highlighted sections on brain function, individual differences, abnormal functioning, and development. To remind you of how language and thought is tied to other psychology subfields and issues, here are some interesting points from throughout the chapter.

WHAT HAPPENS IN THE BRAIN?

- The main language areas are on the left side of the brain for most people—but not all.
- Thinking about images (or smells or tests) activates the same brain areas as if we were actually seeing (or smelling or tasting). Thoughts that involve language activate language areas of the brain.
- When we watch other people do things, mirror neurons in our brain can activate just as though we were doing the same things.

HOW WE DIFFER

- Girls tend to learn to talk earlier than boys. However, the difference soon disappears.
- Babies who learn two languages at home begin talking slightly later than those who learn just one.
- The number of words we have in our language for a certain object or concept (such as a colour) may influence how we can think about that object or concept.

WHEN THINGS GO WRONG

- Damage near Broca's area of the brain can cause us to lose our ability to use grammar.
- Obsessive-compulsive disorder involves unavoidable thoughts called obsessions and irresistible urges, or compulsions, to perform certain behaviours.
- About 1.1 percent of all people in Canada display schizophrenia, a disorder marked by disorganized thoughts and loss of contact with reality.

HOW WE DEVELOP

- Very young infants are able to perceive all the sounds of every language. As time passes, however, we lose the ability to distinguish phonemes of other languages.
- Our ability to learn languages is at its best before school age. After we pass age 13, it is much more difficult for us to learn new languages than it was earlier.
- We naturally tend to use child-directed speech with babies. It may be an evolutionary adaptation that helps humans learn language.
- One of the reasons toddlers don't play hide-and-seek very well is because their theory of mind abilities are still undeveloped.

Psychology Around Us

Differences in Language and Communication

Speaking the Same Language

View this in Action WILEY PLUS www.wileyplus.com

Video Lab Exercise

Everybody says it. Living in this age of cell phones and the Internet, we are witnessing a communication explosion. People are said to be more closely connected than ever, and, correspondingly, the world is supposedly getting smaller. But is this true? Are language and communication in today's world better, or even different, than in the past? Are we becoming one, or is communication across people and the world as complex and flawed as ever?

For this video lab exercise, you will become a communications expert, observing a range of encounters and communications, judging their effectiveness, accounting for the weaknesses and strengths of each, and then working to improve the communications. You will observe two people texting messages, a parent talking to a child, animals vocalizing to each other, a trainer communicating with an animal, and a man and woman having a heart-to-heart.

As you are working on this online exercise, consider the following questions:

- What does this lab exercise suggest about how language and communication develop, within species and across species?
- Do men and women listen differently and/or speak different languages?
- How does language affect thinking, decision making, perception, and behaviour?
- What's going on in the brain while all this communication is happening?

CHAPTER 10

Intelligence

CHAPTER OUTLINE

- What Do We Mean by Intelligence?
- Additional Types of Intelligence
- How Do We Measure Intelligence?
- Is Intelligence Governed by Genetic or Environmental Factors?
- Intelligence *What Happens in the Brain?*
- Extremes in Intelligence *How We Differ*

AS SMART AS THEY LOOK?

How can you tell if someone is intelligent? What sorts of behaviours should you look for? How well they did in school? How much money they earn at work? Perhaps if we had an example to work from . . . someone unmistakably intelligent. What about the character of Sheldon Cooper on TV's *The Big Bang Theory*. Is he intelligent? Well, he certainly thinks so. He sped through school, going to college at the age of 12, and he views community-college grads with disdain: " . . . you thought the opposite of stupid loser was community-college grad?" Sheldon does research in cutting edge physics and is certain he is destined to win a Nobel Prize one day: "Although I will not have time to mention you in my Nobel speech, when I get around to writing my memoirs, I promise you a very effusive footnote, and maybe a signed copy." Indeed, Sheldon is an intelligent character who collects comics and excels in theoretical physics, and yet there are some, well, . . . issues. He is self-centred, arrogant, and socially inept, and at times in social situations he looks particularly stupid. His friends find him extremely frustrating; after living with him for weeks at a remote North Pole research station, his friends admit that they wanted to kill him, even temporarily considering throwing his Kindle outside and locking the door when he went out to get it! He is both brilliant and seriously challenged.

Clearly, Sheldon's character is built around common, if somewhat geeky, conceptions of what intelligence is. Like many other aspects of human behaviour, however, intelligence is a concept that appears simple at first glance, only to become more and more complicated the closer we look at it. Start with the basic question: how do you define intelligence? Most people use "smart" or "stupid" to characterize the people in their lives, and they generally have a great deal of confidence in their assessments. But answer this: when you describe a friend as a generally smart person, how are you assessing smartness? Are you thinking about how your friend performs in all situations, or are you just impressed by how sophisticated her answers are in English class and ignoring the fact that she's just scraping by in chemistry? If you were watching Sheldon Cooper on *Big Bang*, would you be sympathetic to him despite his lack of "street smarts"? And what about Sheldon seems to be "book smart" but lacks common sense? Is Sheldon, book smarts and all, the one you want leading you if your plane crashes on a remote island?

So what do we mean by intelligence? Does it mean the same thing in every instance? How do we understand it, and how do we measure it? To these basic questions we must add several others:

- Can we distinguish between intelligence and talent?
- Are intelligence and wisdom the same thing?

- Are intelligence and creativity related?
- And, finally, how do we value intelligence?

Our answers to such questions will influence how we define intelligence and whether we decide that anyone is particularly high in intelligence. ■

What Do We Mean By Intelligence?

LEARNING OBJECTIVE 1

Describe various ways in which intelligence has been defined and summarize the current thinking on whether intelligence is general or specific.

Although Western thinkers as far back in history as Socrates, Plato, and Aristotle have commented on intelligence, it was not until the nineteenth and early twentieth centuries that psychologists and others began to form our present notions about it. In 1921, a group of scholars attended a symposium on the subject of intelligence. In their report, they emphasized that whatever else might be involved, **intelligence** involves the ability to *learn and the ability to meet the demands of the environment effectively*. People who hope to master algebra, for example, must have the capacity to grasp mathematical principles and profit from mathematical instruction, and they must be able to apply what they learn to various problem sets and life situations. As we will see later, we need to be careful about how broadly we apply the "meeting the demands of the environment" criteria for intelligence. Sheldon, one of the main characters in the *The Big Bang Theory* television show, is certainly intelligent, and certainly well adapted to the environment of the field of physics, but he is quite inept in social situations (as evidence, consider "Sheldon's Friendship Flowchart" online to see how he analytically manages his friendships).

intelligence the ability to learn, to meet the demands of the environment effectively, and to understand and control one's mental activities.

"I know that I am intelligent, because I know that I know nothing."
—Socrates, Greek philosopher

Years later, another survey of scholars pointed to these same abilities—learning and meeting the demands of the environment—as keys to intelligence, and added a third: *the ability to understand and control one's mental activities*. This additional mental capacity was termed **metacognition** (Cornoldi, 2010). Sometimes metacognition is understood as the ability to think about one's own thinking. The ancient philosopher Socrates gave us an early example of metacognitive thinking when he proclaimed, "Know thyself." A better example might be that studying is a way of meeting the demands of the academic environment, while knowing when you have studied enough and are ready for a test is a metacognitive skill.

metacognition the ability to understand and control one's mental activities.

Defining intelligence in terms of our ability to learn, to adapt to the demands of our environment, and to reflect on and understand our own mental processes makes intuitive sense. However, this definition encompasses a wide variety of notions about what intelligence might be. To develop a more precise definition, let's begin by considering a very basic question: is intelligence just one thing, or is it a combination of many different skill sets? All current theories of intelligence consider this question in one way or another.

PSYCHOLOGY AROUND US But Is He Really Smart?

In 2011, IBM supercomputer Watson played *Jeopardy!* against the two greatest human players—Brad Rutter, who has earned the most money on the program, and Ken Jennings, who holds the record for consecutive wins. In fact, the supercomputer won, and won big. Watson had a final dollar amount of $77,147 compared with Jennings' $24,000 and Rutter's $21,600.

Obviously, the challenge for Watson's programmers wasn't the issue of knowledge. Watson's hard drive included Wikipedia, encyclopedias, dictionaries, and millions of pages of additional source material. Instead, the hard part was helping Watson figure out how to respond to the puns, clever turns of phrase, and unique stylings of the "answers" provided by *Jeopardy!*.

In other words, whereas we think the smart part of playing *Jeopardy!* comes from knowing a lot about everything, the tricky part for Watson was to learn to understand and respond to natural language—something a young child can do. Even more interesting, the hardest "answers" for Watson were often the simplest, with the fewest words. The supercomputer just didn't have the context to narrow its choices.

Watson's undertaking seemed to please most viewers in one way or another. On the one hand, computer experts came away believing that the Watson prototype can form the basis for computers to become more directly responsive to natural language commands. On the other hand, everyday folks were comforted in knowing that as long as Watson thinks Toronto is a U.S. city, we don't have to get ready for our robot overlords quite yet.

Is Intelligence General or Specific?

Suppose you were joining a challenging mountain-climbing expedition. Which of your team members do you think would be more likely to complete the climb successfully: a generally smart person, or a person who had mastered, one by one, a large number of important tasks associated with mountain climbing? That is, is intelligence largely the result of a single, general factor, or does it come from a cluster of different, more focused abilities?

Spearman and the *g* Factor Charles Spearman (1863–1945) was a psychologist/philosopher and British army officer who also became an influential figure in the study of intelligence. Spearman helped to develop a tool for analyzing intelligence, called factor analysis. Factor analysis is a statistical method for determining whether different items on a test correlate highly with one another, thus forming a unified set, or cluster, of items. In the case of intelligence tests, for example, people who do well on vocabulary items also tend to do well on other verbal items, such as reading comprehension. Taken together, all of the test items relating to words and reading form a verbal-reasoning cluster that can be used to assess a person's overall verbal-reasoning skill. On Western intelligence tests, other clusters include those related to logical, spatial, and mechanical reasoning.

factor analysis a statistical method for determining whether certain items on a test correlate highly, thus forming a unified set, or cluster, of items.

***g* factor** a theoretical general factor of intelligence underlying all distinct clusters of mental ability; part of Spearman's two-factor theory of intelligence.

***s* factor** a theoretical specific factor uniquely tied to a distinct mental ability or area of functioning; part of Spearman's two-factor theory of intelligence.

While Spearman granted that some people have a particular strength in one area or another, he also noticed that those who scored high on one cluster tend to score high on other clusters as well. As he put it, "A bright child tends to score higher on all aspects of an intelligence test than a dull one." Thus, he hypothesized that a general factor, the *g* factor, of intelligence, underlies all distinct clusters of mental ability. At the same time, he believed that each cluster of intelligence is further affected by a *specific factor*, an *s* factor, which is uniquely tied to that particular area of functioning (**Figure 10-1**) (Spearman, 1937, 1927, 1923, 1904).

To illustrate this *two-factor view* of intelligence, think again about Sheldon Cooper on *The Big Bang Theory*. There is certainly some variability in some areas of Sheldon's knowledge. At the same time, there are many areas where Sheldon is very knowledgeable—an assumption consistent with the existence of a general intelligence.

Over the years, many theorists have embraced Spearman's notion of a *g* factor, and researchers have repeatedly found indications that such a factor may indeed be at work (Castejon, Perez, & Gilar, 2010; Johnson et al., 2004). These theorists typically agree that the *g* factor "is not merely book learning, a narrow academic skill, or test-taking smarts. Rather, it reflects a broader and deeper capability for comprehending our surroundings—'catching on,' 'making sense' of things, or 'figuring out' what to do" (Gottfredson, 1997, p. 13).

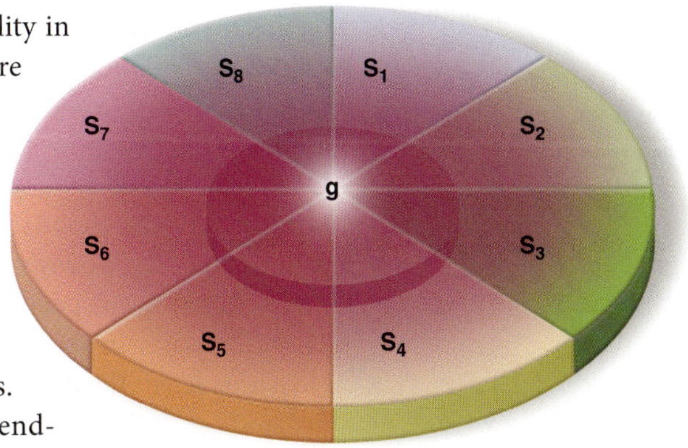

FIGURE 10-1 Spearman's two-factor theory of intelligence. In Spearman's model, the *g* factor of intelligence represents a broad and deep capability that underlies all other specific mental abilities, or the *s* factors.

Thurstone and Primary Mental Abilities Although many theorists initially accepted and indeed continue to embrace Spearman's notion of a *g* factor of intelligence, the idea of such a general factor was controversial in Spearman's day and remains so to the present.

TABLE 10-1 Thurstone's 7 Factors of Intelligence

Factor	Examples
Verbal comprehension	Vocabulary, reading, comprehension, verbal analogies, etc.
Word fluency	The ability to quickly generate and manipulate a large number of words with specific characteristics, as in anagrams or rhyming tests
Numerical skill	The ability to quickly and accurately carry out mathematical operations
Spatial ability	Spatial visualizations as well as ability to mentally transform spatial figures
Associative memory	Rote memory
Perceptual speed	Quickness in perceiving visual details, anomalies, similarities, etc.
Reasoning	Skill in a variety of inductive, deductive, and arithmetic reasoning tasks

Who was the smartest person ever? It depends on your criteria. Although Albert Einstein's name has become synonymous with the term "brilliance," his cognitive functioning was below average in certain ways. Viewed as the ultimate absent-minded professor, he once had to call the dean's office at the Princeton Institute for Advanced Study to ask for directions to his home—located a block from campus (how is that for "adapting to the environment?").

An early critic of Spearman's ideas was Lewis L. Thurstone (1887–1955), a pioneer in psychological measurement and statistics. He argued that intelligence is made up of seven distinct mental abilities: verbal comprehension, word fluency, numerical skill, spatial ability, associative memory, perceptual speed, and reasoning (Thurstone, 1938; see **Table 10-1**). Thurstone termed these factors **primary mental abilities**.

Observing differences from person to person, Thurstone argued that each of the primary mental abilities on his list was distinct, not simply a reflection of general underlying intelligence. And, in fact, his initial work seemed to suggest that these abilities were not related. However, recognizing this theory as a direct challenge to the notion of the *g* factor, Spearman and others used factor analyses to reevaluate Thurstone's ideas. They detected at least a slight tendency of those who scored high in one mental ability to score high in another (Spearman, 1939). So, Thurstone's work did not fully dispel the notion of the *g* factor.

Despite the limitations of Thurstone's theory, the idea of distinct areas of intelligence has continued to drive theorizing about intelligence, even among those who believe that a *g* factor is at least partly involved in intellectual functioning. Let's turn next to the work of three modern theorists who have carried on Thurstone's quest to identify separate components of intelligence.

primary mental abilities seven distinct mental abilities identified by Thurstone as the basic components of intelligence.

Current Multifactor Theories of Intelligence

Most of the early theorists on intelligence agreed with Spearman that intelligence has a *g* factor at its core. Today's psychologists increasingly question the *g* factor, or at least place more emphasis on specific abilities, or *s* factors, that may affect intellectual performance. Three theorists in particular—Howard Gardner, Robert Sternberg, and Stephen Ceci—have broadened the definition of intelligence and deemphasized the *g* factor.

Howard Gardner's Theory of Multiple Intelligences Are you equally successful in every academic subject? If you are like most people, you probably do better in some areas than others. If you are a good academic student, are you also a good artist? Musician? Cook? Do you know someone who does not do well on academic tests, but nevertheless seems intelligent? Perhaps this person has strong leadership skills, social intuition, street smarts, or a razor-sharp sense of humour.

Who's more intelligent? According to Howard Gardner's theory of multiple intelligences, these three extraordinary individuals each have a different kind of intelligence. For Neil Young, it's musical intelligence. For award-winning author Margaret Atwood, it's linguistic intelligence. And for physicist Stephen Hawking, it's mathematical intelligence.

theory of multiple intelligences theory that there is no single, unified intelligence, but instead several independent intelligences arising from different portions of the brain.

Psychologist Howard Gardner, influenced in part by the work of Thurstone, has advanced the **theory of multiple intelligences**, which argues that there is not a single unified intelligence (Gardner, 2011, 2008, 2004; Gardner & White, 2010). Instead, Gardner believes that there are several independent intelligences. Drawing on research from the fields of neuroscience and developmental, evolutionary, and cognitive psychology, he claims that the different intelligences come from different areas of the brain. In support of this view, he notes that damage to specific areas of the brain does not necessarily lead to a universal collapse of mental functioning. Rather, some types of functioning may be affected while others remain intact.

Gardner's research regarding people of exceptional ability has also contributed to the notion of multiple and independent intelligences. His work with individuals with *savant syndrome*, for example, seems consistent with this view. Individuals with savant syndrome often score low, sometimes extremely low, on traditional intelligence tests, yet possess startling ability in a specific area. Some have little verbal ability but are able to compute numbers with the speed of a calculator, others can draw with great skill, and still others have a keen memory for music. Stephen Wiltshire is a savant with autism who has phenomenal artistic skills. On YouTube, you can watch him drawing a fully-detailed picture to scale of 4 square miles of Rome, Italy after observing it for the first time from a helicopter for just 12 minutes (www.metacafe.com/watch/4200256/autistic_savant_stephen_wiltshire_draws_rome_from_memory/).

Table 10-2 outlines the eight basic intelligences identified by Gardner: linguistic, logical-mathematical, musical, spatial, bodily-kinesthetic, interpersonal, intrapersonal, and naturalistic. In addition, Gardner has raised the possibility that there may be two additional

TABLE 10-2 Gardner's Multiple Intelligences

Type of Intelligence	Characteristics	Possible Vocations
Linguistic	Sensitivity to the sounds and meaning of words	Author, journalist, teacher
Logical/mathematical	Capacity for scientific analysis and logical and mathematical problem solving	Scientist, engineer, mathematician
Musical	Sensitivity to sounds and rhythm; capacity for musical expression	Musician, composer, singer
Spatial	Ability to perceive spatial relationships accurately	Architect, navigator, sculptor, engineer
Bodily/kinesthetic	Ability to control body movements and manipulate objects	Athlete, dancer, surgeon
Interpersonal	Sensitivity to the emotions and motivations of others; skillful at managing others	Manager, therapist, teacher
Intrapersonal	Ability to understand one's self and one's strengths and weaknesses	Leader in many fields
Naturalistic	Ability to understand patterns and processes in nature	Biologist, naturalist, ecologist, farmer

Source: Adapted from Gardner, 1993.

intelligences: spiritual intelligence, which enables persons to focus on cosmic and spiritual issues, and existential intelligence, which is needed to consider ultimate issues, such as the meaning of life.

Although Gardner's theory has roots in Thurstone's ideas, it is, in fact, different from Thurstone's theory in several ways. First, Thurstone held that the mental functions he identified *collectively* constitute intelligence. He did not believe, as Gardner does, that each factor is itself an "intelligence." Further, Gardner believes that the various intelligences are best measured in the contexts in which they occur. Thus, assessments conducted in real-world settings where the intelligences they are trying to tap are actually used are more useful than paper-and-pencil examinations for assessing several of the intelligences (Tirri & Nokelainen, 2008). Finally, Gardner's definition of multiple intelligences includes an important cultural component: each intelligence, he suggests, reflects "the ability to solve problems, or to create products, that are valuable within one or more cultural settings" (Gardner, 1993).

Because the various intelligences are thought to emanate from different areas, or modules, of the brain, Gardner's theory is often called a *modular model* of mental functioning (Gardner, 1993). Nevertheless, according to Gardner, the various intelligences can influence one another. For example, in addition to a well-developed musical intelligence, a cellist might need a high bodily-kinesthetic intelligence to physically handle the instrument, and a high interpersonal intelligence to work in perfect harmony with other players in an orchestra.

Critics of Gardner's ideas, however, maintain that still deeper relationships exist among the various intelligences and mental functions (Gardner & Traub, 2010). There is not much data supporting the existence of the distinct intelligences that Garner suggests. Validating studies demonstrating that the different intelligences can be consistently and distinctly measured have yet to be accomplished (Sternberg & Grigerenko, 2004). As well, when measured, most of Gardner's intelligences correlate positively with general intelligence measures, which calls into question just how distinct Gardner's intelligences are (Visser et al., 2006). Not all human abilities have to be called intelligence.

triarchic theory of intelligence Sternberg's theory that intelligence is made up of three interacting components: internal, external, and experiential components.

Robert Sternberg's Triarchic Theory of Intelligence Psychologist Robert Sternberg has proposed a **triarchic theory of intelligence** (Mandelman et al., 2010; Sternberg, 2010, 2003). Sternberg shares Gardner's view that intelligence is not a unitary mental function. According to Sternberg, however, intelligence is made up not of numerous independent intelligences, but of three interacting components, as shown in **Figure 10-2**, called internal, external, and experiential components. These are sometimes referred to as the analytic, creative, and practical components.

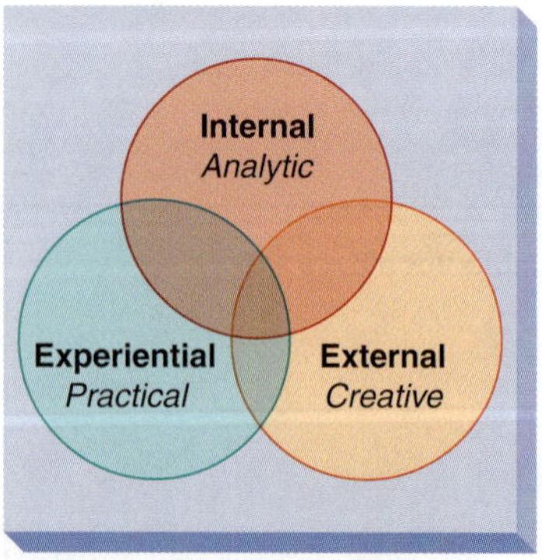

FIGURE 10-2 Sternberg's triarchic theory of intelligence. Robert Sternberg proposes that there are three components to intelligence, not multiple independent ones. In his model, intelligence is related to the successful interaction among these three: the internal (analytic), the external (creative), and the experiential (practical) components.

- *Internal (analytic)* This component of intelligence relates to the internal processing of information: acquiring information; planning, monitoring, and evaluating problems; or carrying out directions. The internal aspect of intelligence is the one most often measured by today's intelligence tests—the sort of intelligence needed for straightforward tasks and problems that we confront at school or work or in life.
- *External (creative)* Sternberg notes that some tasks are novel and so require a special way of thinking. Travelling to Russia for the first time, for example, requires more creative thinking than walking down a local street in your home town. Among other things, a traveller would have to figure out how to get through Russian customs, find his or her way to a hotel, and order meals in restaurants—all, perhaps, without knowing the language. This component of intelligence clearly requires creativity, and it also must interact with the internal component of intelligence to bring about successful results.
- *Experiential (practical)* This type of thinking helps us adapt to or improve our environments or select new environments. Let's say you move into a new home and find that the neighbours make a lot of noise when you are trying to go to sleep. At first, you might try to solve the problem by moving to another bedroom in the

house (adapting to the environment). If this doesn't work, you might try installing soundproof windows or complaining to the neighbours or to the landlord (changing the environment). And, finally, if that doesn't work, you might decide to move to another house (selecting a new environment).

Sternberg suggests that practical intelligence often relies on *tacit knowledge*, "action-oriented knowledge, acquired without direct help from others, that allows individuals to achieve goals they personally value" (Sternberg et al., 1995, p. 916). A successful business-person who earned only average grades in school has probably acquired considerable tacit knowledge, or "know-how," by working in the business environment and figuring out what is needed to get the work done. Not surprisingly, research shows that tacit knowledge is related to job success (Joia et al., 2010; Sternberg, 2003).

Sternberg argues that effective interactions among the internal, external, and experiential components are key to achieving successful intelligence—an advantageous balance between adapting to, shaping, and selecting problems encountered within one's environment. Because each intellectual component in Sternberg's theory actively relates to the others, his model is considered more dynamic, or interactive, than Gardner's. There is also more research evidence in support of Sternberg's theory. A number of studies have been able to measure and distinguish among the components of the triarchic theory of intelligence (Sternberg et al., 2000).

Stephen Ceci's Bioecological Theory of Intelligence Psychologist Stephen Ceci has proposed the bioecological model of intelligence, which holds that intelligence is "a function of the interactions between innate potential abilities, environmental context (ecology), and internal motivation" (**Figure 10-3**) (Barnett & Ceci, 2005; Ceci et al., 1997). According to Ceci, each person's innate abilities derive from a system of biological factors, or "resource pools." These resource pools are independent of each other, and each is responsible for different aspects of one's information-processing capabilities. Further, Ceci claims that a person's innate abilities will develop based more or less on how they interact with the individual's environmental resources, or context.

bioecological model of intelligence Ceci's theory that intelligence is a function of the interactions among innate potential abilities, environmental context, and internal motivation.

Consider, for example, a child whose biological resource pool endows her with the potential to succeed in math. Her abilities might lead to early successes in arithmetic, prompting her parents to provide environmental changes—her own computer, special enrichment opportunities in math, and so forth—that will help her to further develop her innate math potential. This encouraging environmental context will likely lead to further successes, which in turn may lead to additional environmental changes, such as enrollment in a special school.

Finally, according to the bioecological model, individuals must be internally *motivated* to fulfill their innate abilities and take advantage of their particular environments. When people feel motivated in certain areas, they tend to focus on their intellectual skills in those areas and to seek out environmental resources that are relevant. In an interesting study, Ceci found that men who were successful at race track betting and who produced complicated strategies for predicting winning horses did not demonstrate sophisticated thinking in other areas of functioning (Ceci & Liker, 1986). Clearly, such men were motivated to win serious money at the race track, and so developed complex intellectual processing and personal environmental opportunities (expertise) that might lead to that particular result.

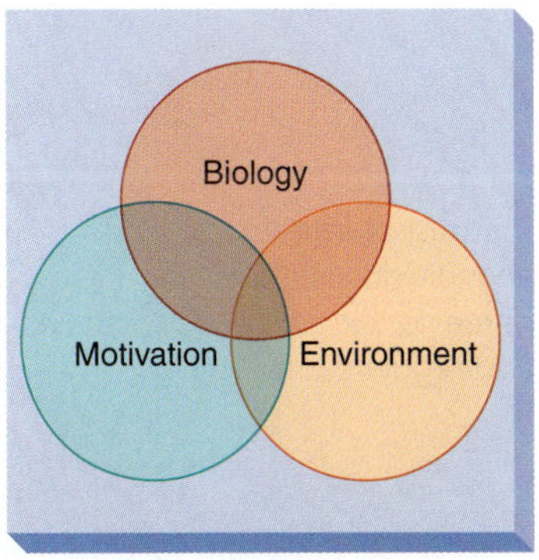

FIGURE 10-3 Ceci's bioecological model of intelligence. Stephen Ceci proposes that intelligence is the product of interaction among biological, environmental, and motivational resources, and that each resource is responsible for a different aspect of intelligence.

Where Are We Today?

Obviously, many theories on the nature of intelligence have been proposed and investigated. Is there a basic view upon which today's theorists agree? On the one hand, it would be fair to say that the majority do believe that intelligence *includes* a *g* factor—an overriding intellectual ability (Hunt, 2011; Larsen et al., 2008). On the other hand, few current theorists believe that the *g* factor is the best theory of intelligence. Most consider specific abilities (verbal, numerical, spatial skills, for example) and special factors (motivation, context, experience, and the like) to also be important in the expression of intelligence. The *g* factor is at work in every task that we confront in life, while the specific abilities and special factors come into play for some tasks but not others. This prevailing view is called a *hierarchical model* of intelligence (Castejon et al., 2010; Lubinski, 2004).

> "Knowing others is intelligence; knowing yourself is true wisdom. Mastering others is strength; mastering yourself is true power."
> —*Tao Te Ching, Chinese philosopher*

Because the *g* factor seems to play a role across all kinds of tasks, it is, of course, desirable to have a high degree of general intelligence. But the *g* factor alone will not consistently lead to outstanding performances or successes in school, work, or other areas of life. Conversely, verbal ability, high motivation, or proper environment alone rarely guarantees high intellectual achievement. Intelligence truly appears to be a complex, multifaceted phenomenon.

Before You Go On www.wiley.com/go/comer

What Do You Know?

1. Identify and define the two factors in Spearman's model of intelligence.
2. How does Thurstone's theory of primary mental abilities differ from Gardner's theory of multiple intelligences?
3. Name four of Gardner's intelligences. What are some of the concerns about Gardner's definition of intelligence(s)?
4. What are the three components of the triarchic theory of intelligence, and how do they contribute to mental functioning?
5. What are the main features that interact to produce intelligence in Ceci's theory?

SCAN TO GET THE ANSWERS

What Do You Think?

How would you define intelligence? Apply one or two of the theories to yourself and to one or two other people you know well. Do the theories fit with your general assumptions about intelligence?

Additional Types of Intelligence

LEARNING OBJECTIVE 2

Discuss several proposed types of intelligence that go beyond intellectual functioning.

The ideas and work that we have encountered so far consider a wide range of intellectual skills. But have they captured all aspects of intelligence? A growing number of theorists are focusing on the role of intelligence in emotions, social functioning, wisdom, creativity, and personality.

Emotional Intelligence

emotional intelligence an individual's ability to perceive, express, assimilate, and regulate emotion.

The concept of emotional intelligence is rather new—researchers began to actively study it in the 1990s. **Emotional intelligence** refers to an individual's ability to perceive, express, and assimilate emotion, and to regulate emotion in the self and others (Cherniss, 2010; Roberts et al., 2010; Goleman, 1995). Emotionally intelligent people are thought to be self-aware, sensitive to how they feel and how their feelings change, and able to manage their emotions so that they are not overwhelmed by them. People with well-developed emotional intelligence also tend to be empathic, knowing how to comfort and encourage others. Not surprisingly, they often succeed in their careers and marriages, as parents, and as leaders (Brackett et al., 2011; Martin, 2008).

If we grant the existence of emotional intelligence, then the question arises: can it be measured? In fact, researchers have devised a number of ways to measure it (Roberts et al., 2010). One test is the *Multifactor Emotional Intelligence Scale* (Maul, 2011; Mayer et al., 2003; Salovey et al., 2003). This test measures 12 emotional abilities that are, in turn, grouped into four "branches of abilities"—perceiving, facilitating, understanding, and managing emotion.

Although some theorists believe that certain individuals are inherently more skilled than others in the emotional sphere, other theorists argue that emotional intelligence can be learned and they call for schools and businesses to offer systematic instruction in the understanding and management of emotions (Alegre, 2011).

Emotional intelligence and acting. Their abilities to perceive and regulate emotions in themselves and in others enable successful actors to portray a wide range of characters. Jim Carrey, for example, has an exceptionally broad range of facial and emotional expressions he can draw on while acting.

Social Intelligence

Most people know someone who displays remarkable social savvy, a person who can walk right into a party or a meeting and just take over the room. Such people seem to know intuitively what is important to others, how to charm their way out of difficult situations, and how to gain the affection of everyone with whom they interact. Would you say these individuals are highly intelligent? Some theorists would say yes (Murphy & Hall, 2011; Goleman, 2006). Specifically, they would say that these individuals are high in *social intelligence.*

The notion of social intelligence is older than that of emotional intelligence. In fact, early in the twentieth century, the learning pioneer Edward Thorndike (whom you may remember from Chapter 7) suggested that intelligence consists of three facets: the ability to understand and manage ideas (abstract intelligence), concrete objects (mechanical intelligence), and people (social intelligence) (Thorndike, 1920). By social intelligence, Thorndike meant "the ability to understand and manage men and women, boys and girls—to act wisely in human relationships." Other theorists have described social intelligence more simply as the ability to get along with others. Either way, it is clearly an important asset, not only in interpersonal relationships, but also at school and work and in leadership roles (Furnham, 2009, 2008; Bass, 2002).

Social intelligence for profit. People with high social intelligence seem to have a natural grasp of what is important to others and an ability to help other people "open up." *The Hour*'s George Stroumboulopoulus uses his social intelligence to achieve professional success.

Wisdom

In myth, art, and popular culture, we often encounter characters who do not possess much formal education but who seem to have an insightful appreciation of life and the world. They are generally portrayed as experienced in the ways of the world; little about life appears to surprise them. These people are considered to possess *wisdom*, the ability to make sound judgments about important, difficult, or uncertain situations and to choose the best course of action (Karelitz, Jarvin, & Sternberg, 2010; Fowers, 2005, 2003). Are intelligence and wisdom the same thing?

Robert Sternberg (2010, 2008, 2003) believes that wisdom is a special version of intelligence, and has developed the *balance theory of wisdom* to account for this special capacity. Recall that in Sternberg's triarchic theory, intelligence consists of three aspects—analytic, creative, and practical—with practical intelligence involving the ability to effectively apply one's experiences and learning to everyday decisions. According to Sternberg, wisdom is

PSYCHOLOGY AROUND US Social Limits

Katniss Everdeen is a teenage girl forced to participate in a reality show in which teenagers must hunt and kill each other to entertain the masses. Katniss is the heroine of author Suzanne Collins' dystopian young adult novel, *The Hunger Games*. Katniss is unquestionably brilliant when it comes to hunting and survival. She's a particularly deadly archer, and she is smart enough to know how to get an edge up in the competition by destroying the food supply of wealthy rivals who aren't used to going hungry.

That said, as ultracompetent as she is at surviving, she struggles with managing relationships. When her fellow tribute Peeta starts to show signs of interest in her, she has no idea how to respond other than to treat it as gamesmanship and strategy. Katniss is so locked in to the idea of being a survivor that she can't remember how to form a human bond with someone else.

primarily (though not entirely) the product of practical intelligence. He says that wisdom is the application of tacit knowledge—"know-how"—to solve problems in such a way that a common good is achieved and a balance maintained among the interests of the individual, the community, and society. Sternberg distinguishes wisdom from other expressions of practical intelligence by noting that wisdom involves a particular concern for the community at large and a careful balancing of interests.

More than any other dimension of intelligence, wisdom may be associated with age. When people are asked to name someone in their lives whom they consider to be wise, they are more likely to point to a grandparent, an uncle or aunt, or a parent, rather than to a teenager or young adult. Why? Because it typically takes years and repeated experiences to appreciate the needs of the community, the advantages of compromise solutions, the drawbacks of self-serving decisions, and the delicate art of balancing multiple perspectives (Ardelt, 2011; Nair, 2003). That is, it takes time and experience to acquire a high degree of wisdom. However, not all older people are wise, and some younger people are wise; although there is a strong correlation between age and wisdom, age does not *cause* wisdom.

Creativity

creativity the ability to produce ideas that are both original and valuable.

Creativity is the ability to produce ideas that are both original and valuable (Kaufman & Sternberg, 2010). Like wisdom, creativity reflects collective, as well as personal, values. Societies benefit from the creativity of their members; indeed, creativity plays a key role in technological, scientific, and artistic advances. Thus, it is not surprising that different cultures define and appreciate creativity in different ways (Lubart, 2010; Runco, 2010, 2004). Creativity often requires verbal and mathematical skills in Western culture, for example, while it depends more on the ability to appreciate and interact with nature in some other cultures (Runco, 2004).

Psychologists who study creativity and intelligence typically believe that a high intellectual aptitude is necessary but not sufficient for creativity (Kim et al., 2010; Silvia, 2008). People who score high on intelligence tests tend to score high on tests of creativity, but beyond a certain point (that is, beyond an intelligence test score of about 120), the correlation between intelligence and creativity diminishes. Research has shown, for example, that on average, exceptionally creative architects, musicians, scientists, and engineers do not score higher on intelligence tests than do their less creative colleagues (MacKinnon & Hall, 1972). Thus, it appears that there is more to creativity than what intelligence tests measure.

Theorists and researchers have pointed to various personal qualities as being key to creativity (Cramond et al., 2010; Sternberg, 2010, 2003). At the top of the list is *intrinsic motivation*, an internal drive to create. Also cited frequently are *imagination*—an ability and willingness to reexamine problems in new ways—and a *game personality*, one that tolerates ambiguity, risk, and initial failure. Other useful qualities important to creative thought include complex thinking, broad attention, expertise in relevant fields, broad interests, high energy, independence, and self-confidence. Finally, divergent thinking is often seen as a key part of creativity. Measures of divergent thinking include seeing how many different ways people can think about simple objects or events. For example, how many different uses can you think of for a brick? The more uses you can come up with in two minutes, the higher your scores on other measures of creativity are likely to be (Runco, 1991).

Creativity around the world. Different cultures encourage different kinds of creativity. A woman who can decorate a customer's hand with a beautiful henna design in India (*left*) is considered highly creative and intelligent in her country, while a Canadian programmer who addresses his firm's production needs by developing a complex computer model (*right*) is called a "creative genius" by his colleagues.

Investigators have also found that creative thinking is, in fact, nurtured, inspired, and refined by creative environments (Beghetto et al., 2010; Sternberg, 2010). Creative environments share several qualities: they encourage people to be innovative; are relatively free of criticism; and provide freedom, creative role models, sufficient resources, and time to think and explore. Artist communities and schools for the performing arts aspire to be environments of this kind. Some such communities and schools succeed in this regard, while others become more demanding and competitive than nurturing. In addition, a creative environment need not be large or formal; it can exist in a supportive home, a positive work setting, or a comfortable class.

Creative environment? Dancers at the National Ballet of Canada are immersed in a creative environment.

Personality Characteristics

Even the earliest researchers of intelligence noted a relationship between intelligence and personality, our unique patterns of experiencing and acting in the world. Although intelligence tests often seek to separate intellectual functioning from personal style, many theorists argue that the division is artificial, that personality characteristics are inherent to intellectual functioning (Feist, 2010; Mayer, 2009, 2008). Indeed, David Wechsler, a pioneer in intelligence testing, considered intelligence to be a manifestation of personality (Wechsler, 1961). He thought that emotional, motivational, and other personal characteristics (such as interest and volition) must be key components of any meaningful notion of intelligence.

Following Wechsler's lead, a number of today's theorists think of intelligence as the cognitive part of personality (Murphy & Hall, 2011; Furnham & Monsen, 2009). Others propose a complex reciprocal relationship between intelligence and personality, with intellectual, emotional, and motivational variables repeatedly affecting each other in day-to-day behaviour (Hennessey, 2010; Mayer, 2008). Consistent with such notions, studies have found that negative emotional and motivational states can impair intellectual performance to some degree, especially when the intellectual tasks demand attention or quick recall. Conversely, certain personality factors, such as self-efficacy (the belief that one can master a demanding task) and a high need to achieve, often enhance performance on intellectual tasks (Freund & Holling, 2011; Lounsbury et al., 2009, 2003).

Before You Go On

www.wiley.com/go/comer

What Do You Know?

6. What is emotional intelligence and how is it measured?
7. How does Robert Sternberg describe wisdom in relation to his triarchic theory of intelligence?
8. What are some factors that affect creativity?

What Do You Think?

Suppose you were given the job of making up a test to assess social intelligence. What kinds of questions would you include on the test?

SCAN TO GET THE ANSWERS

How Do We Measure Intelligence?

LEARNING OBJECTIVE 3

Identify important considerations in the construction of intelligence tests, discuss the history of intelligence testing, and describe some criticisms of intelligence tests.

For better or for worse, the history of intelligence theory is completely intertwined with the history of intelligence testing. That is, both the theories psychologists propose and the tests they devise affect how they understand intelligence. It was only about a century ago that researchers and statisticians first fashioned standardized tests and statistical methods with which to assess intelligence. In the West, one of the oldest and most enduring approaches to understanding and assessing intelligence is the psychometric approach. The **psychometric approach** attempts to measure intelligence with carefully constructed psychological tests, called *intelligence tests*. The psychometric approach is also used to construct measures for other human individual difference dimensions such as personality.

psychometric approach an approach to defining intelligence that attempts to measure intelligence with carefully constructed psychological tests.

Before examining in detail some of the ways people have measured intelligence throughout history, it's worthwhile to think about what qualities make a good intelligence test. Knowing how psychologists build and use intelligence tests will help you make up your own mind about what these tests mean. Keep in mind, though, that much of the reason we are able to think about intelligence in such a sophisticated way today is that we have benefited from the insights and mistakes of the theorists and researchers we will be discussing later.

Intelligence Test Construction and Interpretation

Intelligence test constructors typically assume a comparative view of test scores. That is, intelligence is typically measured by comparing one person's test scores with another's. There is no absolute or independent standard of intelligence against which to compare intelligence test scores (i.e., there is no mental dipstick to use to know someone's intelligence with absolute certainty). Because of this comparative approach, a number of cautions or limits on how we think about and use intelligence measures arise. First, a test must function the same in different groups of people (so that individuals do not get different scores just because they are from different ethnic groups or different parts of the country). Second, similar items on a test must relate both to one another and to the material of interest (to the things the test is supposed to predict, like school grades). To ensure that intelligence tests are grounded in sound scientific principles, psychologists design tests that adhere to three basic criteria: standardization, reliability, and validity (Bowden et al., 2011; Canivez & Watkins, 2010).

standardization the use of uniform procedures in administering and scoring a test.

normal distribution a symmetrical, bell-shaped distribution in which most scores are in the middle, with smaller groups of equal size at either end.

median the score exactly in the middle of a distribution.

mean the average score in a distribution.

mode the score that occurs most frequently in a distribution.

Standardization If you were the only person taking a particular intelligence test, your score would mean very little. For your score to have meaning, it must be compared with the scores of people who have already taken the same test. This group of people is referred to as a standardization or normative *sample*. If all subsequent test-takers follow the same procedures as those used by the standardization or normative sample, then each individual's test score can be compared with the scores of the sample. The process of obtaining meaningful test scores from a standardization or normative sample through the use of uniform procedures is called **standardization**.

Test results from large populations tend to follow particular patterns, called *distributions*. Scores on intelligence tests follow a **normal distribution** (or *normal curve*), a statistical pattern in which most people achieve fairly similar scores at or near the middle of the distribution, while a small number earn low scores and an equally small number earn high scores. In graph form, these results form a bell-shaped pattern, often called a *bell curve* (see **Figure 10-4**).

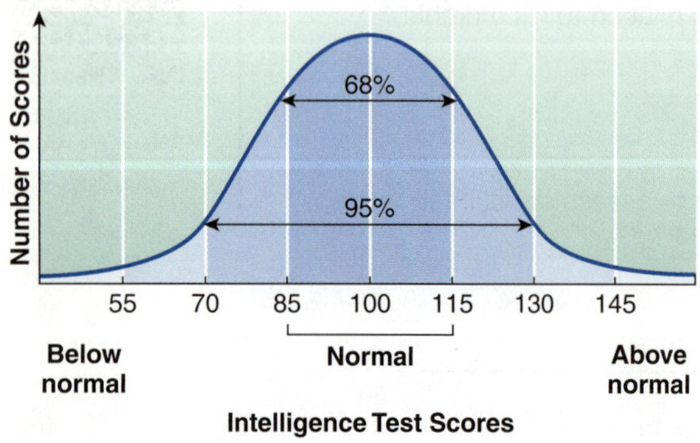

FIGURE 10-4 The bell curve of intelligence scores. The distribution of scores on intelligence tests follows a statistical pattern called the bell curve. Most peoples' scores fall in the middle range, with a small number scoring at the extreme ends.

In a normal distribution, the scores of most people fall in the vicinity of the **median** score (that is, the middle score). The scores that are higher or lower than the median keep declining in number as the scores extend farther and farther from the median. The very lowest and the very highest scores are found at the outer edges of the bell curve. The median score is but one indicator of a population's central tendencies. Others include the **mean**, or the average score, and the **mode**, the score that occurs most frequently in the population. If a sample is properly standardized into a normal distribution, the median, mean, and mode should be the same.

Reliability The second criterion that is needed for a test to be of value is reliability. When a test is reliable, it consistently produces similar scores for the same test-takers over time. Psychologists have developed several ways to show that a test is reliable. One approach (*test-retest reliability*) is to administer it once and then a second time, in either the same version or a version that is slightly different. If the scores on the two administrations agree for each individual, they are said to correlate highly, and the test is considered to be reliable. Another approach (*split-half reliability*) is to divide the items on a single test into two tests, and see whether each individual's scores on the two halves of the test correlate highly. Whatever the approach, the higher the statistical correlation between scores, the greater the reliability. Remember from Chapter 2 that a correlation can vary from a value of −1.00 to +1.00. To be reliable, a test must produce very similar results when administered to the same people within a short period of time (so that we can assume little has changed between testing sessions). A correlation between the first and second test administration scores that is up near +1.00 indicates that the test is stable or *reliable*.

reliability the degree to which a test produces the same scores over time.

Validity A test with a high degree of reliability does not necessarily have high validity. Validity is the extent to which a test accurately measures or predicts what it is supposed to measure or predict. Suppose, for example, we use a broken scale to weigh the residents of a town and we weigh each resident multiple times. Assuming that, for each person, the scale repeatedly yields the same weight, the resulting weights would be said to have a high degree of reliability. The results, however, would have low validity because the weights offered by the broken scales are not accurate; that is, although everyone's weight would be uniformly reported, no one's reported weight would be correct. We would not know how much anyone actually weighs.

validity the extent to which a test accurately measures or predicts what it is supposed to measure or predict.

How can we determine the validity, or accuracy, of a test? Often we can simply look at the test's content. If you were to administer a test on Chinese grammar to assess students' mastery of French, the test would not demonstrate much content validity. By contrast, if you were taking flying lessons and your instructor tested you on your understanding of the instrument panel and other kinds of relevant information, the test would demonstrate high content validity.

content validity the degree to which the content of a test accurately represents what the test is intended to measure.

We can also assess the validity of tests by correlating test scores with an external criterion that we have some confidence in—a correlation called a validity coefficient. If, for example, we believe that intelligent people will perform better at school (because of their higher intelligence), then we expect individuals' scores on a particular intelligence test to correlate with their school grades. The higher the validity coefficient, the more valid the test. A test need not just measure current performance. When high scores on an intelligence test continue to successfully predict high grades later in life, it is said to display high predictive validity (Gow et al., 2011).

validity coefficient a correlation coefficient that measures validity by correlating a test score with some external criterion.

predictive validity the extent to which scores on a particular test successfully predict the things it is supposed to predict.

History of Intelligence Testing

The first systematic attempts to measure intelligence were developed during the second half of the nineteenth century. The most influential approaches were those of Francis Galton in England and Alfred Binet in France. Later, in the United States, Lewis Terman and David Wechsler made important contributions.

Galton and "*Psychophysical Performance*" Profoundly affected by the work of his half-cousin Charles Darwin, Francis Galton (1822–1911) sought to apply Darwin's ideas about evolution to the study of intelligence. He believed that by studying intellectual development, he could learn more about the evolution of the human species in general, and the inheritance of intelligence in particular (Hunt, 2010; Fancher, 2009, 2004). In particular, Galton sought to understand why some people appear to be more intelligent than others. If he could understand the evolutionary factors at work in such differences, he reasoned, then steps could be taken to improve the species.

Galton, who believed in a general intelligence factor, proposed that two qualities distinguish more gifted from less gifted people: a kind of psychic energy and a heightened sensitivity to external stimuli. His theory, termed the *theory of psychophysical performance*, held that people with more energy can perform more work and, in turn, develop greater intelligence. In addition, inasmuch as people gather information from their five senses, individuals who have more highly developed senses can take in more information (Kaufman, 2000). To more accurately gauge intelligence, Galton developed tests of an individual's sensory processing, motor skills, and reaction time.

"Intelligence is not to make no mistakes, but quickly to see how to make them good."
—*Bertholt Brecht, playwright*

Galton's work influenced many theorists. James McKean Cattell, in particular, later designed 50 psychophysical tests, expecting that the tests would support and extend Galton's ideas (Sokal, 2010; Tulsky et al., 2003). Cattell tested skills, such as how fast people can move their arm over a specified distance and how many letters in a series they can remember. Ironically, Cattell's tests eventually helped to discredit Galton's notions rather than support them by supporting the idea that there is more than one general form of intelligence.

In his doctoral dissertation, one of Cattell's students, Clark Wissler, hypothesized that people would perform consistently well or consistently poorly across the various psychophysical tests, and that those who did consistently well would display a higher level of general intelligence than those who performed poorly (Wissler, 1961). However, Wissler found that a given person's various test performances did not necessarily correlate either with each other or with academic performance. To determine whether each research participant's performances on various psychophysical tests were in fact correlated, Wissler used *correlation coefficients*—a statistical method developed by Galton. Thus, the use of Galton's own statistical tool eventually helped to challenge his theory. Although in general, his psychophysical theory of intelligence was not supported, certain of his specific physical measures have been found to relate to other measures of intelligence.

Intelligence testing pioneers. Alfred Binet (pictured) and Theodore Simon developed the first standardized intelligence test for use in sorting new arrivals into the Paris school system, following the passage of mandatory school attendance laws.

Alfred Binet and the Binet-Simon Intelligence Test At the same time that Galton and his followers were developing psychophysical theories and tests, Alfred Binet (1857–1911), along with his collaborator Theodosius Simon, were viewing intelligence and its measurement in a different way.

In 1904, the French government mandated compulsory education, and the Minister of Public Instruction in Paris formed a commission to devise a way to distinguish children with mental retardation from those who were unsuccessful in school for other reasons, such as behavioural problems. The idea was to assign intellectually capable children to regular classes and place those with mental retardation in special classes. To help determine the most appropriate type of class for each child, Binet and Simon devised the first widely applied intelligence tests (Hunt, 2010).

Binet shared with Galton the notion of a general intelligence factor. However, regarding the psychophysical theory as "wasted time," he argued that the basis of intelligence is "judgment, otherwise called good sense, practical sense, initiative, the faculty of adapting one's self to circumstances. To judge well, to comprehend well, to reason well, these are the essential activities of intelligence." In short, Binet viewed intelligence as the "ability to demonstrate memory, judgment, reasoning, and social comprehension."

The tasks on Binet's intelligence test focused largely on language abilities, in contrast to the many non-verbal tasks devised by Galton. Binet also introduced the idea of mental age, the intellectual age at which a child is actually functioning. **Mental age** does not necessarily match chronological age. A child's mental age is indicated by the chronological age typically associated with his or her level of intellectual performance. Thus, the typical

mental age the intellectual age at which a person is functioning, as opposed to chronological age.

11-year-old has a mental age of 11. A more intelligent 11-year-old, however, might have a mental age of 13, while a less intelligent 11-year-old might have a mental age of 9.

Binet did not believe his intelligence test necessarily measured a child's *inborn* level of intelligence. His goal was simply to predict a student's likelihood of success in school. And, in fact, he did find a strong correlation between performance on his test and performance in school. The test also correlated with scores on *achievement tests*—tests of knowledge about particular school subjects—although at a lower magnitude.

It is worth noting that Binet refused to use test scores to rank children. He felt that intelligence is too complex a phenomenon to draw meaningful conclusions about the *relative* intelligence among most children. It would be unfair to say, he argued, that one child of average intelligence, as measured by his test, was more intelligent than another child of average intelligence. However, Binet's concerns did not stop others from extending his test in ways that he neither anticipated nor advocated.

Lewis Terman and the Stanford-Binet Intelligence Test Interest in Binet's work spread throughout the world, and Stanford University professor Lewis Terman (1877–1956) adapted the Binet-Simon intelligence test for use in the United States. He realized that some of the test items, originally developed to test French children, needed to be changed to better assess the intelligence of children in the United States. The age norms, for example, did not apply to the American school children in Terman's sample. This was an important early recognition of the influence of culture in intelligence testing. Terman called his new test the Stanford-Binet Intelligence Test (Simonton, 2010; Raid & Tippin, 2009).

In developing his version of Binet's test, Terman decided to state the results not simply in terms of mental age, but as a measure that would relate mental to chronological age. Thus, the famous **intelligence quotient**, or **IQ**, was devised. To arrive at this measure of intelligence, Terman calculated the ratio of mental age to chronological age and multiplied that ratio by 100 (to remove the decimal point). Thus, returning to our earlier examples, the 11-year-old with average intelligence would earn an IQ of 100 (11/11 × 100), the more intelligent child would post an IQ of 118 (13/11 × 100), and the less intelligent child's IQ would be 82 (9/11 × 100).

intelligence quotient (IQ) Terman's measure of intelligence; the ratio of a child's mental age to his or her chronological age, multiplied by 100.

In addition to adapting Binet's test for use in American schools, Terman had a larger goal—a goal that today is considered reprehensible. He was an advocate of the nineteenth century *eugenics movement*, which sought to discourage people deemed as "unfit" from reproducing, while encouraging "fit" individuals to have children (Leslie, 2000). He believed that his IQ test could help determine the "fitness" of individuals to reproduce. He stated, "[T]he children of successful and cultured parents test higher than children from wretched and ignorant homes for the simple reason that their heredity is better." More generally, Terman believed that his test demonstrated that some groups of people are inherently less intelligent than others (Hegarty, 2007; Feldhusen, 2003).

Working with agencies in the United States government, Terman also administered his test to newly arrived immigrants and to almost two million World War I army recruits. His student, Arthur Otis, developed non-verbal tasks for non-English speaking individuals. Some psychologists at the time believed that the results of these alternative versions of the intelligence test proved the inferiority of people whose origins were not Anglo-Saxon. In fact, the mass testing of immigrants helped lead to a 1924 law that greatly lowered the number of people allowed to enter the United States from Southern and Eastern Europe, while increasing the number from Northern and Western Europe. This is a vivid example of how non-scientific thinking (for example, prejudice and racism) can sometimes influence scientific thinking and political decision making. Despite such misuse of the early Stanford-Binet test, it remained for many years

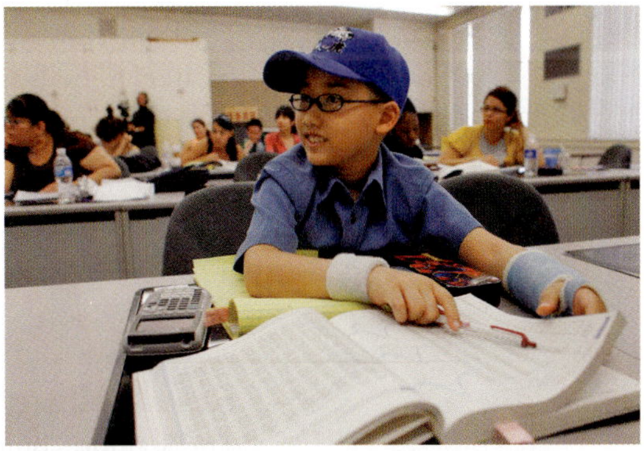

A high IQ. Michael Kearney graduated high school at 6 years of age, junior college at age 8, and received his first degree (a Bachelor's degree in Anthropology) at age 10.

As a result of eugenics research, two Canadian Provinces (Alberta in 1928 and British Columbia in 1933) enacted laws requiring individuals deemed "mentally retarded" or "mentally ill" to be sterilized. Nazi practices during World War II led to public distaste for eugenics, but these laws were not repealed in Canada until 1972.

the leading intelligence testing instrument in the United States and Canada.

David Wechsler and the WAIS As a young man inducted into the army during World War I, David Wechsler (1896–1981) was trained to administer and score the Stanford-Binet and other intelligence tests of the time. Over the course of his work, he came to recognize two key problems with the tests (Kaufman, 2009, 2000).

First, he realized that the distinction between mental and chronological age becomes less informative when testing adults. While it may be true that a considerable difference in intelligence may be evident between an 8-year-old and a 13-year-old, a five-year difference between adults tends to be meaningless. How much difference is there, for example, between the mental ability of a typical 30-year-old and a typical 35-year-old? Not much. Second, Wechsler, who was born in Romania and whose family emigrated to the United States when he was 6 years old, recognized the need for greater fairness when testing people who did not speak English or who spoke it poorly.

Over the course of his professional life, Wechsler devised a number of intelligence tests that took such problems into account. The first such test—the *Wechsler-Bellevue Intelligence Scale*—was published in 1939. Different versions of Wechsler's tests continue to be published by his associates to the present day (Watkins, 2010; Hartman, 2009). The best known of these tests are the *Wechsler Adult Intelligence Scale* (*WAIS*) and the *Wechsler Intelligence Scale for Children* (*WISC*). **Figure 10-5** shows sample items from the WAIS.

Wechsler borrowed much from the Stanford-Binet and other tests; however, his tests were less dominated by tasks requiring verbal ability. There are 12 subtests on the current 4th edition of the WAIS, some requiring verbal ability and others requiring non-verbal reasoning. Each individual who takes the test receives subtest scores, which are grouped into two main categories—a verbal score (further divided into a verbal comprehension and a working memory index) and a performance score (further divided into a perceptual organization and a processing speed index). The individual also receives an overall score that Wechsler associated with the *g* factor. Wechsler also discarded the old formula for calculating an IQ score. Although he still called a person's overall score an *intelligence quotient*, or *IQ*, he derived the score from a normal distribution (discussed earlier in this chapter), rather than from a ratio. Essentially, he would compare individual scores to scores obtained over a very large sample of individuals. Using the normal distribution, Wechsler could see how much individual scores differenced from or deviated from (were higher or lower than) the general estimate of the population average. This change in IQ score generation has been adopted in most other intelligence tests.

Wechsler's tests resulted from his clinical experience, not from a clear theoretical position. However, he did come to develop a broad view of what intelligence means. In particular, he believed that it is more than success on test scores. To him, intelligence is at work as individuals try to manage the day-to-day aspects of life, interact with others, and perform at work. Wechsler's broad view of intelligence has gained momentum over the years. Indeed, as we suggested earlier, it lies at the centre of most current theories of intelligence.

How Well Do Intelligence Tests Predict Performance?

The Stanford-Binet and the WAIS have very high degrees of reliability (Hunt, 2010). The correlation coefficient for retakes of each test is about +.90. Furthermore, repeated measurements of IQ across the lifespan tend to correlate very highly (Gow et al., 2011; Larsen et al., 2008). Today's leading intelligence tests are also highly correlated with school

Wechsler Adult Intelligence Scale (WAIS) Sample Items

Test	Description	Example
Verbal Scale		
Information	Taps general range of information	On which continent is France?
Comprehension	Tests understanding of social conventions and ability to evaluate past experience	Why do people need birth certificates?
Arithmetic	Tests arithmetic reasoning through verbal problems	How many hours will it take to drive 150 miles at 50 miles per hour?
Similarities	Asks in what way certain objects or concepts are similar; measures abstract thinking	How are a calculator and a typewriter alike?
Digit span	Tests attention and rote memory by orally presenting series of digits to be repeated forward or backward	Repeat the following numbers backward: 2 4 3 5 1 8 6
Vocabulary	Tests ability to define increasingly difficult words	What does repudiate mean?
Performance scale		
Digit symbol	Tests speed of learning through timed coding tasks in which numbers must be associated with marks of various shapes	Shown: 1 2 3 4 Fill in: 4 2 1 3 
Picture completion	Tests visual alertness and visual memory through presentation of an incompletely drawn figure; the missing part must be discovered and named	Tell me what is missing: 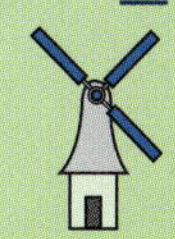
Block design	Tests ability to perceive and analyze patterns presenting designs that must be copied with blocks	Assemble blocks to match this design: 
Picture arrangement	Tests understanding of social situations through a series of comic-strip-type pictures that must be arranged in the right sequence to tell a story	Put this picture in the right order: 
Object assembly	Tests ability to deal with part/whole relationships by presenting puzzle pieces that must be assembled to form a complete object	Assemble the pieces into a complete object: 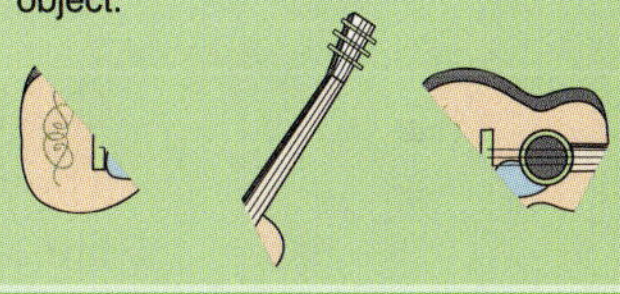

FIGURE 10-5 Items similar to those on the WAIS. The widely used WAIS gives separate scores for verbal intelligence and performance, as well as an overall intelligence score.

Source: Harcourt Assessment, Inc.

performance—a validity coefficient of about +.50 (Lynn & Meisenberg, 2010; Sternberg et al., 2001). The correlations are even higher between IQ scores and the number of years of schooling that people complete (Ceci, 1991). These findings are especially relevant considering that IQ tests were originally designed to assess for school performance.

PSYCHOLOGY AROUND US Cramming at an Early Age

To gain admission to some prestigious private schools, children as young as 4 years are required to take the Wechsler Preschool and Primary Scale of Intelligence (WPPSI). This test is a revision of the more commonly used intelligence tests for older children (WISC) and adults (WAIS). The WPPSI, now in its third edition, is intended to measure the basic components of intelligence, just as its cousins try to do with older persons.

But evidence indicates that the WPPSI is quite unreliable (unlike the WISC and WAIS). The more often preschoolers take the test, the higher they will score. It is also particularly sensitive to practice effects. All of this calls into question the test's usefulness as an admissions test for access to exclusive private schools.

In fact, the biggest controversy surrounding the WPPSI has focused on parents' attempt to game the test by hiring psychologists to administer the test to their young children beforehand. Many parents acquire versions of the WPPSI to train their children, and some also have the children attend test prep services. In at least one high-profile case, a mother sued her child's preschool for $19,000, saying that the preschool had not adequately prepared her child for the WPPSI. Apparently, the preschool had merely provided a playroom where the child could interact and paint and hang out with other children. Of course, in the old days, that's what preschools were all about.

Research suggests you are just as likely to win a Nobel prize if you have an IQ of 130 as if you have an IQ of 180. (Sulloway, 1996)

Of course, IQ tests are meant to do more than predict school (or preschool!) performance. When we talk about IQ, though, we often think about it in terms of defining general mental ability. After all, we still measure IQ for adults far past school age. This is so even though most of the tasks on any IQ test relate most strongly to school performance. Although these tasks are highly relevant to the types of challenges encountered in school—math, store of knowledge, reasoning—it is unclear to what degree they measure the many other types of intelligence that we have described in this chapter.

So what does IQ mean outside the classroom? Performance on intelligence tests correlates to some degree with other areas of functioning in life, such as occupational and social achievements, income, and health-related behaviours (Hunt, 2011; Cramond et al., 2010; Lubinski, 2004). In a massive undertaking, researchers administered the same intelligence test to every 11-year-old child in Scotland in 1932 and 1947, and then followed the children's development and achievements as they moved through the lifespan (Deary et al., 2004). Performance on the IQ test at this young age was found to correlate to some degree with better health throughout life, greater independence during old age, and a longer lifespan. It would appear, then, that IQ testing does have some relevance beyond the school ages. However, it is important to recall that these relationships are correlational. We do not know that higher intelligence *caused* any of these outcomes.

Cultural Bias and Stereotypes in Intelligence Testing

Though widely used and respected, intelligence tests are subject to many criticisms, both fair and unfair. One set of concerns involves *cultural bias* (Tomes, 2010; Wicherts & Dolan, 2010). As mentioned earlier, different cultures may have different ideas of intelligence. For example, Western intelligence tests emphasize abilities, such as logic, mathematical skill, and verbal fluency rather than emphasizing abilities, such as getting along with others and fitting in with one's environment—abilities that are important in Chinese notions of intelligence. Such differences obviously make comparing intelligence across cultures challenging.

Is Intelligence an Important Part of Diagnosing Learning Disabilities?

Intelligence tests have historically played a central role in defining and diagnosing learning disabilities. Children with learning disabilities have difficulty processing certain types of information. These include, but are not limited to: language processing; phonological processing (recall chapter 9); visual spatial processing; processing speed; memory and attention; and executive functions (e.g., planning and decision making) (Learning Disabilities Association of Canada, 2002).

The current standard definition of learning disability that shapes education assessment, practice, and policy has two parts. The American Department of Education definition states that a learning disability may exist if "1. The child does not achieve commensurate with his or her age and ability when provided with appropriate educational experiences, and 2. The child has a severe discrepancy between achievement and intellectual ability in one or more areas relating to communication skills and mathematical abilities" (USDE, 1977, p. 65083). The current Canadian definition is similar, defining a learning disability as reflecting a discrepancy between assessed intelligence and achievement, and viewing it as reflecting a cognitive

processing disorder or condition with processing deficits (Kozey & Siegel, 2008).

Lee Gunderson and Sandra Scarr at the University of British Columbia are among many psychologists concerned about the effects associated with this discrepancy definition of learning disabilities (2001). They point out that intelligence tests play a central, sometimes provincially-mandated, role in determining if a discrepancy exists that would indicate the presence of a learning disability. The discrepancy in question is between a score on an intelligence test and either scores on an educational achievement test battery or school grades. The reasoning is that if a child is not achieving in school to the level that would be anticipated based upon their intelligence test score, then she may have a learning disability (that would be identified with a more specific learning assessment). Once the child's learning issues are identified, a specialized program of instruction or individual program plan can be created to addresses the child's challenges and draws on his strengths to assist him to achieve educationally.

Scarr and Gunderson have no concerns about this, but point out that the discrepancy approach also leads to children who are not achieving educationally but whose intelligence test scores are also low not being considered for learning disabilities. They point out that children with low reading scores and with or without low intelligence test scores benefit equally from reading disability programs (Siegel, 1992). In one study, the children with lower intelligence scores actually showed greater reading improvements in a reading program than did students without low intelligence scores (Yule, 1973). Scarr and Gunderson suggest that we focus on all students who need help with learning, rather than limiting program access to those with intelligence/achievement discrepancies.

Scarr and Gunderson state that ESL (English as a second language) students with learning issues are particularly likely to be missed, as their incomplete fluency in English can suppress their scores on intelligence tests (as such tests rely heavily on fluency in English, or in whatever language in which the test was constructed). ESL children with learning disabilities may not show the required discrepancy because their intelligence test scores are suppressed by their lack of fluency in the test language. As a result, many ESL students with learning disabilities do not receive educational assistance that would benefit them.

Finally, Scarr and Gunderson warn of something called the Matthew effect. Named by sociologist Robert Merton (1968) the effect is based on a passage from the Gospel of Matthew: "For to all those who have, more will be given, and they will have an abundance; but from those who have nothing, even what they have will be taken away (Matthew 25:29)." The passage is taken to mean that the rich get richer and the poor get poorer. In terms of reading, Keith Stanovich (1986) points out that reading competence plays an increasingly important role in both school performances across all subjects and in intelligence test performance. As a consequence, children with unaddressed reading issues will have intelligence test scores that fall back further and further from those of their peers as they move through their elementary school years. If their reading issues are not picked up early, the Matthew effect will drive down their intelligence test scores over their elementary years, making it less likely that a diagnostic discrepancy will be there to be picked up. As a result, rich (good) readers get better while poor readers get poorer and are less and less likely to get the assistance they need to stop their reading (and achievement and academic self-confidence) slide.

Scarr and Gunderson conclude that we should move away from our consistent use of intelligence tests as part of the process of identifying children with learning disabilities. Instead, they suggest that we move to a more direct assessment of learning abilities so that we do not withhold support and treatment from children who would benefit from it.

Furthermore, problems are not limited to comparing people from different countries, but extend to comparing members of different subcultures within a single country. For example, although Wechsler made considerable efforts to standardize the WAIS and make it as unbiased as possible, critics noted several curious oversights in earlier versions of the test. Many of its problem-solving questions reflected learning experiences and opportunities more commonly encountered in middle-class settings. For instance, the quality of the education experiences provided middle-class children is higher, and they acquire vocabularies at home and school

TABLE 10-3 Sample Items from the Chitling Test

1. A "handkerchief head" is: (a) a cool cat, (b) a porter, (c) an Uncle Tom, (d) a hoddi, (e) a preacher.
2. Which word is most out of place here? (a) splib, (b) blood, (c) gray, (d) spook, (e) black.
3. Cheap chitlings (not the kind you purchase at a frozen food counter) will taste rubbery unless they are cooked long enough. How soon can you quit cooking them to eat and enjoy them? (a) 45 minutes, (b) 2 hours, (c) 24 hours, (d) 1 week (on a low flame), (e) 1 hour.
4. If you throw the dice and 7 is showing on the top, what is facing down? (a) 7, (b) snake eyes, (c) boxcars, (d) little Joes, (e) 11.
5. "Jet" is: (a) an East Oakland motorcycle club, (b) one of the gangs in "West Side Story," (c) a news and gossip magazine, (d) a way of life for the very rich.
6. "Bird" or "Yardbird" was the "jacket" that jazz lovers from coast to coast hung on: (a) Lester Young, (b) Peggy Lee, (c) Benny Goodman, (d) Charlie Parker, (e) "Birdman of Alcatraz."
Find the whole test here: http://wilderdom.com/personality/intelligenceChitlingTestShort.html

that are more representative of the vocabulary skills assumed by intelligence test developers (Hunt, 2011; Ford, 2008). In addition, until the most recent revisions of the WAIS, every time a picture of a person was used for a test item, the picture was of a Caucasian person.

stereotype vulnerability or threat a phenomenon in which people in a particular group perform poorly because they fear that their performance will conform to a negative stereotype associated with that group.

In part to point out the culture-specific nature of intelligence testing, sociologist Adrian Dove created the Dove Counterbalance General Intelligence Test (now called the Chitling Test; see **Table 10-3**). Dove intended the test to be at least partly a satire of the notion that a culture-free intelligence test could ever be developed. Dove's test helps us to clearly see that all intelligence tests are grounded in particular cultural perspectives. It is likely that there will always be culture-based disagreements about intelligence tests and about what knowledge and skills are important.

Most people interested in the construction of intelligence tests have abandoned the idea of totally unbiased tests, and instead try to design tests that do not put particular cultures at an absolute disadvantage. The Progressive Matrices Test attempts to achieve this goal in part by emphasizing abstract, non-verbal skills, for example. However, there are still cultural and education influences on scores for this measure (Owen, 1992). As such, the test is acknowledged to not be culture free, but it is somewhat more culture fair than other intelligence tests. **Figure 10-6** shows some sample items from that test.

FIGURE 10-6 Item similar to the Progressive Matrices Test. This test emphasizes abstract, non-verbal skills. Here the respondent chooses which of the numbered boxes below finishes the sequence above. (Box #6 is the correct answer.)

A related testing issue involves **stereotype vulnerability or threat**, which occurs when people in a particular group perform poorly because they fear that their performance will conform to a negative stereotype associated with their group. Several studies have found that simply suggesting to students that they will not do well on a test because of their gender or race can lower their test scores (Owens & Massey, 2011; Steele & Aronson, 2004, 1995). In one particularly interesting study, researchers were able to use stereotype threat to manipulate the performance of Asian women on a math test (Ambady et al., 2004, 2001; Shih, Pittinsky, & Ambady, 1999). Some participants were encouraged to focus on their female identity, and they tended to perform less well on the test (in keeping with the stereotype that women are not good at math). Other participants had their attention focused on their Asian identity, and they tended to perform better (in keeping with the stereotype that Asians are good at math). Those given no encouragement to think about their gender or racial heritage still showed the above effects, depending on whether they were tested in a room with males (implicitly drawing attention to the females' gender) or with non-Asian students (implicitly drawing attention to their racial heritage). Finally, these effects were reduced if the participants read a prepared "scientific" article which stated that the stereotypes (females bad at math and Asians good at math) were not true (Smith & White, 2002).

As psychologists' awareness and ability to detect bias grows, they are becoming increasingly able to construct tests that are more sensitive and more effective. We have, for example, already noted the efforts of developers of the WAIS to make their tests less culture-specific. Overall bias can be assessed both at the general level we have discussed here and also at a more detailed level. During test construction, today's tests are also assessed for *item bias*; if individuals from a particular gender or ethnic group miss an item with high frequency, that item is considered for elimination from the test. Similarly, certain questions may become less culturally relevant even for the majority culture over time and must be exchanged for questions that better reflect current conditions. It appears that ongoing efforts to assess and challenge these sorts of bias have been somewhat successful in rendering generally non-biased testing (Ford, Moore, & Whiting, 2006; Whiting & Ford, 2006).

The power of stereotype vulnerability or threat. In one study, Asian women who were encouraged to focus largely on their female identity performed poorly on a math test, while those who were led to focus on their Asian identity performed well on the math test.

If you are interested in reading more about the good and not so good history of psychological efforts to measure intelligence, we recommend a book by Stephen Jay Gould, a now deceased Harvard paleontologist, called *The Mismeasure of Man* (1996). In addition to examining the history of IQ test development, this book also looks at early attempts to determine intelligence levels by measuring head size or cranial capacity.

Is Human Intelligence Increasing?

We have observed that the median score on intelligence tests, such as the Stanford-Binet and the WAIS, is set at 100. To keep the median score at 100, the tests periodically must be *restandardized*. People taking the WAIS today, for example, are taking a version that has been reconstructed—not the version that David Wechsler designed originally.

Upon reviewing test scores over time, researchers have noticed something startling: intelligence test scores from around the industrialized world seem to be increasing, even though scores from other kinds of educational tasks and tests, such as college aptitude tests, are dropping (Nettelbeck & Wilson, 2004). Studies indicate that an average IQ score of 100 from 70 years ago would equate to a score of only 76 today. This puzzling phenomenon has been named the Flynn effect, after New Zealand researcher James Flynn (2007), who first discovered it in data from at least 14 nations (**Figure 10-7**).

Flynn effect an observed rise in average IQ scores throughout the world over time.

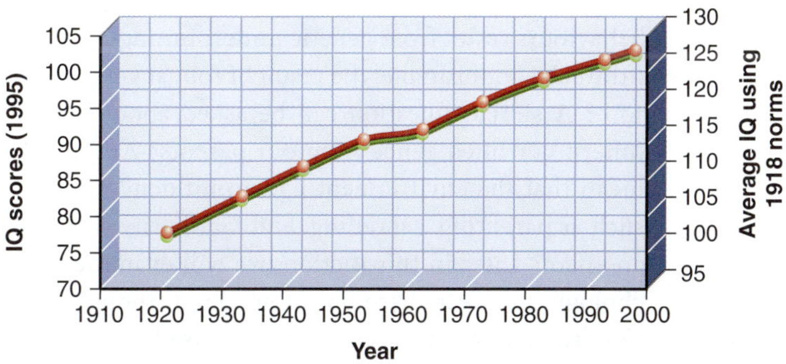

FIGURE 10-7 The Flynn effect. Flynn demonstrated that intelligence scores have increased from 1918 to 1995. The right axis of the graph shows that if the 1918 scales were used today, the average IQ score in the United States would be 125. The left axis shows that if the 1995 scales were used, the average IQ score in 1918 would equate to a score of 76 today. Source: Adapted from Flynn, J. R. (1998). IQ gains over time: Toward finding the causes. In U. Neisser (Ed.), The rising curve: Long-term gains in IQ and related measures (p. 37). Washington, DC: American Psychological Association. Copyright © by the American Psychological Association. Reprinted by permission of the author.

Researchers do not fully understand why intelligence scores have increased over time (Ceci & Kanaya, 2010; Weiss, 2010). One possibility is that there is something wrong with the basic procedures, content, or nature of standardized intelligence tests. A more widely embraced explanation holds that intelligence is changeable and that, on average, people today exhibit higher intelligence than people did in the past. Such improvements in intelligence might be related to improvements in education around the world, better nutrition, the development of more stimulating environments, reductions in childhood disease, or evolutionary shifts in genetic inheritance (Mingroni, 2007, 2004). It is also worth noting that some theorists believe that rising intelligence test performance is due to the greater test-writing sophistication and test-taking motivation of today's students (Neisser, 1997).

Before You Go On

www.wiley.com/go/comer

What Do You Know?

9. What three basic criteria are central to designing an intelligence test?
10. What was the original purpose of Binet's intelligence test? How did he measure intelligence?
11. How does mental age differ from chronological age?
12. How does Terman's definition of IQ differ from that of Wechsler?
13. What are the components of the WAIS and WISC intelligence tests? Give a couple of examples of what is measured on each component.
14. What are some of the ways in which intelligence tests have been shown to be culturally biased?
15. What does the concept of stereotype threat suggest about the situations in which people are tested?
16. What are some proposed causes of the Flynn effect?

SCAN TO GET THE ANSWERS

What Do You Think?

How would you design a culture-free intelligence test?

Is Intelligence Governed by Genetic or Environmental Factors?

LEARNING OBJECTIVE 4

Review the contributions of heredity and environment to intelligence, and explain how emphasizing one factor or the other can affect social policy.

As you saw in Chapter 3, the nature–nurture debate centres on the question of whether particular qualities and behaviours result from genetic underpinnings or from the environment. Is a happy and healthy baby, for example, the result of robust genes, effective parental care and attention, or both? A similar question can be asked about intelligence. Do we inherit our intelligence from our parents? And if we do, does that mean that the environment has no influence, or can experiences, such as parenting, schooling, and familiarity with test taking, have an effect? Later in this section, we will examine how various psychologists answer these questions. First, though, we will consider important social questions that are raised by the search to identify the origin of intelligence.

Statistically, firstborn children appear to represent a majority of Nobel prize winners, classical music composers, and eminent psychologists. Later born appear to more likely become leaders and may, on average, be more creative (Plucker, 2003).

What Are the Social Implications of the Nature–Nurture Debate?

If genes were clearly identified as the main determinant of intelligence, what might some of the social consequences be? For some, such a finding might be taken to justify claims that

Environmental impact. Research indicates that a stimulating environment can help facilitate the intellectual development of children, whereas a deprived environment often has a negative impact.

particular individuals or groups of people are inherently superior to others. Such people might even seek to create a social structure that assigns people to classes according to their parentage and restricts certain classes to particular social roles.

On the other hand, what if the environment were found to be more decisive in determining intelligence? Children from disadvantaged environments would be expected to lead disadvantaged lives and display, on average, lower intelligence, but then again, their environments and their intellectual level could potentially be improved. But would people who possessed environmental advantages be willing to share them with those who were deprived?

Other difficult questions involving the nature–nurture debate and intelligence have been asked with respect to gender, ethnicity, and race. Perhaps the clearest example of the serious social consequences of such questions was the Nazi claim in the early twentieth century that Aryans (Indo-Europeans who were supposedly Nordic in appearance and of German ancestry) were superior to all other groups. Although Nazi scientists failed to support this assertion, their efforts demonstrated that there will always be people who wish to use possible genetic differences in intelligence as a basis for oppressing and controlling people.

The Bell Curve Controversy

Consider a more recent example of the social implications of the nature–nurture debate concerning intelligence. In 1994, two researchers published a book that ignited a firestorm of controversy regarding the issue of intelligence. In *The Bell Curve*, Richard Herrnstein and Charles Murray surveyed research on the origins and nature of intelligence, and also reported their own analyses. Based on this large amount of data, the authors drew several controversial conclusions. Many psychologists, educators, and researchers argue that many of the authors' conclusions do not follow from the data. The conclusions offered by Herrnstein and Murray were:

1. Conventional IQ tests accurately measure intelligence.
2. IQ is an important predictor of many measures of success in life, including success at school, work, parenting, and income. Higher IQ also predicts the avoidance of welfare dependence and criminality.
3. Given such correlations, people who are high in intelligence form a cognitive elite—they reach the upper levels of society—whereas those with lower IQs fall toward the bottom.
4. Given their predictive powers, intelligence tests can and should be used as a *gating* mechanism, to allow those with high IQs access to opportunities.
5. IQ is largely heritable, passed on through the genes from one generation to the next.

6. There are clear racial and ethnic differences in intelligence.
7. It is likely, although not certain, that at least some of this difference between groups is due to genetic factors.

Herrnstein and Murray went on to argue for greater acceptance of these ideas and benign recognition of the limitations of individuals with lower IQs, making greater efforts help them in areas of life where lower intelligence holds them back. As you might imagine, the debate over the book's conclusions and implications remains heated today. As noted above, most psychologists and researchers argue that many of the authors' conclusions do not follow from the data, and may instead reflect the authors' ideology (Nisbett, 2009; Flynn, 2008, 2000). Furthermore, according to many critics, even if some of the authors' conclusions are justified, the social policies they recommend on the basis of those conclusions are still unfair and racist (Richards, 2004).

A related controversy within Canadian psychology circulates around the work of Phillipe Rushton at the University of Western Ontario. At the height of the nature–nurture debates, Rushton (1994, 1995, 2008) argued that races could be ranked in terms of a number of characteristics, including intelligence, with Asians, as a group, scoring highest, blacks the lowest, and whites in between. Rushton's work has been severely criticized, not just because of its harmful nature, but also because it is not based on solid scientific evidence. For example, intelligence is correlated with socio-economic status (parents with means can provide richer intellectual environments) and race is correlated with poverty (in North America, blacks on average have a lower standard of living than whites; Weizmann et al., 1990).

Many researchers dismissed Rushton's claims and were not interested in further investigating an area seen as unworthy of further work. David Suzuki, the well-known Canadian scientist and environmentalist, dedicated an episode of his CBC radio show Quirks and Quarks to having researchers report on their work, carefully examining and refuting all of Rushton's claims (CBC Radio, 1989). Suzuki also publically debated Rushton at the University of Western Ontario (CBC Television, 1989). In that debate, Suzuki again refuted Rushton's claims and argued strongly that Rushton's views were racist, that his work was not science, and that Rushton's grants should be cancelled and he should be fired. The result was a test of university academic freedom, which appropriately states that academic researchers' university positions are protected in the event that they engage in research that is unpopular. Rushton had his teaching reduced and his access to student research pools restricted, but he kept his job and has continued to conduct research. His university publicly apologized for any pain caused by his views and agreed to monitor his future lectures (Helwig, 1989; Platiel & Strauss, 1989; Tenzen, 1989).

To be clear, it is important to remember three things about the sorts of claims made by Rushton. First, you should not accept them at face value, but critically search out and evaluate the scientific data related to the claims and to criticisms of those claims. Second, you should keep in mind that average race-related differences in intelligence scores could reflect differences in environmental opportunity (poverty), issues with the tests used to assess intelligence, or other issues not directly related to intelligence. Finally, you need to keep in mind that average differences at the population level, whether related to race and intelligence test scores or gender and spatial reasoning, tell you nothing useful when predicting the intelligence or spatial skills of individuals within those populations. Let's examine what scientists actually have learned and not learned about the nature–nurture debate on human intelligence.

Genetic Influences on Intelligence

A variety of studies suggest that genetic factors play a major role in intelligence. In particular, studies of twins and other relatives and research in molecular biology point to genes as a key contributor.

Family Studies Twins have received particular attention from intelligence researchers. If genetic factors are at work in intelligence, identical twins (who share all their genes) should have more similar intelligence test scores than fraternal twins (who share only about half of their genes). This expectation has been supported consistently by research (Bratko et al., 2010; Plomin & Spinath, 2004). Studies have found, on average, a correlation of +.86 between the intelligence test scores of identical twins, compared with a correlation of +.60 between the scores of fraternal twins.

The heritability of intelligence. Twin studies suggest that genetics play a major role in intelligence. There is a higher correlation in IQ scores for identical twins in contrast to all other family comparisons.

Do such findings mean that intelligence is related *primarily* to genes? Not necessarily. It turns out that parents treat identical twins more alike than fraternal twins. In fact, family studies find that identical twins are treated the most alike of all siblings, followed by same-gender fraternal twins and then different-gender twins. Perhaps, then, the more closely related intelligence scores found among identical twins are, at least in part, a reflection of more similar interactions with parents.

To help sort out the relative influence of heredity and environment, we might want to look at IQ scores for identical twins who have been raised apart from one another. If genetic factors are important determinants of intelligence, then the scores should remain closely related. Thus, researchers have looked at the IQ scores of identical twins who were adopted at birth and placed in separate homes. The correlation between the scores of these separated identical twins is +.75 (Plomin & Spinath, 2004), an impressive statistic that seems to reflect once again the influence of genetic factors. At the same time, this correlation is not as large as the +.86 correlation for the IQ scores of identical twins who are raised together, a difference that we might attribute to those twins' shared environments.

Another approach to the heredity and intelligence question is to examine the relationships between the IQ scores of adopted children and those of their biological and adoptive parents. If heredity is more influential than environment, the IQ scores of adopted children should be more similar to those of their biological parents than to those of their adoptive parents. If environment matters more, we should find the children's IQ scores closer to their adoptive parents' scores than to the scores of their biological parents (Plomin & Spinath, 2004).

Researchers have found, on average, a correlation of +.22 between the scores of adopted children and the scores of their biological parents, and a correlation of +.19 between the children's scores and those of their adoptive parents (Plomin & Spinath, 2004). On the one hand, the children's IQ scores are somewhat related to the scores of their biological parents (correlation of +.22), indicating a possible genetic influence. On the other hand, this correlation is not especially large, nor is it significantly higher than the +.19 correlation found between the scores of the children and those of their adoptive parents. This pattern of findings indicates once again that the nature–nurture question is not a simple one to answer.

All of these family studies suggest that genes play a role in intelligence, but exactly how much of a role? Scientists have sought to answer this question by examining the specific data from many studies and arriving at an overall estimate of the heritability of intelligence. **Heritability** refers to the overall extent to which differences among people are attributable to genes. Evaluating the data from studies of twins and other relatives, researchers have determined that the heritability of intelligence is approximately 50 percent (Plomin & Spinath, 2004). It is important to note that the concept of heritability is used to explain the differences between groups of people, not to provide information about a single individual. Thus, the finding that the heritability of intelligence is around 50 percent does not mean that 50 percent of a particular individual's intelligence is inherited. Rather, it suggests that 50 percent of all differences or variabilities observed in a population's intelligence test scores are due to genetic factors.

heritability the overall extent to which differences among people are attributable to genes.

heritability coefficient a correlation coefficient used to indicate the contribution of heredity to some characteristic, such as intelligence.

The statistical measure used to indicate the contribution of heredity to intelligence (or to any other characteristic) is the **heritability coefficient**, a number ranging from 0.00 to +1.00. A coefficient of 0.00 means that heredity has no impact on variations observed among people, whereas a coefficient of +1.00 means that heredity is the sole influence on the characteristic under investigation. The heritability coefficient for Huntington's Disease, in which genetic factors are totally responsible for the emergence of the disorder, is +1.00. In contrast, as we have just observed, the heritability coefficient for intelligence is +0.50—a figure that holds in studies conducted around the world, from Canada to the United States to Russia, Japan, and India (Plomin & Spinath, 2004).

Nature or Nurture: Which Is More Important? It is easy to get caught up in the debate about just how much of intelligence is due to nature and how much is due to nurture. It is helpful to keep in mind a quote attributed to the great Canadian psychologist Donald Hebb. When asked by a journalist to specify how much of intelligence is due to nature and how much to nurture, Hebb reportedly replied, "Which contributes more to the area of a rectangle, its length or its width?" (Meaney, 2004). Which contributes more is really the wrong question to ask. Better to try to figure out how these two general categories of factors interact and influence intelligence. Sandra Scarr (1991) suggested that nature (heredity) may set upper and lower limits on the level of intelligence a child may develop. This range of possible outcomes is called the **reaction range**. Scarr suggested that our nature sets general limits on our intellectual achievement, but it is our nurturing environments that determine where in our reaction range we end up. The main advantage of this theory is that it focuses directly on the interaction of both nature and nurture. It helps to account for children from poor backgrounds who do well, and for children from enriched environments who do not do so well.

reaction range the upper and lower level of intelligence or other outcomes made possible by a child's genetic nature.

Environmental Influences on Intelligence

If the heritability of intelligence is 50 percent, then environmental factors are responsible for the remaining 50 percent of differences in intelligence among people. The term *environment* can have a narrow or broad meaning. It can refer to our home setting, neighbourhood, extended family, school, or socioeconomic group. It even can refer to biological events and experiences that a fetus confronts in its mother's uterus. Or, it can refer to the sum of all such contexts. Four environmental influences have received particular attention in the study of intelligence: family and home, culture, occupation, and schooling.

Animal studies suggest that organisms perform better on learning and intelligence tests when they are mildly hungry (Miller, 1957).

Family and Home Environment The first overtly social environment to which we are exposed in life and the one that dominates our childhood is the family and home. Our parents' childrearing methods and other characteristics, our interactions with siblings, the objects in our houses, family trips—these are all parts of our family and home environment. Do such environmental factors affect children's intelligence?

Research has suggested a link between family and home environment and children's intelligence scores. A number of studies, for example, have examined the IQ scores of biological siblings and adoptive siblings. These investigations have found that when biological siblings are raised apart, the correlation between their IQ scores is +.22. In contrast, when children from different families are adopted and raised together, the correlation between their IQ scores is +.32 (Plomin & Spinath, 2004). If family and home environment did not affect intelligence levels, we would expect a near-zero correlation between the IQ scores of adoptive siblings. Instead, they display a higher correlation than that displayed by biological siblings who are raised apart.

Cultural Influences Most definitions of intelligence include how well people adapt to their environments. This criterion raises an important question: does the definition of

THINGS STUDENTS WANT TO KNOW

Can Parents Improve Their Children's Intelligence?

Early theories held that an individual's intellectual capacity was totally fixed at birth. The many examples presented throughout this chapter of how the environment can affect intelligence certainly challenge this early assumption. In particular, we now know that interventions of various kinds can improve intellectual functioning.

Two researchers, Robert Bradley and Bettye Caldwell, have examined the impact of the home environment on intelligence and identified several parenting approaches that may help raise the IQ scores of preschoolers (Bradley, Caldwell, & Corwyn, 2003; Bradley & Caldwell, 1984). In fact, these researchers claim that such approaches are better predictors of IQ scores than factors such as socio-economic class or family structure. Current research seems to support their assertions (Sidhu et al., 2010).

The parent to-do list includes:

- Be emotionally and verbally responsive and involved with your child: comment on and talk about what she is looking at and noticing, draw your child's attention to things around her.
- Avoid too much restriction and punishment: within reason, allow your child to explore his environment and do things for himself.
- Organize the physical environment and the child's activity schedule: have an area of your home that is set up for the child and is child friendly.
- Provide appropriate play materials: they do not have to be expensive child play toys, just things to challenge your child and encourage activity and exploration.
- Provide a variety of forms of daily stimulation: build in some play time with your child and, when she is older, with other children. Where possible, include your child in outings to local stores or even just for walks around your neighbourhood.

intelligence change across different cultural environments? Many researchers say yes, the definition of intelligence varies from culture to culture (Smith, 2010; Georgas, 2003).

Note that this is different from asking whether people from different parts of the world (or from different racial or ethnic groups) have different levels of intelligence. That question relates more to the idea of comparing general intelligence. Instead, here we are more concerned with comparing specific skill sets that constitute intelligence in different cultures. Researchers have found that the values of a society or cultural group often have powerful effects on the intellectual skills of its members. Rice farmers in Liberia, for example, are particularly skilled at estimating quantities of rice (Cole, Gay, & Glick, 1967); and children in Botswana, with much story experience, have good memories for the details of stories (Dube, 1982). These specific skills would improve individuals' ability to survive and thrive within their cultures, and thus would be valued components of intelligence within each culture. Such principles can apply within subcultures as well; as the example at the beginning of the chapter demonstrates, a knowledge of theoretical physics and obscure comic hero trivia are prized abilities in some subcultures within Western culture.

Societal needs and intelligence. An individual's particular expression of intelligence is often tied to the survival needs of his or her society. Rice farmers, such as these field workers during rice harvest, are often highly skilled at estimating quantities of rice and are admired for their high intelligence.

Most of the assumptions about intelligence that we have looked at so far are Western-oriented. Western views of intelligence tend to be influenced by the Western value of individualism, while some other cultures place more emphasis on the community as a whole. Moreover, Westerners tend to equate high intelligence with rapid mental processing, whereas other cultures may value depth of thinking, even if it occurs at a slower rate (Sternberg, 2007; Sternberg et al., 1981). One study found that Taiwanese-Chinese theorists typically point to five factors at the root of intelligence:

(1) a general cognitive factor; (2) interpersonal intelligence (knowing about others); (3) intrapersonal intelligence (knowing about oneself); (4) intellectual self-assertion (advocating for your own intellectual achievements); and (5) intellectual self-effacement (being humble about your intellectual achievements) (Yang & Sternberg, 1997). While the first three qualities are similar to factors in some Western definitions of intelligence, the final two are not. Also, Westerners often believe that intelligence further involves verbal skill and the ability to solve practical problems, features absent from the Chinese list.

Occupational Influences Researchers consistently have found a relationship between intelligence and job complexity. People of higher intelligence tend to work in more complex jobs (Hunt, 2011; Ganzach, 2003; Ganzach & Pazy, 2001). An obvious explanation for this relationship is that individuals of higher intelligence can handle complex jobs more readily than less intelligent people and so are more likely to obtain and succeed in such positions.

Which causes which? People in complex jobs, such as this engineer working in a telecommunications control room, are often highly intelligent. Does their high intelligence qualify them for more complex work, or does the complex work increase their intelligence? Research supports both explanations.

Studies also suggest, however, that complex work may itself improve intelligence. In one study, for example, interviews with 3,000 men in various occupations seemed to indicate that more complex jobs lead to more "intellectual flexibility and independent judgment among employees" (Schooler, 2001; Kohn & Schooler, 1973). A job that requires workers to organize and interpret detailed financial data, for example, may help produce more intellectual depth than one requiring workers to simply add up customer bills.

Why would more complex jobs enhance intellectual skills? Perhaps because holders of such jobs are forced to acquire a greater amount of complex information and knowledge (Kuncel et al., 2010, 2004)—the very kinds of information and knowledge that are measured on intelligence tests. The complexity factor may also help explain differences in IQ scores between urban and rural populations. A few generations ago, studies found that urban residents scored, on average, six IQ points higher than rural residents (Terman & Merrill, 1937; Seashore, Wesman, & Doppelt, 1950). One possible explanation for this difference is the greater complexity of the urban environment. More recently, the difference declined to about two points (Kaufman & Doppelt, 1976; Reynolds et al., 1987). It could be that changes in rural environments—less isolation, increased travel, mass communication, Internet access, improvements in schools, and increased use of technology on farms—have raised the level of complexity in these environments and, in turn, brought the IQ scores of rural citizens closer to those of city residents.

Times are changing. An elderly farmer in Sweden sits in the doorway of his barn while working out his agricultural needs on a laptop. Some psychologists believe that the increased use of technology on farms helps account for the recent closing of the gap between the IQ scores of urban and rural populations.

School Influences Researchers have determined that schooling is both a cause and consequence of intelligence (Shayer & Adhami, 2010; Fish, 2002; Sangwan, 2001). Children with higher intelligence test scores are more likely to be promoted from grade to grade, less likely to drop out of school, and more likely to attend college. In turn, schooling helps change mental abilities, including those measured on intelligence tests.

Researchers Stephen Ceci and Wendy Williams (2010, 2007, 1997) have demonstrated some interesting ties between intelligence scores and the amount of time spent in school. Students' IQ scores tend to rise during the school year and drop when schooling is discontinued or during summer vacation. Students who complete high school perform higher on intelligence tests than those who leave school early. And young children whose birthdays just make the cut-off for beginning school early earn higher intelligence scores than those of almost identical age who miss the cut-off and remain at home for an extra year.

"When schools flourish, all flourishes."
—Martin Luther, German theologian and reformer

Why might schooling help improve intelligence scores? In part because schools provide the opportunity both to acquire information (Who wrote *Moby Dick*? What is a square root, and how do you calculate it?) and to develop "systematic problem-solving, abstract thinking, categorization, sustained attention to material of little intrinsic interest, and repeated manipulation of basic symbols and operations"—skills measured on intelligence tests (Neisser, 1998, p.16).

Researchers have also shown that the *quality* of the school environment affects intellectual performance. In financially poor schools, children tend to learn less, and in turn, tend to score significantly lower on IQ tests (Johnson, 2010; Nisbett, 2009). One researcher reported that when students from a poor school in Georgia moved to Philadelphia, their IQ scores improved (Lee, 1961). Clearly, such findings argue for better schools so that each child can work in as enriching an environment as possible.

Schooling and intellectual performance. Schools are not all equal in their ability to meet children's learning needs. On average, children who attend financially poor schools perform less well on intelligence tests.

Group Differences in IQ Scores

Recall that at the beginning of this section we discussed *The Bell Curve*, in which the authors argued that group differences in IQ may be due largely to genetic factors. We went on to discuss findings that intelligence is, indeed, heritable, but that environment plays a significant role as well. Let us now look more closely at group differences in IQ scores.

There are two trends on which most researchers of group differences in intelligence agree (Sackett & Shen, 2010; Lynn, 2008; Fish, 2002). First, racial groups do indeed differ in their average scores on intelligence tests. Second, high-scoring people (and groups) are more likely to attain high levels of education and income. In one review conducted decades ago, 52 researchers agreed that the IQ bell curve for Americans is centred around a score of 100 for white Americans and 85 for African Americans, with scores for different subgroups of Hispanic Americans falling in between (Avery et al., 1994). Similarly, a review by Wes Darou (1992) of counselling services within the Canadian International Development Agency indicates that Aboriginal Canadians score, on average, 15 to 20 points lower on intelligence tests than their non-Aboriginal contemporaries. Likewise, researchers have noted that European New Zealanders tend to outscore native Maori New Zealanders, Israeli Jews outscore Israeli Arabs, and people with good hearing outscore the hearing impaired (Zeidner, 1990). What can we make of such trends?

Two important issues about group differences can be clarified by means of an analogy offered by geneticist Richard Lewontin (2001, 1982, 1976; Feldman & Lewontin, 2008). Suppose you start with 100 plant seeds from the same source and divide them into two groups. You plant one group of seeds in a flowerpot filled with poor soil and the other group in a flowerpot filled with fertile soil. What differences would you expect between the groups of seeds as they grow into plants? As shown in **Figure 10-8**, you should see two kinds of variation: variation between the two groups and variation within each group. When evaluating these variations, we need to keep in mind two principles that also apply to evaluating group differences in intelligence scores:

1. *Environment contributes to variation between the groups.* The plants growing in poor soil vary from the ones growing in good soil, even though all of the plants came from the same mixture of seed. For example, the plants raised in poor soil are, on average, shorter than those raised in fertile soil. This difference is probably attributable to the environment. In short, optimal environments tend to produce optimal plants, and deficient environments tend to produce less successful plants. Similarly,

FIGURE 10-8 Lewontin's plant analogy of intelligence. If two groups of plants start out from the same source of seeds (genetics), but one group is given a better environment, the differences in height between the two groups would be mainly determined by environmental conditions. The analogy applies when evaluating group differences in IQ scores.

on average, groups that now display lower average IQ scores have been raised in worse environments than the groups with higher scores.

2. *An average variation between groups cannot be applied to individuals within each group.* In our plant example, even though on average the plants growing in poor soil are shorter than those growing in good soil, some of the poor-soil plants will be taller than others. Some will probably even be taller than the average plant in the good soil. These differences probably are attributable to normal genetic variation, since all the plants in a given pot share the same environment.

Again, this principle applies to people as well as plants. You cannot deduce anything about the intelligence of one person based on the mean scores of that individual's group. Even Herrnstein and Murray (1994), the authors of *The Bell Curve*, granted that "millions of Blacks have higher IQs than the average White." It is essential to realize that knowing someone's group membership tells you nothing about that person's actual intelligence. Failing to distinguish between individual performance and group norms can mislead people, produce incorrect expectations, and cause social injustices—and is essentially prejudicial.

With this analogy in mind, let us return to the question of IQ scores and group differences. Lorenzo Cherubini and his colleagues at Brock University have looked in detail at the situation of Aboriginal education policy and practice in Ontario. They note that there is a significant gap between the levels of school success of Aboriginal and non-Aboriginal students, with Aboriginal students twice as likely to drop out and fail to complete or take much longer to complete secondary school. He argues that equal education opportunities do not just consist of attending the same schools, but require that Aboriginal children and youth work in school systems that acknowledge and celebrate Aboriginal values and heritage. This will ensure that positive identity and commitment to education and learning will be a more consistent part of the Aboriginal student experience (Cherubini et al., 2010).

Such research suggests that public policy aimed at making more equitable resources available throughout society would lead to more similar intelligence test scores across different groups (Biswas-Diener, 2011; Williams et al., 2004). Of course, this raises yet another important question: do efforts to equalize educational experiences and other environmental resources actually improve intelligence? We will consider next the effects of *environmental enrichment*—providing disadvantaged children with more stimulating environments at home and at school.

Does Environmental Enrichment Make a Difference?

Studies have indicated that young children from poor families typically receive less intellectual stimulation than do children from wealthier homes (Arnold & Doctoroff, 2003). They have, on average, far fewer books and educational toys, for example, and their parents read to them less. Only half of preschoolers from families on public assistance have alphabet books, compared with 97 percent of children from wealthy homes (Mason et al., 1990; McCormick & Mason, 1986). It appears that their early environmental limitations may place poor children at a severe disadvantage when it comes to developing intellectual and academic skills.

We can see this problem particularly clearly in institutional settings such as orphanages and in foster homes. (Beckett et al., 2010; Nelson et al., 2009, 2007). During the early 1980s, psychologist J. McVicker Hunt (1982) conducted work in a poor Iranian orphanage. In an effort to improve the lives of children in the orphanage and, in turn, improve their development, he offered a program of "tutored human enrichment." He found that such early interventions did indeed help improve the cognitive functioning of the children. In other work, however, he clarified that early instruction of this kind helps to improve the intellectual capacities only of children who have been living in deprived environments, not of those who have already been living in enriched environments.

Getting a head start. Two toddlers enjoy the individualized attention provided by their teacher and their ultra-stimulating classroom environment in a Head Start program in Mississippi.

Based on findings such as Hunt's, Project Head Start, a United States federally-funded preschool program, was launched in 1965. The program, which has served more than 22 million disadvantaged children since its inception and now serves around one million each year, aims to enhance children's performances in school and beyond by helping to develop their cognitive and social skills as early as possible (USDHHS, 2011; Olsen & DeBoise, 2007; Ripple et al., 1999). The program continues to enjoy significant community and political support.

Does Head Start work? Researchers have assessed its success by comparing children enrolled in the program with same-aged counterparts who are not enrolled. Studies indicate that programs such as Head Start do indeed produce at least short-term cognitive gains among disadvantaged children (USDHHS, 2011; Arnold & Doctoroff, 2003). Two investigations found, for example, that by mid-adolescence, children who participated in early childhood educational programs were more than a grade ahead of a matched control group of children who had not been in the programs (Zigler & Berman, 1983; Lazar & Darlington, 1982). The early education participants also scored higher on various tests of scholastic achievement. More recent studies typically tell a similar story (Sassi, 2011).

Head Start and similar programs also appear to increase children's readiness for school, thus reducing the need for children to repeat grades or to be placed in special-education classes. Although some research suggests that the IQ changes and academic benefits resulting from these early education programs may diminish over time, other studies indicate that, at the very least, the programs enhance emotional intelligence, instill a more positive attitude toward learning, reduce school dropouts, and even decrease later criminality (USDHHS, 2011; Siegler, 2003).

Is There Really a Mozart Effect?

For the past 20 years, a notion has been floating around that listening to the music of Mozart and other classical composers will significantly increase a person's intelligence, and that the earlier in life one is exposed to such music, the greater the intellectual impact. The phenomenon is called the "Mozart effect," and it has spurred many parents to surround their young children with such music. In some families, the composer's music is even introduced during the prenatal months. The idea of a Mozart effect is exciting and even inspiring. But there is one small problem. It has no basis in fact (Pietschnig et al., 2010). So where did the notion come from?

Back in 1993, a research team investigated whether performances by participants on a test of abstract spatial reasoning could be influenced by listening to classical music (Rauscher, Shaw, & Ky, 1993). The participants were administered three different spatial tests—one after listening to a sonata by Mozart, another after listening to repetitive

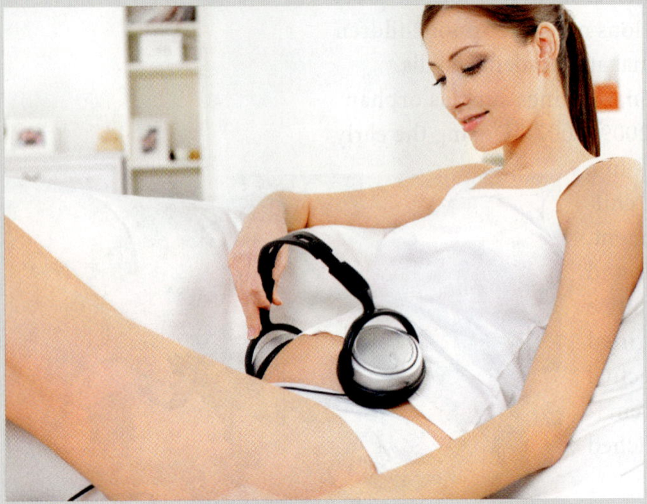

relaxation music, and a third after sitting in silence. The researchers found that the spatial test scores of the participants rose nine points after they had listened to Mozart. Almost immediately, exciting reports about the Mozart phenomenon spread throughout the world.

It is critical to note that the effect of this music on the participants' performances was temporary—15 minutes at most. Moreover, there was no effect on any other kind of intellectual task or on general intelligence. But such details were lost as the findings worked their way into the media. Hundreds of news stories, and later, books, proclaimed the *permanent* impact of classical music—particularly Mozart's music—on *general learning* and on *general intelligence*. The governor of the State of Georgia even proposed in his 1998 state budget that $105,000 be allocated to provide every child in the state with a CD of classical music.

Over the past decade, many studies have been conducted on the relationship between music and cognitive functioning (Pietschnig et al., 2010). The findings have been mixed, although some suggest that music, perhaps by its effects on mood and on arousal, can sometimes have temporary and modest effects on certain kinds of cognitive performances (Thompson, Husaine, & Schellenberg, 2001). But none of these studies has even come close to suggesting that classical music—by Mozart or anyone else—actually makes you smarter.

Early intervention programs can extend beyond school settings. They can include going into the homes of young children; working with their parents; adding stimulating toys, books, and tools to the home; and otherwise enriching the home and community environments. It appears that such home-bound programs often help increase children's cognitive achievements. In fact, evaluation work contributed to by Mike Boyes from the University of Calgary (and one of the authors of this book) shows that earlier intervention programs, such as Healthy Families programs that identify and offer support to new, at-risk families in the form of weekly visits from a healthy family home visitor, have been successful in getting children and their families onto a better starting track toward intellectual and educational success. These programs reduce child welfare involvement and improve both child and parent functioning (Elnitsky et al., 2003). Another extensive research project has clarified that enrichment-intervention programs of various kinds achieve greater success when they (1) begin earlier in life and continue; (2) are more intensive (more hours per day and more days per year); and (3) include programs for maintaining positive attitudes and behaviours (Pungello et al., 2010; Ramey & Ramey, 2007).

Before You Go On

www.wiley.com/go/comer

What Do You Know?

17. What are the main arguments of *The Bell Curve?*
18. About what percentage of intelligence is thought to be genetically determined, and what evidence supports this claim?
19. What types of environmental factors have been shown to affect intelligence?

What Do You Think?

Considering the material you have read about test construction, heritability, and cultural differences, what type of learning environment would maximize the intelligence of all individuals?

SCAN TO GET THE ANSWERS

Intelligence — WHAT HAPPENS IN THE BRAIN?

LEARNING OBJECTIVE 5

Describe how brain size, number of neurons, processing speed, brain activity, and cortical thickness relate to intelligence.

So far in this chapter, we have explored several important questions concerning the nature, measurement, and sources of intelligence. We now add another question: what happens in the brain when we exhibit intelligence? Have researchers, for example, detected relationships between specific brain activities or specific brain structures and intelligence? To answer this question, let's look at four areas of investigation: brain size, brain speed, brain activity, and cortical thickness (Reynolds et al., 2008; Vernon et al., 2000).

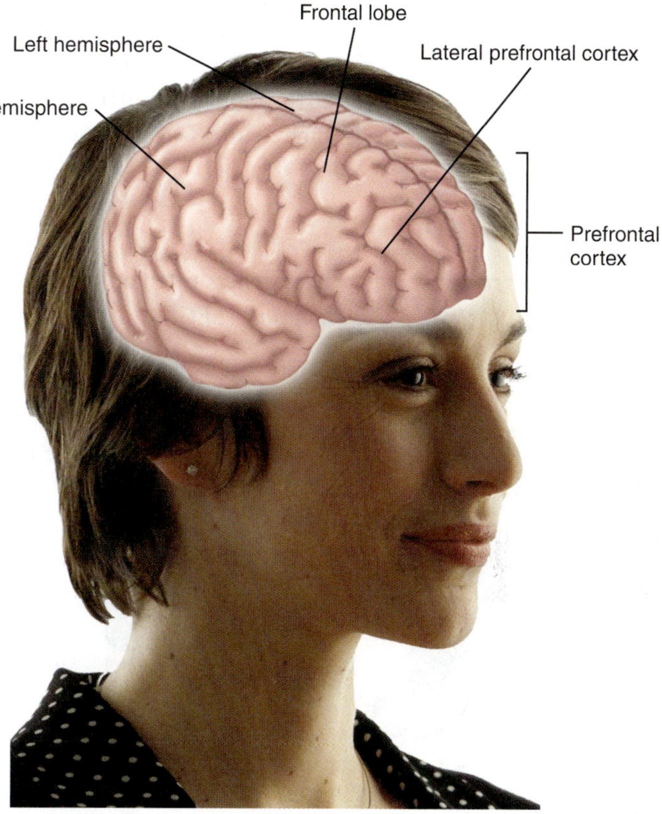

Brain Size, Number of Neurons, and Intelligence

Researchers have been exploring correlations between brain size and intelligence since the mid-nineteenth century (Ash & Gallup, 2008; Galton, 1948, 1888). Philippe Rushton has done some work here as well (Rushton, 2009). Initially, limitations in technology hampered meaningful outcomes. For example, researchers could only study the brains of corpses, which certainly put a damper on testing their intelligence. Today's neuroimaging technologies, however, allow scientists to measure brain size and brain activity in living people.

Some neuroimaging findings over the past few decades have indeed suggested a possible correlation between brain size and mental functioning, but most studies of this issue fail to support this notion (Choi et al., 2008; Vernon et al., 2000). As we noted in Chapter 4, the overall size of the brain appears to be more closely related to the size of the body than to intelligence. The main exception to this is people with extremely small or extremely large brains, each of whom are more likely to exhibit mental deficiencies than are people whose brain sizes fall within the normal range (Tramo et al., 1998).

PSYCHOLOGY AROUND US When Smaller Is Better

Sherlock Holmes once deduced the intelligence of a man by trying on his hat: "[The hat] came right over the forehead and settled upon the bridge of his nose. 'It is a question of cubic capacity,' said [Holmes]; 'a man with so large a brain must have something in it.'" As it turns out, however, human brains have shrunk over the last 30,000 years (Geary, 2005). Not because we are getting dumber (fans of the movie *Idiocracy* should quiet down now), but because our brains are becoming more efficient.

Another potential reason for our shrinking brains is that our bodies are smaller than they once were. When you are more compact, you don't need as much brain space to regulate your movement and involuntary activities.

And there may be yet one more reason for the downward trend in brain size—"crowdsourcing." Greater decreases in brain size appear to be correlated with increased population density. Some scientists believe that an individual brain doesn't need to be as big because people can rely on each other to help solve problems of living. In effect, we become part of a social network and approach problems as a unit, so more of our brain becomes devoted to social organizations rather than to holding onto the instincts that we once needed to survive (Geary, 2005).

Regardless of brain size, does the total number of neurons in a brain predict intellectual functioning? Apparently not. After all, there are, on average, 16 percent more neurons in male brains than female brains, but most research has found no difference in IQ scores between men and women. On the other hand, intelligence may be related to the number of neurons in particular brain regions. Studies have suggested, for example, that general intelligence may be tied to the number of neurons in the brain's frontal lobes (Glascher et al., 2010; Tang et al., 2010; Tranel et al., 2008). All other things being equal, people with more such neurons seem to perform better on intelligence tests.

Brain Speed and Intelligence

Researchers often analyze the bioelectrical activity of the brain by using an *electroencephalogram (EEG)*, a device that places sensors on the outside of an individual's head and records *brain waves*. EEG research has allowed investigators to see whether intelligence is correlated with brain speed—the speed with which the brain responds successfully to various stimuli, tasks, and events (Sternberg, 2003; Deary & Stough, 1997, 1996).

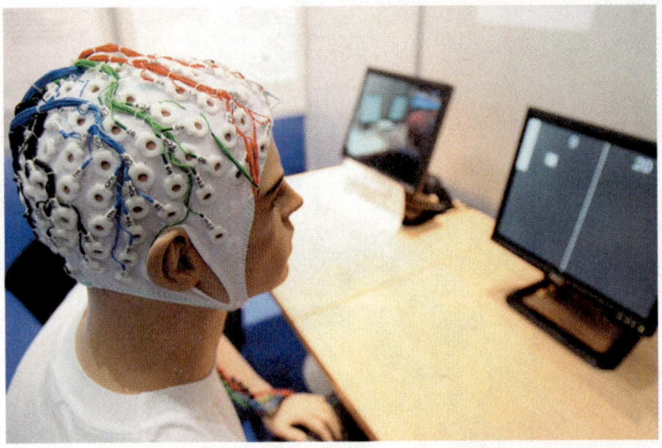

Speedier brains? People who score higher on intelligence tests tend to perceive correct images more quickly, as indicated by EEG readings.

One procedure, for example, involves the speed at which people process stimuli that are flashed before their eyes. In a typical study, the experimenter briefly flashes an incomplete stimulus on one side of a screen, then quickly flashes a more complete stimulus on the other side. Viewers are asked to indicate which side the complete image appeared on. It typically takes only a fraction of a second to correctly answer this question. Still, some people are quicker than others, and those who perceive the correct image more quickly (as indicated by their EEG readings) tend to score higher on intelligence tests (especially on perceptual tasks) than those whose reactions are a bit slower. In short, more intelligent people may be physiologically wired to acquire and use information more quickly than others.

nerve conduction velocity (NCV) the speed with which electrical impulses are transmitted along nerve fibres and across synapses.

In a related line of research, several investigators have found significant correlations between IQ scores and **nerve conduction velocity (NCV)**, the speed with which electrical impulses are transmitted along nerve fibres and across synapses (Sternberg, 2003; Vernon et al., 2000; Reed & Jensen, 1992). Both the NCV and EEG findings fit well with studies showing that highly intelligent people are, on average, able to make decisions more quickly than less intelligent people (Demaree et al., 2010; Tulsky & O'Brien, 2008).

Brain Activity and Intelligence

Another biological approach to the study of intelligence examines how active people's brains are when solving intellectual problems. A *positron emission tomography (PET)* scan is a type of neuroimaging technology that can reveal where and how actively the brain is metabolizing, or breaking down, glucose at any given moment. Very active areas of the brain show up as red and orange on a PET scan's colour-coded pictures, while less active areas show up as green and blue. PET scans have generally revealed lower activity in the brains of people who are performing well on an intellectual task and higher activity in the brains of those who are performing poorly (Raichle, 2005; Haier, 2003; Posner et al., 2009, 2002). Thus, some researchers suggest that the brains of higher-performing people do not need to work as hard as the brains of lower-performing people—that is, their brains are more efficient (Grabner et al., 2003; Neubauer & Fink, 2010, 2003).

Although high intellectual performance seems to be related to an overall reduction in brain activity, PET scans have revealed that particular areas of brain activity are at work during certain types of intellectual tasks. Investigator John Duncan and his colleagues conducted a PET scan on 13 men and women while they were taking an intelligence test

(Duncan, 2001; Duncan et al., 2000). They found that for each individual, the brain activity during the test was concentrated in the left lateral prefrontal cortex and the right lateral prefrontal cortex—brain regions located toward the front and outer sides of the brain's two hemispheres. When a test-taker was performing verbal tasks on the test, the *left* lateral prefrontal cortex was activated. (Remember from Chapters 4 and 9 that language is processed predominantly in the left hemisphere of the brain.) During spatial tasks, both the left lateral prefrontal cortex and the right lateral prefrontal cortex were activated. It is worth noting that the prefrontal cortex, which sends and receives information to and from numerous other brain sites, may help people keep track of several thoughts at the same time, solve problems, produce new ideas, and filter out unimportant information.

While such studies are interesting, keep in mind that they do not clarify the causal relationships at work. Do people of higher intelligence display less brain activity overall, despite experiencing more activity in the prefrontal cortex, because they are smart, for example, or are people smart because their brain activity is more efficient? Or are both brain activity and intelligence related to yet a third causal factor that researchers have yet to discover?

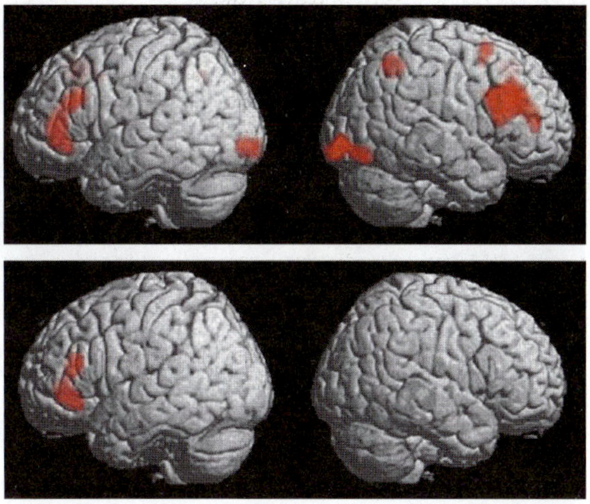

The prefrontal cortex and performance on intelligence tests. The study by John Duncan and his colleagues (2000) found that the left lateral prefrontal cortex is active during the performance of a range of cognitive tasks. These PET scans from the study reveal that the left and right lateral prefrontal cortices are both active during spatial tasks (top row), while activity during verbal tasks tends to centre in the left lateral prefrontal cortex (bottom row).

Cortical Thickening and Intelligence HOW WE DEVELOP

We have seen that various brain features, such as the number of neurons, brain speed, and brain activity, may be tied to intelligence. A related issue is whether *brain development* is related to the development of intelligence. A highly publicized study by researcher Philip Shaw and his colleagues sought to answer this question (Shaw et al., 2008, 2006).

In a longitudinal study, the Shaw (2008, 2006) team performed brain scans on 309 children and teenagers between the ages of 6 and 19 years, with each participant scanned every two years. The scans revealed that throughout childhood and adolescence, individuals display changes in the thickness of the *cortex*—the folded outer layer of the brain—changes that have implications for the development of intelligence (Karama et al., 2011).

Using a neuroanatomical MRI scan (where MRI brain scan data are further analyzed by computer program to provide detailed 3-D information about the cellular structure of brain areas), the study found that children begin with a thin cortex, which thickens over the years and then begins to thin down and continues thinning through adolescence. These changes in thickness are consistent with what is known about *neural pruning* during development. As we observed in Chapter 3, the brains of very young children produce a large number of neural synapses and neurons. Then, as the children grow older, their brains prune down the neural connections that are not being used, and perhaps reduce the actual number of neurons as well, leaving the individuals with a much lower number of connections and, perhaps, neurons, in their teenage and adult years. It is believed that a thick cortex may reflect a higher number of neural connections and neurons, whereas a thin cortex may reflect a lower number; so as adolescence approaches and pruning occurs, the cortex becomes thinner.

At one time, the Guinness Book of World Records listed Kim Ung-yong as the person in the world with the highest IQ. Kim Ung-yong scored 210 on the Stanford-Binet and reportedly began to study differential calculus at the age of 3.

The study further found this pattern of changes in cortical thickness to be clearest in the prefrontal regions, the brain areas whose activity has been tied closely to intellectual activity. Thus, it appears that the development of intelligence may involve a process of synaptic and neural growth and then pruning, particularly in the prefrontal cortex—a process that is reflected by changes in cortical thickness throughout childhood and adolescence.

Moving up the ladder. As children develop, they move toward greater intellectual independence—for example, from a child who is read stories by her father to a young woman who produces and reads her own reports. Over the same period of time, the individual's brain is undergoing synaptic pruning and other key changes.

Beyond this general picture, Shaw and his colleagues (2008, 2006) found that the participants who were most intelligent showed a pattern of cortical thickening and thinning that was different from the pattern shown by participants with lower intelligence. That is, the highly intelligent individuals began with a rather thin cortex during early childhood, and the cortex gradually thickened until the age of 11 or 12, at which time thinning began and continued into the late teenage years. In contrast, the participants with lower intelligence began with a somewhat thicker cortex, which then further thickened until the age of 8, at which time the thinning began. Assuming that all of this reflects growth and pruning of synapses and perhaps of neurons as well, particularly in the prefrontal cortex, it may be that the processes of growth and pruning unfold over a much longer developmental span in highly intelligent people than they do in less intelligent individuals, perhaps because more complex and sophisticated neural circuits are being constructed (Vedantam, 2006).

Are such brain changes over the course of childhood and adolescence genetically predetermined? Once again, the answer is "Not necessarily." We observed in Chapter 3 that the formation and pruning of neural networks are closely tied to interactions with the environment. Moreover, earlier in this chapter, we observed that enriching the environments of deprived young children often increases their intellectual performances. It could be that people with particularly high intelligence tend to be raised in rich social and learning environments, and that this kind of environmental stimulation contributes heavily to the pattern of cortical thickness change that such individuals displayed in the study by Shaw and his colleagues (2008, 2006).

Before You Go On

www.wiley.com/go/comer

What Do You Know?

20. How are brain size and number of neurons related to intelligence?
21. How do researchers measure the speed of information processing in the brain? How is this related to intelligence?
22. Is efficient processing linked to relatively lower or relatively higher activity in the brain?
23. What is the role of cortical thickness in the development of intelligence?

SCAN TO GET THE ANSWERS

What Do You Think?

Can you think of any other ways to explain why the brains of people who are performing better on intelligence tests are often less active than those of people who are doing poorly?

Extremes in Intelligence

HOW WE DIFFER

LEARNING OBJECTIVE 6

Discuss mental retardation and giftedness.

Earlier in the chapter, we mentioned that intelligence, as measured by IQ tests, follows a normal distribution—that is, a distribution shaped like a bell curve. At either end of this curve are a small number of people who score either much lower or much higher than the people who make up the large middle. At the lower end are people who are diagnosed with mental retardation, and at the higher end are those who are intellectually gifted (**Figure 10-9**).

Making music. A young man with Down syndrome is the percussionist in a community orchestra (left), while a child prodigy sings opera to an appreciative audience at a school for the arts (right).

Mental Retardation (Intellectual Disability)

Most individuals demonstrate sufficient levels of intelligence to survive on their own and to manage their daily lives. But the intellectual and adaptive functioning of some people is well below that of most other people. These individuals are said to display **mental retardation**, a combination of general intellectual functioning that is well below average and poor adaptive behaviour (APA, 2000). That is, in addition to having an IQ score of 70 or below, many of these individuals experience great difficulty in areas such as communication, home living, self-direction, work, and safety (APA, 2000). Some psychologists now prefer the term *intellectual disability* to mental retardation, so we will use the terms interchangeably in our discussion (National Center on Birth Defects and Developmental Disabilities, 2005).

mental retardation term describing individuals who display general intellectual functioning that is well below average and, at the same time, poor adaptive behaviour.

We have already observed that IQ tests and scores may be biased in various ways. It is certainly plausible that diagnoses of mental retardation based on such tests can be subject to error (Tomes, 2010; Toth & King, 2010). Thus, to properly diagnose mental retardation, mental-health professionals must observe the functioning of an individual in his everyday environment, taking both the person's background and the community's standards into account.

The most consistent sign of intellectual disability is very slow learning (Toth & King, 2010; Hodapp & Dykens, 2003). Other areas of difficulty include attention, short-term memory, planning, and language (Schalock et al., 2010; Edgin, Pennington, & Mervis, 2010). These difficulties vary, of course, according to the level of mental retardation.

The American Psychiatric Association (2000) describes four levels of mental retardation: mild (IQ 50–55 to approximately 70), moderate (IQ 35–40 to 50–55), severe (IQ 20–25 to 35–40), and profound (IQ below 20–25). Because of the biases already noted in IQ assessments and scores (especially as they relate to community, linguistic, and cultural

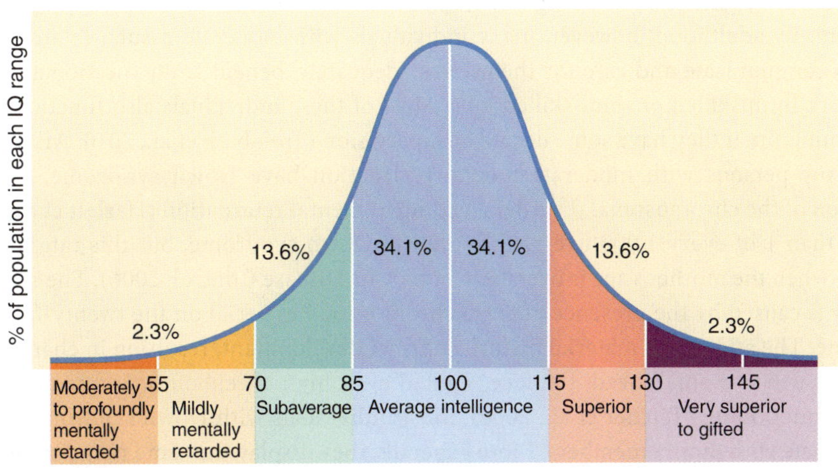

FIGURE 10-9 Extreme scores in intelligence. A small but equal number of people score at the extreme low and extreme high end of the IQ range. (Source: Anastasi & Urbina, 1997)

diversity), the American Association of Mental Retardation prefers to identify degrees of mental retardation according to the level of support the person needs—intermittent, limited, extensive, or pervasive.

Mild Retardation Around 80 to 85 percent of all people with mental retardation fall into the category of mild retardation (Dusseljee et al., 2011; Harris, 2010; APA, 2000). They are sometimes called "educable retarded" because they can profit from education and can support themselves as adults. Mild mental retardation is not usually recognized until children enter school. These individuals have reasonable language, social, and play skills, but they need assistance when under stress—a limitation that becomes increasingly apparent as academic and social demands increase. Often the intellectual performance of individuals with mild mental retardation improves with age; some even stop meeting the criteria for the label after they leave school (Toth & King, 2010; Sturmey, 2008). Their jobs tend to be unskilled or semi-skilled.

Severe retardation and special needs. A 7-year-old lies by his teacher at a training centre in China for children with disorders such as severe mental retardation, autism, and cerebral palsy.

Research has linked mild mental retardation mainly to familial factors, particularly poor and unstimulating environments, inadequate parent–child interactions, and insufficient learning experiences during a child's early years (Martin 2010; Sturmey, 2008). In addition, studies suggest that a mother's moderate drinking, drug use, or malnutrition during pregnancy may lower her child's intellectual potential (Hart et al., 2010; Stein et al., 1972).

Moderate, Severe, and Profound Retardation WHEN THINGS GO WRONG Although mild mental retardation is considered a variation in human functioning by many psychologists, the other levels of retardation—moderate, severe, and profound—are viewed by most as disorders. Moreover, whereas the primary factors in intellectual disability seem to be related to cultural and familial factors, moderate, severe, and profound levels of retardation are caused largely by factors such as genetically based chromosomal and metabolic abnormalities, significant prenatal alcohol or drug use by mothers, prenatal maternal infections such as rubella and syphilis, complications during or after delivery, and injuries and severe infections during early childhood (Martin, 2010; Sturmey, 2008).

In fact, severe and profound levels of mental retardation often appear as part of larger syndromes that include severe physical handicaps. The physical problems are often even more limiting than the individual's low intellectual functioning, and in some cases can be fatal. Given such causes, moderate, severe, and profound levels of retardation are typically viewed as neurological disorders.

Around 10 percent of persons with mental retardation receive a label of *moderate retardation*. They receive their diagnosis early in life, typically demonstrating clear deficits in language development and play during their preschool years. By middle school, significant delays in the acquisition of reading and number skills and deficits in adaptive skills become apparent. By adulthood, however, many individuals with moderate mental retardation are able to communicate and care for themselves adequately, benefit from vocational training, and work in unskilled or semi-skilled jobs. Most of these individuals also function well in the community if they have some degree of supervision (Trembath et al., 2010; APA, 2000).

Down syndrome an inherited disorder, usually caused by the presence of extra chromosomal material on the twenty-first chromosome, that results in mental retardation.

Many persons with moderate mental retardation have **Down syndrome**, the most common of the chromosomal disorders leading to mental retardation (Hazlett et al., 2010). Fewer than 1 of every 1,000 live births result in Down syndrome, but this rate increases greatly when the mother's age is over 35 (Centers for Disease Control, 2006). The syndrome usually is caused by the presence of extra chromosomal material on the twenty-first chromosome. The additional material disturbs normal development, resulting in characteristic features such as a small head, flat face, slanted eyes, high cheekbones, and reduced intellectual functioning (Teicher et al., 2008). Most individuals with Down syndrome are very affectionate with family members. More generally they display the same range of personality characteristics as people in the general population (Fidler, 2006).

Approximately 3 to 4 percent of people with mental retardation meet the criteria for *severe retardation*. They typically demonstrate basic motor and communication deficits during infancy. Many have an increased vulnerability to brain seizure disorder. They usually require careful supervision, profit from vocational training to some degree, and can perform only basic work tasks in structured and sheltered settings. Most are able to function well in the community if they live in group homes, in community nursing homes, or with their families (Cain et al., 2010; Bebko & Weiss, 2006; APA, 2000).

Around 1 to 2 percent of people with mental retardation receive a diagnosis of *profound retardation*. Their limitations are very noticeable at birth or early infancy. With training, the individuals may develop or improve basic skills such as walking, some talking, and feeding themselves. They require a very structured environment, with close supervision and considerable help, including a close relationship with a caregiver, to develop adequately (Cain et al., 2010; Sturmey, 2008; APA, 2000).

Giftedness

Psychologists do not agree on how to define *giftedness* (Sternberg, Jarvin, & Grigorenko, 2011) Some use IQ tests as the sole criterion, defining the top 1 or 2 percent of the tested population as gifted. For example, Lewis Terman defined gifted people as those with IQ scores above 140, and in a famous longitudinal study, he followed a group of gifted research participants over the course of their lifetime (Simonton, 2010; Leslie, 2000; Terman, 1925).

Other researchers and educators have added criteria such as school success or career achievement to IQ scores when defining giftedness. Indeed, many of the participants in Terman's study, who became known as the "Termites," achieved extraordinary success as scientists, scholars, businessmen, and professionals (Seagoe, 1975).

Other definitions of intelligence have led to still other definitions of giftedness. Howard Gardner, whom we discussed earlier in the chapter, suggests that people can be gifted with high intelligence in any one of the multiple intelligences he has identified. He would consider a highly talented athlete or musician to be as gifted as a math or verbal whiz (Gardner, 1993).

Researchers have tried to look for common characteristics among gifted people (Sternberg et al., 2011). They have come up with several:

Educating the gifted. A gifted 9-year-old girl sits in her college algebra class in Nashville, Tennessee. The algebra is apparently a snap for her, but getting in and out of the adult-sized desk chair can be a problem.

- *Environment can contribute to giftedness.* Many gifted people are raised in nurturing and stimulating environments. Terman's Termites, for example, were typically members of upper socio-economic families, and they received many years of education. It is worth noting that, contrary to stereotype, most gifted children are not pushed by demanding parents. Families do, however, tend to centre much attention on such children. Typically, the parents first recognize the budding giftedness of their children and then support it by providing high-level intellectual or artistic stimulation. Parents of highly gifted children also tend to have higher expectations of themselves, model hard work for their children, and grant the children high degrees of independence (Winner, 2000).
- *Gifted people are often intrinsically motivated.* It appears that children who are gifted at piano playing, violin playing, chess, bridge, athletics, and the like typically experience a deep, intrinsic motivation to master such domains and subject themselves to many hours of deliberate practice. Perhaps the high motivation of these children drives them and sustains their practice efforts. However, research has failed to show that gifted abilities necessarily precede extensive practice. Does this mean that a person of average intelligence and above-average motivation can readily become a concert pianist or astrophysicist? No. Other research indicates that hard work, intensive training, perseverance, and practice alone rarely lead to giftedness.

In short, motivation and hard work seem to be necessary, but not sufficient, requirements for the development of giftedness (Winner, 2000).

- *Some people gifted in academic or other forms of intelligence may not be equally gifted with social and emotional intelligence.* Some psychologists have observed that gifted children often display disproportionate social and emotional difficulties, especially during adolescence. Many are socially isolated and introverted. In fact, a number of academically gifted children try to hide their giftedness in an attempt to fit in with others. Girls seem more likely than boys to do this (Winner, 2000).

Before You Go On www.wiley.com/go/comer

What Do You Know?

24. What are the four levels of mental retardation, and which is most common?
25. What are some causes of mental retardation?
26. Is high IQ the only criterion for giftedness?

What Do You Think?

How might environment produce the effect of mental retardation? Do you think this effect could be reversed? If so, how? If not, why?

SCAN TO GET THE ANSWERS

Summary

What Do We Mean by Intelligence?

LEARNING OBJECTIVE 1 Describe various ways in which intelligence has been defined and summarize the current thinking on whether intelligence is general or specific.

- Scholars early in the twentieth century defined *intelligence* as the ability to learn and to meet the demands of the environment effectively. Later, other scholars added to this definition the ability to understand and control one's mental activities, called metacognition.
- A central issue in defining intelligence is whether it is a single, general factor or a cluster of different abilities. Charles Spearman hypothesized that a general factor, or *g* factor, underlies all mental abilities, while Lewis Thurstone argued that intelligence is made up of seven distinct *primary mental abilities*.
- Although most theorists today agree that intelligence does include a *g* factor, modern theorists such as Howard Gardner, Robert Sternberg, and Stephen Ceci have tended to deemphasize the *g* factor and focus on specific abilities, or *s* factors.

Additional Types of Intelligence

LEARNING OBJECTIVE 2 Discuss several proposed types of intelligence that go beyond intellectual functioning.

- Other theorists have broadened the definition of intelligence further to include emotional intelligence, social intelligence, wisdom, creativity, and personality.

How Do We Measure Intelligence?

LEARNING OBJECTIVE 3 Identify important considerations in the construction of intelligence tests, discuss the history of intelligence testing, and describe some criticisms of intelligence tests.

- The *psychometric approach* to studying intelligence attempts to measure intelligence with carefully constructed psychological tests.
- To ensure that intelligence tests are grounded in sound scientific principles, psychologists design tests that adhere to three basic criteria: *standardization*, *reliability*, and *validity*.
- Early pioneers of intelligence testing include Francis Galton, who proposed the theory of psychophysical performance, and Francis Binet, who developed a test to predict children's success in school.
- Adapting Binet's work for use in the United States, Lewis Terman constructed the Stanford-Binet Intelligence Test and devised the *intelligence quotient* (*IQ*).
- David Wechsler broadened the usefulness of intelligence testing by developing the Wechsler Adult Intelligence Scale (WAIS), along with several other tests.
- Both the Stanford-Binet and the WAIS have high degrees of reliability. Performance on intelligence tests also correlates highly with school performance, and to some degree with other areas of functioning in life, such as occupational achievements.
- Although widely used, intelligence tests are subject to several criticisms. One issue involves the culture-specific

nature of the tests, which may produce bias. A related problem is *stereotype threat*.

- Intelligence test scores from around the world have increased over time, a phenomenon known as the *Flynn effect*. Possible explanations include potential problems with the procedures, content, or nature of the tests and improvements in education, nutrition, health, or environments.

Is Intelligence Governed by Genetic or Environmental Factors?

LEARNING OBJECTIVE 4 Review the contributions of heredity and environment to intelligence, and explain how emphasizing one factor or the other can affect social policy.

- The nature–nurture debate as applied to intelligence has important social implications, exemplified by the controversial book *The Bell Curve*, whose authors argued that group differences in IQ are likely due at least in part to genetic factors.
- Family studies and research in molecular biology have indicated that heredity does play a major role in intelligence. Researchers estimate that the heritability of intelligence is about 50 percent.
- Environmental factors that affect intelligence include family and home, overall culture, occupation, and schooling.
- Group differences in IQ scores enable us only to make distinctions between groups, not to reach any conclusions about an individual within a group.
- Studies have confirmed that environmental enrichment for members of disadvantaged groups is effective in producing at least short-term cognitive gains.

Intelligence *What Happens in The Brain?*

LEARNING OBJECTIVE 5 Describe how brain size, number of neurons, processing speed, brain activity, and cortical thickness relate to intelligence.

- Neuroimaging studies suggest that overall brain size is not correlated with intelligence. The number of neurons in certain brain regions, such as the frontal lobes, may be related to intellectual functioning.
- The speed with which the brain responds to stimuli, which can be measured by means of EEGs and *nerve conduction velocity* (*NCV*), also correlates with intelligence.
- PET scans, which show what areas of the brain are active at a particular moment, have generally revealed lower activity in the brains of people performing well on an intellectual task and higher activity in the brains of people performing poorly. This suggests that the brains of the higher performers may be more efficient.
- It appears that the development of intelligence involves a process of neuron growth and then neuron pruning, particularly in the prefrontal cortex—a process that is reflected by a distinct pattern of change in cortical thickness throughout childhood and adolescence.

Extremes In Intelligence *How We Differ*

LEARNING OBJECTIVE 6 Discuss mental retardation and giftedness.

- The two extremes of intelligence, as measured by IQ tests, are represented by mental retardation and giftedness.
- Mental retardation is classified as mild (IQ 50–70), moderate (IQ 35–49), severe (IQ 20–34), and profound (IQ below 20).
- Home environmental causes of intellectual disability include poor and unstimulating environments and inadequate parent–child interactions. These causes have been associated in particular with mild retardation, though they may also be at work in more severe cases.
- Other causes of retardation include genetically based chromosomal abnormalities, certain prenatal conditions in the mother, complications at delivery, and injuries and infections during early childhood. These causes have been associated in particular with moderate to profound levels of retardation.
- *Down Syndrome* is a genetic abnormality resulting in mental retardation.
- Psychologists do not agree on how to define giftedness, but often identify gifted persons as having IQs at the top 1 or 2 percent of the tested population.
- Environment can contribute to giftedness, and gifted people are often highly motivated. However, academically gifted people may not be equally gifted with social and emotional intelligence.

Key Terms

bioecological model of intelligence 373
content validity 379
creativity 376
Down syndrome 404
emotional intelligence 374
factor analysis 369
Flynn effect 387
g factor 369
heritability 391
heritability coefficient 392
intelligence 368
intelligence quotient (IQ) 381
mean 378
median 378
mental age 380

mental retardation 403
metacognition 368
mode 378
nerve conduction velocity (NCV) 400
normal distribution 378
predictive validity 379
primary mental abilities 370
psychometric approach 378
reaction range 392
reliability 379
s factor 369
standardization 378
stereotype vulnerability or threat 386
theory of multiple intelligences 371
triarchic theory of intelligence 372
validity 379
validity coefficient 379

TYING IT TOGETHER

The study of intelligence is closely connected to the study of all other areas of psychology. Throughout this chapter, we have stressed how intelligence interfaces with psychology's various subfields, including our highlighted sections on brain function, individual differences, abnormal functioning, and development. To remind you of how intelligence is tied to other psychology subfields and issues, here are some interesting points from throughout the chapter.

WHAT HAPPENS IN THE BRAIN?

- A larger number of neurons in particular brain areas, such as the frontal lobes, may be associated with higher intellectual functioning.
- How fast the brain responds to stimuli also correlates with intelligence. It may be that some people are wired to acquire information more quickly than others.
- PET scans have shown that the brains of people performing well on an intellectual task are less active than those of people performing poorly—that is, the brains of the high-performing people may not need to work as hard.

HOW WE DIFFER

- Intelligence, as measured by IQ tests, follows a distribution shaped like a bell curve. At one end of this curve are those diagnosed with mental retardation, and at the other are those considered intellectually gifted.
- Mental retardation involves a combination of lower general intellectual functioning and poorer adaptive behaviour. The most consistent sign of mental retardation is very slow learning.
- Mild retardation, the most common kind, is linked primarily to home environmental causes, such as poor and unstimulating environments during early life.
- Often, intellectual giftedness is defined only in terms of IQ scores and doesn't take other forms of intelligence into account. Thus, an intellectually gifted person may be quite low in emotional or social intelligence.

WHEN THINGS GO WRONG

- Most psychologists view moderate, severe, and profound levels of intellectual disability as mental disorders.
- Biological factors are primarily responsible for moderate, severe, and profound retardation. Severe and profound retardation often are part of larger syndromes that include severe physical handicaps.
- Although children with moderate retardation display significant delays in school, special-education programs can help them to succeed in many areas. By adulthood, they can generally function well at work and in the community with supervision.

HOW WE DEVELOP

- As noted in Chapter 3, children's brains actually lose neurons and synapses as the children grow into adolescence. This developmental process is reflected in a thinning of the cortex.
- The developmental pattern of cortical thickening and thinning is different in more intelligent children than in less intelligent children. In highly intelligent children, the process takes longer.
- These brain changes may be the result of environmental interactions, genetic factors, or both. Indeed, we know that enriching the environment of deprived children can improve their intellectual performance.

Psychology Around Us

General Intelligence versus Specific Intelligence

Who's More Intelligent?

View this in Action
WILEY PLUS
www.wileyplus.com

Video Lab Exercise

After reading this chapter, you can appreciate that defining and measuring intelligence is one of psychology's most controversial, complex, and challenging tasks. Where do you stand on the issue of intelligence? On what basis do you conclude that someone is intelligent? And how do your notions of intelligence compare to those proposed by the various theorists and researchers in this chapter?

In this video lab exercise, you will look at people in action and decide if they are intelligent, how they are intelligent, and why you believe they are intelligent. Over the course of your work, you will come to appreciate even more the difficulties—some would say the misguidedness—at work in the field of intelligence and intelligence testing. In addition, along the way, this lab exercise will help you to appreciate the power, impact, and dangers of intelligence labels.

As you are working on this online exercise, consider the following questions:

- How do your assessments of intelligence compare to each of the leading theories on intelligence?
- Are cognitive, emotional, and creative intelligence related?
- Does intelligence increase over the course of a person's life? Can it increase once a person reaches adulthood?
- Is intelligence related to wisdom? conscientiousness? achievement? likeability? social perceptions and expectations?

CHAPTER 11

Motivation

CHAPTER OUTLINE

- Theories of Motivation
- Biological Motivations: Hunger
- Biological Motivations: Sex
- Psychological Motivations: Affiliation and Achievement

"I DON'T WANT TO DIE, BUT I ACCEPT THAT IT CAN HAPPEN."

Who might say something like that? Someone going in for risky surgery? Someone going into battle? How about someone engaging in an extreme sport? Scuba diving used to be considered an extreme sport, but now almost anyone can do it. How about extreme snowboarding or skiing as seen in the X-Games? There are certainly more options for broken limbs and other injuries in the X-Games, but death? . . . Not particularly likely. How about bungee jumping or skydiving? Sometimes bungee cords break or chutes fail to open, but with good equipment and instruction, how dangerous is it?

The quote at the top of the page refers to Buildings, Antennas, Spans, and Earth (cliff) or BASE jumping. Caitlin Forsey (2009) wrote her University of British Columbia Master's thesis on the sport (in which her boyfriend participates). BASE jumping involves a parachute, but you jump from a fixed object (i.e., a building, antenna, bridge, or cliff). It differs from skydiving in other ways as well. BASE jumpers need a chute that opens much faster than a regular skydiving chute because they often jump from objects at or below 150 metres (as compared to the minimum 600 metres by very experienced skydivers). BASE jumpers do not carry a reserve chute—if their main chute does not work, there is no time to even think about opening another. Skydivers carry an automatic activation device (AAD) designed to open their chute if they get too close to the ground and they have not yet opened it themselves. BASE jumpers usually start their jumps so close to the ground that an AAD would be pointless. Skydivers typically have between 3 and 5 minutes of "canopy time" after their chutes open. This provides a safety cushion if things go a bit wrong. BASE jumpers have only about 10 to 15 seconds of canopy time—hardly enough to make any adjustments at all. As a consequence, they also need specially designed rapid deployment chutes so they do not eat up their whole 10- to 15-second canopy time safety window.

Sound like fun? BASE jumping is a growing sport, not that we are recommending it! Finally, if you are thinking it would be impossible to imagine there being a sport with any more associated risk than BASE jumping, search YouTube for "Wingsuit Flying, BASE jumping, and/or Loic Jean-Albert." We are not going to say anymore; you have to see it. Sports like BASE jumping make you wonder what motivates an individual to engage in such odd behaviour. Is it an adrenaline rush? Most certainly. Do people enjoy tempting fate?

Psychologists define **motivation** as a condition that directs behaviour (Reeve, 2005). This behaviour is usually directed toward a goal. For any given circumstance, your behaviour is probably the consequence of a combination of several **motives**—your needs or desires. If you consider the many behaviours you engage in throughout your day-to-day life, your motivations are sometimes related to the fulfillment of basic biological needs, but more often they are the result of complicated factors involving past experience and learning.

motivation an internal state or condition that directs behaviour.

motive a need or desire.

Motivation differs a lot from person to person. Your fellow students differ in their motivation to study. This accounts for some of the variation in performance within classes. The reasons for these differences are very complex and often difficult to investigate scientifically. Variation in the degree to which people experience biological drives is also evident and has been the subject of much investigation. In particular, relatively large differences in food intake and sexual behaviour are obvious among humans in the absence of any abnormality.

BASE jumping. Thrill-seekers put on a specially-designed parachute to jump off a cliff, a building, or a bridge.

BASE jumpers are likely motivated by a number of things. Maybe they feel a need for the rewards of attention, social recognition, and fame, and have learned that BASE jumping is one way to get those rewards. Or perhaps the jumps themselves are why they do it. Contestants may want to be pushed to do their best, even if it is in a field few people enter. Most likely, we would need a combination of reasons to explain this behaviour.

In this chapter, we will see that psychologists have developed a number of theories that explain how our motivation drives and guides our behaviour. Researchers have discovered a great deal about how body and brain signals work to motivate us to fulfill some of our basic biological motives. We will take a look at how even common biological motives, such as hunger, can interact with our experiences and thoughts to lead to specific behaviours. We will discuss how these processes develop and what happens when things go wrong—when we become motivated to do things that aren't in our best interests. ■

Theories of Motivation

LEARNING OBJECTIVE 1

Briefly explain each of the five major theories of motivation.

So how do psychologists explain people's behaviour? They have devised several theories of motivation, each of which takes a different approach to explaining what compels individuals to act as they do (**Table 11-1**). However, no single theory has yet been able to provide a complete explanation of what motivates us to engage in our many different behaviours.

instincts inborn behavioural tendencies, activated by stimuli in our environments.

Instinct Theory

Instinct theory maintains that behaviours originate from a set of behavioural blueprints, or **instincts** (Fancher, 1996). Instinctive behaviours are inborn and activated

TABLE 11-1 Major Theories of Motivation

Theory	Approach
Instinct	Behaviour is motivated by instincts that are inborn and that are activated by environmental stimuli
Drive reduction	Behaviour is motivated by biological needs to maintain the body in a state of balance or equilibrium
Arousal	Behaviour is motivated by the need to achieve optimum levels of arousal
Incentive	Behaviour is motivated by internal (intrinsic) or external (extrinsic) incentives or rewards
Hierarchy of needs	Behaviour is motivated by the current most basic need, when different motives compete; basic survival needs must be satisfied first before we are motivated to satisfy higher level needs such as belonging and self-esteem

by particular environmental stimuli. A good example of instinctual motivation can be observed in the maternal behaviour of female rats. Virgin female rats typically ignore or avoid unfamiliar rat pups. In some instances, virgin females will even commit infanticide. However, if they are given a longer period of exposure to the infant rat pups, they may actually start to act as foster mothers (Peters, Sist, & Kristal, 1991). The same rat that reacted with indifference or violence when exposed to pups prior to giving birth will engage in a rich repertoire of maternal behaviour once her own babies are born. She will build a nest, and lick, groom, retrieve, huddle over, and nurse her pups. These behaviours are not learned by the animal, nor are there any external incentives for engaging in them. They occur automatically as a result of changes in hormone levels that coincide with delivering a litter of rat pups (Kinsley et al., 2008).

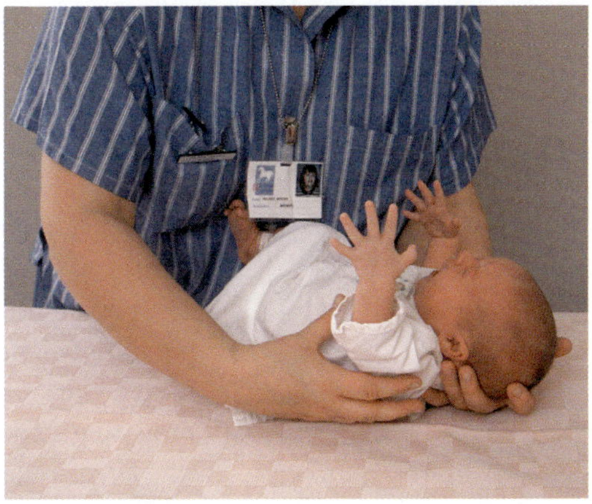

The moro reflex. A nurse checks the moro reflex of a 1-day-old girl. In this reflex, babies react to loud noises or to a sense of being dropped by throwing their arms outward and bringing them together as if trying to grasp something.

Many of our own basic motives are inborn. Some of the most critical for survival, such as eating, are present at birth (Colson, Meek, & Hawdon, 2008). Although the range of foods considered to be rewarding changes substantially from the time we are babies until our adult lives (infants will readily eat baby food and formula, both of which adults typically consider bland and unappealing), the basic motivation to eat when hungry persists throughout life.

Humans are also naturally motivated to form social contacts. As we saw in Chapter 5, babies are born with a well-developed sense of smell that lets them recognize the particular scent of their mothers (Porter & Winberg, 1999). We are also born with reflexes that allow us to engage in primitive social behaviour. The rooting reflex, discussed in Chapter 3, for example, involves turning the head and using the mouth to search for a nipple. Rooting not only helps a baby to eat, but it allows the infant to seek contact with other people. Along with the ability to recognize their mothers by smell, rooting enables babies to start establishing close relationships with their mothers (Swain et al., 2007). As the baby grows, new abilities emerge, such as smiling, laughing, reaching arms out to be carried, and talking. All of these further encourage the formation of social bonds, thus increasing the chance of survival (Messinger & Fogel, 2007; Broad, Curley, & Keverne, 2006). As with eating, the nuances of this basic motivation change as we grow. For example, instead of seeking mother love, we seek romantic love. The motivation to be socially connected remains strong throughout life, however.

Challenging a theory. This bungee jumper takes off from a bridge and begins a wild—and seemingly dangerous—free fall, challenging instinct theory along the way.

Although instinct theory can explain some of our behaviour and a substantial proportion of animal behaviour, instincts don't account for all behaviour, even in relatively simple creatures, such as rats (Clark, Broadbent, & Squire, 2008). In fact, studies on learning and memory would be impossible to carry out on laboratory animals if all of their behaviour was innate; the animals would never need to learn or remember anything.

Instinct theory also has trouble explaining differences among individuals (Bevins, 2001). Among humans, for example, some of us seek out experiences that others avoid or even find painful. Consider adventurers who have climbed Mount Everest, a gruelling and dangerous activity. Conversely, some individuals avoid experiences that others find rewarding and pleasurable. Catholic priests and nuns, for example, forego marriage and biological parenthood to fulfill their obligations to their church. Clearly, these behaviours are not driven by instincts. We need other explanations for these motivations.

Drive-Reduction Theory

homeostasis a tendency of the body to maintain itself in a state of balance or equilibrium.

Drive-reduction theory is another attempt to account for motivation on the basis of internal biological factors. This theory is based on the concept of **homeostasis**, a tendency of the body to maintain itself in a state of balance or equilibrium (**Figure 11-1**). When an external factor alters the state of balance in the organism, a motivation arises to correct that balance (Stricker & Zigmond, 1986). A simple example of this can be seen in the response of the body to heat. When the temperature rises, your body perspires and you lose water. The perspiration evaporates and cools the surface of the skin, helping to maintain the temperature balance in the body. In addition, you may feel motivated to take actions that will hasten your return to an ideal body temperature, such as shedding some layers of clothing or getting a cool drink.

Drive-reduction theory works well to explain behaviours related to biological needs, such as cooling off when we are too hot. We engage in many behaviours, however, that do not appear to be motivated by a need to keep the body in a state of equilibrium (Schneider et al., 2007). In fact, some human behaviour is designed to do just the opposite. Some people seek out adventurous situations that are designed to thrill and even terrorize for entertainment. Amusement park owners make millions of dollars every year providing an outlet for this sort of interest. It's difficult to explain the motivation to go on the West Edmonton Mall's Mindbender roller coaster or the Behemoth roller coaster at Canada's Wonderland in terms of a need to restore the body to a state of equilibrium. Instead, the main purpose is to experience excitement by throwing riders suddenly *out* of a state of emotional equilibrium. That type of thrill-seeking behaviour may be better described in terms of another theory.

Where both instinct and drive reduction theory have problems is with the idea of voluntary decision making as part of motivation. We are capable of over-riding our physiological motivational processes and doing things simply because we want to (Binswanger, 1991). To address this shortfall, we need to add a few more concepts to our discussion of motivational factors.

Arousal Theory

Arousal theory maintains that motivation comes from a need to achieve an appropriate level of arousal (Jones, 2003). This theory is different from drive-reduction theory in that the motivation doesn't always arise from a need to reduce arousal back to a neutral state. While some situations, such as hunger or thirst, can elevate our arousal to uncomfortable

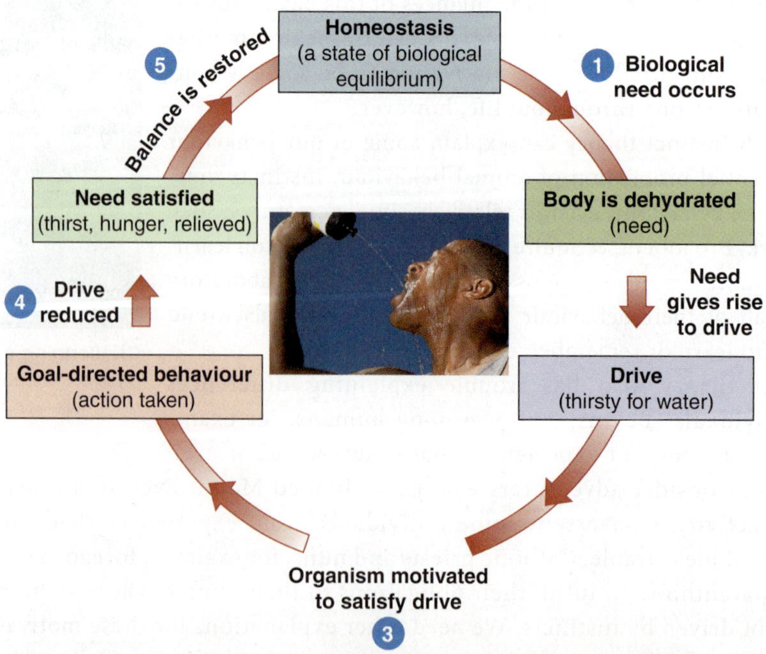

FIGURE 11-1 Drive-reduction theory. When external factors alter our body's normal state of equilibrium, we are motivated to behave in ways that restore the balance.

levels that we try to reduce (for example, by seeking food or drink), arousal theory states that we can also be motivated to elevate our arousal levels if they fall too low. Such underarousal may stimulate us to seek out interesting and exciting situations (Maggini, 2000).

Arousal theory explains a number of behaviours that instinct and drive-reduction theories cannot. Consider the millions of dollars earned every year by paparazzi and the tabloids. Even though a rich knowledge in the latest celebrity gossip is unlikely to enhance your reputation, and could even cause embarrassment if your interest is discovered by co-workers or others, many of us seek out gossip because we are generally curious. Curiosity often motivates us to seek out information, even if there is no other goal involved. Arousal theory would describe the behaviour of people who follow celebrity gossip as an attempt to elevate our levels of arousal and interest.

You may have noticed arousal-increasing behaviours in your dog. Your dog might explore new surroundings, watch a television show, or sniff another dog, for no apparent reason except to satisfy his curiosity. Scientists have long recognized that rodents also engage in behaviour that does not appear to be goal-directed. As you read in Chapter 7, for example, if rats are exposed to a maze, they will navigate the apparatus, and even learn its spatial characteristics, without receiving rewards or punishments (Hughes, 2007). They appear to explore just because they find it interesting.

Challenging another theory. People riding the Behemoth rollercoaster at Canada's Wonderland demonstrate the limits of drive-reduction theory.

In addition to providing motivation, our arousal levels can systematically affect our performance on tasks we undertake. The Yerkes-Dodson law states that ideal performance on a task occurs when our arousal level is right for the difficulty of the task. Task difficulty and arousal seem to be inversely related (**Figure 11-2**). That is, our performance on difficult tasks is optimal at low to medium arousal states, while our performance on easy tasks is optimal at medium to high arousal states. This may be related to the fact that difficult tasks require more intense concentration that may be disrupted by highly arousing circumstances. Imagine, for example, that you are trying to finish writing a term paper. You may find it easier to focus on your writing if you are not highly aroused by a deadline looming only a few hours away. If, however, you are trying to read some really boring material (something other than this book, of course), you may need to periodically raise your arousal levels with snacks, stretch breaks, and the like, to help you focus on the task.

Yerkes-Dodson law law stating that ideal performance on a task occurs when the arousal level is optimized to the difficulty level.

intrinsic motivation engaging in a behaviour simply for the satisfaction that is part of doing it.

incentives external motives that indirectly indicate reward.

extrinsic motivation engaging in a behaviour due to the influence of factors outside ourselves.

Incentive Theory

Some behaviours are intrinsically motivating, which means that engaging in the behaviour is satisfying in and of itself (Schmitt & Lahroodi, 2008). For the rats described earlier, exploring mazes seems to be intrinsically motivating. For some people, taking thrill-seeking rides is intrinsically motivating. Although they may never skydive, they occasionally like a rollercoaster ride for the pleasure they get out of doing so.

Other behaviours are driven by external motives, or incentives. Behaviour that is motivated by external incentives is known as extrinsically motivated. Rats can be extrinsically motivated: they learn their way through a maze more quickly if provided with an incentive, such as food or a way to escape something unpleasant (such as water), than they do when no incentives are involved (Komaki, 2004).

Even when our motivation to behave in a certain way involves instinct, a drive to maintain homeostasis, or a motive to achieve an optimal level of arousal, it's clear that incentives play a major role in most human behaviour. *Incentive theory* highlights the influence of external stimuli in behaviour, suggesting that external rewards, such as public acclaim or financial prizes, contribute to the motivation of some BASE jumpers. A good deal of your

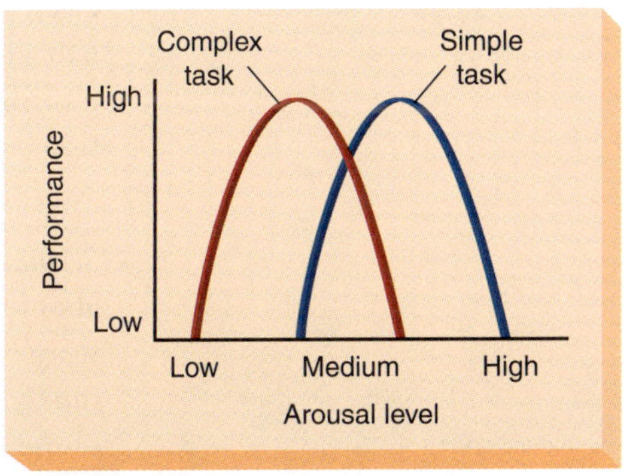

FIGURE 11-2 The Yerkes-Dodson law. Our optimal performance on tasks is inversely related to our arousal level. We perform difficult tasks best when our arousal level is low to medium and simple, or boring ones best when our arousal level is medium to high.

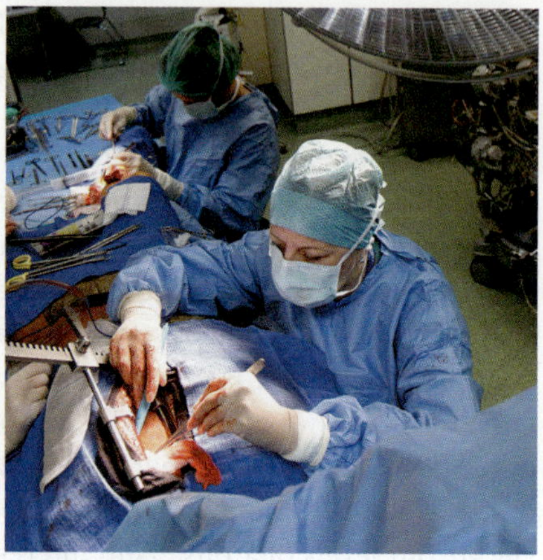

The Yerkes-Dodson law in action. The worker on the left uses a knife to cut bread at a restaurant in Italy, while the surgeon on the right uses her sharp instrument to perform open-heart surgery. According to the Yerkes-Dodson law, a high level of physical arousal will help the restaurant worker's performance but probably not the surgeon's.

PSYCHOLOGY AROUND US Goalie Psychology

The Yerkes-Dodson law has obvious applications to sports. Athletes who fail to get sufficiently "psyched up" or aroused may never even get into the game. On the other hand, getting too "revved up" or over-aroused might lead to "choking." Ryan Gelinas and Krista Munroe-Chandler at the University of Windsor have examined how this and other psychological issues in motivation can impact the performance of hockey goaltenders (Gelinas & Munroe-Chandler, 2006). They point out that each goalie (and each athlete in general) has an optimal level of arousal at which they perform their best. Some goalies need to get "psyched up" or excited to reach that optimal level, while others need to calm down so as not to become over-aroused. High levels of arousal, especially when associated with anxiety, lead to muscle tension that can slow a goalie down. It can also narrow the goalie's attentional field, making it less likely that they will take in all the information needed to properly position him or herself in the net. The aim for goaltenders is to keep themselves in the "zone" of optimal arousal so that they can consistently perform at their best throughout the game.

own behaviour as a student is probably also motivated by external factors, such as the desire to achieve high grades, graduate on time, and obtain a good job.

Incentives can be either primary or secondary, and they can be rewarding or punitive.

- *Primary incentives* are rewards or punishments that are innate; we do not have to learn to either like or dislike them. Food is a primary reward, and pain is a primary punishment, for example. Most humans instinctually find food rewarding and electric shock punishing. For that reason, these stimuli are likely to influence our behaviour. There is an adaptive, or evolutionary, component to primary rewards and punishments. Typically, stimuli that increase our chances of survival and reproduction, such as food and sex, are rewarding, while those that are potentially harmful, such as anything painful, are punishing.

- *Secondary incentives* are cues that are viewed as rewarding as a result of learning about their association with other events. For example, most people are motivated to work to earn money. Money, in and of itself, is not rewarding. It becomes motivating to us when we learn its association with the rewarding goods, such as food, that money can buy.

Although money is generally considered to be a strong motivator, its effects differ greatly from person to person. Why is this? Scientists attribute the different motivational power of certain cues to *incentive salience*, how noticeable or important a particular incentive is to us (Berridge, 2007). Incentives can become more salient and more motivating after they become associated with specific emotions (Robinson & Berridge, 2001). Consider our motivation to work hard at a job. The first time we receive a paycheque, the things we purchase with the money may lead to happiness. This association of money with happiness may, in turn, motivate us to engage in behaviours designed to improve the chance of earning even more money, such as working harder. Alternatively, if our first work experience is a very negative one that becomes associated with boredom and unhappiness, our drive to pursue happiness through hard work is less likely to expand. We may seek to avoid work altogether, or we may be motivated to look for a better and more gratifying job. Particularly for complex behaviours, such as working at a job, there can be many incentives that motivate different individuals. Some people work to avoid punishment, such as homelessness and shame, for example, while others work to receive rewards, such as money and pride.

The big payoff. Although Canadian poker star Daniel Negreaunu has consistently won big on the world poker tour, the money he wins is not, in itself, rewarding. Rather, it is what the money can buy, the prestige attached to winning so much, and the pride the big payoff instills in him.

Motivational theories that focus on incentives often take into consideration the distinction between "liking" and "wanting" (Berridge & Kringelbach, 2008). "Liking" refers to our experience of reward or pleasure that happens *at the moment* we are engaging in a particular behaviour, while "wanting" refers to the anticipation of an experience that we expect will cause us pleasure. Having a pleasurable experience in the past often leads to wanting to repeat that experience again in the future. If you really like your first live concert, you might want more like it. You might even become motivated to travel to other cities, just to attend concerts.

Neuroscientists have found that overlapping, but distinct, regions of our brains are involved in liking and wanting (Litman, 2005). Pleasure, or liking, is typically associated with systems of the brain that produce *opiates*. Opiates, such as endorphins, are naturally-occurring neurochemicals that contribute to our feelings of pleasure. Eating, drinking, and sex—biological motivations that we discuss later in this chapter—are all associated with a release in opiates. Other experiences, such as intense physical exercise (for example, long distance running) can also stimulate the release of brain opiates, producing a phenomenon called "runner's high" (Boecker et al., 2008).

In addition to activating the brain-opiate system, rewarding stimuli typically stimulate the release of the neurotransmitter dopamine (Berridge & Kringelbach, 2008; Arias-Carrión & Pöppel, 2007). As discussed in Chapter 4, dopamine is present in two major systems of the brain. One region is mostly important for movement and is affected by Parkinson's disease (Lang & Obeso, 2004), while the other is important for reinforcement learning. The latter system consists of dopamine neurons in a region of the midbrain, called the ventral tegmental area, that send their axons to two key areas in the front of the brain: the *nucleus accumbens* and the *prefrontal cortex* (**Figure 11-3**). As we noted in Chapter 4, the nucleus accumbens is highly active in the experience of

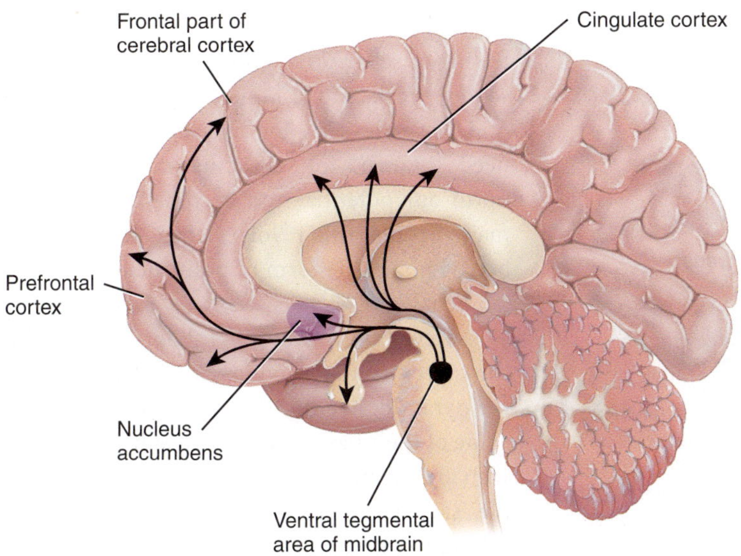

FIGURE 11-3 **Reward pathways in the brain.** Rewarding stimuli typically trigger dopamine neurons in the ventral tegmental area of the brain. The axons of these neurons project to the nucleus accumbens and the prefrontal cortex, activating rewarding and pleasurable feelings, while others project into the cingulated cortex.

rewarding and pleasurable feelings (Carlezon & Thomas, 2009). The pathways of dopamine neurons from the ventral tegmental area to the nucleus accumbens and prefrontal cortex are not only activated during the reward experience, but they appear to be critical for future behaviour directed toward that reward. In other words, the dopamine system plays a critical role in "wanting."

Although incentive theory explains how our behaviour is shaped by external stimuli, not all of our behaviour is motivated by wanting a reward or avoiding a punishment. Integrating incentive theory with other motivation theories is necessary to explain the complexity of motivation. For example, drive-reduction theory explains that eating to reduce the feeling of hunger maintains homeostasis, and incentive theory explains the rewarding feelings associated with what you eat and the incentive to eat that food again in the future.

Multiple Motivations: Hierarchy of Needs

As we have seen, a combination of factors, including innate and learned motives, interact to drive behaviour. Psychologists have also recognized that different motives can compete with one another (LaGraize et al., 2004). For instance, you might find it particularly difficult to concentrate on completing a homework assignment if you are really thirsty. The relative strength of certain motives and their ability to supersede one another led humanist psychologist Abraham Maslow to describe motives, or needs, in terms of a *hierarchy* (Maslow, 1978). **Figure 11-4**, which you also studied in Chapter 1, shows Maslow's hierarchy of needs.

The most basic needs, such as the need to eat or drink, are at the bottom of the hierarchy pyramid. Unless these needs are satisfied, we find it difficult to generate motivation to engage in other behaviours. Above the basic needs are the safety needs: the need to feel secure and stable. It's important to realize that a balance exists between the first and second tier on the pyramid. It would not make sense for us to drink tainted water when waiting would be safer. That doesn't happen often, because water is usually not a matter of life or death in Western culture. But humans, as well as other animals, will often take great risks to obtain food and water if they can't be obtained in a safer setting.

Above safety needs is the need to feel love and to belong to a social group. This need motivates us to seek companionship in the form of friends and romantic partners. It motivates the creation of families and the formation of clubs and other social organizations. Social needs vary considerably from species to species. The tree shrew, for example, lives a solitary life and only interacts with other tree shrews for purposes of mating. The mother tree shrew doesn't even sleep with her own babies. Humans vary from person to person, but as a species, we are highly social and our need for human contact is often a very strong motivator of our behaviour.

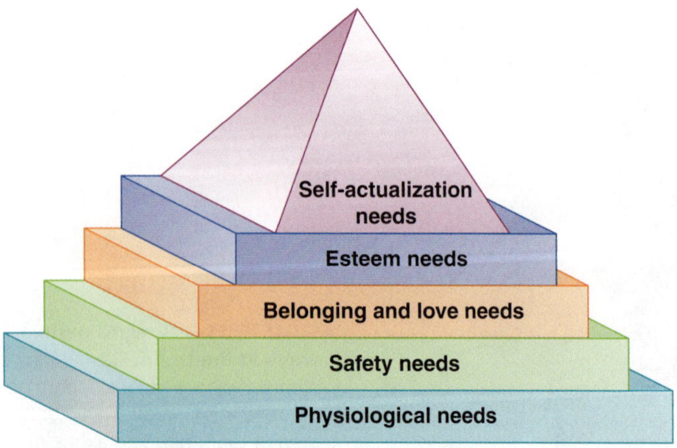

FIGURE 11-4 Maslow's hierarchy of needs. A combination of needs, both innate and learned, drive our behaviour and sometimes are in competition. Maslow identified the relative strengths of these needs and arranged them in a hierarchy. Basic survival needs at the base of the pyramid are the strongest and must be satisfied first before we are motivated to achieve our higher needs.

Above the need to belong socially rests the need for a feeling of self-worth. This need motivates us to achieve at school, work, and at home. Finally, at the top of the pyramid rests the need for self-actualization. As our highest need, the need for self-actualization motivates us to live up to our potential and become the best we can be. For many people, this involves engaging in selfless, altruistic behaviour, in the form of political activism or humanitarian behaviour.

According to Maslow's theory, it is difficult to meet this need without having satisfied the needs below it on the pyramid. Even so, many people sacrifice fulfillment of some of their basic needs to meet higher needs. Physicians who are members of Doctors without Borders, for example, sacrifice their safety needs to fulfill their needs for self-actualization.

Before You Go On

www.wiley.com/go/comer

What Do You Know?

1. What are some examples of instinctive motivations among humans?
2. How does drive-reduction theory differ from arousal theory?
3. What is intrinsic motivation and how does it differ from extrinsic motivation?
4. Give an example of a primary incentive and a secondary incentive.
5. What are the lowest level needs in the hierarchy of needs?

SCAN TO GET THE ANSWERS

What Do You Think?

Consider one of your favourite leisure-time activities, such as reading novels, playing videogames, or playing a sport. Whatever the activity, describe how each of the motivational theories discussed in this chapter would explain why you do it. Does any one theory best describe your motivation?

Biological Motivations: Hunger

LEARNING OBJECTIVE 2

Summarize the factors that affect our levels of hunger and our eating behaviour.

As noted, the drive to eat is biologically ingrained or instinctual. Even newborn babies show interest in feeding soon after they are born. The biological drive to eat remains in place throughout our lives, since we need to eat to live. A person can generally last only about 40 days without food (Lieberson, 2004). Eating is not simply a matter of following an instinctive pattern of behaviour to satisfy an inborn drive, however. Instead, a number of other factors play a role in motivating how much, what, when, and even where we are motivated to eat. First, let's explore what we know about the biology of eating.

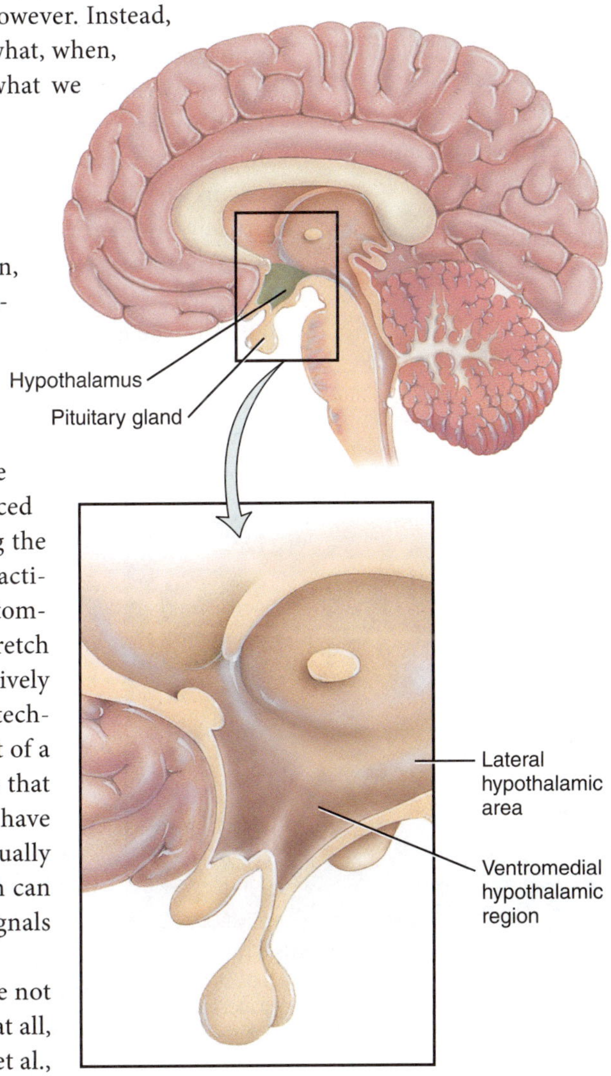

Hunger — WHAT HAPPENS IN THE BRAIN?

A number of stimuli contribute to hunger signals in our brain, including how full our stomachs are, the levels of nutrients circulating in our bloodstreams, and interacting with both of those signals, the activities of key parts of our brains.

Stomach Signals As you may have experienced, an empty stomach can trigger feelings of hunger. Physicians treating obese patients take advantage of the fact that physical signals produced by stretch receptors in the stomach are important for informing the brain to stop eating. These cues, called *satiety* signals, can be activated by surgically placing a balloon in the stomach. Since the stomach space is already partially occupied by the balloon, the stretch receptors will be activated even when the person eats a relatively small meal (Fernandes et al., 2007; Rigaud et al., 1995). Another technique that works on a similar principle is the surgical placement of a band around the stomach or physically stapling the stomach so that it is much smaller (Bowne et al., 2006). Many individuals who have undergone these procedures first lose weight, but then eventually gain it back, suggesting that, although signals from the stomach can influence the degree to which we are motivated to eat, these signals aren't the only mediators (Christou, Look, & Maclean, 2006).

Indeed, it turns out that satiety signals from the stomach are not even the most important hunger clues. People with no stomach at all, as a result of surgery for cancer, still experience hunger (Kamiji et al.,

2009). Also, as you may have experienced, eating a small amount of food often stimulates additional hunger.

Chemical Signals Eating occurs as a result of a complex interplay between hunger and satiety. Considerable evidence suggests that cues related to the metabolism of food can signal hunger or satiety (Erlanson-Albertsson, 2005; Wynne, Stanley, & Bloom, 2004). Some of these cues are related to levels of different chemicals produced in our blood when our bodies digest food. Two of the most well-researched of these are *glucose*, also known as blood sugar, and lipids, the products produced when our bodies break down fats from food. There are receptors for both glucose and *lipids* in the brain, which can influence hunger (Levin et al., 2004; Meister, 2000). Injections of glucose into the bloodstream, for instance, can reduce eating in experimental animals (Novin, Sanderson & Vanderweele, 1974).

leptin a protein produced by fat cells that is important for regulating the amount of food eaten over long periods of time.

The protein **leptin** is another signal that appears to be important for regulating the amount of food eaten over long periods of time. Leptin is released from our fat cells as they grow larger. When receptors in the brain sense high levels of leptin, they in turn send signals that inhibit us from eating (Dhillon et al., 2006; Hommel et al., 2006). Obese animals and obese humans may be insensitive to leptin. Some evidence suggests that although they have higher blood levels of leptin than normal-weight individuals, they have fewer leptin receptors in their brains, which may prevent the signal to stop eating from being generated soon enough (Bjornhelm et al., 2007; Farooqi et al., 2007).

lateral hypothalamus (LH) a region of the hypothalamus important in signalling thirst and hunger.

ventromedial region of the hypothalamus (VMH) a region of the hypothalamus important in signalling satiety.

Brain Signals Within the brain, the hypothalamus is a key mediator of eating. As you can see in the brain illustration on the previous page, specific subregions in the hypothalamus have been linked to both hunger and satiety. The **lateral hypothalamus (LH)** is important for hunger. Rodents with damage to this area dramatically undereat; they need to be force-fed or they will starve to death (Petrovich et al., 2002). A nearby brain region, the **ventromedial region of the hypothalamus (VMH)**, has been shown to play an important role in satiety. Destruction of this region leads to overeating and obesity in rats (see **Figure 11-5**). Humans who develop brain tumours in the VMH also increase their food intake and become markedly heavier (Yadav et al., 2009). A genetic condition in humans, known as Prader-Willi syndrome, is associated with an insatiable appetite leading to obesity. This condition is believed to arise, at least in part, from dysfunction of the hypothalamus (Hinton et al., 2006; Holland et al., 1993).

The identification of these two brain regions as important for feeding behaviour led to the formation of the *dual-centre theory of motivation*. This idea proposes that activity in one area serves to inhibit the area that serves the opposite function. For example, an empty stomach and low blood glucose may stimulate the LH to motivate us to eat, while at the same time, inhibiting satiety signals from the VMH. Once the stretch receptors are activated and blood-glucose reaches a certain level, the VMH would once again become active and it would inhibit the LH.

FIGURE 11-5 The VMH and obesity. The rat on the left had its ventromedial hypothalamus destroyed, which led to overeating and a dramatic increase in its body weight compared to the normal weight rat in the picture.

Subsequent research, however, has shown that these brain regions influence eating in a more complicated way through the action of a hormone called *insulin* (Plum, Belgardt, & Brüning, 2006; Woods et al., 2006). The VMH appears to be important for modulating the levels of insulin in the blood. Insulin helps the body to metabolize and use glucose. Damage to the VMH can increase insulin levels. High insulin levels, in turn, cause our fat cells to store more glucose and grow. Studies of animals with lesions or damage in the VMH show that they experience increases in fat deposits, regardless of the amount of food they eat (Yadav et al., 2009). So, it is not just a matter of the VMH failing to provide these animals with a satiety signal. They are actually short on blood sugar, or glucose. Because they store energy from glucose as fat more rapidly than undamaged animals, the signals of satiety, such as an increase in blood-glucose level, don't occur. As a result, the animals continue eating.

As we have stressed throughout this book, however, it's important to remember that no single area of the brain acts alone, especially in a complex behaviour such as eating. Along with the hypothalamus, several additional brain regions participate in eating. Our ability to taste food certainly plays a role in eating, for example. As described in Chapter 5, taste information is processed in the regions of the prefrontal cortex. Disgust cues related to the presentation of unpalatable food involve the insular cortex, a region situated close to the prefrontal cortex (Roman, Lin, & Reilly, 2009; Roman & Reilly, 2007).

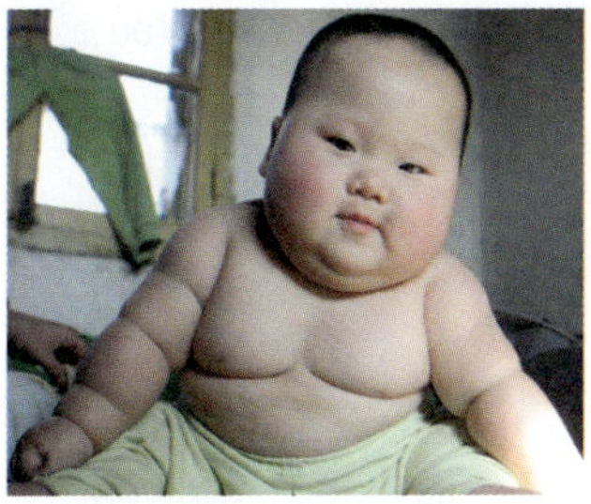

Prader-Willi Syndrome causes unstoppable appetite.

Not only are many areas of the brain involved in eating, but the brain circuitry involved in our eating behaviour is also active in a variety of motivational situations. Pathways important for general reward, punishment, and disgust under other circumstances interact with brain regions that specifically process visual, olfactory, and gustatory information to modulate eating (Rolls, 2007; De Araujo et al., 2003). For example, the same part of our brain that is active when we are enjoying the lovely scent of a flower might also be involved when we are enticed by the aroma wafting from a nearby bakery.

Hunger HOW WE DIFFER

In addition to our basic biological need to eat, several psychological factors affect how hungry we feel and how much we eat. People are often motivated to eat—sometimes to eat a great deal—even when they are not particularly hungry. Cultural and social influences also affect our eating behaviour.

Culture plays a role not only in the types of foods that we enjoy and what times of the day we prefer to eat, but also in how much we eat. For example, in Korea, where a meal often consists of many communal side dishes, it is considered proper etiquette to try a little food from each. People in India often skip breakfast, but in Ireland, breakfast is a large meal, often including porridge, eggs, and bacon. Food is also strongly associated with social interactions. Studies have shown that people eat considerably more when they are in a social setting, particularly when it is a relatively large gathering, compared to when eating alone (Lumeng & Hillman, 2007). People with schedules that involve business meetings and social engagements over meals are likely to eat more than those whose schedules do not include meetings at mealtimes, for example. This may be due to the fact that meals take longer with more participants, as well as the fact that people may pay less attention to restricting their diets when they are engaged in conversation (Pliner et al., 2006).

Some researchers have also suggested that we each have an individual **body weight set point**. Researchers have long recognized that as adults, our weights tend to stabilize near a certain general level. We may fluctuate in a small range around that weight, but we typically return to the original set point, even after major deviations from it (Pasquet & Apfelbaum, 1994). This is particularly evident when people diet. A reduction in body weight is often followed by a rebound back toward the original weight, which is why so many dieters fail to achieve lasting weight loss. This isn't always the case, however. Some people do undergo dramatic weight changes in one direction or another and maintain their new weights for a considerable period of time. People who maintain a lower body weight typically make permanent changes in their eating habits and persistently monitor their weight (Dansinger et al., 2005; Warziski et al., 2008; Dansinger et al., 2005).

body weight set point a weight that individuals typically return to even after dieting or overeating.

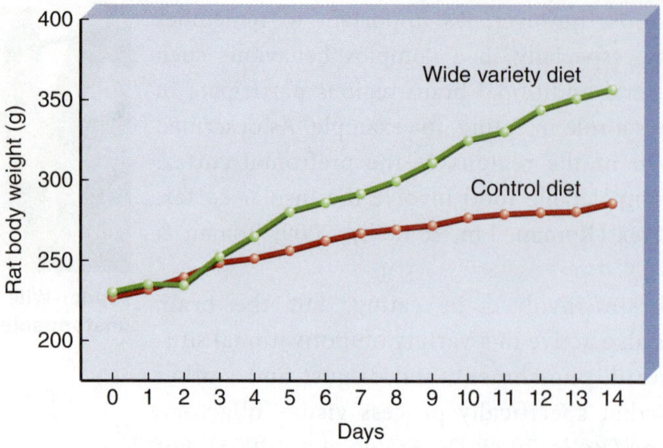

FIGURE 11-6 Food variety and obesity. Research suggests that body weight set point is not the only factor determining the amount of food eaten by humans or animals. When rats are given a wide variety of highly palatable foods, they will eat more and become obese (Sclafani & Springer, 1976).

Other research suggests, however, that body weight set point is not the only factor at play in determining how much we eat. John Pinel at the University of British Columbia points out that set point alone is not a very useful tool for predicting weight. He states that from an evolutionary point of view, our ancestors were not concerned with overeating but with the lack of consistent food. Consequently, when food was available, our ancestors ate a lot to build up fat stores in case the next meals were some time away. Stopping eating so as to maintain a set point weight would not have been adaptive (Pinel, Assand, & Lehman, 2000). Pinel also indicates that another set point prediction, that having people consume a high-calorie drink before eating should reduce food intake, has not been shown to be effective in reducing food intake at meals (Lowe, 1993). Finally, the ability of learning, taste preference, and social factors to overwhelm set point controls on food intake also argue against the set point theory. Just think of the number of times you found room, when full, for a favourite dessert or for a favourite food (Pinel, Assand, & Lehman, 2000). So, there is a lot more to weight maintenance than set point theory.

"A man seldom thinks with more earnestness of anything than he does of his dinner."
—*Samuel Johnson, writer*

The availability of food is an important additional factor in eating behaviour. Many individuals in societies such as much of North America, where food is plentiful, find their weights steadily creeping up over the years (Philipson, 2001). This can be seen with laboratory rodents, too. Presenting them with a wide array of highly palatable foods will cause more eating and weight gain (**Figure 11-6**) (Hagan et al., 2003). This suggests that a firm body weight set point doesn't exist in experimental animals or humans. When presented with highly palatable food and a diminishing level of activity, most people have a tendency to put on weight as they age.

Hunger and Eating Disorders

WHEN THINGS GO WRONG

We have seen that our motivation to eat is very complex, affected not only by intricate biological processes, but also by psychological, social, and cultural influences. As with any complex system, we face the potential for problems in our eating behaviour. Two of the most common problems include obesity, often related to too much eating, and eating disorders, which often involve eating too little.

obesity overweight characterized as a body mass index of over 30.

body mass index (BMI) weight-to-height ratio.

Obesity Obesity, a condition of extreme overweight, is determined on the basis of a weight-to-height ratio, called the body mass index (BMI). Adults with a BMI of 30 or higher are considered obese, and those with BMIs between 25 and 30 are categorized as *overweight* (Health Canada, 2003). Obesity is a major health problem in North America.

Twenty-three percent of the adult Canadian population is obese (Health Canada, 2006). Being overweight or obese is associated with a variety of health problems, most notably diabetes and heart disease (Poirier et al., 2006; Huang, 2005). In addition to the physical risks they face, obese people are also more likely than those of normal weight to suffer from mood disorders, such as depression and anxiety. As the box on page 425 describes, obese people are also often the victims of discrimination.

Some people become obese as a result of medical conditions. Researchers estimate, however, that medical conditions cause only about 1 to 5 percent of all cases of obesity and seem to be the result of a biological abnormality unrelated to overeating (Harvey et al., 2005). In the vast majority of people, obesity is caused by overeating.

Why is overeating so common? One answer to this question may be found by considering the evolutionary perspective. Early people evolved under conditions of unpredictable food availability. At times when food was plentiful, after a successful hunt or during a time when weather conditions led to an abundance of edible plants, it was surely advantageous to overeat in preparation for subsequent food deprivation. Overeating led to fat storage that increased the chances of survival throughout periods when food was scarce. In many of today's developed cultures, especially in North America, where inexpensive high-calorie food is readily available, this built-in adaptive mechanism is being activated in a chronic and maladaptive way. Intermittent overeating followed by periods of fasting has been replaced by chronic, continuous overeating.

The problem of overeating has intensified over the past few decades, as the food and restaurant industries have increased the size of portions and prepared foods have become a mainstay of the North American diet. Consider the fact that in 1955, when McDonald's restaurants opened, a regular size adult's soft drink was 199 ml (7 ounces). In the new millennium, a child-sized serving of soft drink is 355 ml, and adults can choose from 473-, 621- or 946-ml beverages (Young & Nestle, 2007). Burger King offers a Triple Whopper® sandwich that is 1,160 calories, more than half the recommended daily calorie allotment for an average adult male (Burger King, 2009; Department of Health and Human Services & Department of Agriculture, 2005).

Consumer behaviour research strongly suggests that North Americans appreciate large-size portions because they appear to be a good value (Ledikwe, Ello-Martin, & Rolls, 2005). However, it's very difficult to regulate the amount of food you ingest when the portions are so much larger than those recommended for maintaining a healthy weight. The

Bigger portions, bigger waists. The size and calorie count of meals and drinks at fast food restaurants have increased dramatically over the past several decades.

massive oversizing of portions so common today has, for many of us, led to an increase in energy intake, as measured in calories, without a corresponding change in energy expenditure. As a result, people gain weight.

Once people become accustomed to ingesting very large amounts of food, scaling back to sensible-sized portions can feel like deprivation. Many nutritionists often suggest that dieters eat their food from smaller plates to avoid feeling that the reduced portions are meager. This trick alone is typically not sufficient to support a substantial weight loss, however.

You can calculate your body mass index using Health Canada's online calculator: www.hc-sc.gc.ca/fn-an/nutrition/weights-poids/guide-ld-adult/bmi_chart_java-graph_imc_java-eng.php

In fact, billions of dollars are spent every year on dieting programs and products that are designed to help overweight individuals lose weight and keep it off (Cleland et al., 1997). However, diet programs are often unsuccessful for long-term weight change. For this reason, many experts suggest that the best way to combat obesity is to prevent its occurrence in the first place (Bendelius, 2004; Mogan, 1984). Some approaches to obesity prevention may be suggested by identifying the risk factors for developing obesity. Why are some people more prone to obesity than others? The answer seems to involve multiple factors.

One substantial contributor to obesity is genes. Adoption and twin studies have shown that a good deal of the variation in obesity can be attributed to genetics. Adopted individuals studied tend to have the body mass indexes that more closely resemble the BMIs of their biological parents than those of their adoptive parents (Sørensen et al., 1992; Moll, Burns, & Lauer, 1991). Moreover, identical twins separated at birth are as similar in body weight as those that were raised together (Price & Gottesman, 1991). This strongly suggests that genetics play a major role in determining obesity. Scientists do not completely understand exactly how our genes might predispose us to become obese. Some possibilities include inheriting a larger than normal number of fat cells, a lower metabolic rate (the speed at which we break down and burn the calories in food), or, as we saw earlier in the chapter, an abnormal leptin gene (Bjornhelm et al., 2007; Farooqi et al., 2007).

Genes or environment? Research clearly suggests that obesity is related to genes, but there is also evidence that the eating habits of parents and other family members can play a major role in the development of this problem.

Genetics alone cannot explain the rise in obesity over the past few decades in this country, however. Genes may predispose people to become overweight, but the environment must be conducive to overeating in order for them to realize this potential. As we have seen, social and cultural factors contribute to our eating behaviour. The social aspect of overeating is evident in recent findings that humans are much more likely to gain weight if they have an overweight friend, even if that person lives far away and the number of shared meals is minimal (Christakis & Fowler, 2007). One explanation for this correlation is that having overweight friends produces less resistance to gaining weight, perhaps because weight gain becomes associated with the positive stimulus of friendship. Obesity (especially among women) is also much more common among members of lower socio-economic groups than in higher socio-economic groups (McLaren, 2007). Researchers have suggested that this may be the result of less education about nutrition, fewer healthy food choices (the cost and availability of healthy food), and less social pressure to be thin (Monteiro et al., 2004).

Although obesity can significantly reduce the quality of life, people can be overweight for decades before the negative health effects become evident. Eating disorders on the other end of the spectrum, those that involve eating too little, can lead rather abruptly to emergency situations, and even death.

anorexia nervosa eating disorder in which individuals undereat and have a distorted body image of being overweight.

Anorexia Nervosa and Bulimia Nervosa Anorexia nervosa is a condition in which individuals are preoccupied with the notion that they are fat or will become fat, and have a distorted image of being overweight (when they are not). To combat these thoughts, people with anorexia engage in extreme dieting, often eating fewer than 500 calories per day (Sadock & Sadock, 2008). The restricted eating associated with anorexia generally leads to extreme weight loss, which can be very dangerous. People who lose too much weight are at greater risk for illnesses and imbalances in their blood chemistry. In as many as 10 percent of cases, anorexic weight loss leads to death (Steinhausen, 2002).

It's important to realize that there are major differences between people who diet, even those who do so continuously, and those with anorexia. People with anorexia have a distorted body image. Even when they are dangerously thin, they still think of themselves as fat and often cannot be convinced to increase their calorie intake. They may use laxatives or exercise to burn off the small number of calories they take in. If they are female (as most—90 percent—are) their periods stop or do not start with maturity due to the lack of nutrition.

The Social Stigma Against Obesity

Fighting a social stigma. Participants protest at a rally against size discrimination, seeking to speak out against the taunting and discrimination that plagues many obese people.

Obesity is acceptable and even considered to be desirable in some cultures. For example, in the African nation of Mauritania, parents have been known to force feed their daughters with high-calorie food to make them gain weight so that they will be more attractive to prospective suitors. While this practice may be on its way out, given that nation's recent recognition that obesity is unhealthy, Mauritanians certainly hold a different standard of beauty from the ideals prevalent in North America.

In North America, the media often dictate a certain standard of beauty, particularly for women. Young, slender women are considered desirable. The thin standard of beauty is becoming more and more extreme. Top female models and beauty pageant queens weigh 23 percent less than the average woman, compared to 8 percent less twenty-five years ago (Sheppird, 2009). Ironically, as the ideal weight is dropping, the weight of people in the general population is going up (CDC, 2009).

A study found that people describe obese individuals as less attractive than thinner people, and ascribe a number of other unfavourable characteristics to people who are obese (Puhl et al., 2008). Although overweight people are often considered to be "friendly" and "happy," they are also judged more often as "lazy," "stupid," and "incompetent" than are people of normal weight (Puhl et al., 2008; Friedman et al., 2005). Obese individuals are more often turned down for jobs (NAAFA, 2009). This discrimination can even affect normal-weight individuals associated with obese people. One study looked at the hiring rate of normal-weight job applicants who happened to be sitting next to an obese person just before their interview (Hebl & Mannix, 2003). They were less likely to be hired! Perhaps unsurprisingly, obese people are also more likely than normal-weight people to suffer from depression and anxiety (Friedlander et al., 2003).

In recent years, several organizations have attempted to combat this prejudice by supporting the obese and lobbying the government to pass laws against obesity discrimination. There are no national antiweight discrimination laws yet within Canada. Our Supreme Court did rule that airlines could not charge passengers who are functionally disabled by obesity extra for their flights, even if they require two seats (Air Canada v. Canadian Transportation Agency, 2008). It will be interesting to see what, if any, new laws are proposed in this area, or if discrimination based on weight will be added to Canadian employment discrimination laws.

Anorexia can begin as early as puberty (Hudson et al., 2007). Statistics suggest that about 1 in 300 young women in Canada has anorexia (Government of Canada, 2006; Hoek, 2007). It is much more common in females than males, although recent years have seen an increase in the number of males diagnosed with the condition (Hudson et al., 2007).

The causes of anorexia are complex, but it is most common in cultures where food is prevalent and social pressure exists for people to be thin (Makino, Tsuboi, & Dennerstein, 2004). Similarly, many theorists have noted, with alarm, that today's media and fashion industry glamorize dangerously thin models. Anorexia often coexists with other anxiety disorders, such as obsessive-compulsive disorder (Health Canada, 2002), which we discussed in Chapter 9, suggesting that anorexia is just one of several possible outlets for a more general psychological disturbance.

Treatment of anorexia may involve hospitalization if extreme weight loss occurs. Patients receive nutritional counselling to help restore a healthy weight. In addition, cognitive-behavioural therapy is used, which attempts to help patients develop a healthier body image (Berkman et al., 2006). Adolescents with anorexia may also benefit from family therapy (Keel & Haedt, 2008).

bulimia nervosa eating disorder in which individuals binge and then engage in purging-type behaviour.

Bulimia nervosa is a disorder in which individuals consume excessive calories and then go to extremes to prevent those calories from contributing to weight gain. People with bulimia typically rid themselves of excess food by inducing vomiting or diarrhea or by engaging in intensive exercise (Sigel, 2008). This cycle of bingeing followed by purging defines bulimia. Although people with anorexia often engage in bulimic behaviour to prevent weight gain, most people with bulimia do not appear to be underweight. Some are even overweight (Probst et al., 2004). Like anorexia, bulimia is more common among females than males. Studies suggest that about 1 out of 100 young women in Canada have bulimia (Government of Canada, 2006; Hoek, 2007).

The causes of bulimia are difficult to pinpoint. Like anorexia, bulimia is associated with other psychological disturbances, including OCD (Godart et al., 2007; Kaye et al., 2004). A significant number of people with bulimia also engage in other damaging behaviours, such as cutting themselves (Favaro et al., 2008).

Dangerous trend. After the death of Brazilian model Ana Carolina Reston in 2006, the fashion industry has been criticized for using increasingly thin models, like this one. Reston was only 21 and weighed just 88 pounds when she died of complications from anorexia nervosa.

Unlike anorexia, bulimia is somewhat less likely to be fatal (Health Canada, 2002). However, it can produce unwanted medical and dental problems, such as constipation from overuse of laxatives and tooth decay from excessive vomiting (Cremonini et al., 2009; Aranha, de Paula Eduardo, & Cordás, 2008). The psychological effects of bulimic behaviour can be even more damaging than the physical ones. Because people with bulimia are generally ashamed of their binge–purge behaviours, they generally carry out these behaviours privately and make attempts to hide the evidence and keep their condition a secret. This secrecy, as well as the syndrome itself, often contribute to anxiety and depression (Pettersen, Rosevinge, & Ytterhus, 2008; Hayaki, Friedman, & Brownell, 2002).

Treatment of bulimia requires that patients admit that the problem exists and talk openly about it. Effective treatments for bulimia include behavioural modification, in which healthier eating behaviours are rewarded, and cognitive therapy, which attempts to help people with bulimia develop healthier views of themselves and their eating patterns (Wilson & Shafran, 2005; Bailer et al., 2004). Antidepressant drug treatments have also been found to be effective, particularly when combined with behavioural or cognitive therapy (Romano et al., 2002).

Young people with concerns about eating disorders (involving themselves or a friend or relative) can get help in several ways. First, if you or your friend or relative is a student at a college or university, the student counselling or health or wellness centre on campus will be able to arrange contact with a counsellor or therapist, or arrange for a referral to a local counselling or resource centre. A general practitioner (family doctor) will also be able to arrange a referral to someone who can talk about eating disorders and offer services. Finally, you can find out about local eating disorder resources through the Canadian National Eating Disorder Information

Centre (www.nedic.ca). Even if you are just concerned about someone in your life who you think might be struggling with an eating disorder, it is worth seeking some support and some ideas about how you can be supportive.

Before You Go On www.wiley.com/go/comer

What Do You Know?

6. Describe three main categories of biological hunger signals.
7. What non-biological factors affect our eating behaviour?
8. What is obesity and what factors can contribute to it?
9. What are the characteristics of anorexia nervosa and bulimia nervosa?

SCAN TO GET THE ANSWERS

What Do You Think?

As a public-health effort to combat obesity, several U.S. states and locations have begun to require restaurants to provide calorie and other nutritional information about food on their menus. What are some potential advantages and disadvantages of providing this information to diners?

Biological Motivations: Sex

LEARNING OBJECTIVE 3

Describe factors that affect our sexual motivation and behaviour.

Another basic motivation is sex. From an evolutionary perspective, engaging in sexual behaviour is highly adaptive; the continuation of the species depends on it. However, most sexual behaviour does not occur with the goal of procreating in mind. Actually, the opposite seems to be true. Humans often engage in sexual behaviour while taking steps to avoid conception. Humans, as well as other animals, seek out and engage in sexual behaviour because it is a primary drive—it's pleasurable and rewarding.

Sex: Psychological and Social Factors

Although there is a basic biological instinct to engage in sexual activity, sexual motivation is strongly governed by social cues. In some species of animals, only select members of the social group reproduce. Among honeybees, for example, only the queen bee of each hive reproduces, while the other bees work to maintain the living environment (Wenseleers et al., 2004). In other groups, such as marmoset monkeys, dominant females in a social group procreate, and the other females help to raise the dominant's babies. Subordinate females must wait until a change occurs in the social order (perhaps the dominant will get old and sick and lose her rank) before they can reproduce (Barrett, Abbott, & George, 1993).

Among humans, cultural factors play an important role in determining our choice and number of sexual partners, our range of sexual practices, and the age at which sexual activity typically begins. For instance, some societies, such as certain Nigerian tribes, practise polygamy, an arrangement in which men have multiple wives. Other societies, such as the Naxi of China, practise polyandry, an arrangement in which women have multiple male sexual partners (Yan, 1986).

Societies also vary in the sexual practices that are considered taboo or unacceptable. For example, in Canada, young people have a range of protections that are in force up to their eighteenth birthday. It is not possible for a 14- or 15- year-old to have consensual sex with anyone who is more than five years older. The age moves up to 18 years of age if exploitation (prostitution, pornography, etc.) is involved. In contrast, in some Middle Eastern countries, the earliest age of marriage (and its consummation) is 9 years old (Admon, 2009; Norman-Eady, Reinhart, & Martino, 2003).

Of national concern. Winston Blackmore shares a laugh with six of his daughters and some of his grandchildren. Blackmore is the religious leader of the controversial polygamous community of Bountiful, located near Creston, B.C.

Some sexual taboos seem to be almost universal, however, suggesting that they may be rooted in human evolution. One example of this is the incest taboo. In most cultures, incest, or having sex with close relatives, is forbidden (with rare exceptions, such as ancient Egypt, when it was deemed necessary to preserve a royal bloodline). It's illegal for siblings to marry in most countries throughout the world. In one case in Germany, for example, a biological brother and sister who were brought up separately, then met and fell in love as young adults were sentenced to prison after marrying (Connolly, 2007).

Why is sex between siblings so universally forbidden? From an evolutionary viewpoint, there are at least two possible reasons. First, procreation between closely related individuals increases the likelihood of passing on defective genes, particularly recessive ones. Early societies that forbade incest may have been genetically stronger than those that did not. Second, incest taboos put pressure on societies to interact with neighbouring cultures. Historically, this meant that tribal elders would bargain about marrying their children to one another. In the process, the two tribes might increase general commerce and enhance the access to food and other forms of wealth for both groups (Leavitt, 1989; Johnson & Earle, 1987). According to these views, avoiding sex with close relatives enhances the chances for survival of a group of people. Cultural regulation of our biological drive toward sexual behaviour may also have emerged because it serves the purpose of promoting our survival as a group.

Although norms vary from culture to culture, as we have seen, all cultures do approve certain sexual practices while condemning others. Within nations, many religious, ethnic, and other subcultural groups also influence the sexual behaviour of their members. In many societies, sex is not acceptable unless the couple's relationship is considered legitimate, in many cases until marriage (Cavendish, 2010). In North America, the sexual revolution of the 1960s and 1970s loosened many social restrictions on premarital sex. Today, over 95 percent of people in the United States have sex before marriage (Finer, 2007) and about 14 percent of Canadian couples living together are unmarried (Canadian Council on Social Development, 2001). The number of young adults with multiple sexual partners has also increased. By the time most individuals reach their early 20s, they have had three to four sexual partners (Mosher, Chandra, & Jones 2005). Some sexual behaviours, such as homosexual relationships, are becoming more widely accepted. Canada has a national law allowing for marriage among same-sex couples, and increasingly strong enforcement of laws against discrimination based on sexual orientation (Larocque, 2006).

Sex: What Happens in the Body and Brain

Changes in societal views of sex grew, in part, from psychology research on sexual behaviour. One of the most influential sex researchers was biologist Alfred Kinsey. Early in his career, as a junior faculty member, Kinsey was assigned to teach a course in basic sex practices along with a team of all male instructors (Moore, Davidson, & Fisher, 2010). Realizing that many of his college students were uneducated about basic sexual practices, Kinsey switched his field of study from insect behaviour to human sexual behaviour in the 1940s (Bullough, 2004). He then undertook a massive project, interviewing thousands of people to collect data on the sexual practices of ordinary Americans. Kinsey's work was widely publicized and led to the realization that many "normal" Americans engaged

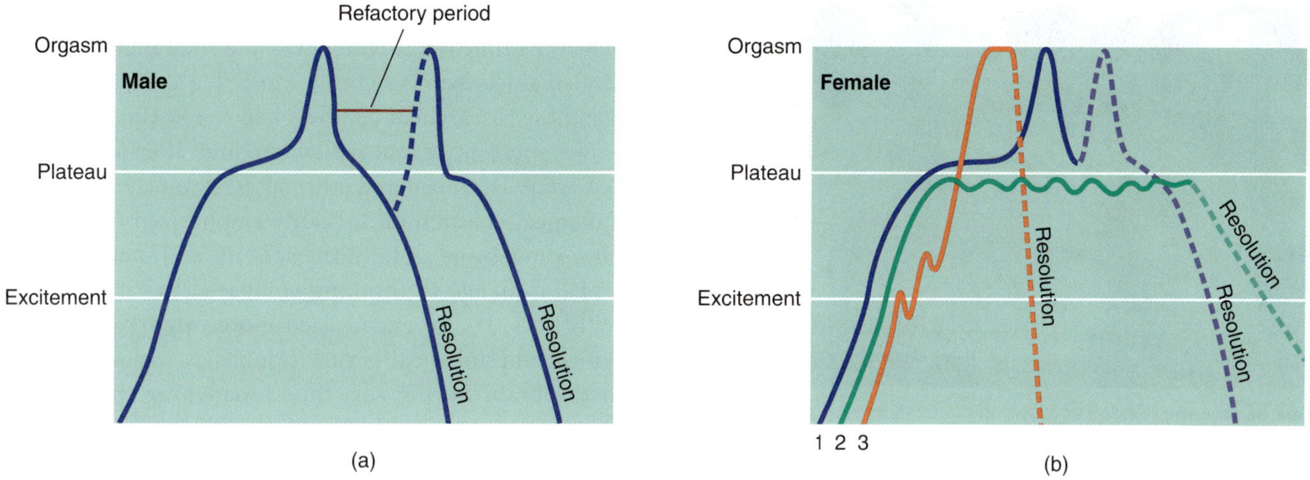

FIGURE 11-7 Human sexual responses. Masters and Johnson identified four phases in sexual response. Part (a) illustrates the typical pattern in males. Women experience greater variability in their sexual response. Part (b) shows three female patterns.

in sexual behaviour that was not considered to be conventional at the time, including oral sex, anal sex, and having multiple partners (Brown & Fee, 2003). Kinsey's work helped to lessen taboos about discussing these sexual practices, because people realized they were not uncommon.

Sex: What Happens in the Body During the 1950s and 1960s, researchers William Masters and Virginia Johnson brought the study of sexual behaviour into the laboratory. Masters and Johnson recorded some of the first physiological data in humans during sex. They studied the sexual responses of both men and women and described four general, and somewhat modestly described, phases of the human sexual response, as shown in **Figure 11-7** (Masters & Johnson, 1966).

- *Excitement* This is the beginning of arousal and it can last up to several hours. Heart rate quickens, though not constantly over a long period of time.
- *Plateau* At this phase, breathing and pulse rates increase. Muscles tense and a flush may appear across the chest.
- *Orgasm* Muscle tension and blood pressure reach a peak. This is quickly followed by climax, which is a series of muscle contractions (the intensity varies, particularly among women).
- *Resolution* Muscles relax and heart rate returns to normal. While men have a refractory period after an orgasm, during which they cannot ejaculate, women may have additional orgasms.

In the 1970s, sex therapist Helen Kaplan incorporated an additional element to the beginning of the sexual response cycle. Kaplan believed that *desire*—basically, whether or not you're "in the mood"—was a necessary condition to motivate an individual to become excited (Kaplan, 1977). The research of Masters and Johnson and those that followed, such as Kaplan, was particularly influential to North American society, because it encouraged women to enjoy sex, which was previously considered to be inappropriate (Weiss, 2000). Masters and Johnson's research also dispelled myths about aging and sexual behaviour. Prior to their research, the conventional view was that sexual behaviour was the realm of young to middle-aged adults, and that after a certain age, sexual behaviour was minimal, if not physically impossible. As a result of Masters and Johnson's research, as well as others that followed, the current view is that sexual behaviour can continue throughout old age, providing a person remains physically healthy and has a willing partner (Waite et al., 2009; DeLamater & Karraker, 2009).

Sex at any age. Sexual activity can continue into old age as long as partners are willing.

Although the work of the early sex researchers was highly controversial at the time it was conducted and their methods have been questioned since then (Cochran, Mosteller, & Tukey, 1953), the publicity these researchers received had the lasting effects of increasing awareness of sexual behaviour and altering societal standards of what is considered normal (Gagnon, 1975). This early psychological research on sexuality emphasized that sexual behaviour is a wholesome and healthy activity, and that idea represented a major change in thinking compared to earlier, more restrictive attitudes. It also encouraged more extensive research into our typical physiological sexual responses, including what happens in the brain during sex, thus broadening the field of acceptable research.

Sex WHAT HAPPENS IN THE BRAIN? Reproductive hormones are clearly important factors in modulating sexual behaviour (Raskin et al., 2009; Kudwa et al., 2006; Berman, 2005). In males, the testes and adrenal glands produce male sex hormones collectively referred to as *androgens*. In females, the ovaries produce the female sex hormones (*estrogen* and *progesterone*). Even though androgens are referred to as male sex hormones, they are produced by the adrenal glands of females too. Like all other hormones, these molecules are released in the blood stream and travel throughout the body. In men, blood levels of androgens, particularly testosterone, are linked positively to sex drive (Bancroft, 2005; Simon et al., 2005). On average, sex drive in males declines with advancing age as testosterone levels drop, although as we have seen, aging does not preclude sexual interest and activity (Feldman et al., 2002). In women, the story appears to be a bit more complicated—estrogen levels are important for the physiological aspects of the sexual response (Frank et al., 2008) as well as in determining feelings about one's attractiveness (Durante et al., 2009). However, sex drive also appears to be simulated, at least in part, by androgens in women.

In order for testosterone to enhance motivation for sex, it needs to act upon the brain. Sex hormones are all small molecules that readily cross the blood–brain barrier to act on many regions of the brain. One subregion of the hypothalamus, the medial preoptic area, is especially responsive to testosterone. This area is rich in sex hormone receptors and is important for sexual behaviour (Dugger et al., 2007). Again, as with hunger, motivating

THINGS STUDENTS WANT TO KNOW

How does Viagra work?

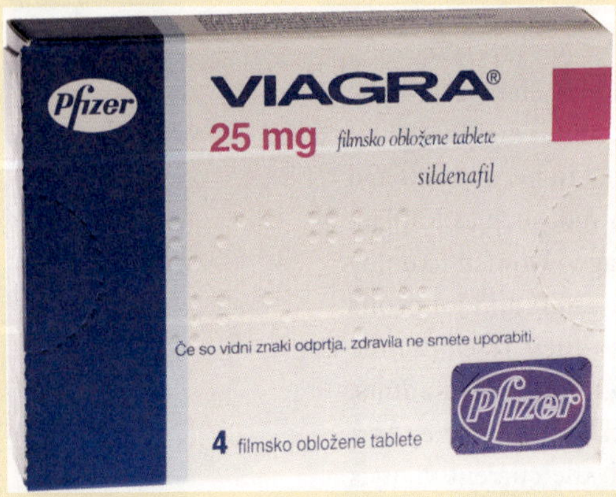

Viagra is one of a group of medications called phosphodiesterase type 5 or PDE-5 inhibitors. Basically, during sexual stimulation in males, the muscles that inhibit blood flow into the penis relax. This allows more blood to flow into the tissues of the penis, causing them to become engorged and the penis to become erect. PDE-5 inhibitors block the actions of those chemicals that counter the relaxation process, allowing for longer, firmer erections. Viagra does not actually cause erections, as sexual arousal is still required. What this also means is that taking Viagra will not cause an erection in day-to-day situations (unless day-to-day situations already turn you on). It also means that Viagra does not increase sexual desire...it only increases the results of sexual arousal (Drewes, George, & Khan, 2003).

people to have sex is not as simple as activating a single brain region. For humans, as well as for less complex animals, many brain regions are involved in sexual arousal and behaviour (Toates, 2009) and different regions are activated during different phases of the sexual response. Most research has focused on the excitement phase. Neuroimaging studies of people while they are viewing erotic films show that the hypothalamus, amygdala, prefrontal cortex, striatum, and ventral tegmental area are all activated (Miyagawa et al., 2007; Karama et al., 2002). These latter three regions are important components of the brain's reward system. The brain's reward system is also activated when we look at photos of our romantic partner's faces, suggesting that this area is importantly involved in responding to rewarding stimuli that are not necessarily erotic (Fisher et al., 2005). During the orgasm phase, one study in males found that in addition to the ventral tegmental area, the cerebellum is activated (Holstege et al., 2003). While the involvement of the cerebellum in this phase of sexual activity remains a mystery, there may be links to the role of this brain region in emotional processing.

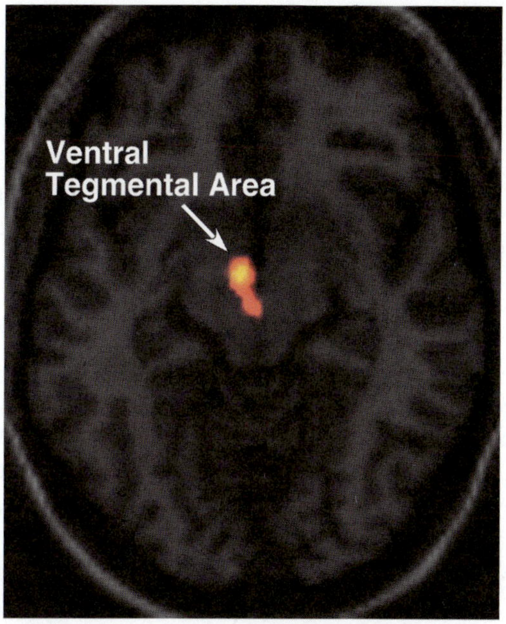

The brain, sexual arousal, and rewards. Gazing at a photo of one's romantic partner activates the ventral tegmental area (VTA), (shown in yellow on this fMRI image). The VTA is activated during early-stage, intense romantic love, as well as when looking at photos of loved ones for which there is no sexual interest, showing that this brain area is associated with learning about rewarding stimuli in general.

Neuroimaging studies show that we can get aroused just by watching sexual behaviour. When people view videos of sex acts, or merely imagine them, parts of their brains associated with the *mirror neuron system*, such as the parietal and frontal lobes, are activated (Mouras et al., 2008; Shmuelof & Zohary, 2007; Gallese et al., 1996). As described in Chapter 9, the mirror neuron system is made up of areas of the brain that, when we watch another person engage in a specific activity, are activated in the same way as when we actually do the same activity ourselves (Rizzolatti & Craighero, 2004). Thus, watching other people engage in sexual behaviour activates some of the same regions of the viewer's brain that would be active if the viewer were actually having sex. This activation makes viewers feel sexually aroused simply from watching.

Even if we do not consciously see an erotic picture or film, we can become aroused. In one study, researchers presented a series of photos to participants. Some of the photos were sexual, and these were rapidly shown and removed before the viewer was consciously aware. Even though viewers did not remember seeing anything, neuroimaging showed activation of regions of the brain associated with arousal and reward (Childress et al., 2008). Sexual behaviour is essential for survival of the species, and the rapid activation of brain regions by subtle sexual cues ensures that we are motivated to have sex.

Sex HOW WE DIFFER

Gender Identity Before we consider individual differences in sexuality, we need to address the most basic of differences in this domain: whether or not we are male or female. Early in prenatal life, it's impossible to tell whether the fetus is a boy or girl (unless a chromosomal analysis is done). After a certain developmental stage, if the fetus is genetically male (its sex chromosomes are XY), it will develop testes. In the absence of testes, the fetus will develop ovaries. In other words, development of a female fetus is a default program that happens if the signals to masculinize are not present (Bull, 1983).

The testes release *testosterone*, which travels throughout the body. In certain organs, this hormone is converted to one of two other hormones, *dihydrotestosterone* (*DHT*), or surprisingly, to estrogen. DHT is important for masculinizing the external genitalia—this is the hormone that causes a male fetus to grow a penis. Testosterone can be converted to estrogen in the central nervous system, and some evidence suggests that estrogen, along with testosterone, then *masculinizes* the brain: they set up brain functioning that is, on average, characteristic of male brains. Since estrogen is considered to be a female reproductive hormone, its involvement in *masculinization* seems contradictory, leading scientists to recognize that the traditional view of estrogen as the female sex hormone and testosterone as the male sex hormone was probably an oversimplification (Breedlove & Hampson, 2002). Estrogen's role in masculinization also raises the question of why the female fetus, which produces estrogen directly from its ovaries, doesn't end up with a masculinized brain. The answer to this question is that female fetuses are protected against their own estrogen and the estrogen produced by the mother, because they make a protein that binds to estrogen and prevents it from masculinizing the brain (Puts, Jordan, & Breedlove, 2006).

Masculinization of the brain occurs in the hypothalamus, the brain region important for coordinating reproductive hormone release from the pituitary. Masculinization also occurs in brain regions important for non-reproductive behaviours, such as those important for regulating aggression. Exposure to specific hormones during fetal life may also determine whether humans identify with being a male or female. Indeed, girls with a medical condition that exposes them during the fetal stage to masculine levels of hormones may later engage in play behaviour that is more like boys than it is like girls (Hines & Kaufman, 1994).

In some cases, babies arrive with ambiguous genitalia, and the issue of gender identity isn't readily resolved. Sometimes an XX baby, because of the hormones it was exposed to in utero, will be born with an enlarged clitoris that resembles a penis. Other times, an XY baby will arrive with a smaller than normal penis. People with ambiguous genitalia are now referred to as intersex (Roughgarden, 2004). This term has largely replaced the old name hermaphrodite. After determining the genetic sex of the baby, physicians and parents need to make decisions about how to proceed.

In the past, psychologists and healthcare providers believed that gender identity is determined mostly by the environment (Leaper, 2000). In other words, if a child is treated like a boy (or girl), then he/she will grow up to identify with that gender. As a result, several individuals with ambiguous genitalia received treatment to make their external genitalia appear to be more "normal." For example, boys without fully developed penises underwent surgery and were raised as girls. In some cases, this treatment backfired and the surgically created "girls" grew up very unhappy with their gender assignment and eventually underwent treatment to live the remainder of their lives as males (Reiner & Gearheart, 2004). What is very clear at this point is that the influences that determine gender outcomes are a very complex mix of genetics, hormones, and social influences. Physicians are not as clear as they once were that physical appearances should always be followed when deciding a child's sex in cases of uncertainty (Zucker, 2002).

Different needs and preferences. Given gender differences regarding sexual needs, attraction, arousal, and fantasies, a couple's thoughts may be in different places at moments like this.

Gender Differences in Sexuality Although each person has unique preferences, beliefs, and behaviours, there do seem to be some differences between men and women when it comes to what they want in sex. Men and women differ in characteristics they perceive as attractive in a mate and in the stimuli that arouse them. Their fantasies and desired numbers of partners may also differ.

Evolutionary psychologists suggest that much of how heterosexual men and women interact with the opposite sex is the result of thousands of years of evolution designed to maximize our chances of survival and reproductive success. Men desire youthful, attractive mates because those attributes signal good odds for reproductive success; women are attracted to men who are dependable and strong because they will most likely be able to protect and care for children (Miller, 2000).

In addition to what makes someone attractive, men and women also differ in what arouses them. Men, on average, are aroused more quickly than women by visual stimuli (Stoléru et al., 1999). Women, on the other hand, respond more strongly than men do to physical contact and verbal expression. This may be because arousal in women is more often influenced by their relationship with a partner, as well as their own self-image, than it is in men (Peplau, 2003).

Even women's sexual fantasies are more commitment-oriented (Ellis & Symons, 1990) and they tend to have fewer fantasies than men (Byers, Purdon, & Clark, 1998). In one study, surveyors asked college students, "Have you had sex with over a thousand different partners in your imagination?" Males in the study were four times more likely than females to say yes (Ellis & Symons, 1990). The frequency of men's arousal and the number of their fantasies have led many psychologists to conclude that men generally have a higher sex drive. In fact, men tend to rate their own sex drives as higher than women rate theirs (Baumeister, Catanese, & Vohs, 2001).

It's important to realize that reported gender differences in sexual desire and sexual activity may reflect biases in reporting. On surveys and during interviews, women may downplay their sexual desires and behaviours because of perceived social constraints. Conversely, males may be more likely to exaggerate such feelings and behaviours to fulfill imagined expectations for men. There is no question that women and men are judged differently by society when it comes to sex. In movies, for example, women with high sex drives are often portrayed as dangerous or emotionally unstable, while men with low sex drives are often the subject of ridicule. These perceptions may influence the way that people respond to questions about their sex lives. In reality, though, women and men may be more alike than researchers once thought. Recent studies of university undergraduates have not found significant differences between women and men in their desired number of partners (Miller et al., 2002; Fenigstein & Preston, 2007).

Sexual Orientation Most people are **heterosexual**; they are sexually attracted to members of the opposite sex. The proportions of the population that identify as **homosexual** (gay or lesbian)—people who are sexually attracted to members of their own sex—vary depending on how the questions are asked. Estimates of the number of people who identify as homosexual vary. One large study (Laumann, 1994) suggested that about 2.8 percent of males and 1.4 percent of females primarily identify as homosexual. A more carefully designed study was conducted by Chris Bagley at the University of Calgary. Bagley argued that how you ask questions about sexual orientation and how you sample the population affects your results (for example, it is likely that there are higher proportions of gay and lesbian individuals in cities). In his study, Bagley also took extra steps to make it very clear that all data gathered would carefully protect anonymity. Based on the results, Bagley suggested that the rate of homosexuality in urban settings may be as high as 10 to 15 percent (Bagley & Tremblay, 1988). Homosexuality is increasingly being recognized as a part of the diversity of life. The American Psychological Association removed homosexuality from its Diagnostic and Statistical Manual of Mental Disorders in 1973. Why are some people attracted to members of the opposite sex while others are attracted to members of the same sex? Arguments about this topic have been heated and often reflect a nature–nurture debate.

heterosexual sexual attraction to members of the opposite sex.

homosexual sexual attraction to members of one's own sex.

Alfred Kinsey believed that sexual orientation was on a continuum, with many people fitting between the two extremes of exclusively heterosexual and exclusively homosexual (Kinsey, Pomeroy, & Martin, 1948). According to this idea, each person contains a certain proportion of heterosexuality and homosexuality. It follows, then, that if a person living as a homosexual is, in fact, at least part heterosexual, intervention can cause the person to increase the heterosexual-to-homosexual ratio—that is, to emphasize in his or her life heterosexual behaviours and thoughts (Murphy, 1992; Pattison & Pattison, 1980).

Kinsey's theory is controversial, but it does suggest that sexual orientation is changeable. Based on this idea, numerous organizations have devised treatment programs to "convert" homosexuals to heterosexuality—that is, to emphasize heterosexual behaviours and thoughts in his or her life (Murphy, 1992; Pattison & Pattison, 1980). In fact, in the late 1960s, the Masters and Johnson Institute sponsored such a program and reported conversions among the majority of participants (Masters & Johnson, 1979). These findings

Turnim-Man: When "Girls" Become Men

One way that human sexuality differs between people is the extent to which their sexuality is thought to be fixed from birth. Some individuals carry a genetic mutation that leads to a lack of the enzyme necessary for conversion of testosterone to DHT. Genetically male individuals with *5-alpha reductase deficiency* are born with feminized external genitalia. They are often raised as girls, but once puberty sets in and secondary sex characteristics develop, it becomes evident that they are not becoming women. Voices deepen, facial hair develops, and the external genitalia enlarge. This genetic condition is relatively rare in open societies, but clusters of 5-alpha reductase deficiency exist in closed communities in which most individuals are related genetically. One such community is located in Papua New Guinea. Perhaps because this condition is more common (Imperato-McGinlay et al., 1991) and also because medical treatments are scarce in this region, the people have developed an acceptance of 5-alpha reductase deficiency individuals. Even if they were raised as girls, they often transition into manhood without significant psychological difficulties. In Papua New Guinea there is even a special name for these people—Turnim-man (one language of Papua New Guines is pidgin English, and it's not difficult to discern what this name means). The relative ease with which the "Turnim-man" accept manhood probably occurs because the brain has already been masculinized by estrogen and the community is accepting of individuals moving from girlhood to manhood. It's not surprising, however, that such transitions are more difficult in western societies, where gender differences are often emphasized and medical intervention to correct whatever is considered to be "abnormal" has been prevalent.

have not been supported, and current research strongly suggests that homosexuality is biologically based and cannot be "cured." If anything, such attempts can be damaging to the individual, since they typically produce feelings of shame and embarrassment (Cramer et al., 2008; Haldeman, 1994).

Additional evidence that homosexuality is a natural, biological phenomenon comes from repeated observations of homosexual behaviour throughout the animal kingdom. Homosexuality has been reported in both male and female birds (including one celebrated case of a homosexual penguin at the Central Park Zoo in New York City), as well as among bonobos, a type of chimpanzee (Roughgarden, 2004; Smith, 2004).

Although the exact influences leading to sexual orientation remain unknown, considerable evidence suggests that sexual orientation has a biological basis. Researchers have studied the intertwined influences of genes, hormones, and anatomical brain differences.

- *Genes* Studies suggest a strong genetic influence on sexual orientation. In other words, homosexuality tends to run in families (Bailey & Pillard, 1991; Buhrich, Bailey, & Martin, 1991). The correlation is greatest among monozygotic, or identical, twins. If one twin is homosexual, the other is also likely to have that orientation. Some evidence suggests this link exists even if the twins are raised apart (Eckert et al., 1986). As with many other traits, however, genetics do not completely determine sexual orientation; even among pairs of identical twins who share the same genes, some pairs differ in orientation (Långström et al., 2008). Researchers have therefore considered other biological factors.
- *Hormones* Some studies suggest that some homosexual males may experience different hormone levels before birth compared to heterosexual males. Studies have shown that having an older brother increases the odds of male homosexuality. With each additional older brother, the likelihood of homosexuality increases (Blanchard, 2004; Blanchard, 2001). In the case of younger brothers with homosexual orientations, some researchers suggest that the mother's immune system may sometimes react to male sex hormones while she is carrying a male fetus, such that in

Gay marriage and the law. The relationship between the law and psychology is not always clear. Research is increasingly showing that homosexuality is a natural human phenomenon. Societal acceptance is increasing, and Canada has taken a positive step by legalizing gay marriages.

subsequent pregnancies, maternal antibodies will lessen the "masculinizing" action of hormones on the brain of the younger brother. Although this hypothesis cannot account for the majority of homosexual individuals, studies examining brain differences support the possibility that prenatal hormone exposure may be an important factor for some individuals (Rahman, 2005; Williams et al., 2000).

- *Brain anatomy* A sex difference exists in the anterior, or front, part of the hypothalamus. This region is twice as large in heterosexual men as it is in women (Orikasa, Kondo, & Sakuma, 2007). A similar size difference exists in this brain region between heterosexual men and homosexual men. The anterior hypothalamuses of homosexual men are, on average, more similar in size to those of women than to those of heterosexual men, suggesting that individual differences in masculinizing factors (most likely hormones) may contribute to changes in brain anatomy that ultimately lead to homosexual or heterosexual behaviour (LeVay, 1991).

Society is gradually becoming less discriminatory and more understanding of homosexuality. In 2006 a Statistic Canada study (2007) found that about 45,000 Canadian couples are in a same-sex relationship, one-fifth of them married. The Canadian population's view of gay marriage is split along age lines, with the majority of younger Canadians supporting it and the majority of Canadians over 60 years of age opposed to it (Angus Reid Strategies, 2009).

> "The State has no place in the bedrooms of the Nation."
> —*Pierre Elliott Trudeau*

Sex WHEN THINGS GO WRONG

Although sexual activity brings great pleasure to most people, it can pose significant problems for some. A number of sexual problems or disorders may occur, such as sexual dysfunctions, paraphilias, gender identity disorder, and medical problems.

Sexual Dysfunctions Sexual dysfunctions are disorders in which people cannot respond normally in key areas of sexual functioning, making it difficult or impossible to enjoy sexual intercourse. As you read earlier, the human sexual response consists of several phases. Sexual dysfunctions typically affect one or more of these phases.

sexual dysfunctions disorders in which people cannot respond normally in key areas of sexual functioning, making it difficult or impossible to enjoy sexual intercourse.

Sexual aversion disorder centres on how much sexual desire a person experiences. People with *sexual aversion disorder* find sex distinctly unpleasant or repulsive. Indeed, sexual overtures may sicken, disgust, or frighten them. Aversion to sex is relatively uncommon, particularly among men (Wincze et al., 2008; Maurice, 2007).

Issues in the bedroom. Sexual issues and incompatibilities can place great strain on relationships.

Two sexual dysfunctions affect the excitement phase of the sexual response cycle: female sexual arousal disorder (once referred to as "frigidity") and male erectile disorder (once called "impotence"). Women with a *female sexual arousal disorder* are persistently unable to attain or maintain proper lubrication or genital swelling during sexual activity (Basson, 2007; Heiman, 2007). Estimates of its prevalence vary, but most studies agree that more than 10 percent of women experience these symptoms (Laumann et al., 2005, 1999, 1994; Bancroft et al., 2003). Men with *male erectile disorder* persistently fail to attain or maintain an adequate erection during sexual activity. This problem occurs in about 10 percent of the male population (Laumann et al., 2005, 1999), most over the age of 50 (Cameron et al., 2005). However, research by William Fisher at the University of Western Ontario and his colleagues (Rosen et al., 2004) shows that half of all adult men experience erectile difficulty during intercourse at least some of the time.

Dysfunctions of the orgasm phase of the sexual response cycle are rapid ejaculation, male orgasmic disorder, and female orgasmic disorder. A man suffering from *rapid* or *premature ejaculation* persistently reaches orgasm and ejaculates with very little sexual stimulation before, on, or shortly after penetration, and before he wishes to. As many as 30 percent of men in North America experience rapid ejaculation at some time (Jannini & Lenai, 2005). Research suggests that men of any age may suffer from rapid ejaculation (Althof, 2007). A man with *male orgasmic disorder* is repeatedly unable to reach orgasm or is very delayed in reaching orgasm after normal sexual excitement. The disorder occurs in 8 percent of men (Hartmann & Waldinger, 2007; Laumann et al., 2005, 1999). Similarly, women with *female orgasmic disorder* rarely reach orgasm or generally experience a very delayed orgasm. Studies indicate that 10 percent or more of women have never had an orgasm, either alone or during intercourse, and at least another 9 percent rarely have orgasms (LoPiccolo, 2004, 1995; Bancroft et al., 2003). In contrast, half of all women experience orgasm in intercourse at least fairly regularly (LoPiccolo & Stock, 1987).

Each of the sexual dysfunctions may be caused by a combination of biological and psychological factors. In the biological realm, for example, abnormal hormone activity can adversely affect sexual functioning and various medications can interfere with sex drive and behaviour. Problematic psychological factors include feelings of depression, anxiety, or anger; inaccurate beliefs about sex; and stressors such as job pressure or relationship problems. Masters and Johnson (1970) found two psychological factors to be particularly common among men with sexual dysfunctions: *performance anxiety* and *spectator role*. They found that once some men experience erectile or orgasmic problems, they start to worry about the possibility of failing to have erections or orgasms during their sexual encounters (performance anxiety). As a result, instead of relaxing during such encounters, they keep observing themselves and their performances. They become judges and spectators rather than sexually aroused participants, and their ability to engage in sexual activity declines.

Today's treatments for sexual dysfunctions can be traced to the publication of Masters and Johnson's landmark book *Human Sexual Inadequacy* in 1970. Their *sex therapy* program has grown into a complex approach that now includes a combination of cognitive-behavioural, couple, and family techniques (Leiblum, 2007; Bach et al., 2001). In recent years, drug therapies have been added to the sex treatment approaches, triggered by the enormous success of drugs such as *sildenafil* (trade name Viagra) in the treatment of male erectile disorder (see earlier discussion of how Viagra works).

paraphilias disorders in which people have repeated and intense sexual urges or fantasies, or display sexual behaviours in response to objects or situations that society considers inappropriate.

Paraphilias **Paraphilias** are disorders in which people have repeated and intense sexual urges or fantasies or display sexual behaviours in response to objects or situations that society considers inappropriate. Some of the most common paraphilias are fetishism, exhibitionism, voyeurism, pedophilia, and sexual sadism. For most paraphilias, men with the disorders greatly outnumber women.

People with *fetishism* display recurrent intense sexual urges or behaviours that involve the use of a non-living object. The object—women's underwear, shoes, and boots are particularly common—may be touched, smelled, worn, or used in some other way while the individual masturbates or has intercourse (Marshall et al., 2008).

A person (almost always male) with *exhibitionism* has recurrent urges to expose his genitals to another person, almost always a member of the opposite sex. He rarely attempts to initiate sexual activity with the person to whom he exposes himself; rather, he wants to produce shock or surprise. Sometimes an exhibitionist will expose himself in a particular neighbourhood at particular hours. In one survey of 2,800 men, 4.3 percent reported that they perform exhibitionistic behaviour (Långström & Seto, 2006).

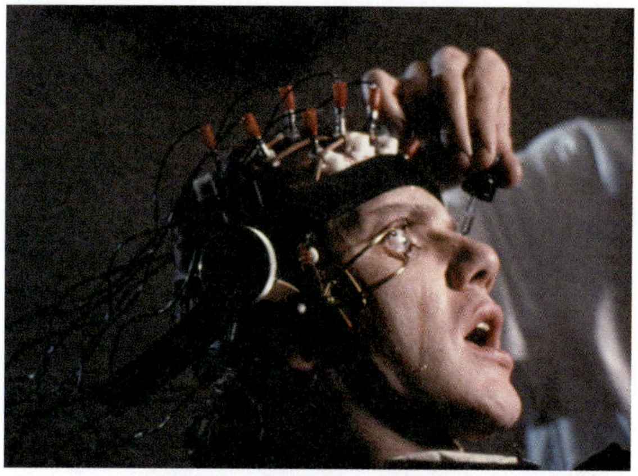

Sexual sadism and the cinema. In a famous scene from the movie *A Clockwork Orange*, Alex, a sexual sadist, is forced to watch violent images while experiencing severe stomach cramps, in the hope that he will develop an aversion to sexually violent acts.

An individual with *voyeurism* has recurrent and intense urges to secretly observe unsuspecting people as they undress or to spy on couples having intercourse. The person may also masturbate during the act of observing or when thinking about it afterward, but does not generally seek to have sex with the observed person.

People with *pedophilia* gain sexual gratification by watching, touching, or engaging in sexual acts with prepubescent children, usually 13 years old or younger. Some individuals with this disorder are aroused by material such as children's underwear ads; others seek out child pornography; and some are driven to actually watch, fondle, or engage in sexual activities with children (Durkin & Hundersmarck, 2008). Both boys and girls can be pedophilia victims, but research suggests that two-thirds of victims are girls (Doctor & Neff, 2001).

Some people with pedophilia also exhibit distorted thinking, such as "It's all right to have sex with children as long as they agree" (Roche & Quayle, 2007). Similarly, it is not uncommon for pedophiles to blame the children for adult–child sexual contacts or to assert that the children benefited from the experience (Durkin & Hundersmarck, 2008).

Most pedophilic offenders are imprisoned or forced into treatment if they are caught (Stone et al., 2000). Clearly, they are committing child sexual abuse when they have sexual contact with a child. Canada created a National Sex Offender Registry to assist law enforcement in tracking the whereabouts of sex offenders, even after their release from prison. Unlike the United States, the information in the registry is not available to the public, although police forces will sometimes warn communities when an offender with a high risk to re-offend is released back to a community.

A person with *sexual sadism* is intensely sexually aroused by the thought or act of inflicting suffering on others by dominating, restraining, blindfolding, cutting, strangling, mutilating, or even killing the victim. Many carry out sadistic acts with a consenting partner; some, however, act out their urges on non-consenting victims (Marshall et al., 2008). A number of rapists and sexual murderers, for example, exhibit sexual sadism. The key to their arousal is the suffering they cause to their victims.

A number of explanations have been proposed for the various paraphilias, but none has received much research support (Abramowitz, 2008). Moreover, none of the current treatments for these disorders has met with clear success (Roche & Quayle, 2007).

Gender Identity Disorder Most people feel like and identify themselves as males or females—an identity that is consistent with the gender to which they are born. But psychologists have come to appreciate that many people do not experience such gender clarity. They have *transgender experiences*—a sense that their actual gender identity is different from the gender category to which they were born physically, or that it lies outside the usual male versus female categories (Carroll, 2007). Many of today's psychologists believe

Nina Arsenault. Artist Nina Arsenault is described as Canada's most famous transgendered person. She had written and lectured extensively (*The Silicone Diaries* and *I Am Barbie*) about her experiences (over 60 surgeries and procedures) in transforming herself from a man to a woman.

that, in many cases, transgender feelings reflect alternative, rather than disordered, ways of experiencing one's gender identity. And, indeed, a number of people with transgender experiences come to terms with their gender inconsistencies, blend gender in some way, and become comfortable with their atypical gender identity. However, others experience extreme unhappiness with their given gender and may seek treatment. These individuals receive a diagnosis of *gender identity disorder*. There is significant concern as to whether this category of behaviour warrants the label disorder (classifying it as a form of mental illness). It has been proposed that it be replaced with the term Gender Dysphoria in the next edition of the Diagnostic and Statistical Manual of Mental Illness (APA, 2010). We will continue to use the currently published term for now, but indicate that a change seems to be on the way. People with gender identity disorder would like to get rid of their primary and secondary sex characteristics—many of them find their own genitals repugnant—and acquire the characteristics of the other sex. Men with the disorder outnumber women by around 2 to 1 (APA, 2000).

Some children experience gender identity disorder (Carroll, 2007; Zucker, 2005). Like adults with this disorder, the children feel uncomfortable about their assigned sex and deeply desire to be members of the opposite sex. Surveys of mothers indicate that about 1 to 2 percent of young boys wish to be a girl, and 3 to 4 percent of young girls wish to be a boy (Carroll, 2007; Zucker & Bradley, 2005). This childhood pattern usually disappears by adolescence or adulthood, but in some cases it develops into adult gender identity disorder (Cohen-Kettenis, 2001).

The causes of gender identity disorder are not understood. In addition, treatment for the disorder has been very controversial. Many adults with this disorder receive *hormone treatments* to change their sexual characteristics (Andreasen & Black, 2006; Hepp et al., 2002; Bradley, 1995). Physicians prescribe *estrogen* for male patients, causing breast development, loss of body and facial hair, and change in body fat distribution. Similarly, women with gender identity disorder are treated with *testosterone*. For other individuals, however, this is not enough, and they pursue one of the most hotly debated practices in medicine: *sex-change* or *sexual reassignment surgery* (Andreasen & Black, 2006; Hepp et al., 2002). For men, the operation itself includes amputation of the penis, creation of an artificial vagina, and face-changing plastic surgery. For women, surgery may include a bilateral mastectomy and hysterectomy. Studies in Europe have suggested that 1 of every 30,000 men and 1 of every 100,000 women may seek sex-change surgery (Carroll, 2007; Bakker et al., 1993). In the United States, more than 6,000 persons may have undergone this surgical procedure (Doctor & Neff, 2001). The numbers in Canada are less clear. Some clinicians consider such surgery to be a humane solution, while others believe that sexual reassignment is an inappropriate approach for a complex disorder (Olsson & Moller, 2003).

Medical Problems: Sexually Transmitted Infections (STIs) Sexual activity is not without risks. People who have sex without contraception face the risk of unintended or unwanted pregnancies. Unprotected sex also leaves participants at risk of contracting sexually transmitted infections (STIs), including HIV, the virus linked to AIDS. Other common STIs include chlamydia, which is the most frequently reported; gonorrhea; genital herpes; and human papillomavirus (HPV—linked to genital warts and higher rates of cervical cancer as well as anal, penile, vaginal, and vulvar cancers). Most individuals with an STI have no symptoms. Using condoms can greatly reduce the chances of contracting most STIs, and women younger than 26 years of age can receive a vaccine to protect against most of the HPV strains that cause cervical cancers. However, abstaining from sex is the only way to entirely prevent infection (CDC, 2008; Markowitz et al., 2007). In 2007, the Canadian federal government committed $300 million to assist provinces in providing the HPV vaccine to girls in late elementary school (Public Health Agency of Canada, 2008). Provinces provided the vaccine to girls in grades 5 to 9 (depending on province or territory). The proportion of girls in the target age range actually vaccinated varied from 53 to 87 percent (Colucci, Hryiuk, & Savage, 2009). Health Canada has recently approved the use of HPV vaccine for boys and recommends it be given between 9 and 26 years of age (Health Canada, 2010).

A signature moment. An important turning point in changing the public's attitudes toward AIDS and its victims came in 1991, when the enormously popular and respected professional basketball player Magic Johnson announced at this press conference that he had been diagnosed HIV positive.

Half of all new cases of HIV are contracted before the age of 25 (CDC, 2001). Because of the public health threats posed by HIV/AIDS, as well as other STIs and teen pregnancies, sex education for secondary school students has become an important priority in Canada (SIECCAN, 2009). Sex education programs generally take one of two major approaches. One, called comprehensive sex education, includes teaching about contraception and safer sex measures, such as condom use, to prevent sexually transmitted infections. The other approach provides less information on the specifics of contraception and disease prevention, focusing instead on promoting abstinence from intercourse, generally until marriage.

Many political and religious organizations support abstinence programs, suggesting that the detailed information provided in comprehensive programs actually encourages sexual activity among teens (Gaul, 2007). Proponents of comprehensive education respond that research evidence does not support the claim that sex education increases sexual activity (Trenholm et al., 2007). In fact, teenagers in either type of program are just as likely to engage in sex (Brückner & Bearman, 2005).

Promoters of comprehensive programs further point out that abstinence education takes a negative, disapproving view of premarital sex. They note that feelings of shame and embarrassment about sexual activity can actually increase the likelihood of *unprotected* sex (Kay & Jackson, 2008; Brückner & Bearman, 2005). Planning ahead for contraception and condom use is more often associated with open attitudes about sexual activity than with feelings of guilt. The first large analysis of the effectiveness of comprehensive sex education found that it reduces teen pregnancy by 50 percent, compared to either abstinence-only education or no sex education at all (Kohler, Manhart & Lafferty, 2008). The American Psychological Association says that well-rounded sex education also reduces the risk of HIV infection, whereas abstinence-only programs may actually increase the risk of getting HIV (APA, 2005).

Before You Go On

www.wiley.com/go/comer

What Do You Know?

10. What aspects of sexual behaviour are affected by our cultural standards?
11. What are the phases of the sexual response cycle described by Masters and Johnson and what happens at each one?
12. What biological factors has research found to be related to sexual orientation?
13. Identify four kinds of sexual problems or disorders and give an example of each.
14. How do comprehensive sex education and abstinence education differ?

SCAN TO GET THE ANSWERS

What Do You Think?

Describe the specific cultural standards for sexual behaviour that affect your peer group.

Psychological Motivations: Affiliation and Achievement

LEARNING OBJECTIVE 4

Describe factors that influence our psychological motivations for affiliation and achievement.

In the previous sections, we talked about biological motivations. Recall Maslow's hierarchy of needs though and you will see that we are also motivated by non-biological needs. The need to belong and the need for self-worth are psychological motivations that are just as important to our health and happiness. These motivations make sense when we consider that humans live in tightly-knit social groups, and as such our connection to our social group and our sense of worth within our group is very important.

Just as it may be difficult to focus on achieving in school if you are hungry, your focus may be affected if the more basic psychological need of *affiliation*, or belonging, is not met.

Affiliation

Affiliation is defined as the need to form attachments to other people for support, guidance, and protection. Going to college or university is, for many students, their first experience away from home for a prolonged period of time. Suddenly, you are on your own, without the support and comfort of your family. Those first few weeks can be quite stressful, until students become acquainted with their new surroundings and meet new people.

affiliation the need to form attachments to other people for support, guidance, and protection.

Being part of a social group, whether it is a family or a group of friends or an organization, helps us define who we are and allows us to feel secure about our place in the world. This need has evolved from the evolutionary advantage that groups had in being able to provide food and protection, compared to individuals living alone (Diener & Seligman, 2002).

From the moment we are born, we seek a connection with others. As we learned previously, instinct theory explains that infants automatically seek out their mother's breast, and this rooting reflex reinforces the infant's chances of survival. As we develop, relationships with friends, and later with significant others, help to raise our self-esteem. Men and women in long-term, healthy relationships have less depression and live longer (Holt-Lunstad, Birmingham, & Jones, 2008). Even elderly spouses who provide more care to each other live longer than those who are less considerate of each other (Kaplan & Kronick, 2006).

Trying to make gang membership less attractive. In an effort to reduce gang recruitments, the Young Warriors Network runs a number of programs aimed at reducing gang recruitment and strengthening community ties within Canada First Nations youth.

Affiliation WHEN THINGS GO WRONG Our motivation to belong may also explain why some individuals remain in abusive relationships and join gangs. The fear of social exclusion is a powerful motivator. In fact, when people feel excluded, the anterior cingulate cortex in the frontal cortex is activated (Eisenberger, Lieberman, & Williams, 2003). Recall that this same area responds to physical pain.

The need to be affiliated with others is routinely exploited as a means of punishment or torture during war and even in prisons. So profound is our motivation to be around others that the effects of long-term isolation are not only disturbing, they often lead to permanent psychological damage. One study of inmates at a prison (Haney, 2008) found that months of isolation can literally cause a person to become catatonic, or competely non-responsive. Another study of over 200 interviews of prisoners who had been confined to solitary cells found that one-third became psychotic, losing contact with reality (Grassian, 1983).

Affiliation with others is an essential psychological need. When we are denied contact with other humans, we are not only unable to satisfy biological needs but we also lose our motivation to pursue our highest level needs: self-worth and self-actualization. We are no longer driven to achieve.

Achievement

The fact that you are reading this book means that you are motivated to go to school, study, and obtain a degree. You may even pursue additional degrees or you may graduate and find a job. No matter what path you take, to satisfy the needs at the top of Maslow's pyramid, self-worth and self-actualization, you need to feel competent, engage with others, and possess control over your own life. **Self-determination** theory suggests that competence, relatedness, and autonomy are instinctive, and that they give purpose and meaning to life (Ryan & Deci, 2002). Not all psychologists agree with this theory, though. As you will see later in this section, other cultures, such as the Chinese, place less importance on autonomy, instead valuing collective effort.

self-determination instinctive feelings of competence, relatedness, and autonomy that give purpose to life.

As you might expect, incentives often play a role in motivating us to achieve. In school, you may be motivated intrinsically by curiosity to learn new information. In other words, the behaviour may be engaging in and of itself. Or you may be motivated extrinsically by incentives. For instance, your reason for studying hard in this course may be because you are hoping to be rewarded with an A at the end of the semester. When achievement is motivated by incentives, it is often associated with competition. People who place too much value on rewards are more likely to suffer when they fail (Sheldon et al., 2004). If they succeed, they may think that the reward, and not their motivation, was the reason for their success. In contrast, psychologists associate intrinsic motivation with the qualities of self-determination theory: competence, relatedness, and autonomy. When you strive to do well for yourself, you enjoy yourself more (Blumenfeld, Kempler, & Krajcik, 2006). See "Your Brain and Behaviour: Motivating Ourselves to Run a Marathon" on the following pages for a display of what happens in the brain when we strive to achieve in the realm of physical exercise.

Achievement HOW WE DEVELOP Social, or non-biological, motivations, especially those that involve incentives, are not present at birth, but are learned. In fact, often, incentive motivations involve inhibiting basic biological drives to obtain the reward. Consider a restaurant server trying to earn money. If the server acted on biological instincts and ate the food off the customer's plate, then it would be difficult to keep the job and earn money.

Delaying gratification is especially important for some of the goals you set as a student. Earning a degree takes a long period of time, during which you often set aside immediate pleasures, such as social activities, in favour of studying. This type of self-control isn't present in very small children, but instead develops over time. The ability to delay gratification requires not just an understanding of the relative worth of the rewards, but also an ability to control impulses. Impulse control also develops over time. While playing, toddlers often get into physical fights over sharing toys, whereas preschool and kindergarten-age children react this way less and less frequently.

Developmental psychologists have tested the ability to delay gratification in the laboratory by offering children of varying ages

Tying It Together: **Your Brain and Behaviour**

Motivating Ourselves to Run a Marathon

A marathon is a 42.16 km (26.2 mile) race that generally requires months of preparation. Many people follow strict regimens to help them prepare. Runners eagerly sign up for marathons all across the world, in all kinds of weather. What might motivate people to run?

When we are motivated to run for personal achievement, the reward learning pathway—the brain regions involved in basic biological reward, such as the ventral tegmental area, the nucleus accumbens, and the prefrontal cortex—is engaged. In addition, areas that are important for storing the memories of our past running experiences, such as the hippocampus and neocortex, are likely to be involved. The prefrontal cortex is also important for enabling us to attend to our goals and respond flexibly to changes in the terrain as we run. Will we beat our personal best?

Questions

1 **Which region of the brain is most strongly activated by attending to goals and responding to changes in the environment?**

2 **What does it mean to say that exercise has beneficial effects on the brain as well as on other parts of the body?**

3 **In which region of the brain is increased blood flow after aerobic exercise particularly evident?**

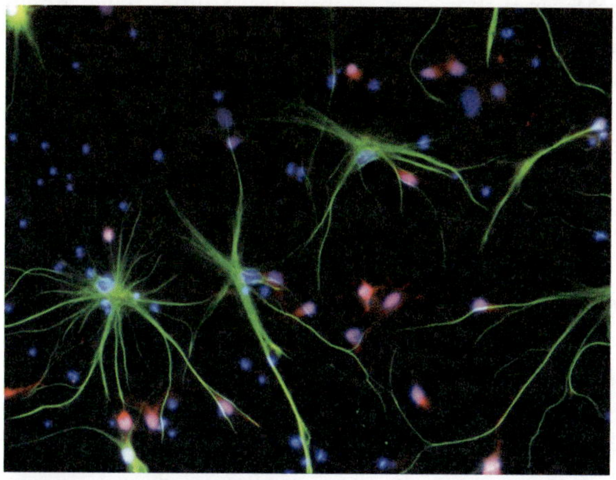

REAPING THE BENEFITS

Long-term exercise increases the number of glial cells (shown here stained with green fluorescent dyes) in the prefrontal cortex, a brain region important for reward learning and cognitive function. Glial cells assist with synaptic function and provide growth factors to sustain neurons, so an increase in their number may improve prefrontal function, potentially enhancing the rewards of running.

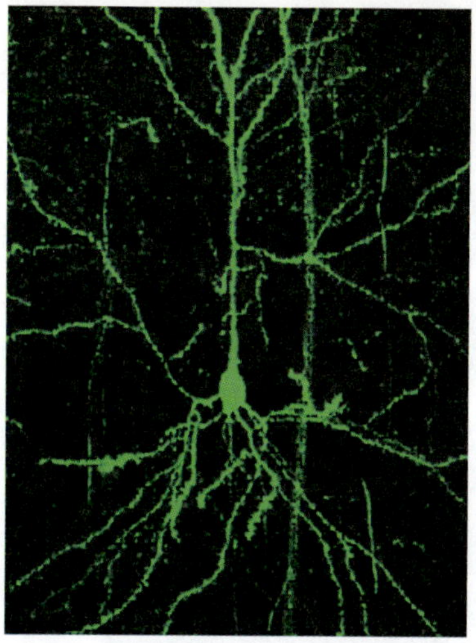

GROWING NEURONS WHILE YOU BUILD MUSCLE

One of the long-term benefits of getting in shape by running is that exercise stimulates the growth of new dendrites and new synaptic connections in the neocortex (shown here in this temporal lobe pyramidal neuron stained with a fluorescent dye). More connections likely translate into greater brain function, enhancing learning and memory.

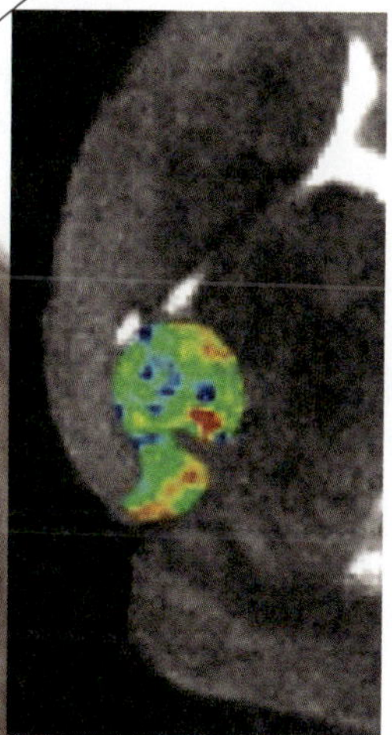

GETTING THE BLOOD FLOWING

Aerobic exercise increases our heart rate, which sends more blood throughout our body as well as to the brain. Increased blood flow in runners is particularly evident in the hippocampus, shown here in colours on this brain scan. Since the hippocampus is important for anxiety regulation, increased blood flow may contribute to the calming and mood-elevating effects often associated with exercise.

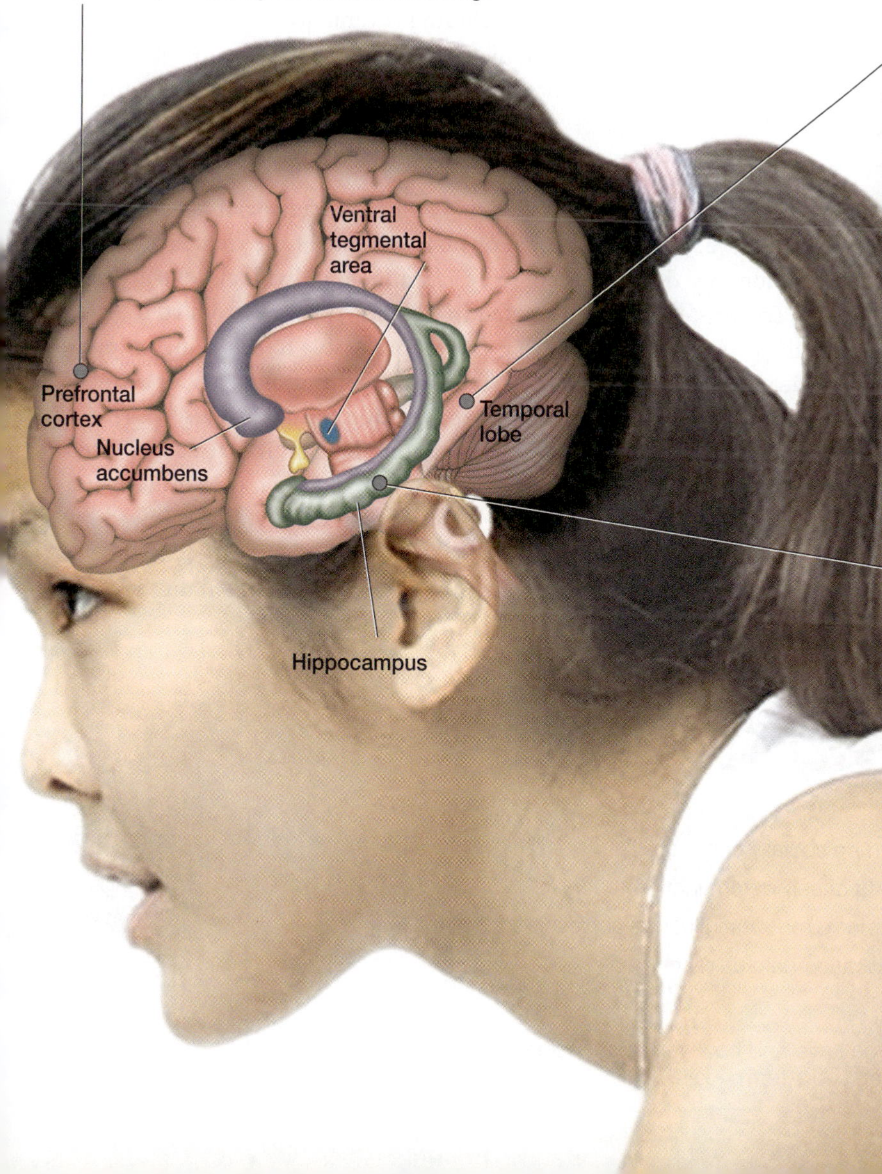

Collectivist achievement. This barn raising in Brampton, Ontario around 1900 is evidence of what communities could do when they got together to help each other out.

the choice of getting a reward right away or waiting some amount of time to get a better reward. For example, researchers might offer a child the choice of receiving a single M&M immediately, or getting a whole bag of M&Ms if they wait 30 minutes. Studies have shown that children display a wide range of abilities to delay gratification; some are much more able to do so than others (Lemmon & Moore, 2007). Related research also suggests that the ability to delay gratification in a laboratory setting may be predictive of success in other realms, including in academic and social settings (Mischel, Shoda, & Rodriguez, 1989).

One likely explanation for the fact that very young children lack the skills necessary to work toward long-term goals and delay instant gratification along the way is that their brains are not yet developed in key areas related to these tasks. The prefrontal cortex is not yet myelinated in children, and the adult levels of synapses connecting them to other neurons are not reached until after puberty. The prefrontal cortex is not only important for mediating reward signals, but also for planning and carrying out complicated tasks that involve several steps toward the achievement of a long-term goal. This may provide some explanation for the common observation that, compared to adults, teenagers are more likely to engage in risky behaviour, jeopardizing their futures for instant gratification.

You may find that as you get older, it is easier to set your sights on goals far in the future, including several years away. You realize that your actions in the here and now will contribute to your situation in the future. These are mature thought processes that cannot occur without an intact prefrontal cortex.

Achievement HOW WE DIFFER Just as psychological and social factors influence our motivation to achieve, so does culture. For instance, one of the elements of self-determination theory, autonomy, does not seem to be essential to individuals who are part of collectivist cultures (Triandis, 2002). As we noted in Chapter 1, people from collectivist cultures tend to view achieving as a cooperative group as preferable to achieving on one's own. Individuals may be motivated to succeed to make their organization, team, or country proud, for example, rather than to garner individual recognition for themselves.

Motivation, whether biological or psychological, is complex and inextricably linked with other cognitive processes, such as memory and emotion. In trying to understand why we do the things we do, it is important to remember that society and culture play important roles as well. Whether undertaking the challenge BASE jump or trying to ace a psychology course, our behaviours illustrate that our survival is dependent on the need for purpose.

Before You Go On

www.wiley.com/go/comer

What Do You Know?

15. Why are we motivated to be socially connected?
16. What are the components of self-determination theory?
17. How do intrinsic and extrinsic motives influence achievement?
18. How does delay of gratification help us reach goals?

What Do You Think?

Describe a long-term goal you have and how you might achieve that goal by dividing it into several smaller, short-term goals.

SCAN TO GET THE ANSWERS

Summary

Theories of Motivation

LEARNING OBJECTIVE 1 Briefly explain each of the five major theories of motivation.

- Several theories offer explanations for our motivation, but no single theory can explain all our behaviour.
- Instinct theory, which suggests that environmental cues stimulate inborn behavioural instincts, best explains motivation that serves basic biological drives, such as eating, drinking, and sex.
- Drive-reduction theory suggests that internal homeostatic mechanisms produce balance within the body by reducing arousal stemming from unmet basic biological needs.
- Arousal theory explains why we sometimes seek to increase arousal levels. The Yerkes-Dodson law proposes that task performance is best if our arousal level matches that needed for a task.
- Incentive learning produces extrinsic motivation to engage in experiences that do not fulfill basic biological drives. Primary and secondary incentives may both be involved. Different incentives motivate different people. Incentive motivation involves brain systems associated with pleasure, incentive learning, and the neurochemical opiate dopamine.
- Maslow proposed that we are motivated by a hierarchy of needs, in which basic survival needs must be satisfied before higher-level needs for belonging, achievement, and self-actualization.

Biological Motivations: Hunger

LEARNING OBJECTIVE 2 Summarize the factors that affect our levels of hunger and our eating behaviour.

- Hunger, our motivation to eat, is created by the interaction of signals from our stomachs, levels of food-related chemicals in our blood, and brain activity, particularly in the hypothalamus.
- Culture and individual differences interact with our basic biological need for food to determine what foods we will eat, when and with whom we like to eat, and how much we eat.
- Obesity is a major public health problem in North America. It is usually caused by overeating, which can result from an interaction between genes and the environment.
- Anorexia nervosa is an eating disorder in which individuals believe they are fat and eat too little. Bulimia nervosa is an eating disorder in which people binge on food, then purge themselves of the food before it can add weight to their bodies.

Biological Motivations: Sex

LEARNING OBJECTIVE 3 Describe factors that affect our sexual motivation and behaviour.

- Sexual practices driven by sexual motivation vary widely as a result of cultural influences.
- Research consistently shows much variety in normal sexual behaviour throughout healthy adulthood.
- Testosterone and other hormones affect our motivation toward sexual behaviour. Many parts of our brains become active during sexual arousal and behaviour.
- Four types of sexual problems that may affect human sexual behaviour are: sexual dysfunctions, paraphilias, gender identity disorder, and medical problems.
- Sex education programs for teens attempt to reduce their risks of sexually-transmitted infections and pregnancy. Two approaches are comprehensive sex education and abstinence programs.

Psychological Motivations: Affiliation and Achievement

LEARNING OBJECTIVE 4 Describe factors that influence our psychological motivations for affiliation and achievement.

- Affiliation represents our need to interact with others, not only for survival, but also for self-worth.
- Isolation puts people at risk of psychological impairments.
- Self-determination theory suggests that we need competence, relatedness, and autonomy to realize our potential.
- Achievement through intrinsic motivation does not involve incentives.
- Individuals who are able to delay gratification can focus on goals and ignore distractions.

Key Terms

affiliation 440
anorexia nervosa 424
body mass index (BMI) 422
body weight set point 421
bulimia nervosa 426
extrinsic motivation 415
heterosexual 433
homeostasis 414

homosexual 433
incentives 415
instincts 412
intrinsic motivation 415
lateral hypothalamus (LH) 420
leptin 420
motivation 411
motive 411
obesity 422
paraphilias 436
self-determination 441
sexual dysfunction 435
ventromedial region of the hypothalamus (VMH) 420
Yerkes-Dodson law 415

TYING IT TOGETHER

The study of motivation is closely connected to the study of all other areas of psychology. Throughout this chapter, we have stressed how motivation interfaces with psychology's various subfields, including our highlighted sections on brain function, individual differences, abnormal functioning, and development. To remind you of how motivation is tied to other psychology subfields and issues, here are some interesting points from throughout the chapter.

WHAT HAPPENS IN THE BRAIN?

- Rewards can lead our brains to release natural pain-killing neurochemicals called opiates, the same ones responsible for the so-called "runner's high."
- Damage to different parts of the hypothalamus can lead to either severe overeating or undereating.
- When we see erotic videos or pictures, mirror neurons in the brain activate just as though we were having sex ourselves.

HOW WE DIFFER

- We eat more in social settings, with other people, than we do when we are alone.
- Men are more likely to fantasize about having lots of sexual partners, but the number of partners men and women say they would like to have in real life is close to the same.
- People in collectivist societies value achievement that contributes to one's groups more highly than individual achievements.

WHEN THINGS GO WRONG

- One-quarter of Canadian adults are obese.
- Restricted eaters, people who use external cues such as calorie counts to control their eating, are more likely than non-restricted eaters to binge after they've eaten a small amount of a high-calorie food.
- Long-term isolation from other people can lead people to develop severe psychological problems.
- At least 10 percent of men experience erectile disorder and at least 10 percent of women experience sexual arousal disorder.

HOW WE DEVELOP

- Even as young children, people vary in their ability to delay immediate gratification in exchange for larger rewards later. Some can do it, while some cannot.
- Delaying immediate gratification to achieve long-term goals may get easier with age for most children and teens because parts of their brain associated with planning are still developing.

Psychology Around Us

Eating, Body Satisfaction, and Eating Disorders

You Are What You Eat?

View this in Action WILEY PLUS www.wileyplus.com

Video Lab Exercise

In certain respects, eating is the simplest human motive to understand: we must eat or we will die. Yet, it also has become the most complex of human needs in Western society because, for women, eating is intertwined with issues such as self-concept, self-control, mood, and social engagement. Indeed, some have argued that it is almost impossible to grow up female in Western society and not have a range of upsetting, self-destructive, and deflating attitudes toward food and eating.

In this video exercise, you will observe several individuals involved in situations that relate to eating and weight. You will compare the needs and attitudes of the individuals; consider the impact of their attitudes on eating behaviour, self-image, mood, and the like; and search for the sources of such attitudes. You will also come to appreciate that the food attitudes of "normal" females in Western society and females with eating disorders are remarkably similar.

As you are working on this online exercise, consider the following questions:

- Do the psychological and biological eating needs of women in Western society complement each other, or do they conflict?
- Given the attitudes of women in Western society toward food and eating, why is obesity a major problem?
- Why do most diets fail?
- Why is the prevalence of eating disorders on the rise in Western society?

CHAPTER 12

Emotion

CHAPTER OUTLINE

EMOTION IN THE DRIVER'S SEAT

"Road-Rage Victim Fine Young Man," trumpeted the headline to a story detailing how an outburst of violent emotion had sparked a fatal chain of events that resulted in the death of Silas O'Brian, a 21-year-old man from Aldergrove, British Columbia.

On March 13, 2008, Silas and two friends had spent the earlier part of their evening at a youth gathering at the Cloverdale church and were getting ready to head out to the Seattle airport for a trip to Hawaii. It is not entirely clear what happened, but the three friends were driving a white Silverado truck. They had tried to pass another truck, but the driver of that truck became so incensed that he followed the Silverado, pulled up beside it, and forced it into the ditch.

The three young men got out of the truck, climbed out of the ditch, and spoke briefly with the driver of a second car that had stopped to see if they were all right. Moments later, the truck that had forced them into the ditch came speeding back, aiming right for the three friends as they stood on the road. Silas's two friends managed to get out of the way, but Silas was struck and killed. The other truck sped off. We have no account of the emotions of the driver who struck Silas. Road rage is a descriptive term, but it does not provide us with an understanding of the emotional factors within the driver that give rise to such horrific behaviour.

Ten months later Brent Parent was arrested and charged with dangerous driving causing death, dangerous driving, failure to stop, and failure to offer assistance. His trial was set for September 2011. We may not understand what gave rise to this incident of road rage, but we can look at what we do understand about emotion and the factors that influence it.

Road rage has been defined as an incident in which an angry or impatient motorist or passenger intentionally injures or kills or threatens to injure or kill another motorist, passenger, or pedestrian (Smart et al., 2007; Rathbone & Huckabee, 1999). Although anger is a common and often adaptive human experience, the explosive and dangerous anger on display in cases of road rage shows how extreme, powerful, and even uncontrollable human emotions can become in certain circumstances.

Of course, anger and rage are not the only emotions people experience, and more often than not, experiencing an emotion does not lead to tragic consequences. In fact, today alone you have undoubtedly experienced several different emotions—perhaps happiness, surprise, or fear—and you may even be experiencing clear, readily-identified emotions as you read this chapter (hopefully boredom is not one of them). What exactly happens when we experience an emotion? Where do emotions come from? Are emotions meaningful, or are they just noise cluttering up our better judgment?

Might even negative emotions be good for us? We will address all these issues in this chapter, but first we will examine a more basic question: what is emotion? ■

What Is Emotion?

LEARNING OBJECTIVE 1

Define emotion and discuss the components, measurement, and functions of emotion.

How would you define emotion? Despite all the attention psychologists give to emotion, they have had difficulty agreeing on exactly what an emotion is. Over 500 words in the English language refer to various aspects or forms of emotions, from *affect*, to *mood*, to *feeling*. Perhaps it is not surprising that a unified definition has eluded scientists (Averill, 1980). Nevertheless, psychologists continue to believe that human emotion is among psychology's most important topics.

Components of Emotion

emotion an intrapersonal state that occurs in response to either an external or an internal event and typically involves a physiological component, a cognitive component, and a behavioural component.

Most of today's theorists define an **emotion** as an individual state that occurs in response to either an external or an internal event and that typically involves three separate but intertwined components:

1. A *physiological component*—changes in bodily arousal, such as increased heart rate, body temperature, and respiration.
2. A *cognitive component*—the subjective appraisal and interpretation of one's feelings and one's surrounding environment.
3. A *behavioural component*—the expression of emotion through verbal or non-verbal channels, such as smiling, frowning, whining, laughing, reflecting, or slouching.

Let's look more closely at each of these components. Remember, though, that when we experience an emotion, all three are at work.

Physiological Component The physiological component of emotion refers to the bodily arousal we feel when experiencing a particular emotion, whether it is positive or negative. When you are nervous about giving a class presentation or going out on a first date, for example, you may notice that your heart beats faster, your hands sweat, and your mouth becomes dry. These physical manifestations of anxiety are produced by your *autonomic nervous system (ANS)*, shown in **Figure 12-1**. As described in Chapter 4, the ANS is responsible for regulating various bodily functions and the activity of specific organs, glands, and muscles. Other physiological changes that might occur as we experience an emotion include increased blood pressure, increased blood sugar, pupil dilation, and the inhibition of intestinal action.

Emotional ingredients. Blue Jay closer Kevin Greg in a "discussion" with the home plate umpire over his interpretation of the strike zone. Greg is showing physical signs of emotion, cognitive components (at least as reflected in what he is saying), and behavioural components.

Because emotions vary in intensity, some emotions may be accompanied by several physiological changes, while others may involve only a few. If, for example, you are anxious about going out with someone for the first time, you will likely experience less intense and fewer physiological reactions than if you are trying to escape from a fire in a crowded concert hall. The reason for these differences has to do with the *sympathetic nervous system*, the subdivision of the ANS that mobilizes internal resources and primes the organism to take swift action for survival—the *fight-or-flight*

Sympathetic Nervous System Prepares the Body for Actions		Parasympathetic Nervous System Returns the Body to Normal State
Pupils dilate	**Eyes**	Pupils constrict
Salivation decreases	**Mouth**	Salivation increases
Perspires; goose bumps	**Skin**	Dries up; no goose bumps
Breathing rate increases	**Lungs**	Breathing rate decreases
Accelerates	**Heart**	Slows
Release stress hormones	**Adrenal glands**	Decrease release of stress hormones
Decreased motility	**Digestion**	Increased motility
Blood vessels constrict; blood sugar increases	**Blood**	Blood vessels dilate; blood sugar drops
Perspire	**Palms**	Dry up

FIGURE 12-1 Emotion and the autonomic nervous system. The physiological changes we experience in emotion are controlled by the autonomic nervous system. The sympathetic branch arouses the body in situations of anxiety or danger. The parasympathetic branch returns the body to its normal state.

response. When waiting for a new date to arrive, your heart may beat faster and your palms may sweat because that is your body's way of signifying the importance of the situation to you. When you need to flee a burning building, however, more emotional arousal and energy are needed, and the body produces a more intense physiological response (Friedman & Silver, 2007). Like fear and anxiety, emotions such as happiness, excitement, and surprise also involve activation of the sympathetic nervous system. Here, too, the intensity of the physiological arousal and the number of bodily changes depend on the nature of the situation.

Following an intense physiological reaction, the other component of the ANS, the *parasympathetic nervous system*, works to calm the body down and attempts to conserve energy by returning the organism to a normal state. Later, we will see how various areas of the brain and the endocrine system are involved in each of these processes.

Cognitive Component The cognitive component of emotion refers to both the evaluative thoughts people have about their emotional experiences (such as "I am afraid") and the appraisal of the events that are producing the emotions. Our interpretation of an event not only helps bring about an emotional reaction, but also influences how intensely we will experience that emotion. Consider the event of coming face to face with a grizzly bear. If the grizzly bear is just a cub and is safely behind a protective barrier at the Calgary Zoo, you will probably appraise the situation as pleasant and experience an emotion such as happiness. If, however, a full-grown grizzly bear were to appear in front of you on a hiking trail in the Canadian Rockies, you would likely appraise the situation as life-threatening and experience, among other emotions, very intense fear.

In addition to appraising the situation that gives rise to a particular emotion, people also interpret and evaluate the emotion itself, further shaping how they experience that emotion. If you love to ride roller coasters, you will most likely interpret the bodily arousal you feel while going into a big drop as excitement and thrill. If, in contrast, you dread roller coasters but are talked into riding one by friends, you will likely label that same bodily arousal as fear.

Behavioural Component When you experience an emotion, you not only have particular thoughts and bodily sensations, but also express and reveal that emotion. You do so through body language, such as facial expressions, gestures, and body posture, as well as through verbal expression. For example, happiness is almost universally expressed with a smile (Leppänen & Hietanan, 2007). Conversely, someone who is frustrated may cross his

PSYCHOLOGY AROUND US Expressing Emotion in a Digital World

On September 19, 1982, a critical moment in the evolution of emotional expression occurred. At Carnegie Mellon University, members of the computer science department began using the latest brand-new thing—an online bulletin board—to communicate among themselves. The problem was, every now and then a discussion would explode into violent debate because someone had posted a joke or sarcastic comment that was misinterpreted as serious by other members of the board. In response, the board users decided that they needed a symbol of some kind that digital communicators could use to indicate when they were, in fact, kidding. The users considered various symbols including (#) and \-/, before board user Scott Fahlman invented a symbol that you might find to be familiar: :-). Thank goodness for this invention. As a result of the "emoticon," no one ever has to worry again that the emotion behind their emails, texts, or tweets will be misinterpreted. :-).

arms and shrug his shoulders; someone who is angry may clench her teeth and furrow her eyebrows; and a person who is sad may frown, slump, and avoid eye contact. You can no doubt think of many more examples.

Research suggests that most people are able to accurately identify several facial expressions. Paul Ekman, a pioneer in the study of emotion and facial expressions, conducted a series of studies in which participants were asked to identify which emotion an individual was experiencing on the basis of the individual's facial cues (Cohn, Ambadar, & Ekman, 2007; Ekman, 2003; Ekman & Friesen, 1975). Ekman and his colleagues found that research participants can typically identify six fundamental emotions: anger, sadness, happiness, surprise, fear, and disgust. In fact, some research suggests that the ability to identify the facial expressions for these emotions is genetically programmed (Izard, 2009, 1997, 1977).

If you asked people whether they preferred to feel fear or vicarious (observed in others) love, the answer would be obvious—right? Then consider this: the adjusted box office revenues of the top 25 horror films surpass those of the top 25 romances by over a billion dollars—even with Titanic, the highest-grossing movie of all time, included among the romances. (MPAA)

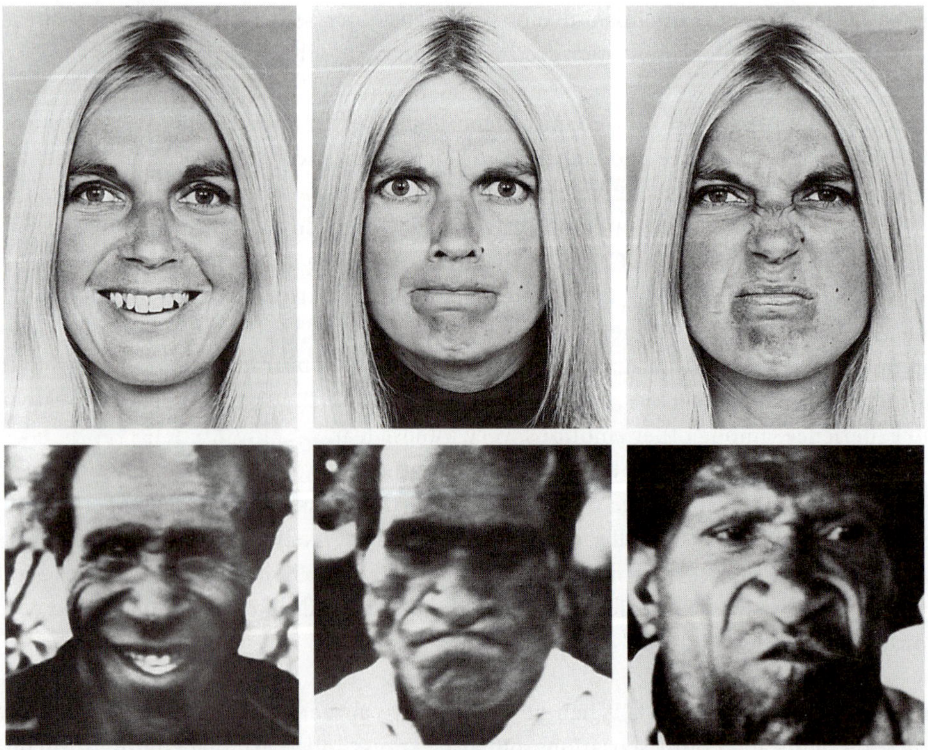

Universal recognition. In one study, Paul Ekman travelled to parts of New Guinea where he found that members of the Fore tribe could readily identify the emotions of happiness, anger, and disgust expressed on a Westerner's face (*top row*). Similarly, he found that college students in the United States easily recognized the same emotions when they were expressed on a Fore tribe member's face (*lower row*).

This would explain why even people from different countries and cultures readily recognize the same emotions depicted in photographs of facial expressions (Ekman et al., 1987; Ekman & Friesen, 1986).

Although less fundamental to emotional expression than non-verbal emotional behaviours, verbal expression of emotion is also important (Rimé, 2007). Studies asking respondents to recall a recently experienced emotion from memory found that more than 90 percent of them had already talked with someone about that experienced emotion (Luminet et al., 2000). And, when it comes to emotions, once people get started, it's hard for them to stop talking; after someone discloses an emotional experience to another person, that person often discusses it with yet a third person. Researchers Veronique Christophe and Bernard Rimé (2001, 1997) reported that this so-called *secondary social sharing* occurs in more than two-thirds of cases. The likelihood of sharing experiences increases with the intensity of the reported emotion.

An interesting aspect of behavioural expressions of emotion is that just by pretending to express the emotion, people may begin to experience that emotion—a phenomenon you will come across again later in this chapter. It is worth noting here because it suggests a strong interdependency among the three components of emotion. As we shall soon see, this complex relationship makes the development of a comprehensive theory of emotion a daunting endeavour.

Measurement of Emotions

Researchers typically use three kinds of information to measure an individual's emotions: (1) behavioural displays of emotion, (2) self-reports of emotion, and (3) physiological reactions.

Behavioural displays of emotion are most often observed by objective raters. These displays typically include obvious acts, such as fighting, fleeing, or making sexual advances. Behavioural displays may also include facial expressions. Researchers often observe behavioural displays in role-playing situations. The researchers attempt to evoke particular emotional responses from participants by showing them a film, giving them a small gift, or manipulating them in some other way (Isen, 2008, 2004, 1993), and then measure how well the participants perform on tasks of various kinds.

Self-ratings are the most widely used approach to measuring a person's emotional experience. The use of such measures is based on the premise that the best way to evaluate emotional states is to simply ask individuals how they are feeling. Many questionnaires and surveys have been published that ask people to provide ratings for how happy, afraid, content, anxious, or depressed they are. The *Positive and Negative Affect Schedule* (*PANAS*), for example, is a measure of various emotional states (Watson & Tellegen, 1985). It contains a list of adjectives, such as *cheerful*, *angry*, *sad*, *happy*, and *timid*, and asks individuals to rate how much they are feeling each emotional state on a scale from 1 ("very slightly") to 5 ("extremely"). Self-report scales such as this offer a fast and convenient measure of emotional experiences. However, self-reports may be inaccurate at times, as they provide only a limited picture of a person's total emotional experience and rely on a person's ability to properly identify and describe an emotional experience. In addition, self-reports do not work well with children.

In recent years, researchers have developed several techniques for measuring an individual's *psychophysiological reactions* to stimuli, and have begun using such measures to assess emotional experiences (Santerre & Allen, 2007; Bradley, Cuthbert, & Lang, 1991). This approach is based on the premise that emotions vary biologically from one another, although this approach does involve some inference and assumes that there are distinct physiological patterns associated with particular emotions (Bradley & Lang, 2007, 2000). These new tools allow the measurement of emotion to go beyond questionnaire-based assessments and may provide a more thorough and accurate report of many of the processes involved in the experience of emotion (Sloan, 2004). Psychophysiological approaches include facial electromyography and assessments of heart rate, skin conductance, and the startle reflex.

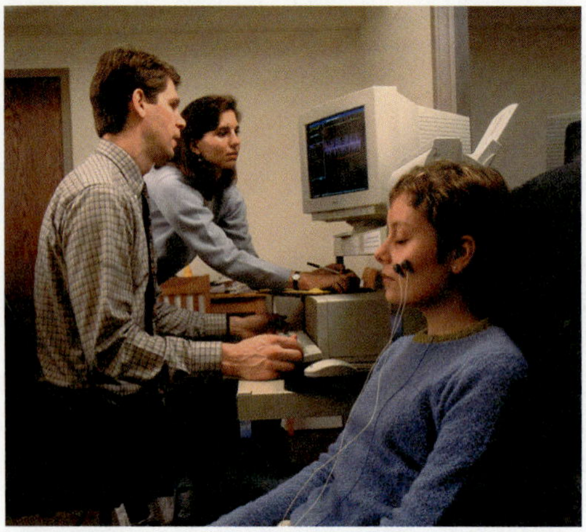

Detecting facial changes. EMG measurements indicate that each emotion is accompanied by a distinct set of facial muscle contractions.

- *Facial electromyography (EMG)* When a person is exposed to an emotionally-charged stimulus, such as a pleasant or unpleasant picture, certain facial muscles contract. A facial EMG measures these contractions. Studies have found that emotional reactions to unpleasant stimuli, such as pictures of mutilated bodies, are often associated with greater activity of the muscles used in frowning. That is, when we are exposed to distressing stimuli, we tend to lower and contract our eyebrows (Sloan et al., 2002; Lang et al., 1993). Conversely, when individuals are shown pleasant stimuli, such as scenic images, they display heightened activity of the facial muscles responsible for smiling.
- *Heart rate* Reductions in heart rate have been observed when individuals are presented with unpleasant/fearful stimuli, whereas pleasant stimuli are associated with accelerations in heart rate (Löw et al., 2008; Bradley & Lang, 2000: Bradley, Cuthbert, & Lang, 1990).
- *Skin conductance* We tend to perspire when we are emotionally aroused. One technique developed to detect and measure emotional arousal involves placing a large electrode on part of the palm of a person's hand and determining from readings of the electrode how well the skin of the hand conducts electrical activity. This technique measures what is called the galvanic skin response—or the electrical resistance of the skin—and reflects increased perspiration, so a higher conductance reading means greater arousal of emotions. Readings of skin conductance are a very useful indicator of emotional arousal (either positive or negative) and of sympathetic nervous system activity.
- *Startle reflex* An additional physiological indicator of emotional reactivity is the startle reflex, an involuntary movement (an eye blink, for example) that is brought on by the onset of a sudden stimulus, such as a loud burst of noise. Researchers usually measure startle reflexes by placing tiny electrodes on the muscle just below a person's eye, and assessing the magnitude of involuntary eye blinks that occur when people are startled while viewing pleasant and unpleasant pictures. Studies have revealed that eye blinks that occur while people are viewing unpleasant pictures are more pronounced than those that occur while they are viewing pleasant pictures (Bradley et al., 2007, 1990; Mallan & Lipp, 2007; Bradley, Cuthbert, & Lang, 1991). This would suggest that the underlying physiological aspects of emotion vary with type of emotional response, although this is still an inference.

Although psychophysiological measures of emotion are in some respects more valid and reliable indicators of emotional states than behavioural displays and self-ratings, most investigators of emotion agree that the complexity of emotion is best measured by using multiple approaches. This also acts as a check on the possibility that we have inferred the presence of physiological reactions that may not actually be so unique. Thus, the integration of all three types of measures provides the richest picture of a person's overall emotional experience.

Functions of Emotions

Since ancient times, philosophers have often considered emotion inferior to reason, but modern researchers who study emotion have emphasized its positive effects. William James (1842–1910), perhaps the most influential emotion researcher of the last 150 years, declared that, without emotion, consciousness and cognition would be "void of human significance" (1890, p. 471). Emotions provide colour to our every experience and lie at the heart of what makes life worth living. Can you imagine riding a roller coaster without experiencing exhilaration (or fear)? How about watching your favourite movie, holding a newborn or a pet, playing your favourite sport, or spending time with your best friends without feeling some happiness or satisfaction? Without emotions, our enjoyable activities and experiences might not seem very rewarding. Clearly emotions play a large role in the meaning we take from our experiences. In this area emotions can serve cognitive, behavioural, and social functions.

Cognitive Functions One function of emotions is to help us organize our memories. As we discussed in Chapter 8 and in the box below on emotional decision making, for example, memories associated with emotional content are much easier to recall (Abercrombie et al., 2008). Emotions also help us to prioritize our concerns, needs, or goals in a given moment (Morris, 1992). The information we gain from noticing our emotions may help us form judgments and make decisions (Gohm & Clore, 2002). A strong feeling of fear when you are preparing to withdraw money from an ATM at night in a dark and scary area of town will make it easy for you to decide to find a better location for your banking. As the box on emotional decision making describes, our emotions also guide our judgments in far more everyday circumstances.

> "Human behavior flows from three main sources: desire, emotion, and knowledge."
> —*Plato, Greek philosopher*

Behavioural Functions Emotions, whether positive or negative, can not only help us perform cognitive tasks, such as remembering relevant information, prioritizing our goals, and making decisions, they can also organize our behaviour. Generally speaking, we act to minimize our experience of negative emotions and maximize our experience

Emotional Decision Making

Wary of strangers. Children often rely unconsciously on their emotional states when making decisions about people, particularly strangers, in social situations.

Emotions were once thought to be unimportant to rational decisions, but it appears that in many situations emotions may, in fact, provide more guidance than our conscious evaluations, even when individuals are unaware of them (LeDoux, 1996).

Consider the case of Boswell, a man with amnesia so severe that he could not retain any newly acquired knowledge for longer than 60 seconds (Tranel & Damasio, 1993). He could not remember the faces of the caregivers, professionals, or family members who visited him regularly over the 15 years of his amnesia. Nevertheless, he preferred some of his regular caregivers over others. By manipulating Boswell's experiences with his daily caregivers so that one acted as a "good guy," another as a "bad guy," and a third as a "neutral guy," researchers discovered that the emotional content of his daily encounters helped guide Boswell's behaviour. He preferred the good and neutral guys to the bad guy. The researchers concluded that Boswell's emotions served an adaptive function; they unconsciously protected him from "bad guys" who might do him harm.

In everyday life, most of us also experience and are influenced by similar "gut" feelings or intuitions of which we may not be consciously aware. Children often seem to be particularly well-tuned to such feelings, especially about strangers. And adults often unconsciously rely on their emotional states when they make "snap" decisions about people in social situations. In fact, if we are asked to remember an encounter with a stranger, most of us have less difficulty recalling how we felt about that individual than remembering the person's hair colour or clothing (Zajonc, 1980).

Unconscious emotional processing is not always a good thing. Although it may offer protection against menacing social situations, it can also exacerbate social problems by leading to prejudice (DeSteno et al., 2004). One study, for example, demonstrated that angry emotions increase the likelihood of participants agreeing with prejudiced statements about unfamiliar social groups, or *outgroups* (Greenwald & Banaji, 1995). So, while it often makes sense to pay attention to our gut feelings about individuals, it is also important to apply rational thought as we move through life forming judgments and making decisions.

"Let's do this again next week." Emotions can be viewed as messengers that predict particular action tendencies. A day at the beach brings this family so much joy, they are likely to repeat the activity again and again.

of positive emotions. Such actions can involve basic behaviours, including diverting our attention away from unpleasant or disgusting images in favour of more neutral or positive images, as well as more complex behaviours, such as procrastination. You have probably noticed a correlation between how terrible you believe the experience of working on a homework assignment will be and how long you delay starting that assignment. In contrast, it is very easy to find time for tasks that we find enjoyable or pleasurable, such as spending time with a partner, and these tasks are hard to delay. In this way, our emotions can help us organize our behaviours (although admittedly in ways that sometimes run counter to what is in our best interest).

Some theorists describe emotions as indicators that serve a valuable information function, telling us how to respond appropriately to events in our environments (Frijda, 2007, 1986; Parrott, 2004, 2001). Many theorists also believe that particular emotions are associated with predictable patterns of behaviour, sometimes called *action tendencies*, that help us to adapt and survive in our social and physical environments (Frijda, 2007, 1986; Gross, 1998; Lang, Bradley, & Cuthbert, 1998). Specific action tendencies associated with key emotions include the following:

- *Happiness* results when people engage in rewarding behaviours or positive interactions. Because they feel happiness and joy, they will likely continue to engage in those behaviours or interactions. Happiness and joy also signal to people that particular goals have been attained (Carver, 2004; Fredrickson, 2001).
- *Embarrassment* often evokes forgiveness and motivates reconciliation and adherence to social norms (Parrott, 2004, 2001; Keltner & Kring, 1998). Consider, for example, that you tell one friend you are busy studying and then, when another friend asks you to go to a movie you want to see, you change your mind about studying and go to the movie. You run into the first friend at the movie. Embarrassment may not only lead you to apologize profusely, but also help to ensure that you will not do such a potentially hurtful thing again. Similarly, guilt directs people's awareness toward their transgressions and may trigger conciliatory efforts, personal change, and self-improvement.
- *Anger* signals the presence of injustice and prompts aggression, as well as other self-protective behaviours (Mayer & Salovey, 2004, 1997).
- *Anxiety* directs a person's attention toward potential threats and motivates appropriate action to avoid or cope with them (Öhman, 2000).
- *Sadness* may signal the loss of positive relationships and help people to seek needed support and assistance from others (Oatley & Jenkins, 1996; Campos et al., 1989).

Research suggests that the avoidance of negative emotion is typically a more powerful motivator than the achievement of positive emotion (Cacioppo & Berntsen, 1994).

Social Functions Another important function of emotions appears to be coordination of relationships. Emotions form the foundations of relationships by helping us develop a sense that we like and trust another person. In one study, for example, viewers assigned more positive ratings of friendliness and competence to people who showed a sincere smile in their yearbook photographs than to those whose pictures had fake smiles or no smiles (Harker & Keltner, 2001).

Emotions, even when they are negative, can also improve the quality of our relationships. Research suggests, for example, that the more married couples talk about their feelings, the happier they are (Gottman & Levenson, 1988). In contrast, keeping our emotions inside may get in the way of our ability to form lasting relationships. One study found that participants who habitually kept their emotions to themselves were more likely to report problems with closeness and sharing in intimate relationships than people who talked about their emotions (Gross & John, 2003).

Before You Go On

www.wiley.com/go/comer

What Do You Know?

1. What system produces the bodily arousal associated with emotions?
2. What three types of information are most commonly used by researchers to measure emotions?
3. Name four physiological indicators of emotional state.
4. What are the major functions of emotion?

SCAN TO GET THE ANSWERS

What Do You Think?

Think about the road-rage incident described in our opening example and describe what you think the physiological, cognitive, and behavioural components of the various drivers might have been.

Theories of Emotion

LEARNING OBJECTIVE 2

Discuss the major theories of emotion, and identify the pathways through which emotions are experienced according to each theory.

How do emotions occur? What causes them? How have they evolved in the human species? How do they develop in individuals as they move from infancy to adulthood? And what's going on in the brain while all this is happening? These are the core questions for understanding emotions, and we will turn to them next.

Since the birth of psychology, a number of theories have been proposed to explain how emotions occur and what causes them. The most prominent of these theories are: the James-Lange theory, the Cannon-Bard theory, the Schacter and Singer two-factor theory, the cognitive-mediational theory, and the facial-feedback theory. Each theory proposes a different story of the sequence of an emotional episode and each emphasizes a particular component of emotion (physiological, cognitive, or behavioural). In addition, evolutionary theory has important things to say about the origins of emotion.

James-Lange Theory

As we observed earlier, William James was the earliest and one of the most influential psychologists to study emotion. James took issue with the conventional common-sense explanation of emotion, which suggests that an event triggers an emotion, which leads to physiological changes, followed by a behavioural response to the situation. Looking at the road rage example that began this chapter, the common-sense explanation would suggest that the driver in our opening story became angry in response to Silas O'Brian's friend's driving. As a result, we can imagine that his heart started beating faster and his face became flushed and red. Once he experienced this high arousal, he began blocking O'Brian's car.

James (1884, 1890) argued that emotions actually work differently. He suggested that an emotion begins with (1) the perception of an environmental situation or event, followed by (2) the elicitation of physiological and behavioural changes, which are then (3) processed by the cortex and converted into felt emotion. In other words, the driver in our story did not become angry and then, as a result, experience high physiological arousal; instead, he experienced high physiological arousal and interpreted it as anger.

James believed that our physiological response to a stimulus occurs prior to, and provides the basis for, the experience of a particular emotion.

In 1885, a Danish physiologist, Carl Lange (1834–1900), published a theory of emotion that was very similar to James's. Both theorists believed that there is no emotion to experience unless it is driven by a physiological component (Davidson, Jackson, & Kalin, 2000). Their views are collectively referred to as the **James-Lange theory of emotion**.

James-Lange theory of emotion a theory proposing that felt emotions result from physiological changes, rather than being their cause.

Although the two theories are very similar, they do have a few key differences. Whereas James believed there is a place for cognition in the context of an emotional episode, Lange viewed mental activity as having little to do with emotion. Lange (1885) postulated instead that the *vasomotor centre*, a collection of nerves and muscles that cause the blood vessels to constrict or dilate, is the root cause of all emotion: "We owe all the emotional side of our mental life, our joys and sorrows, our happy and unhappy hours, to our vasomotor system" (p. 80). **Figure 12-2** compares the James-Lange theory with the two theories that we will turn to next, the Cannon-Bard theory and the Schachter and Singer two-factor theory.

Cannon-Bard Theory

The James-Lange theory of emotion produced quite a stir in the fields of psychology and physiology, and much research was published disputing various aspects of the theory. The leading critic of the James-Lange theory was Harvard psychologist Walter Cannon (1871–1945). Central to Cannon's criticism was the James-Lange theory's notion that *visceral organs*—that is, our internal organs in which physiological arousal occurs, such as the heart—can produce complex emotional experiences. Pointing to a number of research findings, Cannon disputed the accuracy of the James-Lange theory on five different points (1927):

1. *Total separation of the visceral organs from the central nervous system does not alter emotional behaviour*. Cannon cited research on dogs and cats whose vasomotor centres had been disconnected from their central nervous systems. Even without the vasomotor centre that Lange believed to be of utmost importance, cats and dogs continued to display aggression and rage in the usual way (Bard, 1934). Similarly, more recent studies indicate that most human patients with spinal cord injuries continue to experience emotional excitability that is similar to their functioning prior to injury; some actually report an increase in the intensity of particular emotions (Bermond et al., 1991; Chwalisz, Diener, & Gallager, 1988).

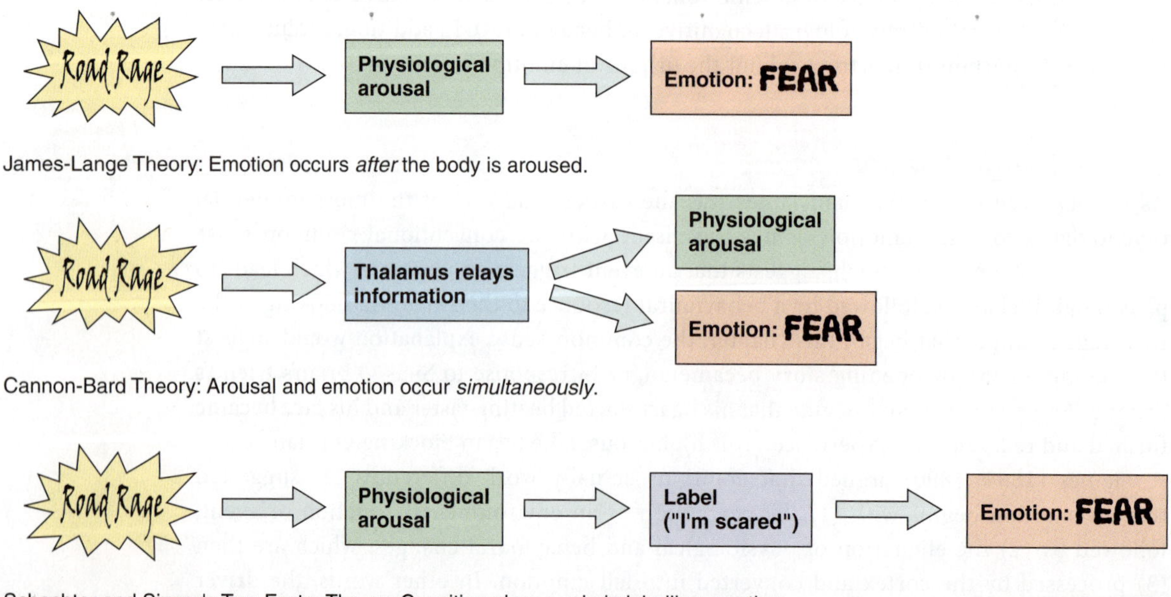

FIGURE 12-2 Three major theories of emotion. The three major theories of emotion have different ways of accounting for how a victim of road rage would react emotionally.

2. *The same visceral changes often occur in different emotional states and in non-emotional states.* Recall that the arousal associated with emotions arises from the sympathetic nervous system. Cannon argued that, because the activity of the sympathetic nervous system is typically general and non-specific, several emotions probably share similar patterns of visceral activity. Cannon further noted that certain non-emotional events, such as fever, produce patterns of sympathetic nervous system activity that are similar to the patterns that accompany emotions, although they are not experienced as emotions.

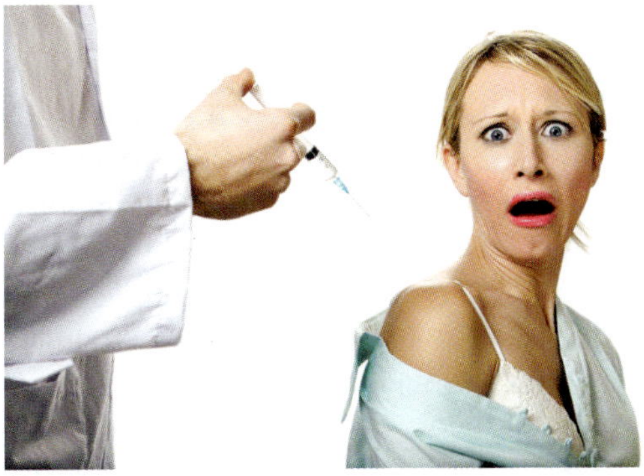

Theories of emotion. The timing of and relationships among the situations we find ourselves in, our internal physiological arousal, and our interpretations of what our circumstances mean to us are all part of the various theories of emotion.

3. *The viscera are rather insensitive structures.* According to Cannon, "We can feel the thumping of the heart because it presses against the chest wall, we can also feel the throbbing of the blood vessels because they pass through tissues well supplied with sensory nerves . . . [but], normally, the visceral processes are extraordinarily undemonstrative" (1927, p. 111).

4. *Visceral changes are too slow to be the source of emotional feeling.* Cannon argued that the amount of time it takes for the body's vasomotor system to communicate with the brain and send impulses back to the rest of the body is too slow "to be the occasion for the appearance of affective states" (1927, p. 112).

5. *Artificially inducing visceral changes does not produce strong emotions.* Citing research by the Spanish psychologist Gregorio Marañon (1924), Cannon pointed out that the injection of adrenaline, a stimulant, into the bloodstream of research participants, which activates the sympathetic nervous system and produces visceral changes characteristic of intense emotions, does not lead to discrete and identifiable emotional reactions.

Following his critique of the James-Lange theory, Cannon (1927) offered his own explanation of emotion, which was later elaborated on by Philip Bard (1934). This theory, often referred to as the **Cannon-Bard theory of emotion**, states that when we perceive an emotionally stirring event, the *thalamus*, a key brain structure, simultaneously relays information about the event to both the sympathetic nervous system and to the parts of the brain that are active in thought and decision making. As a result, the subjective experience of emotion and the activation of the sympathetic nervous system (that is, bodily arousal) occur simultaneously (see Figure 12-2 again). According to the Cannon-Bard theory, the driver in our story would have simultaneously experienced both rage and physiological arousal when he perceived Silas O'Brian's car approaching him and trying to pass.

Cannon-Bard theory of emotion a theory proposing that the subjective experience of emotion and the activation of the sympathetic nervous system (that is, bodily arousal) occur simultaneously.

PSYCHOLOGY AROUND US "I Know How You Feel"

"If changes in blood pressure and skin temperature can reliably distinguish between the emotions of anger, fear, sadness, joy, and disgust, and if machines . . . can detect these bodily changes, then why can we not build machines that know how we feel—that read our emotions? Imagine sensors built into the steering wheel of a car to read the driver's heart rate and skin temperature. Imagine sensors built into the handles of bicycles, pilot simulators, joysticks, golf clubs, and utensils. . . .

Actually, soon you will not need to imagine such technological inventions, as scientists in the new field of 'affective computing' are hard at work building such devices. One particularly interesting invention is the 'emotion mouse.' It functions like an ordinary computer mouse, except it [also monitors] heart rate, skin temperature, hand movements, and electrical skin conductance. The computer monitors the data collected by the emotion mouse and analyzes this data to infer the user's emotional state.

If a computer can read a user's emotions, then a computer gains the potential capacity for adjusting to its user. A computer game can be made more or less challenging, a tutorial can be adjusted to decrease fear or to increase joy, or an online counseling session can provide emotional feedback regarding the feelings of a client at different points in the conversation." (Reeve, 2008, 2001, p. 440)

Schachter and Singer's Two-Factor Theory

In 1962, Stanley Schachter and Jerome Singer, American social psychologists, published a landmark study that helped change psychology's understanding of emotion. According to Schachter and Singer (1962), earlier theories had neglected to consider the influence of cognition, or thought processes, in our emotional experiences. Physiological differences alone are too subtle to define specific emotional states, said these researchers; it is our cognitive appraisal of the immediate situation that provides a label ("I am afraid") for our bodily feelings.

Schachter and Singer's two-factor theory of emotion a theory proposing that an emotional state is a function of both physiological arousal and cognition.

According to **Schachter and Singer's two-factor theory of emotion**, "It is the cognition which determines whether the state of physiological arousal will be labeled as 'anger,' 'joy,' 'fear,' or 'whatever'" (Schachter & Singer, 1962, p. 380). Schachter and Singer suggested that, although physiological arousal is *necessary* for an emotion to occur—in fact it determines the intensity of the emotional experience—it's up to our cognitive faculties to determine our specific emotional state (see Figure 12-2).

If we were to apply Schachter and Singer's two-factor theory to our opening case, we would assume that the severity of the driver's actions was determined by his level of physiological arousal. If his arousal had been mild or moderate, he might have appraised the situation differently ("Another driver pushing a bit too hard") and might have responded in a mildly angry or frustrated way (perhaps cursing in the privacy of his car or raising his middle finger at the other vehicle). Instead, however, we would presume that he experienced intense physiological arousal and appraised the situation in a way that led to anger ("That driver is purposely trying to tick me off"), making him respond in ways that ultimately had fatal consequences.

Schachter and Singer's two-factor theory also suggests that, when the cause of our physical arousal is not immediately clear to us, we use cues from our surroundings to help us identify a cause. This can lead to mislabelling physical arousal from a non-emotional source as an emotion. Schacter and Singer (1962) conducted a well-known experiment at the University of Minnesota to test this idea (see **Figure 12-3**). They told undergraduate research participants that the study was examining the effects of a vitamin supplement (they called it *Suproxin*) on vision.

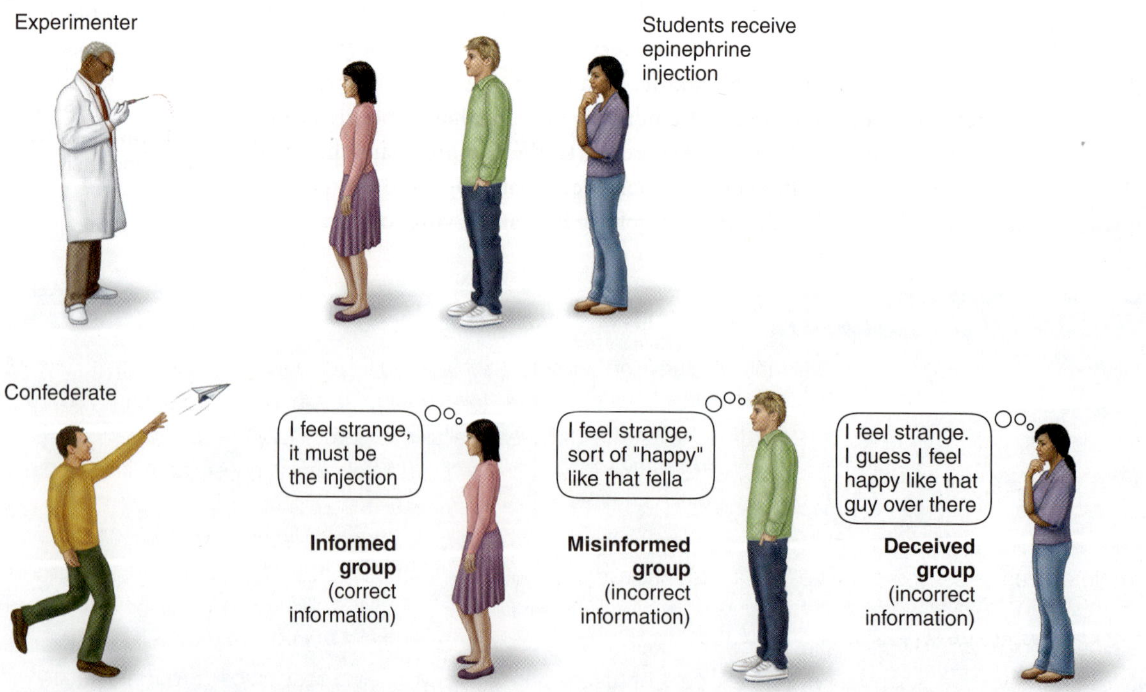

FIGURE 12-3 Testing the two-factor theory. In the absence of correct information, participants in the deceived and misinformed groups who received the epinephrine injection concluded that they were feeling happy, like the confederate who had acted euphoric.

When the students arrived at the lab, they were met by an experimenter and told that they would be receiving a small injection of Suproxin and then would complete several vision tests. The participants then received an injection of either epinephrine (adrenalin) or a placebo (saline solution). By producing physiological arousal, the epinephrine injections mimicked sympathetic nervous system activation. Among those who received epinephrine, one-third (the *informed group*) were told they might experience side effects, such as palpitations, trembling, and facial flushing; one-third (the *deceived group*) were told they would experience no side effects; and one-third (the *misinformed group*) were told they would experience side effects that were not in fact likely to occur, such as headaches. All the participants in the placebo group were told they would have no side effects from their injections. After the participants were given the drug, a confederate of the experimenters' entered the room and acted either euphoric or angry. These manipulations allowed Schachter and Singer to create a scenario in which participants experienced bodily arousal either with or without plausible explanations for it.

As Schachter and Singer's two-factor theory had predicted, students who received an epinephrine injection but were not given a proper explanation for their bodily arousal (the deceived and misinformed groups) later reported feelings of anger or euphoria when they encountered an angry or euphoric confederate (acting that way on the instructions of the experimenter). In contrast, students in the epinephrine condition who were told to anticipate various symptoms of sympathetic nervous system activity (informed group) did not experience anger or euphoria—they were immune to any effects of the arousal manipulation. Clearly, the label of an emotion is influenced by whether or not a person has an appropriate explanation for the arousal.

Schachter and Singer's two-factor theory served to redirect the focus of emotion research toward the role of cognitive factors. Indeed, a number of studies have since provided indirect evidence for their two-factor theory. In a classic study conducted by Don Dutton of the University of British Columbia, for example, male participants were

Echoes of the Capilano Bridge study. The couple on the left pose for wedding pictures on the Caplilano Suspension Bridge in North Vancouver. This wooden-boarded, not-so-sturdy footbridge stands high above the water and near the sounds of water pouring over the top of the Capilano dam. If asked, they might well talk more about their strong feelings for each other rather than any fear induced by the swaying bridge and sounds of rushing water. What about the couple on the right on their much smaller, sturdier bridge?

approached by an attractive female (a confederate of the researchers) and asked to complete questionnaires. Males approached by the woman while crossing the Capilano Suspension Bridge in British Columbia—a long, narrow footbridge constructed of wooden boards and wire cables suspended about 30 metres (100 feet) above a river and near very dramatic falls—later reported being more attracted to the female confederate than males who met the same woman on a wider, sturdier bridge only about 3 metres (10 feet) above the river (Dutton & Aron, 1974). The researchers concluded that the men on the shaky Capilano Bridge had experienced anxious arousal because of the height of the bridge and had misinterpreted this arousal as sexual attraction—findings consistent with Schachter and Singer's two-factor theory.

Cognitive-Mediational Theory

One theory that built on Schachter and Singer's ideas was developed by Richard Lazarus, an influential psychologist at the University of California, Berkeley. As we shall see in Chapter 15, Lazarus spent much of his career investigating the role of appraisal in people's reactions to stress (Lazarus, 2007; Lazarus et al., 1965; Lazarus & Alfert, 1964). Eventually, Lazarus came to believe that appraisal must play a similar role in emotional experiences to that which it plays in stress reactions. Unlike Schachter and Singer's two-factor theory, Lazarus's theory holds that appraisal affects not only how people interpret physical arousal, but also the level of arousal itself. As such, the **cognitive-mediational theory of emotion** views cognitive interpretations of events as playing a still broader role in the experience of emotion.

cognitive-mediational theory of emotion a theory proposing that cognitive interpretations, particularly appraisals, of events are the keys to experiences of emotion.

In one of his early studies, for example, Lazarus and his colleagues had participants watch stressful films (featuring, for example, skin-piercing rituals among Australian tribesmen) while their autonomic nervous system activity was measured and their subjective reports of stress were recorded. Some of the viewers were told "the people in this film were not hurt or distressed by what is happening," while others were told, "many of the people you see in this film suffered severe pain and infection from these rituals." By influencing the way the participants construed what was happening in the films, Lazarus and his colleagues found they could greatly alter the participants' physiological activity and subjective stress reactions while viewing. That is, appraisal serves as a *cognitive mediator* between environmental stimuli and people's reaction to those stimuli (Lazarus, 2007, 1993).

Facial-Feedback Theory

We mentioned earlier, in discussing the behavioural component of emotion, that people may begin to experience an emotion just by pretending to express it. Related to this observation is the **facial-feedback theory of emotion**, which is derived from Charles Darwin's early (1872) notion that muscular activity can either strengthen or lessen the experience of emotion. According to the current facial-feedback perspective, our subjective experiences of emotion are influenced by sensory feedback we receive from the activity of our facial muscles, our **facial efference** (Izard, 2007, 1997, 1977; Tomkins, 1962). Thus, facial expressions not only express a given emotion, but also intensify the physiological experience of that emotion.

facial-feedback theory of emotion a theory proposing that subjective experiences of emotion are influenced by sensory feedback from facial muscular activity, or facial efference.

facial efference sensory feedback from facial muscular activity.

In one study, for example, participants were directed to move their facial muscles into certain positions, without directly being told which emotions they were expressing. The facial changes produced significant changes in their autonomic nervous system arousal, as indicated by increases in their heart rates, skin conductance, and finger temperatures (Ekman, Levenson, & Friesen, 1983). In a related study, research participants held pens in their mouths while rating the funniness of cartoons (Strack, Martin, & Stepper, 1988). This approach enabled the experimenters to manipulate the participants' facial expressions without calling attention to their facial activity or to the emotions normally associated with that activity. People directed to hold the pen in their teeth made a face similar to a smile, while those directed to hold the pen with their lips were unable to smile (**Figure 12-4**).

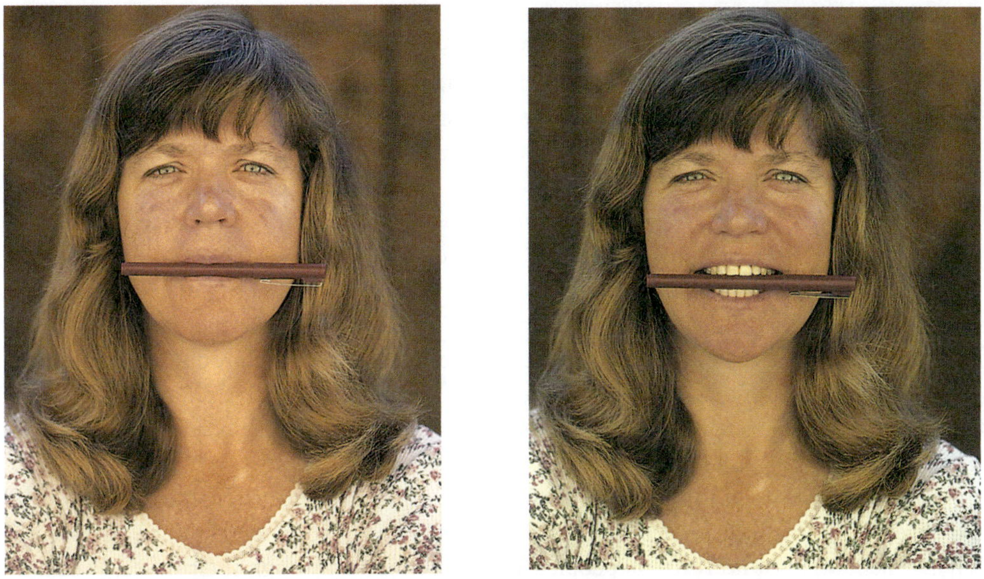

FIGURE 12-4 Testing the facial-feedback theory. When you hold a pen between your teeth, you activate facial muscles that are associated with a smile and you are more likely to report pleasant feelings than if you held the pen between your lips (Strack, Martin, & Stepper, 1988).

Sure enough, individuals who held the pen in their teeth found the cartoons funnier than those who held the pen in their lips.

The facial-feedback theory of emotion has also been supported by studies of the *Duchenne smile*, named after French neurologist Guillaume Duchenne. Duchenne observed that smiles reflecting genuine emotion involve the activity of certain muscles near the mouth and the eyes, whereas more artificial "social smiles" involve only muscles near the mouth (see **Figure 12-5**). One experiment found that participants who displayed genuine Duchenne smiles while viewing a positive film clip displayed greater physiological arousal and experienced more positive emotion than other participants (Soussignan, 2002).

Check this out for yourself. Have several friends hold a pen in their lips for 2 minutes and then ask them to rate their level of happiness on a 1 to 10 point scale. Have another group of friends hold a pen in their teeth for 2 minutes and then rate their happiness on the same scale. Which group had the highest average happiness ratings?

How might facial expressions produce physiological arousal and the subjective experience of emotion? Several explanations have been proposed. It may be that facial expressions serve as *relays* between an emotionally stirring event and a resulting subjective experience of emotion. Indeed, psychologist Silvan Tomkins (1962) argued that emotionally-stirring stimuli activate an inborn, almost reflexive "affect program" that sends signals throughout the body by motor and circulatory pathways, bypassing the parts of the brain involved in cognition. The body reacts to these signals in forms, such as facial expressions (smiles,

"A smile is the universal welcome."
—Max Eastman, American writer

FIGURE 12-5 Genuine versus artificial smiles. Real or Duchenne smiles reflect genuine emotion and involve muscles near the mouth and the eyes (*left*). Social or artificial smiles involve only muscles near the mouth (*right*).

frowns) and other activities, which then supply sensory feedback to the brain, producing the experience of an emotion. Tomkins (1992, 1980) further argued that receptors in the face change position when people contract their facial muscles and that this sensory information is also sent to the brain, ultimately leading to a felt emotion.

Another theory is that patterns of facial muscle activity change the temperature of blood entering the brain, and by doing so affect neuron activity in the brain, eventually producing particular emotional states. In one study, researchers had research participants repeat a series of vowel sounds—*i*, *e*, *o*, *a*, *ü*, *ah*, and *u*—while measuring blood temperature in the participants' brains and asking them to provide a general rating of their emotional state (pleasant versus unpleasant, for example) (Zajonc, Murphy, & Inglehart, 1989). The researchers hypothesized that the pronunciation of *e* and *ah* would produce muscular patterns similar to that of a smile and an expression of surprise, respectively. Similarly, the long *u* sound, *ü*, was expected to mimic aspects of facial expressions associated with negative emotions.

The results showed that facial efference of this kind did indeed produce negative and positive feelings, as well as corresponding changes in brain blood temperature. Apparently, saying the long *u* sound restricts people's ability to breathe through their noses. Breathing through the nose generally cools our blood before it reaches our brains. Because participants in the Zajonc study were breathing less through their noses, they experienced a rise in brain blood temperature and, along with that, a rise in negative emotions. In contrast, the pronunciation of *e* and *ah* increases nose breathing, allowing the cooling of blood travelling to the brain, and ultimately produces positive emotional experiences—a pattern also confirmed by participants in this study.

It is important to note that none of the theories just discussed seems to explain emotion completely. As psychologist Robert Zajonc has said, "It is unlikely that all emotions have the same etiology, are characterized by the same affective and cognitive processes, . . . or have the same underlying neuroanatomical structure and neurochemical actions" (Zajonc et al., 1989, p. 412). Thus, one emotional experience may result largely from a singular source, such as physiological arousal, cognitive appraisal, or facial expression, while others may be the product of a combination of these factors.

Negative emotions. Zajonc claimed that negative emotions may result from a rise in brain blood temperature.

Evolutionary Theory

Over the past 50 years, a number of theorists have suggested that emotions are innate, prewired responses that have evolved over millions of years from lower species to humans (Izard, 2007; Cosmides & Tooby, 2000; Plutchik, 1980). This perspective is based on the evolutionary theory of Charles Darwin, described in Chapters 1 and 4.

In 1872, having noted the similarities in emotional expression across and within species throughout the world, Darwin published *The Expression of the Emotions in Man and Animals*. Here he argued that emotional expression in both people and animals serves a *communicative* function that is essential to survival. Emotional expressions may, for example, warn others of danger, dissuade enemies from attacking, or signal sexual receptiveness (Seyfarth & Cheney, 2003; LeDoux, 1996).

Evolutionary psychologists argue that certain emotions have been passed down through the generations because they have played an integral role in the survival of our species (Nesse & Ellsworth, 2009; Nesse, 1990). It may even be that each emotion corresponds to a particular situation that has occurred repeatedly throughout the course of evolution, and that each emotion increases an individual's ability to cope with the adaptive challenges that arise in such a situation (see **Table 12-1**). For example, organisms that experienced fear when confronted by predators most likely survived at a much higher rate than those that experienced calm during such interactions. Over time, as this situation was repeated, fear became a characteristic response to danger and, eventually, an

TABLE 12-1 Evolutionary Links Between Emotion and Behaviour in Humans and Other Animals

Situation	Emotion	Survival Function
Threat	Fear, terror, anxiety	Fight, flight
Obstacle	Anger, rage	Biting, hitting
Potential mate	Joy, ecstasy, excitement	Courtship, mating
Loss of valued person	Sadness, grief	Crying for help
Sudden novel object	Surprise	Stopping, attending

Source: Plutchik, 1980.

innate, prewired, and automatic response. Such patterns of emotionality have been genetically passed on to us from generations of ancestors, making our lives much easier than if we were required to learn about every aspect of our environmental surroundings without their guidance.

Much of the research support for an evolutionary explanation of emotion centres on the universal and innate nature of facial expressions of emotion. As we observed earlier, Paul Ekman and his colleagues have conducted a series of studies on facial expressions of emotion (Cohn et al., 2007; Ekman, 2003; Ekman & Friesen, 1971). They found that individuals from many different cultural and language backgrounds, when presented with photographs of different facial expressions, are fairly accurate at selecting the emotions being expressed. Individuals from places such as Estonia, Ethiopia, Turkey, and Japan, for example, similarly recognize facial expressions of happiness, anger, fear, disgust, surprise, and sadness (Ekman et al., 1987). One study even found that the inhabitants of isolated villages in Papua, New Guinea—who had never seen a photograph, magazine, film, or television—recognized facial expressions of emotion with the same degree of accuracy as individuals from countries exposed to Western media (Ekman & Friesen, 1971).

Based on such research on the universality of certain facial expressions and the evolution of emotion, a number of theorists have suggested that some innate, **basic emotions** are preprogrammed into all people, regardless of culture or country of origin. Tomkins (1962) has proposed that there are eight basic emotions: surprise, interest, joy, rage, fear, disgust, shame, and anguish. Other notable theorists have proposed similar lists (Frijda, 1986; Plutchik, 1980; Izard, 1977). Indeed, it appears that infants typically display the facial expressions of such fundamental emotions very early in life (Izard, 1994). Even children who are born without sight display facial expressions similar to those of sighted children of the same age (Galati et al., 2003; Goodenough, 1932).

basic emotions a group of emotions preprogrammed into all humans regardless of culture.

Before You Go On

www.wiley.com/go/comer

What Do You Know?

5. What is the key idea in the James-Lange theory of emotion?
6. What are Cannon's arguments disputing this idea?
7. What element did Schachter and Singer's two-factor theory add to explanations of what determines emotional experience?
8. What is facial efference?
9. What does it mean to say that emotions have been shaped by natural selection?

SCAN TO GET THE ANSWERS

What Do You Think?

Recall a powerful emotional experience you have had. Which of the theories of emotion detailed in this chapter seems to best explain your experience? Is one theory sufficient?

Emotion HOW WE DEVELOP

LEARNING OBJECTIVE 3

Contrast the cognitive theory of emotional development with the differential emotions theory.

We have discussed several ideas about how emotions evolved in the human species, but what about how emotions develop in each individual as that person grows from infant to adult? Next, we will discuss two contrasting theories of emotional development. One holds that emotions unfold as a consequence of neural and cognitive development, while the other argues that emotions themselves help spur neural growth and the development of cognitive processes. As you will see, research on facial expressions, which we discussed in the preceding section, plays a role in both theories.

Lewis's Cognitive Theory of Emotional Development

Developmental psychologist Michael Lewis has proposed a cognitive theory of emotional development suggesting that most emotions can be experienced and expressed only *after* particular cognitive abilities have developed. According to Lewis (2008, 2007, 2005, 1992), children are born with a limited capacity for emotional experience—a capacity that expands enormously over the first three years of life, culminating eventually in the development of a full range of emotions.

As you may have observed, newborn infants often vacillate between only a few *mood states*, appearing either distressed (when hungry, tired, lonely, or in need of changing) or content (when satiated, rested, and secure). Although they display startle reactions in the presence of sudden, loud noises, and show signs of hunger at the sight of food, their emotional responses remain rather undifferentiated until certain milestones in their cognitive development have been achieved. According to Lewis, those key cognitive milestones include the abilities to perceive and discriminate stimuli, to recall memories of past events and compare them with current situations, and to be aware of themselves and compare themselves with others (Lewis, 2008, 2007, 2005, 1992).

By the time babies are 3 months of age, their emotional repertoire has expanded to include happiness and excitement at the sight of familiar objects and faces, and sadness at the loss of positive stimuli, such as a parent's attention. In addition, infants begin to demonstrate disgust during this time, characterized by spitting out unpleasant-tasting objects (Lewis, 2000). Between 4 and 6 months, infants begin to express anger when they are frustrated and surprise when confronted with situations that are unexpected.

By 7 to 8 months of age, most infants display fearfulness. According to Lewis (2000), fearfulness emerges only after infants develop the ability to compare a fear-eliciting event with an internal representation of a similar event that was previously encountered. When, for example, 8-month-old children see an adult, they compare the adult's face with their internal representations or memories of adult faces that they have previously encountered. Based on this comparison, they determine whether the adult is a stranger, and so someone to fear, or a familiar person who can be trusted. Thus, by 8 months of age, after they have developed the cognitive abilities to recall and compare stimuli, most infants exhibit the fundamental emotions—anger, sadness, happiness, surprise, fear, and disgust—identified in studies of facial expressions (Ekman & Friesen, 1986, 1975).

For the next year of life, an infant's emotional development remains stable. No new emotions emerge, although those in the current repertoire are enhanced. From 18 to 24 months, however, children reach the cognitive milestone of paying attention to themselves, and this eventually gives rise to *objective self-awareness*, an ability to look at themselves as objects, with a clear understanding that they are separate from other people (Lewis, 2000). Such cognitive development enables them to experience so-called *emotions of self-consciousness*, such as envy, empathy, and embarrassment.

A final cluster of emotions emerge between the second and third year of life, following the achievement of another cognitive milestone—the capacity to compare one's behaviour against external or internal standards, which eventually include such points of comparison as parents, teachers, and personal ideals (Lewis, 2008, 2007, 1992). These emotions, which Lewis calls *self-conscious evaluative emotions*, include pride, shame, and guilt. Although emotional development continues well into adolescence and beyond, and is further shaped by external factors such as cultural rules, the most significant growth and achievement of emotional milestones is complete by 3 years of age.

Izard's Differential Emotions Theory

Emotion researcher Carroll Izard suggests that emotions, rather than emerging as a result of cognitive development, actually help trigger the achievement of social and cognitive milestones. In his **differential emotions theory**, Izard argues that emotions have evolved largely to help individuals develop and that emotions aid in the successful completion of various stages of development (Izard, 2007, 1991, 1977; Abe & Izard, 1999). Indeed, in Izard's view, emotions evolved largely to help individuals develop.

differential emotions theory a theory holding that particular emotions or sets of emotions become more prominent during specific life stages as they serve stage-related developmental processes.

During the third or fourth month of life, for example, the emotional experiences of an infant and caregiver play off each other more and more, giving rise to two emotional milestones of infancy: the ability to regulate emotions and the formation of attachment bonds with caregivers. The infant's achievement of these emotional milestones, in turn, triggers the emergence of exploratory behaviours. Feeling secure that their parents are nearby and available, infants increasingly are able to examine their surroundings. Similarly, Izard argues that emotional interactions of one kind or another eventually help trigger the achievement of such later cognitive and social milestones as the acquisition of moral standards, the ability to make social comparisons, the emergence of a self-concept, and the ability to think abstractly (Izard, 2007; Abe & Izard, 1999).

Before You Go On

www.wiley.com/go/comer

What Do You Know?

10. What cognitive milestones did Lewis identify as keys to emotional development in infants?
11. In Izard's view, what is the developmental relationship between cognition and emotion?

What Do You Think?

Imagine a toddler showing interest and happiness as she examines her reflection in a mirror with her mother nearby. How would you explain her emotions in terms of Lewis's cognitive-mediational theory? Izard's differential emotions theory?

SCAN TO GET THE ANSWERS

Emotion

WHAT HAPPENS IN THE BRAIN?

LEARNING OBJECTIVE 4

Identify the main brain structures that have been associated with emotion.

We noted earlier that evolution has helped shape human emotions in the same way that thousands of years of natural selection have helped mold and re-mold the human brain, enabling it to adapt to an ever-changing environment. The brain has not evolved as a single unified entity; rather, different parts have evolved at different times, each at its own pace. Thus, the brain structures involved in emotion are located in several different regions of the brain, rather than in a unified "emotion centre." The cluster of brain structures that are activated when we are confronted by a bear, for example, is different from the cluster of structures that springs into action when we feel lust or love toward someone.

Recent neuroscience research suggests that when people with an interest in politics view or listen to political statements, there is significant more activity in the pleasure and rewards centres of their brains than in the brains of those not interested in politics. (Gozzi, Zamboni, Kruegef, and Grafman, 2010)

Early Theories

As we observed earlier, Walter Cannon (1927, 1929) and Phillip Bard (1928, 1929, 1934) were among the first to propose that the brain plays a key role in the production of emotional states. Their view was supported by research in which they removed structures from the brains of cats, piece by piece, trying to pinpoint the area responsible for rage. They found that the removal of the *hypothalamus* affected this emotional response more than the removal of any other structure, and they concluded that this brain structure was the emotion centre of the brain (see **Figure 12-6**). They proposed that emotional stimuli first pass through sensory channels, such as vision and hearing, to the *thalamus*, a brain structure located above the hypothalamus. As we saw in Chapter 5, the thalamus serves as a relay station for a great deal of incoming information in the brain. For example, every sense except smell passes its information through the thalamus on its way for higher level processing. According to Cannon and Bard, the thalamus also sends the emotional information simultaneously to the hypothalamus and to the *cerebral cortex*, the region of the brain responsible for complex functions. The hypothalamus processes this information and produces a bodily response, while the cerebral cortex converts the information into a feeling—the conscious experience of emotion.

In 1937, an anatomy researcher named James Papez expanded Cannon and Bard's theory by suggesting that incoming sensory information is actually split by the thalamus into two *streams of information.* A *stream of thinking* is sent to the cerebral cortex for processing, while a *stream of feeling* is routed to the hypothalamus. The two streams eventually are reunited in the hypothalamus and a full emotional experience is produced (Dalgleish, 2004; LeDoux, 1996).

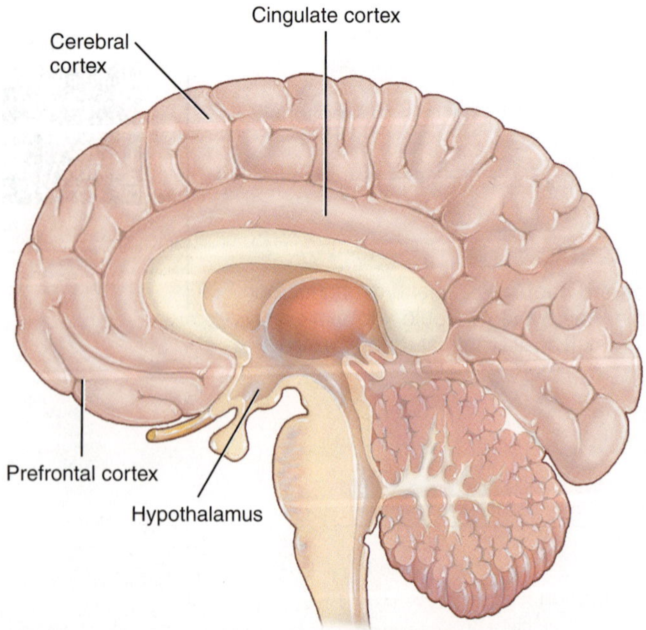

FIGURE 12-6 Brain structures linked to emotion. This figure indicates several of the brain parts that have been tied to emotion by various theories.

Conducting research during the same period as Papez, two other scientists, Heinrich Klüver and Paul Bucy, found evidence that the brain's *temporal lobes* also play a key role in emotion. In the course of research on vision, these two researchers found that monkeys whose temporal lobes had been removed became unusually tame and fearless (i.e., they lost their typical wariness) (Klüver & Bucy, 1937). Although Klüver and Bucy had not been investigating emotions per se, their finding suggested that much of the processing of emotional stimuli may take place in the temporal lobes.

In 1949, Paul MacLean coined the term *limbic system* to describe a system of brain structures that work together in creating emotions. The limbic system includes the thalamus, hypothalamus, hippocampus, cingulate cortex, amygdala, and prefrontal cortex—some of the same structures of interest to earlier emotion researchers. Because the limbic system includes many structures that are also present in less complex mammals, MacLean believed that the limbic system continues to be responsible for primitive brain functions, such as emotion, and that it, in fact, evolved to help humans control their emotional functioning.

Current Research

Although MacLean's notion that the limbic system plays an important role in emotions has been supported by numerous studies, recent research indicates that his ideas were not entirely correct. Research now specifies that the limbic system alone does not control emotion. Instead, as mentioned at the beginning of this section, emotional processes are controlled by a number of areas throughout the brain (Cain & LeDoux, 2008; Schiller et al., 2008; LeDoux, 1996).

Recently, considerable research has focused on the roles of the amygdala and the cerebral cortex in the experience of emotion, particularly the emotion of fear. In fact, according to the influential neuroscientist Joseph LeDoux (2008, 1996), the amygdala is "the hub" of fear in the brain. This almond-shaped structure located in front of the hippocampus is believed to have a direct connection with the thalamus, which allows for almost instantaneous processing of fear-related stimuli (see **Figure 12-7**). For example, if you were to stumble upon a snake while on a hiking trail or if you have stock and the market takes a 1,000-point drop, your thalamus would send the visual information directly to your amygdala, which would immediately produce bodily arousal and begin to prepare your body for danger. At the same time, the thalamus would also send the visual image of the snake to the visual centre of your cerebral cortex, which would process the information and then send that additional assessment to the amygdala as well. In a sense, the initial activation of the amygdala enables your brain to initiate a fear response before you even have a chance to think about the snake or stock value loss in front of you! As you may notice, this order of events is consistent with the early James-Lange theory that perceptions of environmental events produce physiological arousal and behavioural changes prior to the processing of that information by the cerebral cortex.

Most people with phobias—severe, sometimes disabling fears—can't remember what happened to cause their fear. LeDoux's theory suggests they might not remember because they responded so quickly. They might have an emotional memory of the event but no cognitive memory they can access.

Current research repeatedly highlights the importance of the amygdala in the conditioning and recognition of fear. It appears, for example, that individuals with damage to their amygdalas do not easily learn fear responses to various stimuli in the laboratory, while people whose amygdalas are intact readily learn these responses (Angrilli et al., 2008, 1996; Bechara et al., 1995). Moreover, in other research, it has been found that the amygdala becomes active when individuals look at pictures of faces depicting fear, but not when they observe faces depicting happiness (Morris et al., 1996). Conversely, people whose amygdalas are damaged cannot recognize facial expressions of fear, even though their ability to recognize facial expressions of other emotions remains intact (Berntson et al., 2007; Adolphs et al., 1994).

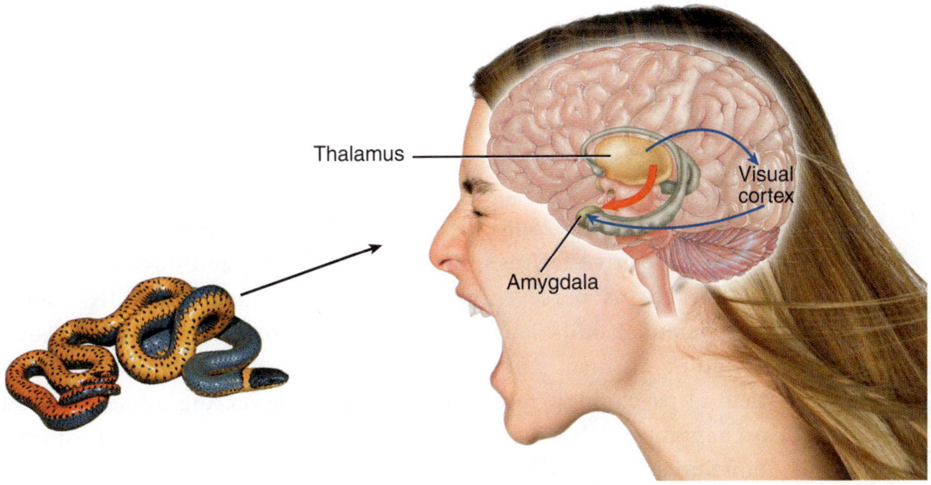

FIGURE 12-7 The brain's shortcut for fear. When sensory input arrives at the thalamus, the thalamus sends it along a fast route to the amygdala and along a slower route to the visual cortex. The shortcut direct to the amygdala allows us to react instantly before thinking (LeDoux, 2008, 1996).

Whereas the amygdala seems to be devoted primarily to fear, it appears that the *prefrontal cortex*, an area of the cerebral cortex, plays a role in the production of a range of both positive and negative emotions. One neuroimaging study found, for example, that participants displayed heightened activity in the right prefrontal cortex when they experienced negative emotions and in their left prefrontal cortex when they experienced positive emotions (Sutton & Davidson, 2000; Sutton et al., 1997). Similarly, other studies indicated that participants with damage to the left brain had a greater incidence of depression than did individuals with damage to the right brain. Still other research found that when people who were very anxious about social situations anticipated giving a public speech, the right prefrontal cortex showed increased activation (Davidson et al., 2000). This pattern of findings has led some researchers to wonder whether positive and negative emotions might be governed by two independent brain systems. Further explorations in this area might help explain why some people appear to be characteristically positive and upbeat—and often, as a result, more extroverted and risk-taking—while other people have a more depressive or negative outlook on life.

Research is also beginning to suggest that the prefrontal cortex may further be involved in *coordinating* emotional responses. Whereas the amygdala is responsible for the rapid processing of emotional information, particularly fear-related stimuli, the prefrontal cortex may serve the role of an emotional guide, turning emotional impulses into carefully planned and deliberate actions (Cain & LeDoux, 2008; LeDoux, 1996).

Before You Go On www.wiley.com/go/comer

What Do You Know?

12. What did Cannon and Bard identify as the emotion centre of the brain, and why?
13. How did MacLean combine the findings of earlier research?
14. According to recent research, what region of the brain is especially important in the experience of fear?

What Do You Think?

Why do you think identifying the parts of the brain responsible for emotion was difficult for early researchers? Why is such research more doable today?

SCAN TO GET THE ANSWERS

What About Positive Emotions?

LEARNING OBJECTIVE 5

Identify some factors that influence whether or not a person is happy.

After reading about the work of early emotion researchers, you may think that psychologists have a great deal to say about unpleasant or negative emotions, such as fear, anxiety, anger, and sadness, but less to say about how people experience pleasant, positive emotions, including happiness, pride, and excitement. The past decade, however, has witnessed a striking rise in research on positive emotions, particularly happiness. As you will recall from Chapter 1, a major new trend in the field of psychology is to focus on positive psychology (Seligman, 2007; Seligman & Steen, 2005). *Positive psychology* is the study and enhancement of positive feelings, including happiness and optimism; positive traits, such as perseverance and wisdom; positive abilities, such as interpersonal skills; and virtues that enhance the well-being of society, including altruism and tolerance. Consistent with this important new field of psychology, researchers are now conducting numerous studies on happiness. We have learned that it is indeed one of the most important and adaptive of human emotions.

In fact, regarding happiness, the news seems to be quite good. Research indicates that people's lives are, in general, more upbeat than psychologists used to think. In fact, most people around the world say they are happy—including most of those who are poor, unemployed, elderly, and disabled (**Table 12-2**) (Becchetti & Santoro, 2007; Pugno, 2007; Wallis, 2005). Of course, happiness involves different things for different people.

"For me, music making is the most joyful activity possible, the most perfect expression of any emotion."
—Luciano Pavarotti, Italian opera tenor

Consider the following results:

- Wealthy people appear only slightly happier than those of modest means (Easterbrook, 2005; Diener et al., 1993).
- Although early studies suggested only a minimal relationship between age and happiness (Myers & Diener, 1997; Inglehart, 1990), more recent studies have found that, provided they remain healthy, people over 65 actually report more happiness and less negative emotion than do younger people (Mroczek & Spiro, 2007, 2005; Mroczek, 2004).

TABLE 12-2 Happiness Levels Around the World, 2000–2008

How Much People Enjoy Their Lives as a Whole, on a Scale of 0 to 10			
Iceland	8.5	France	6.5
Denmark	8.4	Vietnam	6.5
Colombia	8.1	Greece	6.4
Switzerland	8.1	Japan	6.4
Mexico	8.0	Peru	6.4
Finland	7.8	China	6.3
Australia	7.7	Philippines	6.3
Norway	7.7	Iran	6.0
Sweden	7.7	South Africa	6.0
Canada	**7.6**	Bolivia	5.9
Argentina	7.5	India	5.9
Ireland	7.5	Dominican Republic	5.7
Netherlands	7.5	Ecuador	5.7
Brazil	7.4	Ghana	5.7
Costa Rica	7.3	Lebanon	5.6
New Zealand	7.3	Hungary	5.5
Germany	7.2	Kosovo	5.5
Spain	7.2	Turkey	5.5
Venezuela	7.2	Russia	5.4
United Arab Emirates	7.1	Bosnia	5.3
Britain	7.1	Kenya	5.2
Guatemala	7.0	Egypt	5.1
Malta	7.0	Afghanistan	4.7
Saudi Arabia	7.0	Iraq	4.3
United States of America	7.0	Pakistan	4.3
Belize	6.9	Chad	4.2
Chile	6.8	Togo	4.1
Italy	6.8	Angola	4.0
Israel	6.7	Zimbabwe	3.3
Jamaica	6.6	Tanzania	3.2

Source: Adapted from Veenhoven, R., *Average happiness in 144 nations 2000–2008*, World Database of Happiness, Rank Report 2009-1c. Retrieved from: worlddatabaseofhappiness.eur.nl

PRACTICALLY SPEAKING Measuring Your Emotional Well-Being

Think about what you have been doing and experiencing during the past four weeks. Then report how much you experienced each of the following feelings, using the scale below. For each item, select a number from 1 to 5, and write that number on the line next to the feeling:

1 Very rarely or never

2 Rarely

3 Sometimes

4 Often

5 Very often or always

____ Positive (1)	____ Unpleasant (9)
____ Negative (2)	____ Happy (10)
____ Good (3)	____ Sad (11)
____ Bad (4)	____ Angry (12)
____ Pleasant (5)	____ Afraid (13)
____ Contented (6)	____ Loving (14)
____ Interested (7)	____ Depressed (15)
____ Stressed (8)	____ Joyful (16)

A Pleasant feelings: Add up your scores on items 1, 3, 5, 6, 7, 10, 14, and 16 (8 items), and place your score here: ________

B Unpleasant feelings: Add up your scores on items 2, 4, 8, 9, 11, 12, 13, and 15 (8 items), and place your score here: ________

Pleasant feelings

8–13	Extremely low pleasant feelings
14–18	Very low
19–23	Low
24–27	Moderate
28–30	High
31–35	Very high
36–40	Extremely high pleasant feelings

Unpleasant feelings

8–11	Extremely low unpleasant feelings
12–16	Very low
17–20	Low
21–25	Moderate
26–28	High
29–31	Very high
32–40	Extremely high unpleasant feelings

Your happiness balance

Besides your overall pleasant feelings and unpleasant feelings scores, you can also examine the relation between the two, in what is called "hedonic balance," or the amount of pleasant feelings you experience minus the amount of unpleasant feelings.

Subtract your Unpleasant Feelings Score from your Pleasant Feelings Score and put your answer here: ________

Balance scores

24 to 32	Very happy
16 to 23	Happy
5 to 15	Slightly happy
4 to –3	Neutral, mixed
–4 to –12	Somewhat unhappy
–13 to –23	Very unhappy
–24 to –32	Extremely unhappy

Individual emotion items

Besides the summed scores and their balance score, you can also examine individual items.

You ought to be feeling general positive feelings, such as "good" or "positive," the majority of the time, unless some bad event has just occurred in your life. If you are not feeling positive, good, or pleasant most of the time, and only experience these feelings rarely, you should examine why.

Similarly, you should be experiencing negative feelings a minority of the time. If you feel stressed sometimes, but not often, you may feel that this is acceptable. But for some feelings, such as "depressed" and "angry," it is usually most beneficial to feel these emotions only rarely or very rarely.

Do any of your individual emotions stand out? That is, which of the positive feelings do you have less often? If you are interested and positive most of the time, this is a very good sign. When you examine your negative feelings, are there any that you feel substantially more often? If you are frequently afraid, angry, sad, depressed, or stressed, are there steps you can take to reduce those emotions?

If you are unsure what your pattern of responses is telling you or if you are concerned about what you see, you could visit the student wellness or counselling centre on your campus and talk with someone there about your concerns.

Source: Reprinted with permission from Ed Diener and Robert Biswas-Diener, *Happiness: Unlocking the Mysteries of Psychological Wealth* (Malden, MA: Blackwell Publishing, 2008), pp. 237–239.

- Over 90 percent of people with quadriplegia say they are glad to be alive, and overall, people with spinal cord injuries report feeling only slightly less happy than other people (Diener & Diener, 1996).

No age limit. People who are happy when younger tend to remain happy as they age. On average, older people are as likely as younger people to be happy, and perhaps more likely.

Men and women are equally likely to declare themselves satisfied or very happy. Overall, only one person in ten reports being "not too happy" (Myers, 2000; Myers & Diener, 1996), and only one in seven reports waking up unhappy (Wallis, 2005).

People might avoid the extreme ends of the 10-point scale due to social desirability (Fisher & Dubé, 2005) or not wanting to appear non-average. On the other hand, some people are indeed happier than others. Those who are generally happy seem to remain happy from decade to decade, regardless of job changes, moves, and family changes (Becchetti & Santoro, 2007; Myers & Diener, 1996). Such people adjust to negative events and return to their usual cheerful state within a few months (Diener et al., 2007, 1992). Conversely, unhappy people are not cheered much in the long term, even by positive events. Some theorists believe that people have a "happiness set point" to which they consistently return, despite life's ups and downs. However, this notion is not always supported by research (Diener et al., 2007; Lucas, 2007).

Some studies suggest that one's sense of happiness may have a genetic component (Roysamb, 2006; Lykken & Tellegen, 1996). Indeed, one of the most dominant factors in determining happiness may be temperament. Twin studies have found that identical twins' ratings of happiness are generally similar, and other researchers have reported that the single best predictor of future happiness is past happiness (Diener & Lucas, 1999). These findings may suggest that a temperamental predisposition to look at life optimistically is more important than an individual's life situation.

Research also indicates that happiness is linked to our personality characteristics and our typical ways of cognitively interpreting events (Diener et al., 2007; Stewart et al., 2005; Diener, 2000). Happy people are, for example, generally optimistic, outgoing, curious, and tender-minded. They also tend to possess high self-esteem, be spiritual, be goal directed, and have a sense of perseverance and of control over their lives (Peterson et al., 2007; Sahoo et al., 2005; Diener & Seligman, 2002).

A longitudinal study published in the journal Science *found that highly optimistic people had a 55 percent reduced risk of death from any cause and a 23 percent reduced risk of heart problems, compared with highly pessimistic people* (Giltay et al., 2004).

It appears that good relationships are related to happiness and satisfaction. Married people tend to be happier than single people (although this effect may be stronger for men than for women) (Myers, 2000; DeNeve, 1999). And in what may or may not be surprising news to you, college students who have close friends and significant others are happier than college students who do not (Diener & Seligman, 2002).

Before You Go On

www.wiley.com/go/comer

What Do You Know?

15. Why do some researchers suggest that we may have a happiness "set point"?
16. What are some of the life circumstances positively related to happiness and satisfaction?

What Do You Think?

How would you advise a friend who asked you for tips on how he or she could be happier?

SCAN TO GET THE ANSWERS

The Range of Emotional Experience — HOW WE DIFFER

LEARNING OBJECTIVE 6

Identify and discuss the emotional dimensions on which people may differ.

There are as many emotional experiences as there are people. Do you know anyone who experiences emotions in exactly the same way you do? Probably not. People experience their emotions in a variety of ways. In extreme cases, these differences may even amount to psychological disturbances. Let's examine both differences in how people experience emotion and psychological disturbances of emotion, and conclude with a discussion of current research in the field of positive emotions.

Same situation, different emotions. As the faces and body language of these soccer fans reveal, people often react to the same situation very differently.

Some researchers suggest that patterns in the variations in which people experience emotions may have important implications for how we adapt to circumstances in our environments. As we discussed in Chapter 10, for example, people high in *emotional intelligence*—the ability to recognize, produce, and understand emotions—can use emotions to promote their intellectual and emotional growth, as well as for purposes of reasoning, problem solving, and emotion management (Grewal, Brackett, & Salovey, 2006; Mayer & Salovey, 2004, 1997).

Before we can make use of our emotions, however, we must feel them. Researchers have identified some common patterns in how different people experience emotions, as well as differences among individuals in our ability to regulate our emotions. Psychologists have also investigated gender and cultural differences in emotion.

Features of Emotional Responding

A good deal of research has focused on three features of our emotional responding: the clarity of our emotions, the attention we pay to them, and the intensity with which we feel emotions. In different individuals, these three characteristics combine into identifiable clusters or patterns of emotional responding.

Emotional Clarity *Clarity* in understanding one's emotions has been described as the ability to accurately identify and distinguish one's emotions (Barrett et al., 2001). If we vaguely experience our emotions as being either pleasant or unpleasant, we cannot develop clear strategies for reducing or enhancing particular emotions or for navigating particular social circumstances (Gohm, 2003). If, however, we are able to accurately identify and distinguish emotions (say, guilt and anger), we can better understand the causes of those emotions, the context in which they occur, and the most appropriate responses to make in particular situations (Barrett et al., 2007, 2001).

Attention to Emotions A process closely related to emotional clarity is *attention to emotion*, which has been described as a person's tendency to take notice of, value, and focus on his emotions and moods (Gohm, 2003). People who are aware of and attend more to their emotions typically have greater access to them and greater ability to use them in positive and meaningful ways. Conversely, persons who tend to ignore emotions or deem them irrelevant are less able to identify or control them (Gohm, 2003). Through instruction and practice, individuals can become more skilled at attending to their emotions, but such improvements may be limited by the individuals' inborn sensitivity to visceral and other physiological changes that occur within their bodies (Larsen, 2000).

Emotional Intensity Emotional intensity refers to the characteristic strength with which an individual typically experiences emotions. Of course, the magnitude of our emotions is related to the magnitude of the emotional stimuli that we encounter. Nevertheless, some individuals may react intensely to a mild experience (say, a bad grade on a minor homework assignment), while others may barely respond to situations that most individuals would find extremely upsetting (such as a failing grade in a required class). Research has confirmed that individuals who report heightened levels of emotional intensity display stronger emotional responses to the same emotional stimulus than do individuals who report low intensity (Larsen & Diener, 1987).

emotional intensity the characteristic strength with which an individual typically experiences emotion.

Touched by music. The pure ecstasy on the face of this gentleman as he listens to a musical recording suggests that he may generally display high degrees of emotional intensity, attentiveness, and recognition—the so-called "hot" cluster of emotional responding.

Many theorists believe that emotional intensity is a stable trait that generalizes across different kinds of emotions (Charles & Piazza, 2007; Bachorowski & Braaten, 1994; Larsen & Diener, 1987). In support of this notion, studies have found that people who react to positive daily life events with strong positive emotions (say, great joy) also tend to react to negative life events with strong negative emotions (such as intense anger), while those who react to positive events with mild positive emotions react to negative life events with mild negative emotions (Larsen, Diener, & Emmons, 1986; Diener et al., 1985).

Some people who experience emotions very intensely worry that their emotions are too influential and try to dampen their mood states, especially when they are experiencing negative emotions (Gohm, 2003). Such people may also find it uncomfortable to focus too long on their emotions. Conversely, individuals who experience low levels of emotional intensity often find it hard to identify their feelings and may therefore have less access to the useful information provided by emotions. Perhaps not surprisingly, some theorists believe *moderate* emotional intensity to be the ideal level in most circumstances. All this suggests that people vary in terms of how they typically experience emotions, and researchers have studied that variability directly.

PSYCHOLOGY AROUND US Fearless

Psychologists have devoted many studies to people who experience intense fear. They have also conducted research on individuals who are afraid but nevertheless act bravely—people often called *courageous* (Rachman, 2004, 1989). But they have almost ignored people who experience no fear at all—individuals who go through life untouched by anxiety of any kind. Yet, they are out there. Consider the real-life case of SM, a woman referred to by these initials to protect her identity (Feinstein et al., 2011). At first glance, SM seems to be a typical, everyday 44-year-old mother. In fact, however, she was born with two tiny, symmetrical black holes where her amygdala should be. As a result, SM demonstrates complete and absolute fearlessness. Scientists have taken her to haunted houses and horror films. There, SM might exhibit a little curiosity, but she is otherwise unaffected. SM claims to be afraid of snakes, but if scientists take her to a pet store, she can pet or hold snakes with no problem. The woman has been the victim of multiple crimes and has been threatened with both a knife and a gun. Once, she was almost killed. Yet she demonstrates no lasting trauma from any of the crimes, and remembers feeling more or less calm during each situation.

Regulation of Emotions Let's look more closely at the regulation of emotions. Because emotions have "the capacity to either enhance or undermine effective functioning," reducing or otherwise regulating them is often necessary (Thompson, 1994, p. 25). When, for example, emotions occur at inopportune times, are too intense, or run counter to one's goals, dampening them through some form of emotion regulation may be the most desirable response. In fact, we often exert considerable control over our emotions, using various strategies to help influence what emotions we have, when we have them, and how we experience them (Hien et al., 2009; Gross & John, 2003; Gross, 1998).

Efforts to regulate emotions begin very early in life and continue throughout the lifespan (Cicchetti, Ganiban, & Barnett, 1991). Theorists have suggested that the presence or absence of stressors early in a person's life, the person's temperament, and the models available in the person's family and in social settings may influence how that person comes to perceive and experience emotions. Depending on such factors, individuals may develop either adaptive or maladaptive styles of regulation (Linehan & Dexter-Mazza, 2008; Linehan, 1993).

emotion dysregulation unhealthy attempts to regulate emotion.

Unhealthy attempts to regulate one's emotions are referred to as **emotion dysregulation** (Chapman, Leung, & Lynch, 2008; Linehan, 1993). Dysregulation occurs when efforts at regulation inadvertently prevent us from effectively adapting to our life circumstances or negatively influence our overall well-being. Someone who tries to control her emotions by *suppressing* them may find the strategy helpful in the short run, particularly when it decreases the intensity of a strongly negative emotion. Continuing to suppress emotions in situation after situation, however, may eventually backfire, reducing the person's ability to adjust to life circumstances or to attain goals (Cole & Hall, 2008; Carver & Scheier, 1998).

It is often difficult to specify what constitutes adaptive or maladaptive emotional regulation, because emotions depend so much on context. Although suppression of emotions is often a bad thing, there are some occasions when emotions should be suppressed, or at least modulated. For example, even though sharing private information about ourselves often helps us develop intimacy with someone, too much disclosure can on occasion lead to distress and ambivalence on the listener's part (Christophe & Rimé, 1997). Indeed, most of us can recall instances in which we felt very uncomfortable when people we hardly knew shared a little bit too much about themselves. Research indicates that relationships benefit from an emphasis on positive emotion in the early stages. Over time, though, the rules change, and our friendships depend on a balance of positive and negative information. In one study, strangers were found to focus on happiness-related topics when interacting, while friends focused on both happiness- and anger-related topics (Clark & Taraban, 1991).

> "A real gentleman, even if he loses everything he owns, must show no emotion."
> —*Fyodor Dostoevsky, Russian writer*

Gender Differences in Emotion

One of the more enduring stereotypes in Western society is that women are inherently more "emotional" than men (Fischer & Manstead, 2000). Whereas men traditionally have been seen as "calm, cool, and rational" in emotional situations, women have been viewed as being more emotionally intense and more likely to express their feelings openly. Consistent with these stereotypical views, women typically report that they express emotions more than men do, and that they experience emotions more intensively (John & Gross, 2007; Gross & John, 1998; Grossman & Wood, 1993). In one self-report study, for example, female participants reported experiencing more intense emotions than male participants did, as well as expressing more positive and negative emotions (Gross & John, 1998). Such differences between the genders also have been reported when researchers observe the social interactions, facial expressions, and verbalizations of males and females (Brody, 1999; Dimberg & Lundquist, 1990).

display rules cultural expectations that prescribe how, when, and by whom emotions should be expressed.

At first glance, while these findings seem to support the stereotypical view that women are biologically more emotional than men, alternative interpretations are certainly possible. It may be, for example, that when women report experiencing and expressing their emotions more intensely than men, they are being influenced by **display rules**—cultural expectations that prescribe how, when, and by whom emotions should be expressed. In families and society at large, for example, expressions of anger are more socially acceptable for males than for females. Similarly, as we shall see in Chapter 14, society deems it more acceptable for females to express nurturing emotions such as love and warmth (Safdar et al., 2009: Brody, 1999).

One study found that women more often conform to *feminine* display rules, including the suppression of negative emotions and the expression of positive emotions, whereas men more often conform to *masculine* display rules, such as the suppression of positive emotions and the expression of negative emotions (Simpson & Stroh, 2004). Another study found a relationship between participants' acceptance of societal norms and their experiences of emotionality (Grossman & Wood, 1993). For example, female participants who believed that women should experience emotions more intensely than men do tended to actually experience their own emotions with greater intensity than male participants did.

It appears that when cultural display rules are removed from the equation, many of the male–female differences in emotionality disappear. For example, studies have found fewer differences between the emotional experiences of men and women in countries with a greater focus on female empowerment and male–female equality. In such countries, males and females show similar emotional intensities (Fischer et al., 2004). In short, it may be that men and women are actually wired for similar patterns of emotionality, but have learned from society to experience and express their emotions differently.

Narrowing the gender gap. Although research indicates that women, on average, may experience and express emotions more intensely than men, that gender difference seems to be fading. Upon receiving their medals at the 2004 Olympic Games, German canoers Christian Gille and Thomasz Wylenzek expressed their joy, pride, and relief with the same flow of tears (*left*) as that displayed by 2008 Olympic gold medal pole vaulter Elena Isinbaeva of Russia (*right*).

Cultural and Ethnic Differences in Emotion

Emotionality does not vary from culture to culture as much as one might expect. Earlier, we observed that people from cultures across the world tend to display emotions with the same facial expressions and to interpret facial expressions of emotionality in a consistent way. It is true that some cultures do differ in the *language* of emotionality; for example, in Gidjingali, an Australian aboriginal language, only one word, *gurakadj*, is available to describe a range of fearful emotions, from terror, horror, and dread to apprehension and timidity; and in Ecuador, the Quichua people lack any word at all for remorse (Tousignant, 1984; Hiatt, 1978). Despite these sorts of differences, there is considerable overlap from culture to culture with respect to the primary categories used to classify emotions.

In Japan, pharmaceutical companies had a hard time making headway with treatments for mild depression because the Japanese considered depression a bad word. In response, companies changed their marketing language to target depression as a medical illness called kokoro no kaze *("cold of the soul"). Physician referrals for depression skyrocketed 46 percent between 1999 and 2003.* (Schulz, 2004)

When differences between cultural groups are observed, they commonly are due to differences in display rules. Early research, for example, found that Japanese and American participants differed in how the presence of another person affected their expression of negative emotion. When they were left alone, both Japanese and American participants displayed similar expressions of anger, disgust, fear, and sadness in reaction to a negative stimulus. However, when an experimenter remained seated in the room, the Americans continued to exhibit expressions of negative emotions, while the Japanese participants masked their negative emotions with smiles.

The Japanese participants in this study were probably conforming to a culture-specific display rule that prohibits the expression of negative emotions in the presence of a higher-status individual. In Japan's collectivist society, group harmony, cohesion, and cooperation are valued first and foremost, with individual needs and individualistic traits, such as uniqueness and autonomy, considered secondary (Matsumoto et al., 1998). Thus, the Japanese participants in this study may have been smiling in the presence of the experimenter to display harmony and respect for the experimenter's status (Safdar et al., 2009; Ekman, 1972; Friesen, 1972).

Dialects and Facial Expressions of Emotion: Does Your Face Have an Accent?

As we have seen in this chapter, there is strong evidence that certain basic facial expressions are expressed and recognizable on most faces cross-culturally. However, are there any cultural variations in the expression and reading of facial expressions? Well, just as there are different accents among the speakers of a particular language (think of English spoken in Ontario and in Newfoundland, or French in Quebec and in France) it may well be that there are different dialects in the facial expression of emotion.

In one study, Martin Beaupré and Ursula Hess (2004) from the University of Quebec in Montreal examined the abilities of French Canadians, Chinese Canadians, and African Canadians to identify facial expressions of happiness, anger, fear, disgust, and shame on a range of Canadian faces. They found that most participants were adept at recognizing most emotional expressions, in line with Darwin's and Ekman's views that the facial expression of emotions is universal. However, French Canadians in the study were slightly better at identifying shame and sadness, while all participants most often correctly noted fear when expressed in an African Canadian face. The researchers suggest that these results show both cultural similarities and cultural differences in experience in reading certain facial expression of emotion, and that some types of faces are better at expressing certain types of emotions.

In another study, these same researchers (Elfenbein, Beaupré, Lévesque, & Hess, 2007) looked very closely at the facial muscles used to express particular emotions among French-speaking participants from Quebec and Gabon (the

Facial dialects. Can you see the dialect differences (the facial accents) in the expressions of emotion in these pictures? (From Elfenbein, Beaupré, Lévesque, & Hess, 2007).

Gabonese Republic in West Central Africa). Participants were asked to show certain facial expressions of emotion as if they were displaying them to friends, so that they would display the emotions as they typically do within their cultural group. By closely examining the actual muscles used to produce each facial expression, the researchers were able to see cultural differences (or facial dialects) in the expression of serenity, shame, and contempt, and also for anger, sadness, surprise, and happiness, but not for fear, disgust, or embarrassment. The pictures at left show some of these differences or dialect effects.

In the study looking directly at facial dialects (Elfenbein, Beaupré, Lévesque, & Hess, 2007), these researchers coached French-speaking participants from Quebec and Gabon to display facial expressions using as close to a standard pattern of facial muscles as they could manage. They then had other participants "read" all the facial expressions produced. Despite the efforts to standardize facial expressions and remove the facial dialect effects, the researchers found that participants were more accurate in their reading of those facial expressions from their own cultural community that had shown differences in the second study. So even when efforts were made to remove facial "accents," they were still visible and usable by participants familiar with them. Do you think your face has an accent? Grab a mirror and have a look!

Before You Go On

www.wiley.com/go/comer

What Do You Know?

17. What is emotional clarity?
18. What factors may influence the techniques people use to control their emotions?
19. What are display rules and how do they affect emotional differences?

What Do You Think?

Build your own emotional profile by estimating your levels of emotional intelligence, clarity, attention, intensity, and regulation. How easy or difficult do you believe it would be to change your emotional profile?

SCAN TO GET THE ANSWERS

Disorders of Emotion

WHEN THINGS GO WRONG

LEARNING OBJECTIVE 7

Describe how malfunctions in emotional processes are related to psychological disorders.

Earlier, we observed that people differ from one another in the clarity, attention, intensity, and regulation of their emotions. It turns out that extreme manifestations of these features of emotion may contribute to psychological disturbances of one kind or another.

- *Clarity of emotions* Researchers have found that people who are largely unable to identify and describe their emotions, commonly referred to as *alexithymia*, often confuse their emotions with symptoms of medical problems and develop numerous bodily fears and health complaints (Cox et al., 1994).

Mixed emotions. Leaving home to attend a college or university that is far away is likely to leave most people with mixed emotions—happy and excited to be starting a new chapter of your life, but sad to be leaving friends and family behind.

- *Attention to emotions* People who attend to their emotions too much, a pattern called *hypervigilance*, tend to be more anxious than other people (Vujanovic et al., 2007; Swinkels & Giuliano, 1995). Because of their heightened self-focus, they keep noticing signs of arousal that other people are not even aware of, and they repeatedly appraise such arousal in ways that cause them constant worry.
- *Intensity of emotions* People who experience too little emotion may be incapable of caring deeply for and relating effectively with other people. An extreme form of this problem is found among individuals with *antisocial personality disorder*, a pattern that we will be examining more in Chapters 13 and 16. People who display this pattern seem to experience little or no guilt or anxiety, and thus are more likely to violate the needs of other people and are less likely to learn from the adverse consequences of their actions (Cleckley, 1941). Indeed, studies reveal that when such persons are exposed in the laboratory to unpleasant stimuli, they experience little emotion intensity at all (Patrick, 1994; Patrick, Bradley, & Lang, 1993).
- *Mixed emotions* We often think of emotions as opposing pairs. For example, you might be either sad *or* happy, angry *or* calm. Common experience tells us, however, that often we experience *mixed emotions*, degrees and combinations of emotions that lie in between such pairs of opposites. As you have seen in this chapter, positive and negative emotional experiences may reflect activation of different areas of the brain, particularly different areas of the prefrontal cortex (LeDoux, 1995). If so, it seems to imply that we could indeed feel both positive and negative emotions simultaneously.

Studies demonstrate clearly that such mixed emotions exist (Larsen, McGraw, & Cacioppo, 2001). In one experiment, for example, researchers found that participants felt both happy and sad simultaneously after they had received both a smaller reward and a smaller loss than they had expected (Larsen et al., 2004). Perhaps not surprisingly, researchers have also found that we are most likely to experience mixed emotions in emotionally complex situations (Larsen et al., 2007, 2004). For example, on finding out you have been accepted to an out-of-province university that you really wanted to attend, you might feel delighted with the acceptance but sad to be leaving friends behind.

- *Regulation of emotions* People who cannot regulate their emotions often develop self-defeating ways of trying to bring order to their emotional lives (Bradley, 2000). As you will see in Chapter 13, for example, people with *borderline personality disorder* experience a severe inability to regulate their intense emotions. They may show impulsivity or even resort to self-mutilation in what many theorists view as dysfunctional attempts to regulate their intense emotional reactions (Nock & Prinstein, 2004; Gratz, 2003; APA, 2000).

Similarly, research suggests that women with bulimia nervosa (discussed in Chapter 11) experience their emotions as particularly dysregulated, leading many theorists to conclude that binge-eating and purging behaviour represent maladaptive attempts by those

PSYCHOLOGY AROUND US Overregulated

Clearly, poor regulation of one's emotions can lead to all kinds of problems. But overregulation—too much control—is no bargain either. Researchers at the University of Minnesota showed a group of college students a pair of particularly disgusting movie scenes—a scene in a dirty public toilet in *Trainspotting* and a projectile vomiting scene from *Monty Python's The Meaning of Life* (Vohs et al., 2011). The experimenters instructed half of the students in the study to suppress their emotional reactions to the movie, but allowed the other half to react however they pleased. After watching the movie scenes, the student participants were told they were going to play an online game in which they could blast an opponent with noise. The participants who had been asked to suppress their emotions earlier now opted to blast their opponents with substantially louder noise than did the non-suppressing participants. It appears that overregulation of emotions may catch up with people sooner or later.

individuals to deal with their chaotic emotions (Safer, Telch, & Agras, 2001; Westen & Harnden-Fischer, 2001).

Given that emotional irregularities can disrupt functioning so severely, many observers believe that all psychological disorders involve some degree of disturbance in emotional functioning (Gard & Kring, 2009; Yuan & Kring, 2009; Kring & Bachorowski, 1999). For certain psychological disorders, however, emotional disturbances seem to be the central and defining features of the problem. These disorders, sometimes called *emotional disorders*, include the *anxiety disorders* and *mood disorders*.

Anxiety Disorders

Some people experience such levels of disabling fear and anxiety that they cannot lead normal lives. They are said to have an *anxiety disorder*. Anxiety disorders are collectively the most prevalent of all mental disorders, and we will discuss them further in Chapter 15. Four prominent disorders of this kind are *phobias*, *generalized anxiety disorder*, *panic disorder*, and *obsessive-compulsive disorder*.

The most common phobic object in the world is the spider. An intense fear of these arthropods is called arachnophobia.

You already came across phobias in Chapter 7. A **phobia** is a persistent and unreasonable fear of a particular object, activity, or situation. Everyone has areas of special fear, and it is normal for a person to be upset by some things more than other things. A phobia, however, is more intense, persistent, and disruptive than such common fears (APA, 2000).

phobia a persistent and unreasonable fear of a particular object, activity, or situation.

People with **generalized anxiety disorder** experience excessive anxiety under most circumstances. They seem to worry all the time. They also seem to have a cognitive bias that leads them to interpret almost every situation as threatening (Beck & Weishaar, 2011).

generalized anxiety disorder an anxiety disorder in which people feel excessive anxiety and worry under most circumstances.

Individuals with **panic disorder** experience repeated *panic attacks*. These short bouts of panic occur suddenly and feature palpitations of the heart, tingling in the hands or feet, shortness of breath, sweating, hot and cold flashes, trembling, chest pains, faintness, and dizziness. Panic-prone people are more attentive to their bodily sensations than other individuals, experience more intense bodily sensations, and are more inclined to misinterpret their sensations (Nardi et al., 2008, 2001). Indeed, during a panic attack many people fear they will die, go crazy, or lose control (Health Canada, 2002).

panic disorder an anxiety disorder in which people experience periodic, short bouts of panic, called panic attacks.

As noted in Chapter 9, *obsessions* are persistent thoughts or images that seem to invade a person's consciousness. *Compulsions* are repetitive and rigid behaviours that people feel they must perform. A diagnosis of **obsessive-compulsive disorder (OCD)** is made when obsessions or compulsions are excessive, cause great distress, take up much time, and interfere with daily functions (Health Canada, 2002). In this disorder, the obsessions cause intense anxiety, and the compulsions are aimed at preventing or reducing this anxiety.

obsessive-compulsive disorder (OCD) an anxiety disorder in which obsessions or compulsions feel excessive or unreasonable, cause great distress, take up much time, or interfere with daily functions.

Mood Disorders

Most people's moods are transient. Their feelings of happiness or sadness rise and fall in response to daily events. In contrast, the moods of people with mood disorders last a long time, colour all of their interactions with the world, and interfere with normal functioning (Health Canada, 2002).

Everyone is vulnerable. A number of well-known Canadians have openly discussed their struggles with depression, including actor Jim Carrey, poet Leonard Cohen, and singers/songwriters Oscar Lopez and Alanis Morissette. It can happen to anyone.

depression a persistent sad state in which life seems dark and its challenges overwhelming.

mania a persistent state of euphoria or frenzied energy.

unipolar depression a mood disorder that includes only depression.

bipolar disorder a mood disorder in which periods of mania alternate with periods of depression.

Depression and *mania* are the key emotions in mood disorders. **Depression** is a markedly sad state in which life seems dark and its challenges overwhelming. **Mania**, the opposite of depression in many ways, is a state of frenzied energy in which people may have an exaggerated belief that they can do and accomplish anything. Mania is a much more intense emotion than happiness, the positive emotion that we looked at earlier. Most people with a mood disorder suffer only from depression, a pattern called **unipolar depression**. Others experience periods of mania that alternate with periods of depression, a pattern called **bipolar disorder** (Health Canada, 2002). Given what you have read in this chapter, you probably won't be surprised to hear that a variety of factors—cognitive, behavioural, and biochemical, as well as emotional—combine to produce these disorders. We will be looking at them in greater detail in Chapter 16.

Before You Go On

www.wiley.com/go/comer

What Do You Know?

20. Extreme variations of which individual differences in emotion have been linked to psychological disorders?
21. List and describe four major anxiety disorders.
22. List four mood disorders.

SCAN TO GET THE ANSWERS

What Do You Think?

Analyze a character from a film you have seen or a book you have read who has one of the disorders described in this chapter. Is the information provided in the text consistent with what you know of the character?

Summary

What Is Emotion?

LEARNING OBJECTIVE 1 Define emotion and discuss the components, measurement, and functions of emotion.

- An *emotion* is an intrapersonal state that occurs in response to an external or internal event and includes three components: a *physiological component*, a *cognitive component*, and a *behavioural component*.
- To measure emotion, researchers typically use three kinds of information: *behavioural displays of emotion*, *self-reports of emotion*, and *physiological reactions*.
- Emotions serve many functions. They add colour to our lives, give us information about important events in the environment, stir us to action when necessary, and help us to coordinate relationships with others.

Theories of Emotion

LEARNING OBJECTIVE 2 Discuss the major theories of emotion, and identify the pathways through which emotions are experienced according to each theory.

- The conventional *common sense explanation of emotion* holds that an event triggers an emotion, which leads to physiological changes, followed by a response to the situation.
- In contrast, the *James-Lange theory* proposes that the emotion we feel results from bodily and behavioural responses to environmental stimuli, rather than causing those responses.
- According to the *Cannon-Bard theory*, physiological arousal by itself cannot produce complex emotional experiences. Rather, the perception of an emotionally stirring event simultaneously sends messages to parts of the brain responsible for the subjective experience of emotion and physiological arousal.
- *Schachter and Singer's two-factor theory* holds that an emotional state is a function of both physiological arousal and cognition.
- Building on Schachter and Singer's two-factor theory, *cognitive-mediational theory* proposes that cognitive interpretations, and particularly appraisals, of events are in fact the keys to the experience of emotions.
- The *facial-feedback theory* of emotion, based on the ideas of Darwin, holds that facial expressions that occur in response to stimuli provide feedback to the brain that helps to shape emotional experience.
- *Evolutionary theorists* believe that emotions have been shaped by natural selection and that certain emotions have been passed down because of their role in the survival of our species.

Emotion *How We Develop*

LEARNING OBJECTIVE 3 Contrast the cognitive theory of emotional development with the differential emotions theory.

- According to Lewis's *cognitive theory of emotional development*, emotions unfold in infants as a consequence of neural and cognitive development, with the most significant development achieved by the age of 3 years.
- In contrast, Izard's *differential emotions theory* holds that emotions, rather than emerging as a result of cognitive development, actually help to trigger cognitive development. In this view, emotions serve stage-related developmental processes.

Emotion *What Happens in the Brain?*

LEARNING OBJECTIVE 4 Identify the main brain structures that have been associated with emotion.

- Early researchers Cannon and Bard believed that emotional stimuli are routed by the *thalamus* to the *cerebral cortex* and the *hypothalamus*, which they considered the emotion centre of the brain.
- Papez noted that the process was more complex and proposed that the *cingulate cortex* and the *hippocampus* are also involved, providing integration functions.
- Klüver and Bucy found evidence that the *temporal lobes* play a role in the processing of emotional stimuli.
- MacLean proposed that a collection of brain areas, which he called the *limbic system*, is responsible for primitive brain functions, such as emotion.
- Considerable current research has focused on the roles of the *amygdala* and the *cerebral cortex* in the experience of emotion.

What About Positive Emotions?

LEARNING OBJECTIVE 5 Identify some factors that influence whether or not a person is happy.

- Researchers have tended to focus on negative emotions, in part because of difficulties in measuring positive emotions.
- Identifying what makes people happy can be difficult. Research has shown that good relationships, employment, goal-directed behaviour, religious belief, and good health are among the things that can make people happy. In particular, though, temperament and personality predict happiness.

The Range of Emotional Experience *How We Differ*

LEARNING OBJECTIVE 6 Identify and discuss the emotional dimensions on which people may differ.

- Individuals show important differences in *emotional intelligence*, *emotional clarity*, *attention to emotions*, *emotional intensity*, and *regulation of emotions*, and also display patterns of emotional responsiveness that remain relatively stable across situations.
- Women often report being more emotionally expressive than men and experiencing emotions more intensely. However, these gender differences are highly influenced by cultural *display rules* and may not reflect inherent patterns of emotionality.
- Emotionality does not vary greatly from culture to culture, although there may be differences in display rules and the language of emotionality.

Disorders of Emotion *When Things Go Wrong*

LEARNING OBJECTIVE 7 Describe how malfunctions in emotional processes are related to psychological disorders.

- Extremes in the intensity, clarity, attention to, regulation of, and expression of emotion may contribute to psychological disturbances.
- Anxiety disorders, characterized by excessive emotions of fear or worry, include *phobias*, *generalized anxiety disorder*, *panic disorder*, and *obsessive-compulsive disorder*.
- Mood disorders include *depression*, marked by an inescapable sad mood, and *mania*, a maladaptive extreme version of happiness. Depression is very common. Research shows that, as with normal emotions, both cognitive and biological factors contribute to mood disorders.

Key Terms

TYING IT TOGETHER

The study of emotion is closely connected to the study of all other areas of psychology. Throughout this chapter, we have stressed how emotion interfaces with psychology's various subfields, including our highlighted sections on brain function, individual differences, abnormal functioning, and development. To remind you of how emotion is tied to other psychology subfields and issues, we have selected some interesting points from throughout the chapter.

WHAT HAPPENS IN THE BRAIN?

- The amygdala plays a key role in the onset of emotions, particularly fear. Its activation enables the brain to initiate a fear reaction before other brain areas even start to process the fear-arousing situation.
- People whose amygdalas are damaged cannot recognize other people's facial expressions of fear.
- The prefrontal cortex plays a key role in both positive and negative emotions. Negative emotions may be linked to high activity in the right prefrontal cortex, while positive emotions may be tied to greater activity in the left prefrontal cortex.
- Whereas the amygdala is responsible for the rapid processing of emotional information, the prefrontal cortex may serve as more of an emotional coordinator and guide, turning emotional impulses to deliberate actions.

HOW WE DIFFER

- People differ in how clearly they can identify their emotions, how attentive they are to their emotions, and how intense their emotions feel.
- People seem to display either a hot, cool, overwhelmed, or cerebral emotional style, based on their levels of emotional clarity, their attention to their emotions, and the intensity with which they feel emotions.
- Women may not really be all that much more emotional than men. Rather, individuals may follow social *display rules* about the appropriateness of their particular gender expressing emotions.
- Our culture helps determine the display rules we follow. In one study, American and Japanese participants displayed similar expressions of anger, disgust, and fear when alone. However, when seated with an experimenter, the Japanese individuals masked their negative emotions, while the Americans continued to express their negative feelings.
- Women are at least twice as likely as men to experience severe depression.

WHEN THINGS GO WRONG

- Over 12 percent of adults in Canada display one or more of the anxiety disorders, such as phobias, generalized anxiety disorder, panic disorder, and obsessive-compulsive disorder.
- Almost 5 percent of adults in Canada display severe depression each year and an additional 3 percent experience mild depression.
- The various emotional disorders have each been tied to abnormalities in a particular brain circuit. The panic disorder circuit, for example, apparently includes the amygdala and hypothalamus, and the depression circuit includes the amygdala, prefrontal cortex, hippocampus, and cingulate cortex.
- The various emotional disorders have also each been linked to cognitive factors, such as misinterpretations of bodily sensations in panic disorder, and biased and illogical thinking in depression.

HOW WE DEVELOP

- The range of emotions in newborns is largely undifferentiated. Infants vacillate largely between general distress and general contentment.
- Babies express happiness, excitement, and disgust by 3 months of age, anger by 4 to 6 months, and fearfulness by 7 to 8 months.
- Children experience emotions of self-consciousness, such as envy, empathy, and embarrassment, by 18 to 24 months of age, and self-conscious evaluative emotions such as pride, shame, and guilt by 24 to 30 months.
- Some research suggests that the achievement of various cognitive stages enables certain emotions to emerge, while other research finds that the emergence of various emotions helps trigger cognitive and social development, such as the development of moral standards and a self-concept.

Psychology Around Us

The Role of Arousal in Emotion

Identifying (and Misidentifying) Your Emotions

View this in Action WILEY PLUS www.wileyplus.com

Video Lab Exercise

Stanley Schachter and Jerome Singer's classic study of emotions showed that cognitive interpretations of one's own arousal are a key part of the emotional experience. This video lab exercise will help you experience and appreciate their important findings first-hand.

The exercise requires two different sessions. In one session, you will sit down at your computer while in a caffeine-free, arousal-free state. While in this state, you will look at upsetting or uplifting videos and photos and rate your emotions throughout these observations. For the other session, you will sit down at your computer immediately after you have, in the normal course of your life, stimulated your brain and body with exercise, coffee, energy drinks, or the like (whichever is your usual stimulator of choice). You will then observe a set of comparable upsetting or uplifting videos and photos and again rate your emotions during your observations.

Over the course of the exercise, you will feel and react the same way that the participants did in Schachter and Singer's study, and you will come to appreciate first-hand the principles of the two-factor theory. Most importantly, you will better recognize the separate roles played by physical arousal, cognitive interpretation, and behaviour in the experience of emotions.

As you are working on this online exercise, consider the following questions:

- Why was Schachter and Singer's research so stunning to the field and to the public when it was first published?
- How does the two-factor theory of emotion compare to the other theories of emotion?
- Does the two-factor theory apply to some emotions or some levels of emotionality more than to others?
- Schachter and Singer's study had important methodological advantages over this lab exercise. What were they and why did this exercise have to take a somewhat different route?

CHAPTER 13

Personality

CHAPTER OUTLINE

- The Psychodynamic Perspective
- The Humanistic Perspective
- The Trait Perspective
- The Situationist and Interactionist Perspectives
- Biological Foundations of Personality
- Personality *How We Differ*
- Personality Disorders *When Things Go Wrong*
- Personality Assessment

NOT SO IDENTICAL TWINS

Michele Renard is a city girl, raised in the Jewish faith in Montreal. Cécile Corriveau was raised in the Catholic faith in the suburbs. Talking to them as they sit side-by-side in a room on campus, you can tell they grew up in different communities. Dark-haired Michele is dressed in the somber shades of urban chic, while Cécile sports sculpted hair, straightened teeth, and a white fur-lined jacket. Cécile has a car, while Michele does not.

The two students are at neighbouring universities in Montreal, Quebec. They share a birthday, they are exactly the same height, and they both love hip-hop.

The most important thing they share is the same Métis mother. Separated shortly after birth and given up for adoption, for most of their lives they had no idea that somewhere out there was an identical twin.

But they have many similarities in spite of growing up in different homes. They are both night people, they both love to dance, they both want to have a boy and a girl (in that order), and they both use Pantene® shampoo. They are both "B" students, even though Michele attended a top private school and Cécile went to public school. And the subject that gives them both the most trouble? Math. They look remarkably alike, but they are not exactly alike. Michele has a birthmark over her right eyebrow, and Cécile had to wear braces for five years. Plus, Michele says she's a little more outgoing than Cécile, who admits she's a very shy person.

What makes us who we are? How do we explain the striking similarities between Michele and Cécile? Are they an interesting coincidence, or do they reveal something fundamental about the nature of personality?

Personality refers to the unique characteristics that account for our enduring patterns of inner experience and outward behaviour. Personality involves a collection of stable states and characteristics and varies from one individual to another. Thus, in psychology the study of personality is much more concerned with individual differences than are other areas in the discipline.

You probably do a lot of thinking about personality. Have you ever taken an online quiz to figure out which movie celebrity or superhero you most resemble? Maybe you have filled out a quiz in *Cosmopolitan* or *Cosmo* to determine how much of a pushover you are. Maybe you have also spent time thinking and talking about the similarities and differences among your friends' personalities. Thinking about people's unique characteristics allows us to try to understand their behaviour and to try to predict how they might react in a given situation.

personality the unique characteristics that account for enduring patterns of inner experience and outward behaviour.

Psychological research has historically argued for a divide between explanations of nature and nurture when attempting to account for personality development. Increasingly, however, psychologists and biologists have come to acknowledge that environmental experience and biological mechanisms work together to shape personality. In this chapter, we will first explore key historic perspectives on personality—the *psychodynamic*, *humanistic*, *trait*, *situationist*, and *interactionist* perspectives.

We then look at the important role played by genetic predispositions in personality and what researchers have discovered about the contributions of *both* genetic and environmental factors. Next, we examine whether personality differs depending on gender and culture. And, finally, we describe various personality disorders and consider how psychologists assess personality in individuals. ■

FIGURE 13-1 Freud's view of the mind. According to Freud, the mind has three levels of consciousness. The content stored in the unconscious level is especially important for personality development.

The Psychodynamic Perspective

LEARNING OBJECTIVE 1
Summarize the main ideas of the psychodynamic view of personality development.

As you read in Chapters 1 and 6, the psychodynamic model emphasizes the unconscious, often dark desires that have to be held in check. Recall also from those chapters that the model was formulated by the Viennese neurologist Sigmund Freud (1856–1939) at the beginning of the twentieth century. In Freud's view, the personality forms as a result of struggles between primal needs and social or moral restraints. Many other theorists who follow Freud's key principles differ from him in certain ways. However, they share his basic notion that personality and behaviour are shaped by interacting, or *dynamic*, underlying forces. Thus, all such theories, including Freud's, are referred to as *psychodynamic*.

The Structure of Personality

Central to Freud's ideas are his views of the conscious and unconscious mind. To Freud, the mind is a little like an iceberg. Only the top of the massive entity is visible to the outside world (see **Figure 13-1**). Three levels of consciousness contain the information stored in our minds, but most of that information is not available to normal awareness.

1. The topmost level is the *conscious* mind, composed of the thoughts and feelings that we are aware of at any given moment.
2. The second level, just below the surface, is the *preconscious*, which contains thoughts, memories, and ideas that can be easily brought into the conscious mind if attended to. For example, your mother's birthday or your plans for this evening remain in your preconscious until you require the information, at which point the information is transferred into your conscious awareness.
3. The deepest level, the *unconscious*, contains most of the content of our minds. We are unaware of this content and cannot become aware of it except under special circumstances. The unconscious is particularly important to the development of personality.

Freud identified three central forces in personality development: basic instinctual drives (which he called the *id*), rational thoughts (the *ego*), and moral limits (the *superego*).

The **id** is present at birth and represents basic instinctual needs and desires, such as those related to eating, sleeping, sex, and comfort. These impulses are governed by the *pleasure principle*; that is, they constantly strive for gratification. Freud believed that most of these basic impulses have sexual overtones and that sexual energy, which he called *libido*, fuels the id. Due to the simple nature of the id's needs and its urgent demand for satisfaction, the id is often described as immature and childlike. The id resides largely in the unconscious and is not readily available to consciousness.

id according to psychoanalytic theory, the personality element representing basic instinctual drives, such as those related to eating, sleeping, sex, and comfort.

As children grow older, they begin to learn that their id impulses cannot always be satisfied. The **ego** develops as a result of this learning. The ego works under the *reality principle*—the awareness that it is not always possible or acceptable to have all wants and desires met. Much like the id, the ego is responsible for satisfying impulses, but instead of demanding immediate and direct gratification, the ego first assesses what is realistically possible and what the social consequences of gratification might be. Freud essentially saw the ego as the rational, problem-solving force that constantly strives to keep id-based impulses from bursting forth in a destructive manner. From this description, you might conclude that the ego is largely a product of the conscious mind, but Freud believed that it works both consciously and unconsciously.

ego according to psychoanalytic theory, a personality element that works to help satisfy the drives of the id while complying with the constraints placed on behaviour by the environment.

The **superego** also forms during childhood. It is in charge of determining which impulses are acceptable to express openly and which are unacceptable. The superego develops as children observe the behaviours of those in their families and their culture. As children, we *internalize*—or unconsciously adopt—the values and norms embodied in those behaviours and begin to evaluate ourselves with respect to them. The superego's standards of right and wrong comprise our moral code and remain stable over the course of our lives. Our superego might therefore be thought of as our *conscience*—an entity that leads us to feel guilt and sometimes even anxiety. Like the ego, the superego resides in both the conscious and the unconscious mind.

superego according to psychoanalytic theory, a personality element in charge of determining which impulses are acceptable to express openly and which are unacceptable; develops as we observe and internalize the behaviours of others in our culture.

According to Freud, the ego acts as a mediator between the id and superego. That is, it balances the powerful desires of the id with the moral standards of the superego. Freud believed that the three forces are always in conflict to some degree. Usually, the conflict takes place at an unconscious level. What if these conflicts are not resolved? Personality problems and even psychological disorders may result if a person is not able to find acceptable compromises.

Freud's Psychosexual Stages

HOW WE DEVELOP

Freud believed that as the id, the ego, and the superego work with and against one another, children move through stages that result in the development of personality. The two drives that influence these stages most strongly are *sexuality* and *aggression*. To Freud,

TABLE 13-1 Freud's Psychosexual Stages

Stage	Erogenous Zone	Key Conflict or Experience	Symptoms of Fixation
Oral (0–18 months)	Mouth	Weaning	Dependency on pleasures of the mouth; also general dependence on mother
Anal (18 months–3 years)	Anus	Toilet training	Excessive neatness, orderliness, stubbornness, stingy, controlling
Phallic (3–6 years)	Genitals	Attraction to opposite-sex parent	Sexual role rigidity or confusion
Latency (6 years–puberty)	None	Repression of sexual impulses; identification with same-sex parent	No fixations for this stage
Genital (puberty–adult)	Genitals	Establishing mature sexual relations and emotional intimacy	Sexual dysfunction and unsatisfactory relationships

Oral personality in the making? Freud proposed that individuals whose nurturance needs are not adequately met during infancy may become fixated and develop an oral personality style. They may, for example, be inclined to suck their thumbs even during later childhood, chew their nails, smoke cigarettes, and show signs of dependence.

these drives are the most likely to cause internal conflict because they are the ones that most often fall under social and moral constraints and are most likely to be left unsatisfied. Accordingly, the stages of development are termed **psychosexual stages**. Several are named after specific *erogenous zones*, or pleasure-producing areas of the body. As shown in **Table 13-1**, Freud labelled the stages *oral*, *anal*, *phallic*, *latency*, and *genital*.

Freud believed that the psychosexual stages function as learning periods. Children must successfully complete, or *resolve*, the issues of each stage to form a healthy personality. As children move into a new stage, they must cope with new demands from the social environment and conflicting internal feelings. If they do not successfully resolve the conflicts that arise, they may become *fixated*, or mentally stuck at that stage of development. Freud hypothesized that a fixation may affect all subsequent development.

psychosexual stages according to psychoanalytic theory, stages in the development of personality; the stages—labelled oral, anal, phallic, latency, and genital—are primarily influenced by sexuality and aggression.

neurosis an abnormal behaviour pattern caused by unresolved conflicts between the id, ego, and superego.

Freud linked fixation at different psychosexual stages to the development of distinct, sometimes abnormal, personality characteristics. For instance, Freud believed that a boy in the phallic stage focuses on his penis and a girl on her lack of a penis (so-called *penis envy*). A boy entering the phallic stage also begins to feel sexual attraction toward his mother and jealous rage toward her love interest, his father. Freud called these feelings the *Oedipus complex*, after the character in Greek mythology that inadvertently killed his father and married his mother. At the same time, the boy fears that his father will punish him for his feelings, perhaps by cutting off his source of sexual function, his penis (so-called *castration anxiety*). These feelings, of course, are unconscious, and the child's attempts to resolve the conflicts they create also occur largely at the unconscious level. If children fail to resolve such conflicts, they may suffer from **neuroses**, Freud's term for abnormal behaviour patterns characterized by anxiety, depression, and other such symptoms.

Anxiety and Defence Mechanisms

defence mechanisms unconscious tactics employed by the ego to protect the individual from anxiety.

We have seen that internal psychological conflict, often resulting in anxiety, is central to personality development in psychoanalytic theory. Because humans cannot constantly live in an unsettled state of anxiety, they must have some effective methods for handling it—methods for keeping the id forces in check. This realization forms the basis for one of Freud's major contributions to how human beings think about themselves: **defence mechanisms**. Freud described defence mechanisms as unconscious tactics employed by our

TABLE 13-2 Some Common Defence Mechanisms

Mechanism	Description	Example
Repression	Keeping unpleasant memories or thoughts buried in the unconscious	Forgetting the details of a tragic accident
Denial	Refusing to recognize an unpleasant reality	Refusing to admit an addiction: "I don't have a problem"
Rationalization	Creating a socially acceptable excuse to justify unacceptable behaviour	Justifying cheating on taxes because "everyone does it"
Reaction formation	Not acknowledging unacceptable impulses and overemphasizing their opposite	Overpraising a sibling's accomplishment even though you resent his/her success
Projection	Transferring one's unacceptable qualities or impulses to others	Not trusting a co-worker but believing the co-worker does not trust you
Displacement	Diverting one's impulses to a more acceptable target	Yelling at family members after being yelled at by your boss
Sublimation	Channelling socially unacceptable impulses into acceptable activities	Redirecting aggressive behaviour by becoming a professional fighter
Regression	Reverting to immature ways of responding	Throwing a tantrum when frustrated
Identification	Enhancing self-esteem by imagining or forming alliances with others	Joining groups for their prestige value
Intellectualization	Ignoring troubling emotional aspects by focusing on abstract ideas or thoughts	Discussing various economic theories while ignoring the pain of losing your job

egos to protect us from anxiety by dealing with id impulses. **Table 13-2** lists and describes some defence mechanisms.

repression the most basic defence mechanism; the process of keeping unpleasant memories or thoughts buried deep within the unconscious mind.

denial a defence mechanism; the process of refusing to recognize an existing situation.

Repression is the most basic defence mechanism. This strategy keeps unpleasant memories or thoughts buried deep within our unconscious minds, protecting us from the difficult and painful process of facing them. Another frequently used defence mechanism, and one that has entered into our common vocabulary, is denial. This occurs when a person simply refuses to recognize an existing situation. A person who gambles constantly, for example, may claim that she doesn't really gamble that much or that, even if she does, it isn't a problem and she can quit anytime. It's important to remember that, as stated above, defence mechanisms are unconscious tactics. Thus, the gambler in our example is not consciously making excuses for her behaviour when she practises denial. Examples of other defence mechanisms are described in the table.

PSYCHOLOGY AROUND US Denial in Folktales

In *The Emperor's New Clothes*, two rogues come to town with a promise to weave a most beautiful cloth, so fine that it can be seen only by a very wise man. The emperor, who is very vain and especially fond of clothes, requests a suit to be made of this extraordinary material and pays the two rogues handsomely. . . . As time passes, courtiers are sent [by the emperor] to report on the weaving, and eventually the emperor himself goes to see the new suit of clothes.

[In fact] no cloth was being woven. Nevertheless, after each visit by the royal court, the beauty of the cloth was praised; that is, the non-existence of the cloth was denied. Each viewer attributed his difficulty in seeing the cloth to his own stupidity, believing that if he were smarter, he would be able to see the (non-existent) cloth. The denial is carried to an extreme when the emperor rides through the town in a grand procession, wearing the new suit. The townspeople praise the beauty of the new clothes. [Finally] a little child . . . looks at the emperor and cries aloud, "But he hasn't got anything on!" . . . The defence of denial, quite inappropriate for grown men, is exposed by a youngster . . . . (Cramer, 2006)

Evaluating Freud's Theories

The popularity of psychoanalytic theory was at its highest in the mid-twentieth century. Even today, many of Freud's ideas continue to influence the development of the field (Dumont, 2010; Solms, 2007, 2004). However, since the mid-twentieth century, when the

A guilty conscience. Preschool children start to show that they feel guilty when they cause damage or harm.

popularity of psychoanalytic theory was at its highest, Freud's theories have come under significant criticism in the scientific community. Such criticism is largely due to the fact that the key principles of psychoanalytic theory are based on observations that cannot be directly tested by scientific methods.

Freud based his theories on the cases of patients he treated in his private practice as a neurologist. When presented with puzzling symptoms, Freud pieced together clues from the patient's childhood to try to identify the cause. For example, one of his patients—a 5-year-old boy called Little Hans—had developed an intense fear of horses (Freud, 1909, 1961). Freud came to believe that the boy's anxiety was a product of his psychosexual development related to his relationship with his father. In a lengthy summary of his treatment of Hans, Freud described his procedure for helping the father and son learn to address the repressed feelings that were leading to Hans's anxiety.

Freud's case studies, such as that of Little Hans, are effective at characterizing and classifying certain types of observed behaviours. Indeed, Freud's theories can provide an explanation for almost any type of observed behaviour. For example, we might say that a man who keeps getting into fist fights is redirecting angry, unresolved feelings of aggression toward his parents onto his various acquaintances in life. At the same time, we might say that another man, who is unhappy but not hostile, is repressing those same feelings of aggression. In both cases, we have explained the man's behaviour (or non-behaviour). But recall that psychologists seek to predict as well as to describe and explain. Based only on the knowledge that a particular man has unresolved feelings of aggression toward his parents, could we predict whether or not he will be prone to hostile and fighting relationships? Probably not. This lack of predictive power is a key weakness of psychoanalytic theory.

Additionally, many of Freud's observations were based on a very small and select population of upper-class individuals from nineteenth-century Vienna. This raises questions about the theory's cross-cultural validity and highlights the fact that Freud's ideas were based on his particular—and at times narrow—views of sexuality, parenting norms, and his especially narrow views of gender roles.

At the same time, Freud's supporters argue that it is unfair to criticize psychoanalytic theory for not holding up to scientific testing when it was never intended to act as a predictive model. Rather, Freud's fundamental claim was that individuals can find meaning from looking into their past (Rieff, 1979).

On the positive side, many general aspects of Freud's theory remain relevant today, such as the idea that our relationships with our parents can influence how we form intimate emotional relationships in adulthood (Black & Schutte, 2006). In addition, some studies on defence mechanisms suggest that they are observable and can have important functions in both development and psychological disorders (Bouchard & Thériault, 2003; Perry et al. 1998).

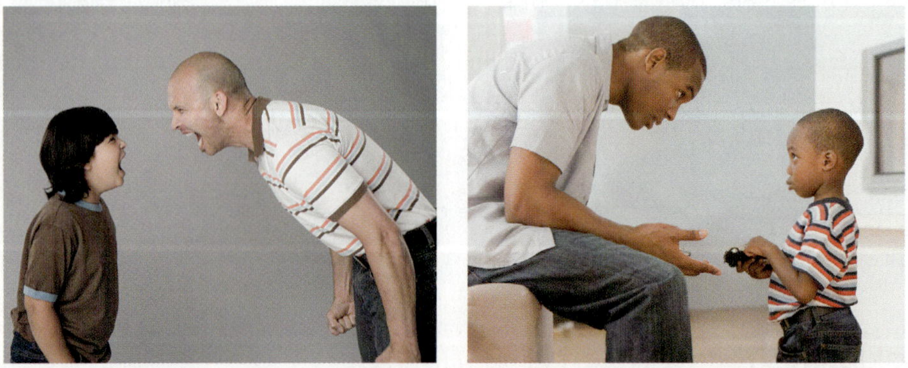

Setting the stage. Freud was among the first theorists to hold that parent–child relationships influence how people feel about themselves and how they handle intimacy as adults. It is obvious which of the interactions pictured here represents a healthier approach to correcting a child's mistakes, according to Freud.

Perhaps most importantly, Freud's ideas spurred the first inquiries into the functioning of the conscious and unconscious aspects of the mind and how they relate to behaviour. The study of the unconscious mind has accelerated in the last two decades. As you learned in Chapters 6 and 8, numerous studies indicate that much of the information processed by the mind remains unconscious, and people rely on a variety of automatic processes to function in the world.

Moving beyond inferiority. Adler proposed that a child's inevitable experiences of helplessness produce early feelings of inferiority, which can lead to a lifelong sense of inferiority or to a lifelong quest for completeness and superiority.

Other Psychodynamic Theories

Over time, some of Freud's followers split away to form their own schools of thought, becoming what are called *neo-Freudians*. Three of Freud's most notable followers were Alfred Adler, Carl G. Jung, and Karen Horney. The theories of the neo-Freudians departed from Freud's in important ways. But, as you read earlier, each held on to Freud's basic belief that human functioning is shaped by interacting, or *dynamic*, psychological forces.

Alfred Adler Alfred Adler (1870–1937) believed that social needs and conscious thoughts are more important to human behaviour than sexual needs and other unconscious motivations. Adler was particularly interested in how feelings of *inferiority* motivate behaviour. In Adler's view, almost everyone has some feelings of inferiority stemming from childhood experiences of helplessness. People often make special efforts to compensate for or mask those painful feelings. Adler focused, in particular, on how feelings of inferiority are channelled into a quest for superiority. Although Adler's school of *individual psychology* has not had a major impact on personality theory, his ideas about how the need for power shapes human behaviour have gained momentum in contemporary research (Watts, 2000).

The positive drives of personality. One-hundred-year-old artist Frances Dunham Catlett speaks about her work at a reception celebrating her "century of creativity." Carl Jung believed that unconscious drives toward joy and creativity are powerful forces in personality.

Carl Jung Carl G. Jung (1875–1961), unlike Adler, agreed with Freud's views on the importance of the unconscious. However, he added a new dimension: the collective unconscious. In Jung's system, the unconscious has two parts. The *personal unconscious*, formed from individual experiences, is similar to the unconscious as seen by Freud. The *collective unconscious*, however, is not a private entity like the personal unconscious. Instead, it is a cumulative storehouse of inherited memories shared by all humankind. Jung called these shared memories *archetypes*. According to Jung, archetypes are reflected in symbols and images that appear in the art, literature, and religions of all cultures. The archetype of the hero, for example, can be found in the stories of almost any cultural tradition, while an archetype of mother and stepmother can be seen throughout children's fairy tales (Robertson, 1995).

Jung's *analytical psychology* also differed from psychoanalytic theory in the emphasis placed on sexuality and aggression. Jung acknowledged the importance of these forces, but argued that the unconscious also includes drives toward joy, creativity, and internal harmony (Wilde, 2011). Indeed, the search for harmony is a central theme of Jung's theory (Singer & Kimbles, 2004). He believed that each of us seeks to integrate the mind's various conscious and unconscious elements into a coherent whole, which he termed the *self*.

Karen Horney Karen Horney (1885–1952), another neo-Freudian, accepted many of the basic principles of psychoanalysis. but went on to develop her own orientation and school of psychoanalytic training. Horney agreed with Freud that anxiety-provoking experiences in childhood can lead to lasting psychological problems, but she was particularly interested in what she called *basic anxiety*, which develops in children who experience extreme feelings of isolation and helplessness. Basic anxiety, in Horney's view, sets the stage for later neuroses.

Perhaps Horney's greatest disagreement with Freud related to the role of cultural influences on behaviour. To Freud, the basic conflicts that shape development are universal, but Horney observed distinct differences in personality structure between patients from Europe and those from the United States. She came to believe that cultural differences play a more important role in development than traditional psychoanalytic theory acknowledged. Horney rejected Freud's theories about penis envy, suggesting that what Freud was really detecting was women's envy of men's power—power that came from cultural norms, not inherent differences (Hitchcock, 2005).

PRACTICALLY SPEAKING Jung in the Business World

In the 1940s, a mother–daughter team, Katharine Cook Briggs and Isabel Briggs Myers, created the Myers-Briggs Type Indicator (MBTI). Today it is one of the most well-known personality tests. Employers in various job fields, employment agencies, and job counsellors administer the questionnaire to several million individuals each year (Wilde, 2011; Furnham, 2008). The test is popular because it describes how we interact with our environment as well as with other people. This knowledge can be extremely useful for a manager in charge of a team of employees from diverse backgrounds, for example. As well, it can be very helpful for individuals in organizational settings to help them figure out why their interactions with their co-workers typically go the way they do.

The MBTI is based on Carl Jung's theory of personality types, and it describes personality in terms of individual preferences for perceiving and judging the world (Kennedy & Kennedy, 2004). Do you prefer a more social or solitary environment? How do you interpret the information you take in? When you make a decision, do you first think about it logically or emotionally? Are you open to several possibilities? Your answers describe your basic preferences and, theoretically, reveal a lot about the kinds of jobs you would most enjoy (Wilde, 2011; Myers et al., 1998). Knowing your preferences may also provide clues about your strengths and weaknesses at work. One thing the MBTI cannot inform you or a prospective employer about is your abilities (McCrae & Costa, 1989); it cannot tell you how well you will perform a particular job.

Most psychologists warn against basing career decisions only on the MBTI (Gardner & Martinko, 1996; Abella & Dutton, 1994). Although the test may inform you that you meet the criteria of an introverted type, this does not mean that you should avoid that sales job you were coveting. Your categorization as an introvert does not mean that you are totally lacking in extraversion qualities, nor does it mean that you cannot behave in an extraverted manner when the social/work situation calls for it. Moreover, success at the job depends on many variables beyond extraversion or other such personality traits. And finally, for most jobs, a variety of different approaches can lead to success.

Recall earlier discussions about the difference between correlation and causation. Remember that *correlation does not imply causation*; that is, simply because variables are correlated it does not mean that one of the variables *causes* the other. So even though you may have a number of characteristics that indicate you might be an introvert, this does not mean that these characteristics will cause you to succeed in one line of work over another; these characteristics simply tell us that, in general, introverts excel in certain types of jobs.

Before You Go On

www.wiley.com/go/comer

What Do You Know?

1. In Freudian theory, how does a neurotic personality develop?
2. What is repression?
3. What are some common criticisms of psychoanalytic theory?
4. How did Jung's idea of the unconscious differ from Freud's?

SCAN TO GET THE ANSWERS

What Do You Think?

Why do you think the concept of defence mechanisms has been embraced by so many theorists (even those who are not psychodynamic) and by the public?

The Humanistic Perspective

LEARNING OBJECTIVE 2

Describe the humanistic theories of Abraham Maslow and Carl Rogers.

Psychodynamic theorists, particularly Freud, generally believe that personality development is driven by forces beyond our control. Humanistic psychologists offer a different view. As you first saw in Chapter 1, they emphasize people's potential and highlight each person's consciousness, free will, and other special human qualities. Let's consider the ideas of two key humanistic theorists: Abraham Maslow (1908–1970) and Carl Rogers (1902–1987).

Abraham Maslow

Chapter 1 pointed out that Abraham Maslow believed humans are basically good. In each of us, according to Maslow, is an urge to grow and fulfill our potential. Personality arises from people's striving to meet their needs (Leontiev, 2008). As you saw in Chapters 1 and 11, these needs are arranged hierarchically, beginning with the need for basic physiological necessities, such as food and shelter, and becoming increasingly complex. Only after our basic needs have been met can we address more subtle needs and strive to attain more complex things. Our highest-level need is **self-actualization**—the need to fulfill our full and special potential as human beings. Maslow described self-actualization as "the full use and exploitation of talents, capacities, [and] potentialities" (1970, p. 150). He suggested that psychologists had become overly focused on biological drives and needs, overlooking the role of high-level processes and the need for more complex forms of fulfillment.

self-actualization the need of humans to fulfill their full and special potential; the highest level of need in Maslow's hierarchy of needs.

Unlike Freud, Maslow believed that more could be learned from individuals who were healthy and well-adjusted than from those who were experiencing psychological problems. In fact, he based his notion of self-actualized individuals on notable historical figures who appeared to lead rich and healthy lives: Albert Einstein and Eleanor Roosevelt, for example (Peterson & Park, 2010). The characteristics that define self-actualized people are the ability to recognize the needs and desires of others, the willingness to respond to the uniqueness of people and situations rather than responding in mechanical or fixed ways, an emotionally deep connection with a few people, spontaneity and creativity, and the ability to resist the urge to conform while still responding to reality.

Some of Maslow's ideas have been taken up by psychologist Mihaly Csikszentmihalyi (2003, 1998). Csikszentmihalyi studied *peak experiences*—moments in which people

Candidates for self-actualization. Maslow proposed that self-actualized people also recognize the needs of others and seek to address them. He believed that full self-actualization was rare. However, well-known people like Bill Gates, Bono, and Gandhi are considered to be self-actualized because of their worldwide humanitarian undertakings However, it is important to note that many people who recognize and seek the needs of others are not self-actualized; consider the case of the volunteer hospice worker who gives selflessly of her time and energy simply to help others.

experience intense clarity of perception, feelings of joy and excitement, and a suspended sense of time and reality. Maslow thought that such moments usually occur when a person becomes totally engrossed in an activity, such as when we hear a beautiful piece of music or experience the beauty of nature. Csikszentmihalyi's writings on peak experiences reflect psychologists' growing interest in **positive psychology**, the study of positive experiences and healthy mental functioning that we discussed in Chapter 12 (Baumgardner & Crothers, 2009; Seligman & Csikszentmihalyi, 2000).

positive psychology an area of psychology focusing on positive experiences and healthy mental functioning.

PSYCHOLOGY AROUND US "In the Zone"

When a golfer like Canadian Stephen Ames is in the zone, his mind and body are harmonized before the swing so the swing happens without any thought or effort. . . .[He] can access his peak performance throughout the round. In this zone state, golfers feel as if they are in a trance, in a heightened sense of awareness—total calm, ease and effortlessness, and mental clarity.

Other athletes also experience the zone. Ted Williams commented that when he was in the zone, he felt as if the baseball was stopped at the plate, waiting for him to swing at it. When Michael Jordan was in the zone, making one of his spectacular leaps, he felt as if he would never come down. John Brody, the San Francisco 49ers quarterback, perceived the opposing line stopped when he was in the zone. He felt as if he had all day to throw the football downfield (King, 1997).

Carl Rogers

Carl Rogers, like Maslow, believed that human nature is fundamentally positive and that people strive for self-actualization (Rogers, 2008, 1963). However, Rogers based his theory of personality around the concept of the *self* rather than around a hierarchy of needs. For Rogers, **self-concept** is a pattern of perception that remains consistent over time and can be used to characterize an individual. Our self-concept is related both to how we see ourselves and to how others see us. Because self-concept develops in part based on how we are perceived by others, as children we need **unconditional positive regard**—acceptance without terms or conditions—from parents or other adults to develop healthy self-concepts.

self-concept a pattern of self-perception that remains consistent over time and can be used to characterize an individual.

unconditional positive regard acceptance without terms or conditions.

The idea of unconditional positive regard became a central part of Rogers's therapeutic practice. He believed that, over the course of development, many children form *conditions of worth*, a perception that they must meet certain standards in order to gain the love of their parents or other important figures. These conditions of worth, often rigid or harsh in nature, can hold over into adulthood and act as a negative force that prevents a person from reaching his full potential. The implications for therapy are clear. In Roger's *client-centred therapy*, discussed in Chapter 1, he worked with clients to create an atmosphere of openness, honesty, and absence of judgment, regardless of the specific type of psychological problems the persons were experiencing. He believed that only in such an atmosphere can individuals begin to put aside the conditions of worth that lie at the root of their personal maladaptive functioning (Rogers, 1995).

Evaluating Humanistic Theories

Many critics fault the humanistic theories for their overly positive focus, saying that they are simplistic and that they ignore the role of psychological dysfunction in society. In addition, it has been difficult for researchers to conduct controlled studies on such abstract concepts as self-actualization and unconditional positive regard (Wilkins, 2000). However, humanistic theories have had a pervasive influence on the field of psychology. As mentioned above, and elsewhere in the textbook, researchers in positive psychology are giving new attention to questions about how human beings can achieve their full potential for happiness. It remains to be seen how humanistic psychology will contribute to this ongoing discussion.

Before You Go On

www.wiley.com/go/comer

What Do You Know?

5. What is self-actualization?
6. According to Rogers, what happens if children fail to regularly receive unconditional positive regard?
7. What is a key criticism of humanistic theory?

What Do You Think?

What do you think are the key qualities of a fully self-actualized person? Who might match your characterization?

SCAN TO GET THE ANSWERS

The Trait Perspective

LEARNING OBJECTIVE 3

Summarize the leading trait theories, and describe how the five-factor theory has evolved from the work of Gordon Allport and Hans Eysenck.

Suppose you were asked to describe your best friend's personality. What would you say? You might use words such as *funny*, *caring*, and *outgoing*. Indeed, an early investigation revealed that there are 4,500 words to describe personality in the English language alone (Allport & Odbert, 1936). Many of these words describe personality traits. **Personality traits** are tendencies to behave in certain ways that remain relatively constant across situations. More precisely, personality traits describe our general dispositions, and those dispositions lead to our behaviours. If people are generally enthusiastic, for example, they may display their trait of enthusiasm by approaching their homework with good cheer or singing out as they walk down the street.

personality traits tendencies to behave in certain ways that remain relatively constant across situations.

Many of today's personality theories are based on the premise that people's personalities are made up of collections of traits. Of course, as many theorists point out, it is often difficult to pinpoint aspects of an individual's personality that are entirely consistent across time and situations.

Human beings are natural trait theorists. It appears, though, that we are likely to explain our own behaviour in situational terms and others' behaviour in terms of personality traits. (This tendency, called the *fundamental attribution error*, is discussed further in Chapter 14.) For example, you didn't finish your paper because you were busy studying for two tests in your other classes. That guy over there didn't finish his paper because he was lazy or disorganized. Thinking about others' behaviour in terms of traits helps make their behaviour predictable and gives us a sense of how our interactions with them might go.

It is also important to note that some researchers, including Hans Eysenck, use a biological explanation for the structure of personality. Although we will discuss his theory in the trait section, Eysenck's theory is also biological in nature.

PSYCHOLOGY AROUND US Blameless, but Consistent

People may not be inclined to point to their personalities to explain their own behaviours, especially their negative behaviours. But they do seem to think that they behave consistently, even when that is not the case. Political scientist Greg Markus collected information about the political behaviours and beliefs of a large group of people in 1973 and again in 1982. Markus found that the people in his study became more conservative as they got older. But, once they changed in this way, they tended to remember themselves as having been more conservative in the past. Only a third of the people he studied were able to accurately remember their past political beliefs—their memory distortions were always in the direction of their current beliefs. For example, people who had previously been in favour of marijuana legalization, but who changed their minds, downplayed the degree to which they were ever for it in the first place. The moral of the study: most of us are probably much more inconsistent than we or others think.

It was trait theorists such as Gordon Allport (1897–1967) and Hans Eysenck (1916–1997) who first proposed that *central traits* affect a broad range of behaviour. Among researchers, it is difficult to pinpoint a standard definition for *central traits*. Generally speaking, however, trait theorists make several assumptions:

1. People have innate tendencies to respond to situations in certain ways (traits).
2. These tendencies can be linked together to form broad habits (central traits).
3. Such principles can be used to form the foundation of a scientifically testable theory.

"I am what is mine. Personality is the original personal property."
—*Norman O. Brown, American writer and philosopher*

Everyone has a number of traits. You may be cheerful, friendly, lazy, disorganized, and talkative. According to the early trait theorists, however, only a few of your traits dominate your behaviours, while others are at work less often. You may be cheerful in most situations, at work, home, and school, and from taking out the garbage to playing basketball (central trait), but lazy only when it comes to cleaning your house. We will look at the ideas of Allport and Eysenck next. Then we will move on to the influential *five-factor theory* of personality.

Gordon Allport

The influential personality theorist Gordon Allport believed that psychoanalysis "may plunge too deep, and that psychologists would do well to give full recognition to *manifest* motives before probing the unconscious" (1968, pp. 383–384). Unlike Freud, Allport did not believe that behaviour is necessarily related to unconscious tensions; rather, he argued that our behaviour can be quite healthy and organized. Over the course of his long and distinguished career, Allport emphasized the unity and uniqueness of the individual, and he believed that the present is more important than the past in understanding personality. Allport conducted detailed case studies that sought to reveal the unique collection of traits at play for each individual. Because much of his work was based on case studies, his ideas have sometimes been criticized by other trait theorists who use empirical investigations to identify the traits that run through large populations (Crandall, 1980). Nevertheless, his work on personality factors provided the starting point for many empirical studies.

Hans Eysenck and Factor Analysis

The British psychologist Hans Eysenck was a strong proponent of using reliable statistical measures to test psychological principles. To Eysenck, it was vital to develop a theory that could be scientifically tested. As a result, he strove to develop adequate measures of personality traits and, specifically, measures of their biological foundations. He hoped that eventually theorists would be able to identify clear correlations between traits and behaviours and underlying biological systems.

The fictional detective Sherlock Holmes was asked by his friend Dr. Watson how he had deduced that a certain man was intellectual. "For answer Holmes clapped the [man's] hat upon his head. It came right over the forehead and settled upon the bridge of his nose. 'It is a question of cubic capacity,' said he; 'a man with so large a brain must have something in it.'"
—*A. Conan Doyle,* Adventure of the Blue Carbuncle

Eysenck made particular use of *factor analysis*—which, as you may recall from Chapter 10, is a statistical method for analyzing correlations among variables. The use of factor analysis marked a significant turning point in the scientific study of personality theory. In the past, psychologists such as Freud and Allport had relied on case studies (one person at a time) and on their own intuition to form ideas about personality structure. Although factor analysis can also be influenced by the decisions and interpretations of a given researcher, the method provides a much more objective way of identifying relationships between variables.

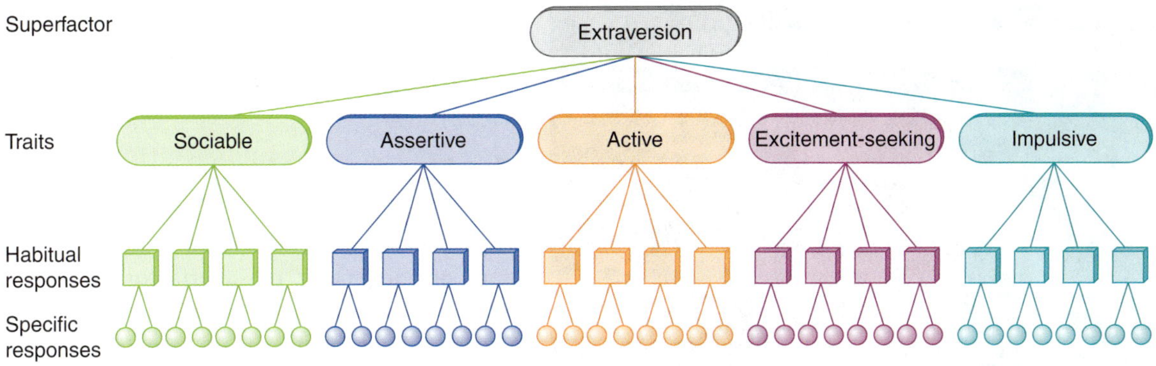

FIGURE 13-2 Eysenck's model of personality. Eysenck used factor analysis to identify traits that cluster together. He described three basic trait clusters, which he called superfactors. Each superfactor, such as extraversion shown here, is made up of specific traits, and in turn each trait is made up of habitual and specific responses.

Eysenck used factor analysis to identify traits that cluster together to form fundamental dimensions of personality, which he called superfactors (**Figure 13-2**). Eysenck eventually identified three basic superfactors:

superfactor a fundamental dimension of personality made up of a related cluster of personality traits.

- *Extraversion*—the degree to which a person is outgoing and enjoys interacting with others. An *extravert* has personality traits such as impulsiveness, sociability, and assertiveness. At the other end of the spectrum, an *introvert* displays traits such as thoughtfulness, reliability, and passivity.
- *Neuroticism*—the degree to which a person tends to experience negative emotions, also known as *mental instability*.
- *Psychoticism*—the degree to which a person is vulnerable to developing the serious disorders known as *psychoses*, in which contact with reality is lost in key ways.

Eysenck saw each of these superfactors—and the individual character traits of which each is composed—as existing on a continuum, with each person displaying a certain degree or level of each superfactor.

Although Eysenck depended on factor analysis to determine how personality traits cluster together, he needed more basic data to make factor analyses possible. To get that data, he gathered information on the traits themselves through the use of questionnaires on which people were asked to rate themselves on a number of trait related behaviours. He administered his *Eysenck Personality Questionnaire* to people in hundreds of countries. The results indicated that his superfactors correspond to basic personality types in similar ways across many cultures (Eysenck, 2002, 1992, 1990).

Because Eysenck believed that personality traits were biologically based, he also studied the biological basis of personality traits. His belief in the biological roots of personality has been supported by a number of studies. Several investigations of twins, for example, involved comparing the personalities of identical twins and suggested that genetics play a significant role in how individuals score on the extraversion superfactor (Pergadia et al., 2006; Heath, Cloninger, & Martin, 1994). A number of studies of hormones, blood pressure, and brain activity support the notion that biological factors are linked to the superfactors at least to some degree (Eysenck, 1990).

Eysenck's work has had an enormous influence on personality theory and research. His early emphasis on empirical research set the stage for much of the current research on personality, which relies very strongly on factor anayses. Moreover, Eysenck's personality tests have been translated into many languages, and his ideas and findings have influenced such diverse fields as education, aesthetics, politics, and psychopathology. Finally, he was one of the first psychologists to systematically investigate the possible biological basis of personality traits, an area of investigation that, as we shall see, has become a significant force in the field (Stelmack, 1997).

Spotting the superfactors. The fundamental dimensions of personality cited in the five-factor model and other theories of personality are each on display in this photo of people passing through an airport waiting area. Can you identify examples of these key trait categories?

The Five-Factor Model

A number of factor analysis studies have derived more than three higher-order dimensions of personality, or superfactors (Poropat, 2009; Boyle, 2008; Saggino & Kline, 1996). The **five-factor theory** identifies five major trait categories, popularly known as *the Big Five* (see **Figure 13-3**): *agreeableness* (versus disagreeableness); *extraversion* (versus introversion); *neuroticism* or *emotional instability* (versus stability); *conscientiousness* or *dependability* (versus irresponsibility); and *openness to experience or imaginativeness* (versus unimaginativeness). A helpful way to memorize these five factors is with the acronym OCEAN (openness, conscientiousness, extraversion, agreeableness, and neuroticism).

five-factor theory an empirically derived trait theory that proposes five major trait categories: agreeableness/disagreeableness, extraversion/introversion, neuroticism/stability, conscientiousness/irresponsibility, and openness to experience/unimaginativeness.

If you look closely, you will notice that Eysenck's dimensions of extraversion and neuroticism are also found among the Big Five superfactors. His third dimension, *psychoticism*, however, does not appear in the five-factor model. That dimension was originally thought by Eysenck to serve as a marker of psychotic tendencies, and people with schizophrenia were indeed found to score high on this dimension. However, many people who score high on Eysenck's psychoticism dimension do not become psychotic and, in fact, they also display particular traits that are found within the Big Five superfactors of agreeableness and conscientiousness (Saggino, 2000).

Despite such differences, Eysenck would probably be happy to learn that trait theory has been reenergized in recent years, thanks largely to the popularity of the five-factor theory. Although some theorists argue that additional factors should be added to the list of five, a great many researchers believe that individual differences in personality can indeed be captured by the five broad categories of this theory (Ewen, 2010; Boyle, 2008; McCrae & Costa, 2003). Because of the theory's popularity with researchers, a significant body of relevant research has accumulated (Zuckerman, 2011; Cooper & Sheldon, 2002). This research has attempted to answer questions about both the validity and the usefulness of the five-factor approach. Most of the research discussed next thus relates directly to the five-factor theory, although some applies to trait theories in general.

Big Five Traits	Low Scorers	High Scorers
1 Openness	Practical Uncreative Incurious Conforming	Imaginative Creative Curious Independent
2 Conscientiousness	Disorganized Careless Lazy Late	Organized Careful Disciplined Punctual
3 Extraversion	Retiring Passive Sober Reserved	Sociable Active Fun-loving Affectionate
4 Agreeableness	Ruthless Suspicious Critical Uncooperative	Soft-hearted Trusting Lenient Helpful
5 Neuroticism	Calm Unemotional Secure Self-satisfied	Anxious Emotional Insecure Self-pitying

FIGURE 13-3 The five-factor model of personality. Studies using factor analysis have identified five broad categories of traits, known as the Big Five. Many researchers believe that individual differences in personality can be captured by these five categories.

Evaluating Trait Theories

A number of questions have been addressed by research into trait theories. First, do traits apply to a variety of cultures? As we mentioned, Eysenck found that his superfactors described basic types across a number of countries. In addition, there is growing evidence that people in many cultures display personality types that can be captured by at least three of the Big Five superfactors and sometimes by all five (Correa & Rogers, 2010; Nye et al., 2008; Saucier, Hampson, & Goldberg, 2000; De Raad et al., 1998).

A second question concerns the power that personality exerts over our behaviour. Consider an interesting study conducted to determine whether people are "naturally" expressive or inexpressive (DePaulo et al., 1992). To evaluate people's ability to control their expressiveness, the experimenters asked subjects to act either very expressively or very inexpressively while discussing a topic. Interestingly, even when asked to feign expressiveness, naturally inexpressive people showed less expression than did expressive people in their natural state. Similarly, when naturally expressive subjects were asked to act inexpressively, they were still more expressive than naturally inexpressive individuals. Clearly, traits are often quite powerful. Even when people try to behave in a manner that conflicts with a particular trait, they may have trouble doing so.

Another benefit of conscientiousness. An elderly teacher carefully demonstrates to a student how to operate woodwork equipment both safely and productively. Studies indicate that, on average, conscientious people live longer than less responsible individuals.

A third question is whether traits, and the behaviours they produce, remain stable across situations. The answer appears to be sometimes yes and sometimes no. In a classic investigation conducted in the early 1980s, investigators observed college students and rated their levels of *conscientiousness*, based on behaviours ranging from being punctual to completing assignments on time and tidying their rooms (Mischel & Peake, 1982). The researchers found that levels of conscientiousness were relatively stable across *similar* situations, but not particularly consistent across very different situations. That is, persons who are punctual for class will likely be punctual for dates, because those situations and their demands are similar. However, individuals who are punctual may not necessarily keep their rooms clean. Although both of these situations require conscientiousness, the situations are quite different, leading to inconsistent displays of conscientiousness for some people.

Yet another question is whether traits, and the behaviours they dictate, are stable over time. Studies indicate that personality traits are more stable over a short period of time than over a span of years (Srivastava et al., 2003). People who conscientiously show up on time for an appointment today are likely to be punctual for appointments next week and next month. But today's punctuality is not as likely to predict punctuality a year or two from now.

Similarly, traits often show inconsistency across a person's lifespan, especially as individuals travel from childhood to adulthood (Fleeson, 2007, 2001). For example, people who score high on the *openness* superfactor (adventurous, imaginative, and untraditional) during their teenage years may display less openness in their fifties. Researchers disagree on why such lifespan changes occur. Some believe that they reflect intrinsic, biologically based maturation (McCrae, 2002), while others hold that they have more to do with changes in an individual's social environment (Srivastava et al., 2003). Either way, it is worth noting that once a person reaches adulthood, lifespan fluctuations seem to lessen, and traits become increasingly stable across the adult years (Roberts & Del Vecchio, 2000; Caspi & Roberts, 1999).

The predictive value of a model is another issue of concern to researchers. Although trait theories do not necessarily claim to serve as a device for predicting what will happen in a person's life, it is tempting to apply them in this way. In fact, the idea that personality factors may be able to predict broad outcomes dates back many years. One longitudinal investigation found that the Big Five superfactor *conscientiousness* helps to predict the length of a person's life (Kern & Friedman, 2008). In this study, a large number of children were followed for 70 years by several researchers. When the children were 11 years old, their parents and teachers rated them on various personality dimensions, and subsequent records were kept about these individuals and the causes of their eventual deaths. It turned out that, on average, those who had been rated as conscientious lived significantly longer than those who had not been rated as conscientious. To explain this finding, the researchers speculated that conscientiousness is related to a broad pattern of health-related behaviours, such as not smoking and not drinking—behaviours that add up over a lifetime. Similarly, research has suggested that certain personality attributes may be predictive of marital satisfaction. One study found, for example, that high agreeableness greatly increases the chances of having a happy and satisfying marriage (Botwin et al., 1997) as do conscientiousness, emotional stability, and intellectual openness.

> "Confidence is what you have before you understand the problem."
> —*Woody Allen, screenwriter and comedy actor*

Finally, researchers have been interested in whether traits are inherited. As suggested earlier, case studies of monozygotic, or identical, twins who have been reared apart seem to suggest that genetic factors can have a strong influence on personality. In addition, a growing number of empirical studies indicate that heredity plays a role in many dimensions of personality (Krueger et al., 2008; Plomin & Caspi, 1999). Based on such studies, the heritability of personality traits has been estimated at around 40 percent (Pervin, Cervone, & John, 2005). In short, it appears that there may be a strong genetic contribution to personality.

Before You Go On

www.wiley.com/go/comer

What Do You Know?

8. Who are Gordon Allport and Hans Eysenck, and what were their contributions to the trait perspective?
9. What is factor analysis, and how is it tied to trait theories?
10. What are the Big Five personality factors?
11. How stable are traits over time and across situations?

SCAN TO GET THE ANSWERS

What Do You Think?

Think of three famous people and predict how they each might score on the major trait categories of the five-factor model.

The Situationist and Interactionist Perspectives

LEARNING OBJECTIVE 4

Describe and differentiate the situationist and interactionist views of personality.

Traits obviously play an important role in behaviour. As we have just seen, traits can be predictive, powerful, and consistent forces in our lives. But are traits the single key to behaviour? It seems not. As we have also just observed, traits show more consistency and are more predictive in the short run than in the long run and across similar situations than across dissimilar situations. Clearly, there is more to behaviour than traits alone. Personality theorists have wrestled with the relative importance of traits and situational factors, and as you will see, many have come to the conclusion that both are important (Fleeson, 2007).

The Situationist Perspective

Over the years, as research identified the limits of trait theory and indicated the importance of situational factors, a number of personality theorists began to embrace a view called **situationism**—the notion that behaviour is governed primarily by the variables in a given situation rather than by internal traits (Mischel, 2004). These theorists acknowledged that personality factors come into play when people are making choices, reacting to events, or displaying other behaviours. Nevertheless, the theorists argued, situational "pushes" and "pulls" rule in most instances.

situationism the view that behaviour is governed primarily by the variables in a given situation rather than by internal traits.

The behaviourist B. F. Skinner, discussed in Chapter 7, could be said to have viewed personality from a situationist perspective. Indeed, Skinner believed that human behaviour was completely shaped by environmental factors. What we call *personality*, Skinner saw as simply a certain consistency in what he called *response tendencies*. By that, Skinner meant that we approach life in a certain way because some of our behaviours have been rewarding to us in the past while other behaviours have not. That is, we tend to favour, or repeat, responses that have previously helped us gain a desired outcome or avoid an undesired one. Whereas a trait theorist might look at your presence in college or university as some combination of intelligence, conscientiousness, and perhaps a little neuroticism, Skinner would say that you studied because you found academic achievement to be rewarding or because studying served to keep your parents happy. Because these outcomes were sufficiently motivating, you developed a general response tendency to persist at studying, which led you to respond consistently and successfully in academic situations (Evans, 1968).

The famous behaviourist B. F. Skinner cited Freud more than he cited any other psychologist in his works. Skinner once applied to be psychoanalyzed at a Boston institute but was turned down because of a long waiting list.

Situationism has a strong appeal. As we already mentioned, human beings appear predisposed to explain their own behaviour in situational terms, although they tend to explain others' behaviour in terms of traits. How often have you responded "it depends" when somebody has asked how you would handle a situation? Certainly, we do not like to think of ourselves as "trait machines"—robots who behave as if we were preprogrammed.

At the same time, however, we must note that there really can be no such thing as *pure* situational factors in human behaviour (Ewen, 2010). Consider, for instance, Skinner's perspective on reward. As you saw in Chapter 7, Skinner defined a *reinforcer* as something that leads you to engage more often in a behaviour. In other words, what is a reinforcer to you may not be a reinforcer to someone else. Theorists argue that even in the context of reinforcement principles, it is still *people* who choose, manipulate, interpret, and react to the situations—or reinforcements—they meet. It's hard to believe, for example, that a particular student puts off every single essay assignment until the very last minute because her reinforcers always line up in that direction. Ultimately, even as we acknowledge the power and influence of situations, we must acknowledge the power and influence of people and their personalities. Thus, it is not surprising that many situationist theorists, including Walter Mischel, the perspective's early leader, came to believe that the most appropriate models are those that try to integrate both personality variables and situational factors to explain behaviour, eventually moving to an interactionist perspective of personality.

The Interactionist Perspective

Interactionism focuses on interactions between people and situations. At the centre of the interactionist model is the idea that people influence the situations they encounter. According to this model, the choices you make, such as being at your present college/university or enrolled in your present classes, are functions of underlying personality traits. Let's say, for example, introversion leads you to choose a school with really small classes—a choice that you suspect would make it more comfortable for you to participate in class—or a school with really large classes—a choice that you believe would make it easier for you to go unnoticed in class. Such choices are likely to result in self-fulfilling prophecies. If you choose the school with big classes, for example, the large class sizes will indeed help ensure that you can remain quiet in class and continue your introverted style. This idea that individual and situational variables interact suggests a way of moving beyond the trait-versus-situation controversy.

interactionism a view emphasizing the relationship between a person's underlying personality traits and the reinforcing aspects of the situations in which they choose to put themselves.

One of the leading interactionist theories is cognitive psychologist (and Alberta-born) Albert Bandura's *social-cognitive theory* (Bandura, 2008, 2006, 1986). Bandura is famous for introducing the concepts of modelling and self-efficacy to the study of human behaviour and personality. As you will recall, *modelling*, also known as *observational learning*, is a process by which people, especially as young children, learn to respond to particular situations by observing and imitating the behaviour of others. *Self-efficacy* refers to people's personal beliefs about their ability to achieve the goals they pursue. The higher your self-efficacy, the more likely you are to pursue a goal and, ultimately, to be reinforced by the outcome of your efforts (Maddux & Volkmann, 2010).

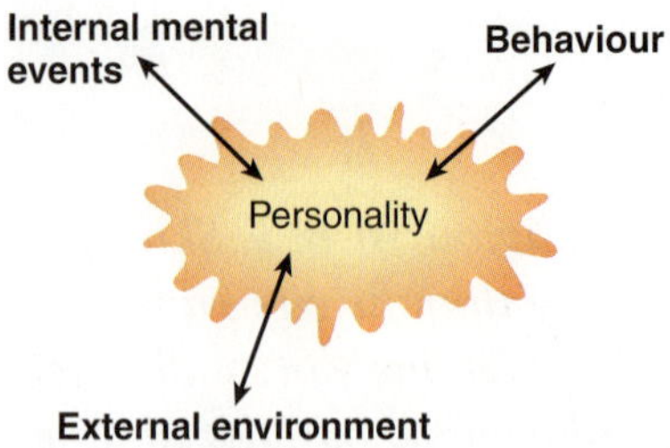

FIGURE 13-4 Bandura's theory of reciprocal determinism. In Bandura's view, personality is determined by the interaction of the external environment, internal mental events, and behaviour.

How do these concepts influence personality? Through a process Bandura called *reciprocal determinism*. In Bandura's way of thinking, the external environment, internal mental events (such as one's beliefs and expectations), and behaviour all interact with one another, as shown in **Figure 13-4**. How, for example, might your current presence in college/university be explained? Bandura might note that as a child you observed your parents or friends studying or working hard, and as a result you engaged in similar behaviour when you entered the school environment. Perhaps you were praised by teachers or your parents for good grades, which reinforced that behaviour. You may in turn have developed a confident belief that you were a good student and curious about and open to new experiences, and your high level of self-efficacy may have led you to persist in behaviours (listening, completing your homework, studying) that further led to desired reinforcements (praise, good grades, positive self-image).

The major advantage of this perspective over other theories of personality is that Bandura's theory, with its special emphasis on observable variables, such as models, behaviours, goals, and outcomes, is readily testable. There is a vast amount of data linking both modelling and self-efficacy to personality development and change across the lifespan (Hoyle, 2010; Borgen & Betz, 2008; Walsh, 2007).

With an interactionist perspective in mind, personality researchers have recently uncovered a new kind of consistency in human affairs: not trait consistency, not situation consistency, but *disposition-situation* consistency. They have discovered that interactive effects between dispositions (traits) and situations are common, and that disposition-situation relationships often show stability (Ewen, 2010; Mischel, 2004; Shoda & Lee Tiernan, 2002). Such stability would be reflected by the statement, "Tamara is more outgoing than her sister when she decides to go for a run, but less outgoing than her sister when visiting a museum in order to please her friends."

Influence of Movies and TV on Personality and Behaviour

Film and television are powerful mediums in the entertainment industry. The stories conveyed in movies and TV shows can make us laugh, cry, or even get angry. But can they fundamentally affect our personality or influence how we act? This is a subject of much debate among parents, psychologists, government organizations, and broadcasters.

Guy Paquette at Université Laval analyzed the amount of violence shown on television in Canada from 1993 to 2001. He found that despite broadcasters stating a desire to offer less violent programming, the overall number of violent acts and the number of violent acts per hour increased steadily over the period of the study. He further noted that a substantial proportion of that violence was broadcast before 7 P.M., thus increasing the likelihood that children would be exposed to it (Paquette, 2004). In another study, movie clips of violent acts were shown to university students to see whether the brain's response to aggression changes with repeated viewing. The researchers found that a region of the brain partly responsible for regulating aggression was less active after repeated exposure to violence (Kelly et al., 2007). Such findings have appropriately raised concern among scientists and the public. At the same time, it is important to recognize that although the average North American views 200,000 dramatized acts of violence by the age of 18, most university- or college-aged individuals are far from violent (Finley, 2007). In short, as we noted in Chapter 7, TV and movie viewing may indeed have a potential relationship to aggressive behaviour, and perhaps to other undesirable behaviours as well, but other factors, such as parental and peer influences, may play an even more powerful role (Kim et al., 2006; Collins, 2005).

TV programs and films appear to have at least some influence on harmful and risky behaviour, but can they also affect us in a positive way? A study of the effect of the movie *Super Size Me*—a film about overeating in which the filmmaker, Morgan Spurlock, lived only on McDonald's food for one month—showed that undergraduates who viewed the film were more conscientious about their food choices afterward (Cottone & Byrd-Bredhenner, 2007). However, the study did not examine whether long-term, permanent changes in eating behaviour occurred.

Film and television are frequently blamed for negatively influencing the behaviour of children and adolescents, and such attributions may indeed have merit. At the same time, however, personality and behaviour are complex, and a variety of genetic and environmental factors interact to influence who we are. In most cases, the content of movies and TV shows probably plays only a supporting role. As well, once again, recall that *correlation does not imply causation.*

Before You Go On

www.wiley.com/go/comer

What Do You Know?

12. What is the situationist view of personality, and what theorists played key roles in promoting it?
13. What is the interactionist view of personality, and how does Bandura's social-cognitive theory fit into this perspective?

What Do You Think?

How might Skinner and Bandura each view someone's failure to quit smoking?

SCAN TO GET THE ANSWERS

Biological Foundations of Personality

LEARNING OBJECTIVE 5

Discuss the heritability of personality traits and some of the neural systems that may be involved in the expression of personality.

You have just seen that the trait-versus-situation debate has moved toward an interactionist view. As we mentioned earlier, the traditional nature–nurture debate has changed in much the same way. In recent years, many researchers have been trying to understand the *relative* contributions of genetic and environmental factors to the development of personality. Other researchers have been investigating what brain structures and other neurological factors affect personality patterns. Let's see what they have found.

Separated at birth. Identical twins Gerald Levy and Mark Newman were separated at birth and did not meet or know of each other's existence until adulthood. In the interim, they had both become firemen and developed a range of very similar personality characteristics, mannerisms, interests, and hobbies.

How Much Do Genetic Factors Contribute to Personality?

HOW WE DEVELOP

As we have seen throughout this book, situations in which twins are separated very early in life and raised in different families afford researchers a unique opportunity to study the separate effects of genetics, shared family and social environments, and non-shared environments. Perhaps the most famous of these twin adoption studies is the *Minnesota Study of Twins Reared Apart* (MISTRA) (Johnson et al., 2007; Bouchard & Pedersen, 1999). This investigation focused on 59 pairs of identical twins who had been raised in different families and 47 pairs of fraternal twins raised in the same household. Recall that identical twins have exactly the same genetic structure, while fraternal twins are no more genetically similar than non-twin siblings.

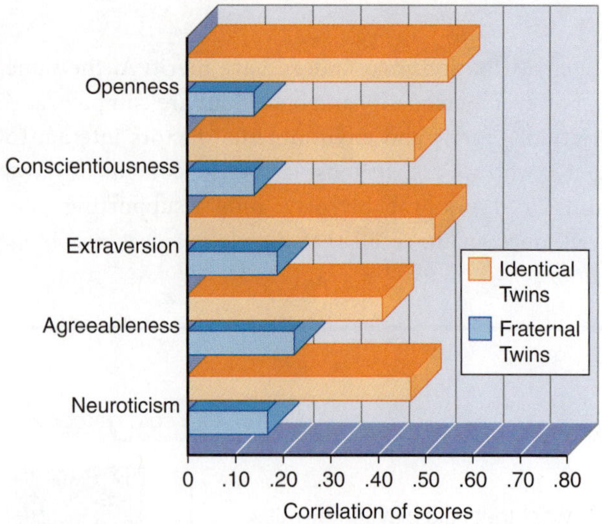

FIGURE 13-5 Heritability of the Big Five traits among twins. Studies comparing identical twins (who share 100 percent of their genes) and fraternal twins reveal that the Big Five personality traits have a strong genetic component (Loehlin, 1992).

The twins who participated in the study spent six days taking personality and intelligence tests. The identical twins proved to be substantially more similar on every psychological dimension than the fraternal twins, even though the identical twins had been raised in separate homes and families. These results suggest that shared environments are less important than genetic factors to the development of temperament and many personality traits, although shared environments certainly do contribute (Zawadzki et al., 2001).

Some broad traits appeared to have particularly strong genetic links (see **Figure 13-5**). For example, in twin studies of personality, the superfactor *agreeableness* from the Big Five scale had an estimated heritability coefficient of .40, and the heritability coefficient (which ranges from 0 to 1.0) of the superfactor *openness* was estimated to be .55 (Bouchard, 2004). Among more specific traits, the heritability coefficient for *warmth* was estimated to be .23, while that for *excitement* was estimated to be .36 (Jang et al., 1998; Loehlin, 1992).

Some researchers have suggested that certain behavioural tendencies, which are expressions of personality, may also have an inherited component. For instance, genetic factors may contribute to an individual's tendency to watch television (Prescott et al., 1991). Even more complex behaviours, such as the tendency to get a divorce (McGue & Lykken, 1992) and to develop alcoholism (Froehlich et al., 2000; Pickens et al., 1991), have been found to be partially heritable. Of course, no single gene is at work in traits or in behaviours such as these. More likely, multiple genes interact and affect an individual's broad biological systems, and these systems contribute to the traits or behaviours in question.

The Minnesota Twin Study has been embraced by the media for its straightforward findings. It is easy, though, to misinterpret the meaning of heritability statistics. Based on their findings, for example, the study's authors estimated that the *heritability coefficient* of IQ is close to .70 (other studies suggest that it is closer to .50). Does this mean that IQ is 70 percent genetic and 30 percent environmental? No. As noted in Chapter 10, the heritability coefficient is related to the total variance in a population, not to the variance within a given individual. That is, a heritability coefficient of .70 means that 70 percent of all differences observed in the tested *population* are due to genetic factors rather than to environmental differences.

Whatever the genetic pathway, even strong proponents of a genetic model recognize that environmental experiences also play a critical role (Zuckerman, 2011). Recall that Eysenck considered personality traits to be biologically-based and proposed that the superfactor *psychoticism* served as a marker of psychotic tendencies, such as schizophrenia. Even Eysenck, however, discovered that persons who are predisposed to high levels of psychoticism will not necessarily develop schizophrenia. Their environmental experiences help determine whether they will become disabled by their genetic disposition or channel that disposition into more productive behaviours.

Personality WHAT HAPPENS IN THE BRAIN?

Twin studies, as we have seen, suggest links between genes and personality. But these studies do not provide precise information about what biological systems affect personality patterns. The search for such systems dates back to Franz Joseph Gall (1758–1828). Gall developed the theory of **phrenology**, a method of assessing a person's mental and moral qualities by studying the shape of the skull. He believed he could pinpoint specific parts of the brain that were responsible for distinct personality qualities by feeling the bumps they raised on the skull (see **Figure 13-6**). The practice became quite widespread between 1820 and 1850 (Gall, 1833).

phrenology a method of assessing a person's mental and moral qualities by studying the shape of the person's skull.

While Gall's techniques were later shown to be inaccurate, his ideas about the localization of brain functions and the role of the brain in personality continue to influence

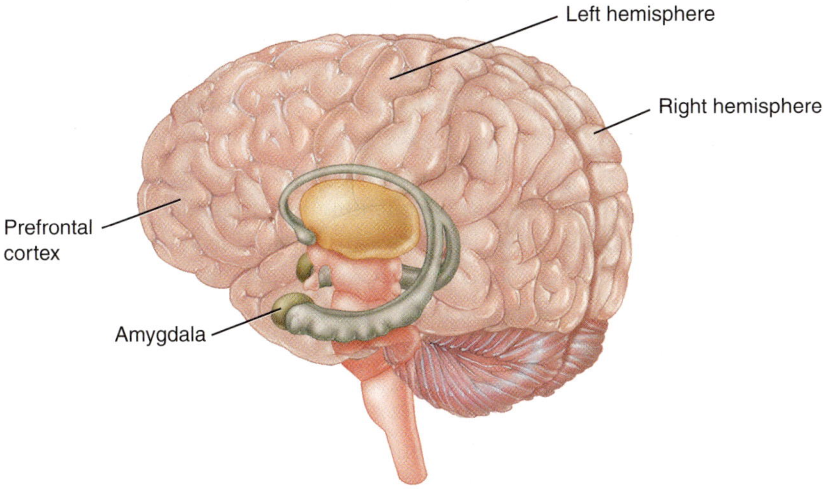

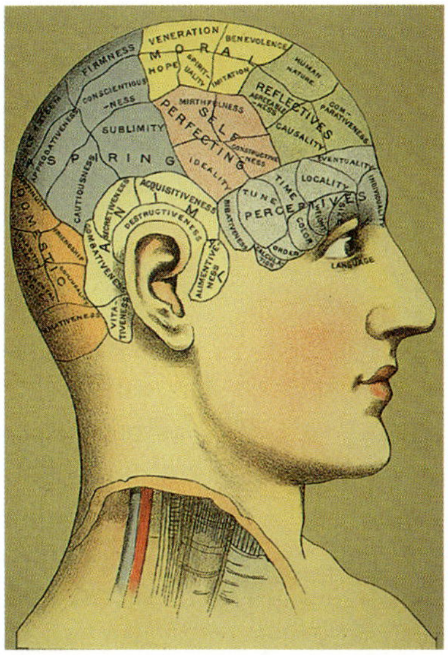

FIGURE 13-6 Bumps, lumps, and personality. Franz Gall proposed that personality could be determined by measuring the bumps on a person's skull, and he diagrammed the areas associated with particular personality traits. While his assumptions were wrong, his idea that some brain functions are localized is true.

neurological science (Novella, 2000). Many researchers are currently attempting to uncover how brain structures, neurotransmitters, and other factors influence personality (Strelau, 2010; Joseph, 2007). Much of this research focuses on specific personality traits, but a new line of study is also examining higher-order personality variables, such as moral inclinations and self-concept (Paprzycka, 2010).

PSYCHOLOGY AROUND US Hardwired for Gossip?

Ever wonder why you you are so curious about and even fascinated by reality TV, the exploits of Charlie Sheen, or the various *Trailer Park Boys*? According to some scientists, we may be built that way. In one study (Anderson et al., 2011), researchers showed a group of participants a set of neutral, unfamiliar faces, and then shared a piece of made-up gossip about each of the faces. The gossip could be negative, positive, or neutral. The researchers then showed the faces to the participants once again, but this time the faces were mixed in with other faces. When the faces were presented in this new manner, the researchers measured where the eye glances of the participants wandered. It turned out that their eyes focused on the faces that had nasty gossip attached to them much more than on faces that had been associated with positive or neutral gossip. All of which suggests to some observers that reality TV may be so successful partly because we are built to want to watch it.

Research on Neural Systems and Personality Many studies suggest that certain *brain structures* help to regulate personality. As we have observed in previous chapters (Chapter 12, for example), the amygdala, a structure in the limbic system, plays a key role in emotionality, motivation, and the processing of negative stimuli, especially stimuli that activate fear and avoidance responses (Haas et al., 2007; Adolphs, Russell, & Tranel, 1999). Brain imaging studies have shown that people with damage to the amygdala have difficulty becoming conditioned to fear stimuli (Le Doux, 1999). The damage may prevent the amygdala from responding to stimuli that normally excite fearful responses in people without amygdala damage. Such studies have spurred a number of psychologists to theorize that children who display an inhibited personality—characterized by shyness and fear of the unfamiliar—may have amygdalas that are *too easily* activated, causing the children to be aroused too readily by unfamiliar situations (Schwartz, Snidman, & Kagan, 1999).

Cerebral hemisphere dominance may also contribute in subtle ways to personality. Some studies have hinted that people whose right hemisphere is dominant experience more negative emotions and traits while those whose left hemisphere is dominant display more positive emotions and traits (Davidson, 1998). One study found, for example, that participants who were generally sad and withdrawn displayed less activity in the left side of their prefrontal cortex—the part of the brain responsible for planned actions and thought and, in part, for emotional reactions to stress (Davidson & Fox, 1989). Moreover, the link between hemisphere dominance and personality may appear at a very early age. Psychologists have studied the brains of infants who show high levels of distress when separated from their mothers. Results indicate that such infants tend to display heightened activity in the right-side prefrontal cortex (Harman & Fox, 1997).

Neurotransmitter activity has also been linked to some personality variables. As mentioned earlier in this book, the neurotransmitter dopamine helps regulate the "pleasure pathway" (Dreher et al., 2009; Volkow & Fowler, 2000). It is central to the brain's reward systems. High dopamine activity in the reward centres, for example, has been associated with positive emotions, high energy, and lack of inhibition, while low activity of this neurotransmitter has been linked to anxiety, inhibition, and low energy levels (Zuckerman, 2007, 1995). Similarly, low serotonin activity has been associated with depression, violent behaviour, and impulsivity (Knutson et al., 1998).

Hormonal activity, too, has been tied to personality. The important hormone cortisol, secreted by the adrenal cortex to help regulate reactions to threatening experiences, has also been tied to personality. As you read in Chapter 3, for example, Jerome Kagan conducted a famous study of inhibited children in 1994. He measured the blood cortisol levels of children as they were reacting to stressful situations. Recall that cortisol is an important hormone that helps regulate reactions to threatening experiences. Kagan found that the children with inhibited temperaments tended to have higher cortisol stress reactions to unfamiliar situations. Recall that temperament (as discussed in Chapter 3) is a way to describe early-appearing stable tendencies toward particular emotional states (called reactivity) and the ability to manage these states.

Organizing Research Findings Numerous studies have looked at the link between biological processes and personality, yielding findings that are complex and often confusing. One of the most compelling methods for organizing these findings has been suggested by the researchers Lee Anna Clark and David Watson, who grouped personality types into three broad categories of temperament, similar to the superfactors proposed by Eysenck and the Big Five theorists (Watson et al., 2008; Clark & Watson, 1999).

- *Negative emotionality* Individuals who have high levels of negative emotionality are thought to experience more negative emotions and see the world as distressing, whereas those low on this dimension are relatively peaceful and have higher levels of satisfaction.
- *Positive emotionality* Measures of positive emotionality are thought to represent a person's engagement with their environment. High scorers are social individuals who lead active lives and exhibit enthusiasm, while low scorers are shyer and have less energy and self-confidence.
- *Disinhibition versus constraint* The disinhibition/constraint dimension reflects how we regulate our various emotions. People high in disinhibition have difficulty controlling their emotional responses and tend to be impulsive, living for the moment. People high in constraint live more careful and controlled lives.

"Don't you just love being with someone who's recklessly impulsive?"
—*Homer Simpson, The Simpsons*

"Actually, it's aged me terribly."
—*Marge Simpson, Homer's wife*

Note that negative emotionality and positive emotionality are two separate dimensions. These two types of emotionality are not necessarily at opposite ends of a spectrum. A person may score high on both, low on both, or high on one and low on the other.

Scores on the three dimensions are broadly related to particular lifestyle patterns (see **Figure 13-7**). Individuals high in negative emotionality are more likely to experience feelings such as anger, contempt, and guilt, while those high in positive emotionality tend to experience positive emotions such as joy, excitement, and pride. Some problematic lifestyle patterns may be found among individuals who score high on the disinhibition dimension.

Temperament	Low Scorers	High Scorers	Biological Roots
1 **P**ositive emotionality	Shy, less energetic Low self-esteem and confidence	Lead active social lives Enthusiastic and engaged with environment	High dopamine activity
2 **N**egative emotionality	Have higher life satisfaction Experience more positive emotions	Experience more negative emotions See life as distressing	Low serotonin activity
3 **D**isinhibition versus restraint	Live in a careful, controlled manner	Impulsive; have difficulty controlling emotional responses	Low serotonin and dopamine activity; high testosterone levels

FIGURE 13-7 The biology of personality. Clark and Watson grouped the findings from personality studies into three dimensions of temperament. Research evidence suggests that biological processes are at the root of these temperament dimensions.

These individuals, who are high in impulsivity and do not act with long-term consequences in mind, tend to get poorer grades in school, perform more poorly in their jobs, and engage in riskier activities, such as drinking and using illegal drugs (Carré et al., 2009). Interestingly, "morning people" are more likely to be high in positive emotionality, while many "night owls" are high on the disinhibition dimension (Clark & Watson, 1999).

Interpreting Research Findings Although research findings suggest links between brain functioning and personality, we must, as always, take care in interpreting these findings. The links just discussed are not usually straightforward, and personality traits are never the result of a single biological process. The activity of one neurotransmitter—say, serotonin—is, at most, *partially* responsible for the regulation of a trait or emotion. Clearly, the relationships between biology and personality that have been discovered represent only a small portion of the complex neurological system.

In addition, it is important to remember that the patterns of brain activity that we have observed have not been shown to provide a causal explanation of traits. Particular biological processes associated with personality may themselves be the results of environment and experience. As you have seen, for example, studies indicate that life experiences, even very early ones, may affect both biological make-up and personality patterns, present and future. One study of rhesus monkeys found that baby monkeys who had endured high levels of abuse and rejection by their mothers displayed lower levels of serotonin activity in adulthood. Moreover, the lower their level of serotonin activity in adulthood, the more likely they were to abuse their own offspring (Maestripieri et al., 2006). Clearly, environmental factors, even at an early age, greatly affect the neurobiological system, and that impact can be enduring.

In summary, we must be very careful about the conclusions we draw from genetic and neurological personality research. First, we must keep in mind that the brain operates as a system, and personality reflects activity in a number of regions, as well as the expression of multiple genes (Bouchard, 2004). Second, we must recall that one gene may interact with other genes and affect a variety of personality dimensions (Livesley, Jang, & Vernon, 2003). Third, we need to recognize that the environment affects the operation and impact of both genetic and biological processes. Those processes in turn affect how individuals interact with their environment. Given the complex, bidirectional relationships that occur between traits, biological factors, the environment, and behaviour, the only certain conclusion that can be drawn is that much more research is needed before we can truly understand the nature and causes of personality (Maruszewski et al., 2010).

Before You Go On

www.wiley.com/go/comer

What Do You Know?

14. What do we mean when we say that the Big Five dimension of openness has a heritability coefficient of .55?
15. What is thought to be the role of the amygdala in the development of inhibited personalities?
16. What are the three categories of temperament proposed by Clark and Watson?
17. Why is it necessary to be careful in interpreting research findings associating particular personality traits with particular biological substances or structures?

SCAN TO GET THE ANSWERS

What Do You Think?

Many of the same brain structures are involved in both emotion and personality. Discuss what you think this suggests about the relationship between emotion and personality.

Personality HOW WE DIFFER

LEARNING OBJECTIVE 6

Explain how gender and cultural differences can affect personality.

So far we have focused on ideas about how personality unfolds. Let's turn now to the question of group differences in personality. Are male and female personalities inherently different? Do personalities differ among different cultures and subcultures? We will examine these questions next.

Gender Differences

The 1992 book *Men Are from Mars, Women Are from Venus* has sold more than six million copies in North America and been translated into 40 languages. The book's premise that men and women are entirely different clearly struck a responsive chord. But how accurate is this notion?

Research into Gender Differences A number of studies suggest that the widespread belief in inherent personality differences between men and women may be no more than a myth. Recent broad reviews of studies on gender differences in personality, cognitive abilities, and leadership have found that the similarities between men and women far outnumber the differences (Hyde, 2008, 2007, 2005). Differences among individuals of each gender are much larger than differences between males and females (Costa, Terracciano, & McCrae, 2001).

Beyond all this, gender researchers have begun to note the importance of context in investigations of psychological gender differences. The situational and social context of a study—for instance, the male-to-female ratio in the experimental room—can greatly influence the nature and size of observed gender differences (Bussey & Bandura, 1999; Eagly & Wood, 1999). Many psychologists rightly stress that incorrect conclusions about certain gender differences can perpetuate stereotypes and improperly affect men and women at work, at home, and in their professional lives (Barnett & Rivers, 2004).

Nevertheless, we must be clear that some consistent sex differences have been documented. For example, women, on average, tend to be more accurate than men at assessing emotion in other people (McClure, 2000). The psychologist Carol Gilligan—who, along with Karen Horney, was one of the first theorists to focus on how women differ psychologically from men—argues that women and men, in fact, are most comfortable with different perspectives on the world, although she also emphasizes that one perspective is not superior to the other, and both men and women are capable of adopting the other's perspective (Gilligan, 2004). Gilligan, whom you first met in Chapter 3, believes that women are more attuned to interpersonal (relational) concerns when making moral decisions, while men are more likely to base such decisions on laws or abstract principles. Building on this idea, she has found that men, on average, score higher on traits that reflect individuality and autonomy, while women score higher on ones that emphasize social connectedness and empathy (Gilligan, 1982). Similarly, some investigations have indicated that women tend to display more nurturing behaviours (Feingold, 1994).

After statistically comparing the results of many studies relating to gender differences in personality, psychologist Janet Hyde (2008, 2005) found only a handful of variables on which females and males differed consistently. Those that she did find, however, seem to be important. Levels of aggression—particularly physical aggression—were somewhat higher among males. In addition, males were quite different from females on measures of motor performance and sexuality, and males and females had strikingly different attitudes about sex in casual, uncommitted relationships—men were more open to sex in such instances. As we noted in Chapter 11, the data on gender differences in sexual attitudes may be influenced by research participants' awareness that society expects men and women to behave in certain ways sexually. Still, it is clear that, overall, differences in aggression and attitudes may lead to significant differences in the expression of personality.

A caring life. Operating against the stereotype that females are consistently more nurturing than males, animal shelter worker Sam Wheeler has devoted much of his life to loving and caring for unfortunate dogs and cats.

Why Do Gender Differences in Personality Exist? Knowing about gender differences is similar to looking at the results of a personality assessment—both provide descriptions but do little to explain *why* certain patterns exist and what those patterns may say about future behaviour. A number of theories attempt to explain the personality differences observed in men and women.

One theory explains these differences in socio-cultural terms. After all, a person's self-concept, life goals, and values all develop in a social context. According to **social role theory**, girls and boys develop different personal styles, behaviours, and skills based largely on the division of labour between the sexes and the resulting differences in gender role expectations (Eagly & Koenig, 2006; Eagly, 1987). In other words, males and females develop the personality attributes that are best suited for the roles that they typically occupy. Some theorists believe that play behaviour in childhood helps teach gender roles and expectations. Young boys are expected to play competitive games, for example, and often are given aggressive-type action figures as toys. Girls, in contrast, are encouraged to play games that emphasize nurturing and interacting with peers.

social role theory theory that gender differences occur because girls and boys develop different behaviours and skills based largely on differences in gender role expectations.

Family and social relationships may also contribute to the development of personality differences between boys and girls. As children interact with their families and peers, they form ideas about gender role expectations based on how those other individuals react to their behaviours. It is particularly important that the reactions of others teach children what behaviours and ideas are not appropriate to their gender role (Henley, 1977). A little boy may, for example, face disapproval if he plays with dolls rather than action figures.

Broad cultural practices, often a reflection of religious and philosophical beliefs, are also significant in the development of male–female differences. Traditionally, men held a position of higher power than women in most societies, and this power structure had a "trickle-down" effect on smaller units of behaviour. Women, for example, often were limited to certain roles, such as child rearing, domestic work, and particular occupations (nurse, teacher, secretary). It may be that women were more likely to develop certain personality traits as a result of these constraints. Consider, for example, the superior abilities of women, on average, to read emotions and to perform in the social realm. Individuals who are in positions of less power or privilege may need to develop their skills at recognizing

PSYCHOLOGY AROUND US Trying to Break Free of Social Roles

Efforts to break free from social roles can take a toll on individuals. Thus, even the best-intended role breakers can only go so far. Perhaps you have noticed, for example, that some men are willing to support a female friend by going to a female-oriented movie or a flower show, but the same guys are much less likely to hold a friend's purse. And on those occasions when men do go that extra mile, they are often left in an uncomfortable emotional state.

Researchers Jennifer K. Bosson and Joseph A. Vandello (2011) asked men to engage in a braiding task—half of them braided a length of rope, and half of them braided hair. Afterward, the men were given the choice of punching a bag or working a puzzle. The men who braided hair overwhelmingly opted to punch a bag. In another condition, men who were not allowed to punch a bag or engage in other aggressive behaviours reported high anxiety levels. In essence, according to Bosson and Vandello, if the men didn't get an opportunity to reassert some gender-stereotyped behaviour, their sense of manliness became threatened.

interpersonal cues and spotting the emotions of those in power to better address their own needs (Eagly & Koenig, 2006; Tavris, 1991; Eagly 1987). They can use such skills as they try to make sure their own needs are met.

A number of theorists further propose that cultural norms influence how men and women form their self-schemas. As we discussed in Chapter 3, *schemas* are ways we organize knowledge. A *self-schema* is an individual's cognitive framework for the knowledge he has about himself. When we need to process new information about ourselves or our interactions, we refer to these schemas for guidance. A number of studies suggest that men are more likely to have self-schemas that emphasize autonomy and independence, while women are more likely to have collectivist or relationship-based schemas (Bekker & van Assen, 2008). One team of researchers further hypothesized that an individual's self-esteem would be directly related to how well he lived up to gender-dependent schemas—a hypothesis supported by a study they conducted (Josephs, Markus, & Tarafodi, 1992). Research participants who were led to believe that they equalled or surpassed most of their peers in gender-specific skills and abilities had consistently higher levels of self-esteem.

In addition to such socio-cultural factors, biological factors may play a role in gender differences in personality. In Chapter 4, for example, we discussed the nature and importance of *hemispheric lateralization* in the brain. It turns out that males and females may exhibit different degrees of hemispheric lateralization. Male brains tend to be more functionally lateralized than female brains: in male brains, one hemisphere is relatively dominant for various kinds of processing, while female brains appear to be more integrated (Everhart et al., 2001; Saucier & Elias, 2001). Still other studies have found that the sex hormones, testosterone and estrogen, which are available in different amounts and often act differently in males and females, have major influences on behaviour and personal tendencies, leading many theorists to believe that they also contribute to gender differences in personality (Hines, 2004; Dabbs et al., 2001, 1997).

In male–female conversations, women laugh 126 percent more often than men.

In summary, it is true that, on the one hand, many of our society's beliefs about male–female personality differences are incorrect or overstated. A number of psychologists worry that the Mars–Venus myth of massive gender differences serves to perpetuate harmful misconceptions. Highlighting differences between men and women, for example, may support prejudicial beliefs and discriminatory practices against women (Hyde, 2005). On the other hand, it is also true that that there is potential danger in not acknowledging the real differences that do exist between the genders. Such denial, argue a number of theorists, may serve to downplay the unique strengths and gifts of each gender. Perhaps the most appropriate response to this debate was offered by the psychologist Diane Halpern, past-president of the American Psychological Association. There may be limited differences between males and females, Halpern stated, but "differences are not deficiencies" (Halpern, 2000).

Differences Among Cultural Groups

Around the world, each culture is characterized by its own values, beliefs, and to some degree, patterns of behaviour. These features help guide members of the cultural group, teaching them what they should value in life, how they should treat others in their group, and how they should view themselves in relation to society. Cultures also form their own ideas about what is important in life, and these ideas can vary widely. For example, the term *self-esteem,* so important in North American culture, is not even found in a number of languages. Clearly, people who live in a society that does not emphasize self-esteem are less likely than North Americans to spend their lives striving for it. Similarly, in North America and Western Europe, a person's goals and life path are often influenced by the culture's emphasis on autonomy and accomplishment, whereas in Asian cultures there is greater emphasis on contributing to a community and honouring one's family (Kim, Pemng, & Chiu, 2008).

Some of the most comprehensive cross-cultural research has focused on personality development in individualist and collectivist cultures. As we observed in Chapter 12, most collectivist cultures consider the needs of the group more important than the needs of the individual. With this orientation comes heightened emphasis on the role of individuals within their family and on social relationships in general. In turn, individuals are more likely to strive to help maintain the social order and to exhibit humility in social interactions (Triandis, 2001; Triandis et al., 1990). Collectivist values are particularly found in African, Latin American, Asian, and Middle Eastern cultures (Buda & Elsayed-Elkhouly, 1998).

> "Nurture shapes nature."
> —*Albert Bandura, psychologist*

In contrast, individualist cultures value individual achievement, freedom, and success. The self is seen as independent, and each individual is thought to possess a set of psychological qualities that are distinct from those of others. Unlike collectivist cultures, individualist cultures consider individual attainment more important than the needs and values of others. Indeed, competition between individuals is valued. Countries known for this type of structure are Canada, Great Britain, the United States, and Australia.

Cross-cultural psychologists have uncovered some interesting personality variations between collectivist and individualist cultures (Correa & Rogers, 2010; Oyserman et al., 2002; Schmitt et al., 2007). One large, multi-nation study found that people in collectivist cultures tend to score higher on measures of agreeableness, for example, while people from individualist cultures score higher on measures of extraversion and openness (Hofstede & McCrae, 2004).

Happiness and success may also be defined differently from culture to culture. In collectivist societies, contentment is related to harmony in interpersonal relationships, and this emphasis affects behaviour (Kitayama, Markus, & Kurokawa, 2000). Interpersonal behaviours are tailored to the feelings and needs of others (Kashima et al., 1992). A strong sense of reciprocity and a responsibility to return favours shapes personal styles, behaviours, life goals, and measures of success. In such a culture, a sense of accomplishment comes not from individual achievements but from strong commitment to family, community, or company.

In contrast, people in more individualist cultures are less constrained by a tightly knit social network and enjoy greater personal freedom. They value their privacy and place a premium on individual human rights. Interestingly, some studies have found that people in individualist cultures report greater happiness than those in collectivist cultures (Kuppens, Realo, & Diener, 2008; Diener, Diener, & Diener, 1995). At the same time, however, individualist societies have higher rates of divorce, homicide, and stress-related disease than collectivist ones (Triandis 2001; Popenoe, 1993; Triandis et al., 1988).

People's sense of their own personalities also differs across cultures. Individuals in collectivist cultures, for example, do not use traits to describe themselves as often as those in individualist cultures. Studies have shown that when students are asked to complete the phrase "I am . . . ," those from North America are more likely to answer using a personal trait (say, "I am friendly" or "I am honest"), while those from cultures with a collectivist orientation are more likely to describe themselves in a social manner (for example, "I am a member of the psychology department") (Cousins, 1989; Triandis, 2001, 1989). In light of such findings, some have argued that Western personality measures, such as the Big Five superfactors, are of limited usefulness in studying behaviour in collectivist cultures (Church & Katigbak, 2000).

"Different people bring out different aspects of one's personality."
—*Trevor Dunn, musician and composer*

The interplay of culture and personality is also evident when people move from one environment to another. As people become entrenched in a new cultural context, they typically absorb the norms and values of the society. Indeed, research has revealed that when individuals move from a collectivist culture to an individualist one, their personal and behavioural patterns change. One study, for example, looked at the personality traits of Chinese students who were enrolled in universities in North America (McCrae et al., 1998). Those students who had been in North America the longest, and had presumably been more exposed to Western culture, showed higher levels of extraversion and had personality profiles more similar to those of other North Americans.

Different values, different personalities. The different ways in which these business meetings are being conducted in North America and Japan reflect the different values and personalities at work in individualist and collectivist cultures. Goals and personal styles in an individualist culture emphasize striving for autonomy, individual achievement, and high self-esteem. In contrast, those on display in a collectivist culture emphasize the community, cooperation, and honouring one's family.

Interestingly, some people who come from bicultural backgrounds seem to develop the ability to "frame switch"—that is, to change back and forth between cultural frameworks as they interpret experiences. This suggests that they may have internalized the belief systems of both cultures (Hong et al., 2000). It is not yet clear what implications frame switching has for the ties between culture and personality. This is, however, an important question as the world moves each day toward greater cultural integration.

Socio-economic class, impulsivity, and behaviour. Research suggests that impulsive boys from poor neighbourhoods may be more likely to engage in delinquent behaviours than impulsive boys from wealthier communities.

Culture, Socio-economic Environment, and Personality

A key aspect of culture is the socio-economic environment. Even in the most prosperous nations, there are distinct differences in living conditions between those in the lowest and those in the highest income brackets. These differences have actually increased across the world in recent years (Autor, Katz, & Kearney, 2006). Although the relationship between socio-economic conditions and personality traits has received relatively little attention, investigations conducted to date suggest that it is an important topic (Caspi, 2002; Caspi, Bem, & Elder, 1989). At the very least, it appears that living conditions have a direct impact on how and whether certain personality traits translate into behaviours.

For example, Yessine and Bonta (2009) examined the trajectories of delinquent Aboriginal youth in Manitoba. Data from the study indicated that chronically high offending youth were more likely to live in impoverished and unstable circumstances, to engage in substance use, and to experience negative peer interactions, suggesting that disorganized environments interact with individual characteristics to increase risk. Indeed, a second study directly assessed the impulsivity of a population of 13-year-old males (Lynam et al., 2000). The teens in the study came from a mixture of backgrounds, from wealthy households to poverty-stricken neighbourhoods. Their socio-economic status was found to clearly link with the outcomes of individual differences in impulsivity. Among boys who lived in poor neighbourhoods, those who displayed high levels of impulsivity were much more likely to engage in delinquent behaviours than those who displayed low levels of impulsivity. In contrast, among boys from high socio-economic status neighbourhoods, behavioural differences between those with low and high impulsivity were negligible. To explain these findings, the investigators reasoned that poor neighbourhoods produce many more triggers for delinquent acts, whereas community structures in affluent neighbourhoods may offer limited opportunities for antisocial activities. In short, particular personality characteristics will result in particular behaviours only if certain situational triggers also are in place.

Before You Go On

www.wiley.com/go/comer

What Do You Know?

18. What personality differences between men and women have researchers identified?
19. How does social role theory explain these differences?
20. What are some of the primary differences between the values of collectivist and individualist cultures, and how do these differences affect personality?
21. How does the socio-economic environment affect personality?

SCAN TO GET THE ANSWERS

What Do You Think?

Think about the personality traits of a number of people you know. Include people of different gender and different cultural or subcultural groups. Do personalities seem to differ more on a group level or on an individual level among these acquaintances? How would you explain your observation?

Personality Disorders

WHEN THINGS GO WRONG

LEARNING OBJECTIVE 7

Define personality disorder, and describe some of the key features of this disorder.

PSYCHOLOGY AROUND US The Roommate

Karen and I met when I placed an ad in a newspaper for a new roommate. At first, I thought we were having fun living together. Then one night, about two months after she moved in, I was getting ready to go out with a friend, and Karen demanded to know where I was going. She wanted to know who I was seeing, what I was doing, and then she tried to make me feel guilty for going out. . . .

When I came home that night, it was really scary. There was a little blood on the floor, and it made a trail that led to her bedroom door. When I banged on the door to see if she was all right, she said that she'd accidentally cut herself making a sandwich, and everything was fine.

Dealing with her was starting to take a lot out of me. Then she started dating this guy, Eric, and I thought things were getting better. Karen was spending almost no time at home, and when I did see her, she would gush about how incredibly happy she was. . . .

I should have seen what was coming next, but, like an idiot, I didn't. Eric left her, and she was totally my problem again. She stayed home and cried for days at a time. She made me take care of her, telling me she was too depressed to do anything for herself. She even fantasized about the violent things she would do to Eric when she felt up to it. . . . After Eric, there was Ahmad, then James, then Stefan. Always the same story, always the same ending. And always with me in the middle. . . .

What does this description tell us about Karen? Was she the victim of emotionally distressing circumstances? Or was her self-destructive behaviour the result of dysfunctional personal characteristics? It appears that Karen's initial positive feelings and excitement about someone new in her life were invariably followed by a turbulent phase of emotional outbursts and an eventual falling out. This pattern suggests that Karen may have a **personality disorder**, an inflexible pattern of inner experience and outward behaviour that causes distress or difficulty with daily functioning. Such patterns are enduring and differ markedly from the experiences and behaviours usually expected of people (APA, 2000).

personality disorder an inflexible pattern of inner experience and outward behaviour that causes distress or difficulty with daily functioning.

As we suggested earlier in this chapter, each of us has a distinct personality and specific personality traits. Yet, for most of us, this distinct personality is also flexible. We are affected by situational factors, and we learn from our experiences. As we interact with our environment, we try out various responses to see which are more effective. This flexibility is missing in people who have a personality disorder.

Disregarding others. Alleged Ponzi-schemer and fraudster Milowe Brost, from Calgary, Alberta, is in custody, charged with defrauding thousands of investors of more than $300 million.

Personality disorders usually become evident during adolescence or early adulthood, although some begin during childhood (APA, 2000). There is no specific data on the rate of personality disorders in Canada (Health Canada, 2002). American data suggests that the rate is somewhere between 9 and 13 percent of the general population (O'Connor, 2008; Lenzenweger et al., 2007). As in Karen's case, the effects of a personality disorder can sometimes be so subtle that they are initially unnoticeable. It may take multiple encounters over time for the maladaptive symptoms to become recognizable. Nevertheless, they have a significant impact on the individual's functioning in school, at work, and in social and romantic relationships (Berenson et al., 2011; Mason & Kreger, 2010).

Based on her roommate's description, Karen appears to be emotionally volatile, particularly when it comes to her relationships. Especially in the early stages of a relationship, she tends to see the men in her life as "perfect," but they inevitably fall from grace. Karen also appears to have a high sensitivity to feeling abandoned, which leads to emotional outbursts. She may even cut herself or cause some other harm as a way of dealing with that negative emotion. Her outbursts and moodiness are off-putting to the roommate and most others in her life. All these features suggest that Karen may be displaying **borderline personality disorder**. Borderline personality disorder is characterized by severe instability in mood and self-concept, which in turn contributes to a high level of instability in relationships (APA, 2000). Borderline personality disorder is often thought of as an emotion dysregulation disturbance (Sherry & Whilde, 2008; Berenbaum et al., 2003; Linehan & Dexter-Mazza, 2008) and will be discussed further in Chapter 16.

borderline personality disorder a personality disorder characterized by severe instability in emotions and self-concept and high levels of volatility.

antisocial personality disorder a personality disaorder characterized by extreme and callous disregard for the feelings and rights of others.

Individuals with **antisocial personality disorder**, most of whom are male, show an extreme and callous disregard for the feelings and rights of others. They typically exhibit impulsivity, egocentrism, and recklessness, along with a superficial charm. Dishonesty and deceit are at the root of their relationships. Indeed, they often form relationships with the intent of exploiting others for material gain or personal gratification. Many are irritable, aggressive, and quick to start fights, and a large number commit criminal acts (APA, 2000). A large study by Dan Offord (1933–2004) at McMaster University suggests that approximately 1.7 percent of the Canadian population shows signs of antisocial personality disorder at any one time (Offord et al., 1996). Another study by Rodger Bland in the department of psychiatry at the University of Alberta suggests that the incidence of this disorder is about 3.7 percent (Bland, Orn, & Newman, 1988). Moreover, cross-cultural

TABLE 13-3 The Major Personality Disorders

Marked by Odd or Eccentric Behaviour
Paranoid: Exaggerated suspicion and distrust of others; assumption that others' motives are hostile; highly guarded and emotionally withdrawn
Schizoid: Detachment from social relationships; flat emotional expression; cold or indifferent to others
Schizotypal: Behaviour that is odd or peculiar; unusual cognitive or perceptual experiences; acute discomfort with close relationships
Involve Dramatic or Emotional Behaviour
Antisocial: Extreme disregard for others; relationships are dishonest, deceitful, and exploitive; typically impulsive and reckless
Borderline: Severe instability in emotion and self-concept; impulsive and self-destructive behaviour
Histrionic: Excessive need to be noticed and be the centre of attention; emotions shallow and changeable; engagement with others superficial
Narcissistic: Characterized by high degree of self-interest and self-importance; callous attitude toward others
Characterized by High Levels of Fear and Anxiety
Avoidant: Extreme feelings of inadequacy; avoidance of social activities; inhibited personal relationships; hypersensitive to criticism
Dependent: Excessive need to be cared for by others; clinging and submissive behaviour; difficulty making decisions
Obsessive-compulsive: Preoccupied with perfectionism and control at the expense of flexibility or enjoyment; excessive devotion to work and productivity

Source: DSM-IV-TR, APA, 2000.

research has shown that similar antisocial patterns of symptoms are found in both Eastern and Western cultures (Zoccolillo et al., 1999).

Many theorists have attempted to uncover the origins of personality disorders, and have highlighted factors such as the roles of biological predispositions, early experiences of abuse and neglect, and the pressures of poverty or otherwise harsh social environments (Arens et al., 2011; Bollini & Walker, 2007; Linehan & Dexter-Mazza, 2008; Millon & Grossman, 2007; Patrick, 2007). Generally, however, these disorders are not well understood.

> "Personality disorders . . . are the only things left in psychiatry where people think you are bad."
> —*Gary Flaxenberg, psychiatrist*

The American Psychiatric Association's diagnostic and classification system (DSM-IV-TR) identifies 10 personality disorders, which are described briefly in **Table 13-3**. You will read more about these personality disorders in Chapter 16, particularly *antisocial personality disorder* and *borderline personality disorder*—the two that have received the most clinical and research attention. At that time, you will come to appreciate just how disabling and disruptive the disorders can be, in part because they are so resistant to treatment.

School Shootings and Videogames

On the December 6, 1989, one of the deadliest shootings in Canadian history occurred at Montreal's École Polytechnique, when a young man killed 14 women students, injured 10 other women and four men, and then shot himself. The gunman claimed that feminists had ruined his life. Attempts to interpret motives for this and other shootings led researchers to focus on issues of violence against women (Mancini Billson, 2005), as well as the role of previous child abuse and its relationship to violent behaviour (Denmark et al., 2005), the role of bullying and victimization (Reid & Sullivan, 2009), the role of violence in the media, and the socio-political roles of poverty and isolation in society (O'Grady et al., 2010). The aftermath of the shootings at the École Polytechnique contributed to the passage of the Firearms Act in 1995, leading the way toward more stringent gun control laws in Canada (Rathjen & Charles, 1999). Investigators have also discovered that most school shootings are premeditated and carefully planned (Robertz, 2007).

For its part, the media has regularly tied school shootings, such as the American shootings at Columbine high school, to the playing of videogames—the two students who orchestrated the Columbine killings were, for example, avid players of Doom. But, it turns out that the behaviour of student-killers is not so easily explained. Three

Unthinkable. One of many memorials held for victims of the Montreal École Polytechnique shootings.

years after Columbine, the American Secret Service and the Department of Education published a joint report that looked at 37 school shootings over the past three decades. They concluded that only 12 percent of the school shooters had any interest in videogames (Vossekuil et al., 2002).

If videogames are not a major factor in most school shootings, what are the causes of these violent outbursts? Recent studies of the relationship between school shootings and videogames have found that family violence is more of a risk factor than fictional violence (Ferguson, 2008; Kutner & Olson, 2008). Low self-esteem, depression, and antisocial personality patterns are also factors. In addition, as we observed earlier in this book, adolescent shooters are often the victims of bullying or rejection, and some fantasize for quite a while about revenge for "perceived offenses" (Robertz, 2007).

In light of the these school shootings and other such incidents, reports (Leavitt et al., 2007) recommend increased awareness of the warning signs of potential attacks, such as a student describing plans to hurt others on a website. The hope is that identifying and addressing problems early on may prevent students with mental health problems from reaching a point where there is no turning back.

Before You Go On

www.wiley.com/go/comer

What Do You Know?

22. What is a personality disorder?
23. What are the 10 personality disorders recognized by DSM-IV-TR?

What Do You Think?

Personality disorders are popular subjects of fiction. Think about films or television programs that you have seen, and try to find examples of characters who may be displaying personality disorders.

SCAN TO GET THE ANSWERS

Personality Assessment

LEARNING OBJECTIVE 8

Describe the two major types of personality tests, and give examples of each.

Go to almost any pop-culture Internet site or flip open any newspaper or popular magazine and you will likely find evidence of people's desire to understand, describe, and use personality traits. Horoscopes, personality quizzes, and even clairvoyants offer personality-based analyses and advice to thousands of people worldwide. The fact that devices such as horoscopes have been shown to be unreliable has done little to diminish their popularity.

Of course, there are also more formal tools for assessing personality, and these tools are used in a variety of important contexts. Clinicians use personality assessment tools to learn more about their clients' problems. Researchers may use them to conduct personality research or to help select participants for their studies. Employers and job counsellors often use such tools to help predict the suitability of potential employees for various positions. Scores on traits such as conscientiousness have, for example, been used to predict absenteeism, misconduct, and termination (Organ & Ryan, 1995). The personality tests used most frequently by these professionals are *personality inventories* and *projective tests*.

Personality Inventories

You have very likely taken a personality inventory at some time in your life. **Personality inventories** are questionnaires that require individuals to respond to a series of true–false or agree–disagree statements designed to measure various aspects of personality. These types of assessments are sometimes called self-report inventories because they depend on information that respondents supply about themselves. Today's most widely used personality inventories are the *Minnesota Multiphasic Personality Inventory 2 (MMPI-2)* and the *NEO (Neuroticism, Extraversion, Openness) Personality Inventory*. Both are considered relatively accurate and consistent. They are favoured by clinicians, employers, and other professionals largely because they are easy to administer and to score, and do not require subjective interpretations by test administrators. Each test requires individuals to respond to hundreds of statements that cover a broad range of feelings, behaviours, and inclinations (Boyle, Matthews, & Saklofske, 2008). Because of this scope, the inventories provide a summary, or *profile*, of the various traits that comprise a personality.

personality inventory a paper-and-pencil questionnaire designed to assess various aspects of personality.

PRACTICALLY SPEAKING Evaluating Personality Quizzes

Are you dating a person with a narcissistic personality? What is your "pizza personality"? What kind of podcast are you? Personality quizzes fascinate and entertain millions of people. Magazines as varied as *Cosmopolitan* and *Chatelaine* publish personality quizzes all the time, and the Internet has numerous websites dedicated to helping you to better understand yourself.

Below are some of the pop-culture quiz types that you are most likely to come across:

- *Scenario quizzes* ask the question: When this happens, how do you react? Popular topics are love and relationships. The claim is that the answers you choose can reveal personal qualities that you may not normally attribute to yourself.
- *Preference quizzes* pose questions on a variety of topics, from your favourite colour to how you write to what time of day you like best. The claim here is that your answers illustrate enduring and broad traits such as extraversion or creativity.
- *Relational quizzes* ask you open-ended questions about how you would react to specific, imaginary events. For example, "If you saw someone being robbed, what would you do?" The claim behind these quizzes is that your responses can tell you a lot about your values and your self-concept, or how you see yourself. But do they really do this? Consider for a moment how scientists construct tests.

Psychologists and other researchers go through a rigorous process to construct tests by relying heavily on solid test construction and knowledge of scoring, validation, and statistics. They first determine the construct; that is, what they want to measure (e.g., trait, ability, attitude, disorder, etc.). They then devise a method for testing and create the individual test items; this process is always related to a particular empirically-supported theory. Typically, once tests are constructed, researchers and specialists in the area review the test (this is formally known as a peer review process) and suggest changes. Once the test is determined to be ready to be assessed, it is administered to a sample of people. Following this, a series of statistical analyses are run on the individual item data to assess whether the test is measuring what it is intended to measure. The test is then edited and tested on a new sample of people. A final series of statistical analyses are run to see if the test represents all of the people in the population it is intended to be measuring (i.e., all age groups, socio-economic classes, gender, cultures, etc.).

A writer for a magazine, without any specialized knowledge on a given topic, is the one who typically devises the "tests" in magazines. For this reason, almost all psychologists recommend treating such pop-culture personality quizzes as entertainment at most. They may be fun, but they typically emerge from the minds of enterprising individuals or organizations, rarely undergo testing or research of any kind, and usually are without any predictive capacity. As a result, they are therefore misleading. Always keep in mind that you should not base important decisions on the results of such quizzes, and that forming insights or views about yourself based on the results of the tests is likely to be a big mistake.

The *Minnesota Multiphasic Personality Inventory 2 (MMPI-2)* is one of the most widely-used personality test (Butcher, 2011; Weiner & Greene, 2008). It is often used to assess abnormal personality characteristics and inclinations. A person's responses on this test are believed to reveal thoughts, emotions, and attitudes; personality characteristics; and possible psychological disorders. The inventory is composed of 567 items and takes approximately 60 to 90 minutes to complete.

The items were empirically derived. This means that many possible test items were administered to people with various personal styles and psychological disorders, and their responses were analyzed to determine which items had predictive value and which patterns of responses corresponded to particular personality styles and diagnostic groups. It is important to note that the test questions do not necessarily have to make intuitive sense, but are instead kept on the test if they have predictive value. For example, if most people who score high on extraversion choose "green" as their favourite colour, then the question, "What is your favourite colour?" has predictive validity and would remain on the test (even though it may not, on the face of it, have anything to do with personality).

If you would like to evaluate your personality using a version of this measure, go to www.personalitytest.net/ipip/ipipneo120.htm.

Unlike the MMPI-2, the *NEO (Neuroticism, Extraversion, Openness) Personality Inventory Revised (NEO-PI-R)* does not attempt to assess maladaptive aspects of personality. It is structured to evaluate 30 traits that comprise three of the five superfactors of the five-factor theory of personality.

PSYCHOLOGY AROUND US The Story Behind the Story

Earlier, you read about one of the field's most widely used and popular personality tests, the Myers-Briggs Type Indicator (MBTI), which is used especially in the business field (see page 494). You might have assumed that this instrument, which applies the principles of Carl Jung's personality theory, was developed by skilled and learned psychologists. However, you would be wrong.

The MBTI was created by a mother and her daughter, neither of whom was a psychologist. The story began when Katharine Briggs met Clarence "Chief" Myers, the boyfriend (and later the husband) of her daughter Isabel. Struck by how different Chief was from anyone in her family, Katharine became interested in personality types. She began reading biographies. From those readings, she identified a list of traits on which people differ. Later, she discovered the work of Carl Jung and adapted her categories to better conform to his constructs. Each person, Katharine believed, could be characterized somewhere along the dimensions of personality that she had identified.

Katharine and Isabel worked feverishly to find applications for their personality typology. Isabel, for example, wrote a mystery novel where the solution hinged on her mother's ideas. She also began teaching herself the fundamentals of test construction, statistics, and psychological assessment. Katharine and Isabel hoped to produce a test that would guide employment opportunities for the massive influx of women entering the workforce during World War II. Eventually, a major test-publishing company took interest in their work, and the rest, as they say, is history.

Despite the popularity of personality inventories, some significant concerns have been raised about their use as indicators of personality. First, the tests rely on self-reports, a source of information that may not always be accurate (Feliciano & Gum, 2010; Gold & Castillo, 2010; Weiner & Green, 2008). If we are not fully aware of our own behaviour patterns, preferences, or interests, our self-reports may not reflect our actual personal style. In one study, for example, extraverted people scored high on the extraversion scale of a personality inventory, but neurotic people did not score high on the neuroticism scale (a less socially desirable trait) of the same inventory (Spain et al., 2000).

Another concern is that personality tests may not always be used and applied properly. Some employers, for example, use measures of conscientiousness to predict an applicant's potential job performance. But some jobs are not well suited for conscientious people, at least not overly-conscientious people (Hogan & Hogan, 1993). An individual's performance on a job that emphasizes speed or quantity of output may be hindered by extensive checking and rechecking, for example.

Still another concern is that test-takers may tailor their answers on personality inventories to try to create a good impression—a phenomenon known as **socially desirable responding** (Viswesvaran & Ones, 1999). The problem of socially desirable responding was, in fact, anticipated by the creators of the MMPI. They included certain questions, called *validity items*, in the questionnaire to assess the likelihood that a respondent would purposely give an answer that was socially desirable rather than accurate. Suppose, for example, that an individual keeps answering "true" to such items as "I smile at everyone I meet" and "false" to "I get angry sometimes." It is assumed that these responses, and perhaps many others as well, are instances of socially desirable responding. In such cases, test scorers may disregard or adjust the respondents' personality scores.

socially desirable responding tailoring answers on personality inventories to try to create a good impression.

The use of personality tests as part of the hiring process has a long history. However, early personality tests were not demonstrated to be particularly good (reliable or valid) at predicting who the best candidate for a job should be. As a consequence, in the United States there were a number of successful lawsuits claiming that hiring decisions based on older personality tests were unfair (Rothstein & Goffin, 2006). In Canada, there was much less litigation. Currently, there are a number of better designed personality tests that do, in fact, meet legally defensible criteria for use as pre-employment selection tools (Rothstein & Goffin, 2006). Within Canada, the use of such tests is regulated by bodies such as human rights commissions, which limit the types of personal information employers can ask prospective employees to questions (including personality test questions) that are directly relevant to the job for which they are applying. Tests must be carefully constructed to ensure they meet these criteria and also show appropriate levels of reliability and validity (Eisenbraun, 2006).

Projective Tests

Projective tests are quite different from personality inventories (see **Figure 13-8**). These tests are commonly used by psychoanalytic clinicians and researchers and are intended to tap into a person's unconscious mind to detect personality styles and conflicts hidden beneath the surface. The most widely-used and famous projective test is the *Rorschach Inkblot Test*. During the test, participants are presented with a set of 10 inkblots and asked to explain what they see. The ambiguous shapes of the inkblots are intended to force participants to *project* structure and meaning onto the images, and the participants' responses are thought to reveal underlying psychological themes and personality issues. For example, a person who sees images of animals or weapons in the inkblots is often thought to be grappling with underlying aggressive urges.

projective test a personality assessment device intended to tap a person's unconscious by presenting the person with an ambiguous stimulus and asking the person to interpret what the stimulus means.

Some clinicians believe that the Rorschach test provides useful suggestions that can enhance the effectiveness of therapy (Cashel, 2002). It is widely agreed in the scientific community, however, that projective tests, such as the Rorschach, display low validity, or

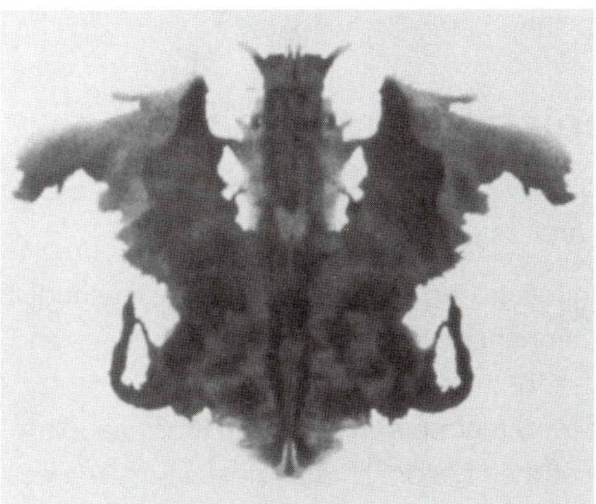

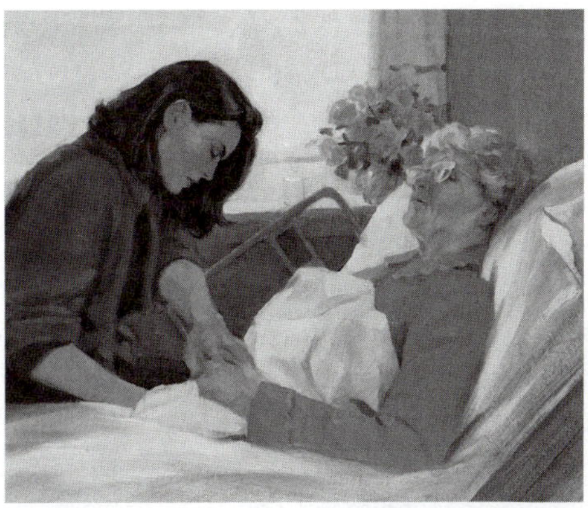

FIGURE 13-8 Projective tests. Clinicians often use tests that consist of vague shapes or situations to help assess personality. Shown here is an inkblot similar to those used in the Rorschach Inkblot Test and a picture similar to the ones used in the Thematic Apperception Test.

accuracy (Bornstein, 2007; Butcher, 2010; Wood et al., 2002). Scoring of the tests depends heavily on interpretations by the test administrators—interpretations that may be affected by the assessor's professional biases or level of expertise. In addition to problems with validity, many have concerns about the reliability, or consistency, of projective tests. Studies have shown that individuals who take a Rorschach test today may offer responses that are very different from those they offered when they took the test last week, leading to different personality assessments. Look again at the sample in Figure 13-8. You can probably see why the Rorschach test might present difficulties.

An alternative and commonly-used type of projective test is the *Thematic Apperception Test (TAT)*. This tool, created in the 1930s by psychologist Henry Murray, is made up of ambiguous black-and-white drawings of people in various situations. Test-takers are asked to describe and make up a story about each drawing. The uses and criticisms of the TAT are similar to those of the Rorschach. Although some systematic scoring procedures exist, most clinicians rely on their own judgments when analyzing an individual's TAT responses (Masling, 2004; Pinkerman et al., 1993). Additionally, it is difficult to know for certain that the stories created by individuals reflect how they are actually feeling; they may instead represent the individuals' projections of how they believe they should be feeling (Lilienfeld et al., 2000).

Before You Go On

www.wiley.com/go/comer

What Do You Know?

24. How do personality inventories differ from projective assessment techniques?
25. What is socially desirable responding and how is it addressed in the MMPI-2?
26. What are some problems with projective assessment techniques?

What Do You Think?

There are so-called personality tests all over the Internet. Which ones have you come across? Why are most such tests uninformative and often misleading?

SCAN TO GET THE ANSWERS

Summary

The Psychodynamic Perspective

LEARNING OBJECTIVE 1 Summarize the main ideas of the psychodynamic view of personality development.

- Personality refers to the unique characteristics that account for enduring patterns of inner experience and outward behaviour.
- Sigmund Freud's psychoanalytic theory of personality depended to a large extent on his ideas about the conscious and unconscious mind. Most of the content of our minds, in Freud's view, is in the unconscious.
- Freud proposed three central forces in personality development: the id, the ego, and the superego.
- In Freud's view, personality develops as children pass through a series of psychosexual stages. Each stage is characterized by strong conflicts between the id, the ego, and the superego. Failure to resolve these conflicts can result in neuroses.
- Conflicts result in anxiety, and Freud believed that we use unconscious tactics called defence mechanisms to protect ourselves from this anxiety.
- Other psychodynamic theories include those of Alfred Adler, Carl G. Jung, and Karen Horney.

The Humanistic Perspective

LEARNING OBJECTIVE 2 Describe the humanistic theories of Abraham Maslow and Carl Rogers.

- Humanistic theorists, including Abraham Maslow and Carl Rogers, emphasized people's basic goodness and their ability to fulfill their potential.
- Maslow proposed that personality arises from people's striving to meet their needs. Human needs are arranged hierarchically, with self-actualization at the top level.
- Rogers based his theory of personality on his ideas about the importance of self-concept. He believed that

children need unconditional positive regard to develop healthy self-concepts.

The Trait Perspective

LEARNING OBJECTIVE 3 Summarize the leading trait theories, and describe how the five-factor theory has evolved from the work of Gordon Allport and Hans Eysenck.

- Personality traits are tendencies to behave in certain ways that remain relatively constant across situations. Trait theorists such as Gordon Allport and Hans Eysenck first proposed that central traits affect a broad range of behaviour.
- Allport conducted detailed case studies that sought to reveal the unique collection of traits at play for each individual.
- Eysenck, using factor analysis, identified three personality superfactors: extraversion, neuroticism, and psychoticism.
- Other trait theorists proposed the five-factor theory, which identified five major trait categories: agreeableness, extraversion, neuroticism, conscientiousness, and openness to experience.
- Although traits play an important role in behaviour, they can be inconsistent over time and across different situations.

The Situationist and Interactionist Perspectives

LEARNING OBJECTIVE 4 Describe and differentiate the situationist and interactionist views of personality.

- Situationism holds that behaviour is governed primarily by the variables in a given situation rather than by internal traits. The behaviourist B. F. Skinner could be said to have viewed personality from this perspective.
- Interactionism focuses on interactions between persons and situations. Albert Bandura's social-cognitive theory is an example of interactionist theory. In Bandura's view, the environment, internal mental events, and behaviour all interact to affect behaviour through the process of reciprocal determinism.

Biological Foundations of Personality

LEARNING OBJECTIVE 5 Discuss the heritability of personality traits and some of the neural systems that may be involved in the expression of personality.

- Twin studies, such as the Minnesota Study of Twins Reared Apart, suggest that many personality traits have strong genetic links.
- Certain brain structures, neurotransmitters, and hormones have been associated with personality variables.
- In interpreting links between genes, physiological factors, and personality, it is important to remember that the relationships are complex and multidirectional.

Personality *How We Differ*

LEARNING OBJECTIVE 6 Explain how gender and cultural differences can affect personality.

- Research has found many more similarities than differences between men's and women's personalities. Nevertheless, some consistent differences have been identified.
- Socio-cultural factors are thought to play an important role in gender differences in personality. According to social role theory, for example, boys and girls develop different behaviours and skills based largely on the division of labour between the sexes and the resulting differences in gender role expectations.
- Cross-cultural research into personality has focused on personality development in individualist and collectivist cultures. Some traits observed in these cultures reflect differing cultural values.
- The relationship between socio-economic conditions and personality traits has received relatively little attention. However, the investigations that have been conducted suggest that at the very least, living conditions have a direct impact on how and whether certain personality traits translate into behaviours.

Personality Disorders *When Things Go Wrong*

LEARNING OBJECTIVE 7 Define personality disorder, and describe some of the key features of this disorder.

- A personality disorder is an inflexible pattern of inner experience and outward behaviour that causes distress or difficulty with daily functioning.
- The American Psychiatric Association outlines 10 personality disorders in its guide for therapists.

Personality Assessment

LEARNING OBJECTIVE 8 Describe the two major types of personality tests, and give examples of each.

- Personality inventories are questionnaires that require individuals to respond to a series of true–false or agree–disagree statements designed to measure various aspects of personality.
- Two widely-used personality inventories are the Minnesota Multiphasic Personality Inventory 2 (MMPI-2) and the NEO (Neuroticism, Extraversion, Openness) Personality Inventory Revised (NEO-PI-R). The MMPI-2 is typically used to assess abnormal personality characteristics and inclinations. The NEO-PI-R evaluates traits associated with the five-factor theory of personality.
- Projective tests are intended to tap into people's unconscious minds by having them interpret ambiguous stimuli. In the case of the Rorschach Inkblot Test, the stimuli are inkblots. In the case of the Thematic Apperception Test (TAT), they are black-and-white drawings.

Key Terms

TYING IT TOGETHER

The study of personality is closely connected to the study of all other areas of psychology. Throughout this chapter, we have stressed how personality interfaces with psychology's various subfields, including our highlighted sections on brain function, individual differences, abnormal functioning, and development. To remind you of how personality is tied to other psychology subfields and issues, we have selected some interesting points from throughout the chapter.

WHAT HAPPENS IN THE BRAIN?

- Phrenologists in the nineteenth century believed that the shapes of people's skulls could reveal their personal and moral characteristics.
- Some studies suggest that, on average, people whose right brain hemisphere is dominant tend to be less extraverted than people with a dominant left hemisphere.
- People with high dopamine activity in their brain's reward learning pathway tend to be less inhibited, less anxious, and more energetic than those with lower dopamine activity in that pathway.

HOW WE DIFFER

- Personality similarities between men and women far outnumber the differences between them.
- Two variables on which males and females tend to differ are aggression and interpersonal sensitivity. On average, males are more aggressive and females are more empathic.
- People from collectivist cultures tend to display more agreeableness. Those from individualistic cultures tend to be more extraverted and success-oriented.

WHEN THINGS GO WRONG

- An excessive need to be noticed, taken care of, or avoid social contacts may each reflect a type of personality disorder: histrionic, dependent, and avoidant, respectively.
- Most online "personality tests" are, at most, a form of entertainment. Typically, they offer inaccurate and useless information about one's personality or one's clinical problems.
- "Neurosis" was Freud's term for psychological dysfunction marked by anxiety, depression, or other such symptoms. The term has no official status in the clinical field today.

HOW WE DEVELOP

- Identical twins tend to be more similar on many personality characteristics than are fraternal twins. This is true even if the identical twins have been raised apart.
- Particularly strong ties have been found between genetic inheritance and the traits of openness, extraversion, neuroticism, and agreeableness.
- Freud warned of life-long fixation at an early stage of development for individuals whose oral, anal, or phallic needs were not adequately met during childhood.

Psychology Around Us

The Five-Factor Personality Model in Action

Spotting Personality Traits

One of the leading models of personality is the five-factor model, which holds that people's personalities can be represented by their scores on five superfactors, each of which consists of numerous specific trait categories. Let's begin by identifying different personalities.

In this video lab exercise, you will observe friends interacting in multiple situations. One of your jobs is to spot the specific traits of each individual and determine the individual's corresponding scores on each of the superfactors. While doing this, you will also examine whether the identified personality traits can be better accounted for by situational factors, distinguish trait-caused behaviours from situation-caused behaviours, and consider the role of culture and gender in personality. By the end of the exercise, you will appreciate that personality assessments are far from exact, regardless of whether you are applying a formal personality model or your own implicit personality theory.

View this in Action WILEY PLUS www.wileyplus.com

Video Lab Exercise

As you are working on this online exercise, consider the following questions:

- Can the trait-versus-situation question ever be firmly resolved in evaluating personality?
- Which personality traits seem most likely to be tied to genetic inheritance?
- How might the brain regulate personality?
- How can we know when an individual's personality profile actually reflects a broad personality disorder?

CHAPTER 14

Social Psychology

CHAPTER OUTLINE

- Social Cognition: Attitudes
- Social Cognition: Attributions
- Social Forces
- Social Relations
- Social Functioning *What Happens in the Brain?*
- Disorders of Social Functioning *When Things Go Wrong*

SOCIAL PSYCHOLOGY AT THE STANLEY CUP FINALS

On June 15, 2011, the Vancouver Canucks lost to the Boston Bruins in game seven of the Stanley Cup final. During the Vancouver home games, thousands of fans gathered in the streets around the arena and watched the games on large screens (as people had done during the Winter Olympics). Following previous games (all Vancouver wins), the crowds had been boisterous but controlled. Following the seventh-game loss, some members of the crowd began to get out of hand. Bottles were tossed at the big screens, porta-potties were tipped over, and the first of what would eventually be a total of 17 cars (including two police cars) were turned over and set ablaze. Fights broke out and 140 people were reported injured, including nine police officers. Transit in the area was shut down, and people attending a musical (*Wicked*) at a nearby theatre were told to wait in the theatre for several hours until the riot subsided. Rioters moved through downtown Vancouver, smashing windows and looting stores. Eventually the rioters were dispersed at about midnight.

At the time of this writing, about 100 people had been arrested in relation to the riot. However, that number is likely to increase as there was also a *virtual* riot: social media videos and photos taken on cell phones were posted in the days following the disturbance. The various sites asked that anyone recognizing a rioter provide his or her name so that it could be passed along to the police and additional rioters could be charged. It has been suggested that the actions of the social media "mob" demanding charges and justice were in some ways similar to the actions of the mob of rioters, but debate on that comparison continues.

The actions of people in and after such events are of particular interest to social psychologists. Many "rioters" were otherwise regular citizens, and yet they behaved in uncharacteristic ways during the riot. Social psychologists study the social forces involved in this sort of behaviour.

The British poet John Donne's famous words, "No man is an island," highlight the interconnectedness of humankind. We live in a world of approximately 7 billion people, and each and every day we influence and are influenced by others. Social psychologists devote themselves to the study of human interconnectedness. Unlike many areas of psychology that focus on areas of individual difference, such as personality, social psychology is based on the belief that "it is not so much the kind of person a man is, as the kind of situation in which he finds himself that determines how he will act" (Milgram, 2004, p. 101).

We might think of social psychology in a general way as the scientific study of how people are affected by other people. This informal definition covers considerable territory. Many aspects of an individual's functioning may be affected by others—thoughts, feelings, and behaviours may

The social impact. Many Vancouverites went downtown the morning after the Stanley Cup riot to help clean up.

each reflect the influence of the social environment. Moreover, the influence of others may be direct or indirect.

Consider the Vancouver riot again. As they responded to the events of that evening, people either worsened or improved the plight of others in innumerable ways. You will read about some of these events later in the chapter. The events in Vancouver affected not only the city's residents, but also people who watched the events unfold on television or over the Internet, causing viewers to reflect on the sometimes thin nature of social bonds and civility.

Given the many ways in which people can affect one another, the pioneering psychologist Gordon Allport (1954), whom we also discussed in the previous chapter, offered a more detailed definition of social psychology that is embraced by most people in the field. That is, **social psychology** seeks to understand, explain, and predict how our thoughts, feelings, and behaviour influence and are influenced by the actual, imagined, or implied presence of others (Allport, 1985).

social psychology an area of psychology that seeks to understand, explain, and predict how people's thoughts, feelings, and behaviours are influenced by the actual, imagined, or implied presence of others.

social cognition the way in which people perceive and interpret themselves and others in their social world.

Which pieces of this definition should social psychologists focus on? Over the years, certain topics have received particular attention. Many social psychologists have concerned themselves with **social cognition**—how people perceive and interpret themselves and others in their social world. They have examined, for example, the attitudes people hold and the attributions that people make. Other social psychologists have paid more attention to social forces and social interactions. We will discuss each of these areas on the following pages, and then examine what happens in the brain during social functioning. We will conclude the chapter with a description of disorders of social behaviour. ■

Social Cognition: Attitudes

LEARNING OBJECTIVE 1

Explain how attitudes form and change and what role they play in behaviour.

There are few things in our world that we do not evaluate in some form or another. On some evaluations, people tend to agree. For example, most people believe that natural disasters (wildfires) are bad, that horror movies are scary, and that Sidney Crosby is an extraordinary hockey player. On other topics, people are more divided—such as the proper role of government in people's lives, the best ice cream flavour, and the advisability of legalizing drugs. Psychologists refer to our relatively stable and enduring (within individuals) evaluations of things and people as **attitudes** (Albarracin et al., 2005).

attitudes relatively stable and enduring evaluations of things and people.

ABC model of attitudes a model proposing that attitudes have three components: the affective component, the behavioural component, and the cognitive component.

According to the **ABC model of attitudes**, attitudes have three components, as shown in **Figure 14-1** (van den Berg et al., 2006; Eagly & Chaiken, 1998):

- The *affective* component—how we feel toward an object.
- The *behavioural* component—how we behave toward an object.
- The *cognitive* component—what we believe about an object.

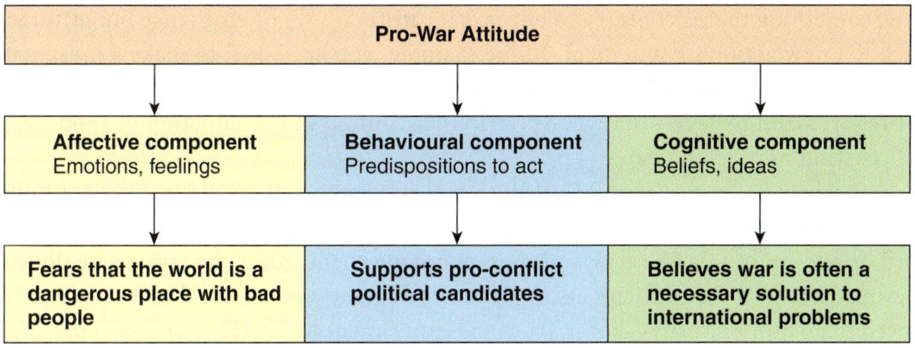

FIGURE 14-1 The ABC model of attitudes.

Before September 11, 2001, many North Americans held the attitude that their everyday world was safe from terrorism. They felt secure (affective component), went to work each day confident that terrorism would not touch their lives (behavioural component), and believed they were safe (cognitive component). General surveys of Canadians indicate that 94 percent of us are satisfied with our level of personal safety (Statistics Canada, 2005). Similarly, in the weeks leading up to the Stanley Cup finals, it seemed, from the nightly turnout around the arena, that most residents of Vancouver felt that their downtown area was safe and secure, even when filled with thousands of hockey fans. We do not have data, but it is certainly clear that attitudes can change. We will explain how that can happen later in this section; but first, let's discuss how attitudes form in the first place.

Attitudes HOW WE DEVELOP

Early in life, parents play a major role in shaping children's beliefs and opinions about things and people (Day et al., 2006). As we observed in Chapter 3, socialization is the process by which children acquire beliefs and behaviours considered desirable or appropriate by the family to which they belong. You are reading this textbook right now because you have been socialized in a number of ways—perhaps to believe in the value of a post-secondary education or the need for hard work to achieve your goals. This socialization may have occurred by direct transmission (your parents lecturing you about these values) or in subtler ways. Perhaps your mother or father praised you for your grades or punished you for not doing your homework. Over time, you might generalize these individual experiences into an overall attitude about the value of what you are doing.

As children mature, their peers, their teachers, and the media also begin to significantly influence their attitudes (Prislin & Wood, 2005). Children observe their classmates and take note of the rewards and punishments those students reap from their behaviour. If a child sees a classmate rejected by the rest of the class for making disparaging remarks about a particular ethnic group, for example, the child may develop an attitude that such remarks are inappropriate and unacceptable. Similarly, seeing a favourite television character get whatever he wants by bullying people might foster an attitude that aggression is an acceptable way to achieve one's goals.

Shaping attitudes. Many school-age children today support recycling. What influences in the media and the general culture may have helped to shape this child's attitude?

How Do Attitudes Change?

Once we have internalized a particular attitude—that is, once we have made it our own—how rigid and long lasting is that attitude? Can people experience a change of heart? In a classic social psychology experiment in the late 1950s, researchers Leon Festinger and J. Merrill Carlsmith (1959) demonstrated that when we are subtly manipulated into doing or saying something that is contrary to our private attitudes, we often change our attitudes to match the new action or statement. If, for example, you are asked to make a presentation in favour of a west coast salmon fishing ban when in fact you oppose such a ban, you may later report—and believe—that your position has shifted in the direction of support for a west coast salmon fishing ban.

In their study, Festinger and Carlsmith had research participants engage in a number of repetitive and boring tasks, such as spending an hour slowly turning square pegs on a board or adding spools to a tray and then removing them. After the tasks were done, the experimenters told the participants that the experiment was over and that they would be allowed to go home shortly—but in truth the experiment had just begun! Each participant was next told that a new group of individuals would soon arrive—individuals who would be performing the same tedious tasks but would be told ahead of time that the tasks were actually "fun" and "intriguing." The experimenter further asked each participant to help out by describing the upcoming tasks as fun and exciting to one of the new individuals. (All of the new individuals were in fact *confederates*, that is, collaborators with the experimenters.) In almost all cases, the participants agreed to prepare the new individuals for an enjoyable experience. In addition, some of the participants were told they would be paid $1 (or about $8 today—a small amount of money) for helping out in this way, while others were told they would receive $20 ($160 in today's dollars).

After presenting the positive spiel about the tedious tasks to the new individuals, the participants were interviewed by the experimenters about how enjoyable they themselves actually believed the tasks to be. This was, in fact, Festinger and Carlsmith's central area of interest. Many of the participants reported that they actually had found the tasks to be quite enjoyable! Even more fascinating, it was those who had been paid $1 for "talking up" the tasks who reported the tasks to be most enjoyable—not those who had been paid $20 (see **Figure 14-2**).

How could participants come to find the mind-numbing tasks of this study enjoyable? Why did those paid less money to convince someone else that the tasks were enjoyable find the tasks *more* enjoyable than those paid more money to do so? Theorists have offered two possible answers to these questions.

cognitive dissonance a state of emotional discomfort people experience when they hold two contradictory beliefs or hold a belief that contradicts their behaviour.

Cognitive Dissonance Theory Festinger (1957) proposed that when we hold two contradictory beliefs, or when we hold a belief that contradicts our behaviour, we experience a state of *emotional discomfort*, or **cognitive dissonance**. This state is so unpleasant that we are motivated to reduce or eliminate it. One way of removing dissonance is to modify our existing beliefs. In Festinger and Carlsmith's study, cognitive dissonance theory would hold that the conflict between the participants' initial attitudes about the tasks (that the tasks were boring and trivial) and their later behaviour (telling someone that the tasks were enjoyable) resulted in cognitive dissonance, and this unpleasant state motivated them to change their attitudes about the tasks in positive directions (that is, to believe they actually did enjoy the task, or at least that they found it less unpleasant).

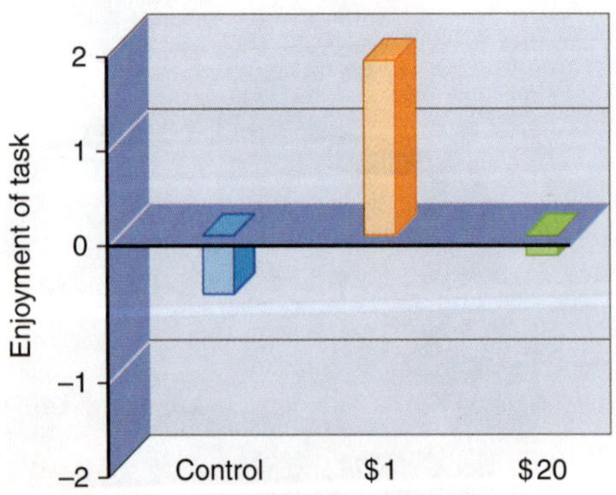

FIGURE 14-2 Cognitive dissonance. After describing a boring task as fun, participants in Festinger and Carlsmith's study were asked to rate their own enjoyment of the task on a scale of −5 to +5. Those paid $1 ($8 in 2012 dollars) for praising the task rated the task as more enjoyable than those paid $20 ($160 dollars in 2012) for praising it.

But what about the differing results for the participants in the $1 condition and those in the $20 condition? According to dissonance theory, the participants in the $20 condition experienced less dissonance because they had sufficient justification for their behaviour. Since they were well paid to say that the tasks were enjoyable, they could tell themselves, "I said the experiment was fun because I got money for saying it." (Twenty dollars would buy quite a bit more in the late 1950s than it does today.) Thus, these participants experienced little or no discrepancy between their attitudes and their behaviour. In contrast, those who received only $1 for their positive statements had insufficient justification for their behaviour and so experienced a marked discrepancy and uncomfortable feelings of dissonance. These participants managed to reduce the uncomfortable feelings by modifying their beliefs about the tasks—that is, by later reporting (and indeed, believing) "the tasks really were kind of interesting."

Festinger's theory of cognitive dissonance has received support from literally hundreds of studies (Cooper et al., 2005, 2004). Furthermore, it has significant implications for many events and strategies in real life. For example, a growing number of today's parents financially reward their children for working on their homework. The parents' hope is that such rewards will move doing homework ahead of attractive alternatives, such as texting, listening to iPods, or playing computer games, and that the children will come to willingly complete and even enjoy homework. However, cognitive dissonance theory warns that such strategies are likely to backfire. Children who are given explicit financial rewards—especially sizeable ones—will likely know exactly why they are doing their homework. That is, they will experience little or no dissonance between their attitude toward homework ("homework is really boring!") and their act of doing homework. In turn, they will not be inclined to change their unfavourable view about doing homework.

Serious dissonance. The contradiction between this nurse's professional commitment to fight cancer and her smoking behaviour may produce noxious feelings of dissonance. To reduce these feelings, she may adopt a belief such as, "I have an addiction to smoking that overrides my better judgment."

The Self-Perception Alternative Cognitive dissonance theory fits some instances of attitude change, but not others. In many cases, we seem to form and change attitudes in the absence of internal discomfort. You might think, for example, that you are alert, but after yawning, you might decide, "I'm tired"—not because of a need to reduce emotional tension brought about by the discrepancy between the attitude ("I'm alert") and the behaviour (a yawn), but simply because the yawn was informative. Thus, psychologist Daryl Bem developed the **self-perception theory** of attitude change (Bem, 1972). This theory minimizes the role of emotional discomfort and suggests that when we are *uncertain* of our attitudes, we simply infer what our attitudes are by observing our own behaviour, in much the same way as outsiders might observe us. According to Bem, our behaviours are often clues from which we deduce our attitudes—we might decide we like roller coasters because we keep riding them, or we might decide we hate spinach because we keep spitting it out whenever we try it.

self-perception theory a theory suggesting that when people are uncertain of their attitudes, they infer what the attitudes are by observing their own behaviour.

Which is correct—the cognitive dissonance or the self-perception explanation of attitude change? Historically, this has been a source of great debate in social psychology; however, research has clarified that each may be right, but one may be more relevant in particular situations than the other (Cooper et al., 2004; Petty et al., 2003; Fazio et al., 1977). Festinger's theory of cognitive dissonance seems more applicable to situations in which we behave in ways that are strikingly out of character for us, whereas Bem's self-perception theory may be at work in situations where we behave only slightly out of character or our attitudes are not all that clear to begin with.

Do Attitudes Influence Behaviour?

If we know someone's attitudes, does that mean we can predict that person's behaviour? It turns out that the attitudes people express are not necessarily related to how they actually behave (Fazio & Roskos-Ewoldsen, 2005; Cooper et al., 2004; Eagly & Chaiken, 1998). In the 1930s, a time when many Americans held very negative attitudes toward Asians, sociologist Richard LaPiere conducted a field study in which he had a Chinese couple travel across the United States and visit over 250 hotels and restaurants (LaPiere, 1934). Although managers at over 90 percent of the establishments indicated in a mailed questionnaire that they would not serve Chinese guests, only one of the establishments visited by the Chinese couple actually refused them service. In fact, most of the hotels and restaurants provided above-average service, indicating that attitudes do not necessarily predict behaviour.

"Believe what I do, not what I say." Many people who endorse healthful eating and better fitness on surveys actually consume huge quantities of junk food in their daily meals.

Of course, sometimes attitudes do predict behaviour. Research has uncovered various factors that affect the extent to which attitudes will predict behaviours (Fabrigar et al., 2006; Fazio & Roskos-Ewoldsen, 2005; Cooper et al., 2004). One of the leading factors is *attitude specificity*. The more specific an attitude, the more likely it is to predict behaviour. If a young woman specifically loves Lady Gaga, for example, she is more likely to download her new song the first day it is released than someone who loves pop music more broadly. Another factor is *attitude strength*. Stronger attitudes predict behaviour more accurately than weak or vague attitudes.

Are People Honest About Their Attitudes?

One reason that attitudes fail to consistently predict behaviours is that people often *misrepresent* their attitudes. In fact, analyses of most self-report questionnaires—the tools usually used by researchers to measure attitudes—cannot distinguish genuine attitudes from false ones (Carels et al., 2006; Cobb, 2002; Rosenberg, 1969). Why would people misrepresent their attitudes? There appear to be several reasons.

The Social Desirability Factor Often, people state attitudes that are *socially desirable* rather than accurate. A person who privately does not trust people of a particular ethnic background, for example, may not acknowledge having this attitude for fear of being judged unfavourably by others. To eliminate the social desirability factor and measure people's attitudes, psychologists have sometimes employed the *bogus pipeline* technique (Jones & Sigall, 1971). Here, a research participant is connected to a non-functioning device that looks like a polygraph (lie-detector machine) and is told that the device can detect deception. When individuals are connected to such a device, they are more likely to report their attitudes truthfully (Nier, 2005; Roese & Jamieson, 1993).

In one bogus pipeline study, investigators asked students about socially sensitive issues, such as how frequently they drank, smoked, had sex, and used illicit drugs (Tourangeau et al., 1997). Participants in one group were hooked up to a device and told that it could detect inaccurate answers. This belief apparently made the participants more honest. The students hooked up to the machine reported performing socially sensitive behaviours relatively frequently. Control participants, who were not hooked up to the device, answered in more socially desirable ways, reporting lower frequencies of the behaviours in question. Following completion of their participation in a bogus pipeline study like this one, all participants must, ethically, be debriefed. That is, the nature and purpose of the study must be explained to them and they must be told that their honesty was not actually being monitored during the study.

"We have all had the experience of finding that our reactions and perhaps even our deeds have denied beliefs we thought were ours."
—*James Baldwin, writer and civil rights activist*

Implicit Attitudes Another problem that researchers run into when trying to measure attitudes is that people are not always *aware* of their true attitudes (Bassili & Brown, 2005). In their own minds, employers may believe that applicants of all ethnicities deserve a fair interview process. But when interviewing individuals from ethnic backgrounds other than their own, the same employers may, in fact, engage in less eye contact, maintain greater physical distance, and offer less interview time than when interviewing applicants whose backgrounds are similar to their own. In such cases, the employers may have difficulty trusting people of different backgrounds, but this attitude has not reached their conscious awareness (Baron & Banaji, 2006; Bassett et al., 2005; Greenwald et al., 2002, 1998). When attitudes such as these lie below the level of conscious awareness, they are called **implicit attitudes**.

implicit attitude an attitude of which the person is unaware.

The finding that people have implicit attitudes is reminiscent of the following observation by the famous Russian writer Fyodor Dostoyevsky:

> *Every man has reminiscences which he would not tell to everyone but only his friends. He has other matters in his mind which he would not reveal even to his friends, but only to himself, and that in secret. But there are other things which a man is afraid to tell even to himself, and every decent man has a number of such things stored away in his mind.*

As you might imagine, measuring attitudes that the holder is not aware of presents a challenge for researchers. To get at implicit attitudes, researchers have employed the *Implicit Association Test (IAT)*, which uses a person's reaction times to help gauge her implicit attitudes. The IAT consists of three stages.

1. First, a person is exposed to two broad categories—say, "dog" and "cat." The person is asked to categorize certain words as belonging in the "dog" category or the "cat" category—for example, fire hydrant and litter box.
2. Next, the person is asked to complete a different task in which they must categorize words as either pleasant or unpleasant. These words are again fairly obvious, such as "poison" and "happiness."
3. Finally, the categories are combined in a third task, and the person is asked to identify a series of words as either more dog-related/pleasant or more cat-related/unpleasant; the categories are later reversed to be cat/pleasant and dog/unpleasant. The assumption is that if a person implicitly believes that dogs are more desirable than cats, the person should be quicker to identify pleasant words during the dog/pleasant combination, because the association between pleasant things and dogs is stronger. It will take this person slightly longer to make the dog/unpleasant association because it requires more effort. Similarly, cat people should respond quicker to the cat/pleasant combination.

If you want to see how an Implicit Association Test works, go online to www.implicit.harvard.edu and take one for yourself. You can be part of a research study with tens of thousands of participants.

You might find this logic convoluted and hard to accept. However, researchers have found that many Caucasian Americans who characterize themselves as not prejudiced have quicker reaction times to Caucasian American/pleasant and African American/unpleasant identifications than to Caucasian American/unpleasant and African American/pleasant ones. Such implicit attitudes appear to be stable over time, and they have been useful predictors of both subtle indicators of discomfort, such as turning one's eyes away during a conversation with someone of another race, and overt acts of racism, such as the use of slurs, physical violence, and snubbing (Rudman & Ashmore, 2007). Researchers have also used the IAT to detect bias against elderly people, overweight people, women, and other groups.

Bertram Gawronski and his colleagues at the University of Western Ontario have investigated different approaches to reducing both implicit and explicit components of prejudiced beliefs. They find that diversity training and guided exposure to the groups toward which prejudiced beliefs are directed work to reduce explicit prejudiced beliefs, while fear reduction and other emotion-focused interventions work best to reduce implicit aspects of prejudice (Gawronski et al., 2008; Sritharan & Gawronski, 2010).

Gawronski's main point is that simple, one-element efforts to reduce prejudice do not work. Instead he argues that a multiple component effort would be more effective if it focused on several of the following options: listening to persuasive messages arguing against prejudiced views toward a particular group; having people write arguments supporting an unprejudiced perspective; and trying to reduce the affective reaction associated with a particular group by presenting information about them in neutral or non-affect associated situations. Gawronski's research has demonstrated that combinations of these

Racial bias. In the aftermath of Hurricane Katrina, newspapers carried many photos of desperate people taking food from local food stores. The news caption that accompanied the photo on the left (of an African American) stated that the man had just finished "looting a grocery store," whereas the one that accompanied the photo on the right (white Americans) said that the two individuals had just finished "finding bread and soda at a local grocery store."

sorts of approaches result in more positive changes in participants' prejudicial cognitions and emotions (Gawronski et al., 2010).

Stereotypes and Prejudice

In the wake of Hurricane Katrina, millions of people began reaching out with contributions and charity to help the suffering people in Louisiana, Alabama, and Mississippi. It was during a special charity drive, which aired on all the major television networks, that controversial rap star Kanye West made a highly provocative statement about the disaster:

> *I hate the way they portray us in the media. You see a black family, it [the media] says, "they're looting." You see a white family, it says, "they're looking for food." And, you know, it's been five days [waiting for federal help] because most of the people are black....*

stereotypes generalized impressions about a person or a group of people based on the social category they occupy.

prejudice negative stereotypical attitudes toward individuals from another group.

In part, West was talking about *stereotypes*. Most of us are familiar with the notion of **stereotypes**—generalized impressions about people or groups of people based on the social category they occupy. Stereotypes can be based on age, race, region of origin, political or religious beliefs, or any other group characteristic.

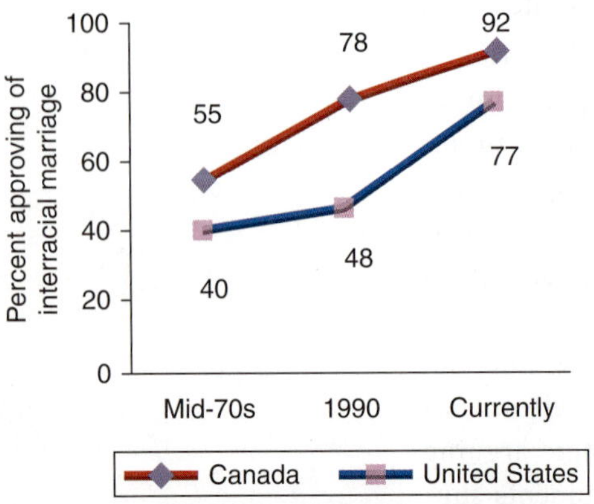

FIGURE 14-3 Prejudice over time. Canadians have expressed greater approval of interracial marriage over the last 40 years, yet studies show that subtle biases remain (Bibby, 2007).

Although stereotypes may be positive or negative, there is little doubt that there is a strong relationship between stereotypes and **prejudice**—negative attitudes toward individuals from another group. Research by Reginald Bibby, a sociologist at Lethbridge University in Alberta, suggests that prejudice in the form of overt racism and sexism has decreased over time in both the United States and Canada, but has always been and continues to be lower in Canada (see **Figure 14-3**). However, despite these reductions reflecting Canada's greater acceptance of diversity, subtle biases remain (Sue et al., 2007; Dovidio et al., 2002). For example, as noted earlier, many Caucasian individuals who characterize themselves as not prejudiced respond to the Implicit Association Test in a way that suggests they have some implicit negative attitudes toward African Americans and African Canadians. Likewise, there has been a long history in Canada of prejudice and negative attitudes toward our Aboriginal population, with negative effects on the overall health of members of that population (Bourassa, McKay, & Hampton, 2004).

Psychologists believe that the human tendency to identify with a group is one of the main contributors to stereotypes and prejudice. As humans, we generally categorize ourselves in terms of similarities to some people and differences from others. Understanding ourselves as members of a particular group (our *in-group*) offers us some insight into who we are. Similarly, perceiving people outside our group as members of other groups (*out-groups*) gives us information—not necessarily valid information—about who they are. As we will discuss in more detail later, human beings appear to have a cognitive predisposition to see things associated with themselves as good and things not associated with themselves as less good (Fiske, 2010).

Evolutionary psychologists suggest that stereotypes and prejudice may have had some adaptive value, as our ancestors probably prized being able to quickly recognize members of their own tribe based on superficial information. Early humans needed to quickly identify other figures as friends or foes, and general appearance would have been an easy way to accomplish this goal. Evolutionary psychologists also suggest that we may be prewired to think of people whom we perceive to be different from us as inferior, which may cause or justify our decisions to exclude or demean them (Fiske, 2000).

A view called the *realistic conflict theory* relies on somewhat more recent history to explain how prejudice comes into play (Jackson, 1993). According to this theory, the amount of actual conflict between particular in-groups and out-groups determines the degree of prejudice or discrimination between those groups. An example is the difficult history of conflict between white Americans and African Americans. Given that history, proponents of realistic conflict theory might have predicted that the media would indeed discriminate against impoverished African-American survivors of Hurricane Katrina, as Kanye West and others later claimed they did.

Rather than focusing on historical antecedents, another view, the **social identity theory**, emphasizes social cognitive factors that come into play in prejudice (Tajfel & Turner, 2004). Social identity theory proposes that prejudice emerges through three processes:

social identity theory a theory that emphasizes social cognitive factors in the onset of prejudice.

1. *Social categorization*, in which a person affiliates with a particular group as a way of figuring out how to act and react in the world.
2. *Social identity*, in which the person forms an identity within the group.
3. *Social comparison*, in which the group member compares the group favourably with other groups, and in turn derives a sense of positive well-being from looking at himself as superior in some way.

In one of his early studies, Tajfel (1981; Jenkins, 2008) randomly assigned study participants to two groups and then had them decide how to divide a sum of money between two people indentified only by their group membership and an ID number. Participants typically showed what Tajfel called an in-group bias by giving more of the money to the person in their group than the person in the other group. Even with no group interaction, the effects of social categorization, social identity, and social comparison can be seen in this result. Now think back to the in- and out-group environment that was very evident in high school, and see if you can recall examples of social behaviour that reflect the three central factors of social identity theory.

Attitudes and the Power of Persuasion

Earlier, we discussed how attitudes form and change. Advertisers have taken a strong interest in these processes. In fact, billions of advertising dollars are devoted each year to helping people develop particular attitudes toward products or services. If you wouldn't dream of using any computer but a MacBook Pro®, or if you much prefer Coke® over Pepsi® (or vice versa), that attitude probably has been created in part through persuasion—the advertiser's best efforts to convince you that its product is far superior to anyone else's and that you must have it. Politicians running for office, interest groups looking to increase their influence, and any number of others also use persuasive techniques regularly. Indeed, most of us have had occasion to try to persuade someone else to come around to our way of thinking.

PSYCHOLOGY AROUND US When Prophecies Fail

Radio evangelist Harold Camping made a prediction that there would be a second coming on May 21, 2011, followed by the end of the world on October 21, 2011. Thousands of followers travelled the country, giving up life savings and exhorting others to repent before the world's end. As you might have guessed if you're reading this book, we are all still here.

Prophets of Armageddon and the end of the world are nothing new. What is interesting is what happens when someone makes such a prediction and it doesn't come true. In the 1950s, psychologists Leon Festinger and Stanley Schacter infiltrated an apocalyptic cult that had been predicting the earth was going to be destroyed by a flood on December 21, 1954. The leader of the cult, Dorothy Martin, said that an alien race would stop by in their flying saucers on the appointed day and save the true believers. The psychologists watched to see what would happen to the beliefs of the followers when (if?) the flying saucers didn't show.

What they found shocked them. After a few awkward hours of waiting, Martin reported she had received a telepathic message indicating that her followers had done such a good job spreading their message, the earth was saved—there was no need for rescue. Martin merely edited the beliefs slightly to accommodate the new information. Even more interesting, her followers became more devout than ever and more convinced that Martin had been right all along.

For persuasion to occur, a few elements must be present (Petty & Cacioppo, 1986). There must be, of course, a *message*, somebody to transmit the message (the *source*), and somebody to receive it (the *receiver*). In attempting to make a message persuasive, the source can use methods that follow either a central route or a peripheral route (**Figure 14-4**).

Central Route versus Peripheral Route The *central route* to persuasion emphasizes the content of the message, using factual information and logical arguments to persuade. This method requires a fair amount of effort on the receiver's part and is more commonly used for matters of some significance (Petty & Cacioppo, 1986). If you were trying to decide whether to buy a Mac or a PC, you might be willing to spend considerable time in careful deliberation of all the facts. After all, a computer is an expensive item and an important purchase. You might not be as interested in thinking hard about whether to buy Coke® or Pepsi®, however, or about which brand of shampoo to purchase.

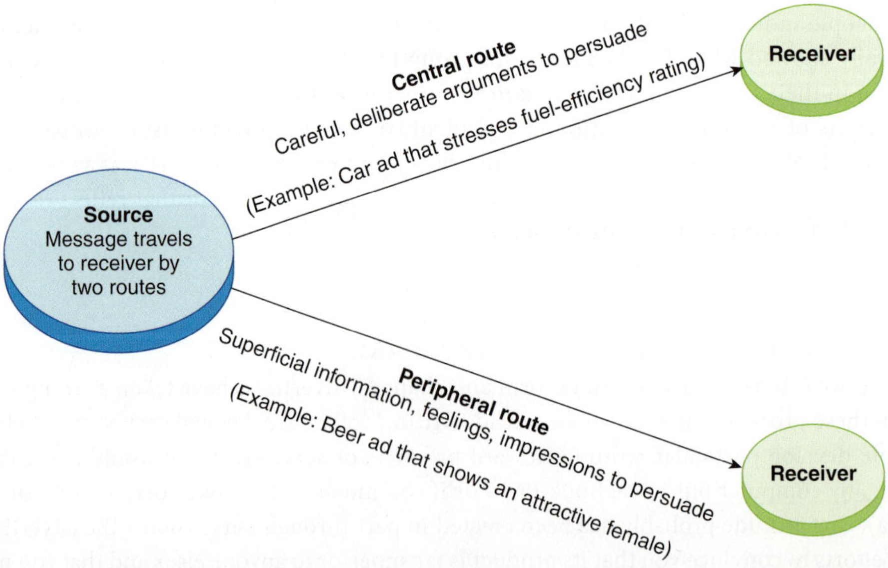

FIGURE 14-4 Two routes to persuasion.

The *peripheral route* relies on more superficial information. When you respond to peripheral appeals, you are responding to such factors as how attractive the spokesperson is and how amusing or engaging the message is (Petty & Cacioppo, 1986). As might be expected, decisions based on central routes to persuasion are more likely to last than decisions based on the peripheral route.

Aids to Persuasion Beyond the route chosen, a number of other factors can also make a message more or less persuasive. Characteristics of the *source* are important (Petty & Cacioppo, 1986). We are more likely to be persuaded by a source who is rated as more knowledgeable or more likable, for example. In addition, if we think of the source as more similar to us, we are more likely to be persuaded by the message. (This is part of the reason why political candidates often try to emphasize their middle-class groundedness by speaking in shopping malls and grocery stores.) Finally, at least in some instances, people are more likely to find a source credible and persuasive when the source presents both sides of an issue (Murphy et al., 2003).

Sometimes the key to persuasion rests on an interaction between audience characteristics and source characteristics, as shown in work by Sleey Chaiken when she was working at the University of Toronto (Chaiken, 1980). If, for example, a source is trying to win the favour of an intelligent or highly motivated audience, an emphasis on logic and on supporting data is more likely to carry the day. If addressing a less intelligent or less interested audience, however, the source might have more success with a glossy, superficial presentation and a good haircut.

A number of *specific techniques* can further improve the chances of successfully persuading others. We will mention only a few here. You have probably been exposed to some of these strategies (and you may even have used some of them).

- The *foot-in-the-door technique* involves getting someone to agree to a small request and then following up with a much larger one (Guéguen, 2002). The idea is that the person will be inclined to grant the second request because of having granted the first one. For example, you might first ask to borrow your parents' car for an hour, and then later ask to borrow it for the weekend.
- The *door-in-the-face technique* reverses this behaviour. The technique involves making an absurd first request that will obviously be turned down, and following it with a more moderate request (Rodafinos, Vucevic, & Sideridis, 2005). A teenager might ask her parents, "Will you buy me a motorcycle?," and then follow up with "Just kidding, but can I borrow $50?" as the parents sigh in relief.

Tools of persuasion. The organization People for the Ethical Treatment of Animals (PETA) has run many campaigns to persuade consumers to stop eating meat and become vegetarian. Which of the above approaches is more likely to help change the minds of meat eaters—the scantily dressed model who holds a sign while posing inside a cage (*left*) or the spokesperson who systematically presents facts and figures on the merits of a vegetarian lifesyle (*right*)?

Sigmund Freud's nephew, Edmund Bernays, is credited with helping to create modern advertising. Bernays applied psychoanalytic theory to link products with emotions. For example, told by psychoanalysts that women smoked less than men because cigarettes were phallic symbols of men's power, Bernays designed campaigns in the 1920s presenting smoking as a women's rights issue, calling cigarettes "torches of freedom." Smoking among women skyrocketed.

- *Appeals to fear* can be powerful. We frequently see these appeals in antismoking campaigns and the like (Sprinkle, 2006). In order to work, however, an appeal to fear must make receivers truly believe that something bad will happen to them if they don't comply with the source's request.

Barriers to Persuasion Other strategies can interfere with persuasion. Again, we will mention only a few.

- Forewarning an audience that you will be trying to persuade them of something will immediately raise their defenses. Although listeners in this situation may make subtle shifts toward your way of thinking, they are unlikely to change their attitudes as much as individuals who are not told that they are about to hear a persuasive speech.
- Beginning with a weak argument instead of a strong one can make subsequent arguments seem weaker. A child arguing for an advance on their allowance and arguing by saying they want the money to buy some candy might lead the parent to interpret a subsequent argument—that the child gave money to a friend at school who had no lunch—as more of an excuse than a valid argument.

Before You Go On

www.wiley.com/go/comer

What Do You Know?

1. What are the three components of attitudes, according to the ABC model?
2. How do cognitive dissonance theory and self-perception theory differ in their explanation of attitude change?
3. Why do people sometimes misrepresent their attitudes?
4. How does social identity theory explain prejudice?
5. What are the central and peripheral routes to persuasion?

SCAN TO GET THE ANSWERS

What Do You Think?

Watch a television advertisement or select a print ad and critique it according to the material in this section. For example, does the advertisement use the central or the peripheral route? Was that a good route for the advertiser to choose, considering the product being advertised?

Social Cognition: Attributions

LEARNING OBJECTIVE 2

Discuss how people make attributions to explain their own behaviour and the behaviour of others.

There has been much debate about the exact nature of the looting that happened in the wake of the Vancouver Canucks' 2011 Stanley Cup loss. It appears that some looters were simply taking advantage of the situation to steal whatever they could carry. It is clear, however, that many of the looters would never have considered breaking into a store if they had not found themselves caught up in a crowd-based post-game party atmosphere.

As the riot spread, many people began recording events in cell-phone pictures and movies, some for souvenirs but many to aide in the identification and police apprehension of rioters and fighters. Across Canada in the days following the riot, individuals formed distinct opinions as they tried to understand the unrest that they were witnessing or hearing about. Did it all occur at the instigation of people practised in how to incite mob violence? Were the people involved just normal Canadians who unfortunately got caught up in the moment? How should those involved in the riots be understood and treated? What can or should be done to restore Vancouver's reputation as a beautiful and exciting tourist destination city? And what might we need to do to restore our image of ourselves as Canadians, given that we prefer to think of ourselves as kind and law-abiding?

In many ways, we are all lay psychologists, continually trying to explain what we see in our social worlds so that we can make sense of events and predict what will happen in the future. We attempt to figure out *why* people, including ourselves, do things. Social psychologists refer to these causal explanations as **attributions**, and they are interested in what influences our attributions and how such attributions affect our subsequent decisions, feelings, and behaviours (Silvera & Laufer, 2005; Stewart, 2005).

attributions causal explanations of behaviour.

PSYCHOLOGY AROUND US Careful Deliberations?

Our criminal justice system is based on the idea that someone is innocent until proven guilty. But what do we do if our brains don't go along with that principle? According to two lawyers, Janice Nadler and Mary-Hunter McDonnell, most social psychology experiments suggest that our tendency to blame others is based on quick, unconscious, intuitive, and broad assessments of their character and their general motives in life, rather than on careful assessments of all relevant details surrounding an event or crime. Even obvious innocence may be overlooked if observers don't like an accused person.

To help emphasize this point, the lawyers conducted a study in which they developed a series of vignettes. For each vignette, a single detail was altered. For example, in a vignette about an accidental fire triggered by the storage of fertilizer, some participants were told that the protagonist in the story had been storing the fertilizer to raise orchids, whereas other participants were told the protagonist had been storing it for the eventual manufacture of methamphetamine. That one detail made all the difference in how careless, irresponsible, and blameworthy the participants judged the protagonist to be. If the protagonist was perceived to be a bad guy making meth, participants found him more to blame for the fire, even if the vignette pointed to the roles played by other factors or persons. In short, if people don't like someone or his general motives, they tend to consider the individual more blameworthy and guilty of carelessness, even if those issues are largely irrelevant to the case at hand (Nadler & McDonnell, 2012).

Dispositional and Situational Attributions

Attributions may fall into one of two categories. *Dispositional*, or *internal*, attributions focus on peoples' traits as the cause of their behaviour (Manusov & Spitzberg, 2008). In contrast, *situational*, or *external*, attributions focus on environmental factors as the cause of behaviour. If you fail an examination, you might make a dispositional attribution that you failed because you were not smart enough. Instead, however, you might tell yourself that the test was unfair and that your neighbour's music was so loud the night before that you couldn't get a good night's sleep—situational attributions.

What determines whether we make dispositional or situational attributions? Research suggests that when explaining *other* people's behaviour, we tend to rely more heavily on dispositional attributions. In a famous study in the 1960s, researchers had participants read a speech that expressed either support for or opposition to Cuban leader Fidel Castro. They then asked each participant to rate the extent to which the speechwriter was pro-Castro (Jones & Harris, 1967). Participants who read a speech supportive of Castro naturally rated the speechwriter as pro-Castro, and those who read a speech critical of Castro naturally rated the speechwriter as anti-Castro. These were dispositional attributions; the participants reasoned that the speeches reflected internal characteristics of the speechwriters. But then the participants were told that the speechwriters had been randomly assigned to write either a pro- or anti-Castro speech. In other words, the participants were given a reason to make a situational attribution rather than a dispositional one. Remarkably, even then, the participants rated speechwriters who had written supportive speeches as very pro-Castro and speechwriters who had written critical speeches as very anti-Castro (see **Figure 14-5**).

Social psychologist Lee Ross (2001, 1977) has referred to our reliance on dispositional attributions to explain the behaviour of other people as the **fundamental attribution error**.

fundamental attribution error the tendency to use dispositional attributions to explain the behaviour of other people.

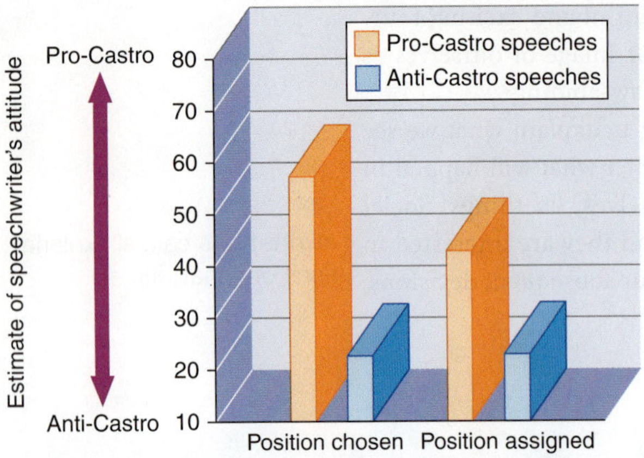

FIGURE 14-5 The fundamental attribution error. Even when told that pro-Castro or anti-Castro speechwriters had been randomly assigned their positions, research participants assumed that each speechwriter truly believed what he or she had written (Jones & Harris, 1967).

When we are almost hit by a speeding driver, we are likely to conclude that the driver is reckless and irresponsible, even though, in fact, she might have been racing to the hospital to see a stricken child. When we meet a woman who is not very talkative, we may conclude that she is shy and introverted, when in fact she might be a normally friendly sort who has a terrible cold. When a waiter provides unsatisfactory service, we may assume that he is disorganized, even though the fault may lie in the restaurant's kitchen or in the policies of management (Cowley, 2005).

In contrast, as we have already suggested, we tend to rely more heavily on situational attributions when explaining our own behaviour. Recall our earlier discussion of dispositional versus situational attributions. If your favourite team loses an important game, you might decide they are not good enough to succeed (dispositional attribution), or you might decide they lost due to poor field conditions and bad refereeing (situational attributions).

The Actor–Observer Effect

actor–observer effect the discrepancy between how we explain other people's behaviour (dispositionally) and how we explain our own behaviour (situationally).

Social psychologists refer to the discrepancy between how we explain other people's behaviour and how we explain our own behaviour as the **actor–observer effect** (Jones & Nisbett, 1971). The idea is that as *actors*, we tend to make situational attributions about our behaviours; and as *observers*, we tend to make dispositional attributions (**Figure 14-6**). Several explanations have been offered as to why this is so. For one thing, as actors, we have information about ourselves that observers don't have. We know from experience, for example, that we don't act the same way in every situation. For another thing, observers tend to focus on the actor, while actors need to focus more on situations. Think about a baseball game. As a fan (observer), you might watch the batter closely. But if you were the batter (actor), you'd need to pay attention to the ball, the other players, and many other aspects of your surroundings. Interestingly, if people are shown videotapes of their own behaviour—that is, if they become observers—they tend to make more dispositional attributions about the causes of their behaviour (Storms, 1973). That is, the video enables them to switch from actors to observers, and their explanations for their behaviours switch correspondingly.

As an example of the actor–observer effect, consider a class exercise developed by social psychologist Susan Fiske (2010). She tells her students, "Rate on a scale from 1 (low) to 10 (high) to what extent each of the following are reasons you chose your college [or university]."

- I had a wish to please my parents.
- I desired to get away from home.
- I wanted to go where my friends went.
- I liked the location of my college or university.
- I decided to go to a prestigious college.
- I was looking to find a marriage partner.
- I wanted a good social life.

After the students have completed these ratings, Fiske instructs them, "Next rate all the reasons that the *typical* student at your college picked it."

Take a break from reading, and think about how you decided to go to the college or university you are now attending by answering Fiske's questions for yourself. What sorts of factors did you consider while pondering your decision? Are you attending school close to home? away from home? at a university or a college? Why this school? What do you hope

FIGURE 14-6 The actor–observer effect. We tend to explain our own behaviour in terms of external factors (situational attributions), and others' behaviour in terms of their internal characteristics (dispositional attributions).

to achieve? After you have considered these questions, answer the same questions in terms of why you think the typical student at your college/university picked it.

Now compare your ratings of your reasons for attending your college/university with your ratings of other students' reasons by turning the page and reading about other student's post-secondary education choices. Did your ratings follow a pattern? If you are like most of the students in Fiske's classes, you thought the reasons on the list described the typical student's decision better than they described yours. If that's the case, your ratings illustrate the actor–observer effect. Each of the reasons on the list is a dispositional attribution, relating to something internal to the person. As Fiske observes, "People see themselves as having rich, deep, and adaptive personalities, able to express almost any [behaviour] or its opposite, depending on the circumstances. *Other* people, of course, are ruled by their personalities" (Fiske, 2010, p. 116).

Exceptions to the Rule

Despite the trend just described, we do not *always* attribute other people's behaviours to their personalities. When we know that just about everyone would react the same way in a given situation, we will likely conclude that a person's behaviour in that situation is situationally caused (Malle, 2006). When most persons are robbed at gunpoint, for example, they (wisely) hand over their money. Thus, a particular robbery victim's surrender of money will usually be attributed to the powerful situational factors.

Researchers have found that depressed individuals sometimes have a more realistic perception of themselves and their abilities, a phenomenon known as depressive realism, or the sadder-but-wiser hypothesis (Cummins & Nistico, 2002).

Similarly, if we are given detailed information about situational pressures, we may attribute the behaviour of other people to situational factors. Think back, once again, to the events surrounding Hurricane Katrina. Initially, most television viewers assumed that all New Orleans residents who had stayed at home rather than evacuate to another city were stubborn, or foolish, or both. However, when information later revealed that thousands of the city's residents were too poor to own a car and that all public transportation systems had shut down, most viewers shifted to a situational explanation for the residents' behaviour. On the other hand, some of the Vancouver rioters who came forward and asked for forgiveness for their bad decisions during the riot were given a bit of a rough ride in both the mainstream and the social media.

By the same token, we do not *always* attribute our own behaviour to situational factors. Let's say, for example, that you do poorly on an examination and complain that the questions were "too hard" and the grading unfair. You are, as we would expect, making a situational attribution for your poor performance. But suppose you get a good mark on the next examination. Will you explain your success by pointing out how easy the exam questions were or how generous the grading was? Not likely.

Post-Secondary Education Decisions

Compare your answers regarding your post-secondary decision to those found in general research on that question.

While 50 to 60 percent of secondary school students say they would like to go on to a university or college, only about 30 percent actually apply (Cheung, 2007). Many decide to go to a college. The majority of those who go on to college or university are female (55%). Fifty percent have secondary school grades between 75 and 85 percent (Academica Group, 2011). Eighty percent of university and college applicants say they are attending for career development and preparation purposes. A majority of students look for programs that interest them and that have a positive reputation, although 17 percent of students elect to attend their local college or university as they are unable to afford to travel to school. Less than half of students indicate that the university's or college's overall reputation is a factor in their decision to attend, while about half suggest that teaching reputation (not research) is very important to them.

The institution's reputation for providing positive student experiences and readily-employable graduates are also significant factors for more than half of students surveyed (Cheung, 2007; Academica Group, 2011). So, you likely see that you share many of your reasons for attending college or university with your fellow students. But don't worry, there are still lots of ways to be unique.

Consistent with this point, social psychologists have noted that when we explain our own behaviour, we are able, and often likely, to fluctuate between situational and dispositional attributions, depending on which puts us in a better light. In other words, we tend to attribute our successes to internal causes and our failures to external ones—a phenomenon referred to as the **self-serving bias** (Johnston & Lee, 2005; Miller & Ross, 1975). Research also has indicated that the direction of our attributions can be influenced by factors such as our moods and emotions, motives, prejudices and stereotypes, and cultural background (Forgas & Locke, 2005; Lieberman et al., 2005; Sadler et al., 2005; Sherman et al., 2005).

self-serving bias the tendency people have to attribute their successes to internal causes and their failures to external ones.

Before You Go On

www.wiley.com/go/comer

What Do You Know?

6. How do dispositional and situational attributions differ?
7. What is the fundamental attribution error?
8. What are some exceptions to the actor–observer effect?

What Do You Think?

How do you think empathy might influence the actor–observer effect?

SCAN TO GET THE ANSWERS

Social Forces

LEARNING OBJECTIVE 3

Describe the power of conformity and obedience in shaping people's behaviour.

As bad as conditions were in the last-resort shelters after Hurricane Katrina, they were even worse in the New Orleans Convention Center. A small group of people decided to make their way to this facility, even though it had not been designated a shelter. Others followed, until the convention centre was filled with thousands of displaced souls. Those people waited for days for food and support to come. However, because the convention centre had never been formally designated a shelter, federal and state agencies did not even know anyone was there. Not until days later, when television and news reporters "found" those in the centre, were they included in the city's relief efforts.

Given the chaos and uncertainty in the aftermath of Hurricane Katrina, it is understandable that people would look for any sign of what to do or how to get help. The fact that a small group of people decisively sought shelter at the convention centre, even in the absence of any information about whether that was a good choice or not, was more than sufficient to influence many other people to seek shelter there. Even in more normal situations, *social forces* such as these exert a powerful influence on our behaviours and beliefs. Often, for example, people conform to the behaviours and opinions of others, especially when those behaviours and opinions reflect a majority position. We will discuss the social forces of conformity and obedience in this section. First, though, let's examine the related topics of *norms* and *social roles conformity* and *obedience*.

PSYCHOLOGY AROUND US More Than Tiredness

Yawning is contagious. Try it. If you have someone in the room with you right now, yawn (or fake a yawn), and see what happens (it's even more fun if you can pull it off with a group of people). Although this effect hasn't been studied specifically in humans, researchers at Emory University were able to trigger enhanced yawning in chimpanzees by showing them film footage of other chimpanzees yawning. The effect was twice as big if the chimpanzees in the movie were familiar to the chimpanzees watching the movie. Psychologists are not sure what's going on here. Is it conformity? Social modelling? Peer pressure? Many social psychologists believe that contagious yawning may be a way of binding ourselves to other members of our group—that is, the sharing of an experience. So if you yawn and a friend or colleague yawns right along with you, don't worry—you're not boring each other; you're sharing a moment.

Norms and Social Roles

Recall that, in the aftermath of Vancouver's 2011 Stanley Cup loss, people around the country learned that a growing number of "sports fans" (many of the riot participants arrived downtown after the game was over to join whatever social event was going to happen) were burning cars and breaking into stores. Such reports made most people feel very unsettled. One reason for their discomfort was that such behaviours seemed to represent a breakdown of social values and compassion. Another reason was that the behaviours defied people's social expectations. Respectable citizens are not supposed to break into stores and carry off goods, and sports fans are supposed celebrate or mourn their team's accomplishments without setting fire to vehicles. These expectations arise from the norms and roles of our society.

Norms Society is filled with rules about how everyone is supposed to act. These conventions, referred to as **norms**, provide order and predictability. Some norms are *explicit*, or stated openly. We all know, for example, that we are supposed to stop our car when we come to a red light. Other norms are *implicit*. These norms are not openly stated, but we are still aware of them. You probably weren't taught as a child to face the front of an elevator, for instance, but when is the last time you stepped into an elevator where all the passengers had their backs to the doors?

norms social rules about how members of a society are expected to act.

We can also classify norms as descriptive or injunctive (Larimer et al., 2005, 2004; Larimer & Neighbors, 2003; Eagly & Karau, 2002). *Descriptive norms* are agreed-on expectations about what members of a group *do*, while *injunctive norms* are agreed-on expectations about what members of a group *ought to do*. Consider the behaviour of museum patrons, for example. The pristine appearance of the typical museum, along with signs throughout the building, regularly reminds patrons not to litter in this setting. Virtually all museum goers abide by this rule, making it a descriptive norm (Kallgren, Reno, & Cialdini, 2000; Cialdini et al., 1991). On the other hand, littering instead of recycling is not doing something people increasingly think we ought to do, and so it is an injunctive norm.

People are more likely to abide by injunctive norms if the norms are called to their attention. For example, people walking through a neighbourhood with litter cans and anti-littering signs are more likely to become aware of and follow the community's injunctive

Pictorial reminder. This sign along a Newfoundland highway reminds drivers of the deadly physics of hitting a moose with your car. It also helps remind people of the community's injunctive norm to drive responsibly. Such reminders often have a beneficial impact.

anti-littering norm. In one study of this phenomenon, researchers passed out handbills to pedestrians. Each pedestrian received a handbill promoting either the importance of not littering, the wisdom of saving electricity by turning off lights, or the responsibility of each citizen to vote (Cialdini et al., 1991). Only 10 percent of the pedestrians who had been given the anti-littering pamphlet crumpled and threw the handbill to the ground after they had finished reading it, compared with 20 percent of those who had been given the "lights out" or "voting" handbill.

Social Roles A **social role** is a set of norms ascribed to a person's social position—expectations and duties associated with the individual's position in the family, at work, in the community, and in other settings (Glass, 2005; Alexander & Wood, 2000; Sarbin & Allen, 1968). The role of police officers, for example, is to maintain law and order. The role of parents is to nurture, rear, and teach their children and prepare them for life outside the family.

social role a set of norms ascribed to a person's social position—expectations and duties associated with the individual's position in the family, at work, in the community, and in other settings.

Roles often have a positive impact on people and society. Indeed, they are critical for the smooth functioning of society. They can, however, also confine people. Just as many actors complain of being "typecast" and prevented from demonstrating their versatility, people in various positions are often limited by their prescribed social roles. Many observers argue, for example, that traditional Western gender roles are oppressive for women.

When individuals in a particular group try to step out of the social roles assigned to members of that group, they may be met with negative reactions and evaluations (Morfei et al., 2004). For example, traditional Western gender roles ascribe more *communal* characteristics to women—that is, ones associated with the welfare of other people—and more *agentic* characteristics to men—that is, those associated with assertiveness, control, and confidence (Mosher & Danoff-Burg, 2008, 2005; Eagly & Koenig, 2006). In short, women in the West are expected to be caring and men to be assertive and self-assured.

Gossiping About People We Don't Even Know

As we noted in Chapter 11, some observers believe that, as a society, we like gossip. In earlier eras, people relied on word of mouth or newspapers to find out what their fellow humans were doing. Today we have the Internet, where gossip sites provide many followers with updated postings of the latest goings-on in Hollywood (KCET, 2007). What is Lindsay Lohan up to these days? Is Charlie Sheen ever going to work again?

Just what makes our society so preoccupied with celebrity happenings? Some researchers suggest that this interest has evolutionary roots (McAndrew, 2008). A shared focus on the comings and goings of others may have helped bond us together into social groups, and over time, strong group affiliation probably helped to enhance safety, improve the chances of successfully bearing and raising children, and the like, thus ensuring continuation of the species (Dunbar, 2004). But why celebrities? According to some theorists, humans have come to view anyone they see frequently as an important member of their social group, even if they don't actually know the person—and we certainly see celebrities frequently. In addition, since modern society is quite mobile, celebrities may be the "friends" we have most in common with the people around us, thus providing a source of conversation and affiliation in our social groups (McAndrew, 2008).

In addition, gossip may serve to teach and enforce social norms (Baumeister, Zhang, & Vohs, 2004). Recall, for example, when Dany Heatley, then a hockey player with the Atlanta Thrashers, crashed his car while speeding and killed his friend and teammate Dan Snyder. There is a social norm that seriously pushing the limits of safe vehicle operation is inappropriate, even if you are a talented hockey player and especially when someone dies as a result. Young Canadian drivers, and especially young male drivers, got a close look at this norm by observing the negative press and comments aimed at Heatley's behaviour leading to his friend's death.

Although few people want to admit that they are a gossip (McAndrew, 2008), it appears that many of us want—and may even need—to talk about other people, even ones we don't know.

Women are often judged harshly when they step outside their gender role. Women who leave their children with the male ex-spouse following a divorce are judged more harshly than men who leave their children with their female ex-spouse. One study found, for example, that when a female manager was described to research participants as "successful," the individuals rated the woman as more hostile, selfish, quarrelsome, and subjective than successful male managers (Heilman, Block, & Martell, 1995). It is small wonder that women's advancement in the business world has often been limited (Abele, 2003).

In 2006, 73.5 percent of Canadian women between 16 and 64 years of age participated in the paid workforce (compared to 82.5 percent of men, Canadian Labour Congress, 2007). As well, women are 1.6 times more likely to earn a bachelor's degree than men (Canadian Education Statistics Council, 2007). Nevertheless, on average, women occupy lower-ranking positions and earn less income than men, with women employed full-time earning an average of 73 cents for every dollar earned on average by men (though this may be partially influenced by time in position; Canadian Human Rights Commission, 2010). In Fortune 500 companies, women constitute only 0.4 percent of the Chief Executive Officers (CEOs) and 4 percent of the five highest earning officers (Catalyst, 2000).

Roles and Situational Demands: The Stanford Prison Experiment Social roles affect not only how others think about us, but also how we think about ourselves and how we act toward others. In 1971, Philip Zimbardo and his colleagues at Stanford University studied the power of roles in a study famously known as *The Stanford Prison Experiment*, although it did not actually follow an experimental design (Zimbardo, 2006, 1972; Haney, Banks, & Zimbardo, 1973). The basement of the university's psychology department was converted into a mock prison, and 24 male students were randomly assigned to play the roles of either prisoners or guards for what was supposed to be two weeks. "Guards" were given batons, uniforms, and mirrored sunglasses and were told that it was their responsibility to run the prison. "Prisoners" wore smocks and small chains around their ankles and were referred to by assigned numbers instead of by name. To the researchers' horror, within hours the "guards" had settled comfortably into their new roles and had begun humiliating their "prisoner" peers. Some actually tormented the prisoners, imposed physical punishments on them, and denied bathroom privileges and food to prisoners who were "out of line." The study was clearly out of hand. With Zimbardo realizing he was acting more like a warden than a researcher, the study raised many ethical questions and the researcher shut it down after just six days.

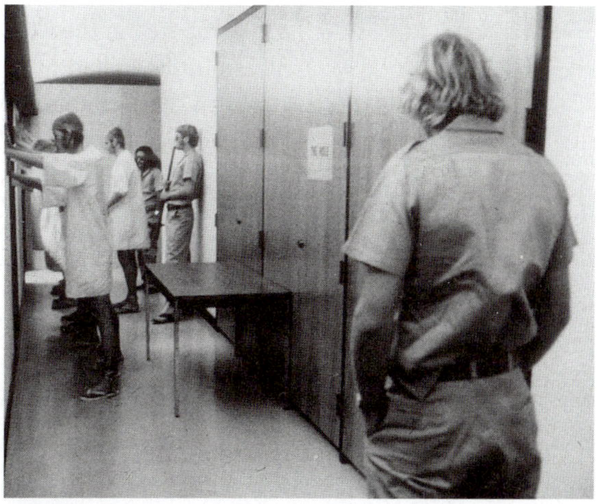

The power of social role playing. In the famous Stanford University prison study, most of the students who were assigned to play prison guards engaged in at least some abuses of power, while those assigned to prisoner roles typically became passive, depressed, and disorganized.

The Stanford Prison Experiment raised many ethical concerns in the field of psychology, primarily because the participants experienced clear psychological pain—both the prisoners, who were abused psychologically, and the guards, who were confronted with the fact that they were capable of cruelty and even sadism. Many researchers have challenged the legitimacy of the study and believe that its costs outweighed its benefits. As you read in Chapter 2, there are now ethical guidelines and review procedures that all researchers must follow when conducting studies—guidelines and procedures that would make it impossible for this same study to be conducted today. That aside, the study did underscore the power and potential dangers of certain social roles.

Roles, Gender, and Social Skills HOW WE DIFFER There is a popular belief in Western society that, on average, women are more skilled socially than men, more sensitive emotionally, more expressive, and more focused on social relationships. In fact, research has supported this belief over the years. In a wide range of social psychology studies, it has been found, for example, that female participants tend to read non-verbal social cues more accurately than male participants, are more expressive with their faces and bodies during interactions, feel more empathy for the emotional experiences of others, and act friendlier in group discussions. For their part, male participants tend to focus more narrowly on the tasks at hand in group activities than do female participants, emerge as leaders (as opposed to social facilitators) in group activities, and adopt more authoritarian and less participative styles when they take on leadership roles (Eagly & Koenig, 2006).

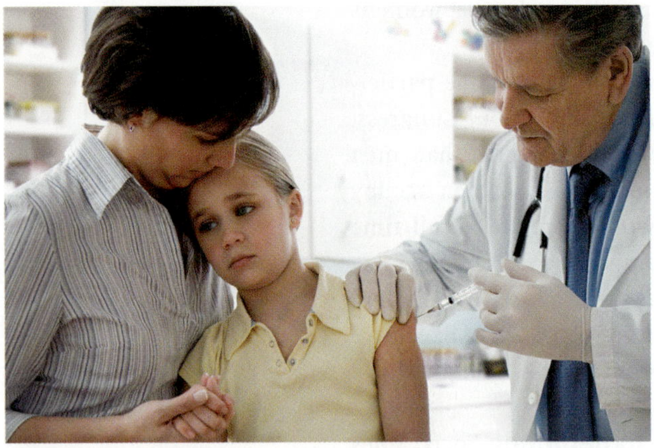

Special social skills? The mother in this photo demonstrates heightened sensitivity and other social skills, while the male physician focuses on the task at hand without paying much attention to the child's social needs. Why are gender differences in social skills less pronounced today than in years past?

Why is this gender difference in the social realm? Although researchers have not fully sorted out the issue, one of the most common explanations points to social roles (Eagly & Wood, 2006). As we observed above, traditional Western gender roles ascribe more communal characteristics to women—including expectations that they should be friendly, unselfish, concerned about others, and emotionally expressive—and more agentic characteristics to men—including expectations that they will be assertive, independent, and controlling. According to social role theory, people are inclined to behave in ways that are consistent with the expectations tied to their roles. Moreover, over the course of their lives, as people enact their social roles, their skills in the assigned realm become sharper and their corresponding attitudes more deeply ingrained. This would suggest that women are socialized to be more interested in and as a consequence, become skilled in the social realm than men typically do.

Of course, as you are well aware, traditional gender roles have been undergoing considerable change in recent decades. Enormous numbers of women, for example, have competed in the work world and many men have taken on domestic and caretaking responsibilities and adopted more people-oriented attitudes and concerns. Not surprisingly, along with these changes in roles and expectations, social psychologists have been finding fewer and smaller gender differences in their studies of social skill, empathy, leadership, and the like. To be sure, such differences still exist in many research undertakings, as social role theory would predict, but there is clearly a shift occurring. It is also important to keep in mind that average group differences (e.g., men have more spatial ability than women on average) do not allow you to make attributions about individuals in either group (e.g., it is inappropriate to say that an individual man will have superior spatial skills as many men do not and many women do have superior spatial abilities).

Conformity

conformity the tendency to yield to social pressure.

Conformity is the tendency to yield to real or imagined group pressure. Investigators have been studying conformity for more than 60 years. Early work on this phenomenon was done by social psychologist Theodore Newcomb (1943). In a classic study, Newcomb examined the political views of students at Bennington College as they progressed through school. Although Bennington College is well known for the politically liberal leanings of many of its faculty members, during the Great Depression in the 1930s it was attended largely by children from conservative families. Newcomb found that as the students progressed through college, immersed in the Bennington culture, their political views grew more and more liberal. Moreover, these liberal views endured well into late adulthood, confirmed by interviews conducted 25 and 50 years later (Alwin, Cohen, & Newcomb, 1991; Newcomb et al., 1967). Laboratory studies tell a similar story, especially the classic work conducted by social psychologist Solomon Asch.

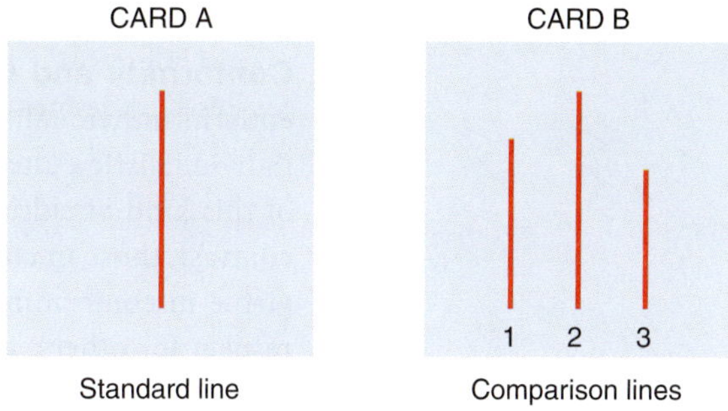

FIGURE 14-7 The perceptual judgment task in Asch's conformity study. Asch's participants were asked which line (1, 2, or 3) was the same length as the standard line. Despite the obvious and correct choice (line 2), when the confederates gave the wrong answer, almost 75 percent of the participants conformed and gave the wrong answer, too.

The Asch Studies Imagine that you agree to participate in a psychology experiment on "perceptual judgments." You and six other participants are seated around a table—you are seated second from the end—and the experimenter presents two cards to the group. The card on the left, Card A, displays a single vertical line, whereas the card on the right, Card B, displays three vertical lines of various lengths (see **Figure 14-7**). The experimenter asks each participant which of the three lines on Card B is equal in length to the line on Card A. When it is your turn, you immediately recognize that the second line on Card B matches the one on Card A. Thus, after the five participants seated ahead of you indicate that the second line on Card B is equal in length to the line on Card A, you do the same. Another set of cards is presented, and again everyone agrees. The straightforward task is moving along easily and comfortably.

Then something odd happens. On the third round, you again readily note which line on Card B matches the line on Card A—it's pretty clear that it's line 3 this time—but you are shocked to hear that the first person called upon by the experimenter answers, "line 1." You think to yourself "he needs an eye exam," but then the second person responds the same as the first. You rub your eyes, blink, and squint, but still you see that it's line 3 that matches the length of the line on Card A. After the five people ahead of you have all selected line 1, it is your turn to respond. What will you say?

In fact, this classic study, conducted by social psychologist Solomon Asch (1955), was not about perceptual judgments at all, but rather was an investigation of conformity. In the study, the other "participants" were actually confederates, coached by the experimenter to give uniformly wrong answers on the third round and thereafter. Asch found that when the responses of the confederates were incorrect, almost 75 percent of the real participants conformed to the group norm and gave an incorrect response.

Asch also varied the procedures in his experiment to reveal what group features might affect this "tyranny of the majority" (Martin & Hewstone, 2001), and others have followed with similar work. One key factor is group *unanimity*. The presence of even one dissenting group member dramatically reduces the likelihood that participants will conform to an incorrect group norm (Prislin & Wood, 2005). The *size* of the group also affects its influence. Groups with fewer than four members, for example, do not seem to bring about a powerful conformity effect (Asch, 1955; see **Figure 14-8**). Many laboratory studies on conformity have been conducted since Asch's pioneering undertaking (Abrams et al., 2005, 2000, 1990). The findings of most such studies are similar to Asch's—they demonstrate the strong effects of social pressure.

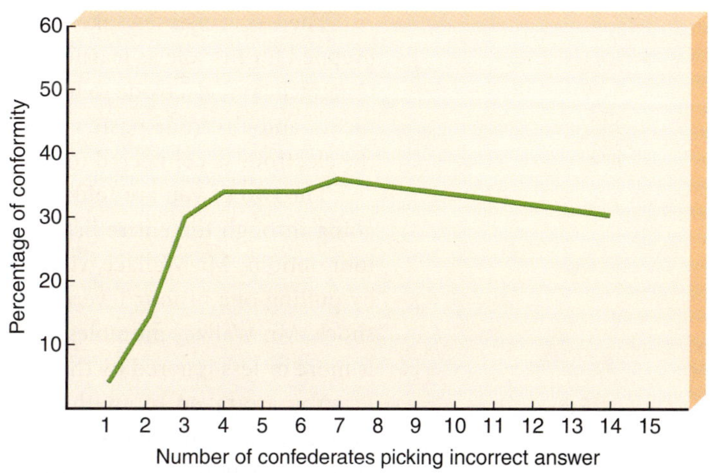

FIGURE 14-8 Group size and conformity. A key factor in conformity is group size. Asch found that the conformity effect is not strong when the group's size is less than four members (Asch, 1955).

Conformity and Culture HOW WE DIFFER Conformity is viewed very differently in individualistic and collectivistic cultures (Markus & Kitayama, 1994). People in individualistic cultures often consider conformity to be a bad thing. Typically, members of this kind of culture want to stand out and be different—to have their own identity. In contrast, those in collectivistic cultures usually value fitting in with other people. They see virtue in conforming to social norms and view conformity as an indication of maturity, respect for others, and appropriate self-control. In fact, the Korean word for conformity means inner strength and maturity (Kim & Markus, 1999).

When ordering food in a restaurant, people in North America, an individualistic society, order whatever they desire (Kim & Masters, 1999). They may say, for example, "I'll have a Caesar salad, but light on the croutons and with the dressing on the side." However, in Korea, a collectivistic culture, that kind of restaurant etiquette is unthinkable. It would be seen as an inability to get along with others and an insensitivity to the needs of the waiter. Thus, as you might expect, whenever Asch-like studies are conducted in collectivistic cultures, the participants show even higher rates of conformity than do participants in the North American studies (Bond & Smith, 1996).

Obedience

In the Asch studies of conformity, there were no leaders in the groups—just peers. In addition, there were no consequences for incorrect responses. No fines were imposed, nobody was hurt, and nobody had to account for or defend their decisions. But what about situations in which people are working under an authority figure, or in which they must pay a price for making an incorrect decision? Classic work by researcher Stanley Milgram offers important, and unsettling, insights into situations of this kind. Milgram studied **obedience**, which occurs when people follow direct commands, usually given by an authority figure.

obedience the act of following direct commands, usually given by an authority figure.

Milgram's Experiment Milgram's (1963) study is perhaps the most famous and controversial experiment in the history of psychology (Blass, 2007, 2004). Imagine that you have agreed to participate in this experiment. You arrive at the designated location and are met by a stern-looking man in a lab coat. The man introduces you to the mild-mannered "Mr. Wallace" and explains that the two of you are participating in a study of the effects of punishment on learning. One of you will be randomly assigned the role of "teacher," and the other, the role of "learner." You are then given the "teacher" role. Although you are not aware of it, the assignment of roles has not been random at all. "Mr. Wallace" is a collaborator in league with the experimenter who is really only interested in your behaviour.

The experimenter takes the two of you to an adjacent room, where Mr. Wallace is prepped for his role as learner. He is told to roll up his right shirt sleeve, and the investigator attaches an electrode to his wrist. His arm is strapped down "to prevent excessive movement," and electrode paste is applied "to prevent blisters or burns." You are informed that the electrode is connected to a shock generator in the other room (**Figure 14-9**).

The two of you are told that you (as the teacher) will recite a list of word pairs. After going through the entire list, you will recite only the first word of each pair, followed by four options. Mr. Wallace will indicate which option is the correct match for the first word by pulling one of four levers. If the response is incorrect, you will administer an electric shock. Mr. Wallace mumbles something about having a heart condition, but that comment is more or less ignored by the experimenter.

You are taken to another room, unable to see Mr. Wallace, and are seated in front of a metallic, box-shaped instrument, covered with knobs and switches and labelled "Shock Generator." You notice that each switch on the shock generator's control panel is identified by a voltage—ranging from 15 volts to 450 volts—and a label—ranging from "slight shock"(15 volts) to "danger: extreme shock" (375 volts) to "XXX" (450 volts).

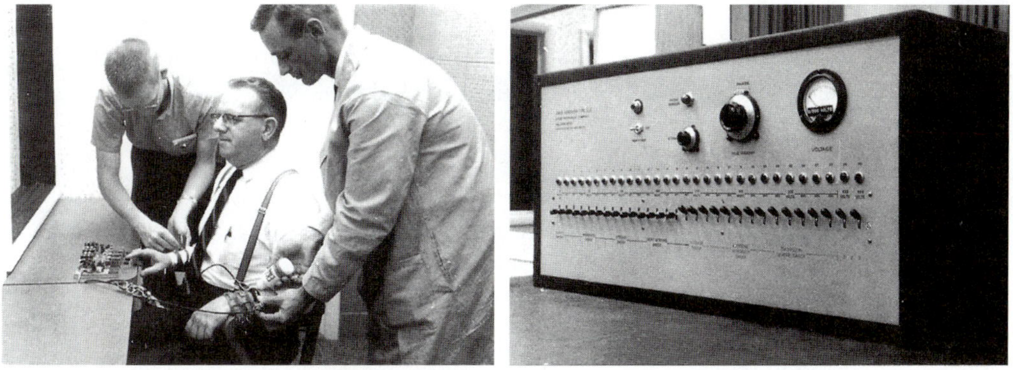

FIGURE 14-9 **Milgram's obedience experiment.** The photo above shows Milgram's shock generator and the "teacher" helping the experimenter strap the "learner" into the shock apparatus. Most people believe that they would not administer shocks to a person crying out in protest, but Milgram's experiment found otherwise.

The experimenter explains that whenever you push down a switch, Mr. Wallace will receive the corresponding shock, and this shock will stop as soon as you push the switch back up.

You are to communicate with Mr. Wallace through a microphone intercom, as the rooms are "partially soundproof." When he responds by pulling one of the four levers, one of four lights on top of the shock generator will light up. You are to administer a shock to Mr. Wallace whenever he responds incorrectly. With each successive incorrect response, you are to move up one switch on the shock generator, administering what the labels suggest are increasingly powerful—and dangerous—shocks.

After Mr. Wallace offers his first incorrect response, you flick the switch identified as "15 volts." The machine springs to life, with bright red lights flashing and an ominous buzzing noise filling the air. As Mr. Wallace continues to offer incorrect responses, you are instructed to administer increasingly powerful shocks. Through the wall, you can hear Mr. Wallace moan and say things, such as "Get me out of here!" Any time you express reluctance to go on, the experimenter confidently states "Please continue" or even, "You have no choice; you must go on." After a while, Mr. Wallace stops responding to your word prompts. The experimenter tells you to treat the failure to respond as an incorrect response and administer another shock (you're up to 450 volts, or "XXX," by now). Mr. Wallace lets out an agonized scream and yells, "Let me out of here! I have heart problems!" You hear and feel Mr. Wallace banging on the adjacent wall. Then he is completely silent. There are no further responses to your word prompts or to the shocks you administer.

As you are reading about this study, you are probably saying to yourself that you would have refused to go on with the experiment very early on. Most people who learn about this study have that reaction. Indeed, before the study became widely known, its procedures were described to psychologists, and they predicted that only 1 percent of participants would continue with the experiment all the way through 450 volts (Milgram, 1963). Astonishingly, Milgram found that 65 percent of the participants continued with the experiment all the way through the 450 volts label, and no participant stopped before the 300-volt mark (see **Figure 14-10**). As well, more recent replications of parts of the study (as the whole study would not receive ethics clearance today) show that things have not changed, and under similar circumstances participants would still behave as Milgram's initial participants behaved (Burger, 2008).

"Obedience is due only to legitimate powers."
—Jacques Rousseau, French philosopher and writer

The Milgram Controversy It is no wonder that Milgram's study is one of psychology's most controversial. The study revealed something profoundly disturbing about human nature—namely, that we are inclined to obey authority, even if it means behaving in ways we would never predict we would behave. Milgram demonstrated that it is not just a cruel

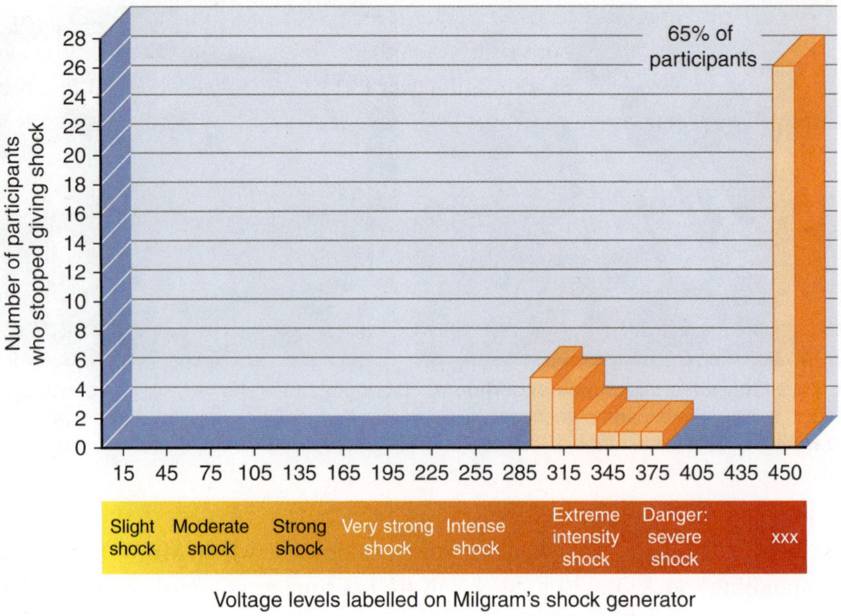

FIGURE 14-10 The results of Milgram's obedience experiment. Milgram found that no participant stopped administering shocks before the 300-volt mark, and that the vast majority (65 percent) continued administering shocks to the highest level (Milgram, 1963).

and sadistic fringe of the population that can inflict pain and suffering on innocent victims; two-thirds of the population might hurt others if ordered to do so by an authority figure.

Milgram (1974) went on to explain the atrocities committed by Nazi Germany within the context of his remarkable findings, although a number of theorists have questioned the appropriateness of such a leap (Miller, 2004).

> "I was just following orders."
> —*Adolf Eichmann, high-ranking official in Nazi Germany and self-proclaimed Jewish Specialist, at his 1961 war criminal trial*

Initially, many refused to believe that Milgram's findings provided an accurate representation of people's readiness to inflict suffering. Critics attacked the experiment on various grounds. Most notably, the participants in the original study were all male. Some speculated that women might be less inclined to obey commands to inflict pain on others. Additionally, a number pointed out that the study had been conducted at Yale University. Had it been carried out at a less prestigious locale, they argued, the participants might have been less likely to obey the experimenter's commands. Finally, many questioned the ethical implications of the research.

Follow-up Studies Milgram spent the years following the publication of his controversial findings conducting variations of the original experiment to further clarify the nature of obedience (Milgram, 1974). To the surprise of many people, he found that female participants were no more likely to defy an experimenter's commands than the male participants in the original experiment. Milgram also set up an alternative site for his experiment, the "Research Associates of Bridgeport"—supposedly a commercial organization that was not connected with Yale. In this variation, the percentage of people who kept administering shocks through 450 volts was somewhat lower than in the original experiment, but still considerable—around 50 percent, compared with the original 65 percent.

Milgram's experiments and subsequent replications demonstrated just how ready people are to obey authority, but they also clarified that certain factors *reduce* people's willingness to obey (Lüttke, 2004).

- If a confederate served as "co-teacher" with the research participant and refused to continue, over 90 percent of the real participants followed suit and disobeyed as well.
- The *salience* of a victim's suffering—its obviousness—affected participants' obedience. Participants in Milgram's studies were, for example, less likely to obey when they could see the look on Mr. Wallace's face with each successive shock.

- A participant's *proximity* to the victim affected obedience. When Milgram's participants were seated in the room with Mr. Wallace, only about 40 percent of them continued to obey through 450 volts. Still fewer (30 percent) were obedient in a condition that had them placing Mr. Wallace's hand on a shock plate to administer the shock.

Of course, there are many occasions in life where it is quite useful, and even advantageous, to obey commands. During military maneuvers, surgical procedures, theatre productions, and sporting competitions, for example, a lack of obedience may result in chaos or disaster. However, Milgram's study demonstrates the dark side of obedience. In a letter to another social psychologist, Milgram wrote, "Certainly, obedience serves numerous productive functions, and you may wonder why I focus on its destructive potential. Perhaps it is because this [the holocaust] has been the most striking and disturbing expression of obedience in our time" (Blass, 2004).

Before You Go On www.wiley.com/go/comer

What Do You Know?

9. What are norms and what is their function in society?
10. What did Solomon Asch's experiments on conformity reveal?
11. What is the central difference between the concepts of conformity and obedience?

What Do You Think?

In both Asch's and Milgram's experiments, the presence of another person who would either go against the group or refuse to obey the authority figure made it more likely that the research participant would do so as well. How would you explain this phenomenon?

SCAN TO GET THE ANSWERS

Social Relations

LEARNING OBJECTIVE 4

Review major concepts in the areas of group dynamics, helping behaviour, aggression, and interpersonal attraction.

Many social psychologists have been interested in social relations. Some have studied *group dynamics*—how membership or participation in a group influences our thoughts and behaviours. Still others have attempted to determine when people choose to help others and when they ignore others' needs. Other social psychologists have examined aggression and interpersonal attraction, trying to understand why people behave aggressively and how people come to like or love others in their social world.

Group Dynamics

A **group** is an organized, stable collection of individuals in which the members are aware of and influence one another and share a common identity. Group members are thus *interdependent*—that is, the behaviour of one group member affects the behaviour of the other members. Let's consider several topics related to groups and group dynamics: *group productivity, the social facilitation effect, social loafing, group polarization,* and *groupthink.*

group an organized, stable collection of individuals in which the members are aware of and influence one another and share a common identity.

Group Productivity One issue of interest to social psychologists is what makes groups productive. Not surprisingly, they have found that the optimal group size for productivity depends on the task at hand (Steiner, 1972).

- When a group is performing an *additive task*, its members must perform parallel actions. For example, to clear a property of snow after a storm, all members of a work crew must shovel snow. For such tasks, group productivity increases directly with group size.

- In contrast, when a group is faced with a *conjunctive task*, the members are only as productive as the weakest member. If, for example, group members are hiking together up a mountain, they can travel only as fast as the slowest person in the group. In this situation, a greater number of group members does not necessarily yield better performance.
- A *disjunctive task* requires a single solution. In such undertakings, the most competent person in the group is likely to provide the solution. Larger groups are typically more productive for disjunctive tasks, because a larger group is more likely to have a superstar member who can solve the problem at hand. Often large groups start by brainstorming for a solution to a task or problem. Asking group members to generate as many possible ideas or solutions as they can without being in any way critical of ideas proposed by others is a wonderful way to gather a broad range of possible solutions, and increases the likelihood that a useful solution will be found.
- *Divisible tasks* involve the simultaneous performance of several different activities. When groups confront such tasks, no single person works on all phases of the undertaking; thus, the different strengths of group members complement one another. For divisible tasks, larger groups tend to be more productive, provided someone or a part of the group manages or coordinates the activities of different parts of the group as they work on the components of the larger group task.

Social Facilitation In many instances, our performance is enhanced when we are in the presence of others. This is one of the oldest observations in social psychology. In the late 1890s, psychologist Norman Triplett noted that cyclists tend to go faster when in the presence of other cyclists than when alone—even when they are not in competition with one another. To test his hypothesis that the presence of others can enhance individual performance, Triplett (1898) conducted an experiment in which he had children wind a fishing reel either all alone or side-by-side with other children. Triplett found that children winding side-by-side worked substantially quicker than children winding by themselves. This phenomenon was later labelled **social facilitation**. Its study was expanded to include not just physical tasks, but also mental tasks, such as solving puzzles and doing math problems (Bond and Titus, 1983).

social facilitation an effect in which the presence of others enhances performance.

As social facilitation has been studied over the years, researchers have learned that people's performance in the presence of others is more complicated than Triplett first believed. Psychologist Robert Zajonc (1965) proposed that the presence of others elevates our arousal level, which in turn facilitates performance on simple, well-learned tasks, but interferes with performance on complicated tasks. In fact, research evidence supports this suggestion. For some tasks, and for some people, performing in the presence of others can impair—rather than enhance—performance (Uziel, 2007; Strauss, 2002; Aiello & Douthitt, 2001). Zajonc's theory has received support from numerous studies and observations of both humans and animals (Bargh, 2001; Platania & Moran, 2001; Zentall & Levine, 1972).

Improving each other's performance. Without realizing it, these two friends probably run faster when they jog together than when they each jog alone—the result of social facilitation.

In recent years, theorists have focused less on the mere presence of others and more on individuals' *interpretations* of and *reactions* to the presence of others (Aiello & Douthitt, 2001; Bond, 2000; Bond & Titus, 1983). If, for example, individuals do not like or trust other persons in their group, their own contributions to a group project may suffer. In addition, if people believe that other group members are disregarding their ideas or efforts, their own performance in the group may decline (Fiske, 2010; Paulus et al., 2002, 1993).

Social Loafing Groups are often formed in hopes that an interconnected body of people can energize and motivate every individual member. However, these hopes are not always realized. How many times, when working in a group, have you noticed that one or two of the group members are not pulling their weight? **Social loafing**—also known as *free riding*—refers to the phenomenon in which people exert less effort on a collective task than they would on a comparable individual task (Liden et al., 2004; Latane et al., 1979).

social loafing a phenomenon in which people exert less effort on a collective task than they would on a comparable individual task; also known as free riding.

Social loafing seems to most often rear its ugly head in large groups (Liden et al., 2004). It is most likely to occur when certain group members lack motivation to contribute, feel isolated from the group, calculate the cost of contributing as too high, or view their own contributions as unnecessary (Chidambaram & Tung, 2005; Shepperd, 1995, 1993). Research suggests that people from Western cultures are more inclined to display social loafing than people from Eastern cultures, and men are more likely to do so than women (Fiske, 2004).

Fortunately, social loafing can be minimized. When, for example, groups are highly *cohesive*—when group members all desire and value membership in the group—the social loafing phenomenon all but disappears (Hoigaard et al., 2006; Liden et al., 2004). Additionally, social loafing is reduced when group members are each explicitly reminded of their uniqueness and importance (Asmus & James, 2005), when they are given specific and challenging goals (Ling et al., 2005), when the output of each member is publicly identified (Williams et al., 1981), and when the members are given clear norms and comparison standards for their work (Hoigaard et al., 2006; Paulus et al., 2002). Finally, alertness tends to decrease social loafing, whereas fatigue tends to increase it (Hoeksema-van Orden, Gaillard, & Buunk, 1998).

Social loafing. Social loafers leave the work of a collective task to others in the group.

Group Polarization Have you ever begun talking about one of your favourite bands with a group of friends with similar musical tastes, and found yourself liking the band even more by the end of the conversation? When an initial tendency of individual group members is intensified following group discussion, **group polarization** occurs (Abrams et al., 2001; Isenberg, 1986). This phenomenon is not simply an example of conformity. With group polarization, the attitudes and inclinations of the individual group members are already in place, and they become more intense and more extreme as a result of the group interaction (Cooper et al., 2004).

group polarization the intensification of an initial tendency of individual group members brought about by group discussion.

Group polarization has been studied most often with regard to racial and ethnic bias and social and political attitudes (Prislin & Wood, 2005; Billings et al., 2000). When, for example, researchers have placed individuals with highly prejudiced attitudes in a group to discuss racial issues, the attitudes of the individuals tend to become still more prejudiced (Myers & Bishop, 1970). In similar work, it has been found that the attitudes of women with moderate leanings toward feminism become more strongly feminist following group discussions (Myers, 1975).

Groupthink Groups often come together to solve specific problems and make decisions. We noted earlier that group cohesiveness can prevent social loafing—but sometimes, groups can become *too* cohesive and single-minded, and the group's decision making can lead to disaster. A classic example occurred in the early 1960s, when the Kennedy administration in the United States government was determined to overthrow the communist government that Fidel Castro had instituted in Cuba. The U.S. government had trained a small group of Cuban exiles as part of a military operation to overthrow Castro. Proponents of the plan predicted that once this small militia touched down in Cuba at the Bay of Pigs, the Cuban citizens would rise up and join them. Instead, the operation collapsed, with no support from the Cuban people and no further help from the U.S. government. As a result of the failed invasion, anti-American sentiment around the globe increased, as did Castro's

A consequence of groupthink? In 2003 the space shuttle Columbia disintegrated during re-entry over Texas, killing all seven crew members. Just two days before the disaster, a NASA engineer had warned his supervisors of possible catastrophes on re-entry, but his message was not forwarded up the chain of command. How might groupthink have been involved in this mishandling of the warning?

influence in Latin America and Cuba's ties with the Soviet Union. There is evidence that no-one within Kennedy's inner circle raised any concerns about the viability of the plan. There was a strong sense of shared certainty that the Cubans would rise up and support the small invasion force (Janis, 1972).

Psychologist Irving Janis (1972), after examining the flawed decision-making process that went into the Bay of Pigs invasion, attributed the fiasco to **groupthink**, which he defined as a form of faulty group decision making that occurs when group members strive too hard for unanimity. The goal of achieving a consensus among all group members overrides the need to realistically appraise alternative courses of action. Clearly, groupthink can have undesired consequences (Henningsen et al., 2006; Baron, 2005; Whyte, 2000).

groupthink a form of faulty group decision making that occurs when group members strive for unanimity and this goal overrides their motivation to realistically appraise alternative courses of action.

Janis identified a number of conditions that set the stage for groupthink: (1) strong similarity in group members' backgrounds and ideologies, (2) high group cohesiveness, (3) high perceived threat, (4) elevated stress, (5) insulation from outside influence, and (6) a directive leader. Group members experience an illusion of invulnerability and have an unquestioned belief in the group's inherent morality. Typically, group members exert direct pressure against any member who expresses strong disagreement, and members protect the group from information that might shatter the shared conviction that their decisions are effective and moral (Janis, 1982).

Groupthink may have been operating within the Canadian government and across English Canada in the days leading up to the 1995 Quebec sovereignty referendum. After having the premiers of all provinces other than Quebec unite and refuse to pass amendments to the Canadian Constitution Repatriation Act, they also ignored René Lévesque's prediction that things would not go well in the next vote on sovereignty in Quebec. Within English-speaking Canada, warnings were ignored and there was surprise when the referendum was only defeated by the narrowest of margins (with 49.42 percent of Quebecers voting to secede from Canada, while 50.58 percent voted to remain within Canada). Similarly, it has been suggested that some of the decisions made by the Bush administration following the 9/11 terrorist attack in New York also fit the profile of groupthink (Yetiv, 2003, 2011). Of course, without detailed information about how decisions were arrived at, it is often hard to determine whether or not groupthink played a role in the outcome.

PSYCHOLOGY AROUND US Space Disasters and Groupthink

"On the morning of January 28, 1986, the space shuttle Challenger blasted off from the Kennedy Space Center in Florida. Seventy-three seconds after lift-off, the Challenger exploded, killing all seven astronauts on board . . . Following the explosion . . . information came to light about the faulty decision-making processes. . . . that [had] led to the decision to launch. Some engineers had expressed concerns about the design of the O-ring seal in the solid-fuel rocket, which could allow hot gases to leak through the joint and thereby spark an explosion. However . . . these concerns were ignored. . . .

"Unfortunately little was learned from this tragic accident because many of these same errors contributed to the loss of the Columbia space shuttle, and its seven astronauts, on February 1, 2003 [The shuttle was trying to return to earth after a 16-day mission in space]. Research now shows that prior to the Columbia disaster, some NASA engineers had grave concern about the shuttle's ability to return to earth following some tile damage it [had] experienced on lift-off. On January 28, just days before the Columbia tragedy, a landing gear specialist at NASA sent an email expressing his concerns about the tile damage. . . . However, high-level NASA administrators viewed the damage to the shuttle as minor—not a serious threat—and refused to respond. . . ." (Sanderson, 2010)

Having identified the phenomenon of groupthink, Janis went on to propose measures that a group can take to safeguard against it. First, the leader of the group should encourage members to air objections and doubts, and should accept criticisms of the group's judgments. Additionally, various group members should be assigned the role of "devil's advocate," arguing against the group's favoured position. Finally, outside experts should be invited to group meetings and encouraged to challenge the group's core views and decisions.

Research conducted since Janis first proposed his theory suggests that groupthink is a complicated phenomenon—probably more complicated than Janis initially realized. The conditions that he believed set the stage for groupthink do not always result in unwarranted unanimity (Baron, 2005). Nor do his proposed safeguards always prevent groupthink. At the same time, research and observations clearly indicate that the phenomenon of groupthink is widespread. Not only does it often affect decision making in important policy-setting groups, as Janis recognized, but it also influences decision making in mundane and temporary groups and groups working on trivial matters (Baron, 2005; Eaton, 2001; Whyte, 2000).

Helping Behaviour

When people are in need, many people offer help as an expression of **altruism** (concern for or acting to help others without any expectation of compensation or reciprocation) or of another social motive. In mid-May 2011, after one-third of the town of Slave Lake in Northern Alberta was burned by a rapidly moving wildfire, offers of accommodation, assistance, and aide poured in from across Canada. Residents of Slave Lake, while devastated by their losses, felt supported and cared for by their fellow Canadians. Other examples of altruism that have inspired others include Terry Fox's run for cancer and Rick Hansen's Man in Motion world tour in support of spinal cord research. Both of these selfless accomplishments have led to many more altruistic activities, with many people across Canada and around the world participating in Terry Fox runs.

altruism self-sacrificing behaviour carried out for the benefit of others.

Why Do We Help? Altruism refers to self-sacrificing behaviour carried out for the benefit of others. To be altruistic, behaviour must be motivated by concern for persons in need, without concern for oneself (Post, 2005; Puka, 2004). Thus, engaging in self-sacrificing behaviour to avoid a sense of guilt or donating to charity for tax purposes would not be considered altruistic behaviour. Such acts, which are motivated by a desire to reduce one's own personal distress or to receive rewards, are sometimes called *egoistic helping behaviours* (Batson et al., 2004, 1997; Khalil, 2004).

When we engage in helping behaviour, our motives can be entirely altruistic, entirely egoistic, or some combination of the two. Surveys have revealed that in the *immediate* aftermath of the 9/11 terrorist attacks, actions such as giving blood, money, and goods and offering prayers were associated with both altruistic and egoistic motives (Piferi et al., 2006). People's motivations for giving ranged from wanting to ease the suffering of others, to hoping to reduce their own attack-induced distress and seeking to reassure themselves that other people would help them if they were in need. In contrast, *sustained* giving after the attacks—that is, giving after one or more years—may have been more consistently associated with altruistic motives (Piferi et al., 2006).

Research further indicates that certain factors increase the likelihood of altruistic behaviour. When people empathize and identify with the individuals in need, they are more likely to behave altruistically (Batson et al., 2004, 1997; Batson & Weeks, 1996). Similarly, people tend to display more altruism when they take the perspective of victims (Mikulincer et al., 2005; Underwood & Moore, 1982). Not surprisingly, then, people who are generally trusting and outward-looking and who form secure attachments in their relationships are most likely to perform altruistic behaviours (Mikulincer et al., 2005; Mikulincer & Shaver, 2005). As you can see, it is often quite difficult to identify and understand the specific motives that drive people's helping behaviour, and especially to determine if their

Responding to tragedy. Almost immediately after a series of terrorist bombs ripped through passenger trains in Madrid, Spain in 2004, killing 191 people and injuring 1800 others, Spanish citizens such as these began lining up to donate blood to the victims. Altruism? Possibly. But social psychologists point out that egoistic motives may also be at work during the early reactions to tragedies of this kind.

behaviour can be seen to be truly selfless and thus truly altruistic. Questions about the existence and nature of altruism have been taken up as central interests by psychologists working in the area of positive psychology (Bateson, Ahmad, & Lishner, 2009).

Bystander Effect (or Bystander Apathy) Imagine you are in a life-threatening situation and desperately need the help of others. If you could choose, would you prefer that one or two people were nearby or that a large number of people were present? If you are like most people, you probably would prefer the larger number. After all, that would mean more potential helpers. In fact, however, this may be the more dangerous choice. It turns out that, in many circumstances, the more people present in a situation where help is required, the less likely it is that any one person will give that help (Fischer et al., 2006; Garcia et al., 2002; Batson, 1991).

On March 13, 1961, a woman named Kitty Genovese was stabbed to death over the course of 30 minutes in the New York borough of Queens, while at least 38 neighbours and other onlookers failed to intervene. This famous murder was followed by a public outcry demanding an explanation for the lack of intervention by others, including a *New York Times* article with the headline: "Thirty-Eight Who Saw Murder Didn't Call the Police" (Gansberg, 1964). Initially, many observers concluded that these 38 bystanders must have had a host of personality flaws that prevented them from helping. But were they really callous and uncaring?

Social psychologists John Darley and Bibb Latané were less interested in the personality traits of these onlookers than with features of the situation that might have kept them from providing help. In a series of studies examining the impact of the presence of others on helping behaviour, Darley and Latané repeatedly demonstrated that we are, in fact, more likely to intervene when we are *alone* than when others are also present. In one of their studies, for example, participants found themselves in a situation where they smelled smoke (faked by the experimenters) while either alone or in the presence of others. When other people were present in the room, fewer than 40 percent of the participants got up to report the smoke. In contrast, 75 percent of the participants reported smelling smoke when no one else was in the room (see **Figure 14-11**) (Latané & Darley, 1968). In another experiment by the two researchers, participants were placed in a situation in which they overheard a person (actually an actor) in another room having a seizure. The more people the participants believed could also hear the individual having the seizure, the less quickly they acted to help (Darley & Latané, 1968).

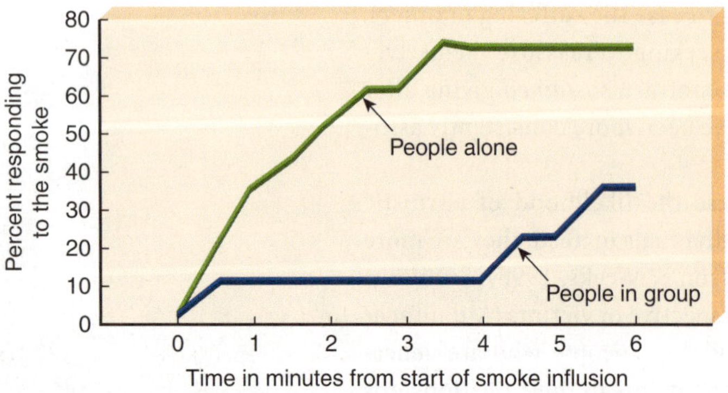

FIGURE 14-11 Bystander intervention. People are more likely to intervene to help when they are alone than in a group. In the presence of others, people feel less compelled to act, a phenomenon called bystander effect (Darley & Latané, 1968).

This phenomenon has been termed *bystander effect*. If your car is broken down in the rain at the side of the road and no-one is stopping to help, you may be experiencing the effects of bystander apathy first hand (and you may be glad for having a CAA membership). Researchers in addition to Darley and Latané have observed group apathy of this kind under a wide variety of conditions, including situations in which a person's belongings were seemingly stolen in a library (Shaffer et al., 1975), graffiti was written on an elevator wall (Chekroun & Brauer, 2002), and drunk driving was about to take place (Rabow et al., 1990).

What must occur for bystanders to intervene on someone else's behalf? Apparently, several steps are involved (Fischer et al., 2006; Darley, 2000; Latané &

Darley, 1970). Bystanders must: (1) notice the event, (2) interpret the event as an emergency, (3) feel personal responsibility for acting, (4) consider what form of assistance is needed, and (5) implement action (Fischer et al., 2011).

Some theorists have focused on the third step, *feeling a sense of personal responsibility*, as the key to bystander apathy (Garcia, Garcia, & Lila, 2009). They suggest that the presence of a large number of people in an emergency situation creates a *diffusion of responsibility* (Freeman, Walker, Borden, & Latane, 1975). When others are present, we feel that we do not bear the full burden of responsibility, and thus we feel less compelled to act. We may also assume that someone else must be taking action. This was exactly what many individuals concluded as they observed bodies of Hurricane Katrina victims floating past them or decaying in the streets of New Orleans—they concluded that other people would soon be collecting the bodies. Of course, when everyone in a crisis assumes that others will be taking responsibility for constructive action, no one intervenes. In extreme cases, such as that of Kitty Genovese, tragedy can result.

Diffusion of responsibility. People are less likely to stop and help an apparently lost child if they are part of a large crowd than if they are walking alone on a street. Why? When many others are present, we are not as likely to feel the full burden of responsibility.

Finally, research is just starting into issues of bystander reactions to violence within virtual realities, such as shared and online video games and worlds. Early work suggests that similar forces are at work shaping the behaviours of virtual bystanders as they do for bystanders in the "real" world (Rovira et al., 2009).

Aggression

In social psychological terms, aggression describes a broad category of behaviours, including physical and verbal attacks, intended to do harm to another. Aggression appears to have at least some biological underpinnings. Twin studies indicate that identical twins are more likely to share the trait of violent temper than fraternal twins, suggesting a genetic component (Baker et al., 2007; Miles & Carey, 1997; Rowe et al., 1999). High levels of the hormone testosterone have been linked with higher levels of aggression, as have low levels of the neurotransmitter serotonin. Indeed, the persons most likely to be involved with violent crime are muscular young men with below-average intelligence, high levels of testosterone, and low levels of serotonin (Dabbs et al., 2001).

aggression a broad range of behaviours intended to harm others.

That said, under the right circumstances, we are all capable of aggressive acts. One major hypothesis explaining aggression in humans—the *frustration-aggression hypothesis*—holds that we become aggressive in response to frustration (Dollard et al., 1939). As suggested in Chapter 12, any emotional stressor that impedes our progress or prevents achievement of some goal elicits frustration. Aggression, then, might be a cue to push harder to achieve that goal.

The frustration-aggression hypothesis was later expanded to include the notion that any unpleasant event, ranging from experiencing a bad odour or an annoying sound to hearing bad news, leads to activation of the sympathetic nervous system (Berkowitz, 1989). Recall from Chapter 12 that activation of the sympathetic nervous system is associated with both anger and fear and with the fight-or-flight response. This theory suggests that if you have translated this activation to aggressive (fight) behaviour in the past, and the outcome has had a desired effect, you will continue to engage in that aggressive behaviour (Friedman & Silver, 2007).

Relational aggression. On average, women are more likely than men to express their anger with relational aggression (for example, ignoring the person who has angered them).

Other factors influencing aggression probably result from both biology and environment (**Figure 14-12**). For example, as we have observed previously, men tend to be more aggressive than women—at least in some respects. Women are more likely to engage in acts of *relational*

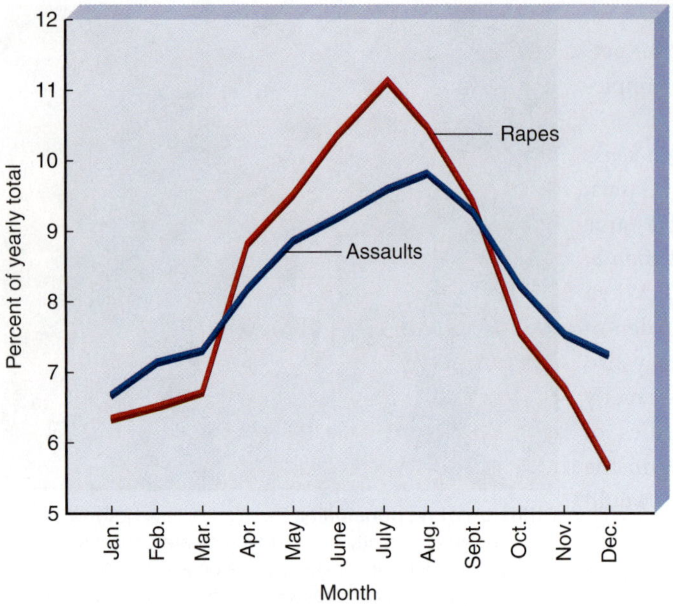

FIGURE 14-12 Aggression by time of year. Studies of data in North America and Europe over the last hundred years show that aggression is highest in the hottest months of the year (Anderson, 1989).

aggression, such as snubbing, gossiping, and otherwise excluding others as a means of venting frustration or anger (Archer, 2005). However, men are more likely to engage in *direct aggression*, which includes direct physical and verbal abuse. In fact, the vast majority of violent offenders are male (Halpern, 2000). Because this gender disparity shows up very early in childhood, it may be at least partially attributable to biological gender differences. However, it is probably also affected by social norms within our society, where men are permitted more than women to express anger and act aggressively.

Alcohol has also been found to increase aggressive behaviour for both biological and psychological reasons (Giancola, 2002). The effects of the drug may reduce inhibitions and so make people more likely to engage in violence or verbal abuse. However, people have been shown to become more aggressive even if they only think that they have had alcohol to drink, suggesting that they are responding to social expectations about how people act when they have been drinking (Lang et al., 1975; Bushman & Cooper, 1990).

Interpersonal Attraction

Why are we attracted to some people and not others? What's the difference between liking someone and loving someone? These are questions central to the study of interpersonal attraction. Interpersonal attraction operates at three levels: *cognitively*, we think certain things about the other person; *affectively*, we experience particular feelings toward the person; and *behaviourally*, we act in certain ways toward the person (Orbuch & Sprecher, 2003; Berscheid & Walster, 1978).

Liking *Liking* refers to fondness and affection for another person. Research has revealed five key factors that lead to liking someone.

1. *Similarity*—The more similar to us we perceive someone to be, the more likely we are to develop a fondness for that person (Lankau, Riordan, & Thomas, 2005; Bates, 2002). In addition, the more similar people are, the likelier it is that their fondness for one another will last a long time (Byrne, 1971).
2. *Proximity*—We tend to like people whom we encounter frequently more than those we do not encounter often, and we tend to like familiar people more than unfamiliar people (Smith & Weber, 2005; Swap, 1977). How many people who you have shared two or three classes with have become friends?
3. *Self-disclosure*—We tend to initially like people who disclose personal information to us (Dindia, 2000; Taylor et al., 1981), and we tend to disclose more to people whom we initially like (Certner, 1973; Worthy et al., 1969).
4. *Situational factors*—The situations in which we encounter other people greatly affect how much we like them. It has been suggested, for example, that we like people when we experience rewards while in their presence (Lott & Lott, 1974). Furthermore, a shared humorous experience seems to be a powerful way of forging closeness with a stranger (Fraley & Aron, 2004; Lyttle, 2001). The famous playwright Oscar Wilde once said, "Laughter is not at all a bad beginning for a friendship."

> "I do not believe that friends are necessarily the people you like the best. They are merely the people who got there first."
> —*Peter Ustinov, actor*

5. *Physical attractiveness*—People of all ages, even babies, prefer to look at and be near attractive people (Smith & Weber, 2005; Langlois & Stephan, 1981; Dion & Berscheid, 1974). Not surprisingly, then, physical attractiveness may affect likeability.

New approach, same criteria. Two people meet in a speed dating program at Bondi Beach in Australia. Speed dating is a relatively new form of social engagement in which large numbers of men and women are rotated to meet many potential partners over a series of short 3- to 8-minute "dates." What kinds of partners do speed daters choose most often? Those who are attractive and hold attitudes similar to those of the selectors.

What kinds of studies have led researchers to these conclusions? Let's examine a few of the investigations into the last factor mentioned above, physical attractiveness. In a study by social psychologist Elaine Walster and her colleagues (1966), the experimenters randomly paired participants to be dates at a dance. During a break in the dance, the participants were asked to rate how much they liked their partners. Overall, the more attractive the partner, the more likeable the partner was reported to be.

In other studies, an attractive middle-aged person was judged to be more outgoing and more pleasant than a less attractive middle-aged individual (Adams & Huston, 1975); physically attractive college students were found to be more popular than less attractive ones among members of the same sex (Byrne et al., 1968); and attractive grade 5 students were rated as more popular by their classmates than were less attractive students (Cavior & Dokecki, 1970).

Finally, one study examined the joint impact of two factors—physical attractiveness and similarity—on liking (Byrne et al., 1970). The experimenters prearranged lab dates for participants, varying both attractiveness and similarity of attitudes on certain issues. Upon their arrival, the dates were sent to a student lounge to talk for 20 minutes and then instructed to return to the lab. In the laboratory, the experimenters then measured how much the date pairs liked each other by having the participants fill out a questionnaire and by observing how close together the date pair stood when they reentered the lab. It turned out that the measures of liking were indeed related to both how attractive the dates were and how similar their attitudes were.

Loving Whereas liking someone involves a sense of fondness, loving is associated with a more extreme affection. When we *love* someone, we experience a strong, passionate attachment to that person. Some see loving as simply an extreme form of liking—with degree of attraction being the key distinction—whereas others see loving as a qualitatively different phenomenon (Watts & Stenner, 2005; Sternberg, 2004, 1987).

Let's first consider the question of what functions love serves. Freud viewed love as *sublimated sexual energy*—that is, a transformation of sexual desire into a more socially acceptable form (Fenchel, 2006). Evolutionary theorists emphasize love's role in propagating the species (Brumbaugh & Fraley, 2006; Wilson, 1981). According to these theorists, strong passionate attachments have ensured that over time, parents would stay together and raise their children together.

Still other theorists argue that love's most important value is to help provide companionship, emotional support, and even protection throughout the lifespan (Mikulincer et al., 2008; Mikulincer & Goodman, 2006). Loving relationships have in fact been associated with improved health (Levin, 2000). Such relationships provide us with people to confide in—and not being able to confide our troubles to someone has been associated with a host of health problems (Pennebaker, 2004, 2003, 1990; Pennebaker et al., 2004). This may be one reason why recently widowed individuals are more vulnerable to disease than individuals of similar age who have not lost a spouse (Troyer, 2006; Daggett, 2002).

What are the building blocks of love? Decades ago, social psychologist Zick Rubin (1970) emphasized three elements of love: attachment, caring, and intimacy. *Attachment* refers to the individual's need or desire for the physical presence and emotional support of the other person; *caring* is a feeling of concern and responsibility for the person; and *intimacy* involves the desire for close, confidential communication with the other individual.

Using this definition of love, Rubin (1973) designed a self-report scale that he hoped would be able to measure love and distinguish it from liking. The scale included *love* items, such as "If I could never be with ____, I would feel miserable" and "I feel I can confide in ____ about virtually everything," along with *like* items, such as "I think that _____ is usually well-adjusted" and "_____ is the sort of person whom I myself would like to be." In one study, Rubin had dating couples fill out this scale, alone and confidentially, focusing on their date partner in their ratings. He found that friends and lovers both scored high on the like items, but friends did not score high on the love items.

In another study, Rubin had volunteer couples come to his laboratory and sit across from each other while awaiting the start of the experiment. His assistants secretly observed the couples from behind a one-way mirror to determine which ones gazed into each other's eyes, a sign of love according to conventional wisdom. As expected, the partners who had scored high on Rubin's love scale gazed lovingly at each other more than did partners who had scored low on the scale.

triangular theory of love a theory proposed by Robert Sternberg that love is composed of three elements: intimacy, passion, and commitment.

Another psychologist, Robert Sternberg, whom you met back in Chapter 10, has proposed the **triangular theory of love**, which holds that love is composed of *intimacy*, *passion*, and *commitment* (Sternberg & Weis, 2006; Sternberg, 2004, 1986). Here, *intimacy* refers once again to feelings that promote closeness and connection, *passion* involves intense desires for union with the other person, and *commitment* refers to the decision to maintain the relationship across time. According to Sternberg, the extent and quality of each of these three components determines the nature of a particular loving relationship.

In fact, Sternberg distinguishes between eight kinds of relationship, each reflecting a particular combination of the three components (**Figure 14-13**). For example, purely *romantic* love consists of much intimacy and passion with little commitment. In contrast, couples who experience *companionate* love are high on intimacy and commitment but low on passion. Couples who experience *consummate* love are high on all three components; and those with *empty* love are high on commitment only. Sternberg also believes these relationships change over time, peaking at different points.

A number of social psychologists propose that relationships proceed through *stages* as the participants move from the fondness and affection of liking to the intimacy and commitment of loving. One theory, for example, cites four stages: exploration, bargaining, commitment, and institutionalization (Backman, 1990, 1981). In the *exploration* stage, the partners try out the possible rewards and costs of a relationship. During the *bargaining* stage, they implicitly negotiate the terms of the relationship. That is, they "feel out" its ground rules—which behaviours are rewarding, which cost too much, and how the joint benefits of the relationship can be maximized. During the third stage, *commitment*, the partners grow increasingly dependent on each other. Finally, in the *institutionalization* stage, shared expectations emerge, and the relationship is recognized by the partners (and by others) as exclusive. Other theorists have proposed different specific stages, but most agree that relationships do tend to proceed step-by-step as they deepen from liking to loving, with each stop marked by changing understandings, behaviours, and feelings (Yela, 2006; Berscheid, 1983).

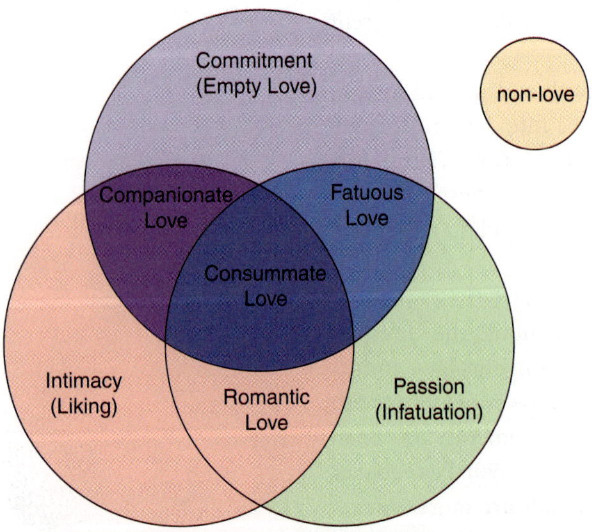

FIGURE 14-13 Sternberg's triangular theory of love. Sternberg's theory (1987) talks about the various possible combinations of intimacy, passion, and commitment and produces eight distinct types of relationship.

What determines *how* we love? Many theorists suggest that the way we express and experience love is a direct outgrowth of our early experiences with caregivers (Hazan & Shaver, 2004, 1994, 1987). For example, as we observed in Chapter 3, young children seem to express one of several kinds of attachment in their relationships with their parents (Ainsworth, 1979). It appears that adults display similar types of attachment in their romantic relationships. Using the attachment model, researchers Cindy Hazan and Phillip Shaver have proposed three types of lovers.

- Those with *secure* attachment styles find it relatively easy to become close to others and are comfortable depending on lovers and being depended on. They do not fear becoming too close or being abandoned.
- Those with *avoidant* attachment styles are somewhat uncomfortable being close to others and have difficulty trusting others and depending on them. In fact, they become nervous when others want to become closer to them.
- Those with *anxious-ambivalent* attachment styles worry that their lovers are less interested in closeness than they are. These insecure individuals are preoccupied with concerns that their partners do not really love them or will not stay with them. Sometimes their demands for security in relationships wind up pushing people away.

In their research, Hazan and Shaver found that approximately 53 percent of adults in relationships display a secure attachment style, 26 percent an avoidant attachment style, and 20 percent an anxious-ambivalent attachment style.

Falling in Limerence

Have you been in love? If yes, what did it feel like? Certainly there are feelings related to intense physical attraction, but what about the psychological aspects of being in new love? Did you think about the object of your affection constantly? Did you intensely fear that the person would reject you? Did you even have an aching feeling in your chest? If so, the reality may have been that you weren't in love—you were in *limerence* (Tennov, 1999).

Based on interviews with over 500 individuals conducted in the 1960s and 1970s, psychologist Dorothy Tennov coined the term *limerence* to describe the ultimate, obsessive form of romantic love. According to Tennov, limerence lasts, on average, two years. A person may experience it many times, only once, or never in a lifetime. The most notable component of limerence is constant, intrusive thinking about the object of affection, whom Tennov referred to as the limerent object, or LO (Reynolds, 1993). Tennov claimed that when people first fall into limerence, they spend about 30 percent of their day thinking about the LO. A few months later, they are thinking about the LO 100 percent of the time (*Time*, 1980).

The reality is, limerence can be problematic. Not only do romantic relationships suffer if one partner is in limerence while the other is not, but friendships and familial relationships can also become strained by the limerent's preoccupation with the LO. Some observers have even compared limerence to substance dependence.

Some psychologists believe that limerence is so disruptive it should be categorized as a psychological disorder for which people should get clinical help. They argue that people in limerence who do seek treatment are often incorrectly diagnosed with generalized anxiety disorder, depression, or obsessive-compulsive disorder (OCD) (Wakin & Vo, 2008).

Some brain research supports the view that limerence is not a usual state. Neuroscientists have found that people who are newly "in love" have activity levels of the neurotransmitter serotonin similar to the levels found in individuals with OCD. In addition, people who have fallen in love within the past six months have elevated levels of the stress hormone cortisol (Anathasawamy, 2004).

What do you think? Is the heart-pounding state that fuels romance novels and movies actually a psychological disorder?

Before You Go On

www.wiley.com/go/comer

What Do You Know?

12. What is groupthink and under what conditions is it most likely to occur?
13. How does altruistic helping behaviour differ from egoistic helping behaviour?
14. How does the presence of other people affect the likelihood that a bystander will intervene on behalf of someone who needs help?
15. What are some of the biological underpinnings of aggressive behaviour?
16. What are the three components of Robert Sternberg's triangular theory of love and how do they interact in relationships?

SCAN TO GET THE ANSWERS

What Do You Think?

Think about a relationship you have had with a friend—someone you really like. Analyze the development of that relationship with reference to some of the key factors discussed in this section.

Social Functioning WHAT HAPPENS IN THE BRAIN?

LEARNING OBJECTIVE 5

Describe the major findings of social neuroscience about regions of the brain particularly important to our social functioning.

Throughout this book, you have seen that with the help of brain-scanning procedures, researchers have tied many areas of psychological functioning, such as memory or emotions, to particular neural circuits—collections of neurons that communicate with each other. The study of social functioning is no different. Indeed, there has been so much work to uncover what happens in the brain when people are thinking and behaving socially that the field of study has been given a special title, *social neuroscience*, and the combination of brain regions that operate together when people function socially has also been given a special name in some circles, the "social brain."

One of the early clues that helped researchers to identify regions of the brain that may be at work in social cognition and behaviour came from evolutionary psychology (Adolphs, 2009, 2003). Beginning with the observation that a unique and critically important area of human functioning is social cognition—particularly the ability to infer what is going on (intentions, feelings, and thoughts) inside the minds of other people—scientists decided to pay special attention to those regions that are newer and/or bigger in human brains than in the brains of other animals. Their suspicion was that these regions may be the ones that play key roles in social functioning.

Not surprisingly, several of the brain regions that, according to brain scans, are very active during social cognition and behaviour are indeed particularly large in the human brain. For example, the *prefrontal cortex*, the part of the frontal cortex that is closest to the front of the head, is much larger in humans than in other animals (see **Figure 14-14**). As we observed in Chapter 4, the entire frontal cortex is somewhat larger in the human brain than in the brains of less complex animals. But the prefrontal cortex is particularly larger (Semendeferi et al., 2002).

Social cognitions and behaviours rely on many of the psychological functions that we have examined throughout this book. They require, for example, rapid identification of social stimuli and signals (for example, recognition of people), rapid retrieval of memories (to help us remember who is a friend and who is a foe), the ability to recognize the perspective of others, anticipation of others' behaviours, experiences of emotion and empathy, and moral and other evaluations of situations (to help us decide, for example, whether prosocial behaviour is in order). Thus, some of the brain regions that are highly active during social

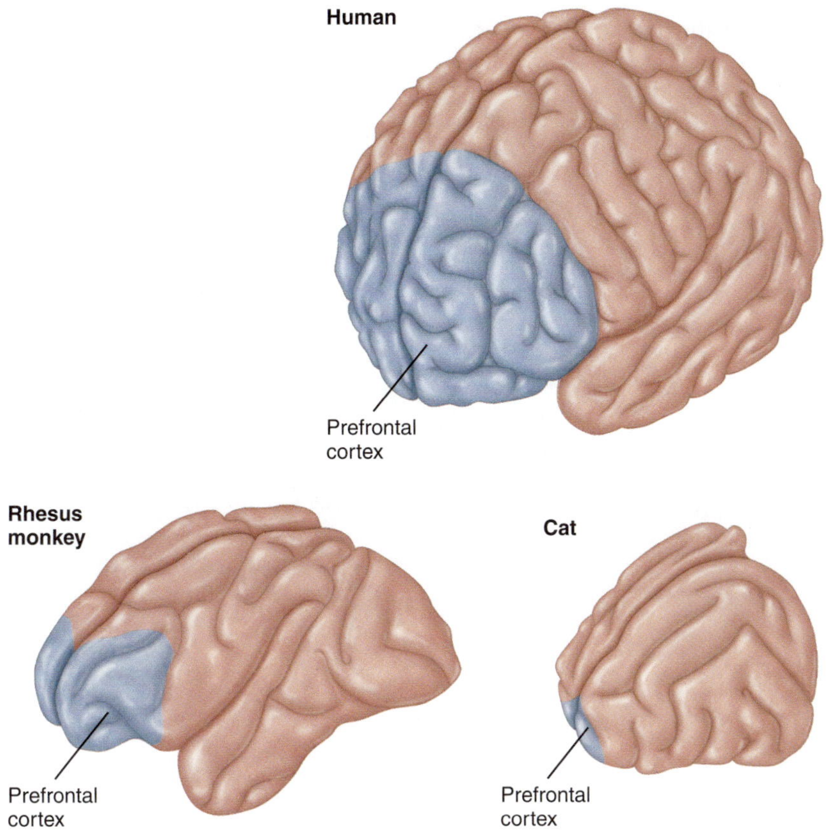

FIGURE 14-14 Across the species. The prefrontal cortex of human beings is larger than that of other animals and is, at the same time, very active during social behaviour, suggesting that it plays an important role in human social functioning.

functioning turn out to be ones related to language and thought, memory, and emotion (Adolphs, 2009). To date, social neuroscientists have identified the following brain regions as among the key players in social functioning:

- *Orbitofrontal cortex*—a subregion of the prefrontal cortex, it is involved in social reasoning, reward evaluation, reading other people, and eliciting emotional states (Stuss et al., 2001).
- *Ventromedial prefrontal cortex*—another subregion of the prefrontal cortex, it plays a key role in the processing of rewards and punishments, interpreting non-verbal social information (such as facial expressions), making social and moral assessments and decisions, and feeling empathy (Koenigs et al., 2007; Shamay-Tsoory et al., 2005).
- *Insula*—a region of the cortex that is located beneath the frontal cortex, it plays a key role in empathy and in reading others. The insula is activated when we observe others in physical or emotional pain and immediately feel that pain ourselves (Keysers & Gazzola, 2007).
- *Amygdala*—a brain region that is located in the temporal lobe, it is, as we have seen, actively involved in the control of emotions. In social functioning, it helps us to identify the emotional facial expressions of other people and to pay particular attention to stimuli that may be unpredictable, potentially rewarding, or potentially punishing (Whalen et al., 2009; Whalen, 1998).

We still have much to learn about how these and other regions operate together to help people function socially. Social neuroscientists are also still trying to identify the precise neural networks that enable us to so readily carry out the social cognitions and behaviours examined throughout this chapter.

PSYCHOLOGY AROUND US The Antisocial Brain: Is Revenge Sweet After All?

Is revenge a good thing? Not usually. But it may be that our brains are wired to enjoy it—at least under certain circumstances. Investigators entertained this possibility after they had research participants observe individuals taking part in a famous decision game called the Prisoner's Dilemma.

In the Prisoner's Dilemma game, two players are separated and accused of a crime. If one person confesses to the crime and the other doesn't, the confessor will get only one year in prison and the silent player will get five years. If both of the players remain silent, they'll each be convicted of a lesser offence and get two years. If they both confess, they each get three years.

In a brain scan study, the participants were hooked up to MRIs and asked to watch confederates play the game. What the researchers found was that if one of the confederates "confessed" and the other didn't, three things happened in the brains of the observing participants: (1) the participants exhibited a strong dislike for the confessor; (2) the participants exhibited less neural activity in pain-related areas of their brains, suggesting they had little empathy for the confessor; and (3) among the male participants, reward centres in their brains lit up like a Christmas tree when they saw the experimenters appear to be applying electric shocks to the hands of the confessor. This was taken to mean that the male participants actually got a positive charge out of seeing the confessors, who had hung their buddies out to dry, get what was coming to them. In other words, for men, it may be that revenge, or the observation of revenge, is indeed sweet—in more than a figurative sense.

Before You Go On

www.wiley.com/go/comer

What Do You Know?

17. What is social neuroscience and what is the "social brain"?
18. Which brain regions have been identified as particularly important to our social functioning?

What Do You Think?

If you were a neuroscientist looking for parts of the brain that are important to social functioning, how would you decide where to look first?

SCAN TO GET THE ANSWERS

Disorders of Social Functioning

WHEN THINGS GO WRONG

LEARNING OBJECTIVE 6

Describe the major features of social phobias, anxiety disorder, avoidant personality disorder, dependent personality disorder, and autism.

Social psychology's various theories and studies all include the implicit notion that people are *socially motivated* (Forgas, Williams, & Laham 2005). That is, they are interested in, concerned about, and influenced by the behaviours, opinions, and feelings of other people; they want to understand others; and they need other people in their lives. Such social needs and behaviours are, however, impaired for some people, leading to significant problems in their relationships and interactions.

Psychologists have identified several types of disorders whose symptoms interfere with the ability to function normally in the social sphere. We have already looked at one such disorder, antisocial personality disorder, in the previous chapter. In two other disorders, social phobia and avoidant personality disorder, individuals are excessively afraid to interact with other people. In contrast, persons with dependent personality disorder have an abnormal need to please and be accepted by others. And finally, those with autism, a severe disorder, are extremely unresponsive to others and uncommunicative, among other symptoms, and are essentially unconnected socially.

Social Anxiety Disorder and Avoidant Personality Disorder

People with a **social anxiety disorder** have severe, persistent, and irrational fears of social situations in which embarrassment may occur. The disorder may be specific, such as a fear of talking in public or writing in front of others, or it may be general, such as a wide-ranging fear of functioning poorly in front of others. This disorder can severely impair how the person participates in groups, relationships, and bystander situations—some of the key social contexts that we have examined in this chapter (Ravindran & Stein, 2011). It appears that around 7 percent of people in countries throughout the Western world—around three women for every two men—currently experience a social anxiety disorder (Alfano & Beidel, 2011; Kessler et al., 2010).

social anxiety disorder a disorder involving severe, persistent, and irrational fears of social situations in which embarrassment may occur.

Words are not always the answer. In 2004, Austrian author Elfriede Jelinek won the Nobel Prize in literature, but her social phobia prevented her from attending the Nobel festivities. Instead, she had to accept the award and present her Nobel lecture by video transmission.

As you will see in Chapter 16, the most influential explanation for social anxiety disorder focuses on dysfunctional social cognitions that people with the disorder seem to hold (Heimberg, Brozovich, & Rapee, 2010). These individuals believe that they are unattractive social beings, that they must perform perfectly in all social situations, and that clumsy social behaviours always lead to terrible consequences, among other beliefs. As a result of these notions, they keep anticipating that social disasters will occur. Moreover, their anxiety levels rise immediately whenever they enter social situations. Research indicates that a number of factors contribute to the development of such beliefs, including genetic factors, trait tendencies, traumatic childhood experiences, and past parent–child interactions (Brozovich & Hemberg, 2011; Kuo et al., 2011; Rosenberg et al., 2010).

People with **avoidant personality disorder** are very uncomfortable and inhibited in social relationships, overwhelmed by feelings of inadequacy, and extremely sensitive to negative evaluation (APA, 2000). They have an extreme fear of being criticized or rejected, so they actively avoid various forms of social contact. Many people with this disorder consider themselves as unappealing or inferior. They may have few or no close friends, though they would certainly like to have intimate relationships. Often, they feel depressed and lonely. It is estimated that between 1 and 2 percent of adults have avoidant personality disorder (Paris, 2010; Mattia & Zimmerman, 2001; APA, 2000).

avoidant personality disorder a disorder involving extreme discomfort and inhibition in social relationships.

Obviously, avoidant personality disorder is similar to social anxiety disorder. In fact, people with one of these disorders often experience the other as well (Cox et al., 2011). A telling difference between the two is that people with social anxiety disorder largely fear social *circumstances*, whereas those with the personality disorder primarily fear close social *relationships* (Kantor, 2010).

Dependent Personality Disorder

Earlier in this chapter, when we examined the famous series of experiments by Stanley Milgram, we observed that people may become excessively obedient under certain circumstances. People with **dependent personality disorder**, however, are excessively obedient under *all* circumstances. They have a wide-ranging, excessive need to be taken care of (APA, 2000). Correspondingly, they are clinging and obedient, and fear separation from their parents, spouses, or friends. At the centre of this disorder is a difficulty with separation. The individuals feel devastated when close relationships end, and they quickly seek out new relationships to fill the void. They may even hold on desperately to relationships with partners who physically or psychologically abuse them (Loas et al., 2011).

dependent personality disorder a disorder involving a pervasive, excessive need to be taken care of and a fear of separation.

People with dependent personality disorder rely on others so much that they cannot make the smallest decision for themselves. They seek help for even the simplest matters, and experience extreme feelings of inadequacy and helplessness. They seldom dispute the opinions of other people, and they allow others to make important decisions for them, including where to live, what job to have, and which neighbours to befriend (Millon, 2011; APA, 2000). Because they are so fearful of rejection, they are extraordinarily sensitive to disapproval and they keep trying to measure up to other people's expectations and wishes, even volunteering for unpleasant or degrading tasks or agreeing to do things that they know are wrong. Over 2 percent of people may display dependent personality disorder (Paris, 2010; Mattia & Zimmerman, 2001).

Autism

autism a severe disorder marked by extreme unresponsiveness, poor communication skills, and very repetitive and rigid behaviours.

Individuals with **autism** are extremely unresponsive to others, uncommunicative, repetitive, and rigid. Their symptoms appear early in life, typically before 3 years of age. As many as 1 in 150 children display the disorder, an estimate that includes cases of autism-like disorders (Mash & Wolfe, 2010; Teicher et al., 2008). The vast majority of children with this disorder remain severely disabled into adulthood.

PSYCHOLOGY AROUND US Lost in His Own World

In retrospect [Susan] can recall some things that appeared odd to her. For example, she remembers that [as a baby] Mark never seemed to anticipate being picked up when she approached. In addition, . . . he showed little interest in toys. In fact, Mark seemed to lack interest in anything. He rarely pointed to things and seemed oblivious to sounds. . . . Mark spent much of his time repetitively tapping on tables, seeming to be lost in his own world.

After his second birthday, Mark's behaviour began to trouble his parents. . . . Mark, they said, would "look through" people or past them, but rarely at them. He could say a few words but didn't seem to understand speech. In fact, he did not even respond to his own name. Mark's time was occupied examining familiar objects, which he would hold in front of his eyes while he twisted and turned them. Particularly troublesome were Mark's odd movements—he would jump, flap his arms, twist his hands and fingers, and perform all sorts of facial grimaces, particularly when he was excited—and what Robert [Mark's father] described as Mark's rigidity. Mark would line things up in rows and scream if they were disturbed. He insisted on keeping objects in their place and would become upset whenever Susan attempted to rearrange the living room furniture.

(Wing, 1976)

Around 80 percent of all cases occur in boys. The vast majority of children with the disorder remain severely disabled into adulthood. In most cases, even the highest-functioning adults with autism continue to have significant problems showing closeness, empathy, and support in their social relationships and communications, and have limited interests and activities (Baron-Cohen & Wheelwright, 2003).

A lack of social responsiveness—including extreme aloofness, little interest in other people, low empathy, and inability to share attention with others—is generally considered the central feature of autism (Boyd et al., 2011; Constantino, 2011). In addition, individuals with the disorder typically have severe language and communication problems (for example, failing to speak, displaying poor language skills, or using odd speech patterns). They may have problems naming objects, employing a proper tone when talking, or using language for conversational purposes. Children with the disorder also may be unable to play in a varied, spontaneous way. They typically fail to include others in their play or to make social experiences part of their play behaviour. More generally, they often fail to see themselves as others see them and make no effort to imitate or be like others (Bodfish, 2011). Finally, the motor movements of people with autism are often unusual. For example, many flap their arms, twist their hands and fingers, rock, and make faces—acts called *self-stimulatory behaviours*. Some individuals also perform *self-injurious behaviours*, such as repeatedly banging their head against a wall, pulling their hair, or biting themselves (Aman & Farmer, 2011).

Asperger's disorder a disorder in which persons have major social impairments, yet have relatively normal intellectual, adaptive, and language skills.

Asperger's Disorder A variation of autism, sometimes referred to as an *autism-spectrum disorder*, is **Asperger's disorder**. Here individuals experience many of the same kinds of social deficits, impairments in expressiveness, and restricted and repetitive behaviours that

Picture of autism. This individual with autism engages in self-stimulatory behaviour (rapidly moving his fingers in front of his eyes), a common behaviour among people with the disorder. This symptom adds to the social impairments that mark autism, such as unresponsiveness to others, limited capacity for imaginative play, poor communication, and severe relationship deficits.

are on display in autism, but at the same time they often have relatively normal intellectual, adaptive, and language skills (Miller & Ozonoff, 2011; Siegel & Ficcaglia, 2006). Individuals with Asperger's disorder often want to fit in and interact with others, but their social limitations make it difficult for them to do so. Instead they may seem awkward and unaware of conventional social rules (ASA, 2006). Although these individuals must contend with deficits throughout their lives, many are—in contrast to those with autism—able to complete a high level of education, such as college or trade school. Many also successfully hold jobs and have satisfying relationships (ASA, 2005).

Causes and Treatments of Autism A variety of explanations have been offered for autism. Some theorists propose that people with the disorder have a key perceptual or cognitive disturbance that makes normal communication and interactions impossible (Pisula, 2010; Frith, 2000). One influential explanation holds, for example, that they fail to develop a *theory of mind*—an awareness that other people base their behaviours on their own beliefs, knowledge, and other mental states, not on information that they have no way of knowing (Hale & Tager-Flusberg, 2005; Frith, 2000). As you will recall from Chapter 9, developing a theory of mind is critical to proper development.

A 1998 study claimed to show an association between the administrations of the MMR (measles, mumps, and rubella) vaccine and increases in the incidence of autism (Wakefield et al., 1998). More recent large-scale studies have failed to show any sign of this relationship (Taylor et al., 1999; Institute of Medicine of the National Academies, 2004). Many questions were asked about the original study and about the credibility of it and its primary author. Very recently, the *British Medical Journal* published an article stating that Wakefield's original article was fraudulent. The most current data does *not* support a connection between autism and the MMR vaccine.

A number of theorists believe that autism and other cognitive limitations have their roots in early biological problems—problems that prevent proper cognitive development. Although a detailed biological understanding of autism has yet to emerge, some promising leads have been found. First, studies of the relatives of people with autism have suggested a *genetic factor* in this disorder. The prevalence of autism is as high as 6 to 8 per 100 among siblings of those with this disorder (Gillis & Romanczyk, 2007), a rate much higher than the general population's. Other studies have also linked autism to *prenatal difficulties* or *birth complications* (Teicher et al., 2008; Rodier, 2000). The chances of developing autism are higher when the mother contracts rubella during pregnancy, comes into contact with toxic chemicals before or during pregnancy, or has complications during labour or delivery.

Other studies have sometimes linked the disorder to *genetic factors*, and certain *brain abnormalities* (Reichenberg et al., 2011; Sakurai et al., 2011; Teicher et al., 2008). The cerebellum has been implicated, for example (Allen, 2011). Apparently abnormal development in this brain region occurs early in the life of people with autism. Similarly, brain scans indicate that many individuals with autism have abnormalities in the brain's limbic system, brain stem nuclei, and amygdala (Bachevalier, 2011; Bauman, 2011). People with autism may also experience reduced activity in the brain's temporal and frontal lobes when they perform language and motor initiation tasks—tasks that, as you will recall, normally involve activity by the brain's left hemisphere (Escalante, Minshew, & Sweeney, 2003).

Although treatment can help people with autism adapt better, no known treatment totally reverses this disorder. The treatments of most help are behavioural therapy, communication training, and parent training. Psychotropic drugs and certain vitamins have also sometimes helped when combined with other approaches (Teicher et al., 2008).

Before You Go On

www.wiley.com/go/comer

What Do You Know?

19. What are the key features of social anxiety disorder, avoidant personality disorder, and dependent personality disorder?
20. Describe some of the ways in which individuals with autism show a lack of responsiveness.

What Do You Think?

Disorders that interfere with social functioning are among the most disabling of problems. Why?

SCAN TO GET THE ANSWERS

Summary

Social Cognition: Attitudes

LEARNING OBJECTIVE 1 Explain how attitudes form and change and what role they play in behaviour.

- *Attitudes* are relatively stable and enduring evaluations of things and people. According to the ABC model, they have affective, behavioural, and cognitive components.
- Parents play a major role in shaping children's attitudes. In older children, peers, teachers, and the media also exert an influence.
- Leon Festinger proposed that people change their attitudes when they experience *cognitive dissonance*—a state of emotional discomfort that arises when a person holds two contradictory beliefs or holds a belief inconsistent with his behaviour.
- The *self-perception theory* of attitude change minimizes the role of emotional discomfort and suggests that people simply infer what their attitudes are by observing their own behaviour.
- The attitudes people express are not necessarily related to their behaviour. In part, this is because people sometimes misrepresent their attitudes. They may wish to express socially desirable attitudes, or they may not be aware of what their *implicit attitudes* really are.
- *Stereotypes* and *prejudice* arise in part from the human tendency to identify with a group. Various explanations of prejudice come from evolutionary theories, realistic conflict theory, and social identity theory.
- People use persuasion techniques to try to influence the attitudes of others. The central route to persuasion emphasizes the content of the message, while the peripheral route depends on more superficial appeals, such as the appearance of the spokesperson.

Social Cognition: Attributions

LEARNING OBJECTIVE 2 Discuss how people make attributions to explain their own behaviour and the behaviour of others.

- *Attributions*, or causal explanations of behaviour, can be *dispositional* (internal) or *situational* (external).
- People tend to attribute their own behaviour to situational factors and the behaviour of others to dispositional factors. The reliance on dispositional factors to explain others' behaviour is the *fundamental attribution error*.
- According to the *actor–observer effect*, this discrepancy exists because people make situational attributions as actors and dispositional attributions as observers.

- People sometimes attribute only their failures to situational factors and attribute their successes to dispositional factors, called the *self-serving bias*.

Social Forces

LEARNING OBJECTIVE 3 Describe the power of conformity and obedience in shaping people's behaviour.

- Society establishes rules, or *norms*, about how people are supposed to act. *Social roles* are sets of norms ascribed to particular social positions. Norms and roles are critical to the smooth functioning of society, but also place limits on individuals.
- *Conformity* is the tendency to yield to real or imagined group pressure. In a famous series of experiments, Solomon Asch found that 75 percent of research participants yielded to implicit group pressure to conform to an incorrect judgment.
- Unlike conformity, *obedience* involves following direct orders, usually from an authority figure. Experiments by Stanley Milgram found that 65 percent of subjects continued to follow orders to administer what they believed to be dangerous electric shocks.

Social Relations

LEARNING OBJECTIVE 4 Review major concepts in the areas of group dynamics, helping behaviour, aggression, and interpersonal attraction.

- The *social facilitation* effect occurs when the presence of others enhances a person's performance. Research shows that this effect holds for simple, well-learned tasks; but the presence of others can impair performance on more complicated tasks.
- With *social loafing*, people in a group exert less effort on a task than they would if performing the task alone.
- *Group polarization* is a phenomenon in which group discussion intensifies the already-held opinions of group members and produces a shift toward a more extreme position.
- Groups with certain characteristics—a strong similarity among members, high group cohesiveness, high-perceived threat, elevated stress, insulation from outside influence, and a directive leader—may become victims of *groupthink*, a faulty decision-making process in which group members strive for unanimity at the expense of realistically appraising alternative courses of action.
- Helping behaviour is of two types: *altruism*, which is motivated by concern for others, and egoistic helping behaviour, which is motivated by a desire to reduce one's own distress or receive rewards.
- People are more likely to engage in helping behaviour when alone than when in the presence of others. Theorists propose that the presence of others may create a diffusion of responsibility, in which no single individual feels personal responsibility for acting.
- *Aggression* describes a broad range of behaviours intended to do harm to another. Aggression has some biological underpinnings. In addition, the frustration-aggression hypothesis proposes that aggression arises in response to frustration.
- Factors that lead to liking another person include similarity, proximity, self-disclosure, situational, and physical attractiveness.
- One description of love includes three elements: attachment, caring, and intimacy. Another, Sternberg's *triangular theory of love*, holds that love is composed of intimacy, passion, and commitment, which combine in varying degrees.
- Similar to young children, adults display three types of attachment in love relationships: secure attachment, avoidant attachment, and anxious-ambivalent attachment.

Social Functioning *What Happens in the Brain?*

LEARNING OBJECTIVE 5 Describe the major findings of social neuroscience about regions of the brain particularly important to our social functioning.

- Social neuroscience is the specialty of neuroscience that studies how the brain works during social functioning. Social functioning is so important and uniquely human that social neuroscientists have given the name "social brain" to the combination of brain areas that are particularly active in social functioning.
- The orbitofrontal cortex, ventromedial prefrontal cortex, insula, and amygdala all have been identified as especially important in social functioning. Researchers continue to try to pinpoint neural connections related to social functioning.

Disorders of Social Functioning *When Things Go Wrong*

LEARNING OBJECTIVE 6 Describe the major features of social phobias, anxiety disorder, avoidant personality disorder, dependent personality disorder, and autism.

- People with *social phobias* have severe, persistent, and irrational fears of social situations in which embarrassment may occur.
- *Avoidant personality disorder* involves extreme discomfort and inhibition in social relationships.
- People with *dependent personality disorder* display a pervasive, excessive need to be taken care of and a fear of separation.
- *Autism* is a severe disorder marked by extreme unresponsiveness, poor communication skills, and very repetitive and rigid behaviours.

Key Terms

ABC model of attitudes 528
actor–observer effect 540
aggression 557
altruism 555
Asperger's disorder 566
attitudes 528
attributions 539
autism 566
avoidant personality disorder 565
cognitive dissonance 530
conformity 546
dependent personality disorder 565
fundamental attribution error 539
group 551
group polarization 553
groupthink 554
implicit attitude 532
norms 543
obedience 548
prejudice 534
self-perception theory 531
self-serving bias 542
social anxiety disorder 565
social cognition 528
social facilitation 552
social identity theory 535
social loafing 553
social psychology 528
social role 544
stereotypes 534
triangular theory of love 560

TYING IT TOGETHER

The study of social psychology is closely connected to the study of all other areas of psychology. Throughout this chapter, we have stressed how social functioning interfaces with psychology's various subfields, including our highlighted sections on brain function, individual differences, abnormal functioning, and development. To remind you of how social psychology is tied to other psychology subfields and issues, we have selected some interesting points from throughout the chapter.

WHAT HAPPENS IN THE BRAIN?

- There has been so much research on the brain's role in social functioning that there is now a branch of neuroscience called *social neuroscience*.
- The prefrontal cortex, much larger in humans than most animals, houses many of the structures important in social functioning.
- High levels of aggression have been linked with a combination of high testosterone activity and low serotonin activity.

HOW WE DIFFER

- Females and males who act outside their society's gender roles may face harsh reactions.
- Studies show that, on average, women in North America are more socially skilled than men.
- People who are trusting and outward-looking and who form secure attachments in their relationships are more likely to perform altruistic behaviours.
- Both men and women are aggressive, but males are, on average, more likely to engage in direct, physical, and verbal aggression. Female aggression is more likely, on average, to be relational, such as snubbing someone.

WHEN THINGS GO WRONG

- Around 7 out of every 100 people in North America experience social anxiety disorder. Another 1 or 2 percent have avoidant personality disorders.
- In contrast, at least 2 percent of the population display dependent personality disorder.
- As many as 1 in every 150 individuals may have autism or an autism-like disorder.

HOW WE DEVELOP

- Part of our socialization as children involves learning our society's norms. Once learned, our norms can influence our behaviour for life.
- Childhood socialization can lead us to develop long-lasting attitudes, including stereotypes and prejudice.
- Although autism is sometimes referred to as a childhood disorder, it is in fact a lifespan disorder for most individuals.

Psychology Around Us

Helping Behaviour and Bystander Apathy

Good Intentions Are Not Enough

View this in Action WILEY PLUS www.wileyplus.com

Video Lab Exercise

Most of us like to think of ourselves as caring people who always stand ready to help those in distress. But, under certain circumstances, many people—indeed, most people—fail to act as helpful bystanders in situations that seem to cry out for the involvement of others. Helping a lost child, coming to the aid of car crash victims, helping someone who is being beaten—these are but a few of the situations in which bystanders—such as you or I—may sometimes fail to act.

Let's see when you are a Good Samaritan and when you are not. In this video lab exercise, you will become a bystander in various situations, and you will see how your prosocial behaviour changes as bystander factors are changed one by one. In a world where we typically think "I would never act that way" upon reading or hearing about undesirable, apathetic behaviours, you will probably be surprised at what you are (or are not) capable of.

As you are working on this online exercise, consider the following questions:

- What factors determine whether bystanders will be apathetic or choose to act?
- What role does diffusion of responsibility play in the bystander apathy phenomenon?
- What defence mechanisms or dissonance principles might apathetic bystanders need to employ later?
- Might there also be personality factors that cause some people to come to the aid of others particularly quickly?

CHAPTER 15

Stress, Coping, and Health

CHAPTER OUTLINE

- What Is Stress?
- Responding to Stress
- Coping with Stress
- Stress and Health
- Posttraumatic Stress Disorder

JUST WORK HARDER

Ashley sits at her desk, unable to concentrate. Her English paper is due on Wednesday, but her computer screen remains blank. She knows she needs to get started, but she is having a hard time. All sorts of thoughts are flying through her head, and each one makes her chest tighten and makes her want to curl up into a ball and shut her eyes.

She has to leave for her job in less than an hour. She desperately needs the bus to be on time. Chris, her boss, has told her that if she is late again, he'll "have to find someone more reliable." And then there is the email she just got from her parents asking—once again—about her grades. She is the first child in her family to go to college, and her parents have been driving her crazy. She's glad that they are so excited, but don't they realize that asking for weekly updates only puts more pressure on her?

In fact, things aren't going so well in some of her classes. She's good at chemistry, but she finds English, especially writing, very difficult. "Just work harder," her parents have told her, as if she weren't trying as hard as she could. Her public speaking class is a disaster: she actually had to leave in the middle of her last speech, fighting back tears.

The more trouble she has, the more she feels like just going out with her friends at night. In fact, she's gone out every night this week, always telling herself, "I'll get started on my paper tomorrow." Even though she knows she can't put her paper off any longer, she has agreed to see a movie tonight after work with some people from school.

Then there is the recent break-up with her boyfriend, Jason. She feels bad about the way their relationship ended. One night when she was late for work and in a panic, he called her and teasingly refused to let her off the phone. After a few minutes, she called him a jerk and hung up on him. It wasn't the first time she had lashed out at him, and even though she tried to apologize the next day, he said he didn't want to deal with her moods anymore.

"All right, let's try to get it together," she tells herself. "Come up with a game plan." She decides to jog to the restaurant, avoiding bus delays and getting some exercise to boot. Moreover, in the few minutes she has before she must leave for work, she forces herself to start typing. Before too long, she has two paragraphs on the screen. At least it's a start. She is finally thinking and acting constructively.

You don't need a textbook to tell you that Ashley is experiencing stress. After all, you have probably been in a similar place—too much to do, too little time, too many expectations, too little certainty about what to do next. Obviously, Ashley feels stress because she has lots of work to do and is running out of time. But she also has feelings of

stress connected to something otherwise pleasant—the opportunity to socialize with friends. Something as minor as an English paper, as pleasant as the prospect of an evening out, or as awful as a life-threatening medical condition can prompt feelings of stress.

Stress affects us both physically and psychologically. Recall how you felt the last time you were stuck in a traffic jam on your way to someplace important. Chances are you had physical and psychological reactions—you may have been frustrated and angry, your stomach may have been tied up in knots, and you may even have pounded on the steering wheel or yelled. Because stress affects us this way, it can damage our health.

The effects of stress on psychological and physical health have made it a subject of major interest. Some researchers are trying to clarify what makes situations stressful. Others are studying how stress affects the body. Still others are trying to figure out what responses help people to cope with stress and lessen its toll. This chapter examines what researchers have learned about the sources and effects of stress. It also looks at ways to deal with stress, noting that certain kinds of behaviour—such as Ashley's jog to work or her decision to simply start writing her paper—can help people reduce stress or cope with it more effectively. ■

What Is Stress?

LEARNING OBJECTIVE 1

Define stress and describe the ways in which people experience stress and the kinds of situations that typically cause stress.

Many people think that stress and emotion are one and the same. They may say, for example, that they're "stressed out" when they really mean they are feeling emotions such as anxiety, depression, or anger. In fact, stress and emotion are related, but they are not the same. Stress often triggers emotional reactions—particularly negative ones—but it has a number of other effects as well. We examine stress in the remainder of this chapter. Let's start with a discussion of what stress is and what brings it on.

You probably use the word *stress* all the time, but have you thought about what it actually means? The term has been defined in various ways, so we will begin our examination of stress with a definition. We will then discuss the ways in which people experience stress and the kinds of situations that cause stress.

stress state brought on by any situation that threatens or appears to threaten a person's sense of well-being, thus challenging the individual's ability to cope.

stressor a situation or circumstance that triggers the stress response.

acute stressor a stressful situation or circumstance that happens in the short term and has a definite endpoint.

chronic stressor a stressful situation or circumstance that is more long term and often lacks a definite endpoint.

Stress and Stressors

Stress is a state brought on by any situation that threatens or appears to threaten a person's sense of well-being, thus challenging the person's ability to cope. A situation or circumstance that triggers the stress response is called a **stressor**. Stressors can be *acute* or *chronic*. An **acute stressor** is short term and has a definite endpoint—for example, a near miss in heavy traffic. A **chronic stressor** is long term and often lacks a definite endpoint—for example, dealing over time with a high-pressure job.

Obviously, our definition of stress is rather broad—literally anything can cause stress. The breadth of the definition takes into account the wide range of situations that people experience as stressful, from daily pressures at work and school to more catastrophic events, such as health crises, natural disasters, and terrorist attacks. At the same time, the definition calls attention to the emotional experience of stress and how individualized stress is.

A number of psychological factors help to determine the degree to which something will cause us to experience stress. In fact, stress is actually derived more from how we *appraise* the situation than it is derived from the situation itself (Lazarus & Folkman, 1984). That is, our appraisal of our ability (or inability) to cope with a situation is an important factor in how much stress we experience. Two people attending a party of mostly strangers may approach the party with differing levels of stress. One person may view the situation as challenging, enjoying the idea of meeting a lot of new people. Another person might instead view the same situation as highly stressful, feeling very threatened by the idea of meeting a large number of people they do not already know. In each instance, each person appraises the situation based on their perceived ability to cope. It is therefore our *perception* of threat that triggers the emotional state we connect to stress. If we do not perceive a situation as threatening, we will not feel particularly stressed. We will look soon at more psychological factors in stress, but before that, let's examine the different ways that people experience stress.

Anxious moments. A trader on the floor of the Toronto Stock Exchange watches the numbers on the board anxiously, waiting desperately for a favourable moment to make his move.

Ways of Experiencing Stress

By definition, people who experience stress feel threatened and challenged. But these threats and challenges come in different forms. Certainly, soldiers in combat, students whose grades are falling, and children whose parents are unhappy with them face different kinds of stress. Psychologists have in fact distinguished between four kinds of stress experience: *frustration*, *pressure*, *conflict*, and *danger*. These kinds of stress are not mutually exclusive.

Feeling Frustrated You finally find a parking spot, and someone pulls into it just ahead of you. You try to register for a course, and it is full. You work hard, but you get a C on the test. Whenever we find ourselves thwarted in the pursuit of a goal, we experience frustration. Life is full of frustration; it is one of our most familiar kinds of stress. Frustration can be caused by acute stressors, such as those in the situations just described, and by chronic stressors. Persons who have chronic illnesses or disabilities, for example, are likely to feel frustrated that they cannot do more. All of these experiences are bound up with the notion of trying to achieve something and having a barrier to our progress. Barriers to progress generate stress.

frustration an emotion people experience when thwarted in pursuit of a goal.

Feeling Pressured We all encounter a certain amount of pressure—the expectation that we should act in a certain way. The pride felt by Ashley's parents over their daughter's admission to college is a source of pressure, and her boss's expectation that she should arrive at work on time is another.

pressure an expectation or demand that someone act in a certain way.

Pressure often comes from within. Some individuals have such high expectations of themselves that they are constantly under self-imposed stress. Think of the sources of pressure in your own life. What standards do you set for yourself academically and socially? Are you driven to achieve in athletics? How much pressure do you experience as a result of such expectations? For some, stress that comes from within is often more difficult to cope with than stress imposed by others. It may not be easy to meet the deadline for turning in a term paper, but at least when you do so, the pressure will be off. By contrast, if you set yourself a rigid standard of perfection, you may never find release from this internal pressure.

Pressure also varies along with the task and situation. One set of studies, for example, demonstrated that participants experienced greater stress when performing complex tasks in front of an audience, but that they performed significantly better without the pressure of an audience (Wan & Huon, 2005; Butler & Baumeister, 1998; Baumeister, 1984).

FIGURE 15-1 Three basic types of conflict that can lead to stress.

Still other research has found a strong correlation between feelings of pressure and symptoms of distress, indicating that perceived discrimination is associated with increased levels of depression and an increased number of medical diagnoses (Todorova et al., 2010).

Feeling Conflicted The stress Ashley feels is not simply the result of pressure from her parents. It also results in part from her desire to do two things at the same time: (1) study to earn good grades and (2) have time to go out with her friends. In situations such as this, we experience conflict—discomfort brought about by two or more goals or impulses that we perceive to be incompatible. There are three basic types of conflict: *approach–approach, avoidance–avoidance*, and *approach–avoidance* (see **Figure 15-1**) (Miller, 1959; Lewin, 1935).

conflict discomfort brought about by two or more goals or impulses perceived to be incompatible.

approach–approach conflict conflict that occurs when a person must choose between two equally desirable options.

avoidance–avoidance conflict conflict that occurs when a person must choose between two equally undesirable options.

approach–avoidance conflict conflict that occurs when any available choice has both desirable and undesirable qualities.

- As its name implies, approach–approach conflict occurs when we must choose between two equally desirable options. Should we have the chocolate cake or the blueberry pie? Should we buy the red backpack or the black one? In many cases, approach–approach conflicts are easy to resolve (you can't really lose with either choice), and so they are not especially stressful.
- Avoidance–avoidance conflicts are somewhat more stressful because here the choice is between two equally undesirable outcomes. Should you clean the garage or do the laundry? You may be tempted to do neither. If you deal with this kind of conflict by deciding to procrastinate, postpone, or avoid the choice, however, you are particularly likely to experience stress (Shafir & Tversky, 2002).
- In an approach–avoidance conflict, any available choice has both desirable and undesirable qualities, rendering us ambivalent and indecisive. In some situations, this sort of conflict may involve only one choice with both positive and negative features. For example, if Ashley were to go out with her friends, she would enjoy herself, but she wouldn't be able to work on her paper. In other situations, more than one option may be involved. Should you buy a car that is expensive but fuel-efficient, for example, or a less expensive gas guzzler? Approach–avoidance conflicts are on display in many of our most agonizing decisions. Often people worry for some time about how to resolve them, and experience considerable stress along the way.

Sports and Pressure

A costly error. A dejected Steve Smith immediately after scoring on his own goal, an error which led to the Edmonton Oilers losing the Stanley Cup Western Conference semi-final game back in 1986.

In the 1986 Western conference semi-finals between the Edmonton Oilers and the Calgary Flames, Oiler Steve Smith made a heartbreaking mistake. The game was tied 2–2 in the third period of the seventh and deciding game, and Smith was carrying the puck out from behind his own net with no-one checking him. He attempted a cross-ice clearing pass that somehow bounced off the back of his own goaltender (Grant Fuhr) and ended up in his own team's net. Calgary knocked the two-time Stanley Cup-winning Oilers out of the playoffs. Smith was devastated. It also happened to be his birthday, and he has since said that now he thinks of the goal every time he blows out his birthday candles.

What happened to Smith and to other athletes who have made mental errors in other high-pressure situations? When does pressure aid athletic performance and when does it impair it? These questions have been the subject of much study. A number of explanations have been offered, but a clear understanding of the effects of pressure on athletes remains elusive (Weinberg & Gould, 2003).

We do know that performance pressure results when athletes feel strongly about the outcome of an event and believe that their own performance will have an impact on that outcome (Wallace, Baumeister, & Vohs, 2005). We also know that this pressure can result in increased physiological and psychological arousal. But researchers cannot predict the precise relationship between such arousal and performance.

For years, psychologists believed that the relationship probably follows the principle of the *Yerkes-Dodson law*. As we observed in Chapter 11, this psychological "law," developed in 1908 by psychologists Robert Yerkes and John Dodson, holds that performances on tasks of any kind increase along with physical or mental arousal—up to a point—but, once an optimal, moderate level of arousal is passed, performances begin to decrease. Applying this law to athletic performances, it is generally believed that if an athlete is not aroused, his or her performance will suffer, and that if he or she is too aroused, performance will also suffer. Optimal performance is thought to occur only in the presence of a moderate level of arousal (Yerkes & Dodson, 1908).

Over the years, research has better supported an alternative version of the Yerkes-Dodson law, particularly in the realm of athletic performance. Recall from Chapter 13 that this alternative model holds that the level of arousal at which optimal performance occurs is a *zone* (not a single point) and varies from athlete to athlete. Some cross-country runners, for example, will perform best if they take naps right before a race, while their teammates will do best if they listen to inspiring music, visualize their opponents, and engage in intense stretching exercises before the race (Hanin, 1997).

A different line of research has suggested that coaches can play a large role in helping athletes cope with performance pressure. Since anxiety tends to be lowest in athletes who believe in their performance abilities and are self-assured, research suggests that coaches can help by facilitating feelings of confidence—by, for example, providing frequent, genuine encouragement and by fostering a positive environment, regardless of whether things have gone well or mistakes have occurred (Weinberg & Gould, 2003). Here again, however, effective methods vary from athlete to athlete.

Feeling Endangered Life-threatening situations understandably produce stress, making us feel endangered. The adrenaline rush we experience when a car in front of us suddenly stops, forcing us to swerve and slam on the brakes, is characteristic of this kind of stress. Similarly, such stress is experienced by people who face combat or are trapped in a fire.

Stress and terror. The aftermath of life-threatening events, like the terrorist attacks of 9/11, might lead some New Yorkers to experience a sense of intense fear at the sight of a plane in the sky, or to cringe at the sound of a bus backfiring.

Natural disasters may also be life threatening and, in turn, stressful. Life-threatening situations created by people may also produce stress. Terrorism leaves individuals with feelings of uncertainty, sadness, and fear, making them vulnerable to the onset of stress disorders (Delahanty, 2007; Bleich et al., 2003; Ursano et al., 2003). Indeed, terrorism may have long-term psychological effects.

Kinds of Stressors

Just as there are different ways of experiencing stress, there are different types of stressors. Indeed, stressors vary widely—from discrete life events to chronic stressors. Moreover, they can be mild, extreme, or anywhere in between. As you will see later in this chapter, what is stressful for one person may not be stressful for another. Still, there are several kinds of events that are likely to produce feelings of stress whenever they are experienced: daily hassles, such as traffic jams; life changes, such as the loss of a job; traumatic events, such as natural disasters; chronic negative situations, such as an enduring illness; and special socio-cultural conditions, such as racism. We will discuss each of these categories in turn, but as you know all too well, they may overlap or intersect.

daily hassles everyday annoyances that contribute to higher stress levels; also known as *micro-stressors*.

Daily Hassles Probably the most familiar sources of stress are **daily hassles** (also called micro-stressors)—the everyday annoyances that leave us feeling upset and at the end of our rope. These stressors can range from minor irritations, such as lost keys or a talkative co-worker, to major problems, such as intense work pressure or conflict with a romantic partner. Some daily hassles seem to be universally upsetting, including time pressures, cash-flow problems, feelings of being cheated after making a purchase, conflicts with romantic partners, mistreatment by friends, and poor evaluations at work.

Over time, daily hassles can add up. They may become particularly stressful when they occur in combination with other stressors, leaving individuals overwhelmed (Boutreyre, Maurel, & Bernaud, 2007; De Longis et al., 1982). A hot day may not be particularly stressful by itself, but combine it with waiting in a long line to renew a driver's licence, a crying child, and a blister on your heel, and you may wind up feeling exasperated and depleted. In fact, data suggest that the accumulation of daily stressors often leads to increased health risks (Seta, Seta, & McElroy, 2002).

It turns out that the impact of daily hassles on health is often greater than that of a major life event (Stuart & Garrison, 2002). This is because ongoing stress may impair our immune system responses, as we shall see later. Indeed, one study found that people who face daily commutes in heavy traffic are particularly likely to miss work because of colds and flu (Novaco, Stokols, & Milanesi, 1990)—illnesses that can result from stress-induced changes in the immune system.

"Get out of my way!" A recently released national poll indicates that Canadians believe that people are worse drivers than they were five years ago (Canadian Automobile Association, 2011).

Researchers have developed several measures of daily hassles. Psychologist Richard Lazarus and his colleagues developed one of the first, the *Daily Hassles Scale*, in which subjects are asked to consider a list of hassles, indicate which ones they had experienced over the past month, and report how stressful each event felt (Kanner et al., 1981). Measuring the impact of daily hassles is difficult, because people vary widely in how they experience and weigh such stressors (Kohn, 1996).

Some daily hassle scales have targeted the experiences of college students (Cardilla, 2008; D'Angelo & Wierzbicki, 2003; Kohn et al., 1990). Such scales have paid special attention to the impact of exams (Edwards & Trimble, 1992; Abella & Heslin, 1989; Folkman & Lazarus, 1985). Feelings of stress tend to be strongest just before an exam and continue (though to a lesser extent) as students wait to receive their grades and as they later try to cope with the results. See **Table 15-1** to review items on the Undergraduate Stress Questionnaire (Crandall, Preisler, & Aussprung, 1992).

TABLE 15-1 Undergraduate Stress Questionnaire

Has this stressful event happened to you at any time during the last two weeks? If it has, please check the space next to it. If it has not, please leave the space blank.	
Lack of money	
Someone broke a promise	
Death (family member or friend)	
Dealt with incompetence at the registrar's office	
Can't concentrate	
Had a lot of tests	
Thought about unfinished work	
Someone did a "pet peeve" of yours	
It's finals week	
Lived with boyfriend/girlfriend	
No sleep	
Applied to graduate school	
Felt need for transportation	
Sick, injury	
Bad haircut	
Victim of a crime	
Had a class presentation	
Job requirements changed	
Applied for a job	
Assignments in all classes due the same day	
Fought with boyfriend/girlfriend	
No time to eat	
Have a hard upcoming week	
Felt some peer pressure	
Lots of deadlines to meet	
Went into test unprepared	
Worked while in school	
Arguments, conflict of values with friends	
Had a hangover	
Problems with computer	
Lost something (especially wallet)	
Death of a pet	
Bothered by having no social support from family	
Performed poorly at a task	
Did worse than expected on a test	
Problem getting home from bar when drunk	
Used a fake ID	
Had an interview	
Had projects, research papers due	
Did badly on a test	
Can't finish everything you need to do	
Heard bad news	
No sex for a while	
Someone cut ahead of you in line	
Had confrontation with an authority figure	
Maintained a long-distance relationship with boyfriend/girlfriend	
Crammed for a test	

(continued)

TABLE 15-1 Undergraduate Stress Questionnaire (Continued)

Parents getting divorced	
Dependent on other people	
Feel unorganized	
Broke up with boyfriend/girlfriend	
Tried to decide on major	
Feeling isolated	
Had roommate conflicts	
Chequebook didn't balance	
Visit from a relative and entertaining them	
Decision to have sex is on your mind	
Car/bike broke down, flat tire, etc.	
Parents controlling with money	
Couldn't find a parking space	
Noise disturbed you while trying to study	
Someone borrowed something without permission	
Had to ask for money	
Got a traffic ticket	
Talked with a professor	
Change of environment (new doctor, dentist, etc.)	
Exposed to upsetting TV show, book, or movie	
Got to class late	
Erratic schedule	
Found out boyfriend/girlfriend cheated on you	
Can't understand your professor	
Tried to get into your major or university/college	
Missed your period and waiting	
Coping with addictions	
Registration for classes	
Stayed up late writing a paper	
Property stolen	
Someone you expected to call did not	
Holiday	
Sat through a boring class	
Favourite sporting team lost	
Thought about the future	

Count the number of check marks. Students with higher scores are more likely to need health care (as measured by going to the student health centre or infirmary) than students with lower scores.

(Crandall, Preisler, & Aussprung, 1992)

Change Another common source of stress is change. Those early weeks in a new school, for example, are usually quite stressful, even if they are also exciting. In the first weeks of college, students need to figure out what classes to take, where classrooms are located, what is expected of them, and where to buy books (as well as how to pay for them). At the same time, they are meeting many new people. Trying to find our way in new relationships can be even more complicated and challenging than finding our way to class.

life changes shifts in life circumstances that require adjustment of some kind.

Life changes—shifts in life circumstances that require adjustment of some kind—were among the first sources of stress ever studied. In 1967, investigators Thomas Holmes and Richard Rahe set out to develop a way to systematically measure how much stress people experience. They compiled a list of 43 events that were likely to change a person's life and therefore cause stress. These events ranged from the death of a spouse, to minor violations of the law, to taking a vacation. Based on ratings by participants, the researchers assigned a point value to each event, ranging from 1 to 100 points, or *life-change units (LCUs)*. The point value for each event corresponded to the amount of upset and adjustment the event typically produced. The death of a spouse received a score of 100 LCUs on the scale, for example, whereas a change in responsibilities at work was 29 LCUs, and taking a vacation came in at 13 LCUs.

Feeling stressed. The first set of midterm exams for first-year post-secondary students are often quite stressful.

With this 43-item list, called the *Social Readjustment Rating Scale (SRRS)*, Holmes and Rahe set about conducting studies on the impact of stress on people's lives. First they had individuals complete the scale to determine how much stress they were under. Participants were asked to check off all those events that had occurred in their lives over a certain time period, usually the past year. Then they added up the total number of life-change units, with the sum indicating the amount of stress the person had been under. A total score of 150 LCUs or less indicated relatively little stress; 150 to 199 indicated mild stress; 200 to 299 suggested moderate stress; and over 300 LCUs pointed to major life stress. Holmes and Rahe claim that those individuals who score over 300 are more likely to experience physical illness than those who score below 150 points. The life events from the SRRS and their ratings are listed in **Table 15-2** on the next page. Notice that a life-changing event need not be an undesirable one. A number of the events on the SRRS are positive, and some can be either positive or negative. A change in living conditions, for example, may reflect a move upward or downward in life.

Think back to our chapter opener. There, we learned that Ashley recently broke up with her boyfriend, an event that would receive a score of 65 LCUs on Holmes and Rahe's scale. In addition, she has been experiencing troubles with her boss (23 LCUs), school pressures (39 LCUs), and new social activities (18 LCUs). Since she is a relatively new student, we can assume that she changed schools (20 LCUs) and residences (19 LCUs) fairly recently. Add in her outstanding personal achievement of being the first in her family to go to college (28 LCUs), and her LCU score totals 212—a moderate level of stress over a short period of time.

We pointed out that the Social Readjustment Rating Scale includes positive as well as negative life events. Nevertheless, the scale has been criticized for looking at many more negative events than positive ones (McLean & Link, 1994). Because of this, the scale may not give a complete picture of the effects of life change on stress levels.

Another shortcoming of the SRRS is that it does not apply equally to all populations. In developing the scale, Holmes and Rahe sampled mostly Caucasian Americans. Fewer than 5 percent of their participants were African Americans, and none were Native Americans. Subsequent research has shown this bias to be particularly problematic because Caucasian Americans and African Americans often rank life events differently. For example, although both groups rank the death of a spouse as the most stressful life event, African Americans rank personal injury or illness and major changes in work responsibilities or living conditions much higher than do Caucasian Americans (Komaroff, Masuda, & Holmes, 1989, 1986). Similarly, certain types of events, such as the death of a family member, loss of a job, credit problems, and change in residence, are generally more stressful for women than for men (Miller & Rahe, 1997).

Even positive changes can be stressful. Even though they are happy events, marriages produce a high degree of stress according to research using the Social Readjustment Rating Scale.

As described by Lawrence Kirmayer of McGill University, over the past decades Canada's Aboriginal population has experienced a broad and unique array of additional stressors. These include residential schools and "60s scoop," in which a great many Aboriginal children were removed from their communities and placed in non-Aboriginal foster

TABLE 15-2 The Social Readjustment Rating Scale

To score your susceptibility to stress on this scale, add up the life change units for the events you experienced in the last year. Scores of 150 or less indicate little stress; 150–199 mild stress; 200–299 moderate stress; and over 300 major life stress.

Life Events	Life Change Units
Death of spouse	100
Divorce	73
Marital separation	65
Jail term	63
Death of a close family member	63
Personal injury or illness	53
Marriage	50
Fired at work	47
Marital reconciliation	45
Retirement	45
Change in health of family member	44
Pregnancy	40
Sex difficulties	39
Gain of a new family member	39
Business readjustment	39
Change in financial state	38
Death of a close friend	37
Change to different line of work	36
Change in number of arguments with spouse	35
Mortgage or loan for major purchase	31
Foreclosure on mortgage or loan	30
Change in responsibilities at work	29
Son or daughter leaving home	29
Trouble with in-laws	29
Outstanding personal achievement	28
Spouse begins or stops work	26
Begin or end school	26
Change in living conditions	25
Revision of personal habits	24
Trouble with boss	23
Change in work hours or condition	20
Change in residence	20
Change in schools	20
Change in recreation	19
Change in church activities	19
Change in social activities	18
Mortgage or loan for lesser purchase (car, major appliance)	17
Change in sleeping habits	16
Change in number of family get-togethers	15
Change in eating habits	15
Vacation	13
Christmas	12
Minor violations of the law	11

Source: Reprinted from Holmes & Rahe (1967). The Social Readjustment Rating Scale. *Journal of Psychosomatic Research*, Vol. III, 213–218. With permission from Elsevier.

homes away from family and Aboriginal culture and community. This has led to a broad range of additional stresses and challenges that are all parts of their social adjustment stress profiles. As a result, the Aboriginal population experiences increased interpersonal problems such as substance abuse, depression, and suicide, as well as increased social problems including high rates of sexual abuse, family violence, and incarceration (Kirmayer, Simpson, & Cargo, 2003).

Life Change and Illness Holmes and Rahe found that the LCU scores of sick people during the year before they became ill were considerably higher than those of healthy people (Holmes & Rahe, 1989, 1967). In fact, as stated above, if a person's life changes totalled more than 300 LCUs over the course of a year, that person was likely to develop a serious health problem.

The SRRS has been revised by researchers over the years (Hobson & Delunas, 2001; Hobson et al., 1998; Miller & Rabe, 1997). Using various scales, studies have tied a variety of life stressors to a wide range of physical problems, from upper respiratory infection to cancer (Baum, Trevino, & Dougall, 2011; Cohen, 2005; Rook, August, & Sorkin, 2011; Taylor, 2004). Generally, the greater the amount of life stress, the higher the likelihood of medical illness. Some researchers have even found a relationship between stress and death. Widows and widowers, for example, have an elevated risk of death during their period of bereavement (Möller et al., 2011).

Life Changes HOW WE DEVELOP

Although feelings of stress may be similar for both young and old people, the life changes that evoke these feelings apparently differ widely from age group to age group. As you have just seen, the most powerful stressors (in decreasing order) on the SRRS, a largely adult scale, are death of a spouse, divorce, marital separation, jail term, death of a close family member, and personal injury or illness. But how does stress affect younger age groups?

Researchers have developed special scales to measure life events and stress among traditional college students (Renner & Mackin, 2002; Crandall et al., 1992). They have found that the most stressful life event for this population is the death of a family member or friend, much like the top life stressor for adults. Beyond this event, however, the leading life stressors for college students are ones that are tied to college life. They are (again in decreasing order) having to take multiple tests, enduring final exam week, applying to graduate school, being a victim of crime, having assignments in a number of different classes due on the same day, and breaking up with a romantic partner.

Moving to still younger individuals, researchers have found that the leading life stressors for children overlap to some degree with those of adults and college students, but, here again, they largely reflect issues unique to childhood (Ryan-Wenger, Sharrer, & Campbell, 2005; Neff & Dale, 1996; Coddington, 1984, 1972; Yamamoto, 1979). Across various scales, the leading stressors for school-aged children are taking tests, having excessive homework, being made fun of or bullied, feeling left out, getting bad grades, getting in trouble, fighting with family members or friends, experiencing the death or illness of someone close, and doing something embarrassing.

It is worth noting that the kinds of life events that produce stress tend to shift as children develop (Vasey et al., 1994). As children move from 5 years old to 12 years old, physical-type events (for example, getting sick) become less stressful, behavioural events (getting into trouble) become more stressful, and psychosocial events (fighting with friends) also become more stressful.

Early separation. This soldier consoles his young daughter prior to his departure for Afghanistan. Research suggests that family military separations of this kind often take an enormous emotional toll on the children who are left behind.

Traumatic events. Major disasters, like the tsunami that hit Japan in March 2011, can traumatize a large proportion of the population.

Finally, focus on particular life stressors seems to change from generation to generation (Ryan-Wenger et al., 2005). For example, in the 1990s, awareness about a number of different childhood events, such as experiences about being bullied and experiencing violence in school, became more recognized as stressors of childhood and therefore became prevalent items on children's life stress scales. Similarly, during the 2000s, several other powerful childhood stressors have emerged, such as cyber bullying, terrorism, and concerns over post-earthquake nuclear meltdowns.

traumatic events unexpected events severe enough to create extreme disruptions.

posttraumatic stress disorder (PTSD) an anxiety disorder experienced in response to a major traumatic event, characterized by lingering, persistent, frightening thoughts or memories of the traumatic events, along with anxiety, depression, and other symptoms.

Traumatic Events Life changes are stressful because they disrupt the routines of our lives. **Traumatic events** are more extreme disruptions—unexpected events that have the power to change the way we view the world. The earthquakes and related tsunamis in Japan in March 2011 are an example of the stress-inducing power of a single, cataclysmic event, as is the wild fire that burned one-third of the community of Slave Lake in Northern Alberta in May 2011. Rape or violent assault can also be traumatizing. Such events can have profound and long-lasting effects. Victims may experience a sense of helplessness, depression, anxiety, numbness, and disorientation (Overmier & Murison, 2005; Carr, 2000). The effects can last for years in some cases.

Some victims of extraordinarily traumatic events develop **posttraumatic stress disorder (PTSD)**, a condition characterized by persistent, frightening thoughts or memories of the traumatic events, along with anxiety, depression, and other symptoms. We will discuss this disorder in more detail later in this chapter.

Although traumatic events are usually of short duration, some can be ongoing. Suffering ongoing physical or sexual abuse or living with an alcoholic partner or parent are examples of long-lasting traumatic events. These, too, can leave victims withdrawn and experiencing recurring mental images, anxiety, and depression (Overmier & Murison, 2005; Carr, 2000).

Chronic Negative Situations A negative situation may become particularly stressful if it continues over a long, perhaps indefinite, period of time (Schmidt et al., 2009). People living in a war zone, for example, confront the fearful possibility of an attack as they go about their daily lives, attending school, shopping, or taking the bus to work. Similarly, people who live in poverty face constant concerns about meeting their basic needs and paying their debts (Freeman, 1984). An ongoing negative home environment—marked by endless arguments with a spouse or child, for example—may produce considerable stress, and so may enduring workplace problems, such as continually feeling underpaid, unappreciated, bored, or in danger of being fired (Rossi et al., 2009; Krantz, Berntsson, & Lundberg, 2005; Lundberg, 2000).

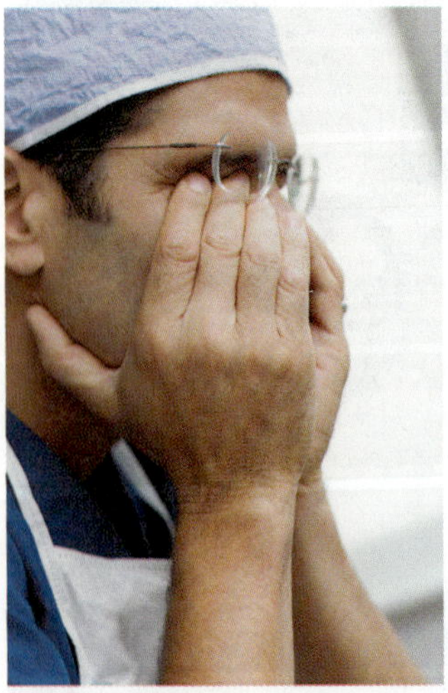

Chronic job stress. Certain jobs produce chronic stress. Research reveals, for example, that physicians, particularly those whose specialties deal largely with life-threatening medical problems, often experience enormous work pressure and strain.

Chronic illnesses can also produce much stress over time. Such illnesses may not only cause pain, but also impose limitations and produce feelings of mortality and uncertainty in people's lives. The patients themselves are not the only ones affected by chronic illnesses; their caregivers also experience stress. Thus, parents of children with special needs—whether enduring illnesses, physical handicaps, intellectual disability, or other conditions—often experience stress. So do the growing numbers of adults who must take care of aging parents or spouses. In fact, research indicates that such caregivers often suffer from depression, drink excessively, are sleep deprived, and engage in fewer healthful behaviours, such as exercise (O'Rourke et al., 2003; Yoon, 2003; Zarit & Gaugler, 2000).

The physical environment may also provide chronic stressors. Chronic noise, for example, often leads to tension and upset (Evans, 2001). Similarly, chronic overcrowding leads to higher bodily arousal and makes it difficult for people to relax (Fleming et al., 1987). Chronic environmental stressors may interact with each other. A noisy roommate, for example, may be both a physical and a social stressor. The roommate's loud music may bombard you and leave you with frequent headaches; at the same time, the tense relationship that develops between the two of you may produce further stress.

Socio-cultural Conditions Socio-cultural conditions, such as those faced by members of ethnic minority groups who confront prejudice regularly, can be sources of stress (Liang et al., 2009). Minority-group members, particularly those in Canada's First Nations and Métis populations, face special challenges and stressors as they try to navigate through the dominant culture. Foreign workers participating in Canada's temporary foreign worker program, for example, have to adjust to new ways of doing things, learn a new language, and often contend with poverty and the stress of a crowded living situation. In addition, members of minority groups often have to try to balance the demands of two cultures—their own culture and that of the dominant culture in which they live. If they are not proficient in the language or nuances of the dominant culture, they may also experience the stress of isolation and of having limited access to the main channels of communication within the dominant culture (Mino, Profit, & Pierce, 2000).

And even when minority group members achieve success in the dominant culture, another source of stress can emerge as individuals find themselves having to assess the role that prejudice and discrimination may have played in their interactions with the dominant culture. For example, consider Jonathan, an Aboriginal Canadian man working in advertising at a large department store. Jonathan's job is to produce advertisements for special sales of fall clothing. His boss, who is Caucasian, doesn't think much of the two ideas Jonathan has proposed and tells him so. In addition to feeling disappointed and perhaps angry about the rejection of his ideas, Jonathan may experience the further stress of wondering whether his boss was reacting to his Aboriginal status or to his ideas. The suspicions, confusion, and resulting vigilance experienced by minority group members as they interact with majority group members, often referred to as *stereotype threat*, is a very real stressor for minority group members, but is often invisible to those in the majority group (Nail, Harton, & Decker, 2003; Profit, Mino, & Pierce, 2000).

Before You Go On

www.wiley.com/go/comer

What Do You Know?

1. What is the difference between an acute stressor and a chronic stressor?
2. What are the four types of stress experiences?
3. Define the three basic types of conflict.
4. What are daily hassles and what is their impact on health?
5. What is the Social Readjustment Rating Scale?

SCAN TO GET THE ANSWERS

What Do You Think?

What kinds of situations do you find especially stressful? How do they compare with what your friends find stressful? What do variations in the experience of stress tell us about stress and stressors?

Responding to Stress

LEARNING OBJECTIVE 2

Describe the physiological, emotional, and cognitive responses to stress, and explain how individual responses to stress differ.

We have looked at the kinds of experiences that cause stress. Let's turn next to what happens to people when they experience stress. Responses to stress fall into three general types: physiological, emotional, and cognitive. As you might expect, people vary greatly in their responses.

Physiological Responses to Stress

WHAT HAPPENS IN THE BRAIN?

Although what happens in the brain is critical to the stress response, responses to stress affect both the brain and the body. Think about how you come to know that you are under stress. Typically, your breathing and heart rate quicken, you begin to sweat, your mouth gets dry, and your stomach tightens. What's happening is that your brain has perceived a challenge and is sending signals to your body to prepare to meet it. This response to stress involves a brain–body reaction. Sweating, dry mouth, and stomach tightness are some of the immediate physical effects of stress, but these effects are actually indicators of more basic physiological responses. We examine these responses next and illustrate them in **Figure 15-2.**

The Fight-or-Flight Response You may remember the discussion of physiologist Walter Cannon's theory of emotion in Chapter 12. Cannon was the first theorist to connect the bodily arousal associated with emotional responses to the need to fight or flee. According to Cannon (1932), the fight-or-flight response is a series of physiological reactions throughout the sympathetic nervous system and the endocrine system that mobilize an organism to either fight or flee an enemy. The process begins in the brain.

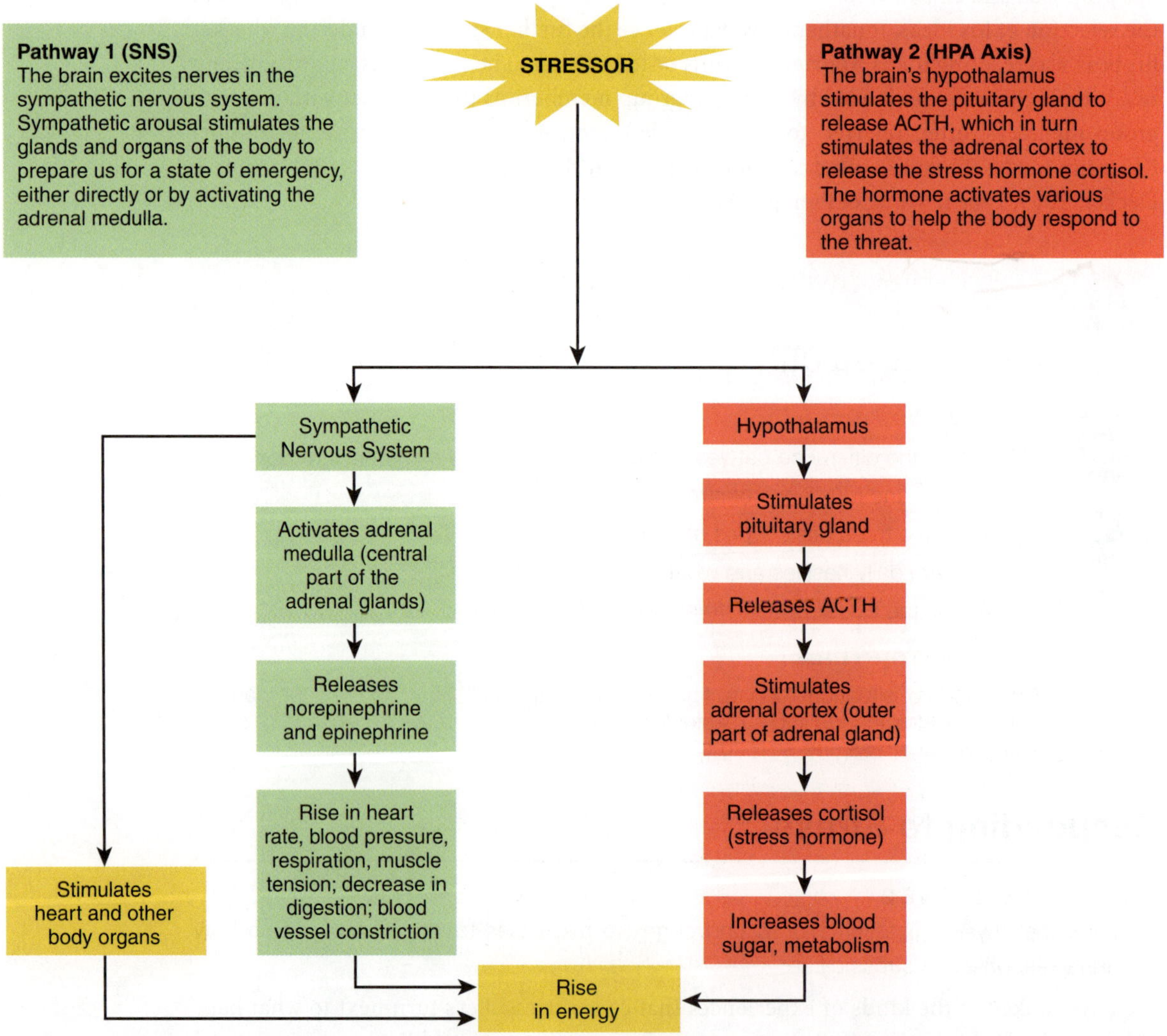

FIGURE 15-2 The physiological response to stress. As shown in this flow chart, the brain sends messages to the endocrine glands and bodily organs through the sympathetic nervous system (SNS) pathway and the hypothalamic-pituitary-adrenal (HPA) axis.

The brain sends messages to the endocrine glands and bodily organs along two different routes. One is through the sympathetic nervous system, which as you recall is a division of the autonomic nervous system (ANS). The other is through the hypothalamic-pituitary-adrenal (HPA) axis (Friedman & Silver, 2007).

Under fire. Riot police were in extreme danger during the riot following the Vancouver Canuck loss during the 2011 NHL playoffs.

When we confront a dangerous situation, within seconds the brain sends messages to the sympathetic nervous system, and these nerves directly stimulate organs of the body (the heart, for example). The nerves also influence organs indirectly by stimulating the adrenal glands (located at the tops of the kidneys), particularly the inner layer of those glands, an area called the *adrenal medulla.* The adrenal medulla, in turn, releases the chemicals epinephrine and norepinephrine (otherwise known as adrenaline and noradrenaline) into the bloodstream, where they are carried to various organs and muscles, further arousing the organism and enabling it to fight or flee. Normally, the biological changes associated with the fight-or-flight response subside around 15 minutes after the threatening situation eases (Friedman & Silver, 2007).

The brain also sends messages through the HPA axis (Jankord & Herman, 2009). When we are confronted by stressors, various brain regions communicate with the hypothalamus, which in turn stimulates the pituitary gland, prompting the gland to release the *adrenocorticotropic hormone (ACTH)* into the bloodstream. ACTH travels to the adrenal glands and interacts with their outer covering, an area called the *adrenal cortex*, causing the release of stress hormones called *cortisol.*

Fight-or-flight, or tend-and-befriend? Females are more likely than males to rely on and take support from social connections and friendships when coping with stressful events.

Cortisol travels to a range of body organs, where, among other activities, it helps elevate blood sugar, supply energy to the organism under stress, and protect the body from inflammation. In this way, cortisol helps prepare individuals who are under stress for their fight-or-flight response (Lupien et al., 2006).

The HPA axis is a slower system than the sympathetic nervous system, taking minutes as opposed to seconds to have a big influence on the body. These two systems (the sympathetic nervous system and the HPA axis), activated in tandem, ensure that the organism is able to mobilize its energy to deal with a crisis, even if it takes a while. As you will see later in the chapter, however, problems can arise if cortisol activity remains high for too long. It can then become harmful, contributing in some cases to high blood pressure, inflammation, anxiety, and depression, among other problems (Kendall-Tackett, 2010; Sher, 2003; Nemeroff, 1998).

> *Some theorists argue that the fight-or-flight response may be a largely male response, and suggest that evolution may have selected a "tend-and-befriend" response to cope with stress in females. Regardless of the mechanism, in general females are more likely to have extensive and well-maintained social networks than are males* (Taylor et al., 2000).

The fight-or-flight response is an early evolutionary adaptation. You can imagine how this kind of reaction might have helped early humans survive. If they suddenly came upon a grizzly bear, they were better able to either overwhelm it or escape in a hurry. But many of the stressors we face today are more subtle and more chronic—homework stress, employment pressures, relationship difficulties, and any number of other conditions. What happens when a stressor is chronic? Hans Selye considered that question in forming his theory of the general adaptation syndrome.

The General Adaptation Syndrome Hans Selye was an Austrian-born endocrinologist who emigrated to Canada in 1939. He is credited with first talking about stress in living creatures (Selye, 1993, 1956, 1936). In his laboratory, Selye exposed animals to a

A Laugh a Day Keeps the Doctor Away?

A different approach. The real Patch Adams, physician and clown, talks here to the sister of a hospitalized child.

In a 1998 film, Robin Williams donned a white coat and a red clown nose and took a new brand of medicine to movie theatres around the world. He was playing real-life physician Patch Adams, who believes that the medical community has failed to embrace the use of laughter and humour to aid in health and healing (Marsh, 2008). While this may be a feel-good sentiment, is there actual support for the notion that laughter is the best medicine?

Research results from medicine and psychology are mixed in their support of a laughter–health link. One study found, for example, that after watching a humorous film, participants who had laughed at and enjoyed the film showed decreases in stress and improvements in their immune system activity (Bennett, 1998). On the basis of such supportive findings, psychologists have offered various explanations for how laughter might improve health (McCreaddie & Wiggins, 2008; Godfrey, 2004). Some such explanations suggest that there is a direct link between laughter and health. One proposal, for example, holds that laughter may increase blood flow, thereby reducing blood pressure. Another proposal argues that 100 laughs can provide an aerobic workout equal to 15 minutes on an exercise bike (Brickey, 2005). Still other scientists suggest that the link between laughter and health is an indirect one. One popular proposal, for example, supported by research conducted by Elsa Marsalis at the University of Toronto, suggests that humour results in greater social support, thereby aiding health, and that humour may help heal by bringing down a person's stress level (Marsalis, McDonald, & Donahue, 2008).

Other research suggests that support for the humour–health link is less clear and perhaps more questionable than first thought. Some studies on this subject have failed to support the link (McCreaddie & Wiggins, 2008; Martin, 2001). Clearer verdicts on the strength of this relationship and on the theories that seek to explain it await the results of some current and future research undertakings.

In the meantime, there is nothing in the literature to suggest laughter is bad for one's health, and many health and humour experts have offered tips on how to increase one's daily quota of good humour. They suggest, for example, browsing through the humour section of a local bookstore; keeping a humour journal filled with funny newspaper headlines, bumper stickers, and notes about humorous events; and reading cartoons daily, making sure to save and post the ones that tickle your funny bone the most (Godfrey, 2004).

variety of stressors. No matter what the stressor—mild shock, pain, restraint, heat, cold—he found that the animals displayed the same pattern of response: a consistent pattern that he labelled *stress* (a term he borrowed from engineers, who use it when they discuss forces that affect the structural integrity of the things they build). Selye believed we respond in much the same ways to stress, whatever its source. This insight was particularly important, because it means that, although our responses to different stressors might vary in degree, we are responding in the same basic way to all of them.

Selye also noticed that if stressors continue, the organism's body progresses through three stages of response: alarm, resistance, and finally, exhaustion. He called this three-stage response to stress the **general adaptation syndrome (GAS)** (see **Figure 15-3**).

general adaptation syndrome (GAS) a three-stage response to stress identified by Hans Selye; the stages are alarm, resistance, and exhaustion.

Stage 1: When an organism is first exposed to a threat, it reacts with *alarm* and becomes aroused physically as it prepares to face the challenge by fighting or fleeing. In short, the first stage of the general adaptation syndrome corresponds to the fight-or-flight response.

Stage 2: If the threat continues, the organism's body undergoes further changes in an attempt to stabilize itself—a second wave of adaptation that Selye called *resistance*.

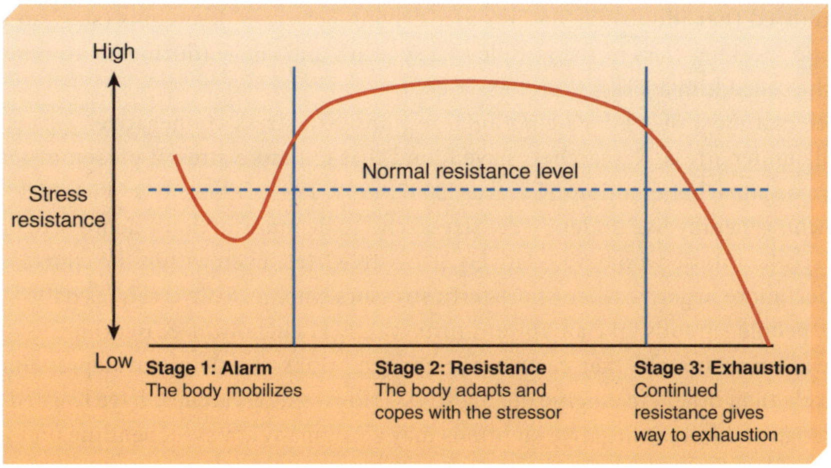

FIGURE 15-3 The general adaptation syndrome. Seyle proposed that the body's physiological response to prolonged stress has three stages.

The organism's level of arousal remains elevated, though slightly lower than during the initial alarm phase, as it adjusts to the stressor. If new stressors are introduced during this stage, the body is less able to marshal the energy needed to address them. According to Selye, this makes the body vulnerable to *diseases of adaptation*—health problems, such as high blood pressure, asthma, and illnesses associated with impaired immune function.

Stage 3: If the organism is exposed to the stressor for still longer periods of time, its resistance gradually gives way to the third stage, *exhaustion*. In this stage, the body is depleted of energy and has little ability to resist. If the threat continues, the organism can suffer organ damage or death.

Students who have gone through final exams often have firsthand experience with Selye's general adaptation syndrome. As the exams approach, most students experience alarm. When they gear up and begin patterns of late-night studying, the students are entering the resistance phase. By the end of the exam period, many students feel as if they are heading toward exhaustion, and, in fact, a number catch colds or develop other illnesses at the end of the school year. If you haven't gone through a final exam period yet, you will soon have a chance to gather your own data on this student experience.

Alarm can save lives. As a wildfire moved closer to Slave Lake, Alberta, in 2011, residents moved into an alarm mode, fleeing the fire as quickly as possible.

Although the principles of Selye's theory are widely accepted today, some theorists have questioned his claim that the stress response is the same no matter what the stressor (Lupien et al., 2007, 2006). They point out that although Selye used many kinds of stressors in his experiments with animals, all were physical—pain, heat, cold, and so forth. This has led some theorists to suggest that the precursors of stress are much more specific than Selye thought, and they vary depending on the type of stress, and in fact those differences are measurable and predictable. As we shall soon see, psychological factors also play an important part in our stress experience.

Emotional Responses to Stress

Bodily arousal is only one dimension of our reaction to stressors. When people feel threatened by an event or situation, they typically experience a change in mood or emotions as well. Let's briefly revisit Ashley, the stressed-out student from the chapter opener. As the stressors in her life mount, Ashley feels increasingly dejected (she wants to curl up in a ball), annoyed (her inquisitive parents are "driving her crazy"), anxious (she had to leave her public speaking class in the middle of a speech), and angry (during an argument with Jason, she called him a jerk).

Note that most of Ashley's emotional responses to stress are negative. This is typical of people under stress. Researchers have found that the more stress a person experiences, the more negative her emotions (Lazarus, 2007, 1999, 1993; D'Angelo & Wierzbicki, 2003). People who generally live under severe stress tend to be more anxious, depressed, or otherwise upset than those who have relatively stress-free lives. Even within the course of a day, people feel more negative when short-term stressors emerge. Conversely, as daily stressors subside, people's moods take an upward turn (van Eck, Nicholson, & Berkhof, 1998).

It was once thought that certain negative emotions—anxiety and depression—were more likely than others to emerge during stress. However, researchers have learned that, in fact, a range of different negative emotions may accompany stress, depending on individuals' personal styles and on the stress-inducing situations. The most common emotional reactions include anxiety, fear, and apprehension; dejection and grief; annoyance, anger, and rage; guilt; shame; disgust; and jealousy (Lazarus, 2007, 1993, 1991; Sher, 2003).

Cognitive Responses to Stress

As we noted at the beginning of the chapter, a key feature of stress is how we *appraise* both the challenging situation and our ability to handle that situation. If asked to speak publicly, for example, one person may be excited and pleased at the opportunity, while another may be fearful and anxious (see "Your Brain and Behaviour: Stressing Out when Speaking in Public" on the following pages). Sometimes, as in the fear of public speaking, this appraisal is stable—that is, people tend to react consistently to the prospect of speaking before a group. In other situations, however, the appraisal depends on the person's present psychological state. We may appraise a missing car key as much more stressful on the day of a final exam than on a less eventful day.

primary appraisal appraisal of a stressor to determine how severe it is; the first stage in Richard Lazarus's description of how people experience stress.

secondary appraisal appraisal of one's personal resources and ability to cope with a stressor; the second stage in Richard Lazarus's description of how people experience stress.

Remember Richard Lazarus and his cognitive-mediational theory of emotions, discussed in Chapter 12? Lazarus believed that emotion is aroused by a combination of two elements—an environmental event and personal factors such as a person's motives and beliefs. In fact, much of his early work was focused specifically on stress, and he identified two steps in how we experience stress (see **Figure 15-4**).

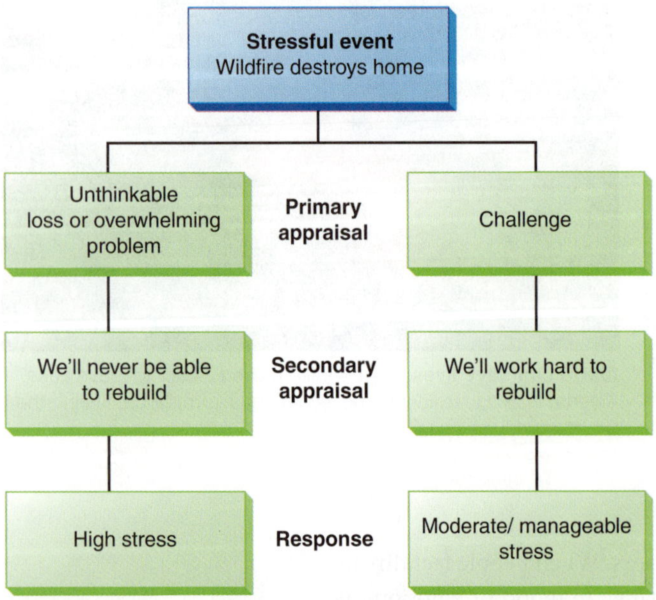

FIGURE 15-4 The cognitive-mediational theory of stress. Our level of stress largely depends on how we appraise a threat and evaluate our abilities to cope with it.

1. In the first step, **primary appraisal**, we examine the stressor and assess how severe it is. We may identify the stressor as a future danger (a threat), a current situation to be confronted and overcome (a challenge), or a loss or harm. The way we appraise the stressor in this first step can have important consequences for how we attempt to deal with it. Ashley, for example, appraised her term paper as a threat to be avoided rather than a challenge to be overcome.
2. In the second step, we evaluate our own resources and ability to cope with the threat, challenge, or loss. This step is called **secondary appraisal**. Perceiving ourselves as lacking the resources to deal with a problem will elevate its threat level. Conversely, by reminding ourselves of what resources we have, we can quickly decrease the threat level. Consider Ashley's more positive attitude when she musters her resources and quickly produces a few paragraphs of her paper.

One common factor in these appraisals is that the degree to which we feel in control of a situation affects how dangerous or stressful it feels. Perceptions of control (or lack of control) can greatly influence our appraisal of a stressor and, in turn, our experience of stress. Persons who believe that they can exert control over a particular stressor will experience less stress than individuals who feel no such control. A study of residents in a nursing home, for example, found that persons who were given more control over their lives (deciding when to attend a movie, for example, or where to receive visitors) experienced less overall stress than residents given little control. Residents with control were twice as likely to still be alive 18 months after the study began (Langer & Rodin, 2004; Rodin & Langer, 1977).

It is important, of course, that our sense of control be realistic. People with life-threatening illnesses such as cancer or heart disease who think that they can control their disease with unproven remedies may feel less stress initially, but they are not likely to be healthier for their efforts. Patients with such illnesses can, however, experience a realistic sense of control (and a lower level of stress) by managing specific aspects of their diseases (seeking out useful medical information, for example), taking part in treatment decisions, controlling some of their emotions, and seeking closer relationships with their loved ones (Thompson et al., 1993).

Individual Responses to Stress

HOW WE DIFFER

It should be clear by now that when it comes down to it, how stressed someone gets in a particular situation often depends on whom we're talking about. You probably have friends who collapse at the slightest hint of trouble, and other friends who are experts in crisis management. Perhaps you have other friends who just let trouble roll off their backs without even a suggestion of worry.

Individuals are unique in many ways. Each of us has a particular biological makeup, a preferred style of interpretation, and a favoured cluster of personality traits. In addition, we each operate within a particular social context. These individual differences profoundly influence our physical, emotional, and cognitive responses to stress. Researchers have spent considerable energy examining four areas of individuality and their relationships to stress: *autonomic reactivity*, *explanatory style*, *personality*, and *social support*.

Autonomic Reactivity and Stress

Earlier, we observed that the autonomic nervous system (ANS), particularly the sympathetic nervous system, plays a key role in stress reactions. When a person confronts a stressor, the ANS stimulates organs throughout the body,

Displaying stress. Each child displays a different reaction to the first day of school: one seems overwhelmed (left), another frustrated and angry (middle), and the other unfazed (right).

Tying It Together: **Your Brain and Behaviour**

Stressing Out when Speaking in Public

If you are like most people, you feel stressed out when you have to give a speech in public. What is happening in the brain while you are feeling this pressure? Although you are not in physical danger, your brain is responding to the presence of an audience as if you were. Brain signals activate the sympathetic nervous system—resulting in increased heart rate, sweaty palms, and a dry mouth. In the brainstem, the locus coeruleus increases arousal by changing activity in its widespread projections throughout the brain. The amygdala and cortex process sensory stimuli that in turn activate stress systems. The hypothalamus sends signals to the pituitary gland to release a hormone that stimulates the adrenal glands (located on top of your kidneys) to release cortisol, the main stress hormone. This hormone helps to mobilize energy stores so that you can cope with the stressor. Finally, the hippocampus and prefrontal cortex recognize elevated levels of cortisol and send inhibitory signals to the hypothalamus to shut down the stress response. Will the audience realize how nervous you are, or will you come across as calm, cool, and collected?

Questions

1 **What is the role of the hypothalamus in responding to a stressor?**

2 **What does it mean to say that the effects of stress on the brain are helpful in the short term but can be harmful in the long term?**

3 **How does the brain response differ when a stressor is rewarding versus not rewarding?**

4 **Where in the brain are the stress hormone receptors that help to restore the brain to its normal state once the stressor has passed?**

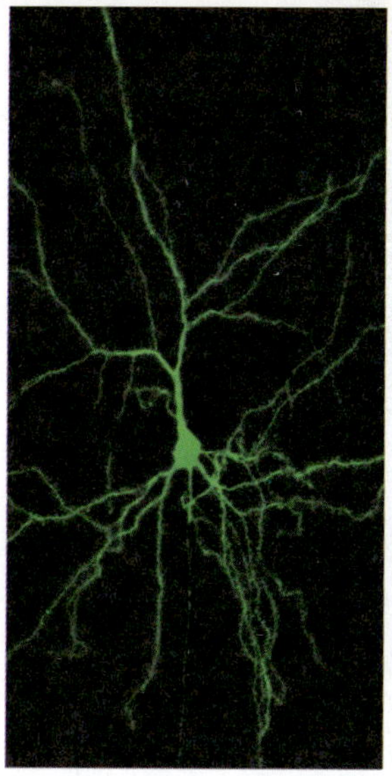

COPING WITH STRESS OVER THE LONG TERM

Activation of stress hormone systems is adaptive in the short term because they can help focus attention and increase energy sources. If negative stress goes on for too long, however, it can become detrimental to the brain. Chronic stress results in a reduction in the size of prefrontal cortex pyramidal neurons (shown here stained with a fluorescent dye) as well as diminished performance on cognitive tasks associated with this brain region.

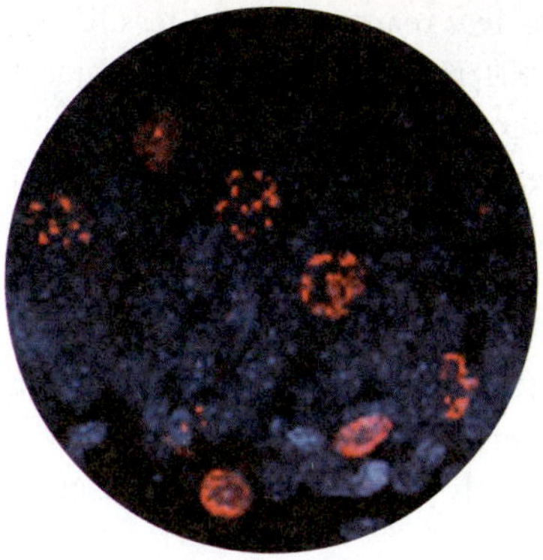

LEARNING TO ENJOY PUBLIC SPEAKING

With repeated experiences, most people find public speaking less frightening and some even begin to enjoy it. When stress has a rewarding component to it, the brain's response switches from negative to positive. Even with elevated stress hormones, neurons are not damaged and they even start to grow. Studies have shown that rewarding stress can stimulate the production of new neurons in the hippocampus (shown here stained with red fluorescent dye).

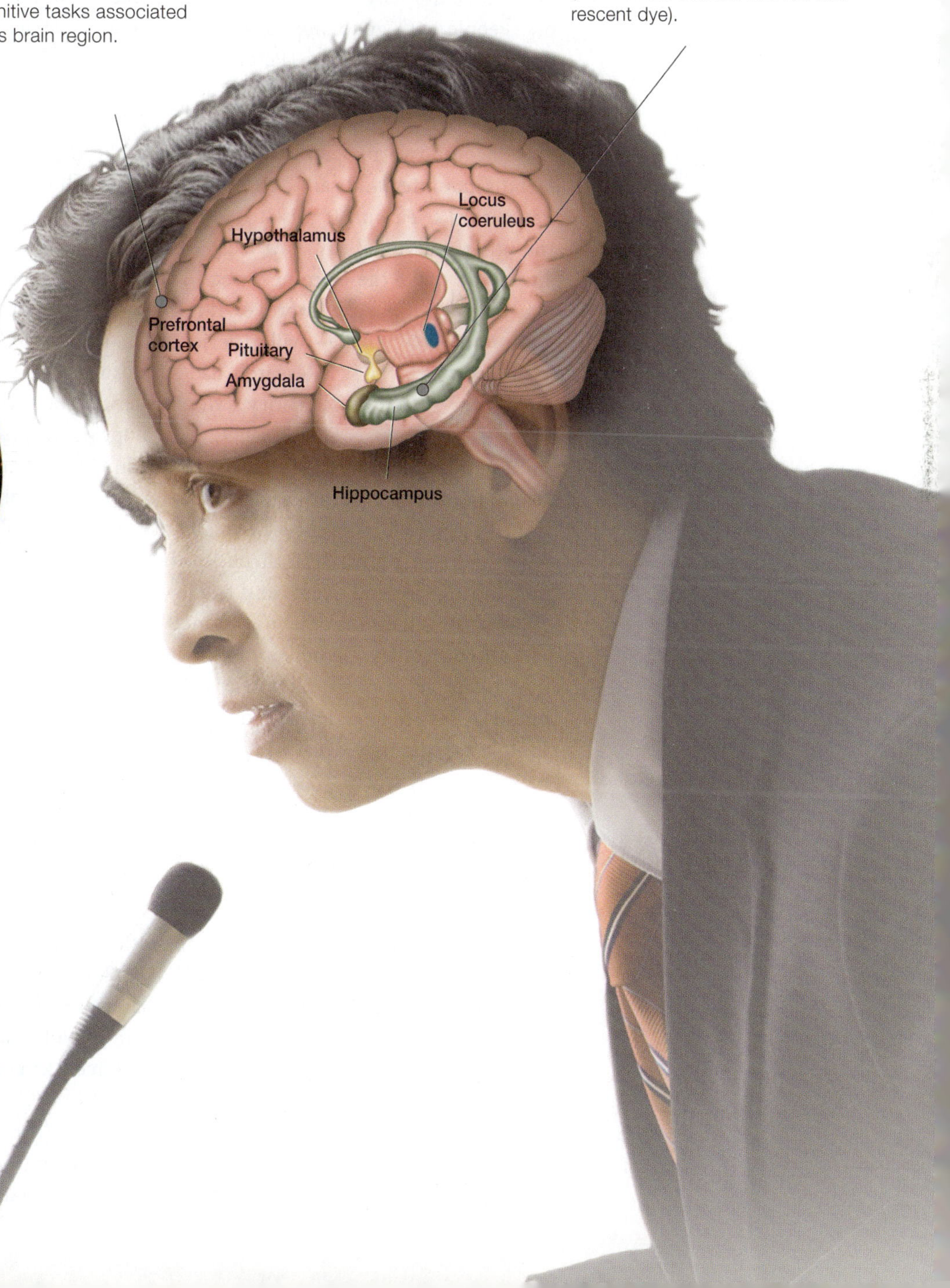

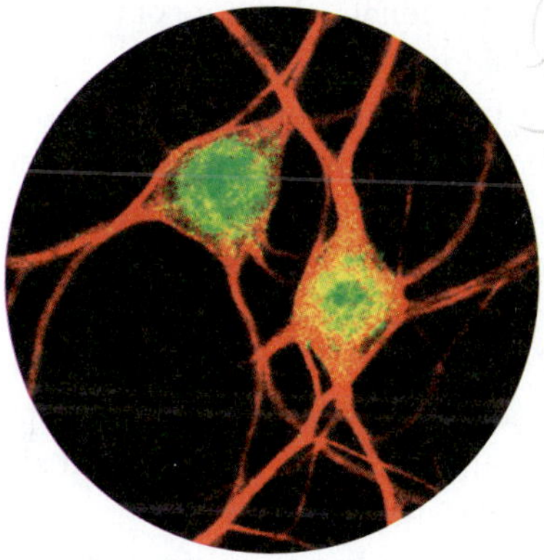

SHUTTING DOWN THE STRESS RESPONSE

To reduce the risks associated with long-term exposure to elevated stress hormones and to enable stress systems to reset themselves for future use with new experiences, the brain has stress hormone receptors (shown here stained with a green fluorescent dye). These receptors, located in the hippocampus, prefrontal cortex, and hypothalamus, work to turn the system off and restore the brain to its normal resting state.

triggering feelings of physical arousal. As you might expect, people differ in how intensely the ANS responds to stressors. In some, the ANS tends to be highly reactive across various situations and springs into action, even in response to mild stressors. In others, the ANS is less reactive and so less likely to respond even to fairly significant stressors. Such basic differences in *autonomic reactivity* may cause some people to experience stress reactions more often or more intensely than other people, even in the face of identical environmental threats (Cohen & Hamrick, 2003; Spielberger, 1985, 1972, 1966).

To illustrate, let's look at cardiovascular responses to stress, which include blood pressure and heart rate. In a number of studies, researchers have measured the cardiovascular reactions of individuals confronting stressors, such as difficult cognitive or social tasks (Sgoifo et al., 2003; Malkoff et al., 1993; Sherwood, 1993). Across a variety of situations, certain participants repeatedly display high-cardiovascular reactivity, while others consistently exhibit low-cardiovascular reactions.

Explanatory Style and Stress The characteristic manner in which we explain events, our *explanatory style*, can make a difference in how we appraise and respond to stressors. People with generally *optimistic* explanatory styles tend to believe that, despite setbacks, things will improve (Peterson & Steen, 2009, 2002). Those with generally *pessimistic* explanatory styles have a gloomier appraisal—they believe that if things can go wrong, they usually will go wrong.

Imagine two people, each failing to make the first-string college soccer team. Both feel disappointed and sad. One says to herself, "I'll never make it. I'm such a dud. I should never have tried out. It was stupid of me to think I was any good at soccer." In contrast, the other individual says, "At least I tried. If I do track in the spring, I can improve my speed and make the team next year. Meanwhile, I'll talk to the coach and find out how I can improve." It is likely that the latter individual—the more optimistic one—will experience less stress than the former.

Some two thousand years ago, the Roman poet Horace wrote, "In times of stress, be bold and valiant."

Research has supported the idea that optimistic and pessimistic explanatory styles influence stress reactions (Chang et al., 2008; Carver & Sheier, 1999). When optimistic research participants appraise stressful situations, they are more likely than pessimists to recognize positive features of the situation and to perceive the situation as manageable (Aspinwall, Richter, & Hoffman, 2001). In turn, those with optimistic explanatory styles typically experience lower levels of stress (Chang, 2002). Similarly, it turns out that optimists are more likely to seek out social support during stressful events and to employ constructive coping techniques (Iwanaga et al., 2004). (We will discuss the importance of social support later in this section.)

Of course, few people are exclusively pessimistic or exclusively optimistic, although they may lean in one direction or other. In fact, some individuals develop an "optimistic brand of pessimism." These individuals believe that things will go wrong but, at the same time, hope that they won't: "I probably will fail to make the soccer team, but maybe I'll get lucky. If I play my best and the others have problems, I might have a chance." Still other people are "defensive pessimists." They anticipate negative outcomes largely to help protect themselves from disappointment (Norem & Illingworth, 2004). Deep down, they hold out hope for the best and so manage to preserve a degree of optimism.

Personality and Stress Our personalities often help set the tone for how we appraise and react to stressors (Vollrath, 2001). People who are generally timid will likely greet a stressor with more alarm than people who are generally bold. Similarly, our ongoing levels of anger, depression, curiosity, and related feelings will influence our stress reactions. Ashley's breakup, for example, appeared to be precipitated by her general tendency to react to stressors by becoming moody and critical.

One personality style that has been studied is the *hardy personality*, sometimes called the *stress-resistant personality* (Maddi, 2007; Bartone, 2003; Oulette & Di Placido, 2001; Kobasa, 1990, 1987). Individuals with such personalities welcome challenges and are willing to commit themselves and take control in their daily lives. Generally, they greet stressors as opportunities for growth rather than as crises, and perceive stressors as less severe than non-hardy individuals. Not surprisingly, hardy persons also seem to experience fewer and less intense feelings of stress (Beasley et al., 2003).

At the other end of the stress continuum are people with personality styles that appear to make them more prone to stress. In the late 1950s, two cardiologists, Meyer Friedman and Raymond Rosenman (1959), reported that many of their heart patients seemed to share similar personality traits: they were consistently angry, cynical, hard-driving, impatient, and time conscious. They were also competitive, ambitious, and in a hurry to do many things at once. Friedman and Rosenman claimed that individuals with this personality style, which they labelled **Type A,** interact with the world in a way that produces continual stress (Jamal & Baba, 2003; Smith & Gallo, 2001; Miller, 2000; Friedman & Rosenman, 1959). In contrast, people who display **Type B** personalities are more relaxed, less aggressive, and less worried about time. People with this personal style are thought to experience lower levels of stress. In fact, most people fall between these two extremes, leaning toward one or the other but showing features of both personality patterns.

Type A a personality type characterized by competitiveness, impatience, and anger and hostility.

Type B a personality type that is less aggressive, more relaxed, and less hostile than Type A.

Researchers later suggested there might be a third personality pattern, **Type C**. People with this personality type are pleasant and peace loving but have a hard time expressing or acknowledging negative feelings (Temoshok et al., 2008; Temoshok, 2003). Although their positive attitudes might be thought to protect them from stress, persons with Type C behaviour patterns are actually particularly vulnerable. When angry, Type C personalities tend to turn the anger inward. They also tend to take losses and relationship problems particularly hard. We will talk more about Type A and Type C personality types when we discuss the relationship between stress and health later in the chapter.

Type C a personality type characterized by difficulty in expressing or acknowledging negative feelings.

Social Support and Stress As we think back to Ashley's struggle at the beginning of the chapter, notice that she seems to be going through her difficulties alone, without much social support. She does not feel free to turn to family members, and she does not appear to have close friends in whom she can confide. In fact, family and social relationships seem to add to her experience of stress. Would Ashley have felt better if she could have turned to family members or friends for support? The answer is yes, according to numerous studies and observations (Taylor, 2008, 2007, 2006).

Want to find out what your personality type is? Go to http://c11.psychtests.com/bin/transfer?req=NDF8Mjk4NnwxNTEzMDU3fDB8MQ==&refempt *to take a short test to find out.*

Social relationships can be paradoxical. On the one hand, as in Ashley's case, negative interactions with relatives and friends can be sources of significant stress (Lepore et al., 1991). On the other hand, studies have resoundingly indicated that social relationships and support help prevent or reduce stress reactions (Cohen & Janicki-Deverts, 2009; Cohen, 2004).

The positive impact of social support on stress was first revealed in animal studies. In a famous investigation, for example, twin goats were subjected to a stressful conditioning task. One goat worked in isolation and the other worked in the presence of its mother. The goat working in isolation reacted with greater anxiety and stress than did its twin (Liddell, 1950). In another study, a group of mice had to "share" a common feeding place, which created a persistent state of territorial conflict (Henry & Cassel, 1969). In one condition, the mice in the group were strangers, while in the other, the mice were from the same litter. The former group showed more signs of stress than did the latter.

Social support can make the difference. A Korean golfer comforts her playing partner as the latter is sizing up a difficult putt on the 18th green of the Women's World Cup of Golf in 2008. The partner went on to sink the putt.

Studies of humans have revealed a similar role for social support in stress reactions (Taylor, 2008, 2007, 2006). It has been found, for example, that when faced with various job stressors, ranging from work overload to job conflict, workers who can rely on their supervisors, co-workers, and spouses for emotional and practical support often experience less distress than workers without such support (Beehr et al., 2003). Other studies suggest that having an intimate, confiding relationship with someone, whether a spouse, close friend, or other individual, provides the strongest kind of social support (Cohen & Wills, 1985).

Why do people who have strong social support seem to experience less stress? Researchers are not sure. Such support may increase people's self-confidence or self-esteem as they confront stressors. It may provide individuals under stress with a greater sense of control or greater optimism that everything will turn out well. Alternatively, social feedback may change people's perspectives as they face stressors, alter their perceptions of threat, or reduce their appraisal of a stressor's importance. Finally, it may be that the reassuring presence of close friends or relatives helps to reduce the kinds of bodily arousal and negative emotions that normally feed stress reactions (Taylor, 2008, 2007, 2006).

Before You Go On

www.wiley.com/go/comer

What Do You Know?

6. How do the sympathetic nervous system and hypothalamic-pituitary-adrenal pathways influence our experience of stress?
7. What happens in each stage of the general adaptation syndrome?
8. What is the difference between primary appraisal and secondary appraisal?
9. How does autonomic reactivity affect how different people experience stress?
10. What are the characteristics of the hardy personality type?

SCAN TO GET THE ANSWERS

What Do You Think?

Can you think of any advantages to having a Type A personality? A Type C personality? Can you think of any disadvantages to having a Type B personality?

Coping with Stress

LEARNING OBJECTIVE 3

Discuss and evaluate several ways in which people cope with stress.

We have seen that a number of individual differences contribute to how stressed we become. Once we feel stressed, we also differ in our efforts to manage the situation. What do you do when you feel stressed? If you feel overloaded or overburdened, do you lie in bed, worrying about all that you have to do, unable to get started? Or do you start making lists and timetables? If you are in a traffic jam, do you pound the steering wheel, or do you instead try to find an interesting radio station or play your favourite CD? Faced with the worrying prospect of a chemistry midterm, do you call a friend to study or light a cigarette?

coping efforts to manage, reduce, or tolerate stress.

Our efforts to manage, reduce, or tolerate stress are called **coping**. Although most people use this term to convey constructive efforts ("I'm coping with the situation"), a coping response may be either adaptive or maladaptive in a given situation (Kleinke, 2007; Folkman & Moskowitz, 2004). For a person faced with failing grades, for example, going out and partying is a less adaptive coping response than spending extra time studying. Each of us has preferred styles of coping that we tend to apply across various situations (Aldwin, 2007; Folkman & Moskowitz, 2004; Carver & Scheier, 2003, 1994). A person may use different coping responses in different situations, however, and some *coping-flexible* individuals are more able than others to depart from their preferred coping styles to meet the demands at hand. Let's look at some of the more common coping styles.

Lashing Out

As stressors pile up, people often say that they feel "as if they're going to explode." Thus, it is not surprising that some individuals do in fact explode—psychologically or physically. They react to stress by lashing out at other people with angry words or behaviours. Around one-quarter of adults report such reactions (Kanner, 1998).

Lashing out often occurs after a series of stressors has taken place. The particular event that triggers an aggressive outburst may seem relatively mild in itself, but for the individual under siege, it is the last straw. Recall how Ashley, the beleaguered student in our case opener, blew up at her boyfriend, Jason, during a phone conversation, calling him names and hanging up on him. Jason's crime? He had refused to let her off the phone. Ordinarily, this teasing might not have elicited such a strong reaction. But Ashley was feeling pressure from her boss, her parents, and the demands of her schoolwork. Ashley's explosive reaction isn't surprising when we consider the cumulative impact of these multiple stressors.

But does it work? In Spain, certain consulting organizations have advised clients such as these men to smash cars (or computers, TVs, or mobile phones) with sledge hammers as a way of fighting stress. The approach has caught on throughout the country, but research has not found that lashing out or venting anger are necessarily effective coping strategies.

Everyone is capable of lashing out at others in the face of stress. For most people, it is an occasional and temporary reaction, performed before they have time to think about things and decide how to act more constructively. For some people, however, lashing out is a characteristic mode of coping. Recall that Ashley had been in the habit of lashing out at Jason. These outbursts were, in fact, a key reason that Jason decided to break up with her.

Angry outbursts, although sometimes understandable, are not typically a constructive way of dealing with stress. Such outbursts may harm relationships, produce psychological or physical damage, and lead to additional stress. Theorists and clinicians once believed that expressions of anger were cathartic, or cleansing—that is, if people expressed their anger and "got their frustrations out of their system," they would feel better and be able to move forward constructively. It turns out, however, that excessive or continuous expressions of anger usually cause further outbursts (Tavris, 2003, 1989). In one study, experimenters induced anger in participants and then directed one group of angry participants to hit a punching bag and the other group of angry individuals to sit quietly (Bushman et al., 1999). Later in the experiment, the "punching bag" participants were found to behave much more aggressively than the "sit quiet" individuals.

In the long term, lashing out can harm or destroy a person's social support network, as in the example of Ashley and Jason. As mentioned earlier, social support is a primary defence against stress. By driving away those who could help with stress-related problems, such as anxiety and depression, a person will likely make those problems worse.

PSYCHOLOGY AROUND US Cursed Response

Want a quick relief from stress? Angry outbursts may not work, but apparently shouting out your favourite curse word can help. Richard Stephens and his research group at Keele University in England had college students put their arms in a bucket of ice water for as long as they could (Stephens et al., 2009). Some of the participants were instructed to shout out curse words of their choosing while holding their arms in the water; others shouted out neutral words only. Which participants do you think were better able to keep their arms immersed in the ice water? That's right: the swearers. In fact, they kept their arms in the water almost a minute longer than the students who repeated neutral words again and again. Why does swearing help? The experimenters theorized that it triggers our fight-or-flight responses, which help us deal with immediate stress and negate the link between fear of pain and pain perception. But be forewarned (or relieved)—swearing has a much greater coping and pain-reduction effect for occasional swearers than for habitual swearers.

Self-Defence

In some instances, people run away from—that is, physically leave—stressors through such actions as dropping a difficult class, changing jobs, or ending a troubled relationship. More commonly, people try to make a "psychological getaway." You may recall Aesop's story of the fox and the grapes. A fox was trying to get some grapes, but they were hanging too high on a vine, and he couldn't reach them. Eventually, after trying for most of the afternoon, the fox gave up, saying, "they're probably sour anyway." Leaving aside the question of why a fox wants grapes in the first place, the fox's behaviour in this story is an example of *reaction formation*—saying or doing the opposite of what one actually believes—one of Freud's defence mechanisms.

"You can avoid reality, but you cannot avoid the consequences of avoiding reality."
—*Ayn Rand, Russian-American writer*

Recall from Chapter 13 that Freud explained such behaviour in psychoanalytic terms. Today, though, the notion of defence mechanisms is widely embraced, even by theorists outside the psychoanalytic model. Many psychologists believe that people often cope with stress—whether consciously or unconsciously—by engaging in defensive behaviours (Cramer, 2001; Erdelyi, 2001). These theorists also agree that the defensive behaviours often involve a high degree of self-deception (Bolger, 1990), but that this self-deception might in fact be adaptive (Taylor et al., 2003).

Although everyone reacts to stressors with defensive behaviours on occasion, some people use such behaviours regularly. In fact, certain individuals display what theorists describe as a *repressive coping style* (Langens & Morth, 2003; Brown et al., 1996). They consistently deny negative feelings and discomfort and try to push such emotions out of awareness.

Is the use of defence mechanisms—whether occasional or continual—a helpful way to cope with stress? Sometimes, it probably is. We can all think of instances when it would be best to simply put something out of our mind, particularly if we don't have any control over the outcome (for example, waiting for our grade on a recent exam). In other instances, however, defensive coping is not constructive. After all, while we spend our time defending and avoiding, the problem typically continues (Holahan & Moos, 1990, 1985). The conflict with a roommate, the course paper that needs writing, and the medical problem that needs attention continue as stressors, and may even intensify.

It is also worth noting that defensive coping can be difficult to achieve. Research has found that people with a repressive coping style often fail to fully repress their feelings of stress (Pauls & Stemmler, 2003; Brown et al., 1996). While research participants were watching an upsetting film, for example, experimenters measured their autonomic nervous system responses. Although participants with a repressive coping style reported feeling less stress than other participants did, their autonomic responses were actually higher (for example, their heart rates and blood pressure were higher throughout the film). It may be that repressive coping behaviours *mask* stress rather than eliminate it. Or perhaps the higher autonomic activity associated with repressive coping indicates that such repression requires considerable physical effort. Either way, it is not surprising that people with this coping style have been found to experience more medical problems than people who use other coping styles do (Coy, 1998).

Self-Indulgence

Many individuals use self-indulgent coping strategies, such as overeating, smoking cigarettes, and consuming drugs and alcohol (Steptoe, 2000). Ashley went partying with her friends, for example, to deal with the stress created by her paper-writing assignment. Such strategies may help people feel better in the short term, but in most instances they fail to change the challenge at hand and so have little long-term benefit. In fact, such responses are often associated with poor adjustment and depression and anxiety (Folkman & Moskowitz, 2004; Aspinwall & Taylor, 1992).

If the problem at hand is transient and simple—recovering from a drive home in a blinding snowstorm, for example—the self-indulgence of having a bowl of ice cream or a beer may indeed help a stressed person to calm down. If, however, the problem is more complex—a term paper due next week—self-indulgence is unlikely to be an effective coping strategy. Eating, drinking, shopping, watching television, or surfing the Internet will not make the problem go away. In fact, it may produce still greater pressure and higher stress: while one indulges, the paper's due date keeps getting closer. Moreover, certain self-indulgent strategies, such as gambling, cigarette smoking, excessive alcohol

PRACTICALLY SPEAKING How Can You Manage Stress?

Mass relaxation. A group of 150 students in Bejing, China receive stress relief training to help them relax during their upcoming college entrance examinations.

Stress is often unavoidable. The traffic jams, life changes, and occasional natural disasters that create stress are not going to miraculously disappear. The issue, then, is how to handle stress. Is there a way to lessen its impact so that cortisol levels, blood pressure, and the like do not soar? The answer, according to many psychologists and studies, is yes (Folkman & Moskowitz, 2004). As this chapter has already begun to suggest, there are quite a few things you can do the next time you anticipate or begin to feel the heart-pounding symptoms of stress.

Exercise, Meditation, and Relaxation

One of the best ways to manage physiological responses to stress is to exercise (Steptoe, 2000). In fact, it appears that people who exercise regularly reap not only physical benefits, such as lowering the activity of stress hormones (Rejeski & Thompson, 2007; Rejeski et al., 1992, 1991), but also psychological benefits, such as increased self-confidence. Similarly, research indicates that some of those who learn to quiet their thoughts and relax their muscles through meditation and relaxation training experience reductions in stress hormone activity, blood pressure, and anxiety levels (Cardoso et al., 2009; Stetter & Kupper, 2002).

Social Support

Seeking the support of others, whether in the form of assistance or a sympathetic ear, is another way to ease the effects of stress. Simply knowing that friends or family will be available when needed is a form of social support (Taylor, 2008, 2007, 2006; Pierce, Sarason, & Sarason, 1996). It appears that social support helps ease the effects of stress in at least two ways—by helping to reduce the actual number and impact of threatening situations and by providing practical, problem-focused assistance when stress does occur.

Religion

For many people, religion is of major help in dealing with stress. As we have observed in this chapter, one reason for this may be the social support that the individuals derive from religion (Folkman & Moskowitz, 2004). Religion and religious communities can, for example, serve as antidotes to feelings of aloneness and may also provide a sense of order as people face the uncertainties of life. In addition, religious beliefs may offer explanations for stressful events that make those events seem less threatening or overwhelming to many people (Packer, 2000).

Self-Disclosure

Self-disclosure, the sharing of emotions and experiences with others, can also help people deal with stress. Up to a point, self-disclosure serves to release stress—consider the phrase "getting things off my chest"—but it is more than simply the venting of emotion. It helps people to channel emotions into a cohesive narrative, making stressors easier to process and deal with (Foa & Kozak, 1986). In addition, by putting fearful, angry, or uncomfortable feelings into language and "bouncing them off" of other people, individuals are forced to think about and perhaps better address those feelings (Smyth & Pennebaker, 2001). Of course, the effectiveness of self-disclosure is tied to the ability of others to understand the problems a person is going through. Rape victims or former prisoners of war, for example, may discover that certain relatives or friends simply cannot comprehend what they are going through. In such cases, the feedback they receive ("Gee, that's really rough, but I am sure you'll feel better soon") may feel empty, unhelpful, and in some cases even painful.

consumption, drug use, and extreme overeating, have serious health effects (Young, 2009, 2004, 1998, 1996).

Constructive Strategies

It is possible, of course, to cope with stress constructively rather than lashing out at others or engaging in self-defence or self-indulgence. Psychologists Richard Lazarus and Susan Folkman (1984) use the terms *problem-focused coping* and *emotion-focused coping* to distinguish between two kinds of constructive strategies. Which of these strategies we are likely to use depends in part on the nature of the problem (Stanton et al., 2009, 2002; Folkman & Moskowitz, 2004). For example, we could try to hit the highway at 4:00 A.M. as a way of dealing with morning traffic, but it is probably more practical to learn how to react calmly and philosophically to rush-hour tie-ups. Conversely, when a tornado watch is posted, figuring out how to calm down may not be as fruitful as deciding whether to leave town or head for the cellar or for higher ground.

problem-focused coping coping strategies focused on dealing directly with the stressor, such as by changing the stressor in some way.

In **problem-focused coping**, the person's efforts are aimed at dealing directly with the stressor in some way. For example, the late-to-work Ashley might ask her boss to assign her to a different work shift so that she has more time to get to work. Or she might look for a new job closer to campus. She might devise a plan to buy a car, so that she can save time travelling to work. Or she might decide that her earlier solution of jogging to work is worth continuing. In any case, by dealing directly with the stressor, she can begin to reduce its effects.

But what about the noisy 2-year-old next door who keeps interrupting your efforts to relax in the backyard? Or the grief we experience resulting from the death of a loved one? These are not stressors that readily yield to a problem-focused approach. When we can exert little control over stressors, we may instead try to change how we feel toward the stressors, thus limiting their negative effects—an approach Lazarus and Folkman call **emotion-focused coping**.

emotion-focused coping coping strategies focused on changing one's feelings about the stressor.

In some cases, emotion-focused coping may involve *cognitive reappraisal*—finding a way to reinterpret the negative aspects of a situation so that they are less upsetting (Harvey, 2008; Lechner et al., 2008; Gross, Richards, & John, 2006; Gross & John, 2003; Wortman et al., 1992). People who are trying to come to terms with the death of a loved one or with some other catastrophic loss often look for ways to find positive meaning or purpose in their loss (Folkman & Moskowitz, 2004). Similarly, people may reinterpret threatening situations as challenges or tests, rather than catastrophes. The loss of a job, for example, might be viewed as a new beginning or new opportunity (Folkman & Moskowitz, 2000).

> "The greatest weapon against stress is our ability to choose one thought over another."
> —*William James, American psychologist and philosopher*

Changing how we think or feel about a stressor can also be a useful tactic for less traumatic stressors, such as tests and traffic jams. Rather than becoming increasingly upset over a traffic jam, for example, you may be able to shrug it off—saying, in effect, "It won't be great if I'm late, but I'll survive."

Before You Go On

www.wiley.com/go/comer

What Do You Know?

11. How can lashing out negatively affect our management of stressors?
12. What is a repressive coping style?
13. Identify and describe two forms of constructive coping.

What Do You Think?

Do you tend to use constructive coping strategies, or do your responses tend to be more maladaptive? Do you adapt your coping style to the situation, or do you tend to use the same style across many different situations? How could you improve your coping style?

SCAN TO GET THE ANSWERS

Stress and Health

LEARNING OBJECTIVE 4

Explain how stress can cause physical illness, and discuss situations in which stress may be beneficial.

We have seen that stress has a profound effect on bodily functioning. Thus, it should come as no surprise that researchers have found strong relationships between stress and health—or, more accurately, between stress and illness (Groer et al., 2010). Scientists' appreciation of this relationship unfolded slowly. Back in the 1930s and 1940s, researchers began to recognize that certain medical illnesses are caused by an interaction of psychological factors (particularly stress-related factors) and biological factors, rather than by biological factors alone. These special illnesses were given the label *psychosomatic* or *psychophysiological diseases.* By the 1960s, a number of medical illnesses were considered psychosomatic diseases. Among the most prominent were ulcers, asthma, tension and migraine headaches, and hypertension (Murison, 2001; Ramadan, 2000; Sriram & Silverman, 1998; Pickering et al., 1996). Although peptic ulcers have since been shown to be bacterial in nature (Marshall, 1994), stress is known to weaken the immune response and thereby increase vulnerability to the development of ulcers (Murison, 2001).

As the list of psychosomatic diseases grew, medical researchers began to suspect that stress might, in fact, be at work in a wide range of medical illnesses, not just in a special few. Their suspicions changed to near certainty when studies revealed that stress often contributes to coronary heart disease (the second leading cause of death, after cancer, in Canada). Researchers continue to investigate how stress is connected to various illnesses, as well as how stress brings about its effects on body systems.

Coronary Heart Disease

Coronary heart disease involves a blocking of the coronary arteries—the blood vessels that surround the heart and are responsible for carrying oxygen to the heart muscle. The term actually refers to several problems, including blockage of the coronary arteries and *myocardial infarction* ("heart attack"). Together, such problems are the second-leading cause of death after cancer in men and women over the age of 45 in Canada, accounting for close to 50,000 deaths each year (Statistics Canada, 2007). Research has shown that most cases of coronary heart disease are related to an interaction of psychological factors, such as job stress, and physiological factors, such as high cholesterol, obesity, hypertension, smoking, and lack of exercise (Bekkouche et al., 2011; Kendall-Tackett, 2010; Statistics Canada, 2007).

Earlier, we discussed the Type A personality, which was identified by two cardiologists, Friedman and Rosenman. These doctors argued that the stress-producing behaviour of people with Type A personalities makes them more likely to develop coronary heart disease (see **Figure 15-5**). In fact, the Type A personality is also known in many circles as the *coronary-prone personality.* People with the more relaxed Type B behaviour pattern exhibit lower levels of stress and less coronary disease. In a pioneering study of more than 3,000 men, Friedman and Rosenman (1974) separated healthy men in their forties and fifties into Type A and Type B groups and then followed their health over a period of eight years. The doctors found that more than twice as many of the Type A men developed coronary heart disease. Subsequent studies found similar correlations among women (Haynes et al., 1980).

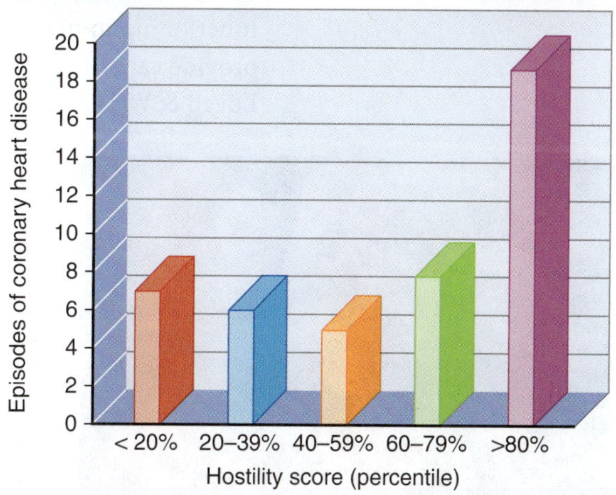

FIGURE 15-5 Type A personality and hostility. A key characteristic of the Type A personality is chronic hostility. People with this personality style interact with others in a way that produces continual high levels of stress and increases their risk of coronary heart disease (Niaura et al., 2002).

Hostility and your heart. It is not surprising that individuals who score high on measures of hostility experience more stress and are at higher risk for heart attacks.

As research continued into the link between Type A behaviour and coronary heart disease, many investigators found that while a connection existed, it was weaker than that reported by Friedman and Rosenman (Gallacher et al., 2003). It now appears that only some of the Type A characteristics are strongly related to heart disease (Ben Zur, 2002; Krantz & McCeney, 2002). In particular, research has identified the importance of negative emotions. Hostility, which includes not just feelings of anger but also enduring cognitive patterns of mistrust and cynicism, seems to be especially important (Smith & Gallo, 2001). People who score high on measures of hostility tend to experience greater stress and to have an increased risk of developing coronary heart disease, as well as other serious medical illnesses (Elovainio et al., 2011; Kendall-Tacket, 2010; Niaura et al., 2002; Miller et al., 1996).

Stress and the Immune System

Research clearly shows that stress can result in various medical disorders. But exactly how does this effect come about? What is it about stress that makes it a threat to health? An area of study called psychoneuroimmunology has tried to answer this question by examining the links between stress, the immune system, and health (Kendall-Tackett, 2010; Kendall-Tackett, 2010; Kiecolt-Glaser et al., 2002).

psychoneuroimmunology an area of study focusing on links between stress, the immune system, and health.

immune system the body's system of organs, tissues, and cells that identify and destroy foreign invaders, such as bacteria and viruses, as well as cancer cells.

lymphocytes white blood cells that circulate through the body and destroy foreign invaders and cancer cells; important components of the immune system.

The immune system is the body's system of organs, tissues, and cells that identify and destroy foreign invaders, such as bacteria and viruses, as well as cancer cells. An important group of cells in the immune system are lymphocytes, white blood cells that circulate through the lymphatic system and the bloodstream. When stimulated by bacterial or viral invaders, lymphocytes act to help the body fight the invaders, often by destroying body cells that have been infected by the invaders.

Researchers believe that severe stress can negatively affect the activity of lymphocytes, slowing them down and thus reducing a person's ability to fight off viral and bacterial infections (see **Figure 15-6**) (Ader et al., 2001; Dhabhar, 2011). In a pioneering study, Roger Bartrop and his colleagues (1977) in New South Wales, Australia, compared the immune systems of 26 people whose spouses had died eight weeks earlier to those of 26 similar participants whose spouses had not died. Blood samples showed that lymphocyte functioning was significantly slower in the bereaved people than in the non-bereaved individuals (Bartrop et al., 1977). Similarly, other studies have shown poor immune system functioning in persons who are exposed to long-term stressors, such as people who must provide care for relatives with Alzheimer's disease (Kiecolt-Glaser et al., 2002, 1996, 1991; Lovell & Wetharall, 2011).

Internal combat. This scanning electron micrograph shows a cancer cell (red) being attacked by natural killer T-cells (yellow).

In short, during periods when healthy people confront unusual levels of stress, their immune systems slow down so that they become susceptible to illness. If stress adversely affects our very capacity to fight off illness, it is not surprising that Holmes and Rahe and other researchers have found a relationship between life stress and a wide range of illnesses. Several factors seem to influence whether and when stress will lead to immune system problems. A number of biochemical changes must occur for stress to have such an impact. Certain behavioural changes, personality styles, and social circumstances may also play a role.

Biochemical Activity Remember that when stressors first appear, the sympathetic nervous system springs into action. Its activity includes an increase in the release of norepinephrine throughout the brain and body. Apparently, beyond supporting the activity of the sympathetic nervous system, norepinephrine can eventually help slow the functioning of the immune system (Carlson, 2008; Groer et al., 2010; Lekander, 2002). During periods of low stress, norepinephrine travels to particular lymphocyte receptors, binds to them, and gives a message for the lymphocytes to increase activity. As stress rises and continues, however, the chemical travels to other receptors on the lymphocytes, binds to them, and gives an inhibitory message—a signal for the lymphocytes to stop their activity. Thus, the release of norepinephrine increases immune functioning at low levels of stress, but it slows down immune functioning in the face of higher and continuing stress.

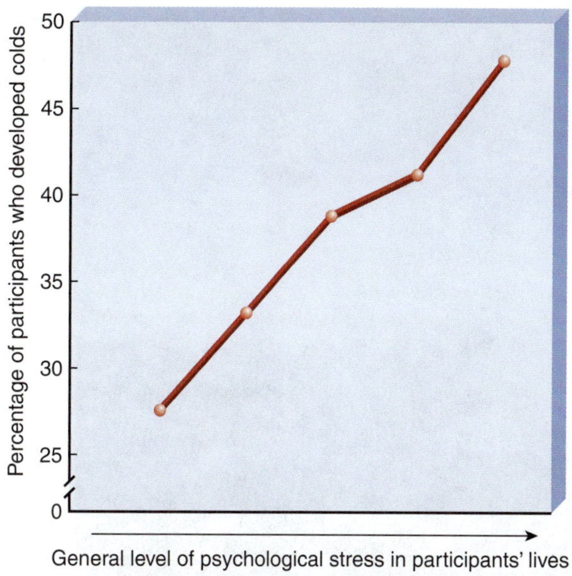

FIGURE 15-6 Stress and the common cold. Researchers have examined the links between stress and illness. One study found that when healthy inoculation volunteers were exposed to a cold virus, those who reported generally the highest levels of stress in their lives were most likely to come down with a cold and to develop worse symptoms (Cohen et al., 1991).

Similarly, the stress hormone cortisol lowers immune system functioning during periods of extended stress. Recall that when people are under stress, their adrenal glands release cortisol. Initially, the release of this hormone stimulates body organs into action. After stress continues for 30 minutes or more, however, the stress hormone travels to particular receptor sites in the body, binds to these sites, and gives inhibitory messages meant to help calm down the stressed body (Manuck et al., 1991). Some of these receptor sites are located on the lymphocytes. When the cortisol binds to such receptors, its inhibitory messages slow down the activity of the immune system (Bellinger et al., 1994; Groer et al., 2010). Again, a chemical that initially helps people to deal with stress eventually acts to slow the immune system.

Another action of cortisol is to stimulate an increase in the production of *cytokines*—proteins that bind to receptors throughout the body and play a key role in the immune system. At early levels of stress, the cytokines help fight infection. But as stress continues, the ongoing production and spread of cytokines leads to inflammation throughout the body (Burg & Pickering, 2011; Burg et al., 2011; Kendall-Tackett, 2010; McEwen, 2002). *Inflammation* is an immune response characterized by swelling, heat, redness, and pain. Chronic inflammation of this kind may contribute to heart disease, stroke, and other illnesses.

Finally, investigators have learned that patterns of immune system responding vary from individual to individual (Marsland et al., 2002). Certain individuals experience more profound immune system slowdowns in the face of stress than other individuals do. Moreover, these individual differences in immune system functioning tend to be consistent across stressful situations. Thus, some stressed persons are more likely than others to develop infections and other diseases. Let's look next at some individual factors that may be responsible for differences in immune system functioning.

Behaviour, Personality, and Social Support Stress may trigger a series of behavioural changes that affect the immune system indirectly (Kalueff & La Porte, 2008). People under chronic stress may, for example, become anxious or depressed, perhaps even develop an anxiety or mood disorder. In turn, they may eat poorly, exercise less, have trouble sleeping, or smoke or drink. Such behaviours are all known to slow down the immune system (Brooks et al., 2011; Kibler et al., 2010; Irwin & Cole, 2005; Kiecolt-Glaser & Glaser, 2002, 1999, 1988).

An individual's personality may also help determine how much the immune system is affected by stress. Studies suggest that people who typically respond to life stress with optimism, effective coping, and resilience tend to experience better immune system functioning and to be better prepared to combat illness (Kern & Friedman, 2011; Kendall-Tackett, 2010; Taylor, 2006, 2004; Williams et al., 2011). Correspondingly, those with "hardy" or resilient personalities tend to remain healthy after stressful events, whereas those whose

Healthy communities. This group of Inuit perform a "blanket toss" ceremony in which they form a ring around a blanket and use it to hurl group members into the air. Communities that share activities and remain close-knit often have lower illness rates than other communities.

personal styles are less hardy are more vulnerable to illness (Bonanno et al., 2010; Ouellett & DiPlacido, 2001).

Several studies have actually noted a relationship between certain personality characteristics and cancer (Hjerl et al., 2003). People exhibiting the Type C behaviour pattern appear to be more at risk for cancer. Recall that people with the Type C personality have trouble acknowledging negative feelings and may be particularly vulnerable to stress. In addition, some studies have found that patients with certain forms of cancer who display a helpless or repressive coping style tend to have less successful recoveries than patients who express their emotions. It is important to note, however, that other studies have found no relationship between personality and cancer outcome (Urcuyo et al., 2005; Garssen & Goodkin, 1999).

Some researchers have identified a connection between religiousness and health. Specifically, studies have found that regular attendance at a place of worship is correlated with a decreased risk of death over a particular period (Ellison et al., 2000). A few studies have also linked spirituality to better immune system functioning (Jackson & Bergeman, 2011; Folkman & Moskowitz, 2004; Koenig & Cohen, 2002). Although the relationship between attendance at a place or worship and health is not well understood, it appears to result at least in part from the social support people receive from others in their religious group.

More generally, research indicates that social support helps to protect us from the effects of stress. People who have little social support and feel lonely tend to experience poorer immune functioning when stressed than other people do (Uchino & Birmingham, 2011; Curtis et al., 2004; Cohen, 2002). Conversely, it appears that social support helps protect people from stress, poor immune system functioning, and illness and helps improve recovery from illness or surgery (Matsumoto & Juang, 2008; Cohen, 2002; Kiecolt-Glaser et al., 2002). Some studies have even suggested that patients with certain kinds of cancer who receive social support or supportive therapy often display better immune system functioning and, in turn, have more successful recoveries than patients without such social help.

The stress-reducing benefits of social support can be seen in the health of people who grow up in close-knit communities. One early study explored the low rate of stress-related illnesses among residents of the town of Roseto, Pennsylvania (Wolf, 1969). The death rate from coronary heart disease in this town was considerably lower than that in the general population, despite the fact that the residents' eating, smoking, and exercise patterns were similar to those in communities with much higher coronary death rates. Clearly, something special was responsible for the residents' good health. That something turned out to be Roseto's positive social environment. An Italian enclave, Roseto was home to extremely close, supportive, and traditional families. Relatives, friends, and local priests were always available to help out with any kind of problem. During the 1970s, Roseto's younger generation began to marry people from other backgrounds and move away. Church attendance also dropped. These social changes resulted in less social support throughout the community. Perhaps not surprisingly, the rate of heart attacks in the community increased (Greenberg, 1978).

The Benefits of Stress

It might be hard to believe, given the litany of problems that we have identified here, but stress can be positive. In fact, when Selye first identified stress as a concept back in 1936, he actually drew a distinction between unpleasant stressors and pleasant stressors. How can a stressor be pleasant? Think about waiting for a call from someone you met at a party last night; it can be stressful, but in an exciting way. Unpleasant stressors, according to Selye, cause **distress**—the kind of unpleasant stress on which we have generally been focusing up to now. Pleasant stressors, in contrast, cause *eustress*.

A key benefit of stress is that it helps promote positive development. Remember in Chapter 3 when we discussed some theorists' notion that parents can actually stunt a baby's development by meeting all the baby's needs, and that there is some optimal level of frustration that facilitates development? Researchers have suggested that similar principles apply across the lifespan. That is, adverse events and the stress that they produce can force you to confront challenges, adapt to your environment, and build up strength and resilience (Tennen & Affleck, 2009, 2002; Tennen, Affleck, & Armeli, 2005; Harvey, 2008).

Stress inoculation? Why is this drill instructor screaming at this poor recruit? The logic behind this time-honoured training technique is that intense stressors experienced during basic training will build mental strength and resilience and make individuals more effective in actual combat.

Today, **eustress** is defined not in terms of the stressor, but in terms of the stress level—it is the optimal level of stress that promotes physical and psychological health (Nelson & Cooper, 2005). But what exactly is an optimal level of stress? We can think about this question in a couple of ways. First, exposing yourself to a smaller level of stress in a controlled situation can improve your performance in a more stressful situation, a process called **inoculation.** If you call one friend to talk through what you want to say to another friend with whom you have been arguing, you are inoculating yourself.

distress stress caused by unpleasant situations or circumstances.

eustress the optimal level of stress needed to promote physical and psychological health.

inoculation exposing oneself to a relatively low level of stress in a controlled situation to improve later performance in a more stressful situation.

As we have seen previously, another way of considering what constitutes an optimal level of stress involves looking at the relationship between stress and performance. As shown in **Figure 15-7**, researchers have found that stress can actually facilitate performance on a task, depending on the complexity of the task.

- *Performance of very easy tasks can benefit from a high level of stress.* For example, the old videogame Tetris® involves very little cognitive complexity and very low stakes, but as the computer starts dropping the pieces faster, it will get your attention and help you stay focused on the game.
- *A moderately difficult task benefits from a moderate level of stress.* Too low, and you won't get excited enough to perform your best. Too high, and you will be more likely to lose your focus or perform poorly.
- *For a complex task, low stress leads to the optimal performance.* Consider that next time you decide to make a complex dinner you have never prepared before for a few friends and don't leave quite enough time to get your house cleaned and everything prepared before they arrive. You might do better ordering out.

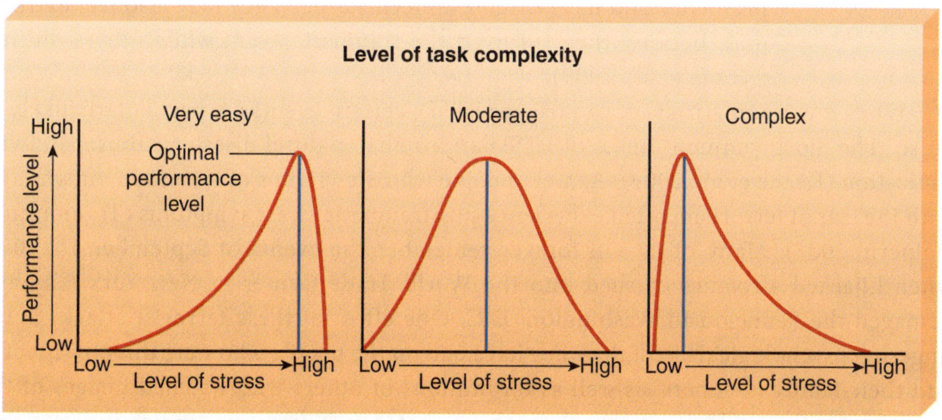

FIGURE 15-7 Stress and performance. Stress can actually benefit performance, depending on the complexity of the task. On very complex tasks, a low level of stress is optimal for performing your best; on very easy tasks, a high stress level helps you stay focused.

Before You Go On

www.wiley.com/go/comer

What Do You Know?

14. How has stress been linked with coronary heart disease?
15. What is the connection between life changes and illness?
16. How does stress affect the immune system?
17. What factors influence whether stress will have this effect?
18. What are some beneficial effects of stress?

SCAN TO GET THE ANSWERS

What Do You Think?

Try to recall five events in your life or in the lives of your family members and friends that suggest a relationship between stress and illness. Having now read this chapter, how might you account for those events and relationships?

Posttraumatic Stress Disorder

WHEN THINGS GO WRONG

LEARNING OBJECTIVE 5

Describe the symptoms and causes of posttraumatic stress disorder, and discuss some risk factors for developing it.

As we have seen, stress, when moderate and handled constructively, can serve us well. But it can also work against us. In addition to leading to physical diseases, it can contribute to various psychological disorders, from depression to sexual dysfunctions. Moreover, it plays a central role in *posttraumatic stress disorder,* or *PTSD,* mentioned earlier in the chapter.

PTSD. Survivors mourn the dozens of teenagers and young adults killed by a lone gunman on July 22, 2011, at Utoeya, a youth camp for Norway's Labour Party.

In posttraumatic stress disorder, persons who have confronted an extraordinarily stressful event—combat, rape, earthquake, airplane crash, automobile accident—experience a number of severe psychological symptoms lasting for months or even years (Keane, Marx, & Sloan, 2009). They have lingering reactions of intense fear and helplessness. They may be battered by memories, dreams, or nightmares connected to the traumatic event and may repeatedly try to avoid activities, thoughts, feelings, or conversations that remind them of the event. Many also feel detached from other people, some lose interest in activities that once brought enjoyment, and some feel dazed. A number of individuals with the disorder are easily startled, develop sleep problems, and have trouble concentrating. They may also feel extreme guilt because they survived the traumatic event while others did not (Keane et al., 2009).

While any traumatic event can trigger PTSD, certain events are particularly likely to do so. The most common causes of PTSD are combat, natural disasters, abuse, and victimization (Keane et al., 2009). As well, people who are victims of terrorism, or who live with the fear of terrorism, often experience posttraumatic stress symptoms (Tramontin & Halpern, 2007). Many of us will forever remember the events of September 11, 2001, when hijacked airplanes crashed into the World Trade Center in New York City and damaged the Pentagon in Washington, D.C. One effect of these terrorist attacks is the lingering psychological effect that they have had on the people who were directly affected and their family members, as well as on millions of others who watched images of the disasters on their television sets throughout that day. Numerous studies indicate that posttraumatic stress reactions were common even in people who simply witnessed the events through the media (Marshall et al., 2007; Schlenger et al., 2002).

Who Develops PTSD?

Almost 10 percent of Canadians experience posttraumatic stress disorder during their lifetimes (Burijon, 2007; Kessler et al., 2005). The disorder can occur at any age, even in childhood (Balaban, 2009). Women are at least twice as likely as men to develop PTSD (Koch & Haring, 2008).

Although anyone who experiences an unusual trauma will be affected by it, only some people develop posttraumatic stress disorder (McNally, 2001). To understand the development of this disorder more fully, researchers have looked at the same stress-related factors that we have examined throughout this chapter—and they have come up with promising leads.

Is anyone immune? Most people who experience extraordinary traumatic events are capable of developing PTSD. Even rescue workers at the site of disasters often develop the disorder. Nevertheless, all things being equal, some people seem particularly prone to PTSD in the aftermath of traumatic events.

Biological Factors As we have observed, stressors trigger biochemical reactions throughout the brain and body. Apparently, in the face of extraordinarily threatening stressors, some people develop particularly strong biochemical reactions—reactions that continue well beyond a short-term fight-or-flight period. It appears that such individuals are more likely than others to experience a posttraumatic stress disorder (Bremner & Charney, 2010; Pace & Heim, 2011; Yehuda, 2009). Consistent with this notion, researchers have found abnormal activity of the stress hormone cortisol and the neurotransmitter norepinephrine in the urine and blood of combat soldiers, rape victims, concentration camp survivors, and survivors of other traumatic events (Burijon, 2007; Delahanty et al., 2005).

Indeed, some studies suggest that people who develop PTSD have exaggerated sympathetic nervous system responses and blunted HPA axis responses to stress (Yehuda, 2001; Yehuda et al., 1998). There is also some evidence that once a posttraumatic stress disorder sets in, the individual's continuing biochemical arousal may eventually shrink the hippocampus, one of the brain areas that helps control the body's stress hormones, thus further locking in the disorder (Carlson, 2008; Mirzaei et al., 2005). At the same time, it is worth noting that, according to some research, people who are more susceptible to developing PTSD may have a smaller hippocampus to begin with (Gilbertson et al., 2002).

Personality Earlier, we observed that people with certain personality styles or coping styles are particularly likely to react to threats with stress and to develop medical problems. Similarly, such styles increase the likelihood of developing a posttraumatic stress disorder (Burijon, 2007; Chung et al., 2005). It turns out, for example, that people with less resilient, or less hardy, personality styles appear more likely to develop a posttraumatic stress disorder than those with more resilient styles (Kunst, 2011; Maddi, 2007). So too are war veterans who had psychological problems before they went into combat (Dikel et al., 2005). In addition, people who typically view life's negative events as beyond their control are more likely than others to develop posttraumatic stress symptoms after criminal assaults (Taylor, 2006; Regehr et al., 1999).

Childhood Experience Studies have also suggested that certain childhood experiences increase the risk of later posttraumatic stress disorders (Alter & Hen, 2009; Rapee & Bryant, 2009). People whose childhoods have been characterized by poverty appear more

Detecting PTSD in children. The Sesame Street Muppet Rosita tells children in New York about "You Can Ask," a program that seeks to identify and deal with stress in children. The program was first formed in the aftermath of the September 11, 2001 terrorist attacks.

likely to develop this disorder when later confronting horrific events. So are people whose parents displayed psychological disorders and who experienced assault, abuse, or catastrophe at a young age (Koch & Haring, 2008; Ozer et al., 2003).

Social Support Finally, the social environment may influence whether victims of traumatic events develop posttraumatic stress disorders. Earlier, we saw that inadequate social support can intensify stress reactions and slow down immune system functioning. Thus, it is not surprising that people with weak social support systems are also more likely to develop a posttraumatic stress disorder after a traumatic event (Charuvastra & Cloitre, 2008; Ozer et al., 2003). For example, rape victims who feel loved, cared for, and accepted by their friends and relatives tend to recover more successfully, as do those treated with dignity by the criminal justice system (Murphy, 2001; Sales et al., 1984).

We will look at posttraumatic stress disorder in greater detail in Chapter 16. In the meantime, the current discussion helps clarify once again that stress is a very powerful force. Moreover, when it is overwhelming or dealt with ineffectively, it can totally disrupt our functioning and our lives.

Before You Go On

www.wiley.com/go/comer

What Do You Know?

19. What are some symptoms of posttraumatic stress disorder?
20. What factors put a person at heightened risk for developing posttraumatic stress disorder following a traumatic event?

What Do You Think?

Try to recall five events in your life or in the lives of your family members and friends that suggest a relationship between stress and illness. Having now read this chapter, how might you account for those events and relationships?

SCAN TO GET THE ANSWERS

Summary

What Is Stress?

LEARNING OBJECTIVE 1 Define stress and describe the ways in which people experience stress and the kinds of situations that typically cause stress.

- Stress is a state brought on by any situation that threatens or appears to threaten a person's sense of well-being, thus challenging the person's ability to cope. A situation that triggers the stress response is a stressor. A stressor may be acute (short term) or chronic (long term).
- People may experience stress as frustration, pressure, conflict, or danger.
- Kinds of stressors include daily hassles, life changes (which can be measured by use of the Social Readjustment Rating Scale), traumatic events, chronic negative situations, and special socio-cultural conditions.

Responding to Stress

LEARNING OBJECTIVE 2 Describe the physiological, emotional, and cognitive responses to stress, and explain how individual responses to stress differ.

- There are two main physiological pathways of stress: the sympathetic nervous system and the hypothalamic-pituitary-adrenal axis. Both lead to activation of the fight-or-flight response, which is an immediate response to a stressor.

- Hans Selye first described the effects of chronic stress, which he called the general adaptation syndrome (GAS). The syndrome has three stages: alarm, resistance, and exhaustion.
- Emotional responses to stress generally involve negative emotions. The more stress a person experiences, the more negative the emotions.
- Cognitive appraisal is an important element in responses to stress. Richard Lazarus identified two steps in this process: *primary appraisal*, in which people assess the severity of the stressor, and *secondary appraisal*, in which they evaluate how well they can cope with it.
- Individuals vary greatly in their responses to stress. Areas of difference include autonomic activity, explanatory style, personality, and availability of social support.

Coping with Stress

LEARNING OBJECTIVE 3 Discuss and evaluate several ways in which people cope with stress.

- Coping describes efforts to manage, reduce, or tolerate stress.
- Dealing with stress by lashing out at others, using defence mechanisms such as repression, and engaging in self-indulgent behaviours such as smoking or drinking alcohol, can be destructive when used in excess.
- More constructive coping strategies include directly confronting a stressor in hopes of changing the situation (*problem-focused coping*) and changing how you feel or think about the stressor to reduce its impact (*emotion-focused coping*).

Stress and Health

LEARNING OBJECTIVE 4 Explain how stress can cause physical illness, and discuss situations in which stress may be beneficial.

- Stress can increase risk for a number of health problems. People with *Type A* personalities are prone to stress and appear to be at greater risk for coronary heart disease than the more relaxed *Type B* personalities. Using the Social Readjustment Rating Scale, researchers have found that stress-producing life changes also increase the risk of illness.
- *Psychoimmunology* is an area of study that examines the links between stress, the immune system, and health.
- Severe stress may interfere with the activity of *lymphocytes*, a component of the immune system that helps the body to overcome invaders, such as bacteria and viruses.
- Stress-related biochemical changes in the body, such as changes in the activity of norepinephrine and cortisol, can eventually slow the functioning of the immune system.
- Behaviour, personality, and social support are additional factors affecting how much the immune system is slowed down by stress.
- Unlike *distress*, or negative stress, eustress offers benefits. Optimal levels of stress can promote the development of resilience and facilitate performance, especially for easy or moderately difficult tasks.

Posttraumatic Stress Disorder

LEARNING OBJECTIVE 5 Describe the symptoms and causes of posttraumatic stress disorder, and discuss some risk factors for developing it.

- Posttraumatic stress disorder is characterized by persistent, frightening thoughts or memories of a traumatic event, along with anxiety, depression, and other symptoms.
- Combat, natural disasters, and abuse and victimization are among the events most likely to cause posttraumatic stress disorder.
- Not everyone affected by unusual trauma develops posttraumatic stress disorder. Factors that affect the likelihood of developing the disorder include biological factors, personality factors, childhood experiences, and the availability of social support.

Key Terms

acute stressor 574
approach–approach conflict 576
approach–avoidance conflict 576
avoidance–avoidance conflict 576
chronic stressor 574
conflict 576
coping 596
daily hassles 578
distress 605
emotion-focused coping 600
eustress 605
frustration 575
general adaptation syndrome (GAS) 588
immune system 602
inoculation 605
life changes 580
lymphocytes 602
posttraumatic stress disorder (PTSD) 584
pressure 575
primary appraisal 590
problem-focused coping 600
psychoneuroimmunology 602
secondary appraisal 590
stress 574
stressor 574
traumatic events 584
Type A 595
Type B 595
Type C 595

TYING IT TOGETHER

The study of stress, coping, and health is closely connected to the study of all other areas of psychology. Throughout this chapter, we have stressed how stress interfaces with psychology's various subfields, including our highlighted sections on brain function, individual differences, abnormal functioning, and development. To remind you of how stress is tied to other psychology subfields and issues, we have selected some interesting points from throughout the chapter.

WHAT HAPPENS IN THE BRAIN?

- In the face of danger or stress, the brain and body respond with a fight-or-flight response, particularly among males.
- The brain reacts to danger or stress by both activating the sympathetic nervous system and setting in motion the HPA axis.
- The brains and bodies of stressed people may progress through three stages: alarm, resistance, and, if the danger continues too long, exhaustion.
- The release of norepinephrine and stress hormones can be helpful and protective when people experience short-term stress, but physically debilitating when people experience high, longer-term stress.

HOW WE DIFFER

- The brains and bodies of women may react to danger or stress with a "tend-and-befriend" response rather than a "fight-or-flight" response.
- People with highly reactive ANSs, pessimistic explanatory styles, Type A personality styles, or weak social supports display, on average, more intense stress reactions than other people.
- Optimists are more likely than pessimists to seek out social support during stressful events and to employ constructive coping techniques.
- Optimists, constructive copers, and resilient people tend to experience better immune system functioning and better health than other people.

WHEN THINGS GO WRONG

- People with high levels of hostility and certain other Type A personality characteristics are at greater risk for coronary heart disease.
- Significant life changes occurring over a limited period of time may contribute to a slowdown in immune system functioning and the onset of various medical problems.
- Almost 10 percent of Canadians experience posttraumatic stress disorder during their lifetimes. The disorder can occur at any age, even in childhood. Women are at least twice as likely as men to develop PTSD.
- People with generally abnormal stress hormone and norepinephrine reactions, weak social supports, or a general sense of helplessness in life appear more likely than other people to develop PTSD in the face of an extraordinary and traumatic event.

HOW WE DEVELOP

- As children move from 5 years old to 12 years old, physical events (e.g., getting sick) feel less stressful to them, while behavioural events (e.g., getting into trouble) and psychosocial events (e.g., fighting with friends) arouse more stress.
- The leading stressors for school-aged children include taking tests, having excessive homework, being bullied or made fun of, feeling left out, getting in trouble, and fighting with family members or friends.
- The leading stressors for college students include having to take multiple tests, enduring finals week, applying to graduate school, being a crime victim, having multiple assignments due on the same day, and breaking up with a boyfriend or girlfriend.
- Children who live in poverty or who experience assault, abuse, or catastrophe have an increased vulnerability to developing PTSD as adults.

Psychology Around Us

Reacting to and Dealing with Stress

Stressing Out

Video Lab Exercise

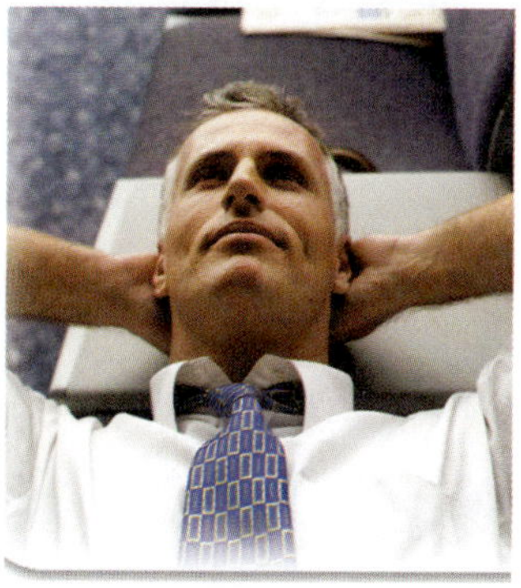

It's hard to fully identify our reactions during a stressful event or to identify our coping mechanisms. We are, after all, too busy feeling stressed and dealing with stressors at hand. In this video lab exercise, however, your involvement with stress will be "virtual," allowing you just enough psychological space to observe your reactions and coping mechanisms at the same time that you are experiencing stress.

While observing various stressful situations and placing yourself firmly in those situations, you will be required to identify the features of your stress reaction. You will also be guided down a decision tree during which you will decide how you would deal and cope with the pressures and frustrations you are confronting. While doing all this, you will compare your reactions and coping mechanisms to those of other people and categorize them using the terms laid out in the chapter. Along the way, you will learn a lot about your personal ways of feeling and coping with stress, and the merits or drawbacks of your approach.

As you are working on this online exercise, consider the following questions:

- What kind of stressors do people confront and what are the components of stress?
- Why do certain situations feel more stressful than others, and why do some people feel more stressed than others by a given situation?
- What's going on in the brain and body as we confront stressors?
- What are the various ways in which people try to manage, reduce, or tolerate stress? Do those approaches work?

CHAPTER 16

Psychological Disorders

CHAPTER OUTLINE

- Defining, Classifying, and Diagnosing Psychological Abnormality
- Models of Abnormality
- Mood Disorders
- Anxiety Disorders
- Schizophrenia
- Other Disorders

DEPRESSED AND LOST

Diane Markos, a 38-year-old single female, struggled with depression. Within a period of three months, she lost 16 pounds and she felt tired all the time. She withdrew from nearly all her usual social activities and she openly acknowledged thoughts of overdosing on pills. Previous psychotherapy and treatment with antidepressant medication had produced no improvement. She was referred to a psychologist for additional treatment.

Diane's changes over the three months occurred shortly after the breakup of a relationship she had been having with a man for approximately two years. She now saw herself as fat, unattractive, and doomed to be alone. Although she had never had a wide circle of friends, the past two years had seen her social contacts become even more limited. Other than the few evenings that she spent with her boyfriend, she had gradually managed to work herself into a life of all work and no play, and she was intensely lonely.

Diane lived alone and worked full-time as a pediatric nurse while pursuing a master's degree part-time in nursing. Although she was a straight-A student, she had numerous interpersonal difficulties with fellow students and instructors. Her relations with co-workers were similarly troubled. Although she had a reputation as a good staff nurse, she had never been able to hold supervisory positions for any length of time without interpersonal conflicts.

Diane's early family history provided some clues to the sources of her current difficulties. As the eldest of three children, she was frequently expected to play the role of caretaker for her younger siblings. She felt that her parents' love was contingent on her playing the role of "mother's little helper." She believed that her sister and brother had been allowed to lead a much more carefree childhood.

In short, Diane saw her past and present as an unhappy life of servitude, rejection, and failure. And she could envision no other scenario for her future. She felt quite hopeless, and her new therapist therefore considered her to be a serious suicidal risk (Spitzer et al., 1983).

Throughout this book we have examined the nature of behaviour and mental functioning, from sensations to memory to personality. Most of our discussions have looked at "typical" functioning. And indeed, our mental life and behaviour are fascinating and complex even when they do not go astray. However, as we have repeatedly observed, functioning often does go astray. We are immediately reminded of this as we read about Diane

Art and psychological disorders. Many of our greatest paintings focus on psychological dysfunction. Two of the most famous are *The Scream*, by Edvard Munch, which brings symptoms of anxiety and panic to life, and *Portrait of Dr. Gachet*, by Vincent van Gogh, about depression.

Markos. Most who hear about Diane would likely agree that her depressed mood, isolated behaviour, and negative thinking are far from functional.

You have already come across the leading psychological disorders while reading the *When Things Go Wrong* sections throughout this book. In this chapter, we will be looking even more closely at the topic of abnormal psychological functioning. First, we will see that although most people believe they know abnormal functioning when they see it, it is, in fact, a difficult concept to define. Then, we will explore the ways in which psychologists classify, assess, and explain the various kinds of abnormal functioning. In the next chapter, we will examine how mental health practitioners try to help the individuals whose behaviours, thoughts, or emotions are dysfunctional—individuals known as *clients* or *patients* when seen in mental health settings. ■

Defining, Classifying, and Diagnosing Psychological Abnormality

LEARNING OBJECTIVE 1

Identify the common features of most definitions of abnormal functioning, and describe how psychological disorders are classified and diagnosed.

Diane Markos's emotions, behaviours, and thoughts appear to be abnormal, the result of states sometimes referred to as *psychological dysfunctioning*, *psychopathology*, *psychological disorders*, or *mental disorders*. The field devoted to the scientific study of psychological disorders is usually called **abnormal psychology**.

abnormal psychology the scientific study of psychological disorders.

Abnormal psychological functioning is a wide-ranging problem, as indicated in **Figure 16-1**. It has been estimated that in a given year, at least 22 percent of the adults in Canada experience serious psychological disturbances (Health Canada, 2002). The numbers and rates in other countries are similar (Kessler et al., 2009, 2007, 2005).

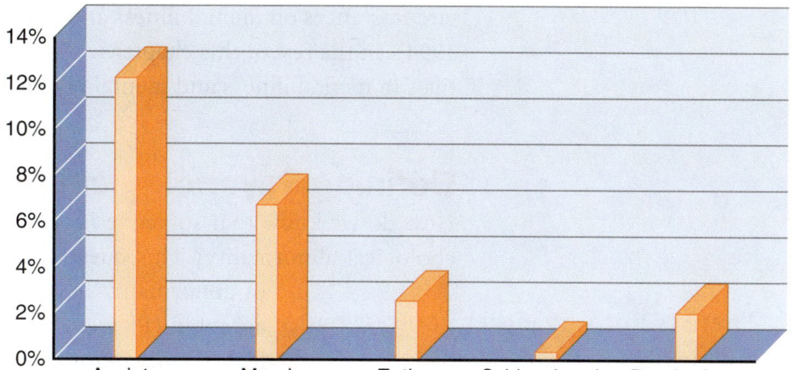

FIGURE 16-1 How many people are diagnosed with mental disorders each year? Nearly one-quarter of the adults in Canada each year experience symptoms that qualify for a diagnosis of at least one mental disorder (Health Canada, 2002).

Furthermore, many people go through periods of great tension, upset, or other forms of psychological discomfort in their lives. At such times, they experience at least some of the distress found in psychological disorders.

What are your thoughts regarding the causes of mental illness? Throughout history humans have speculated about the causes of the abnormal behaviours that seem to be a part of the human condition. In ancient times, there is evidence that "madness" was seen as a sign of demonic possession or of witch or warlock status. In many cases the "cures" were not particularly helpful to the individuals involved, given that they were intended to cast out evil spirits by burning or drowning. Many people did not survive their "cures." In more recent times, things were not much better for the mentally ill. A lack of understanding of the causes of mental illness led to a general belief that afflicted individuals were of inferior character, even less than human (Carson, Butcher, & Mineka, 2000). In the 1700s in the United Kingdom, those families that could afford it often hid their mentally ill relatives away and cared for them in isolation. Those that could not afford this had few options. Many "mad" people were left at places like Bethlehem Hospital in London, where care was minimal and the use of restraints typical. Tours through the hospital to see the mad people were a major source of revenue for the hospital (Reed, 1952).

While many argued for more humanitarian treatment for the mentally ill, reform movements did not really gain any ground until a clear connection was made between physical illness and madness. A condition called general paresis was well-known in medical circles (Beck, 2008). It usually afflicted males between 20 and 40 years of age. Initial symptoms included memory loss (short and long term), impairment of judgment, and decreases in motivation and language. Later symptoms included delusions and hallucinations, inappropriate moods and/or anger, and eventually full-blown dementia, seizures, and death. The symptoms progressed over a few months to at most one or two years and death was inevitable. When it was discovered that general paresis was the result of a sexually transmitted infection, syphilis, two things resulted (Brown, 2008). First, it was possible to treat syphilis and avoid general paresis; second, it clearly showed that the signs of madness could be symptoms of an underlying physical illness. This gave strong support to mental health reform movements such as *moral treatment*, which led to more humane treatment for the mentally ill (Gerard, 1998).

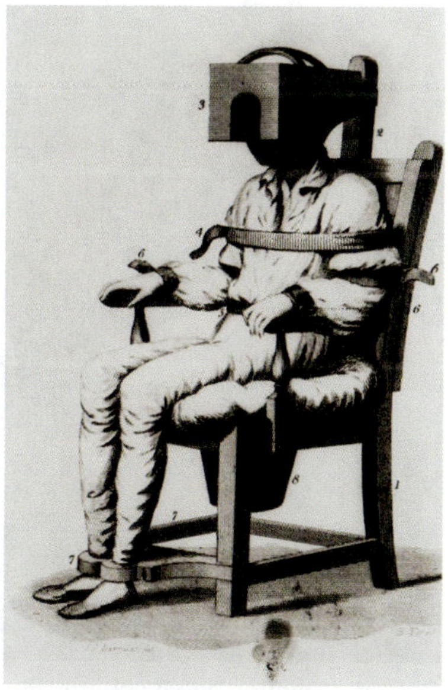

Early interventions. Benjamin Rush, a doctor and signatory to the American constitution, developed the tranquilizing chair shown here. It was believed to calm mental patients by reducing blood flow to the head.

The *medical model* approach to understanding and treating mental illness has been a major influence on our thinking and practices in assisting those struggling with mental illness over the past century. The medical model encourages a search for patterns in the symptoms people present with the goal of first identifying a syndrome—a collection of symptoms, like general paresis—that is recognized and about which one can make predictions. In the case of general paresis, the predictions made about prognosis were accurate but deadly. The next step involves a search for possible causes of the observed symptoms. Hopefully the identification of underlying causes also suggests viable treatments. As we will see later in this chapter and in the next chapter when we look at treatment approaches, the biological basis of the medical model approach to mental illness certainly has significant research support. We will also see, however, that there are serious concerns about the limitations of the medical model. By focusing on physical/biological causes, the medical model takes focus away from the possible roles played by psychological processes and socio-cultural circumstances on mental illness and mental health (Boorse, 1976; Sadler, Hulgus, & Agich, 1994). In the rest of this chapter we will provide you with a sense of these broader perspectives in mental illness and mental health.

Defining Psychological Abnormality

How do we know that someone is functioning abnormally? In other words, what is psychological abnormality? This question is not easy to answer. Although many definitions of abnormality have been proposed over the years, none is universally accepted (Pierre, 2010). Nevertheless, most of the definitions have key features in common, often called "the four Ds": deviance, distress, dysfunction, and danger.

> "There is nothing either good or bad, but thinking makes it so."
> —*William Shakespeare,* Hamlet

- *Deviance* Behaviour, thoughts, and emotions are considered abnormal when they differ from a society's ideas about proper functioning. Judgments of deviance and abnormality vary from society to society. A society that values competition and dominance may embrace aggressive behaviour, whereas one that emphasizes cooperation may consider such behaviour unacceptable and even abnormal (Eller, 2005). Moreover, a society's values may change over time, leading to a new societal view of what is psychologically abnormal. In Western society, for example, a woman's participation in athletics, academia, or business was considered unusual and even inappropriate 100 years ago (Matsumotto, 2001). Today, people in Western cultures value that behaviour.
- *Distress* To be considered abnormal, behaviours, ideas, or emotions usually must also cause distress or unhappiness. Diane Markos feels upset and burdened most of the time by her negative feelings and thoughts and the impact they are having on her life.
- *Dysfunction* Abnormal behaviour also tends to interfere with daily functioning, as opposed to behaviour that is simply eccentric but a part of a person's life. When behaviour upsets people so that they cannot take proper care of themselves, interact well with others, or work effectively, then it is referred to as abnormal. As we saw in the opening case, Diane's behaviours have contributed to social isolation, problems at work, and conflicts at school.
- *Danger* Some people with psychological dysfunctioning become dangerous to themselves or others. If, for example, individuals are consistently hostile or confused, they may put themselves, family members, or friends at risk. Recall that Diane Markos's thoughts of overdosing on pills led her therapist to consider her a serious suicide risk. It is important to note, however, that although danger is often cited as a feature of abnormal psychological functioning, research indicates that it is actually the exception rather than the rule (Hiday & Burns, 2010). Despite popular views, most people who are greatly troubled or even out of touch with reality pose no immediate danger to themselves or anyone else.

Does dysfunction equal abnormality? A Tibetan man set himself on fire to protest China's occupation of Tibet. In this context, such behaviour, while self-harming, does not, by itself, indicate that he is experiencing a psychological disorder.

As our discussion suggests, the current definition of abnormality depends heavily on social norms and values. At the same time, societies often have difficulties distinguishing between an abnormality that requires help and an eccentricity that should not be the concern of other people. We often see or hear about people who behave in ways we consider strange, such as an individual who lives alone with dozens of animals and avoids other people. The behaviour of such individuals is deviant, but unless it leads to clear distress and dysfunction, most clinicians would judge it to be eccentric rather than abnormal (Ernst, 2006).

PSYCHOLOGY AROUND US Just a Bit Different

An eccentric is a person who deviates from common behaviour patterns or displays odd or whimsical behaviour. Eccentrics do not typically suffer from psychological disorders, and eccentricity is not an absolute but a continuum. Whereas the unusual behaviour of persons with disorders is thrust upon them and usually causes them suffering, eccentricity is chosen freely and provides pleasure. In short, "Eccentrics know they're different and glory in it" (Weeks & James, 1995, p. 14).

Some very famous people were eccentrics. Writer James Joyce always carried a tiny pair of lady's bloomers, which he waved in the air to show approval. Emily Dickinson always wore white, never left her room, and hid her poems in tiny boxes. Benjamin Franklin took "air baths" for his health, sitting naked in front of an open window. United States President John Quincy Adams swam nude in the Potomac River each morning. Alexander Graham Bell covered the windows of his house to keep out the rays of the full moon. He also tried to teach his dog how to talk. Writer D. H. Lawrence enjoyed removing his clothes and climbing mulberry trees. Canadian Prime Minister William Lyon Mackenzie King regularly attended seances to consult the spirits of Leonardo da Vinci, Sir Wilfrid Laurier, his mother, and several of his Irish Terrier dogs (all named Pat, with the exception of one named Bob) (Stacey, 1985). Finally, Icelandic singing star Bjork was recently voted "most eccentric celebrity" in a large BBC survey (Brown, 2006).

Given such difficulties, how do psychologists determine which experiences constitute or do not constitute a psychological disorder, and how do they distinguish among various disorders? In large part, they rely upon *classification* and *diagnosis*.

Classifying and Diagnosing Psychological Disorders

A symptom is a physical, behavioural, or mental feature that helps indicate a condition, illness, or disorder. Fatigue is often a symptom of depression, for example. Similarly, poor concentration can be a symptom of anxiety, and hallucinations may indicate schizophrenia (Ernst, 2006). When certain symptoms regularly occur together and follow a particular course, clinicians agree that those symptoms make up a particular mental disorder. A list of such disorders, with descriptions of the symptoms and guidelines for determining when individuals should be assigned to the categories, is known as a *classification system*.

The classification system that is used by most countries throughout the world is the **International Classification of Diseases (ICD)**, published by the World Health Organization. The ICD is now in its tenth edition (ICD-10). The leading classification system in North America is the **Diagnostic and Statistical Manual of Mental Disorders (DSM)**, published by the American Psychiatric Association. The DSM has been revised several times since it was first published in 1952. The current version is called the DSM-IV Text Revision (DSM-IV-TR) (APA, 2000). It lists and describes the symptoms of approximately 400 mental disorders (see **Table 16-1** on the next page). A new version of the DSM, called DSM-5, is planned for publication in 2013 (Regier et al., 2011).

When clinicians decide that a person's symptoms fit the criteria for a particular disorder, they are making a **diagnosis**. Most clinicians in Canada use the DSM to help them diagnose their clients' problems. Assigning a diagnosis suggests that the client's pattern of dysfunction is basically the same as patterns displayed by many other people who show the same pattern of symptoms, has been researched in numerous studies, and has responded

International Classification of Diseases (ICD) the system used by most countries to classify psychological disorders; published by the World Health Organization and currently in its tenth edition (ICD-10).

Diagnostic and Statistical Manual of Mental Disorders (DSM) the leading classification system for psychological disorders in Canada; DSM-IV-TR is the current version.

diagnosis a clinician's determination that a person's cluster of symptoms represents a particular disorder.

TABLE 16-1 Disorders in DSM-IV-TR

Group	Description	Some Disorders Included in this Group
Disorders usually first diagnosed in infancy, childhood, and adolescence	Disorders in this group tend to emerge before adult life.	• Mental retardation • Autism • Asperger's disorder • Learning disorders • Attention-deficit hyperactivity disorder • Conduct disorder • Separation anxiety disorder
Cognitive disorders	These disorders are dominated by impairment in cognitive functioning.	• Alzheimer's disease • Huntington's disease
Substance-related disorders	These disorders are brought about by the use of substances that affect the central nervous system.	• Alcohol use disorders • Opioid use disorders • Amphetamine use disorders • Cocaine use disorders • Hallucinogen use disorders
Psychotic disorders	In this group of disorders, functioning deteriorates until the individual reaches a state of psychosis, or loss of contact with reality.	• Schizophrenia
Mood disorders	Disorders in this group are marked by severe disturbances of mood that cause people to feel extremely and inappropriately sad or elated for extended periods of time.	• Major depressive disorder • Bipolar disorders
Anxiety disorders	Anxiety is the predominant disturbance in this group of disorders.	• Generalized anxiety disorder • Social anxiety disorder • Phobias • Panic disorder • Obsessive-compulsive disorder • Posttraumatic stress disorder
Somatoform disorders	These disorders are marked by physical symptoms that apparently are caused primarily by psychological rather than physiological factors.	• Conversion disorder • Somatization disorder • Hypochondriasis • Body dysmorphic disorder
Dissociative disorders	These disorders are characterized by significant changes in consciousness, memory, identity, or perception without a clear physical cause.	• Dissociative amnesia • Dissociative fugue • Dissociative identity disorder (multiple personality disorder)
Eating disorders	People with these disorders display abnormal patterns of eating that significantly impair their functioning.	• Anorexia nervosa • Bulimia nervosa
Sexual disorders and gender identity disorder	These are disorders in sexual function, behaviour, or preferences.	• Sexual dysfunctions • Paraphilias • Gender identity disorder
Sleep disorders	People with these disorders display chronic sleep problems.	• Primary insomnia • Primary hypersomnia • Sleep-terror disorder • Sleepwalking disorder
Impulse-control disorders	People with these disorders are chronically unable to resist impulses, drives, or temptations to perform certain acts that are harmful to themselves or to others.	• Pathological gambling • Kleptomania • Pyromania • Intermittent explosive disorder
Psychological factors affecting medical condition	These disorders, also called psychophysiological disorders, result from an interaction of psychological and biological factors.	• Ulcer • Asthma • Hypertension • Coronary heart disease
Personality disorders	People with these disorders display pervasive, inflexible, enduring, and deviant personality traits and behaviours.	• Paranoid, schizoid, schizotypal antisocial, borderline, histrionic, narcissistic avoidant, dependent, and obsessive-compulsive personality disorders

to certain kinds of treatment. It helps to ensure that clinicians are acting in a consistent manner and that they are basing their clinical and research decisions on a set of clearly articulated and shared criteria. Clinicians can then apply what is generally known about the disorder to the client with whom they are working.

In addition to carefully comparing a client's symptoms to the specific lists of criteria for the mental disorders described in Table 16-1, clinicians gather data from their clients on each of five dimensions, or what the DSM-IV-TR calls *axes*.

Made for each other. A bride with real scorpions on her gown kisses her groom, who has a real centipede in his mouth. She holds the world record for staying in a cage with 3,400 scorpions for 32 days, he for staying with 1,000 centipedes for 28 days. Eccentric? Yes. Mentally disordered? Probably not.

- Axis I contains the detailed criteria for the principal disorders outlined in Table 16-1. These are usually the reason why the client is seeking assistance (e.g., panic attacks, depression, schizophrenia). The disorders on this axis have a recognizable point of onset (they have not always been there) and a realistic probability of recovery.
- Axis II includes criteria relating to longer-term disorders such as personality disorders, learning disabilities, and developmental disorders, any of which may complicate or influence the expression of any Axis I disorders that may be present.
- Axis III lists any medical or neurological problems that may be important to consider in relation to current or past psychiatric problems. For example, if a person has recurrent asthma attacks, this may be important to consider in relation to any indication of panic attacks on Axis I. Likewise, if a client is reporting delusions (false beliefs), it would be important to know if he is a long-term alcoholic before considering schizophrenia as an Axis I diagnosis. Prescription and recreational drugs used are also considered on this axis.
- Axis IV records any major psychosocial stressors the individual has faced recently, such as recent divorce, death of spouse, job loss, etc.
- Axis V uses a 0 to 100 point detailed general functioning scale that the clinician uses to assess the client's current level of functioning, as well as her highest level of functioning in the past year. This data is useful in making decisions about treatment options, and it also provides information about how quickly the symptoms have arisen and impacted the client's life.

Information gathered on all five axes is used to arrive at a diagnosis and to begin the process of treatment planning.

As we will see later in this chapter, based on her pattern of symptoms, Diane Markos would probably receive a diagnosis of a mood disorder: *major depressive disorder*. A clinician might also take note of the fact that Diane has avoided people and social relationships throughout her life, largely because she fears being judged, and might further assign her a diagnosis of *avoidant personality disorder*. When people qualify for two or more diagnoses, they are said to display **comorbidity**.

comorbidity the condition in which a person's symptoms qualify him for two or more diagnoses.

Although often quite useful, the DSM-IV-TR does not always lead to accurate diagnoses. When an incorrect diagnosis is made, various problems may unfold, including treatments that are misguided (Skodol, Williams, Spitzer, Gibbon, & Kass 1984). We discuss some of the risks of diagnosis for clients in the accompanying box, "Can Assessment and Diagnosis Cause Harm?"

Can Assessment and Diagnosis Cause Harm?

Although mental health terms such as anxiety, depression, and schizophrenia are commonly discussed in the media, public discourse, and even daily conversations, it turns out that accurate diagnoses of these and other psychological disorders are often elusive in the clinical field. It appears that even with effective assessment techniques and carefully researched classification categories, clinicians sometimes arrive at a wrong conclusion or diagnosis (Fernbach et al., 2011).

Indeed, studies have sometimes revealed enormous errors in assessment and diagnosis, particularly in hospitals (Mitchell, 2010). In a famous study, skilled clinicians were asked to reevaluate the diagnoses of 131 patients at a mental hospital in New York (Lipton & Simon, 1985). Whereas 89 of the patients had originally received a diagnosis of schizophrenia when they were hospitalized, only 16 received it upon reevaluation. And while 16 patients initially had been given a diagnosis of mood disorder, 50 received that label on reevaluation.

Beyond the possibility of misdiagnosis, the sheer act of classifying people can lead to unfortunate results. Diagnostic labels can, for example, become self-fulfilling prophecies. When people are diagnosed as having a mental disorder, others may view and react to them in ways that actually make them act more "sick" or disturbed. For example, if a child is labelled as bright, those who interact with that child may do so in ways that actually raise that child's level of academic performance (Rosenthal & Jackson, 1971). Similarly, being told someone is delusional (believing things that are not true) can undermine her credibility when others interact with her. Furthermore, our society attaches a stigma, or negative prejudice, to abnormality (Wahlen, 2007; Rosenberg, 2011). Stereotypic beliefs about what it means to have or to have had a mental disorder can mark or stigmatize those currently or previously struggling with a mental disorder. This can make it less likely that they will seek treatment for fear of the stigmatizing consequences (Barney et al., 2006). People with such labels may find it hard to get a job, particularly one with a high level of responsibility, or to be accepted socially (Roeloffs et al., 2003). In short, such labels may stick for a long time.

Given these problems, some clinicians have argued for doing away with assessment and diagnosis. Others, however, believe that classification and diagnosis are essential to understanding and treating people with psychological difficulties. They suggest that we must simply work to increase what is known about psychological disorders and improve assessment and diagnostic techniques (Corrigan, 2007; Ben-Zeev, Young, & Corrigan, 2010).

Before You Go On

www.wiley.com/go/comer

What Do You Know?

1. Define and explain the "four Ds" of abnormal behaviour.
2. What is the DSM-IV-TR?

What Do You Think?

We talked about the stigmatizing issues associated with being diagnosed with a mental disorder in this section. Think about people you know or people you heard about or read about who were described as "having a mental disorder." What sorts of things did you think or assume about them simply based on this knowledge? Any negative generalizations could become part of the stigma associated with mental disorders.

SCAN TO GET THE ANSWERS

Models of Abnormality

LEARNING OBJECTIVE 2

Describe the major models used by psychologists to explain abnormal functioning.

Over the course of our lives, each of us has developed a perspective that helps us make sense of the things other people say and do. The perspectives that scientists use to explain phenomena are known as *models*, or *paradigms* (Kuhn, 1962). You can think of a model or paradigm as a big idea about how things work. So, for example, a mechanistic paradigm builds on the idea that people are like complex machines and then when something goes

TABLE 16-2 Today's Leading Models of Abnormality

Approaches	Causes of Abnormal Functioning
Neuroscience Approaches	Structural or biochemical malfunctions in the brain
Psychodynamic Approaches	Unconscious conflicts often rooted in childhood
Cognitive-Behavioural Approaches	Abnormal behaviours acquired through a tightly interwoven mix of conditioning, modelling, and cognitive principles
Humanistic and Existential Approaches	Distorted views of self prevent personal growth or decision making
Socio-cultural Approaches	Societal, cultural, social, and family pressures or conflicts
Developmental Psychopathology Approach	Early risk factors combined with poor resilience throughout life stages

wrong it is probably because something in the mechanism is broken. To understand how a clinical theorist explains disorders, we must know which model shapes the theorist's view of abnormal functioning. Thus, in this section we will examine today's most influential clinical models—the neuroscience, psychodynamic, cognitive-behavioural, humanistic-existential, socio-cultural, and developmental psychopathology models (see **Table 16-2**). In the next chapter, we will see how these models inform treatment.

The Neuroscience Model

WHAT HAPPENS IN THE BRAIN?

Neuroscientists view abnormal behaviour as an illness brought about by a malfunctioning brain (Pliszka, 2003). As we have seen throughout the textbook, researchers have discovered connections between certain psychological or neurological disorders and problems in specific structures of the brain. One such disorder is Huntington's disease, a disorder marked by violent emotional outbursts, memory loss, suicidal thinking, involuntary body movements, and absurd beliefs. Huntington's disease has been linked to the loss of cells in the brain region called the *striatum* (Quarrell, 2008).

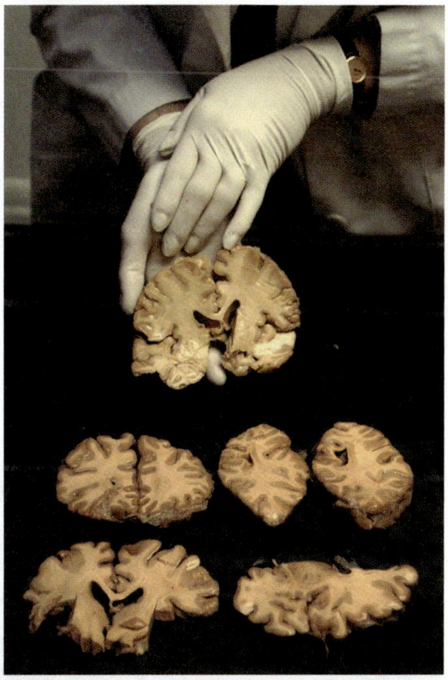

Extreme antisocial disorders and the brain. Forensic psychiatrist Helen Morrison displays slices of the brain of John Wayne Gacy, who murdered at least 33 boys and young men between 1972 and 1978. Post-mortem examinations have not revealed clear links between abnormal brain structure and the extreme antisocial patterns exhibited by Gacy and other serial killers.

Neuroscientists have also linked some mental disorders to deficient or excessive activity of different neurotransmitters. Depression, for example, seems to be related to insufficient activity of the neurotransmitters *norepinephrine* and *serotonin* (Beck & Alford, 2009).

In addition to focusing on neurotransmitters, neuroscience researchers have learned that mental disorders are sometimes related to abnormal hormonal activity in the body's endocrine system (see Chapter 4). Abnormal secretions of the hormone *cortisol*, for example, also have been tied to depression.

What causes these problems with brain anatomy and chemical functioning? Two factors have received particular attention from clinical theorists in recent years: *genetics* and *viral infections*.

Studies suggest that genetic inheritance plays a key role in mood disorders, schizophrenia, intellectual disability, Alzheimer's disease, and other mental disorders. It appears that in most cases, no single gene is responsible for a particular disorder (Oksenberg & Hauser, 2010). Instead, many genes combine to help produce our actions and reactions, both functional and dysfunctional. Moreover, as you have read throughout the textbook, the predispositions set up by such genes often will result in psychological disorders only when the individuals are also exposed to adverse environmental conditions.

Another possible source of abnormal brain structure or biochemical dyfunctioning appears to be viral infections. Some research suggests, for example, that schizophrenia, a disorder marked by hallucinations and other departures from reality, may be related to exposure to certain viruses before birth or during childhood (Fox, 2010). The studies suggest that a damaging virus may enter the brain of a fetus or young child and then remain quiet there until the individual reaches puberty or young adulthood. At that time, activated by hormonal changes, by another infection, or by stressful life events, the virus may set in motion the symptoms of schizophrenia. In addition to schizophrenia, research has sometimes linked viruses to mood and anxiety disorders (Fox, 2010).

Today, the neuroscience model of mental dysfunctioning is highly regarded, and researchers are constantly producing valuable new information about various psychological and neurological disorders (Pliszika, 2003). As you will see in Chapter 17, brain treatments such as psychotropic medications often bring great symptomatic relief where other approaches have failed.

At the same time, some proponents of this model seem to expect that biological factors and brain interventions alone can explain and treat all abnormal behaviours. This view neglects the complex interplay of biological and non-biological factors, such as a person's environmental experiences. Indeed, as we have seen throughout this book, the connections in our brains unfold partly in response to the experiences that we keep having throughout our lives, beginning in the womb.

The Cognitive-Behavioural Model

Cognitive-behavioural theorists propose that psychological disorders result largely from a combination of problematic learned behaviours and dysfunctional cognitive processes. According to this model, such behaviours and thinking processes interact with and mutually influence each other: people use their particular ways of thinking to explain their behaviours and the events in their lives, behaviours may lead to particular thoughts, various cognitions may trigger certain behaviours, and so on. Cognitive-behavioural theorists also view emotions and biological events as key variables. And, indeed, they seek to understand how these variables influence and interact with behaviours and cognitions to help bring about abnormal functioning. Both behavioural and cognitive principles lie at the centre of the model (Butler, Chapman, Forman, & Beck, 2006). Correspondingly, as you will see in Chapter 17, cognitive-behavioural therapists focus largely on behaviours and cognitions in their efforts to help people with psychological disorders by helping them to change their thoughts and behaviours.

To more fully understand the cognitive-behavioural model, it is useful to first examine the behavioural and cognitive components separately. In fact, at one time, the behavioural model stood alone, and behaviourists used only principles of conditioning and modelling to explain abnormal functioning. In the 1960s, however, a number of theorists began calling for a more cognitive-behavioural perspective (Beck, 1975). They argued that human beings engage in unseen *cognitive behaviours*, such as private thoughts and beliefs, which had largely been ignored by behaviourists up to that time. Moreover, they made the important observation that people's cognitions greatly influence and are influenced by their behaviours.

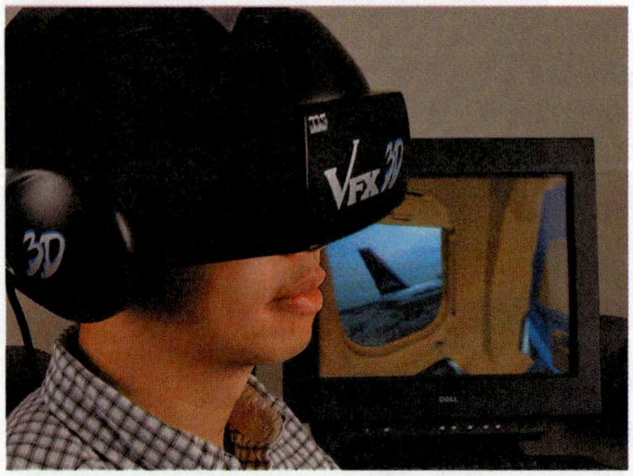

"Virtual" desensitization. Virtual reality software enables phobic clients to more vividly experience their feared objects and situations, such as flying in an airplane, during desensitization.

The Behavioural Perspective As we observed in Chapter 7, behavioural theorists use learning principles to explain human functioning. These principles focus on how the environment changes a person's behaviours. Many learned behaviours are constructive and help people to cope with daily challenges and lead satisfying lives. However, abnormal and undesirable behaviours also can be learned.

According to the behavioural perspective, abnormal behaviours are acquired by the same principles of learning as adaptive behaviours. As you saw in Chapter 7, for example, phobias may occur as a result of *classical conditioning* that pairs a previously neutral object with an unconditioned stimulus that creates fear.

Behavioural theorists also suggest that some of the many behaviours we learn through *operant conditioning* processes of reward and punishment are abnormal ones. For example, some people may learn to abuse alcohol and drugs because initially such behaviours brought feelings of calm, comfort, or pleasure. Others may develop or continue to display disordered eating patterns partly because of praise they receive for a thinner appearance (Wilson, 2011).

Modelling, in which we learn by observing others, can also lead to abnormality. Recall from Chapter 7 the famous study in which children learned from a model to behave aggressively toward a Bobo doll, an inflatable clown (Bandura, Ross, & Ross, 1963). Similarly, children of psychologically dysfunctional people may develop maladaptive reactions because of their exposure to the models presented by their parents (Luyckx et al., 2011).

One of the appeals of behavioural principles is that, in contrast to psychodynamic concepts, they can be tested in the laboratory. Experimenters have used the principles of conditioning to produce clinical symptoms in research participants, suggesting that psychological disorders may in fact develop through learning (Seligman, 1975). Moreover, as you will see in Chapter 17, research has indicated that behavioural interventions can be helpful to people with specific fears, compulsive behaviours, social deficits, intellectual disabilities, and a wide range of other problems (Wilson, 2011).

The Cognitive Perspective According to the cognitive perspective, when people display abnormal patterns of functioning, cognitive problems are to blame. Abnormal functioning can result from several such problems, including *maladaptive beliefs* and *illogical thinking processes*.

The pioneering clinical theorists Albert Ellis (1913–2007) and Aaron Beck proposed that each of us holds broad beliefs about ourselves and our world that help to guide us through life and determine our reactions to the situations we encounter. However, some people's beliefs are unjustified and unhelpful, leading them to act and react in ways that are inappropriate and that reduce their chances of happiness.

Such people may, for example, assume that they are failures if they are not loved or approved of by every person they know. An otherwise successful presentation in the classroom can, for example, make them sad or anxious because one listener seemed bored. Their problematic belief helps set the stage for a life hampered by tension and disappointment.

Think back to Diane Markos, whose case opened this chapter. She held some unjustified beliefs that may have left her particularly vulnerable to depression. Her case study further stated:

> *Many of her [problems] seemed to stem from underlying attitudes . . . such as: "If I care for others, they should/must care for me," or "If something good happens to me, I'll have to pay for it later with pain," or "People either love me or hate me"* (Spitzer et al., 1983, p. 129).

As you saw in Chapter 12, Beck also found that some people continuously think in illogical ways and keep drawing self-defeating and even pathological conclusions (Beck & Weishaar, 2011). He identified several illogical thinking processes—processes that turn out to be very common in depression and anxiety disorders. These include:

- *Selective perception*—seeing only the negative features of an event.
- *Magnification*—exaggerating the importance of undesirable events.
- *Overgeneralization*—drawing broad negative conclusions on the basis of a single insignificant event.

Diane Markos's therapist noted repeated examples of illogical thinking that helped predispose Diane to depressive reactions:

> *When she finally did get a B from her professor, she concluded that she had failed miserably. There was no recognition of any middle ground between total academic success and total academic failure. Moreover, she tended to magnify the importance of events like this as if they were an indictment of her as a total human being* (Spitzer et al., 1983, p. 129).

Cognition and psychological disorders. Social isolation and difficulties in problem solving can make it harder for people to get help with depression.

Anal personality? According to Freud, when an individual's neat and orderly personality is as extreme as this woman's (prior to storing her knickknacks, she organizes them carefully before her and enters each item on a computer file), fixation at the anal stage of development may be operating.

The cognitive perspective has appealed to a wide range of theorists. They embrace a viewpoint that sees *thought* as a key factor in both normal and abnormal behaviour. Research supports this appeal. Investigators have found that people with psychological disorders do, indeed, often display the kinds of beliefs and errors in thinking described in the cognitive theories (Sharf, 2012; Ellis, 2011).

The Psychodynamic Model

The psychodynamic model has its roots in Sigmund Freud's theories. As we observed in Chapter 13, psychodynamic theorists believe that a person's behaviour is determined largely by underlying psychological forces of which the person is not consciously aware. Abnormal behaviours or symptoms are viewed as the consequences of conflicts between these forces or as unconscious attempts to resolve conflicts and lessen painful inner turmoil.

Setting the stage. Object relations theorists believe that early relationships in life, particularly with parents, are a key to adult functioning.

As we pointed out in Chapter 13, Freud proposed that a child's environment may prevent his id, ego, and superego from maturing properly or interacting effectively. When that happens, the child can become *fixated*, or entrapped, at an early stage of development. Such fixations affect all subsequent development and may set in motion abnormal functioning.

Freud would have suggested that the family pressures Diane Markos experienced during her early years caused an imbalance of power among her id, ego, and superego. The demands she experienced forced her to put aside many of her own id needs and to act in a mature, ego-dominated manner beyond her years. Freud would certainly have looked upon such childhood pressures and deprivations as possible roots for her adult depression.

As we also saw in Chapter 13, several of Freud's colleagues disagreed with key aspects of his theories. As a result, there are now a number of different psychodynamic explanations for abnormal functioning (Sharf, 2012). For example, one group of psychodynamic theorists, called *object relations* theorists, believe people are motivated primarily by a need to establish relationships with others, known as *objects*. They propose that severe problems in early relationships may result in abnormal development and psychological problems (Blum, 2010; Kernberg, 2005, 1997).

Freud and his followers helped change the way abnormal functioning is viewed (Wolitzky, 2011). Primarily because of their work, many different kinds of theorists today look for explanations outside biological processes. In addition, Freud and his followers were the first practitioners to demonstrate the value of systematically applying theory and techniques to treatment. However, as you will see in Chapter 17, research has often failed to support the effectiveness of psychodynamic therapies (Prochaska & Norcross, 2010).

The Socio-cultural Model

HOW WE DIFFER

According to many theorists, abnormal behaviour is best understood in light of the social, cultural, and family forces brought to bear on an individual. The unique characteristics of a given society may create special stresses that heighten the likelihood of abnormal functioning in its members. Researchers have, for example, found relationships between abnormal functioning and factors such as widespread social change, socio-economic class membership, cultural background, social networks, and family systems (Cardemil et al., 2011; Tanaka-Matsumi, 2001).

PSYCHOLOGY AROUND US A Mother Knows

On a summer day in 1996, a 3-year-old boy climbed over a barrier at the Brookfield Zoo in Illinois and fell 24 feet onto the cement floor of the gorilla compound. An 8-year-old 160-pound gorilla named Binti-Jua picked up the child and cradled his limp body in her arms. The child's mother, fearing the worst, screamed out, "The gorilla's got my baby!" But Binti protected the boy as if he were her own. She held off the other gorillas, rocked him gently, and carried him to the entrance of the gorilla area, where rescue workers were waiting. Within hours, the incident was seen on video replays around the world, and Binti was being hailed for her maternal instincts (Hauser, 2000).

After this incident, clinical theorists had a field day interpreting the gorilla's gentle and nurturing care for the child, each within his or her preferred theory. Some psychodynamic theorists (and ethological theorists), for example, suggested that the gorilla was expressing the feelings of attachment and bonding already experienced with her own 17-month-old daughter. In contrast, some cognitive-behavioural theorists proposed that the gorilla may have been imitating the nurturing behaviour that she had observed in human models during her own infancy at the zoo. In the meantime, Binti-Jua returned to her quiet and predictable life at the zoo, and the boy fully recovered.

Social Change When a society undergoes major change, the mental health of its members can be greatly affected. Societies undergoing rapid urbanization, for example, usually show a rise in mental disorders. It is not yet known which features of urbanization—overcrowding, technological change, social isolation, migration, and so forth—are most to blame. Similarly, societies in the throes of economic depression often display rises in rates of clinical depression and suicide (SAMHSA, 2011; Hammer, 1993).

Socio-economic Class Studies by Jitender Sareen, Brian Cox, and Murray Stein at the University of Manitoba have found that rates of psychological abnormality, especially severe abnormality, are much higher among members of the lower socio-economic classes than among members of the higher ones (Sareen et al., 2011). Perhaps the special pressures of lower-class life help explain this relationship. Poverty is linked to many stressors, including high rates of crime, unemployment, overcrowding, and even homelessness, as well as inferior medical care and limited educational opportunities. Of course, other factors may account for this relationship. People who suffer from significant mental disorders may be less effective at work, earn less money, and, as a result, drift downward to settle in a lower socio-economic class (Read, 2010; Murali & Oyebode, 2010).

Cultural Factors Many theorists believe that human behaviour, including abnormal behaviour, is understood best by examining an individual's unique cultural context, including the values of that culture and the external pressures faced by members of the culture (Matsumoto & van de Vijer, 2011; Alegria et al., 2009, 2007, 2004). As we have seen throughout this book, the cultural groups that have been studied most often are ethnic and racial minority groups, along with economically disadvantaged persons, women, and homosexual individuals. Each of these groups faces special pressures in society that may help produce feelings of stress and, in some cases, abnormal functioning. Moreover, of course, membership in these groups often overlaps.

The economy and mental health. Thousands of Filipino job seekers line up at a 2009 job fair in Manila. Unemployment and poverty seem to be strongly linked to psychological dysfunction.

Researchers have learned that women are at least twice as likely as men to be diagnosed with depressive and anxiety disorders, although

Pressures of discrimination. In 2009, these dancers performed at an all-day anti-racism concert in Britain entitled "Love Music, Hate Racism." Multicultural research suggests that prejudice and discrimination can contribute to abnormal functioning.

this may be due partially to women being more likely than men to seek treatment (Essau et al., 2010). Suicide rates in the Canadian Aboriginal population are more than twice the sex-specific rates and three times the age-specific rates of non-Aboriginal Canadians (56.3 per year per 100,000 persons for Aboriginal males and 11.8 for Aboriginal females) (McNamee & Offord, 2003). Aboriginal Canadians also display extremely high alcoholism rates (Kirmayer, Brass, & Tait, 2000). In Canada, cultural origins, immigrant status, and Aboriginal status have been liked to varying rates of mental illness and adjustment issues (Kopec et al., 2001; MacMillan et al., 2008). Racial and sexual prejudice and related problems certainly may help explain these differences (Guimón, 2010).

A good example of the role of culture in mental health comes from the work of Michael Chandler (University of British Columbia) and Chris Lalonde (University of Victoria) that we discussed in Chapter 3. They examined the youth suicide rates among a large number of First Nations Band communities in British Columbia. In addition to suicide rates, Chandler and Lalonde gathered data regarding whether each band was or had been engaged in land claim negotiations with the provincial government, whether the band had taken control of education, fire, police, and child welfare services in their community, and whether there was a physical structure in the community dedicated to their cultural heritage. If all of these things were in place, the youth suicide rate was among the lowest in Canada; if none of them were in place, the rates were among the highest in Canada (Chandler, Lalonde, Sokol, & Hallet, 2003). Having a strong, culturally-rich context in which to develop clearly has a significant positive effect on individual mental health and identity development.

Another cultural factor that has received much attention from clinical researchers and therapists in recent years is religion. Researchers have studied possible links between religious faith and mental health and have learned that the two are often correlated. Studies have found, for example, that genuinely spiritual people tend, on average, to be less lonely, pessimistic, depressed, or anxious than other people (Day, 2010). Moreover, as we observed in Chapter 15, such individuals often seem to cope better with major life stressors and appear less likely to abuse drugs or to attempt suicide. Spirituality can be a source of comfort, hope, and meaning, which may at least partially account for this spirituality effect (Koenig, 2010).

Social Networks and Supports Many theorists focus on the social networks in which people operate, including their social and professional relationships. How well do they communicate with others? What kind of signals do they send to or receive from others? Researchers have often found ties between deficiencies in a person's social networks and that person's functioning (Gask et al., 2011; Vega et al., 2011; Paykel, 2006, 2003). They have observed, for example, that people who are isolated and lack social support or intimacy in their lives are more likely to become depressed when under stress and to remain depressed longer than are people with supportive spouses or warm friendships.

family systems theory a theory holding that each family has its own implicit rules, relationship structure, and communication patterns that shape the behaviour of the individual members.

Family Systems According to family systems theory, the family is a system of interacting parts—the family members—who interact with one another in consistent ways and follow rules unique to each family (Goldenberg & Goldenberg, 2011). Family systems theorists believe that the *structure* and *communication* patterns of certain families actually force individual members to react in ways that otherwise seem abnormal. If the members were to behave normally, they would severely strain the family's usual manner of operation and would actually increase their own and their family's turmoil.

Recall, for example, how Diane Markos's family was structured. She was required to be a third parent in the family, which in many ways deprived her of normal childhood experiences and emotions. In turn, she came to view her life as one of "servitude, rejection, and failure," and she experienced ongoing depression.

The Developmental Psychopathology Model

HOW WE DEVELOP

As you read in Chapter 3, developmental psychopathology theorists are interested in how psychological disorders evolve, based on both genetics and early childhood experiences. They also try to understand how those early problematic patterns affect functioning as individuals move through later life stages (Cicchetti, 2010; Santostefano, 2010; Hinshaw, 2008). Developmental psychopathologists compare and contrast abnormal behaviour patterns with more typical ones, attempting to identify risk factors—biological and environmental factors that contribute to negative outcomes. In addition, they seek to identify other factors that can help children avoid or recover from such outcomes.

developmental psychopathology the study of how problem behaviours evolve as a function of a person's genes and early experiences and how these early issues affect the person at later life stages.

risk factors biological and environmental factors that contribute to problem outcomes.

Like other kinds of developmental psychologists, developmental psychopathologists hold that behaviour can be analyzed in a variety of ways. A full accounting of how individuals get off-track (or stay on-track) requires looking at how genetics, early environmental influences, and their own psychological processes all collaborate to form their current pattern and functioning.

Developmental psychologists have contributed two concepts to the field of psychology: *equifinality* and *multifinality* (Fanti & Henrich, 2010; Mitchell et al., 2004). The concept of equifinality holds that individuals can start out from all sorts of different places and yet, through their life experiences, wind up functioning (or dysfunctioning) in similar ways. Multifinality follows the opposite principle. It suggests that children can start from the same point and wind up in any number of different psychological places.

equifinality the idea that different children can start from different points and wind up at the same outcome.

multifinality the idea that children can start from the same point and wind up at any number of different outcomes.

Let's apply these two concepts to *conduct disorder*, a disorder of childhood and adolescence characterized by repeated violations of others' rights, displays of aggression, and destructive behaviour. It appears that various roads may lead to the development of a conduct disorder during adolescence. A child with this disorder may have been born with a difficult temperament, experienced poor parenting, or developed poor social skills, for example (Litschge, Vaughn, & McCrea, 2010). As suggested by the notion of equifinality, regardless of which set of those risk factors is at play, the outcome is often similar.

At the same time, multifinality assures us that not every difficult baby and not every baby with ineffective parents will wind up with a conduct disorder. The vast majority will wind up with no pathology at all. Developmental psychopathologists are very interested in the biological, psychological, or environmental events that help buffer against or negate the impact of risk factors—events that help produce resilience, an ability to recover from or avoid the serious effects of negative circumstances (Dudley et al., 2011; Flouri et al., 2011; Hudziak & Bartels, 2008). In short, according to this viewpoint, it is just as critical to understand what goes right as it is to understand what goes wrong.

resilience the ability to recover from or avoid the serious effects of negative circumstances.

Before You Go On

www.wiley.com/go/comer

What Do You Know?

3. What are the major models used by psychologists to explain abnormal functioning?
4. What major types of brain problems are linked to abnormal functioning?
5. In the view of cognitive-behavioural theorists, what kinds of problems can lead to abnormal functioning?
6. How are the humanistic and existential models similar, and how do they differ?
7. What social and cultural factors have been found to be related to abnormal functioning?

SCAN TO GET THE ANSWERS

What Do You Think?

How would you describe your personal model for explaining why people behave as they do?

Mood Disorders

LEARNING OBJECTIVE 3

Describe and differentiate major depressive disorder and bipolar disorder.

As you saw earlier, there are more than 400 different disorders listed in DSM-IV-TR. In the rest of this chapter, we will look at some of the disorders that are particularly common and that have received considerable study. We begin with mood disorders, which you first encountered in Chapter 15.

Most people's moods come and go. Their feelings of joy or sadness are understandable reactions to daily events and do not affect their lives greatly. The moods of people with mood disorders, in contrast, tend to last a long time. As in Diane Markos's case, the moods colour all their interactions with the world and interfere with normal functioning.

Depression and mania are the key features in mood disorders. **Depression** is a low, sad state in which life seems dark and its challenges seem overwhelming. **Mania**, the opposite of depression, is a state of breathless euphoria, or at least frenzied energy, in which people may have an exaggerated belief that the world is theirs for the taking. Most people with a mood disorder suffer only from depression, a pattern found in **major depressive disorder** or in a less disabling but chronic form of depression called *dysthymic disorder*. Others experience periods of mania that alternate or intermix with periods of depression, a pattern called **bipolar disorder** in its severe form and *cyclothymic disorder* in a less severe but chronic form (Beck & Alford, 2009).

depression a persistent sad state in which life seems dark and its challenges overwhelming.

mania a persistent state of euphoria or frenzied energy.

major depressive disorder a disorder characterized by a depressed mood that is significantly disabling and is not caused by such factors as drugs or a general medical condition.

bipolar disorder a mood disorder in which periods of mania alternate with periods of depression.

Major Depressive Disorder

People more unhappy than usual often say they are "depressed." Typically, they are responding to sad events, fatigue, or unhappy thoughts. This use of the term confuses a perfectly normal mood swing with a clinical syndrome. All of us experience dejection from time to time. Only some experience major depressive disorder. This disorder brings severe and long-lasting psychological pain that may intensify as time goes by. Those who suffer from it may become unable to carry out the simplest of life's activities. Some even try to end their lives.

It is estimated that nearly 5 percent of adults in Canada are diagnosed with major depressive disorder in any given year. Another 3 percent of adults are diagnosed with mild forms of the disorder (Health Canada, 2002). Women are at least twice as likely as men to be diagnosed with depression. It is important to note that this difference between men's and women's rates of depression could also reflect a number of factors, such as: women's greater tendency to seek assistance; men's tendency to deny or pay less attention to their feelings; and women's greater likelihood of carrying the stress of multiple roles as parent, spouse, and employee. These factors can lead to differential diagnosis rates without telling us about the actual underlying rates of disorders like depression among men and women (Nolen-Hoeksema, 2001). Approximately half of people with this disorder recover within six weeks, and 90 percent recover within a year, some without treatment (Kessler, 2002). However, most of them have at least one other episode of depression later in their lives (Taube-Schiff & Lau, 2008).

Depression is the most common health-care topic searched for on the Internet each year (19 percent of searches), followed by allergies/sinuses (16 percent), bipolar disorder (14 percent), and arthritis/rheumatism (10 percent).

The DSM diagnostic criteria for a Major Depressive Episode are listed in **Table 16-3**. Due to space limitations and concerns over currency, as some diagnostic criteria are under review and revision, we have not included the DSM diagnostic criteria for all the disorders we discuss in this chapter. If you are interested in reviewing the diagnostic criteria for other disorders, run a web search using the following criteria: DSM Criteria for "name of disorder." This search will return many websites showing the DSM diagnostic criteria for the disorder in question. Make sure that the site you choose to view clearly states that the criteria it displays are from the DSM (the most recent version is the DSM-IV-TR) and that the site

TABLE 16-3 The Diagnostic Criteria for a Major Depressive Episode from the DSM-IV

Major Depressive Episode
A. Five (or more) of the following symptoms have been present during the same two-week period and represent a change from previous functioning; at least one of the symptoms is either (1) depressed mood or (2) loss of interest or pleasure.
Note: Do not include symptoms that are clearly due to a general medical condition, or mood-incongruent delusions or hallucinations.
(1) depressed mood most of the day, nearly every day, as indicated by either subjective report (e.g., feels sad or empty) or observation made by others (e.g., appears tearful) *Note:* In children and adolescents, can be irritable mood.
(2) markedly diminished interest or pleasure in all, or almost all, activities most of the day, nearly every day (as indicated by either subjective account or observation made by others)
(3) significant weight loss when not dieting or weight gain (e.g., a change of more than 5% of body weight in a month), or decrease or increase in appetite nearly every day *Note:* In children, consider failure to make expected weight gains.
(4) insomnia or hypersomnia nearly every day
(5) psychomotor agitation or retardation nearly every day (observable by others, not merely subjective feelings of restlessness or being slowed down)
(6) fatigue or loss of energy nearly every day
(7) feelings of worthlessness or excessive or inappropriate guilt (which may be delusional) nearly every day (not merely self-reproach or guilt about being sick)
(8) diminished ability to think or concentrate, or indecisiveness, nearly every day (either by subjective account or as observed by others)
(9) recurrent thoughts of death (not just fear of dying), recurrent suicidal ideation without a specific plan, or a suicide attempt or a specific plan for committing suicide

Source: (APA, 2000)

references the DSM as the source of the material. That way you can be reasonably confident that the criteria being shown are accurate.

As we saw in the case of Diane Markos, severe depression has many symptoms other than sadness, and the symptoms often feed into one another. The symptoms span five areas of functioning: emotional, motivational, behavioural, cognitive, and physical.

Feeling blue. Feeling sad is not necessarily depression. Major depressive disorder brings severe and long-lasting psychological pain that may intensify as time goes by.

Characteristics of Depression Most people who are depressed feel sad and dejected. They describe themselves as "miserable" and "empty." They often lose the desire to participate in their usual activities. Almost all report a lack of drive, initiative, and spontaneity. Many depressed people become uninterested in life or wish to die; others wish that they could kill themselves, and some actually try. Suicide represents the ultimate escape from life's activities and pressures. It has been estimated that between 6 and 16 percent of people who suffer from severe depression commit suicide (Taube-Schiff & Lau, 2008).

Depressed people are usually less active and less productive than other people. They spend more time alone and may stay in bed for long periods. They may also move and even speak more slowly than others. Most hold extremely negative views of themselves. They consider themselves inadequate, undesirable, inferior, and perhaps evil. They also blame themselves for nearly every unfortunate event. Another cognitive symptom of depression is pessimism. Sufferers are usually convinced that nothing will ever improve, and they feel helpless to change any aspect of their lives (Mitchell, 2010; Joiner, 2002). Finally, people who are depressed often have physical ailments such as headaches, indigestion, constipation, dizzy spells, and general pain. They may also have disturbances in appetite and sleep (Mitchell, 2010; Neckelmann et al., 2007).

Post-secondary students who seek and receive negative feedback from their roommates feel more depressed than students who do not receive such feedback.

Major depressive disorders often seem to be triggered by stressful events (Brown, 2010; Hammen et al., 2009). In fact, researchers have found that depressed people experience a greater number of stressful life events during the month just before the onset of a depressive episode than do other people during the same period of time (Monroe & Hadjiyannakis, 2002).

Today's leading explanations for major depressive disorder point to either neuroscience, psychological, or socio-cultural factors. Many theorists believe that the various explanations should be combined to more fully understand people with this disorder (Beck & Alford, 2009). We will examine them separately here so that each perspective is clear.

How Do Neuroscientists Explain Depression? WHAT HAPPENS IN THE BRAIN? If people inherit a predisposition to major depressive disorder, we would expect a particularly large number of cases among the close relatives of depressed persons. Twin studies support this expectation (Richard & Lyness, 2006). One investigation, for example, looked at nearly 200 pairs of twins. When a *monozygotic* (*identical*) twin had depression, there was a 46 percent chance that the other twin would have the same disorder. In contrast, when a *dizygotic* (*fraternal*) twin had depression, the other twin had only a 20 percent chance of developing the disorder (McGuffin et al., 1996).

If genetic influences are indeed at work in unipolar depression, what biological factors might ultimately produce the disorder? Researchers have focused most often on abnormal neurotransmitter activity—namely, low activity of norepinephrine and serotonin (Goldstein et al., 2011).

In the 1950s, several pieces of evidence began to point to these neurotransmitters. First, medical researchers discovered that several medications for high blood pressure often caused depression (Ayd, 1956). As it turned out, some of these medications lowered norepinephrine activity and others lowered serotonin. A second piece of evidence was the discovery of the first truly effective antidepressant drugs. These drugs were discovered almost by accident. In 1956, Roland Kuhn, a psychiatrist working in Switzerland, was administering a new trial drug to patients with schizophrenia. The drug did not seem to work, and in fact made symptoms worse in some patients. Kuhn noticed, however, that those patients also with comorbid symptoms of depression showed improvement in their depressive symptoms on the drug. Kuhn tried the drug with patients who were only showing depressive symptoms, and many of them improved dramatically (Cahn, 2006). With these initial observations in hand, researchers soon learned that they could relieve depression by increasing either norepinephrine or serotonin activity (Bunney & Davis, 1965; Schildkraut, 1965).

An enormous number of studies over the past half-century have further supported the notion that major depressive disorder is related to low activity of norepinephrine and/or serotonin. Neuroscience research has also indicated that the body's endocrine system may play a role in depression. People with depression have been found to have high levels of cortisol, the hormone released by the adrenal glands during times of stress (Neumeister et al., 2005). This relationship is not all that surprising, given that stressful events often seem to trigger depression.

How Do Cognitive-Behavioural Theorists Explain Depression? Cognitive-behavioural theorists believe that people with severe depression acquire distinctly negative behaviours and think in dysfunctional ways that help cause and lock in their disorders (Zuckerman, 2011). The two most influential cognitive-behavioural explanations centre on the phenomenon of learned helplessness and on the power of negative thinking.

Learned Helplessness Since the mid-1960s, psychologist Martin Seligman has been developing the *learned helplessness* theory of depression (Gillham et al., 2011; Yu & Seligman, 2002, 2002; Seligman 1992, 1975). It holds that people become depressed when they think (1) that they no longer have control over the rewards and punishments in their lives, and (2) that they themselves are responsible for this helpless state.

Seligman's theory first began to take shape when he was working with laboratory dogs. He found that when dogs were given inescapable shocks, they came to learn that that they have no control over the unpleasant punishments (shocks) in their lives. That is, they learned

PSYCHOLOGY AROUND US Losing Control: Learning to Feel Helpless

Mary was 25 years old and had just begun her senior year in college. . . . Asked to recount how her life had been going recently, Mary began to weep. Sobbing, she said that for the last year or so she felt she was losing control of her life and that recent stresses (starting school again, friction with her boyfriend) had left her feeling worthless and frightened. Because of a gradual deterioration in her vision, she was now forced to wear glasses all day. "The glasses make me look terrible," she said, and "I don't look people in the eye much any more." Also, to her dismay, Mary had gained 20 pounds in the past year. She viewed herself as overweight and unattractive. At times she was convinced that with enough money to buy contact lenses and enough time to exercise she could cast off her depression; at other times she believed nothing would help. . . . Mary saw her life deteriorating in other spheres, as well. She felt overwhelmed by schoolwork and, for the first time in her life, was on academic probation. . . . In addition to her dissatisfaction with her appearance and her fears about her academic future, Mary complained of a lack of friends. Her social network consisted solely of her boyfriend, with whom she was living. Although there were times she experienced this relationship as almost unbearably frustrating, she felt helpless to change it and was pessimistic about its permanence. . . .

(Spitzer et al., 1983, pp. 122–123)

that they were helpless to do anything to change negative situations. You may recall from Chapter 7 that this phenomenon is called *learned helplessness*. Moreover, when later placed in a new situation where they could in fact escape shocks and control their fate, the dogs continued to act as if they were generally helpless. They would just lie in their experimental boxes and accept the shocks. Seligman noted that the effects of learned helplessness greatly resemble the symptoms of human depression, and he proposed that people become depressed after developing a general belief that they have no control over the rewards and punishments in their lives (Seligman & Maier, 1967; Seligman, 1975).

The learned helplessness explanation of depression has been revised somewhat over the past two decades. According to a newer version of the theory, the *attribution-helplessness theory*, when people view events to be beyond their control, they ask themselves why this is so (Taube-Schiff & Lau, 2008; Abramson et al., 2002, 1989, 1978). If they attribute their present lack of control to some *internal* cause (some deficiency in themselves) that is both *global* (a deficiency that is wide-ranging) and *stable* (a deficiency that will continue for a long time), they may well feel helpless to prevent future negative outcomes and they may experience depression. If they make other kinds of attributions, this reaction is unlikely.

Consider a university student whose girlfriend breaks up with him. If he attributes this loss of control to an internal cause that is both global and stable—"It's my fault [internal]; I ruin everything I touch [global], and I always will [stable]"—he then has reason to expect loss of control in the future and may generally experience a sense of helplessness. According to the learned helplessness view, he is a prime candidate for depression. If the student instead attributes the breakup to causes that are more specific ("The way I've behaved the past couple of weeks blew this relationship"), unstable ("I don't usually act like that"), or external ("She never did know what she wanted"), he might not expect to lose control again and would probably not experience helplessness and depression.

Breaking up is hard to do. Having your significant other break up with you can be devastating. According to the attribution-helplessness theory, if a person attributes the break-up to their own internal shortcomings rather than to more specific events, the break-up could cause depression.

Negative Thinking Like Seligman, Aaron Beck believes that negative thinking plays a key role in depression. Beck, however, points to *dysfunctional attitudes*, *errors in thinking*, the *cognitive triad*, and *automatic thoughts* as the keys to the clinical syndrome (Beck & Weishaar, 2011; Beck, 2002, 1991, 1967).

As you read earlier, Beck believes that some people develop *dysfunctional attitudes*, such as "My general worth is tied to every task I perform," and "If I fail, others will feel repelled by me." In addition, as you also observed, Beck believes that those same people often commit errors in their thinking, such as arbitrary inferences or magnification.

cognitive triad a pattern of thinking in which individuals repeatedly interpret their experiences, themselves, and their futures in negative ways that lead them to feel depressed.

automatic thoughts specific upsetting thoughts that arise unbidden.

According to Beck, this steady onslaught of dysfunctional attitudes and illogical thinking eventually triggers extended rounds of negative thinking in these individuals. The thinking typically takes three forms and is therefore termed the **cognitive triad**: the individuals repeatedly interpret (1) *their experiences*, (2) *themselves*, and (3) *their futures* in negative ways that lead them to feel depressed. That is, depressed people interpret their experiences as burdens that repeatedly defeat or deprive them. They view themselves as undesirable, worthless, and inadequate. And they regularly see the future as bleak, as seen in **Figure 16-2**.

Finally, depressed people experience **automatic thoughts**, a steady train of unpleasant thoughts that keep suggesting to them that they are inadequate and that their situation is hopeless. Beck labels these thoughts "automatic" because they seem to just happen, as if by reflex. In the course of only a few hours, depressed people may be visited by hundreds of such thoughts: "I'm worthless. . . . I let everyone down. . . . Everyone hates me. . . . My responsibilities are overwhelming. . . . I've failed as a parent. . . . I'm stupid. . . . Everything is difficult for me. . . . Things will never change."

While it is not entirely clear whether this sort of negative thinking is a cause or a symptom of depression, Beck's explanation has received considerable research support. Several studies confirm, for example, that depressed people hold dysfunctional attitudes, and the more of these attitudes they hold, the more depressed they tend to be (Evans et al., 2005; Whisman & McGarvey, 1995). Moreover, other research has found the cognitive triad at work in depressed people. In various studies, for example, depressed participants have recalled unpleasant experiences more readily than positive ones, rated themselves lower than non-depressed subjects do, and selected pessimistic statements in storytelling tests (for example, "I expect my plans will fail") (Ridout et al., 2003).

How Do Socio-cultural Theorists Explain Depression? Socio-cultural theorists propose that social forces play an important role in the development of major depressive disorder. Their belief is supported by the finding, discussed earlier, that depression is often triggered by outside stressors. In addition, the unavailability of social support seems to play a role in the onset of depression (Brown, 2010; Doss et al., 2008). People who are separated or divorced display three times the depression rate of married or widowed persons, and double the rate of people who have never been married (Weissman et al., 1991). In some cases, a spouse's depression may contribute to a separation or divorce, but more often the interpersonal conflicts and lack of mutual support found in troubled relationships seem to lead to depression (Highet et al., 2005).

People whose lives are isolated and without intimacy seem particularly likely to become depressed at times of stress (Brown, 2010; Kendler et al., 2005). Some highly publicized studies conducted in England several decades ago showed that women who had three or more young children, lacked a close confidante, and had no outside employment were more likely than other women to become depressed after experiencing stressful life events (Brown, 2010; Brown et al., 2005; Brown & Harris, 1978). Studies have also found that depressed people who lack social support remain depressed longer than those who have a supportive spouse or warm friendships (Rao, Hammen, & Poland, 2010; Cowan et al., 2007).

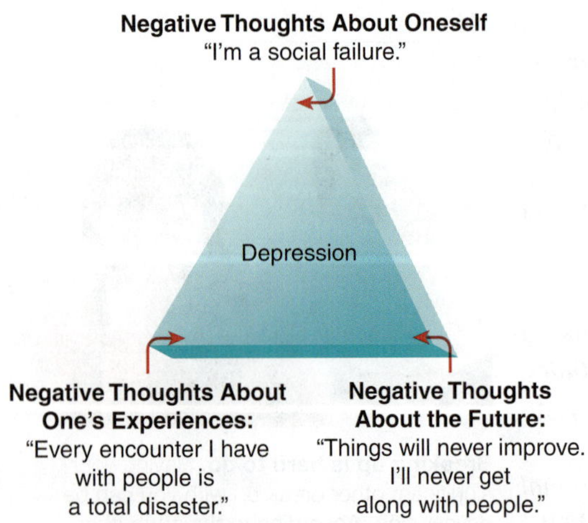

FIGURE 16-2 Cognitive triad of depression. According to Aaron Beck, a regular pattern of these three types of negative thoughts increases vulnerability to depression.

Bipolar Disorders

People with a *bipolar disorder* often describe their lives as an emotional roller coaster. They shift back and forth between extreme moods, experiencing both the lows of depression and the highs of mania. Unlike people sunk in the gloom of depression, those in a state of *mania* experience dramatic and inappropriate rises in mood. The symptoms of mania span the same areas of functioning—emotional, motivational, behavioural, cognitive, and physical—as those of depression, but mania affects these areas in an opposite way.

In mania, people have active, powerful emotions in search of an outlet. Their mood of euphoric joy or extreme agitation is out of all proportion to the actual events in the person's life. In the motivational realm, people with mania seem to want constant excitement, involvement, and companionship. Correspondingly, they move quickly and talk rapidly and loudly.

Top of the world. During manic periods, some people feel invincible . . . like there is nothing they can't succeed at or do.

In the cognitive realm, individuals with mania usually show poor judgment and planning, as if they feel too good or move too fast to consider possible pitfalls. Filled with optimism, they rarely listen when others try to slow them down, interrupt their buying sprees, or prevent them from investing money unwisely. They may also hold an inflated opinion of themselves, and sometimes their self-esteem approaches grandiosity (for example, an exaggerated belief in one's personal importance). Finally, in the physical realm, the individuals feel remarkably energetic. They typically get little sleep, yet feel and act wide awake.

Surveys from around the world indicate that between 1 and 2.6 percent of all adults suffer from a bipolar disorder at any given time (Merikangas et al., 2007). According to most studies, bipolar disorders are equally common in women and men and among all socio-economic classes and ethnic groups.

George Frederic Handel wrote his Messiah in less than a month during a manic episode.

Throughout the first half of the twentieth century, the search for the causes of bipolar disorders made little progress. More recently, neuroscience research has produced some promising clues. There is now strong evidence that a combination of gene abnormalities play a major role in the development of bipolar disorders (Grieco & Edwards, 2010; Schulze & McMahon, 2009). There is also evidence that the disorders may be linked to irregularities in the electrically-charged ions that enable neurons to fire and transmit messages (El-Mallakh, 2004).

Although genes and biological factors appear to play key roles, there is growing evidence that stress and certain kinds of environmental events also must occur in order for episodes of bipolar disorder to unfold. Some studies suggest, for example, that major stress must combine with an individual's genetic predisposition for episodes of bipolar disorder to occur, particularly in early (the first few) episodes (Post & Miklowitz, 2010). Still other studies suggest that certain kinds of positive events (ones involving the attainment of or striving toward goals) are needed for bipolar disorders to unfold in biologically predisposed people. The idea is that individuals predisposed to develop bipolar disorder overreact to the arousal produced by goal-related events and develop the mania-related symptoms of bipolar disorder (Alloy et al., 2011; Bender & Alloy, 2011; Alloy & Abramson, 2010).

Before You Go On

www.wiley.com/go/comer

What Do You Know?

8. What is learned helplessness, and what is its role in depression?
9. What is the cognitive triad?
10. How does bipolar disorder differ from major depression?

What Do You Think?

Which of the explanations described in this section do you think best explains depression? Why?

SCAN TO GET THE ANSWERS

Anxiety Disorders

LEARNING OBJECTIVE 4

Describe the various types of anxiety disorders, and explain some causes of these disorders.

Read through the following example of a conversation between a patient named Bob and his doctor, paying particular attention to what Bob says about his feeling of anxiety.

Bob: *It's been an awful month. I can't seem to do anything. I don't know whether I'm coming or going. I'm afraid I'm going crazy or something.*

Doctor: *What makes you think that?*

Bob: *I can't concentrate. My boss tells me to do something and I start to do it, but before I've taken five steps I don't know what I started out to do. I get dizzy and I can feel my heart beating and everything looks like it's shimmering or far away from me or something—it's unbelievable.*

Doctor: *What thoughts come to mind when you're feeling like this?*

Bob: *I just think, "Oh, Christ, my heart is really beating, my head is swimming, my ears are ringing—I'm either going to die or go crazy."*

Doctor: *What happens then?*

Bob: *Well, it doesn't last more than a few seconds, I mean that intense feeling. I come back down to earth, but then I'm worrying what's the matter with me all the time, or checking my pulse to see how fast it's going, or feeling my palms to see if they're sweating.*

Doctor: *Can others see what you're going through?*

Bob: *You know, I doubt it. I hide it. I haven't been seeing my friends. You know, they say "Let's stop for a beer" or something after work and I give them some excuse—you know, like I have to do something around the house or with my car. I'm not with them when I'm with them anyway—I'm just sitting there worrying. My friend Pat said I was frowning all the time. So, anyway, I just go home and turn on the TV or pick up the sports page, but I can't really get into that either.*

Feeling anxious. Anxiety is a normal part of life—everyone feels anxious sometimes. Anxiety becomes a problem when it interferes with a person's ability to participate fully in society.

Some people suffer such disabling levels of fear and anxiety that they cannot lead a normal life. Their discomfort is too severe or too frequent; it lasts too long; or it is triggered too easily. These people are said to have an *anxiety disorder*. Anxiety disorders are collectively the most common mental disorders in Canada. In any given year, about 12 percent of the adult population suffer from one or another of the anxiety disorders identified by DSM-IV (Health Canada, 2002; Daitch, 2011; Kessler et al., 2010, 2009, 2005).

There are several kinds of anxiety disorders. Individuals with *generalized anxiety disorder* experience persistent feelings of worry and anxiety. People with *social anxiety disorder* display persistent fears of social or performance situations. People with *phobias* have a persistent and irrational fear of a specific object, activity, or situation. Individuals with *panic disorder* have recurrent attacks of terror. Those with *obsessive-compulsive disorder* feel overrun by recurrent thoughts that cause anxiety or by the need to perform repetitive actions to reduce anxiety. And those with *posttraumatic stress disorder (PTSD)* are tormented by fear and related symptoms well after a horrifying event has ended.

Studies find that participants with generally high levels of anxiety are more likely than calmer participants to notice and remember pictures of threatening faces. Attention to happy or neutral faces is about the same in both groups.

Most individuals with one anxiety disorder suffer from a second one as well. Bob Donaldson (the Bob in the example), for example, experiences the excessive worry found in generalized anxiety disorder and the repeated attacks of terror that mark panic disorder.

Generalized Anxiety Disorder

generalized anxiety disorder an anxiety disorder in which people feel excessive anxiety and worry under most circumstances.

People with generalized anxiety disorder experience excessive anxiety under most life circumstances and worry about practically anything (see **Figure 16-3**). Like Bob Donaldson, they typically feel restless, keyed up, or on edge, tire easily, have difficulty concentrating, suffer from muscle tension, and have sleep problems.

Surveys suggest that as many as 4 percent of the North American population have symptoms of this disorder in any given year (Kessler et al., 2010, 2005; Ritter, Blackmore, & Heimberg, 2010). Women diagnosed with the disorder outnumber men 2 to 1. The leading explanations of generalized anxiety disorder come from the cognitive and neuroscience models.

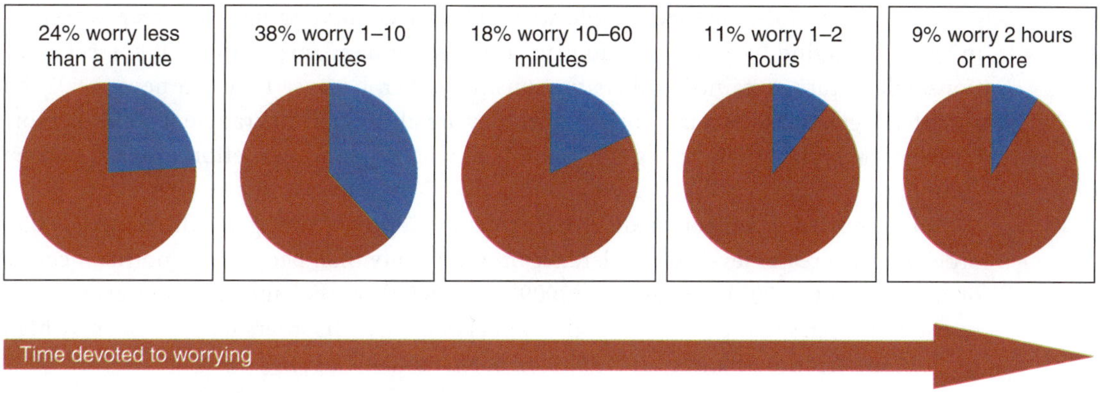

FIGURE 16-3 Some people worry more than others. In one survey, 24 percent of post-secondary students said they spend less than 1 minute at a time worrying about something. In contrast, 9 percent worry for more than 2 hours. (Adapted from Tallis et al., 1994.)

How Do Cognitive Theorists Explain Generalized Anxiety Disorder? As with depression, cognitive theorists suggest that generalized anxiety disorder is caused in part by *dysfunctional assumptions.* Aaron Beck argues that people with generalized anxiety disorder constantly hold silent assumptions that imply they are in imminent danger—for example, "A situation or a person is unsafe until proven to be safe" or "It is always best to assume the worst" (Beck & Weishaar, 2011; Beck & Emery, 1985). Similarly, Albert Ellis (2011, 2002, 1962) claimed that people who are generally anxious hold the following "irrational" assumptions in particular:

- "It is a dire necessity for an adult human being to be loved or approved of by virtually every significant other person in his community."
- "It is awful and catastrophic when things are not the way one would very much like them to be."
- "If something is or may be dangerous or fearsome, one should be terribly concerned about it and should keep dwelling on the possibility of its occurring."
- "One should be thoroughly competent, adequate, and achieving in all possible respects if one is to consider oneself worthwhile."

(Ellis, 1962)

In recent years, some additional cognitive explanations for generalized anxiety disorder have emerged. Sometimes called *new wave cognitive explanations*, each of these explanations builds on the notions of Ellis and Beck and their emphasis on danger (Ritter et al., 2010). According to one such explanation, the *intolerance of uncertainty theory*, certain individuals consider it unacceptable that negative events may occur, even if the possibility of occurrence is very small. Given that life is filled with uncertain events, such individuals may come up against several "unacceptable" events each day. Worrying constantly that unacceptable events are on the verge of happening, the individuals are particularly vulnerable to the development of generalized anxiety disorder (Dugas, Buhr, & Ladouceur, 2004).

Of course, most outcomes in life are uncertain. Think of when you first become attracted to someone and how you feel as you wait for your first text message or first call with that person. Even if you have reason to expect that all will go well, some uncertainty remains. And in a critical social situation of this kind, where anything less than success would feel like failure, that uncertainty may be all that it takes to get you worrying—big time worrying. The worry that you experience in such instances—the sense of sometimes unbearable uncertainty—is, according to this intolerance of uncertainty theory, how people with generalized anxiety disorder feel all the time.

According to this theory, people with generalized anxiety disorder keep worrying in an effort to find "correct" solutions to situations at hand, expecting that correct solutions will restore certainty to the situations. However, because they can never really be sure that a given solution is a correct one, they are always left to grapple with intolerable levels of uncertainty, triggering new rounds of worrying and new efforts to find correct solutions.

In support of this theory, studies have found that people with generalized anxiety disorder display greater levels of intolerance of uncertainty than people with normal degrees of anxiety (Daitch, 2011; Dugas et al., 2009, 2005, 2002). At the same time, however, recent research indicates that people with other kinds of anxiety disorders may also display high levels of intolerance of uncertainty (Nelson & Shankman, 2011).

WHAT HAPPENS IN THE BRAIN?

How Do Neuroscientists Explain Generalized Anxiety Disorder? One important neuroscience explanation of generalized anxiety disorder focuses on *gamma-aminobutyric acid (GABA)*, one of the brain's most common and important neurotransmitters. GABA carries inhibitory messages. That is, when GABA is received at a neuron's receptor, it causes the neuron to stop firing.

In normal fear reactions, key neurons throughout the brain fire more rapidly, triggering the firing of still more neurons and creating a general state of excitability throughout the brain and body. This state is experienced as fear or anxiety. After neuron firing continues for a while, it apparently triggers a *feedback system*—that is, brain and body activities that reduce the level of excitability. Some neurons throughout the brain release the neurotransmitter GABA, which then binds to GABA receptors on certain neurons and instructs those neurons to stop firing. The state of excitability is thereby halted, and the experience of fear or anxiety subsides (Atak, 2010).

Some neuroscientists now believe that a malfunction in this feedback system can cause fear or anxiety to go unchecked (Bremner & Charney, 2010; Roy-Byrne, 2005). In fact, when some investigators have reduced GABA's ability to bind to GABA receptors, they have found that animal subjects react with heightened anxiety. This finding suggests that people with generalized anxiety disorder may have ongoing problems in their anxiety feedback system. Perhaps they have too few GABA receptors, or their GABA receptors do not properly capture the neurotransmitter (Lydiard, 2003).

Recent research further clarifies that the root of generalized anxiety disorder is probably more complicated than GABA alone. Other neurotransmitters may also play important roles (Martin & Nemeroff, 2010). Moreover, as you read in Chapter 12, emotional reactions of various kinds are tied to brain *circuits*—networks of brain structures that work together, triggering each other into action with the help of neurotransmitters and producing particular kinds of emotional reactions. It turns out that the circuit that produces anxiety reactions includes the *prefrontal cortex*, *anterior cingulate*, and *amygdala*. According to several studies, this circuit may function improperly in people with generalized anxiety disorder (Schienle et al., 2011; McClure et al., 2007).

Social Anxiety Disorder

Many people worry about interacting with others or talking or performing in front of others. A number of entertainers, from singer Barbra Streisand to actor Anthony Hopkins, have described major bouts of anxiety before performing. Social fears of this kind are unpleasant and inconvenient, but usually the people who have them manage to function adequately, some at a very high level.

social anxiety disorder an anxiety disorder in which people feel severe, persistent, and irrational fears of social or performance situations in which embarrassment may occur.

People with a **social anxiety disorder**, by contrast, have severe, persistent, and irrational fears of social or performance situations in which embarrassment may occur. The social anxiety may be *narrow*, such as a fear of talking in public or writing in front of others, or it may be *broad*, such as a general fear of functioning poorly in front of others. In both forms, people repeatedly judge themselves as performing less adequately than they actually do.

Public performances. Most people do not enjoy standing up and presenting in front of a class or group of people. People with social anxiety disorder have particularly intense and irrational fears of not only talking or performing in front of others, but even of just being in regular social situations.

A social phobia can interfere greatly with one's life (Ravindran & Stein, 2011). A person who is unable to interact with others or speak in public may fail to perform important responsibilities. One who cannot eat in public may reject dinner invitations or other social opportunities. Since most people with this phobia keep their fears secret, their social reluctance is often misinterpreted as snobbery, lack of interest, or hostility.

Surveys indicate that at least 7.1 percent of people in Western countries—around three women for every two men—experience social anxiety disorder in any given year. Around 12 percent develop this problem at some point in their lives (Alfano & Beidel, 2011; Kessler et al., 2010). It often begins in late childhood or adolescence, and may continue into adulthood.

Research finds that poor people are 50 percent more likely than wealthier people to display a social phobia (Sareen et al., 2011). Moreover, in several studies, minority group participants scored higher than non-minority group participants on surveys of social anxiety (Stein & Williams, 2010; Schultz et al., 2008, 2006).

The most influential explanations for social anxiety disorder have come from cognitive-behavioural theorists and researchers (Heimberg, Brozovich, & Rapee, 2010; Hofmann, 2007; Clark & Wells, 1995). They hold that, like people with generalized anxiety disorder, individuals with this disorder have dysfunctional cognitions that help produce and maintain their symptoms. In the case of social anxiety disorder, those cognitions all centre on the social arena.

According to the cognitive-behavioural explanations, people with this disorder hold a cluster of social beliefs and expectations that severely work against them. These include the following (Hope et al., 2010; Koopmans et al., 1994):

- They hold unrealistically high social standards and so believe that they must perform perfectly in social situations. Given such standards, they cannot develop social goals that are reasonable and achievable.
- They view themselves as unattractive social objects.
- They view themselves as socially unskilled and inadequate.
- They believe that they are in danger of behaving incompetently in social situations.
- They believe that clumsy or inept behaviours in social situations will always lead to terrible consequences.
- They believe that they have no control over feelings of anxiety that emerge during social situations.

Although the poet Emily Dickinson wrote movingly about love, she was not able to interact comfortably with people. She became so reclusive that she sometimes spoke to her visitors from an adjoining room rather than talking to them face to face.

Cognitive-behavioural theorists contend that, as a result of this cluster of dysfunctional notions, individuals with social anxiety disorder keep anticipating that social disasters will occur, and they repeatedly perform "avoidance" and "safety" behaviours to help prevent or minimize such disasters (Rosenberg, Ledley, & Heimberg, 2010). Avoidance behaviours include, for example, talking only to familiar persons at meetings or parties. Safety behaviours include holding on to a podium during a classroom presentation so that their hands don't tremble or wearing make-up to cover up blushing.

Given such beliefs and expectations, the anxiety levels of people with social anxiety disorder rise immediately when they find themselves in social situations. Moreover, because they are convinced that their social inadequacies are the cause of the anxiety, certain that they do not have the social ability to deal with the situation, and concerned that they cannot control their negative arousal, they become consumed with anxiety.

Finally, after the social events have occurred, the individuals keep going over the details of the events in their mind. They overestimate how badly things went and what negative repercussions may unfold. These ruminations serve to keep the events alive and also feed into the individuals' fears about future social situations (Hope et al., 2010; Rosenberg et al., 2010; Moscovitch, 2009; Hofmann, 2007). Cognitive-behavioural theorists often differ, however, on how those variables interact to produce the disorder.

Why do some individuals, and not others, have such dysfunctional cognitions? Researchers have identified a number of factors. These include genetic predispositions, trait tendencies, biological abnormalities, traumatic childhood experiences, and past parent–child interactions (Brozovich & Heimberg, 2011; Kuo et al., 2011; Ledley, Erwin, & Heimberg, 2008). In one study, for example, college students with this disorder recalled that their mothers had been excessively protective throughout their childhoods (Spokas & Heimberg, 2009).

Phobias

phobia a persistent and unreasonable fear of a particular object, activity, or situation.

As you saw in Chapter 7, a **phobia** (from the Greek for "fear") is a persistent and unreasonable fear of a particular object, activity, or situation. Most phobias technically fall under the category *specific phobia*, an intense fear of a specific object or situation. Common specific phobias include intense fears of particular animals or insects, heights, enclosed spaces, thunderstorms, and blood, but as you can see in the box "10 Most Common Phobias" there are others as well. Phobias are common in our society. Surveys suggest that 7.7 percent of people in Canada suffer from at least one specific phobia in any given year (Kessler et al., 2010, 2009; Stern, 1995).

Behavioural principles provide the leading explanations for specific phobias (Gamble et al., 2010). According to behaviourists, *classical conditioning* is one way of acquiring fear reactions to objects or situations that are not really dangerous. Let's say, for example, that a frightening event, such as a lightning strike (*unconditioned stimulus*) naturally elicits a reaction of fear (*unconditioned response*) in an individual. In such a situation, it is possible that a harmless object, such as raindrops (*conditioned stimulus*)—an object that had simply accompanied the frightening event—will come to also elicit a fear reaction (*conditioned response*) in the person. An old but useful learning theory of phobias is

Fear of an animal is the most common specific phobia among women. Fear of heights is the most common one among men.

10 Most Common Phobias

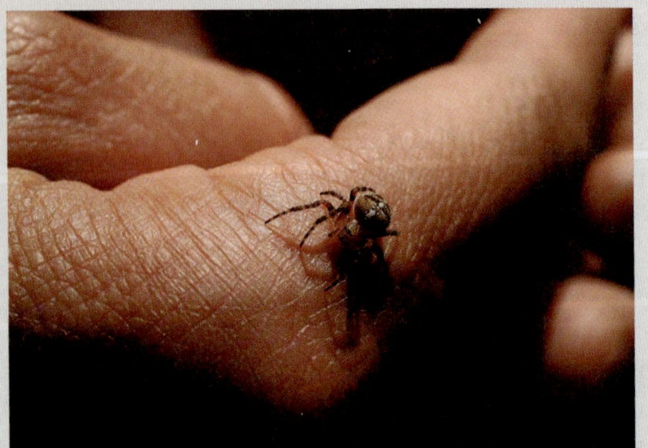

spiders—arachnophobia
heights—acrophobia
public, social places—agoraphobia
social situations—social phobia
flying—aerophobia
enclosed spaces—claustrophobia
thunder—brontophobia
germs—mysophobia
cancer—carcinophobia
death—necrophobia

Sources: Van Wagner, 2007; Melville, 1978

Mowrer's (1950) two-factor theory of phobia learning, which suggests that the fears associated with phobic objects are learned through classical conditioning, while the avoidance behaviours associated with phobias are reinfoerced through operant conditioning. So, for example, a person might develop a social phobia as a fesult of a panic attck in a crowd (classical conditinoing) and then stop going out so as to avoid crowds in future (operant conditioning).

According to behaviourists, another way of acquiring a fear reaction is through *modelling*—that is, through observation and imitation (Bandura & Rosenthal, 1966). A person may observe that others are afraid of certain objects or events and develop fears of the same things. Consider a young boy whose mother is afraid of illnesses, doctors, and hospitals. If she frequently expresses those fears, before long the boy himself may fear illnesses, doctors, and hospitals. Laboratory research has indicated repeatedly that fears can indeed be acquired through classical conditioning or modelling (Wilson, 2011).

panic attacks periodic, short bouts of panic.

panic disorder an anxiety disorder characterized by recurrent and unpredictable panic attacks that occur without apparent provocation.

agoraphobia a phobia that makes people avoid public places or situations in which escape might be difficult or help unavailable should panic symptoms develop.

Panic Disorder

Sometimes an anxiety reaction takes the form of a smothering, nightmarish panic. People experiencing this panic lose control of their behaviour and, in fact, are practically unaware of what they are doing. Anyone can react with panic when a real threat looms up suddenly. A number of people, however, experience **panic attacks**—periodic, discrete bouts of panic that occur suddenly, reach a peak within 10 minutes, and gradually pass. And some of those individuals have panic attacks repeatedly and often unexpectedly without apparent reason, perhaps suffering from **panic disorder**. In addition to panic attacks, people with this disorder experience changes in their thinking or behaviour as a result of the attacks. For example, they may believe that their attacks mean they are having a heart attack or losing their mind.

According to a Greek myth, Pan, the cloven-hoofed god of pastures, flocks, and shepherds, used to take naps in caves or thickets along country roads. When travellers disturbed the foul-looking god, he would let out a horrifying scream. The god's appearance and scream terrified the travellers—a reaction henceforth known as panic.

Panic disorder is often accompanied by **agoraphobia**, a fear of venturing into public places, especially when one is alone. Because of their panic attack history, some sufferers of panic disorder develop a fear of travelling to any location where escape might be difficult or help unavailable should panic symptoms develop.

Around 21 percent of all people in Canada over 15 years of age have suffered from a panic attack at some point in their lives, and about 8 percent of the population report having had a panic attack in the year prior to the survey (Ramage-Morin, 2004). The rate for the past year was highest (11.8 percent) among 15- to 24-year-olds and lowest (4.2 percent) among those over 55 years of age. Women were 1.65 times more likely than men to have experienced a panic attack in the past year (Ramage-Morin, 2004; Kessler et al., 2010, 2009, 2005; APA, 2000). The leading explanation for panic disorder is one that combines neuroscience and cognitive-behavioural principles.

Panic attack. Many people experience difficulty "catching their breath" during a panic attack, which can lead to hyperventilation.

As you read in Chapter 12, neuroscientists have determined that emotional reactions of various kinds are tied to brain circuits. Panic attacks are apparently produced in part by a brain circuit consisting of such areas as the *amygdala*, *hypothalamus*, and *locus ceruleus* (Elkin, 2010; Dresler et al., 2011). Many of today's researchers believe that this brain circuit—including *norepinephrine* and other neurotransmitters at work throughout the circuit—probably functions improperly, producing an excess amount of norepinephrine in people who experience panic disorder (Bremner & Charney, 2010; Burijon, 2007). Partly because of this malfunctioning brain circuit, these people are particularly prone to experience certain bodily sensations, such as breathing discomfort, fullness of the abdomen, and heart palpitations.

According to cognitive theorists, once these individuals experience such bodily sensations, they tend to misinterpret the sensations as signs of a medical catastrophe (Wenzel, 2011; Clark & Beck, 2010; Clark, 1986). Rather than understanding the probable cause of

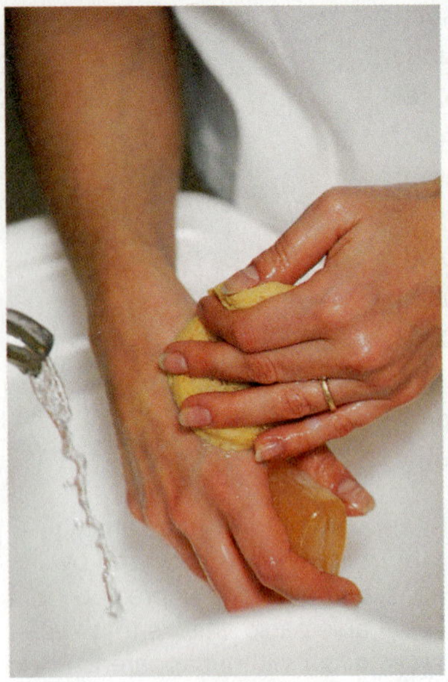

Cleaning compulsions. Cleaning compulsions are very common. People with these compulsions feel compelled to keep cleaning themselves, their clothing, or their homes. The cleaning may follow ritualistic rules and be repeated dozens or hundreds of times a day, making it almost impossible to have a normal life.

unusual or unexpected sensations as "something I ate" or "a fight with the boss," the panic-prone grow increasingly worried about losing control, fear the worst, lose all perspective, and rapidly plunge into panic. Constant concern over the possibility that the "dangerous" sensations may return at any time only increases the likelihood of future panic attacks.

Sufferers consistently appear to experience more bodily sensations than other people do, are more puzzled and troubled by such sensations than other people, and are particularly likely to interpret them as harmful and dangerous (Reinecke et al., 2011; Wilson & Hayward, 2005; McNally, 2001).

Obsessive-Compulsive Disorder

Obsessions are persistent thoughts, ideas, impulses, or images that seem to invade a person's consciousness. **Compulsions** are repetitive and rigid behaviours or mental acts that people feel compelled to perform to prevent or reduce anxiety. A diagnosis of **obsessive-compulsive disorder (OCD)** is called for when obsessions or compulsions are severe, are viewed by the person as excessive or unreasonable, cause great distress, consume considerable time, or interfere with daily functions.

In fact, compulsive acts on display in this disorder are typically responses to obsessive thoughts. One study found that in most cases of OCD, compulsions represent a *yielding* to obsessive doubts, ideas, or urges (Akhtar et al., 1975). For example, a woman who has obsessive fears of contamination may yield to that fear by performing cleaning rituals. The study also found that compulsions sometimes serve to *control* obsessions. A man with obsessive images of sexual events, for example, may try to control those images by filling his mind with compulsive verbal rituals, such as repeated expressions, phrases, or chants. In all such instances, the performance of the compulsive acts reduces the anxiety produced by obsesive thoughts.

obsessions persistent thoughts, ideas, impulses, or images that seem to invade a person's consciousness.

compulsions repetitive and rigid behaviours or mental acts that people feel compelled to perform to prevent or reduce anxiety.

obsessive-compulsive disorder (OCD) a mental disorder associated with repeated, abnormal, anxiety-provoking thoughts and/or repeated rigid behaviours.

As many as 2 percent of people in Canada suffer from obsessive-compulsive disorder in any given year (Health Canada, 2002; Kessler et al., 2010; Björgvinsson & Hart, 2008). The disorder is equally common in men and women and among people of different races and ethnic groups.

Obsessions often take the form of obsessive *wishes* (for example, repeated wishes that one's spouse would die), *impulses* (repeated urges to yell out obscenities at work or in church), *images* (fleeting visions of forbidden sexual scenes), or *doubts* (concerns that one has made or will make a wrong decision). Like obsessions, compulsions take various forms. For example, *cleaning compulsions* are very common. People with these compulsions feel compelled to keep cleaning themselves, their clothing, or their homes. The cleaning may follow ritualistic rules and be repeated dozens or hundreds of times a day, making it almost impossible to have a normal life.

The leading explanations for obsessive-compulsive disorder come from the behavioural and neuroscience models.

PSYCHOLOGY AROUND US Overrun by Cleanliness

Ruth complained that . . . she was spending most of her time engaged in some type of behaviour she felt driven to carry out. In addition, each ritual activity was becoming more involved and time consuming. At the time of the interview, she was washing her hands at least three or four times an hour, showering six or seven times a day, and thoroughly cleaning her apartment at least twice a day. . . . She was obsessed with germs and contamination.

Ruth stated that she felt frustrated and tired most of the time, due to the amount of effort involved in these rituals. She experienced a great deal of pain in her hands because the outer layer of skin was virtually rubbed off. Nonetheless, she felt compelled to thoroughly wash her hands and repeatedly clean her apartment each time she felt that she or her environment was contaminated in some way.

Leon, 1977, pp. 127–132

How Do Cognitive-Behavioural Theorists Explain Obsessive-Compulsive Disorder? According to one cognitive-behavioural theory, people stumble upon their compulsions quite randomly. In a fearful situation, they happen just coincidentally to wash their hands, say, or dress a certain way. When the threat lifts, they link the improvement to that particular action. After repeated accidental associations, they believe that the action is bringing them good luck or actually changing the situation. As a result, they perform the same action again and again in similar situations. The act becomes a key method of avoiding or reducing anxiety (Frost & Steketee, 2001).

The experiments that led Louis Pasteur to the pasteurization process may have been driven in part by his obsession with contamination and infection. Apparently he would not shake hands, and regularly wiped his glass and plate before dining.

Another cognitive-behavioural theory focuses on the relationship between obsessions and compulsions and suggests that people learn to perform compulsive acts specifically because such acts reduce the anxiety aroused by their obsessions. According to this theory, some people are generally more inclined than others to experience repetitive, unwanted, and intrusive thoughts, to blame themselves for such thoughts, and to expect that the thoughts can somehow cause terrible things to happen (Clark & Beck, 2010; Salkovskis, 1999, 1985). To avoid such negative outcomes, they learn to "neutralize" the thoughts—behave in ways meant to put matters right, make amends, and reduce their anxiety.

In support of this cognitive-behavioural explanation, studies have found that people who have obsessive-compulsive disorder do indeed experience intrusive thoughts more often than other people, resort to more neutralizing strategies, and experience reductions in anxiety after using neutralizing techniques (Shafran, 2005; Salkovskis et al., 2003). But why do certain people experience more intrusive thoughts in the first place? This seems to be where the neuroscience explanation comes into play.

WHAT HAPPENS IN THE BRAIN?

How Do Neuroscientists Explain Obsessive-Compulsive Disorder? The neuroscience explanation of this disorder features two lines of brain research. One points to abnormally low activity of the neurotransmitter serotonin, and the other to abnormal activity in key brain structures.

The most important clue to serotonin's role in obsessive-compulsive disorder was the surprising finding by clinical researchers that certain antidepressant drugs help reduce obsessive and compulsive symptoms (Stein & Fineberg, 2007). Since these particular drugs also increase serotonin activity, some researchers have concluded that the disorder may be caused by low serotonin activity (Spooren et al., 2010).

In another line of research, investigators found a link between obsessive-compulsive disorder and abnormal functioning in specific regions of the brain. Particularly important are the *orbitofrontal cortex*, a region in the prefrontal cortex, and the *caudate nuclei*, structures located within the basal ganglia. These regions are part of a brain circuit that usually converts sensory information into thoughts and actions (Craig & Chamberlain, 2010). Based on a variety of studies, many neuroscientists have come to believe that one or both of these brain regions are somewhat overactive in certain people, leading to a constant eruption of troublesome thoughts and actions (Endrass et al., 2011). Additional parts of this brain circuit have been identified in recent years, including the *thalamus*, the *cingulate cortex*, the *striatum's caudate nucleus* and, once again, the *amygdala*. It may be that these regions also play key roles in obsessive-compulsive disorder. The serotonin and brain region abnormalities may be linked. It turns out that serotonin plays a very active role in the operation of the orbitofrontal cortex, caudate nuclei, and other structures in the brain circuit. Thus, low serotonin activity might well disrupt the proper functioning of those brain structures. The hypothesis is that the cingulated cortex and hypothalamus activate the OCD impulses that are inhibited though the caudate nucleus, while the amygdala drives the fear and anxiety components of the OCD response (Shah et al., 2008).

Posttraumatic Stress Disorder (PTSD)

Stress reactions, and the sense of fear they produce, are often at play in psychological disorders. As you have seen, for example, people who experience a large number of stressful events are particularly vulnerable to the onset of depression. In addition, stress plays a more central role in *acute stress disorder* and *posttraumatic stress disorder (PTSD)*.

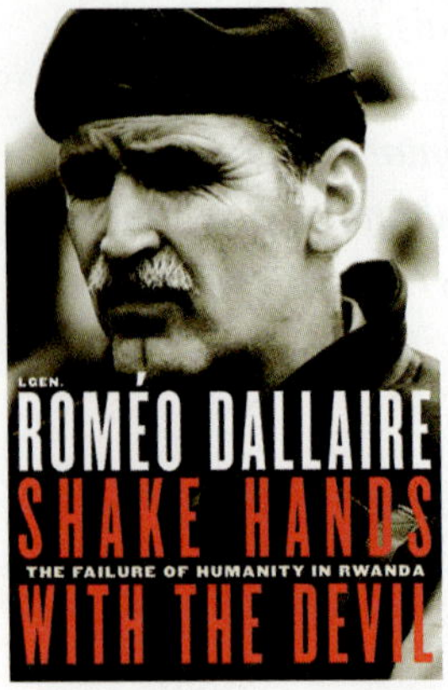

Many events can produce PTSD. Roméo Dallaire wrote about his experiences as Canada's highest ranking officer in Rwanda in his book *Shake Hands with the Devil: The Failure of Humanity in Rwanda (left)*. Dallaire is now a Canadian senator and is working to raise awareness of PTSD. When wildfires engulfed Slave Lake, Alberta, in May 2011 (right), residents had to flee with little or no notice. Many lost their homes and all belongings in the fires. Local service providers are aware of the possibility of PTSD arising as people return to their homes and lives.

Symptoms of Acute Stress Disorder and Posttraumatic Stress Disorder Chapter 15 described the roles of the *autonomic nervous system (ANS)* and the *hypothalamic-pituitary-adrenal (HPA)* axis during everyday stress reactions. Moreover, if a stressful situation is extraordinary and unusually dangerous, we may temporarily experience levels of arousal, anxiety, and depression that are far beyond those everyday stress reactions. Canadian soldiers who served in Afghanistan and residents of Slave Lake, Alberta who had to flee from a wild fire that destroyed a substantial portion of their town are all candidates for PTSD.

For most people, the unusual reactions subside soon after the special danger passes. But for others, the feelings of anxiety and depression, as well as other kinds of symptoms, persist well after the upsetting situation is over. These people are suffering from *acute stress disorder* or *posttraumatic stress disorder*, patterns that arise in reaction to a psychologically traumatic event, such as combat, rape, an earthquake, an airplane crash, or traffic accidents.

acute stress disorder an anxiety disorder in which fear and related symptoms are experienced soon after a traumatic event and last less than a month.

posttraumatic stress disorder (PTSD) an anxiety disorder in which fear and related symptoms continue to be experienced long after a traumatic event.

If the lingering stress symptoms begin within four weeks of the traumatic event and last for less than a month, a diagnosis of **acute stress disorder** is in order (APA, 2000). If the symptoms continue longer than a month, a diagnosis of **posttraumatic stress disorder (PTSD)** is given. The symptoms of PTSD may begin either shortly after the traumatic event or months or even years afterward (McFarlane, 1988; Frueh, 2009).

Studies indicate that as many as 80 percent of all cases of acute stress disorder develop into posttraumatic stress disorder (Burijon, 2007). Aside from the differences in onset and duration, the symptoms of acute stress disorder and PTSD are almost identical. The individuals experience high levels of ongoing anxiety and depression. They may feel overly alert (hyper alertness), be easily startled, have trouble concentrating, and develop sleep problems (Ruzek et al., 2011; Breslau et al., 2005). They may also feel extreme guilt because they survived the traumatic event while others did not.

In addition, people with the stress disorders may be battered by recurring thoughts, memories, dreams, or nightmares connected to the traumatic event (Geraerts, 2010). They tend to avoid all activities that remind them of the event and try to avoid related thoughts, feelings, or conversations (Marx & Sloan, 2005). In addition, people with the stress disorders often feel detached from other people or lose interest in activities that once brought enjoyment. They may feel dazed and have trouble remembering things.

You can see evidence of these symptoms in the recollections of a Vietnam combat veteran years after he returned home, found in the Psychology Around Us box on the next page.

Michael Anton Van Ameringen, at McMaster University, and his colleagues conducted an incidence study looking at stress disorders in Canada. They found a lifetime PTSD prevalence of 9.2 percent in their Canadian sample, as well as a current (at the time of the survey) incidence of 2.4 percent (Van Ameringen et al., 2008; Peterlin et al., 2011; Taylor, 2010; Kessler et al., 2009, 2005). Women are at least twice as likely as men to develop stress

PSYCHOLOGY AROUND US Remembering All Too Well

I can't get the memories out of my mind! The images come flooding back in vivid detail, triggered by the most inconsequential things, like a door slamming or the smell of stir-fried pork. Last night I went to bed, was having a good sleep for a change. Then in the early morning a storm-front passed through and there was a bolt of crackling thunder. I awoke instantly, frozen in fear. I am right back in Vietnam, in the middle of the monsoon season at my guard post. I am sure I'll get hit in the next volley and convinced I will die. My hands are freezing, yet sweat pours from my entire body. I feel each hair on the back of my neck standing on end. I can't catch my breath and my heart is pounding. I smell a damp sulfur smell.

(Davis, 1992)

disorders: around 20 percent of women who are exposed to a serious trauma may develop one, compared to 8 percent of men (Koch & Haring, 2008).

What Causes a Stress Disorder? Clearly, extraordinary trauma can cause a stress disorder. The stressful event alone, however, is not the entire explanation. Certainly, anyone who experiences an unusual trauma will be affected by it, but only some people develop acute stress disorder or posttraumatic stress. To more fully explain the onset of these disorders, researchers from the various models of abnormality point to individuals' biological processes, personalities, childhood experiences, social support systems, and cultural backgrounds.

- *Biological and Genetic Factors* Investigators have learned that traumatic events often trigger physical changes in the brain and body that may lead to severe stress reactions and, in some cases, to stress disorders. They have found, for example, abnormal activity of the hormone *cortisol* and the neurotransmitter *norepinephrine* in the urine, blood, and saliva of combat soldiers, rape victims, concentration camp survivors, and survivors of other severe stresses (Gerardi et al., 2010; Delahanty et al., 2005).
- Evidence from brain studies also shows that once a stress disorder sets in, individuals experience further biochemical arousal, and this continuing arousal may eventually damage key brain areas, particularly the *hippocampus* and, yet again, the *amygdala* (Bremner & Charney, 2010; Yehuda et al., 2010).
- *Personality* Some studies suggest that people with certain personalities, attitudes, and coping styles are particularly likely to develop stress disorders (Burijon, 2007). In the aftermath of Hurricane Hugo in 1989, for example, children who had been highly anxious before the storm were more likely than other children to develop severe stress reactions (Hardin et al., 2002). Research has also found that people who generally view life's negative events as beyond their control tend to develop more severe stress symptoms after sexual or other kinds of criminal assaults than people who feel greater control over their lives (Taylor, 2006).
- *Childhood Experiences* Investigators have found that certain childhood experiences seem to leave some people at risk for later acute and posttraumatic stress disorders. People whose childhoods have been marked by poverty appear more likely to develop these disorders in the face of later trauma. So do people whose family members suffer from psychological disorders; who experienced assault, abuse, or catastrophe at an early age; or who were younger than 10 when their parents separated or divorced (Yehuda et al., 2010; Koch & Haring, 2008).
- *Social Support* It has been found that people whose social and family support systems are weak are also more likely to develop a stress disorder after a traumatic event (Uchino & Birmingham, 2011; Ozer, 2005). Rape victims who feel loved, cared for, valued, and accepted by their friends and relatives recover more successfully. So do those treated with dignity and respect by the criminal justice system (Patterson, 2011).

PSYCHOLOGY AROUND US Canadian Military and PTSD

In March of 2001, in what was likely a suicide attempt, Corporal Christian McEachern drove his SUV directly into the headquarters building at CFB Edmonton. Corporal McEachern had served with Canada's peacekeeping forces in Croatia and Uganda and had been diagnosed with PTSD upon his return. He was eventually tried for this action and found guilty, but was given no jail time. His complaint about the lack of proper services for Canadian Forces personally struggling with PTSD was investigated by Canada's parliamentary ombudsman. The ombudsman found many cases of PTSD among Canada's military personal were going unidentified and untreated (Marin, 2001). A follow-up report in 2008 found that 18 of the 31 recommendations in the original report had not yet been implemented (McFadyen, 2008). Clearly there is still more work to do in dealing with PTSD issues within the Canadian Forces.

Before You Go On

www.wiley.com/go/comer

What Do You Know?

11. What are six types of anxiety disorder?
12. How and why might generalized anxiety disorder be related to uncertainty?
13. What role do conditioning and modelling play in the development of phobias?
14. What individual factors affect who will develop posttraumatic stress syndrome?

SCAN TO GET THE ANSWERS

What Do You Think?

The return home for many soldiers is often difficult. One of the problems they face is trying to find a way to talk about their experiences with friends and relatives; if you haven't experienced war, there's really no way to understand what soldiers go through. What sorts of things can we do to make the return home easier for Canadian soldiers?

schizophrenia a mental disorder characterized by disorganized thoughts, lack of contact with reality, and sometimes hallucinations.

psychosis loss of contact with reality.

positive symptoms in the case of schizophrenia, symptoms that seem to represent pathological excesses in behaviour, including delusions, disorganized thinking and speech, hallucinations, and inappropriate affect.

Schizophrenia

LEARNING OBJECTIVE 5

Describe the features of schizophrenia and some theories of what causes it.

Schizophrenia is a disorder in which people deteriorate into a world of unusual perceptions, odd thoughts, disturbed emotions, and motor abnormalities. People with this disorder experience **psychosis**, a loss of contact with reality. Their ability to perceive and respond to the environment becomes so disturbed that they may not be able to function at home, with friends, in school, or at work. They may have hallucinations (false sensory perceptions) or delusions (false beliefs), or they may withdraw into a private world. Schizophrenia is the most common form of psychosis; however, a number of other disorders also feature psychotic symptoms (see the box "The Case of Andrea Yates").

Approximately 1 of every 100 people in the world suffers from schizophrenia during his or her lifetime (Miller & Mason, 2011; APA, 2000). Equal numbers of men and women receive this diagnosis. Almost 3 percent of all those who are divorced or separated suffer from schizophrenia over the course of their lives, compared with 1 percent of married people and 2 percent of people who remain single.

The symptoms of schizophrenia can be grouped into three categories: *positive symptoms*, *negative symptoms*, and *psychomotor symptoms*.

Positive Symptoms of Schizophrenia

Positive symptoms are "pathological excesses," or bizarre additions, to a person's behaviour. *Delusions*, *disorganized thinking and speech*, *hallucinations*, and *inappropriate affect* are the ones most often found in schizophrenia.

The Case of Andrea Yates

On the morning of June 20, 2001, 36-year-old Andrea Yates called police and explained that she had drowned her five children in the bathtub because "they weren't developing correctly." She recounted the order in which the children had died: first 3-year-old Paul, then 2-year-old Luke, followed by 5-year-old John, 6-month-old Mary, and 7-year-old Noah.

As many as 80 percent of mothers experience "baby blues" soon after giving birth, and between 10 and 30 percent display the clinical syndrome of *postpartum depression*. Postpartum psychosis, by contrast, is an entirely different disorder—one that has become all too familiar to the public in recent times due to cases such as that of Andrea Yates (Doucet et al., 2011; Worley, 2010).

Postpartum psychosis affects about 1 to 2 of every 1,000 mothers who have recently given birth (Posmontier, 2010). The symptoms apparently are triggered by the enormous shift in hormone levels that occur after delivery (Blackmore et al., 2009). Within days or at most a few months of childbirth, the woman develops signs of losing touch with reality, such as delusions (for example, she may become convinced that her baby is the devil); hallucinations (perhaps hearing voices); extreme anxiety, confusion, and disorientation; disturbed sleep; and illogical or chaotic thoughts (for example, thoughts about killing herself or her child).

Women with a history of bipolar disorder, schizophrenia, or major depressive disorder are particularly vulnerable to the disorder (Read & Purse, 2007). In addition, women who have previously experienced postpartum depression or postpartum psychosis have an increased likelihood of developing this disorder after subsequent births (Nonacs, 2007). Andrea Yates, for example, had developed signs of postpartum depression (and perhaps postpartum psychosis) and attempted suicide after the birth of her fourth child. At that time, however, she appeared to respond well to a combination of medications, and so she and her husband later decided to conceive a fifth child (King, 2002).

After the birth of her fifth child, the symptoms did in fact recur, along with features of psychosis. Yates again attempted suicide. Although she was hospitalized twice and treated with various medications, her condition failed to improve. Six months after giving birth to Mary, her fifth child, she drowned all five of her children.

Most clinicians who are knowledgeable about this rare disorder agree that Yates was indeed a victim of postpartum psychosis. Although only a fraction of women with the disorder actually harm their children (estimates run as high as 4 percent), the Yates case reminds us that such an outcome is indeed possible (Posmontier, 2010; Read & Purse, 2007). The case also reminds us that early detection and treatment are critical (Doucet et al., 2011).

After a second trial for murder in 2007, Yates was found *not guilty by reason of insanity* and sent to a high-security mental health facility for treatment. Some months later, she was transferred to a low-security state mental hospital where she continues to receive treatment today.

PSYCHOLOGY AROUND US Drifting into Psychosis

[Laura, a professional dancer, met her husband in Germany, and they later emigrated to the United States.] They had no children...[but Laura] had a dog to whom she was very devoted. The dog became sick and partially paralyzed, and veterinarians felt that there was no hope of recovery. . . . Finally [Laura's husband asked her,] "Are you going to decide to have your dog destroyed or not?" From that time on Laura became restless, agitated, and depressed. . . .

. . . Later Laura started to complain about the neighbors. A woman who lived on the floor beneath them was knocking on the wall to irritate her. According to the husband, this woman had really knocked on the wall a few times; he had heard the noises. However, Laura became more and more concerned about it. . . . Later she . . . started to feel that the neighbors were now recording everything she said; maybe they had hidden wires in the apartment. She started to feel "funny" sensations. There were many strange things happening, which she did not know how to explain; people were looking at her in a funny way in the street. . . . She felt that people were planning to harm either her or her husband. . . . When she looked at television, it became obvious to her that the programs referred to her life. Often the people on the programs were just repeating what she had thought. They were stealing her ideas. She wanted to go to the police and report them.

(Arieti, 1974, pp. 165–168)

delusions blatantly false beliefs that are firmly held despite evidence to the contrary.

Delusions are ideas that are believed wholeheartedly by a person but that have no basis in fact. *Delusions of persecution* are the most common delusions in schizophrenia (APA, 2000). People with this delusion believe that they are being plotted or discriminated against, spied on, slandered, threatened, attacked, or deliberately victimized. Laura, for example, believed that her neighbours were trying to irritate her and that other people were trying to harm her and her husband.

loose associations or **derailment** a common thought disorder of schizophrenia, characterized by rapid shifts from one topic to another.

People with schizophrenia may also exhibit *disorganized thinking and speech*. Many, for example, display **loose associations**, or **derailment**: they rapidly shift from one topic to another, believing that their incoherent statements make sense. One man with schizophrenia, asked about his itchy arms, responded:

> *The problem is insects. My brother used to collect insects. He's now a man 5 foot 10 inches. You know, 10 is my favourite number. I also like to dance, draw, and watch television.*

hallucinations imagined sights, sounds, or other sensory events experienced as if they were real.

Individuals with schizophrenia may also experience **hallucinations**, perceptions that occur in the absence of external stimuli. People who have *auditory hallucinations*, by far the most common kind in schizophrenia, hear sounds and voices that seem to come from outside their heads (APA, 2000).

Yet another positive symptom found in schizophrenia is *inappropriate affect*, emotions that are unsuited to the situation. The individuals may smile when making a serious statement or on being told terrible news, or they may become upset in situations that should make them happy. They may also undergo inappropriate shifts in mood.

negative symptoms in the case of schizophrenia, symptoms that seem to reflect pathological deficits, including poverty of speech, flat affect, loss of volition, and social withdrawal.

catatonia extreme psychomotor symptoms of schizophrenia, including catatonic stupor, catatonic rigidity, and catatonic posturing.

Negative Symptoms of Schizophrenia

Negative symptoms are those that seem to be "pathological deficits," characteristics that are lacking in an individual. *Poverty of speech*, *flat affect*, *loss of volition*, and *social withdrawal* are commonly found in schizophrenia.

Poverty of speech refers to a reduction in speech or speech content. Some people with this negative symptom think and say very little. Others say quite a bit but still manage to convey little meaning. In another negative symptom, *flat affect*, individuals show very little anger, sadness, joy, or other feelings. The faces of these persons are still, their eye contact poor, and their voices monotonous.

Still other persons experience *avolition*, or apathy. They feel drained of energy and interest in normal goals and are unable to start or follow through on a course of action. And, in yet another negative symptom, people with this disorder may *withdraw* from their social environment and attend only to their own ideas and fantasies. Because their ideas are illogical and confused, withdrawal helps distance them still further from reality (Behrendt & Young, 2004; Costello, 1993).

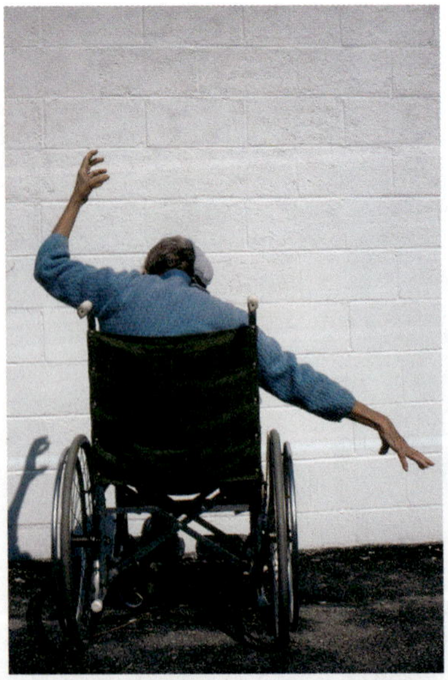

Catatonic posturing. Some people struggling with schizophrenia demonstrate catatonic posturing, where they strike and hold bizarre positions, sometimes for hours.

Psychomotor Symptoms

People with schizophrenia sometimes experience unusual *psychomotor symptoms*—they may move awkwardly or make odd grimaces and gestures. The gestures often seem to have a private, perhaps ritualistic or magical, purpose. The psychomotor symptoms may take extreme forms collectively called **catatonia**. People in a *catatonic stupor*, for example, stop responding to their environment, remaining motionless and silent for long stretches of time. Others exhibit *catatonic rigidity*, maintaining a rigid upright posture for hours and resisting efforts to be moved. Still others display *catatonic posturing*, assuming awkward, bizarre positions (a squatting position, for example) for long periods of time. They may even exhibit *waxy flexibility*, in which they maintain indefinitely postures into which they have been placed by someone else (Weinberger & Harrison, 2011).

An early hypothesis about schizophrenia was that it might divide up into distinct types or versions of the disorder, defined through distinct patterns of symptoms and possibly due to different underlying causes. The five subtypes discussed were paranoid, disorganized, catatonic, undifferentiated, and residual schizophrenia (Noll, 2007). We have already discussed the general symptoms of schizophrenia. The patterns of symptoms believed to be reflected in the different possible subtypes are as follows:

- Paranoid type: The main symptoms in this type are delusions and possibly auditory hallucinations. There is no thought disorder and the delusions centre on being persecuted or on jealousy.
- Disorganized type (also called hebephrenic schizophrenia): the combination of disordered thoughts and flat affect characterize this subtype.
- Catatonic type: As described in the psychomotor symptom section above, this subtype is characterized by immobility or by agitated, purposeless movements.
- Undifferentiated type: Symptoms of schizophrenia are present but not in a combination that allows for categorization in any of the previous other subtypes.
- Residual type: symptoms are present but at a low level of intensity.

There has not been a lot of data (e.g., brain-based differences or treatment outcomes) supporting the existence of these subtypes, and as such there is currently debate as to whether the subtypes should remain in the DSM diagnostic system (APA DSM-V Workgroups, 2010).

How Do Neuroscientists Explain Schizophrenia?

WHAT HAPPENS IN THE BRAIN?

Neuroscience explanations of schizophrenia have received by far the most research support. This is not to say that psychological and socio-cultural factors play no role in the disorder. Rather, a *diathesis-stress* relationship (Walker & Diforio, 1997) may be at work: perhaps people with a biological predisposition (diathesis) develop schizophrenia only if certain kinds of psychological events, personal stress, or societal expectations (stress) are also present.

Genetic Factors Many theorists believe that people inherit a genetic predisposition to schizophrenia (Akbarian, 2010). In support of this notion, studies have found repeatedly that schizophrenia is more common among relatives of people with the disorder than among other individuals (Tamminga et al., 2008). And the more closely related the relatives are to the person with schizophrenia, the greater their likelihood of developing the disorder (see **Figure 16-4**).

Twins, who are among the closest of relatives, have received particular study by schizophrenia researchers. If both members of a pair of twins have a particular trait, they are said to be *concordant* for that trait. If genetic factors are at work in schizophrenia, identical twins (who share all genes) should have a higher concordance rate for this disorder than *fraternal twins* (who share only some genes). This expectation has been supported consistently by research (Higgins & George, 2007). Studies have found that if one identical twin develops schizophrenia, there is a 48 percent chance that the other twin will do so as well at some point in his or her life. If the twins are fraternal, on the other hand, the second twin has approximately a 17 percent chance of developing the disorder.

How might genetic factors lead to the development of schizophrenia? Research has pointed to two kinds of brain abnormalities that could be inherited—*biochemical abnormalities* and *abnormal brain structures*.

Biochemical Abnormalities Over the past four decades, researchers have developed the so-called *dopamine hypothesis* to help explain schizophrenia: certain neurons that use the neurotransmitter dopamine fire too often and transmit too many messages, thus producing the symptoms of the disorder (Busatto et al., 2010; McGowan et al., 2004).

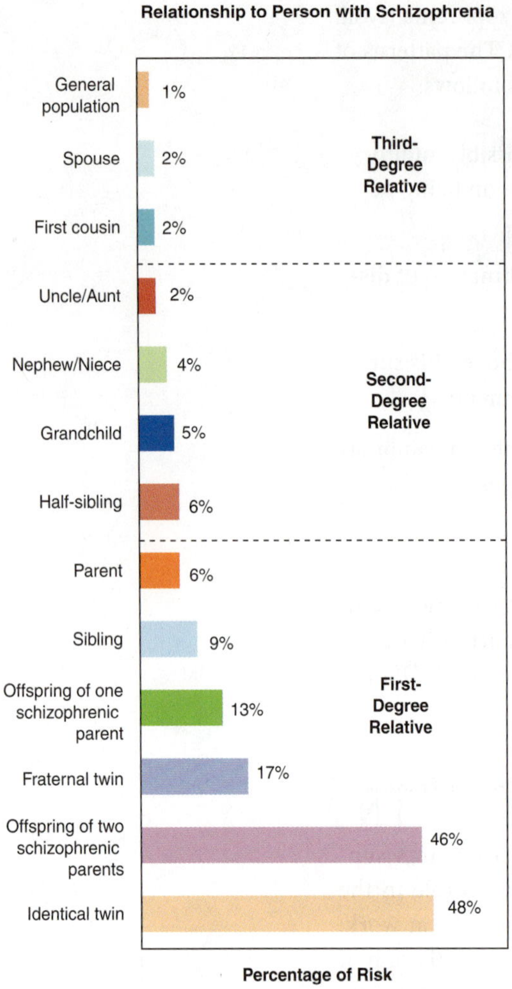

FIGURE 16-4 Family connections. Biological relatives of people with schizophrenia have a higher risk than the general population of developing the disorder during their lifetimes. Closer relatives (who have a more similar genetic makeup) have a greater risk than more distant relatives (Gottesman, 1991, p. 96).

This hypothesis has undergone challenges and adjustments in recent years, but it is still the foundation for present biochemical explanations of schizophrenia.

The first clue that high dopamine activity may contribute to schizophrenia came with the accidental discovery in the 1950s of **antipsychotic drugs**—medications that help remove the symptoms of schizophrenia (Garver, 2006; Healy, 2005). Originally used as anesthetics during surgery, the early drugs were found to also calm agitated psychotic patients. Direct tests followed and a revolution in the treatment of schizophrenia began (Ban, 2007). Clinicians soon learned that these drugs often produce an undesired reaction in patients—muscular tremors like those seen in Parkinson's disease, a disabling neurological illness. Scientists already knew that people who suffer from Parkinson's disease have abnormally low levels of the neurotransmitter dopamine in some areas of the brain, and that lack of dopamine is the reason for their uncontrollable shaking. If antipsychotic drugs produce Parkinsonian symptoms in persons with schizophrenia while removing their psychotic symptoms, perhaps the drugs reduce dopamine activity. And, scientists reasoned further, if lowering dopamine activity helps remove the symptoms of schizophrenia, perhaps schizophrenia is related to excessive dopamine activity.

Many studies have since suggested that messages travelling from dopamine-sending neurons to dopamine receptors on other neurons may be transmitted too easily or too often in people with schizophrenia. This theory is appealing because certain dopamine neurons are known to play a key role in guiding attention (Sikstrom & Soderlund, 2007). People whose attention is severely disturbed by excessive dopamine activity might well be expected to suffer from the problems of attention, perception, and thought found in schizophrenia. Additional studies further suggest that abnormal activity of the neurotransmitters glutamate and serotonin may also play a role in schizophrenia (Bach, 2007).

antipsychotic drugs medications that help remove the symptoms of schizophrenia.

Abnormal Brain Structures During the past decade, researchers have also linked many cases of schizophrenia to abnormalities in brain structure (Brown & Thompson, 2010; Eyler, 2008). Using brain scans, for example, they have found that many people with schizophrenia have enlarged ventricles (the brain cavities that contain cerebrospinal fluid), relatively small temporal lobes and frontal lobes, and abnormal blood flow in certain areas of the brain. In addition, some studies have linked schizophrenia to structural abnormalities of the hippocampus, amygdala, and thalamus (Leube, 2009).

Before You Go On

www.wiley.com/go/comer

What Do You Know?

15. What is a psychosis?
16. What are the positive symptoms of schizophrenia? The negative symptoms? The psychomotor symptoms?
17. What biochemical abnormalities and brain structures have been associated with schizophrenia?

SCAN TO GET THE ANSWERS

What Do You Think?

We noted in this section that if one identical twin develops schizophrenia, there is a 48 percent chance that the other twin will do so as well. Discuss how this might support the diathesis-stress perspective.

Other Disorders

LEARNING OBJECTIVE 6

Discuss the features and possible causes of somatoform, dissociative, and personality disorders.

We have now examined three important categories of psychological disorders: mood disorders, anxiety disorders, and schizophrenia. We will conclude the chapter by looking briefly at three additional disorder categories: somatoform disorders, dissociative disorders, and personality disorders.

Somatoform Disorders

When a physical ailment has no medical cause, the sufferer may be experiencing a somatoform disorder, a pattern of physical complaints with largely psychosocial causes. The individuals do not consciously want or purposely produce their symptoms; they almost always believe that their problems are genuinely medical (Lahmann, Henningsen, & Noll-Hussong, 2010). In some somatoform disorders (conversion disorder, somatization disorder), there is an actual change in physical functioning. In others (hypochondriasis, body dysmorphic disorder), people who are healthy mistakenly worry that there is something physically wrong with them.

somatoform disorder a pattern of physical complaints with largely psychosocial causes; types include *conversion disorder, somatization disorder, pain disorder associated with psychological factors, hypochondriasis,* and *body dysmorphic disorder.*

Conversion Disorder In *conversion disorder*, a psychosocial conflict or need is converted into dramatic physical symptoms that affect voluntary motor or sensory functioning. The symptoms often seem neurological, such as paralysis, blindness, or loss of feeling (APA, 2000). Symptoms may also include muscle tensing, arm or leg twitching, shaking or barking, and other odd behaviours (Tsuruga et al., 2008; Hong, Schonwald, & Stein, 2008; Boogarts, Aldo, & Bloem, 2007). Conversion disorders are diagnosed at least twice as often in women as in men. They usually appear suddenly, at times of extreme stress, and last a matter of weeks. The disorders are thought to be quite rare, occurring in at most 5 of every 1,000 persons (Abbey, 2005).

Somatization Disorder People with *somatization disorder* have many long-lasting physical ailments that have little or no organic basis. These ailments include pain symptoms (such as headaches and chest pain), gastrointestinal symptoms (such as nausea and diarrhea), sexual symptoms (such as erectile or menstrual difficulties), and neurological symptoms (such as double vision or paralysis) (APA, 2000). Sufferers may go from doctor to doctor in search of relief. Some may even seek multiple surgical procedures. They often describe their many symptoms in dramatic and exaggerated terms (Dimsdale & Creed, 2010; Creed, 2009; APA, 2000). Between 0.2 and 2.0 percent of all women in North America may experience this disorder in any given year, compared with fewer than 0.2 percent of men (North, 2005; APA, 2000). The disorder lasts much longer than a conversion disorder, typically for many years (Yutzy, 2007).

PSYCHOLOGY AROUND US Baffling Symptoms

Sheila reported having abdominal pain since age 17, necessitating exploratory surgery that yielded no specific diagnosis. She had several pregnancies, each with severe nausea, vomiting, and abdominal pain; she ultimately had a hysterectomy for a "tipped uterus." Since age 40 she had experienced dizziness and "blackouts," which she eventually was told might be multiple sclerosis or a brain tumour. She continued to be bedridden for extended periods of time, with weakness, blurred vision, and difficulty urinating. At age 43 she was examined for a hernia because of complaints of bloating and intolerance of a variety of foods. She also had additional hospitalizations for neurological, hypertensive, and renal workups, all of which failed to reveal a definitive diagnosis. This pattern is likely reflective of somatization issues.

(Spitzer et al., 1981, p. 185)

Distorting the view. People with body dysmorphic disorder have an extreme obsession with some "flaw" in their appearance—whether the flaw is real or imagined.

Hypochondriasis People who suffer from *hypochondriasis* unrealistically interpret bodily symptoms as signs of a serious illness. Often their symptoms are merely normal bodily changes, such as occasional coughing, sores, or sweating. Between 1 and 5 percent of all people experience hypochondriasis (Abramowitz & Braddock, 2011; APA, 2000). Physicians report seeing many cases (Dimsdale et al., 2011). As many as 7 percent of all patients seen by primary care physicians may display hypochondriasis (Asmundson & Taylor, 2008).

Body Dysmorphic Disorder People who experience *body dysmorphic disorder*, also known as *dysmorphophobia*, become deeply concerned about some imagined or minor defect in their appearance. Most often they focus on wrinkles; spots on the skin; excessive facial hair; swelling of the face; or a misshapen nose, mouth, jaw, or eyebrow (Marques et al., 2011; McKay, Gosselin, & Gupta, 2008). Some worry about the appearance of their feet, hands, breasts, penis, or other body parts. Still others are concerned about bad odours coming from sweat, breath, genitals, or the rectum (Rocca et al., 2010; Phillips & Castle, 2002).

It is common in Western society to worry about appearance (see **Figure 16-5**). Many teenagers and young adults worry about acne, for instance. The concerns of people with body dysmorphic disorder, however, are extreme. Sufferers may severely limit their contacts with other people, be unable to look others in the eye, or go to great lengths to conceal their "defects"—for example, always wearing sunglasses to cover their supposedly misshapen eyes (Didie et al., 2010; Phillips, 2005). As many as half of people with this disorder seek plastic surgery or dermatology treatment, and often they feel worse rather than better afterward (McKay et al., 2008). Up to 5 percent of people in North America—including many college students—may suffer from the disorder (Buhlmann et al., 2010; Ovsiew, 2006; Philips, 2004).

What Causes Somatoform Disorders? Theorists typically explain hypochondriasis and body dysmorphic disorders much as they explain anxiety disorders (Bouman, 2008; Noyes, 2008). Behaviourists, for example, believe that the fears found in the disorders are acquired through classical conditioning or modelling (Marshall et al., 2007). Cognitive theorists suggest that people with the disorders are extremely sensitive to bodily cues and come to misinterpret them (Witthoft & Hiller, 2010; Williams, 2004).

In contrast, the other somatoform disorders—conversion, somatization, and pain disorders—are considered unique and in need of special explanations. Two such explanations are the psychodynamic and socio-cultural explanations. However, these and other explanations offered for somatoform disorders have failed to receive much research support (Kirmayer & Looper, 2007; Yutzy, 2007).

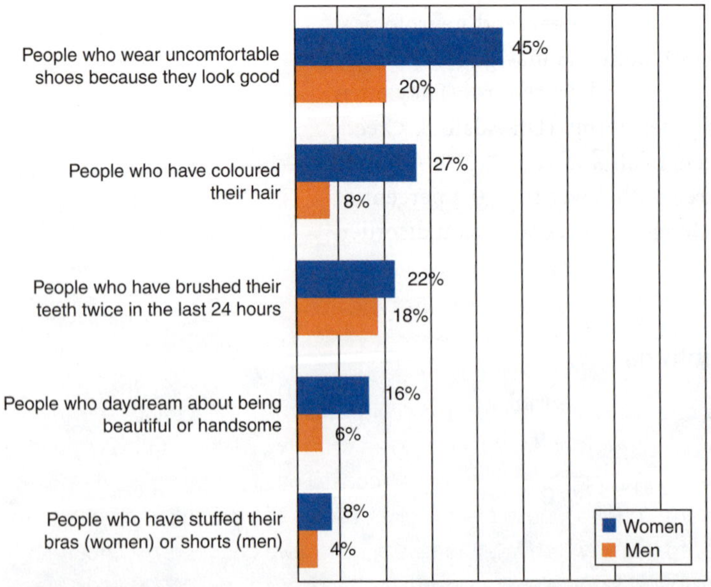

FIGURE 16-5 How do I look? People with body dysmorphic disorder may be extreme, but they're not the only ones who worry about their appearance. Surveys indicate that substantial percentages of people keep trying to change how they look (Noonan, 2003; Branden, 2001).

HOW WE DIFFER

How Do Socio-cultural Theorists Explain Somatoform Disorders? Clinicians often use the term *somatization* when referring to the development of somatic symptoms in response to personal distress, the key feature of somatoform disorders. Somatization of any kind is considered inappropriate in Western countries (So, 2008; Escobar, 2004). Some theorists believe, however, that this position reflects a bias held by Western clinicians—a bias that sees somatic symptoms as an *inferior* (developmentally immature) way of dealing with emotions.

A world-wide view reveals that the transformation of personal distress into somatic complaints is in fact the norm in many non-Western cultures (Draguns, 2006; Kleinman, 1987). In such cultures, somatization is viewed as a socially and medically correct—and less stigmatizing—reaction to life's stressors. Studies have found very high rates of somatization in non-Western medical settings throughout the world, including China, Japan, and Arab countries (Matsumoto & Juang, 2008). Individuals in Latin countries seem to display the greatest number of somatic symptoms (Escobar, 2004, 1995; Escobar et al., 1998, 1992). Even within North America, people from Hispanic cultures display more somatic symptoms in the face of stress than do other populations. Such findings remind us once again that reactions to life's stressors are often influenced by culture. Overlooking this point can lead to knee-jerk mislabels or misdiagnoses.

dissociative disorder a psychological disorder characterized by major loss of memory without a clear physical cause; types include *dissociative amnesia, dissociative fugue,* and *dissociative identity disorder*.

Dissociative Disorders

People sometimes experience a major disruption of their memory. They may, for example, lose their ability to remember new information that they just learned or old information they once knew well. When such a change in memory lacks a physical cause, it is called a **dissociative disorder**. One part of the person's memory seems to be *dissociated*, or separated, from the rest (Barlow, 2011).

Although dissociative disorders are often portrayed in novels, movies, and television shows, many clinicians believe that they are in fact quite rare (Pope et al., 2007). There are several kinds of dissociative disorders, including *dissociative amnesia*, *dissociative fugue*, and *dissociative identity disorder*.

Memory loss. All of us have problems remembering something from time to time, but those with dissociative disorders have major disruptions in memory where one part of their memory seems to be *dissociated* from the rest.

Dissociative Amnesia

People with *dissociative amnesia* are unable to recall important information, usually of an upsetting nature, about their lives (APA, 2000). The loss of memory is much more extensive than normal forgetting and is often triggered by a traumatic event, as in wartime and natural disasters (Hunt, 2010). In most cases, the forgotten material or events eventually return, often without the help of treatment. The 1990s witnessed many reports of past dissociative amnesia in which adults claimed to recall long-forgotten experiences of childhood abuse, as you will see in the box "Repression versus False Memories" below).

Repression versus False Memories

Throughout the 1990s, reports of *repressed childhood memory of abuse* attracted enormous public attention. Adults with this type of *dissociative amnesia* seemed to recover buried memories of sexual and physical abuse from their childhood. A woman might claim, for example, that her father had sexually molested her repeatedly. Or a young man might recall that a neighbour had made sexual advances on many occasions.

Although the number of such claims has declined in recent years, experts remain split on this issue (Birrell, 2011; Haaken & Reavey, 2010). Some believe that recovered memories are just what they appear to be—horrible memories of abuse that have been buried for years in the person's mind. Other experts believe that the memories are actually illusions—false images created by a mind that is confused. Opponents of the repressed memory concept hold that the details of childhood sexual abuse are often remembered all too well, not completely wiped from memory (Loftus & Cahill, 2007). Moreover, they point out that false memories often can be created in the laboratory by tapping into research participants' imaginations (Weinstein & Shanks, 2010).

If the alleged recovery of childhood memories is not always what it appears to be (remember that sometimes the memories are of very real past events), what is it? According to opponents of the concept, it may be a powerful case of suggestibility (Loftus & Cahill, 2007). They hold that the attention paid to the phenomenon by both clinicians and the public has led some therapists to make the diagnosis without sufficient evidence (Haaken & Reavey, 2010). The therapists may actively search for signs of early abuse in clients, and even encourage clients to produce repressed memories (McNally & Garaerts, 2009). Perhaps some clients respond by unknowingly forming false memories of abuse. The apparent memories may then become increasingly familiar to them as a result of repeated therapy discussions of the alleged incidents. Stephen Lindsay at the University of Victoria and Don Read now of Simon Fraser University reviewed the research on this question and describe a series of guidelines for therapy that may involve issues of recovered memory. They indicate that therapists should keep an open mind about their client's history, avoid suggestive questions, not use hypnosis or other memory aids, and keep careful records of any sessions involving memory work (Lindsay & Read, 1995).

Of course, repressed memories of childhood sexual abuse do not emerge only in clinical settings (Geraerts et al., 2009). Many individuals come forward on their own. Opponents of the repressed memory concept explain these cases by pointing to various books, articles, websites, and television shows that seem to validate repressed memories of childhood abuse (Haaken & Reavey, 2010).

It is important to recognize that the experts who question the recovery of repressed childhood memories do not in any way deny the problem of child sexual abuse. In fact, proponents and opponents alike agree that the problem of childhood sexual abuse is all too real and all too common.

Dissociative Fugue People with a *dissociative fugue* not only forget their personal identities and details of their past lives, but also flee to an entirely different location. Some individuals travel a short distance and make few social contacts in the new setting (APA, 2000). In other cases, however, the person may travel far from home, take a new name, and establish a new identity, new relationships, and even a new line of work (APA, 2000).

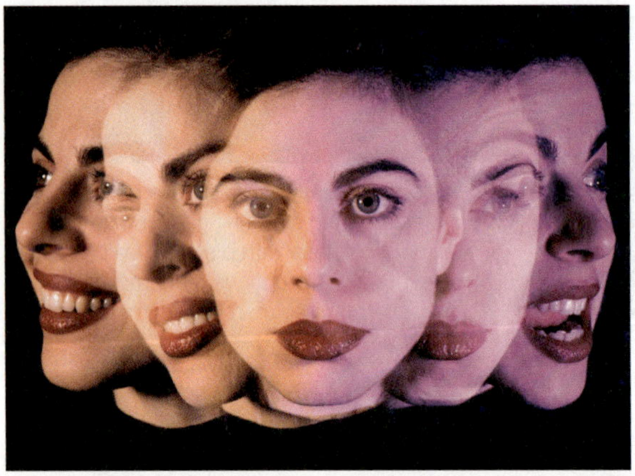

Dissociative Identity Disorder People with *dissociative identity disorder*, previously known as *multiple personality disorder*, develop two or more distinct personalities—called *subpersonalities* or *alternate personalities*—each with a unique set of memories, behaviours, thoughts, and emotions. At any given time, one of the subpersonalities takes centre stage and dominates the person's functioning (Barlow, 2011). Cases of dissociative identity disorder were first reported almost three centuries ago (Rieber, 2006, 2002). Women receive this diagnosis at least three times as often as men (APA, 2000).

PSYCHOLOGY AROUND US The Many Sides of Eric

Dazed and bruised from a beating, Eric, 29, was discovered wandering around a Daytona Beach shopping mall. . . . Transferred six weeks later to Daytona Beach's Human Resources Center, Eric began talking to doctors in two voices: the infantile rhythms of "young Eric," a dim and frightened child, and the measured tones of "older Eric," who told a tale of terror and child abuse. According to "older Eric," after his immigrant German parents died, a harsh stepfather and his mistress took Eric from his native South Carolina to a drug dealers' hideout in a Florida swamp. Eric said he was raped by several gang members and watched his stepfather murder two men.

One day . . . an alarmed counselor watched Eric's face twist into a violent snarl. Eric let loose an unearthly growl and spat out a stream of obscenities. . . . That disclosure of a new personality, who insolently demanded to be called Mark, was the first indication that [the doctors] had been dealing with . . . multiple personality. . . .

. . . Eric gradually unfurled 27 different personalities, including three females. . . . They ranged in age from a fetus to a sordid old man who kept trying to persuade Eric to fight as a mercenary in Haiti.

(*Time*, October 25, 1982, p. 70)

How Do Psychodynamic Theorists Explain Dissociative Disorders? A variety of theories have been proposed to explain dissociative disorders. The psychodynamic explanation, like all other explanations for these disorders, has failed to receive much research support (Merenda, 2008). However, because its explanation of the disorders highlights a key psychoanalytic defence mechanism, it is worth taking note of this viewpoint.

Psychodynamic theorists believe that dissociative disorders are caused by *repression*, the most basic ego defence mechanism. As you read in Chapter 13, psychodynamic theorists believe that people fight off anxiety by unconsciously preventing painful memories, thoughts, or impulses from reaching awareness. Everyone uses repression to a degree, but people with dissociative disorders are thought to repress their memories excessively (Henderson, 2010; Fayek, 2002).

In the psychodynamic view, dissociative amnesia and fugue are *single episodes* of massive repression. In each of these disorders, a person unconsciously blocks the memory of an extremely upsetting event to avoid the pain of facing it (Kikuchi et al., 2010). Repression may be their only protection from overwhelming anxiety.

In contrast, dissociative identity disorder is thought to result from a *lifetime* of excessive repression (Howell, 2011; Wang & Jiang, 2007). Psychodynamic theorists believe that continuous use of repression is motivated by traumatic childhood events, particularly abusive parenting (Baker, 2010). Children who experience such traumas may come to fear the dangerous world they live in and take flight from it by pretending to be another person who is looking on safely from afar. Abused children may also come to fear the impulses that they believe are the reasons for their excessive punishments. Whenever they experience "bad" thoughts or impulses, they unconsciously try to disown and deny them by assigning them to other personalities.

Most of the support for the psychodynamic position is drawn from case histories, which report such brutal childhood experiences as beatings, cuttings, burnings with cigarettes, imprisonment in closets, rape, and extensive verbal abuse (Ross & Ness, 2010). Yet some individuals with dissociative identity disorder do not seem to have experiences of abuse in their background. Moreover, child abuse appears to be far more common than dissociative identity disorder. This has left many critics asking why, if the psychodynamic explanation has merit, do only a small fraction of abused children develop this disorder?

How Does the Neuroscience Approach Explain Dissociative Disorders? The challenge with accepting a psychodynamic explanation of dissociative disorder is that while there are many descriptive terms that seem to prove insight into how dissociative disorders might work (e.g., repression), the terms do not really work as part of causal explanations as there is little in the way of solid scientific support for them. The neuroscience approach does not have a lot to offer in this area as yet (perhaps because things like identity are so neurologically complex), but there have been a number of intriguing findings in recent years. For example, one study used MRI scans to examine the hippocampus and amygdala of individuals with and without dissociative disorder. Both of these brain regions were found to be significantly smaller in those with dissociative disorder. As well, these same regions have been found to be smaller in other individuals with histories of childhood trauma (Vermetten et al., 2006). While this link between the volume of these brain regions and childhood trauma is clear, the role it plays in dissociative disorder has not yet been figured out. Other studies have shown decreased functioning in several emotional processing areas of the brains of individuals struggling with dissociative disorders (Phillips & Sierra, 2003). Finally, PET scans of the brains of individuals with and without dissociative disorders show significant differences in the level of activity in both the sensory cortex and in areas of the brain previously found to be associated with integrated body schemes (Simeon et al., 2000).

What this sort of research is starting to suggest is that it may be possible to begin to identify how some of the complex components of dissociative disorders are drawn out in the brain. This sort of understanding is the first of many steps toward a complete understanding and treatment options.

Personality Disorders

Each of us has a personality—a unique and enduring pattern of inner experience and outward behaviour. We tend to react in our own predictable and consistent ways. Yet, as you saw in Chapter 13, our personalities are also flexible. We learn from experience. As we interact with our surroundings, we try out various responses to see which are more effective. This is a flexibility that people who display a personality disorder do not have.

personality disorder an inflexible pattern of inner experience and outward behaviour that causes distress or difficulty with daily functioning.

A **personality disorder** is a very rigid pattern of inner experience and outward behaviour. The pattern is seen in most of the person's interactions, continues for years, and differs markedly from the experiences and behaviours usually expected of people. Such disorders typically become recognizable in adolescence or early adulthood, although some seem to start during childhood (Westen et al., 2011). It has been estimated that as many as 9 to 13 percent of all adults may have a personality disorder (Paris, 2010; O'Connor, 2008).

DSM-IV-TR identifies 10 personality disorders. Only two of them, the *antisocial* and *borderline personality disorders*, have been studied extensively, partly because they create so many problems for other people.

antisocial personality disorder a personality disorder characterized by extreme and callous disregard for the feelings and rights of others.

Antisocial Personality Disorder Sometimes described as "psychopaths" or "sociopaths," people with **antisocial personality disorder** persistently disregard and violate others' rights (APA, 2000). Aside from substance-related disorders, this is the disorder most closely linked to adult criminal behaviour. Most people with antisocial personality disorder display some patterns of misbehaviour before the age of 15, including truancy, running away, physical cruelty to animals or people, and destroying property (Holmes, Slaughter, & Kashani, 2001).

Antisocial personality disorder was referred to as "moral insanity" during the nineteenth century.

People with antisocial personality disorder lie repeatedly (Patrick, 2007). Many cannot work consistently at a job; they are frequently absent and are likely to quit their jobs altogether. Usually they are also careless with money and frequently fail to pay their debts. They are often impulsive, taking action without thinking of the consequences (Millon, 2011). Correspondingly, they may be irritable, aggressive, and quick to start fights.

Recklessness is another common trait: people with antisocial personality disorder have little regard for their own safety or for that of others, even their children. They are self-centred as well, and likely to have difficulty maintaining close relationships. Usually they develop a knack for gaining personal profit at the expense of other people. The pain or damage they cause seldom concerns them, so clinicians commonly say that they lack a moral conscience (Kantor, 2006). They think of their victims as weak and deserving of being conned or robbed.

Robert Hare of the University of British Columbia has developed and broadly assessed a measure of psychopathy called the Psychopathy Checklist–Revised (PCL-R; Hare, 2003). Hare argues that psychopathy is a more extreme disorder than antisocial personalilty disorder, and he argues that psychopathy should be viewed as a separate disorder. The scale provides subscale scores on aggressive narcisism and socially deviant lifestyle. Scores on the scale correlate well with diagnoses of antisocial personality disorder, but the PCL-R is more speficic. Hare's data indicates that while about 80 percent of individuals in Canadian prisons would meet the DSM criteria for antisocial personality disorder, only 20 percent would meet the PCL-R criteria for psychopathy. The 20 percent identified by the PCL-R are responsible for 50 percent of the most serious crimes (Hare, 1993).

Psychopathy and crime. Half of all serious and repeat rapists and nearly half of all murderers meet the criteria for psychopathy on Robert Hare's PCL-R scale.

Beyond Robert Hare's data, there is no general Canadian data available; however, American surveys indicate that as many as 2 to 3.5 percent of people in the United States meet the criteria for antisocial personality disorder (Paris, 2010; O'Connor, 2008). It is likely that Canadian numbers are similar. The disorder is as much as four times more common among men than women.

Because people with this disorder are often arrested, researchers frequently look for people with antisocial patterns in prison populations (Black et al., 2010). In fact, as many as 30 percent of people in prison may meet the criteria for antisocial personality disorder (O'Connor, 2008).

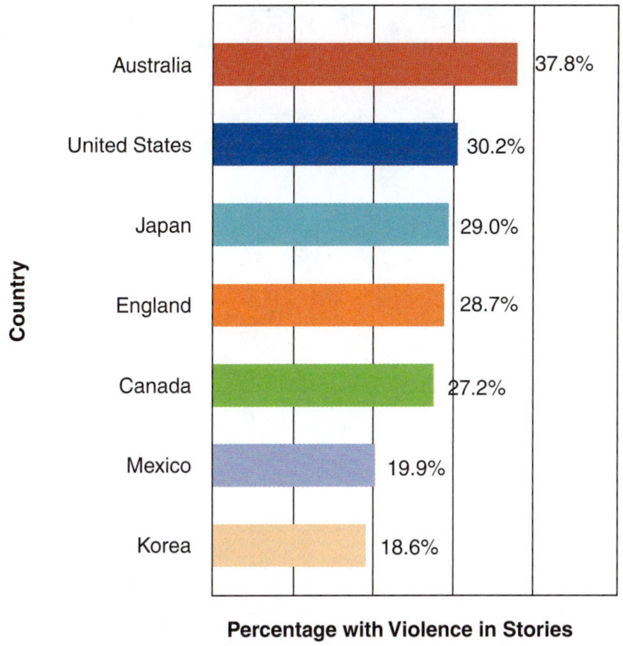

FIGURE 16-6 Antisocial behaviour, country by country. In a cross-cultural study, teenagers described how imaginary characters would respond to conflicts. Almost 40 percent of the respondents from Australia described violent responses, compared to almost 30 percent of respondents from Canada, and fewer than 20 percent of those from Korea. (Adapted from Archer & McDaniel, 1995.)

What Causes Antisocial Personality Disorder? Although the various models provide a range of explanations for antisocial personality disorder, none has managed to account for the broad range of symptoms found in the disorder. However, the behavioural and neuroscience models offer insights about particular symptoms.

According to a number of behavioural theorists, antisocial symptoms may be learned through modelling (Gaynor & Baird, 2007) (see **Figure 16-6**). As evidence, they point to the particularly high rate of antisocial personality disorder found among the parents of people with this disorder (though this could also reflect a genetic aspect of the disorder). Other behaviourists have suggested that some parents unintentionally teach antisocial behaviour by regularly rewarding a child's aggressive behaviour (Kazdin, 2005). When the child misbehaves or becomes violent in reaction to the parents' requests or orders, for example, the parents may give in to restore peace. Without meaning to, they may be teaching the child to be stubborn and perhaps even violent.

Finally, a number of studies suggest that brain factors may play an important role in this disorder. Researchers have found, for example, that people with the disorder display lower serotonin activity than other individuals (Patrick, 2007). Among other things, low serotonin activity has been linked to both impulsivity and aggression—key features of antisocial personality disorder. In addition, deficient functioning has been found in the frontal lobes of persons with this disorder (Morgan & Lilienfield, 2000). Such a deficiency could help explain the poor planning, inferior judgments, and low empathy characteristic of this disorder.

Still other research reveals that people with this disorder often experience less anxiety than other people, and so may lack a key ingredient for learning (Blair et al., 2005). This would help explain why they have so much trouble learning from negative life experiences or tuning in to the emotional cues of others. Why should these individuals experience less anxiety than other people? It appears that many of them tend to respond to warnings or expectations of stress with low brain and bodily arousal (Perdeci et al., 2010; Gaynor & Baird, 2007). Perhaps because of the low arousal, the individuals easily tune out threatening or emotional situations, and so are unaffected by them.

Borderline Personality Disorder People with **borderline personality disorder** display great instability, including major shifts in mood, an unstable self-image, and impulsivity. These characteristics combine to make their relationships very unstable as well (Mason & Kreger, 2010; APA, 2000).

borderline personality disorder a personality disorder characterized by severe instability in emotions and self-concept and high levels of volatility.

People with this disorder swing in and out of very depressive, anxious, and irritable states that last anywhere from a few hours to a few days or more. Their emotions seem to be always in conflict with the world around them. They are prone to bouts of extreme anger, which sometimes result in physical aggression (Koenigsberg et al., 2002; Meyer, Ajchenbrenner, & Bowles, 2005; Zanarini et al., 1998).

Just as often, they direct their impulsive anger inward and inflict bodily harm on themselves—in the form of cutting or mutilating themselves (Whipple & Fowler, 2011). Many try to hurt themselves as a way of dealing with their chronic feelings of emptiness, boredom, and identity confusion.

PSYCHOLOGY AROUND US Self-Injury: Can Pain Relieve Pain?

"Feelings of separation and loneliness bubbled beneath my volcanic surface. Anxiety and lack of self identity swirled in the whirlpool within. It's my fault, I did this, I'm to blame, I shouldn't be here . . .

"Then, I went to work.

"First a cross. . . . In closing, a couple of parallel lines along my wrist. . . .

"My mind screamed from deep inside Dante's Inferno as the neighbors slept soundly in their beds and cats went unstartled. Blood dripped down my arm as a sign of life or something else secretly desired, I don't know. Paper towels spotted with dark red looking like a bad kitchen accident. In time, it was over and whatever psychological pain needed to be transferred to my body was complete.

"I awoke the next day with alternate physical stings and pangs on my arm and my mind in conflict. Had I gone too far? . . . This was not the first time, only the most recent."

(Cooper, 2008)

Suicidal threats and actions are also common. Studies suggest that 75 percent of people with this disorder attempt suicide at least once in their lives. As many as 10 percent actually commit suicide (Gunderson, 2011; Leichsenring et al., 2011).

People with borderline personality disorder frequently form intense, conflict-ridden relationships in which their feelings are not necessarily shared by the other person. They often violate the boundaries of a relationship. Thinking in *dichotomous* (black-and-white) terms, they quickly become furious when their expectations are not met. Yet they remain very attached to the relationships, paralyzed by a fear of being left alone. Sometimes they cut themselves or carry out other self-destructive acts to prevent partners from leaving (Berenson et al., 2011).

Around 2 percent of the general population are thought to suffer from this disorder (Paris, 2010; Sherry & Whilde, 2008). Close to 75 percent of the patients who receive this diagnosis are women (Gunderson, 2011).

What Causes Borderline Personality Disorder? Borderline personality disorder is not well understood. In recent years, however, a number of theorists have combined concepts from each of the leading models of abnormality to form a *biosocial* theory to explain the disorder. According to this view, the disorder actually begins during childhood. It results from a combination of internal forces (for example, difficulty identifying and controlling one's arousal levels and emotions) and external forces (for example, an environment in which a child's emotions are punished or disregarded). If children have difficulties identifying and controlling their emotions, and if their parents further teach them to ignore their intense feelings, the children may never learn how to properly recognize and regulate their emotional arousal or how to tolerate emotional distress. In turn, such children will be at risk for the development of borderline personality disorder (Arens et al., 2011; Linehan & Dexter-Mazza, 2008).

THINGS STUDENTS WANT TO KNOW

How does someone get declared "not criminally responsible on account of mental disorder," and can people use this to "get away with murder"?

First of all, consider a bit of contextual information. Most people with mental disorders are not violent. However, some mental disorders are associated with a greater likelihood of committing violent acts. In general, more serious disorders carry greater risk, and people with delusions may be at elevated risk (Nathan & Labgebucher, 1999).

People with schizophrenia, especially those who suffer from paranoia, may also commit violence. These people experience delusions that make them suspicious, and they feel the need to protect themselves against what they see as real danger (Junginger & McGuire, 2004). When paranoid schizophrenics react to these "dangers," their actions are difficult for others to understand and anticipate because the danger is a delusion. An extreme example of violence among schizophrenics is Theodore Kaczynski, the serial killer more commonly known as the Unabomber, who was diagnosed as paranoid schizophrenic. His paranoia focused on technology, and his violence was directed toward those who were involved with technology. Research on people discharged from mental institutions indicates that the threat of violence is elevated, but not as strongly related to the experience of threatening delusions as previously believed (Appelbaum, Robbins, & Monahan, 2000). Some other very nasty examples from Canadian history are child killer Clifford Olson and murderer Paul Bernado, both of whom meet the criteria for antisocial personality disorder, were convicted of murder, and were classified as dangerous offenders.

But the question asked is not really if insane people can commit violent acts, but whether someone who was not clearly diagnosed as disordered before committing a violent act (a potential crime) could be found not responsible for the crime on account of mental disorder. The concept of insanity, which is used in the U.S. legal system, is not a psychological one; its definition is legal. *Insanity* refers to a condition that excuses people from responsibility and protects them from punishment. From the legal point of view, a person cannot be held responsible for a crime if, at the time of the crime, the person lacked the capacity to distinguish right from wrong or to obey the law. As Regina Schuller of York University and James Ogloff of Simon Fraser University point out, the Canadian legal outcome of "not criminally responsible on account of mental disorder" is not a diagnosis or even a psychological concept; it is simply a legal finding (Schuller & Ogloff, 2001). If a person is found "not criminally responsible by reason of mental disorder," they are neither convicted nor acquitted, and as such they are not formally sentenced. Instead, a court review board decides on the most appropriate arrangement, which could be an absolute discharge, a discharge with conditions (such as probation and/or treatment or medication), or detention in a hospital.

There is an effort underway in Canada to pass something called Tim's law. The effort is being driven by the parents of Tim McLean, who was killed while sleeping at the back of a Greyhound bus and decapitated. The man charged, who has schizophrenia, is named Vincent Li. Li believed God had told him that his own life depended on his killing McLean. Li was found not criminally responsible on account of mental disorder and is currently confined in a mental facility where he is to remain until he is no longer a threat to the community. Tim's law (www.timslaw.ca) would change the possible finding to "not psychologically accountable," which would mean that individuals like Li could be found criminally responsible even with a mental disorder, ensuring that they could be more firmly incarcerated.

Consider Dorothy Joudrie, a Calgary woman who was charged with shooting her husband, Earl. Dorothy, who had been an alcoholic for many years, had been beaten by her husband over a prolonged period, though the beatings had stopped 18 years before the shooting. Claiming she had no memory of the incident and was acting in an automaton state, Dorothy shot Earl six times at close range with a small-calibre handgun. She seemed unaware of her actions, and even Earl said that she looked and sounded very calm during the shooting. At her trial, all of the psychiatrists, even those called by the prosecution, agreed that Dorothy had been in a dissociative state at the time of the shooting. Based on this evidence, the jury found her not criminally responsible for her actions. She was placed in a mental hospital and released within a year, though she continued to undergo treatment until her death.

Another thing to consider is that that only about 1 percent of all indicted defendants use an insanity defence—and the plea is successful only about one-quarter of the time (Lymburner & Roesch, 1999). Despite the number of times we come upon the idea of an insanity defence in the media, it is, in truth, quite rare. Even when the insanity plea is successful, the person rarely walks out of the courtroom a free person; such people generally are confined to mental hospitals.

Before You Go On

www.wiley.com/go/comer

What Do You Know?

18. What distinguishes a pain disorder associated with psychological factors from a conversion or somatization disorder?
19. List and describe three dissociative disorders.
20. Which disorder discussed in this section is most closely linked to adult criminal behaviour?

SCAN TO GET THE ANSWERS

What Do You Think?

Analyze a character from a film you have seen or a book you have read that has one of the disorders described in this section. Is the information provided in the text consistent with what you know of the character?

Summary

Defining, Classifying, and Diagnosing Psychological Abnormality

LEARNING OBJECTIVE 1 Identify the common features of most definitions of abnormal functioning, and describe how psychological disorders are classified and diagnosed.

- The study of psychological disorders is usually called *abnormal psychology*. Abnormal psychological functioning is a wide-ranging problem in this country.
- Definitions of psychological disorders often include the "four Ds"—deviance, distress, dysfunction, and danger.
- *The Diagnostic and Statistical Manual of Mental Disorders (DSM)* (current version DSM-IV-TR) is the leading classification system in North America.

Models of Abnormality

LEARNING OBJECTIVE 2 Describe the major models used by psychologists to explain abnormal functioning.

- Clinicians use several major models to explain abnormal functioning, including the neuroscience, psychodynamic, cognitive-behavioural, humanistic-existential, socio-cultural, and developmental psychopathology models.
- The neuroscience model views abnormal functioning as a result of malfunctions in brain structure or chemical activity. Malfunctions can be caused by injuries or other factors, including genetics or viruses.
- Psychodynamic theorists view abnormal functioning as the result of unconscious conflicts that may have originated in our early development. Freud focused on fixations during the oral, anal, and phallic stages of development, while other theorists have focused on difficulties in ego development or our relationships with others.
- Behavioural theorists propose that abnormal behaviours develop via the same processes as more adaptive behaviours: classical conditioning, operant conditioning, and modelling. Cognitive theorists believe that abnormal functioning can result from disordered thoughts, including basic irrational assumptions, specific upsetting thoughts, and illogical thinking processes.
- Humanists suggest that people are vulnerable to psychological disorders when they develop inaccurate views of their worth or goals in life. Existentialist therapies focus on helping clients discover their personal freedom of choice and take responsibility for making choices.
- According the socio-cultural model, abnormal behaviour is best understood in light of the social, cultural, and family forces brought to bear on an individual. Important factors include social change, socio-economic class membership, cultural background, social networks, and family systems.
- Developmental psychopathology theorists are interested in how psychological disorders evolve, based on both genetics and early childhood experiences, and on how those early patterns affect people's functioning as they move through later life stages.

Mood Disorders

LEARNING OBJECTIVE 3 Describe and differentiate major depressive disorder and bipolar disorder.

- The key features in mood disorders are *depression*—a low, sad state—and *mania*—a state of breathless euphoria. Most people with a mood disorder suffer only from depression.
- People with *major depressive disorder* suffer a variety of symptoms, including feelings of sadness and lack of interest, low levels of activity and productivity, negative views of themselves and their lives, and physical ailments.
- Today's leading explanations for major depressive disorder point to neuroscientific, psychological, or socio-cultural factors. Many theorists believe that the various explanations should be combined.
- People with *bipolar disorder* experience not only the lows of depression, but also the highs of mania. In the manic state, they want constant excitement. They tend to show poor judgment and planning, hold inflated opinions of themselves, and show a great deal of energy.
- Although genes and biological factors appear to play key roles in the development of bipolar disorder, there is growing evidence that stress and certain kinds of environmental events also must occur in order for episodes to unfold.

Anxiety Disorders

LEARNING OBJECTIVE 4 Describe the various types of anxiety disorders, and explain some causes of these disorders.

- As a group, anxiety disorders are the most common mental disorders in North America. Often, people with one type of anxiety disorder have another type as well.
- People with *generalized anxiety disorder* experience persistent feelings of worry and anxiety. Some cognitive theorists suggest that this disorder arises in people who hold certain dysfunctional or irrational assumptions, while others focus on the individual's intolerance of uncertainty. An important neuroscience explanation focuses on gamma-aminobutyric acid, a neurotransmitter involved in fear reactions.

- People with *social anxiety disorder* display severe, persistent, and irrational fears of social or performance situations. Some socio-cultural factors appear to be involved.
- People with *phobias* have a persistent and irrational fear of a specific object, activity, or situation. Behavioural principles, including classical conditioning and modelling, provide the leading explanations for specific phobias.
- People with *panic disorder* have recurrent attacks of terror. These *panic attacks* are sometimes accompanied by *agoraphobia*—a fear of venturing into public places. A neuroscience-cognitive explanation of the disorder focuses on physical sensations produced by malfunctioning brain circuitry, which are then misinterpreted.
- People with *obsessive-compulsive disorder* feel overrun by recurrent thoughts that cause anxiety (obsessions) and by the need to perform repetitive actions to reduce this anxiety (compulsions). While cognitive-behavioural theorists focus on the role of learning in these behaviours, neuroscientists focus on abnormally low levels of serotonin or abnormal functioning in specific brain regions.
- People with *posttraumatic stress disorder (PTSD)* are tormented by fear and related symptoms well after a horrifying event has ended. Although extraordinary trauma causes the disorder, not everyone who experiences such trauma develops PTSD. Differences in biological processes, personalities, childhood experiences, social support systems, and cultural backgrounds also make people more or less likely to respond to trauma by developing the disorder.

Schizophrenia

LEARNING OBJECTIVE 5 Describe the features of schizophrenia and some theories of what causes it.

- *Schizophrenia* is a disorder in which people deteriorate into a world of unusual perceptions, odd thoughts, disturbed emotions, and motor abnormalities. These people experience *psychosis*, a loss of contact with reality.
- Positive symptoms of schizophrenia are "pathological excesses" in behaviour. They include delusions, disorganized thinking and speech, hallucinations, and inappropriate affect.
- Negative symptoms, or "pathological deficits," include poverty of speech, flat affect, loss of volition, and social withdrawal.
- People with schizophrenia also sometimes experience unusual psychomotor symptoms, which in their most extreme form are collectively called *catatonia*.
- Many theorists believe that people inherit a genetic predisposition to schizophrenia. Two kinds of brain abnormalities might be inherited—biochemical abnormalities and abnormal brain structure.
- Although neuroscience explanations of schizophrenia have received by far the most research support, psychological and sociocultural factors may help to bring about schizophrenia in people with a biological predisposition to develop it.

Other Disorders

LEARNING OBJECTIVE 6 Discuss the features and possible causes of somatoform, dissociative, and personality disorders.

- A *somatoform disorder* is a pattern of physical complaints with largely psychosocial causes. In *conversion disorder*, *somatization disorder*, and *pain disorder associated with psychological factors*, there is an actual change in physical functioning. In *hypochondriasis* and *body dysmorphic disorder*, people who are healthy mistakenly worry that there is something physically wrong with them.
- Theorists typically explain hypochondriasis and body dysmorphic disorders much as they explain anxiety disorders, as resulting from classical conditioning, modelling, or misinterpretation of bodily cues. Psychodynamic and socio-cultural explanations have been offered for conversion, somatization, and pain disorders, but these explanations have failed to receive much research support.
- Changes in memory that lack a physical cause are called *dissociative disorders*. In *dissociative amnesia*, people are unable to recall important information about their lives. In *dissociative fugue*, people not only forget their identities and their past lives, but also flee to a different location. In *dissociative identity disorder*, people develop two or more distinct personalities.
- Psychodynamic theorists believe that dissociative disorders are caused by repression, the most basic ego defence mechanism, but this view has not received strong research support.
- People with *antisocial personality disorder* persistently disregard and violate others' rights. Because of their potentially negative behaviour, such as lying, impulsiveness, and recklessness, they are frequently found in prison. According to behavioural theorists, this disorder can be learned through various means. Neuroscience explanations focus on brain factors, such as low serotonin levels, deficient frontal lobe functioning, and low arousal in response to warnings.
- People with *borderline personality disorder* display great instability, including major shifts in mood, an unstable self-image, and impulsivity. This disorder is not well understood, but a recent biosocial theory proposes that it results from a combination of internal and external forces.

Key Terms

abnormal psychology 614
acute stress disorder 642
agoraphobia 639
antipsychotic drugs 648
antisocial personality disorder 654
automatic thoughts 632
bipolar disorder 628
borderline personality disorder 655
catatonia 646
cognitive triad 632
comorbidity 619
compulsions 640
delusions 646
depression 628
developmental psychopathology 627
diagnosis 617
Diagnostic and Statistical Manual of Mental Disorders (DSM) 617
dissociative disorder 651
equifinality 627
family systems theory 626
generalized anxiety disorder 634
hallucinations 646
International Classification of Diseases (ICD) 617
loose associations, or derailment 646
major depressive disorder 628
mania 628
multifinality 627
negative symptoms 646
obsessions 640
obsessive-compulsive disorder (OCD) 640
panic attacks 639
panic disorder 639
personality disorder 654
phobia 638
positive symptoms 644
posttraumatic stress disorder (PTSD) 642
psychosis 644
resilience 627
risk factors 627
schizophrenia 644
social anxiety disorder 636
somatoform disorder 649

TYING IT TOGETHER

The study of psychological disorders is closely connected to all other areas of psychology. Throughout this chapter, we have stressed how this topic interfaces with psychology's other areas, including our highlighted sections on brain function, individual differences, and development. To remind you of how psychological disorders are tied to such areas, here are some interesting points from throughout the chapter.

WHAT HAPPENS IN THE BRAIN?

- Low activity of the neurotransmitter GABA has been linked to several anxiety disorders.
- Low serotonin and low norepinephrine activity have been tied to depression.
- High dopamine activity accompanies schizophrenia.
- Improper functioning of various brain structures and brain circuits has also been linked to psychological disorders.

HOW WE DIFFER

- Poor people experience more psychological disorders than wealthy people.
- Women dignosed with depression and panic disorders outnumber men with these disorders by at least 2 to 1.
- Aboriginal Canadians have higher rates of alcoholism and suicide than any other ethnic or racial group.
- People with high sensitivity to bodily cues are more likely to develop certain anxiety disorders and somatoform disorders.

WHEN THINGS GO WRONG

- Over 400 psychological disorders are listed in the DSM.
- Around 12 percent of adults suffer from one or more of the anxiety disorders, making them the most common psychological disorders in Canada.
- Around 5 percent of adults experience major depressive disorder, whereas 1 percent display bipolar disorder.
- Almost 3 percent of all divorced or separated people suffer from schizophrenia, compared to 1 percent of married persons.

HOW WE DEVELOP

- Traumas and significant losses during childhood increase the likelihood of developing adult depression.
- People who acquire dysfunctional attitudes early in life are more likely to develop generalized anxiety disorder, social anxiety disorder, and depression in adolescence or adulthood.
- Individuals whose childhoods are filled with uncontrollable events are prone to develop depression.
- People who develop resilience in life can overome early risk factors for psychopathology.

Psychology Around Us

Spotting Psychological Disorders

View this in Action WILEY PLUS www.wileyplus.com

Video Lab Exercise

How good are you at identifying psychological dysfunctioning? Can you distinguish a normal mood downswing from a depressive disorder? Can you tell the difference between normal anxiety and anxiety disorders? This video lab exercise will answer those questions, as you play "diagnostician for a day."

In this exercise, you'll consider the video behaviours, emotions, and thoughts of individuals with psychological problems, and, using decision trees, you'll decide whether or not they should receive a clinical diagnosis. As a diagnostician, you'll also get the chance to show off your knowledge of the DSM. Most likely, when all is said and done, you'll come to appreciate that distinguishing between normal and abnormal behaviour is harder than it looks.

As you are working on this online exercise, consider the following questions:

- How useful is the process of diagnosis in general and the application of the DSM in particular?
- What are the limitations and undesired effects of psychological labelling?
- Medical school students often come to believe that they have the diseases they're reading about in their textbooks. This phenomenon is even more common among psychology students as they read about clinical disorders. Why?

CHAPTER 17

Treatment of Psychological Disorders

CHAPTER OUTLINE

- Treatment in Today's World
- Biological Treatments *What Happens In The Brain?*
- Psychodynamic Therapies *How We Develop*
- Behavioural Therapies
- Cognitive-Behavioural Therapies
- Humanistic and Existential Therapies
- Formats of Therapy
- Does Therapy Work?
- Some Final Thoughts About the Field of Psychology

FINDING HIS WAY BACK

February: *He cannot leave the house; Jefferson knows that for a fact. Home is the only place where he feels safe—safe from humiliation, danger, even ruin. If he were to go to work, his co-workers would somehow reveal their contempt for him. A pointed remark, a quizzical look—that's all it would take for him to get the message. If he were to go shopping at the store, before long everyone would be staring at him. Surely others would see his dark mood and thoughts; he wouldn't be able to hide them. He dare not even go for a walk alone in the woods—his heart would probably start racing again, bringing him to his knees and leaving him breathless, incoherent, and unable to get home. No, he's much better off staying in his room, trying to get through another evening of this curse called life. Thank goodness for the Internet. Were it not for his reading of news sites and postings to blogs and online forums, he knows he would be cut off from the world altogether.*

July: *Jefferson's life revolves around his circle of friends—Mikel and Jason from the office, where he was recently promoted to director of customer relations, and Bryant and Darnell, his weekend tennis partners. The gang meets for dinner every week at someone's house, and they chat about life, politics, and their jobs. Particularly special in Jefferson's life is Kyra. They go to movies, restaurants, and concerts together. She thinks Jefferson's just terrific, and Jefferson finds himself beaming whenever she's around. Jefferson looks forward to work each day and to his one-on-one dealings with customers. He's taking part in many activities and relationships and more fully enjoying life.*

Jefferson's thoughts, feelings, and behaviour interfered with all aspects of his life in February. Yet most of his symptoms had disappeared by July. Many factors may have contributed to Jefferson's improvement—advice from friends and family members, a new job or vacation, perhaps a big change in his diet or exercise regimen. Any or all of these things may have been useful, but they could not be considered **treatment**, or **therapy**. Those terms are usually reserved for specific, systematic procedures designed to change abnormal behaviour into more normal behaviour. According to the clinical theorist Jerome Frank, all forms of therapy have three essential features:

treatment, or **therapy** systematic procedures designed to change abnormal behaviour into more normal behaviour.

1. A *sufferer* who seeks relief from the healer.
2. A trained, socially accepted *healer*, whose expertise is accepted by the sufferer and his or her social group.
3. A *series of contacts* between the healer and the sufferer, through which the healer tries to produce certain changes in the sufferer's emotional state, attitudes, and behaviour. The healing process may be brought about primarily by **psychotherapy**—in Frank's words, "by words, acts, and rituals in which sufferer, healer, and—if there is one—group participate jointly." Or it may be accomplished through **biological therapy**, consisting of "physical and chemical procedures" (Frank, 1973, pp. 2–3).

psychotherapy a treatment system in which a client and therapist use words and acts to overcome the client's psychological difficulties.

biological therapy the use of physical and chemical procedures to help people overcome psychological difficulties.

Healers are called *clinicians*, *clinical practitioners*, or *therapists*. You read about the work of *clinical researchers* in Chapter 16. As you saw, they gather information systematically so that they can better describe, explain, and predict psychological disorders. The knowledge that they acquire is then used by clinicians, whose role is to detect, assess, and treat people with psychological disorders.

Getting help. Therapy is a systematic procedure to help people deal with the pathology, adjustment issues, or day-to-day problems that are negatively affecting their lives.

Despite Frank's (1973) straightforward definition, clinical treatment is surrounded by conflict and confusion. In fact, Carl Rogers has been cited as saying that "therapists are not in agreement as to their goals or aims. . . . They are not in agreement as to what constitutes a successful outcome of their work. They cannot agree as to what constitutes a failure. It seems as though the field is completely chaotic and divided" (Comer, 2010).

Some clinicians view abnormality as an illness and so consider therapy a procedure that helps cure the illness. Others see abnormality as a problem in living and therapists as teachers of more functional behaviour and thought. Clinicians even differ on what to call the person who receives therapy. Those who see abnormality as an illness speak of the "patient," while those who view it as a problem in living refer to the "client." Because both terms are so common, this chapter will use them interchangeably.

Despite their differences, most clinicians do agree that large numbers of people need therapy of one kind or another. Later you will encounter evidence that therapy is indeed often helpful. ■

Treatment in Today's World

LEARNING OBJECTIVE 1

Explain who receives treatment for psychological problems today, how they enter treatment, and what general features characterize different types of treatment.

A Canadian Mental Health Association (2005) survey indicates that Canadians view mental health as being as important as their physical health. Other surveys suggest that more than 20 million people—children, adolescents, and adults—in North America receive therapy for psychological problems in the course of a year (NAMI, 2011). The number and variety of problems for which treatments are available have increased during the past 110 years. When Freud and his colleagues first began conducting therapy during the late nineteenth and early twentieth centuries, most of their patients suffered from anxiety or depression. People with schizophrenia and other more severe disorders were considered poor prospects for therapy, and treatment for them was confined to custodial care in institutions (Levin, Hennessy, & Petrila, 2010).

All of that has changed since the 1950s. Anxiety and depression still dominate the therapy picture, as more than three-quarters of Canadians diagnosed with a mental illness each year suffer from one or the other of these two disorder types (Health Canada, 2002). However, people with other kinds of disorders also receive therapy (NIDA, 2011; CDC, 2010; SAMHSA, 2010, 2008; Narrow et al., 1993). People with schizophrenia and people with substance-related disorders, for example, make up a large percentage of the clients in therapy today. Moreover, large numbers of people with milder psychological problems, sometimes called "problems in living," are also in therapy. Surveys suggest that non-disordered reasons for entering therapy largely include problems with marriage, family, job, peer, school, or community relationships (Vessey & Howard, 1993).

Who Seeks Treatment? HOW WE DIFFER

Other characteristics of clients have also changed over the years. Until the middle of the twentieth century, therapy was primarily a privilege of the wealthy, largely because of the high fees that outpatients were required to pay. After all, Freud's fee for one session of therapy was $20 ($160 in today's dollars). The current cost of private outpatient therapy varies by service and location. Provincial psychologists' regulatory groups (e.g., the Ontario College of Psychologists) set the hourly rate for psychological therapy. The hourly rate among provinces typically ranges from $130 to $180. However, with the expansion of third-party coverage (such as Blue Cross) and the emergence of publicly-supported community mental health centres, people at all socio-economic levels now receive both outpatient and inpatient therapy.

Women used to outnumber men in therapy by four to one, partly because they were less reluctant than men to seek help. Lately, however, our society's attitudes and sex-role expectations have been changing, and men are increasingly willing to enter therapy (Addis & Mahalik, 2003). More than one-third of today's therapy patients are male (NIDA, 2011; CDC, 2010). As you will see later in this chapter, however, members of ethnic minority groups tend to seek treatment for their psychological problems less often (Comas-Diaz, 2011, 2006).

Entering and Receiving Treatment

People enter therapy in various ways. Many decide on their own to consult a therapist. Others may do so on the advice of a friend, family member, minister, physician, or other professional with whom they have discussed their difficulties. Still others are forced into treatment. Parents, spouses, teachers, and employers may virtually order people to seek treatment if they are causing disruptions or are in obvious distress; or judges may formally pronounce people mentally disturbed and dangerous and commit them to a mental hospital for treatment.

In most cases, the decision to seek therapy is not easy. Extensive studies indicate that most individuals are aware of their problems well before they look for help. Many wait more than two years after they first become aware that they have a problem. And it is estimated that at least half of the people with psychological disorders never seek treatment (Ndumele & Trivedi, 2011; SoRelle, 2000). Generally speaking, therapy seems to hold greater attraction for those who have a social network of "friends and supporters of therapy"—people who have themselves been clients or who express confidence in therapy as a solution to personal problems (SAMHSA, 2008, 2002; Kadushin, 1969).

The under-use of therapy has a long history. Back in the 1970s, for example, a labour union in the United States, called the United Auto Workers, negotiated a contract in which management agreed to pay the entire cost of both inpatient and outpatient mental health services for a million union members. Yet, after three years, only 1 percent of eligible workers had used the benefit (Brown, 1976). Apparently they and their referral agents (shop foremen, clergy, and the like) were either unaware of the benefit, ignorant of what therapy could do for them, unlikely to think about personal problems in mental health terms, or worried about the stigma that psychological problems might bring in their social set.

The stigma of seeking therapy. Many people don't seek therapy because there is a social stigma against it. Some people believe therapy is for "whiners" and they don't want to be perceived as "weak" by their social set. The truth is that therapy can benefit anyone and it is not a weakness to seek help.

Heather Stuart of Queens University (2010) has reviewed the history of efforts within Canada to reduce the stigma associated with acknowledging and obtaining treatment for mental illness. As far back as the 1950s, efforts were underway to reduce the stigma associated with mental illness and to help Canadians move toward an understanding that many mental illnesses can be treated, and that most can be treated outside of hospital settings. For example, as efforts were underway to reduce the number of mental patients treated in hospitals, there was initial resistance from the public based on unfounded fears regarding public safety if mentally ill people were treated on an outpatient basis. Since that time, there has been a significant reduction in the stigma associated with mental illness. However, perceptions of stigma continue to play a role in people's decisions about whether or not to acknowledge their mental issues and whether or not to seek treatment.

Conducting Treatment: Who, Where, and How

A variety of professionals conduct therapy today. Most are psychologists, psychiatrists, counsellors, and psychiatric social workers. Whatever their profession, these therapists generally see the same kinds of clients. That is, the majority of their clients are people with anxiety, depression, or relationship problems. However, although psychiatrists treat clients with depression, anxiety, and relationship issues, they see a much larger number of patients with schizophrenia, bipolar disorders, and other severe disorders than do psychologists, counsellors, or social workers. The providers of mental health services are concentrated in urban areas across Canada. In fact, there is a shortage of practitioners available to serve the needs of the many people who live in rural areas (Jackson et al., 2007; Smith et al., 2004). Even in the larger centres, some kinds of services are easier to access (e.g., medications through hospital psychiatric or emergency wards) than others (e.g., counselling, therapy, and support) (Kirby & Keon, 2006).

Therapy takes place in all sorts of settings, from public institutions, to schools, to private offices. Most clients, even those who are severely disturbed, are treated as outpatients. They live in the community and make regular visits to the therapist's office or hospital/clinic. Most of the people who receive inpatient treatment, whether in the psychiatric wards of general hospitals or in psychiatric hospitals, have severe psychological problems (Craig & Power, 2010). The Canadian health care system ensures that mental health services and necessary treatments are available to all who need them, either through hospital facilities or outpatient clinics. Therapy offered by psychologists in private practice is usually paid for by the people who seek out such mental health services; however, many workplace health insurance providers offer some coverage for psychological treatment.

Guidelines for admitting individuals to psychiatric facilities, either voluntarily or involuntarily, are provided in the Canadian Mental Health Act (Choy & Mamak, in press). This act includes information on the conditions under which a person can be admitted and detained in hospital against his will, and also outlines the rights of patients in psychiatric facilities.

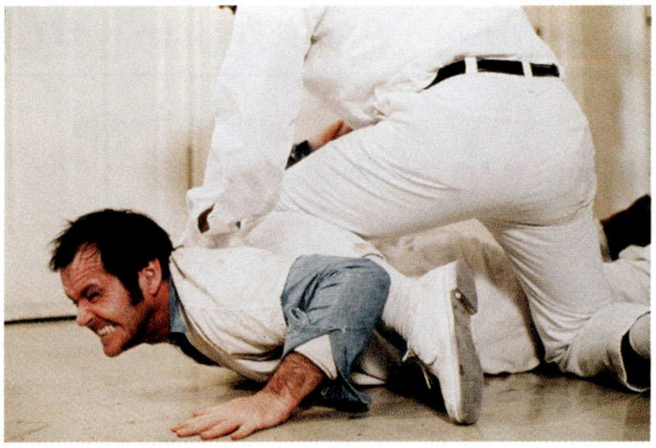

The "crazy house." For many, the perception of psychiatric care continues to be something like the treatment received by the patients portrayed in the well-known movie *One Flew Over the Cuckoo's Nest*. However, the reality is that laws and policies protect Canadians hospitalized with mental illness.

Clinicians have become increasingly concerned about the negative effects of long-term institutionalization. Thus, beginning in the 1960s, they carried out a policy of *deinstitutionalization* that basically continued over the next 40 years. Paul Whitehead of the University of Western Ontario reported this process as being quite variable across Canada. In general terms, the number of psychiatric beds per 1,000 population went from four in 1964 to one in 1975 and the total number of psychiatric beds dropped from 54,801 in 1975 to 20,301 in 1981 (Sealy & Whitehead, 2004).

Hospitalization today usually lasts weeks instead of months or years. When people develop severe psychological disorders, therapists now try to treat them first as outpatients, usually with medications along with other forms of therapy. If this strategy proves ineffective, the patient may be admitted to a hospital for a short period so that the condition can be monitored, diagnosed, and stabilized. As soon as hospitalization has served the purpose of stabilization, the patient is returned to the community.

In theory, this may be a reasonable treatment plan for people with severe psychological disorders. However, as you will see later, community treatment facilities have been so underfunded and understaffed over the years that they have not been able to meet the treatment needs of the majority of severely impaired people. Indeed, many people with severe psychological disorders are currently condemned to an endless cycle of hospital discharges and readmissions and are often homeless (Frankish, Hwang, & Quantz, 2005). According to the Canadian Institute for Health Information (2008), one-third of Canadians released from hospital following treatment for mental illness are readmitted to hospital within a year.

In the clinical field today there are, by some estimates, more than 400 forms of therapy, each practised by clinicians who believe that their chosen methodology is highly effective (Karasu, 1992). Typically, the therapists use principles and techniques that they have been trained in and are consistent with the theories of psychological dysfunction they have been taught.

In Chapter 16, you read about today's leading theories explaining psychological disorders. Proponents of those explanations have proposed corresponding treatment approaches, and clinical practitioners have put those approaches into action as they work with clients. Carl Rogers's humanistic theory, for example, identifies self-awareness and self-actualization as fundamental to good mental health. Correspondingly, therapists who follow his client-centred treatment approach listen to and empathize with clients, expecting that such techniques will help the clients become better aware of themselves and more able to actualize their special human potential. The following sections focus on biological, psychodynamic, behavioural, cognitive-behavioural, and humanistic-existential therapies (see **Table 17-1** on the next page). Recall from our chapter opener, though, that all these forms of therapy have three essential features: a sufferer who seeks relief, a trained healer, and a series of contacts between the two in which the healer tries to bring about changes in the sufferer's emotional state, attitudes, and behaviour.

T[illegible] Comparison of Treatments for Psychological Disorders

	Goals of Therapy	Therapy Techniques	Strengths	Weaknesses
Biological Approaches	Improve structural or biochemical functioning, relieve symptoms	Psychotropic drugs; electroconvulsive therapy (ECT); psychosurgery	• Often effective for people whose problems don't respond to other treatments	• Side effects • Not always effective • May neglect non-biological problems of clients
Psychodynamic Approaches	Discover source of conflicts and resolve them	Free association; therapist analysis of resistance, transference, and dreams; catharsis; and working through problems	• Offered first major alternative to biological treatments • Sees abnormal functioning as rooted in same processes as normal functioning • Model for many other psychological treatments	• Research does not support effectiveness of therapies
Behavioural Approaches	Learn more functional behaviours	Desensitization; aversion therapy; operant conditioning, including token economies; therapist modelling, including social-skills training	• Research often supports effectiveness of treatments	• Effects of treatment may not always last long after treatment stops • May neglect unobservable cognitive processes
Cognitive-Behavioural Approaches	Change harmful thinking patterns to more useful ones	Rational-emotive therapy; cognitive therapy cognitive-behavioural techniques	• Considerable research supports for its application to several disorders	• Dysfunctional thinking may result from, not cause, abnormal functioning
Humanistic and Existential Approaches	Provide support for honest self-appraisal, self-acceptance, and self-actualization	Client-centred and gestalt therapy techniques; existential therapy	• Recognize positive human goals • Recognize distinctly human values and needs	• Unsupportive and limited research to test effectiveness

Before You Go On

www.wiley.com/go/comer

What Do You Know?

1. What trends have changed who tends to receive treatment for psychological disorders?
2. How does inpatient therapy differ from outpatient therapy?
3. What are the three key features common to all forms of therapy?

What Do You Think?

Why do you suppose people tend to wait so long before seeking help for a psychological problem? If you were experiencing some sort of psychological difficulty—say, depression—how do you think you would arrive at the decision to get treatment?

SCAN TO GET THE ANSWERS

Biological Treatments

WHAT HAPPENS IN THE BRAIN?

LEARNING OBJECTIVE 2

Describe the major biological treatments for psychological disorders.

Biological therapies use chemical and physical methods to help people overcome their psychological problems. The practitioners who apply such approaches are usually *psychiatrists*, therapists whose training includes medical school. The three principal kinds of brain interventions are *drug therapy*, *electroconvulsive therapy*, and *psychosurgery*. Drug therapy is by far the most common of these approaches.

Drug Therapy

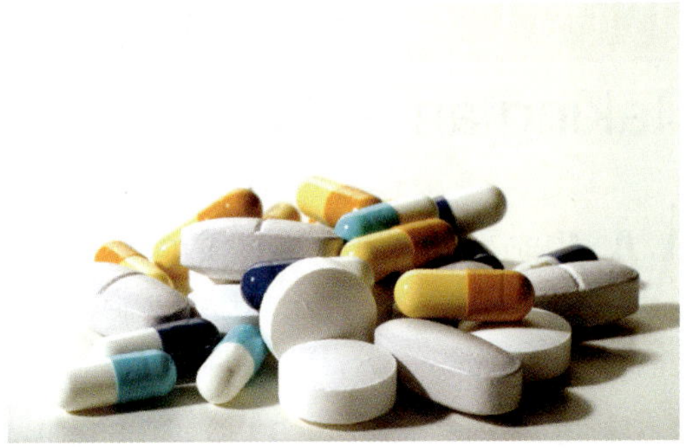

Since the 1950s, researchers have discovered several kinds of effective psychotropic drugs. These drugs act primarily on the brain and, in many cases, significantly reduce the symptoms of psychological disorders (Julien et al., 2011). We have touched on some of these medications throughout this book. Such drugs are now used widely, either as the first-line treatment for a disorder or in conjunction with psychotherapy or other interventions.

As you can see in **Table 17-2**, four major psychotropic drug groups are used in therapy: antianxiety, antidepressant, antibipolar, and antipsychotic drugs. Antianxiety drugs, also called *minor tranquilizers* or *anxiolytics*, help reduce tension and anxiety. Antidepressant drugs help improve the mood of people who are depressed. Antibipolar drugs, also called *mood stabilizers*, help steady the moods of those with a bipolar disorder, the condition marked by mood swings from mania to depression. And antipsychotic drugs help reduce the confusion, hallucinations, and delusions of *psychotic disorders*, the disorders (such as schizophrenia) marked by a loss of contact with reality.

These medications have radically changed the outlook for many people with psychological disorders. However, they do not work for everyone. Moreover, many clinical theorists worry that the drugs are being overused and, at times, misused, in our quick-fix world. Another concern is that some drugs have serious undesired effects. The risks of taking these drugs must be weighed against the good the drugs can do. For example, certain of the *antipsychotic drugs* may produce severe movement abnormalities, including severe shaking, bizarre-looking contractions of the face and body, and extreme restlessness (Geddes et al., 2011). Fortunately, in recent decades, researchers have developed a new group of antipsychotic drugs, called *atypical* antipsychotic drugs. These new drugs are not as likely to produce unpleasant and dangerous effects. In addition, they are often more effective than the conventional antipsychotic drugs (Julien et al., 2011).

Neuroscientists continue to advance in their ability to map the brain and connect its functioning with human behaviour. As progress continues, they believe that they will eventually be able to pinpoint the actions of drugs and their precise areas of impact. The result will be drugs that are more effective and that have fewer harmful or annoying side effects.

psychotropic drugs medications that act primarily on the brain.

antianxiety drugs psychotropic drugs that reduce tension and anxiety.

antidepressant drugs psychotropic drugs that lift the mood of depressed people.

antibipolar drugs psychotropic drugs that help stabilize the moods of people suffering from bipolar disorder.

antipsychotic drugs psychotropic drugs that help correct grossly confused or distorted thinking.

Electroconvulsive Therapy

Another form of biological treatment is electroconvulsive therapy (ECT), a technique first developed in the 1930s. ECT is used primarily for people who have severe depression.

electroconvulsive therapy (ECT) use of electric shock to trigger a brain seizure in hopes of relieving abnormal functioning.

TABLE 17-2 Commonly Prescribed Psychotropic Drugs

Symptom	Type of Medication	Examples
Psychosis (loss of touch with reality)	Antipsychotics Atypical antipsychotics	chlorpromazine (Thorazine) clozapine (Clozaril) risperidone (Risperdal)
Depression	Antidepressants	trazodone (Desyrel) amitriptyline (Elavil) phenelzine (Nardil) fluoxetine (Prozac) paroxetine (Paxil) sertraline (Zoloft) venlafaxine (Effexor)
Mania	Mood stabilizers Antipsychotics	lithium (Lithonate) carbamazepine (Tegretol) valproate (Depakote) olanzapine (Zyprexa)
Anxiety	Anxiolitics Antidepressants	benzodiazepines (Valium, Xanax) fluoxetine (Prozac)

Tying It Together: **Your Brain and Behaviour**

Taking an Antidepressant

When people have symptoms of depression so severe that they interfere with normal functioning, physicians will sometimes prescribe the use of antidepressant medication. Some of the most commonly prescribed antidepressants are selective serotonin reuptake inhibitors (SSRIs); these drugs are known by trade names such as Celexa, Paxil, Prozac, and Zoloft. The primary action of these drugs is to increase the availability of the neurotransmitter serotonin in the brain. Neurons that make serotonin are present in the brainstem raphe nuclei. These neurons send axon projections to the cortex, hippocampus, and amygdala, among other regions. SSRIs have a multitude of effects on these brain regions, although the precise mechanisms by which the drugs alleviate symptoms of depression are not known. How might antidepressant drugs work?

Questions

1 **Which area of the cerebral cortex often shows reduced activity in people who are depressed?**

2 **What does it mean to say that a particular drug is a "serotonin reuptake inhibitor"?**

3 **What is the role of the hippocampus in the recovery of someone taking antidepressant medication to relieve depression?**

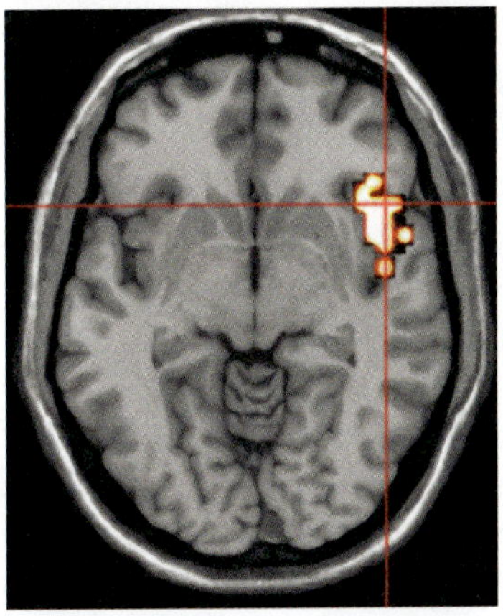

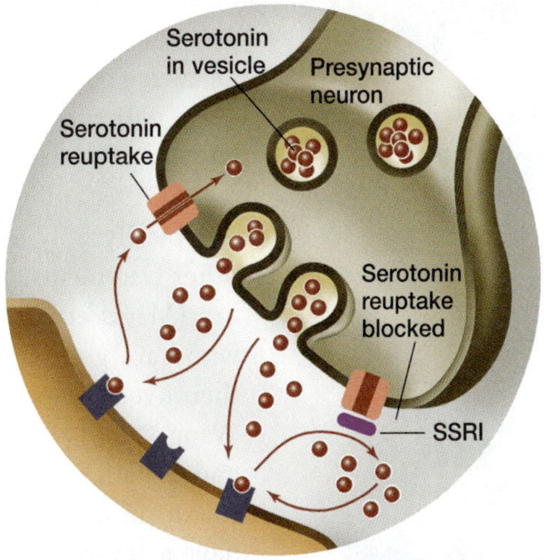

BLOCKING SEROTONIN REUPTAKE

By blocking key receptors, SSRIs prevent the reuptake, or retention, of serotonin by presynaptic neurons (shown in this illustration), thus freeing the neurotransmitter to better activate brain regions that are targets of serotonin axons, including the hippocampus and cerebral cortex. Depression relief, however, usually does not occur until someone has taken the drug for a few weeks, suggesting that some other mechanism may also be responsible for improving mood.

RESTORING BRAIN ACTIVITY TO NORMAL LEVELS

The prefrontal cortex of depressed individuals shows reduced activity and a lower than normal level of blood flow. Some studies suggest that antidepressants ultimately raise activity in this brain region (shown on this brain scan in yellow) and restore blood flow to levels observed in non-depressed individuals. Similar findings have been reported for the amygdala.

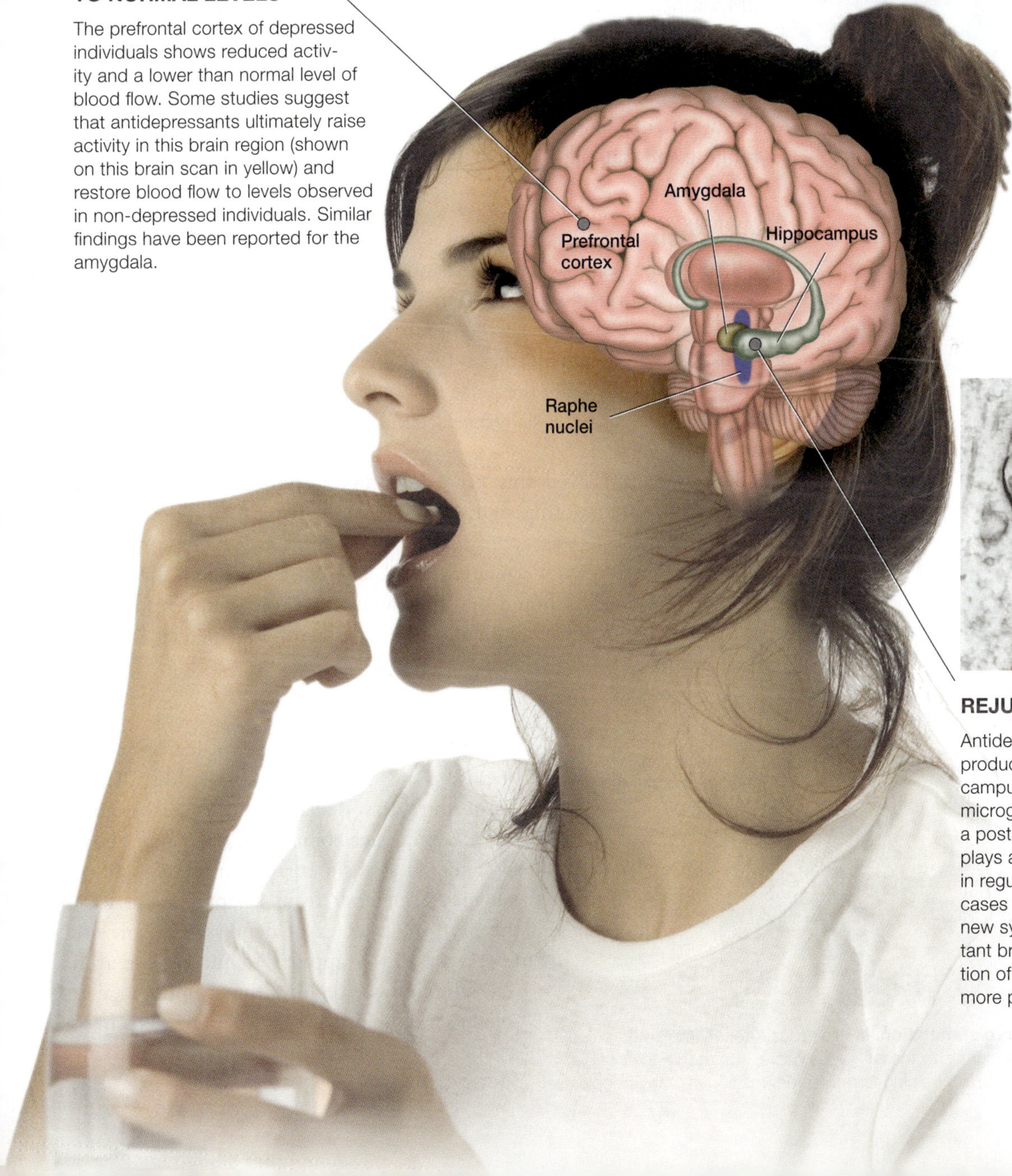

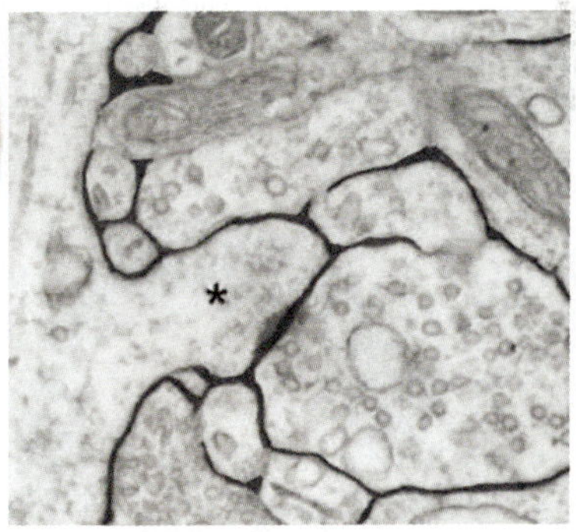

REJUVENATING THE MIND

Antidepressant use stimulates the production of synapses in the hippocampus (shown here in this electron micrograph, with the asterisk indicating a postsynaptic site). The hippocampus plays a role in cognitive function and in regulating anxiety (a feature in many cases of depression). The growth of new synapses may refresh this important brain region, enabling the formation of new connections to support a more positive outlook.

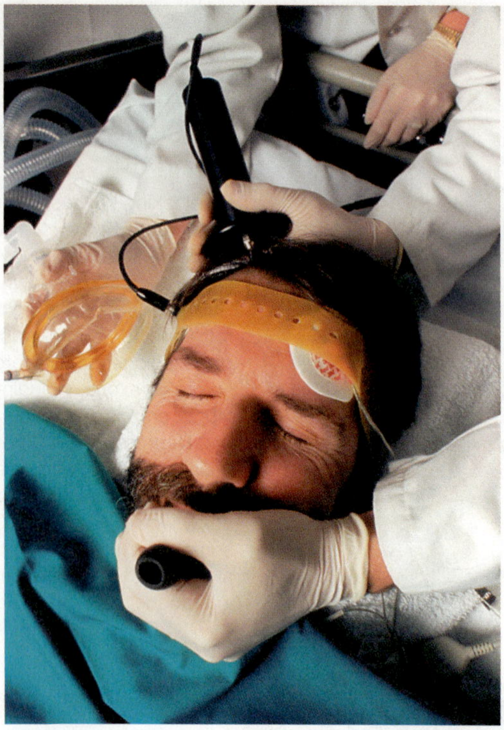

ECT today. As we can see with this patient, today's ECT treatments are conducted with considerable medical care and many safety precautions, and include procedures that help patients sleep throughout the procedure.

ECT is administered in the following manner. First, a strong muscle relaxant and usually a short-acting anesthetic is administered. Next, two electrodes are attached to the patient's forehead, and 65 to 140 volts of electricity are briefly passed through the brain (Endler, 1988). The procedure produces a brain seizure that lasts up to a few minutes. After an average of seven to nine ECT sessions, spaced two or three days apart, many patients feel considerably less depressed. ECT helps approximately 70 percent of depressed patients to improve (Perugi et al., in press).

ECT is administered less often today than it was in the past, and is typically only used in treating depression that has not responded to other treatments. The procedure can negatively affect short-term memory (Merkl et al., 2011). Most such memories return, but some people who have gone through ECT report memory difficulties for the rest of their lives, though this was more common in the past (Hanna et al., 2009; Wang, 2007). With the growing success of antidepressant medications and certain forms of psychotherapy, fewer depressed patients now need this form of treatment. Nevertheless, ECT is still applied when people have a severe depressive episode that does not respond to other forms of treatment, which makes its high success rate all the more impressive.

In recent years, two other biological approaches have been developed that also directly stimulate the brain. These approaches are *vagus nerve stimulation* and *transcranial magnetic stimulation*. They appeal to many patients and clinicians because they are applied without the wide-ranging and traumatic impact of ECT.

vagus nerve stimulation a procedure in a which an implanted device sends electrical signals to the brain through the vagus nerve; used to treat severe depression.

Vagus Nerve Stimulation The vagus nerve, the longest nerve in the human body, runs from the brain stem through the neck down the chest and on to the abdomen. In the procedure of **vagus nerve stimulation**, a surgeon implants a small pacemaker-like device called a *pulse generator* under the skin of the chest. The surgeon then guides a wire, which extends from the pulse generator, up to the neck and attaches it to the left vagus nerve (see **Figure 17-1**). Electrical signals travel periodically from the pulse generator through the wire to the vagus nerve. In turn, the stimulated vagus nerve delivers electrical signals to the brain. These signals affect the mood centres of the brain.

In 1997, Health Canada approved this procedure for treating cases of otherwise intractable epilepsy. In 2001, after noting significant increases in positive mood in epileptics receiving the treatment, it was approved as a long-term treatment for severe treatment-resistant depression (Guberman, 2004; Kennedy et al., 2009). Since this time, some research has found that the vagus nerve stimulation procedure provides significant symptomatic relief in as many as 65 percent of cases (Howland et al., 2011; Nahas et al., 2005).

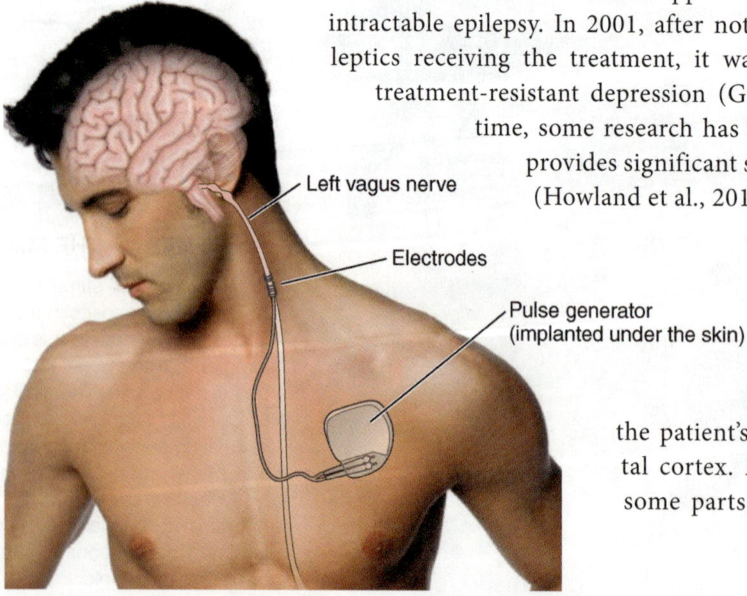

FIGURE 17-1 Vagus nerve stimulation. In this procedure, an implanted pulse generator sends electrical signals to the left vagus nerve. That nerve then delivers electrical signals to the brain, helping to reduce depression in many people.

Transcranial Magnetic Stimulation In the **transcranial magnetic stimulation (TMS)** procedure, first developed in 1985, the clinician places an electromagnetic coil on or above the patient's head. The coil sends a current into the prefrontal cortex. As you may remember from Chapter 16, at least some parts of the prefrontal cortex of depressed people are underactive. TMS appears to increase neuron activity in those regions, thus helping to alleviate severe depression in about 65 percent of patients after it has been administered daily for two to four weeks (Howland et al., 2011;

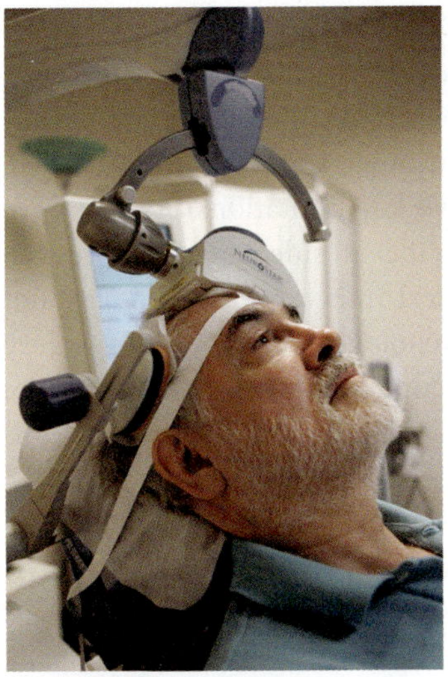

Transcranial magnetic stimulation. TMS is a non-invasive procedure used to treat depression. The electromagnetic coil is placed on the patient's head and sends a current into the prefrontal cortex.

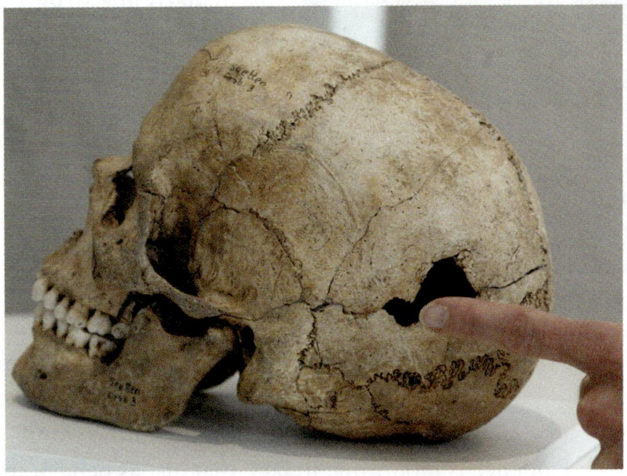

Early roots of psychosurgery? The hole in this 5,100-year-old skull indicates that the individual underwent trephining, cutting away a circular section of the skull. Some historians believe that trephination was done to release the evil spirits that were thought to be responsible for mental dysfunction.

Rosenberg et al., 2011). TMS was approved as a treatment option by Health Canada in 2001 (Kennedy et al., 2009).

transcranial magnetic stimulation (TMS) a procedure in which an electromagnetic coil placed on or above a person's head sends a current into the prefrontal cortex; used to treat severe depression.

psychosurgery brain surgery often used in hopes of relieving abnormal functioning.

trephining prehistoric practice of chipping a hole in the skull as a treatment for various brain conditions.

lobotomy surgical practice of cutting the connections between the frontal lobe and the lower centres of the brain.

deep brain stimulation a procedure in which implanted electrodes deliver constant low stimulation to a small area of the brain; used to treat severe depression, Parkinson's disease, and epilepsy.

Psychosurgery

From time to time throughout the book, we have mentioned psychosurgery—brain-surgery procedures that can help some people with psychological disorders. Actually, the first use of brain surgery as a treatment for mental disorders was trephining, the prehistoric practice of chipping a hole in the skull to treat an injury or other disorder. Evidence indicates that trephining was used not only by prehistoric people, but also by people in classical and medieval times.

Many modern forms of psychosurgery are derived from a past technique known as a lobotomy. In this procedure, the surgeon cuts the connections between the brain's frontal lobes and the lower centres of the brain. Lobotomies were widely used for a few decades after the procedure was developed in the 1930s, particularly in cases of schizophrenia. By the late 1950s, however, it had become clear that lobotomies were not as effective as many psychosurgeons had been claiming. Moreover, many patients who had undergone the surgery later suffered irreversible effects, including seizures, extreme listlessness, stupor, and in some cases death (Barahal, 1958). Thus, use of this procedure declined during the 1960s as less invasive alternative therapies became available (Valenstein, 2010).

Psychosurgery today is much more precise than the lobotomies of the past. It has fewer negative effects, and it is apparently beneficial for some psychological and neurological disorders. One form of psychosurgery that is currently receiving considerable attention is deep brain stimulation—a procedure applied in cases of severe depression, Parkinson's disease, and brain seizure disorder (epilepsy). In deep brain stimulation, a surgeon drills two tiny holes into the patient's skull and implants electrodes in areas of the brain that have been implicated in the disorder. The electrodes are connected to a battery, or "pacemaker," that is implanted in the patient's chest (for men) or stomach (for women). The pacemaker powers the electrodes, sending a steady stream of low-voltage electricity to the problematic brain areas. In many cases, this repeated stimulation readjusts the person's brain activity and, over time, brings significant improvement (Blomstedt et al., 2011; Hamani et al., 2011; Mayberg et al., 2005). Although such implants have offered promising results, at present they are still considered experimental. Thus, they are used infrequently, particularly in cases of depression, and usually only after the severe disorder has continued for years without responding to other forms of treatment.

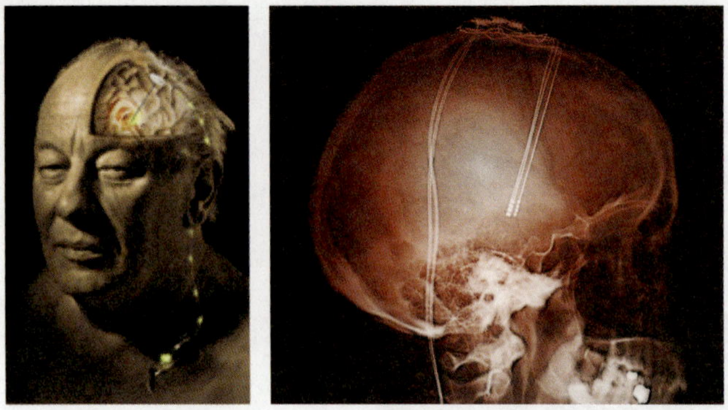

Deep brain stimulation. To treat severe cases of depression, Parkinson's disease, and epilepsy, electrodes are surgically implanted in the patient's brain to deliver constant low stimulation to adjust brain activity.

Biological Treatments in Perspective

Today, biological treatments for psychological disorders, particularly the drug treatments, are highly regarded. They often bring great relief when other approaches have failed. However, the treatments have key limitations. As you have read, they can produce significant side effects. Moreover, more often than not, biological interventions alone are not a sufficient treatment for psychological disorders. To believe otherwise is to neglect the complex interplay of biological and environmental factors that defines all human functioning—normal and abnormal (Kosslyn & Rosenberg, 2004). Indeed, as we have seen throughout the textbook, the connections in our brains unfold partly in response to the environmental experiences that we have all through our lives, beginning in the womb.

Evidence is mounting, in fact, that just as behaviour can respond to changes in our brain chemistry, so too does our brain chemistry respond to changes in behaviour. One study, for example, found that people with depression who responded to psychotherapy came to show brain responses similar to those of healthy, non-depressed individuals. In contrast, depressed individuals who did not respond to psychotherapy continued to show the abnormal brain patterns that typically accompany depression (Okamoto et al., 2006). In short, just as negative experiences can interact with brain activity to produce abnormal functioning, positive experiences can interact with the brain to make our functioning more normal.

Before You Go On

www.wiley.com/go/comer

What Do You Know?

4. What are the three main categories of biological treatments?
5. What are some new methods of direct brain stimulation, and how are they used?

What Do You Think?

Are today's clinicians and their clients too reliant on drugs as a treatment? Why or why not?

SCAN TO GET THE ANSWERS

Psychodynamic Therapies

HOW WE DEVELOP

LEARNING OBJECTIVE 3

Describe the psychodynamic treatments for psychological disorders.

Following the principles of the psychodynamic model, psychodynamic therapists contend that today's emotional disorder is the result of yesterday's emotional trauma. A variety of psychodynamic therapies are now being practised, ranging from classical *Freudian psychoanalysis* to modern therapies such as *short-term psychodynamic therapy* and *relational psychoanalytic therapy*. All share the goals of helping clients to uncover past traumatic events and the inner conflicts that have resulted from them; to resolve, or settle, those conflicts; and to resume interrupted personal development. Psychodynamic therapists of different theoretical persuasions might focus on different conflicts, but they tend to use similar techniques.

Techniques of Psychodynamic Therapies

Psychodynamic therapists try to subtly guide their discussions with clients so that the clients discover their underlying problems for themselves. How do they do this? In part, they rely on such techniques as *free association*, *therapist interpretation*, *catharsis*, and *working through* (Etchegoyen, 2005).

Free Association In psychodynamic therapies, the client is responsible for starting and leading each discussion. The therapist tells the individual to describe any thoughts or feelings that come to mind, even if they seem unimportant. This is the process known as **free association**. The therapist then probes the client's associations in the hope that they will eventually reveal the unconscious events that underlie the individual's problem.

Psychodynamic techniques. In order to help clients come to an appropriate understanding of their underlying problems, psychodynamic therapists interpret what the clients tell them.

Therapist Interpretation Psychodynamic therapists share their interpretations of a client's associations with the client only when they think the individual is ready to hear them. The interpretations of three phenomena—*resistance*, *transference*, and *dreams*—are thought to be of special value.

- *Resistance* Individuals demonstrate **resistance** when they encounter a block in their free associations or change the subject so as to avoid a potentially painful discussion. The therapist remains on the lookout for resistance, which is usually unconscious, and may point it out to the client and interpret it.
- *Transference* Psychodynamic therapists also believe that clients act and feel toward the therapist as they do toward important figures in their lives, past and present. This displacement of feelings is called **transference**. By interpreting transference behaviour, therapists may help individuals better understand how they unconsciously feel toward a parent or some other key person. In the excerpt found in the Psychology Around Us box below, a psychodynamic therapist helps a client to explore her transference.
- *Dream interpretation* Freud (1924) called dreams the "royal road to the unconscious." He believed that repression and other defence mechanisms operate ineffectively during sleep. Thus, a client's dreams can help reveal the person's unconscious instincts, needs, and wishes. Of course the dreams must be correctly interpreted. Freud distinguished a dream's *manifest content* (the consciously remembered dream) from its *latent content* (the symbolic meaning).

free association psychodynamic therapy technique of allowing clients to freely talk about whatever they want.

resistance practice in which clients encounter a block in their free associations or change the subject so as to avoid a potentially painful discussion.

transference process through which clients come to act and feel toward the therapist as they did toward important figures in their childhood.

PSYCHOLOGY AROUND US A Revealing Transfer

Patient: *I get so excited by what is happening here. I feel I'm being held back by needing to be nice. I'd like to blast loose sometimes, but I don't dare.*

Therapist: *Because you fear my reaction?*

Patient: *The worst thing would be that you wouldn't like me. You wouldn't speak to me friendly; you wouldn't smile; you'd feel you can't treat me and discharge me from treatment. But I know this isn't so, I know it.*

Therapist: *Where do you think these attitudes come from?*

Patient: *When I was nine years old, I read a lot about great men in history. I'd quote them and be dramatic. I'd want a sword at my side; I'd dress like an Indian. Mother would scold me. Don't frown, don't talk so much. Sit on your hands, over and over again. I did all kinds of things. I was a naughty child. She told me I'd be hurt. Then at fourteen I fell off a horse and broke my back. I had to be in bed. Mother told me on the day I went riding not to, that I'd get hurt because the ground was frozen. I was a stubborn, self-willed child. Then I went against her will and suffered an accident that changed my life, a fractured back. Her attitude was, "I told you so." I was put in a cast and kept in bed for months.*

(Wolberg, 1967, p. 662)

Catharsis Psychodynamic therapists believe that individuals must experience **catharsis** if they are to resolve internal conflicts and overcome their problems. That is, they must re-experience their past repressed feelings. Emotional catharsis must accompany intellectual insight for genuine progress to be achieved.

catharsis reliving of past repressed feelings as means of settling internal conflicts and overcoming problems.

Catharsis. Patients must re-experience past feelings in order to resolve internal conflicts and overcome their problems. Catharsis must be accompanied by intellectual insight.

Working Through A single session of interpretation and catharsis will not change a person. For deep and lasting insight to be gained, the client and therapists must *work through*, or examine, the same issues over and over, across many sessions, trying on the insights offered through therapy, each time with new and sharper clarity (Brenner, 1987).

Short-Term Psychodynamic Therapies

It should be clear by now that Freud's psychoanalytic therapy takes time. However, over the years the public and health care providers increased their demand for more efficient, time-limited psychotherapies. In Canada the pressure for briefer therapy is also present, though driven more by limits of coverage for therapy either though employee assistance programs or health care insurance providers. As a result, several efforts to make psychodynamic therapy shorter, more efficient, and more cost-effective emerged. In brief versions of psychodynamic therapy, called *short-term psychodynamic therapy*, clients focus on a single problem—a *dynamic focus*—such as excessive dependence on other people (Wolitzky, 2011). The therapist and client centre their discussions on this problem and work only on issues that relate to it. A relatively small number of studies have tested the effectiveness of these short-term psychodynamic therapies. Their findings, however, suggest that the approaches are sometimes quite helpful (Wolitzky, 2011; Present et al., 2008).

Relational Psychoanalytic Therapy

relational psychoanalytic therapy a school of psychodynamic therapy holding that therapists should work to form more equal relationships with clients.

Whereas Freud believed that psychodynamic therapists should take on the role of a neutral, distant expert during a treatment session, a current school of psychodynamic therapy called **relational psychoanalytic therapy** argues that therapists are key figures in the lives of clients—figures whose reactions and beliefs should be directly included in the therapy process (Luborsky et al., 2011). Thus, a key principle of relational psychoanalytic therapy is that therapists should also disclose things about themselves, particularly their own reactions to patients, and try to establish more equal relationships with clients as opposed to the distant analytic relationships typical of standard psychoanalysis.

Psychodynamic Therapies in Perspective

Freud and his followers have had a major impact on treatment. They were the first practitioners to demonstrate the value of systematically applying both theory and techniques to treatment. Moreover, their approaches were the first to clarify the potential of psychological, as opposed to biological, treatment. In fact their ideas have served as a starting point for many other psychological treatments.

Freud's couch.

Carefully conducted research, however, has failed to support the effectiveness of most psychodynamic therapies (Wampold et al., 2011; Neitzel et al., 2003). For the first half of the twentieth century, the value of these approaches was supported mostly by the case studies of enthusiastic clinicians and by uncontrolled research studies. Controlled investigations have been conducted only since the 1950s, and, with the exception of short-term psychodynamic therapies, only a small number of such studies have found psychodynamic therapies to be more effective than no treatment or placebo treatments (Prochaska & Norcross, 2010). Nevertheless, 15 percent of today's clinical psychologists identify themselves as psychodynamic therapists (Sharf, 2012; Prochaska & Norcross, 2010).

Before You Go On www.wiley.com/go/comer

What Do You Know?

6. Contrast three types of psychodynamic therapy.
7. List and describe psychodynamic therapy techniques.

What Do You Think?

Remember Jefferson, in our chapter opener. In treating Jefferson's psychological distress, where might a Freudian psychoanalyst start? Would this analyst be likely to achieve the results described in the time frame identified? Why or why not?

SCAN TO GET THE ANSWERS

Behavioural Therapies

LEARNING OBJECTIVE 4

Describe the behavioural treatments for psychological disorders.

As you read in Chapter 16, behavioural theories and treatments today are usually part of the *cognitive-behavioural model*—the perspective that combines behavioural and cognitive principles to explain and treat psychological disorders. For many years, however, behavioural treatments were applied on their own, and, even today, there are times when behavioural interventions are sufficient to treat certain problems. Thus, in this section we will look at behavioural therapies exclusively. We will then move on to cognitive-behavioural therapies in the next section.

As you may recall from Chapter 16, behaviourists contend that the symptoms of a psychological disorder are learned behaviours acquired through the same conditioning processes that produce normal behaviours. The goal of behavioural therapy is to identify the client's specific problem-causing behaviours and to replace them with more adaptive behaviours. The therapist's attitude toward the client is that of a teacher, rather than a healer. Behavioural techniques fall into three categories: *classical conditioning*, *operant conditioning*, and *modelling*.

Classical Conditioning Techniques

Classical conditioning treatments are intended to change clients' dysfunctional reactions to stimuli. One treatment, described in Chapter 7, is *systematic desensitization*. This step-by-step process is aimed at teaching people with phobias to react with calm instead of fear to the objects or situations they dread (Fishman et al., 2011; Wolpe, 1997, 1995, 1990). Clients first are trained in deep-muscle relaxation, through deep breathing, calming mental imagery, and systematic tensing and releasing of muscles (Chamove, 2005). Next, they construct a *fear hierarchy* in which they list objects or situations associated with their phobia, starting with the least feared and ending with the most feared. For a client with a phobia of elevators, for example, looking at an elevator on the outside of a building a block away might be low on the fear hierarchy. Watching the elevator doors close while inside the elevator might be near the top (see **Figure 17-2**). Finally, either in imagination or physically, clients confront each item on the hierarchy while they are in a state of deep relaxation, starting with the least fearful and then moving on up the list.

Research has repeatedly found that systematic desensitization and other classical conditioning techniques reduce phobic reactions more effectively than placebo treatments or no treatment at all (Olatunji et al., 2011; Kraft & Kraft, 2010). These techniques have also been helpful in treating several other kinds of problems, including sexual dysfunctions, posttraumatic stress disorder, agoraphobia, and asthma attacks (Koch & Haring, 2008). Because desensitization techniques expose individuals to the objects or situations they fear, and because this exposure seems so critical to implement, these and related approaches are often referred to as *exposure* treatments.

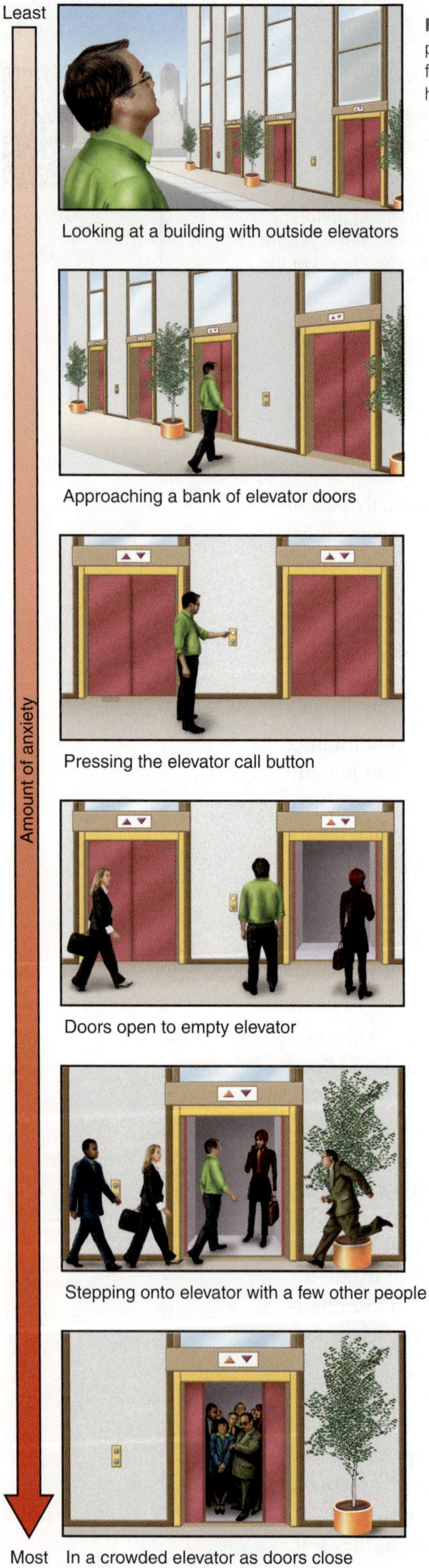

FIGURE 17-2 Fear hierarchy. Systematic desensitization uses classical conditioning principles to reduce a person's fears. Starting with the least stressful situation on his fear hierarchy, a man with a fear of riding in an elevator is exposed to each item on the hierarchy while applying relaxation techniques.

An opposite use of classical conditioning is known as **aversion therapy**. Here, clients *acquire* anxiety responses to stimuli that they have been finding too attractive. This approach has been used with people who want to stop excessive drinking, for example, as shown in **Figure 17-3** (Owen-Howard, 2001). In repeated sessions, the clients may be given an electric shock, a nausea-producing drug, or some other noxious stimulus whenever they reach for a drink. Aversion therapy has also been applied to help eliminate such undesirable behaviours as self-mutilation in autistic children, sexual paraphilias, and smoking (George & Weinberger, 2008; Krueger & Kaplan, 2002). The effects of this approach have, however, typically been short-lived, especially for those individuals who are aware that it is the drugs and not the alcohol, smoking, or other behaviour that is actually causing their nausea (Lancaster et al., 2000).

Operant Conditioning Techniques

In operant conditioning treatments, therapists consistently provide rewards for appropriate behaviour and withhold rewards for inappropriate behaviour. This technique has been employed frequently, and often successfully, with hospitalized patients experiencing psychosis (Kopelowicz, Liberman, & Zarate, 2007; Paul & Lentz, 1977; Ayllon & Azrin, 1965). When such patients talk coherently and behave normally, they are rewarded with food, privileges, attention, or something else they value. Conversely, they receive no rewards when they speak bizarrely or display other psychotic behaviours.

Parents, teachers, and therapists have successfully used operant conditioning techniques to change problem behaviours in children (such as repeated tantrums) and to teach skills to individuals with autism or intellectual disabilities (Soorya et al., 2011; Spiegler & Guevremont, 2003). Rewards in such cases have included food, recreation time, social rewards, and television watching.

Operant conditioning techniques typically work best in institutions or schools, where a person's behaviour can be reinforced systematically throughout the day. Often, a whole ward or classroom is converted into an operant conditioning arena. In many such programs, desirable behaviour is reinforced with tokens that can later be exchanged for food, privileges, or other rewards (Ayllon & Azrin, 1968). Programs of this sort are called **token economy** programs.

Behavioural techniques based on operant conditioning have also been useful for depression (Lazzari, Egan, & Rees, 2011). Recall from Chapter 16 that depression is often associated with a decline in pleasant activities and withdrawal. To deal with these behaviours, therapists may work with depressed individuals to identify activities the clients enjoy and then guide the individuals in adding the activities back into their lives.

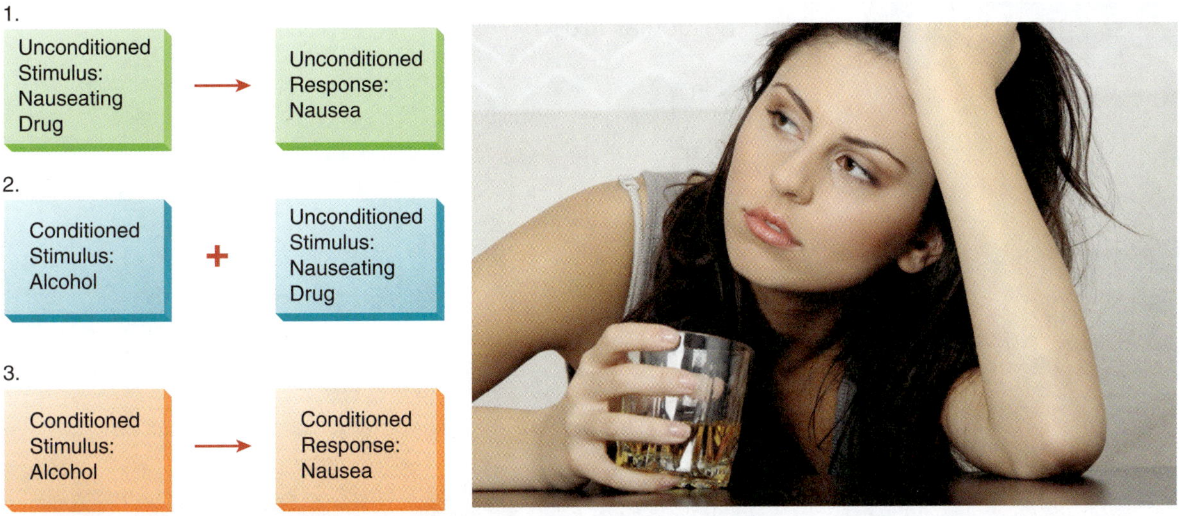

FIGURE 17-3 Aversion therapy. Aversion therapy uses classical conditioning principles to create a negative response to a stimulus a person would like to avoid, such as alcohol. Here a woman has a drink just before the effects of a nauseating drug begin.

Modelling Techniques

Modelling therapy was first developed by the pioneering social learning theorist Albert Bandura (1977, 1969). Here, therapists demonstrate appropriate behaviours for clients. Then the clients, through a process of imitation and rehearsal, acquire the ability to perform the behaviours in their own lives. This procedure has been used to treat phobias, for example. When therapists repeatedly display calm emotions while confronting objects that are feared by phobic clients, many clients are able to overcome their phobias (Rosenthal & Bandura, 1978; Bandura, Adams, & Beyer, 1977).

Behavioural therapists have also used modelling to help people acquire or improve their social skills and assertiveness. In an approach called social skills training, for example, therapists point out the social deficits of clients and then role-play social situations with the clients, typically modelling more appropriate social behaviours for them. Ultimately, the clients practise the behaviours in real-life situations (Corrigan, 1991). In the Psychology Around Us box on the next page, the client is a male college student who has difficulty making dates with women.

aversion therapy therapy designed to help clients to acquire anxiety responses to stimuli that the clients have been finding too attractive.

token economy operant conditioning therapy program in which participants receive tokens (that can be traded for rewards) when they display desired behaviours.

social skills training behavioural therapy technique in which therapists serve as models and teachers to help clients acquire desired social behaviours.

Using a combined strategy of modelling, rehearsal, feedback, and practice, therapists have successfully taught social and assertion skills to shy, passive, or socially isolated people. These techniques can help people who have a pattern of bursting out in rage or violence after building up resentment (rather than asserting themselves) over perceived social slights (Lochman et al., 2010; Fisher et al., 2004). The approach has also been used to improve the social skills of children and adults who experience depression, anxiety, or other psychological problem (Ogden, 2011; Ishikawa et al., 2010; Cooney et al., 1991).

We're all familiar with token economies. The token economies applied in various mental health settings operate just like the star system that most of us were exposed to in elementary school. At school, however, good work was rewarded with stars instead of tokens, and numerous stars added up to a certificate instead of privileges, treats, or other rewards.

Behavioural Therapies in Perspective

Behavioural interventions have been among the most widely researched treatment approaches in the clinical field (Wilson, 2011). Certainly, they lend themselves to research more than the psychodynamic approaches do. The removal of symptoms—the criterion of progress in behavioural therapy—is easier to observe and measure than conflict resolution—the psychodynamic

PSYCHOLOGY AROUND US Acquiring the Social Touch

Client: *By the way, [Pause] I don't suppose you want to go out Saturday night?*

Therapist: *Up to actually asking for the date you were very good. However, if I were the girl, I think I might have been a bit offended when you said, "By the way." It's like your asking her out is pretty casual. Also, the way you phrased the question, you were kind of suggesting to her that she doesn't want to go out with you. Pretend for the moment I'm you. Now, how does this sound: "There is a movie at the Varsity Theater this Saturday that I want to see. If you don't have other plans, I'd very much like to take you."*

Client: *That sounded good. Like you were sure of yourself and liked the girl too.*

Therapist: *Why don't you try it.*

Client: *You know that movie at the Varsity? Well, I'd like to go, and I'd like to take you Saturday, if you don't have anything better to do.*

Therapist: *Well, that certainly was better. Your tone of voice was especially good. But the last line, "if you don't have anything better to do," sounds like you don't think you have too much to offer. Why not run through it one more time.*

Client: *I'd like to see the show at the Varsity, Saturday, and, if you haven't made other plans, I'd like to take you.*

Therapist: *Much better. Excellent, in fact. You were confident, forceful, and sincere.*

(Rimm & Masters, 1979, p. 74)

Behavioural interventions. Time out is a popular behavioural technique for disciplining young children.

criterion of improvement. Moreover, behavioural approaches have been effective for numerous problems, including specific fears, social deficits, and intellectual disabilities (Wilson, 2011, 2008).

At the same time, behavioural therapies have certain limitations. First, the improvements they bring about do not always maintain themselves without further behavioural interventions. Second, behavioural therapies, by themselves, do not appear to be particularly effective with psychological disorders that are broad or vaguely defined. Problems involving generalized anxiety, for example, are unlikely to be alleviated by step-by-step, behaviour-by-behaviour interventions (Wilson, 2011; O'Leary & Wilson, 1987). This is one of the reasons these interventions are now usually combined with cognitive approaches.

Before You Go On

www.wiley.com/go/comer

What Do You Know?

8. What are systematic desensitization and aversion therapy?
9. What principles and procedures are involved in a token economy program?
10. How does social skills training work?

What Do You Think?

Does changing behaviour fully treat people's disorders?

SCAN TO GET THE ANSWERS

Cognitive-Behavioural Therapies

LEARNING OBJECTIVE 5

Describe cognitive-behavioural therapies for psychological disorders.

Working from the assumption that dysfunctional thinking is at the centre of many psychological disorders, cognitive-behavioural therapists try to help people recognize and change their faulty thinking processes. Because different disorders involve different kinds of cognitive dysfunction, therapists may employ a range of cognitive strategies. Most such therapists also use some behavioural techniques to help clients think, behave, and feel better. Thus, their approaches are typically referred to as cognitive-behavioural. Three influential cognitive-behavioural approaches are those of Albert Ellis, Aaron Beck, and the "second-wave" cognitive-behavioural therapists (Hayes, 2004).

rational-emotive behavioural therapy Ellis's therapy technique designed to help clients discover and change the irrational assumptions that govern their emotions, behaviours, and thinking.

cognitive therapy Beck's cognitive therapy technique designed to help clients recognize and change their dysfunctional thoughts and ways of thinking.

Ellis's Rational-Emotive Behavioural Therapy

In line with his belief that irrational assumptions give rise to abnormal functioning, Albert Ellis developed an approach called rational-emotive behavioural therapy (Ellis, 2011, 2005, 1962). Therapists using this approach first help clients identify the irrational assumptions that seem to govern their behavioural and emotional responses. Next, they help clients change those assumptions into constructive ways of viewing themselves and the world. One of the techniques the therapists may use is *cognitive restructuring*, in which clients learn to replace negative interpretations with more positive notions (see **Figure 17-4**).

In his own practice, Ellis would point out to clients their irrational assumptions in a blunt, confrontational, and often humorous way. Then he would model the use of alternative assumptions. After criticizing a young man's perfectionistic standards, for example, he might say, "So what if you did a lousy job on that paper? It's important to realize that one lousy paper simply means one lousy paper, and no more than that!" Ellis gave clients homework assignments requiring them to observe their assumptions at work in their everyday lives. He also required them to think of ways to test the rationality of the assumptions. And, finally, he had them rehearse new assumptions during therapy and apply them at home and work.

Silverman and colleagues (1992) reviewed research that evaluated the effectiveness of rational-emotive therapy. Their findings suggest that this form of therapy has been demonstrated to be an effective means of addressing issues for those who suffer from anxiety or assertiveness issues. For example, clients with social anxiety who are treated with this therapy improve more than socially anxious clients who receive no treatment or placebo treatments (McEvoy, 2007).

FIGURE 17-4 Cognitive restructuring. This cognitive strategy can help clients change self-defeating thinking and, in turn, open the door to new, more positive life experiences.

Beck's Cognitive Therapy

Aaron Beck independently developed a system of therapy that is similar to Ellis's rational-emotive behavioural therapy. Although he named his approach cognitive therapy, Beck has emphasized for decades that he also has clients experiment with new behaviours as a key feature of the approach.

This approach has been used most often with people who are depressed, although it also has been applied to problems ranging from panic disorder to personality disorders (Beck & Weishaar, 2011, 2008). In their work with depressed clients, Beck-like cognitive therapists help clients to identify the negative thoughts and errors in logic that pervade their thinking and help give rise to feelings of depression. The therapists also teach clients to challenge their dysfunctional thoughts, try new interpretations, and apply different ways of thinking in their daily lives. In the following excerpt,

PSYCHOLOGY AROUND US Thinking More Rationally

Therapist: *The point is for you to decide exactly what hypothesis or nutty idea you want to work on for at least ten minutes a day. And, in your case, it would be the idea, again, that it's terrible for you to get rejected by a woman you find attractive. You would take this idea, and ask yourself several basic questions, in order to challenge and dispute it.*

Client: *What kind of questions?*

Therapist: *Usually, four basic questions—though they have all kinds of variations. The first one is, "What am I telling myself?" or, "What silly idea do I want to challenge?" And the answer, in your case, is, "It's terrible if a woman whom I find attractive rejects me." The second question is, "Is this, my hypothesis, true?" And the answer is —?*

Client: *Uh, well, uh. No, it isn't.*

Therapist: *Fine. If you had said it was true, the third question would have been, "Where is the evidence for its being true?" But since you said it isn't true, the third question is, "Where is the evidence that it's not true?" Well —?*

Client: *Well, uh, it's not true because, as we said before, it may be very inconvenient if an attractive woman rejects me, but it's not more, uh, than that. It's only damned inconvenient!*

(Ellis, 1976, pp. 29–30)

Beck guides a depressed 26-year-old graduate student to see the link between the way she interprets her experiences and the way she feels, and to begin questioning the accuracy of her interpretations.

Patient: *I get depressed when things go wrong. Like when I fail a test.*

Therapist: *How can failing a test make you depressed?*

Patient: *Well, if I fail I'll never get into law school.*

Therapist: *So failing the test means a lot to you. . . . Did everyone who failed get depressed enough to require treatment?*

Patient: *No, but it depends on how important the test was to the person.*

Therapist: *Right, and who decides the importance?*

Patient: *I do . . .*

Therapist: *Now what did failing mean?*

Patient: *(Tearful) That I couldn't get into law school.*

Therapist: *And what does that mean to you?*

Patient: *That I'm just not smart enough.*

Therapist: *Anything else?*

Patient: *That I can never be happy.*

Therapist: *And how do these thoughts make you feel?*

Patient: *Very unhappy.*

Therapist: *So it is the meaning of failing a test that makes you very unhappy. [Moreover] you get yourself into a trap—by definition, failure to get into law school equals "I can never be happy."*

(Beck et al., 1979, pp. 145–146)

Around two-thirds of depressed people who are treated with Beck's cognitive approach improve. This is significantly more than those who receive no treatment and about the same as those who receive biological treatments (Beck & Weishaar, 2011; Hollon et al., 2006, 2005, 2002). Research also indicates the effectiveness of Beck-like cognitive therapy in cases of panic disorder and social anxiety disorder.

Depression. Cognitive therapy is effective at identifying the negative thoughts and errors in logic that permeate the thinking of depressed individuals.

Second-Wave Cognitive-Behavioural Therapies

A growing body of research suggests that the kinds of cognitive changes proposed by Ellis, Beck, and other cognitive therapists are not always possible to achieve

(Sharf, 2012). Thus, a new group of cognitive-behavioural therapies, sometimes called *second-wave* cognitive-behavioural therapies, has emerged in recent years (Hollon & DiGiuseppe, 2011). These approaches help clients to *accept* many of their problematic thoughts rather than judge them, act on them, or try fruitlessly to change them. The hope is that by recognizing such thoughts for what they are—just thoughts—clients will eventually be able to let them pass through their awareness without being particularly troubled by them.

One of several disorders to which this kind of approach has been applied is generalized anxiety disorder. As you read in Chapter 16, this disorder is characterized by persistent and excessive feelings of anxiety and endless worrying about numerous events and activities. Second-wave cognitive-behavioural therapists guide clients with generalized anxiety disorder to recognize and then accept their dysfunctional uses of worrying (Newman et al., 2011; Ritter et al., 2010; Wells, 2010). They begin by educating the clients about the role of worrying in their disorder and have them observe their bodily arousal and cognitive responses across various life situations. Over time, the clients come to appreciate the triggers of their worrying, their misconceptions about worrying, and their misguided efforts to control their lives by worrying. As their insights grow, clients are expected to see the world as less threatening (and so less arousing), try out more constructive ways of dealing with arousal, and, perhaps most important, worry less about the fact that they worry so much. Research has begun to indicate that a concentrated focus on worrying of this kind is indeed a helpful addition to the treatment of generalized anxiety disorder (Ritter et al., 2010; Wells, 2010).

One of today's leading second-wave cognitive-behavioural approaches is *mindfulness-based cognitive therapy*, developed by psychologist Steven Hayes and his colleagues as part of their broader treatment approach called *acceptance and commitment therapy* (Antony, 2011; Treanor, 2011; Hayes et al., 2004). Here therapists help clients to become mindful of their streams of thoughts—including their worries—at the very moments they are occurring, and to *accept* such thoughts as mere events of the mind. Once again, by accepting their thoughts rather than trying to eliminate them, the clients are expected to be less upset and affected by them.

Mindfulness-based cognitive therapy has also been applied to other psychological problems such as depression, posttraumatic stress disorder, personality disorders, and substance abuse, often with promising results (Orsillo & Roemer, 2011; Hayes et al., 2004). The approach borrows heavily from a form of meditation called *mindfulness meditation*, which teaches individuals to pay attention to the thoughts and feelings that flow through their minds during meditation and to accept such thoughts in a non-judgmental way.

Cognitive-Behavioural Therapies in Perspective

A model that sees and treats thought as the main cause of normal and abnormal behaviour offers great appeal. Accordingly, therapists from varied backgrounds have come to embrace and use cognitive-behavioural approaches. Moreover, research has supported these approaches. Cognitive-behavioural therapies have proved very effective for treating depression, social anxiety disorder, generalized anxiety disorder, panic disorder, sexual dysfunctions, and a number of other psychological disorders (Beck & Weishaar, 2011; Landon & Barlow, 2004).

But the cognitive-behavioural approaches also have their limitations. First, although disturbed cognitive functioning is found in many psychological disorders, its precise role has yet to be determined. It is not always clear that it is at the *centre* of various disorders. Correspondingly, it is not clear whether it is the behavioural or the cognitive features of the cognitive-behavioural approaches that most powerfully propel these treatments. The assumption of many therapists is that the behavioural features help bring about essential cognitive changes. But it could well be that in many cases and disorders, it is the behavioural changes that are most important. And, finally, although cognitive-behavioural therapies are certainly effective for many problems, they do not help everyone (Sharf, 2012).

Before You Go On

www.wiley.com/go/comer

What Do You Know?

11. What do therapists help clients to do in rational-emotive behavioural therapy?
12. What is cognitive therapy?
13. What are the goals of second-wave cognitive-behavioural therapies?

What Do You Think?

We all sometimes have irrational assumptions, though they don't usually cause psychological disorders. What irrational assumptions and thoughts do you occasionally have?

SCAN TO GET THE ANSWERS

Humanistic and Existential Therapies

LEARNING OBJECTIVE 6

Describe the humanistic and existential therapies for psychological disorders.

Believing that psychological disorders are rooted in self-deceit, humanistic and existential therapists try to help clients look at themselves and their situations more accurately and acceptingly. They expect that clients will then be better able to actualize their full potential as human beings. To achieve this, humanistic and existential therapists usually emphasize present experiences rather than events from the client's past.

Rogers's Client-Centred Therapy

client-centred therapy humanistic therapy designed to help clients experience unconditional positive regard and look at themselves honestly and acceptingly.

Clinicians who practise Carl Rogers's **client-centred therapy** try to create a positive climate in which clients can look at themselves honestly and acceptingly (Raskin et al., 2011). The therapist must display three important qualities throughout the therapy:

- *Unconditional positive regard*—full and warm acceptance for the client.
- *Accurate empathy*—skillful listening, including restatements of the client's own comments.
- *Genuineness*—realness, sincere communication, no professional front or facade.

According to Rogers, clients will feel accepted by their therapists in this kind of atmosphere. They will eventually come to recognize and value their own emotions, thoughts, and behaviours once again. They will then be freed from the insecurities that have been preventing self-actualization (Rogers, 1980). The following interaction shows a therapist using the techniques Rogers advocates:

Client: *In classes I feel that everyone's just waiting for a chance to jump on me. . . . When I meet somebody I wonder what he's actually thinking of me. Then later on I wonder how I match up to what he's come to think of me.*

Therapist: *You feel that you're pretty responsive to the opinions of other people.*

Client: *Yes, but it's things that shouldn't worry me.*

Therapist: *You feel that it's the sort of thing that shouldn't be upsetting, but they do get you pretty much worried anyway.*

Client: *. . . There are lots of little things that aren't true. . . . Things just seem to be piling up, piling up inside of me. . . . It's a feeling that things were crowding up and they were going to burst.*

Therapist: *You feel that it's a sort of oppression with some frustration and that things are just unmanageable.*

Client: *In a way . . .. I'm afraid I'm not very clear here but that's the way it comes.*

Therapist: *That's all right. You say just what you think.*

(Snyder, 1947, pp. 2–4)

Rogers was committed to clinical research, and his commitment helped promote the systematic study of treatment. Client-centred therapy has not performed well in research, however (Sharf, 2008). Although some studies report improvements among people who receive this therapy, most controlled research finds it to be of limited effectiveness. Nevertheless, Rogers's therapy has had a very positive influence on the clinical field (Raskin et al., 2011; Kirschenbaum, 2004). As one of the first major alternatives to psychodynamic therapy, it helped open up the field to new approaches (Prochaska & Norcross, 2007).

An alternative source of unconditional positive regard. Based on the Rogerian principle that unconditional positive regard is highly therapeutic, pet therapy has become a widely applied intervention to help reduce the depression of elderly nursing home residents, medically ill people, and developmentally disabled individuals. In this approach, individuals interact with various kinds of non-judgmental animals.

Gestalt Therapy

Gestalt therapy, another humanistic approach, was developed in the 1950s by clinical theorist Frederick (Fritz) Perls. Gestalt therapists, like client-centred therapists, move clients toward self-recognition and self-acceptance (Yontef & Jacobs, 2011). But unlike client-centred therapists, they often try to do this by challenging and frustrating the clients. Perls's favourite techniques included skillful frustration, role playing, and rules.

- *Skillful frustration* Gestalt therapists consistently refuse to meet their clients' expectations or demands. The aim here is to help the clients to see how often they try to manipulate others into meeting their needs.
- *Role playing* Gestalt therapists often have clients act out various roles. A person may be instructed to be another person, an object, an alternate self, or even a part of the body. Role playing can become very intense, as individuals are encouraged to fully express their feelings. They may cry out, scream, kick, or pound. Eventually they are expected to "own," or accept, feelings that previously made them uncomfortable.
- *Rules* The rules enforced by Gestalt therapists ensure that clients look at themselves closely. In certain versions of this therapy, for example, clients may be required to use "I" language instead of "it" language. They must say, "I am sad" rather than "The situation is depressing."

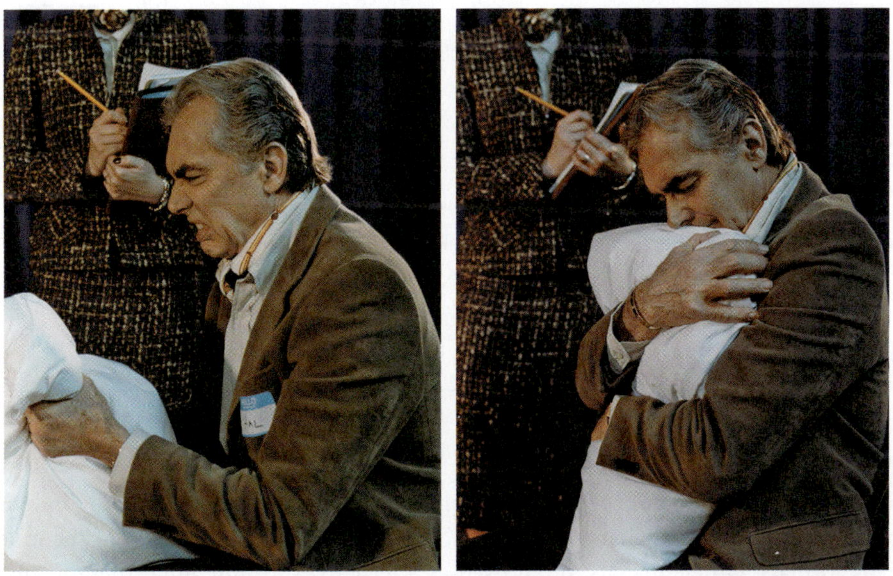

Gestalt techniques. Gestalt therapists often guide clients, such as this man, to express their needs and feelings to an extreme through role playing and other exercises. In this session, the client moves from "strangling" a pillow (left) to banging the pillow, to hugging it (right). The pillow may represent a person about whom the client has mixed feelings.

Because Gestalt therapists believe that subjective experiences and self-awareness defy objective measurement, limited research has been conducted on the approach (Yontef & Jacobs, 2011; Strümpfel, 2006, 2004). Recently, Gestalt techniques have been included in a group of other treatments referred to as *emotion-focused*. These treatments emphasize attention to one's current emotional experiences as a way to reduce anxiety, depression, and other psychological difficulties (Greenberg & Goldman, 2008).

Existential Therapy

Existential therapists encourage clients to accept responsibility for their lives and their problems. They help clients to recognize their freedom so that they may choose different paths and live more meaningful lives (Yalom & Josselson, 2011; Schneider & Krug, 2010). Existential therapists also place great emphasis on the relationship between therapist and client, and try to create an atmosphere of honesty, shared learning, and growth.

Like gestalt therapists, most existential therapists do not believe that experimental methods can properly test the effectiveness of their treatments (Yalom & Josselson, 2011). In fact, they hold that research dehumanizes individuals by reducing them to test measures. Thus, little controlled research has been done to clarify the effectiveness of this approach.

Humanistic and Existential Therapies in Perspective

By recognizing the special challenges of human existence, both humanistic and existential therapists highlight an aspect of psychological life that is typically missing from the other models (Watson et al., 2011; Cain, 2007). In addition, the factors that they say are critical to positive functioning—self-acceptance, personal values, personal meaning, and personal choice—certainly seem to be lacking in many people with psychological disorders. Such virtues aside, the broad issues of human fulfillment at the core of these approaches are hard to research. Only recently have properly controlled studies been conducted. These studies, in fact, suggest that the therapies may be beneficial in some cases (Schneider & Krug, 2010; Cain, 2007; Strümpfel, 2006). This emerging interest in research may soon lead to clearer insights about the approaches.

Before You Go On

www.wiley.com/go/comer

What Do You Know?

14. What are the key characteristics therapists should display in client-centred therapy?
15. What techniques are used in Gestalt therapy?
16. What are the main goals of existential therapy?

What Do You Think?

What kind of clients and what kind of problems do you think would benefit most from humanistic and existential therapies?

SCAN TO GET THE ANSWERS

Formats of Therapy

LEARNING OBJECTIVE 7

Describe commonly used formats of therapy.

individual therapy psychotherapy format in which the therapist sees the client alone; the oldest of the modern formats.

Thus far, our discussions of therapy have centred on treatments conducted by individual therapists with individual clients. In fact, **individual therapy** is the oldest of the modern therapy formats. Other formats, often used as alternatives to individual therapy, include *group therapy*, *family and couple therapy*, and *community treatment*. Therapists may apply their favoured techniques and principles in each of these formats, whether they be psychodynamic, behavioural, or other techniques. In addition, special strategies have been developed for use in the non-individual formats.

Group Therapy

In **group therapy**, a therapist sees several clients who are grappling with psychological problems at the same time. Group therapy became a popular format for treating people with psychological difficulties after World War II, when growing demand for psychological services forced therapists throughout North America and Europe to look for time-saving alternatives to individual therapy (Fehr, 2003). Many therapists now specialize in group therapy, and countless others conduct therapy groups as one aspect of their practice. A survey of clinical psychologists, for example, revealed that almost one-third of them practise group therapy to some degree (Norcross & Goldfried, 2005).

group therapy psychotherapy format in which a therapist sees several clients at the same time.

Typically, group members meet with a therapist and discuss the problems or concerns of one or more of the members (Burlingame & Baldwin, 2011). Groups are often created with particular client populations in mind. For example, there are groups for people with alcoholism, for people who are physically handicapped, and for people who are divorced, abused, or bereaved.

On the basis of his own work and other investigations, a leading group-therapy theorist, Irvin Yalom, suggests that successful forms of group therapy share certain "curative" features (Cox, Vinogradov, & Yalom, 2008; Yalom & Leszcy, 2005):

- *Guidance* Group therapy usually provides information and advice for members.
- *Identification* Group therapy provides models of appropriate behaviour.
- *Group cohesiveness* Group therapy offers an atmosphere of solidarity in which members can learn to take risks and accept criticism.
- *Universality* Members discover that other people have similar problems.
- *Altruism* Members develop feelings of self-worth by helping others.
- *Catharsis* Members develop more understanding of themselves and of others and learn to express their feelings.
- *Skill building* Members acquire or improve social skills.

One kind of group intervention in wide use today is **self-help groups**. These groups are made up of people who have similar problems or who may be at different places in a life process (e.g., supporting a loved one with Alzheimer's) and come together to help and support one another without the direct leadership of a professional clinician (White & Madara, 2011; Mueller et al., 2007). Self-help groups have become increasingly popular over the past few decades.

self-help groups groups consisting of people who have similar problems and come together to help and support one another without the direct leadership of a professional clinician.

Range of formats. Individual therapy (left) used to be the only treatment format for psychological problems. Today, other formats are also used, such as group therapy (middle) and couple therapy (right).

Self-help groups address a wide assortment of issues. Examples include alcoholism and other forms of substance abuse, compulsive gambling, bereavement, overeating, phobias, child abuse, medical illnesses, rape victimization, unemployment, and divorce. Online self-help chat rooms and message boards are often similar to the traditional self-help groups and have themselves exploded in number and popularity in recent years.

Self-help groups are popular for several reasons. Many participants have lost confidence in the ability of clinicians and social institutions to help with their particular problems. For example, Alcoholics Anonymous, the well-known network of self-help groups for people dependent on alcohol, was developed in 1934 in response to the general ineffectiveness of clinical treatments for alcoholism (Tonigan et al., 1995). Still other people are drawn to self-help groups because they find them less threatening and less stigmatizing than therapy groups.

Because groups—from conventional therapy groups to self-help groups—vary so much, it has been difficult to assess their effectiveness. Research does suggest, however, that group therapy is often of help to clients—perhaps as helpful as individual therapy (Burlingame & Baldwin, 2011; Dies, 2003). It appears that candid feedback is usually useful for group members as long as a balance is struck between positive and negative feedback.

Family Therapy

family therapy a format in which therapists meet with all members of a family to help the whole family to change.

Family therapy dates back to the 1950s. In this format, therapists meet with all members of a family, point out problematic behaviours and interactions between the members, and try to help the whole family change (Goldenberg & Goldenberg, 2011). Most family therapists meet with family members as a group, but some choose to see them separately. Either way, the family is viewed as the unit under treatment.

Family therapy. In family therapy, the family is treated as a unit, regardless of whether individual family members are counselled or whether the entire family is counselled together.

Like group therapists, family therapists may follow the principles of any of the major theoretical models. Whatever their orientation, however, most also adhere to some of the principles of family systems theory. As you may recall from Chapter 16, family systems theory holds that each family has its own implicit rules, relationship structure, and communication patterns that shape the behaviour of the individual members, including dysfunctional behaviour. For one family member to change, the family system must change (Barker, 2007).

Family therapies are often helpful to individuals. Research has not fully clarified how helpful, however (Goldenberg & Goldenberg, 2011). Some studies have found that as many as 65 percent of individuals treated with family approaches improve, but other studies have found much lower success rates. Nor has any one type of family therapy emerged as consistently more helpful than the others (Alexander et al., 2002).

Couple Therapy

couple therapy or **marital therapy** therapy format in which a therapist works with two people who are in a long-term relationship.

In **couple therapy**, also known as **marital therapy**, the therapist works with two people who are in a long-term relationship, focusing on the structure and communication patterns in their relationship (Gurman & Snyder, 2011; Baucom et al., 2010, 2009). Often this format of therapy involves a husband and wife, but the couple need not be married or even living together. Similarly, they need not be heterosexual. Indeed, some therapists specialize in working with same-sex couples.

Although some degree of discord occurs in any long-term relationship, there is growing evidence that many adults in our society experience serious marital problems. The divorce rate across North America and Europe is now close to 50 percent of the marriage rate, and has been climbing steadily in recent decades (U.S. Census Bureau, 2011). Currently, 38 percent of Canadian marriages do not survive past the thirtieth anniversary

(Ambert, 2009). Many of those who live together without marrying seem to have similar levels of relationship disharmony (Harway, 2005).

Like group and family therapy, couple therapy may be conducted with any therapy orientation (Baucom et al., 2010; Shadish & Baldwin, 2005). People treated in couple therapy show greater improvements in their relationships than people who fail to receive such treatment, but no one form of couple therapy stands out as more effective than the others (Gurman & Snyder, 2011; Christensen et al., 2010). Two-thirds of treated couples display improved marital functioning. However, fewer than half of those who are treated achieve "distress-free" relationships. One-quarter of all treated couples eventually divorce.

Community mental health in action. This man with both schizophrenia and bipolar disorder is moving into his own apartment, a key step in his recovery.

Community Treatment

At one time, people with psychological disorders, especially severe disorders, had to seek help from distant facilities or institutions. Today, however, a number of **community mental health treatment** programs offer such people services from nearby agencies. Community-based treatments include community mental health centres, community day programs, and group homes and other residential services. Collectively, these agencies often play a major role in the treatment of people with severe psychological disorders, such as schizophrenia (Daly et al., 2010).

community mental health treatment treatment programs that emphasize community care, including an emphasis on prevention.

PSYCHOLOGY AROUND US In Need of Community Care

What happens to persons with schizophrenia and other severe psychological disorders whose communities do not provide the mental health services they need and whose families cannot afford private treatment? Many return to their families and receive medication and support, but little else in the way of treatment (Barrowclough & Lobban, 2008). Around 8 percent receive only custodial care and medication in an alternative institution, such as a nursing home or rest home (Torrey, 2001). As many as 18 percent are placed in privately run residences, such as boarding houses, where supervision often is provided by untrained individuals. Another 31 percent live in totally unsupervised settings, including rundown single-room-occupancy hotels or rooming houses, surviving on government disability payments and spending their days wandering through neighbourhood streets (Burns & Drake, 2011). Over 100,000 become homeless (Kooyman & Walsh, 2011), and at least 100,000 more end up in prisons because their disorders lead them to break the law (Scott, 2010).

A key feature of community treatment is *prevention*. Community clinicians reach out to clients rather than wait for them, an approach that is often very successful (Clanton Harpine, 2011; Juhnke et al., 2011). Community workers identify three types of prevention: *primary*, *secondary*, and *tertiary*.

- *Primary prevention* consists of efforts to improve community functioning and policies. The goal here is to prevent psychological disorders altogether. Community workers may lobby for better child-care facilities in the community, consult with a district school board to help develop a curriculum, offer mental health fairs or workshops on stress reduction, or provide online information and support sites.
- *Secondary prevention* consists of detecting and treating psychological disorders in the early stages, before they reach serious levels. Community workers may teach clergy, teachers, or police how to identify early signs of psychological dysfunction and how to refer people for treatment.

- *Tertiary prevention* aims to provide effective treatment immediately so that moderate or severe disorders do not become chronic problems. Unfortunately, although community agencies are able to offer tertiary care for millions of people with moderate problems, low funding often prevents them from providing care for hundreds of thousands with severe disorders (Althouse, 2010).

Before You Go On

www.wiley.com/go/comer

What Do You Know?

17. What are self-help groups?
18. What is the main assumption of family systems therapy?
19. Describe primary, secondary, and tertiary prevention.

What Do You Think?

Which therapy format appeals to you most? Least? Why? Are certain formats better suited for particular problems or client personalities?

SCAN TO GET THE ANSWERS

Does Therapy Work?

LEARNING OBJECTIVE 8

Summarize research on the effectiveness of therapy.

therapy outcome studies research that looks at the effects of various treatments.

As we noted earlier, as many as 400 forms of therapy are currently practised in North America (Corsini & Wedding, 2011). The most important question to ask about each of them is whether the therapy really helps. **Therapy outcome studies**, which measure the effects of various treatments, typically ask one of four questions:

1. *Is therapy in general effective?* Studies reveal that therapy is often more helpful than no treatment or placebo treatments. Using a statistical technique called *meta-analysis* in which the results from a large number of studies are combined to provide a more general picture of a particular area of interest, one early review combined the results of 375 separate, controlled studies, covering a total of almost 25,000 people seen in a wide assortment of therapies (Smith, Glass, & Miller, 1980; Smith & Glass, 1977). According to this statistical analysis, shown in **Figure 17-5**, the average person who received treatment was better off than 75 percent of the untreated control clients. Other analyses have found similar relationships between treatment and improvement (Sharf, 2012; Bickman, 2005).
2. *How effective are particular therapies?* A number of studies have found that each of the major forms of therapy is of some help to clients—certainly of more help than a placebo treatment (Prochaska & Norcross, 2010; Overholser, Braden, Fisher, 2010). Other research has compared these therapies to one another and found that no one form of therapy generally stands out over all others (Luborsky et al., 2006, 2003, 1975). If different kinds of therapy have similar overall success rates, it may be that they share common features (Sharf, 2012; Bohart & Tallman, 2010). Surveys of highly successful therapists suggest that, regardless of their particular orientations, successful therapists tend to do similar things: (1) they provide feedback to clients; (2) they help clients focus on their own thoughts and behaviour; (3) they pay careful attention to the way they and their clients interact; and (4) they try to build a sense of self-mastery in their clients (Portnoy, 2008; Korchin & Sands, 1983).
3. *Are particular therapies especially effective for certain problems?* Researchers have found that particular therapies are especially effective at treating certain disorders

(Beutler, 2011; Corsini, 2011). Behavioural therapies, for example, seem to be the most effective of all treatments for phobias (Wilson, 2011). Cognitive-behavioural therapies are particularly helpful in cases of social anxiety disorder, generalized anxiety disorder, panic disorder, and depression (Craske, 2010; Pontoski et al., 2010). And drug therapy is the single most helpful treatment for schizophrenia and bipolar disorder (Minzenberg, Yoon, & Carter, 2011). Today's clinicians may also combine two or more approaches when treating particular disorders (Cuijpers et al., 2010). Drug therapy, for example, is often combined with cognitive-behavioural therapy to treat depression or various anxiety disorders, although the superiority of such combinations over the individual approaches has not been supported consistently by research (Otto, McHugh, & Kantak, 2010; Pontoski & Heimberg, 2010). In fact, it is now common for clients to be seen by two therapists—one of them a *psychopharmacologist* (a psychiatrist who prescribes medications) and the other a psychologist, social worker, or other therapist who conducts psychotherapy.

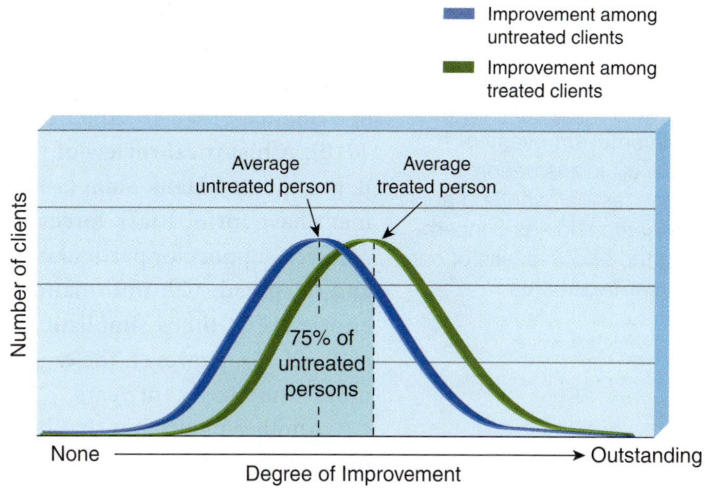

FIGURE 17-5 Is therapy generally effective? An analysis of 375 studies of treatment effectiveness shows that the average person is better off after treatment of any kind than a similar person who does not get treatment.

4. *Is therapy equally effective across race and gender?* Studies conducted in countries across the world have found that members of ethnic and racial minority groups typically show less improvement in clinical treatment, make less use of mental health services, and stop therapy sooner than members of majority groups (Comas-Diaz, 2011, 2006; Ward, 2007). Given such findings, a number of clinicians have developed **culture-sensitive therapies**, which seek to address the unique issues faced by members of cultural minority groups. Clinicians using these approaches typically try to do the following (Brown, 2011; Comas-Diaz, 2011; Wyatt & Parham, 2007):

    - Be aware of the client's cultural values.
    - Be aware of the stress, prejudices, and stereotypes to which minority clients are exposed.
    - Be aware of the hardships faced by the children of immigrants.
    - Help clients recognize the impact of both their own culture and the dominant culture on their self-views and behaviours.
    - Help clients identify and express suppressed anger and pain.
    - Help clients achieve a bicultural balance that feels right for them.
    - Help clients raise their self-esteem—a sense of self-worth that has often been damaged by generations of negative messages.

culture-sensitive therapies approaches that seek to address the unique issues faced by members of cultural minority groups.

Therapies geared to the pressures of being female, called **gender-sensitive**—or **feminist—therapies**, follow similar principles (Calogero et al., 2011). In a related vein, when working with clients who are very religious, many of today's therapists make a point of including spiritual issues in therapy (Aten et al., 2011; Worthington, 2011). They may, for example, encourage clients to use their spiritual resources to help them cope (Galanter, 2010).

gender-sensitive—or feminist—therapies approaches that seek to address the unique pressures of being female.

Obviously, knowledge of how particular therapies fare with particular disorders and particular populations can help therapists and clients alike make better decisions

empirically supported or **evidence-based treatment movement** movement to help clinicians become more familiar with and apply research findings concerning the effectiveness of particular treatments.

about treatment (Beutler, 2011, 2002; Beutler et al., 2011). To help clinicians become more familiar with and apply such research findings, there is a movement in Canada, the United States, the United Kingdom, and elsewhere called the **empirically supported** or **evidence-based treatment movement** (Sharf, 2012; Pope & Wedding, 2011; Lambert, 2010). A historical review of the development of this perspective is provided by Christy Bryceland and Hank Stam (2005) at the University of Calgary. Proponents of this movement have formed task forces that seek to identify which therapies have received clear research support for particular disorders, to propose corresponding treatment guidelines, and to spread such information to clinicians. Critics of the movement worry that such efforts are at times simplistic, biased, and even misleading (Hagemoser, 2009; Westen et al., 2005). However, the empirically supported treatment movement has been gaining momentum in recent years.

Another movement that has been receiving support in recent years is a move toward integration and eclecticism among psychotherapeutic approaches. This move supports the integration of a variety of psychotherapeutic perspectives rather than adherence to a particular orientation. This movement encourages practitioners to integrate diverse approaches and to draw on a variety of perspectives when treating clients (see the Society for the Exploration of Psychotherapy Integration for more information on this topic).

THINGS STUDENTS WANT TO KNOW

How do I find and choose a therapist?

Selecting the right therapist is obviously a very important decision. Even if you seek assistance at the student wellness or counselling centre at your college or university (where treatment is usually free to students) or if you seek a referral to a therapist from your family doctor, a friend or relatives, or your province's College of Psychologists, you still have some choice regarding which of the available therapists you would like to work with.

Here is a list of key questions to consider when selecting a therapist. You should direct some of questions to the potential therapists themselves.

- *Where can you get names of skilled potential therapists?* Ask a professional whom you trust—a psychologist you know, such as your introductory psychology professor, someone at your local student wellness or counselling centre, a family physician, or the like—for recommendations. Many provinces or cities also provide relevant information and lists.
- *What is the professional status of the potential therapists?* Are they clinical psychologists, psychiatrists, social workers, or counsellors? Are they chartered/registered with your province's regulatory college for their profession?
- *What is the experience level of the potential therapists?* What is their overall experience in the field? What is their specific experience and success rate with your kind of problem?
- *What is the treatment orientation of the potential therapists?* Are they psychodynamic, behavioural, cognitive, humanistic, existential, or eclectic? How do they approach problems such as yours?
- *What is the success rate of their treatment orientation for problems such as yours?* Reading this chapter or an abnormal psychology textbook should help you with this question.
- *Do the potential therapists believe in psychotropic medication as part of therapy in certain cases?* Can they arrange for medication consults if needed?
- *How do the potential therapists match up on personal variables that are important to you?* What

are their genders, ages, personalities, and the like? Although such factors do not necessarily affect a therapist's ability to help, you may personally feel that the variables could affect your comfort level or confidence in the therapy process.

- *Once you are in therapy, are you comfortable with the way things are going?* Does the therapist seem attentive, interested, and engaged? Does the therapist's approach continue to make sense to you? Do you feel you are making progress? Don't be afraid to change therapists if, after a reasonable period of time, you are not making progress. In most such instances, you are not failing at therapy. The therapy is failing you!

Before You Go On

www.wiley.com/go/comer

What Do You Know?

20. What does research show about whether or not therapy is generally effective?
21. What do effective therapists have in common?
22. What does research show about the effectiveness of particular therapies for certain problems?
23. Is therapy equally effective across race and gender?

SCAN TO GET THE ANSWERS

What Do You Think?

If a person feels that his or her treatment is not helping, is it likely to be worthwhile for that person to try to change therapists or treatment methods? Why or why not?

Some Final Thoughts About the Field of Psychology

It is ironic that we end this book with chapters on abnormal psychology and its treatments. Early on, we noted that many people automatically think of abnormal psychology when they hear the term *psychology*. But, as you have seen throughout this book, psychology is a broad field that studies all kinds of mental processes and behaviour. And, as you have also observed, all of those processes and behaviours—both normal and abnormal—are rather awe-inspiring. For example, disorders of memory, such as Alzheimer's disease and dissociative identity disorder, are certainly fascinating. But normal acts of memory—our very ability to encode, store, and retrieve so many experiences and pieces of information in the first place—are no less remarkable.

Psychology is a wide-ranging and complex field consisting of many sub-areas, from sensation and perception to social psychology. Each seeks to explain particular aspects of mental functioning from a particular angle. Collectively, these many sub-areas provide us with an impressive understanding of mental processes and behaviour. But it is important to recognize that this understanding is at a very early stage of development. There are many miles to go in our quest to more fully understand the subject matter of psychology.

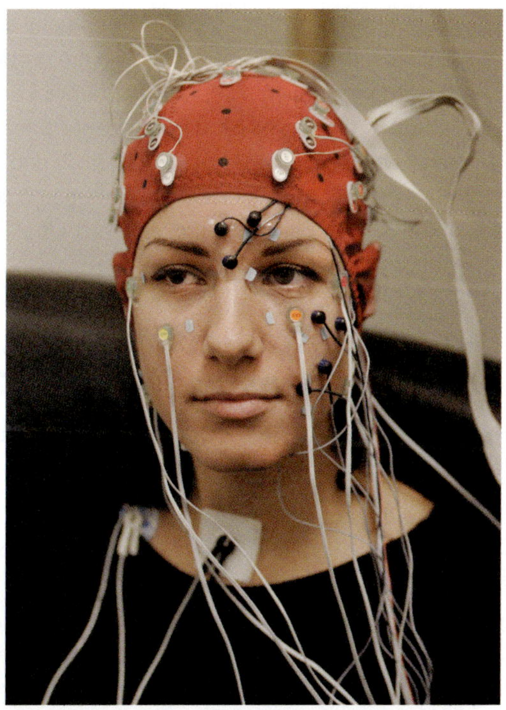

Covering all the angles. To fully understand a mental process such as "intruding thoughts," today's psychologists study the phenomenon at many levels, from measuring the brain waves of individuals while their minds wander (seen here), to determining the possible childhood roots of such thoughts.

Perhaps the most important feature of psychological study today—and one that offers enormous promise for the future—is that the sub-areas are coming together. More and more, they are being viewed as closely connected areas of study. Each helps to inform the others, and all can, collectively, provide a more integrated, complete, and accurate understanding of mental processes and behaviour. It is, for example, no longer a matter of choosing between neuroscience, cognitive psychology, and social psychology to understand how and why people behave (or don't behave) when passing by an accident scene. Rather, we seek to understand how these interacting subfields jointly account for that behaviour. In short, psychology is becoming a truly integrated field. Given this critical course correction, one can only imagine how many insights and breakthroughs regarding mental processes and behaviour lie ahead.

Summary

Treatment in Today's World

LEARNING OBJECTIVE 1 Explain who receives treatment for psychological problems today, how they enter treatment, and what general features characterize different types of treatment.

- More than 20 million North Americans receive therapy for psychological problems in the course of a year. Almost half suffer from anxiety and depression.
- Therapy was once primarily a privilege of the wealthy, but today people at all socio-economic levels receive treatment. Similarly, while women once outnumbered men in therapy by four to one, men today are more willing to enter therapy.
- People may enter therapy on their own or may be forced into treatment. Many never seek treatment at all.
- A variety of professionals conduct therapy, including psychologists, psychiatrists, counsellors, and psychiatric social workers.
- Most clients are treated in the community as outpatients, but some people with severe problems are treated as inpatients in private or public institutions.
- All forms of therapy have three essential features: a sufferer who seeks relief, a trained healer, and a series of contacts between the two in which the healer tries to bring about changes in the sufferer's emotional state, attitudes, and behaviour.

Biological Treatments *What Happens In The Brain?*

LEARNING OBJECTIVE 2 Describe the major biological treatments for psychological disorders.

- *Drug therapy*, *electroconvulsive therapy (ECT)*, and *psychosurgery* are the three major categories of biological treatments.
- Psychotropic drugs, including *antianxiety*, *antidepressant*, *antibipolar*, and *antipsychotic drugs*, have brought relief to many, but they do not work for everyone and may have undesired side effects.
- Electroconvulsive therapy (ECT), used primarily to treat depression, is administered less often today than in the past. Two more recently developed brain stimulation treatments, *vagus nerve stimulation* and *transcranial magnetic stimulation*, have less wide-ranging and traumatic side effects than ECT.
- Psychosurgery today is much more precise than the lobotomies of the past, in which the connections between the frontal lobe and the lower brain centres were severed.
- Biological treatments for psychological disorders, particularly drug treatments, are highly regarded today. However, more often than not, biological interventions alone are not enough.

Psychodynamic Therapies *How We Develop*

LEARNING OBJECTIVE 3 Describe the psychodynamic treatments for psychological disorders.

- Psychodynamic therapies range from classical *Freudian psychoanalysis* to modern therapies. All share the goals of helping clients to uncover past traumatic events and the inner conflicts that have resulted from them, and to resolve those conflicts.
- Psychodynamic therapy techniques include *free association*; therapist interpretation of *resistance*, *transference*, and *dreams*; *catharsis*; and repeatedly *working through* issues.
- Recent developments in psychodynamic therapy include *short-term psychodynamic therapy* and *relational psychoanalytic therapy*.
- The psychodynamic approach has had a lasting influence on the conduct of treatment and was the first to offer an alternative to biological explanations of abnormal functioning. But the effectiveness of psychodynamic therapy is not well supported by research.

Behavioural Therapies

LEARNING OBJECTIVE 4 Describe the behavioural treatments for psychological disorders.

- Behavioural treatments, aimed at replacing abnormal behaviours with more functional ones, are based on learning processes. Behavioural techniques fall into three categories: *classical conditioning*, *operant conditioning*, and *modelling*.

- Systematic desensitization and *aversion therapy* rely on classical conditioning. Systematic desensitization is especially effective in treating phobias, while aversion therapy has been used to treat people who want to eliminate problem behaviours, such as drinking.
- *Token economies* follow the principles of operant conditioning and use rewards to encourage desired behaviours.
- *Social skills training* uses modelling to help clients acquire desired social behaviours.
- Research suggests that behavioural therapies are often effective. They do not always bring lasting change outside therapy, however, and do not appear particularly effective with disorders that are broad or vaguely defined.

Cognitive-Behavioural Therapies

LEARNING OBJECTIVE 5 Describe cognitive-behavioural therapies for psychological disorders.

- Cognitive-behavioural therapists try to help people recognize and change their faulty thinking processes. Most such therapies use some behavioural techniques. Three influential cognitive-behavioural approaches are those of *Albert Ellis*, *Aaron Beck*, and the "*second-wave*" *cognitive-behavioural therapists*.
- Ellis's *rational-emotive behavioural therapy* focuses on helping clients to identify their maladaptive assumptions, test them, and change them.
- Beck's cognitive therapy guides clients to challenge their maladaptive attitudes, automatic thoughts, and illogical thinking. Research supports the effectiveness of cognitive therapy for depression and certain other disorders.
- Second-wave cognitive-behavioural therapies help clients to accept their problem behaviours rather than judge them, act on them, or try fruitlessly to change them.
- The cognitive view is quite popular today, and research suggests that cognitive treatment is often effective. It is still not clear, however, whether psychological disorders create or result from maladaptive thoughts.

Humanistic and Existential Therapies

LEARNING OBJECTIVE 6 Describe the humanistic and existential therapies for psychological disorders.

- Humanistic and existential therapists try to help clients look at themselves and their situations more accurately and acceptingly.
- Therapists practising Carl Rogers' *client-centred therapy* try to provide *unconditional positive regard*, *accurate empathy*, and *genuineness*, so that clients come to value their own emotions, thoughts, and behaviours.
- Gestalt therapists use skillful frustration, role playing, and rules to help clients recognize and accept their needs and goals.
- Existentialist therapies focus on helping clients discover their personal freedom of choice and take responsibility for making choices.
- Only recently have humanistic and existential therapies begun to undergo systematic research. Early research suggests they can be beneficial for some clients.

Formats of Therapy

LEARNING OBJECTIVE 7 Describe commonly used formats of therapy.

- *Individual therapy*, in which practitioners meet with one client at a time, is the oldest of the modern therapy formats.
- In *group therapy*, several clients with similar problems meet with a single therapist at the same time. *Self-help groups* are similar, but conducted without the leadership of a therapist. Both types of groups can be helpful for certain clients.
- *Family therapy* treats all members of a family, together or individually, and therapists usually consider the family as a system.
- Two people in a long-term relationship can seek *couple therapy* to help address issues in their relationship.
- *Community mental health treatment* focuses on preventing abnormal functioning through (1) primary prevention—policies that reduce psychological risk in a community; (2) secondary prevention—treating minor problems before they become serious; and (3) tertiary prevention—providing prompt treatment for moderate and severe disorders so they do not become long-term problems.

Does Therapy Work?

LEARNING OBJECTIVE 8 Summarize research on the effectiveness of therapy.

- In general, receiving therapy is more likely to help people with psychological disorders than going without treatment. Research has found that each of the major forms of therapy is of some help to clients, although research also indicates that particular therapies are often best suited for certain disorders.
- Successful therapists often share similar effective elements in their approaches, regardless of their particular orientations. They provide feedback, help clients focus on their own thoughts and behaviour, pay careful attention to the way they interact with clients, and try to build a sense of self-mastery in their clients.

- Women and members of ethnic minority groups face pressures that sometimes contribute to psychological dysfunctioning. *Culture-sensitive* and *gender-sensitive therapy* approaches help clients become aware of and react adaptively to the gender-related and cultural pressures and issues they face.
- The *empirically supported* or *evidence-based treatment movement* seeks to identify which therapies have received clear research support for particular disorders, to propose corresponding treatment guidelines, and to spread such information to clinicians.

Key Terms

antianxiety drugs 669
antibipolar drugs 669
antidepressant drugs 669
antipsychotic drugs 669
aversion therapy 678
biological therapy 664
catharsis 675
client-centred therapy 684
cognitive therapy 681
community mental health treatment 689
couple therapy or marital therapy 688
culture-sensitive therapies 691
deep brain stimulation 673
electroconvulsive therapy (ECT) 669
empirically supported or evidence-based treatment movement 692
family therapy 688
free association 675
gender-sensitive or feminist therapies 691
group therapy 687
individual therapy 686
lobotomy 673
psychosurgery 673
psychotherapy 664
psychotropic drugs 669
rational-emotive behavioural therapy 681
relational psychoanalytic therapy 676
resistance 675
self-help groups 687
social skills training 679
therapy outcome studies 690
treatment or therapy 664
token economy 678
transcranial magnetic stimulation (TMS) 672
transference 675
trephining 673
vagus nerve stimulation 672

TYING IT TOGETHER

The treatment of psychological disorders is closely connected to all other areas of psychology. Throughout this chapter, we have stressed how treaments interface with psychology's many areas, including our highlighted sections on brain function, individual differences, and development. To remind you of how the subject and practice of treatment are tied to such areas, here are some interesting points from throughout the chapter.

WHAT HAPPENS IN THE BRAIN?

- ECT remains one of the clinical field's most effective treaments for severe depression.
- Psychosurgery traces its roots back to the prehistoric practice of chipping a hole in a person's skull to let demons out.
- Research suggests that successful psychotherapy may produce positive changes in brain activity.
- For anxiety disorders and depression, combinations of drug therapy and psychotherapy do not necessarily help more than either approach alone.

HOW WE DIFFER

- Women in therapy for psychological problems used to outnumber men by two to one. Now the number of women and men in therapy is about equal.
- On average, members of racial and ethnic minority groups across the world show less improvement in clinical treatment, make less use of mental health services, and stop therapy sooner than members of majority groups.
- If inpatient treatment is needed, poorer people and those with poorer insurance coverage are more likely than wealthier people to receive treatment in a public institution.
- Therapy groups and self-help groups often specialize in particular populations, such as bereaved people or compulsive gamblers.

WHEN THINGS GO WRONG

- More than 400 different types of therapies are now practised in North America.
- Behavioural therapy is particularly effective for phobias; cognitive-behavioural therapies for depression, social anxiety disorder, and panic disorder; and drug therapies for schizophrenia and bipolar disorder.
- Group therapy took off after World War II in response to increased client demand.
- Second-wave cognitive-behavioural therapists help excessive worriers by guiding them to stop worrying about the fact that they worry so much.

HOW WE DEVELOP

- Psychodynamic therapists believe that it's common for clients to feel and behave toward their therapists as they did toward important figures in their childhood (transference).
- Psychodynamic therapists believe that patients' current psychological disorders are linked to traumatic childhood experiences.
- Around 15 percent of today's psychotherapists practise psychodynamic therapy.
- Gestalt therapists often prohibit clients from focusing on past experiences.

Psychology Around Us

Treating Psychological Disorders

Therapist for a Day

How do you make yourself feel better when you're down? What kinds of things do other people do to lift their spirits? And how do such informal techniques compare to today's leading treatments for depression, such as cognitive therapy and drug therapy? This video lab exercise will help you answer those questions, as you play "therapist for a day."

In this exercise, you'll consider the interview and therapy responses of depressed individuals and weigh in on how they might respond to today's leading treatments. You'll even get the chance to see and consider how effective "light therapy" might be for *seasonal affective disorder*—depression that occurs and reoccurs only during the winter. Finally, you'll get to consider useful tips for finding an effective therapist and determining his or her appropriateness for a given problem. Along the way, you'll learn a lot about treatment—both informal and formal.

View this in Action
WILEY PLUS
www.wileyplus.com

Video Lab Exercise

As you are working on this online exercise, consider the following questions:

- Which treatments are particularly effective for particular problems?
- Why are some people helped by certain techniques when they're depressed, whereas other people respond to other strategies?
- How might one know when to try to help a depressed friend directly and when to instead suggest formal treatment?
- Are everyday blues, clinical depression, and seasonal affective disorder related or entirely different problems?

APPENDIX A

Statistics in Psychology

descriptive statistics statistics used to describe and summarize data.

inferential statistics statistics used to draw conclusions about research data.

As outlined in Chapter 2, psychology is considered to be a science, given that it relies upon empirical observations of mental processes and behaviour in order to develop and test theories regarding the underlying laws that govern behaviour. Psychologists use statistics to help them summarize and interpret the observations (or data) that they collect in their research. Essentially there are two basic types of statistics used by psychologists: descriptive statistics, which include a variety of procedures used to describe and summarize the data collected, and inferential statistics, which are procedures that allow psychologists to draw conclusions about the data they have collected. This appendix is designed to help you better understand statistics and how psychologists use them.

Descriptive Statistics

Statistics are commonly used in psychology to summarize data that have been collected as part of some research project or study. Such statistical summaries are referred to as descriptive statistics.

To illustrate some common descriptive techniques, consider the following data set:

46	56	50	50	59	44
61	49	50	52	32	43
67	58	51	36	58	46
51	54	53	62	50	39
42	44	51	41	53	57

Assume that the data represent scores obtained from 30 students who have taken their first test in an introductory psychology course.

If the instructor is interested in determining how well the students performed on this test, she might quickly eyeball the scores above. However, nothing may readily jump out at her in terms of things like how well the typical student is doing, what was the lowest score, what was the highest score, and so on.

One of the first things the instructor might want to do to get an idea of what's going on with student performance is to simply sort the data so that the scores are arranged from lowest to highest. Doing so produces a data set like the one in **Table A-1**. Now the instructor can look at the data set to see things like the lowest score earned by a student was 32, a fairly large number of students received scores of 50 and 51, and the highest score earned by a student was 67.

TABLE A-1 Thirty Exam Scores—Sorted

32	36	39	41	42	43
44	44	46	46	49	50
50	50	50	50	51	51
51	52	53	53	54	56
57	58	59	61	62	67

However, this still doesn't tell her a whole lot about her students' performance. To get a better idea of what's going on in this set of data, the instructor might use a number of descriptive techniques to summarize the data (this would especially be the case if there were a larger number of students in the class, such as 500). One common way to summarize such a data set is to create frequency distributions.

Frequency Distributions

There are two major types of frequency distributions: ungrouped frequency distributions and grouped frequency distributions. With an ungrouped frequency distribution, the number of times that each of the unique scores occurs in a data set is calculated. In our example, this would essentially be a count of how many students received a 32, how many received a 36, and so on. To create an ungrouped frequency distribution for the student exam scores, we would need to create a table with two columns—one column containing the various exam scores (sorted from smallest to largest) and another column indicating how frequently each of these scores occurred. **Table A-2** shows an example of an ungrouped frequency distribution for the 30 exam scores.

ungrouped frequency distribution a count of the number of times each specific data point or score appears in a data set.

Using this ungrouped frequency distribution, the instructor can readily see that the exam scores ranged from a low of 32 (with one person receiving that score) to a high of 67 (also with one person receiving this score). In addition, she can determine that seven people earned scores of either 50 or 51.

In the current example there are 21 unique exam scores. While this is a manageable number of categories, there are many instances where there are many more unique scores. As a result, the number of categories in an ungrouped frequency distribution becomes unmanageable. In such cases (and even in the present case, as we will see), you might want to create a grouped frequency distribution instead.

grouped frequency distribution a count of the number of times specific data points fall into a range of values in a data set.

To create a grouped frequency distribution, the instructor first creates a number of ranges, or classes of scores, to serve as the basis of the distribution. In general, there should be between five and 20 classes, and the classes need to be continuous (i.e., the classes need to encompass all of the scores from lowest to highest). **Table A-3** shows an example of a grouped frequency distribution for the 30 exam scores (each with a width of five scores). To complete the grouped frequency distribution, the instructor needs to determine how many of the 30 exam scores fall into each of the classes. For example, only one person had a score between 30 and 34 (i.e., the person who scored 32), so that class has a frequency of 1. There were two scores in the class of scores 35–39 (a 36 and a 39),

TABLE A-2 Ungrouped Frequency Distribution for 30 Exam Scores

Exam Score	Frequency
32	1
36	1
39	1
41	1
42	1
43	1
44	2
46	2
49	1
50	4
51	3
52	1
53	2
54	1
56	1
57	1
58	2
59	1
61	1
62	1
67	1
Total	**30**

TABLE A-3 Grouped Frequency Distribution for 30 Exam Scores

Exam Score Classes	Frequency	Midpoint
30–34	1	32
35–39	2	37
40–44	5	42
45–49	3	47
50–54	11	52
55–59	5	57
60–64	2	62
65–69	1	67
Total	**30**	

FIGURE A-1 Histogram for 30 exam scores.

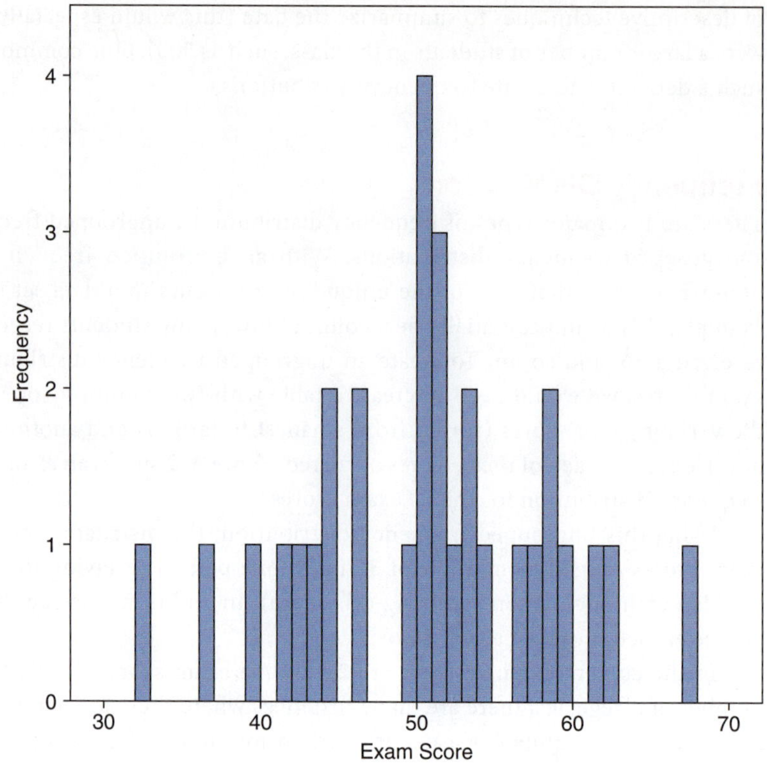

so this class has a frequency of 2. The remainder of the frequencies for the classes are determined in a similar fashion.

Using this grouped frequency distribution, the instructor can identify aspects of the data set, such as there were 11 students who scored between 50 and 54, and there were only three students who scored less than 40.

Frequency distributions can be presented either in tabular format (as we have done in Tables A-2 and A-3) or, following the adage that a picture is worth a thousand words, in some type of graphic form such as a histogram or a frequency polygon. Histograms are commonly used to graphically represent ungrouped frequency distributions. They are similar to bar charts and are constructed using a set of two axes. One axis, the horizontal or x-axis, contains an ordered listing of the various values for the scores from the ungrouped frequency distribution. The other axis, the vertical or y-axis, provides the frequency of those scores. **Figure A-1** shows a histogram based on the ungrouped frequency distribution for the 30 exam scores.

histogram a bar chart showing the number of times specific data points fall into a range of values in a data set.

Frequency polygons are similar to histograms, but they are typically used to graphically represent grouped frequency distributions. Recall that a grouped frequency distribution summarizes the frequency of scores for each of a number of classes or ranges of scores. To create a frequency polygon from a grouped frequency distribution, you need to determine the *midpoint* (i.e., the centre) for each of the classes. In our example, the first class is from 30–34, so the midpoint of that class would be 32 $\left[\frac{(30 + 34)}{2}\right]$, with the remaining midpoints for the classes calculated in a similar way (see Table A-3). These midpoints are then included on the horizontal axis of the frequency polygon, and the frequencies for each of the classes are included on the vertical axis. **Figure A-2** provides a frequency polygon for the grouped frequency distribution for the 30 exam scores.

frequency polygon a line graph depicting a grouped frequency distribution, which is created by connecting the midpoints of each class of data.

Measures of Central Tendency

Another common use of descriptive statistics is to summarize a collection of data with a single number that represents the entire data set. Such numbers are called measures of central tendency. For example, these numbers may be the most frequent number or a number that

measures of central tendency numbers used to summarize data sets.

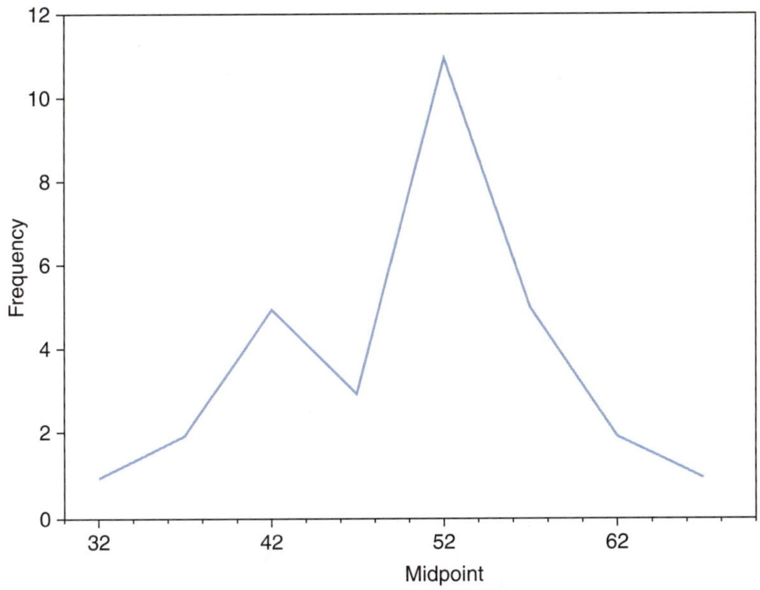

FIGURE A-2 Frequency polygon for 30 exam scores.

is thought to be typical of the data set. The three most common statistical measures of central tendency are the mean, median, and mode.

You most likely are already familiar with the **mean**—it is equivalent to the (arithmetic) average of the data set. As you know, to calculate an average (or the mean of a data set), total the numbers in the data set and divide by the total number of numbers. Returning to our example, to calculate the mean, total the 30 numbers and divide by 30. The total of the 30 scores is 1,505, so the mean (or average) of those scores is $\frac{1{,}505}{30} = 50.1667$.

mean the average value in a data set; the sum of all numbers in the set divided by the total number of items in the set.

Statisticians frequently use formulas to summarize the procedures required to calculate various statistical values (like the mean). The formula for the mean is presented below:

$$\mu = \frac{\Sigma X}{N}$$

where: μ is the symbol for the mean,[1]

Σ is summation notation and indicates the procedure of totalling the individual values in the data set,

X represents the possible values in the data set, and

N represents the number of observations.

While the mean is the average of the set of data, the **median** represents the midpoint or middle in an ordered set of data. That is, to determine the median for a set of data, first order the set of data (from smallest to largest) and then determine the midpoint of that ordered data set. Our 30 exam scores are sorted in Table A-1. Because there is an even number of scores (or observations), the exact midpoint for the data set would be between the 15th and 16th numbers. In cases where the number of observations (or N) is even, calculate the median by taking the average of the two middle numbers in the ordered data set. In our example, the 15th highest score is 50 while the 16th highest score is 51, so for this set of data the median is $50.5\left(\frac{50 + 51}{2}\right)$. In cases where there are an odd number of observations in the data set, the median is simply the middle number in the ordered data set.

median the data set value that represents the midpoint of an ordered set of numbers.

A third measure of central tendency that may be calculated for a set of data is the **mode**, which is the most frequently occurring score or observation. The mode can be easily determined by looking at an ungrouped frequency distribution for the set of data. As Table A-1 shows, the score of 50 was the most frequent score in our data set of 30 exam scores, with

mode the most frequent or most common value in a data set.

[1] μ is the symbol for the mean of a population, whereas $\overline{X}$ is the symbol for the mean of a sample. The distinction between populations and samples is discussed later in this appendix.

four of the 30 students earning that score. So for this set of data, the mode would be 50. In cases where there are multiple scores that each have equally high frequencies, then the data set has multiple modes (for example, if in our data set four people scored 50 and four people scored 58, then the data set would have two modes, 50 and 58).

In summary, for our example set of data we have three measures of central tendency: a mean of 50.1667, a median of 50.5, and a mode of 50. As you can see, for this set of data the three measures of central tendency are similar to one another, and you may wonder which is the "best" measure of central tendency. We will return to this question later in the appendix.

Measures of Variability

measures of variability indicators that tell how different the values are within a data set.

range the difference between the smallest and the largest value in a data set.

variance a calculated indicator of the degree to which values in a data set differ from the mean value of that data set; the average of squared deviations about the mean.

Whereas measures of central tendency provide some idea of a typical number in a set of data, they do not tell us anything about how different the numbers in a set of data are from one another. Statistics that do this are known as **measures of variability**.

The simplest measure of variability for a set of data is the **range**, which is the difference between the largest and the smallest values in a data set. To calculate the range for our 30 exam scores, determine the largest and the smallest score and then to take the difference between them. Referring to Table A-1 the largest score is 67 while the smallest score is 32, so the range of scores is 35 ($67 - 32 = 35$). One advantage of the range is that it is easy to calculate, but it does have a major shortcoming: for any set of data, the range is based only on two scores and, by definition, these are extreme scores (i.e., they are the largest and smallest scores). As such, the size of the range is influenced by any extreme score, and further, the range only provides limited information about how different each of the numbers in a set of data are from one another.

To deal with the shortcomings of the range, there are a couple of related measures of variability: the variance and the standard deviation. Let's say we wanted to calculate, on average, how different each number in a set of data is from the mean. To do this we would have to calculate what is referred to as a *deviation score* for each of the observations (these are calculated by taking the difference between each score and the mean) and then calculate the average of those deviation scores (see **Table A-4**). However, when we follow this procedure a problem arises: to calculate the average of the deviation scores, we have to take the total of those scores and divide this total by the number of scores. Whenever we do this (for any set of scores), the total of the deviation scores will always be 0 (regardless of how different the scores are from one another). Thus, the average of the deviation scores is always 0 for every set of data and, as such, it is not very useful as a possible measure of variability.

Statisticians deal with this problem by calculating another measure of variability, known as the variance. The **variance** is the average of the squared deviation scores. The resulting set of scores has the property that the larger the squared deviation, the further that observation is from the mean. Thus, the larger the variance is for a set of data, the more different the scores are from one another. To calculate the variance for our 30 exam scores, take the average of the squared deviation scores, which gives a variance of 60.94 $\left(60.94 = \frac{1{,}828.167}{30}\right.$; see Table A-4).

The formula for the variance is presented below:

$$\sigma^2 = \frac{\sum(X - \mu)^2}{N}$$

where: σ^2 is the symbol for the variance,[2]

$\sum$ is summation notation and indicates the procedure of totalling the individual squared deviation scores $(X - \mu)^2$, and

N represents the number of observations.

While the variance is a useful measure of variability in that its magnitude reflects how different the numbers in a set of data are from one another, it also has a major shortcoming: the variance is not in the same metric as the original scores. For example, in calculating

[2] σ^2 is the symbol for the variance of a population, whereas s^2 is the symbol for the variance of a sample. The distinction between populations and samples is discussed later in this appendix.

TABLE A-4 Thirty Exam Scores with the Mean, Deviation Score, and Squared Deviation Score

	Exam Score (X)	Mean (μ)	Deviation Score ($X - \mu$)	Squared Deviation Score $(X - \mu)^2$
	32	50.1667	−18.17	330.029
	36	50.1667	−14.17	200.695
	39	50.1667	−11.17	124.695
	41	50.1667	−9.17	84.028
	42	50.1667	−8.17	66.695
	43	50.1667	−7.17	51.362
	44	50.1667	−6.17	38.028
	44	50.1667	−6.17	38.028
	46	50.1667	−4.17	17.361
	46	50.1667	−4.17	17.361
	49	50.1667	−1.17	1.361
	50	50.1667	−0.17	0.028
	50	50.1667	−0.17	0.028
	50	50.1667	−0.17	0.028
	50	50.1667	−0.17	0.028
	51	50.1667	0.83	0.694
	51	50.1667	0.83	0.694
	51	50.1667	0.83	0.694
	52	50.1667	1.83	3.361
	53	50.1667	2.83	8.028
	53	50.1667	2.83	8.028
	54	50.1667	3.83	14.694
	56	50.1667	5.83	34.027
	57	50.1667	6.83	46.694
	58	50.1667	7.83	61.361
	58	50.1667	7.83	61.361
	59	50.1667	8.83	78.027
	61	50.1667	10.83	117.360
	62	50.1667	11.83	140.027
	67	50.1667	16.83	283.360
Totals	**1,505**	**1,505**	**0.00**	**1,828.167**

the variance, we determined the average of the squared deviations, so for our example the variance was approximately 61. However, that 61 is in the metric of *squared* exam scores, not the original exam scores we started with. To have a measure of variability that is in the same metric as the original scores, we calculate the standard deviation—the square root of the variance. In our example of 30 exam scores, the standard deviation is 7.81 ($7.81 = \sqrt{60.94}$). The benefit of using the standard deviation as compared to the variance is that this measure of variability is in the same metric as the original scores.

standard deviation a deviation value that is the square root of the variance; it is a statistical index of how much scores vary within a group.

Frequency Distributions—Again

If we were to obtain a very large number of measurements of one of a variety of human characteristics (e.g., physical characteristics like height or weight or psychological variables like intelligence or anxiety) and plot the frequency of the various values, we would find that the majority of scores fall near the middle of that frequency distribution. Comparatively fewer scores are associated with the more extreme values. Such distributions frequently resemble a theoretical distribution known as a **normal distribution** (sometimes, because of its shape, it may be referred to as a **bell curve**).

normal distribution or **bell curve** a symmetrical, bell-shaped distribution in which most scores are in the middle with smaller groups of equal size at either end.

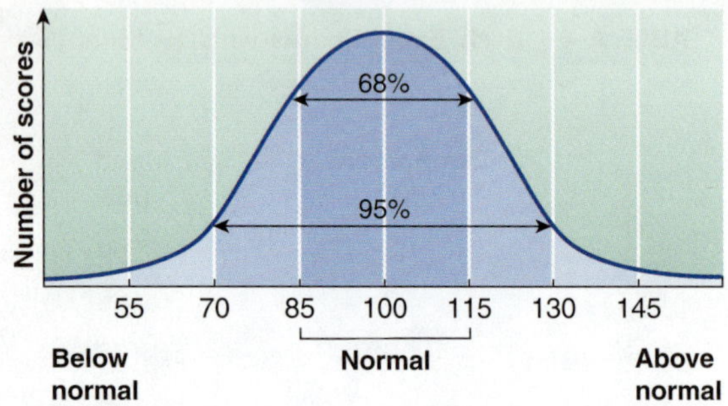

FIGURE A-3 A normal distribution.

Normal distributions all have the same basic shape, but vary depending upon the mean and the standard deviation for the data. For example, scores on the Wechsler Adult Intelligence Scale (WAIS), discussed in Chapter 10, are designed to follow the normal distribution with a mean of 100 and a standard deviation of 15 (see **Figure A-3**).

Once we know that a set of scores (at least theoretically) follows a normal distribution, then we also know certain things about how those scores are distributed. First, the normal distribution is a *symmetrical distribution*—that is, the bottom half of the distribution is the same shape as the top half. Also, with the normal distribution, the three measures of central tendency, the mean, the median, and the mode, all fall in the exact same location. Based on this we know that in the case of WAIS scores that have a mean of 100, 50 percent of individuals will have scores less than 100 and similarly, 50 percent of individuals will have scores greater than 100. Further, theoretically, approximately 68 percent of people will score within plus or minus one standard deviation of the mean (i.e., between 85 and 115), and similarly about 95 percent of people will score within plus or minus two standard deviations of the mean (i.e., between 70 and 130).

positively skewed distribution a distribution where most values occur at the lower end of the scale.

Not all variables follow a normal distribution. In many instances, a large data set may have a comparatively small number of scores that are either very low or very high. For example, consider the distribution of 2010–2011 salaries for players from the Toronto Maple Leafs (Sports City, 2011). In this team, as is common in many teams in the NHL, there are a few premiere players who receive considerably higher than normal salaries, which results in a **positively skewed distribution** (sometimes referred to as a *distribution skewed to the right*). As **Figure A-4** reflects, in situations where the distribution is positively skewed, the average (or mean) for the distribution is considerably larger than the median value since the few extremely large salaries are included in the calculation of the mean. The mode also tends to be less than the median, which is also typical in positively skewed distributions.

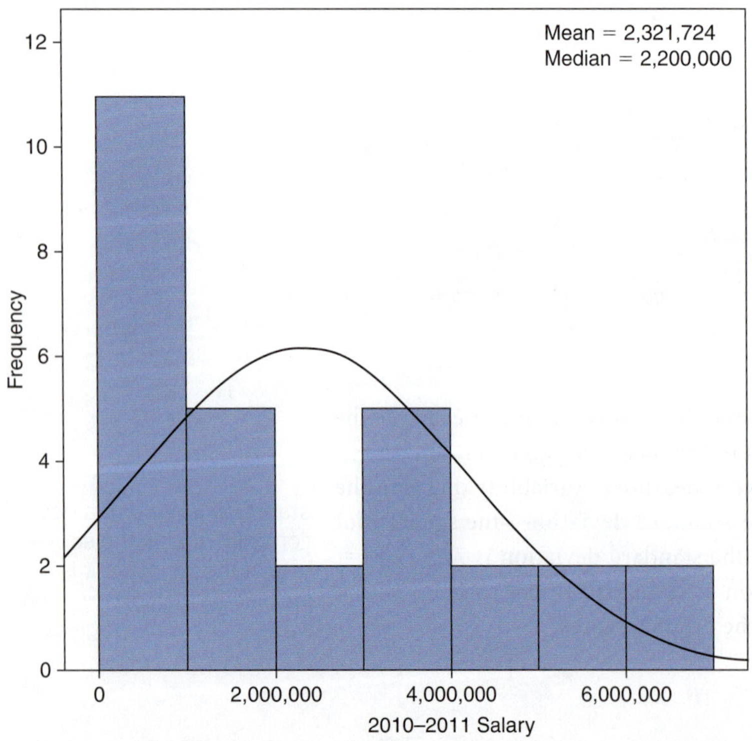

FIGURE A-4 Example of a positively skewed distribution.

In other instances, a distribution of scores may contain comparatively few low scores along with many more higher scores. For example, consider a nine-item true–false quiz that an instructor might give to an introductory psychology class with 250 students. Assume that the test is quite easy, so most of the students do very well. This could result in a distribution of scores such as the one depicted in **Figure A-5**. As you can see, the mean is less than the median (again, this is because the value for the mean is influenced by the comparatively few small scores), which is also

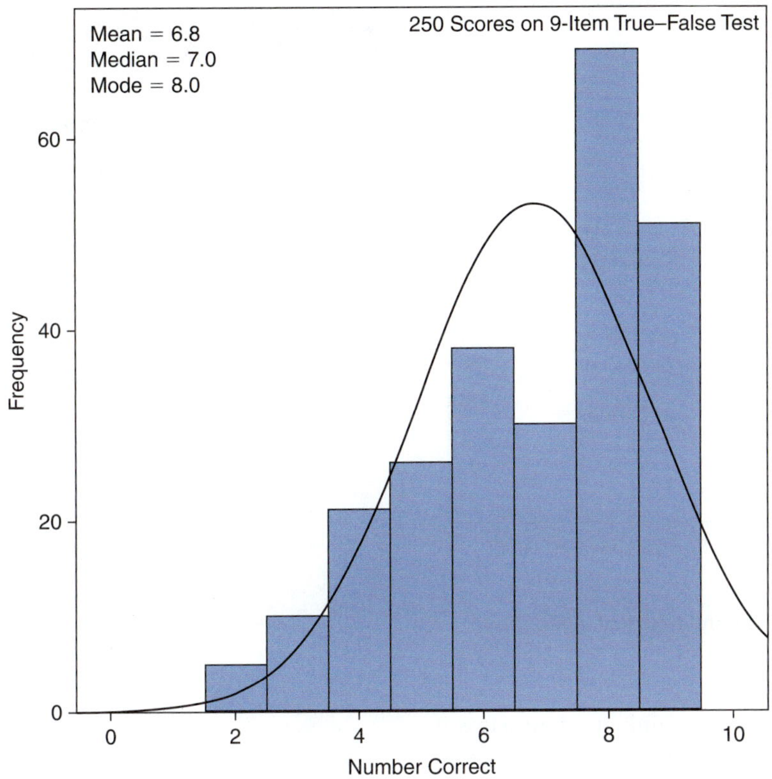

FIGURE A-5 Example of a negatively skewed distribution.

less than the mode. These types of distributions are called negatively skewed distributions (sometimes referred to as a *distribution skewed to the left*).

negatively skewed distribution a distribution where most values occur at the upper end of the scale.

In summary, if a distribution has comparatively few small or high scores, the mean may not be the best measure of central tendency since it is the only measure of central tendency that is influenced by these types of extreme scores. In such cases, the median or mode may be a better, more representative measure of central tendency.

Measures of Association

In many situations, psychologists are interested in studying the relationship between two (or more) variables. For example, what is the relationship between exposure to televised violence and actual physical aggression? Or is there a relationship between exposure to actors smoking in the media (e.g., in movies and television) and the likelihood of a teenager deciding to start smoking? In instances such as these, we can quantify and summarize the degree of relationship or association between variables using descriptive statistics known as measures of association.

measures of association descriptive statistics that quantify and summarize the degree of relationship or association between variables.

Recall our earlier example where we had scores from 30 students on their first psychology test (refer to this variable as *X*). Suppose that we had also asked those same 30 students the following question: "In the week before the test, how many hours did you spend playing video games?" (call this variable *Y*). **Table A-5** provides a listing of these data.

In instances where we have collected data on two variables from a group of individuals, it is possible to represent the relationship between the two variables using a display known as a scatterplot (or scattergram). In this display, values of one of the variables are plotted on the horizontal axis of the graph and the corresponding values of the other variable are plotted on the vertical axis. **Figure A-6** provides a scatterplot of our example data. On average, higher exam scores are associated with students who spent less time playing video games. Similarly, students who received the lower exam scores, on average, spent more time playing video games in the week before the exam.

scatterplot a graph or plot of the values of one variable or measure associated with the values on another variable or measure.

While we can understand the nature of the relationship between two variables using scatterplots, we might want to have an index or number that reflects the nature of that

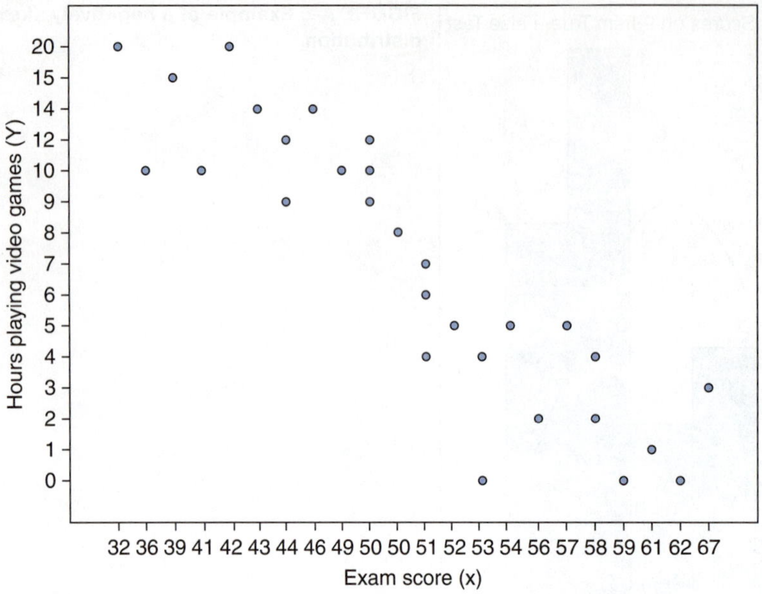

FIGURE A-6 Scatterplot showing exam scores and hours of video game playing.

TABLE A-5 Exam Scores and Hours of Video Game Playing

Student	Exam Score (*X*)	Hours Playing Video Games (*Y*)
1	32	20
2	36	10
3	39	15
4	41	10
5	42	20
6	43	14
7	44	8
8	44	12
9	46	14
10	46	14
11	49	10
12	50	12
13	50	8
14	50	10
15	50	8
16	51	6
17	51	7
18	51	4
19	52	5
20	53	0
21	53	4
22	54	5
23	56	2
24	57	5
25	58	4
26	58	2
27	59	0
28	61	1
29	62	0
30	67	3

Pearson product-moment correlation coefficient a statistic indicating the degree of association or relationship between two variables or measures, ranging from –1 to +1.

positive or **direct relationship** a relationship where as the value of one variable increases, so do values in another associated variable.

negative or **inverse relationship** a relationship where as the value of one variable increases, values in another associated variable decrease.

relationship. The most commonly used measure of association between two variables is the Pearson product-moment correlation coefficient (often symbolized with an *r* and frequently referred to as simply the correlation coefficient). The correlation coefficient provides an index of the degree of (linear) relationship between two variables, with possible values of the coefficient ranging between -1 and $+1$. The value of the correlation coefficient reflects both the *magnitude* of the relationship between the two variables and the *direction* of the relationship between the two variables. Positive values of the correlation coefficient ($r > 0.00$) indicate that there is a positive or direct relationship between the variables. In instances like this, higher values on one of the variables are associated, on average, with higher values on the other variable; similarly, lower values of the one variable are associated, on average, with lower values of the other variable. In cases where the correlation coefficient is negative (i.e., $r < 0.00$), the nature of the relationship between the two variables is referred to as a negative or inverse relationship. In this case, the lower scores on one variable are, on average, associated with higher scores on the other variable and vice versa (as was the case with our example data).

Figure A-7 provides an example of a number of scatterplots depicting varying degrees of relationship between the two variables. The left-most scatterplots reflect instances of positive and negative perfect relationships (i.e., $r = +1$ and $r = -1$). In instances like these, values on one variable change on a one-to-one basis with changes in the other variable and the relationship can be represented with a straight line. Such relationships are rarely observed in real life. As we move to the right in Figure A-7, as the degree of relationship between the variables decreases, the data points in the scatterplot no longer fall on a straight line. Further, with decreases in the degree of relationship, the points in the scatterplot fall farther from the straight line.

As previously mentioned, the value of the correlation coefficient reflects both the *direction* and the *magnitude* of the relationship between the two variables. To interpret the magnitude of the relationship reflected, we need to consider the absolute value of the correlation (i.e., ignoring whether or not it is positive or negative). The closer the absolute value of the correlation coefficient is to 1, the stronger the degree of relationship between the two variables. An alternative way of understanding the magnitude of the relationship is to take the square of the correlation coefficient (i.e., r^2). This value is known as the **coefficient of determination** and indicates the degree to which values on one variable can be predicted by knowing the values of the other variable. For example, if the correlation between number of cigarettes smoked and life expectancy were $r = 0.80$, then we could predict with 64 percent accuracy a person's life expectancy based on how much he or she had smoked.

To calculate the Pearson product-moment correlation coefficient, take the ratio of the covariance between the two variables (which is another measure of association) and divide that by the product of the standard deviations of the two variables. The covariance between two variables (let's call them X and Y) is defined by the following formula:

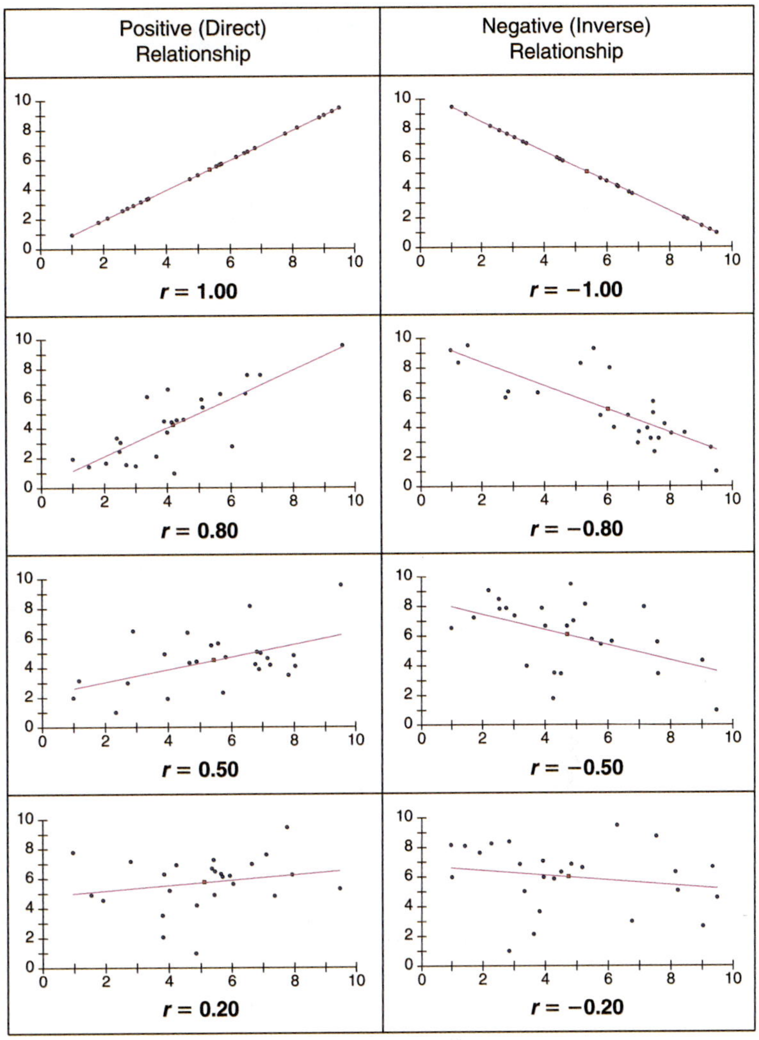

FIGURE A-7 Scatterplots showing various degrees of relationship.

$$\sigma_{XY} = \frac{\sum(X - \mu_X)(Y - \mu_Y)}{N}$$

where: σ_{XY} is the symbol for the covariance,[3]

$\sum$ is summation notation and indicates the procedure of totalling the products of each pair of deviation scores $(X - \mu_X)$ and $(Y - \mu_Y)$, and

N represents the number of observations.

coefficient of determination the degree to which values on one variable can be predicted by knowing the values of the other variable.

Table A-6 shows our example data looking at the relationship between students' exam scores (X) and hours spent playing video games (Y). The table includes the details on the initial calculations required to determine the variances for each of the variables and the covariance between the two variables.

First, consider the covariance between the two variables. The numerator for the covariance is based on the sum of the product of the individual pairs of deviation scores (i.e., $\sum(X - \mu_X)(Y - \mu_Y)$. In this example the total is negative, which reflects the inverse relationship that exists between the students' exam scores and the number of hours they spent playing video games. On average, the students who had higher exam scores, and who therefore also had positive deviation scores for that variable $(X - \mu_X)$, were more likely to have spent less time playing video games, and therefore had negative deviation scores for that variable $(Y - \mu_Y)$. Further, the reverse is true for students who had lower exam scores. When this happens, the covariance between the two variables will be negative and this will result in the correlation

[3] σ_{XY} is the symbol for the covariance of a population, whereas s_{XY} is the symbol for the covariance of a sample. The distinction between populations and samples is discussed later in this appendix.

TABLE A-6 Data Required for Calculating Pearson Correlation Coefficient

Student	Exam Score (X)	Hours Playing Video Games (Y)	$X - \mu_X$	$Y - \mu_Y$	$(X - \mu_X)(Y - \mu_Y)$	$(X - \mu_X)^2$	$(Y - \mu_Y)^2$
1	32	20	−18.17	12.23	−222.24	330.03	149.65
2	36	10	−14.17	2.23	−31.64	200.69	4.99
3	39	15	−11.17	7.23	−80.77	124.69	52.32
4	41	10	−9.17	2.23	−20.47	84.03	4.99
5	42	20	−8.17	12.23	−99.91	66.69	149.65
6	43	14	−7.17	6.23	−44.67	51.36	38.85
7	44	8	−6.17	0.23	−1.44	38.03	0.05
8	44	12	−6.17	4.23	−26.11	38.03	17.92
9	46	14	−4.17	6.23	−25.97	17.36	38.85
10	46	14	−4.17	6.23	−25.97	17.36	38.85
11	49	10	−1.17	2.23	−2.61	1.36	4.99
12	50	12	−0.17	4.23	−0.71	0.03	17.92
13	50	8	−0.17	0.23	−0.04	0.03	0.05
14	50	10	−0.17	2.23	−0.37	0.03	4.99
15	50	8	−0.17	0.23	−0.04	0.03	0.05
16	51	6	0.83	−1.77	−1.47	0.69	3.12
17	51	7	0.83	−0.77	−0.64	0.69	0.59
18	51	4	0.83	−3.77	−3.14	0.69	14.19
19	52	5	1.83	−2.77	−5.07	3.36	7.65
20	53	0	2.83	−7.77	−22.01	8.03	60.32
21	53	4	2.83	−3.77	−10.67	8.03	14.19
22	54	5	3.83	−2.77	−10.61	14.69	7.65
23	56	2	5.83	−5.77	−33.64	34.03	33.25
24	57	5	6.83	−2.77	−18.91	46.69	7.65
25	58	4	7.83	−3.77	−29.51	61.36	14.19
26	58	2	7.83	−5.77	−45.17	61.36	33.25
27	59	0	8.83	−7.77	−68.61	78.03	60.32
28	61	1	10.83	−6.77	−73.31	117.36	45.79
29	62	0	11.83	−7.77	−91.91	140.03	60.32
30	67	3	16.83	−4.77	−80.24	283.36	22.72
Totals (Σ)	**50.167**	**7.767**	**0.00**	**0.00**	**−1,077.83**	**1,828.17**	**909.37**

between the two variables being negative as well, since the covariance serves as the numerator for the correlation.[4] For our example data, the covariance between the two variables is:

$$\sigma_{XY} = \frac{\sum(X - \mu_X)(Y - \mu_Y)}{N} = \frac{-1{,}077.83}{30} = -35.93$$

[4] Note that when there is a positive relationship between the two variables, higher scores on one variable will on average be associated with higher scores on the other variables (thus the product of the corresponding deviation scores will be positive). Additionally, lower scores on one variable will on average be associated with lower scores on the other variable (and in this case, the two corresponding deviation scores will both be negative and therefore their product will be positive). In cases like this, the covariance between the two variables will be a large positive value, which will result in the correlation between the two variables being positive.

The next step in calculating the correlation coefficient is to determine the standard deviation for each of the variables. Recall that the standard deviation for a variable is the square root of the variance. The variance for each of the two variables can be calculated as shown below:

$$\sigma_X^2 = \frac{\Sigma(X - \mu_X)^2}{N} = \frac{1{,}828.17}{30} = 60.94 \text{ and } \sigma_Y^2 = \frac{\Sigma(Y - \mu_Y)^2}{N} = \frac{909.37}{30} = 30.31$$

To obtain the standard deviations for the two variables, take the square roots of the two variances (i.e., $\sigma_X = \sqrt{60.94} = 7.81$ and $\sigma_Y = \sqrt{30.31} = 5.51$). Finally, take the covariance and divide it by the product of the two standard deviations[5]:

$$r = \frac{\rho_{XY}}{\sigma_X \sigma_Y} = \frac{-35.93}{7.81 \times 5.51} = -0.84$$

So, for our 30 students, the correlation between their exam scores and the amount of time spent playing video games is –0.84. In other words, we could predict with about 70 percent accuracy (i.e., 0.84^2) a student's exam score if we knew how many hours that person had spent playing video games. Finally, as discussed in Chapter 2, remember that correlations tell us nothing regarding causality. So even though there is a fairly strong negative relationship between exam scores and video game playing in our example data, we do not know whether one variable causes the other or whether there is some third variable that is responsible for the relationship. So video gaming might reduce exam scores, or low exam scores might increase video gaming, or low exam scores and high amounts of video gaming might both be due to a lack of interest in or commitment to the course in question.

Inferential Statistics

Whereas psychologists (and others) use descriptive statistics to summarize collections of data, they use *inferential statistics* to help them make informed decisions regarding the types of conclusions they can make regarding their research findings. To understand this better, let's begin with some definitions and an example.

Populations and Samples

In most cases, when psychologists conduct research (whether on human participants or animal subjects), what they are doing is collecting observations based on a sample of individuals that is drawn from a larger group or population (see **Figure A-8**). Consider a simple experimental study where a psychologist is interested in testing the effectiveness of a new drug to improve memory. It would be impractical (and very expensive) to test every individual who might take the drug, so the researcher obtains a sample of individuals, studies them, and then draws some type of conclusions based on the results of that study. Let's look at this procedure in more detail.

sample a group or set of people or items drawn from a larger population.

population the entire group of individuals about whom we hope to learn (e.g., the Canadian population consists of all Canadians).

First, consider the underlying population—the group about which the psychologist ultimately wants to make conclusions—from which the psychologist is going to obtain her sample. In the case of testing a drug that supposedly improves (human) memory, we might consider the population to be all adults in North America. Since the psychologist cannot test the effect of the drug on all members of the population, she instead obtains a sample of individuals from that population. Often the ideal type of sample to obtain would be a random sample, in which every member of the population has an equal chance of being selected for the study. However, in many instances it is not possible to obtain a truly random sample. Instead researchers rely on sampling from a group of individuals to which they have access (e.g., first-year psychology students).

random sample a group or set made by randomly selecting people or items from a larger population; like closing your eyes and picking any two socks from your drawer.

[5] This formula for the correlation coefficient is really more of a "definitional" formula and would only be used if the number of observations was small. In most instances, the correlation coefficient is calculated using one of several alternative "calculational" formulas.

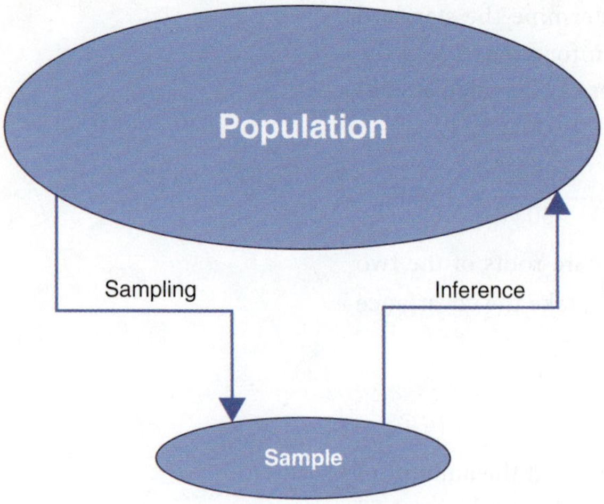

FIGURE A-8 Relationship between population and samples.

Assume that the psychologist has recruited 50 participants for her study. This study will involve two groups: the experimental group, which will receive the drug and then will have their memory tested, and a control group that will consist of participants who are treated exactly the same as the participants in the experimental group with the exception that they will not receive the drug.[6] In conducting the experiment, the researcher might randomly assign 25 participants to each of the two conditions (e.g., participants could be assigned to the experimental vs. control groups based on the results of the flip of a coin). Random assignment helps to ensure that any differences that might have existed between the two groups are evenly distributed between the groups so that the two groups are as similar as possible at the start of the study.

Hypothesis Testing

Assume that memory is assessed in this study with a standard memory test, and the researcher finds that the average score for the experimental group is 50 whereas the average score for the control group is 25. At this point, the psychologist can conclude that, on average, the experimental group had better performance on the memory test than did the control group, which she could attribute to the effect of the drug. However, the more interesting question, and the one that is at the heart of inferential statistics, is whether or not a similar finding would be obtained if the drug were given to other individuals in the population. The answer to this question comes down to the psychologist determining whether or not the difference observed between the two groups in the sample is "big enough" for her to conclude that similar differences would likely occur if the study was conducted again with a different sample of individuals.

hypothesis testing testing a statement or claim about a population using a sample and, in its simplest form, looking at experimental and control group differences.

null hypothesis an assertion that in the underlying population from which the sample was obtained, there is no difference between the average performance of individuals in one group compared to another.

alternative hypothesis an assertion that in the underlying population from which the sample was obtained, there *is* a difference between the average performance of individuals in one group compared to another.

sampling distribution the theoretical distribution of a sample statistic; for example, the difference between two sample means taken from a population.

To address this question, the psychologist can employ a technique known as **hypothesis testing**. With hypothesis testing, the psychologist sets up two hypotheses: the null hypothesis and the alternative hypothesis. Under the **null hypothesis**, the psychologist asserts that in the underlying population from which the sample was obtained, there is no difference between the average performance of individuals who might receive the drug and those who might not receive the drug (in other words, this null hypothesis asserts that the memory drug is *not* effective). The **alternative hypothesis** would be that in the population from which the sample was obtained, the average performance on the memory test for individuals receiving the memory drug would be better than that for individuals not receiving the drug (in other words, asserting that the memory drug *is* effective).

When the psychologist conducts her memory drug study, she obtains her sample of 50 individuals from the underlying population and uses that sample to create two groups. Theoretically, she could have obtained many other, different samples from that population. In this particular study, the researcher finds that there is a 25-point difference between the average memory performance for participants in the control group and those in the experimental group. Now the inferential question is, how likely is it that she would have found a difference of 25 points between the two sample means *if* the null hypothesis was true (i.e., if there really was no difference in peoples' memory between those who receive the memory drug and those who do not)? To determine the likelihood of this finding, the psychologist needs to consider a theoretical distribution known as a **sampling distribution**. In this case, the psychologist would consider a sampling distribution for the difference between two sample means (or averages) that are taken from an underlying population in which there is no difference between the means. The characteristics of this sampling distribution are based on the variability of the sample data and the size of the samples.

[6] In a well-designed study, the participants in the control group would not know that they were in the control group and would be administered some type of placebo (e.g., a sugar pill).

In our example, assume that the standard deviation for scores on the memory test was 20 for the control group and 30 for the experimental group. If the null hypothesis was true, then we would know theoretically that all possible differences between two sample means would be normally distributed with a mean of 0 and a standard deviation of 7.21.[7] Given that we know the characteristics of the theoretical sampling distribution, we can calculate that the likelihood or probability of finding a difference of 25 points between the two sample means would be very low (in fact, it would be less than 1 chance in 1,000). In this case, the psychologist would reject the null hypothesis and could be reasonably confident in concluding that the finding she obtained in her study was not due to chance and that the drug really had some effect on memory performance.

When psychologists test hypotheses using the procedures outlined above, before analyzing their data, they determine what level of risk they would be willing to take in terms of making an incorrect conclusion. Typically psychologists set the risk of drawing an incorrect conclusion at a level of either *less than 5 in 100* times or, if they want to be more certain (and more conservative) *less than 1 in 100* times. These levels translate to what is known as the **significance level**, or the **rejection level**, for the hypothesis test, and are often reported in the literature as finding a significant difference between the groups at $p < 0.05$ or $p < 0.01$. In practice, if a psychologist ends up rejecting the null hypothesis, she concludes that there is evidence to support the alternative hypothesis (e.g., that the memory drug is effective)—what she cannot say, however, is that she has "proven" the alternative hypothesis. This is because we only have information from the one sample and there is still some possibility (albeit a low one) that the sample she obtained did indeed come from a population where the drug had no effect on memory.

significance level or **rejection level** the level of risk researchers would be willing to take in terms of making an incorrect conclusion.

Effect Size

Whereas inferential statistics provide psychologists with tools to determine the likelihood of the finding in the sample being one that would also occur in the population, they do not provide information regarding the magnitude of the study's effect. For example, while a psychologist may use null hypothesis testing to find that there is a significant difference between memory performance for two groups, the hypothesis test does not tell us about the magnitude or size of the difference—it only allows the psychologist to make a statement regarding the probability of the finding. Researchers can use another category of descriptive statistics, namely **effect size** estimates, in conjunction with hypothesis testing to help them assess the magnitude of research findings. An effect size is a standardized measure that reflects the degree of relationship or size of the difference between two or more variables. Further, since effect sizes are standardized, they can be compared across different studies (Field, 2005).

effect size a standardized measure that reflects the degree of relationship or size of the difference between two or more variables.

Two common categories of effect sizes are (1) group difference indices that estimate the magnitude of the difference between two (or more) groups; and (2) strength of association indices that estimate the degree of shared variation between two (or more) variables (Ferguson, 2009). In simple studies that involve examining the difference in average performance between two groups, Cohen's *d* is the most common effect size. Cohen's *d* is the standardized difference between two population means and can be estimated by taking the difference between the two sample means and dividing this by the standard deviation for the data. In the previous memory study example there was a 25-point difference between the two sample means; if we divide that by the standard deviation[8] of the data, then Cohen's *d* equals 0.98 $\left(d = \frac{25}{25.5} = 0.98\right)$. In terms of interpreting effect sizes (specifically Cohen's *d*),

[7] This standard deviation is known as the *standard error of the differences between means* and equals $\sqrt{\frac{20^2}{25} + \frac{30^2}{25}} = 7.21$.

[8] In the case of the example study, the standard deviation of the data is obtained by using the pooled standard deviation, which can be calculated as $s* = \sqrt{\frac{(n_1 - 1)s_1^2 + (n_2 - 1)s_2^2}{n_1 + n_2 - 2}} = \sqrt{\frac{(25 - 1)20_1^2 + (25 - 1)30_2^2}{25 + 25 - 2}} = 25.5$.

a frequently used rule-of-thumb is to define effect sizes as "small, $d = .2$," "medium, $d = .5$," and "large, $d = .8$" (Cohen, 1992). Thus, for the example data, we could conclude that the memory drug has a large effect.

For non-experimental studies, a common effect size that is a measure of association is the Pearson correlation coefficient (i.e., r). In terms of interpreting r as an effect size, Cohen (1992) suggests the following: "small, $r = .1$," "medium, $r = .3$," and "large, $r = .5$." Recall that squaring the correlation coefficient provides the coefficient of determination, which tells us how much of the variability in one variable can be predicted based on scores from the other variable. With this in mind, for non-experimental research, if one could account for 1 percent of the variability, then you would have a small effect; if you could account for 9 percent of the variability, then you would have a medium effect; and if you could account for 25 percent of the variability, you would have a large effect.

Why Statistics Matter

This appendix has hopefully provided you with some insight into several of the basic statistical procedures used by psychologists as tools to summarize and interpret the data they collect as part of their research studies. Students of psychology are often surprised by the degree to which the study of psychology requires at least a basic familiarity with statistics. However, only with this type of understanding will students become better consumers of psychological research and thereby become better able to critically evaluate the claims made by psychologists. In fact, students who choose to major in psychology as undergraduates will most likely require further instruction in statistics. A survey of requirements for undergraduate degrees in psychology showed that the vast majority of universities and colleges require at least one course in statistics (Messer, Griggs, & Jackson, 1999). So if you are interested in pursuing a degree in psychology, you can expect to encounter even more statistics.

Glossary

A

ABC model of attitudes a model proposing that attitudes have three components: the affective component, the behavioural component, and the cognitive component.

abnormal psychology the scientific study of psychological disorders.

absolute pitch the ability to recognize or produce any note on a musical scale.

absolute refractory period a short time after an action potential, during which a neuron is completely unable to fire again.

absolute threshold the minimal stimulus necessary for detection by an individual.

academic psychology a branch of psychology focusing on research and instruction in the various areas or fields of study in psychology.

accommodation one of two ways of acquiring knowledge, defined by Piaget as the alteration of pre-existing mental frameworks to take in new information.

action potential a sudden positive change in the electrical charge of a neuron's axon. Also known as a spike, or firing, action potentials rapidly transmit an excitatory charge down the axon.

activation-synthesis model theory that dreams result from brain's attempts to synthesize or organize random internally generated signals and give them meaning.

actor-observer effect the discrepancy between how we explain other people's behaviour (dispositionally) and how we explain our own behaviour (situationally).

acute stress disorder an anxiety disorder in which fear and related symptoms are experienced soon after a traumatic event and last less than a month.

acute stressor a stressful situation or circumstance that happens in the short term and has a definite endpoint.

adaptive theory of sleep theory that organisms sleep for the purposes of self-preservation, to keep away from predators that are more active at night.

addiction psychological or physical compulsion to take a drug, resulting from regular ingestion and leading to maladaptive patterns of behaviour and changes in physical response.

affiliation the need to form attachments to other people for support, guidance, and protection.

ageusia inability to taste.

aggression a broad range of behaviours intended to harm others.

agoraphobia a phobia that makes people avoid public places or situations in which escape might be difficult or help unavailable should panic symptoms develop.

agrammatism a neurological condition arising from damage to a brain region just anterior to Broca's area, where the patient is incapable of using words in grammatical sequence.

alcoholism long-term pattern of alcohol addiction.

algorithm problem-solving strategy that always leads to a solution.

allele variation of a gene.

alternative hypothesis an assertion that in the underlying population from which the sample was obtained, there *is* a difference between the average performance of individuals in one group compared to another.

altruism self-sacrificing behaviour carried out for the benefit of others.

Alzheimer's disease most common form of dementia, usually beginning with mild memory problems, lapses of attention, and problems in language, and progressing to difficulty with even simple tasks and recall of long-held memories.

amnestic disorders organic disorders in which memory loss is the primary symptom.

amygdala brain area involved in processing information about emotions, particularly fear.

amyotrophic lateral sclerosis (ALS or Lou Gehrig's disease) neurological disease that causes degeneration of motor neurons in the spinal cord, leading to loss of movement and eventual death.

anorexia nervosa eating disorder in which individuals under-eat and have a distorted body image of being overweight.

anosmia inability to smell.

anterograde amnesia ongoing inability to form new memories after an amnesia-inducing event.

antianxiety drugs psychotropic drugs that reduce tension and anxiety.

antidepressant drugs psychotropic drugs that lift the mood of depressed people.

antibipolar drugs psychotropic drugs that help stabilize the moods of people suffering from bipolar disorder.

antipsychotic drugs psychotropic drugs that help correct grossly confused or distorted thinking.

antisocial personality disorder a personality disorder characterized by extreme and callous disregard for the feelings and rights of others.

applied psychology the branch of psychology applying psychological principles to practical problems in other fields, such as education, marketing, or industry.

approach-approach conflict conflict that occurs when a person must choose between two equally desirable options.

approach-avoidance conflict conflict that occurs when any available choice has both desirable and undesirable qualities.

Asperger's disorder a disorder in which persons have major social impairments yet have relatively normal intellectual, adaptive, and language skills.

assimilation one of two ways of acquiring knowledge, defined by Piaget as the inclusion of new information or experiences into pre-existing schemes.

association cortex areas of the neocortex responsible for complex functions, including higher-order sensory processing, thinking, and planning.

associative learning learning that involves forming associations between stimuli.

attachment a close emotional bond to another person, such as a baby to a caregiver.

attention deficit disorder (ADD) a disorder characterized by an inability to pay attention.

attention deficit hyperactivity disorder (ADHD) a disorder characterized by an inability to pay attention, accompanied by excessive activity.

attitudes relatively stable and enduring evaluations of things and people.

attributions causal explanations of behaviour.

autism a severe disorder marked by extreme unresponsiveness, poor communication, and very repetitive and rigid behaviours.

automatic processing encoding of information with little conscious awareness or effort.

automatic thoughts specific upsetting thoughts that occur unbidden.

autonomic nervous system portion of the peripheral nervous system that includes the sympathetic and parasympathetic nervous systems.

availability heuristic judging easily-recalled events as more common.

aversion therapy therapy designed to help clients to acquire anxiety responses to stimuli that the clients have been finding too attractive.

avoidance-avoidance conflict conflict that occurs when a person must choose between two equally undesirable options.

avoidant personality disorder a disorder involving extreme discomfort and inhibition in social relationships.

axon the part of the neuron that carries information away from the cell body toward other neurons.

axon terminal the end of a neuron's axon, from which neurotransmitters are released.

B

babbling babies' production of meaningless sounds.

basic emotions a group of emotions preprogrammed into all humans regardless of culture.

basilar membrane structure in the cochlea where the hair cells are located.

behaviour modification a systematic approach to change behaviour using principles of operant conditioning.

behaviour observable activities of an organism, often in response to environmental cues.

behavioural genetics a subfield of psychology looking at the influence of genes on human behaviour.

behaviourism a branch of psychological thought arguing that psychology should study only directly observable behaviours rather than abstract mental processes.

biases distorted beliefs based on a person's subjective sense of reality.

bioecological model of intelligence Ceci's theory that intelligence is a function of the interactions among innate potential abilities, environmental context, and internal motivation.

biological therapy the use of physical and chemical procedures to help people overcome psychological difficulties.

bipolar disorder a mood disorder in which periods of mania alternate with periods of depression.

body mass index (BMI) weight-to-height ratio.

body weight set point a weight that individuals typically return to even after dieting or overeating.

borderline personality disorder a personality disorder characterized by severe instability in emotions and self-concept and high levels of volatility.

bottom-up processing perception that proceeds by transducing environmental stimuli into neural impulses that move onto successively more complex brain regions.

bounded rationality in many situations, our ability to make clear rational decisions is limited or "bounded" by things like a lack of information, time constraints, or emotions attached to aspects of the problem we are trying to solve.

brainstem the part of the brain closest to the spinal cord that serves basic functions.

Broca's aphasia a neurological condition arising from damage to Broca's area where the patient is unable to produce coherent speech.

Broca's area a region in the frontal lobes near the motor cortex that is important for speech production.

bulima nervosa eating disorder in which individuals binge and then engage in purging-type behaviour.

C

Cannon-Bard theory of emotion a theory proposing that the subjective experience of emotion and the activation of the sympathetic nervous system (that is, bodily arousal) occur simultaneously.

case study study focusing on a single person.

catatonia extreme psychomotor symptoms of schizophrenia, including catatonic stupor, catatonic rigidity, and catatonic posturing.

catharsis reliving of past repressed feelings as means of settling internal conflicts and overcoming problems.

cellular clock theory theory suggesting that we age because our cells have built-in limits on their ability to reproduce.

cephalocaudal pattern a pattern in which growth and development proceed from top to bottom.

cerebellum part of the brain, near the back of the head, important for motor coordination.

child-directed speech speech characterized by exaggerated emotional responses and a slower pace that is common among caregivers communicating with babies and young children.

chromosomes strands of DNA; each human being has 46 chromosomes, distributed in pairs.

chronic stressor a stressful situation or circumstance that is relatively long term and often lacks a definite endpoint.

chunking grouping bits of information together to enhance ability to hold that information in working memory.

circadian rhythm pattern of sleep–wake cycles that in human beings roughly corresponds to periods of daylight and night.

client-centred therapy an approach to therapy founded by Carl Rogers, based on the notion that the client is an equal and positive gains are made by mirroring clients' thoughts and feelings in an atmosphere of unconditional positive regard.

clinical and counselling psychology the study of abnormal psychological behaviour and interventions designed to change that behaviour.

cochlea fluid-filled structure in the inner ear; contains the hair cells.

codominance in a heterozygous combination of alleles, both traits are expressed in the offspring.

coefficient of determination the degree to which values on one variable can be predicted by knowing the values of the other variable.

cognition mental processes of thinking and knowing.

cognitive control the ability to direct thought in accord with one's intentions.

cognitive development changes in thinking that occur over the course of time.

cognitive dissonance a state of emotional discomfort people experience when they hold two contradictory beliefs or hold a belief that contradicts their behaviour.

cognitive-mediational theory of emotion a theory proposing that cognitive interpretations, particularly appraisals, of events are the keys to experiences of emotion.

cognitive neuroscience the study of mental processes and how they relate to the biological functions of the brain.

cognitive psychology the field of psychology studying mental processes as forms of information processing, or the ways in which information is stored and operated in our minds.

cognitive therapy Beck's cognitive therapy technique designed to help clients recognize and change their dysfunctional thoughts and ways of thinking.

cognitive triad a pattern of thinking in which individuals repeatedly interpret their experiences, themselves, and their futures in negative ways that lead them to feel depressed.

cohort-sequential design blended cross-sectional and longitudinal research, designed to look at how individuals from different age groups compare to one another and to follow them over time.

collectivist a culture whose members focus more on the needs of the group and less on individual desires.

community mental health treatment treatment programs that emphasize community care, including an emphasis on prevention.

comorbidity condition in which a person's symptoms qualify him for two or more diagnoses.

compulsions repetitive and rigid behaviours or mental acts that people feel they must perform to prevent or reduce anxiety.

concentration gradient the relative concentration of sodium ions inside and outside of the neuron.

concrete operations Piagetian stage during which children are able to talk about complex relationships, such as categorization and cause and effect, but are still limited to understanding ideas in terms of real-world relationships.

conditioned response (CR) a physical response elicited by a conditioned stimulus; it is usually the same as the unconditioned response.

conditioned stimulus (CS) a neutral stimulus that eventually elicits the same response as an unconditioned stimulus with which it has been paired.

conditioned taste aversion a form of classical conditioning whereby a previously neutral stimulus (often an odour or taste) elicits an aversive reaction after it's paired with illness (nausea).

conduct disorder clinical disorder in children and adolescents associated with emotional and behavioural problems, such as rule-breaking, trouble with limit-setting from authority figures, bullying and fighting with other people, and cruelty.

cones photoreceptors responsive to colours.

confirmation bias tendency to look for information that meets our expectations.

conflict discomfort brought about by two or more goals or impulses perceived to be incompatible.

conformity the tendency to yield to social pressure.

consciousness personal awareness of ongoing mental processes, behaviours, and environmental events.

conservation the understanding that certain properties of an object (such as volume and number) remain the same despite changes in the object's outward appearance.

content validity the degree to which the content of a test accurately represents what the test is intended to measure.

context the original location where you first learned a concept or idea is rich with retrieval cues that will make it more likely you will be able to recall that information later if you are in that same location or context.

continuous reinforcement what occurs when behaviour is reinforced every time it occurs.

control group group that has not been or will not be exposed to the independent variable.

convergence inward movement of the eyes to view objects close to oneself.

convergent evolution the development of similar physical characteristics or behaviours in different species that do not share a common ancestor; occurs because of exposure to similar environmental conditions for different species.

coping efforts to manage, reduce, or tolerate stress.

corpus callosum bundle of axons that allows communication from one side of the neocortex to the other.

correlation predictable relationship between two or more variables.

correlation coefficient statistic expressing the strength and nature of a relationship between two variables.

couple therapy or **marital therapy** therapy format in which a therapist works with two people who are in a long-term relationship.

creativity the ability to produce ideas that are both original and valuable.

critical periods points in development when an organism is extremely sensitive to environmental input, making it easier for the organism to acquire certain brain functions and behaviours.

cross-cultural psychology the study of what is generally or universally true about human beings regardless of culture.

cross-sectional design a research approach that compares groups of different-aged people to one another.

cultural psychology the study of how cognitive processing varies across different populations.

cultural universality behaviours and practices that occur across all cultures.

culture a set of shared beliefs and practices that are transmitted across generations.

culture-sensitive therapies approaches that seek to address the unique issues faced by members of cultural minority groups.

D

daily hassles everyday annoyances that contribute to higher stress levels; also known as *micro-stressors*.

deafness loss or lack of hearing.

debriefing supplying full information to participants at the end of their participation in a research study.

decay theory theory of forgetting, suggesting that memories fade over time due to neglect or failure to access over long periods of time.

decision making evaluating and choosing from among options.

deductive reasoning reasoning proceeding from broad basic principles applied to specific situations.

deep brain stimulation a procedure in which implanted electrodes deliver constant low stimulation to a small area of the brain; used to treat severe depression, Parkinson's disease, and epilepsy.

defence mechanisms unconscious tactics employed by the ego to protect the individual from anxiety.

delusions blatantly false beliefs that are firmly held despite evidence to the contrary.

dementia severe memory problems combined with losses in at least one other cognitive function, such as abstract thinking or language.

dendrites the parts of neurons that collect input from other neurons.

denial a defence mechanism; the process of refusing to recognize an existing situation.

deoxyribonucleic acid (DNA) molecules in which genetic information is enclosed.

dependent personality disorder a disorder involving a pervasive, excessive need to be taken care of and a fear of separation.

dependent variable condition or event that you expect to change as a result of variations in the independent variable.

depolarized regions of postsynaptic membranes have been stimulated by excitatory neurochemicals to open their ion channels and increase the likelihood that the neuron they are part of will initiate an action potential.

depressants class of drugs that slow the activity of the central nervous system.

depression a persistent sad state in which life seems dark and its challenges overwhelming.

descriptive research methods studies that allow researchers to demonstrate a relationship between the variables of interest, without specifying a causal relationship.

descriptive statistics statistics used to describe and summarize data.

developmental psychology the study of changes in behaviour and mental processes over time and the factors that influence the course of those constancies and changes.

developmental psychopathology the study of how problematic behaviours evolve as a function of a person's genetics and early experiences and how those early problematic issues affect the person at later life stages.

diagnosis a clinician's determination that a person's cluster of symptoms represents a particular disorder.

Diagnostic and Statistical Manual of Mental Disorders (DSM) the leading classification system for psychological disorders in Canada; DSM-IV-TR is the current version.

difference threshold or **just noticeable difference** the minimal difference between two stimuli necessary for detection of a difference between the two.

differential emotions theory a theory holding that particular emotions or sets of emotions become more prominent during specific life stages as they serve stage-related developmental processes.

discrete trait trait that results as the product of a single gene pairing.

dishabituation a form of non-associative learning whereby there is a recovery of attention to a novel stimulus following habitation.

display rules cultural expectations that prescribe how, when, and by whom emotions should be expressed.

dissociation a splitting of consciousness into two dimensions.

dissociative amnesia psychological disorder characterized by inability to recall important information, usually of an upsetting nature, about one's life.

dissociative disorders psychological disorder characterized by major loss of memory without a clear physical cause. Types include *dissociative amnesia*, *dissociative fugue*, and *dissociative identity disorder.*

dissociative fugue psychological disorder characterized by loss of memory of personal identity and details of one's past life and flight to an entirely different location.

dissociative identity disorder psychological disorder characterized by the development of two or more distinct personalities.

distress stress caused by unpleasant situations or circumstances.

dominant trait trait that is expressed in a phenotype, no matter whether the genotype is homozygous or heterozygous for the trait.

dopamine neurotransmitter plentiful in brain areas involving movement and rewards.

double-blind procedure study in which neither the participant nor the researcher knows what treatment or procedure the participant is receiving.

Down syndrome an inherited disorder, usually caused by the presence of extra chromosomal material on the twenty-first chromosome, that results in mental retardation.

dyscalculia an inability to readily acquire information about mathematics.

dysexecutive syndrome impairments in the ability to control and direct mental activities.

dyslexia a learning disability that involves deficits in learning to read and write.

E

effect size a standardized measure that reflects the degree of relationship or size of the difference between two or more variables.

effortful processing encoding of information through careful attention and conscious effort.

ego according to psychoanalytic theory, a personality element that works to help satisfy the drives of the id while complying with the constraints placed on behaviour by the environment.

egocentrism flaws in a child's reasoning based on his or her inability to take other perspectives.

electroconvulsive therapy (ECT) use of electric shock to trigger a brain seizure in hopes of relieving abnormal functioning.

emotion an intrapersonal state that occurs in response to either an external or an internal event and typically involves a physiological component, a cognitive component, and a behavioural component.

emotion dysregulation unhealthy attempts to regulate emotion.

emotion-focused coping coping strategies focused on changing one's feelings about the stressor.

emotional intelligence an individual's ability to perceive, express, assimilate, and regulate emotion.

emotional intensity the characteristic strength with which an individual typically experiences emotion.

empirical able to be tested in objective ways.

empirically supported or **evidence-based treatment movement** movement to help clinicians become more familiar with and apply research findings concerning the effectiveness of particular treatments.

encoding a basic activity of memory, involving the recording of information in our brain.

endocrine system the system that controls levels of hormones throughout the body.

endorphins naturally-occurring pain-killing chemicals (neurotransmitters) in the brain.

enkephalins naturally-occurring pain-killing chemicals (neurotransmitters) in the brain.

episodic memory a person's memory of personal events or episodes from his or her life.

equifinality the idea that different individuals can start out from different places and wind up at the same outcome.

equilibrium balance in a mental framework.

eustress the optimal level of stress needed to promote physical and psychological health.

evolution by natural selection the differential likelihood between members of a species in their ability to survive and reproduce.

evolutionary psychology field of study that examines how the process of evolution has shaped the body and brain via the interaction of our genes and the environment to produce our thoughts and behaviours.

executive function the brain's ability to control and manage the mental processing of information.

experiment controlled observation in which researchers manipulate the presence or amount of the independent variable to see what effect it has on the dependent variable.

experimental group group that is exposed to the independent variable.

explicit memory memory that a person can consciously bring to mind, such as one's date of birth.

extinction reduction of a conditioned response after repeated presentations of the conditioned stimulus alone.

extrinsic motivation engaging in a behaviour due to the influence of factors outside ourselves.

F

facial efference sensory feedback from facial muscular activity.

facial-feedback theory of emotion a theory proposing that subjective experiences of emotion are influenced by sensory feedback from facial muscular activity, or facial efference.

factor analysis a statistical method for determining whether certain items on a test correlate highly, thus forming a unified set, or cluster, of items.

family systems theory a theory holding that each family has its own implicit rules, relationship structure, and communication patterns that shape the behaviour of the individual members.

family therapy a format in which therapists meet with all members of a family to help the whole family to change.

fitness the ability of an individual to successfully grow to maturity and have offspring that perpetuate the existence of the species that the individual belongs to.

five-factor theory an empirically derived trait theory that proposes five major trait categories: agreeableness/disagreeableness, extraversion/introversion, neuroticism/stability, conscientiousness/irresponsibility, and openness to experience/unimaginativeness.

fixed interval schedule schedule of reinforcement that occurs every time a specific time period has elapsed.

fixed ratio schedule schedule of reinforcement that occurs after a specific number of responses.

flashbacks recurrence of the sensory and emotional changes after LSD has left the body.

flashbulb memory detailed and near-permanent memories of an emotionally significant event, or of the circumstances surrounding the moment we learned about the event.

Flynn effect an observed rise in average IQ scores throughout the world over time.

forgetting the inability to recall information that was previously encoded into memory.

formal operations Piaget's final stage of cognitive development when the child achieves formal adult reasoning and the ability to think about things that don't have a concrete reality.

fovea centre of the retina, containing only cones, where vision is most clear.

free association psychodynamic therapy technique of allowing clients to freely talk about whatever they want.

free nerve endings sensory receptors that convert physical stimuli into touch, pressure, or pain impulses.

free-radical theory theory suggesting we age because special negatively charged oxygen molecules become more prevalent in our body as we get older, destabilizing cellular structures and causing the effects of aging.

frequency polygon a line graph depicting a grouped frequency distribution, which is created by connecting the midpoints of each class of data.

frontal cortex lobe of the neocortex involved in many functions, including movement and speech production.

frustration an emotion people experience when thwarted in pursuit of a goal.

functional fixedness tendency to view objects as having only one function.

functionalism the belief that mental processes have purpose and focus of study should be on how the mind adapts those purposes to changing environments.

fundamental attribution error the tendency to use dispositional attributions to explain the behaviour of other people.

G

***g* factor** a theoretical general factor of intelligence underlying all distinct clusters of mental ability; part of Spearman's two-factor theory of intelligence.

gate control theory of pain theory suggesting that certain patterns of neural activity can close a "gate" to keep pain information from travelling to parts of the brain where it is perceived.

gender-sensitive therapies or **feminist therapies** approaches that seek to address the unique pressures of being a female.

general adaptation syndrome (GAS) a three-stage response to stress identified by Hans Selye; the stages are alarm, resistance, and exhaustion.

generalized anxiety disorder an anxiety disorder in which people feel excessive anxiety and worry under most circumstances.

genes basic building blocks of our biological inheritance.

genotype a person's genetic inheritance.

Gestalt psychology the field of psychology arguing that we have inborn tendencies to structure what we see in particular ways and to structure our perceptions into broad perceptual units.

glia the cells that, in addition to neurons, make up the nervous system.

group an organized, stable collection of individuals in which the members are aware of and influence one another and share a common identity.

group polarization the intensification of an initial tendency of individual group members brought about by group discussion.

group therapy psychotherapy format in which a therapist sees several clients who have similar problems at the same time.

grouped frequency distribution a count of the number of times specific data points fall into a range of values in a data set.

groupthink a form of faulty group decision making that occurs when group members strive for unanimity and this goal overrides their motivation to realistically appraise alternative courses of action.

gustatory sense sense of taste.

H

habituation process in which individuals pay less attention to a stimulus after it is presented to them over and over again.

hair cells sensory receptors that convert sound waves into neural impulses.

hallucinations imagined sights, sounds, or other sensory events experienced as if they were real.

hallucinogens substances that dramatically change one's state of awareness, causing powerful changes in sensory perception.

Hawthorne effect people who are being observed in studies or at their workplace will improve or change some of their behaviour simply because they are being watched or studied, not in response to an experimental manipulation.

hemispheres halves of the brain.

heritability the overall extent to which differences among people are attributable to genes.

heritability coefficient a correlation coefficient used to indicate the contribution of heredity to some characteristic, such as intelligence.

heterosexual sexual attraction to members of the opposite sex.

heterozygous parents contribute two different alleles to offspring.

heuristic a shortcut thinking strategy.

higher order conditioning what occurs when a previously conditioned stimulus functions as if it were an unconditioned stimulus for further conditioning.

hindbrain the part of the brain closest to the spinal cord that consists of the medulla, the reticular formation, pons, and cerebellum.

hippocampus brain region important for certain types of learning and memory.

histogram a bar chart showing the number of times specific data points fall into a range of values in a data set.

homeostasis a tendency of the body to maintain itself in a state of balance or equilibrium.

homosexual sexual attraction to members of one's own sex.

homozygous both parents contribute the same genetic material for a particular trait.

humanistic psychology theory of psychology that sought to give greater prominence to the special and unique features of human functioning.

Huntington's disease inherited neurological disorder that results in the death of neurons in the striatum.

hyperpolarized areas of a cell have had their negative charge increased in an inhibitory fashion, making it less likely that the cell will generate an action potential.

hypnagogic state a pre-sleep period often characterized by vivid sensory phenomena.

hypnosis a seemingly altered state of consciousness during which individuals can be directed to act or experience the world in unusual ways.

hypothalamus brain structure important for motivation and control of the endocrine system.

hypothesis a general statement about the way variables relate that is objectively falsifiable.

hypothesis testing testing a statement or claim about a population using a sample and, in its simplest form, looking at experimental and control group differences.

hypothetico-deductive reasoning process of modern science where scientists begin with an educated guess about how the world works, and then set about designing small controlled observations to support or invalidate that hypothesis.

I

id according to psychoanalytic theory, the personality element representing basic instinctual drives, such as those related to eating, sleeping, sex, and comfort.

immune system the body's system of organs, tissues, and cells that identify and destroy foreign invaders, such as bacteria and viruses, as well as cancer cells.

implicit attitude an attitude of which the person is unaware.

implicit learning the acquisition of information without awareness.

implicit memory knowledge that we have stored in memory that we are not typically aware of or able to recall at will.

incentives external motives that indirectly indicate reward.

independent variable condition or event that is thought to be a factor in changing another condition or event.

individual therapy psychotherapy format in which the therapist sees the client alone; the oldest of the modern formats.

individualistic a culture that places the wants or desires of the person over the needs of the group.

inductive reasoning reasoning process proceeding from small specific situations to more general truths.

inferential statistics statistics used to draw conclusions about research data.

information processing the means by which information is stored and operates internally.

information-processing model view of memory suggesting that information moves among three memory stores during encoding, storage, and retrieval.

information-processing theory a developmental theory focusing on how children learn, remember, organize, and use information from their environment.

informed consent requirement that researchers give as much information as possible about the purpose, procedures, risks, and benefits of the study so that a participant can make an informed decision about whether or not to participate.

inoculation exposing oneself to a relatively low level of stress in a controlled situation to improve later performance in a more stressful situation.

insight learning a sudden realization of a solution to a problem or leap in understanding new concepts.

insomnia sleep disorder characterized by a regular inability to fall asleep or stay asleep.

instincts inborn behavioural tendencies, activated by stimuli in our environments.

intelligence the ability to learn, to meet the demands of the environment effectively, and to understand and control one's mental activities.

intelligence quotient (IQ) Terman's measure of intelligence; the ratio of a child's mental age to his or her chronological age, multiplied by 100.

interactionism a view emphasizing the relationship between a person's underlying personality traits and the reinforcing aspects of the situations in which they choose to put themselves.

interference theory theory that forgetting is influenced by what happens to people before or after they take information in.

intermittent or **partial reinforcement** a schedule of reinforcement where the behaviour is only followed by reinforcement some of the time.

interneuron neuron that typically has a short axon and serves as a relay between different classes of neurons. In the spinal cord, interneurons communicate with both sensory and motor neurons.

International Classification of Diseases (ICD) the system used by most countries to classify psychological disorders; published by the World Health Organization and currently in its tenth edition (ICD-10).

intrinsic motivation engaging in a behaviour simply for the satisfaction that is part of doing it.

introspection a method of psychological study endorsed by Wundt and his followers involving careful evaluation of mental processes and how they expand simple thoughts into complex ideas.

ion channels pores in the cell membrane that open and close to allow certain ions into and out of the cell.

J

James-Lange theory of emotion a theory proposing that felt emotions result from physiological changes, rather than being their cause.

L

language a set of symbols used to communicate.

language comprehension the process of understanding spoken, written, or signed language.

language production the structured and conventional expression of thoughts through words.

lateral hypothalamus a region of the hypothalamus important in signalling thirst and hunger.

law of effect behaviours leading to rewards are more likely to occur again, while behaviours producing unpleasantness are less likely to occur again.

learned helplessness a situation in which repeated exposure to inescapable punishment eventually produces a failure to make escape attempts.

learning a lasting change caused by experience.

learning curve a graph that shows change in performance on a learning task over time.

learning disability a specific deficiency in one aspect of cognitive function while other aspects function normally.

leptin a protein produced by fat cells that is important for regulating the amount of food eaten over long periods of time.

lexical meaning dictionary meaning of a word.

life changes shifts in life circumstances that require adjustment of some kind.

linguistic relativity hypothesis suggests that the vocabulary available for objects or concepts in a language influences how speakers of that language think about them.

lobotomy surgical practice of cutting the connections between the frontal lobe and the lower centres of the brain.

long-term memory the memory system in which we hold all of the information we have previously gathered available for retrieval and use in a new situation or task.

long-term potentiation (LTP) repeated stimulation of certain nerve cells in the brain greatly increases the likelihood that the cells will respond strongly to future stimulation.

longitudinal design a research approach that follows the same people over a period of time by administering the same tasks or questionnaires and seeing how their responses change.

loose associations or **derailment** a common thought disorder of schizophrenia, characterized by rapid shifts from one topic to another.

lucid dreams dreams in which the sleeper fully recognizes that he or she is dreaming, and occasionally actively guides the outcome of the dream.

lymphocytes white blood cells that circulate through the body and destroy foreign invaders and cancer cells; important components of the immune system.

M

major depressive disorder a disorder characterized by a depressed mood that is significantly disabling and is not caused by such factors as drugs or a general medical condition.

mania a persistent state of euphoria or frenzied energy.

maturation the unfolding of development in a particular sequence and time frame.

mean the average value in a data set; the sum of all numbers in the set divided by the total number of items in the set.

measures of association descriptive statistics that quantify and summarize the degree of relationship or association between variables.

measures of central tendency numbers used to summarize data sets.

measures of variability indicators that tell how different the values are within a dataset.

median the data set value that represents the midpoint of an ordered set of numbers.

meditation technique designed to turn one's consciousness away from the outer world toward one's inner cues and awareness.

medulla part of the brain that controls basic bodily processes and regulates reflexes.

Meissner's corpuscles sensory receptors that convert physical stimuli about sensory touch on the fingertips, lips, and palms.

memory the faculty for recalling past events and past learning.

memory span maximum number of items that can be recalled in correct order.

menopause series of changes in hormonal function occurring in women during their 50s, which lead to the end of the menstrual cycle and reproductive capabilities.

mental age the intellectual age at which a person is functioning, as opposed to chronological age.

mental imagery picturing things in your mind.

mental processes activities of our brain when engaged in thinking, observing the environment, and using language.

mental retardation term describing individuals who display general intellectual functioning that is well below average and, at the same time, poor adaptive behaviour.

mental set tendency to use problem-solving strategies that have worked in the past.

Merkel's discs sensory receptors that convert information about light to moderate pressure on the skin.

metacognition the ability to understand and control one's mental activities.

mirror neurons neurons located in the frontal and parietal cortex, which respond similarly when the individual engages in an activity and when the individual watches someone else engage in the activity.

miscarriage discharge of the fetus from the uterus before it is able to function on its own.

mnemonic devices techniques used to enhance the meaningfulness of information, as a way of making them more memorable.

mode the most frequent or most common value in a data set.

modelling what occurs when an observer learns from the behaviour of another.

monocular cues visual clues about depth and distance that can be perceived using information from only one eye.

morpheme the smallest units of a language that convey meaning.

motivation an internal state or condition that directs behaviour.

motive a need or desire.

motor skills the ability to control our bodily movements.

multifinality the idea that children can start from the same point and wind up in any number of other outcomes.

multiple sclerosis neurological disease that causes a loss of myelin on the axons of neurons.

myelin a fatty, white substance, formed from glial cells, that insulates the axons of many neurons.

myelination development of fatty deposits on neurons that allow electric impulses to pass through neurons more efficiently.

N

narcolepsy sleep disorder marked by uncontrollable urge to fall asleep.

naturalistic observation a study in which researchers directly observe people in a study behaving as they normally do.

negative correlation relationship in which, on average, scores on one variable increase as scores on another variable decrease.

negative punishment removal of a pleasant stimulus as a consequence of a behaviour to decrease the probability of the behaviour being repeated.

negative reinforcement removal of an unpleasant stimulus after a response to increase the probability that the behaviour will reoccur.

negative or **inverse relationship** as the value of one variable increases, values in another associated variable decrease.

negative symptoms in the case of schizophrenia, symptoms that seem to reflect pathological deficits, including poverty of speech, flat affect, loss of volition, and social withdrawal.

negatively skewed distribution a distribution where most values occur at the upper end of the scale.

neocortex the largest portion of the brain, responsible for complex behaviours including language and thought.

nerve conduction velocity (NCV) the speed with which electrical impulses are transmitted along nerve fibres and across synapses.

neurofibrillary tangles twisted protein fibres found within the cells of the hippocampus and certain other brain areas.

neuroimaging techniques that allow for studying brain activity by obtaining visual images in awake humans.

neuron a nerve cell.

neuroscience the study of psychological functions by looking at biological foundations of those functions. Previously known as *psychobiology.*

neurosis an abnormal behaviour pattern caused by unresolved conflicts between the id, ego, and superego.

neurotransmitter receptors proteins in the membranes of neurons that bind to neurotransmitters.

neurotransmitters specialized chemicals that travel across synapses to allow communication between neurons.

non-associative learning learning that does not involve forming associations between stimuli.

non-REM sleep (NREM) Stages 1 through 4 of normal sleep pattern.

non-verbal communication body language.

norepinephrine neurotransmitter important for arousal and attention.

normal distribution a symmetrical, bell-shaped distribution in which most scores are in the middle with smaller groups of equal size at either end.

norms social rules about how members of a society are expected to act.

nucleus accumbens a brain area important for motivation and reward.

null hypothesis an assertion that in the underlying population from which the sample was obtained, there is no difference between the average performance of individuals in one group compared to another.

O

obedience the act of following direct commands, usually given by an authority figure.

obesity overweight characterized as a body mass index of over 30.

object permanence an infant's realization that objects continue to exist even when they are outside one's immediate sensory awareness.

observational learning/social learning occurs without overt training in response to watching the behaviour of others, called models.

obsessions persistent thoughts, ideas, impulses, or images that seem to invade a person's consciousness.

obsessive-compulsive disorder (OCD) a mental disorder associated with repeated, abnormal, anxiety-provoking thoughts and/or repeated rigid behaviours.

occipital cortex lobe of the neocortex at the back of the skull, important for processing very visual information.

odorants airborne chemicals that are detected as odours.

olfactory bulb the first region where olfactory information reaches the brain on its way from the nose.

olfactory receptor neurons sensory receptor cells that convert chemical signals from odorants into neural impulses that travel to the brain.

olfactory sense sense of smell.

operant or **instrumental conditioning** a form of associative learning whereby behaviour is modified depending on its consequences.

operationalize to develop a working definition of a variable that allows you to test it.

operations Piagetian description of a child's ability to hold an idea in his or her mind and mentally manipulate it.

opioids class of drugs derived from the sap of the opium poppy.

optic nerve the bundle of axons of ganglion cells that carries visual information from the eye to the brain.

ossicles tiny bones in the ear called the maleus (*hammer*), incus (*anvil*), and stapes (*stirrup*).

oval window a membrane separating the ossicles and the inner ear, deflection of which causes a wave to form in the cochlea.

overregularization the process by which elementary school children apply learned grammatical rules to improperly "correct" an irregular verb.

P

Pacinian corpuscles sensory receptors that respond to vibrations and heavy pressure.

panic attacks periodic, short bouts of panic.

panic disorder an anxiety disorder characterized by recurrent and unpredictable panic attacks that occur without apparent provocation.

papillae bumps on the tongue that contain clumps of taste buds.

parallel distributed-processing (PDP) (or **connectionist**) **model** theory of memory suggesting that information is represented in the brain as a pattern of activation across entire neural networks.

parasympathetic nervous system the division of the autonomic nervous system active during restful times.

parietal cortex lobe of the neocortex involved in processing information related to touch and complex visual information, particularly about locations.

Parkinson's disease neurological disease that involves the death of dopaminergic neurons in the substantia nigra, leading to tremors, muscle rigidity, and other motor problems.

Pavlovian or **classical conditioning** a form of associative learning whereby a neutral stimulus is paired with a salient stimulus so that eventually the neutral stimulus predicts the salient stimulus.

Pearson product-moment correlation coefficient a statistic indicating the degree of association or relationship between two variables or measures, ranging from -1 to $+1$.

perception recognition and identification of a sensory stimulus.

perceptual constancies our top-down tendency to view objects as unchanging, despite shifts in the environmental stimuli we receive.

perceptual set readiness to interpret a certain stimulus in a certain way.

perfect correlation one in which two variables are exactly related, such that low, medium, and high scores on both variables are always exactly related.

personality the unique characteristics that account for enduring patterns of inner experience and outward behaviour.

personality disorder an inflexible pattern of inner experience and outward behaviour that causes distress or difficulty with daily functioning.

personality inventory a paper-and-pencil questionnaire designed to assess various aspects of personality.

personality traits tendencies to behave in certain ways that remain relatively constant across situations.

phenotype the observable manifestation of a person's genetic inheritance.

phobia a persistent, irrational, or obsessive fear of a specific object, activity, or situation that may arise as a result of fear conditioning.

phoneme the smallest unit of sound in a language, an individual sound.

phonology the study of how individual sounds or phonemes are used to produce language.

photoreceptors the sensory receptor cells for vision, located in the retina.

phrenology an unsubstantiated method of assessing a person's mental and moral qualities by studying the shape of the person's skull.

phylogeny the development of unique species over time.

pituitary gland brain structure that plays a central role in controlling the endocrine system.

placenta nutrient-rich structure that serves to feed the developing fetus.

plasticity change in the nervous system.

polygenic trait trait that manifests as the result of the contributions of multiple genes.

pons part of the brain anterior to the brainstem that includes the locus coeruleus.

population the entire group of individuals about whom we hope to learn (e.g., the Canadian population consists of all Canadians).

positive correlation relationship in which, on average, scores on two variables increase together.

positive psychology an area of psychology focusing on positive experiences and healthy mental functioning.

positive punishment presentation of an unpleasant consequence following a behaviour to decrease the probability of the behaviour being repeated.

positive reinforcement presentation of a pleasant consequence following a behaviour to increase the probability that the behaviour will reoccur.

positive or **direct relationship** as the value of one variable increases, so do values in another associated variable.

positive symptoms in the case of schizophrenia, symptoms that seem to represent pathological excesses in behaviour, including delusions, disorganized thinking and speech, hallucinations, and inappropriate affect.

positively skewed distribution a distribution where most values occur at the lower end of the scale.

postsynaptic potentials electrical events in postsynaptic neurons that occur when a neurotransmitter binds to one of its receptors.

posttraumatic stress disorder (PTSD) an anxiety disorder experienced in response to a major traumatic event, characterized by lingering, persistent, frightening thoughts or memories of the traumatic events, along with anxiety, depression, and other symptoms.

pragmatics the practical aspects of language usage, including speech pace, gesturing, and body language.

preconsciousness level of awareness in which information can become readily available to consciousness if necessary.

predictive validity the extent to which scores on a particular test successfully predict the things they are supposed to predict.

prefrontal cortex portion of the frontal cortex involved in higher-order thinking, such as memory, moral reasoning, and planning.

prejudice negative stereotypical attitudes toward individuals from another group.

prenatal period period of development stretching from conception to birth.

preoperational stage according to Piaget, a developmental stage during which the child begins to develop ideas of objects in the external world and the ability to work with them in his or her mind.

pressure an expectation or demand that someone act in a certain way.

primary appraisal appraisal of a stressor to determine how severe it is; the first stage in Richard Lazarus's description of how people experience stress.

primary mental abilities seven distinct mental abilities identified by Thurstone as the basic components of intelligence.

primary punisher a stimulus that is naturally aversive to an organism.

primary reinforcer a stimulus that has survival value and is therefore intrinsically rewarding.

primary sex characteristics changes in body structure that occur during puberty that have to do specifically with the reproductive system, including the growth of the testes and the ovaries.

priming activation of one piece of information, which in turns leads to activation of another piece, and ultimately to the retrieval of a specific memory.

private speech a child's self-talk, which Vygotsky believed the child uses to regulate behaviour and internal experiences.

proactive interference competing information that is learned before the forgotten material, preventing its subsequent recall.

problem solving determining how to reach a goal.

problem-focused coping coping strategies focused on dealing directly with the stressor, such as by changing the stressor in some way.

projective test a personality assessment device intended to tap a person's unconscious by presenting the person with an ambiguous stimulus and asking the person to interpret what the stimulus means.

proximodistal pattern a pattern in which growth and development proceed from the centre to the extremities.

private speech a child's self-talk, which Vygotsky believed the child uses to regulate behaviour and internal experiences.

psychoactive drugs chemicals that affect awareness, behaviour, sensation, perception, or mood.

psychoanalytic theory psychological theory that human mental processes are influenced by the competition among unconscious forces to come into awareness.

psychology the study of mental processes and behaviours.

psychometric approach an approach to defining intelligence that attempts to measure intelligence with carefully constructed psychological tests.

psychoneuroimmunology an area of study focusing on links between stress, the immune system, and health.

psychosexual stages according to psychoanalytic theory, stages in the development of personality; the stages—labelled oral, anal, phallic, latency, and genital—are primarily influenced by sexuality and aggression.

psychosis loss of contact with reality.

psychosurgery brain surgery, often used in hopes of relieving abnormal functioning.

psychotropic drugs medications that act primarily on the brain.

psychotherapy a treatment system in which a client and therapist use words and acts to overcome the client's psychological difficulties.

puberty development of full sexual maturity during adolescence.

punishment an experience that produces a decrease in a certain behaviour.

R

random sample a group or set made by randomly selecting people or items from a larger population; like closing your eyes and picking any two socks from your drawer.

random selection identifying a sample in such a way that everyone in the population of interest has an equal chance of being involved in the study.

range the difference between the smallest and the largest value in a data set.

rapid eye movement sleep (REM) stage of sleep associated with rapid and jagged brain-wave patterns, increased heart rate, rapid and irregular breathing, rapid eye movements, and dreaming.

rational-emotive behavioural therapy Ellis's therapy technique designed to help clients discover and change the irrational assumptions that govern their emotions, behaviours, and thinking.

reaction range the upper and lower level of intelligence or other outcomes made possible by a child's genetic nature.

recall tasks memory tasks in which people are asked to produce information using no or few retrieval cues.

recessive trait trait that is only expressed if a person carries the same two genetic alleles (e.g., is homozygous for the trait).

reciprocal socialization the transactional relationship between parent and child.

recognition tasks memory tasks in which people are asked to identify whether or not they have seen a particular item before.

reflexes programmed physical reactions to certain cues that do not require any conscious thought to perform.

rehearsal conscious repetition of information in an attempt to make sure the information is encoded.

reinforcement a learning process in which the consequence resulting from a behaviour will increase or decrease the likelihood that the behaviour will occur again.

reinforcer an experience that produces an increase in a certain behaviour.

relational psychoanalytic therapy a school of psychodynamic therapy holding that therapists should work to form more equal relationships with clients.

relative refractory period just after the absolute refractory period during which a neuron can only fire if it receives a stimulus stronger than its usual threshold level.

reliability the degree to which a test produces the same scores over time.

replication repeated testing of a hypothesis to ensure that the results you achieve in one experiment are not due to chance.

representativeness heuristic assumes that individuals share characteristics of category of which they are a member.

repression the most basic defence mechanism; the process of keeping unpleasant memories or thoughts buried deep within the unconscious mind.

Research Ethics Board (REB) research oversight group that evaluates research to protect the rights of participants in the study.

resilience the ability to recover from or avoid the serious effects of negative circumstances.

resistance practice in which clients encounter a block in their free associations or change the subject so as to avoid a potentially painful discussion.

response the way we react to stimuli.

resting potential the electrical charge of a neuron when it is at rest.

restorative theory of sleep theory that we sleep to allow the brain and body to restore certain depleted chemical resources and eliminate chemical wastes that have accumulated during the waking day.

reticular formation a brain structure important for sleep and wakefulness.

retina a specialized sheet of nerve cells in the back of the eye containing the sensory receptors for vision.

retinal disparity the slight difference in images processed by the retinas of each eye.

retrieval a basic activity of memory, involving recovery of information when we need it later.

retrieval cues words, sights, or other stimuli that remind us of the information we need to retrieve from our memory.

retroactive interference learning of new information that disrupts access to previously recalled information.

retrograde amnesia inability to remember things that occurred before an organic event.

reward-deficiency syndrome theory that people might abuse drugs because their reward centre is not readily activated by usual life events.

reward learning pathway brain circuitry that is important for learning about rewarding stimuli.

risk factors biological and environmental factors that contribute to problematic outcomes.

rods photoreceptors most responsive to levels of light and dark.

Ruffini's end-organs sensory receptors that respond to heavy pressure and joint movement.

S

s factor a theoretical specific factor uniquely tied to a distinct mental ability or area of functioning; part of Spearman's two-factor theory of intelligence.

sample a group or set of people or items drawn from a larger population.

sampling distribution the theoretical distribution of a sample statistic; for example, the difference between two sample means taken from a population.

scaffolding developmental adjustments that adults make to give children the help that they need, but not so much that the children fail to move forward.

scatterplot a graph or plot of the values of one variable or measure associated with the values on another variable or measure.

Schachter and Singer's two-factor theory of emotion a theory proposing that an emotional state is a function of both physiological arousal and cognition.

schemas knowledge bases that we develop based on prior exposure to similar experiences or other knowledge bases.

scheme Piaget's proposed mental structures or frameworks for understanding or thinking about the world.

schizophrenia a mental disorder characterized by disorganized thoughts, lack of contact with reality, and sometimes hallucinations.

secondary appraisal appraisal of one's personal resources and ability to cope with a stressor; the second stage in Richard Lazarus's description of how people experience stress.

secondary punisher a stimulus that becomes aversive when associated with a primary punisher.

secondary reinforcer a neutral stimulus that becomes rewarding when associated with a primary reinforcer.

secondary sex characteristics changes that occur during puberty and that differ according to gender, but are not specifically related to sex.

sedative-hypnotic drugs class of drugs, the members of which produce feelings of relaxation and drowsiness.

self-actualization the need of humans to fulfill their full and special potential; the highest-level of need in Maslow's hierarchy of needs.

self-concept a pattern of self-perception that remains consistent over time and can be used to characterize an individual.

self-determination instinctive feelings of competence, relatedness, and autonomy that give purpose to life.

self-help groups groups consisting of people who have similar problems and come together to help and support one another without the direct leadership of a professional clinician.

self-perception theory a theory suggesting that when people are uncertain of their attitudes, they infer what the attitudes are by observing their own behaviour.

self-serving bias the tendency people have to attribute their successes to internal causes and their failures to external ones.

semantic code cognitive representation of information or an event based on the meaning of the information.

semantic memory a person's memory of general knowledge of the world.

semantics the study of how meaning in language is constructed of individual words and sentences.

senile plaques sphere-shaped deposits of a protein known as beta-amyloid that form in the spaces between cells in the hippocampus, cerebral cortex, and certain other brain regions, as well as in some nearby blood vessels.

sensation the act of using our sensory systems to detect environmental stimuli.

sensitive period a time during development after which it becomes more difficult to develop certain capabilities.

sensitization a form of non-associative learning whereby a strong stimulus results in an exaggerated response to the subsequent presentation of weaker stimuli.

sensory adaptation the process whereby repeated stimulation of a sensory cell leads to a reduced response.

sensory memory memory involving detailed, brief sensory image or sound retained for a brief period of time.

sensory receptor cells specialized cells that convert a specific form of environmental stimuli into neural impulses.

sensory transduction the process of converting a specific form of environmental stimuli into neural impulses.

serotonin neurotransmitter involved in activity levels and mood regulation.

shaping introducing new behaviour by reinforcing small approximations of the desired behaviour.

significance level or **rejection level** the level of risk researchers would be willing to take in terms of making an incorrect conclusion.

situationism the view that behaviour is governed primarily by the variables in a given situation rather than by internal traits.

sleep apnea sleep disorder characterized by repeatedly ceasing to breathe during the night, depriving the brain of oxygen and leading to frequent awakenings.

sleep spindles bursts of brain activity lasting a second or two; occur during Stage 2 sleep.

social anxiety disorder an anxiety disorder in which people may feel severe, persistent, and irrational fears of social or performance situations in which embarrassment may occur.

social cognition the way in which people perceive and interpret themselves and others in their social world.

social facilitation an effect in which the presence of others enhances performance.

social identity theory a theory that emphasizes social cognitive factors in the onset of prejudice.

social loafing a phenomenon in which people exert less effort on a collective task than they would on a comparable individual task; also known as free riding.

social neuroscience the study of social functioning and how it is tied to brain activity.

social phobia a disorder involving severe, persistent, and irrational fears of social situations in which embarrassment may occur.

social psychology an area of psychology that seeks to understand, explain, and predict how people's thoughts, feelings, and behaviours are influenced by the actual, imagined, or implied presence of others.

social role a set of norms ascribed to a person's social position; expectations and duties associated with the individual's position in the family, at work, in the community, and in other settings.

social role theory theory that gender differences occur because girls and boys develop different behaviours and skills based largely on the differences in gender role expectations.

social skills training behavioural therapy technique in which therapists serve as models and teachers to help clients acquire desired social behaviours.

socially desirable responding tailoring answers on personality inventories to try to create a good impression.

sociobiologists theorists who believe humans have a genetically innate concept of how social behaviour should be organized.

sodium potassium pump protein molecules in the membrane of cells that push out sodium ions and push in potassium ions.

somatic nervous system all the peripheral nerves that transmit information about the senses and movement to and from the central nervous system.

somatoform disorder a pattern of physical complaints with largely psychosocial causes; types include conversion disorder, somatization disorder, pain disorder associated with psychological factors, hypochondriasis, and body dysmorphic disorder.

somatosensory strip an area of the parietal cortex that processes tactile information coming from our body parts.

sound waves vibrations of the air in the frequency of hearing.

source misattribution remembering information, but not the source it came from; can lead to remembering information from unreliable sources as true.

spacing effect facilitated encoding of material through rehearsal situations spread out over time.

spatial navigation learning learning that involves forming associations among stimuli relevant to navigating in space.

speech the expression of language through sounds.

spinal cord portion of the central nervous system that extends from the base of the brain and mediates sensory and motor information.

spontaneous recovery re-emergence of a conditioned response some time after extinction has occurred.

stage a distinct developmental phase in which organisms behave, think, or respond in a particular way that is qualitatively different from the way they responded before.

standard deviation statistical index of how much scores vary within a group.

standardization the use of uniform procedures in administering and scoring a test.

state-dependent memory memory retrieval facilitated by being in the same state of mind in which you encoded the memory in the first place.

stem cell undifferentiated cell that can divide to replace itself and create new cells that have the potential to become all other cells of the body, including neurons.

stereotype threat a phenomenon in which people in a particular group perform poorly because they fear that their performance will conform to a negative stereotype associated with that group.

stereotypes generalized impressions about a person or a group of people based on the social category they occupy.

stimulants substances that increase the activity of the central nervous system.

stimuli elements of the environment that trigger changes in our internal or external states.

stimulus discrimination what occurs when an organism learns to emit a specific behaviour in the presence of a stimulus, but not in the presence of stimuli similar to the original stimulus.

stimulus generalization when similar stimuli elicit the same response as a conditioned stimulus after classical conditioning has occured.

storage a basic activity of memory, involving retention of information for later use.

stress state brought on by any situation that threatens or appears to threaten a person's sense of well-being, thus challenging the individual's ability to cope.

stressor a situation or circumstance that triggers the stress response.

striatum a brain area that works with the substantia nigra to enable fluid movements.

structuralism the belief that the mind is a collection of sensory experiences and that its study should focus on mental processes rather than explanation of the mechanisms underlying those processes.

subpersonalities alternate personalities developed in dissociative identity disorder, each with a unique set of memories, behaviours, thoughts, and emotions.

substantia nigra brain region important in fluidity of movement and inhibiting movements.

superego according to psychoanalytic theory, a personality element in charge of determining which impulses are acceptable to express openly and which are unacceptable; develops as we observe and internalize the behaviours of others in our culture.

superfactor a fundamental dimension of personality made up of a related cluster of personality traits.

suprachiasmatic nucleus (SCN) a small group of neurons in the hypothalamus responsible for coordinating the many rhythms of the body.

survey study in which researchers give participants a questionnaire or interview them.

sympathetic nervous system the division of the autonomic nervous system activated under conditions of stress.

synapses tiny spaces between the axon terminal of one neuron and the next neuron through which communication occurs.

synaptic pruning developmental reduction of neuronal connections, allowing stronger connections to flourish.

synaptic vesicles membrane-bound spheres in the axon terminals of neurons where neurotransmitters are stored before their release.

syntax the system for using words (semantics) and word order to convey meaning (grammar).

systematic desensitization a process used to condition extinction of phobias through gradual exposure to the feared object or situation.

T

taste buds clusters of sensory receptor cells that convert chemical signals from food into neural impulses that travel to the brain.

telegraphic speech speech that consists of minimalistic sentences. This form of speech characterizes early toddlerhood and is the first evidence of sentence formation.

temperament biologically-based tendencies to respond to certain situations in similar ways throughout our lifetimes.

temporal cortex part of the neocortex important in processing sounds, in speech comprehension, and in recognizing complex visual stimuli, such as faces.

teratogens any environmental agent that causes damage during gestation.

thalamus an area of the brain that serves as a relay station for incoming sensory information.

theories ideas about laws that govern phenomena.

theory of mind an awareness of one's own mental states and the mental states of others.

theory of multiple intelligences theory that there is no single, unified intelligence, but instead several independent intelligences arising from different portions of the brain.

therapy (treatment) systematic procedures designed to change abnormal behaviour into more normal behaviour.

therapy outcome studies research that looks at the effects of various treatments.

threshold the point at which the relative excitatory influence of other neurons succeeds in causing a neuron to initiate an action potential.

token economy operant conditioning therapy program in which participants receive tokens (that can be traded for rewards) when they display desired behaviours.

tolerance mark of physical dependence on a drug, in which a person needs to take incrementally larger doses of the drug to achieve the same effect.

tonotopic map representation in the auditory cortex of different sound frequencies.

top-down processing perception processes led by cognitive processes, such as memory or expectations.

transcranial magnetic stimulation (TMS) a procedure in which an electromagnetic coil placed on or above a person's head sends a current into the prefrontal cortex; used to treat severe depression.

transduction process that involves converting stimulus energy into neural impulses that can be interpreted by the brain.

transference process through which clients come to act and feel toward the therapist as they did toward important figures in their childhood.

traumatic events unexpected events severe enough to create extreme disruptions.

trephining ancient practice of chipping a hole in the skull as a treatment for various brain conditions.

triangular theory of love a theory proposed by Robert Sternberg that love is composed of three elements: intimacy, passion, and commitment.

triarchic theory of intelligence Sternberg's theory that intelligence is made up of three interacting components: internal, external, and experiential components.

tympanic membrane the ear drum.

Type A a personality type characterized by competitiveness, impatience, and anger and hostility.

Type B a personality type that is less aggressive, more relaxed, and less hostile than Type A.

Type C a personality type characterized by difficulty in expressing or acknowledging negative feelings.

U

unconditional positive regard acceptance without terms or conditions.

unconditioned response (UR) a physical response elicited by an unconditioned stimulus; it does not need to be learned.

unconditioned stimulus (US) a stimulus that on its own elicits a response.

unconscious hypothesized repository of thoughts, feelings, and sensations outside human awareness, thought in some theories to have a strong bearing on human behaviour; a state in which information is not easily accessible to conscious awareness.

unconscious state state in which information is not easily accessible to conscious awareness.

ungrouped frequency distribution a count of the number of times each specific data point or score appears in a dataset.

unipolar depression a mood disorder that includes only depression.

V

vagus nerve stimulation a procedure in a which an implanted device sends electrical signals to the brain through the vagus nerve; used to treat severe depression.

validity the extent to which a test accurately measures or predicts what it is supposed to measure or predict.

validity coefficient a correlation coefficient that measures validity by correlating a test score with some external criterion.

variable condition, event, or situation that is studied in an experiment.

variable interval schedule schedule of reinforcement that occurs after varying amounts of time.

variable ratio schedule schedule of reinforcement where the number of responses required for reinforcement is unpredictable.

variance a calculated indicator of the degree to which values in a data set differ from the mean value of that data set; the average of squared deviations about the mean.

ventromedial region of the hypothalamus a region of the hypothalamus important in signalling satiety.

vicarious learning learning that occurs when an individual observes the consequences to another's actions and then chooses to duplicate the behaviour or refrain from doing so.

voluntarism belief that much of behaviour is motivated and that attention is focused for an explicit purpose.

W

wear-and-tear theory theory suggesting we age because use of our body wears it out.

Wernicke's aphasia a neurological condition associated with damage to Wernicke's area where a person cannot understand language.

Wernicke's area a brain region located in the temporal lobe that is important for language comprehension.

withdrawal symptoms unpleasant and sometimes dangerous side effects of reducing intake of a drug after a person has become addicted.

working memory a short-term memory store that can hold five to nine items at once.

Y

Yerkes-Dodson law law stating that ideal performance on a task occurs when the arousal level is optimized to the difficulty level.

Z

zone of proximal development the gap between what a child could accomplish alone and what the child can accomplish with help from others.

zygote a single cell resulting from successful fertilization of the egg by sperm.

References

Abbey, S. E. (2005). Somatization and somatoform disorders. In J. L. Levenson (Ed.), *The Amerian Psychiatric Publishing textbook of psychosomatic medicine* (pp. 271–296). Washington, DC: American Psychiatric Publishing.

Abe, J. A., & Izard, C. E. (1999). The developmental functions of emotions: An analysis in terms of differential emotions theory. *Cognition and Emotion, 13,* 523–549.

Abele, A. E. (2003). The dynamics of masculine-agentic and feminine-communal traits: Findings from a prospective study. *Journal of Personality and Social Psychology, 85*(4), 768–776.

Abella, K., & Dutton, S. (1994). Questions and answers. *Typework, 2.*

Abella, R., & Heslin, R. (1989). Appraisal processes, coping and the regulation of stress-related emotions in a college examination. *Basic and Applied Social Psychology, 10,* 311–327.

Abercrombie, H. C., Chambers, A. S., Greischar, L., & Monticelli, R. M. (2008). Orienting, emotion, and memory: Phasic and tonic variation in heart rate predicts memory for emotional pictures in men. *Neurobiology of Learning and Memory, 90*(4), 644–650.

Abosch, A., & Cosgrove, G. R. (2008). Biological basis for the surgical treatment of depression. *Neurosurgical Focus, 25*(1), E2.

Abramowitz, A. J., & O'Leary, S. G. (1990). Effectiveness of displayed punishment in an applied setting. *Behavior Therapy, 21,* 231–239.

Abramowitz, J. S. (2008). Is nonparaphilic compulsive sexual behavior a variant of OCD? In J. S. Abramowitz, D. McKay, & S. Taylor (Eds.), *Obsessive-compulsive disorder: Subtypes and spectrum conditions.* Oxford, England: Elsevier.

Abramowitz, J. S., & Braddock, A. E. (2011). *Hypochondriasis and health anxiety.* Cambridge, MA: Hogrefe Publishing.

Abrams, D., Hogg, M. A., & Marques, J. M. (2005). A social psychological framework for understanding social inclusion and exclusion. *The social pshychology of inclusion and exclusion* (pp. 1–23). New York, NY: Psychology Press.

Abrams, D., Marques, J. M., Bown, N., & Henson, M. (2000). Pro-norm and anti-norm deviance within and between groups. *Journal of Personality and Social Psychology, 78*(5), 906–912.

Abrams, D., Wetherell, M., Cochrane, S., Hogg, M. A., & Turner, J. C. (2001). Knowing what to think by knowing who you are: Self-categorization and the nature of norm formation, conformity and group polarization. In M. A. Hogg & D. Abrams (Eds.), *Intergroup relations: Essential readings* (pp. 270–288). New York, NY: Psychology Press.

Abrams, D., Wetherell, M., Cochrane, S., Hogg, M. A., et al., (1990). Knowing what to think by knowing who you are: Self-categorization and the nature of norm formation, conformity and group polarization. *British Journal of Social Psychology, 29*(2), 97–119.

Abramson, L. Y., Alloy, L. B., Hankin, B. L., Haeffel, G. J., MacCoon, D. G., & Gibb, B. E. (2002). Cognitive vulnerability—Stress models of depression in a self-regulatory and psychobiological context. In I. H. Gotlib & C. L. Hammen (Eds.), *Handbook of depression* (pp. 268–294). New York: Guilford Press.

Abramson, L. Y., Metalsky, G. I., & Alloy, L. B. (1989). Hopelessness depression: A theory-based subtype of depression. *Psychological Review, 96*(2), 358–372.

Abramson, L. Y., Seligman, M. E., & Teasdale, J. D. (1978). Learned helplessness in humans: Critique and reformulation. *Journal of Abnormal Psychology, 87*(1), 49–74.

Academica Group. (2011). *2010 University and College Applicant Study: Colleges Ontario.* Retrieved from http://www.collegesontario.org/research/external-reports/2010_ucas_ executive_summary.pdf.

Accolla, R., Bathellier, B., Petersen, C. C., & Carleton, A. (2007). Differential spatial representation of taste modalities in the rat gustatory cortex. *The Journal of Neuroscience, 27,* 1396–1404.

Acebo, C., Sadeh, A., Seifer, R., Tzischinsky, O., Hafer, A., & Carskadon, M. A. (2005). Sleep/wake patterns derived from activity monitoring and maternal report for healthy 1 to 5-year-old children. *Sleep, 28,* 1568–1577.

Acosta, M. C., Haller, D. L., & Schnoll, S. H. (2005). Cocaine and stimulants. In R. J. Frances, A. H. Mack, & S. I. Miller (Eds.), *Clinical textbook of addictive disorders (3rd Ed.).* New York, NY: Guilford Press.

Acredolo, L., & Goodwyn, S. (1988). Symbolic gesturing in normal infants. *Child Development, 59,* 450–466.

Adams, G. R., & Huston, T. L. (1975). Social perception of middle-aged persons varying in physical attractiveness. *Developmental Psychology, 11,* 657–658.

Addis, M. E., & Mahalik, J. R. (2003). Men, masculinity, and the contexts of help seeking. *American Psychologist, 58*(1), 5–14.

Ader, R. (2003). Conditioning innumomodulation: Research needs and directions. *Brain, Behavior, and Immunity, 17*(1), S51–S57.

Ader, R., & Cohen, N. (1984). Behavior and the immune system. In W. D. Gentry (Ed.), *Handbook of behavioural medicine.* New York: Guilford.

Ader, R., Felten, D. L., & Cohen, N. (Eds.). (2001). *Psycho-neuroimmunology* (3rd Ed., Vols. 1 & 2). San Diego, CA: Academic Press.

Adlaf, E. M., & Paglia-Boak, A. (2007). *Drug Use Among Ontario Students: OSDUHS Highlights 1977–2007.* Centre for Addiction and Mental Health.

Admon, Y. (2009). *Rising Criticism of Child Bride Marriages in Saudi Arabia.* The Middle East Media Research Institute. Retrieved from: http://memri.org/bin/articles.cgi?Page=archives&Area=ia&ID=IA50209.

Adolf, K. E., & Berger, S. E. (2006). Motor development. In D. Kuhn & R. Siegler (Eds.), *Handbook of child psychology, Vol. 2. Cognition, perception and language* (6th Ed., pp. 161–213). Hoboken, NJ: Wiley.

Adolphs, R. (2009). The social brain: Neural basis of social knowledge. *Annual Review of Psychology, 60,* 693–716.

Adolphs, R. (2003). Cognitive neuroscience of human social behaviour. *Nature Reviews Neuroscience, 4*(3), 165–178.

Adolphs, R., Russell, J., & Tranel, D. (1999). A role for the human amygdala in recognizing emotional arousal from unpleasant stimuli. *Psychological Science, 10,* 167–171.

Adolphs, R., Tranel, D., Damasio, H., & Damasio, A. (1994). Impaired recognition of emotion in facial expressions following bilateral damage to the human amygdala. *Nature,* 372, 669–672.

Aftanas, L. I., & Golosheikin, S. A. (2003). Changes in cortical activity in altered states of consciousness: The study of meditation by high-resolution EEG. *Human Physiology, 29*(2), 143–151.

Aguirre, G. K. (2010). Experimental design and data analysis for fMRI. In S. H. Faro & F. B. Mohamed (Eds.), *fMRI: A guide to functional imaging for neuroscientists* (pp. 55–69). New York: Springer Science+ Business Media.

Aiello, J. R., & Douthitt, E. A. (2001). Social facilitation from Triplett to electronic performance monitoring. *Group Dynamics: Theory, Research, and Practice, 5,* 163–180.

Ainsworth, M. D. S. (2010). Security and attachment. In R. Volpe (Ed.), *The secure child: Timeless lessons in parenting and childhood education* (pp. 43–53). Greenwich, CT: IAP Information Age Publishing.

Ainsworth, M. D. S. (1993). Attachment as related to mother-infant interaction. *Advances in Infancy Research, 8,* 1–50.

Ainsworth, M. D. S. (1985). Patterns of attachment. *Clinical Psychologist, 38*(2), 27–29.

Ainsworth, M. D. S. (1979). Attachment as related to mother-infant interaction. In J. S. Rosenblatt, R. A. Hinde, C. Beer, & M. Busnel (Eds.), *Advances in the study of behavior (Vol. 9).* Orlando, FL: Academic Press.

Ainsworth, M. D S. (1967). *Infancy in Uganda: Infant care and the growth of love.* Baltimore, MD: Johns Hopkins University Press.

Air Canada v. Canadian Transportation Agency (2008). File No. 32729. Supreme Court of Canada (Ottawa).

al Absi, M., & Rokke, P. D. (1991). Can anxiety help us tolerate pain? *The Journal of Pain, 46*, 43–51.

Akbarian, S. (2010). Epigenetics of schizophrenia. In N. R. Swerdlow (Ed.), *Behavioral neurobiology of schizophrenia and its treatment* (pp. 611–628). New York: Springer-Verlag Publishing.

Akhtar, S., Wig, N. H., Verma, V. K., Pershod, D., & Verma, S. K. (1975). A phenomenological analysis of symptoms in obsessive-compulsive neuroses. *British Journal of Psychiatry, 127*, 342–348.

Albarracin, D., Zanna, M. P., Johnson, B. T., & Kumkale, G. T. (2005). Attitudes: Introduction and scope. *The handbook of attitudes* (pp. 3–19). Mahwah, NJ: Lawrence Erlbaum Associates Publishers.

Aldwin, C. M. (2007). *Stress, coping, and development: An integrative perspective* (2nd Ed.). New York, NY: Guilford Press.

Aldwin, C. M., Yancura, L. A., & Boeninger, D. K. (2010). Coping across the life span. In M. E. Lamb, A. M. Freund, & R. M. Lerner (Eds.), *The handbook of life-span development*, vol 2: *Social and emotional development* (pp. 298–340). Hoboken, NJ: John Wiley & Sons.

Alegre, A. (2011). Parenting styles and children's emotional intelligence: What do we know? *The Family Journal, 19*(1), 56–62.

Alegria, A. A., Petry, N. M., Hasin, D. S., Liu, S., Grant, B. F., & Blanco, C. (2009). Disordered gambling among racial and ethnic groups in the US: Results from the national epidemiologic survey on alcohol and related conditions. *CNS Spectrums, 14*(3), 132–142.

Alegria, M., Mulvaney-Day, N., Torres, M., Polo, A., Cao, Z., & Canino, G. (2007). Prevalence of psychiatric disorders across Latino subgroups in the United States. *American Journal of Public Health, 97*(1), 68–75.

Alegria, M., Takeuchi, D., Canino, G., Duan, N., Shrout, P., Meng, X. L., et al. (2004). Considering context, place and culture: The National Latino and Asian American Study. *International Journal of Methods in Psychiatric Research, 13*(4), 208–220.

Alessio, A., Bonilha, L., Rorden, C., Kobayashi, E., Min, L. L., Damasceno, B. P., et al. (2006). Memory and language impairments and their relationships to hippocampal and perirhinal cortex damage in patients with medial temporal lobe epilepsy. *Epilepsy & Behavior, 8*(3), 593–600.

Alessio, A., Kobayashi, E., Damasceno, B. P., Lopes-Cendes, I., & Cendes, F. (2004). Evidence of memory impairment in asymptomatic individuals with hippocampal atrophy. *Epilepsy & Behavior, 5*(6), 981–987.

Alexander, J. F., Sexton, T. L., & Robbins, M. S. (2002). The developmental status of family therapy in family psychology intervention science. In H. A. Liddle, D. A. Santiseban, R. F. Levant, & J. H. Bray (Eds.), *Family psychology: Science-based interventions* (pp. 17–40). Washington, DC: American Psychological Association.

Alexander, M. G., & Wood, W (2000). Women, men, and positive emotions: A social role interpretation. In A. H. Fischer (Ed.), *Gender and emotion: Social psychological perspectives* (pp. 189–210). New York, NY: Cambridge University Press.

Alfano, C. A., & Beidel, D. C. (Eds.). (2011). *Social anxiety in adolescents and young adults: Translating developmental science into practice*. Washington, DC: American Psychological Association.

Allan, R.W. (1998). Operant-respondent interactions. In W. O'Donohue (Ed.), *Learning and behaviour therapy.* Boston: Allyn & Bacon.

Allen, B. (2011). The use and abuse of attachment theory in clinical practice with maltreated children. *Trauma, Violence, and Abuse, 12*, 13–22.

Allen, S., & Daly, K. (2007). *The effects of father involvement: An updated research summary of evidence*. Father Involvement Research Alliance, Centre for Families, Work & Well-Being, University of Guelph 2007. Retrieved from http://www.fira.ca/cms/documents/29/Effects_of_Father_Involvement.pdf.

Alloy, L. B., & Abramson, L. Y. (2010). The role of the behavioral approach system (BAS) in bipolar spectrum disorders. *Current Directions in Psychological Science, 19*(3), 189–194.

Alloy, L. B., Urošević, S., Abramson, L. Y., Jager-Hyman, S., Nusslock, R., Whitehouse, W. G., & Hogan, M. (2011). Progression along the bipolar spectrum: A longitudinal study of predictors of conversion from bipolar spectrum conditions to bipolar I and II disorders. *Journal of Abnormal Psychology,* No Pages.

Allport, G. W. (1985). The historical background of social psychology. In G. Lindzey & E. Aronson (Eds.), *Handbook of Social Psychology* (Vol. 1, 3rd Ed., pp. 1–46). New York, NY: Random House.

Allport, G. W. (1968). *The Person in Psychology*. Boston, MA: Beacon Press.

Allport, G. W. (1954). *The nature of prejudice Oxford.* England: Addison-Wesley.

Allport, G. W., & Odbert, H. S. (1936). Traitnames. A psycho-lexical study. *Psychological Monographs, 47*, 171.

Alter, M. D., & Hen, R. (2009). Serotonin, sensitive periods, and anxiety. *Stress-induced and fear circuitry disorders: Advancing the research agenda for DSM-V* (pp. 159–173). Arlington, VA: American Psychiatric Publishing, Inc.

Althof, S. E. (2007). Treatment of rapid ejaculation: Psychotherapy, pharmacotherapy, and combined therapy. *Principles and practice of sex therapy (4th Ed.)* (pp. 212–240). New York, NY: Guilford Press.

Althouse, R. (2010). Jails are nation's largest institutions for mentally ill. *The National Psychologist, 19*(6), 1–5.

Alwin, D. F., Cohen, R. L., & Newcomb, T M. (1991). *Political Attitudes over the Life-Span: The Bennington Women After Fifty Years*. Madison, WI: The University of Wisconsin Press.

Aman, M. G., & Farmer, C. A. (2011). Self-injury, aggression, and related problems. In E. Hollander, A. Kolevzon & J. T. Coyle (Eds.), *Textbook of autism spectrum disorders* (pp. 179–187). Arlington, VA: American Psychiatric Publishing, Inc.

Ambady, N., Paik, S. K., Steele, J., Owen-Smith, A., & Mitchell, J. P. (2004). Deflecting negative self-relevant stereotype activation: The effects of individuation. *Journal of Experimental Social Psychology, 40*(3), 401–408.

Ambady, N., Shih, M., Kim, A., & Pittinsky, T. L. (2001). Stereotype susceptibility in children: Effects of identity activation on quantitative performance. *Psychological Science, 12*(5), 385–390.

Ambert, A. M. (2009). Divorce: Facts, causes and consequences, Vanier Institute of the Family. Retrieved from http://www.vifamily.ca/node/72.

Amedi, A., Merabet, L. B., Bermpohl, F., & Pascual-Leone, A. (2005). The Occipital Cortex in the Blind: Lessons About Plasticity and Vision. *Current Directions in Physiological Science, 14*(6), 306–311.

American Psychiatric Association DSM-V Work Groups. (2010). *Proposed Revisions – Schizophrenia and Other Psychotic Disorders*. Retrieved from http://www.dsm5.org/ProposedRevisions/Pages/SchizophreniaandOtherPsychoticDisorders.aspx.

American Psychiatric Association. (2000). *Diagnostic and statistical manual of mental disorders DSM-IV-R (4th Ed.)*. Washington, DC: American Psychiatric Association.

American Psychological Association. (2009). *Center for workforce studies*. Washington, DC.

American Psychological Association. (2008). *Graduate study in psychology*. Washington, DC.

American Psychological Association. (2005). Resolution In Favor of Empirically Supported Sex Education and HIV Prevention Programs for Adolescents. Retrieved from http://www.apa.org/ releases/sexed_resolution.pdf.

American Society of Plastic Surgeons. (2008). *2008 Quick Facts*. Retrieved from http://www.plasticsurgery.org/Media/stats/2008-quick-facts-cosmetic-surgery-minimally-invasive-statistics.pdf.

Ames, E. W., & Chisholm, K. (2001). Social and emotional development in children adopted from institutions. In D. B. Bailey Jr., J. T. Bruer, F. J. Symons, & J. W. Lichtman, (Eds.), *Critical thinking about critical periods*. Baltimore, MD, US: Paul H Brookes Publishing.

Amsterdam, B. (1972). Mirror self-image before age two. *Developmental Psychobiology, 5*(4), 297–305.

Anastasi, A., & Urbina, S. (1997). *Psychological testing* (7th Ed.). Upper Saddle River, NJ: Prentice Hall.

Anathaswamy, A. (2004). Hormones converge for couples in love. New Scientist. Retrieved from http://www.newscientist.com/article/dn4957-hormones-converge-for-couples-in-love.html.

Andersen, M. L., Santos-Silva, R., Bittencourt, L. R. A., & Tufik, S. (2010). Prevalence of erectile dysfunction complaints associated with sleep disturbances in Sao Paulo, Brazil: A population-based survey. *Sleep Medicine, 11*(10), 1019–1024.

Anderson, C. A. (1989). Temperature and aggression: Ubiquitous effects of heat on occurrence of human violence. *Psychological Bulletin, 106*(1), 74–96.

Anderson, C., & Platten, C. R. (2011). Sleep deprivation lowers inhibition and enhances impulsivity to negative stimuli. *Behavioural Brain Research, 217*(2), 463–466.

Anderson, D. (1994). Breaking the tradition on college campuses: Reducing drug and alcohol misuse. Fairfax, VA: George Mason University Press.

Anderson, E., Siejel, E. H., Bliss-Moreau, E., & Barrett, L. F. (2011). The visual impact of gossip. *Science, 332*(6036), 1446–1448.

Anderson, S. W., Bechara, A., Damasio, H., Tranel, D., & Damasio, A. R. (1999). Impairment of social and moral behavior related to early damage in human prefrontal cortex. *Nature Neuroscience, 2*(11), 103–107.

Andreasen, N. C., & Black, D. W. (2006). *Introductory textbook of psychiatry (4th Ed.).* Washington, DC: American Psychiatric Publishing.

Angell, J. R. (1903). A preliminary study of the localization of sound. *Psychological Review, 10*, 1–18.

Angier, N. (2001, May 20). Bully for you. Why push comes to shove. *New York Times*, Sect. 4. p. 1.

Angrilli, A., Bianchin, M., Radaelli, S., Bertagnoni, G., & Pertile, M. (2008). Reduced startle reflex and aversive noise perception in patients with orbitofrontal cortex lesions. *Neuropsychologia, 46*(4), 1179–1184.

Angrilli, A., Mauri, A., Palomba, D., Flor, H., Birbaumer, N., Sartori, G., & di Paola, F. (1996). Startle reflex and emotion modulation impairment after a right amygdala lesion. *Brain: A Journal of Neurology, 119*, 1991–2000.

Angulo, M. C., Le Meur, K., Kozlov, A. S., Charpak, S., & Audinat, E. (2008). GABA, a forgotten gliotransmitter. *Progress in Neurobiology, 86*, 297–303.

Angus Reid Strategies. (2009). *Same Sex marriage.* Retrieved from http://www.visioncritical.com/public-opinion/3719/canada_more_open_to_same_sex_ marriage_than_us_uk/.

Antony, M. M. (2011). Recent advances in the treatment of anxiety disorders. *Canadian Psychology/Psychologie Canadienne, 52*(1), 1–9.

APA. (2010). *Gender Dysphoria.* American Psychiatric Association. Retrieved from http://www.dsm5.org/ProposedRevision/Pages/GenderDysphoria.aspx.

Apicella, C. L., Feinberg, D. R., & Marlowe, F. W. (2007). Voice pitch predicts reproductive success in male hunter-gatherers. *Biology Letters, 3*(6),682–684.

Apostolova, L. G., & Cummings, J. L. (2008). Neuropsychiatric aspects of Alzheimer's disease and other dementing illnesses. In S. C. Yudofsky & R. E. Hales (Eds.), *The American psychiatric publishing textbook of neuropsychiatry and behavioral neurosciences (5th Ed.).* Washington, DC: American Psychiatric Publishing.

Appelbaum, P. S., Robbins, P. C., & Monahan, J. (2000). Violence and Delusions: Data from the MacArthur Violence Risk Assessment Study. *American Journal of Psychiatry, 157*, 566–572.

Arahna, A. C. C., de Paula Eduardo, C., & Cordas, T. A. (2008). Eating disorders. Part I: Psychiatric diagnosis and dental implications. *Journal of Contemporary Dental Practice, 9*, 73–81.

Archer, D., & McDaniel, P. (1995). Violence and gender: Differences and similarities across societies. In R. B. Ruback & N. A. Weiner (Eds.), *Interpersonal violent behaviors: Social and cultural aspects.* New York: Springer.

Archer, J. (2005). Are women or men the more aggressive sex? In S. Fein, G. R. Goethals, & M. J. Sandstrom (Eds.), *Gender and aggression: Interdisciplinary perspectives.* Mahwah, NJ: Erlbaum.

Ardelt, M. (2011). Wisdom, age, and well-being. In K. W. Schaie & S. L. Willis (Eds.), *Handbook of the psychology of aging* (7th Ed., pp. 279–291). San Diego, CA: Elsevier Academic Press.

Arens, E. A., Grabe, H., Spitzer, C., & Barnow, S. (2011). Testing the biosocial model of borderline personality disorder: Results of a prospective 5-year longitudinal study. *Personality and Mental Health, 5*(1), 29–42.

Arias-Carrión, Ó., & Pöppel, E. (2007). Dopamine, learning, and reward-seeking behavior. *Acta Neurobiologiae Experimentalis (Warsaw), 67*(4), 481–488.

Arieti, S. (1974). *Interpretation of schizophrenia.* New York: Basic Books.

Armstrong, V., Brunet, P. M., Chao, H., Nishimura, M., Poole, H. L., & Spector, F. J. (2006). What is so critical?: A commentary on the reexamination of critical periods. *Development and Psychobiology, 45*, 326–331.

Arnold, D. H., & Doctoroff, G. L. (2003). The early education of socioeconomically disadvantaged children. *Annual Review of Psychology, 54*, 517–545.

Artero, S., Ancelin, M., Portet, F., Dupuy, A., Berr, C., Dartigues, J., Tzourio, C., Rouaud, O., Poncet, M., Pasquier, F., Auriacombe, S., Touchon, J., & Ritchie, K. (2008). Risk profiles for mild cognitive impairment and progression to dementia are gender specific. *Journal of Neurology, Neurosurgery & Psychiatry, 79*(9), 979–984.

Asch, S. E. (1955). Opinions and social pressure. *Scientific American*, 31–35.

Aschersleben, G., Hofer, T., & Jovanovic, B. (2008). The link between infant attention to goal-directed action and later theory of mind abilities. *Developmental Science, 11*(6), 862–868.

Aserinsky, E. (1996). Memories of famous neuropsychologists: The discovery of REM sleep. *Journal of the History of the Neurosciences, 5*(3), 213–227.

Ash, J., & Gallup Jr., G. G. (2008). Brain size, intelligence, and paleocli-matic variation. In G. Geher & G. Miller (Eds.), *Mating intelligence: Sex, relationships, and the mind's reproductive system* (pp. 313–335). Mahwah, NJ: Lawrence Erlbaum Associates Publishers.

Aslin, R. N., Jusczyk, P. W., & Pisoni, D. B. (2000). Speech and auditory processing during infancy: Constraints on and precursors to language. In D. Kuhn & R. S. Siegler (Eds.), *Handbook of Child Psychology, Volume 2, Cognition, Perception, and Language* (5th Ed., p. 147–198). New York, NY: John Wiley & Sons, Inc.

Asmundson, G. J. G., & Taylor, S. (2008). Health anxiety and its disorders. In M. Hersen & J. Rosqvist (Eds.), *Handbook of psychological assessment, case conceptualization, and treatment, Vol. 1: Adults* (pp. 701–727). Hoboken, NJ: John Wiley & Sons.

Asmus, C. L., & James, K. (2005). Nominal group technique, social loafing, and group creative project quality. *Creativity Research Journal, 17*(4), 349–354.

Aspinwall, L. G., Richter, L., & Hoffman III, R. R. (2001). Understanding how optimism works: An examination of optimists' adaptive moderation of belief and behavior. *Optimism & pessimism: Implications for theory, research, and practice* (pp. 217–238). Washington, DC: American Psychological Association.

Aspinwall, L. G., & Taylor, S. E. (1992). Modeling cognitive adaptation: A longitudinal investigation of the impact of individual differences and coping on college adjustment and performance. *Journal of Personality and Social Psychology, 63*(6), 989–1003.

Astington, J. W., & Baird, J. A., Eds. (2005). *Why language matters for theory of mind.* New York: Oxford University Press.

Atack, J. R. (2010). GABAA receptor subtype-selective modulators as potential nonsedating anxiolytics. In M. B. Stein, & T. Steckler (Eds.), *Behavioral neurobiology of anxiety and its treatment* (pp. 331–360). New York: Springer Science + Business Media.

Aten, J. D., McMinn, M. R., & Worthington, E. L., Jr. (2011). *Spiritually oriented interventions for counseling and psychotherapy.* Washington, DC: American Psychological Association.

Atkinson, R. C. (Dec. 2001). *Achievement versus aptitude tests in college admissions.* Presentation at University of California at Los Angeles.

Atkinson, R. C. (1975). Mnemotechnics in second-language learning. *American Psychologist, 30*(8), 821–828.

Atkinson, R. C., & Shiffrin, R. M. (1968). Chapter: Human memory: A proposed system and its control processes. In K. W. Spence & J. T. Spence (Eds.), *The psychology of learning and motivation* (Volume 2, pp. 89–195). New York: Academic Press.

Augustine, K. (2007). Near-death experiences with hallucinatory features. *Journal of Near-Death Studies, 26*(1), Fall, 3–31.

Auld, J. M. (2007). Review of hypnosis and communication in dental practice. *Australian Journal of Clinical & Experimental Hypnosis, 35*(2), 248–250.

Autism Society of America (ASA). (2006). *Asperger's syndrome.* Retrieved from www.autism-society.org.

Autism Society of America (ASA). (2005). *Asperger's syndrome.* Retrieved from www.autism-society.org.

Autor, D., Katz, L., & Kearney, M. (2006). The polarization of the U.S. labor market. *American Economic Review, 96*, 189–194.

Averill, J. R. (1980). A constructivist view of emotion. In R. Plutchik & H. Kellerman (Eds.), *Theories of emotion* (Vol. 1, pp. 305–340). New York, NY: Academic Press.

Axelrod, F. B. (2004). Familial dysautonomia. *Muscle & Nerve, 29*, 352–363.

Ayd, F. J., Jr. (1956). A clinical evaluation of Frenquel. *Journal of Nervous and Mental Disease 124*, 507–509.

Ayllon, T., & Azrin, N. (1968). *The token economy: A motivational system for therapy and rehabilitation East Norwalk,* CT: Appleton-Century-Crofts.

Ayllon, T., & Azrin, N. H. (1965). The measurement and reinforcement of behavior of psychotics. *Journal of the Experimental Analysis of Behavior, 8*(6), 357–383.

Baars, B. J. (2003). How brain reveals mind: Neuroimaging supports the central role of conscious experience. *Journal of Consciousness Studies, 10,* 100–114.

Baars, B. J. (1986). *The cognitive revolution in psychology.* New York, NY: Guilford Press.

Baars, B. J., Banks W P., & Newman J. B. (Eds.). (2003). *Essential sources in the scientific study of consciousness.* Cambridge, MA: MIT Press.

Baars, B. J., & Gage, N. M. (2010). *Cognition, brain, and consciousness: Introduction to cognitive neuroscience (2nd Ed.).* San Diego, CA, US: Elsevier Academic Press.

Baccus, J. (2004). The strange death of Sir Francis Bacon: The do's and don'ts of appellate advocacy in the WTO. *Legal Issues of Economic Integration, 31,* 13–24. Retrieved from http://www.worldtradelaw.net/articles.htm#bacchus.

Bach, A. K., Wincze, J. P., & Barlow, D. H. (2001). Sexual dysfunction. *Clinical handbook of psychological disorders: A step-by-step treatment manual (3rd Ed.)* (pp. 562–608). New York, NY: Guilford Press.

Bach, P. A. (2007). Psychotic disorders. In D. W. Woods & J. W. Kanter (Eds.), *Understanding behavior disorders: A contemporary behavioral perspective.* Reno, NV: Context Press.

Bachevalier, J. (2011). The amygdala in autism spectrum disorders. In E. Hollander, A. Kolevzon & J. T. Coyle (Eds.), *Textbook of autism spectrum disorders* (pp. 363–374). Arlington, VA: American Psychiatric Publishing, Inc.

Bachorowski, J. & Braaten, E. B. (1994). Emotional intensity: Measurement and theoretical implications. *Personality and Individual Differences, 17,* 191–199.

Backhaus, J., Hoeckesfeld, R., Born, J., Hohagen, F., & Junghanns, K. (2008). Immediate as well as delayed post learning sleep but not wake-fulness enhances declarative memory consolidation in children. *Neurobiology of Learning & Memory, 89,* 76–80.

Backman, C. W. (1990). Attraction in interpersonal relationships. In M. Rosenberg & R. H. Turner (Eds.), *Social Psychology: Sociological Perspectives* (pp. 235–268). New Brunswick, NJ: Transaction Publishers.

Backman, C. W. (1981). Attraction in interpersonal relationships. In M. Rosenberg & R. Turner (Eds.), *Social Psychology: Sociological Perspectives.* New York, NY: Basic Books.

Bäckman, L., & Nyberg, L. (Eds.). (2010). *Memory, aging and the brain: A festschrift in honour of lars-göran nilsson.* New York, NY, US: Psychology Press.

Baddeley, A. D. (2010). Long-term and working memory: How do they interact? In L. Backman, & L. Nyberg (Eds.), *Memory, aging and the brain: A festschrift in honour of lars-göran nilsson* (pp. 7–23). New York, NY, US: Psychology Press.

Baddeley, A. D. (1966). Short-term memory for word sequences as a function of acoustic, semantic and formal similarity (PDF). *Quarterly Journal of Experimental Psychology, 18*(4), 362–365.

Baddeley, A. D., & Hitch, G. (1974). *Working memory.* In G. H. Bower (Ed.), *The psychology of learning and motivation: Advances in research and theory* (Vol. 8, pp. 47–89). New York: Academic Press.

Baer, L., Rauch, S. L., Ballantine, H. T., Jr., Martuza, R., Cosgrove, R., Cassen, E., Giriunas, I., Manzo, P. A., Dimino, C., Jenike, M. A. (1995). Cingulotomy for intractable obsessive-compulsive disorder. Prospective long-term follow-up of 18 patients. *Archivaes of General Psychiatry, 52*(5), 384–392.

Bagley, C., & Tremblay, P. (1988) On the prevalence of homosexuality and bisexuality in a random community survey of 750 men aged 18 to 27. *Journal of Homosexuality, 36*(2), 1–18.

Bailer, U., de Zwaan, M., Leisch, F., Strnad, A., Lennkh-Wolfsberg, C., El-Giamal, N., et al. (2004). Guided self-help versus cognitive-behavioral group therapy in the treatment of bulimia nervosa. *The International Journal of Eating Disorders, 35*(4), 522–537.

Bailey, J. M., & Pillard, R. C. (1991). A genetic study of male sexual orientation. *Archives of General Psychiatry, 48*(12), 1089–1096.

Baillargeon, R. (2004). Infants' reasoning about hidden objects: Evidence for event-general and event-specific expectations. *Developmental Science, 7,* 391–424.

Baillargeon, R. (1987). Object permanence in 3- and 4-month-old infants. *Developmental Psychology, 23,* 655–664.

Baird, A. A. (2010). The terrible twelves. In P. D. Zelazo, M. Chandler, & E. Crone (Eds.), *Developmental social cognitive neuroscience* (pp. 191–207). New York: Psychology Press.

Baker, K. (2010). From "it's not me" to "it was me, after all": A case presentation of a patient diagnosed with dissociative identity disorder. *Psychoanalytic Social Work, 17*(2), 79–98.

Baker, L. A., Jacobson, K. C., Raine, A., Lozano, D. I., & Bezdjian, S. (2007) Genetic and environmental bases of childhood antisocial behavior: A multi-informant twin study. *Journal of Abnormal Psychology, 116,* 219–235.

Baker, T. B., Japuntich, S. J., Hogle, J. M., McCarthy, D. E., & Curtin, J. J. (2006). Pharmacologic and behavioral withdrawal from addictive drugs. *Current Directions in Psychological Science, 15,* 232–236.

Bakin, J. S., South, D. A., & Weinberger, N. M. (1996). Induction of receptive field plasticity in the auditory cortex of the guinea pig during instrumental avoidance conditioning. *Behavioral Neuroscience, 110,* 905–913.

Bakker, A., van Kestren, P. J., Gooren, L. J. G., & Bezemer, P. D. (1993). The prevalence of transsexualism in the Netherlands. *Acta Psychiatrica Scandinavica, 87,* 237–238.

Balaban, V. (2009). Assessment of children. Effective treatments for PTSD: Practice guidelines from the international society for traumatic stress studies (2nd Ed.) (pp. 62–80). New York, NY: Guilford Press.

Balaraman, S. (1962). Color vision research and the trichromatic theory: a historical review. *Psychological Bulletin, 59,* 434–448.

Ball, J. (2010). Culture and Early Childhood Education. Encyclopaedia on Early Childhood Education. Retrieved from http://www.ecdip.org/docs/pdf/Politics%20of%20Comparison%20CEECD%20final%20distribute.pdf.

Ball, J. (2008). Promoting equity and dignity for aboriginal children in Canada. *Choices, 14*(7), 5–27.

Ball, J. (2004). *Early Childhood Development Programs as Hook and Hub: Promising Practices in First Nations Communities.* University of Victoria, School of Child and Youth Care, Early Childhood Development Intercultural Partnerships Programs.

Ball, J., & Moselle, K. (2007). *Fathers' contributions to children's well-being.* Commissioned brief overview of research for the Public Health Agency of Canada.

Ball, J., & Simpkins, M. (2004). The community within the child. *American Indian Quarterly 28,* (3 and 4), 480–498.

Ban, T. A. (2007). Fifty years chlorpromazine: a historical perspective. *Journal of Neuropsychiatric Disease and Treatment, 3*(4), 495–500.

Bancroft, J. (2005). The endocrinology of sexual arousal. *The Journal of Endocrinology, 186*(3), 411–427.

Bancroft, J., Loftus, J., & Long, J. S. (2003). Distress about sex: A national survey of women in heterosexual relationships. *Archives of Sexual Behavior, 32*(3), 193–208.

Bandura, A. (2008). Reconstrual of "free will" from the agentic perspective of social cognitive theory. In J. Baer, J. C. Kaufman, & R. F. Baumeister (Eds.), *Are We Free? Psychology and Free Will* (86–127). New York, NY: Oxford University Press.

Bandura, A. (2006). Toward a psychology of human agency. *Perspectives on Psychological Science, 1,* 164–180.

Bandura, A. (1986). Social foundations of thought and action: A social cognitive theory. Englewood Cliffs, NJ: Prentice Hall.

Bandura, A. (1978). Social learning theory of aggression. *The Journal of Communication, 28*(3), 12–29.

Bandura, A. (1977). Self-efficacy: Toward a unifying theory of behavioral change. *Psychological Review, 84*(2), 191–215.

Bandura, A. (1969). *Principles of behavior modification.* Oxford, England: Holt, Rinehart, & Winston.

Bandura, A., & Rosenthal, T. (1966). Vicarious classical conditioning as a function of arousal level. *Journal of Personal and Social Psychology, 3,* 54–62.

Bandura, A., Adams, N. E., & Beyer, J. (1977). Cognitive processes mediating behavioral change. *Journal of Personality and Social Psychology, 35*(3), 125–139.

Bandura, A., Ross, D. & Ross, S. A. (1963). Imitation of film-mediated aggressive models. In R. J. Huber, C. Edwards, & D. Henning Bownton (Eds.), *Cornerstones of Psychology-Readings in the History of Psychology* (pp. 215–227). Asia: Thomson Learning Inc.

Bandura, A., Ross, D., & Ross, S. A. (1961). Transmission of aggression through imitation of aggressive models. *Journal of Abnormal and Social Psychology, 63*, 575–582.

Bandura, A., Roth, D., & Ross, S. (1963). Imitation of film-mediated aggressive models. *Journal of Abnormality and Social Psychology, 66*, 3–11.

Banks, M. S., & Salapatek, P. (1983). Infant Visual Perception. In M. M. Haith & J. J. Campos (Eds.), *Handbook of Psychology* (pp. 435–571). New York, NY: Wiley.

Barahal, H. S. (1958). 1000 prefrontal lobotomies: A five to ten year follow-up study. *Psychiatric Quarterly, 32*, 653–690.

Barash, D. P. (1979). *The whispering within: Evolution and the origin of human nature.* New York, NY: Viking Press/Penguin Books.

Bard, P. (1934). The neuro-humoral basis of emotional reactions. In C. Murchinson (Ed.), *Handbook of general experimental psychology* (pp. 264–311). Worcester, MA: Clark University Press.

Bard, P. (1929). The central representation of the sympathetic nervous system: As indicated by certain physiological observations. *Archives of Neurology and Psychiatry, 22*, 230–246.

Bard, P. (1928). A diencephalic mechanism for the expression of rage with special reference to the central nervous system. *American Journal of Physiology, 84*, 490–513.

Bargh, J. A. (2001). The psychology of the mere. In J. A. Bargh & D. K. Apsley (Eds.), *Unraveling the Complexities of Social Life: A Festschrift in Honor of Robert B. Zajonc* (pp. 25–37). Washington, D.C.: American Psychological Association.

Barker, P. (2007). *Basic Family Therapy* (5th Ed.). Oxford: Blackwell.

Barlow, D. H. (2002). Anxiety and its disorders: The nature and treatment of anxiety and panic (2nd Ed.). New York, NY: Guilford Press.

Barlow, M. R. (2011). Memory for complex emotional material in dissociative identity disorder. *Journal of Trauma & Dissociation, 12*(1), 53–66.

Barnabé-Heider, F., & Frisén, J. (2008). Stem cells for spinal cord repair. *Cell Stem Cell., 3*, 16–24.

Barnes, L. L., Wilson, R. S., Bienias, J. L., Schneider, J. A., Evans, D. A., & Bennett, D. A. (2005). Sex differences in the clinical manifestations of alzheimer disease pathology. *Archives of General Psychiatry, 62*(6), 685–691.

Barnett, R., & Rivers, C. (2004). Same difference: How gender myths are hurting our relationships, our children, and our jobs. New York, NY: Basic Books.

Barnett, S. M., & Ceci, S. J. (2005). The role of transferable knowledge in intelligence. *Cognition and intelligence: Identifying the mechanisms of the mind* (pp. 208–224). New York, NY: Cambridge University Press.

Barney, L. J., Griffiths, K. M., Jorm, A. F., & Christensen, H. (2006). Stigma about depression and its impact on help-seeking intentions. *Australian and New Zealand Journal of Psychiatry, 40*(1), 51–54.

Barnier, A. J., & Council, J. R. (2010). Hypnotizability matters: The what, why, and how of measurement. In S. J. Lynn, J. W. Rhue, & I. Kirsch (Eds.), *Handbook of clinical hypnosis (2nd Ed.)* (pp. 47–77). Washington, DC, US: American Psychological Association.

Barnier, A. J., McConkey, K. M., & Wright, J. (2004). Posthypnotic amnesia for autobiographical episodes: Influencing memory accessibility and quality. *International Journal of Clinical and Experimental Hypnosis, 52*, 260–279.

Baron, A. S., & Banaji, M. R. (2006). The development of implicit attitudes: Evidence of race evaluations from ages 6 and 10 and adulthood. *Psychological Science, 17*(1), 53–58.

Baron, R. S. (2005). So right it's wrong: Groupthink and the ubiquitous nature of polarized group decision making. In M. P. Zanna (Ed.), *Advances in Experimental Social Psychology, Vol. 37* (pp. 219–253). San Diego, CA: Elsevier Academic Press.

Baron-Cohen, S., & Wheelwright, S. (2003). The Friendship Questionnaire: An investigation of adults with Asperger syndrome or high-functioning autism, and normal sex differences. *Journal of Autism and Developmental Disorders, 33*, 509–517.

Barrett, J., Abbott, D. H., & George, L. M. (1993). Sensory cues and the suppression of reproduction of subordinate female marmoset monkeys. *Journal of Reproduction and Fertility, 97*(1), 301–310.

Barrett, L. F., Gross, J. J., Christensen, T. C., & Benvenuto, M. (2001) Knowing what you're feeling and knowing what to do about it: Mapping the relation between emotion differentiation and emotion regulation. *Cognition and Emotion, 15*, 713–724.

Barrett, L. F., Mesquita, B., Ochsner, K. N., & Gross, J. J. (2007). The experience of emotion. *Annual Review of Psychology, 58*, 373–403.

Barrowclough, C., & Lobban, F. (2008). Family intervention. In K. T. Mueser & D. V. Jeste (Eds.), *Clinical handbook of schizophrenia* (pp. 214–225). New York: Guilford Press.

Bartone, P. T. (2003). Hardiness as a resilience resource under high stress conditions. *Promoting capabilities to manage posttraumatic stress: Perspectives on resilience* (pp. 59–73). Springfield, IL: Charles C. Thomas Publisher.

Bartoshuk, L. M., Duffy, V. B., & Miller, I. J. (1994). PTC/PROP tasting: anatomy, psychophysics, and sex effects. *Physiology Behavior, 56*, 1165–1171.

Bartoshuk, L. M., Duffy, V. B., Reed, D., & Williams A. (1996). Supertasting, earaches and head injury: genetics and pathology alter our taste worlds. *Neuroscience and Biobehavioral Reviews, 20*, 79–87.

Bartrop, R. W., Lockhurst, E., Lazarus, L., Kiloh, L. G., & Penny, R. (1977). Depressed lymphocyte function after bereavement. *Lancet, 1*, 834–836.

Bartzokis, G., Lu, P. H., Tingus, K., Mendez, M. F., Richard, A., Peters, D. G., & Mintz, J. (2010). Lifespan trajectory of myelin integrity and maximum motor speed. *Neurobiology of Aging, 31*(9), 1554–1562.

Basak, C., Boot, W. R., Voss, M. W., & Kramer, A. F. (2008). Can training in a real-time strategy video game attenuate cognitive decline in older adults? *Psychology and Aging, 23*(4), 765–777.

Bass, B. M. (2002). Cognitive, social, and emotional intelligence of transformational leaders. In R. E. Riggio, S. E. Murphy & F. J. Pirozzolo (Eds.), *Multiple intelligences and leadership* (pp. 105–118). Mahwah, NJ: Lawrence Erlbaum Associates Publishers.

Bassett, R. L., Van Nikkelen-Kuyper, M., Johnson, D., Miller, A., Carter, A., & Grimm, J. P. (2005). Being a good neighbor: Can students come to value homosexual persons? *Journal of Psychology and Theology, 33*(1), 17–26.

Bassili, J. N., & Brown, R. D. (2005). Implicit and explicit attitudes: Research, challenges, and theory. In D. Albarracín, B. T. Johnson & M. P. Zanna (Eds.), *The handbook of attitudes* (pp. 543–574). Mahwah, NJ: Lawrence Erlbaum Associates Publishers.

Basson, R. (2007). Sexual desire/arousal disorders in women. *Principles and practice of sex therapy (4th Ed.)* (pp. 25–53). New York, NY: Guilford Press.

Bastien, C. (2011). Insomnia: Neurophysiological and neuropsychological approaches. *Neuropsychology Review, 21*(1), 22–40.

Bates, J. E. (1989). Concepts and measures of temperament. In G. A. Kohnstamm, J. E. Bates, & M. K. Rothbart (Eds.), *Temperament in childhood* (pp. 3–26). Oxford, England: John Wiley & Sons, Inc.

Bates, J. E., Schermerhorn, A. C., & Goodnight, J. A. (2010). Temperament and personality through the life span. In M. E. Lamb, A. M. Freund, & R. M. Lerner (Eds.), *The handbook of life-span development,* vol. 2: *Social and emotional development* (pp. 208–253). Hoboken, NJ: John Wiley & Sons.

Bates, R. (2002). Liking and similarity as predictors of multi-source ratings. *Personnel Review, 31*(5), 540–552.

Batson, C. D. (1991). *The altruism question: Towards a social psychological answer.* Hillsdale, NJ: Lawrence Erlbaum Associates.

Batson, C. D., Ahmad, N., & Lishner, D. A. (2009). Empathy and Altruism. In C.R. Snyder and S.J. Lopez (Eds), *Handbook of Positive Psychology* (pp. 417–426). New York: Oxford University Press.

Batson, C. D., Ahmad, N., & Stocks, E. L. (2004). Benefits and liabilities of empathy–induced altruism. In A. G. Miller (Ed.), *The social psychology of good and evil* (pp. 359–385). New York, NY: Guilford Press.

Batson, C. D., Sanger, K., Garst, E., Kang, M., Rubchinsky, K., & Dawson, K. (1997). Is empathy-induced helping due to self-other merging? *Journal of Personality and Social Psychology, 73*, 495–509.

Batson, C. D., & Weeks, J. L. (1996). Mood effects of unsuccessful helping: Another test of the empathy-altruism hypothesis. *Personality and Social Psychology Bulletin, 22*, 148–157.

Battmer, R. D., Linz, B., & Lenarz, T. (2009). A review of device failure in more than 23 years of clinical experience of a cochlear implant program with more than 3,400 implantees. *Otology & Neurotology, 30*, 455–463.

Baucom, B. R., Atkins, D. C., Simpson, L. E., & Christensen, A. (2009). Prediction of response to treatment in a randomized clinical trial of couple therapy: A 2-year follow-up. *Journal of Consulting and Clinical Psychology, 77*(1), 160–173.

Baucom, D. H., Epstein, N. B., Kirby, J. S., & LaTaillade, J. J. (2010). Cognitive-behavioral couple therapy. In K. S. Dobson (Ed.), *Handbook of cognitive-behavioral therapies* (3rd Ed., pp. 411–444). New York: Guilford Press.

Bauer, R. A. (1952). *The new man in Soviet psychology*. Cambridge, MA: Harvard University Press.

Baum, A., Trevino, L. A., & Dougall, A. L. (2011). Stress and the cancers. In R. J. Contrada & A. Baum (Eds.), *The handbook of stress science: Biology, psychology, and health* (pp. 411–423). New York: Springer Publishing Co.

Bauman, M. L. (2011). Neuroanatomy of the brain in autism spectrum disorders. In E. Hollander, A. Kolevzon & J. T. Coyle (Eds.), *Textbook of autism spectrum disorders* (pp. 355–361). Arlington, VA: American Psychiatric Publishing, Inc.

Baumeister, R. F. (1984). Choking under pressure: Self-consciousness and paradoxical effects of incentives on skillful performance. *Journal of Personality and Social Psychology, 46*(3), 610–620.

Baumeister, R. F., Catanese, K. R., & Vohs, K. D. (2001). Is there a gender difference in strength of sex drive? Theoretical views, conceptual distinctions, and a review of relevant evidence. *Personality and Social Psychology Review, 5,* 242–273.

Baumeister, R. F., Zhang, L., & Vohs, K. D. (2004). Gossip as cultural learning. *Review of General Psychology, 8*(2), 111–121.

Baumgardner, S. R., & Crothers, M. K. (2009). *Positive psychology*. Upper Saddle River, NJ: Prentice Hall/Pearson Education.

Baumrind, D. (1991). The influence of parenting style on adolescent competence and substance use. *The Journal of Early Adolescence, 11,* 56–95.

Baumrind, D., Larzelere, R. E., & Owens, E. B. (2010). Effects of preschool parents' power assertive patterns and practices on adolescent development. *Parenting: Science and Practice, 10*(3), 157–201.

Baun, K. (2009) Stigma Matters: The Media's Impact on Publiuc Perceptions of Mental Illness. *Ottawa Life Magazine*. Retrieved from http://www.ontario.cmha.ca/admin_ver2/maps/olm_stigma_matters_200902.pdf, accessed.

Beach, J., & Bertrand, J. (2009). Early childhood programs and the education system, *Paediatric Child Health, 14*(10), 666–668.

Bear, M. F., Connors, B. W., & Paradiso, M. A. (2007). *Neuroscience: Exploring the Brain (3rd Ed)*. Baltimore: Lippincott Williams & Wilkins.

Beasley, M., Thompson, T., & Davidson, J. (2003). Resilience in responses to life stress: The effects of coping style and cognitive hardiness. *Personality and Individual Differences, 34*(1), 77–95.

Beaupre, M. G., & Hess, U. (2004). Cross-Cultural Emotion Recognition among Canadian Ethnic Groups. *Journal of Cross-Cultural Psychology, 36*(3), 355–370.

Becchetti, L., & Santoro, M. (2007). The income-unhappiness paradox: A relational goods/Baumol disease explanation. In P. L. Porta & L. Bruni (Eds.), *Handbook on the economies of happiness*. Northampton, MA: Edward Elgar Publishing.

Bechara, A., Tranel, D., Damasio, H., Adolphs, R., Rockland, C., & Damasio, A. R. (1995). Double dissociation of conditioning and declarative knowledge relative to the amygdala and hippocampus in humans. *Science, 269,* 1115–1118.

Beck, A. T. (2002). Cognitive models of depression. In R. L. Leahy & E. T. Dowd (Eds.), *Clinical advances in cognitive psychotherapy: Theory and applications*. New York, NY: Springer.

Beck, A. T. (1991). Cognitive therapy: A 30-year retrospective. *American Psychologist, 46*(4), 368–375.

Beck, A. T. (1975). *Cognitive Therapy and the Emotional Disorders*. International Universities Press Inc.

Beck, A. T. (1967). Depression: Clinical, experimental and theoretical aspects. New York, NY: Harper & Row.

Beck, A. T., & Alford, B. A. (2009) *Depression: Causes and treatment*. Philadelphia, PA: University of Pennsylvania Press.

Beck, A. T., & Emery, G. (1985). *Anxiety disorders and phobias: A cognitive perspective*. New York: Basic Books.

Beck, A. T., Emery, G., & Greenberg, R. L. (1985). Differentiating anxiety and depression: A test of the cognitive content-specificity hypothesis. *Journal Abnormal Psychology, 96,* 179–183.

Beck, A. T., Rush, A. J., Shaw, B. F., & Emery, G. (1979). *Cognitive therapy of depression*. New York: Guilford Press.

Beck, A. T., & Weishaar, M. (2011). Cognitive therapy. In R. J. Corsini & D. Wedding (Eds.), *Current Psychotherapies, 9th Ed.* Florence, KY: Cengage Learning.

Beck, A. T., & Weishaar, M. E. (2008). Cognitive therapy. In R. J. Corsini & D. Wedding (Eds.), *Current psychotherapies (8th edition)*. Belmont, CA: Brooks Cole.

Beck, B. J. (2008). Mental disorders due to a general medical condition. In T. A. Stern, J. F. Rosenbaum, M. Fava, J. Biederman, & S. L. Rauch (Eds.), *Massachusetts General Hospital Comprehensive Clinical Psychiatry,* 1st Ed. Philadelphia, Pa: Mosby Elsevier.

Beckett, C., Castle, J., Rutter, M., & Sonuga-Barke, E. (2010). Institutional deprivation, specific cognitive functions, and scholastic achievement: English and Romanian adoptees (ERA) study findings. *Monographs of the Society for Research in Child Development, 75*(1), 125–142.

Bédard, P., & Sanes, J. N. (2009). Gaze and hand position effects on finger movement related human brain activation. *Journal of Neurophysiology, 101*(2), 834–842.

Bedinghaus, T. (2010). Top 5 milestones in vision development. In *About. Com Guide*. Retrieved from http://vision.about.com/od/childrens-vision/tp/vision_develop.htm.

Beehr, T. A., Farmer, S. J., Glazer, S., Gudanowski, D. M., & Nair, V. N. (2003). The enigma of social support and occupational stress: Source congruence and gender role effects. *Journal of Occupational Health Psychology, 8*(3), 220–231.

Beghetto, R. A., & Kaufman, J. C. (2010). Broadening conceptions of creativity in the classroom. In R. A. Beghetto & J. C. Kaufman (Eds.), *Nurturing creativity in the classroom* (pp. 191–205). New York: Cambridge University Press.

Behrendt, R. P., & Young, C. (2004). Hallucinations in schizophrenia, sensory impairment, and brain disease: A unifying model. *Behavioral and Brain Sciences, 27,* 771–787.

Beilin, H. (1992). Piaget's enduring contribution to developmental psychology. *Developmental Psychology, 28,* 191–204.

Bekker, M. H. J. & van Assen, Marcel, A. L. M. (2008). Autonomy-connectedness and gender. *Sex Roles, 59*(7–8), 532–544.

Bekkouche, N. S., Holmes, S., Whittaker, K. S., & Krantz, D. S. (2011). Stress and the heart: Psychosocial stress and coronary heart disease. In R. J. Contrada & A. Baum (Eds.), *The handbook of stress science: Biology, psychology, and health*. New York: Springer Publishing Co.

Bellinger, D. L., Madden, K. S., Felten, S.Y, & Felten, D. L. (1994). Neural and endocrine links between the brain and the immune system. In C. S. Lewis, C. O'Sullivan, & J. Barraclough (Eds.), *The psychoimmunology of cancer: Mind and body in the fight for survival*. Oxford, England: Oxford University Press.

Bem, D. J. (1972). Self-perception theory. In L. Berkowitz (Ed.), *Advances in Experimental Social Psychology, Vol. 6*. New York: Academic Press.

Benarroch, E. E. (2011). The midline and intralaminar thalamic nuclei: Anatomic and functional specificity and implications in neurologic disease (Update). *Neurology, 74.*

Benarroch, E. E. (2008). The midline and intralaminar thalamic nuclei: Anatomic and functional specificity and implications in neurologic disease. *Neurology, 71,* 944.

Bendelius, J. (2004). Prevention: the best way to help our kids avoid the obesity epidemic. *School Nurse News, 21*(3), 32–33.

Bender, R. E., & Alloy, L. B. (2011). Life stress and kindling in bipolar disorder: Review of the evidence and integration with emerging biopsychosocial theories. *Clinical Psychology Review, 31*(3), 383–398.

Benjamin Jr., L. T. (2007). *A brief history of modern psychology*. Malden, MA: Blackwell Publishing.

Benjamin Jr., L. T. (Ed.). (1997). A history of psychology: Original sources and contemporary research (2nd Ed.). New York, NY: Mcgraw-Hill Book Company.

Benloucif, S., Guico, M. J., Reid, K. J., Wolfe, L. F., L'hermite-Balériaux, M., & Zee, P. C. (2005). Stability of melatonin and temperature as circadian phase markers and their relation to sleep times in humans. *Journal of Biological Rhythms, 20*(2), 178–188.

Bennett, M. P. (1998). The effect of mirthful laughter on stress and natural killer cell cytotoxicity US: ProQuest Information & Learning).

Dissertation Abstracts International: Section B: The Sciences and Engineering, 58(7), 3553.

Bensafi, M., Sobel, N., & Khan, R. M. (2007). Hedonic-specific activity in piriform cortex during odor imagery mimics that during odor perception. *Journal of Neurophysiology, 98*, 3254–3262.

Benton, A. (2000). *Exploring the History of Neuropsychology*. Oxford University Press.

Ben-Zeev, D., Young, M. A., & Corrigan, P. W. (2010). DSM-V and the stigma of mental illness. *Journal of Mental Health, 19*(4), 318–327.

Ben-Zur, H. (2002). Associations of type A behavior with the emotional traits of anger and curiosity. *Anxiety, Stress & Coping: An International Journal, 15*(1), 95–104.

Benzies, K., Magill-Evans, J., Harrison, M.J., MacPhail, S., & Kimak, C. (2008). Strengthening new fathers' skills in interaction with their 5-month-old infants: Who benefits from a brief intervention? *Public Health Nursing, 25*, 431–439.

Berenbaum, H., & Barch, D. (1995). The categorization of thought disorder. *Journal of Psycholinguist Research, 24*, 349–376.

Berenbaum, H., Raghavan, C., Huynh-Nhu, L., Vernon, L. L., & Gomez, J. J. (2003). A taxonomy of emotional disturbances. *Clinical Psychology: Science and Practice, 10*, 206–226.

Berenson, K. R., Downey, G., Rafaeli, E., Coifman, K. G., & Paquin, N. L. (2011). The rejection–rage contingency in borderline personality disorder. *Journal of Abnormal Psychology, 120*(3), 681–690.

Berger, K. T. (1988). *Zen Driving*. Ballentine Books.

Berk, L. E. (2008). *Infants, Children, and Adolescents, 6e*. Boston: Allyn & Bacon.

Berk, L.E. (1994). Why children talk to themselves. *Scientific American, 271*(5), 78–83.

Berkman, N. D., Bulik, C. M., Brownley, K. A., Lohr, K. N., Sedway, J. A., Rooks, A., et al. (2006). Management of eating disorders. Evidence report/technology assessment No. 135. *AHRQ Publication No. 06-E010*.

Berkowitz, L. (1989). Frustration-aggression hypothesis: Examination and reformulation. *Psychological Bulletin, 106*, 59–73.

Berman, J. R. (2005). Physiology of female sexual function and dysfunction. *International Journal of Impotence Research, 17*(1), S44–51.

Bermond, B., Nieuwenhuyse, B., Fasotti, L., & Schuerman, J. (1991). Spinal cord lesions, peripheral feedback, and intensities of emotional feelings. *Cognition & Emotion, 5*, 201–220.

Bermudez, P., Lerch, J. P., Evans, A. C., & Zatorre, R. J. (2009). Neuroanatomical correlates of musicianship as revealed by cortical thickness and voxel-based morphometry. *Cerebral Cortex, 19*, 1583–1596.

Berntson, G. G., Bechara, A., Damasio, H., Tranel, D., & Cacioppo, J. T. (2007). Amygdala contribution to selective dimensions of emotion. *Social Cognitive Affective Neuroscience, 2*(2), 123–129.

Berr, C., Wancata, J., & Ritchie, K. (2005). Prevalence of dementia in the elderly in Europe. *Eur. Neuropsyhopharmacology, 15*(4), 463–471.

Berridge, K. C. (2007). The debate over dopamine's role in reward: The case for incentive salience. *Psychopharmacology, 191*(3), 391–431.

Berridge, K. C., & Kringelbach, M. (2008). Affective neuroscience of pleasure: Reward in humans and animals. *Psychopharmacology, 199*(3), 457–480.

Berry, J. W. (1992). *Cross-cultural psychology, research and applications*. New York, NY: Cambridge University Press.

Berry, J., Hastings, E., West, R., Lee, C., & Cavanaugh, J. C. (2010). Memory aging: Deficits, beliefs, and interventions. In J. C. Cavanaugh, C. K. Cavanaugh, J. Berry & R. West (Eds.), *Aging in america, vol 1: Psychological aspects* (pp. 255–299). Santa Barbara, CA, US: Praeger/ABC-CLIO.

Berscheid, E. (1983). Interpersonal attraction. In. G. Lindzey & E. Aronson (Eds.), *Handbook of Social Psychology (3rd Ed.)*. Reading, MA: Addison-Wesley.

Berscheid, E., & Walster, E. H. (1978). Interpersonal attraction. In G. Lindzey & E. Aronson (Eds.), *Handbook of Social Psychology* (Vol. 2, pp. 413–484). New York, NY: Random House.

Berson, D. M. (2003). Strange vision: ganglion cells as circadian photoreceptors. *Trends in Neuroscience, 26*(6), 314–320.

Bertini, M., Ferrara, M., De Gennaro, L., Moroni, F., De Gasperis, M., Babiloni, C., Rossini, P. M., Vecchio, F., & Curcio, G. (2007). Directional information flows between brain hemispheres during presleep wake and early sleep stages. *Cerebral Cortex, 17*(8), 1970–1978.

Beutler, L. E. (2011). Prescriptive matching and systematic treatment selection. In J. C. Norcross, G. R. VandenBos, & D. K. Freedheim (Eds.), *History of psychotherapy: Continuity and change* (2nd Ed., pp. 402–407). Washington, DC: American Psychological Association.

Beutler, L. E. (2002). The dodo bird is extinct. *Clinical Psychology: Science and Practice, 9*(1), 30–34.

Bevins, R. A. (2001). Novelty seeking and reward: Implications for the study of high-risk behaviors. *Current Directions in Psychological Science, 10*(6), 189–193.

Beyerstein, B. (2004). Do we really use only 10 percent of our brains? *Scientific American*. Retrieved from http://www.scientificamerican.com/article.cfm?id=do-we-really-use-only-10.

Bialystok, E., & Craik, F. I. M. (2010). Structure and process in life-span cognitive development. In W. F. Overton & R. M. Lerner (Eds.), *The handbook of life-span development*, vol 1.: *Cognition, biology, and methods* (pp. 195–225). Hoboken, NJ: John Wiley & Sons.

Bibby, R. (2007). *Racial Intermarriage: Canada and the U.S.* Project Canada Press Release #9, University of Lethbridge. Retrieved from http://www.reginaldbibby.com/images/PC_9_RACIAL_INTERMARRIAGE_AUG2907.pdf.

Bickman, L. (2005). A common factors approach to improving mental health services. *Mental Health Services Research, 7*(1), 1–4.

Billings, L. S., Vescio, T. K., & Biernat, M. (2000). Race-based social judgment by minority perceivers. *Journal of Applied Social Psychology, 30*(2), 221–240.

Bindschaedler, C., Peter-Favre, C., Maeder, P., Hirsbrunner, T., & Clarke, S. (2011). Growing up with bilateral hippocampal atrophy: From childhood to teenage. *Cortex, 47*, 931–944.

Binswanger, H. (1991). Volition as cognitive self-regulation. *Organizational Behavior and Human Decision Processes, 50*(2), 154–178.

Birrell, P. (2011). Review of Memory matters: Contexts for understanding sexual abuse recollections. *Journal of Trauma & Dissociation, 12*(1), 107–109.

Bisaga, A. (2008). Benzodiazepines and other sedatives and hypnotics. In H. D. Kleber & M. Galanter (Eds.), *The American Psychiatric Publishing textbook of substance abuse treatment (4th Ed.)*. Arlington, VA: American Psychiatric Publishing.

Bissette, G., Seidler, F. J., Nemeroff, C. B., & Slotkin, T. A. (1996). High affinity choline transporter status in Alzheimer's disease tissue from rapid autopsy. In R. J. Wurtman, S. Corkin, J. H. Growdon, & R. M. Nitsch (Eds.), *The neurobiology of Alzheimer's disease*. New York, NY: New York Academy of Sciences.

Biswas-Diener, R. (Ed.). (2011). *Positive psychology as social change*. New York: Springer Science + Business Media.

Bitterman, M. E. (2006). Classical conditioning since pavlov. *Review of General Psychology, 10(4)*, 365–376.

Bjorgvinsson, T., & Hart, J. (2008). Obsessive-compulsive disorder. In M. Hersen & J. Rosqvist (Eds.), *Handbook of psychological assessment, case conceptualization, and treatment, Vol. 1: Adults* (pp. 237–262). Hoboken, NJ: John Wiley & Sons.

Björkman, B., Arnér, S., & Hydén, L. C. (2008). Phantom breast and other syndromes after mastectomy: Eight breast cancer patients describe their experiences over time: a 2-year follow-up study. *The Journal of Pain, 9*, 1018–1025.

Björnholm, M., Münzberg, H., Leshan, R. L., Villanueva, E. C., Bates, S. H., Louis, G. W., & Myers, Martin G., Jr. (2007). Mice lacking inhibitory leptin receptor signals are lean with normal endocrine function. *The Journal of Clinical Investigation, 117*(5), 1354–1360.

Black, K. A., & Schutte, E. D. (2006) Recollections of being loved: Implications of childhood experiences with parents for young adults' romantic relationships. *Journal of Family Issues, 27*, 1459–1480.

Blackburn, E. H. (1991). Structure and function of telomeres. *Nature, 350*(6319), 569–573.

Blagrove, M., Bell, E., & Wilkinson, A. (2010). Association of lucid dreaming frequency with stroop task performance. *Dreaming, 20*(4), 280–287.

Black, D. W., Gunter, T., Loveless, P., Allen, J., & Sieleni, B. (2010). Antisocial personality disorder in incarcerated offenders: Psychiatric comorbidity and quality of life. *Annals of Clinical Psychiatry, 22*(3), 113–120.

Blackmore, E. R., Craddock, N., Walters, J., & Jones, I. (2009). Is the perimenopause a time of increased risk of recurrence in women with a history of bipolar affective postpartum psychosis? A case series. *Archives of Women's Mental Health, 11*(1), 75–78.

Blair, J., Mitchell, D., & Blair, K. (2005). *The psychopath: Emotion and the brain.* Malden, MA: Blackwell Publishing.

Blakemore, S., Burnett, S., & Dahl, R. E. (2010). The role of puberty in the developing adolescent brain. *Human Brain Mapping, 31*(6), 926–933.

Blanchard, R. (2004). Quantitative and theoretical analyses of the relation between older brothers and homosexuality in men. *Journal of Theoretical Biology, 230*(2), 173–187.

Blanchard, R. (2001). Fraternal birth order and the maternal immune hypothesis of male homosexuality. *Hormonal Behavior, 40*(2), 105–114.

Bland, R. C., Orn, H., & Newman, S. C. (1988). Lifetime prevalence of psychiatric disorders in Edmonton. *Acta Psychiatrica Scandinavica Supplement, 338*, 24–32.

Blass, T. (2007). Unsupported allegations about a link between Milgram and the CIA: Tortured reasoning in a question of torture. *Journal of the History of the Behavioral Sciences, 43*, 199–203.

Blass, T. (2004). The man who shocked the world: The life and legacy of Stanley Milgram. New York, NY: Basic Books.

Bleich, A., Gelkopf, M., & Solomon, Z. (2003). Exposure to terrorism, stress-related mental health symptoms, and coping behaviors among a nationally representative sample in Israel. *Journal of the American Medical Association, 290*(5), 612–620.

Bliss, T. V., & Lomo, T. (1973). Long-lasting potentiation of synaptic transmission in the dentate area of the anaesthetized rabbit following stimulation of the perforant path. *The Journal of Physiology, 232*, 331–356.

Bliwise, D. L. (2010). The pit (of sleeplessness) and the pendulum (of regulation). *Sleep Medicine, 11*(1), 7–8.

Blomstedt, P., Sandvik, U., Hariz, M. I., Fytagoridis, A., Forsgren, L., Hariz, G., & Koskinen, L. D. (2011). Influence of age, gender and severity of tremor on outcome after thalamic and subthalamic DBS for essential tremor. *Parkinsonism & Related Disorders, 17*(8), 617–620.

Blomstedt, P., Sjoberg, R. L., Hansson, M., Bodlund, O., & Hariz, M. I. (2011). Deep brain stimulation in the treatment of depression. *Acta Psychiatrica Scandinavica, 123*(1), 4–11.

Bloom, L. (1970). Language development: Form and function in emerging grammars. Cambridge, MA: MIT Press.

Blum, H. P. (2010). Object relations in clinical psychoanalysis. *The International Journal of Psychoanalysis, 91*(4), 973–976.

Blum, K., Braverman, E. R., Holder, J. M., Lubar, J. F., Monastra, V. J., Miller, D., et. al. (2000). Reward deficiency syndrome: A biogenetic model for the diagnosis and treatment of impulsive, addictive, and compulsive behaviors. *Journal of Psychoactive Drugs, 32* (Suppl.), 1–68.

Blumberg, M. S., & Seelke, A. M. H. (2010). The form and function of infant sleep: From muscle to neocortex. In M. S. Blumberg, J. H. Freeman & S. R. Robinson (Eds.), *Oxford handbook of developmental behavioral neuroscience* (pp. 391–423). New York, NY: Oxford University Press.

Blumenfeld, P., Kempler, T., & Krajcik, J. (2006). Motivation and cognitive engagement in learning environments. In R. K. Sawyer (Ed.), *The Cambridge handbook of the learning sciences* (pp. 475–488). Cambridge, MA: Cambridge University Press.

Bock, P. (2005). Infant science: How do babies learn to talk. *Pacific Northwest: The Seattle Times Magazine,* March 6, 2005.

Bodfish, J. W. (2011). Restricted repetitive behaviors. In E. Hollander, A. Kolevzon & J. T. Coyle (Eds.), *Textbook of autism spectrum disorders* (pp. 169–177). Arlington, VA: American Psychiatric Publishing, Inc.

Boecker, H., Sprenger T., Spilker, M. E., Henriksen, G., Koppenhoefer, M., Wagner, K. J., Valet, M., Berthele, A., & Tolle, T. R. (2008). The runner's high: Opioidergic mechanisms in the human brain. *Cerebral Cortex, 18*(11), 2523–2531.

Bohart, A. C., & Tallman, K. (2010). Clients: The neglected common factor in psychotherapy. In B. L. Duncan, S. D. Miller, B. E. Wampold, & M. A. Hubble (Eds.), *The heart and soul of change: Delivering what works in therapy* (2nd Ed., pp. 83–111). Washington, DC: American Psychological Association.

Boldyrev, A. A., & Johnson, P. (2007). Free radicals and cell signaling in Alzheimer's disease. *Journal of Alzheimer's Disease, 11*(2), 141.

Bolger, N. (1990). Coping as a personality process: A prospective study. *Journal of Personality and Social Psychology, 59*, 525–537.

Bollinger, T., Bollinger, A., Oster, H., & Solbach, W. (2010). Sleep, immunity, and circadian clocks: A mechanistic model. *Gerontology, 56*(6), 574–580.

Bollini, A. M., & Walker, E. F. (2007). Schizotypal personality disorder. In W. O'Donohue, K. A. Fowler, & S. O. Lilienfeld (Eds.), *Personality Disorders: Toward the DSM-V* (pp. 81–108). Thousand Oaks, CA: Sage Publications.

Bonanno, G. A., Brewin, C. R., Kaniasty, K., & La Greca, A. M. (2010). Weighing the costs of disaster: Consequences, risks, and resilience in individuals, families, and communities. *Psychological Science in the Public Interest, 11*, 1–49.

Bonanno, G. A., & Mancini, A. D. (2010). Beyond resilience and PTSD: Mapping the heterogeneity of responses to potential trauma. *Psychological Trauma: Theory, Research, Practice, and Policy,* No Pages.

Bond, C. F. Jr. (2000). Social facilitation. In A. E. Kazdin (Ed.), *Encyclopedia of Psychology, vol. 7* (pp. 338–440). Washington, D.C.: American Psychological Association.

Bond, C. F., & Titus, L. J. (1983). Social facilitation: A meta analysis of 241 studies. *Psychological Bulletin, 94*, 265–292.

Bond, R., & Smith, P. B. (1996). Culture and conformity: A meta-analysis of studies using Asch's (1952b, 1956) line judgment task. *Psychological Bulletin, 119*, 111–137.

Boogaarts, H. D., Abdo, W. F., & Bloem, B. R. (2007). "Recumbent" gait: relationship to the phenotype of "astasia–abasia"? *Movement Disorders, 22*(14), 2121–2122.

Boorse, C. (1976). What a theory of mental health should be. *Journal for the Theory of Social Behaviour, 6*(1), 61–84.

Bord-Hoffman, M. A., & Donius, M. (2005). Loss in height: When is it a problem? *AAACN Viewpoint, 1*, 14–15.

Borgen, F. H., & Betz, N. E. (2008). Career self-efficacy and personality: Linking career confidence and the healthy personality. *Journal of Career Assessment, 16*(1), 22–43.

Bornstein, M. H., Tal, J., Rahn, C., Galperin, C. Z., Pecheux, M., Lamour, M., Azuma, H., Toda, S., Ogino, M., & Tamis-LeMonda, C. S. (1992). Functional analysis of the contents of maternal speech to infants of 5 and 13 months in four cultures: Argentina, France, Japan, and the United States. *Developmental Psychology, 28*, 593–603.

Bornstein, R. F. (2007). Might the Rorschach be a projective test after all? Social projection of an undesired trait alters Rorschach oral dependency scores. *Journal of Personality Assessment, 88*(3), 354–367.

Bosson, J. K., & Vandello, J. A. (2011). Precarious manhood and its links to action and aggression. *Current Directions in Psychological Science, 20*(2), 82–86.

Botton, A. (2006). *The Architecture of Happiness.* Pantheon: London, England.

Botvinick, M., Nystrom, L. E., Fissell, K., Carter, C. S., & Cohen, J. D. (1999). Conflict monitoring versus selection-for-action in anterior cingulate cortex. *Nature, 402*, 179–181.

Botwin, M. D., Buss, D. M., & Shackelford, T. K. (1997). Personality and mate preferences: Five factors in mate selection and marital satisfaction. *Journal of Personality, 65*, 107–136.

Bouchard, G., & Thériault, V. J. (2003). Defense mechanisms and coping strategies in conjugal relationships: An integration. *International Journal of Psychology, 38*(2), 79–90.

Bouchard, T., Jr. (2004). Genes, environment, and personality. *Science, 264*, 1700–1701.

Bouchard, T., & Pedersen, N. (1999). Twins reared apart: Nature's double experiment. In M. LaBuda & E. Grigorenko (Eds.), *On the Way to Individuality: Current Methodological Issues in Behavior Genetics* (pp. 71–93). Commack, NY: Nova Science Press.

Bouman, T. K. (2008). Hypochondriasis. In J. S. Abramowitz, D. McKay, & S. Taylor (Eds.), *Obsessive-compulsive disorder: Subtypes and spectrum conditions.* Oxford, UK: Elsevier.

Bourassa, C., McKay, K., & Hampton, M. (2004). Racism, sexism, and colonialism: The impact on the health of aboriginal women in Canada. *Canadian Women Studies, 24*(1), 23–29.

Bourne, L. E., Dominowski, R. L., & Loftus, W F. (1979). *Cognitive processes.* Englewood Cliffs, NJ: Prentice Hall.

Bouteyre, E., Maurel, M., & Bernaud, J-L. (2007). Daily hassles and depressive symptoms among first year psychology students in France:

The role of coping and social support. *Stress and Health: Journal of the International Society for the Investigation of Stress, 23,* 93–99.

Bowden, S. C., Saklofske, D. H., & Weiss, L. G. (2011). Invariance of the measurement model underlying the Wechsler adult intelligence scale-IV in the United States and Canada. *Educational and Psychological Measurement, 71*(1), 186–199.

Bower, G. H. (2008). The evolution of a cognitive psychologist: A journey from simple behaviors to complex mental acts. *Annual Review of Psychology, 59,* 1–27.

Bower, G. H. (1981). Mood and memory. *American Psychologist, 36*(2), 129–148.

Bowlby, J. (1999). *Attachment: Attachment and loss* (vol. 1, 2nd Ed.). New York: Basic Books.

Bowlby, J. (1969). *Attachment and loss, Vol. 1: Attachment.* New York: Basic Books.

Bowlby, J. (1958). The nature of the child's tie to his mother. *International Journal of Psycho-Analysis, XXXIX,* 1–23.

Bowne, W. B., Julliard, K., Castro, A. E., Shah, P., Morgenthal, C. B., Ferzli, G. S., et al. (2006). Laparoscopic gastric bypass is superior to adjustable gastric band in super morbidly obese patients. *Archives of Surgery, 141,* 683–689.

Boyd, B. A., Conroy, M. A., Asmus, J., & McKenney, E. (2011). Direct observation of peer-related social interaction: Outcomes for young children with autism spectrum disorders. *Exceptionality, 19*(2), 94–108.

Boyd, R. (2004). Fact or fiction?: Waking a sleepwalker may kill them. *Scientific American, 1.*

Boyle, G. J. (2008). Critique of the five-factor model of personality. In G. J. Boyle, G. Matthews, & D. H. Saklofske (Eds.), *The SAGE Handbook of Personality Theory and Assessment, Vol 1: Personality Theories and Models* (pp. 295–312). Sage Publications.

Boyle, G. J., Matthews, G., & Saklofske, D. H. (2008). *The SAGE handbook of personality theory and assessment: Personality measurement and testing (Volume 2).* Sage Publications.

Brach, J. S., FitzGerald, S., Newman, A. B., Kelsey, S., Kuller, L., VanSwearingen, J. M., & Kriska, A. M. (2003). Physical activity and functional status in community-dwelling older women. *Archives of Internal Medicine, 163,* 2565–2571.

Brackett, M. A., Rivers, S. E., & Salovey, P. (2011). Emotional intelligence: Implications for personal, social, academic, and workplace success. *Social and Personality Psychology Compass, 5*(1), 88–103.

Braddick, O. J., O'Brien, J. M. D., Wattam-Bell, J., Atkinson, J., Hartley, T., & Turner, R. (2001) Brain areas sensitive to coherent visual motion. *Perception, 30*(1), 61–72.

Bradley, M. M., & Lang, P. J. (2007). Emotion and motivation. In J. T. Cacioppo, L. G. Tassinary, & G. G. Berntson (Eds.), *Handbook of psychophysiology (3rd Ed.)* (pp. 581–607). New York, NY: Cambridge University Press.

Bradley, M. M., & Lang, P. J. (2000). Measuring emotion: Behavior, feeling, and physiology. In R. D. Lane & L. Nadel (Eds.), *Cognitive neuroscience of emotion* (pp. 242–276). New York, NY: Oxford University Press.

Bradley, M. M., Cuthbert, B. N., & Lang, P. J. (1991). Startle and emotion: Lateral acoustic probes and the bilateral blink. *Psychophysiology, 28,* 285–295.

Bradley, M. M., Cuthbert, B. N., & Lang, P. J. (1990). Startle reflex modification: Emotion or attention? *Psychophysiology, 27,* 513–522.

Bradley, R. H., & Caldwell, B. M. (1984). The HOME inventory and family demographics. *Developmental Psychology, 20*(2), 315–320.

Bradley, R. H., Caldwell, B. M., & Corwyn, R. F. (2003). The child care HOME inventories: Assessing the quality of family child care homes. *Early Childhood Research Quarterly, 18*(3), 294–309.

Bradley, R., Conklin, C. Z., & Westen, D. (2007). Borderline personality disorder. In W. O'Donohue, K. A. Fowler, & S. O. Lilienfeld (Eds.), *Personality Disorders: Toward the DSM-V* (pp. 167–201). Sage Publications.

Bradley, S. D., Angelini, J. R., & Lee, S. (2007). Psychophysiological and memory effects of negative political ads: Aversive, arousing, and well remembered. *Journal of Advertising, 36*(4), 115–127.

Bradley, S. J. (2000). Affect regulation and the development of psychopathology. New York: Guilford Press.

Bradley, S. J. (1995). Psychosexual disorders in adolescence. In J. M. Oldham & M. B. Riba (Eds.), *American Psychiatric Press review of psychiatry (Vol. 14).* Washington, DC: American Psychiatric Press.

Braffman, W., & Kirsch, I. (2001). Reaction time as a predictor of imaginative suggestibility and hypnotizability. *Contemporary Hypnosis, 18*(3), 107–119.

Branden, N. (2001). *The psychology of self-esteem: A revolutionary approach to self-understanding that launched a new era in modern psychology.* San Francisco, CA: Jossey-Bass.

Bratko, D., Butkovic, A., & Chamorro-Premuzic, T. (2010). The genetics of general knowledge: A twin study from Croatia. *Personality and Individual Differences, 48*(4), 403–407.

Braun, A. R., Guillemin, A., Hosey, L., & Varga, M. (2001). The neural organization of discourse: An H215o-PET study of narrative production in English and American sign language. *Brain, 124*(10), 2028–2044.

Breedlove, S. M., & Hampson, E. (2002). Sexual differentiation of the brain and behavior. In J. Becker, S. M. Breedlove, D. Crews, & M. McCarthy (Eds.), *Behavioral endocinology 2nd edition* (pp. 75–115). Cambridge, MA: MIT Press.

Breland, K., & Breland, M. (1961). The misbehavior of organisms. *American Psychologist, 16,* 681–684.

Bremner, J. D., & Charney, D. S. (2010). Neural circuits in fear and anxiety. In D. J. Stein, E. Hollander, & B. O. Rothbaum (Eds.), *Textbook of anxiety disorders* (2nd Ed., pp. 55–71). Arlington, VA: American Psychiatric Publishing.

Brenner, C. (1987) Working through: 1914–1984. *The Psychoanalytic Quarterly, 56,* 88–108.

Breslau, N., Roth, T., Burduvali, E., Kapke, A., Schults, L., & Roehrs, T. (2005). Sleep in lifetime posttraumatic stress disorder: A community-based polysomnographic study: Correction. *Archives of General Psychiatry, 62*(2), 172.

Bretherton, I. (1992). The origins of attachment theory: John Bowlby and Mary Ainsworth. *Developmental Psychology, 28,* 759–775.

Brickey, M. (2005). *52 steps to grow young.* Columbus, OH: New Resources Press.

Brislin, R. W., & Keating, C. F. (1976). Cultural differences in the perception of a three-dimensional ponzo illusion. *Journal of Cross-Cultural Psychology, 7,* 397–412.

Broad, K. D., Curley, J. P., & Keverne, E. B. (2006). Mother-infant bonding and the evolution of mammalian social relationships. *Philosophical Transactions of the Royal Society of London, Series B, Biological sciences, 361*(1476), 2199–2214.

Broca, P. P. (1861). Loss of speech, chronic softening and partial destruction of the anterior left lobe of the brain. *Bulletin de la Société Anthropologique, 2,* 235–238.

Brody, L. R. (1999). *Gender, emotion and the family.* Cambridge, MA: Harvard University Press.

Brookmeyer, R., Johnson, E., Ziegler-Graham, K., & Arrighi, H. M. (2007). Forecasting the global burden of Alzheimer's disease. *Alzheimer's and Dementia, 3*(3), 186–191.

Brooks, L., McCabe, P., & Schneiderman, N. (2011). Stress and cardiometabolic syndrome. In R. J. Contrada & A. Baum (Eds.), *The handbook of stress science: Biology, psychology, and health* (pp. 399–409). New York: Springer Publishing Co.

Brosnan, S. F., & De Waal, F. B. (2003). Monkeys reject unequal pay. *Nature, 425,* 297–299.

Brown, A. S. (March 1991). A review of the tip-of-the-tongue experience. *Psychological Bulletin, 109*(2), 204–223.

Brown, A. S. & Susser, E. S. (2002). In utero infection and adult schizophrenia. *Mental Retardation and Developmental Disabilities Research Reviews, 8,* 51–57.

Brown, B. S. (1976). Obstacles to treatment for blue-collar workers. *New dimensions in mental health.* Washington, DC: U.S. Department of Health, Education, and Welfare.

Brown, D. E. (1991). *Human Universals.* New York, NY: McGraw-Hill.

Brown, G. G., & Thompson, W. K. (2010). Functional brain imaging in schizophrenia: Selected results and methods. In N. R. Swerdlow (Ed.), *Behavioral neurobiology of schizophrenia and its treatment* (pp. 181–214). New York: Springer-Verlag Publishing.

Brown, G. W. (2010). Psychosocial origins of depressive and anxiety disorders. In D. Goldberg, K. S. Kendler, & P. J. Sirovatka (Eds.),

Diagnostic issues in depression and generalized anxiety disorder: Refining the research agenda for DSM-V (pp. 303–331). Washington, DC: American Psychiatric Association.

Brown, G. W., & Harris, T. O. (1978). *Social origins of depression: A study of psychiatric disorder in women.* London: Tavistock.

Brown, J. (2006). Björk tops BBC list of the world's most eccentric celebrities, *The Idependent.* Retrieved from http://www.independent.co.uk/news/media/bjoumlrk-tops-bbc-list-of-the-worlds-most-eccentric-celebrities-522245.html.

Brown, L. F., Davis, L. W., LaRocco, V. A., & Strasburger, A. (2010). Participant perspectives on mindfulness meditation training for anxiety in schizophrenia. *American Journal of Psychiatric Rehabilitation, 13*(3), 224–242.

Brown, L. L., Tomarken, A. J., Orth, D. N., Loosen, P. T., Kalin, N. H., & Davidson, R. J. (1996). Individual differences in repressive-defensiveness predict basal salivary cortisol levels. *Journal of Personality and Social Psychology, 70*(2), 362–371.

Brown, L. S. (2011). Client diversity in psychotherapy. In J. C. Norcross, G. R. VandenBos, & D. K. Freedheim (Eds.), *History of psychotherapy: Continuity and change* (2nd Ed., pp. 475–483). Washington, DC: American Psychological Association.

Brown, T. M., & Fee, E. (2003). Sexual behavior in the human male. *American Journal of Public Health, 93*(6).

Brown, W. M., Cronk, L., Grochow, K., Jacobson, A., Liu, C. K., Popović, Z., & Trivers, R. (2005). Dance reveals symmetry especially in young men. *Nature, 438*(7071), 1148–1150.

Brozovich, F. A., & Heimberg, R. G. (2011). A treatment-refractory case of social anxiety disorder: Lessons learned from a failed course of cognitive-behavioral therapy. *Cognitive and Behavioral Practice, 18*(3), 316–325.

Bruckner, H., & Bearman, P. S. (2005). After the Promise: The STD consequences of adolescent virginity pledges. *Journal of Adolescent Health, 36,* 272–278.

Brumbaugh, C. C., & Fraley, R. C. (2006). The evolution of attachment in romantic relationships. In M. Mikulincer, & G. S. Goodman (Eds.), *Dynamics of romantic love: Attachment, caregiving, and sex* (pp. 71–101). New York, NY: Guilford Press.

Bruner, J. (1986). *Actual minds, possible worlds.* Cambridge, MA: Harvard University Press.

Bruner, J. (1983). *Child's talk: Learning to use language.* New York, NY: Norton.

Bryan, W. L., & Harter, N. (1897). Studies in the psychology of the telegraphic language. *Psychological Review, 4,* 27–53.

Bryceland, C., & Stam, H. J. (2005). Empirical validation and professional codes of ethics: Description or prescription? *Journal of Constructivist Psychology, 18,* 131–155.

Buchsbaum, G., & Gottschalk, A. (1983). Trichromacy, opponent colours coding and optimum colour information transmission in the retina. *Proceedings of The Royal Society of London, Series B, Containing Papers of a Biological Character, 220,* 89–113.

Buck, L. B. (1996). Information coding in the vertebrate olfactory system. *Annual Reviews in the Neurosciences, 19,* 517–544.

Buda, R., & Elsayed-Elkhouly, S. M. (1998). Cultural differences between Arabs and Americans: Individualism-collectivism revisited. *Journal of Cross-Cultural Psychology, 29,* 487–492.

Buhlmann, U., Glaesmer, H., Mewes, R., Fama, J. M., Wilhelm, S., Brahler, E., & Rief, W. (2010). Updates on the prevalence of body dysmorphic disorder: A population-based survey. *Psychiatry Research, 178*(1), 171–175.

Buhrich, N., Bailey, M. J., & Martin, N. G. (1991). Sexual orientation, sexual identity, and sex-dimorphic behaviors in male twins. *Behavior Genetics, 21*(1), 75–96.

Bull, J. J. (1983). *Evolution of sex determining mechanisms.* Menlo Park, California: Benjamin/ Cummings Pub. Co., Advanced Book Program.

Bullough, V. L. (2004). Sex will never be the same: The contributions of Alfred C. Kinsey *Archives of Sexual Behavior, 33*(3), 277–286.

Bunney, W. E., & Davis, J. M. (1965). Norepinephrine in depressive reactions: A review. *Archives of General Psychiatry, 13*(6), 483–493.

Burg, M. M., & Pickering, T. G. (2011). The cardiovascular system. In R. J. Contrada & A. Baum (Eds.), *The handbook of stress science: Biology, psychology, and health* (pp. 37–45). New York: Springer Publishing Co.

Burg, M. M., Soufer, A., Lampert, R., Collins, D., & Soufer, R. (2011). Autonomic contribution to endothelin-1 increase during laboratory anger-recall stress in patients with coronary artery disease. *Molecular Medicine (Cambridge, Mass.), 17*(5–6), 495–501.

Burger King. (2009). Burger King USA Nutritionals. Retrieved from http://www.bk.com/Nutrition/PDFs/NutritionalBrochure.pdf.

Burger, J. M. (2008). Replicating Milgram: Would people still obey today? *American Psychologist, 64*(1), 20–27.

Burgess, J. L. (2001). Phosphine exposure from a methamphetamine laboratory investigation. *Journal of Toxicology and Clinical Toxicology, 39,* 165.

Burijon, B. N. (2007). *Biological bases of clinical anxiety.* New York, NY: W. W. Norton & Company.

Burlingame, G. M., & Baldwin, S. (2011). Group therapy. In J. C. Norcross, G. R. VandenBos, & D. K. Freedheim (Eds.), *History of psychotherapy: Continuity and change* (2nd Ed., pp. 505–515). Washington, DC: American Psychological Association.

Burns, T., & Drake, B. (2011). Mental health services for patients with schizophrenia. In D. R. Weinberger & P. J. Harrison (Eds.), *Schizophrenia* (3rd Ed.). Hoboken, NJ: Blackwell-Wiley.

Busatto, G. F., Zanetti, M. V., Schaufelberger, M. S., & Crippa, J. A. S. (2010). Brain anatomical abnormalities in schizophrenia: Neurodevelopmental origins and patterns of progression over time. In W. F. Gattaz & G. Busatto (Eds.), *Advances in schizophrenia research 2009* (pp. 113–148). New York: Springer Science + Business Media.

Bush, G., Valera, E. M., & Seidman, L. J. (2005). Functional neuroimaging of attention-deficit/hyperactivity disorder: a review and suggested future directions. *Biological Psychiatry, 57,* 1273–1284.

Bushman, B. J., Baumeister, R. F., & Stack, A. D. (1999). Catharsis, aggression, and persuasive influence: Self-fulfilling or self-defeating prophecies? *Journal of Personality and Social Psychology, 76*(3), 367–376.

Bushman, B. J., & Cooper, H. M. (1990). Effects of alcohol on human aggression: An integrative research review. *Psychological Bulletin, 107*(3), 341–354.

Bushnik, T. (2003). Learning, earning and leaving: The relationship between working while in high school and dropping out. *Education, skills and learning - Research papers.* Statistics Canada Catalogue no. 81-595-MIE, No. 4.

Buss, D. M. (2009). The great struggles of life: Darwin and the emergence of evolutionary psychology. *American Psychologist, 64*(2), 140–148.

Buss, D. M. (Ed.) (2005). *The handbook of evolutionary psychology.* Hoboken, NJ: John Wiley & Sons.

Buss, D. M. (1999). Evolutionary psychology: The new science of the mind. Boston, MA: Allyn & Bacon.

Bussey, K., & Bandura, A. (1999). Social cognitive theory of gender development and differentiation. *Psychological Review, 106,* 676–713.

Butcher, J. N. (2011). *A beginner's guide to the MMPI-2 (3rd Ed.)* Washington, DC: American Psychological Association.

Butcher, J. N. (2010). Personality assessment from the nineteenth to the early twenty-first century: Past achievements and contemporary challenges. *Annual Review of Clinical Psychology, 6,* 1–20.

Butler, A. C., Chapman, J. E., Forman, E. M., & Beck, A. T. (2006). The empirical status of cognitive-behavioral therapy: a review of meta-analyses. *Clinical Psychological Review, 26* (1), 17–31.

Butler, C. (2011). Meditation and mindfulness may give your brain a boost. *The Washington Post, 134*(72).

Butler, E. A., Egloff, B., Wilhelm, F. H., Smith, N. C., Erickson, E. A., & Gross, J. J. (2003). The social consequences of expressive suppression. *Emotion, 3*(1), 48–67.

Butler, J. L., & Baumeister, R. F. (1998). The trouble with friendly faces: Skilled performance with a supportive audience. *Journal of Personality and Social Psychology, 75*(5), 1213–1230.

Butterworth, B. (2010). Foundational numerical capacities and the origins of dyscalculia. *Trends in Cognitive Sciences, 14*(12), 534–541.

Butterworth, B, Varma S, & Laurillard D. (2011). Dyscalculia: from brain to education. *Science, 332*(6033), 1049–1053.

Byers, E. S., Purdon, C., & Clark, D. A. (1998). Sexual intrusive thoughts of college students. *Journal of Sex Research, 35,* 359–369.

Byrne, D. (1971). *The attraction paradigm.* New York, NY: Academic Press.

Byrne, D., Ervin, C., & Lamberth, J. (1970). Continuity between the experimental study of attraction and real-life computer dating. *Journal of Personality and Social Psychology, 16,* 157–165.

Byrne, D., London, O., & Reeves, K. (1968). The effects of physical attractiveness, sex, and attitude similarity on interpersonal attraction. *Journal of Personality, 36,* 259–271.

Cacioppo, J. T., & Berntson, G. G. (1994). Relationship between attitudes and evaluative space: A critical review, with emphasis on the separability of positive and negative substrates. *Psychological Bulletin, 115*(3), 401–423.

Cahill, L., Prins, B., Weber, M., & McGaugh, J. L. (1994). Beta-adrenergic activation and memory for emotional events. *Nature, 371*(6499), 702–704.

Cahn, C. (2006). Obituary: Roland Kuhn, 1912–2005. *Neuropsychopharmacology, 31,* 1096.

Cain, C. K., & LeDoux, J. E. (2008). Emotional processing and motivation: In search of brain mechanisms. In A. J. Elliot (Ed.), *Handbook of approach and avoidance motivation* (pp. 17–34). New York, NY: Psychology Press.

Cain, D. J. (2007). What every therapist should know, be and do: Contributions from humanistic psychotherapies. *Journal of Contemporary Psychotherapy, 37*(1), 3–10.

Cain, N., Davidson, P., Dosen, A., Garcia-Ibañez, J., Giesow, V., Hillery, J., & Torr, J. (2010). An international perspective of mental health services for people with intellectual disability. In N. Bouras & G. Holt (Eds.), *Mental health services for adults with intellectual disability: Strategies and solutions* (pp. 37–53). New York: Psychology Press.

Calder, A. J., Beaver, J. D., Davis, M. H., van Ditzhuijzen, J., Keane, J., & Lawrence, A. D. (2007). Disgust sensitivity predicts the insula and pallidal response to pictures of disgusting foods. *The European Journal of Neuroscience, 25,* 3422–3428.

Caley, L., Syms, C., Robinson, L., Cederbaum, J., Henry, M. Shipkey, N. (2008). What human service prossions know and want to know about fetal alcohol syndrome. *Canadian Journal of Clinical Pharmacology, 15,* e117–e123.

Calogero, R. M., Tantleff-Dunn, S., and Thompson, J. K. (Eds.). (2011). *Self-objectification in women: Causes, consequences, and counteractions.* Washington, DC: American Psychological Association.

Cameron, A., Rosen, R. C., & Swindle, R. W. (2005). Sexual and relationship characteristics among an internet-based sample of U.S. men with and without erectile dysfunction. *Journal of Sex & Marital Therapy, 31*(3), 229–242.

Cameron, H. A., & McKay, R. D. (2001). Adult neurogenesis produces a large pool of new granule cells in the dentate gyrus. *Journal of Comparative Neurology, 435,* 406–417.

Campos, J. J., Campos, R. G., & Barrett, K. C. (1989). Emergent themes in the study of emotional development and emotion regulation. *Developmental Psychology, 25*(3), 394–402.

Canadian Automobile Association. (July, 2011). *Bad driving habits on the rise.* Retrieved from http://www.caa.ca/newsroom/newsroom-releases-details-e.cfm?newsItem=50&yearToShow=2011.

Canadian Council on Animal Care. (1989). *Ethics of animal investigation.* Retrieved from C:\Users\MCB\Documents\Comer - Wiley Project\Chapter 2\CCAC Programs-Guidelines-CCAC Policy Statements-Ethics of Animal Investigation.mht.

Canadian Council on Social Development. (2001). *A profile of Canadian families.* Retrieved from http://www.ccsd.ca/factsheets/family/families.pdf.

Canadian Education Statistics Council. (2007). *Education indicators in Canada: Report of the Pan-Canadian Education Indicators Program.* Catalogue no. 81-582-XPE. Retrieved from http://www.statcan.gc.ca/pub/81-582-x/81-582-x2007001-eng.htm.

Canadian Human Rights Commission. (2010). *Equal pay for work of equal value: Employers' guide.* Retrieved from http://www.chrc-ccdp.ca/publications/employers_responsibility-eng.aspx.

Canadian Institute for Health Information. (2008). *Hospital mental health services in Canada, 2005–2006.* Ottawa.

Canadian Institutes of Health Research, Natural Sciences and Engineering Research Council of Canada, Social Sciences and Humanities Research Council of Canada. (1998; with 2000, 2002 and 2005 amendments). *Tri-council policy statement: Ethical conduct for research involving humans.* Retrieved from http://www.pre.ethics.gc.ca/english/policystatement/introduction.cfm.

Canadian Labour Congress. (2007). *Women in the workforce: Still a long way to go.* Retrieved from http://www.chrc-ccdp.ca/publications/employers_responsibility-eng.aspx.

Canadian Mental Health Association. (2005). *Physical and mental health equally important to Canadians.* Retrieved from http://www.cmha.ca/bins/content_page.asp?cid=6-20-21-386.

Canadian Psychological Association. (2000). *Canadian code of ethics for psychologists.* CPA, Ottawa.

Canadian Public Health Association: Assessment toolkit for Bullying. (2004). *Harassment and peer relations at school: Definitions – Bullying.* Retrieved from http://www.cpha.ca/uploads/progs/_/safeschools/assessment_toolkit_e.pdf.

Canadian Study of Health and Aging Working Group. (2000). The incidence of dementia in Canada. *Neurology, 55*(1), 66–73.

Canadian Wireless and Telecommunications Association. (2010). *New web site will help teach teens to practice safe texting.* Retrieved from http://cwta.ca/CWTASite/english/whatsnew_download/nov19_10.html.

Canivez, G. L., & Watkins, M. W. (2010). Exploratory and higher-order factor analyses of the Wechsler adult intelligence scale-fourth edition (WAIS-IV) adolescent subsample. *School Psychology Quarterly, 25*(4), 223–235.

Cannon, W B. (1932). *Effects of strong emotions.* Oxford: Univ. Chicago Press.

Cannon, W B. (1929). *Bodily changes in pain, hunger, fear, and rage,* Vol. 2. New York, NY: Applet on.

Cannon, W. B. (1927). The James-Lange theory of emotions: A critical examination and an alternative theory. *The American Journal of Psychology, 39*(1), 106–124.

Cardemil, E. V., Moreno, O., & Sanchez, M. (2011). One size does not fit all: Cultural considerations in evidence-based practice for depression. In W. David, A. Rubin, C. G. Beevers (Eds.), *Treatment of depression in adolescents and adults* (pp. 221–243). John Wiley and Sons.

Cardena, E., & Gleaves, D. H. (2007). Dissociative disorders. In M. Hersen, S. M. Turner, & D. C. Beidel (Eds.), *Adult psychopathology and diagnosis (5th Ed.).* Hoboken, NJ: John Wiley & Sons Inc.

Cardilla, K. (2008). Personality vulnerabilities, coping, and depression: A multi-method daily diary study of college students' coping with daily hassles. US: ProQuest Information & Learning). *Dissertation Abstracts International: Section B: The Sciences and Engineering, 69*(5), 3294.

Cardoso, R., Souza, E., & Camano, L. (2009). Meditation in health: Definition, operationalization, and technique. *Stress and quality of working life: The positive and the negative* (pp. 143–166). Charlotte, NC: Information Age Publishing.

Carels, R. A., Cacciapaglia, H. M., Rydin, S., Douglass, O. M., & Harper, J. (2006). Can social desirability interfere with success in a behavioral weight loss program? *Psychology & Health, 21*(1), 65–78.

Carey, B. (2009). The afterlife of near-death. *The New York Times, 158*(54), 559.

Carlezon, W. A., Jr., & Thomas, M. J. (2009). Biological substrates of reward and aversion: A nucleus accumbens activity hypothesis. *Neuropharmacology, 56* (Suppl.1), 122–132.

Carlson, N. R. (2009). *Physiology of Behavior (10th Ed).* New York: Pearson Education Inc.

Carlson, N. R. (2008). Foundations of physiological psychology (7th edition). Boston MA: Pearson.

Carlsson, A. & Lindqvist, M. (1963). Effect of chlorpromazine o haloperidol on formation of 3-methoxytyramine and normetanephrine in mouse brain. *Acta Pharmcol Toxicol (Copenh), 20,* 140–144.

Carpendale, J. I. M., & Lewis, C. (2010). The development of social understanding: A relational perspective. In W. F. Overton & R. M. Lerner (Eds.), *The handbook of life-span development,* vol. 1: *Cognition, biology, and methods* (pp. 584–627). Hoboken, NJ: John Wiley.

Carr, V. S. (2000). Stress effects of earthquakes. In G. Fink (Ed.), *Encyclopedia of stress, Vol. 2* (1–4). New York, NY: Academic Press.

Carré, J. M., Putnam, S. K., & McCormick, C. M. (2009). Testosterone responses to competition predict future aggressive behaviour at a cost to reward in men. *Psychoneuroendocrinology, 34*(4), 561–570.

Carroll, R. A. (2007). Gender dysphoria and transgender experiences. In S. R. Leiblum (Ed.), *Principles and practice of sex therapy (4th Ed.)* (pp. 477–508). New York, NY: Guilford Press.

Carskadon, M. A. (Ed.). (2002). *Adolescent sleep patterns: Biological, social and psychological influences*. New York, NY: Cambridge University Press.

Carson, R. C., Butcher, J. N., & Mineka, S. (2000). *Abnormal psychology and modern life* (11th Edition). Boston: Allyn & Bacon.

Carter, C. (2010). *Science and the near-death experience: How consciousness survives death.* Rochester, VT: Inner Traditions International.

Carter, C. S., Botvinick, M. M., & Cohen, J.D. (1999). The contribution of the anterior cingulate cortex to executive processes in cognition. *Nature Reviews Neuroscience, 10*, 49–57.

Cartwright, R. D. (2010). The twenty-four hour mind: The role of sleep and dreaming in our emotional lives. New York, NY: Oxford University Press.

Carver, C. S. (2004). Self-regulation of action and affect. In R. F. Baumeister & K. D. Vohs (Eds.), *Handbook of self-regulation: Research, theory, and applications* (pp. 13–39). New York, NY: Guilford Press.

Carver, C. S., & Scheier, M. (2003). Optimism. *Positive psychological assessment: A handbook of models and measures* (pp. 75–89). Washington, DC: American Psychological Association. doi:10.1037/ 10612–005.

Carver, C. S., & Scheier, M. (1999). Optimism. In C. R. Snyder (Ed.), *Coping: The psychology of what works.* New York, NY: Oxford University Press.

Carver, C. S., & Scheier, M. F. (1998). *On the self-regulation of behavior*. New York, NY: Cambridge University Press.

Carver, C. S., & Scheier, M. F. (1994). Situational coping and coping dispositions in a stressful transaction. *Journal of Personality and Social Psychology, 66*(1), 184–195.

Cashel, M. L. (2002). Child and adolescent psychological assessment: Current clinical practices and the impact of managed care. *Professional Psychology: Research and Practice, 33*(5), 446–453.

Caspi, A. (2002). Social selection, social causation, and developmental pathways: Empirical strategies for better understanding how individuals and environments are linked across the life course. In L. Pulkkinen & A. Caspi (Eds.), *Paths to Successful Development; Personality in the Life Course* (pp. 281–301). Cambridge, UK: Cambridge University Press.

Caspi, A. (1998). Personality development across the life course. In W. Damon & N. Eisenberg (Eds.), *Handbook of child psychology: Vol. 3, Social emotional, and personality development* (5th Ed., pp. 311–388). New York, NY: John Wiley & Sons, Inc.

Caspi, A., & Roberts, B. W. (1999). Personality change and continuity across the life course. In L. A. Pervin & O. P. John, *Handbook of Personality Theory and Research* (Vol. 2, pp. 300–326). New York, NY: Guilford Press.

Caspi, A., Bem, D. J., & Elder, G. H., Jr. (1989). Continuities and consequence of interactional styles across the life course. *Journal of Personality, 57*, 375–406.

Castejon, J. L., Perez, A. M., & Gilar, R. (2010). Confirmatory factor analysis of project spectrum activities: A second-order g factor or multiple intelligences? *Intelligence, 38*(5), 481–496.

Catalyst. (2000). Census of women corporate officers and top earners. New York, NY: Catalyst.

Catrambone, R. (1998). The subgoal learning model: creating better examples so that students can solve novel problems. *Journal of Experimental Psychology: General, 127*, 355–376.

Cavallini, E., Pagnin, A., & Vecchi, T. (2003). Aging and everyday memory: The beneficial effect of memory training. *Archives of Gerontology and Geriatrics, 37*(3), 241–257.

Cavendish, M. (2010). *Sex and society*. Tarrytown, NY: Marshal Cavendish Reference.

Cavior, N., & Dokecki, P. R. (1971). Physical attractiveness of self concept: A test of mead's hypothesis. *Proceedings of the Annual Convention of the American Psychological Association, 6*, 319–320.

Cavior, N., & Dokecki, P. R. (1970). *Physical attractiveness and interpersonal attraction among fifth grade boys: A replication with Mexican children.* Paper presented at the meeting of the Southwestern Psychological Association: St. Louis, Mo.

Cawthon, R. M., Smith, K. R., O'Brien, E., Sivatchenko A., & Kerber, R. A. (2003). Association between telomere length in blood and morality in people aged 60 years or older. *Lancet, 361*, 393–395.

CDC (Centers for Disease Control and Prevention). 2010. Listeriosis (Listeria) and pregnancy. *Pregnancy.* Retrieved from http://www.cdc.gov/ncbdd/pregancy_gateway//infections-listeria.html.

Ceci, S. J. (2003). Cast in six ponds and you'll reel in something: Looking back on 25 years ofresearch. *American Psychologist, 58*(11), 855–864.

Ceci, S. J. (1991). How much does schooling influence general intelligence and its cognitive components? A reassessment of the evidence. *Developmental Psychology, 27*(5), 703–722.

Ceci, S. J., & Kanaya, T. (2010). "Apples and oranges are both round": Furthering the discussion on the Flynn effect. *Journal of Psychoeducational Assessment, 28*(5), 441–447.

Ceci, S. J., & Liker, J. (1986). A day at the races: A study of IQ, expertise, and cognitive complexity. *Journal of Experimental Psychology, 115*, 255–266.

Ceci, S. J., & Williams, W. M. (2010). The mathematics of sex: How biology and society conspire to limit talented women and girls. New York: Oxford University Press.

Ceci, S. J., & Williams, W M. (2007). Little g: Prospects and constraints. *European Journal of Personality, 21(5)*, 716–718.

Ceci, S. J., & Williams, W. M. (1997). Schooling, intelligence, and income. *American Psychologist, 52*(10), 1051–1058.

Ceci, S. J., Fitneva, S. A., & Gilstrap, L. L. (2003). Memory development and eyewitness testimony. In A. Slater & G. Bremner (Eds.), *An introduction to developmental psychology* (pp. 283–310) Malden, MA: Blackwell Publishing.

Cenci, M. A. (2007). Dopamine dysregulation of movement control in L-DOPA-induced dyskinesia. *Trends in Neurosciences, 30*, 236–243.

Centers for Disease Control and Prevention (CDC). (2009). *Health, United States, 2008*, Table 75. Retrieved from: http://www.cdc.gov/nchs/data/hus/hus08.pdf#075.

Centers for Disease Control and Prevention (CDC). (2008). *Sexually transmitted disease surveillance, 2007.* Atlanta, GA: U.S. Department of Health and Human Services.

Centers for Disease Control and Prevention (CDC). (2001). *Young people at risk: HIV/AIDS among America's youth*. Retrieved from: www.cdc.gov/hiv/pubs/facts/youth.pdf.

Centre for Addiction and Mental Health. (2004). *Canadian campus survey*. Retrieved from http://www.camh.net/Research/Areas_of_research/Population_Life_Course_Studies/canadian_campus0905.pdf.

Certner, B. C. (1973). Exchange of self-disclosures in same-sexed groups of strangers. *Journal of Consulting and Clinical Psychology, 40*, 292–297.

Cetas, J. S., Saedi, T., & Burchiel, K. J. (2008). Destructive procedures for the treatment of nonmalignant pain: A structured literature review. *Journal of Neurosurgery, 109*, 389–404.

Chaiken, S. (1980). Heuristic versus systematic information processing and the use of source versus message cues in persuasion. *Journal of Personality and Social Psychology, 39*, 752–756.

Challis, G. B., & Stam, H. J. (1002). A longitudinal study of the development of anticipatory nausea and vomiting in cancer chemotherapy patients: The role of absorption and autonomic perception. *Health Psychology, 11*, 181–189.

Chan, B. L., Witt, R., Charrow, A. P., Magee, A., Howard, R., Pasquina, P. (2007). Mirror therapy for phantom limb pain. *New England Journal of Medicine, 357*, 2206–2207.

Chan, S. M. (2010). Aggressive behavior in early elementary school children: Relations to authoritarian parenting, children's negative emotionality and coping strategies. *Early Child Development and Care, 180*(9), 1253–1269.

Chan, S. W., & Blackburn, E. H. (2002). New ways not to make ends meet: telomerase, DNA damage proteins and heterochromatin. *Oncogene, 21*, 553–563.

Chandler, M. J., & Carpendale, J. I. (1998). Inching toward a mature theory of mind. In M. D. Ferrari & R. J. Sternberg (Eds.), *Self-awareness: Its nature and development* (pp. 148–190). New York, NY: Guilford Press.

Chandler, M. J. & Lalonde, C. E. (2008). Cultural continuity as a moderator of suicide risk among Canada's first nations. In L. J. Kirmayer & G. G. Valaskakis (Eds), *Healing traditions: The mental health of aboriginal peoples in Canada*. Vancouver, BC: UBC Press.

Chandler, M. J., Lalonde, C. E., Sokol, B., & Hallett, D. (2003). *Personal persistence, identity development, and suicide: A study of native and non-native north American adolescents. Monographs of the Society for Research in Child Development*, *68*(2), No. 273.

Chang, E. C. (2002). Optimism-pessimism and stress appraisal: Testing a cognitive interactive model of psychological adjustment in adults. *Cognitive Therapy and Research, 26*(5), 675–690.

Chang, R., Chang, E. C., Sanna, L. J., & Hatcher, R. L. (2008). Optimism and pessimism as personality variables linked to adjustment. *The SAGE handbook of personality theory and assessment, vol 1: Personality theories and models* (pp. 470–485). Thousand Oaks, CA: Sage Publications, Inc.

Changeux, J. (2011). The epigenetic variability of memory: Brain plasticity and artistic creation. In S. Nalbantian, P. M. Matthews & J. L. McClelland (Eds.), *The memory process: Neuroscientific and humanistic perspectives* (pp. 55–72) Cambridge, MA: MIT Press.

Chansonneuve, D. (2007). Addictive behaviours among aboriginal people in Canada. *The Aboriginal Healing Foundation*. Retrieved from http://www.ahf.ca/downloads/addictive-behaviours.pdf.

Chao, R. (2001). Extending research on the consequences of parenting style for Chinese Americans and European Americans. *Child Development, 2*, 1832–1843.

Chapman, A. L., Leung, D. W., & Lynch, T. R. (2008). Impulsivity and emotion dysregulation in borderline personality disorder. *Journal of Personality Disorders, 22*(2), 148–164.

Charles, E. P., & Rivera, S. M. (2009). Object permanence and method of disappearance: Looking measures further contradict reaching measures. *Developmental Science, 12*(6), 991–1006.

Charles, S. T., & Piazza, J. R. (2007). Memories of social interactions: Age differences in emotional intensity. *Psychology and Aging, 22*(2), 300–309.

Charuvastra, A., & Cloitre, M. (2008). Social bonds and posttraumatic stress disorder. In S. Fiske, D. L. Schacter, & R. Sternberg (Eds.), *Annual review of psychology (Vol. 59)*. Palo Alto, CA: Annual reviews.

Chein, J. M., Moore, A. B., & Conway, A. R. A. (2011). Domain-general mechanisms of complex working memory span. *NeuroImage, 54*(1), 550–559. doi: 10.1016/j.neuroimage.2010.07.067

Chekroun, P., & Brauer, M. (2002). The bystander effect and social control behavior: The effect of the presence of others on people's reactions to norm violations. *European Journal of Social Psychology, 32*(6), 853–866.

Chelli, D., & Chanoufi, B. (2008). Fetal audition: Myth or reality? *Journal de gynecologie, obstetrique et biologie de la reproduction, 37*(6), 554–558.

Chen, G., Zou, X., Watanabe, H., van Deursen, J. M., & Shen, J. (2010). CREB binding protein is required for both short-term and long-term memory formation. *The Journal of Neuroscience, 30*(39), 13066–13077. doi: 10.1523/JNEUROSCI.2378-10.2010.

Chen, X., Rubin, K. H., Cen, G., Hastings, P.D., Chen, H., and Stewart, S. (1999). In M. E. Hertzig and E.A. Farber (Eds), *Progress in child psychiatry and child development 1999*. Taylor and Francis.

Chen, Y. R., Swann, A. C., & Burt, D. B. (1996). Stability of diagnosis in schizophrenia. *American Journal of Psychiatry, 153*(5), 682–686.

Cherniss, C. (2010). Emotional intelligence: Toward clarification of a concept. *Industrial and Organizational Psychology: Perspectives on Science and Practice, 3*(2), 110–126.

Chess, S., & Thomas, A. (1996). *Temperament: Theory and practice*. New York: Brunner-Mazel.

Cheung, A. (2007). *Education decisions of Canadian youth: A synthesis report on access to postsecondary education*. Prepared for The Higher Education Quality Council Of Ontario. Retrieved from https://ospace.scholarsportal.info/bitstream/1873/9175/1/276409.pdf.

Chidambaram, L., & Tung, L. L. (2005). Is out of sight, out of mind? An empirical study of social loafing in technology-supported groups. *Information Systems Research, 16*(2), 149–168.

Childress, A. R., Ehrman, R. N., Wang, Z., Li, Y., Sciortino, N., Hakun, J., et al. (2008). Prelude to passion: Limbic activation by "unseen" drug and sexual cues. *PLoS ONE, 3*(1), e1506.

Chin, J. H., Ma, L., MacTavish, D., & Jhamandas, J. H. (2007). Amyloid beta protein modulates glutamate-mediated neurotransmission in the rat basal forebrain: Involvement of presynaptic neuronal nicotinic acetylcholine and metabotropic glutamate receptors. *Journal of Neuroscience, 27*(35), 9262–9269.

Chisholm, K., Carter, M. C., Ames, E. W., & Morison, S. J. (1995). Attachment security and indiscriminately friendly behavior in children adopted from Romanian orphanages. *Development and Psychopathology, 7*(2), 283–294.

Choi, Y. Y., Shamosh, N. A., Cho, S. H., DeYoung, C. G., Lee, M. J., Lee, J., et al. (2008). Multiple bases of human intelligence revealed by cortical thickness and neural activation. *Journal of Neuroscience, 28*(41), 10323–10329.

Chomsky, N. (2005). Editorial: Universals of human nature. *Psychotherapy and Psychosomatics, 74*(5), 263–268.

Chomsky, N. (1964). The development of grammar in child language: Formal discussion. *Monographs of the Society for Research in Child Development, 29*, 35–39.

Chomsky, N. (1959). A review of B. F. Skinner's verbal behavior. *Language, 35*, 26–58.

Choy, A., & Mamak, M. (in press). The Psychiatrist and Psychologist as Consultant to Law Enforcement. In H. Bloom, The Hon. Mr. Justice R. Schneider, & S. Hucker, S. (Eds.), *Psychiatry and the law in Canada*. Centre for Addiction and Mental Health & Irwin Law.

Christakis, N. A., & Fowler, J. H. (2007). The spread of obesity in a large social network over 32 years. *New England Journal of Medicine*, 357, 370–379.

Christensen, A., Atkins, D. C., Baucom, B., & Yi, J. (2010). Marital status and satisfaction five years following a randomized clinical trial comparing traditional versus integrative behavioral couple therapy. *Journal of Consulting and Clinical Psychology, 78*(2), 225–235.

Christman, S. D., & Propper, R. E. (2010). Episodic memory and interhemispheric interaction: Handedness and eye movements. In G. M. Davies, & D. B. Wright (Eds.), *Current issues in applied memory research* (pp. 185–205). New York, NY, US: Psychology Press.

Christophe, V., & Rimé, B. (2001). Exposure to the social sharing of emotion: Emotional impact, listener responses and secondary social sharing. In W. G. Parrott (Ed.), *Emotions in social psychology: Essential readings* (pp. 239–250). New York, NY: Psychology Press.

Christophe, V., & Rimé, B. (1997). Exposure to the social sharing of emotion: Emotional impact, listener responses and secondary social sharing. *European Journal of Social Psychology, 27*(1), 37–54.

Christou, N. V., Look, D., & Maclean, L. D. (2006). Weight gain after short- and long-limb gastric bypass in patients followed for longer than 10 years. *Annals of Surgery, 244*(5), 734–740.

Chudler, E. H. (2011). *Milestones in neuroscience research*. Retrieved from http://faculty.washington.edu/chudler/hist.html.

Chung, M. C., Dennis, I., Easthope, Y., Werrett, J., & Farmer, S. (2005). A multiple-indicator multiple-case model for posttraumatic stress reactions: Personality, coping, and maladjustment. *Psychosomatic Medicine, 67*(2), 251–259.

Church, A. T., & Katigbak, M. S. (2000). Trait psychology in the Philippines. *American Behavioral Scientist, 44*, 73–94.

Chwalisz, K., Diener, E., & Gallagher, D. (1988). Autonomic arousal feedback and emotional experience: Evidence from the spinal cord injured. *Journal of Personality and Social Psychology, 54*, 820–828.

Cialdini, R. B., Kallgren, C. A., & Reno, R. R. (1991). A focus theory of normative conduct: A theoretical refinement and reevaluation of the role of norms in human behavior. In M. P. Zanna (Ed.), *Advances in Experimental Social Psychology (Vol. 24)* (pp. 201–234). New York: Academic Press.

Cicchetti, D. (2010). A developmental psychopathology perspective on bipolar disorder. In D. J. Miklowitz & D. Cicchetti (Eds.), *Understanding bipolar disorder: A developmental psychopathology perspective* (pp. 1–32). New York: Guilford Press.

Cicchetti, D., & Rogosch, F. A. (1996). Equifinality and multifinality in developmental psychopathology *Development and Psychopathology, 8*(4), 597–600.

Cicchetti, D., Ganiban, J., & Barnett, D. (1991). Contributions from the study of high-risk populations to understanding the development of emotion regulation. In J. Garber & K. A. Dodge (Eds.), *The development of emotion regulation and dysregulation* (pp. 15–48). New York, NY: Cambridge University Press.

Clanton H. E. (2011). *Group-centered prevention programs for at-risk students*. New York: Springer Science + Business Media.

Clark, D. A., & Beck, A. T. (2010). *Cognitive therapy of anxiety disorders: Science and practice* New York: Guilford Press.

Clark, D. M. (1986). A cognitive approach to panic. *Behaviour Research and Therapy, 24*(4), 461–470.

Clark, D. M., & Wells, A. (1995). A cognitive model of social phobia. In R. G. Heimberg, M. R. Liebowitz, D. A. Hope, & F. R. Schneier (Eds.), *Social phobia: Diagnosis, assessment, and treatment* (pp. 69–93). New York: Guilford Press.

Clark, J. J. (2010). Life as a source of theory: Erik Erikson's contributions, boundaries, and marginalities. In T. W. Miller (Ed.), *Handbook of stressful transitions across the lifespan* (pp. 59–83). New York: Springer Science + Business Media.

Clark, L., & Watson, D. (1999). Temperament: A new paradigm for trait psychology. In L. A. Pervin & O. P. John (Eds.), *Handbook of Personality* (2nd. Ed., pp. 399–423). New York, NY: Guilford Press.

Clark, M. S., & Taraban, C. (1991). Reactions to and willingness to express emotion in communal and exchange relationships. *Experimental Social Psychology, 27*(4), 324–336.

Clark, R. E., Broadbent, N. J., & Squire, L. R. (2008). The hippocampus and spatial memory: Findings with a novel modification of the water maze. *Journal of Neuroscience, 27*(25), 6647–6654.

Cleckley, H. (1941). The mask of sanity; an attempt to reinterpret the so-called psychopathic personality. St. Louis, MO: Mosby

Cleland, R., Graybill, D., Hubbard, V., Khan, L., Stern, J., Wadden, T., Weinsier, R., & Yanovski, S. (1997). Commercial weight loss products and programs: What consumers stand to gain and lose. *Public Conference on the Information Consumers Need to Evaluate Weight Loss Products and Programs.* Retrieved from http://www.ftc.gov/os/1998/03/weightlo.rpt.htm#1.%20Consumers%20Are%20Not.

Clément, M-E., & Chamberland, C. (2007). Physical violence and psychological aggression towards children: Five-year trends in practices and attitudes from two population surveys. *Child Abuse and Neglect, 31*(9), 1001–1011.

Clements, A. M., Rimrodt, S. L., Abel, J. R., Blankner, J. G., Mostofsky, S. H., Pekar, J. J., Denckla, M. B., & Cutting, L. E. (2006). Sex differences in cerebral laterality of language and visuospatial processing. *Brain Language, 98,* 150–158.

Clements, C. M., & Sawhney, D. K. (2000). Coping with domestic violence: Control attributions, dysphoria, and hopelessness. *Journal of Traumatic Stress, 13,* 219–240.

Cobb, M. D. (2002). Unobtrusively measuring racial attitudes: The consequences of social desirability effects. ProQuest Information & Learning: US. *Dissertation Abstracts International Section A: Humanities and Social Sciences, 62*(8), 2869.

Cochran, W. G., Mosteller, F., & Tukey, J. W. (1953). Some statistical problems of the Kinsey Report. *Journal of the American Statistical Association, 48,* 673–716.

Coddington, R. D. (1984). Measuring the stressfulness of a child's environment. In J. H. Humphrey (Ed.), *Stress in Childhood.* New York, NY: AMS Press.

Coddington, R. D. (1972). The significance of life events as etiologic factors in the disease of children, II: A study of a normal population. *Journal of Psychosomatic Research, 16,* 205–213.

Code, C., Hemsley, G., & Herrmann, M. (1999). The emotional impact of aphasia. *Seminars in Speech and Language, 20*(1), 19–31.

Cohen, J. (1992). A power primer. *Psychological Bulletin, 112*(1), 155–159. doi:10.1037/0033-2909.112.1.155

Cohen, R. (1987). Suddenly, I'm the adult. *Psychology Today, 21* (May), 70–71.

Cohen, S. (2005). Psychological stress, immunity and upper respiratory infections. In G. Miller & E. Chen (Eds.), *Current directions in health psychology.* Upper Saddle River, NJ: Pearson.

Cohen, S. (2004). Social relationships and health. *American Psychologist, 59*(8), 676–684.

Cohen, S. (2002). Psychosocial stress, social networks, and susceptibility to infection. In H. G. Koenig & H. J. Cohen (Eds.), *The link between religion and health: Psychoneuroimmunology and the faith factor* (pp. 101–123). New York, NY: Oxford University Press.

Cohen, S., & Hamrick, N. (2003). Stable individual differences in physiological response to stressors: Implications for stress-elicited changes in immune related health. *Brain, Behavior, and Immunity, 17*(6), 407–414.

Cohen, S., & Janicki-Deverts, D. (2009). Can we improve our physical health by altering our social networks? *Perspectives on Psychological Science, 4*(4), 375–378.

Cohen, S., & Wills, T. A. (1985). Stress, social support, and the buffering hypothesis. *Psychological Bulletin, 98*(2), 310–357.

Cohen, S., Alper, C. M., Doyle, W J., Adler, N., Treanor, J. J., & Turner, R. B. (2008). Objective and subjective socioeconomic status and susceptibility to the common cold. *Health Psychology, 27(2),* 268–274.

Cohen, S., Doyle, W. J., Turner, R. B., Alper, C. M., & Skoner, D. P. (2003). Emotional style and susceptibility to the common cold. *Psychosomatic Medicine, 65,* 652–657.

Cohen, S., Tyrell, D. A. J., & Smith, A. P. (1991). Psychological stress and susceptibility to the common cold. *The New England Journal of Medicine, 325,* 606–612.

Cohen-Kettenis, P. (2001). Gender identity disorder in DSM? *Journal of the American Academy of Child & Adolescent Psychiatry, 40*(4), 391.

Cohn, J. F., Ambadar, Z., & Ekman, P. (2007). Observer-based measurement of facial expression with the facial action coding system. In J. A. Coan & J. J. B. Allen (Eds.), *Handbook of emotion elicitation and assessment* (pp. 203–221). New York, NY: Oxford University Press.

Cole, M., Gay, J., & Glick, J. (1967). A cross-cultural study of clustering in free recall. *Psychonomic Bulletin, 1*(2), 18.

Cole, P. M., & Hall, S. E. (2008). Emotion dysregulation as a risk factor for psychopathology. In T. P. Beauchaine & S. P. Hinshaw (Eds.), *Child and adolescent psychopathology* (pp. 265–298). Hoboken, NJ: John Wiley & Sons, Inc.

College of Ontario Psychologists. (2010). *Member search.* Retrieved from https://members.cpo.on.ca/members_search/new.

Collins, A. (2002). *In the Sleep Room: The Story of CIA Brainwashing Experiments in Canada.* Toronto: Key Porter Books.

Collins, R. L. (2005). Sex on television and its impact on American youth: Background and results from the RAND television and adolescent sexuality study. *Child and Adolescent Psychiatric Clinics of North America, 14*(3), 371–385.

Colson, S. D., Meek, J. H., & Hawdon, J. M. (2008). Optimal positions for the release of primitive neonatal reflexes stimulating breastfeeding. *Early Human Development, 84*(7), 441–449.

Colucci, R., Hryiuk, W., & Savage, C. (2009). *HPV vaccination programs In Canada: Are we hitting the mark? Report card on cancer in Canada.* Cancer Advocacy Coalition, Canada. Retrieved from http://www.canceradvocacy.ca/reportcard/2008/HPV%20Vaccination%20Programs%20in%20Canada.pdf.

Colvin, M. K., & Gazzaniga, M. S. (2007). Split-brain cases. In S. Schneider & M. Velman (Eds.), *The Blackwell companion to consciousness* (pp. 181–193). Malden, MA: Blackwell Publishing.

Comas-Diaz, L. (2011). Multicultural psychotherapies. In R. J. Corsini & D. Wedding (Eds.), *Current psychotherapies* (9th Ed.). Florence, KY: CENGAGE Learning.

Comas-Diaz, L. (2006). Cultural variation in the therapeutic relationship. In C. D. Goodheart, A. E. Kazdin, & R. J. Sternberg (Eds.), *Evidence-based psychotherapy: Where practice and research meet* (pp. 81–105). Washington, DC: American Psychological Association.

Compas, B. E. (2004). Processes of risk and resilience during adolescence: Linking contexts and individuals. In R. M. Lerner, & L. Steinberg (Eds.), *Handbook of adolescent psychology (2nd Ed.)* (pp. 263–296). Hoboken, NJ: John Wiley & Sons Inc.

Confer, J. C., Easton, J. A., Fleischman, D. S., Goetz, C. D., Lewis, D. M. G., Perilloux, C., & Buss, D. M. (2010). Evolutionary psychology: Controversies, questions, prospects, and limitations. *American Psychologist, 65*(2), 110–126.

Connolly, K. (2007). Brother and sister fight German's incest laws. *The Guardian*, Tuesday, February 27, 2007.

Connolly, T., & Zeelenberg, M. (2002). Regret in decision making. *Current Directions in Psychol Science, 11,* 212–216.

Connor-Greene, P. A. (2007). Observation or interpretation: Demonstrating unintentional subjectivity and interpretive variance. *Teaching of Psychology, 34*(3), 167–171.

Conrad. R., & Hull, A. J. (November 1964). Information, acoustic confusion and memory span (PDF). *British Journal of Psychology,* 55, 429–432.

Constantino, J. N. (2011). Social impairment. In E. Hollander, A. Kolevzon & J. T. Coyle (Eds.), *Textbook of autism spectrum disorders* (pp. 139–145). Arlington, VA: American Psychiatric Publishing, Inc.

Cooney, N. L., Kadden, R. M., Litt, M. D., & Getter, H. (1991). Matching alcoholics to coping skills or interactional therapies: Two-year follow-up results. *Journal of Consulting and Clinical Psychology, 59*(4), 598–601.

Cooper, J., Kelly, K. A., & Weaver, K. (2004). Attitudes, norms, and social groups. In M. B. Brewer & M. Hewstone (Eds.), *Social Cognition* (pp. 244–267). Malden, MA: Blackwell Publishing.

Cooper, J., Mirabile, R., & Scher, S. J. (2005). Actions and attitudes: The theory of cognitive dissonance. In T. C. Brock & M. C. Green (Eds.), *Persuasion: Psychological Insights and Perspectives, 2nd Ed* (pp. 63–79). Thousand Oaks, CA: Sage Publications.

Cooper, M. L., & Sheldon, M. S. (2002). Seventy years of research on personality and close relationships: Substantive and methodological trends over time. *Journal of Personality, 70,* 783–812.

Cooper, R. P., & Aslin, R. N. (1994). Developmental differences in infant attention to the spectral properties of infant-directed speech. *Child Development, 65,* 1663–1677.

Cooper, S. (2008). Self-cutting. *Orato, Online Magazine.* July 30, 2008.

Cooper, S. J. (2005). Donald O. Hebb's synapse and learning rule: a history and commentary. *Neuroscience and Biobehavioral Reviews, 28,* 851–874.

Corkin, S. (1984). Lasting consequences of bilateral medial temporal lobectomy: Clinical course and experimental findings. *Seminars in Neuroscience, 4,* 249–259.

Corbetta, M., & Shulman, G. L. (2002). Control of goal-directed and stimulus-driven attention in the brain. *Nature Reviews Neuroscience, 3,* 215–229.

Corbetta, M., Kincade, M. J., Lewis, C., Snyder, A. Z., & Sapir, A. (2005). Neural basis and recovery of spatial attentional deficits in spatial neglect. *Nature Neuroscience 8,* 1424–1425.

Coren, S. (2010a). *Born to bark: My adventures with an irrepressible and unforgettable dog.* New York: Free Press.

Coren, S. (2010b). *Dogs all-in-one for dummies.* New Jersey: Wiley & Sons.

Coren, S. (2008a). *The Modern Dog.* New York: Free Press.

Coren, S. (2008b). *Why do dogs have wet noses?* Kids Can Press.

Coren, S. (2006a). *Why does my dog act that way? A complete guide to your dog's personality.* New York: Free Press.

Coren, S. (2006b). *The Intelligence of Dogs.* New York: Free Press.

Coren, S. (2003). *The pawprints of history: Dogs and the course of human events.* New York: Free Press.

Coren, S. (1998). *Why We Love The Dogs We Do.* New York: Free Press.

Coren, S. (1997). *What Do Dogs Know?* New York: Free Press.

Coren, S. (1996). *Sleep thieves: An eye-opening exploration into the science and mysteries of sleep.* New York: Free Press.

Coren, S. (1993). *The left-hander syndrome: The causes and consequences of left-handedness.* Vintage Books.

Coren, S., Ward, L. M., & Enns, J. T. (2004). *Sensation and perception* (6th Ed.). New Jersey: Wiley & Sons.

Corina, D. (1998) Aphasia in users of signed languages. In P. Coppens, Y. Lebrun, & A. Basso (Eds.), *Aphasia in atypical populations.* Mahwah, NJ: Lawrence Erlbaum Associates.

Cornoldi, C. (2010). Metacognition, intelligence, and academic performance. In H. S. Waters & W. Schneider (Eds.), *Metacognition, strategy use, and instruction* (pp. 257–277). New York: Guilford Press.

Correa, A. A., & Rogers, R. (2010). Cross-cultural applications of the PAI. In M. A. Blais, M. R. Baity, & C. J. Hopwood (Eds.), *Clinical applications of the personality assessment inventory* (pp. 135–148). New York: Routledge/Taylor & Francis Group.

Corrigan, P. W. (2007). How clinical diagnosis might exacerbate the stigma of mental illness. *Social Work, 52*(1), 31–39.

Corrigan, P. W. (1991). Social skills training in adult psychiatric populations: A meta-analysis, Journal of Behavior Therapy and Experimental Psychiatry, *22*(3), 203–210.

Corsini, R. J., & Wedding, D. (Eds.). (2011). *Current psychotherapies* (9th Ed.). Florence, KY: CENGAGE Learning.

Cosmides, L., & Tooby, J. (2000). Evolutionary psychology and the emotions. In M. Lewis & J. M. Haviland-Jones (Eds.), *Handbook of Emotions, Second Edition* (pp. 91–115). New York, NY: The Guilford Press.

Costa, P. T., Jr., Terracciano, A., & McCrae, R. R. (2001). Gender differences in personality traits across cultures: Robust and surprising findings. *Journal of Personality and Social Psychology, 81,* 322–331.

Costa-Mattioli, M., Sossin, W. S., Klann, E., & Sonenberg, N. (2009). Translational control of long-lasting synaptic plasticity and memory. *Neuron, 61,* 10–26.

Costello, C. G. (1993). *Symptoms of schizophrenia.* John Wiley and Sons.

Cottone, E., & Byrd-Bredbenner, C. (2007). Knowledge and Psychosocial effects of the film Super Size Me on young adults. *Journal of the American Dental Association, 107*(7).

Courage, M. L., Howe, M. L., Ilkowska, M., Engle, R. W., Kossowska, M., Orehek, E., . . . Brzezicka, A. (2010). Individual differences in working memory and higher-ordered processing: The commentaries. In A. Gruszka, G. Matthews & B. Szymura (Eds.), *Handbook of individual differences in cognition: Attention, memory, and executive control* (pp. 419–436). New York, NY: Springer Science + Business Media. doi: 10.1007/978-1-4419-1210-7_25.

Cousins, S. D. (1989). Culture and selfhood in Japan and the U.S. *Journal of Personality and Social Psychology, 56,* 124–131.

Cousteau, J. Y., & Diole, P. (1973). *Octopus and squid: The soft intelligence.* London, Cassell.

Covington, M. A., He, C., Brown, C., Naçi, L., McClain, J. T., Fjordbak, B. S., Semple, J., & Brown, J. (2005). Schizophrenia and the Structure of language: the linguist's view. *Schizophrenia Research, 77,* 85–98.

Covino, N. A., & Pinnell, C. M. (2010). Hypnosis and medicine. In S. J. Lynn, J. W. Rhue & I. Kirsch (Eds.), *Handbook of clinical hypnosis (2nd Ed.)* (pp. 551–573). Washington, DC: American Psychological Association.

Cowan, M. J., Freedland, K. E., Burg, M. M., Saab, P. G., Youngblood, M. E., Cornell, C. E., Powell, L. H., & Czajkowski, S. M. (2007). Predictors of treatment response for depression and inadequate social support—The ENRICHD randomized clinical trial. *Psychotherapy and Psychosomatics, 77*(1), 27–37.

Cowan, N., & Chen, Z. (2009). How chunks form in long-term memory and affect short-term memory limits. In A. S. C. Thorn & M. P. A. Page (Eds.), *Interactions between short-term and long-term memory in the verbal domain* (pp. 86–107). New York, NY: Psychology Press.

Cowley, E. (2005). Views from consumers next in line: The fundamental attribution error in a service setting. *Journal of the Academy of Marketing Science, 33*(2), 139–152.

Cox, B. J., Kuch, K., Parker, J. D. A., Shulman, I. D., & et al. (1994). Alexithymia in somatoform disorder patients with chronic pain. *Journal of Psychosomatic Research, 38*(6), 523–527.

Cox, B. J., Turnbull, D. L., Robinson, J. A., Grant, B. F., & Stein, M. B. (2011). The effect of avoidant personality disorder on the persistence of generalized social anxiety disorder in the general population: Results from a longitudinal, nationally representative mental health survey. *Depression and Anxiety, 28*(3), 250–255.

Cox, P. D., Vinogradov, S., & Yalom, I. D. (2008). Group therapy. In R. E. Hales, S. C. Yudofsky, & G. O. Gabbard (Eds.), *The American psychiatric publishing textbook of psychiatry* (5th Ed., pp. 1329–1373). Arlington: American Psychiatric Publishing.

Coy, T. V. (1998). The effect of repressive coping style on cardiovascular reactivity and speech disturbances during stress. US: ProQuest Information & Learning). *Dissertation Abstracts International: Section B: The Sciences and Engineering, 58*(8), 4512.

Craig, K. J., & Chamberlain, S. R. (2010). The neuropsychology of anxiety disorders. In D. J. Stein, E. Hollander, & B. O. Rothbaum (Eds.), *Textbook of anxiety disorders* (2nd Ed., pp. 87–102). Arlington, VA: American Psychiatric Publishing.

Craig, T., & Power, P. (2010). Inpatient provision in early psychosis. In P. French, J. Smith, D. Shiers, M. Reed, & M. Rayne (Eds.), *Promoting recovery in early psychosis: A practice manual* (pp. 17–26). Hoboken, NJ: Wiley-Blackwell.

Craik, F. I. M., & Lockhart, R. S. (1972). Levels of processing: A framework for memory research. *Journal of Verbal Learning & Verbal Behavior, 11*(6), 671–684.

Cramer, P. (2006). *Protecting the self: Defense mechanisms in action.* New York: Guilford Press.

Cramer, P. (2001). The unconscious status of defense mechanisms. *American Psychologist, 56,* 762–763.

Cramer, R. J., Golom, F. D., LoPresto, C. T., & Kirkley, S. M. (2008). Weighing the evidence: Empirical assessment and ethical implications of conversion therapy. *Ethics & Behavior, 18*(1), 93–114.

Cramond, B., Kim, K. H., & VanTassel-Baska, J. (2010). The relationship between creativity and intelligence. In J. C. Kaufman, & R. J. Sternberg (Eds.), *The Cambridge handbook of creativity* (pp. 395–412). New York: Cambridge University Press.

Crandall, C. S., Preisler, J. J., & Aussprung, J. (1992). Measuring life event stress in the lives of college students: The Undergraduate Stress Questionnaire (USQ). *Journal of Behavioral Medicine, 15*, 627–662.

Crandall, J. E. (1980). Adler's concept of social interest: Theory, measurement, and implications for adjustment. *Journal of Personality and Social Psychology, 39*(3), 481–495.

Craske, M. G. (2010). Evaluation. In *Cognitive-behavioral therapy* (pp. 115–126). Washington, DC: American Psychological Association.

Creed, F. (2009). Somatization and pain syndromes. In E. A. Mayer & M. C. Bushnell (Eds.), *Functional pain syndromes: Presentation and pathophysiology* (pp. 227–244). Seattle, WA: IASP Press.

Cremonini F., Camilleri M., et al. (2009). Associations among binge eating behaviour patterns and gastrointestinal symptoms: A population-based study. *International Journal of Obesity, 33*, 342–353.

Crisp, M. (2001, April 8). Sticks & stones: "New Kid" puts comic spin on a serious situation. *Sunday News* (Lancaster, PA), p. H-1.

Crisp, S. (2010). How much sleep do children need? *NetDoctor.* London, England: Hearst Digital Network.

Critchley, H. D., Elliott, R., Mathias, C. J., & Dolan, R. J. (2000). Neural activity relating to generation and representation of galvanic skin conductance responses: A functional magnetic resonance imaging study. *Journal of Neuroscience, 20*, 3033–3040.

Crowley, S. J., Acebo, C., & Carskadon, M. A. (2007). Sleep, circadian rhythms, and delayed phase in adolescence. *Sleep Medicine, 8*, 602–612.

Csikszentmihalyi, M. (2003). *Good business: Leadership, flow, and the making of meaning.* New York, NY: Penguin Books.

Csikszentmihalyi, M. (1998). Finding flow: The psychology of engagement with everyday life. Basic Books.

Cuffe, S. P., McKeown, R.E., Addy, C. L., & Garrison, C. Z. (2005, February). Family psychosocial risk factors in a longitudinal epidemiological study of adolescents. *Journal of American Academic Child Adolescent Psychiatry, 44*, 121–129.

Cuijpers, P., van Straten, A., Hollon, S. D., & Andersson, G. (2010). The contribution of active medication to combined treatments of psychotherapy and pharmacotherapy for adult depression: A metaanalysis. *Acta Psychiatrica Scandinavica, 121*(6), 415–423.

Cukan, A. (2001, March 8). *Confronting a culture of cruelty.* General feature release. United Press International.

Cummings, M. J. (2003). Shakespeare and medicine. Retrieved from http://www.cummingsstudyguides.net/xMedicine.html.

Cummins, R. A., Nistico, H. (2002). Maintaining life satisfaction: The role of positive cognitive bias. *Journal of Happiness Studies,* 3, 37–69.

Cuninkova, L., & Brown, S. A. (2008). Peripheral circadian oscillators: Interesting mechanisms and powerful tools. *Molecular and biophysical mechanisms of arousal, alertness, and attention* (pp. 358–370). Malden, MA: Blackwell Publishing.

Cunningham-Owens, D. G. (2000). The challenges of diagnosis and continuing patient assessment. *International Journal of Psychiatric Clinical Practice, 4*(Suppl. 1), S13–S18.

Curcio, C. A., Sloan, K. R., Kalina, R. E., & Hendrickson, A. E. (1990). Human photoreceptor topography. *Journal of Comparative Neurology, 292*(4), 497–523.

Curtis, R., Groarke, A. M., Coughlan, R., & Gsel, A. (2004). The influence of disease severity, perceived stress, social support and coping in patients with chronic illness: A 1-year follow-up. *Psychology, Health, and Medicine, 9*(4), 456–475.

Curzi-Dascalova, L., & Challamel, M. J. (2000). Neurophysiological basis of sleep development. In G. M. Loughlin, J. L. Carroll, & C. L. Marcus (Eds.), *Sleep and breathing in children: A developmental approach* (pp. 3–37). New York, NY: Marcel Dekker.

Cynkar, A. (2007, June). The changing gender composition of psychology. *Monitor on Psychology, 38*(6), 46.

Czigler I., & Winkler I. (Eds.). (2010). *Unconscious memory representations in perception.* Amsterdam, Netherlands: John Benjamins Publishing Company.

Dabbs Jr., J. M., Bernieri, F. J., Strong, R. K., Campo, R., & Milun, R. (2001). Going on stage: Testosterone in greetings and meetings. *Journal of Research of Personality, 35*(1), 27–40.

Dabbs, Jr., J. M., & Hargrove, M. (1997). Age, testosterone, and behavior among female prison inmates. *Psychosomatic Medicine, 59*, 477–80.

Dabbs Jr., J. M., Riad, J. K., Chance, S. E. (2001). Testosterone and ruthless homicide. *Personality and Individual Differences, 31*(4), 599–603.

Daggett, L. M. (2002). Living with loss: Middle-aged men face spousal bereavement. *Qualitative Health Research, 12*(5), 625–639.

Daitch, C. (2011). *Anxiety disorders: The go-to guide for clients and therapists.* New York: W. W. Norton.

Dakin, R., & Montgomerie, R. (2011- in press). Peahens prefer peacocks displaying more eyespots, but rarely. *Animal Behaviour,* 1–8.

Dalgleish, T. (2004). The emotional brain. *Nature Reviews: Neuroscience, 5*, 582–589.

Dally, J. M., Emery, N. J., & Clayton, N. S. (2006). Food-caching western scrub-jays keep track of who was watching when. *Science, 312*(5780), 1662–1665.

Dalton, P. (2000). Psychophysical and behavioral characteristics of olfactory adaptation. *Chemical Senses, 25*, 487–92.

Daly, A., Doherty, D. T., & Walsh, D. (2010). Reducing the revolving door phenomenon. *Irish Journal of Psychological Medicine, 27*(1), 27–34.

Daly, M., & Wilson, M. (1988). Evolutionary social psychology and family homicide. *Science, 242*, 519–524.

Damasio, A. (2010). *Self comes to mind: Constructing the conscious brain.* New York: Pantheon.

Damasio, A. R., & Geschwind, N. (1984). The neural basis of language. *Annual Review of Neuroscience, 7*, 127–147.

Damasio, H., Grabowski, T., Frank, R., Galaburda, A. M., & Damasio, A. R. (1994). The return of Phineas Gage: Clues about the brain from a famous patient. *Science, 264*, 1102–1105.

Damasio, H., Tranel, D., Grabowski, T., Adolphs, R., & Damasio, A. (2004). Neural systems behind word and concept retrieval. *Cognition, 92*, 179–229.

Damsa, C., Kosel, M., & Moussally, J. (2009). Current status of brain imaging in anxiety disorders. *Current Opinion in Psychiatry, 22*(1), 96–110.

Danovi, S. A. (2010). Circadian rhythms: In the heat of the night. *Nature Reviews Neuroscience, 11*(12), 788.

Dansinger, M. L., Gleason, J. A., Griffith, J. L., Selker, H. P., & Schaefer, E. J. (2005). Comparison of the Atkins, Ornish, Weight Watchers, and Zone diets for weight loss and heart disease risk reduction: A randomized trial. *Journal of the American Medical Association, 293*(1), 43–53.

Darley, J. M. (2000). Bystander phenomenon. In A. E. Kazdin (Ed.), *Encyclopedia of Psychology, vol. 1* (pp. 493–495). Washington, D.C.: American Psychological Association.

Darley, J. M., & Latane, B. (1968). Bystander intervention in emergencies: Diffusion of responsibility. *Journal of Personality and Social Psychology, 8*, 377–383.

Darwin, C. R. (1872). The expression of emotions in man and animals. London: John Murray.

Darwin, C. R. (1859). *The Origin of the Specie.* Retrieved from http://darwin-online.org.uk/pdf/1859_origin_PC_Virginia-Francis-F373.pdf.

Davey, G. (2011). *Introduction to applied psychology.* Hoboken, NJ: Wiley-Blackwell.

Davidson, R. J. (1998). Affective style and affective disorders: Perspectives from affective neuroscience. *Cognition and Emotion, 12*, 307–330.

Davidson, R. J., & Fox, N. A. (1989). Frontal brain asymmetry predicts infants' response to maternal separation. *Journal of Abnormal Psychology, 98*, 127–131.

Davidson, R. J., Jackson, D. C., & Kalin, N. H. (2000). Emotion, plasticity, context, and regulation: Perspectives from affective neuroscience. *Psychological Bulletin, 126*, 890–909.

Davies, I. R., & Corbett, G. G. (1997). A cross-cultural study of colour grouping: Evidence for weak linguistic relativity. *British Journal of Psychology, 88*, 493–517.

Davis, J. N. (1997). Birth order, sibship size, and status in modern Canada. *Human Nature, 8*(3), 205–230.

Davis, M. (1992). Analysis of aversive memories using the fear potentiated startle paradigm. In N. Butters & L. R. Squire (Eds.), *The neuropsychology of memory* (2nd Ed.). New York, NY: Guilford Press.

Dawson, T. L. (2002). New tools, new insights: Kohlberg's moral judgement stages revisited. *International Journal of Behavioral Development, 26*(2), 154–166.

Day, D. M., Peterson-Badali, M., & Ruck, M. D. (2006). The relationship between maternal attitudes and young people's attitudes toward children's rights. *Journal of Adolescence, 29*(2), 193–207.

De Araujo, Ivan E. T., Rolls, Edmund T., Kringelbach, Morten L., McGlone, F., & Phillips, N. (2005). Taste-olfactory convergence, and the representation of pleasantness of flavour, in the human brain. *European Journal of Neuroscience, 18*, 2059–2068.

de Haan, A. D., Prinzie, P., & Deković, M. (2010). How and why children change in aggression and delinquency from childhood to adolescence: Moderation of overreactive parenting by child personality. *Journal of Child Psychology and Psychiatry, 51*(6), 725–733.

De Longis, A., Coyne, J. C., Dakof, G., Folkman, S., & Lazarus, R. S. (1982). Relationships of daily hassles, uplifts, and major life events to health status. *Health Psychology, 1*, 119–136.

De Raad, B., Perugini, M., Hrebickova, M., & Szarota, P. (1998). Lingua franca of personality: Taxonomies and structures based on the psycholexical approach. *Journal of Cross-Cultural Psychology, 29*, 212–232.

de Villers-Sidani, E., Chang, E. F., Bao, S., & Merzenich, M. M. (2007). Critical Period Window for Spectral Tuning Defined in the Primary Auditory Cortex (A1) in the Rat. *The Journal of Neuroscience, 27*, 180–189.

De Vries, R. (1969). Constancy of genetic identity in the years three to six. *Monograph of the Society for Research in Child Development, 34* (Serial No. 127).

Debiec, J., LeDoux, J. E., & Nader, K. (2002). Cellular and systems reconsolidation in the hypocampus. *Neuron, 36*, 527–538.

DeCasper, A. J., & Spence, M. J. (1986). Prenatal maternal speech influences newborns' perception of speech sounds. *Infant Behavior and Development, 9*, 133–150.

DeFelipe, J. (2002). Sesquicentenary of the birthday of Santiago Ramón y Cajal, the father of modern neuroscience. *Trends in Neurosciences, 25*, 481–484.

Del Bigio, M. R. (1995). The ependyma: A protective barrier between brain and cerebrospinal fluid, *Glia, 14*(1), 1–13.

Dela Cruz, A. M. (2010). Alberta Aboriginal Head Start in urban and northern communities: longitudinal study pilot phase. *Chronic Diseases in Canada, 30*(2). Retrieved from http://www.phac-aspc.gc.ca/publicat/cdic-mcbc/30-2/ar_01-eng.php.

Delahanty, D. L., Nugent, N. R., Christopher, N. C., & Walsh, M. (2005). Initial urinary epinephrine and cortisol levels predict acute PTSD symptoms in child trauma victims. *Psychoneuroendocrinology, 30(2)*, 121–128.

DeLamater, J., & Karraker, A. (2009). Sexual functioning in older adults. *Current Psychiatry Reports, 11*(1), 6–11.

Delaney, P. F., Sahakyan, L., Kelley, C. M., & Zimmerman, C. A. (2010). Remembering to forget: The amnesic effect of daydreaming. *Psychological Science, 21*(7), 1036–1042.

Demaree, H. A., Burns, K. J., & DeDonno, M. A. (2010). Intelligence, but not emotional intelligence, predicts Iowa gambling task performance. *Intelligence, 38*(2), 249–254.

Dement, W. C., & Vaughan, C. (1999). The promise of sleep: A pioneer in sleep medicine explores the vital connection between health, happiness, and a good night's sleep. New York, NY: Dell.

Demo, D. H., Allen, K. R., & Fine, M. A. (Eds.). (2000). *Handbook of family diversity*. New York, NY: Oxford University Press.

Denes, G., & Pizzamiglio, L. (1999). *Handbook of clinical and experimental neuropsychology*. Southwick, W. Sussex, UK: The Psychology Press.

DeNeve, K. M. (1999). Happy as an extraverted clam? The role of personality for subjective well-being. *Current Directions in Psychological Science, 8*(5), 141–144.

Denmark, F. L., Krauss, H. H., Wesner, R. W., Midlarsky, E., & Gielen, U. (2005). *Violence in schools: Cross national and cross-cultural perspectives*. New York, NY: Springer Science & Business Media.

Denver, J. Y., Lane, S. M., & Cherry, K. E. (2010). Recent versus remote: Flashbulb memory for 9/11 and self-selected events from the reminiscence bump. *The International Journal of Aging & Human Development, 70*(4), 275–297. doi: 10.2190/AG.70.4.a

Department of Health and Human Services and U.S. Department of Agriculture, 2005.

Department of Justice. (2007). *Methamphetamine report for federal-provincial-territorial ministers responsible for justice*. Retrieved from http://www.justice.gc.ca/eng/dept-min/pub/meth/sum-som.html#executive.

DePaulo, B. M., Blank, A. L., Swaim, G. W., & Hairfield, J. G. (1992). Expressiveness and expressive control. *Personality and Social Psychology Bulletin, 18*, 276–285.

Desphande, S. (1988). *That Long Silence*. London: Virago Press.

DeSteno, D., Dasgupta, N., Bartlett, M. Y., & Cajdric, A. (2004). Prejudice from thin air: The effect of emotion on automatic intergroup attitudes. *Psychological Science, 15*(5), 319–324.

DeValois, R. L., & DeValois, K. K. (1975). Neuronal coding of color. In E.C. Carterette & M.P. Friedman (Eds.), *Handbook of perception: Vol. V, Seeing*. New York: Academic Press.

Devenport, J. L., Kimbrough, C. D., & Cutler, B. L. (2009). Effectiveness of traditional safeguards against erroneous conviction arising from mistaken eyewitness identification. In B. L. Cutler (Ed.), *Expert testimony on the psychology of eyewitness identification* (pp. 51–68). New York, NY: Oxford University Press. doi: 10.1093/acprof:oso/9780195331974.003.003

Dhabhar, F. S. (2011). Effects of stress on immune function: Implications for immunoprotection and immunopathology. In R. J. Contrada & A. Baum (Eds.), *The handbook of stress science: Biology, psychology, and health*. New York: Springer Publishing Co.

Dhillon, H., Zigman, J. M., Ye, C., Lee, C. E., McGovern, R. A., Tang, V., et al. (2006). Leptin directly activates SF1 neurons in the VMH, and this action by leptin is required for normal body-weight homeostasis. *Neuron, 49*(2), 191–203.

Dick, A. O. (1974). Iconic memory and its relation to perceptual processing and other memory mechanisms. *Perception & Psychophysics, 16*(3), 575–596.

Didie, E. R., Kuniega-Pietrzak, T., & Phillips, K. A. (2010). Body image in patients with body dysmorphic disorder: Evaluations of and investment in appearance, health/illness, and fitness. *Body Image, 7*(1), 66–69.

Diefendorff, J. M., & Mehta, K. (2007). The relations of motivational traits with workplace deviance. *Journal of Applied Psychology, 92*, 967–977.

Diekelmann, S., & Born, J. (2010a). The memory function of sleep. *Nature Reviews Neuroscience, 11*(2), 114–126.

Diekelmann, S., & Born, J. (2010b). Slow wave sleep takes the leading role in memory reorganization. *Nature Reviews Neuroscience, 11*(3), 218.

Diener, E. (2000). Subjective well-being: The science of happiness and a proposal for a national index. *American Psychologist, 55*(1), 34–43.

Diener, E., & Biswas-Diener, R. (2008). *Happiness: Unlocking the Mysteries of Psychological Wealth*. Malden, MA: Blackwell Publishing.

Diener, E., & Diener, C. (1996). Most people are happy. *Psychological Science, 7*(3), 181–185.

Diener, E., Diener, M., & Diener, C. (1995). Factors predicting the subjective well-being of nations. *Journal of Personality and Social Psychology, 69*, 851–864.

Diener, E., Larsen, R. J., Levine, S., & Emmons, R. A. (1985). Frequency and intensity: The underlying dimensions of affect. *Journal of Personality and Social Psychology, 48*, 1253–1265.

Diener, E., & Lucas, R. E. (1999). Personality and subjective well-being. In D. Kahneman, E. Diener, & N. Schwarz (Eds.), *Well-being: The foundations of hedonic psychology* (pp. 213–229). New York, NY: Russell Sage Foundation.

Diener, E., Sandvik, E., & Larsen, R. (1985). Age and sex effects for emotional intensity. *Developmental Psychology, 21*, 542–546.

Diener, E., Sanvik, E., Pavot, W., & Fujita, E. (1992). Extraversion and subjective well-being in a U.S. national probability sample. *Journal of Research in Personality, 26*(3), 205–215.

Diener, E., Sanvik, E., Seidlitz, L., & Diener, M. (1993). The relationship between income and subjective well-being: Relative or absolute? *Social Indicators Research, 28*(3), 195–223.

Diener, E., & Seligman, M. E. P. (2002). Very happy people. *Psychological Science, 13*(1), 81–84.

Dienes, Z., Brown, E., Hutton, S., Kirsch, I., Mazzoni, G., & Wright, D. B. (2009). Hypnotic suggestibility, cognitive inhibition, and dissociation. *Consciousness and Cognition: An International Journal, 18*(4), 837–847.

Dies, R. R. (2003). Group psychotherapies. In A. S. Gurman & S. B. Messer (Eds.), *Essential psychotherapies: Theory and practice* (2nd Ed.). New York, NY: Guilford Press.

Dietrich, C., Swingley, D., & Werker, J. F. (2007). Native language governs interpretation of salient speech sound differences at 18 months. *Proceedings of the National Acadamy Sciences, USA, 104*, 27–31.

Dietrich, S., Hertrich, I. and Ackermann, H. (2010). *Visual cortex doing an auditory job: Enhanced spoken language comprehension in blind subjects.* Paper presented at the Neuroscience Conference, San Diego, CA, November.

Dijksterhuis, A. (2004). I like myself but I don't know why: Enhancing implicit self-esteem by subliminal evaluative conditioning. *Journal of Personality and Social Psychology, 86*, 345–355.

Dikel, T. N., Engdahl, B., & Eberly, R. (2005). PTSD in former prisoners of war: Prewar, wartime, and postwar factors. *Journal of Traumatic Stress, 18*(1), 69–77.

Dillof, M. (2010). Mysteries in broad daylight: A strange case of unconscious shoplifting. *Blog Catalog*, July 6.

Dimberg, U., & Lundquist, L. (1990). Gendeer differences in facial reactions to facial expressions. *Biological Psychology, 30*, 151–159.

Dimsdale, J. E., & Creed, F. H. (2010). The proposed diagnosis of somatic symptom disorders in *DSM-V* to replace somatoform disorders in *DSM-IV*—A preliminary report. *Journal of Psychosomatic Research, 68*(1), 99–100.

Dimsdale, J. E., Sharma, N., & Sharpe, M. (2011). What do physicians think of somatoform disorders? *Psychosomatics: Journal of Consultation Liaison Psychiatry, 52*(2), 154–159.

Dindia, K. (2000). Sex differences in self-disclosure, reciprocity of self-disclosure, and self-disclosure and liking: Three meta-analyses reviewed. In S. Petronio (Ed.), *Balancing the Secrets of Private Disclosures* (pp. 21–35). Mahwah, NJ: Lawrence Erlbaum Associates Publishers.

Dion, K. K., & Berscheid, E. (1974). Physical attractiveness and peer perception among children. *Sociometry, 37*, 1–12.

Di Pietro, J. (2000). Baby and the brain: Advances in child development. *Annual Review of Public Health 2000, 21*, 455–471.

Djordjevic, J., Jones-Gotman, M., De Sousa, K., & Chertkow, H. (2008). Olfaction in patients with mild cognitive impairment and Alzheimer's disease. *Neurobiology of Aging, 29*, 693–706.

Dobbing, J., & Sands, J. (1973). Quantitative growth and development of human brain. *Archives of Disease in Childhood, 48*(10), 757–767.

Doctor, R. M., & Neff, B. (2001). Sexual disorders. In H. S. Friedman (Ed.), *Specialty articles from the encyclopedia of mental health.* San Diego, CA: Academic Press.

Dodgen, C. E. (2005). Nicotine dependence: Understanding and applying the most effective treatment interventions. Washington, DC: American Psychological Association.

Doetsch, F. (2003). The glial identity of neural stem cells. *Nature Neuroscience, 6*, 1127–1134.

Dogu, O., & Pressman, M. R. (2011). Identification of sleepwalking gene(s): Not yet, but soon? *Neurology, 76*(1), 12–13.

Dohrenwend, B., Pearlin, L., Clayton, P., Hamburg, B., Dohrenwend, B. P., Riley, M., & Rose, R. (1982). Report on stress and life events. In G. R. Elliott & C. Eisdorfer (Eds.), *Stress and Human Health: Analysis and Implications of Research.* New York, NY: Springer.

Doidge, N. (2007). *The Brain That Changes Itself: Stories of Personal Triumph from the frontiers of brain science.* New York: Viking.

Dollard, J., Miller, N. E., Doob, L. W., Mowrer, O. H., & Sears, R. R. (1939). *Frustration and aggression.* New Haven, CT: Yale University.

Doss, B. D., Mitchell, A. E., & De la Garza-Mercer, F. (2008). Marital distress. In M. Hersen & J. Rosqvist (Eds.), *Handbook of psychological assessment, case conceptualization, and treatment, Vol. 1: Adults* (pp. 563–589). Hoboken, NJ: John Wiley & Sons.

Dossenbach, M., & Dossenbach, H.D. (1998). *All about animal vision.* Blackbirch Press.

Doty, R. I. (1986). Odor-guided behavior in mammals. *Experentia, 42*, 257–271.

Doucet, S., Jones, I., Letourneau, N., Dennis, C., & Blackmore, E. R. (2011). Interventions for the prevention and treatment of postpartum psychosis: A systematic review. *Archives of Women's Mental Health, 14*(2), 89–98.

Dovidio, J. F., Gaertner, S. L., Kawakami, K., & Hodson, G. (2002). Why can't we all just get along? Interpersonal biases and interracial distrust. *Cultural Diversity and Ethnic Minority Psychology, 8*, 88–102.

Doweiko, H. E. (2006). *Concepts of chemical dependency (6th Ed.).* Belmont, CA: Thomson Brooks/Cole.

Drachman, D. A. (2006). Aging of the brain, entropy, and Alzheimer disease. *Neurology, 67*, 1340–1352.

Draguns, J. G. (2006). Culture in psychopathology—psychopathology in culture: Taking a new look at an old problem. In T. G. Plante (Ed.), *Mental disorders of the new millennium, Vol. 2: Public and social problems.* Westport, CT: Praeger Publishers.

Drake, C. L. , Roehrs, T., Richardson, G., Walsh, J. K., & Roth, T. (2004). Shift work sleep disorder: Prevalence and consequences beyond that of symptomatic day workers. *SLEEP, 27*(8).

Dreher, J., Kohn, P., Kolachana, B., Weinberger, D. R., & Berman, K. F. (2009). Variation in dopamine genes influences responsivity of the human reward system. *PNAS Proceedings of the National Academy of Sciences of the United States of America, 106*(2), 617–622.

Dresler, T., Hahn, T., Plichta, M. M., Ernst, L. H., Tupak, S. V., Ehlis, A., et al. (2011). Neural correlates of spontaneous panic attacks. *Journal of Neural Transmission, 118*(2), 263–269.

Drewes, S. E., George, J., & Khan, F. (2003). Molecules of interest: Recent findings on natural products with erectile-dysfunction activity. *Phytochemistry, 62*(7), 1019–1025.

Drummond, M. (2011). Men's bodies throughout the life span. In C. Blazina & D. S. Shen-Miller (Eds.), *An international psychology of men: Theoretical advances, case studies, and clinical innovations* (pp. 159–188). New York: Routledge/Taylor & Francis Group.

Dubé, A. A., Duquette, M., Roy, M., Lepore, F., Duncan, G., & Rainville, P. (2009). Brain activity associated with the electrodermal reactivity to acute heat pain. *NeuroImage, 45*, 169–180.

Dube, E. F. (1982). Literacy, cultural familiarity, and "intelligence"as determinants of story recall. In U. Neisser (Ed.), *Memory observed: Remembering in natural contexts* (pp. 274–292). New York, NY: Freeman.

Dudai, Y. (2011). The engram revisited: On the elusive permanence of memory. In S. Nalbantian, P. M. Matthews & J. L. McClelland (Eds.), *The memory process: Neuroscientific and humanistic perspectives* (pp. 29–40). Cambridge, MA: MIT Press.

Dudley, K. J., Li, X., Kobor, M. S., Kippin, T. E., & Bredy, T. W. (2011). Epigenetic mechanisms mediating vulnerability and resilience to psychiatric disorders. *Neuroscience and Biobehavioral Reviews, 35*(7), 1544–1551.

Duesbury, E. M. (2011). *The counselor's guide for facilitating the interpretation of dreams: Family and other relationship systems perspectives.* New York, NY: Routledge/Taylor & Francis Group.

Dugas, M. J., Buhr, K., & Ladouceur, R. (2004). The role of intolerance of uncertainty in etiology and maintenance. In R. G. Heimberg, C. L. Turk, & D. S. Mennin (Eds.), *Generalized anxiety disorder: Advances in research and practice.* New York, NY: Guilford Press.

Dugas, M. J., Buhr, K., & Ladouceur, R. (2002). The role of intolerance of uncertainty in the etiology and maintenance of generalized anxiety disorder. In R. G. Heimberg, C. L. Turk, & D. S. Mennin (Eds.), *Generalized anxiety disorder: Advances in research and practice.* New York: Guilford Press.

Dugas, M. J., Francis, K., & Bouchard, S. (2009). Cognitive behavioural therapy and applied relaxation for generalized anxiety disorder: A time series analysis of change in worry and somatic anxiety. *Cognitive Behaviour Therapy, 38*(1), 29–41.

Dugas, M. J., Marchand, A., & Ladouceur, R. (2005). Further validation of a cognitive-behavioral model of generalized anxiety disorder: Diagnostic and symptom specificity. *Journal of Anxiety Disorders, 19*(3), 329–343.

Dugger, B. N., Morris, J. A., Jordan, C. L., & Breedlove, S. M. (2007). Androgen receptors are required for full masculinization of the ven-tromedial hypothalamus (VMH) in rats. *Hormones and Behavior, 51*(2), 195–201.

Dumont, F. (2010). *A history of personality psychology: Theory, science, and research from Hellenism to the twenty-first century.* New York: Cambridge University Press.

Dunbar, R. I. M. (2009). The social brain hypothesis and its implications for social evolution. *Annals of Human Biology, 36*(5), 562–572.

Dunbar, R. I. M. (2004). Gossip in evolutionary perspective. *Review of General Psychology, 8*(2), 100–110.

Dunbar, R. I. M., Barett, L., & Lycett, J. (2007). *Evolutionay Psychology.* One-World Publications: Oxford.

Dunbar, R. I. M., & Shultz S. (2007). Evolution in the social brain. *Science, 317*(5843), 1344–1347.

Duncan, J. (2001). Frontal lobe function and the control of visual attention. In J. Braun, C. Koch & J. L. Davis (Eds.), *Visual attention and cortical circuits* (pp. 69–88). Cambridge, MA: The MIT Press.

Duncan, S. C., Duncan, T. E., & Strycker, L. A. (2006). Alcohol use from ages 9 to 16: A cohort-sequential latent growth model. *Drug and Alcohol Dependence, 81*(1), 71–81.

Dupont, R. L., & Dupont, C. M. (2005). Sedatives/hypnotics and ben-zodiazepines. In R. J. Frances, A. H. Mack, & S. I. Miller (Eds.), *Clinical textbook of addictive disorders (3rd Ed.)*. New York, NY: Guilford Press.

Durante, K. M., & Li, N. P. (2009). Oestradiol level and opportunistic mating in women. *Proceedings of the Royal Society of London: Biology Letters, 5*(2), 19–182.

Durkin, K. F., & Hundersmarck, S. (2008). Pedophiles and child molesters. *Extreme deviance* (pp. 144–150). Thousand Oaks, CA: Pine Forge Press/Sage Publications Co.

Dusseljee, J. C. E., Rijken, P. M., Cardol, M., Curfs, L. M. G., & Groenewegen, P. P. (2011). Participation in daytime activities among people with mild or moderate intellectual disability. *Journal of Intellectual Disability Research, 55*(1), 4–18.

Dutton, D. G., & Aron, A. P. (1974). Some evidence for heightened sexual attraction under conditions of high anxiety. *Journal of Personality and Social Psychology, 23*, 510–517.

Dworak, M., McCarley, R. W., Kim, T., Kalinchuk, A. V., & Basheer, R. (2010). Sleep and brain energy levels: ATP changes during sleep. *The Journal of Neuroscience, 30*(26), 9007–9016.

Eagly, A. H. (1987). Sex differences in social behavior: A social-role interpretation. Hillsdale, NJ: Lawrence Erlbaum Associates.

Eagly, A. H., & Chaiken, S. (1998). Attitude structure and function. In D. T. Gilbert, St. T. Fiske, & G. Lindzey (Eds.), *The handbook of social psychology* (4th Ed., pp. 269–322). New York, NY: McGraw-Hill.

Eagly, A. H., & Karau, S. J. (2002). Role congruity theory of prejudice toward female leaders. *Psychological Review, 109*, 573–598.

Eagly, A. H., & Koenig, A. M. (2006). Social role theory of sex differences and similarities: Implication for prosocial behavior. In K. Dindia, & D. J. Canary (Eds.), *Sex differences and similarities in communication, 2nd Ed* (pp. 161–177). Mahwah, NJ: Lawrence Erlbaum Associates Publishers.

Eagly, A. H., & Wood, W. (2006). Three ways that data can misinform: Inappropriate partialling, small samples, any anyway, they're not playing our song. *Psychological Inquiry, 17*(2), 131–137.

Eagly, A. H., & Wood, W. (1999). The origins of sex differences in human behavior: Evolved dispositions versus social roles. *American Psychologist, 54*, 408–423.

Earleywine, M. (2007). *Pet politics: Marijuana and the costs of prohibition.* New York, NY: Oxford University Press.

Easterbrook, G. (2005). The real truth about money. *Time, 165*(3), A32–A34.

Eaton, J. (2001). Management communication: The threat of group-think. *Corporate Communications, 6*(4), 183–192.

Ebbinghaus, H. (1913). *On memory: A contribution to experimental psychology.* New York: Teachers College.

Eberhart-Phillips, J. E., Frederick, P. D., & Baron, R. C. (1993). Measles in pregnancy: A descriptive study of 58 cases. *Obstetrics and Genecology, 26*, 127–133.

Eckert, E. D., Bouchard, T. J., Bohlen, J., & Heston, L. L. (1986). Homosexuality in monozygotic twins reared apart. *The British Journal of Psychiatry, 148*, 421–425.

Edelstein, B. A., Stoner, S. A., & Woodhead, E. (2008). Older adults. In M. Hersen & J. Rosqvist (Eds.), *Handbook of Psychological Assessment, Case Conceptualization and Treatment, Volume 1, Adults.* Hoboken, NJ: John Wiley & Sons, Inc.

Edery-Halpern, G., & Nachson, I. (2004). Distinctiveness in flashbulb memory: Comparative analysis of five terrorist attacks. *Memory, 12*(2), 147–157.

Edgin, J. O., Pennington, B. F., & Mervis, C. B. (2010). Neuropsychological components of intellectual disability: The contributions of immediate, working, and associative memory. *Journal of Intellectual Disability Research, 54*(5), 406–417.

Edin, F., Macoveanu, J., Olesen, P., Tegnér, J., & Klingberg, T. (2007). Stronger synaptic connectivity as a mechanism behind development of working memory-related brain activity during childhood. *Journal of Cognitive Neuroscience, 19*(5), 750–760.

Edwards, J. M., & Trimble, K. (1992). Anxiety, coping, and academic performance. *Anxiety, Stress, and Coping, 5*, 337–350.

Edwards, W. (1977). How to Use Multiattribute Utility Measurement for Social Decision Making. *IEEE Transactions on Systems, Man and Cybernetics, 17*, 326–340.

Edwards, W., & Newman, J. R. (1986). Multiattribute Evaluation. In H. R. Arkes & K. R. Hammond (Eds.), *Judgment and Decision Making: An Interdisciplinary Reader* (pp. 17–34). New York, NY: Cambridge University Press.

Eimas, P. D. (1975). Developmental studies in speech perception. In L. B. Cohen & P. Salapatek (Eds.), *Infant Perception: From Sensation to Cognition* (pp. 193–231). New York, NY: Academic Press.

Eimas, P. D., Siqueland, E. R., Jusczyk, P., & Vigorito, J. (1971). Speech perception in infants. *Science, 171*, 303–306.

Einstein, G. O., & McDaniel, M. A. (2010). Prospective memory and what costs do not reveal about retrieval processes: A commentary on Smith, Hunt, McVay, and McConnell (2007). *Journal of Experimental Psychology: Learning, Memory, and Cognition, 36*(4), 1082–1088. doi: 10.1037/a0019184

Einstein, G. O., & McDaniel, M. A. (2005). Prospective memory: Multiple retrieval processes. *Current Directions in Psychological Science, 14*(6), 286–290. doi: 10.1111/j.0963-7214.2005.00382.x

Einstein, G. O., & McDaniel, M. A. (1990). Normal aging and prospective memory. *Journal of Experimental Psychology: Learning, Memory, and Cognition, 16*(4), 717–726. doi: 10.1037/0278-7393.16.4.717

Eisenberger, N. I., Lieberman, M. D., & Williams, K. D. (2003). Does rejection hurt? An FMRI study of social exclusion. *Science, 302*, 290–292.

Eisenbraun, G. A. (2006). *The pros and cons of personality testing in the workplace.* LawNow, Feb–March. Retrieved from http://findarticles.com/p/articles/mi_m0OJX/is_4_30/ai_n25001715.

Ekman, P. (2003). Emotions revealed: Recognizing faces and feelings to improve communication and emotional life. New York: Times Books.

Ekman, P. (1972). Universal and cultural differences in facial expressions of emotions. In J. Cole (Ed.), *Nebraska Symposium on Motivation, 1971: Vol. 19.* Lincoln, NE: University of Nebraska Press.

Ekman, P., & Friesen, W. V. (1986). A new pan-cultural facial expression of emotion. *Motivation and Emotion, 10*, 159–168.

Ekman, P., & Friesen, W. V. (1975). *Unmasking the face: A guide to recognizing emotions from facial clues.* Oxford, England: Prentice Hall.

Ekman, P., & Friesen, W. V. (1971). Constants across cultures in the face and emotion. *Journal of Personality and Social Psychology, 17*(2), 124–129.

Ekman, P., Friesen, W. V., O'Sullivan, M., Chan, A., et al. (1987). Universals and cultural differences in the judgments of facial expressions of emotion. *Journal of Personality and Social Psychology, 53*, 712–717.

Ekman, P., Levenson, R. W., & Friesen, W. V. (1983). Autonomic nervous system activity distinguishes among emotions. *Science, 221*, 1208–1210.

El-Mallakh, R., & Huff, M. O. (2001). Mood stabilizers and ion regulation. *Harvard Review of Psychiatry, 9*(1), 23–32.

El-Sheikh M. (Ed.). (2011). *Sleep and development: Familial and socio-cultural considerations.* New York, NY: Oxford University Press.

Elfenbein, H. A., Beaupré, M., Lévesque, M., & Hess, U. (2007). Toward a dialect theory: Cultural differences in the expression and recognition of posed facial expressions. *Emotion, 7*(1), 131–146.

Elisha, P. (2011). Psyche and soma in the work of Sigmund Freud: Theoretical foundations. In P. Elisha (Ed.), *The conscious body: A psychoanalytic exploration of the body in therapy* (pp. 65–97). Washington, DC: American Psychological Association.

Elkin, D. (2010). *Introduction to clinical psychiatry.* McGraw-Hill Professional.

Elkind, D. (2007). *The hurried child: Growing up too fast too soon (25th anniversary Ed.).* Cambridge, MA: Da Capo Press.

Elkind, D. (1978). Understanding the young adolescent. *Adolescence, 13*(49), 127–134.

Eller, J. D. (2005). *Violence and culture: A cross cultural and interdisciplinary perspective.* Thopmpson/Wadsworth.

Elliott, J. (2007, February 26). *Professor researches cell phone usage among college students.* Retrieved from http://www.physorg.com/ news 91732046.html.

Ellis, A. (2011). Rational emotive behavior therapy. In R. J. Corsini & D. Wedding (Eds.), *Current psychotherapies* (9th Ed.). Florence, KY: CENGAGE Learning.

Ellis, A. (2008). Rational emotive behavior therapy. In R. J. Corsini & D. Wedding (Eds.), *Current psychotherapies (8th edition)*. Belmont, CA: Thomson Brooks/Cole.

Ellis, A. (2005). Rational-emotive therapy. In R. Corsini & D. Wedding (Eds.), *Current psychotherapies* (7th Ed., pp. 166–201). Boston, MA: Thomson/Brooks-Cole.

Ellis, A. (2002). The role of irrational beliefs in perfectionism. In G. L. Flett & P. L. Hewitt (Eds.), *Perfectionism: Theory, research, and treatment* (pp. 217–229). Washington, DC: American Psychological Association.

Ellis, A. (1962). *Reason and emotion in psychotherapy*. Secaucus, NJ: Lyle Stuart.

Ellis, B. J., & Symons, D. (1990). Sex differences in sexual fantasy: An evolutionary psychological approach. *Journal of Sex Research, 27*, 527–555.

Ellison, C. G., Hummer, R. A., Cormier, S., & Rogers, R. G. (2000). Religious involvement and mortality risk among african american adults. *Research on Aging, 22*(6), 630–667.

Elovainio, M., Merjonen, P., Pulkki-Raback, L., Kivimaki, M., Jokela, M., Mattson, N., & Keltikangas-Jarvinen, L. (2011). Hostility, metabolic syndrome, inflammation and cardiac control in young adults: The young Finns study. *Biological Psychology, 87*(2), 234–240.

Elrod, S. S. (2010). Seniors Return to Retirement Jobs. *Senior Citizen Journal*, November 18.

Ely, R. (1997). Language and literacy in the school years. In J. Berko Gleason (Ed.), *The development of language* (4th Ed, pp. 398–439). Boston, MA: Allyn and Bacon.

Empson, J. (2002). *Sleep and dreaming (3rd edition)*. Palgrave MacMillian.

Endler, N. S. (1988). The origins of electroconvulsive therapy. *Convulsive Therapy, 4*, 5–23.

Endrass, T., Kloft, L., Kaufmann, C., & Kathmann, N. (2011). Approach and avoidance learning in obsessive-compulsive disorder. *Depression and Anxiety, 28*(2), 166–172.

Engmann, B., & Reuter, M. (2009). Spontaneous perception of melodies – hallucination or epilepsy? *Nervenheikunde* (April 28), 217–221.

Erdelyi, M. H. (2010). The ups and downs of memory. *American Psychologist, 65*(7), 623–633. doi: 10.1037/a0020440

Erdelyi, M. H. (2001). Defense processes can be conscious or unconscious. *American Psychologist, 56*, 761–762.

Erikson, E. H. (1985). *The life cycle completed: A review*. New York, NY: W.W Norton & Co.

Erikson, E. H. (1984). Reflections on the last stage—and the first. *Psychoanalytic Study of Children, 39*, 155–165.

Erikson, E. H. (1959). Identity and the life cycle: Selected papers. *Psychological Issues, 1*, 1–171.

Erlacher, D., & Schredl, M. (2010). Practicing a motor task in a lucid dream enhances subsequent performance: A pilot study. *The Sport Psychologist, 24*(2), 157–167.

Erlanson-Albertsson, C. (2005). Appetite regulation and energy balance. *Acta Paediatrica (Norway), Supplement, 94*(448), 40–1.

Ernst, M., & Hardin, M. (2010). Neurodevelopment underlying adolescent behavior: A neurobiological model. In P. D. Zelazo, M. Chandler, & E. Crone (Eds.), *Developmental social cognitive neuroscience* (pp. 165–189). New York: Psychology Press.

Ernst, W. (2006). *Histories of the normal and the abnormal: social and cultural histories of norms and normativity*. New York: Routledge.

Erten-Lyons, D., Woltjer, R. L., Dodge, H., Nixon, R., Vorobik, R., Calvert, J. F., Leahy, M., Montine, T., & Kaye, J. (2009). Factors associated with resistance to dementia despite high alzheimer disease pathology. *Neurology, 72(4)*, 354–360.

Escalante, P. R., Minshew, N. J., & Sweney, J.A. (2003). Abnormal brain lateralization in high-functioning autism. *Journal of Autism and Developmental Disorders, 33*, 539–543.

Escobar, J. I. (2004, April 15). Transcultural aspects of dissociative and somatoform disorders. *Psychiatric Times, 21*(5), 10.

Escobar, J. I. (1995). Transcultural aspects of dissociative and somatoform disorders. *Psychiatric Clinics of North America, 18*(3), 555–569.

Escobar, J. I., Canino, G., Rubio-Stipec, M., & Bravo, M. (1992). Somatic symptoms after a natural disaster: A prospective study. *American Journal of Psychiatry, 149*(7), 965–967.

Escobar, J. I., Gara, M., Silver, R. C., Waitzkin, H., Holman, A., & Compton, W. (1998). Somatisation disorder in primary care. *British Journal of Psychiatry, 173*, 262–266.

Espie, C. A. (2002). Insomnia: Conceptual issues in the development, persistence, and treatment of sleep disorders in adults. *Annual Review of Psychology, 53*, 215–243.

Essau, C. A., Lewinsohn, P. M., Seeley, J. R., & Sasagawa, S. (2010). Gender differences in the developmental course of depression. *Journal of Affective Disorders, 127*(1–3), 185–190.

Etaugh, C. (2008). Women in the middle and later years. In F. L. Denmark & M. A. Paludi (Eds.), *Psychology of women: A handbook of issues and theories* (2nd Ed.). Westport, CT: Praeger Publishers/ Greenwood Publishing Group.

Etchegoyen, H. (2005). *The Fundamentals of Psychoanalytic Technique*. Karnac Books Ed., New Ed.

Eun, B. (2010). From learning to development: A sociocultural approach to instruction. *Cambridge Journal of Education, 40*(4), 401–418.

Evans, G. W. (2001). Environmental stress and health. In A. Baum, T. A. Revenson & J. E. Singer (Eds.), *Handbook of Health Psychology* (pp. 365–385). Mahwah, New Jersey: Lawrence Erlbaum Associates.

Evans, J., Heron, J., Lewis, G., Araya, R., & Wolke, D. (2005). Negative self-schemas and the onset of depression in women: Longitudinal study. *British Journal of Psychiatry, 186*(4), 302–307.

Evans, R. I. (1968). *BF Skinner: The man and his ideas*. Dutton, New York.

Everhart, D. E., Shucard, J. L., Quatrin, T., & Shucard, D. W. (2001). Sex-related differences in event-related potentials, face recognition, and facial affect processing in prepubertal children. *Neuropsychology, 15*, 329–341.

Ewen, R. B. (2010). *An introduction to theories of personality* (7th Ed.). New York: Psychology Press.

Eyler, L. T. (2008). Brain imaging. In K. T. Mueser & D. V. Jeste (Eds.), *Clinical handbook of schizophrenia* (pp. 35–43). New York: Guilford Press.

Eysenck, H. J. (2002). The dynamics of anxiety & hysteria: An experimental application of modern learning theory to psychiatry. New Brunswick, NJ: Transaction Publishers.

Eysenck, H. J. (1992). Four ways five-factors are not basic. *Personality and Individual Differences, 13*, 667–673.

Eysenck, H. J. (1990). Biological dimensions of personality. In L. A. Pervin (Ed.), *Handbook of Personality: Theory and Research* (pp. 244–276). New York, NY: Guilford.

Eysenck, M. W., Matthews, G., Nęcka, E., Chuderski, A., Schweizer, K., & Szymura, B. (2010). Individual differences in attention: The commentaries. In A. Gruszka, G. Matthews, & B. Szymura (Eds.), *Handbook of individual differences in cognition: Attention, memory, and executive control* (pp. 283–292). New York: Springer Science + Business Media.

Faas, A. E., Spontón, E. D., Moya, P. R., & Molina, J. C. (2000). Differential responsiveness to alcohol odor in human neonates: Efects of maternal consumption during gestation. *Alcohol, 22*(1), 7–17.

Fabrigar, L. R., Petty, R. E., Smith, S. M., & Crites Jr., S. L. (2006). Understanding knowledge effects on attitude-behavior consistency: The role of relevance, complexity, and amount of knowledge. *Journal of Personality and Social Psychology, 90*(4), 556–577.

Fancher, R. E. (2009). Scientific cousins: The relationship between Charles Darwin and Francis Galton. *American Psychologist, 64*(2), 84–92.

Fancher, R. E. (2004). The concept of race in the life and thought of Francis Galton. In A. S. Winston (Ed.), *Defining difference: Race and racism in the history of psychology* (pp. 49–75). Washington, DC: American Psychological Association.

Fancher, R. E. (1996). *Mind in conflict. pioneers in psychology* (pp. 393–394). New York, NY: W. W. Norton & Company, Inc.

Fanselow, M. S., & Poulos, A. M. (2005). The neuroscience of mammalian associative learning. *Annual Review of Psychology, 56*, 207–234.

Fanti, K. A., & Henrich, C. C. (2010). Trajectories of pure and co-occurring internalizing and externalizing problems from age 2 to age 12: Findings from the national institute of child health and human development study of early child care. *Developmental Psychology, 46*(5), 1159–1175.

Farah, M. (2011). Overcorrecting the neuroenhancement discussion. *Addiction, 106*, 1190.

Farah, M. J., Levinson, K. L., & Klein, K. L. (1995). Face perception and within-category discrimination in prosopagnosia. *Neuropsychologia, 33*, 661–674.

Farbman, A. I. (1997). Injury-stimulated neurogenesis in sensory systems. *Advances in Neurology, 72,* 157–161.

Farooqi, I. S., Wangensteen, T., Collins, S., Kimber, W., Matarese, G., Keogh, J. M., et al. (2007). Clinical and molecular genetic spectrum of congenital deficiency of the leptin receptor. *The New England Journal of Medicine, 356(3),* 237–247.

Farry, A., & Baxter, D. (2010). *The incidence and prevelance of spinal cord injury in Canada: Overview and extimates based on current evidence.* The Rick Hansen Institute and Urban Futures, Vancouver.

Favaro, A., Santonastaso, P., Monteleone, P., Bellodi, L., Mauri, M., Rotondo, A., et al. (2008). Self-injurious behavior and attempted suicide in purging bulimia nervosa: associations with psychiatric comorbidity. *Journal of Affective Disorders, 105(1–3),* 285–289.

Fayek, A. (2002). Analysis of a case of psychogenic amnesia: The issue of termination. *Journal of Clinical Psychoanalysis, 11*(4), 586–612.

Fazio, R. H., & Roskos-Ewoldsen, D. (2005). Acting as we feel: When and how attitudes guide behavior. In T. C. Brock & M. C. Green (Eds.), *Persuasion: Psychological Insights and Perspectives, 2nd Ed.* (pp. 41–62). Thousand Oaks, CA: Sage Publications.

Fazio, R. H., Zanna, M. P., & Cooper, J. (1977). Dissonance and self perception: An integrative view of each theory's proper domain of application. *Journal of Experimental Social Psychology, 13,* 464–479.

Fedotchev, A. I. (2011). Modern nondrug methods of human sleep regulation. *Human Physiology, 37*(1), 113–120.

Fehr, S. S. (2003). *Group therapy: A practical guide (2nd Ed).* New York: Haworth Press.

Feinberg, D. R., Jones, B. C., Law Smith, M. J., Moore, F. R., DeBruine, L. M., Cornwell, R. E., Hillier, S. G., & Perrett, D. I. (2006). Menstrual cycle, trait estrogen level, and masculinity preferences in the human voice. *Hormonal Behavior, 49*(2), 15–22.

Feingold, A. (1994). Gender differences in personality: A meta-analysis. *Psychological Bulletin, 116,* 429–456.

Feinstein, J. S., Adolphs, R., Damsio, A., & Tranel, D. (2011). The human amygdala and the induction and experience of fear. *Current Biology, 21*(1), 34–38.

Feist, G. J. (2010). The function of personality in creativity: The nature and nurture of the creative personality. In J. C. Kaufman & R. J. Sternberg (Eds.), *The Cambridge handbook of creativity* (pp. 113–130). New York: Cambridge University Press.

Feldhusen, J. F. (2003). Lewis M. Terman: A pioneer in the development of ability tests. In B. J. Zimmerman & D. H. Schunk (Eds.), *Educational psychology: A century of contributions* (pp. 155–169). Mahwah, NJ: Erlbaum.

Feldman, D. H. (2003). Cognitive development in childhood. In R. M. Lerner, M. A. Easterbrooks & J. Mistry (Eds.), *Handbook of psychology: Developmental psychology, vol. 6* (pp. 195–210). Hoboken, NJ: John Wiley & Sons Inc.

Feldman, H. A., Longcope, C., Derby, C. A., Johannes, C. B., Araujo, A. B., Coviello, A. D., et al. (2002). Age trends in the level of serum testosterone and other hormones in middle-aged men: Longitudinal results from the Massachusetts male aging study. *Journal of Clinical Endocrinology & Metabolism, 87*(2), 589–598.

Feldman, M. W., & Lewontin, R. C. (2008). Race, ancestry, and medicine. In B. A. Koenig, S. S. Lee, & S. S. Richardson (Eds.), *Revisiting race in a genomic age* (pp. 89–101). Piscataway, NJ: Rutgers University Press.

Feldman, R. S. (2009). *The liar in your life: The way to truthful relationships.* New York: Twelve.

Feldman, R. S., Forrest, J. A., & Happ, B. R. (2002). Self-presentation and verbal deception: Do self-presenters lie more? *Basic and Applied Social Psychology, 24,* 163–170.

Feliciano, L., & Gum, A. M. (2010). Mood disorders. In D. L. Segal, & M. Hersen (Eds.), *Diagnostic interviewing* (pp. 153–176). New York: Springer Publishing Co.

Fenchel, G. H. (2006). *Psychoanalytic reflections on love and sexuality.* Lanham, MD: University Press of America.

Fenigstein, A., & Preston, M. (2007). The desired number of sexual partners as a function of gender, sexual risk and the meaning of "ideal." *Journal of Sex Research.*

Fenson, L., Dale, P. S., Reznick, J. S., Bates, E., Thal, D. J., & Pethick, S. J. (1994). Variability in early communicative development. *Monographs of the Society for Research in Child Development, 59,* 1–185.

Ferguson, C. J. (2009). An effect size primer: A guide for clinicians and researchers. *Professional Psychology: Research and Practice, 40*(5), 532–538. doi:10.1037/a0015808

Ferguson, C. J. (2008). The school shooting/violent video game link: Causal Relationship or moral panic? *Journal of Investigative Psychology and Offender Profiling, 5,* 25–37.

Fernald, A., Taeschner, T., Dunn, J., Papousek, M., Boysson-Bardies, B., & Fukui, I. (1989). A cross-language study of prosodic modifications in mothers' and fathers' speech to preverbal infants. *Journal of Child Language, 16,* 477–502.

Fernandes, M., Atallah, A. N., Soares, B. G., Humberto, S., Guimarães, S., Matos, D., et al. (2007). Intragastric balloon for obesity. *Cochrane Database of Systematic Reviews (Online), 1,* CD004931.

Fernbach, P. M., Darlow, A., & Sloman, S. A. (2011). Asymmetries in predictive and diagnostic reasoning. *Journal of Experimental Psychology, 140*(2), 168–185.

Ferraro, R., Shiv, B., & Bettman, J. R. (2005). Let us eat and drink, for tomorrow we shall die: Effects of mortality salience and self-esteem on self-regulation in consumer choice. *Journal of Consumer Research, 32,* 65–75.

Festinger, L. (1957). *A Theory of Cognitive Dissonance.* Stanford, CA: Stanford University Press.

Festinger, L. & Carlsmith, J. M. (1959). Cognitive consequences of forced compliance. *Journal of Abnormal and Social Psychology, 58,* 203–210.

Field, A. (2005). Meta-analysis. In J. Miles, P. Gilbert, J. Miles, P. Gilbert (Eds.) , *A handbook of research methods for clinical and health psychology* (pp. 295–308). New York, NY: Oxford University Press.

Field, A. P. & Nightingale, Z. C. (2009). Test of time: What if little Albert had escaped? *Clinical Child Psychology and Psychiatry, 14,* 311–319.

File, S. E., Gonzalez, L. E., & Gallant, R. (1998). Role of the basolateral nucleus of the amygdala in the formation of a phobia. *Neuropsychopharmacology, 19,* 397-405.

Finckh, U. (2001). The dopamine D2 receptor gene and alcoholism: Association studies. In D. P. Agarwal & H. K. Seitz (Eds.), *Alcohol in health and disease.* New York, NY: Marcel Dekker.

Finer, L. B. (2007). Trends in premarital sex in the United States, 1954–2003. *Public Health Reports, 122,* 73–78.

Fink, B., Neave, N., Manning, J. T., & Grammer, K. (2006). Facial symmetry and judgements of attractiveness, health and personality. *Personality and Individual Differences, 41,* 491–499.

Finke, R. A. (1989). *Principles of Mental Imagery.* Cambridge, MA: MIT Press.

Finley, L. L. (2007). *The Encyclopedia of Juvenile Violence.* Westport, CT: Greenwood Publishing Group.

Finnegan, L. P., & Kandall, S. R. (2008). Perinatal substance abuse. In H. D. Kleber & M. Galanter (Eds.), *The American Psychiatric Publishing textbook of substance abuse treatment (4th Ed.).* Washington, DC: American Psychiatric Publishing.

Fioravante, D., & Byrne, J. H. (2011). Protein degradation and memory formation. *Brain Research Bulletin, 85*(1–2), 14–20.

Fischer, A. H., & Manstead, A. S. R. (2000). The relation between gender and emotions in different cultures. In A. H. Fischer (Ed.), *Gender and emotion: Social psychology perspectives* (pp. 71–94). New York, NY: Cambridge University Press.

Fischer, A. H., Rodriguez Mosquera, P. M., van Vianen, A. E. M., & Manstead, A. S. R. (2004). Gender and culture differences in emotion. *Emotion, 4*(1), 87–94.

Fischer, P., Greitemeyer, T., Pollozek, F., & Frey, D. (2006). The unresponsive bystander: Are bystanders more responsive in dangerous emergencies? *European Journal of Social Psychology, 36*(2), 267–278.

Fischer, P., Krueger, J. I., Greitemeyer, T., Vogrincic, C., Kastenmüller, A., Frey, D., Heene, M., Wicher, M., & Kainbacher, M. (2011). The bystander-effect: A meta-analytic review on bystander intervention in dangerous and non-dangerous emergencies. *Psychological Bulletin, 137*(4), 517–537.

Fish, J. M. (Ed.) (2002). *Race and intelligence: Separating science from myth.* Mahwah, NJ: Lawrence Erlbaum Associates Publishers.

Fisher, H., Aron, A., & Brown, L. L. (2005, Dec. 5). Romantic love: an *f*MRI study of a neural mechanism for mate choice. *Journal of Comparative Neurology, 493*(1), 58–62.

Fisher, L., Ames, E. W., Chisholm, K., & Savoie, L. (1997). Problems reported by parents of Romanian orphans adopted to British Columbia. *International Journal of Behavioral Development, 20*(1), 67–82.

Fisher, P. H., Masia-Warner, C., & Klein, R. G. (2004). Skills for social and academic success: A school-based intervention for social anxiety disorder in adolescents. *Clinical Child and Family Psychological Review, 7*(4), 241–249.

Fisher, R. J., & Dubé, L. (2005). Gender differences in responses to emotional advertising: A social desirability perspective. *Journal of Consumer Research, 31*(4), 850–858.

Fishman, D. B., Rego, S. A., & Muller, K. L. (2011). Behavioral theories of psychotherapy. In J. C. Norcross, G. R. VandenBos, & D. K. Freedheim (Eds.), *History of psychotherapy: Continuity and change* (2nd Ed., pp. 101–140). Washington, DC: American Psychological Association.

Fiske, S. T. (2010). Social beings: Core motives in social psychology, Second Edition. Hoboken, NJ: John Wiley & Sons.

Fiske, S. T. (2004). *Social beings: A core motives approach to social psychology*. Hoboken, NJ: John Wiley & Sons, Inc.

Fiske, S. (2000). Stereotyping, prejudice, and discrimination at the seam between the centuries: Evolution, culture, mind, and brain. *European Journal of Social Psychology, 30*, 299–322.

Fitch, M. T., & Silver, J. (2008). CNS injury, glial scars, and inflammation: Inhibitory extracellular matrices and regeneration failure. *Experimental Neurology, 209*, 294–301.

Fleeson, W. (2007). Situation-based contingencies underlying trait-content manifestation in behavior. *Journal of Personality, 75(4)*, 825–862.

Fleeson, W. (2001). Towards a structure- and process-integrated view of personality: Traits as density distributions of states. *Journal of Personality and Social Psychology, 80*, 1011–1027.

Fleischman, D. A., Wilson, R. S., Gabrieli, J. D. E., Bienias, J. L., & Bennett, D. A. (2004). A longitudinal study of implicit and explicit memory in old persons. *Psychology and Aging, 19*(4), 617–625. doi: 10.1037/0882-7974.19.4.617

Fleming, I., Baum, A., Davidson, L., Rectanus, E., & McArdle, S. (1987). Chronic stress as a reactivity factor in physiologic reactivity to challenge. *Health Psychology, 11*, 221–237.

Flouri, E., Hickey, J., Mavroveli, S., & Hurry, J. (2011). Adversity, emotional arousal, and problem behaviour in adolescence: The role of non-verbal cognitive ability as a resilience promoting factor. *Child and Adolescent Mental Health, 16*(1), 22–29.

Flynn, J. R. (1998). IQ gains over time: Toward finding the causes. In U. Neisser (Ed.), *The rising curve: Long-term gains in IQ and related measures* (p. 37). Washington, DC: American Psychological Association.

Foa, E., & Kozak, M. (1986). Emotional processing of fear: Exposure to corrective information. *Psychological Bulletin, 99*, 20–35.

Focus Adolescent Services (FAS). (2008). *Teen Violence*. online: Focusas.com.

Fodor, J. A. (2007). The revenge of the given. In B. P. McLaughlin, & J. Cohen (Eds.), *Contemporary debates in philosophy of mind* (pp. 105–116). Malden, MA: Blackwell Publishing.

Fodor, J. A. (2006). Précis of the modularity of mind. In J. L. Bermúdez (Ed.), *Philosophy of psychology: Contemporary readings* (pp. 513–523). New York, NY: Routledge/Taylor & Francis Group.

Fodor, J. A. (1968). Psychological explanation: An introduction to the philosophy of psychology. New York, NY: Random House.

Fogel, S. M., Smith, C. T., Higginson, C. D., & Beninger, R. J. (2011). Different types of avoidance behavior in rats produce dissociable post-training changes in sleep. *Physiology & Behavior, 102*(2), 170–174.

Foldvary, N., Nashold, B., Mascha, E., Thompson, E. A., Lee, N., McNamara, J. O., et al. (2000). Seizure outcome after temporal lobectomy for temporal lobe epilepsy: A Kaplan-Meier survival analysis. *Neurology, 54*(3), 630–634.

Folkman, S., & Lazarus, R. S. (1985). If it changes it must be a process: Study of emotion and coping during three stages of a college examination. *Journal of Personality and Social Psychology, 48*, 150–170.

Folkman, S., & Moskowitz, J. T. (2004). Coping: Pitfalls and promise. *Annual Review of Psychology, 55*, 745–774.

Folkman, S., & Moskowitz, J. T. (2000). Stress, positive emotion, and coping. *Current Directions in Psychological Science, 9*(4), 115–118.

Folkman, S., & Moskowitz, J. T. (2000). Positive affect and the other side of coping. *American Psychologist, 55*, 647–654.

Fontana, D. (2007). Meditation. In M. Velmans & S. Schneider (Ed.), *The Blackwell companion to consciousness*. Malden, MA: Blackwell Publishing.

Ford, D. Y. (2008). Intelligence testing and cultural diversity: The need for alternative instruments, policies, and procedures. In J. L. Van Tassel-Baska (Ed.), *Alternative assessments with gifted and talented students* (pp. 107–128). Waco, TX: Press.

Ford, D. Y., Moore, J. L., III, & Whiting, G. W. (2006). Eliminating deficit orientations: Creating classrooms and curriculums for gifted students from diverse cultural backgrounds. In M. G. Constantine & D. W. Sue (Eds.), *Addressing racism Facilitating cultural competence in mental health and educational settings* (pp. 173–193). Hoboken, NJ: John Wiley & Sons.

Ford, D. Y., & Whiting, G. W. (2006). Under-representation of diverse students in gifted education: Recommendations for nondiscriminatory assessment (part 1). *Gifted Education Press Quarterly, 20*(2), 2–6.

Forgas, J. P. (2008). Affect, cognition, and social behavior: The effects of mood on memory, social judgments, and social interaction. In M. A. Gluck, J. R. Anderson, & S. M. Kosslyn (Eds.), *Memory and mind: A festschrift for Gordon H. Bower* (pp. 261–279). Mahwah, NJ: Lawrence Erlbaum Associates Publishers.

Forgas, J. P., & Locke, J. (2005). Affective influences on causal inferences: The effects of mood on attributions for positive and negative interpersonal episodes. *Cognition & Emotion, 19*(7), 1071–1081.

Forgas, J. P., Williams K. D., & Laham S. M. (Eds.). (2005). *Social motivation: Conscious and unconscious processes*. New York, NY: Cambridge University Press.

Forsey, C. A. (2009) *"I don't want to die but I accept that it can happen": Taking risks and doing gender among BASE jumpers*. Masters Thesis, University of British Columbia. Retrieved from https://dspace.library.ubc.ca/bitstream/handle/2429/12601/ubc_2009_fall_forsey_caitlin.pdf?sequence=1.

Förstl, H., & Kurz, A. (1999). Clinical features of Alzheimer's disease. *European Archives of Psychiatry and Clinical Neuroscience, 249*(6), 288–290.

Fossel, M., Blackburn, G., & Woynarowski, D. (2010). *The immortality edge: Realize the secrets of your telomeres for a longer healthier life*. Hoboken, NJ: John-Wiley and Sons.

Foster, J. D. (2009, March, 16). *Mass murder is nothing to fear*. Message posted to Psychology Today. Retrieved from http://www.psychologytoday.com/blog/the-narcissus-in-all-us/200903/mass-murder-is-nothing-fear.

Fowler, M. (2008). *Restraint and handling of wild and domestic animals, 3rd edition*. Blackwell Publishing.

Fox, D. (2010). The insanity virus. *Discover, 31*(5).

Fozard, J., Wolf, E., Bell, B., Farland, R., & Podolsky, S. (1977). Visual perception and communication. In J. Birren & K. Schaie (Eds.), *Handbook of the psychology of aging*. New York, NY: Van Nostrand Reinhold.

Fraley, B., & Aron, A. (2004). The effect of a shared humorous experience on closeness in initial encounters. *Personal Relationships, 11*, 61–78.

Frank, J. D. (1973). *Persuasion and healing* (Rev. Ed.). Baltimore, MD: Johns Hopkins University Press.

Frank, J., Mistretta, P., & Will, J. (2008). Diagnosis and treatment of female sexual dysfunction. *American Family Physician, 77*(5), 635–642.

Frankish, C., Hwang, S., & Quantz, D. (2005). Homelessness and health in Canada: Research lessons and priorities. *Canadian Journal of Public Health, 96*(2), 23–29.

Franklin, R. J., & French-Constant, C. (2008). Remyelination in the CNS: from biology to therapy. *Nature Reviews Neuroscience, 9*, 839–855.

Franks, K. M., & Isaacson, J. S. (2005). Synapse specific downregulation of NMDA receptors by early experience: A critical period for plasticity of sensory input to olfactory cortex. *Neuron, 7*, 101–114.

Fredericks, L. E. (2001). The use of hypnosis in surgery and anesthesiology: Psychological preparation of the surgical patient. Springfield, IL: Charles C. Thomas Publisher.

Fredrickson, B. L. (2001). The role of positive emotions in positive psychology: The broaden-and-build theory of positive emotions. *American Psychologist, 56*(3), 218–226.

Freed, W. J. (2000). *Neural transplantation: An introduction*. Cambridge, MA: The MIT Press.

Freedman, *J. L. (2002). Media violence and its effect on aggression: Assessing the scientific evidence*. University of Toronto Press, Scholarly Publishing Division.

Freedman, V. A., Aykan, H., & Martin, L. G. (2001). Aggregate changes in severe cognitive impairment among older Americans: 1993 and 1998. *Journal of Gerontology, 56B*, S100–S111.

Freeman, H. L. (1984). Housing. In. H. L. Freeman (Ed.), *Mental Health and the Environment* (pp. 197–225). London: Churchill Livingston.

Freeman, S., Walker, M. R., Borden, R., & Latané, B. (1975). Diffusion of responsibility and restaurant tipping: cheaper by the bunch. *Personality and Social Psychology Bulletin, 1*(4), 584–587.

Freud, S. (1961). The infantile genital organization: An interpolation into the theory of sexuality. *Standard Edition, 19*, 141–145.

Freud, S. (1924). The loss of reality in neurosis and psychosis. In *Sigmund Freud's collected papers* (Vol. 2, pp. 272–282). London: Hogarth Press.

Freud, S. (1909). Analysis of a phobia in a five-year-old boy. *Standard Edition, 10*, 5–149.

Freud, S. (1900). The Interpretation of Dreams.

Freund, P. A., & Holling, H. (2011). Who wants to take an intelligence test? Personality and achievement motivation in the context of ability testing. *Personality and Individual Differences, 50*(5), 723–728.

Frey, K. S., Hirschstein, M. K., Snell, J. L., Edstrom, L. V., MacKenzie, E. P., & Broderick, C. J. (2005). Reducing playground bullying and supporting beliefs: An experimental trial of the Steps to Respect program. *Developmental Psychology, 41*, 479–491.

Friedlander, S. L., Larkin, E. K., Rosen, C. L., Palermo, T. M., & Redline, S. (2003). Decreased quality of life associated with obesity in school-aged children. *Archives of Pediatrics & Adolescent Medicine, 157*(12), 1206–1211.

Friedman, H. S., & Silver, R. C. (Eds.) (2007). *Foundations of Health Psychology*. New York: Oxford University Press.

Friedman, K. E., Reichmann, S. K., Costanzo, P. R., Zelli, A., Ashmore, J. A., Musante, G. J., et al. (2005). Weight stigmatization and ideological beliefs: relation to psychological functioning in obese adults. *Obesity research, 13*(5), 907–916.

Friedman, M., & Rosenman, R. H. (1959). Association of a specific overt behavior pattern with increases in blood cholesterol, blood clotting time, incidence of arcus senilis and clinical coronary artery disease. *Journal of the American Medical Association, 169*, 1286–1296.

Friedman, M., & Rosenman, R. (1974). *Type A behavior and your heart*. New York, NY: Knopf.

Friesen, W. V. (1972). Cultural differences in facial expressions in a social situation: An experimental test of the concept of display rules. Unpublished doctoral dissertation. San Francisco, CA: University of California.

Frijda, N. H. (2007). *The laws of emotion*. Mahwah, NJ: Lawrence Erlbaum Associates.

Frijda, N. H. (1986). *The emotions*. Cambridge, MA: Cambridge University Press.

Frith, C. (2003). The scientific study of consciousness. In M. A. Ron & T.W. Robbins (Eds.), *Disorders of brain and mind 2*. New York, NY: Cambridge University Press.

Frith, U. (2000). Cognitive explanations of autism. In K. Lee (Ed.), Childhood cognitive development: The essential readings. Essential readings in developmental psychology. Malden, MA: Blackwell.

Froehlich, J. C., Zink, R. W., Li, T., & Christian, J. C. (2000). Analysis of heritability of hormonal responses to alcohol in twins: Beta-endorphin as a potential biomarker of genetic risk for alcoholism. *Alcoholism: Clinical and Experimental Research, 24*(3), 265–277.

Frost, R. O., & Steketee, G. (2001). Obsessive-compulsive disorder. In H. S. Friedman (Ed.), *Specialty articles from the encyclopedia of mental health*. San Diego: Academic Press.

Frueh, B. C. (2009). Delayed-onset post-traumatic stress disorder among war veterans in primary care clinics. *British Journal of Psychiatry, 194*(6), 515–520.

Fry, C. J. (1988). Left-handedness and tongue-rolling ability. *Perceptual and Motor Skills, 67*(1), 168–170.

Fulton, J. F. (1938). *Physiology of the nervous system*. New York: Oxford University Press.

Furnham, A. (2009). The validity of a new, self-report measure of multiple intelligence. *Current Psychology: A Journal for Diverse Perspectives on Diverse Psychological Issues, 28*(4), 225–239.

Furnham, A. (2008). Personality and intelligence at work: Exploring and explaining individual differences at work. Hove: Psychology Press/ Taylor & Francis (UK).

Furnham, A., & Monsen, J. (2009). Personality traits and intelligence predict academic school grades. *Learning and Individual Differences, 19*(1), 28–33.

Gadsden, V., & Ray, A. (2003). Father's role in children's academic achievement and early literacy. *ERIC Clearinghouse on Early Education and Parenting*. Retrieved from http://www.ericdigests.org/2004-3/role.html

Gagnon, J. H. (1975). Sex research and social change. *Archives of Sexual Behavior, 4*(2).

Gahlinger, P. M. (2000). A comparison of motion sickness remedies in severe sea conditions. *Wilderness and Environmental Medicin, 11*(2), 136–167.

Gais, S., Hüllemann, P., Hallschmid, M., & Born, J. (2006). Sleep-dependent surges in growth hormone do not contribute to sleep-dependent memory consolidation. *Psychoneuroendocrinology, 31*(6), 786–791.

Galanter, E. (1962). Contemporary Psychophysics. In R. Brown, E. Galanter, E. H. Hess, & G. Mander (Eds), *New Directions in Psychology*. NY: Holt, Rinehart and Winston.

Galati, D., Sini, B., Schmidt, S., & Tinti, C. (2003). Spontaneous facial expressions in congenitally-blind and sighted children aged 8–11. *Journal of Visual Impairment and Blindness, 97*, 418–428.

Galef, B. G., Jr., & Laland, K. N. Social learning in animals: empirical studies and theoretical models. *Bioscience, 55*, 489–499.

Galef, B. G., Jr., Dudley, K. E., & Whiskin, E. E. (2008). Social Learning of food preferences in "dissatisfied" and "uncertain" Norway rats. *Animal Behaviour, 75*, 631–637.

Galanter, M. (2010). Review of *religion and spirituality in psychiatry*. *The American Journal of Psychiatry, 167*(7), 871–872.

Galanter, M. (2010). Spirituality in psychiatry: A biopsychosocial perspective. *Psychiatry: Interpersonal and Biological Processes, 73*(2), 145–157.

Gall, F. J. (1833) The anatomy and physiology of the nervous system in general, and of the brain in particular, with observations upon the possibility of ascertaining the several intellectual and moral dispositions of man and animal, by the configuration of their heads. *The American Journal of the Medical Sciences*, Southern Society for Clinical Investigation.

Gallacher, J. E. J., Sweetnam, P. M., Yarnell, J. W G., Elwood, P. C., & Stansfeld, S. A. (2003). Is type A behavior really a trigger for coronary heart disease events? *Psychosomatic Medicine, 65*(3), 339–346.

Gallese, V., Fadiga, L., Fogassi, L., & Rizzolatti, G. (1996). Action recognition in the premotor cortex. *Brain. 119*(2), 593–609.

Gallup, G. G. (1970). Chimpanzees: Self-recognition. *Science, 167*, 86–87.

Galton, F. (1948). Co-relations and their measurement, chiefly from anthropometric data, 1888. In W. Dennis (Ed.), *Readings in the history of psychology* (pp. 336–346). East Norwalk, CT: Appleton-Century-Crofts.

Gamble, A. L., Harvey, A. G., & Rapee, R. M. (2010). Specific phobia. In D. J. Stein, E. Hollander, & B. O. Rothbaum (Eds.), *Textbook of anxiety disorders (2nd Ed.)* (pp. 525–541). Arlington, VA: American Psychiatric Publishing, Inc.

Gangestad, S. W., & Thornhill, R. (1998). Menstrual cycle variation in women's preferences for the scent of symmetrical men. *Proceedings of the Royal Society of Biological Sciences, 265*(1399), 927–933.

Gansberg, M. (1964, March 27). Thirty-eight who saw murder didn't call the police. *New York Times*.

Gantt, W. H. (1980). Review of the shaping of a behaviorism (B.F. Skinner). *The Pavlovian Journal of Biological Science, 15*, 42–44.

Garbarino, J. (2011). *The positive psychology of personal transformation: Leveraging resilience for life change*. New York: Springer Science +Business Media.

Garcia, E., García, F., & Lila, M. (2009). Public responses to intimate partner violence against women: The influence of perceived severity and personal responsibility. *The Spanish Journal of Psychology, 12*(2), 648–656.

Garcia, E., Godoy-Izquierdo, D., Godoy, J. F., Perez, M., & Lopez-Chicheri, I. (2007). Gender differences in pressure pain threshold in a repeated measures assessment. *Psychology: Health, & Medicine, 12*, 567–579.

Garcia, J., & Koelling, R. A. (1971). The use of ionizing rays as a mammalian olfactory stimulus. In H. Autrum et al. (Eds.), *Handbook of sensory physiology: Volume 4*. New York: Springer-Verlag.

Garcia, J., Lasiter, P. S., Bermudez-Rattoni, F., & Deems, D. A. (1985). A general theory of aversion learning. *Annals of the New York Academy of Sciences, 443*, 8–21.

Garcia, S. M., Weaver, K., Moskowitz, G. B., & Darley, J. M. (2002). Crowded minds: The implicit bystander effect. *Journal of Personality and Social Psychology, 83*(4), 843–853.

García-García, F., De, L. H., Juárez-Aguilar, E., Regalado-Santiago, C., Millán-Aldaco, D., Blanco-Centurión, C., & Drucker-Colín, R. (2011).

Growth hormone improves hippocampal adult cell survival and counteracts the inhibitory effect of prolonged sleep deprivation on cell proliferation. *Brain Research Bulletin, 84*(3), 252–257.

Garcia-Rill, E., Charlesworth, A., Heister, D., Ye, M., & Hayer, A. (2008). The developmental decrease in REM sleep: The role of transmitters and electrical coupling. *Sleep: Journal of Sleep and Sleep Disorders Research, 31*(5), 673–690.

Gard, D. E., & Kring, A. M. (2009). Emotion in the daily lives of schizophrenia patients: Context matters. *Schizophrenia Research*.

Gardner, H. (2011). Changing minds: How the application of the multiple intelligences (MI) framework could positively contribute to the theory and practice of international negotiation. In F. Aquilar & M. Galluccio (Eds.), *Psychological and political strategies for peace negotiation: A cognitive approach* (pp. 1–14). New York: Springer Science Business Media.

Gardner, H. (1993). *Multiple intelligences: The theory in practice.* New York: Basic Books.

Gardner, H., & Traub, J. (2010). A debate on "multiple intelligences." In D. Gordon (Ed.), *Cerebrum 2010: Emerging ideas in brain science* (pp. 34–61). Washington, DC: Dana Press.

Gardner, H., & White, J. (2010). Is the theory of multiple intelligences valid? In B. Slife (Ed.), *Clashing views on psychological issues* (16th Ed., pp. 198–216). New York: McGraw-Hill.

Gardner, W. L., & Martinko, M. J. (1996). Using the Myers-Briggs Type Indicator to study managers: A literature review and research agenda. *Journal of Management, 22*(1), 45–83.

Gariepy, J-L., & Blair, C. (2008). A biological window on psychological development. *Developmental Psychobiology, 50*, 1–3.

Garlow, S. J. (2002). Age, gender, and ethnicity differences in patterns of cocaine and ethanol use preceding suicide. *American Journal of Psychiatry, 159*(4), 615–619.

Garoff-Eaton R. J., Slotnick S. D., Schacter D. L. (2006). Not all false memories are created equal: The neural basis of false recognition. *Cerebral Cortex, 16*, 1645–1652.

Garssen, B., & Goodkin, K. (1999). On the role of immunological factors as mediators between psychosocial factors and cancer progression. *Psychiatric Research, 85*(1), 51–61.

Garver, D. L. (2006). Evolution of antipsychotic intervention in the schizophrenic psychosis. *Current Drug Targets, 7*(9), 1205–1215.

Garvey, C. (1974). Requests and responses in children's speech. *Journal of Child Language, 2*, 41–60.

Gask, L., Aseem, S., Waquas, A., & Waheed, W. (2011). Isolation, feeling 'stuck' and loss of control: Understanding persistence of depression in British Pakistani women. *Journal of Affective Disorders, 128*(1–2), 49–55.

Gaston, K. E. (1978). Interocular transfer of a visually mediated conditioned food aversion in chicks. *Behavioral Biology, 24*, 272–278.

Gathercoal, K. A., Mcminn, L., Peterson, M., & Schenk, J. (2010). Female and male psychologists in academic administration: Resource control and perceived influence. *Academic Leadership: The Online Journal, 8*(3). Retrieved from http://www.academicleadership.org/article/print/Female_and_Male_Psychologists_in_Academic_Administration_Resource_Control_and_Perceived_Influence.

Gaul, M. (2007). Testimony on D.C. public schools sex education. *Family Research Council.* Retrieved from: http://www.frc.org/get.cfm?i=TS07L01.

Gawande, A. (2008). The itch. *The New Yorker*, June 30.

Gawronski, B., Deutsch, R., Mbirkou, S., Seibt, B., & Strack, F. (2008). When "just say no" is not enough: Affirmation versus negation training and the reduction of automatic stereotype activation. *Journal of Experimental Social Psychology, 44*, 370–377.

Gaynor, S. T., & Baird, S. C. (2007). Personality disorders. In D.W. Woods & J. W. Kanter (Eds.), *Understanding Behavior Disorders: A Contemporary Behavioral Perspective.* Reno, NV: Context Press.

Gazzaniga, M. S. (2010). Neuroscience and the correct level of explanation for understanding mind: An extraterrestrial roams through some neuroscience laboratories and concludes earthlings are not grasping how best to understand the mind–brain interface. *Trends in Cognitive Sciences, 14*(7), 291–292.

Gazzaniga, M. S. (2009). Two brains: My life in science. In P. Rabbitt (Ed.), *Inside Psychology* (pp. 101–116). Oxford: Oxford University Press.

Gazzaniga, M. S. (2005). Forty-five years of split-brain research and still going strong. *Nature Reviews Neuroscience, 6*, 653–659.

Gazzaniga, M. S. (1995). On neural circuits and cognition. *Neural Computation, 7*(1), 1–12.

Gazzaniga, M. S. (1995). Principles of human brain organization derived from split-brain studies. *Neuron, 14*, 217–228.

Gazzaniga, M. S. (1995). The visual analysis of shape and form. *The cognitive neurosciences* (pp. 339–350). Cambridge, MA: MIT Press.

Geary, D. C. (2005) *The Origin of Mind.* American Psychological Association.

Geddes, J. R., Stroup, T. S., & Lieberman, J. A. (2011). Comparative efficacy and effectiveness in the drug treatment of schizophrenia. In D. R. Weinberger & P. J. Harrison (Eds.), *Schizophrenia* (3rd Ed.). Hoboken, NJ: Blackwell-Wiley.

Gehrmann, J. (1996). Microglia: a sensor to threats in the nervous system? *Research in Virology, 147*(2–3), 79–88.

Geldard, F. A. (1972). *The human senses (2nd Ed.).* New York: Wiley.

Gelinas, R. & Munroe-Chandler, K. (2006). Psychological skills for successful ice hockey goaltenders. *Athletic Insight: The Online Journal of Sport Psychology, 8*(2), Retrieved from http://athleticinsight.com/Vol8Iss2/HockeyPDF.pdf.

Genesee, F., Hamers, J., Lambert, W. E., Mononen, L., Setiz, M., & Starck, R. (1978). Language processing in bilinguals. *Brain and Language, 5*(1), 1–12.

Georgas, J. (2003). Cross-cultural psychology, intelligence, and cognitive processes. In J. Georgas, L. G. Weiss, F. J. R. van de Vijver, & D. H. Saklofske (Eds.), *Culture and children's intelligence: Cross-cultural analysis of the WISC-III* (pp. 23–37). San Diego, CA: Academic Press.

George, T. P., & Weinberger, A. H. (2008). Nicotine and tobacco. In H. D. Kleber & M. Galanter (Eds.), *The American Psychiatric Publishing textbook of substance abuse treatment* (4th Ed.). Arlington, VA: American Psychiatric Publishing.

Geraerts, E. (2010). Posttraumatic memory. In G. Rosend & B. C. Frueh (Eds.), *Clinician's guide to posttraumatic stress disorder* (pp. 77–95). Hoboken, NJ: John Wiley & Sons.

Geraerts, E., Lindsay, D. S., Merckelbach, H., Jelicic, M., Raymaekers, L., Arnold, M. M., & Schooler, J. W. (2009). Cognitive mechanisms underlying recovered-memory experiences of childhood sexual abuse. *Psychological Science, 20*(1), 92–98.

Gerard, D. L. (1998). Chiarugi and Pinel considered: Soul's brain/person's mind. *Journal of the History of the Behavioral Sciences, 33*(4), 381–403.

Gerardi, M., Rothbaum, B. O., Astin, M. C., & Kelley, M. (2010). Cortisol response following exposure treatment for PTSD in rape victims. *Journal of Aggression, Maltreatment & Trauma, 19*(4), 349–356.

Gerbner, G., Gross, L. Morgan, M., & Signorielli, N. (1994). Growing up with television: The cultivation perspective. In J. Bryant & D. Zillmann (Eds.), *Media effects: Advances in theory and research* (pp. 17–41). Hillsdale, NJ: Erlbaum.

Gernsbacher, M. A., & Kaschak, M. P. (2003). Neuroimaging studies of language production and comprehension. *Annual Review of Psychology, 54*, 91–114.

Gershoff, E. T. (2002). Parental corporal punishment and associated child behaviors and experiences: A meta-analytic and theoretical review. *Psychological Bulletin, 128*, 539–579.

Gershon, I. (2010). *The breakup 2.0: Disconnecting over new media.* Ithica, NY: Cornell University Press, Sage House.

Gfeller, J. D., & Gorassini, D. R. (2010). Enhancing hypnotizability and treatment response. In S. J. Lynn, J. W. Rhue, & I. Kirsch (Eds.), *Handbook of clinical hypnosis (2nd Ed.)* (pp. 339–355). Washington, DC: American Psychological Association.

Giancola, P. R. (2002). Alcohol-related aggression in men and women: The influence of dispositional aggressivity. *Journal of Studies on Alcohol, 63*(6).

Gibbons, D. E., & Lynn, S. J. (2010). Hypnotic inductions: A primer. In S. J. Lynn, J. W. Rhue & I. Kirsch (Eds.), *Handbook of clinical hypnosis (2nd Ed.)* (pp. 267–291). Washington, DC: American Psychological Association.

Gibbs, J. C., Basinger, K. S., Grime, R. L. & Snarey, J. R. (2007). Moral judgment development across cultures: Revisiting Kohlberg's universality claims. *Developmental Review, 27*, 443–500.

Gigerenzer, G. (2004). Fast and frugal heuristics: The tools of founded rationality. In D. J. Koehler & N. Harvey (Eds.), *Blackwell handbook of judgment and decision making* (pp. 62–88). Malden, MA: Blackwell Publishing.

Gigerenzer, G., & Goldstein, D. G. (1996). Reasoning the fast and frugal way: Models of bounded rationality. *Psychological Review, 103*, 650–669.

Gilbertson, M. W., Shenton, M. E., Ciszewski, A., Kasai, K., Lasko, N. B., Orr, S. P., & Pitman, R. K. (2002). Smaller hippocampal volume predicts pathologic vulnerability to psychological trauma. *Nature Neuroscience, 5*(11), 1242–1247.

Gilchrist, A. L., & Cowan, N. (2010). Conscious and unconscious aspects of working memory. In I. Czigler, & I. Winkler (Eds.), *Unconscious memory representations in perception* (pp. 1–35) Amsterdam, Netherlands: John Benjamins Publishing Company.

Giedd, J. N. (2009). Linking adolescent sleep, brain maturation, and behavior. *Journal of Adolescent Health, 45*(4), 319–320.

Gilligan, C. (2004). Recovering psyche: Reflections on life-history and history. *The Annual of Psychoanalysis, 32,* 131–147.

Gilligan, C. (1993). *In a different voice.* Cambridge, MA: Harvard University Press.

Gilligan, C. (1982). In a different voice: Psychological theory and women's development. Cambridge, MA: Harvard University Press.

Gillham, J., Adams-Deutsch, Z., Werner, J., Reivich, K., Coulter-Heindl, V., Linkins, M., & Seligman, M. E. P. (2011). Character strengths predict subjective well-being during adolescence. *The Journal of Positive Psychology, 6*(1), 31–44.

Gillis, J. M., & Romanczyk, R. G. (2007). Autism spectrum disorders and related developmental disabilities. In M. Hersen & A. M. Gross (Eds.), *Handbook of clinical psychology (Vol.2).* Hoboken, NJ: John Wiley & Sons.

Giltay, E. J., Geleijnse, J. M., Zitman, F. G., Hoehstra, T, & Schouten, E. G. (2004). Dispositional optimism and all-cause and cardiovascular mortality in a prospective cohort of elderly Dutch men and women. *Archives of General Psychiatry, 61*, 1126–1135.

Ginandes C. S. (2006). Six players on the inner stage: Using ego state therapy with the medically ill. *International Journal of Clinical and Experimental Hypnosis, 54*(2), 113–129.

Gingras, Y. (2002). The costs of dropping out of high school. *Pan-Canadian Education Research Agenda Symposium Report.* Retrieved from http://cesc-csce.ca/ pceradocs/ 2000/ 00Gingras_e.pdf.

Gingrich, K. J., & Byrne, J. H. (1985). Simulation of synaptic depression, posttetanic potentiation, and presynaptic facilitation of synaptic potentials from sensory neurons mediating gill-withdrawal reflex in Aplysia. *Journal of Neurophysioliogy, 53*, 652–669.

Gioia, G. (2007). *Expert: Millions get concussions.* Retrieved from philly.com.

Girden, E. R., & Kabacoff, R. I. (2011). *Evaluating research articles: From start to finish* (3rd Ed.). Thousand Oaks, CA: Sage Publications.

Gläscher, J., Rudrauf, D., Colom, R., Paul, L. K., Tranel, D., Damasio, H., & Adolphs, R. (2010). Distributed neural system for general intelligence revealed by lesion mapping. *PNAS Proceedings of the National Academy of Sciences of the United States of America, 107*(10), 4705–4709.

Glaser, J., & Kihlstrom, J. F. (2005). Compensatory automaticity: Unconscious volition is not an oxymoron. In R. R. Hassin, J. S. Uleman, & J. A. Bargh (Eds.), *The new unconscious. Oxford series in social cognition and social neuroscience.* New York, NY: Oxford University Press.

Glaser, V., Carlini, V. P., Gabach, L., Ghersi, M., de Barioglio, S. R., Ramirez, O. A., . . . Latini, A. (2010). The intra-hippocampal leucine administration impairs memory consolidation and LTP generation in rats. *Cellular and Molecular Neurobiology, 30*(7), 1067–1075. doi: 10.1007/s10571-010-9538-4

Glass, J. (2005). Sociological perspectives on work and family. In S. M. Bianchi, L. M. Casper, & B. R. King (Eds.), *Work, Family, Health, and Well-Being* (pp. 215–229). Mahwah, NJ: Lawrence Erlbaum Associates Publishers.

Glassenberg, A. N., Feinberg, D. R., Jones, B. C., Little, A. C., & Debruine, L. M. (2010). Sex-dimorphic face shape preference in heterosexual and homosexual men and women. *Archives of Sexual Behavior, 39*(6), 1289–1296.

Godart, N. T., Perdereau, F., Rein, Z., Berthoz, S., Wallier, J., Jeammet, P., et al. (2007). Comorbidity studies of eating disorders and mood disorders. Critical review of the literature. *Journal of Affective Disorders, 97(1–3),* 37–49.

Gödde, G. (2010). Freud and nineteenth-century philosophical sources on the unconscious. In A. Nicholls, & M. Liebscher (Eds.), *Thinking the unconscious: Nineteenth-century german thought* (pp. 261–286). New York, NY: Cambridge University Press.

Godfrey, J. R. (2004). Toward optimal health: The experts discuss therapeutic humor. *Journal of Women's Health, 13(5),* 474–479.

Goff, D. C., & Coyle, J. T. (2001). The emerging role of glutamate in the pathophysiology and treatment of scizophrenia. *American Journal of Psychiatry, 158*, 1367–1377.

Gohm, C. L. (2003). Mood regulation and emotional intelligence: Individual differences. *Journal of Personality and Social Psychology, 84*, 594–607.

Gohm, C. L., & Clore, G. L. (2002). Four latent traits of emotional experience and their involvement in well-being, coping, and attributional style. *Cognition and Emotion, 16*, 495–518.

Gold, S. N., & Castillo, Y. (2010). Dealing with defenses and defensiveness in interviews. In D. L. Segal, & M. Hersen (Eds.), *Diagnostic interviewing* (pp. 89–102). New York, US: Springer Publishing Co.

Goldberg, A. E. (2008). Universal grammar? Or prerequisites for natural language? *Behavioral and Brain Sciences, 31*, 522–523.

Goldberg, R. F., Perfetti, C.A., & Schneider, W. (2006). Perceptual knowledge retrieval activates sensory brain regions. *Journal of Neuroscience, 26*, 4917–4921.

Goldenberg, I., & Goldenberg, H. (2011). Family therapy. In R. J. Corsini & D. Wedding (Eds.), *Current psychotherapies* (9th Ed.). Florence, KY: CENGAGE Learning.

Goldin-Meadow, S. (1999). The role of gesture in communication and thinking. *Trends in Cognitive Sciences, 3*, 419–429.

Goldstein, D. J., Potter, W. Z., Ciraulo, D. A., & Shader, R. I. (2011). Biological theories of depression and implications for current and new treatments. In D. A. Ciraulo & R. I. Shader (Eds.), *Pharmacotherapy of depression* (2nd Ed., pp. 1–32). New York: Springer Science + Business Media.

González, A. R. A., Escobar-Córdoba, F., & Castañeda, G. C. (2007). Factores de riesgo para violencia y homicidio juvenil/Risk factors for juvenile violence and homicide. *Revista Colombiana de Psiquiatria, 36*(1), 78–97.

González, J., Barros-Loscertales A., Pulvermüller F., Meseguer V., Sanjuán A., Belloch V., Avila C. (2006). Reading cinnamon activates olfactory brain regions. *Neuroimage, 32*, 906–912.

Gonzalez, T. (2010). Review of why kids kill: Inside the minds of school shooters. *Professional School Counseling, 13*(5), 281–282.

Goodenough, F. L. (1932). Expression of the emotions in a blind-deaf child. *Journal of Abnormal and Social Psychology, 27*, 328–333.

Goodwin, C. J. (2011). *Research in psychology: Methods and design* (6th Ed.). Hoboken, NJ: John Wiley & Sons.

Gopnik. A., & Astington, J. W. (1988). Children's understanding of representational change and its relation to the understanding of false belief and the appearance reality distinction. *Child Development, 59*, 26–37.

Gorman, T. (1996). Television: Glorioius past, uncertain future. *Statistics Canada*, 63F0002XPB No. 6.

Goto, Y., & Grace, A. A. (2008) Limbic and cortical information processing in the nucleus accumbens. *Trends in Neurosciences,* 31, 552–558.

Gottesman, I. I. (1991). Schizophrenia Genesis: The Origin of Madness. New York: Freeman.

Gottman, J. M., & Levenson, R. W. (1988). The social psychophysiology of marriage. In P. Noller & M. A. Fitzpatrick (Eds.), *Perspectives on marital interaction* (pp. 182–200). Multilingual Matters: Clevedon.

Goubet, N., Strasbaugh, K., & Chesney, J. (2007). Familiarity breeds content? Soothing effect of a familiar odor on full-term newborns. *Journal of Developmental and Behavioral Pediatrics, 28*, 189–194.

Gould, E. (2007). How widespread is adult neurogenesis in mammals? *Nature Reviews Neuroscience,* 8, 481–488.

Gould, S. J., & Lewontin, R. C. (1979). The sandrels of San Marco and the Panglossian paradigm: A critique of the adaptation programme. *Proceedings of the Royal Society of London, Series B, 205*, 581–598.

Gourine, A. V., Kasymov, V., Marina, N., Tang, F., Figueiredo, M., Lane, S., Teschemacher, A. G., Spyer, K. M., Deisseroth, K., & Kasparov, S. (2010). Astroctes control breathing through pH-dependent release of ATP. *Science, 329*(5991), 571–575.

Government of Canada. (2006). *The Human Face of Mental Health and Mental Illness in Canada 2006.*

Gow, A. J., Johnson, W., Pattie, A., Brett, C. E., Roberts, B., Starr, J. M., & Deary, I. J. (2011). Stability and change in intelligence from age 11 to ages 70, 79, and 87: The Lothian birth cohorts of 1921 and 1936. *Psychology and Aging, 26*(1), 232–240. doi: 10.1037/a0021072

Gozzi, M., Zamboni, G., Kruegef, F., & Grafman, J. (2010). Interest in politics modulates neural activity in the amygdala and ventral striatum. *Human Brain Mapping, 31*(11), 1763–1771.

Grahn, J. A., Parkinson, J. A., & Owen, A. M. (2008). The cognitive functions of the caudate nucleus. *Progress in Neurobiology, 86*, 141–155.

Grassian, S. (1983). Psychopathological Effects of Solitary Confinement. *American Journal of Psychiatry, 140*, 1450–1454.

Gratz, K. L. (2003). Risk factors for and functions of deliberate self-harm: An empirical and conceptual review. *Clinical Psychology: Science and Practice, 10*(2), 192–205.

Gray, J. A. (1970). The psychophysiological basis of introversion-extraversion. *Behavioral Research Therapy, 8*, 249–266.

Gray, J. A., & McNaughton, N. (2000). *The neuropsychology of anxiety (2nd Ed.).* New York, NY: Oxford University Press.

Graziano, M. S. (2006). The organization of behavioral repertoire in motor cortex. *Annual Review of Neuroscience, 29*, 105–134.

Greely, H., Sahakian, B., Harris, J., Kessler, R.C., Gazzaniga, M., Campbell, P., & Farah, M. J. (2008). Towards responsible use of cognitive-enhancing drugs by the healthy. *Nature, 456*, 702–705.

Green, J. P. (2010). Hypnosis and smoking cessation: Research and application. In S. J. Lynn, J. W. Rhue & I. Kirsch (Eds.), *Handbook of clinical hypnosis (2nd Ed.)* (pp. 593–614). Washington, DC: American Psychological Association.

Greenberg, J. (1978). The Americanization of Roseto. *Science News, 113*, 378–382.

Greenberg, L., & Goldman, R. N. (2008). *Emotion-focused couples therapy.* Washington, D.C.: American Psychological Association.

Greene, J. (2003). From neural "is" to moral "ought:" What are the moral implications of neuroscientfic moral psychology? *Neuroscience, 4*, 847–850.

Greenwald, A. G., & Banaji, M. R. (1995). Implicit social cognition: Attitudes, self-esteem, and stereotypes. *Psychological Review, 102*, 4–27.

Greenwald, A. G., Banaji, M. R., Rudman, L. A., Farnham, S. D., Nosek, B. A., & Mellott, D. S. (2002). A unified theory of implicit attitudes, stereotypes, self-esteem, and self-concept. *Psychological Review, 109*(1), 3–25.

Greenwald, A. G., McGhee, D. E., & Schwartz, J. L. K. (1998). Measuring individual differences in implicit cognition: The implicit association test. *Journal of Personality and Social Psychology, 74*, 1464–1480.

Gregoski, M. J., Barnes, V. A., Tingen, M. S., Harshfield, G. A., & Treiber, F. A. (2011). Breathing awareness meditation and LifeSkills training programs influence upon ambulatory blood pressure and sodium excretion among african american adolescents. *Journal of Adolescent Health, 48*(1), 59–64.

Grewal, D., Brackett, M., & Salovey, P. (2006). Emotional intelligence and the self-regulation of affect. In D. K. Snyder, J. Simpson, & J. N. Hughes (Eds.), *Emotion regulation in couples and families: Pathways to dysfunction and health* (pp. 37–55). Washington, DC: American Psychological Association.

Grieco, R., & Edwards, L. (2010). *The other depression: Bipolar disorder* (2nd Ed.). New York: Routledge/Taylor & Francis Group.

Groer, M., Meagher, M. W., & Kendall-Tackett, K. (2010). An overview of stress and immunity. *The psychoneuroimmunology of chronic disease: Exploring the links between inflammation, stress, and illness* (pp. 9–22). Washington, DC: American Psychological Association.

Gross, C. G. (2005). Processing the facial image: a brief history. *American Psychologist, 60*, 755–763.

Gross, J. J. (1998). The emerging field of emotion regulation: An integrative review. *Review of General Psychology, 2*, 271–299.

Gross, J. J., & John, O. P. (2003). Individual differences in two emotion regulation processes: Implications for affect, relationships, and well-being. *Journal of Personality and Social Psychology, 85*(2), 348–362.

Gross, J. J., & John, O. P. (1998). Mapping the domain of expressivity: Multimethod evidence for a hierarchical model. *Journal of Personality and Social Psychology, 74*(1), 170–191.

Gross, J. J., Richards, J. M., & John, O. P. 2006. Emotion regulation in everyday life. In D. K. Snyder, J. A. Simpson, & J. N. Hughes (Eds.), *Emotion Regulation in Families: Pathways to Dysfunction and Health* (pp. 13–25). Washington, DC: American Psychological Association.

Grossmann, K., Grossmann, K., Fremmer-Bombik, E., Kindler, H., Scheuerer-Englisch, H., Zimmermann, P. (2002). The uniqueness of the child-father attachment relationship: Fathers' sensitive and challenging play as a pivotal variable in a 16-year longitudinal study. *Social Development, 11*(3), 301–337.

Grotenhermen, F. (2002). Review of therapeutic effects. *Cannabis and Cannabinoids: Pharmacology, Toxicology and Therapeutic Potential.* New York City: Haworth Press.

Gruneberg, M. M., & Sykes, R. N. (1993). The generalisability of confidence—accuracy studies in eyewitnessing. *Memory, 1*(3), 185–189.

Grusec, J. E., & Ungerer, J. (2003). Effective socialization as problem solving and the role of parenting cognitions. In L. Kuczynski (Ed.,), *Handbook of dynamics in parent–child relations* (pp. 211–228). Thousand Oaks, CA: Sage.

GSS (General Social Survey). (2007). *Job satisfaction in the United States.* Chicago, IL: National Opinion Research Center.

Guberman, A. (2004). Vagus nerve stimulation in the treatment of epilepsy. *Canadian Medical Association Journal, 171(10)*, 1165–1166.

Guéguen, N. (2002). Foot-in-the-door technique and computer-mediated communication, *Computers in Human Behavior, 18*(1), 11–15.

Guevara, R. E. (2008). A 13-year retrospective study on listeriosis in Los Angeles County, 1992-2004. *Dissertation Abstracts International: Section B: The Sciences and Engineering, 69*(1-B), 203.

Guimon, J. (2010). Prejudice and realities in stigma. *International Journal of Mental Health, 39*(3), 20–43.

Gumustekin, K., Seven, B., Karabulut, N., Aktas, O., Gursan, N., Aslan, S., Keles, M., Varoglu, E., & Dane, S. (2004). Effects of sleep deprivation, nicotine, and selenium on wound healing in rats (Abstract). *International Journal of Neuroscience, 114*(11), 1433–1442.

Gunderson, J. G. (2011). Borderline personality disorder. *The New England Journal of Medicine, 364*(21), 2037–2042.

Gunderson, L., & Scarr, S. (2001). The evils of the use of IQ tests to define learning disabilities in first and second language learners. *The Reading Teacher, 55*(1), 48–55.

Gunzelmann, G., Moore, L. R., Gluck, K. A., Van Dongen, H. P. A., & Dinges, D. F. (2011). Fatigue in sustained attention: Generalizing mechanisms for time awake to time on task. In P. L. Ackerman (Ed.), *Cognitive fatigue: Multidisciplinary perspectives on current research and future applications* (pp. 83–101). Washington, DC: American Psychological Association.

Gurman, A. S., & Snyder, D. K. (2011). Couple therapy. In J. C. Norcross, G. R. VandenBos, & D. K. Freedheim (Eds.), *History of psychotherapy: Continuity and change* (2nd Ed., pp. 485–496). Washington, DC: American Psychological Association.

Guttorm, T. K., Leppänen, P. H., Poikkeus, A. M., Eklund, K. M., Lyytinen, P., & Lyytinen, H. (2005). Brain event-related potentials (ERPs) measured at birth predict later language development in children with and without familial risk for dyslexia. *Cortex* (Elsevier Science), *41*(3), 291–303.

Haaken, J., & Reavey, P. (2010). Why memory still matters: Disturbing recollections. In J. Haaken & P. Reavey (Eds.), *Memory matters: Contexts for understanding sexual abuse recollections* (pp. 1–13). New York: Routledge/Taylor & Francis Group.

Haas, B. W., Omura, K., Constable, R. T., & Canli, T. (2007). Emotional conflict and neuroticism: Personality-dependent activation in the amygdala and subgenual anterior cingulate. *Behavioral Neuroscience, 121*(2), 249–256.

Haber, S. N., (2003). The primate basal ganglia: parallel and integrative networks. *Journal of Chemical Neuroanatomy, 26*(4), 317–330.

Hagan, M. M., Chandler, P. C., Wauford, P. K., Rybak, R. J., & Oswald, K. D. (2003). The role of palatable food and hunger as trigger factors in an animal model of stress induced binge eating. *The International Journal of Eating Disorders, 34*(2), 183–197.

Hagelin, J., Carlsson, H.-E., Hau, J. (2003). An overview of surveys on how people view animal experimentation: Some factors that may influence the outcome. *Public Understanding of Science, 12*(1), 67–81.

Hagemoser, S. D. (2009). Braking the bandwagon: Scrutinizing the science and politics of empirically supported therapies. *Journal of Psychology: Interdisciplinary and Applied, 143*(6), 601–614.

Haldeman, D. C. (1994). The practice and ethics of sexual orientation conversion. *Journal of Consulting and Clinical Psychology, 62*(2), 221–227.

Hale, C. M., & Tager-Flusberg, H. (2005). Social communication in children with autism: The relationship between theory of mind and discourse development. *Autism, 9*(2), 157–178.

Hall, C. W., & Webster, R. E. (2002). Traumatic symptomatology characteristics of adult children of alcoholics. *Journal of Drug Education, 32*(3), 195–211.

Hall, W. D., & Lucke J. C. (2010). The enhancement use of neuropharmaceuticals: more skepticism and caution needed. *Addiction, 105*, 2041–2043.

Halle, M. (1990). Phonology. In D. N. Osherson and H. Lasnick (Eds.), *An Invitation to Cognitive Science, Vol. 1: Language*. Cambridge MA: MIT Press.

Halliday, G. (2004). Dreamwork and nightmares with incarcerated juvenile felons. *Dreaming, 14*(1), 30–42.

Halpern, D. F. (2000). *Sex Differences in Cognitive Abilities* (3rd Ed.). Mahwah, NJ: Lawrence Erlbaum Associates.

Hamani, C., Diwan, M., Raymond, R., Nobrega, J. N., Macedo, C. E., Brandao, M. L., & Fletcher, P. J. (2011). Reply to: Electrical brain stimulation in depression: Which target(s)? *Biological Psychiatry, 69*(4), e7–e8.

Hamann, S. B., Ely, T. D., Hoffman, J. M., & Kilts, C. D. (2002). Ecstasy and agony: Activation of the human amygdale in positive and negative emotion. *Psychological Science, 13*(2), 135–141.

Hambree, R. (1988). Correlates, causes, effects, and treatments of test anxiety. *Review of Educational Research, 58*(1), 47–77.

Hambrick, D. Z., & Engle, R. W. (2003). The role of working memory in problem solving. In J. E. Davidson & R. J. Sternberg (Eds.), *The psychology of problem solving* (pp. 176–206). New York, NY: Cambridge University Press.

Hammen, C., Kim, E. Y., Eberhart, N. K., & Brennan, P. A. (2009). Chronic and acute stress and the prediction of major depression in women. *Depression and Anxiety, 26*(8), 718–723.

Hammer, T. (1993). Unemployment and mental health among young people: A longitudinal study. *Journal of Adolescence, 16*(4), 407–420.

Hammond, D. C. (2008). Hypnosis as sole anesthesia for major surgeries: Historical & contemporary perspectives. *American Journal of Clinical Hypnosis, 51*(2), 101–121.

Haney, C., Banks, C., & Zimbardo, P. (1973). Interpersonal dynamics in a simulated prison. *International Journal of Criminology & Penology, 1*, 69–97.

Haney, M. (2008). Neurobiology of stimulants. In H. D. Kleber & M. Galanter (Eds.), *The American Psychiatric Publishing textbook of substance abuse treatment (4th Ed.)*. Washington, DC: American Psychiatric Publishing.

Hanin, Y. L. (1997). Emotions and athletic performance: Individual zones of optimal functioning. *European Yearbook of Sport Psychology, 1*, 29–72.

Hanna, D., Kershaw, K., & Chaplin, R. (2009). How specialist ECT consultants inform patients about memory loss. *Psychiatric Bulletin, 33*(11), 412–415.

Hardin, S. B., Weinrich, S., Weinrich, M., Garrison, C., Addy, C., & Hardin, T. L. (2002). Effects of a long-term psychosocial nursing intervention on adolescents exposed to catastrophic stress. *Issues in Mental Health Nursing, 23*(6), 537–551.

Hare, R. D. (2003). *Psychopathy checklist-revised technical manual, 2nd Ed.* Toronto: Multihealth Systems, Inc.

Hare, R. D. (1993) *Without Conscience: The Disturbing World of Psychopaths Among Us*. New York: Pocket Books.

Harker, L., & Keltner, D. (2001). Expressions of positive emotion in women's college yearbook pictures and their relationship to personality and life outcomes across adulthood. *Journal of Personality and Social Psychology, 80*(1), 112–124.

Harlow, J. M. (1868). Recovery from the passage of an iron bar through the head. *Publications of the Massachusetts Medical Society, 2*, 327–347.

Harlow, J. M. (1848). Passage of an iron rod through the head. *Boston Medical and Surgical Journal, 39*, 389–393. (Republished in Neylan, T. C. (1999). Frontal lobe function: Mr. Phineas Gage's famous injury. *Journal of Neuropsychiatry and Clinical Neuroscience, 11*, 281–283.)

Harman, C., & Fox, N. A. (1997). Frontal and attentional mechanisms regulating distress experience and expression during infancy. In N. A. Krasnegor, G. R. Lyon, & P. S. Goldman-Rakic (Eds.), *Development of the Prefrontal Cortex: Evolution, Neurobiology, and Behavior* (pp. 191–208). Baltimore, MD: Paul H Brookes Publishing.

Harrell, W. A. (1981). Verbal aggressiveness in spectators at professional hockey games: The effects of tolerance of violence and amount of exposure to hockey. *Human Relations, 34*(8), 643–655.

Harris, B. (1979). Whatever happened to Little Albert? *American Psychologist, 34*(2), 151–160.

Harris, J. C. (2010). *Intellectual disability: A guide for families and professionals*. New York: Oxford University Press.

Harrison, R. V. (2008). Noise-induced hearing loss in children: A 'less than silent' environmental danger. *Paediatric Children's Health, 13*(5), 377–382.

Harrison, Y., & Horne, J. A. (2000). The impact of sleep deprivation on decision making: A review. *Journal of Experimental Psychology: Applied, 6*, 236–249.

Hart, B., & Risley, T. R. (1995). Meaningful differences in everyday experiences of young American children. Baltimore, MD: Paul Brookes.

Hart, C., Ksir, C., & Oakley, R. (2010). *Drugs, society, and human behavior.* New York, NY: McGraw-Hill.

Hartman, D. E. (2009). Test review: Wechsler adult intelligence scale IV (WAIS IV): Return of the gold standard. *Applied Neuropsychology, 16*(1), 85–87.

Hartmann, U., & Waldinger, M. D. (2007). Treatment of delayed ejaculation. *Principles and practice of sex therapy (4th Ed.)* (pp. 241–276). New York, NY: Guilford Press.

Harvey, J. H. (2008). Growth through loss and adversity in close relationships. *Trauma, recovery, and growth: Positive psychological perspectives on posttraumatic stress* (pp. 125–143). Hoboken, NJ: John Wiley & Sons Inc.

Harvey, N. L., Srinivasan, R. S., Dillard, M. E., Johnson, N. C., Witte, M. H., Boyd, K., et al. (2005). Lymphatic vascular defects promoted by Prox1 haploinsufficiency cause adult-onset obesity. *Nature genetics, 37*(10), 1072–1081.

Harway, M. (Ed.). (2005). *Handbook of couples therapy*. New York, NY: Wiley.

Hassin, R. R. (2005). Nonconscious control and implicit working memory. In R. R. Hassin, J. S. Uleman, & J. A. Bargh (Eds.), *The new unconscious* (pp. 196–222). New York, NY: Oxford University Press.

Hauser, M. D. (2000). Morals, apes, and us; when Binti the gorilla rescued a small boy who fell into her enclosure at a Chicago zoo, did she know she was doing a good deed? Can animals learn to share, cooperate, and punish? *Discover, 21*(2), 50–55.

Hawkins, R. D., Cohen, T. E., & Kandel, E. R. (2006). Dishabituation in Aplysia can involve either reversal of habituation or superimposed sensitization. *Learning & Memory, 13*, 397–403.

Hawkley, L. C., Berntson, G. G., Engeland, C. G., Marucha, P.T., Masi, C. M., & Cacioppo, J. T. (2005). *Canadian Psychology/Psychologie Canadienne, 46*(3), 115–125.

Hawley, W. R., Grissom, E. M., & Dohanich, G. P. (2011). The relationships between trait anxiety, place recognition memory, and learning strategy. *Behavioural Brain Research, 216*(2), 525–530. doi: 10.1016/j.bbr.2010.08.028

Haxel, B. R., Grant, L., & Mackay-Sim, A. (2008). Olfactory dysfunction after head injury. *The Journal of Head Trauma Rehabilitation, 23*, 407–413.

Hayaki, J., Friedman, M. A., & Brownell, K. D. (2002). Shame and severity of bulimic symptoms. *Eating Behaviors, 3*(1), 73–83.

Hayatbakhsh, M. R., Najman, J. M., McGee, T. R., Bor, W., & O'Callaghan, M. J. (2009). Early pubertal maturation in the prediction of early adult substance use: A prospective study. *Addiction, 104*(1), 59–66.

Haydon, P. G., Blendy, J., Moss, S. J., & Jackson, R. F. (2009). Astrocytic control of synaptic transmission and plasticity: a target for drugs of abuse? *Neuropharmacology, 56*(1), 83–90.

Hayes, S. C. (2004). Acceptance and commitment therapy, relational frame theory, and the third wave of behavioral and cognitive therapies. *Behavior Therapy, 35*(4), 639–665.

Hayes, S. C., Follette, V. M., & Linehan, M. M. (Eds.). (2004). *Mindfulness and acceptance: Expanding the cognitive-behavioral tradition.* New York: Guilford Press.

Haynes, S. G., Feinleib, M., & Kannel, W B. (1980). The relationship of psychosocial factors to coronary heart disease in the framingham study: III. Eight-year incidence of coronary heart disease. *American Journal of Epidemiology, 111*(1), 37–58.

Hazan, C., & Shaver, P. R. (2004). Attachment as an organizational framework for research on close relationships. In H. T. Reis, & C. E. Rusbult (Eds.), *Close relationships: Key readings* (pp. 153–174). Philadelphia, PA: Taylor & Francis.

Hazan, C., & Shaver, P. R. (1994). Attachment as an organizational framework for research on close relationships. *Psychological Inquiry: 5*(1), 1–22.

Hazan, C., & Shaver, P. R. (1994). Deeper into attachment theory. *Psychological Inquiry, 5*(1), 68–79.

Hazan, C., & Shaver, P. (1987). Romantic love conceptualized as an attachment process. *Journal of Personality and Social Psychology, 52*(3), 511–524.

Hazlett, H. C., Hammer, J., Hooper, S. R., & Kamphaus, R. W. (2011). Down syndrome. In S. Goldstein & C. R. Reynolds (Eds.), *Handbook of neurodevelopmental and genetic disorders in children* (2nd Ed., pp. 362–381). New York: Guilford Press.

Headey, B. (2008). Life goals matter to happiness: A revision of set-point theory. *Social Indicators Research, 86*(2), 213–231.

Health Canada. (2010). *Human Papillomavirus (HPV), it's your life.* Health Canada and the Public Health Agency of Canada. Retrieved from http://www.hc-sc.gc.ca/hl-vs/alt_formats/pdf/iyh-vsv/diseases-maladies/hpv-vph-eng.pdf.

Health Canada. (2009). *Canadian alcohol and drug use monitoring survey.* Retrieved from http://www.hc-sc.gc.ca/hc-ps/drugs-drogues/stat/_2009/summary-sommaire-eng.php.

Health Canada. (2008). *Canadian tobacco use monitoring survey.* Retrieved from http://www.hc-sc.gc.ca/hc-ps/tobac-tabac/research-recherche/stat/_ctums-esutc_2008/ann-eng.php.

Health Canada. (2006). *2004 canadian community health survey (CCHS): Nutrition.* Retrieved from http://www.hc-sc.gc.ca/fn-an/alt_formats/hpfb-dgpsa/pdf/surveill/cchs-guide-escc-eng.pdf.

Health Canada. (2005). *STOP fetal alcohol syndrome/fetal alcohol effects now!* Retrieved from http://www.hc-sc.gc.ca/fniah-spnia/pubs/famil/_preg-gros/stop-arret-syndrome/index-eng.php.

Health Canada. (2003). *Canadian guidelines for body weight classification in adults.* Retrieved from http://www.hc-sc.gc.ca/fn-an/alt_formats/hpfb-dgpsa/pdf/nutrition/weight_book-livres_des_poids-eng.pdf.

Health Canada. (2002). *A report on mental illness in Canada.* Retrieved from http://www.phac-aspc.gc.ca/publicat/miic-mmac/pdf/men_ill_e.pdf accessed.

Healy, A. F., Kosslyn, S. M., & Shiffrin, R. M. (Eds.) (1992). *From learning processes to cognitive processes.* Hillsdale, NJ: Lawrence Erlbaum.

Healy, D. (2005). *Psychiatric drugs explained, 4th Ed.* Britain: Elsevier Limited.

Heath, A. C., Madden, P. A., Cloninger, C. R., & Martin, N. G. (1994). Genetic and environmental structure of personality. In C. R. Cloninger (Ed.), *Personality and Psychopathology.* Washington, D.C.: American Psychiatric Press.

Hebb, D. (1949). *The Organization of Behavior: A Neuropsychological Theory.* New York: Wiley.

Hebl, M. R., & Mannix, L. M. (2003). The weight of obesity in evaluating others: A mere proximity effect. *Personality and Social Psychology Bulletin, 29*(1), 28–38.

Hedden, T., & Gabrieli, J. D. E. (2004). Insights into the ageing mind: A view from cognitive neuroscience. *Nature Reviews Neuroscience, 5*(2), 87–96. doi: 10.1038/nrn1323

Heider, E. R. (1972). *Universals in color naming and memory.*

Heilman, M. E., Block, C. J., & Martell, R. F. (1995). Sex stereotypes: Do they influence perceptions of managers? *Journal of Social Behavior and Personality, 10,* 237–252.

Heiman, J. R. (2007). Orgasmic disorders in women. *Principles and practice of sex therapy (4th Ed.)* (pp. 84–123). New York, NY: Guilford Press.

Heimberg, R. G., Brozovich, F. A., & Rapee, R. M. (2010). A cognitive-behavioral model of social anxiety disorder: Update and extension. In S. G. Hofmann & P. M. DiBartolo (Eds.), *Social Anxiety: Clinical, developmental, and social perspectives.* New York: Academic Press.

Heller, A. C., Amar, A. P., Liu, C. Y., & Apuzzo, M. L. (2006). Surgery of the mind and mood: A mosaic of issues in time and evolution. *Neurosurgery, 59,* 720–733.

Hellman, K., Hernandez, P., Park, A., & Abel, T. (2010). Genetic evidence for a role for protein kinase A in the maintenance of sleep and thalamocortical oscillations. *Sleep: Journal of Sleep and Sleep Disorders Research, 33*(1), 19–28.

Henderson, H. A., & Wachs, T. D. (2007). Temperament theory and the study of cognitive-emotion interactions across development. *Developmental Review, 27,* 396–427.

Henderson, V. (2010). Diminishing dissociative experiences for war veterans in group therapy. In S. S. Fehr (Ed.), *101 interventions in group therapy* (rev. Ed., pp. 217–220). New York: Routledge/Taylor & Francis Group.

Henley, N. M. (1977). *Body politics: Power, sex, and nonverbal communication.* Englewood Cliffs, NJ: Prentice Hall.

Hennessey, B. A. (2010). The creativity—motivation connection. In J. C. Kaufman & R. J. Sternberg (Eds.), *The Cambridge handbook of creativity* (pp. 342–365). New York: Cambridge University Press.

Henningsen, D. D., Henningsen, M. L. M., Eden, J., & Cruz, M. G. (2006). Examining the symptoms of groupthink and retrospective sense-making. *Small Group Research, 37*(1), 36–64.

Henry, J. P., & Cassel, J. C. (1969). Psychosocial factors in essential hypertension: Recent epidemiologic and animal experimental evidence. *American Journal of Epidemiology, 90*(3), 171–200.

Hepp, U., Klaghofer, R., Burkhard, K., & Buddeberg, C. (2002). Treatment history of transsexual patients: A retrospective follow-up study. *Nervenarzt, 73*(3), 283–288.

Herd, S. A., Banich, M. T., & O'Reilly, R. C. (2006) Neural mechanisms of cognitive control: An integrative model of stroop task performance and FMRI data. *Journal of Cognitive Neuroscience, 18,* 22–32.

Herdt, G. (2010). Sex/gender, culture, and development: Issues in the emergence of puberty and attraction. In C. M. Worthman, P. M. Plotsky, D. S. Schechter, & C. A. Cummings (Eds.), *Formative experiences: The interaction of caregiving, culture, and developmental psychobiology* (pp. 356–374). New York: Cambridge University Press.

Hergenhahn, B. R. (2009). *An Introduction to the History of Psychology* (6th Ed.). Belmont, CA: Thomson Wadsworth.

Hergenhahn, B. R. (2005). *An introduction to the history of psychology.* (5th Ed.). Belmont, CA: Thomson Wadsworth.

Hertrich, I., Dietrich, S., Moos, A., Trouvain, J., Ackermann, H. (2009). Enhanced speech perception capabilities in a blind listener are associated with activation of fusiform gyrus and primary visual cortex. *Neurocase: The Neural Basis of Cognition, 15*(2), 163–170.

Hertzman, C. (2009) The state of child development in Canada: Are we moving toward, or away from, equity from the start? *Paediatric Children's Health, 14*(10), 673–676.

Herxheimer, A., & Petrie K. J. (2002). Melatonin for the prevention and treatment of jet lag (Cochrane Review). *The Cochrane Library, 2.* Oxford: Update Software.

Hiatt, L. R. (1978). Classification of the emotions. In L. R. Hiatt (Ed.), *Australian aboriginal concepts* (pp. 182–187). Princeton, NJ: Humanities Press.

Hiday, V. A., & Burns, P. J. (2010). Mental illness and the criminal justice system. In T. L. Scheid, & T. N. Brown (Eds.), *A handbook for the study of mental health: Social contexts, theories, and systems* (2nd Ed., pp. 478–498). New York: Cambridge University Press.

Hien, D., Litt, L. C., Cohen, L. R., Miele, G. M., & Campbell, A. (2009). Emotion regulation. *Trauma services for women in substance abuse treatment: An integrated approach* (pp. 55–74). Washington, DC: American Psychological Association.

Higgins, E. S., & George, M. S. (2007). *The neuroscience of clinical psychiatry: The pathophysiology of behavior and mental illness.* Philadelphia, PA: Wolters Kluwer/Lippincott Williams & Wilkins.

Higgins, S. T., Heil, S. H., & Lussier, J. P. (2004). Clinical implications of reinforcement as a determinant of substance use disorders. *Annual Review of Psychology, 55,* 431–461.

Highet, N., Thompson, M., & McNair, B. (2005). Identifying depression in a family member: The carers' experience. *Journal of Affective Disorders, 87*(1), 25–33.

Hilgard, E. R. (1992). Dissociation and theories of hypnosis. In E. Fromm & M.R. Nash (Eds.), *Contemporary hypnosis research.* New York, NY: Guilford Press.

Hilgard, E. R. (1991). Suggestibility and suggestions as related to hypnosis. In J. F. Schumaker (Ed.), *Human suggestibility: Advances in theory, research, and application.* Florence, KY: Taylor & Frances/Routledge.

Hilgard, E. R. (1982). Hypnotic susceptibility and implications for measurement. *International Journal of Clinical and Experimental Hypnosis, 30*(4), 394–403.

Hill, D. E., Yeo, R. A., Campbell, R. A., Hart, B., Vigil, J., & Brooks, W. (2003). Magnetic resonance imaging correlates of attention-deficit/hyperactivity disorder in children. *Neuropsychology, 17,* 496–506.

Hines, M. (2004). In A. Eagly, A. Beall, & R.Sternberg (Eds.) *The Psychology of Gender (2nd Ed.).* New York, NY: Guilford Press.

Hines, M., & Kaufman, F. R. (1994) Androgen and the development of human sex-typical behavior: Rough-and-tumble play and sex of preferred playmates in children with congenital adrenal hyperplasia (CAH). *Child Development, 65*(4), 1042–1053.

Hines, T. (1987). Left brain/right brain mythology and implications for management and training. *The Academy of Management Review, 12*(4).

Hinshaw, S. P. (2008). Developmental psychopathology as a scientific discipline: Relevance to behavioral and emotional disorders of childhood and adolescence. In T. P. Beauchaine & S. P. Hinshaw (Eds.), *Child and adolescent psychopathology*. Hoboken, NJ: John Wiley & Sons, Inc.

Hinshaw, S. P. (2002). Process, mechanism, and explanation related to externalizing behavior in developmental psychopathology. *Journal of Abnormal Child Psychology, 30*, 431–446.

Hinton, E. C., Holland, A. J., Gellatly, M. S., Soni, S., & Owen, A. M. (2006). An investigation into food preferences and the neural basis of food-related incentive motivation in Prader-Willi syndrome. *Journal of Intellectual Disability Research, 50*(9), 633–642.

Hirata, S. (2009). Chimpanzee social intelligence: selfishness, altruism, and the mother-infant bond. *Primates, 50*, 2–11.

Hirshfiled, S., Remien, R. H., Humberstone, M., Walavalkar, I., & Chiasson, M. A., (2004). Substance use and high-risk sex among men who have sex with men: A national online study in the USA. *AIDS Care, 16*(8), 1036–1047.

Hitchcock, S. T. (2005). *Karen Horney: Pioneer of feminine psychology*. Women in Medicine series, Chelsea House Publishers.

Hitti, M. (2004). Brain chemicals suggest marijuana's effects. *WebMD*. Retrieved from my.webmd.com/content/ Article/94/102660.htm.

Hjerl, K., Andersen, E. W., Keiding, N., Mouridsen, H. T., Mortensen, P. B., & Jorgensen, T. (2003). Depression as a prognostic for breast cancer mortality. *Journal of Consultation and Liaison Psychiatry, 44*(1), 24–30.

Hobson, C. J., & Delunas, L. (2001). National norms and life-event frequencies for the revised social readjustment rating scale. *International Journal of Stress Management, 8*(4), 299–314.

Hobson, C. J., Kamen, J., Szostek, J., Nethercut, C. M., Tiedmann, J. W., & Wojnarowicz, S. (1998). Stressful life events: A revision and update of the Social Readjustment Rating Scale. *Interational Journal of Stress Management, 5*(1), 1–23.

Hobson, J. A. (2009). REM sleep and dreaming: Towards a theory of protoconsciousness. *Nature Reviews Neuroscience, 10*(11), 803–813.

Hobson, J. A. (2005). Sleep is of the brain, by the brain and for the brain. *Nature, 437*, 1254–1256.

Hobson, J. A., & McCarley, R. W. (1977). The brain as dream state generator: An activation-synthesis hypothesis of the dream process. *American Journal of Psychiatry, 134*, 1335–1348.

Hobson, J. A., Pace-Schott, E., & Stickgold, R. (2003). Dreaming and the brain: Toward a cognitive neuroscience of conscious states. In E. F. Pace-Schott, M. Solms, M. Blagrove, & S. Harnad (Eds.), *Sleep and dreaming: Scientific advances and reconsiderations* (pp. 1–50). New York, NY: Cambridge University Press.

Hobson, J. A., Sangsanguan, S., Arantes, H., & Kahn, D. (2011). Dream logic—The inferential reasoning paradigm. *Dreaming, 21*(1), 1–15.

Hobson, J. A., Stickgold, R., & Pace-Schott, E. F. (1998). The neuropsychology of REM sleep dreaming. *Neuroreport: An International Journal for the Rapid Communication of Research in Neuroscience, 9*(3), R1–R14.

Hochman, J. (2010). The eidetic: An image whose time has come? *Journal of Mental Imagery, 34*(1–2), 1–9.

Hochman, J. (2001). A basic online search on the eidetic with PsycINFO, MEDLINE and ERIC. *Journal of Mental Imagery, 25*(1–2), 99–215.

Hoeft, F., Hernandez, A., McMillon, G., Taylor-Hill, H., Martindale, J. L., Meyler, A., Keller, T. A., Siok, W. T., Deutsch, G. K., Just, M. A., Whitfield-Gabrieli, S., & Gabrieli, J. D. (2006). Neural basis of dyslexia: a comparison between dyslexic and nondyslexic children equated for reading ability. *Journal of Neuroscience, 26*, 10700–10708.

Hoek, H. W. (2007). Incidence, prevalence and mortality of anorexia and other eating disorders. *Current Opinion in Psychiatry, 19*(4), 389–394.

Hoeksema-van Orden, C. Y. D., Gaillard, A. W. K., & Buunk, B. P. (1998). Social loafing under fatigue. *Journal of Personality and Social Psychology, 75*, 1179–1190.

Hoffmann, J. P. (2002, May). The community context of family structure and adolescent drug use. *Journal of Marriage and Family, 64*, 314–330.

Hofmann, S. G. (2007). Cognitive factors that maintain social anxiety disorder: A comprehensive model and its treatment implications. *Cognitive Behaviour Therapy, 36*(4), 193–209.

Hofmann, W., Friese, M., Schmeichel, B. J., & Baddeley, A. D. (2011). Working memory and self-regulation. In K. D. Vohs, & R. F. Baumeister (Eds.), *Handbook of self-regulation: Research, theory, and applications (2nd Ed.)* (pp. 204–225). New York, NY: Guilford Press.

Hofstede, G., & McCrae, R. R. (2004). Culture and personality revisited: Linking traits and dimensions of culture. *Cross-Cultural Research, 38*, 52–88.

Hogan, J., & Hogan, R. (1993). *The ambiguity of conscientiousness.* Paper presented at the 8th annual conference of the Society for Industrial and Organizational Psychology, San Francisco.

Hoigaard, R., Säfvenbom, R., & Tonnessen, F. E. (2006). The relationship between group cohesion, group norms, and perceived social loafing in soccer teams. *Small Group Research, 37*(3), 217–232.

Holahan, C. J., & Moos, R. H. (1990). Life stressors, resistance factors, and improved psychological functioning: An extension of the stress resistance paradigm. *Journal of Personality and Social Psychology, 58*(5), 909–917.

Holahan, C. J., & Moos, R. H. (1985). Life stress and health: Personality, coping, and family support in stress resistance. *Journal of Personality and Social Psychology, 49*(3), 739–747.

Holcomb, T. F. (2010). Transitioning into retirement as a stressful life event. In T. W. Miller (Ed.), *Handbook of stressful transitions across the lifespan* (pp. 133–146). New York: Springer Science + Business Media.

Holland, A. J., Treasure, J., Coskeran, P., Dallow, J., Milton, N., & Hillhouse, E. (1993). Measurement of excessive appetite and metabolic changes in Prader-Willi syndrome. *International Journal of Obesity and Related Metabolic Disorders, 17*, 527–532.

Hollon, S. D, & DiGiuseppe, R. (2011). Cognitive theories of psychotherapy. In J. C. Norcross, G. R. VandenBos, & D. K. Freedheim (Eds), *History of psychotherapy: Continuity and change* (2nd Ed.) (pp. 203–241). Washington, DC: American Psychological Association.

Hollon, S. D., Haman, K. L., & Brown, L. L. (2002). Cognitive behavioral treatment of depression. In I. H. Gotlib & C. L. Hammen (Eds.), *Handbook of depression* (pp. 383–403). New York, NY: Guilford Press.

Holmes, D. (1990). The evidence for repression: An examination of sixty years of research. In J. Springer (Ed.), *Repression and dissociation: Implications for personality, theory, psychopathology, and health* (pp. 85–102). Chicago: University of Chicago Press.

Holmes, J. (1993). *John Bowlby and attachment theory*. New York, Routledge.

Holmes, S. E., Slaughter, J. R., & Kashani, J. (2001). Risk factors in childhood that lead to the development of conduct disorder and antisocial personality disorder. *Child Psychiatry & Human Development, 31*(3), 183–193.

Holmes, T. H., & Rahe, R. H. (1989). The social readjustment rating scale. In T. H. Holmes & E. M. David (Eds.), *Life change, life events, and illness: Selected papers*. New York, NY: Praeger.

Holmes, T. H., & Rahe, R. H. (1967). The social readjustment rating scale. *Journal of Psychosomatic Research., 11*, 213–218.

Holstege, G., Georgiadis, J. R., Paans, A. M., Meiners, L. C., & Graaf, F. H. (2003). Brain activation during human male ejaculation. *Experimental Brain Research, 23*(27), 9185–9193.

Holt-Lunstad, J., Birmingham, W., & Jones, B. Q. (2008). Is there something unique about marriage? The relative impact of marital status, relationship quality, and network social support on ambulatory blood pressure and mental health. *Annals of Behavioral Medicine, 35*(2), 239–244.

Holyoak, K. J., & Morrison (2005). Analogy. In K. J. Holyoak & R. G. Morrison (Eds.), *The Cambridge Handbook of Thinking and Reasoning* (pp. 409–414). New York, NY: Cambridge University Press.

Holzman, L. (2009). *Vygotsky at work and play*. Oxford, UK: Routledge.

Hommel, J. D., Trinko, R., Sears, R. M., Georgescu, D., Liu, Z. W., Gao, X. B., Thurmon, J. J., Marinelli, M., & DiLeone, R. J. (2006). Leptin receptor signaling in midbrain dopamine neurons regulates feeding. *Neuron 51*, 801–810.

Homstol, L. (2011). *Applications of learning theory to human-bear conflict: The efficacy of aversive conditioning and conditioned taste aversion.* Master thesis completed in partial fulfillment of the degree of Master of Science, Biological Sciences, University of Alberta.

Hong, J., Schonwald, A., & Stein, M. T. (2008). Barking vocalizations and shaking movements in a 13-year old girl. *Journal of Developmental and Behavioral Pediatrics, 29*(2), 135–137.

Hong, Y., Morris, M. W., Chiu, Y., & Benet-Martinez, V. (2000). Multicultural minds: A dynamic constructivist approach to culture and cognition. *American Psychologist, 55,* 709–717.

Hope, D. A., Burns, J. A., Hayes, S. A., Herbert, J. D., & Warner, M. D. (2010). Automatic thoughts and cognitive restructuring in cognitive behavioral group therapy for social anxiety disorder. *Cognitive Therapy and Research, 34*(1), 1–12.

Hopkin, K. (2010). Some nerve. *The Scientist, 24*(9), 52.

Horn, M. (2005). Rude awakening: What to do with the sleepwalking defense. *Boston College Law Review, 46,* 149–182.

Horne, J. (2010). Primary insomnia: A disorder of sleep, or primarily one of wakefulness? *Sleep Medicine Reviews, 14*(1), 3–7.

Hovakimyan, M., Haas, S. J., Schmitt, O., Gerber, B., Wree, A., & Andressen, C. (2008). Mesencephalic human neural progenitor cells transplanted into the adult hemiparkinsonian rat striatum lack dopaminergic differentiation but improve motor behavior. *Cells Tissues Organs,* 188, 373–383.

Hoveida, R., Alaei, H., Oryan, S., Parivar, K., & Reisi, P. (2011). Treadmill running improves spatial memory in an animal model of alzheimer's disease. *Behavioural Brain Research, 216*(1), 270–274. doi: 10.1016/j.bbr.2010.08.003

Howell, E. F. (2011). *Understanding and treating dissociative identity disorder: A relational approach.* New York: Routledge/Taylor & Francis Group.

Howes, C. (1999). Attachment relationships in the context of multiple caregivers. In J. Cassidy, & P. R. Shaver (Eds.), *Handbook of attachment: Theory, research, and clinical applications* (pp. 671–687). New York, NY: Guilford Press.

Howland, R. H., Shutt, L. S., Berman, S. R., Spotts, C. R., & Denko, T. (2011). The emerging use of technology for the treatment of depression and other neuropsychiatric disorders. *Annals of Clinical Psychiatry, 23*(1), 48–62.

Hoyle, R. H. (Ed.). (2010). *Handbook of personality and self-regulation.* Hoboken, NJ: Wiley-Blackwell.

Huang, P. L. (2005). Unraveling the links between diabetes, obesity, and cardiovascular disease. *Circulation Research, 96,* 1129–1131.

Hubel, D. H., & Wiesel, T. N. (1959). Receptive fields of single neurones in the cat's striate cortex. *The Journal of Physiology, 148,* 574–591.

Hublin, C., Kaprio, J., Partinen, M., & Koskenvuo, M. (2001). Parasomnias: Co-occurrence and genetics. *Psychiatric Genetics, 11*(2), 65–70.

Hublin, C., Kaprio, J., Partinen, M., & Koskenvuo, M. (1999). Limits of self-report in assessing sleep terrors in a population survey. *Sleep: Journal of Sleep Research & Sleep Medicine, 22*(1), 89–93.

Hudson, R. F., High, L., & Al Otaiba, S. (2007). Dyslexia and the brain: What does current research tell us? *The Reading Teacher, 60*(6), 506–515.

Hudziak, J., & Bartels, M. (2008). Genetic and environmental influences on wellness, resilience, and psychopathology: A family-based approach for promotion, prevention, and intervention. In J. J. Hudziak (Ed.), *Developmental psychopathology and wellness: Genetic and environmental influences.* Washington, DC: American Psychiatric Publishing, Inc.

Hughes, D. A. (2009). *Attachment-focused parenting: Effective strategies to care for children.* New York: W W Norton.

Hughes, L. F., McAsey, M. E., Donathan, C. L., Smith, T., Coney, P., & Struble, R. G. (2002). Effects of hormone replacement therapy on olfactory sensitivity: Cross-sectional and longitudinal studies. *Climacteric, 5,* 140–150.

Hughes, R. N. (2007). Neotic preferences in laboratory rodents: Issues, assessment, and substrates. *Neuroscience and Biobehavioral reviews, 31*(3), 441–464.

Hulit, L. M., & Howard, M. R. (1997). *Born to talk: An introduction to speech and language development (2nd Ed).* Boston: Annyn & Bacon.

Hunt, E. (2011). *Human intelligence.* New York: Cambridge University Press.

Hunt, N. C. (2010). *Memory, war and trauma.* New York, NY: Cambridge University Press.

Huttenlocher, J., Haight, W., Bryk, A., Seltzer, M., & Lyons, T. (1991). Early vocabulary growth: Relation to language input and gender. *Developmental Psychology, 27*(2), 236–248.

Hyde, J. S. (2008, Spring). Men are from earth, women are from earth: The gender similarities hypothesis. *General Psychologist, 43*(1).

Hyde, J. S. (2007). New directions in the study of gender similarities and differences. *Current Directions in Psychological Science, 16*(5), 259–263.

Hyde, J. S. (2005). The gender similarities hypothesis. *American Psychologist, 60,* 581–592.

Hyde, M., & Power, D. (2006). Some ethical dimensions of cochlear implantation for deaf children and their families. *Journal of Deaf Studies and Deaf Education, 11,* 102–111.

Hyman Jr., I. E., & Kleinknecht, E. E. (1999). False childhood memories: Research, theory, and applications. In L. M. Williams & V. L. Banyard (Eds.), *Trauma & memory* (pp. 175–188). Thousand Oaks, CA: Sage Publications.

Hymowitz, N. (2005). Tobacco. In R. J. Frances, A. H. Mack, & S. I. Miller (Eds.), *Clinical textbook of addictive disorders (3rd Ed.).* New York, NY: Guilford Press.

Iadecola, C., & Nedergaard, M. (2007). Glial regulation of the cerebral microvasculature. *Nature Neuroscience. 10,* 1369–1376.

IMHRO. (2009). International Mental Health Research Organization. Retrieved from www.schizophrenia.com/szfacts.htm.

Imperato-McGinley, J., Miller, M., Wilson, J. D., Peterson, R. E., Shackleton, C., Gajdusek, D. C. (1991). A cluster of male pseudoher-maphrodites with 5 alpha-reductase deficiency in Papua New Guinea. *Clinical Endocrinology (Oxford), 34*(4), 293–298.

Inglehart, R. (1990). *Culture shift in advanced industrial society.* Princeton, NJ: Princeton University Press.

Ingram, D. (1986). Phonological development: Production. In P. Fletcher & M. Garman (Eds.), *Language acquisition* (2nd Ed., pp. 223–239). New York, NY: Cambridge University Press.

Inhelder, B., & Piaget, J. (1979). Procedures et structures [Procedures and structures]. *Archives de Psychologie, 47,* 165–176.

Institute of Medicine of the National Academies. (2004). *Immunization safety review: Vaccines and autism.* National Academy of Sciences, Washington, D.C.

Irwin, M. (2001). Neuroimmunology of disordered sleep in depression and alcoholism. *Neuropsychopharmacology, 25*(5), S45–S49.

Irwin, M. R., & Cole, J. C. (2005). Depression and psychonueroimmunology. In K. Vedhara & M. Irwin (Eds.), *Human psychoneuroimmunology.* Oxford, England: Oxford University Press.

Isacson, O., & Kordower, J. H. (2008). Future of cell and gene therapies for Parkinson's disease. *Annals of Neurology, 2,* S122–S138.

Isen, A. M. (2008). Positive affect and decision processes: Some recent theoretical developments with practical implications. In C. P. Haugtvedt, P. M. Herr, & F. R. Kardes (Eds.), *Handbook of consumer psychology* (pp. 273–296). New York, NY: Taylor & Francis Group/Lawrence Erlbaum Associates.

Isen, A. M. (2004). Some perspectives on positive feelings and emotions: Positive affect facilitates thinking and problem solving. In A. Manstead, N. Frijda, & A. Fischer (Eds.), *Feelings and emotions: The Amsterdam symposium* (pp. 263–281). New York, NY: Cambridge University Press.

Isen, A. M. (1993). Positive affect and decision making. In M. Lewis & J. M. Haviland (Eds.), *Handbook of emotions* (pp. 261–277). New York, NY: Guilford Press.

Isenberg, D. J. (1986). Group polarization: A critical review and meta-analysis. *Journal of Personality and Social Psychology, 50,*1141–1151.

Ishikawa, S., Iwanaga, M., Yamashita, B., Sato, H., & Sato, S. (2010). Long-term effects of social skills training on depressive symptoms in children. *Japanese Journal of Educational Psychology, 58*(3), 372–384.

Ivanenko, A., & Johnson, K. P. (2010). Sleep disorders. In M. K. Dulcan (Ed.), *Dulcan's textbook of child and adolescent psychiatry* (pp. 449–461). Arlington, VA: American Psychiatric Publishing, Inc.

Iwanaga, M., Yokoyama, H., & Seiwa, H. (2004). Coping availability and stress reduction for optimistic and pessimistic individuals. *Personality and Individual Differences, 36*(1), 11–22.

Izard, C. E. (2009). Emotion theory and research: Highlights, unanswered questions, and emerging issues. *Emotion Theory and Research, 60,* 1–25.

Izard, C. E. (2007). Basic emotions, natural kinds, emotion schemas, and a new paradigm. *Perspectives on Psychological Science, 2,* 260–280.

Izard, C. E. (1997). Emotions and facial expressions: A perspective from differential emotions theory. In J. A. Russell & J. M. Fernandez-Dols (Eds.), *The psychology of facial expression* (pp. 57–77). New York, NY: Cambridge University Press.

Izard, C. E. (1994). Innate and universal facial expressions: Evidence from developmental and cross-cultural research. *Psychological Bulletin, 115*, 288–299.

Izard, C. E. (1991). *The psychology of emotions*. New York, NY: Plenum.

Izard, C. E. (1977). *Human emotions*. New York, NY: Plenum Press.

Jaakkola, J. J., & Gissler, M. (2004). Maternal smoking in pregnancy, fetal development, and childhood asthma. *American Journal of Public Health, 94*, 136–140.

Jackson, B. R., & Bergeman, C. S. (2011). How does religiosity enhance well-being? The role of perceived control. *Psychology of Religion and Spirituality, 3*(2), 149–161.

Jackson, H., Judd, F., Komiti, A., Fraser, C., Murray, G., Robins, G., & Wearing, A. (2007). Mental health problems in rural contexts: What are the barriers to seeking help from professional providers? *Australian Psychologist, 42*(2), 147–160.

Jackson, J. W. (1993) Realistic group conflict theory: A review and evaluation of the theoretical and empirical literature. *The Psychological Record, 43*(3), 395–413.

Jacobs, A. K. (2008). Components of evidence-based interventions for bullying and peer victimization. In R. G. Steele, T. D. Elkin, & M. C. Roberts (Eds.), *Handbook of evidence-based therapies for children and adolescents: Bridging science and practice*. New York, NY: Spriger.

Jacobson, C. F., Wolf, J. B., & Jackson, T. A. (1935). An experimental analysis of the functions of the frontal association areas in primates. *Journal of Nervous and Mental Disease, 82*, 1–14.

Jacoby, L. L., Bishara, A. J., Hessels, S., & Toth, J. P. (2005). Aging, subjective experience, and cognitive control: Dramatic false remembering by older adults. *Journal of Experimental Psychology: General, 134*(2), 131–148.

Jamal, M., & Baba, V.V. (2003). Type A behavior, components, and outcomes: A study of canadian employees. *International Journal of Stress Management, 10*(1), 39–50.

James, W. (1890). *The principles of psychology* (Vols. 1 & 2). New York, NY: Holt.

James, W. (1884). What is emotion? *Mind, 19*, 188–205.

James, W. D., Berger, T., et al. (2006). *Andrews' diseases of the skin: Clinical dermatology*. Saunders Elsevier.

Janca, A., Aarli, J.A., Prilipko, L., Dua, T., Saxena, S., & Saraceno, B. (2006). WHO/WFN survey on neurological services: a world-wide perspective. *Journal of the Neurological Sciences, 247*, 29–34.

Jang, K., McCrae, R., Angleitner, A., Riemann, R., & Livesley, W. (1998). Heritability of facet-level traits in a cross-cultural twin sample: Support for a hierarchical model of personality. *Journal of Personality and Social Psychology, 74*, 1556–1565.

Janis, I. L. (1982). *Groupthink*. Boston, MA: Houghton Mifflin.

Janis, I. (1972). Victims of groupthink: A psychological study of foreign-policy decisions and fiascoes. Boston, MA: Houghton Mifflin.

Jankord, R., & Herman, J. P. (2009). Limbic regulation of hypothalamo-pituitary-adrenocortical function during acute and chronic stress. *Stress, neurotransmitters, and hormones: Neuroendocrine and genetic mechanisms* (pp. 63–74). New York, NY: New York Academy of Sciences; Wiley-Blackwell.

Jankovic, J., & Aguilar, L. G. (2008). Current approaches to the treatment of Parkinson's disease. *Neuropsychiatric Disease and Treatment, 4*, 743–757.

Jannini, E., & Lenai, A. (2005). Ejaculatory disorders; Epidemiology and current approaches to definition, classification and subtyping. *World Journal of Urology, 23*, 68–75.

Jansson-Fröjmark, M., Harvey, A. G., Lundh, L., Norell-Clarke, A., & Linton, S. J. (2011). Psychometric properties of an insomnia-specific measure of worry: The anxiety and preoccupation about sleep questionnaire. *Cognitive Behaviour Therapy, 40*(1), 65–76.

Jastrow, J. (1929). Review of J. B. Watson, Ways of behaviorism, psychological care of infant and child, battle of behaviorism. *Science, 69*, 455–457.

Jaussent, I., Dauvilliers, Y., Ancelin, M., Dartigues, J., Tavernier, B., Touchon, J., . . . Besset, A. (2011). Insomnia symptoms in older adults: Associated factors and gender differences. *The American Journal of Geriatric Psychiatry, 19*(1), 88–97.

Jay, T. (1999). *Why we curse:Aa neuro-psycho-social theory of speech*. Philadelphia, PA: John Benjamins Publishing Co.

Jefferson, D. J. (2005). America's most dangerous drug. *Newsweek, 146*(6), 40–48.

Jefferson, T., Herbst, J. H., & McCrae, R. R. (1998). Associations between birth order and personality traits: Evidence from self-report and observer ratings. *Journal of Research in Personality, 32*, 498–502.

Jeneson, A., Kirwan, C. B., Hopkins, R. O., Wixted, J. T., & Squire, L. R. (2010). Recognition memory and the hippocampus: A test of the hippocampal contribution to recollection and familiarity. *Learning & Memory, 17*(1), 63–70. doi: 10.1101/lm.1546110

Jenkins, R. (2008). *Social identity*. Oxon, UK: Routledge.

Jensen, L. A. (Ed.). (2011). *Bridging cultural and developmental approaches to psychology: New syntheses in theory, research, and policy*. New York: Oxford University Press.

Jensen, M. P. (2010). Chronic pain. In A. F. Barabasz, K. Olness, R. Boland & S. Kahn (Eds.), *Medical hypnosis primer: Clinical and research evidence* (pp. 25–32). New York, NY: Routledge/Taylor & Francis Group.

Jessen, K. R., & Mirsky, R. (2005). The origin and development of glial cells in peripheral nerves. *Nature Reviews Neuroscience, 6*(9), 671–682.

Johannsdottir, K. R., & Herdman, C. M. (2010). The role of working memory in supporting drivers' situation awareness for surrounding traffic. *Human Factors, 52*(6), 663–673.

Johansson, C. B., Momma, S., Clarke, D. L., Risling, M., Lendahl, U., & Frisen J. (1999). Identification of a neural stem cell in the adult mammalian central nervous system. *Cell, 96* (1), 25–34.

John, O. P., & Gross, J. J. (2007). Individual differences in emotion regulation. In J. J. Gross (Ed.), *Handbook of emotion regulation* (pp. 351–372). New York, NY: The Guilford Press.

Johnson, A. L. (2011). Psychoanalytic theory. In D. Capuzzi, & D. R. Gross (Eds.), *Counseling and psychotherapy (5th Ed.)* (pp. 59–76). Alexandria, VA: American Counseling Association.

Johnson, A., & Earle, T. (1987). *The evolution of human societies*. Stanford, CA: Stanford University Press.

Johnson, C. H., Elliott, J., Foster, R., Honma, K. I., & Kronauer, R. (2004). Fundamental properties of circadian rhythms. In J. C. Dunlap, J. J. Loros, et al. (Eds.), *Chronobiology: Biological timekeeping*. Sunderland, MA: Sinauer Associates, Inc.

Johnson, J. G., Cohen, P., Smailes, E. M., Kasen, S., & Brook, J. S. (2002). Television viewing and aggressive behavior during adolescence and adulthood. *Science, 295*, 2468–2471.

Johnson, J. S., & Newport, E. L. (1989). Critical period effects in second language learning: The influence of maturational state on the acquisition of English as a second language. *Cognitive Psychology, 21*, 60–99.

Johnson, W. (2010). Review of intelligence and how to get it: Why schools and cultures count. *Gifted Child Quarterly, 54*(1), 72.

Johnson, W., Bouchard Jr., T. J., McGue, M., Segal, N. L., Tellegen, A., Keyes, M., et al. (2007). Genetic and environmental influences on the verbal-perceptual-image rotation (VPR) model of the structure of mental abilities in the Minnesota study of twins reared apart. *Intelligence, 35*(6), 542–562.

Johnston, C., & Lee, C. M. (2005). Children's attributions for their own versus others' behavior: Influence of actor versus observer differences. *Journal of Applied Developmental Psychology, 26*(3), 314–328.

Johnston, L. D., O'Malley, P. M., Bachman, J. G., & Schulenberg, J. E. (2007). *Monitoring the future national results on adolescent drug use: Overview of key findings, 2006* (NIH Publication No. 07-6202). Bethesda, MD: National Institute on Drug Abuse.

Johnston, V. S. (2006). Mate choice decisions: The role of facial beauty. *Trends in Cognitive Sciences, 10*(1), 9–13.

Joia, L. A., & Lemos, B. (2010). Relevant factors for tacit knowledge transfer within organisations. *Journal of Knowledge Management, 14*(3), 410–427.

Joiner, T. E., Jr. (2002). Depression in its interpersonal context. In I. H. Gotlib & C. L. Hammen (Eds.), *Handbook of depression* (pp. 295–313). New York: Guilford Press.

Jolly, J. L., Treffinger, D. J., Inman, T. F., & Smutny, J. F. (Eds.). 2011. *Parenting gifted children: The authoritative guide from the National Association for Gifted Children*. Waco, TX: Prufrock Press.

Jones, B. E. (2003). Arousal systems. *Frontiers in Bioscience, 8*, 438–451.

Jones, E. E., & Harris, V. A. (1967). The attribution of attitudes. *Journal of Experimental Social Psychology, 3*, 1–24.

Jones, E. E., & Nisbett, R. E. (1971). *The Actor and the Observer: Divergent Perceptions of the Causes of Behavior*. Morristown, NJ: General Learning Press.

Jones, E. E., & Sigall, H. (1971). The bogus pipeline: A new paradigm for measuring affect and attitude. *Psychological Bulletin, 76*, 349–364.

Jones, E. G. (2007). Neuroanatomy: Cajal and after Cajal. *Brain Research Reviews*, 55, 248–55.

Jones, P. E. (1995). Contradictions and unanswered questions in the genie case: A fresh look at the linguistic evidence. *Language and Communication, 15*, 261–280.

Jones, S. R., Fernyhough, C., & Larøi, F. (2010). A phenomenological survey of auditory verbal hallucinations in the hypnagogic and hypnopompic states. *Phenomenology and the Cognitive Sciences, 9*(2), 213–224.

Jonides, J., Lewis, R. L., Nee, D. E., Lustig, C. A., Berman, M. G., & Moore, K. S. (2008). The mind and brain of short-term memory. *Annual Review of Psychology, 59*, 193–224.

Jonides, J., Sylvester, C. C., Lacey, S. C., Wager, T. D., Nichols, T. E., & Awh, E. (2003). Modules of working memory. In R. H. Kluwe, G. Lüer, & F. Rösler (Eds.), *Principles of learning and memory* (pp. 113–134). Cambridge, MA: Birkhäuser.

Joseph, S. V. (2007). A study of the amplitudes and latencies of the brain stem and cortical auditory evoked potentials (AEP) in relation to the personality dimension of extraversion*. ProQuest Information & Learning: US. *Dissertation Abstracts International: Section B: The Sciences and Engineering, 68*(6), 4133.

Josephs, R. A., Markus, H., & Tarafodi, R. W. (1992). Gender and self-esteem. *Journal of Personality and Social, 63*, 391–402.

Juhnke, G. A., Granello, D. H., & Granello, P. F. (2011). *Suicide, selfinjury, and violence in the schools: Assessment, prevention, and intervention strategies*. Hoboken, NJ: John Wiley & Sons.

Julien, R. M. (2008). *A primer of drug action: A comprehensive guide to the actions, uses, and side effects of psychoactive drugs* (11th Ed.). Portland: Worth Publishers.

Julien, R. M., Advokat, C. D., & Comaty, J. E. (2011). *Primer of drug action* (12th Ed.). New York: Worth Publishers.

Julien, R. M., Advokat, C. D., & Comaty, J. E. (2008). A primer of drug action: A comprehensive guide to the actions, uses, and side effects of psychoactive drugs (11th Ed). New York, NY: Worth Publishers.

Junginger, J., & McGuire, L. (2004). Psychotic motivation and the paradox of current research on serious mental illness and rates of violence. *Schizophrenia Bulletin, 30*, 21–30.

Just, M. A., & Carpenter, P. A. (2002). A capacity theory of comprehension: Individual differences in working memory. In T. A. Polk & C. M. Seifert (Eds.), *Cognitive modeling* (pp. 131–177). Cambridge, MA: MIT Press.

Kabat-Zinn, J. (2005). Wherever you go, there you are: Mindfulness meditation in everyday life. New York, NY: Hyperion.

Kadushin, C. (1969). *Why people go to psychiatrists*. Oxford, UK: Atherton Press.

Kagan, J. (2010). Emotions and temperament. In M. H. Bornstein (Ed.), *Handbook of cultural developmental science* (pp. 175–194). New York: Psychology Press.

Kagan, J. (2008). Behavioral inhibition as a risk factor for psychopathology. In T. P. Beauchaine, & S. P. Hinshaw (Eds.), *Child and adolescent psychopathology* (pp. 157–179). Hoboken, NJ: John Wiley & Sons Inc.

Kagan, J. (2001). Biological constraint, cultural variety, and psychological structures. In A. Harrington (Ed.), *Unity of knowledge: The convergence of natural and human science* (pp. 177–190). New York, NY: New York Academy of Sciences.

Kagan, J., & Snidman, N. (2004). *The long shadow of temperament*. Cambridge: Harvard University Press.

Kahneman, D., & Tversky, A. (1979). Prospect theory: An analysis of decision making under risk. *Econometrica, 47*, 263–292.

Kakigi, R., Hoshiyama, M., Shimojo, M., Naka, D., Yamasaki, H., Watanabe, S., Xiang, J., Maeda, K., Lam, K., Itomi, K., & Nakamura, A. (2000). The somatosensory evoked magnetic fields. *Progress in Neurobiology, 61*, 495–523.

Kallgren, C. A., Reno, R. R., & Cialdini, R. B. (2000). A focus theory of normative conduct: When norms do and do not affect behavior. *Personality and Social Psychology Bulletin, 26*, 1002–1012.

Kallio, S., & Revonsuo, A. (2003). Hypnotic phenomena and altered states of consciousness: A multilevel framework of description and explanation. *Contemporary Hypnosis, 20*(3), 111–164.

Kalsbeek, A., Fliers, E., Hofman, M. A., Swaab, D. F., & Buijs, R. M. (2010). Vasopressin and the output of the hypothalamic biological clock. *Journal of Neuroendocrinology, 22*(5), 362–372.

Kalueff A. V., & La Porte J. L. (Eds.) (2008). *Behavioral models in stress research*. Hauppauge, NY: Nova Biomedical Books.

Kamiji, M. M., Troncon, L. E., Suen, V. M., & de Oliveira, R. B. (2009). Gastrointestinal transit, appetite, and energy balance in gastrec-tomized patients. *The American Journal of Clinical Nutrition, 89*(1), 231–239.

Kandel, E. R. (2001). The molecular biology of memory storage: a dialogue between genes and synapses. *Science, 294*, 1030–1038.

Kannape, O. A., Schwabe, L., Tadi, T., & Blanke, O. (2010). The limits of agency in walking humans. *Neuropsychologia, 48*(6), 1628–1636.

Kanner, A. D., Coyne, J. C., Schaefer, C., & Lazarus, R. S. (1981). Comparison of two modes of stress measurement: Daily hassles and uplifts versus major life events. *Journal of Behavioral Medicine, 4*,1–39.

Kanner, B. (1998, February). Are you normal? Turning the other cheek. *American Demog.*

Kanner, B. (1998, May). Are you normal? Creatures of habit. *American Demog.*

Kanner, B. (1995) *Are You 'Normal'?: Do You Behave Like Everyone Else?* New York, NY: St. Martin's Press.

Kant, I. (2003). Anthropology from a pragmatic point of view. *The history of psychology: Fundamental questions* (pp. 127–140). New York, NY: Oxford University Press.

Kantor, M. (2010). The essential guide to overcoming avoidant personality disorder. Santa Barbara, CA: Praeger/ABC–CLIO.

Kantor, M. (2006). The psychopathy of everyday life. In T. G. Plante (Ed.), *Mental disorders of the new millennium, Vol. 1: Behavioral issues*. Westport, CT: Praeger Publishers.

Kaplan, H. S. (1977). Hypoactive sexual desire. *Journal of Sex & Marital Therapy, 3*(1), 3–9.

Kaplan, H., & Dove, H. (1987). Infant development among the ache of eastern paraguay. *Developmental Psychology, 23*(2), 190–198.

Kaplan, R. M., & Kronick, R. G. (2006). Marital status and longevity in the United States population. *Journal of Epidemiology & Community Health, 60*(9), 760–765.

Karama, S., Colom, R., Johnson, W., Deary, I. J., Haier, R., Waber, D. P., & Evans, A. C. (2011). Cortical thickness correlates of specific cognitive performance accounted for by the general factor of intelligence in healthy children aged 6 to 18. *NeuroImage, 55*(4), 1443–1453.

Karama, S., Lecours, A. R., Leroux, J., Bourgouin, P., Beaudoin, G., Joubert, S., et al. (2002). Areas of brain activation in males and females during viewing of erotic film excerpts. *Human Brain Mapping, 16*(1), 1–13.

Karasu, T. B. (1992) *Wisdom in the practice of psychotherapy*. New York, NY: Basic Books.

Karelitz, T. M., Jarvin, L., & Sternberg, R. J. (2010). The meaning of wisdom and its development throughout life. In W. F. Overton, & R. M. Lerner (Eds.), *The handbook of life-span development, vol. 1: Cognition, biology, and methods* (pp. 837–881). Hoboken, NJ: John Wiley & Sons.

Karni, A., Tanne, D., Rubenstien, B. S., Askenasy, J. J. M., et al., (1994). Dependence on REM sleep of overnight improvement of a perceptual skill. *Science, 265*(5172), 679–682.

Kashima, Y., Siegal, M., Tanaka, K., & Kashima, E. S. (1992). Do people believe behaviours are consistent with attitudes? Towards a cultural psychology of attribution processes. *British Journal of Social Psychology, 31*, 111–124.

Kassam, A., & Patten, S. B. (2006). Canadian trends in benzodiazepine & zopiclone use. *Canadian Journal of Clinical Pharmacology, 13*(1), e121–e127.

Katzir, T., & Pare-Blagoev, J. (2006). Applying cognitive neuroscience research to education: The case of literacy. *Educational Psychologist, 41*(1), 53–74.

Kauert, G., & Iwersen-Bergmann, S. (2004). Illicit drugs as cause of traffic crashes, focus on cannabis. *Sucht (German Journal of Addiction Research and Practice), 50*(5), 327–333.

Kaufman, A. S. (2000a). Intelligence tests and school psychology: Predicting the future by studying the past. *Psychology in the Schools, 37*(1), 7–16.

Kaufman, A. S. (2000b). Wechsler, David. In A. E. Kazdin (Ed.), *Encyclopedia of psychology, vol. 8* (pp. 238–239). Washington, DC: American Psychological Association.

Kaufman, J. C., & Sternberg, R. J. (Eds.). (2010). *The Cambridge handbook of creativity*. New York: Cambridge University Press.

Kaufman J. C. (Ed.). (2009). Intelligent testing: Integrating psychological theory and clinical practice. New York: Cambridge University Press.

Kaufman, L., & Rock, I. (1989). The moon illusion thirty years later. In M. Hershenson (Ed.), *The moon illusion* (pp. 193–234). Hillsdale, NJ: Lawrence Erlbaum Assoc.

Kay, J. F, & Jackson, A (2008). Sex, lies, and stereotypes: How abstinence-only programs harm women and girls. New York, NY: Legal Momentum.

Kaye, W. H., Bulik, C. M., Thornton, L., Barbarich, N., Masters, K. (2004). Comorbidity of anxiety disorders with anorexia and bulimia nervosa. *American Journal of Psychiatry, 161*(12), 2215–2221.

Kazdin, A. E. (2005). *Parent management training: Treatment for oppositional, aggressive, and antisocial behavior in children and adolescents.* New York: Oxford University Press.

Kazdin, A. E., & Benjet, C. (2003). Spanking children: Evidence and issues. *Current Directions in Psychological Science, 12*(3), 99–103.

KCET. (2007, May 24). *Life & times transcript.* Retrieved from http://www.kcet.org/lifeandtimes/archives/200705/ 20070524.php.

Kean, M.-L. (1977). The linguistic interpretation of aphasic syndromes: Agrammatism in Broca's aphasia, an example. *Cognition, 5*(1), 9–46.

Keane, M. (2008, September 29). Texting overtakes voice in mobile phone usage. Retrieved from http://www.wired.com/epicenter/2008/09/texting-overtak/.

Keane, T. M., Marx, B. P., & Sloan, D. M. (2009). Post-traumatic stress disorder: Definition, prevalence, and risk factors. *Post-traumatic stress disorder: Basic science and clinical practice* (pp. 1–19). Totowa, NJ: Humana Press.

Keates, J., & Stam, H. J. (2009). The disadvantaged psychological scene: Educational experiences of women in early Canadian psychology. *Canadian Psychology, 50*(4), 273–282.

Keel, P. K., & Haedt, A. (2008). Evidence-based psychosocial treatments for eating problems and eating disorders. Journal of Clinical Child and Adolescent Psychology : The Official Journal for the Society of Clinical Child and Adolescent Psychology, 37(1), 39–61.

Keller, C., Siegrist, M., & Gutscher, H. (2006). The role of the affect and availability of heuristics in risk communication. *Risk Analysis, 26*, 631–639.

Keller, F. S. (1973). *The Definition of Psychology* (2nd Ed.). Englewood Cliffs, NJ: Prentice Hall.

Kellman, P. J., & Arterberry, M. E. (1998). *The cradle of knowledge: Development of perception in infancy.* Cambridge, MA: MIT Press.

Kelly, C. R., Grinband, J., & Hirsch, J. (2007). Repeated exposure to media violence is associated with diminished response in an inhibitory frontolimbic network. *PLoS ONE,* 2(12), e1268.

Kelman, L. (2007). The triggers or precipitants of the acute migraine attack. *Cephalalgia, 27*, 394–402.

Keltner, D., & Kring, A. M. (1998). Emotion, social function, and psychopathology. *Review of General Psychology, 2*, 320–342.

Kendall-Tackett, K. (2010). Depression, hostility, posttraumatic stress disorder, and inflammation: The corrosive health effects of negative mental states. *The psychoneuroimmunology of chronic disease: Exploring the links between inflammation, stress, and illness* (pp. 113–131). Washington, DC: American Psychological Association.

Kendler, K. S., Myers, J., & Prescott, C. A. (2005). Sex differences in the relationship between social support and risk for major depression: A longitudinal study of opposite-sex twin pairs. *American Journal of Psychiatry, 162*(2), 250–256.

Kennedy, Q., Mather, M., & Carstensen, L. L. (2004). The role of motivation in the age-related positivity effect in autobiographical memory. *Psychological Science, 15*(3), 208–214.

Kennedy, R. B., & Kennedy, D. A. (2004). Using the Myers-Briggs Type Indicator in career counseling. *Journal of Employment Counseling, 41*, 38–44.

Kennedy, S. H., et al. (2009). Canadian Network for Mood and Anxiety Treatments (CANMAT) Clinical guidelines for the management of major depressive disorder in adults, IV, neurostimulation therapies. *Journal of Affective Disorders, 117*, 544–553.

Kensinger, E. A., & Corkin, S. (2003). Memory enhancement for emotional words: Are emotional words more vividly remembered than neutral words? *Memory & Cognition, 31*(8), 1169–1180.

Kensinger, E. A., Ullmann, M. T., & Corkin, S. (2001). Bilateral medial temporal lobe damage does not affect lexical or grammatical processing. Evidence from amnesic patient H.M. *Hippocampus, 11*(4), 347–360.

Keon, W. J. (2009). Early childhood education and care: Canada's challenges and next steps. *Paediatrics & Child Health, 14*(10), 660–661.

Kern, M. L., & Friedman, H. S. (2011). Personality and pathways of influence on physical health. *Social and Personality Psychology Compass, 5*(1), 76–87.

Kern, M. L., & Friedman, H. S. (2008). Do conscientious individuals live longer? A quantitative review. *Health Psychology, 27*(5), 505–512.

Kernberg, O. F. (2005). Object relations theories and technique. In E. S. Person, A. M. Cooper, & G. O. Gabbard (Eds.), *The American Psychiatric Publishing textbook of psychoanalysis* (pp. 57–75). Washington, DC: American Psychiatric Publishing.

Kernberg, O. F. (1997). Convergences and divergences in contemporary psychoanalytic technique and psychoanalytic psychotherapy. In J. K. Zeig (Ed.), *The evolution of psychotherapy: The third conference.* New York, NY: Brunner/Mazel.

Kesselring, T., & Muller, U. (2010). The concept of egocentrism in the context of Piaget's theory. *New Ideas in Psychology.* No Pages.

Kessels, R. P. C., & Postma, A. (2002). Verbal interference during encoding and maintenance of spatial information in working memory. *Current Psychology Letters: Behaviour, Brain & Cognition, 9*, 39–46.

Kessler, R. C., Adler, L. A., Barkley, R., Biederman, J., Conners, C. K., Faraone, S. V., et al. (2005). Patterns and predictors of attention-deficit/hyperactivity disorder persistence into adulthood: Results from the National Comorbidity Survey Replication. *Biological Psychiatry, 57*(11), 1442–1451.

Kessler, R. C., Amminger, G. P., Aguilar-Gaxiola, S., Alongo, J., & Lee, S. (2007). Age of onset of mental disorders: A review of recent literature. *Curent Opinions in Psychiatry, 20*(4), 359–364.

Kessler, R. C., Berglund, P., Demler, O., Jin, R., & Walters, E. E. (2005). Lifetime prevalence and age-of-onset distributions of DSM-IV disorders in the National Comorbidity Survey Replication. *Archives of General Psychiatry, 62*, 593–602.

Kessler, R. C., Chiu, W. T., Demler, O., Merikangas, K. R., & Walters, E. E. (2005). Prevalence, severity, and comorbidity of 12-month DSM-IV disorders in the National Comorbidity Survey Replication. *Archives of General Psychiatry, 62*, 617–627.

Kessler, R. C., Ruscio, A. M., Shear, K., & Wittchen, H. (2009). Epidemiology of anxiety disorders. In M. B. Stein, & T. Steckler (Eds.), *Behavioral neurobiology of anxiety and its treatment* (pp. 21–35). New York: Springer Science + Business Media.

Keysers, C., & Gazzola, V. (2007). Integrating simulation and theory of mind: From self to social cognition. *Trends in Cognitive Sciences, 11*(5), 194–196.

Khalil, E. L. (2004). What is altruism? *Journal of Economic Psychology, 25*(1), 97–123.

Kibler, J. L., Joshi, K., & Hughes, E. E. (2010). Cognitive and behavioral reactions to stress among adults with PTSD: Implications for immunity and health. In K. Kendall-Tackett (Ed.), *The psychoneuroimmunology of chronic disease: Exploring the links between inflammation, stress, and illness* (pp. 133–158). Washington, DC: American Psychological Association.

Kiecolt-Glaser, J. K., Dura, J. R., Speicher, C. E., Trask, O. J., & Glaser, R. (1991). Spousal caregivers of dementia victims: Longitudinal changes in immunity and health. *Psychosomatic Medicine, 53*, 345–362.

Kiecolt-Glaser, J. K., & Glaser, R. (2002). Depression and immune function: Central pathways to morbidity and mortality. *Journal of Psychsomatic Research, 53*, 873–876.

Kiecolt-Glaser, J. K. & Glaser, R. (1999). Psychoneuroimmunology and cancer: Fact or fiction? *European Journal of Cancer, 35*, 1603–1607.

Kiecolt-Glaser, J. K., & Glaser, R. (1988). Behavioral influences on immune function: Evidence for the interplay between stress and health. In *Stress and coping across development* (pp. 189–205). Hillsdale, NJ: Erlbaum.

Kiecolt-Glaser, J. K., Glaser, R., Gravenstein, S., Malarkey, W. B., & Sheridan, J. (1996). Chronic stress alters the immune response to influenza virus vaccine in older adults. *Proceedings of the National Academy of Sciences, USA, 93*, 3043–3047.

Kiecolt-Glaser, J., McGuire, L., Robles, T. F., & Glaser, R. (2002). Psychoneuroimmunology and psychosomatic medicine: Back to the future. *Psychosomatic Medicine, 64*(1), 15–28.

Kihlstrom, J. F. (2007). Consciousness in hypnosis. In P. D. Zelazo, M. Moscovitch, & E. Thompson (Eds.), *The Cambridge handbook of consciousness*. New York, NY: Cambridge University Press.

Kihlstrom, J. F. (2006). Repression: A unified theory of a will-o'-the-wisp. *Behavioral and Brain Sciences, 29*(5), 523.

Kihlström, J. F. (2001). *Dissociative disorders*. New York, NY: Kluwer Academic/Plenum.

Kihlstrom, J. F., Beer, J. S., & Klein, S. B. (2003). Self and identity as memory. In M. R. Leary & J. P. Tangney (Eds.), *Handbook of self and identity* (pp. 68–90). New York, NY: Guilford Press.

Kihlstrom, J. F., Dorfman, J., & Park, L. (2007). Implicit and explicit memory and learning. In M. Velmans & S. Schneider (Eds.), *The Blackwell companion to consciousness*. Malden, MA: Blackwell Publishing.

Kihlstrom, J. F., Mulvaney, S., Tobias, B. A., & Tobis, I. P. (2000). The emotional unconscious. In E. Eich, J. F. Kihlstrom, et al. (Eds.), *Cognition and Emotion*, London, England: Oxford University Press.

Kim, H., & Markus, H. R. (1999). Deviance or uniqueness, harmony or conformity? A cultural analysis. *Journal of Personality and Social Psychology, 77*, 785–800.

Kim, J. L., Collins, R. L., Kanouse, D. E., Elliott, M. N., Berry, S. H., Hunter, S. B., Miu, A., & Kunkel, D. (2006). Sexual readiness, household policies, and other predictors of adolescents' exposure to sexual content in mainstream entertainment television. *Media Psychology, 8*(4), 449–471.

Kim, T. Y., Hon, A. H. Y., & Lee, D. R. (2010), Proactive personality and employee creativity: The effects of job creativity requirement and supervisor support for creativity. *Creativity Research Journal, 22*(1), 37–45.

Kim, Y.-H., Peng, S., & Chiu, C.-Y. (2008). Explaining self-esteem differences between Chinese and North Americans: Dialectical self (vs. Self-consistency) or lack of positive self-regard. *Self and Identity, 7*(2), 113–128.

Kimmel, S. R. & Ratliff-Schaub, K. (2007). Growth and development. In R. E. Rakel (Ed.), *Textbook of Family Medicine*, 7th Ed. Philadelphia, Pa: Saunders Elsevier.

Kimura, D. (2000). *Sex and cognition*. Cambridge, MA: A Bradford Book/ The MIT Press.

King, J. A. (1997, January). Golf in the zone state: Attaining your peak performance. *The Club Golfer*.

King, L. (2002, March 19). Interview with Russell Yates. *Larry King Live, CNN*.

Kinsley, C. H., Bardi, M., Karelina, K., Rima, B., Christon, L., Friedenberg, J., et al. (2008). Motherhood induces and maintains behavioral and neural plasticity across the lifespan in the rat. *Archives of Sexual Behavior, 37*(1), 43–56.

Kirby, M. J. L., & Keon, W. J. (2006). *Out of the shadows at last: Transforming mental health, mental illness and addiction services in Canada*. The standing senate committee on social affairs, science and technology final report on mental health, mental illness and addiction. Retrieved from http://www.parl.gc.ca/Content/SEN/Committee/391/soci/rep/pdf/rep02may06part1-e.pdf .

Kirmayer, L., Simpson, C., & Cargo, M. (2003) Healing traditions: Culture, community and mental health promotion with Canadian Aboriginal peoples. *Australasian Psychiatry, 11*, 15–23.

Kirmayer, L. J., & Looper, K. J. (2007). Somatoform disorders. In M. Hersen, S. M. Turner, & D. C. Beidel (Eds.), *Adult psychopathology and diagnosis* (5th Ed., pp. 410–472). Hoboken, NJ: John Wiley & Sons.

Kirmayer, L. J., Tait, C. L. & Simpson, C. (2009). The mental health of Aboriginal peoples in Canada: Transformations of identity and community. In L. J. Kirmayer & G. G. Valaskakis (Eds), *Healing traditions: The mental health of Aboriginal peoples in Canada*. Vancouver, BC: UBC Press.

Kirschenbaum, H. (2004). Carl Rogers's life and work: An assessment on the 100th anniversary of his birth. *Journal of Counseling and Development, 82*(1), 116–124.

Kirschner, P. A., & Karpinski, A. C. (2010). Facebook and academic performance. Computers in Human Behavior, 26, 1237–1245.

Kitayama, S., Markus, H. R., & Kurokawa, M. (2000). Culture, emotion, and well-being: Good feelings in Japan and the United States. *Cognition and Emotion, 14*, 93–124.

Kleber, H. D., & Galanter, M. (Eds.). (2008). *The American Psychiatric Publishing textbook of substance abuse treatment (4th Ed.)*. Washington, DC: American Psychiatric Publishing.

Klein, G. (2004). *The power of intuition: How to use your gut feelings to make better decisions at work*. Crown Business.

Klein, J. (2011). *A vending machine for crows: An experiment in corvid learning*. Retrieved from http://www.wireless.is/projects/cros/.

Klein, N. (2007). *The shock doctrine: The rise of disaster capitalism*. New York, NY: Metropolitan Books.

Kleiner, S., & Condor, B. (2007). *The good mood diet:Feel great while you lose weight*. New York, NY: Springboard Press.

Kleinke, C. L. (2007). What does it mean to cope? *The praeger handbook on stress and coping (vol.2)* (pp. 289–308). Westport, CT: Praeger Publishers/Greenwood Publishing Group.

Kleinman, A. (1987). Anthropology and psychiatry: The role of culture in cross-cultural research on illness. *British Journal of Psychiatry, 151*, 447–454.

Kluger, J. (2007, October 29). *The power of birth order*. Time.

Klüver, H., & Bucy, P. C. (1939). Preliminary analysis of functions of the temporal lobes of monkeys. *Archives of Neurology and Psychiatry, 42*, 979–1000.

Klüver, H., & Bucy, P. C. (1937). "Psychic blindness" and other symptoms following bilateral temporal lobectomy in rhesus monkeys. *American Journal of Physiology, 119*, 352–353.

Knudson, E. I. (2004). Sensitive periods in the development of the brain and behavior. *Journal of Cognitive Neuroscience, 16*, 1412–1425.

Knutson, B., Wolkowitz, O., Cole, S., Chan, T., Moore, E., Johnson, R., et al. (1998). Selective alteration of personality and social behavior by serotonergic intervention. *American Journal of Psychiatry, 155*, 373–379.

Kobasa, S. C. O. (1990). Stress-resistant personality. *The healing brain: A scientific reader* (pp. 219–230). New York, NY: Guilford Press.

Kobasa, S. C. O. (1987). Stress responses and personality. *Gender and stress* (pp. 308–329). New York, NY: Free Press.

Koch, W. J., & Haring, M. (2008). Posttraumatic stress disorder. In M. Hersen & J. Rosqvist (Eds.), *Handbook of psychological assessment, case conceptualization, and treatment, Vol. 1: Adults* (pp. 263–290). Hoboken, NJ: John Wiley & Sons.

Koenig, H. G., & Cohen, H. J. (2002). Psychosocial factors, immunology, and wound healing. *The link between religion and health: Psychoneuroimmunology and the faith factor* (pp. 124–138). New York, NY: Oxford University Press.

Koenigs, M., Young, L., Adolphs, R., Tranel, D., Cushman, F., Hauser, M., et al. (2007). Damage to the prefontal cortex increases utilitarian moral judgements. *Nature, 446*(7138), 908–911.

Koenigsberg, H. W., Harvey, P. D., Mitropoulou, V., et al. (2002). Characterizing affective instability in borderline personality disorder. *American Journal of Psychiatry, 159*(5), 784–788.

Koffka, K. (*1935). Principles of Gestalt psychology*. New York: Harcourt, Brace, & World.

Kohlberg, L. (2008). The development of children's orientations toward a moral order: I. sequence in the development of moral thought. *Human Development, 51*(1), 8–20.

Kohlberg, L. (1994). The claim to moral adequacy of a highest stage of moral judgment. In B. Puka (Ed.), *The great justice debate: Kohlberg criticism* (pp. 2–18). New York, NY: Garland Publishing.

Kohlberg, L. (1981). *The philosophy of moral development: Moral stages and the idea of justice. Essays on moral development, Volume 16*. Harper and Row.

Kohlberg, L. (1963). The development of children's orientations toward a moral order: I. sequence in the development of moral thought. *Vita Humana, 6*(1–2), 11–33.

Kohler, P. K., Manhart, L. E., & Lafferty, W. E. (2008). Abstinence-only and comprehensive sex education and the initiation of sexual activity and teen pregnancy. *Journal of Adolescent Health, 42*(4), 324–326.

Kohn, P. M. (1996). On coping adaptively with daily hassles. In M. Zeidner and N. S. Endler (Eds.), *Handbook of coping: Theory, research, applications*. New York, NY: John Wiley & Sons, Inc.

Kohn, P. M., Lafreniere, K., & Gurevitch, M. (1990). The inventory of college students' recent life experiences: A decontaminated hassle scale for a special population. *Journal of Behavioral Medicine, 13,* 619–630.

Koivisto, H. U. K. (1999). Factors influencing children's food choice. *Annals of Medicine, Suppl, 1,* 26–32.

Kolb, B., & Whishaw, I. Q. (2009). *Fundamentals of human neuropsychology (6th Ed.).* New York, NY: Worth Publishers.

Komaki, J. (2004). Water can induce better spatial memory performance than food in radial maze learning by rats. *Japanese Psychological Research, 46*(1), 65–71.

Komaroff, A. L., Masuda, M., & Holmes, T. H. (1989). The Social Readjustment Rating Scale: A comparative study of Black, white, and Mexican Americans. In T. H. Holmes and E. M. David (Eds.), *Life change, life events, and illness.* New York, NY: Praeger.

Komaroff, A. L., Masuda, M., & Holmes, T. H. (1986). The Social Readjustment Rating Scale: A comparative study of Negro, white, and Mexican Americans. *Journal of Psychosomatic Research., 12,*121–128.

Komiyama, O., Wang, K., Svensson, P., Arendt-Nielsen, L., Kawara, M., & De Laat, A. (2009). Ethnic differences regarding sensory, pain, and reflex responses in the trigeminal region. *Clinical Neurophysiology, 120,* 384–389.

Koob, G. F., & LeMoal, M. (2008). Addiction and the brain antireward system. In S. Fiske, D. L. Schacter, & R. Sternberg (Eds.), *Annual review of psychology—Volume 59.* Palo Alto, CA: Annual reviews.

Koopmans, P. C., Sanderman, R., Timmerman, I., Emmelkamp, P. M. G. (1994). The Irrational Beliefs Inventory (IBI): Development and psychometric evaluation. *European Journal of Psychological Assessment, 10*(1), 15–27.

Kooyman, I., & Walsh, E. (2011). Societal outcomes in schizophrenia. In D. R. Weinberger & P. J. Harrison (Eds.), *Schizophrenia* (3rd Ed.). Hoboken, NJ: Blackwell-Wiley.

Kopasz, M., Loessl, B., Hornyak, M., Riemann, D., Nissen, C., Piosczyk, H., & Voderholzer, U. (2010). Sleep and memory in healthy children and adolescents—a critical review. *Sleep Medicine Reviews, 14*(3), 167–177.

Kopec, J., Williams, J. I., To, T., et al. (2001). Cross-cultural comparisons of health status in Canada using the Health Utilities Index. *Ethnicity and Health, 6*(1), 41–50.

Kopelowicz, A., Liberman, R. P., & Zarate, R. (2007). Psychosocial treatments for schizophrenia. In P. E. Nathan & J. M. Gorman (Eds.), *A guide to treatments that work* (3rd Ed., pp. 243–269). New York: Oxford University Press.

Korchin, S. J., & Sands, S. H. (1983). Principles common to all psychotherapies. In C. E. Walker (Ed.), *The handbook of clinical psychology.* Homewood, IL: Dow Jones-Irwin.

Kosslyn, S. M., & Rosenberg, R. S. (2004).*Psychology: The brain, the person, the world* (2nd Ed.). Essex, England: Pearson Education Limited.

Kosten, T. R., George, T. P., & Kleber, H. D. (2005). The neurobiology of substance dependence: Implications for treatment. In R. J. Frances, A. H. Mack, & S. I. Miller (Eds.), *Clinical textbook of addictive disorder* (3rd edition). New York, NY: Guilford Press.

Kosten, T. R., Sofuoglu, M., & Gardner, T. J. (2008). Clinical management: Cocaine. In H. D. Kleber & M. Galanter (Eds.), *The American Psychiatric Publishing textbook of substance abuse treatment* (4th edition). Washington, DC: American Psychiatric Publishing.

Kraft, D., & Kraft, T. (2010). Use of in vivo and in vitro desensitization in the treatment of mouse phobia: Review and case study. *Contemporary Hypnosis, 27*(3), 184–194.

Krantz, D. S., & McCeney, M. K. (2002). Effects of psychological and social factors on organic disease: A critical assessment of research on coronary heart disease. *Annual Review of Psychology, 53(*1), 341–369.

Krantz, G., Berntsson, L., Lundberg, U. (2005). Total workload, work stress, and perceived symptoms in Swedish male and female white-collar employees. *European Journal of Public Health, 15,* 209–214.

Krebs, D. L., & Denton, K. (2006). Explanatory Limitations of Cognitive-Developmental Approaches to Morality. *Psychological Review, 113,* 672–675.

Kring, A. M., & Bachorowski, J. (1999). *Emotions and psychopathology, 13*(5), 575–599.

Krippner, S. (1990.) *Dreamtime and Dreamwork: Decod ing the Language of the Night.* Los Angeles: Jeremy P. Tarcher.

Kroger, J., Martinussen, M., & Marcia, J. E. (2010). Identity status change during adolescence and young adulthood: A meta-analysis. *Journal of Adolescence, 33*(5), 683–698.

Krubitzer, L. (1995). The organization of neocortex in mammals: Are species really so different? *Trends in Neurosciences, 18,* 408–418.

Krueger, R. F., South, S., Johnson, W., & Iacono, W. (2008). The heritability of personality is not always 50%: Gene-environment interactions and correlations between personality and parenting. *Journal of Personality, 76*(6), 1485–1522.

Krueger, R. G., & Kaplan, M. S. (2002). Behavioral and psychopharmacological treatment of the paraphilic and hypersexual disorders. *Journal of Psychiatric Practices, 8*(1), 21–32.

Krüetzen, M., Mann, J., Heithaus, M. R., Connor, R. C., Bejder, L. & Sherwin, W B. (2005). Cultural transmission of tool use in bottlenose dolphins. *Proceedings of the National Academy of Sciences USA, 102,* 8939–8943.

Ksir, C., Hart, C. L., & Oakley, R. (2008). *Drugs, society, and human behavior (12th Ed.).* Boston, MA: McGraw-Hill.

Kuboshima-Amemori, S,. & Sawaguchi, T. (2007). Plasticity of the primate prefrontal cortex. *Neuroscientist, 13,* 229–240.

Kudwa, A. E., Michopoulos, V., Gatewood, J. D., & Rissman, E. F. (2006). Roles of estrogen receptors alpha and beta in differentiation of mouse sexual behavior. *Neuroscience, 138*(3), 921–928.

Kuhn, T. S. (1962). *The structure of scientific revolutions.* Chicago, IL: University of Chicago Press.

Kuncel, N. R., Ones, D. S., & Sackett, P. R. (2010). Individual differences as predictors of work, educational, and broad life outcomes. *Personality and Individual Differences, 49*(4), 331–336.

Kunst, M. J. J. (2011). Affective personality type, post-traumatic stress disorder symptom severity and post-traumatic growth in victims of violence. *Stress and Health: Journal of the International Society for the Investigation of Stress, 27*(1), 42–51.

Kuo, J. R., Goldin, P. R., Werner, K., Heimberg, R. G., & Gross, J. J. (2011). Childhood trauma and current psychological functioning in adults with social anxiety disorder. *Journal of Anxiety Disorders, 25*(4), 467–473.

Kuppens, P., Realo, A., & Diener, E. (2008). The role of positive and negative emotions in life satisfaction judgment across nations. *Journal of Personality and Social Psychology, 95*(1), 66–75.

Kutner, L., & Olson, C. (2008). Grand theft childhood: The surprising truth about violent video games and what parents can do. New York, NY: Simon & Schuster.

Kyle, J. G. (1980). Auditory deprivation from birth—Clarification of some issues. *British Journal of Audiology, 14,* 34–36.

Labbé, E. E. (2011). Psychology moment by moment: A guide to enhancing your clinical practice with mindfulness and meditation. Oakland, CA: New Harbinger Publications.

Lack, L. C., & Bootzin, R. R. (2003). Circadian rhythm factors in insomnia and their treatment. In M. L. Perlis & K. L. Lichstein (Eds.), *Treating sleep disorders: Principles and practice of behavioral sleep medicine.* New York, NY: John Wiley & Sons, Inc.

Lagercrantz, H., & Changeux. J. P. (2009). The emergence of human consciousness: from fetal to neonatal life. *Pediatric Research, 65,* 255–260.

LaGraize, S. C., Borzan, J., Rinker, M. M., Kopp, J. L., & Fuchs, P. N. (2004). Behavioral evidence for competing motivational drives of nociception and hunger. *Neuroscience Letters, 372*(1/2), 30–34.

Lahey, B. B., & Waldman, I. D. (2007). Personality dispositions and the development of violence and conduct problems. In D. J. Flannery, A. T. Vazsonyi, & I. D. Irwin (Eds.), *The Cambridge handbook of violent behavior and aggression.* New York, NY: Cambridge University Press.

Lahey, B. B., Kupfer, D. L., Beggs, V. E., & Landon, D. (1982). Do learning-disabled children exhibit peripheral deficits in selective attention? An analysis of eye movements during reading. *Journal of Abnormal Child Psychology, 10,* 1–10.

Lahmann, C., Henningsen, P., & Noll-Hussong, M. (2010). Somatoforme schmerzen—Ein uberblick. [somatoform pain disorder—Overview]. *Psychiatria Danubina, 22*(3), 453–458.

Lakhan, S. E. (2007). Neuropsychological generation of source amnesia: An episodic memory disorder of the frontal brain. *Journal of Medical Chemistry.* Retrieved from http://www.scientificjournals.org/journals2007/ articles/1038.html.

Lalasz, R. (2011). Is something wrong with the scientific method? Part 1. *Cool green science (The conservation blog of the Nature Conservancy)*, January 21.

Lalonde, J. K., Hudson, J. I., Gigante, R. A., & Pope Jr., H. G. (2001). Canadian and American psychiatrists' attitudes toward dissociative disorders diagnoses. *Canadian Journal of Psychiatry, 46*(5), 407–412.

Lambert, M. J. (2010). *Prevention of treatment failure: The use of measuring, monitoring, and feedback in clinical practice.* Washington, DC: American Psychological Association.

Laming, P. R., Syková, E., Reichenbach, A., Hatton, G. I., & Bauer, H. (2011). *Glial cells: Their role in behaviour*. Cambridge University Press.

Lancaster, T., Stead, L., Silagy, C., & Sowden, A. (2000). Effectiveness of interventions to help people stop smoking: findings from the *Cochrane Library. British Medical Journal, 321*, 355.

Landon, T. M., & Barlow, D. H. (2004). Cognitive-behavioral treatment for panic disorder: Current status. *Journal of Psychiatric Practices, 10*(4), 211–226.

Landsberger, H. A. (1958). *Hawthorne revisited.* Ithaca, NY: Cornell University.

Lang, A. R. et al. (1975). Effects of alcohol on aggression in male social drinkers. *Journal of Abnormal Psychology, 84*, 508–518.

Lang, P. J., Bradley, M. M., & Cuthbert, B. N. (1998). Emotion, motivation, and anxiety: Brain mechanisms and psychophysiology. *Biological Psychiatry, 44*, 1248–1263.

Lang, P. J., Greenwald, M. K., & Bradley, M. M. (1993). Looking at pictures: Affective, facial, visceral, and behavioral reactions. *Psycho-physiology, 30*, 261–273.

Lange, C. G. (1885). The mechanism of the emotions. Paper originally published in 1885 and reprinted in B. Rand (Ed.), *The classical psychologists* (pp. 672–684). Boston, MA: Houghton Mifflin (1921).

Langens, T A., & Morth, S. (2003). Repressive coping and the use of passive and active coping strategies. *Personality and Individual Differences, 35*(2), 461–473.

Langer, E. J., & Rodin, J. (2004). The effects of choice and enhanced personal responsibility for the aged: A field experiment in an institutional setting. *The interface of social and clinical psychology: Key readings* (pp. 339–348). New York, NY: Psychology Press.

Langlois, J. H., & Stephan, C. W. (1981). Beauty and the beast: The role of physical attractiveness in the development of peer relations and social behavior. In S. S. Brehm, S. M. Kassin, & F. X. Gibbons (Eds.), *Developmental social psychology*. New York, NY: Oxford University Press.

Långström, N., Rahman, Q., Carlström, E., Lichtenstein, P. (2008). Genetic and environmental effects on same-sex sexual behavior: A population study of twins in Sweden. *Archives of Sexual Behaviour, 39*(1), 75–80.

Långström, N., & Seto, M. C. (2006). Exhibitionist and voyeuristic behavior in a Swedish national population survey. *Archives of Sexual Behavior, 35*, 27–35.

Lankau, M. J., Riordan, C. M., & Thomas, C. H. (2005). The effects of similarity and liking in formal relationships between mentors and protégés. *Journal of Vocational Behavior, 67*(2), 252–265.

Lanting, C. P., de Kleine, E., & van Dijk, P. (2009). Neural activity underlying tinnitus generation: results from PET and fMRI. *Hearing Research, 255*, 1–13.

LaPiere, R. (1934). Attitudes versus actions. *Social Forces, 13*, 230–237.

Lareau, A. (2003). *Unequal childhoods: Class race and family life*. University of California Press.

Larimer, M. E., Kilmer, J. R., & Lee, C. M. (2005). College student drug prevention: A review of individually-oriented prevention strategies. *Journal of Drug Issues, 35*(2), 431–456.

Larimer, M. E., & Neighbors, C. (2003). Normative misperception and the impact of descriptive and injunctive norms on college student gambling. *Psychology of Addictive Behaviors, 17*(3), 235–243.

Larimer, M. E., Turner, A. P., Mallett, K. A., & Geisner, I. M. (2004). Predicting drinking behavior and alcohol-related problems among fraternity and sorority members: Examining the role of descriptive and injunctive norms. *Psychology of Addictive Behaviors, 18*(3), 203–212.

Larocque, S. (2006). *Gay Marriage: The Story of a Canadian Social Revolution*. Toronto: James Lorimer & Company.

Larry, L. L., Young Owl, M., & Kersting, M. P. (2005), *The Cambridge Dictionary of Human Biology and Evolution.* Cambridge & New York: Cambridge University Press.

Larsen, J. T., McGraw, A. P., & Cacioppo, J. T. (2001). Can people feel happy and sad at the same time? *Journal of Personality and Social Psychology, 81*(4), 684–696.

Larsen, J. T., McGraw, A. P., Mellers, B. A., & Cacioppo, J. T. (2004). The agony of victory and thrill of defeat: Mixed emotional reactions to disappointing wins and relieving losses. *Psychological Science, 15*(5), 325–330.

Larsen, J. T., To, Y. M., & Fireman, G., (2007). Children's understanding and experience of mixed emotions. *Psychological Science, 18*(2), 186–191.

Larsen, R. J. (2000). Toward a science of mood regulation. *Psychological Inquiry, 11*, 129–141.

Larsen, R. J., & Diener, E. (1987). Affect intensity as an individual difference characteristic: A review. *Journal of Research in Personality, 21*, 1–39.

Larsen, R. J., Diener, E., & Emmons, R. A. (1986). Affect intensity and reactions to daily life events. *Journal of Personality and Social Psychology, 51*, 803–814.

Larson, E. B., Wang, L., Bowen, J. D., McCormick, W. C., Teri, L., Crane, P., & Kukull, W. (2006). Exercise is associated with reduced risk of incident dementia among persons 65 years of age and older. *Annals of Internal Medicine, 144*, 73–81.

Lashley, K. S. (1948). Brain mechanisms and intelligence, 1929.

Lashley, K. S. (1929). Brain mechanisms and intelligence: A quantitative study of injuries to the brain. Chicago, IL: University of Chicago Press.

Laslo, P., Lipski, J., Nicholson, L. F., Miles, G. B., & Funk, G. D. (2001). GluR2 AMPA receptor subunit expression in motoneurons at low and high risk for degeneration in amyotrophic lateral sclerosis. *Experimental Neurology*, 169, 461–471.

Latane, B., & Darley, J. M. (1970). *The unresponsive bystander: Why doesn't he help?* Englewood Cliffs, NJ: Prentice Hall.

Latane, B., & Darley, J. M. (1968). Group inhibition of bystander intervention in emergencies. *Journal of Personality and Social Psychology, 10*, 215–221.

Latane, B., Williams, K., & Harkins, S. G. (1979). Many hands make light the work: The cause and consequences of social loafing. *Journal of Personality and Social Psychology, 37*, 822–832.

Laumann, E. O., Paik, A., & Rosen, R. C. (1999). Sexual dysfunction in the United States: Prevalence and predictors. *Journal of the American Medical Association, 281*(6), 537–544.

Laumann, E. O., Gagnon , J. H., Michael, R. T., & Michaels, S. (1994). *The social organization of sexuality: sexual practices in the United States.* CSG Enterprises and Stuart Michaels.

Laumann, E. O., Nicolosi, A., Glasser, D. B., Paik, A., Gingell, C., Moreira, E., et al. (2005). Sexual problems among women and men aged 40–80 years: Prevalence and correlates identified in the Global Study of Sexual Attitudes and Behaviors. *International Journal of Impotence Research, 17*, 39–57.

Lavie, P. (2001). Sleep-wake as a biological rhythm. *Annual Review of Psychology, 52*, 277–303.

Lawford, B. R., Young, R. McD., Rowell, J. A., Gibson, J. N., et al. (1997). Association of the D2 dopamine receptor A1 allele with alcoholism: Medical severity alcoholism and type of controls. *Biological Psychiatry, 41*, 386–393.

Lazarus, R. S. (2007). Stress and emotion: A new synthesis. In A. Monat, R. S. Lazarus, & G. Reevy (Eds.), *The Praeger handbook on stress and coping (vol.1)* (pp. 33–51). Westport, CT: Praeger Publishers/ Greenwood Publishing Group.

Lazarus, R. S. (1999). *Stress and emotion: A new synthesis.* New York, NY: Springer Publishing Co.

Lazarus, R. S. (1993). From psychological stress to the emotions: A history of changing outlooks. *Annual Review of Psychology, 44*, 1–21.

Lazarus, R. S. (1993). Why we should think of stress as a subset of emotion. *Handbook of stress: Theoretical and clinical aspects (2nd Ed.)* (pp. 21–39). New York, NY: Free Press.

Lazarus, R. S. (1991). Progress on a cognitive-motivational-relational theory of emotion. *American Psychologist, 46*(8), 819–834.

Lazarus, R. S., & Alfert, E. (1964). The short-circuiting of threat by experimentally altering cognitive appraisal. *Journal of Abnormal and Social Psychology, 69*, 195–205.

Lazarus, R. S., Opton, E. M., Jr., Nomikos, M. S., & Rankin, N. O. (1965). The principle of short-circuiting of threat: Further evidence. *Journal of Personality, 33*, 622–635.

Lazarus, R. S., & Folkman, S. (1984). *Stress, appraisal, and coping*. New York: Springer.

Lazzari, C., Egan, S. J., & Rees, C. S. (2011). Behavioral activation treatment for depression in older adults delivered via videoconferencing: A pilot study. *Cognitive and Behavioral Practice,* No Pages.

Leahey, T. H. (2005). Mind as a scientific object: A historical-philosophical exploration. In C. E. Erneling, & D. M. Johnson (Eds.), *The mind as a scientific object: Between brain and culture* (pp. 35–78). New York, NY: Oxford University Press.

Leahey, T. H. (2000). *A History of Psychology*. (5th Ed.) Upper Saddle River, NJ: Prentice Hall.

Leaper, C. (2000) The social construction and socialization of gender during developmnet. In P. H. Miller and E. K. Schlonick, (Eds), *Towards a feminist developmental psychology* (pp. 127–152). New York: Routledge.

Learning Disabilities Association of Canada. (2002). *Official definition of learning disabilities*. Retrieved from www.ldac-acta.ca/en/learn-more/ld-defined.html.

Leavitt, G. C. (1989). Disappearance of the incest taboo: A cross-cultural test of general evolutionary hypotheses. *American Anthropologist, 91*(1), 116–131.

Leavitt, M. O., Spellings, M., & Gonzales, A. R. (2007). *Report to the President on Issues Raised by the Virginia Tech Tragedy*. Washington, D.C.

Lechner, S. C., Stoelb, B. L., & Antoni, M. H. (2008). Group-based therapies for benefit finding in cancer. *Trauma, recovery, and growth: Positive psychological perspectives on posttraumatic stress* (pp. 207–231). Hoboken, NJ: John Wiley & Sons Inc.

Ledikwe, J. H., Ello-martin, J. A., & Rolls, B. J. (2005). Portion sizes and the obesity epidemic. *Journal of Nutrition, 135*, 905–909.

Ledley, D. R., Erwin, B. A., & Heimberg, R. G. (2008). Social anxiety disorder. In W. E. Craighead, D. J. Miklowitz, & L. W. Craighead (Eds.), *Psychopathology: History, diagnosis, and empirical foundations* (pp. 198–233). Hoboken, NJ: John Wiley & Sons.

LeDoux, J. E. (2008). Remembrance of emotions past. In M. H. Immordino-Yang (Ed.), *The Jossey-Bass reader on the brain and learning* (pp. 151–179). San Francisco, CA: Jossey-Bass.

LeDoux, J. E. (2007). The amygdala. *Current Biology, 17*, R868–874.

LeDoux, J. E. (2003). The emotional brain, fear, and the amygdala. *Cellular and Molecular Neurobiology,* 23(4–5), 727–738.

LeDoux, J. E. (2000). Emotion circuits in the brain. *Annual Review of Neuroscience, 23*, 155–184.

LeDoux, J. E. (1999). The power of emotions. In R. Conlan (Ed.), *States of mind: new discoveries about how our brains make us who we are*. New York: John Wiley & Sons, Inc.

LeDoux, J. E. (1998). Where the wild things are. *The emotional brain* (pp. 225–266). New York, NY: Simon & Schuster.

Ledoux, J. E. (1996). The emotional brain: The mysterious underpinnings of emotional life. New York, NY: Simon and Schuster.

LeDoux, J. E. (1995). Emotions: Clues from the brain. *Annual Review of Psychology, 46*, 209–235.

LeDoux, J. E., & Doyère, V. (2011). Emotional memory processing: Synaptic connectivity. In S. Nalbantian, P. M. Matthews & J. L. McClelland (Eds.), *The memory process: Neuroscientific and humanistic perspectives* (pp. 153–171). Cambridge, MA, US: MIT Press.

Lee, E., Mishna, F., & Brennenstuhl, S. (2010). How to critically evaluate case studies in social work. *Research on Social Work Practice, 20*(6), 682–689.

Lee, M. G., Hassani, O. K., & Jones, B. (2005). Discharge of identified orexin/hypocretin neurons across the sleep-waking cycle. *The Journal of Neuroscience, 25*(28), 6716–6720.

Legault, G., Delay, S., & Madore, A. (2010). Identification of a rapid eye movement sleep window for learning of the win-shift radial arm maze task for male sprague-dawley rats. *Journal of Sleep Research, 19*(4), 508–515.

Lehrer, J. (2007). *Proust was a Neuroscientist*. Houghton Mifflin Harcourt.

Leiblum, S. R. (2007). Sex therapy today: Current issues and future perspectives. *Principles and practice of sex therapy (4th Ed.)* (pp. 3–22). New York, NY: Guilford Press.

Leichsenring, F., Leibing, E., Kruse, J., New, A. S., & Leweke, F. (2011). Borderline personality disorder. *The Lancet, 377*(9759), 74–84.

Leitch, K. K. (2007). *Reaching for the top: A report by the advisor on healthy children & youth*. Her Majesty the Queen in Right of Canada, represented by the Minister of Health Canada, 2007. Retrieved from http://www.hc-sc.gc.ca/hl-vs/pubs/child-enfant/advisor-conseillere/index eng.php.

Lekander, M. (2002). Ecological immunology: The role of the immune system in psychology and neuroscience. *European Psychiatry, 7*(2), 98–115.

Lemmon, K., & Moore, C. (2007). The development of prudence in the face of varying future rewards. *Developmental Science, 10*(4), 502–511.

Lemonick, M. D. (2007). Why we get disgusted. *Time Magazine,* May 24, 2007.

Lenz, F. A., Casey, K. L., Jones, E. G., & Willis, W. (2010). *The human pain system*. Cambridge University Press.

Lenzenweger, M. F., Lane, M. C., Loranger, A. W., & Kessler, R. C. (2007). DSM-IV personality disorders in the national comorbidity survey replication. *Biological Psychiatry, 62*, 553–564.

Leon, G. R. (1977). *Case histories of deviant behavior* (2nd Ed.). Boston, MA: Allyn & Bacon.

Leontiev, D. A. (2008). Maslow yesterday, today, and tomorrow. *Journal of Humanistic Psychology, 48*(4), 451–453.

Lepore, S. J., Evans, G. W., & Palsane, M. N. (1991). Social hassles and psychological health in the context of chronic crowding. *Journal of Health and Social Behavior, 32*(4), 357–367.

Leppänen, J. M., & Hietanen, J. K. (2007). Is there more in a happy face than just a big smile? *Visual Cognition, 15*(4), 468–490.

Leslie, M. (2000). The vexing legacy of Lewis Terman. *Stanford Magazine,* July/August 2000, 1–21.

Leube, D. (2009). S25-04 The neural basis of disorganized symptoms in schizophrenia. *European Psychiatry, 24*(1), S141.

Leuner, B., Glasper, E. R., & Gould, E. (2010). Parenting and plasticity. *Trends in Neurosciences, 33*(10), 465–473.

Leuner, B., & Gould, E. (2010). Structural plasticity and hippocampal function. *Annual Review of Psychology, 61*, 111–140.

Leuner, B., Gould, E., & Shors, T. J. (2006) Is there a link between adult neurogenesis and learning? *Hippocampus, 16*(3), 216–224.

Levay, S. (1991). A difference in hypothalamic structure between heterosexual and homosexual men. *Science, 253*, 1034–1037.

Leventhal, E. A., Leventhal, H., Shacham, S., & Easterling, D. V. (1989). Active coping reduces reports of pain from childbirth. *Journal of Consulting and Clinical Psychology, 57*, 365–371.

Levi-Montalcini, R. (1988). *In praise of imperfection: my life and work*. New York, NY: Basic Books.

Levin, J. (2000). A prolegomenon to an epidemiology of love: Theory, measurement, and health outcomes. *Journal of Social & Clinical Psychology, 19*(1), 117–136.

Levin, B. E., Routh, V. H., Kang, L., Sanders, N. M., & Dunn-Meynell, A. (2004). Neuronal glucosensing: What do we know after 50 years? *Diabetes, 53*(10), 2521–2528.

Levin, B., Hennessy, K. D., & Petrila, J. (2010.) *Mental health services: a public health perspective, 3rd Ed*. Oxford University Press, New York.

Levinson, D. J. (1986). Conception of adult development. *American Psychologist, 41*(1), 3–13.

Levinson, D. J. (1984). The career is in the life structure, the life structure is in the career: An adult development perspective. In M. B. Arthur, L. Bailyn, D. J. Levinson, & H. Shepard (Eds.), *Working with careers*. New York: Columbia University School of Business.

Levinson, D. J. (1977). Toward a conception of adult life course. In N. Smelser & E. H. Erikson (Eds.), *Themes of love and work in adulthood*. Cambridge, MA: Harvard University Press.

Levinson, D. J. (1977). The mid-life transition. *Psychiatry, 40*, 99–112.

Levinson, D. J., & Levinson, J. D. (1996). *Seasons of a woman's life*. New York: Alred A. Knopf.

Lewin, K. (1935). *A dynamic theory of personality*. New York, NY: McGraw-Hill.

Lewis, M. (2010). The emergence of consciousness and its role in human development. In W. F. Overton, & R. M. Lerner (Eds.), *The handbook of life-span development, vol 1: Cognition, biology, and methods* (pp. 628–670). Hoboken, NJ: John Wiley & Sons Inc.

Lewis, M. (2008). The emergence of human emotions. *Handbook of emotions (3rd Ed.)* (pp. 304–319). New York, NY: Guilford Press.

Lewis, M. (2007). Self-conscious emotional development. In J. L. Tracy, R. W. Robins, & J. P. Tangney (Eds.), *The self-conscious emotions: Theory and research* (pp. 134–149). New York, NY: The Guilford Press.

Lewis, M. (2005). Origins of the self-conscious child. In W. R. Crozier, & L. E. Alden (Eds.), *The essential handbook of social anxiety for clinicians* (pp. 81–98). Hoboken, NJ: John Wiley & Sons, Inc.

Lewis, M. (2000). The emergence of human emotions. In M. Lewis & J. M. Haviland-Jones (Eds.), *Handbook of Emotions, Second Edition* (pp. 265–280). New York, NY: The Guilford Press.

Lewis, M. (1992). *Shame: The exposed self.* New York, NY: Free Press.

Lewis, M., & Brooks-Gunn, J. (1979). *Social cognition and the acquisition of self.* New York, NY: Plenum.

Lewis, T. L., & Maurer, D. (2005). Multiple sensitive periods in human visual development: evidence from visually deprived children. *Developmental Psychobiology, 46,* 163–183.

Lewis-Harter, S. (2000). Psychosocial adjustment of adult children of alcoholics. A review of the recent empirical literature. *Clinical Psychology Review, 20*(3), 311–337.

Lewontin, R. C. (1976). Science and politics: An explosive mix. *PsycCRITIQUES, 21*(2), 97–98.

Li, Q. (2005). *Cyberbullying in schools: Nature and extent of Canadian adolescents experience.* Paper presented at the conference of the American Educational research Association, Montreal.

Li, S. (2010). Neuromodulation of fluctuations of information processing: Computational, neural, and genetic perspectives. In P. C. M. Molenaar, & K. M. Newell (Eds.), *Individual pathways of change: Statistical models for analyzing learning and development* (pp. 23–35). Washington, DC: American Psychological Association.

Li, W., Howard, J. D., Parrish, T. B., & Gottfried, J. A. (2008). Aversive learning enhances perceptual and cortical discrimination of indiscriminable odor cues. *Science, 319,* 1842–1845.

Lian, J., Goldstein, A., Donchin, E., & He, B. (2002). Cortical potential imaging of episodic memory encoding. *Brain Topography, 15*(1), 29–36.

Liang, C. T. H., Alvarez, A. N., Juang, L. P., & Liang, M. X. (2009). The role of coping in the relationship between perceived racism and racism-related stress for asian americans: Gender differences. *Asian American Journal of Psychology,* S(1), 56–69.

Liddell, H. S. (1950). Animal origins of anxiety. *Feelings and emotions; the mooseheart symposium* (pp. 181–188). New York, NY: McGraw-Hill.

Liden, R. C., Wayne, S. J., Jaworski, R. A., & Bennett, N. (2004). Social loafing: A field investigation. *Journal of Management, 30*(2), 285–304.

Lieberman, M. D., Jarcho, J. M., & Obayashi, J. (2005). Attributional inference across cultures: Similar automatic attributions and different controlled corrections. *Personality and Social Psychology Bulletin, 31*(7), 889–901.

Lieberson, A. D. (2004). How long can a person survive without food? *Scientific American.* Retrieved from http://www.scientificamerican.com/article.cfm?id=how-long-can-a-person-sur.

Liem, D. G., & Mennella, J. A. (2003). Heightened sour preferences during childhood. *Chemical Senses, 28,* 173–180.

Lilienfeld, S., Lynn, S., Namy, L., & Wolf, N. (2008). *Psychology: From Inquiry to Understanding.* Boston: Pearson, Allyn & Bacon.

Lilienfeld, S. O., Wood, J. M., & Garb, H. N. (2000). The scientific status of projective techniques. *Psychological Science in the Public Interest, 1,* 27–66.

Lindsay, D. S., Hagen, L., Read, J. D., Wade, K. A., & Garry, M. (2004). True photographs and false memories. *Psychological Science, 15*(3), 149–154.

Lindsay, S. D., & Read, J. D. (1995). "Memory work" and recovered memories of childhood sexual abuse: scientific evidence and public, professional, and personal issues. *Psychology, Public Policy, and Law, 1*(4), 846–908.

Linehan, M. M. (1993). Cognitive-behavioral treatment of borderline personality disorder. New York, NY: The Guilford Press.

Linehan, M. M., & Dexter-Mazza, E. (2008). Dialectical behavior therapy for borderline personality disorder. In D. H. Barlow (Ed.), *Clinical handbook of psychological disorders: A step-by-step treatment manual (4th Ed.)* (pp. 365–420). New York, NY: The Guilford Press.

Ling, K., Beenen, G., Ludford, P., Wang, X., Chang, K., Li, Z., Cosley D., Frankowski, D., Terveen, L., Rashid, A. M., Resnick, P., & Kraut, R. (2005). Using social psychology to motivate contributions to online communities. *Journal of Computer-mediated Communication, 10,* article 10.

Linville, P. W., Fischer, G. W., & Fischhoff, B. (1993). AIDS risk perceptions and decision biases. In J. B. Pryor & G. D. Reeder (Eds.), *The Social psychology of HIV infection.* Hillsdale, NJ: Lawrence Erlbaum Associates.

Lipsitt, L. P., Pederson, L. J., & Delucia, C. A. (1966). Conjugate reinforcement of operant responding in infants. *Psychonomic Science, 4*(2), 67–68.

Lipton, A. A., & Simon, F. S. (1985). Psychiatric diagnosis in a state hospital: Manhattan State revisited. *Hospital and Community Psychiatry,* 36(4), 368–373.

Litman, J. (2005). Curiosity and the pleasures of learning: Wanting and liking new information. *Cognition & Emotion, 19*(6), 793–814.

Litschge, C. M., Vaughn, M. G., & McCrea, C. (2010). The empirical status of treatments for children and youth with conduct problems: An overview of meta-analytic studies. *Research on Social Work Practice, 20*(1), 21–35.

Liu, H., Xu, Y., & Larson, C. R. (2009). Attenuation of vocal responses to pitch perturbations during Mandarin speech. *Journal of the Acoustical Society of America, 125*(4), 2299–2306.

Livesley, W., Jang, K., & Vernon, P. (2003). Genetic Basis of Personality Structure. In I. B. Weiner (Series Ed.), T. Millon, & M. J. Lerner (Vol. Eds.), *Handbook of Psychology: Vol. 5. Personality and Social Psychology* (pp. 59–84).

Llinás, R. R., & Ribary, U. (2001). Consciousness and the brain: The thalamocortical dialogue in health and disease. *Annals of the New York Academy of Sciences, 929,* 166–175.

Lloyd, M., Burghardt, A., Ulrich, D. A., & Angulo-Barroso, R. (2010). Physical activity and walking onset in infants with down syndrome. *Adapted Physical Activity Quarterly, 27*(1), 1–16.

Loas, G., Cormier, J., & Perez-Diaz, F. (2011). Dependent personality disorder and physical abuse. *Psychiatry Research, 185*(1–2), 167–170.

Lochman, J. E., Barry, T., Powell, N., & Young, L. (2010). Anger and aggression. In D. W. Nangle, D. J. Hansen, C. A. Erdley, & P. J. Norton (Eds.), *Practitioner's guide to empirically based measures of social skills* (pp. 155–166). New York: Springer Publishing Co.

Locke, E. A. (2007). The case for inductive theory building. *Journal of Management, 33*(6), 867–890.

Loehlin, J. C. (1992). *Genes and environment in personality development.* Newbury Park, CA: Sage.

Loessl, B., Valerius, G., Kopasz, M., Hornyak, M., Riemann, D., & Voderholzer, U. (2008). Are adolescents chronically sleep-deprived? An investigation of sleep habits of adolescents in the southwest of Germany. *Child: Care, Health and Development, 34,* 549–556.

Loewenstein, R. J. (2007). Dissociative identity disorder: Issues in the iatrogenesis controversy. In D. Spiegel, E. Vermetten, & M. Dorahy (Eds.), *Traumatic dissociation: Neurobiology and treatment.* Washington, DC: American Psychiatric Publishing.

Loewi, O. (1957). On the background of the discovery of neurochemical transmission. *Journal of Mount Sinai Hospital, 24,* 1014–1016.

Loftus, E. F. (2005). Planting misinformation in the human mind: A 30-year investigation of the malleability of memory. *Learning & Memory, 12*(4), 361–366.

Loftus, E. F., & Cahill, L. (2007). Memory distortion: From misinformation to rich false memory. In J. S. Nairne (Ed.), *The foundations of remembering: Essays in honor of Henry L. Roediger, III.* New York: Psychology Press.

Loftus, E. F., & Loftus, G. R. (1980). On the permanence of stored information in the human brain. *American Psychologist, 35*(5), 409–420.

Loftus, E. F., Miller, D. G., & Burns, H. J. (1978). Semantic integration of verbal information into a visual memory. *Journal of Experimental Psychology: Human Learning and Memory, 4*(1), 19–31.

Logsdon, A. (2011). Early child development (Your baby's first six month early child development). *About.com Guide: Learning disabilities.* Retrieved from http:/learningdisabilities/.about.com/od/infancyandearlychildhood.

Logue, D. M., Abiola, I. O., Rains, D., Bailey, N. W., Zuk, M., & Cade, W. H. (2010). Does signalling mitigate the cost of agonistic interactions? A test in a cricket that has lost its song. *Proceedings in Biological Science, 227,* 2571–2575.

López-Muñoz, F.; Boya, J., Alamo, C. (2006). Neuron theory, the cornerstone of neuroscience, on the centenary of the Nobel Prize award to Santiago Ramón y Cajal. *Brain Research Bulletin, 70*(4–6), 391–405.

LoPiccolo, J. (2004). Sexual disorders affecting men. *Handbook of primary care psychology* (pp. 485–494). New York, NY: Oxford University Press.

LoPiccolo, J. (1995). Sexual disorders and gender identity disorders. In R. J. Comer, *Abnormal Psychology* (2nd edition). New York: WH. Freeman.

LoPiccolo, J., & Stock, W. E. (1987). Sexual function, dysfunction, and counseling in gynecological practice. In Rosenwaks, F. Benjamin, & M. L. Stone (Eds.), *Gynecology*. New York: Macmillan.

Lorenz, K. (2002). Critique of the modern ethologists' attitude. In M. H. Johnson, Y. Munakata, & R. O. Gilmore (Eds.), *Brain development and cognition: A reader* (2nd Ed.). Malden, MA: Blackwell Publishing.

Lorenz, K. (1971). *Studies in animal and human behaviour: II. trans. R. Martin* Oxford, UK: Harvard University Press.

Lorenz, K. (1970). *Studies in animal and human behaviour: I. trans. R. Martin* Oxford, UK: Harvard University Press.

Lorusso, L. (2010). Review of Aristotele e il cervello: Le teorie del piugrande biologo dell'antichita nella storia del pensiero scientifico. *Journal of the History of the Neurosciences, 19*(2), 203–206.

Lott, A. J., & Lott, B. E. (1974). The role of reward in the formation of positive interpersonal attitudes. In T. L. Huston (Ed.), *Foundation of Interpersonal attraction* (pp. 171–189). New York, NY: Academic Press.

Lourenç, O., & Machado, A. (1996). In defense of Piaget's theory: A reply to 10 common criticisms. *Psychological Review, 103*, 143–164.

Lovell, B., Moss, M., & Wetherell, M. A. (2011). Perceived stress, common health complaints and diurnal patterns of cortisol secretion in young, otherwise healthy individuals. *Hormones and Behavior, 60*(3), 301–305.

Lövheim, H., Sandman, P., Karlsson, S., & Gustafson, Y. (2009). Sex differences in the prevalence of behavioral and psychological symptoms of dementia. *International Psychogeriatrics, 21*(3), 469–475.

Löw, A., Lang, P. J., Smith, J. C., & Bradley, M. M. (2008). Both predator and prey: Emotional arousal in threat and reward. *Psychological Science, 19*(9), 865–873.

Lowe, M. R. (1993). The effects of eating on dieting behavior: A three factor model. *Psychologial Bulletin, 114*, 100–121.

Lowry, C. A., Hale, M. W., Evans, A. K., Heerkens, J., Staub, D. R., Gasser, P. J., & Shekhar, A. (2008). Serotonergic systems, anxiety, and affective disorder: focus on the dorsomedial part of the dorsal raphe nucleus. *Annals of the New York Academy of Sciences, 1148*, 86–94.

Lu, L., & Shih, J. (1997). Personality and happiness: Is mental health a mediator? *Personality and Individual Differences, 22*, 249–256.

Lubart, T. (2010). Cross-cultural perspectives on creativity. In J. C. Kaufman & R. J. Sternberg (Eds.), *The Cambridge handbook of creativity* (pp. 265–278). New York: Cambridge University Press.

Luborsky, E. B., O'Reilly-Landry, M., & Arlow, J. A. (2011). Psychoanalysis. In R. J. Corsini & D. Wedding (Eds.), *Current psychotherapies* (9th Ed.). Florence, KY: CENGAGE Learning.

Luborsky, L. B., Barrett, M. S., Antonuccio, D. O., Shoenberger, D., & Stricker, G. (2006). What else materially influences what is represented and published as evidence? In J. C. Norcross, L. E. Beutler, & R. F. Levant (Eds.), *Evidence-based practices in mental health: Debate and dialogue on the fundamental questions* (pp. 257–298). Washington, DC: American Psychological Association.

Luborsky, L., Rosenthal, R., Diguer, L., Andrusyna. T. P., Levitt, J. T., Seligman, D. A., Berman, J. S., & Krause, E. D. (2003). Are some psychotherapies much more effective than others? *Journal of Applied and Psychoanalytic Studies, 5*(4), 455–460.

Luborsky, L., Singer, B., & Luborsky, L. (1975). Comparative studies of psychotherapies. *Archives of General Psychiatry*, 32, 995–1008.

Lucas, R. E. (2007). Adaptation and the set point model of subjective wellbeing: Does happiness change after major life events? *Current Directions in Psychological Science, 16*(2), 75–79.

Luchins, A. S. (1942). Mechanization in problem solving. *Psychological Monographs, 54*(248).

Luh, C. W. (1922). The conditions of retention. *Psychological Monographs, 31*.

Lumeng, J. C., & Hillman, K. H. (2007). Eating in larger groups increases food consumption. *Archives of Disease in Childhood, 92*(5), 384–387.

Luminet, O., Bouts, P., Delie, F., Manstead, A. S. R., & Rimé, B. (2000). Social sharing of emotion following exposure to a negatively valenced situation. *Cognition and Emotion 14*(5), 661–688.

Lundberg, U. (2000). Workplace stress. In G. Fink (Ed.), *Encyclopedia of Stress, Vol. 3* (pp. 684–692). New York, NY: Academic Press.

Lundqvist, T. (2005). Cognitive consequences of cannabis use: Comparison with abuse of stimulants and heroin with regard to attention, memory and executive functions. *Pharmacology, Biochemistry and Behavior, 81*, 330–391.

Luo, L., & Craik, F.I.M. (2008). Aging and memory: A cognitive approach. *Canadian Journal of Psychiatry, 53*(6), 346–353.

Lupien, S. J., Maheu, F., Tu, M., Fiocco, A., & Schramek, T. E. (2007). The effects of stress and stress hormones on human cognition: Implications for the field of brain and cognition. *Brain and Cognition, 65*(3), 209–237.

Lupien, S. J., Ouelle-Morin, I., Hupback, A., Walker, D., Tu, M. T., & Buss, C. (2006). Beyond the stress concept: Allostatic load—a developmental biological and cognitive perspective. In D. Cicchetti (Ed.), *Handbook Series on Developmental Psychopathology* (pp. 784–809). New York, NY: John Wiley & Sons.

Lüttke, H. B. (2004). Experimente unter dem milgram-paradigma. [experiments within the milgram paradigm.]. *Gruppendynamik Und Organisationsberatung, 35*(4), 431–464.

Luyckx, K., Tildesley, E. A., Soenens, B., Andrews, J. A., Hampson, S. E., Peterson, M., & Duriez, B. (2011). Parenting and trajectories of children's maladaptive behaviors: a 12-year prospective community study. *Journal of Clininical Childhood and Adolescent Psychology, 40*(3), 468–478.

Lydiard, R. B. (2003). The role of GABA in anxiety disorders. *The Journal of Clinical Psychiatry (Supplement), 64*(3), 21–27.

Lykken, D., & Tellegen, A. (1996). Happiness is a stochastic phenomenon. *7*(3), 186–189.

Lymburner, J. A., & Roesch, R. (1999). The insanity defense: Five years of research (1993–1997). *International Journal of Law and Psychiatry, 22*, 213–240.

Lynam, D., Caspi, A., Moffitt, T., Wikstrom, P., Loeber, R., & Novak, S. (2000) The interaction between impulsivity and neighborhood context on offending: The effects of impulsivity are stronger in poorer neighborhoods. *Journal of Abnormal Psychology, 109*, 563–574.

Lynch, G., Larson, J., Staubli, U., Ambros-Ingerson, J., & Granger, R. (1991). Long-term potentiation and memory operations in cortical networks. In R. G. Lister & H. J. Weingartner (Eds.), *Perspectives on cognitive neuroscience* (pp. 110–131). New York, NY: Oxford University Press.

Lynch, S. K., Turkheimer, E., D'Onofrio, B. M., Mendle, J., Emery, R. E., Slutske, W. S., & Martin, N. G. (2006). A genetically informed study of the association between harsh punishment and offspring behavioral problems. *Journal of Family Psychology, 20*, 190–198.

Lynn, R., & Meisenberg, G. (2010). National IQs calculated and validated for 108 nations. *Intelligence, 38*(4), 353–360.

Lynn, S. J., Rhue J. W. and Kirsch I. (Eds.). (2010). *Handbook of clinical hypnosis (2nd Ed.)*. Washington, DC: American Psychological Association.

Lynn, S. J., & Kirsch, I. (2006). Smoking cessation. In S. J. Lynn & I. Kirsch, *Essentials of clinical hypnosis: An evidence-based approach. Dissociation, trauma, memory, and hypnosis book series*. Washington, DC: American Psychological Association.

Lyttle, J. (2001). The effectiveness of humor in persuasion: The case of business ethics training. *Journal of General Psychology, 128*(2), 206–216.

MacLean, P. D. (1954). The limbic system and its hippocampal formation: Studies in animals and their possible application to man. *Journal of Neurosurgery, 11*, 29–44.

MacLeod, C. (2010). Hebb award winner 2010: When learning met memory. *Canadian Journal of Experimental Psychology, 64*(4) 227–240.

Macleod, M. D., Saunders, J., & Chalmers, L. (2010). Retrieval-induced forgetting: The unintended consequences of unintended forgetting. In G. M. Davies, & D. B. Wright (Eds.), *Current issues in applied memory research* (pp. 50–71). New York, NY: Psychology Press.

MacMillan, H. L., Jamieson, E., Walsh, C. A., Wong, M. Y.-Y., Faries, E. J., McCue, H., MacMillan, A. B., & Offord, D. R. (2008). First Nations women's mental health: Results from an Ontario survey. *Archives of Women's Mental Health, 11*(2), 109–115.

Macmillan, M. (2008). Phineas Gage – Unravelling the myth. *The Psychologist* (British Psychological Society), *21*(9), 828–831.

MacNamara, Á., Button, A., & Collins, D. (2010). The role of psychological characteristics in facilitating the pathway to elite performance. *The Sport Psychologist, 24*, 52–73.

MacQueen,G., Marshall, J., Perdue, M., Siegel, S., & Bienenstock, J. (1989). Pavlovian conditioning of rat mucosal mast cells to secrete rat mast cell protease II. *Science, 243*, 83–86.

Maddi, S. R. (2007). The story of hardiness: Twenty years of theorizing, research, and practice. *The praeger handbook on stress and coping (vol.2)* (pp. 327–340). Westport, CT: Praeger Publishers/ Greenwood Publishing Group.

Maddux, J. E., & Volkmann, J. (2010). Self-efficacy. In R. H. Hoyle (Ed.), *Handbook of personality and self-regulation* (pp. 315–331). Hoboken, NJ: Wiley-Blackwell.

Maestripieri, D., Higley, J., Lindell, S., Newman, T., McCormack, K., & Sanchez, M. (2006). Early maternal rejection affects the development of monoaminergic systems and adult abusive parenting in rhesus macaques (Macaca mulatta). *Behavioral Neuroscience, 120,* 1017–1024.

Magee, J. C., & Teachman, B. A. (2007). Why did the white bear return? Obsessive-compulsive symptoms and attributions for unsuccessful thought suppression. *Behavior Research and Therapy, 45,* 2884–2898.

Maggini, C. (2000). Psychobiology of boredom. *CNS Spectrums, 5*(8), 24–27.

Maguire, E. A., Gadian, D. G., Johnsrude, I. S., Good, C. D., Ashburner, J., Frackowiak, R. S., & Frith, C. D. (2000). Navigation-related structural change in the hippocampi of taxi drivers. *Proceedings of the National Academy of Sciences USA, 97,* 4398–4403.

Main, M., Hesse, E., & Kaplan, N. (2005). Predictability of attachment behavior and representational processes at 1, 6, and 19 years of age: The Berkeley longitudinal study. In K. E. Grossmann, K. Grossmann, & E. Waters (Eds.), *Attachment from infancy to adulthood: The major longitudinal studies* (pp. 245–304). New York: Guilford Press.

Main, M., & Solomon, J. (1990). Discovery of a new, insecure-disorganized/ disoriented attachment pattern. In T. B. Brazelton & M. Yogman (Eds.), *Affective development in infancy* (pp. 121–160). Norwood, NJ: Ablex.

Makino, M., Tsuboi, K., & Dennerstein, L. (2004). Prevalence of eating disorders: A comparison of western and non-western countries. *Medscape General Medicine 6*(3), 49.

Maldonado, J. R., & Spiegel, D. (2007). Dissociative disorders. In S. C. Yudofsky, J. A. Bourgeois, & R. E. Hales (Eds.), *The American Psychiatric Publishing Board prep and review guide for psychiatry*. Washington, DC: American Psychiatric Publishing.

Malkoff, S. B., Muldoon, M. F., Zeigler, Z. R., & Manuck, S. B. (1993). Blood platelet responsivity to acute mental stress. *Psychosomatic Medicine, 55*(6), 477–482.

Mallan, K. M., & Lipp, O. V. (2007). Does emotion modulate the blink reflex in human conditioning? Startle potentiation during pleasant and unpleasant cues in the picture-picture paradigm. *Psychophysiology, 44,* 737–748.

Malle, B. F. (2006). The actor-observer asymmetry in causal attribution: A (surprising) meta-analysis. *Psychological Bulletin, 132,* 895–919.

Mancini Billson, J. (2005). After the Montreal masscre: gender and the pervasiveness of violence. In J. Mancini Billson, & C. Fluehr-Lobban (Eds.), *Female well-being: toward a global theory of social change.* St. Martin's Press: New York: NY.

Mandelman, S. D., Tan, M., Kornilov, S. A., Sternberg, R. J., & Grigorenko, E. L. (2010). The metacognitive component of academic self-concept: The development of a triarchic self-scale. *Journal of Cognitive Education and Psychology, 9*(1), 73–86.

Mandler, J. M. (2004). *Foundations of the mind.* New York: Oxford.

Manelis, A., Hanson, C., & Hanson, S. J. (2011). Implicit memory for object locations depends on reactivation of encoding-related brain regions. *Human Brain Mapping, 32*(1), 32–50.

Mannen, T., Iwata, M., Toyokura, Y., & Nagashima, K. (1982). The Onuf's nucleus and the external anal sphincter muscles in amyotrophic lateral sclerosis and Shy-Drager syndrome. *Acta Neuropathologica. 58,* 255–260.

Manuck, S. B., Cohen, S., Rabin, B. S., Muldoon, M. F., & Bachen, E. A. (1991). Individual differences in cellular immune responses to stress. *Psychological Science, 2,* 1–5.

Manusov, V., & Spitzberg, B. H. (2008). Attributes of attribution theory: Finding good cause in the search for theory. In D. O. Braithwaite & L. A. Baxter (Eds.), *Engaging theories in interpersonal communication* (pp. 37–49). Thousand Oaks, CA: Sage Publications.

Mar, R. A., Tackett, J. L., & Moore, C. (2010). Exposure to media and theory-of-mind development in preschoolers. *Cognitive Development, 25*(1), 69–78.

Marañon, G. (1924). Contribution a l'etude de l'action emotive de l'adrenaline. *Rev. Francmse Endocrinol, 2,* 301–325.

Maratsos, M. (2000). More overregularizations after all: New data and discussion on Marcus, Pinker, Ullman, Hollander, Rosen & Xu. *Journal of Child Language, 27,* 183–212.

Marcia, J. E. (2010). Life transitions and stress in the context of psychosocial development. In T. W. Miller (Ed.), *Handbook of stressful transitions across the lifespan* (pp. 19–34). New York: Springer Science + Business Media.

Marcia, J. E. (2007). Theory and measure: The identity status interview. In M. Watzlawik, & A. Born (Eds.), *Capturing identity: Quantitative and qualitative methods* (pp. 1–14). Lanham: University Press of America.

Marcia, J. E. (2002). Identity and psychosocial development in adulthood. *Identity, 2,* 7–28.

Marcia, J. E. (1994). The empirical study of ego identity. In H. A. Bosma, T. L. G. Graafsma, H. D. Grotevant, & D. J. de Levita (Eds.), *Identity and development: An interdisciplinary approach* (pp. 67–80). Thousand Oaks, CA: Sage Publications.

Marin, A. (2001). *Report to the Minster of National Defence: Special report on the systematic treatment of CF members with PTSD.* Retrieved from http://www.ombudsman.forces.gc.ca/rep-rap/sr-rs/pts-ssp/doc/pts-ssp-eng.pdf.

Markowitz, L. E., Dunne, E. F., Saraiya, M., Lawson, H. W., Chesson, H., & Unger, E. R. (2007). Quadrivalent human papillomavirus vaccine: Recommendations of the Advisory Committee on Immunization. *Morbidity and Mortality Weekly Report, 56*(10).

Markowitsch, H. J., Welzer, H., & Emmans, D. (2010). *The development of autobiographical memory.* New York, NY: Psychology Press.

Markus, H. R., & Kitayama, S. (1994). A collective fear of the collective: Implications for selves and theories of selves. *Personality and Social Psychology Bulletin, 20,* 568–579.

Markus, H. R., Plaut, V. C., & Lachman, M. E. (2004). Well-being in America: Core features and regional patterns. In O. G. Brim, C. D. Ryff, & R. C. Kessler (Eds.), *How healthy are we?: A national study of well-being at midlife* (pp. 614–650). Chicago, IL:University of Chicago Press.

Marques, L., LeBlanc, N., Weingarden, H., Greenberg, J. L., Traeger, L. N., Keshaviah, A., & Wilhelm, S. (2011). Body dysmorphic symptoms: Phenomenology and ethnicity. *Body Image, 8*(2), 163–167.

Marsalis, E., McDonald, L., & Donahue, P. (2008). The role of coping humor in the physical and mental health of older adults. *Aging and Mental Health, 12*(6), 713–718.

Marsh, E. J. (2007). Retelling is not the same as recalling: Implications for memory. *Current Directions in Psychological Science, 16,* 16–20.

Marsh, J. (2008). Playing doctor: An interview with Patch Adams. *Greater Good Magazine, 4(4).* Retrieved from http://greatergood.berkeley.edu/greatergood/2008spring/Q_A054.html

Marshall, B. J. (1994). Heliobacter pylori. *American Journal of Gastroenterology, 71,* 269–279.

Marshall, M. J. (2002). *Why spanking doesn't work: Stopping this bad habit and getting the upper hand on effective discipline.* Bonneville Books.

Marshall, R. D., Bryant, R. A., Amsel, L., Suh, E. J., Cook, J. M., & Neria, Y. (2007). The psychology of ongoing threat: Relative risk appraisal, the September 11 attacks, and terrorism-related fears. *American Psychologist, 62*(4), 304–316.

Marshall, W. L., Serran, G. A., Marshall, L. E., & O'Brien, M. D. (2008). Sexual deviation. *Handbook of psychological assessment, case conceptualization, and treatment, (Vol. 1): Adults* (pp. 590–615). Hoboken, NJ: John Wiley & Sons Inc.

Marsland, A. L., Bachen, E. A., Cohen, S., Rabin, B., & Manuck, S. B. (2002). Stress, immune reactivity and susceptibility to infectious disease. *Physiology & Behavior, 77*(4–5), 711–716.

Martin, E. I., & Nemeroff, C. B. (2010). The biology of generalized anxiety disorder and major depressive disorder: Commonalities and distinguishing features. In D. Goldberg, K. S. Kendler, & P. J. Sirovatka (Eds.), *Diagnostic issues in depression and generalized anxiety disorder: Refining the research agenda for DSM-V* (pp. 45–70). Washington, DC: American Psychiatric Association.

Martin, J. A. (2010). Genetic causes of mental retardation. In R. C. Dryden-Edwards & L. Combrinck-Graham (Eds.), *Developmental disabilities from childhood to adulthood: What works for psychiatrists in community and institutional settings* (pp. 127–142). Baltimore, MD: Johns Hopkins University Press.

Martin, J. H. (2003). *Neuroanatomy: Text and atlas*. McGraw-Hill.

Martin, N. (2009). The roles of semantic and phonological processing in short-term memory and learning: Evidence from aphasia. In A. S. C. Thorn & M. P. A. Page (Eds.), *Interactions between short-term and long-term memory in the verbal domain* (pp. 220–243). New York, NY: Psychology Press.

Martin, R., & Hewstone, M. (2001). Conformity and independence in groups: Majorities and minorities. In M. A. Hogg & R. S. Tindale (Eds.), *Blackwell Handbook of Social Psychology: Group Processes* (pp. 209–234). Malden, MA: Blackwell.

Martin, R. A. (2001). Humor, laughter, and physical health: Methodological issues and research findings. *Psychological Bulletin, 127*(4), 504–519.

Martinez, A. (1992). *Scientific knowledge about television violence*. Canadian Radio-television and Telecommunications.

Maruszewski, T., Fajkowska, M., & Eysenck, M. W. (2010). Introduction: An integrative view of personality. In T. Maruszewski, M. Fajkowska, & M. Eysenck (Eds.), *Personality from biological, cognitive, and social perspective: Warsaw lectures in personality and social psychology*. Clifton Corners, NY: Eliot Werner Publications.

Marx, B. P., & Sloan, D. M. (2005). Peritraumatic dissociation and experimental avoidance as predictors of posttraumatic stress symptomatology. *Behavioral Research and Therapy, 43*(5), 569–583.

Masataka, N. (1998). Motherese in Japanese sign language by 6-month-old hearing infants. *Developmental Psychology, 34*, 241–246.

Mash, E. J., & Wolfe, D. A. (2010). *Abnormal child psychology*, 4th edition. Belmont, CA: Wadsworth CENGAGE Learning.

Mashour, G. A., Walker, E. E., & Martuza, R. L. (2005). Psychosurgery: Past, present and future. *Brain Review, 48*(3), 409–418.

Masling, J. (2004). A storied test. *PsycCRITIQUES* [np].

Maslow, A. (1970). *Motivation and personality* (rev. Ed.). New York, NY: Harper & Row.

Mason, P. T., & Kreger, R. (2010). Stop walking on eggshells: Taking your life back when someone you care about has borderline personality disorder (2nd Ed.). Oakland, CA: New Harbinger Publications.

Masters, W. H., & Johnson, V. E. (1979). *Homosexuality in perspective*. Boston, MA: Little, Brown.

Masters, W. H., & Johnson, V.E. (1970). *Human sexual inadequacy*. Boston, MA: Little, Brown.

Masters, W. H., & Johnson, V. E. (1966). *Human sexual response*. Oxford, England: Little, Brown.

Mather, M. (2009). When emotion intensifies memory interference. In B. H. Ross (Ed.), *The psychology of learning and motivation (vol 51)* (pp. 101–120). San Diego, CA: Elsevier Academic Press. doi: 10.1016/S0079-7421(09)51003-1

Mathew, R. J., Wilson, W. H., Humphreys, D., Lowe, J. V., et al. (1993). Depersonalization after marijuana smoking. *Biological Psychiatry, 33*(6), 431–441. doi: 10.1016/0006-3223(93)90171-9

Matsumoto, D. R. (2001). *Handbook of culture and psychology*. New York, NY: Oxford University Press.

Matsumoto, D., & Juang, L. (2008). *Culture and psychology* (4th Ed.). Australia: Thomson Wadsworth.

Matsumoto, D., Takeuchi, S., Andayani, S., Kouznetsova, N., & Krupp, D. (1998). The contribution of individualism vs. collectivism to cross-national differences in display rules. *Asian Journal of Social Psychology, 1*, 147–165.

Matsumoto, D., & van de Vijver, F. J. R. (Eds.). (2011). *Cross-cultural research methods in psychology*. New York: Cambridge University Press.

Matthews, P. M. (2011). The mnemonic brain: Neuroimaging, neuropharmacology, and disorders of memory. In S. Nalbantian, P. M. Matthews & J. L. McClelland (Eds.), *The memory process: Neuroscientific and humanistic perspectives* (pp. 99–127). Cambridge, MA: MIT Press.

Mattia, J. I., & Zimmerman, M. (2001). Epidemiology. In W. J. Livesley (Ed.), *Handbook of personality disorders: Theory, research, and treatment*. New York, NY: Guilford Press.

Maul, A. (2011). The factor structure and cross-test convergence of the Mayer–Salovey–Caruso model of emotional intelligence. *Personality and Individual Differences, 50*(4), 457–463.

Maurer, D., & Lewis, T. (2001). Visual acuity: The role of visual input in inducing postnatal change. *Clinical Neuroscience Research, 1*, 239–247.

Maurer, D., & Salapatek, P. (1976). Developmental changes in the scanning of faces by young infants. *Child Development, 47*, 523–527.

Maurice, W. L. (2007). Sexual desire disorders in men. *Principles and practice of sex therapy (4th Ed.)* (pp. 181–211). New York, NY: Guilford Press.

Mayberg, H. S., Lozano, A. M., Voon, V., McNeely, H. E., Seminowicz, D., Hamani, C., et al. (2005). Deep brain stimulation for treatment-resistant depression. *Neuron, 45*, 651–660.

Maybery, M. T., & Do, N. (2003). Relationships between facets of working memory and performance on a curriculum-based mathematics test in children. *Educational and Child Psychology, 20*(3), 77–92.

Mayer, J. D., & Salovey, P. (2004). What is emotional intelligence? In P. Salovey, M. A. Brackett, & J. D. Mayer (Eds.), *Emotional intelligence: Key readings on the Mayer and Salovey model* (pp. 29–59). Port Chester, NY: Dude Publishing.

Mayer, J. D., & Salovey, P. (1997). What is emotional intelligence? In P. Salovey & D. Sluyter (Eds.), *Emotional development and emotional intelligence: Educational implications* (pp. 3–31). New York, NY: Basic Books.

Mayer, S. J. (2005). The early evolution of Jean Piaget's clinical method. *History of Psychology, 8*, 262–382.

Mayhew, D. R., Brown, S. W., & Simpson, H. M. (2002). *The alcohol crash problem in Canada*. Traffic Injury Research Foundation of Canada for Transport Canada. Retrieved from http://www.tc.gc.ca/media/documents/roadsafety/tp11759e_2000.pdf.

Mayr, E. (2001). *What evolution is*. Basic Books: New York.

Mazzoni, G., Heap, M., & Scoboria, A. (2010). Hypnosis and memory: Theory, laboratory research, and applications. In S. J. Lynn, J. W. Rhue, & I. Kirsch (Eds.), *Handbook of clinical hypnosis (2nd Ed.)* (pp. 709–741). Washington, DC: American Psychological Association.

McAndrew, F. T. (2008, October). The science of gossip: Why we can't stop ourselves. *Scientific American*. Retrieved from http://www.sciam.com/article.cfm?id=the-science-of-gossip.

McCain, M., & Mustard, F. (1999). *Reversing the real brain drain: Early Years Study*. Ontario Children's Secretariate, Toronto. Retrieved from http://www.founders.net/fn/bios.nsf/c85b89504068a23f8525673300768a53/46254872cb9d894c852568f00052b616!OpenDocument.

McClelland, J. L. (2011). Memory as a constructive process: The parallel distributed processing approach. In S. Nalbantian, P. M. Matthews & J. L. McClelland (Eds.), *The memory process: Neuroscientific and humanistic perspectives* (pp. 129–155). Cambridge, MA: MIT Press.

McClure, E. B. (2000). A meta-analytic review of sex differences in facial expression processing and their development in infants, children, and adolescents. *Psychological Bulletin, 126*, 424–453.

McClure, E. B., Monk, C. S., Nelson, E. E., Parrish, J. M., Adler, A., Blair, R. J., Fromm, S., Charney, D. S., Leibenluft, E., Ernst, M., & Pine, D. S. (2007). Abnormal attention modulation of fear circuit function in pediatric generalized anxiety disorder. *Archives of General Psychiatry, 64*(1), 97–106.

McCrae, R. R. (2002). The maturation of personality psychology: Adult personality development and psychological well-being. *Journal of Research in Personality, 36*(4), 307–317.

McCrae, R. R., & Costa, P. T. (2003). *Personality in adulthood: A five-factor theory perspective* (2nd Edition). New York, NY: Guilford.

McCrae, R. R., & Costa, P. T. (1989). Reinterpreting the Myers-Briggs Type Indicator from the perspective of the five-factor model of personality. *Journal of Personality, 57*(1), 17–40.

McCrae, R. R., Yik, M. S. M., Trapnell, P. D., Bond, M. H., & Paulhus, D. L. (1998). Interpreting personality profiles across cultures: Bilingual, acculturation and peer rating studies of Chinese undergraduates. *Journal of Personality and Social Psychology, 74*,1041–1055.

McCreaddie, M., & Wiggins, S. (2008). The purpose and function of humour in health, health care, and nursing: A narrative review. *Journal of Advanced Nursing, 61*(6), 584–595.

McCrink, K., & Wynn, K. (2004). Large-number addition and subtraction by 9-month-old infants. *Psychological Science, 15*(11), 776–781.

McDonald, J. H. (2010). Tongue rolling. In J. H. McDonald, *Myths of Human Genetics*. University of Delaware.

McDonald, R. V., & Siegel, S. (2004) The potential role of drug-onset cues in drug dependence and withdrawal. *Experimental and Clinical Psychopharmacology, 12*, 23–26.

McEvoy, P. M. (2007). Effectiveness of cognitive behavioural group therapy for social phobia in a community clinic: A benchmarking study. *Behavior Research Therapy, 45*(12), 3030–3040.

McEwen, B. S. (2002). Protective and damaging effects of stress mediators: The good and bad sides of the response to stress. *Metabolism, 51*(Suppl 1), 2–4.

McEwen, D. P., Jenkins, P. M., & Martens, J. R. (2008). Olfactory cilia: our direct neuronal connection to the external world. *Current Topics in Developmental Biology, 85*, 333–370.

McFadyen, M. (2008). *A long road to recovery battling operational stress injuries: Second review of the department of national defence and Canadian forces actionon operational stress injuries.* Retrieved from http://www.ombudsman.forces.gc.ca/rep-rap/sr-rs/osi-tso-3/doc/osi-tso-3-eng.pdf.

McGaugh, J. L. (2006). Make mild moments memorable: Add a little arousal. *Trends in Cognitive Sciences, 10*(8), 345–347. doi: 10.1016/j.tics.2006.06.001

McGaugh, J. L. (2003). *Memory and emotion: The making of lasting memories.* New York, NY: Columbia University Press.

McGaugh, J. L. (1999). The perseveration-consolidation hypothesis: Mueller and pilzecker, 1900. *Brain Research Bulletin, 50*(5–6), 445–446.

McGowan, S., Lawrence, A. D., Sales, T., Quested, D., & Grasby P. (2004). Presynaptic dopaminergic dysfunction in schizophrenia: A positron emission tomography [18F] fluorodopa study. *Archives of General Psychiatry, 61*, 134–142.

McGrath, R. E. (2011). *Quantitative models in psychology.* Washington, DC: American Psychological Association.

McGue, M., & Lykken, D. T. (1992). Genetic influence on risk of divorce. *Psychological Science, 3*(6), 368–373.

McGuffin, P., Katz, R., Watkins, S., & Rutherford, J. (1996). A hospital-based twin register of the heritability of DSM-IV unipolar depression. *Archives of General Psychiatry, 53*, 129–136.

McKay, D., Gosselin, J. T., & Gupta, S. (2008). Body dysmorphic disorder. In J. S. Abramowitz, D. McKay, & S. Taylor (Eds.), *Obsessive compulsive disorder: Subtypes and spectrum conditions.* Oxford, UK: Elsevier.

McKee, A. C., Cantu, R. C., Nowinski, C. J., Hedley-Whyte, E. T., Gavett, B. E., Budson, A. E., Santini, V. E., Lee, H.-Y., Kubilus, C. A., & Stern, R. A. (2009). Chronic traumatic encephalopathy in athletes: progressive tauopathy following repetitive head injury. *Journal of Neuropathology & Experimental Neurology, 68*(7), 709–735.

McKelvie, S. J., & Drumheller, A. (2001). The availability heuristic with famous names: A replication. *Perceptual and Motor Skills, 92*, 507–516.

McLaren, A. (1990) *Our Own Master Race: Eugenics in Canada, 1885–1945.* Toronto: Oxford University Press.

McLaren, L. (2007). Socioeconomic status and obesity. *Epidemiologic Reviews, 29*, 29–48.

McLaughlin, C.V., & Williams, V. (2009). Normal sleep in children and adolescents. *Child and Adolescent Psychiatric Clinics of North America, 18*(4), 799–811.

McLean, D. E., & Link, B. G. (1994). Unraveling complexity: Strategies to refine concepts, measures, and research designs in the study of life events and mental health. *Stress and mental health: Contemporary issues and prospects for the future* (pp. 15–42). New York, NY: Plenum Press.

McNally, R. J. (2001). Vulnerability to anxiety disorders in adulthood. In R. E. Ingram & J. M. Price (Eds.), *Vulnerability to psychopathology: Risk across the lifespan* (pp. 304–321). New York, NY: Guilford Press.

McNally, R. J., & Geraerts, E. (2009). A new solution to the recovered memory debate. *Perspectives on Psychological Science, 4*(2), 126–134.

McNamee, J. E., & Offord, D. R. (2003). *Canadian task force on preventive health care (2001).* Retrieved from http://www.canadiancrc.com/Canadian_Task_Force_Preventive_Health_Care_suicide.aspx.

McVicker Hunt, J. M. (1982). Toward equalizing the developmental opportunities of infants and preschool children. *Journal of Social Issues, 38*(4), 163–191.

Mech, L. D., & Boitani, L. (2003). *Wolves: behavior, ecology, and conservation.* Chicago, IL: University of Chicago Press.

Mecklinger, A., Brunnemann, N., & Kipp, K. (2011). Two processes for recognition memory in children of early school age: An event-related potential study. *Journal of Cognitive Neuroscience, 23*(2), 435–446. doi: 10.1162/jocn.2010.21455

Meister, B. (2000). Control of food intake via leptin receptors in the hypothalamus. *Vitamins and Hormones, 59*, 265–304.

Mellers, B. A., Schwartz, A., & Cooke, A. D. (1998). Judgment and decision making. *Annual Review of Psychology, 49*, 447–477.

Mellers, B. A., Schwartz, A., Ho, K., & Ritov, L. (1997). Decision affect theory: Emotional reactions to the outcomes of risky options. *Psychological Science, 8*, 423–429.

Mellinger, D. I. (2010). Hypnosis and the treatment of anxiety disorders. In S. J. Lynn, J. W. Rhue & I. Kirsch (Eds.), *Handbook of clinical hypnosis (2nd Ed.)* (pp. 359–389). Washington, DC: American Psychological Association.

Meltzer, M. (2007). Leisure and innocence: The eternal appeal of the stoner movie. *Slate.*

Melville, J. (1978). *Phobias and obsessions.* New York: Penguin.

Melzack, R.(1999). From the gate to the neuromatrix. *The Journal of Pain, Suppl 6*, S121–126.

Memmert, D. (2011). Creativity, expertise, and attention: Exploring their development and their relationships. *Journal of Sports Sciences, 29*(1), 93–102.

Mennella, J. A., Johnson, A., & Beauchamp, G. K. (1995). Garlic ingestion by pregnant women alters the odor of amniotic fluid. *Chemical Senses, 20*, 207–209.

Merenda, R. R. (2008). The posttraumatic and sociocognitive etiologies of dissociative identity disorder: A survey of clinical psychologists. *Dissertation Abstracts International: Section B: The Sciences and Engineering, 68*(8–B), 55–84.

Merikangas, K. R., Akiskal, H. S., Angst, J., Greenberg, P. E., Hirschfeld, R. M. A., Petukhova, M., et al. (2007). Lifetime and 12-month prevalence of bipolar spectrum disorder in the National Comorbidity Survey Replication. *Archives of General Psychiatry, 64*(5), 543–552.

Merkl, A., Schubert, F., Quante, A., Luborzewski, A., Brakemeier, E., Grimm, S., & Bajbouj, M. (2011). Abnormal cingulate and prefrontal cortical neurochemistry in major depression after electroconvulsive therapy. *Biological Psychiatry, 69*(8), 772–779.

Messer, W. S., Griggs, R. A., & Jackson, S. L. (1999). A national survey of undergraduate psychology degree options and major requirements. *Teaching Of Psychology, 26*(3), 164–171. doi:10.1207/S15328023TOP260301.

Messinger, D., & Fogel, A. (2007). The interactive development of social smiling. *Advances in Child Development and Behavior, 35*, 327–366.

Mesulam, M. M. (1981). A cortical network for directed attention and unilateral neglect. *Annals of Neurology, 10*, 309–325.

Meyer, B., Ajchenbrenner, M., & Bowles, D. P. (2005). Sensory sensitivity, attachment experiences, and rejection responses among adults with borderline and avoidant features. *Journal of Personality Disorders, 19*(6), 641–658.

Meyer-Luehmann, M., Spires-Jones, T., Prada, C., Garcia-Alloza, M., de Calignon, A., Rozkalne, A., Koenigsknecht-Talboo, J., Holtzman, D. M., Bacskai, B. J., & Hyman, B. T. (2008). Rapid appearance and local toxicity of amyloid-P plaques in a mouse model of alzheimer's disease. *Nature, 451*(7179), 720–724.

Michel, G. F., & Tyler, A. N. (2005). Critical period: A history of the transition from questions of when, to what, to how. *Development and Psychobiology, 46*, 156–162.

Mikulincer, M., & Shaver, P. R. (2005). Attachment security, compassion, and altruism. *Current Directions in Psychological Science, 14*(1), 34–38.

Mikulincer, M., Shaver, P. R., & Gillath, O. (2008). A behavioral systems perspective on compassionate love. *The science of compassionate love: Theory, research, and applications* (pp. 225–256). Wiley-Blackwell.

Mikulincer, M., Shaver, P. R., Gillath, O., & Nitzberg, R. A. (2005). Attachment, caregiving, and altruism: Boosting attachment security increases compassion and helping. *Journal of Personality and Social Psychology, 89*(5), 817–839.

Miles, D. R., & Carey, G. (1997). Genetic and environmental architecture on human aggression. *Journal of Personality and Social Psychology, 72*(1), 207–217.

Milgram, S. (2004). *Obedience to authority*. New York: Perennial Classics. [Original work published in 1974].

Milgram, S. (1974). *Obedience to Authority: An Experimental View*. New York, NY: Harper and Row.

Milgram, S. (1973). The perils of obedience . *Harper's, 247*(1483), 62–77.

Milgram, S. (1963). Behavioral study of obedience. *Journal of Abnormal and Social Psychology, 67,* 371–378.

Miller, A. G. (2004). What can the Milgram obedience experiments tell us about the holocaust? Generalizing from the social psychology laboratory. In A. G. Miller (Ed.), *The Social Psychology of Good and Evil* (pp. 193–239). New York, NY: Guilford Press.

Miller, D. B., & O'Callaghan, J. P. (2005). Aging, stress and the hippocampus. *Ageing Research Review, 4,* 123–140.

Miller, D. T., & Ross, M. (1975). Self-serving biases in the attribution of causality: Fact or fiction? *Psychological Bulletin, 82,* 213–225.

Miller, F. D., & Gauthier, A. S. (2007). Timing is everything: making neurons versus glia in the developing cortex. *Neuron, 54,* 357–369.

Miller, G., Tybur, J. M., & Jordan, B. D. (2007). Ovulatory cycle effects on tip earnings by lap dancers: Economic evidence for human estrus? *Evolution and Human Behavior, 28,* 375–381.

Miller, G. A. (1978). The acquisition of word meaning. *Child Development, 49,* 999–1004.

Miller, G. A. (1956). The magical number seven, plus or minus two: Some limits on our capacity for processing information. *Psychological Review, 63*(2), 81–97.

Miller, G. F. (2000). *The Mating Mind: How sexual choice shaped the evolution of human nature.* Heinemann, London.

Miller, J. S., & Ozonoff, S. (2011). Asperger's syndrome. In E. Hollander, A. Kolevzon & J. T. Coyle (Eds.), *Textbook of autism spectrum disorders* (pp. 77–88). Arlington, VA: American Psychiatric Publishing, Inc.

Miller, L. C., Putcha, A., & Pederson, W. C. (2002). Men's and women's mating preferences: Distinct evolutionary mechanisms? *Current Directions in Psychological Science, 11,* 88–93.

Miller, M. A., & Rahe, R. H. (1997). Life changes scaling for the 1990s. *Journal of Psychosomatic Research, 43*(3), 279–292.

Miller, N. E. (1959). Liberalization of basic S-R concepts: Extensions to conflict behavior, motivation, and social learning. In S. Koch (Ed.), *Psychology: A study of a Science, Vol. 2.* New York, NY: McGraw-Hill.

Miller, R., & Mason, S. E. (2011). *Diagnosis: Schizophrenia—A comprehensive resource for consumers, families, and helping professionals* (2nd Ed.). New York: Columbia University Press.

Miller, T. Q. (2000). Type A behavior. In G. Fink (Ed.), *Encyclopedia of Stress, Vol. 3* (pp. 623–624). New York, NY: Academic Press.

Miller, T. Q., Smith, T. W., Turner, C. W., Guijarro, M. L., & Hallet, A. J. (1996). A meta-analytic review of research on hostility and physical health. *Psychological Bulletin, 119,* 322–348.

Millon, T. (2011). Disorders of personality: Introducing a DSM/ICD spectrum from normal to abnormal (3rd Ed.). Hoboken, NJ: John Wiley & Sons.

Millon, T., & Grossman, S. (2007). Moderating severe personality disorders: A personalized psychotherapy approach. Hoboken, NJ: John Wiley & Sons Inc.

Mills, J. A. (1998). Control: A history of behaviourism. New York: New York University Press.

Milner, B., Corkin, S., & Teuber, H. L. (1968). *Neuropsychologia, 6,* 215–234.

Mindell, J. A., & Owens, J. A. (2003). *A clinical guide to pediatric sleep: diagnosis and management of sleep problems.* Lippincott Williams & Wilkins.

Mino, I., Profit, W. E., & Pierce, C. M., (2000). Minorities and stress. In G. Fink (Ed.), *Encyclopedia of stress, Vol. 3* (pp. 771–776). New York, NY: Academic Press.

Minzenberg, M. J., Yoon, J. H., & Carter, C. S. (2011). Schizophrenia. In R. E. Hales, S. C. Yudofsky, & G. O. Gabbard (Eds.), *Essentials of psychiatry* (3rd Ed., pp. 111–150). Arlington, VA: American Psychiatric Publishing.

Mirescu, C., & Gould, E. (2006). Stress and adult neurogenesis. *Hippocampus, 16,* 233–238.

Mirzaei, S., Gelpi, E., Roddrigues, M., Knoll, P., & Gutierrez-Lobos, K. (2005). Progress in post-traumatic stress disorder research. In T. A. Corales (Ed.), *Focus on posttraumatic stress disorder research* (pp. 157–177). Hauppauge, NY: Nova Science Publishers.

Mischel, W. (2004). Toward an integrative science of the person. *Annual Review of Psychology, 55,* 1–22.

Mischel, W., & Peake, P. K. (1982). Beyond deja vu in the search for cross-situational consistency. *Psychological Review, 89,* 730–755.

Mischel, W., Shoda, Y., & Rodriguez, M. L. (1989). Delay of Gratification in Children. *Science, 244*(4907), 933–938.

Mitchell, A. J. (2010). Overview of depression scales and tools. In A. J. Mitchell & J. C. Coyne (Eds.), *Screening for depression in clinical practice: An evidence-based guide* (pp. 29–56). New York: Oxford University Press.

Mitchell, C. M., Kaufman, C. E., Beals, J., et. al. (2004). Equifinality and multifinality as guides for prevention interventions: HIV risk/protection among American Indian young adults. *Journal of Primary Prevention, 25*(4), 491–510.

Mittal, B. V., Desai, A. P., & Khade, K. R. (1991). Methyl alcohol poisoning: an autopsy study of 28 cases. *Journal of Posy Graduate Medicine, 37*(1) 9–13.

Miyagawa, Y., Tsujimura, A., Fujita, K., Matsuoka, Y., Takahashi, T., Takao, T., et al. (2007). Differential brain processing of audiovisual sexual stimuli in men: comparative positron emission tomography study of the initiation and maintenance of penile erection during sexual arousal. *NeuroImage, 36*(3), 830–842.

Mogan, J. (1984). Obesity: prevention is the treatment. *Patient Education and Counseling, 6*(2), 73–76.

Mojet, J., Christ-Hazelhof, E., & Heidema, J. (2001). Taste perception with age: generic or specific losses in threshold sensitivity to the five basic tastes? *Chemical Senses, 26*(7), 845–860.

Moll, P. P., Burns, T. L., & Lauer, R. M. (1991). The genetic and environmental sources of body mass index variability: The Muscatine ponderosity family study. *The American Journal of Human Genetics, 49,* 1243–1255.

Moller, J., Bjorkenstam, E., Ljung, R., & Yngwe, M. A. (2011). Widowhood and the risk of psychiatric care, psychotropic medication and all-cause mortality: A cohort study of 658,022 elderly people in Sweden. *Aging & Mental Health, 15*(2), 259–266.

Monroe, S. M., & Hadjiyannakis, K. (2002). The social environment and depression: Focusing on severe life stress. In I. H. Gotlib & C. L. Hammen (Eds.), *Handbook of depression: Research and treatment* (pp. 314–340). New York: Guilford Press.

Monteiro, C. A., Moura, E. C., Conde, W. L., & Popkin, B. M. (2004). Public Health Reviews: Socioeconomic status and obesity in adult populations of developing countries: a review. *Bulletin of the World Health Organization, 84*(12), 940–946.

Moorcroft, W. H. (2003). *Understanding sleep and dreaming.* New York: Springer.

Moore, J. (2010). Philosophy of science, with special consideration given to behaviorism as the philosophy of the science of behavior. *The Psychological Record, 60*(1), 137–150.

Moore, N. B., Davidson, J. K., Sr., & Fisher, T. D., Ed. (2010). *Speaking of sexuality: Interdisciplinary readings.* New York: Oxford University Press.

Morales, A. C., & Fitzsimons, G. J. (2007). Product contagion: changing consumer evaluations through physical contact with "disgusting" products. *Journal of Marketing Research, 44*(2), 272–283.

Morfei, M. Z., Hooker, K., Carpenter, J., Mix, C., & Blakeley, E. (2004). Agentic and communal generative behavior in four areas of adult life: Implications for psychological well-being. *Journal of Adult Development, 11*(1), 55–58.

Morgan, A. B., & Lilienfeld, S. O. (2000). A meta-analytic review of the relation between antisocial behavior and neuropsychological measures of executive function. *Clinical Psychology Review, 20,* 113–136.

Morgan, M. A., Romanski, L. M., & LeDoux, J. E. (1993). Extinction of emotional learning: contribution of medial prefrontal cortex. *Neuroscience Letters, 163,* 109–113.

Moriceau, S., & Sullivan, R. M. (2006). Maternal presence serves as a switch between learning and attraction in infancy. *Nature Neuroscience, 9,* 1004–1006.

Morison, S. J., Ames, E. W., Chisholm, K. (1995). The development of children adopted from Romanian orphanages. *Merrill-Palmer Quarterly: Journal of Developmental Psychology, 41*(4), 411–430.

Morris, J. S., Frith, C. D., Perrett, D. I., Rowland, D., et al. (1996). A differential neural response in the human amygdala to fearful and happy facial expressions. *Nature, 383*(6603), 812–815.

Morris, R. G. (1990). Toward a representational hypothesis of the role of hippocampal synaptic plasticity in spatial and other forms of learning. *The Cold Spring Harbor Symposia on Quantitative Biology, 55*, 161–173.

Morris, W. N. (1992). A functional analysis of the role of mood in affective systems. In M. S. Clark (Ed.), *Emotion* (pp. 256–293). Thousand Oaks, CA: Sage Publications, Inc.

Morton, J., & Johnson, M. H. (1991). Conspec and Conlern—A Two-Process Theory of Infant Face Recognition. *Psychological Review, 98*, 164–181.

Moscovitch, D. A. (2009). What is the core fear in social phobia? A new model to facilitate individualized case conceptualization and treatment. *Cognitive and Behavioral Practice, 16*(2), 123–134.

Moser, E. I., Kropff, E., & Moser, M. B. (2008). Place cells, grid cells, and the brain's spatial representation system. *Annual Review of Neuroscience, 31*, 69–89.

Mosher, C. E., & Danoff-Burg, S. (2008). Agentic and communal personality traits: Relations to disordered eating behavior, body shape concern, and depressive symptoms. *Eating Behaviors, 9*(4), 497–500.

Mosher, C. E., & Danoff-Burg, S. (2005). Agentic and communal personality traits: Relations to attitudes toward sex and sexual experiences. *Sex Roles, 52*(1–2), 121–129.

Mosher, W. D., Chandra, A., & Jones, J. (2005). Sexual behavior and selected health measures: men and women 15–44 years of age, United States, 2002. Advance Data From Vital Health Statistics (362).

Mouras, H., Stolérus, M. V., Pélégrini-Issac, M., Rouxel, R., Grandjean, B., Glutron, D., Bittoun, J. (2008). Activation of mirror-neuron system by erotic video clips predicts degree of induced erection: an *f*MRI study. *Neuroimage, 42*, 1142–1150.

Mowrer, O. H. (1950). *Learning theory and personality dynamics: selected papers*. New York: Ronald P. Co.

Mowry, M., Mosher, M., & Briner, W. (2003). Acute physiologic and chronic histologic changes in rats and mice exposed to the unique hallucinogen Salvinorin A. *Journal of Psychoactive Drugs, 35*(3), 379–382.

Mroczek, D. K. (2004). Positive and negative affect at midlife. In O. G. Brim, C. D. Ryff, & R. C. Kessler (Eds.), *How healthy are we? A national study of well-being at midlife* (pp. 205–226). Chicago, IL: University of Chicago Press.

Mroczek, D. K., & Spiro III, A. (2007). Personality change influences mortality in older men. *Psychological Science, 18*(5), 371–376.

Mroczek, D. K., & Spiro III, A. (2005). Change in life satisfaction during adulthood: Findings from the Veterans affairs normative aging study. *Journal of Personality and Social Psychology, 88*(1), 189–202.

Mueller, S. E., Petitjean, S., Boening, J., & Wiesbeck, G. A. (2007). The impact of self-help group attendance on relapse rates after alcohol detoxification in a controlled study. *Alcohol Alcoholism, 42*(2), 108–112.

Mueser, K. T., Crocker, A. G., Frisman, L. B., Drake, R. E., Covell, N. H., & Essock, S. M. (2006). Conduct disorder and antisocial personality disorder in persons with severe psychiatric and substance use disorders. *Schizophrenia Bulletin, 32*(4), 626–636.

Muise, A., Christofides, E., & Desmarais, S. (2009). More information that you ever wanted: does Facebook bring out the green-eyed monster of jealousy? *Cyber Psychology and Behavior, 12*(4), 441–444.

Mukerjee, M. (1997). Trends in animal research. *Scientific American, 86*.

Muller, U., & Racine, T. P. (2010). The development of representation and concepts. In W. F. Overton & R. M. Lerner (Eds.), *The handbook of life-span development,* vol. 1: *Cognition, biology, and methods* (pp. 346–390). Hoboken, NJ: John Wiley & Sons.

Mulvany, M. K., & Mebert, C. J. (2007). Parental corporal punishment predicts behaviour problems in early childhood. *Journal of Family Psychology, 21*, 389–397.

Munger, B. L., & Ide, C. (1988). The structure and function of cutaneous-sensory receptors. *Archives of Histology and Cytology, 51*, 1–34.

Murali, V., & Oyebode, F. (2010). Poverty, social inequality and mental health. Bhattacharya, Rahul, Cross, Sean, Bhugra, Dinesh (Eds), *Clinical topics in cultural psychiatry* (pp. 84–99). London, England: Royal College of Psychiatrists.

Murison, R. (2001). Is there a role for psychology in ulcer disease? *Integrative Physiological and Behavioral Science, 3*(1), 75–83.

Murphy, J. G., McDevitt-Murphy, M. E., & Barnett, N. P. (2005). Drink and be merry? Gender, life satisfaction, and alcohol consumption among college students. *Psychology of Addictive Behaviors, 19*, 184–191.

Murphy, N. A., & Hall, J. A. (2011). Intelligence and interpersonal sensitivity: A meta-analysis. *Intelligence, 39*(1), 54–63.

Murphy, P. K., Long, J. F., Holleran, T. A., & Esterly, E. (2003). Persuasion online or on paper: a new take on an old issue. *Learning and Instruction, 13*(5), 511–532.

Murphy, T. (1992). Redirecting sexual orientation: Techniques and justifications. *Journal of Sex Research, 29*, 501–523.

Murphy, W. J. (2001). The Victim Advocacy and Research Group: Serving a growing need to provide rape victims with personal legal representation to protect privacy rights and to fight gender bias in the criminal justice system. *Journal of Social Distress and the Homeless, 10(1)*, 123–138.

Murray, J., & Farrington, D. P. (2010). Risk factors for conduct disorder and delinquency: Key findings from longitudinal studies. *The Canadian Journal of Psychiatry/La Revue Canadienne De Psychiatrie, 55*(10), 633–642.

Myers, D. G. (2000). The funds, friends, and faith of happy people. *American Psychologist, 55*(1), 56–67.

Myers, D. G. (1975). Discussion-induced attitude polarization. *Human Relations, 28*(8), 699–714.

Myers, D. G., & Bishop, G. D. (1970). Discussion effects on racial attitudes. *Science, 169*, 778–779.

Myers, D. G., & Diener, E. (1997 November). The science of happiness. *Current*, 3–7.

Myers, D. G., & Diener, E. (1996). The pursuit of happiness. *Scientific American*, 70–72.

Myers, I., McCaulley, M., Quenk, N. L., & Hammer, A. L. (1998). *Manual: A guide to the development and use of the Myers-Briggs type indicator. (3rd Ed)*. Palo Alto, CA: Consulting Psychologists Press.

Myrick, H., & Wright, T. (2008). Clinical management of alcohol abuse and dependence. In H. D. Kleber & M. Galanter (Eds.), *The American psychiatric publishing textbook of substance abuse treatment (4th Ed.)*. Washington, DC: American Psychiatric Publishing.

Nader, K. (2003). Memory traces unbound. *Trends in Neuroscince, 26*(2), 65–72.

Nadler, J., & McDonnell, M.-H. (2011). Moral character, motive, and the psychology of blame *Cornell Law Review*, Forthcoming, Northwestern Public Law Research Paper No. 11–43. Retrieved from SSRN: http://ssrn.com/abstract=1814309

Nagy, T. F. (2011). *Essential ethics for psychologists: A primer for understand and mastering core issues.* Washington, DC: American Psychological Association.

Nahas, Z., Marangell, L. B., Husain, M. M., Rush, A. J., Sackeim, H. A., Lisanby, S. H., et al. (2005). Two-year-outcome of vagus nerve stimulation (VNS) for treatment of major depressive episodes. *Journal of Clinical Psychiattry, 66*(9), 1097–1104.

Nail, P. R., Harton, H. C., & Decker, B. P. (2003). Political orientation and modern versus aversive racism: Tests of Dividio and Gaertner's (1998) integrated model. *Journal of Personality and Social Psychology, 84*, 754–770.

Naish, P. L. N. (2010). Hypnosis and hemispheric asymmetry. *Consciousness and Cognition: An International Journal, 19*(1), 230–234.

Nakamichi, N., Kato, E., Kojima, Y., & Itoigawa, N. (1998). Carrying and washing of grass roots by free-ranging Japanese macaques at Katsuyama. *Folia Primatologica, Basel, 69*, 35–40.

Nakano, T., Watanabe, H., Homae, F., & Taga, G. (2009). Prefrontal cortical involvement in young infants' analysis of novelty. *Cerebral Cortex, 19*, 455–463.

Nakano, T. , Watanabe, H. , Homae, F. , Asakawa, K. and Taga, G. , (2006). *Brain imaging of habituation and dishabituation in young infants.* Paper presented at the annual meeting of the XVth Biennial International Conference on Infant Studies, Westin Miyako, Kyoto, Japan.

NAMI (National Alliance on Mental Illness). (2011). *Mental illness: Facts and numbers.* Arlington, VA: Author.

Nardi, A. E., Valença, A. M., Nascimento, I., Freire, R. C., Veras, A. B., de-Melo-Neto, V. L., Lopes, F. L., King, A. L., Soares-Filho, G., Mezzasalma, M. A., Rassi, A., & Zin, W. A. (2008). A caffeine challenge test in panic disorder patients, their healthy first-degree relatives and healthy controls. *Depression and Anxiety, 25*(10), 847–853.

Nardi, A. A., Valença, A. M., Nascimento, I., Mezzasalma, M. A., & Zin, W. A. (2001). Hyperventilation in panic disorder and social phobia. *Psychopathology, 34*(3), 123–127.

Narrow, W. E., Regier, D. A., Rae, D. S., Manderscheid, R. W., et al. (1993). Use of services by persons with mental and addictive disorders: Findings from the National Institute of Mental Health epidemiologic catchment area program. *Archives of General Psychiatry, 50*(2), 95–107.

Nash, J. M. (1997). Addicted. *Time*, 68–76.

Nathan, P. E., & Langenbucher, J. W. (1999). Psychopathology: Description and classification. *Annual Review of Psychology, 50*, 79–108.

National Association to Advance Fat Acceptance. (2009). *Weight discrimination laws*. Retrieved from: http://www.naafaonline.com/dev2/education/laws.html.

National Center on Birth Defects and Developmental Disabilities. (2005). *Intellectual disability*. Retrieved from http://www.cdc.gov/ncbddd/dd/mr3.htm.

National Coalition for Visual Health. (2008). *Our vision of visual health*. Retrieved from http://www.visionhealth.ca/projects/documents/NCVH% 20Handout.pdf.

National Institute of Neurological Disorders and Stroke (NINDS). (2006). *Narcolepsy fact sheet*. Bethesda, MD.

National Institute on Drug Abuse (NIDA). (2010). *NIDA InfoFacts: Marijuana*. Retrieved from http://www.nida.nih.gov/infofacts/marijuana.html.

Ndumele, C. D., & Trivedi, A. N. (2011). Effect of copayments on use of outpatient mental health services among elderly managed care enrollees. *Medical Care, 1*.

Neckelmann, D., Mykletun, A., & Dahl, A. A. (2007). Chronic insomnia as a risk factor for developing anxiety and depression. *Sleep, 30*(7), 873–880.

Nee, D. E., Berman, M. G., Moore, K. S., & Jonides, J. (2008). Neuroscientific evidence about the distinction between short- and long-term memory. *Current Directions in Psychological Science, 17*(2), 102–106.

Neff, E. J. A., & Dale, J. C. (1996). Worries of school-age children. *Journal of the Society of Pediatric Nurses, 1*, 27–32.

Neisser, U. (Ed.) (1998). *The rising curve: Long-term gains in IQ and related measures*. Washington, DC: American Psychological Association.

Neisser, U. (1967). *Cognitive psychology*. New York, NY: Applet on Century-Crofts.

Neitzel, M. T., Bernstein, D. A., Kramer, G. P. & Milich, R. (2003). *Introduction to Clinical Psychology* (6th Ed). Englewood Cliffs, New Jersey: Prentice-Hall.

Nelson, B. D., & Shankman, S. A. (2011). Does intolerance of uncertainty predict anticipatory startle responses to uncertain threat? *International Journal of Psychophysiology, 81*(2), 107–115.

Nelson, D., & Cooper, G. (2005). Stress and health: A positive direction. Stress and Health: Journal of the International Society for the Investigation of Stress, 21, 73–75.

Nelson, J. K., & Bennett, C. S. (2008). Introduction: Special issue on attachment. *Clinical Social Work Journal, 36*, 3–7.

Nelson, K. R., Mattingly, M., Lee, S. A., & Schmitt, F. A. (2006). Does the arousal system contribute to near death experience? *Neurology, 66*(7), 1003–1009.

Nesse, R. M. (1990). Evolutionary explanations of emotions. *Human Nature, 1*, 261–289.

Nesse, R. M., & Ellsworth, P. C. (2009). Evolution, emotions, and emotional disorders. *American Psychologist, 64*(2), 129–139.

Nestler, E. J. (2004). Molecular mechanisms of drug addiction. *Neuropharmacology, 1*, 24–32.

Neubauer, A. C., & Fink, A. (2010). Neuroscientific approaches to the study of individual differences in cognition and personality. In A. Gruszka, G. Matthews, & B. Szymura (Eds.), *Handbook of individual differences in cognition: Attention, memory, and executive control* (pp. 73–85). New York: Springer Science + Business Media.

Neuman, Y., & Nave, O. (2010). Why the brain needs language in order to be self-conscious. *New Ideas in Psychology, 28*(1), 37–48.

Neuschatz, J. S., Preston, E. L., & Toglia, M. P. (2005). Comparison of the efficacy of two name-learning techniques: Expanding rehearsal and name-face imagery. *American Journal of Psychology, 118*, 79–101.

Neumeister, A., Charney, D. S., & Drevets, W. C. (2005). Hippocampus, VI: Depression and the hippocampus. *American Journal of Psychiatry, 162*(6), 1057.

Newcomb, T. M. (1943). *Personality and social change*. New York, NY: Dryden.

Newcomb, T. M., Koening, K. E., Flacks, R., & Warwick, D. P. (1967). *Persistence and change: Bennington College and its students after 25 years*. New York, NY: John Wiley & Sons, Inc.

Newman, G. E., Keil, F. C., Kuhlmeier, V. A., & Wynn, K. (2010). *PNAS Proceedings of the National Academy of Sciences of the United States of America, 107*(40), 17140–17145.

Newman, M. G., Castonguay, L. G., Borkovec, T. D., Fisher, A. J., Boswell, J. F., Szkodny, L. E., & Nordberg, S. S. (2011). A randomized controlled trial of cognitive-behavioral therapy for generalized anxiety disorder with integrated techniques from emotion-focused and interpersonal therapies. *Journal of Consulting and Clinical Psychology, 79*(2), 171–181.

Niaura, R., Todaro, J. F., Stroud, L., Spiro III, A., Ward, K. D., & Weiss, S. (2002). Hostility, the metabolic syndrome, and incident coronary heart disease. *Health Psychology, 21*(6), 588–593.

Nicholls, A. (2010). The scientific unconscious: Goethe's post-Kantian epistemology. In A. Nicholls & M. Liebscher (Eds.), *Thinking the unconscious: Nineteenth-century German thought*. New York: Cambridge University Press.

NIDA (National Institute on Drug Abuse). (2011). *NIDA InfoFacts: Treatment statistics*. Bethesda, MD: Author.

Niedermeyer E., & da Silva, F. L. (2004). *Electroencephalography: Basic Principles, Clinical Applications, and Related Fields*. Lippincot Williams & Wilkins.

Nier, J. A. (2005). How dissociated are implicit and explicit racial attitudes? A bogus pipeline approach. *Group Processes & Intergroup Relations, 8*(1), 39–52.

Nilsson, B. (1979). The occurrence of taste buds in the palate of human adults as evidenced by light microscopy. *Acta Odontologica Scandinavica, 37*, 253–258.

Nilsson, L. G. (2003). Memory function in normal aging. *Acta Neurologica Scandinavica, 107* (Suppl 179), 7–13.

Nisan, M., & Kohlberg, L. (1982). Universality and variation in moral judgment: A longitudinal and cross-sectional study in Turkey. *Child Development, 53*(4), 865–876.

Nisbett, R. E. (2009). Intelligence and how to get it: Why schools and cultures count. New York: W. W. Norton.

Nishina, A., Juvonen, J., & Witkow, M. R. (2005). Sticks and stones may break my bones, but names will make me feel sick. The psychosocial, somatic, and scholastic consequences of peer harassment. *Journal of Clinical Child and Adolescent Psychology, 34*(1), 37–48.

Nishitani, S., Miyamura, T., Tagawa, M., Sumi, M., Takase, R., Doi, H., Moriuchi, H., & Shinohara, K. (2009). The calming effect of a maternal breast milk odor on the human newborn infant. *Neuroscience Research, 63*, 66–71.

Nock, M. K., & Prinstein, M. J. (2004). A functional approach to the assessment of self-mutilative behavior. *Journal of Consulting and Clinical Psychology, 72*, 885–890.

Nolen-Hoeksema, S. (2001). Gender differences in depression. *Current Directions in Psychological Science, 10*(5), 173–176.

Noll, R. (2007). *The encyclopaedia of schizophrenia and other psychotic disorders*. Facts on File, New York.

Nonacs, R. M. (2007). Postpartum depression. *eMedicine Clinical Reference*. Retrieved from http:/www.emedicine.com/med/topic 3408.htm.

Noonan, H. W. (2003). *Personal Identity*. New York: Routledge.

Norcross, J. C., & Goldfried, M. R. (Eds.). (2005). *Handbook of psychotherapy integration* (2nd Ed.). New York, NY: Oxford University Press.

Norem, J. K., & Illingworth, K. S. S. (2004). Mood and performance among defensive pessimists and strategic optimists. *Journal of Research in Personality, 38*(4), 351–366.

Norgren, R., Hajnal, A., & Mungarndee, S. S. (2006). Gustatory reward and the nucleus accumbens. *Physiology & Behavior, 89*, 531–535.

Norman-Eady, S., Reinhart, C., & Martino, P. (2003). *Statutory rape laws by state*. OLR Research Report. Retrieved from: http://www.cga.ct.gov/2003/olrdata/jud/rpt/2003-R-0376.htm.

North, C. S. (2005). Somatoform disorders. In E. H. Rubin & C. F. Zorumski (Eds.), *Adult psychiatry* (2nd Ed., pp. 261–274). Oxford, UK: Blackwell Publishing.

Northcutt, R. G., & Kaas, J. H. (1995). The emergence and evolution of mammalian neocortex. *Trends in Neuroscience. 18*(9), 373–379.

Nosek, M., Kennedy, H. P., Beyene, Y., Taylor, D., Gilliss, C., & Lee, K. (2010). The effects of perceived stress and attitudes toward menopause and aging on symptoms of menopause. *Journal of Midwifery & Women's Health, 55*(4), 328–334.

Novaco, R. W., Stokols, D., & Milanesi, L. (1990). Objective and subjective dimensions of travel impedance as determinants of commuting stress. *American Journal of Community Psychology, 18*, 231–257.

Novella, S. (2000). Phrenology: History of a pseudoscience. *The New England Journal of Skepticism*. Retrieved from http://www.theness.com/index.php/phrenology-history-of-a-pseudoscience.

Novick, L. R., & Bassok, M. (2005). Problem solving. In K. J. Holyoak & R. G. Morrison (Eds.), *The Cambridge handbook of thinking and reasoning* (pp. 321–350). New York, NY: Cambridge University Press.

Novin, D., Sanderson, J. D., & Vanderweele, D. A. (1974). The effect of isotonic glucose on eating as a function of feeding condition and infusion site. *Physiology & Behavior, 13*(1), 4.

Noyes, R. (2008). Hypochondriasis. In M. Gelder, N. Andreasen, J. Lopez-Ibor, & J. Geddes (Eds.), *New Oxford textbook of psychiatry, vol. 2,* (2nd Ed.). New York: Oxford University Press.

NSDUH. (2008). *National survey on drug use*. Washington, DC: Department of Health and Human Services, Substance Abuse and Mental Health Services Administration, Office of Applied Studies.

Numazaki, M., & Tominaga, M. (2004). Nociception and TRP Channels. *Current Drug Targets: CNS and Neurological Disorders, 3*, 479–485.

Nunn, J. A., Gregory, L. J., Brammer, M., Williams, S. C. R., Parslow, D. M., Morgan, M. J., Morris, R. G., Bullmore, E. T., Baron-Cohen, S., & Gray, J. A. (2002). Functional magnetic resonance imaging of synesthesia: Activation of V4/V8 by spoken words. *Nature Neuroscience, 5*(4), 371–375.

Nutravite. (2006). Most married Canadian burdened with a snoring partner. Poll conducted by Ipsos Reid for Nutravite. Retrieved from http://www.nutravite.com/news/october.htm.

Nye, C. D., Roberts, B. W., Saucier, G., & Zhou, X. (2008). Testing the measurement equivalence of personality adjective items across cultures. *Journal of Research in Personality, 42*(6), 1524–1536.

O'Brien, C. P. (2008). The CAGE questionnaire for detection of alcoholism: A remarkably useful but simple tool. *Journal of the American Medical Association, 300*(17), 2054–2056.

O'Connor, B. P. (2008). Other personality disorders. In M. Hersen & J. Rosqvist (Eds.), *Handbook of psychological assessment, case conceptualization, and treatment, Vol 1: Adults* (pp. 438–462). Hoboken, NJ: John Wiley & Sons, Inc.

O'Connor, T., Sadleir, K. R., Maus, E., Velliquette, R. A., Zhao, J., Cole, S. L., . . . Vassar, R. (2008). Phosphorylation of the translation initiation factor eIF2alpha increases BACE1 levels and promotes amyloidogenesis. *Neuron, 60*(6), 988–1009.

O'Craven, K. M., & Kanwisher, N. (2000). Mental imagery of faces and places activates corresponding stimulus-specific brain regions. *Journal of Cognitive Neuroscience, 12*, 1013–1023.

O'Hara, D. (2010). Inductive reasoning comes to science. *Birth Story,* December 15, 2011.

O'Keefe, J. (1990). A computational theory of the hippocampal cognitive map. *Progress in Brain Research, 83*, 301–312.

O'Leary, K. D., & Wilson, G. T. (1987). *Behavior therapy: Application and outcome (2nd Ed.).* Englewood Cliffs, NJ: Prentice-Hall, Inc.

O'Rourke, N., Cappeliez, P., & Guindon, S. (2003). Depressive symptoms and physical health of caregivers of persons with cognitive impairment: Analysis of reciprocal effects over time. *Journal of Aging and Health, 15*(4), 688–712.

Oakley, D. A., & Halligan, P. W. (2010). Psychophysiological foundations of hypnosis and suggestion. In S. J. Lynn, J. W. Rhue & I. Kirsch (Eds.), *Handbook of clinical hypnosis (2nd Ed.)* (pp. 79–117). Washington, DC: American Psychological Association.

Oatley, K., & Jenkins, J. M. (1996). *Understanding emotions.* Malden, MA: Blackwell Publishing.

Oberauer, K., & Kliegl, R. (2006). A formal model of capacity limits in working memory. *Journal of Memory and Language, 55*, 601–626.

Oda, A. Y. (2007). David Elkind and the crisis of adolescence: Review, critique, and applications. *Journal of Psychology and Christianity, 26*(3), 251–256.

Offord, D. R., Boyle, M. H., Campbell, D., Goering, P., Lin, E., Wong, M., Racine, Y. A. (1996) One-year prevalence of psychiatric disorder in Ontarians 15 to 64 years of age. *Canadian Journal of Psychiatry, 41*, 559–565.

Ogawa, S., Tank, D. W., Menon, R., Ellermann, J. M., Kim, S.-G., Merkle, H., & Ugurbil, K. (1992). Intrinsic signal changes accompanying sensory stimulation: functional brain mapping with magnetic resonance imaging. *Proceedings of the National Academy of Sciences, 89*, 5951–5955.

Ogden, T. (2011). Sosial ferdighetsopplaring for barn og ungdom. [Social skills training for children and adolescents.]. *Tidsskrift for Norsk Psykologforening, 48*(1), 64–68.

O'Grady, W., Parnaby, P. F., & Schikschneit, J. (2010).Guns, gangs, and the underclass: A constructionist analysis of gun violence in a Toronto high school. *Canadian Journal of Criminology and Criminal Justice, 52*(1), 55–77.

Öhman, A. (2000). Fear and anxiety: Evolutionary, cognitive, and clinical perspectives. In M. Lewis & J. M. Haviland-Jones (Eds.), *Handbook of emotions, 2nd Ed.* (pp. 573–593). New York, NY: Guilford Press.

Okamoto, Y., Kinoshita, A., Onoda, K., Yoshimura, S., Matsunaga, M., Takami, H., Yamshita, H., Ueda, K., Suzuki, S., & Yamawaki, S. (2006). Functional brain basis of cognition in major depression. *Japanese Journal of Psychonomic Science. 25*, 237–243.

Okie, S. (2005). Medical marijuana and the Supreme Court. *New England Journal of Medicine, 353*(7), 648–651.

Oksenberg, J. R., & Hauser, S. L. (2010). Mapping the human genome with newfound precision. *Annals of Neurology, 67*(6), A8–A10.

Olatunji, B. O., Huijding, J., de Jong, P. J., & Smits, J. A. J. (2011). The relative contributions of fear and disgust reductions to improvements in spider phobia following exposure-based treatment. *Journal of Behavior Therapy and Experimental Psychiatry, 42*(1), 117–121.

Olness, K., & Kohen, D. P. (2010). Childhood problems. In A. F. Barabasz, K. Olness, R. Boland & S. Kahn (Eds.), *Medical hypnosis primer: Clinical and research evidence* (pp. 33–39). New York, NY: Routledge/Taylor & Francis Group.

Olsson, S. E., & Moller, A. R. (2003). On the incidence and sex ratio of transsexualism in Sweden. *Archives of Sexual Behavior, 32*(4), 381–386.

Ophira, E., Nassb, C., & Wagner, A. D. (2009). Cognitive control in media multitaskers. *Proceedings of the National Academy of Sciences, 106*, 15583–15587.

Oppenheimer, D. M. (2004). Spontaneous discounting of availability in frequency judgment tasks. *Psychological Science, 15*, 100–105.

Orbuch, T. L., & Sprecher, S. (2003). Attraction and interpersonal relationships. In J. Delamater (Ed.), *Handbook of social psychology* (pp. 339–362). New York, NY: Kluwer Academic/Plenum Publishers.

Organ, D., & Ryan, K. (1995). A meta-analytic review of attitudinal and dispositional predictors of organizational citizenship behavior. *Personnel Psychology, 48*, 775–802.

Orikasa, C., Kondo, Y., & Sakuma, Y. (2007). Transient transcription of the somatostatin gene at the time of estrogen-dependent organization of the sexually dimorphic nucleus of the rat preoptic area. *Endocrinology, 148*, 1144–1149.

Orne, M. T. (*1951*). The mechanisms of hypnotic age regression: An experimental study. *Journal of Abnormal and Social Psychology, 46*, 213–225.

Ornstein, P. A., & Light, L. L. (2010). Memory development across the life span. In W. F. Overton & R. M. Lerner (Eds.), *The handbook of life-span development,* vol. 1: *Cognition, biology, and methods* (pp. 259–305). Hoboken, NJ: John Wiley & Sons.

Orsillo, S. M., & Roemer, L. (2011). *The mindful way through anxiety: Break free from chronic worry and reclaim your life.* New York: Guilford Press.

Orzeł-Gryglewska, J. (2010). Consequences of sleep deprivation. *International Journal of Occupational Medicine and Environmental Health, 23*(1), 95–114.

Oshima, T., & Kondo, T. (1998). Forensic pathological observations on fatal injuries to the brain stem and/or upper cervical spinal cord in traffic accidents. *Journal of Clinical Forensic Medicine, 5*(3), 129–134.

Otto, M. W., McHugh, R. K., & Kantak, K. M. (2010). Combined pharmacotherapy and cognitive-behavioral therapy for anxiety disorders:

Medication effects, glucocorticoids, and attenuated treatment outcomes. *Clinical Psychology: Science and Practice, 17*(2), 91–103.

Ouellette, S. C., & DiPlacido, J. (2001). Personality's role in the protection and enhancement of health: Where the research has been, where it is stuck, how it might move. In A. Baum, T. A. Revenson, & J. E. Singer (Eds.), *Handbook of health psychology*. Mahwah, NJ: Lawrence Erlbaum.

Overholser, J. C., Braden, A. , & Fisher, L. (2010). You've got to believe: core beliefs that underlie effective psychotherapy, *Journal of Contemporary Psychotherapy, 40*, 185–194.

Overmier, B. J., & Murison, R. (2005). Trauma and resulting sensitization effects are modulated by psychological factors. *Psycho-neuroendocrinology, 30*, 965–973.

Overton, W. F., & Lerner, R. M. (Eds.). (2010). *The handbook of lifespan development*, vol. 1: *Cognition, biology, and methods*. Hoboken, NJ: John Wiley & Sons.

Ovsiew, F. (2006). Hysteria in neurological practice: The somatoform and dissociative disorders. In D. V. Jeste & J. H. Friedman (Eds.), *Psychiatry for neurologists* (pp. 67–80). Totowa, NJ: Humana Press.

Owen-Howard, M. (2001). Pharmacological aversion treatment of alcohol dependence. I. Production and prediction of conditioned alcohol aversion. *American Journal of Drug and Alcohol Abuse, 27*(3), 561–585.

Owens, J., & Massey, D. S. (2011). Stereotype threat and college academic performance: A latent variables approach. *Social Science Research, 40*(1), 150–166.

Oyserman, D., Coon, H. M., & Kemmelmeier, M. (2002a). Rethinking individualism and collectivism: Evaluation of theoretical assumptions and meta-analyses. *Psychological Bulletin, 128*, 3–72.

Oyserman, D., Kemmelmeier, M., & Coon, H. M. (2002b). Cultural Psychology, a new look: Reply to Bond (2002), Fiske (2002), Kityama (2002), and Miller (2002). *Psychological Bulletin, 128*, 110–117.

Ozer, E. J. (2005). The impact of violence on urban adolescents: Longitudinal effects of perceived school connection and family support. *Journal of Adolescent Research, 20*(2), 167–192.

Ozer, E. J., Best, S. R., Lipsey, T. L., & Weiss, D. S. (2003). Predictors of posttraumatic stress disorder and symptoms in adults: A meta-analysis. *Psychology Buletin., 129*(1), 52–73.

Öztekin, I., McElree, B., Staresina, B. P., & Davachi, L. (2009). Working memory retrieval: Contributions of the left prefrontal cortex, the left posterior parietal cortex, and the hippocampus. *Journal of Cognitive Neuroscience, 21*(3), 581–593.

Pace, T. W. W., & Heim, C. M. (2011). A short review on the psychoneuroimmunology of posttraumatic stress disorder: From risk factors to medical comorbidities. *Brain, Behavior, and Immunity, 25*(1), 6–13.

Packer, S. (2000). Religion and stress. In G. Fink (Ed.), *Encyclopedia of Stress, Vol. 3* (pp. 348–355). New York, NY: Academic Press.

Page, R. M., & Brewster, A. (2009). Depiction of food as having druglike properties in televised food advertisements directed at children: Portrayals as pleasure enhancing and addictive. *Journal of Pediatric Health Care, 23*(3), 150–158.

Paine, S., Gander, P. H., & Travier, N. (2006). The epidemiology of Morningness/Eveningness: Influence of age, gender, ethnicity, and socioeconomic factors in adults (30–49 years). *Journal of Biological Rhythms, 21*(1), 68–76.

Palkovitz, R., Copes, M. A., & Woolfolk, T. N. (2001). It's like ... you discover a new sense of being: Involved fathering as an evoker of adult development. *Men & Masculinities, 4*(1), 49–69.

Palumbo, S. R. (1978). Dreaming and memory: A new information processing model. New York, NY: Basic Books.

Panko, T. L. (2005). *Pathways from childhood conduct problems to adult criminality*. Student paper at Rochester Institute of Technology.

Pantalony, D. (1997). *Prism, pendulum and chronograph-philosophers at the University of Toronto*. retrieved from http://www.psych.utoronto.ca/museum/biblio.htm.

Paprzycka, K. (2010). Is neurobiology of personality inevitable? A philosophical perspective. In T. Maruszewski, M. Fajkowska, & M. W. Eysenck (Eds.), *Personality from biological, cognitive, and social perspectives* (pp. 13–27). Clinton Corners, NY: Eliot Werner Publications.

Paquet, L. B. (2000). *Legion Magazine*. Retrieved from http://www.legionmagazine.com/en/index.php/2000/09/our-place-in-space.

Paquette, G. (2004) Violence on Canadian television networks. *Canadian Child and Adolescent Psychiatric Review, 13*(1), 13–15.

Paris, J. (2010). Estimating the prevalence of personality disorders in the community. *Journal of Personality Disorders, 24*(4), 405–411.

Park, D., & Gutchess. A. (2006). The cognitive neuroscience of aging and culture. *Current Directions in Psychological Science, 15*, 105–108.

Park, D. C., & Reuter-Lorenz, P. (2009). The adaptive brain: Aging and neurocognitive scaffolding. *Annual Review of Psychology, 60*,173–196.

Park, D. C., Lautenschlager, G., Hedden, T., Davidson, N. S., Smith, A. D., & Smith, P. (2002). Models of visuospatial and verbal memory across the adult life span. *Psychology & Aging, 17*(2), 299–320.

Parke, R. D. (1995). Fathers and families. In M. H. Bornstein (Ed.), *Handbook of parenting, vol. 3: Status and social conditions of parenting* (pp. 27–63). Mahwah, NJ: Lawrence Erlbaum Associates.

Parke, R. D., & Deur, J. L. (1972). Sciedule of punishment and inhibition of aggression in children. *Developmental Psychology, 7*, 266–269.

Parker, E. S., Cahill, L., & McGaugh, J. L. (2006) A case of unusual autobiographical remembering. *Neurocase, 12*, 35–49.

Parrott, W. G. (2004). The nature of emotion. In M. B. Brewer & M. Hewstone (Eds.), *Emotion and motivation* (pp. 5–20). Malden, MA: Blackwell Publishing.

Parrott, W. G. (2001). Implications of dysfunctional emotions for understanding how emotions function. *Review of General Psychology, 5*, 180–186.

Pasquet, P., & Apfelbaum, M. (1994). Recovery long-term. *American Journal of Physiology*, 861–863.

Paton, C., & Beer, D. (2001). Caffeine: The forgotten variable. *International Journal of Psychiatry in Clinical Practice, 5*(4), 231–236.

Patrick, C. J. (2007). Antisocial personality disorder and psychopathy. In W. O'Donohue, K. A. Fowler, & S. O. Lilienfeld (Eds.), *Personality Disorders: Toward the DSM-V* (pp. 109–166). Thousand Oaks, CA: Sage Publications.

Patrick, C. J. (1994). Emotion and psychopathy: Startling new insights. *Psychophysiology, 31*(4), 319–330.

Patrick, C. J., Bradley, M. M., & Lang, P. J. (1993). Emotion in the criminal psychopath: Startle reflex modulation. *Journal of Abnormal Psychology, 102*(1), 82–92.

Patterson, D. (2011). The linkage between secondary victimization by law enforcement and rape case outcomes. *Journal of Interpersonal Violence, 26*(2), 328–347.

Patterson, D. R. (2010). *Clinical hypnosis for pain control*. Washington, DC: American Psychological Association.

Patterson, F. G. P., & Matevia, M. L. (2001). Twenty-seven years of Project Koko and Michael. In M. Biruté, F. Galdikas, N. Erickson Briggs, L. K. Sheeran, G. L. Shapiro, & J. Goodall (Eds.), *All apes great and small: african apes* (pp. 165–176). Springer.

Pattison, E., & Pattison, M. (1980). "Ex-gays": Religiously mediated change in homosexuals. *American Journal of Psychiatry, 137*, 1553–1562.

Paul, G. L., & Lentz, R. (1977). *Psychosocial treatment of the chronic mental patient*. Cambridge, MA: Harvard University Press.

Pauls, C. A., & Stemmler, G. (2003). Repressive and defensive coping during fear and anger. *Emotion, 3*(3), 284–302.

Paulsen, J. S. (2009). Functional imaging in Huntington's disease. *Experimental Neurology*. Jan 3. [Epub ahead of print].

Paulsen, O., & Sejnowski, T. J. (2000). Natural patterns of activity and long-term synaptic plasticity. *Current Opinion in Neurobiology, 10*(2), 172–179.

Paulus, P. B., Dugosh, K. L., Dzindolet, M. T., Coskun, H., & Putnam, V.L. (2002). Social and cognitive influences in group brainstorming: Predicting production gains and losses. In W. Stroebe & M. Hewston (Eds.), *European Review of Social Psychology (Vol. 12*, pp. 299–325). Chichester: John Wiley & Sons, Inc.

Paulus, P. B., Dzindolet, M. T., Poletes, G., & Camacho, L. M. (1993). Perception of performance in group brainstorming: The illusion of group productivity. *Personality and Social Psychology Bulletin, 19*, 78–79.

Paus, T., Zijdenbos, A., Worsley, K., Collins, D. L., Blumenthal, J., Giedd, J. N., et al. (1999). Structural maturation of neural pathways in children and adolescents: In vivo study. *Science, 283*(5409), 1908–1911.

Pause, B. M., Sojka, B., Krauel, K., Fehm-Wolfsdorf, G., & Ferstl, R. (1996). Olfactory information processing during the course of the menstrual cycle. *Biological Psychology, 44*, 31–54.

Paykel, E. S. (2003). Life events and affective disorders. *Acta Psychiatrica Scandinavica, 108*, 61–66.

Paykel, E. S. (2003). Life events: Effects and genesis. *Psychological Medicine, 33*(7), 1145–1148.

Payne, J. W., & Bettman, J. R. (2004). Walking with the scarecrow: The Information-processing approach to decision research. In D. J. Koehler & N. Harvey (Eds.), *Blackwell handbook of judgment and decision making* (pp. 110–132). Malden, MA: Blackwell Publishing.

Pederson, D. R., & Moran, G. (1996). Expressions of the attachment relationship outside of the strange situation. *Child Development, 67*, 915–927.

Pennebaker, J. W. (2004). Theories, therapies, and taxpayers: On the complexities of the expressive writing paradigm. *Clinical Psychology: Science and Practice, 11*(2), 138–142.

Pennebaker, J. W. (2003). The social, linguistic and health consequences of emotional disclosure. In J. Suls & K. A. Wallston (Eds.), *Social Psychological foundations of health and illness* (pp. 288–313). Malden, MA: Blackwell Publishing.

Pennebaker, J. (1990). *Opening up: The healing power of confiding in others.* New York, NY: William Morrow.

Pennebaker, J. W., Kiecolt-Glaser, J., & Glaser, R. (2004). Disclosure of traumas and immune function: Health implications for psychotherapy. In R. M. Kowalski & M. R. Leary (Eds.), *The interface of social and clinical psychology: Key readings* (pp. 301–312). New York, NY: Psychology Press.

Peplau, L. A. (2003). Human sexuality: how do men and women differ? *Current Directions in Psychological Science, 12*, 37–41.

Perani, D., Paulesu, E., Galles, N. S., Dupoux, E., Dehaene, S., Bettinardi, V. Cappa, S. F., Fazio, F., & Mehler, J. (1998). The bilingual brain. Proficiency and age of acquisition of the second language. *Brain, 121*, 1841–1852.

Perdeci, Z., Gulsun, M., Celik, C., Erdem, M., Ozdemir, B., Ozdag, F., & Kilic, S. (2010). Aggression and the event-related potentials in antisocial personality disorder. *Klinik Psikofarmakoloji Bülteni/Bulletin of Clinical Psychopharmacology, 20*(4), 300–306.

Pereira, A. C., Huddleston, D. E., Brickman, A. M., Sosunov, A. A., Hen, R., McKhann, G. M., Sloan, R., Gage, F. H., Brown, T. R., & Small, S. A. (2007). An in vivo correlate of exercise-induced neurogenesis in the adult dentate gyrus. *Proceedings of the National Academy of Sciences of the United States of America, 104*, 5638–5643.

Peretz, I., Cummings, S., & Dubé, M. P. (2007). The genetics of congenital amusia (tone deafness): a family-aggregation study. *American Journal of Human Genetics, 81*, 582–588.

Pergadia, M., Madden, P., Lessov, C., Todorov, A., Bucholz, K., Martin, N., & Heath, A. (2006). Genetic and environmental influences on extreme personality dispositions in adolescent female twins. *Journal of Child Psychology and Psychiatry, 47*, 902–915.

Perluigi, M., Di Domenico, F., Giorgi, A., Schinina, M. E., Coccia, R., Cini, C., & Calabrese, V. (2010). Redox proteomics in aging rat brain: Involvement of mitochondrial reduced glutathione status and mitochondrial protein oxidation in the aging process. *Journal of Neuroscience Research, 88*(16), 3498–3507.

Perneczky, R., Drzezga, A., Boecker, H., Ceballos-Baumann, A. O., Granert, O., Förstl, H., Kurz, A., & Häussermann, P. (2008). Activities of daily living, cerebral glucose metabolism, and cognitive reserve in Lewy body and Parkinson's disease. *Dementia and Geriatric Cognitive Disorders*, 26, 475–481.

Perry, J. C., Hoglend, P., Shear, K., Valliant, G. E., Horowitz, M., Kardos, M. E., Bille, H., & Kagan, D. (1998). Field trial of a diagnostic axis for defense mechanisms for DSM-IV. *Journal of Personality Disorders, 12*, 56–68.

Perugi, G., Medda, P., Zanello, S., Toni, C., & Cassano, G. B. (2011 in press). Episode length and mixed features as predictors of ect nonresponse in patients with medication-resistant major depression. *Brain Stimulation.*

Pervin, L. A., Cervone, D., & John, O. P. (2005). *Personality: Theory and research* (9th Ed.). New York, NY: John Wiley & Sons, Inc.

Peterlin, B. L., Rosso, A. L., Sheftell, F. D., Libon, D. J., Mossey, J. M., & Merikangas, K. R. (2011). Post-traumatic stress disorder, drug abuse and migraine: New findings from the national comorbidity survey replication (NCS-R). *Cephalalgia, 31*(2), 235–244.

Peters, L. C., Sist, T. C., & Kristal, M. B.(1991). Maintenance and decline of the suppression of infanticide in mother rats. *Physiology and Behavior, 50*(2), 451–456.

Peterson, C., Grant, V., & Boland, L. D. (2005). Childhood amnesia in children and adolescents: Their earliest memories. *Memory, 13*(6), 622–637.

Peterson, C., & Park, N. (2010). What happened to self-actualization?: Commentary on Kenrick et al. *Perspectives on Psychological Science, 5*, 320–322.

Peterson, C., Ruch, W., Beermann, U., Park, N., & Seligman, M. E. P. (2007). Strengths of character, orientations to happiness, and life satisfaction. *Journal of Positive Psychology, 2*(3), 149–156.

Peterson, C., & Steen, T. A. (2009). Optimistic explanatory style. *Oxford handbook of positive psychology (2nd Ed.)* (pp. 313–321). New York, NY: Oxford University Press.

Peterson, C., & Steen, T. A. (2002). Optimistic explanatory style. *Handbook of positive psychology* (pp. 244–256). New York, NY: Oxford University Press.

Petrescu, N. (2008). Loud music listening. *McGill Journal of Medicine, 11*, 169–176.

Petrie, K., Conaglen, J. V., Thompson, L., & Chamberlain, K. (1989). Effect of melatonin on jet lag after long haul flights. *British Medical Journal, 298*, 705–707.

Petrovich, G. D., Setlow, B., Holland, P. C., & Gallagher, M. (2002). Amygdalo-hypothalamic circuit allows learned cues to override satiety and promote eating. *Journal of Comparative Physiology, 22*(19), 8748–8753.

Pettersen, G., Rosenvinge, J. H., & Ytterhus, B. (2008). The "double life" of bulimia: patients' experiences in daily life interactions. *Eating Disorders, 16*(3), 204–211.

Petty, R. E., & Cacioppo, J. T. (1986). *Communication and persuasion: central and peripheral routes to attitude change.* New York: Springer-Verlag.

Petty, R. E., Wheeler, S. C., & Tormala, Z. L. (2003). Persuasion and attitude change. In T. Millon & M. J. Lerner (Eds.), *Handbook of psychology: Personality and social psychology, Vol. 5* (pp. 353–382). Hoboken, NJ: John Wiley & Sons Inc.

Phelps, M. E. (2006). *PET: physics, instrumentation, and scanners.* Springer.

Phillips, K. A. (2005). Placebo-controlled study of pimozide augmentation of fluoxetine in body dysmorphic disorder. *American Journal of Psychiatry, 162*(2), 377–379.

Philips, K. A. (2004). Body dysmorphic disorder: recognizing and treating imagined ugliness. *World Psychiatry, 3*(1), 12–17.

Phillips, K. A., & Castle, D. J. (2002). Body dysmorphic disorder. In D. J. Castle & K. A. Phillips (Eds.), *Disorders of body image.* Petersfield, UK: Wrightson Biomedical Publishing, Ltd.

Philipson, T. (2001). The world-wide growth in obesity: an economic research agenda. *Health Economics, 10*, 1–7.

Phillips, J. L. (1975). *The origins of intellect: Piaget's theory.* London: W. H. Freeman and Company.

Phillips, M. L., & Sierra, M. (2003). Depersonalization disorder: a functional neuroanatomical perspective. *Stress, 6*(3), 157–165.

Phinney, J. S., & Baldelomar, O. A. (2011). Identity development in multiple cultural contexts. In L. A. Jensen (Ed.), *Bridging cultural and developmental approaches to psychology: New syntheses in theory, research, and policy* (pp. 161–186). New York, NY: Oxford University Press.

Piaget, J. (2003). PART I: Cognitive development in children: Piaget: development and learning. *Journal of Research in Science Teaching, 40*, S8–S18.

Piaget, J. (2000). *Studies in reflecting abstraction.* (R. L. Campbell, Trans). Hove: Psychology Press.

Piaget, J. (1985). *The equilibration of cognitive structures: The central problem of intellectual development* (T. Brown & K. Thampy, Trans). Chicago, IL: University of Chicago Press.

Piaget, J. (1981). *Intelligence and Affectivity.* Basic Books, New York.

Piaget, J. (1972). *[Essay on operative logic. (2nd Ed.).]* Dunod: 75661 Paris Cedex 14.

Piaget, J. (1965). *The moral judgment of the child.* New York, NY: Free Press.

Piaget, J., le Cozannet, R., & Samson, D. (2009). La causalite chez l'enfant (children's understanding of causality). *British Journal of Psychology, 100*, 207–224.

Pickens, R., Svikis, D., McGue, M., Lykken, D., Heston, L., & Clayton, P. (1991). Heterogeneity in the inheritance of alcoholism. *Archives of General Psychiatry, 48,* 19–28.

Pickering, T. G., Devereux, R. B., James, G. D., Gerin, W., Landsbergis, P., Schnall, P. L., & Schwartz, J. E. (1996). Environmental influences on blood pressure and the role of job strain. *Journal of Hypertension, 14,* S179–S185.

Pierce, G. R., Sarason, I. G., & Sarason, B. R. (1996). Coping and social support. In M. Zeidner & N. S. Endler (Eds.), *Handbook of coping, theory, research, applications* (pp. 434–451). New York, NY: John Wiley & Sons, Inc.

Pierpaoli, W. (Ed.). (2005). *Reversal of aging: Resetting the pineal clock.* New York, NY: New York Academy of Sciences.

Pierre, J. M. (2010). Hallucinations in nonpsychotic disorders: Toward a differential diagnosis of "hearing voices." *Harvard Review of Psychiatry, 18*(1), 22–35.

Pietschnig, J., Voracek, M., & Formann, A. K. (2010). Mozart effect–Shmozart effect: A meta-analysis. *Intelligence, 38*(3), 314–323.

Piferi, R. L., Jobe, R. L., & Jones, W. H. (2006). Giving to others during national tragedy: The effects of altruistic and egoistic motivations on long-term giving. *Journal of Social and Personal Relationships, 23,* 171–184.

Pinel, J. P. J., Assanand, S., & Leman, D. R. (2000). Hunger, eating, and ill health. *American Psychologist, 55,* 1105–1116.

Pinker, S., & Jackendoff, R. (2005). The faculty of language: What's special about it? *Cognition, 95,* 201–236.

Pinkerman, J. E., Haynes, J. P., & Keiser, T. (1993). Characteristics of psychological practice in juvenile court clinics. *American Journal of Forensic Psychology, 11,* 3–12.

Piper, A., & Merskey, H. (2004). The persistence of folly: A critical examination of dissociative identity disorder. Part I. The excesses of an improbable concept. *Canadian Journal of Psychiatry, 49*(9), 592–600.

Piskulic, D., Olver, J. S., Norman, T. R., & Maruff, P. (2007). Behavioural studies of spatial working memory dysfunction in schizophrenia: a quantitative literature review. *Psychiatry Research, 150,* 111–121.

Pisula, E. (2010). The autistic mind in the light of neuropsychological studies. *Acta Neurobiologiae Experimentalis, 70*(2), 119–130.

Platania, J., & Moran, G. P. (2001). Social facilitation as a function of mere presence of others. *Journal of Social Psychology, 141*(2), 190–197.

Pliner, P., Bell, R., Hirsch, E. S., & Kinchla, M. (2006). Meal duration mediates the effect of "social facilitation" on eating in humans. *Appetite, 46*(2), 189–198.

Pliszka, S. R. (2003). *Neuroscience for the mental health professional.* New York, NY: The Guildford Press.

Plomin, R., & Caspi, A. (1999). Behavioral genetics and personality. In L. A. Pervin & O. P. John (Eds.), *Handbook of personality: Theory and research.* New York, NY: Guilford Press.

Plum, L., Belgardt, B. F., & Brüning, J. C. (2006). Central insulin action in energy and glucose homeostasis. *Insulin, 116*(7).

Plutchik, R. (1980). *Emotion: A psychoevolutionary synthesis.* New York, NY: Harper & Row.

Poirier, P., Giles, T. D., Bray, G. A., Hong, Y., & Stern, J. S. (2006). Obesity and cardiovascular disease: Pathophysiology, evaluation, and effect of weight loss: An update of the 1997 American Heart Association Scientific Statement on Obesity and heart Disease from the Obesity Committee of the Council on Nutrition, Physical Activity, and Metabolism. *Circulation, 113,* 898–918.

Polan, H. J., & Hofer, M. A. (1998). Olfactory preference for mother over home nest shavings by newborn rats. *Developmental Psychobiology, 33*(1), 5–20.

Pollak, S. D., Nelson, C. A., Schlaak, M. F., Roeber, B. J., Wewerka, S. S., Wiik, K. L., & Gunnar, M. R. (2010). Neurodevelopmental effects of early deprivation in postinstitutionalized children. *Child Development, 81*(1), 224–236.

Ponti, G., Peretto, P., Bonfanti, L., & Reh, T. A. (2008). Genesis of neuronal and glial progenitors in the cerebellar cortex of peripuberal and adult rabbits. *PLoS ONE, 3*(6), e2366.

Pontoski, K. E., & Heimberg, R. G. (2010). The myth of the superiority of concurrent combined treatments for anxiety disorders. *Clinical Psychology: Science and Practice, 17*(2), 107–111.

Pontoski, K. E., Heimberg, R. G., Turk, C. L., Coles, M. E. (2010) Psychotherapy for social anxiety disorder. In D. J. Stein, E. Hollander, & B. O. Rothbaum (Eds.), *Textbook of anxiety disorders* (2nd Ed.) (pp. 501–521). Arlington, VA: American Psychiatric Publishing, Inc.

Pope, H. G., Jr., Poliakoff, M. B., Parker, M. P., Boynes, M., & Hudson, J. I. (2007). Is dissociative amnesia a culture-bound syndrome? findings from a survey of historical literature. *Psychological Medicine: A Journal of Research in Psychiatry and the Allied Sciences, 37*(2), 225–233.

Pope, K., & Wedding, D. (2011). Contemporary challenges and controversies. In R. J. Corsini & D. Wedding (Eds.), *Current psychotherapies* (9th Ed.). Florence, KY: CENGAGE Learning.

Popenoe, D. (1993). American family decline 1960–1990: A review and appraisal. *Journal of Marriage and the Family, 55,* 527–544.

Popper, K. (1963). Conjectures and refutations: The growth of scientific knowledge. London: Routledge & Kegan Paul.

Popper, K. R. (1959). *The logic of scientific discovery.* Oxford: Basic Books.

Porges, S. W., & Carter, C. S. (2010). Neurobiological bases of social behavior across the life span. In M. E. Lamb, A. M. Freund, & R. M. Lerner (Eds.), *The handbook of life-span development,* vol. 2: *Social and emotional development* (pp. 9–50). Hoboken, NJ: John Wiley & Sons.

Poropat, A. E. (2009). A meta-analysis of the five-factor model of personality and academic performance. *Psychological Bulletin, 135*(2), 322–338.

Porsolt, R. D. (2000). Animal models of depression: utility for transgenic research. *Reviews in the Neurosciences, 11,* 53–58.

Porter, R., & Winberg, J. (1999). Unique salience of maternal breast odors for newborn infants. *Neuroscience & Biobehavioral Reviews, 23*(3), 439–449.

Porter, R. H., & Winberg, J. (1999). Unique salience of maternal breast odors for newborn infants. *Neuroscience and Biobehavioral Reviews, 23*(3), 439–449.

Portnoy, D. (2008). Relatedness: Where existential and psychoanalytic approaches converge. In K. J. Schneider (Ed.), *Existential-integrative psychotherapy: Guideposts to the core of practice* (pp. 268–281). New York, NY: Routledge/Taylor & Francis Group.

Posmontier, B. (2010). The role of midwives in facilitating recovery in postpartum psychosis. *Journal of Midwifery & Women's Health, 55*(5), 430–437.

Posner, M., Petersen, S. F., Fox, P. T., & Raichle, M. E. (2009). Localization of cognitive operations in the human brain (1988). In *Foundations of psychological thought: A history of psychology* (pp. 279–294). Thousand Oaks, CA: Sage Publications.

Post, R. M., & Miklowitz, D. J. (2010). The role of stress in the onset, course, and progression of bipolar illness and its comorbidities: Implications for therapeutics. In D. J. Miklowitz & D. Cicchetti (Eds.), *Understanding bipolar disorder: A developmental psychopathology perspective* (pp. 370–413). New York: Guilford Press.

Post, S. G. (2005). Altruism, happiness, and health: It's good to be good. *International Journal of Behavioral Medicine, 12*(2), 66–77.

Postle, B. R. (2003). Context in verbal short-term memory. *Memory & Cognition, 31*(8), 1198–1207.

Powis, T. (1990). Paying for the past: A brainwashing victim seeks compensation. *Macleans,* March 19.

Prescott, C., Johnson, R. C., & McArdle, J. (1991). Genetic contributions to television viewing. *Psychological Science, 2,* 430–431.

Present, J., Crits-Christoph, P., Gibbons, M. B. C., Hearon, B., Ring-Kurtz, S., Worley, M., et al. (2008). Sudden gains in the treatment of generalized anxiety disorder. *Journal of Clinical Psychology, 64*(1), 119–126.

Price, G. R., Holloway, I., Räsänen, P., Vesterinen, M., & Ansari, D. (2007). Impaired parietal magnitude processing in developmental dyscalculia. *Current Biology, 17,* R1042–R1043.

Price, R. A., & Gottesman, I. I. (1991). Body fat in identical twins reared apart: Roles for genes and environment. *Behavior Genetics, 21*(1), 22903–22903.

Prinstein, M. J., Dodge K. A. (Eds.) (2008). *Understanding peer influence in children and adolescents.* New York, NY: Guilford Press.

Prislin, R., & Wood, W. (2005). Social influence in attitudes and attitude change. In D. Albarracín, B. T. Johnson, & M. P. Zanna (Eds.), *The Handbook of Attitudes* (pp. 671–705). Mahwah, NJ: Lawrence Erlbaum Associates Publishers.

Probst, M., Goris, M., Vandereycken, W., Pieters, G., Vanderlinden, J., Van Coppenolle, H., et al. (2004). Body composition in bulimia nervosa patients compared to healthy females. *European Journal of Nutrition, 43*(5), 288–296.

Prochaska, J. O., & Norcross, J. C. (2010). *Systems of psychotherapy: A transtheoretical analysis* (7th Ed.). Pacific Grove, CA: Brooks/Cole.

Prochaska, J. O., & Norcross, J. C. (2007). *Systems of psychotherapy: A transtheoretical analysis* (6th Ed.). Pacific Grove, CA: Brooks/Cole.

Profit, W. E., Mino, I., & Pierce, C. M. (2000). Stress in blacks. In G. Fink (Ed.), *Encyclopedia of stress, Vol. 1* (pp. 324–330). New York, NY: Academic Press.

Public Health Agency of Canada. (2011). *Aboriginal Head Start in urban and northern communities (AHSUNC) AHSUNC program celebrates 15 years of success!* Retrieved from http://www.phac-aspc.gc.ca/hp-ps/dca-dea/prog-ini/ahsunc-papacun/index-eng.php.

Public Health Agency of Canada. (2008). Publicly funded immunization programs in Canada—Routine schedule for infants and children (including special programs and catch-up programs). Retrieved from www.phac-aspc.gc.ca/im/ptimprog-progimpt/table-1-eng.php.

Public Health Agency of Canada. (2007). *Population Health Fund Project: Father involvement for healthy child outcomes: partners supporting knowledge development and transfer.* Retrieved from www.phac-aspc.gc.ca/.

Pugno, M. (2007). The subjective well-being paradox: A suggested solution based on relational goods. In P. L. Porta & L. Bruni (Eds.), *Handbook on the economics of happiness.* Northampton: MA: Edward Elgar Publishing.

Puhl, R. M., Moss-Racusin, C. A., Schwartz, M. B., & Brownell, K. D. (2008). Weight stigmatization and bias reduction: perspectives of overweight and obese adults. *Health education research, 23*(2), 347–358.

Puka, B. (2004). Altruism and character. In D. K. Lapsley & D. Narvaez (Eds.), *Moral development, self, and identity* (pp. 161–187). Mahwah, NJ: Lawrence Erlbaum Associates Publishers.

Pungello, E. P., Kainz, K., Burchinal, M., Wasik, B. H., Sparling, J. J., Ramey, C. T., & Campbell, F. A. (2010). Early educational intervention, early cumulative risk, and the early home environment as predictors of young adult outcomes within a high-risk sample. *Child Development, 81*(1), 410–426.

Puts, D. A., Jordan, C. L., & Breedlove, S. M. (2006). Defending the brain from estrogen. *Nature Neuroscience, 9*(2), 155–156.

Qiu, A., Crocetti, D., Adler, M., Mahone, E. M., Denckla, M. B., Miller, M. I., & Mostofsky, S. H. (2009). Basal ganglia volume and shape in children with attention deficit hyperactivity disorder. *The American Journal of Psychiatry, 166,* 74–82.

Quarrell, O. (2008). *Huntington's Disease.* London, UK: Oxford University Press.

Quinnell, T. G., Farooqi, I. S., Smith, I. E., & Schneerson, J. M. (2007). Screening the human prepro-orexin gene in a single-centre narcolepsy cohort. *Sleep Medicine, 8*(5), 498–502.

Quirk, G. J. (2006). Extinction: new excitement for an old phenomenon. *Biological Psychiatry, 60,* 317–318.

Quirk, G. J., Garcia, R., & González-Lima, F. (2006). Prefrontal mechanisms in extinction of conditioned fear. *Biological Psychiatry, 60,* 337–343.

Raaijmakers, J. G. W., & Shiffrin, R. M. (2002). Models of memory. In H. Pashler & D. Medin (Eds.), *Stevens handbook of experimental psychology (3rd Ed.), vol. 2: Memory and cognitive processes* (pp. 43–76). Hoboken, NJ: John Wiley & Sons, Inc.

Raaijmakers, J. G., & Shiffrin, R. M. (1992). Models for recall and recognition. *Annual Review of Psychology, 43,* 205–234.

Rabow, J., Newcomb, M. D., Monto, M. A., & Hernandez, A. C. (1990). Altruism in drunk driving situations: Personal and situational factors in intervention. *Social Psychology Quarterly, 53*(3), 199–213.

Rachman, S. J. (2004). Fear and courage: A psychological perspective. *Social Research: An International Quarterly, 71*(1), 149–176.

Rachman, S. J. (1989). *Fear and courage.* New York: W. H. Freeman.

Rafii, M. S., & Aisen, P. S. (2009). Recent developments in Alzheimer's disease therapeutics. *BMC Medicine, 7,* 7.

Rahman, Q. (2005). The neurodevelopment of human sexual orientation. *Neuroscience and Biobehavioral Rreviews, 29*(7), 1057–1066.

Raid, G. H., & Tippin, S. M. (2009). Assessment of intellectual strengths and weaknesses with the Stanford-Binet intelligence Scales—Fifth edition (SB5). In J. A. Naglieri & S. Goldstein, *Practitioner's guide to assessing intelligence and achievement* (pp. 127–152). Hoboken, NJ: John Wiley & Sons.

Rainville, P., Duncan, G. H., Price, D. D., Carrier, B., & Bushnell, M. C. (1997). Pain affect encoded in human anterior cingulate but not somatosensory cortex. *Science, 277*(5328), 968–971.

Rainville, P., Hofbauer, R. K., Bushnell, M. C., Duncan, G. H., & Price, D. D. (2002). Hypnosis modulates activity in brain structures involved in the regulation of consciousness. *Journal of Cognitive Neuroscience, 14*(6), 887–901.

Ramachandran, V. S. (2005). Plasticity and functional recovery in neurology. *Clinical Medicine, 5,* 368–373.

Ramachandran V. S., & Rogers-Ramachandran, D. (1996). Synaesthesia in phantom limbs induced with mirrors. *Proceedings of the Royal Society of Biological Sciences, 263*(1369), 377–386.

Ramadan, N. M. (2000). Migraine. In G. Fink (Ed.), *Encyclopedia of stress* (pp. 757–770). San Diego, CA: Academic Press.

Ramage-Morin, P. L. (2004). *Panic disorder and coping, supplement to health reports, Volume 15.* Statistics Canada, Catalogue 82–003. Retrieved from http://www.statcan.gc.ca/pub/82-003-s/2004000/pdf/7445-eng.pdf.

Ramirez, J. J., Poulton, W. E., Knelson, E., Barton, C., King, M. A., & Klein, R. L. (2011). Focal expression of mutated tau in entorhinal cortex neurons of rats impairs spatial working memory. *Behavioural Brain Research, 216*(1), 332–340. doi: 10.1016/j.bbr.2010.08.013

Ramponi, C., Richardson-Klavehn, A., & Gardiner, J. M. (2007). Component processes of conceptual priming and associative cued recall: The roles of preexisting representation and depth of processing. *Journal of Experimental Psychology: Learning, Memory & Cognition, 33,* 843–862.

Rao, U., Hammen, C. L., & Poland, R. E. (2010). Longitudinal course of adolescent depression: Neuroendocrine and psychosocial predictors. *Journal of the American Academy of Child & Adolescent Psychiatry, 49*(2), 141–151.

Rapee, R. M., & Bryant, R. A. (2009). Stress and psychosocial factors in onset of fear circuitry disorders. *Stress-induced and fear circuitry disorders: Advancing the research agenda for DSM-V* (pp. 195–214). Arlington, VA: American Psychiatric Publishing, Inc.

Raskin, K., de Gendt, K., Duittoz, A., Liere, P., Verhoeven, G., Tronche, F., et al. (2009). Conditional inactivation of androgen receptor gene in the nervous system: Effects on male behavioral and neuroen-docrine responses. *The Journal of Neuroscience: The Official Journal of the Society for Neuroscience, 29*(14), 4461–4470.

Raskin, N. J., Rogers, C., & Witty, M. (2011). Person-centered therapy. In R. J. Corsini & D. Wedding (Eds.), *Current psychotherapies* (9th Ed.). Florence, KY: CENGAGE Learning.

Raskind, W. H. (2001). Current understanding of the genetic basis of reading and spelling disability. *Learning Disability Quarterly, 24*(3), 141–157.

Ratey, J. J. (2001). A user's guide to the brain: Perception, attention, and the four theaters of the brain. New York, NY: Random House.

Rathbone, D. B., & Huckabee, J. C. (1999). *Controlling Road Rage.* AAA Foundation for Traffic Safety.

Rathjen, H., & Charles, M. (1999). *From the Montreal Massacre to gun control.* Toronto: McClelland & Stewart.

Rauchs, G., Desgranges, B., Foret, J., & Eustache, F. (2005). The relationships between memory systems and sleep stages. *Journal of Sleep Research, 14,* 123–140.

Ravindran, L. N., & Stein, M. B. (2011). Pharmacotherapy for social anxiety disorder in adolescents and young adults. In C. A. Alfano, & D. C. Beidel (Eds.), *Social anxiety in adolescents and young adults: Translating developmental science into practice* (pp. 265–279). Washington, DC: American Psychological Association.

Rawson, R. A., & Ling, W. (2008). Clinical management: Methamphetamine. In H. D. Kleber & M. Galanter (Eds.), *The American psychiatric publishing textbook of substance abuse treatment(4th Ed.).* Washington, DC: American Psychiatric Publishing.

Read, J. P, Beattie, M., Chamberlain, R., & Merrill, J. E. (2008). Beyond the "binge" threshold: Heavy drinking patterns and their association with alcohol involvement indices in college students. *Addictive Behaviors, 33*(2), 225–234.

Read, J. (2010). Can poverty drive you mad? 'Schizophrenia', socio-economic status and the case for primary prevention. *New Zealand Journal of Psychology, 39*(2), 7–19.

Read, K., & Purse, M. (2007, March 22). Postpartum psychosis: Linked to bipolar disorder. *About.com*. Retrieved from http://bipolar.about.com/od/relateddisorders/a/postpartumpsych.htm.

Reddy, L., & Kanwisher, N. (2006). Coding of visual objects in the ventral stream. *Current Opinion in Neurobiology, 16*, 408–414.

Redelmeier, D. A., Katz, J., & Kahneman, D. (2003). Memories of colonoscopy: a randomized trial. *Pain, 104*, 187–194.

Reed, R. R. Jr.(1952). *Bedlam on the Jacobean Stage*. Cambridge, MA: Harvard University Press.

Reeve, J. M. (2008). *Understanding motivation and emotion* (5th Ed.). Hoboken, NJ: John Wiley & Sons.

Reeve, J. M. (2005). *Understanding motivation and emotion* (4th Ed.). Hoboken, NJ: John Wiley & Sons.

Reeve, J. M. (2001). *Understanding motivation and emotion* (3rd Ed.). Fort Worth, TX: Harcourt College Publications.

Regehr, C., Cadell, S., & Jansen, K. (1999). Perceptions of control and long-term recovery from rape. *Ameican. Journal of Orthopsychiatry, 69*(1), 110–115.

Regier, D. A., Narrow, W. E., Kuhl, E. A., & Kupfer, D. J. (Eds.). (2011). *The conceptual evolution of DSM-5*. Arlington, VA: American Psychiatric Publishing.

Reichenberg, A., Gross, R., Kolevzon, A., & Susser, E. S. (2011). Parental and perinatal risk factors for autism. In E. Hollander, A. Kolevzon & J. T. Coyle (Eds.), *Textbook of autism spectrum disorders* (pp. 239–246). Arlington, VA: American Psychiatric Publishing, Inc.

Reid, J. A., & Sullivan, C. J. (2009). A latent class typology of juvenile victims and exploration of risk factors and outcomes of victimization. *Criminal Justice and Behavior, 36*(10), 1001–1024.

Reid, P. J. (2009). Adapting to the human world: Dogs' responsiveness to our social cues. *Behavioral Processes, 80*, 325–333.

Reiff, P. (1979). *Freud: The Mind of a Moralist*. University of Chicago Press.

Reinecke, A., Cooper, M., Favaron, E., Massey-Chase, R., & Harmer, C. (2011). Attentional bias in untreated panic disorder. *Psychiatry Research, 185*(3), 387–393.

Reiner, W. G., & Gearheart, J. P. (2004). Discordant sexual identity in some genetic males with cloacal extophy assigned to female sex at birth. *New England Journal of Medicine, 350*, 333–341.

Reissig, C. J., Strain, E. C., & Griffiths, R. R. (2009). Caffeinated energy drinks—A growing problem. *Drug and Alcohol Dependence, 99*(1–3), 1–10.

Rejeski, W. J., Gregg, E., Thompson, A., & Berry, M. (1991). The effects of varying doses of acute aerobic exercise on psychophysiological stress responses in highly trained cyclists. *Journal of Sport & Exercise Psychology, 13*(2), 188–199.

Rejeski, W. J., & Thompson, A. (2007). Historical and conceptual roots of exercise psychology. *Essential readings in sport and exercise psychology* (pp. 332–347). Champaign, IL: Human Kinetics.

Rejeski, W. J., Thompson, A., Brubaker, P. H., & Miller, H. S. (1992). Acute exercise: Buffering psychosocial stress responses in women. *Health Psychology, 11*(6), 355–362.

Rekers, G. A. (1992). Development of problems of puberty and sex roles in adolescence. In C. E. Walker, & M. C. Roberts (Eds.), *Handbook of clinical child psychology, Second Edition*. Oxford, England: John Wiley & Sons, Inc.

Remler, D. K., & Van Ryzin, G. G. (2011). *Research methods in practice: Strategies for description and causation*. Thousand Oaks, CA: Sage Publications.

Renner, M. J., & Mackin, R. S. (2002). A life stress instrument for classroom use. *Handbook for teaching introductory psychology: Vol. 3: With an emphasis on assessment* (pp. 236–238). Mahwah, NJ: Lawrence Erlbaum Associates Publishers.

Resnick, R. A. (2000). The Dynamic Representation of Scenes. *Visual Cognition,7*, 17–42.

Resnick, R. A., O'Regan, J. K., & Clark, J. J. (1997). To see or not to see: the need for attention to perceive changes in scenes. *Psychological Science, 8*, 368–373.

Revonsuo, A. (2010). *Consciousness: The science of subjectivity*. New York, NY: Psychology Press.

Reynolds, S. E. (1993). "Limerence": A new word and concept. *Psychotherapy: Theory, Research and Practice, 20*(1), 107–111.

Reznick, J. S., & Goldfield, B. A. (1992). Rapid change in lexical development in comprehension and production. *Developmental Psychology, 28*, 406–413.

Rheingold, H. (2000). *They have a word for it: A lighthearted lexicon of untranslatable words & phrases*. Louisville, KY: Sarabande Books, Inc.

Rial, R. V., Akaârir, M., Gamundí, A., Nicolau, C., Garau, C., Aparicio, S., . . . Esteban, S. (2010). Evolution of wakefulness, sleep and hibernation: From reptiles to mammals. *Neuroscience and Biobehavioral Reviews, 34*(8), 1144–1160.

Richard, I. H., & Lyness, J. M. (2006). An overview of depression. In D. V. Jeste & J. H. Friedman (Eds.), *Psychiatry for neurologists* (pp. 33–42). Totowa, NJ: Humana Press.

Richardson, A. (2011). Memory and imagination in romantic fiction. In S. Nalbantian, P. M. Matthews & J. L. McClelland (Eds.), *The memory process: Neuroscientific and humanistic perspectives* (pp. 277–296). Cambridge, MA: MIT Press.

Richardson, R. D. (2006). *William James: In the maelstrom of American modernism*. Boston, MA: Houghton Mifflin Company.

Ridout, N., Astell, A. J., Reid, I. C., Glen, T., & O'Carroll, R. E. (2003). Memory bias for emotional facial expressions in major depression. *Cognition and Emotion, 17*(1), 101–122.

Rieber, R. W. (2006). *The bifurcation of the self: The history and theory of dissociation and its disorders*. New York: Springer Science + Business Media.

Rieber, R. W. (2002). The duality of the brain and the multiplicity of minds: Can you have it both ways? *History of Psychiatry 13*(49, pt1), 3–18.

Rigaud, D., Trostler, N., Rozen, R., Vallot, T., & Apfelbaum, M. (1995). Gastric distension, hunger, and energy intake after balloon implantation in severe obesity. *International Journal of Obesity and Related Metabolic Disorders: Journal of the International Association for the Study of Obesity, 19*(7), 489–495.

Rimé, B. (2007). The social sharing of emotion as an interface between individual and collective processes in the construction of emotional climates. *Journal of Social Issues, 63*, 307–322.

Rimm, D. C., & Masters, J. C. (1979). *Behavior therapy: Techniques and empirical findings* (2nd Ed.). New York, NY: Academic Press.

Ripple, C. H., Gilliam, W. S., Chanana, N., & Zigler, E. (1999). Will fifty cooks spoil the broth? The debate over entrusting head start to the states. *American Psychologist, 54*(5), 327–343.

Ritter, M. R., Blackmore, M. A., & Heimberg, R. G. (2010). Generalized anxiety disorder. In D. McKay, J. S. Abramowitz, & S. Taylor (Eds.), *Cognitive-behavioral therapy for refractory cases: Turning failure into success* (pp. 111–137). Washington, DC: American Psychological Association.

Rizzolatti, G., & Craighero, L. (2004). The mirror-neuron system. *Annual Review of Neuroscience. 27*, 169–192.

Rizzolatti, G., & Fabbri-Destro, M. (2008). The mirror system and its role in social cognition. *Current Opinions in Neurobiology, 18*, 179–184.

Roberson-Nay, R., & Brown, R. C. (2011). Neurodevelopmental aspects of social anxiety. In C. A. Alfano & D. C. Beidel (Eds.), *Social anxiety in adolescents and young adults: Translating developmental science into practice* (pp. 53–71). Washington, DC: American Psychological Association.

Roberts, B. W., & DelVecchio, W. F. (2000). The rank-order consistency of personality from childhood to old age: A quantitative review of longitudinal studies. *Psychological Bulletin, 126*, 3–25.

Roberts, B. W., Helson, R., & Klohnen, E. C. (2002). Personality developmental and growth in women across 30 years: Three perspectives. *Journal of Personality, 70*, 79–102.

Roberts, B. W., Walton, K. E., & Viechtbauer, W. (2006). Patterns of mean-level change in personality traits across the life course: A meta-analysis of longitudinal studies. *Psychology Bulletin, 132*, 1–25.

Roberts, R. D., MacCann, C., Matthews, G., & Zeidner, M. (2010). Emotional intelligence: Toward a consensus of models and measures. *Social and Personality Psychology Compass, 4*(10), 821–840.

Roberts, S. C., Little, A. C., Gosling, L. M., Jones, B. C., Perrett, D. I., Carter V., & Petrie, M. (2005). MHC assortative facial preferences in humans. *Biology Letters, 1*, 400–403.

Robertson, D. W., Low, P. A., & Polinsky, R. J. (Eds.) (1996). *Primer on the Autonomic Nervious System*. Academic Press.

Robertson, R. (1995). *Jungian archetypes: Jung, Goedel, and the history of archetypes*. Main, MA: Nicolas-Hays.

Robertz, F. J. (2007). Deadly dreams. *Scientific American Mind, 18*(4), 52–59.

Robinson, T. E., & Berridge, K. C. (2001). Incentive-sensitization and addiction. *Addiction (England), 96*(1), 103–114.

Rocca, P., Aimetti, M., Giugiario, M., Pigella, E., Romano, F., Crivelli, B., & Bogetto, F. (2010). The complaint of oral malodour: Psychopathological and personality profiles. *Psychotherapy and Psychosomatics, 79*(6), 392–394.

Roche, B., & Quayle, E. (2007). Sexual disorders. In D. W. Woods & J. W. Kanter (Eds.), *Understanding behavior disorders; A contemporary behavioral perspective*. Reno, NV: Context Press.

Rodafinos, A., Vucevic, A., & Sideridis, G. (2005). The effectiveness of compliance techniques: foot in the door versus door in the face. *The Journal of Social Psychology,* 145, 237–239.

Rodier, P. M. (2000, February). The early origins of autism. *Scientific American*, 56–63.

Rodin, J., & Langer, E. J. (1977). Long-term effects of a control-relevant intervention with the institutionalized aged. *Journal of Personality and Social Psychology, 35*(12), 897–902.

Roeloffs, C., Sherbourne, C., Unützer, J., Fink, A., Tang, L., & Wells, K. B. (2003). Stigma and depression among primary care patients. *General Hospital Psychiatry, 25*(5), 311–315.

Roese, N. J., & Jamieson, D. W. (1993). Twenty years of bogus pipeline research: A critical review and meta-analysis. *Psychological Bulletin, 114,* 363–375.

Rogers, C. R. (2008). The actualizing tendency in relation to 'motives' and to consciousness. In B. E. Levitt (Ed.,), *Reflections on human potential: Bridging the person-centered approach and positive psychology* (pp. 17–32). Ross-on-Wye: PCCS Books.

Rogers, C. R. (1995). *Client centered therapy*. Constance.

Rogers, C. R. (1980). *A way of being*. Houghton Mifflin.

Rogers, C. R. (1963). Actualizing tendency in relation to "motives" and to consciousness. In M. R. Jones (Ed.), *Nebraska symposium on motivation* (pp. 1–24). Oxford: University of Nebraska Press.

Rogers, P. (2005). Caffeine and health. *Psychologist, 18*(1), 9.

Rogoff, B. (*1990). Apprenticeship in thinking: cognitive development in social context*. Oxford: Oxford University Press.

Rolls, E. T. (2007). Sensory processing in the brain related to the control of food intake. *The Proceedings of the Nutrition Society, 66*(1), 96–112.

Roman, C., & Reilly, S. (2007). Effects of insular cortex lesions on conditioned taste aversion and latent inhibition in the rat. *The European Journal of Neuroscience, 26*(9), 2627–2632.

Roman, C., Lin, J., & Reilly, S. (2009). Conditioned taste aversion and latent inhibition following extensive taste preexposure in rats with insular cortex lesions. *Brain Research, 1259,* 68–73.

Romanelli, P., Esposito, V. (2004). The functional anatomy of neuropathic pain. *Neurosurgery Clinics of North America, 15*(3), 257–268.

Romano, S. J., Halmi, K. A., Sarkar, N. P., Koke, S. C., & Lee, J. S. (2002). A placebo-controlled study of fluoxetine in continued treatment of bulimia nervosa after successful acute fluoxetine treatment. *American Journal of Psychiatry, 159,* 96–102.

Rook, K. S., August, K. J., & Sorkin, D. H. (2011). Social network functions and health. In R. J. Contrada, & A. Baum (Eds.), *The handbook of stress science: Biology, psychology, and health* (pp. 123–135). New York: Springer Publishing Co.

Rosen, R. C., Fisher, W. A., Eardley, I. Niederberger, C., Nadel, A., & Sand, M. (2004). The multinational Men's Attitudes to Life Events and Sexuality (MALES) study: I. Prevalence of erectile dysfunction and related health concerns in the general population. *Current Medical Research and Opinion, 20*(5), 607–617.

Rosenberg, A., Ledley, D. R., & Heimberg, R. G. (2010). Social anxiety disorder. In D. McKay, J. S. Abramowitz, & S. Taylor (Eds.), *Cognitive-behavioral therapy for refractory cases: Turning failure into success* (pp. 65–88). Washington, DC: American Psychological Association.

Rosenberg, M. J. (1969). The conditions and consequences of evaluation apprehension. In R. Rosenthal & R.S. Rosnow (Eds.), *Artifact in behavioral research*. New York, NY: Academic Press.

Rosenberg, O., Isserles, M., Levkovitz, Y., Kotler, M., Zangen, A., & Dannon, P. N. (2011). Effectiveness of a second deep TMS in depression: A brief report. *Progress in Neuro-Psychopharmacology & Biological Psychiatry, 35*(4), 1041–1044.

Rosenstein, D., & Oster, H. (1988). Differential facial responses to four basic tastes in newborns. *Child Development, 59,* 1555–1568.

Rosenthal, R., & Jackson, L. (1971). Pygmalion in the classroom. *The Urban Review, 3*(1), 16–20.

Rosenthal, T. L., & Bandura, A. (1978). Psychological modeling: Theory and practice. In S. L. Garfield & A. E. Bergin (Eds.), *Handbook of psychotherapy and behavior change: An empirical analysis* (2nd Ed., pp. 621–658). New York, NY: Wiley.

Rosenzweig, M. R. (1996). Aspects of the search for neural mechanisms of memory. *Annual Review of Psychology, 47,* 1–32.

Ross, C. A., & Ness, L. (2010). Symptom patterns in dissociative identity disorder patients and the general population. *Journal of Trauma & Dissociation, 11*(4), 458–468.

Ross, L. D. (2001). Getting down to fundamentals: Lay dispositionism and the attributions of psychologists. *Psychological Inquiry, 12,* 37–40.

Ross, L. (1977). The intuitive psychologist and his shortcomings: Distortions in the attribution process. In L. Berkowitz (Ed.), *Advances in experimental social psychology* (Vol. 10). New York: Academic Press.

Rossano, M. J. (2002). Evolutionary psychology: The science of human behaviour and evolution. New Jersey: John Wiley & Sons.

Rossi, A. M., Quick, J. C., & Perrewe, P. L. (Eds.) (2009). *Stress and quality of working life: The positive and the negative*. Charlotte, NC: Information Age Publishing.

Rothbart, M. K., Derryberry, D., & Hershey, K. (2000). Stability of temperament in childhood: Laboratory infant assessment to parent report at seven years. In V. J. Molfese & D. L. Molfese (Eds.), *Temperament and personality development across the lifespan*. Mahwah, NJ: Lawrence Erlbaum Associates.

Rothstein, M. G., & Goffin, R. D. (2006). The use of personality measures in personnel selection: What does current research support? *Human Resource Management Review, 16,* 155–180.

Roughgarden, J. (2004). Evolutions rainbow: diversity, gender, and sexuality in nature and people. Berkeley, CA: University of California Press.

Rovee-Collier, C., Hayne, H., & Columbo, M. (2001). *The development of implicit and explicit memory*. Philadelphia: John Benjamins Publishing Company.

Rovira, A., Swapp, D., Spanlang, B., & Slater, M. (2009). The use of virtual reality in the study of people's responses to violent incidents. *Frontiers of Behavioral Neuroscience, 3,* 59. Retrieved from http://www.ncbi.nlm.nih.gov/pmc/articles/PMC2802544/.

Rowe, D. C., Almeida, D. M., & Jacobson, K. C. (1999). School context and genetic influences on aggression in adolescence. *Psychological Science, 10*(3), 277–280.

Roy-Byrne, P. P. (2005). The GABA-benzodiazepine receptor complex: Structure, function, and role in anxiety. *Journal of Clinical Psychiatry, 66*(Suppl. 2), 14–20.

Roysamb, E. (2006). Personality and well-being. *Handbook of personality and health* (pp. 115–134). New York, NY: John Wiley & Sons Ltd.

Rubenzer, S. J. (2008). The standardized field sobriety tests: a review of scientific and legal issues. *Law and Human Behavior, 32*(4), 293–313.

Rubin, Z. (1973). *Liking and Loving*. New York: Holt, Rinehart & Winston.

Rubin, Z. (1970). Measurement of romantic love. *Journal of Personality and Social Psychology, 16:* 265–273.

Rubino, G. (2011). Couples without children vs. couples with children. *eHow: Relationships & Family*. Retrieved from http://www.ehow.com/info_7904316_couples-children-vs-couples-children.html.

Rudman, L. A., & Ashmore, R. D. (2007). Discrimination and the Implicit Association Test. *Group Processes and Intergroup Relations, 10,* 359–372.

Rudy, D., & Grusec, J. E., (2001). Correlates of authoritarian parenting in individualist and collectivist cultures and implications for understanding the transmission of values. *Journal of Cross-Cultural Psychology, 32,* 202–212.

Runco, M. A. (2010). Divergent thinking, creativity, and ideation. In J. C. Kaufman, & R. J. Sternberg (Eds.), *The Cambridge handbook of creativity* (pp. 413–446). New York: Cambridge University Press.

Rupke, S. J., Blecke, D., & Renfrow, M. (2006). Cognitive therapy for depression. *American Family Physician, 73,* 83–86.

Rushton, J. P. (2009). Brain size as an explanation of national differences in IQ, longevity, and other life-history variables. *Personality and Individual Differences*. No Pages.

Rutter, M., Sonuga-Barke, E., & Castle, J. (2010). Investigating the impact of early institutional deprivation on development: Background and research strategy of the English and Romanian adoptees (ERA) study. *Monographs of the Society for Research in Child Development, 75*(1), 1–20.

Ruzek, J. I., Schnurr, P. P., Vasterling, J. J., & Friedman, M. J. (Eds.). (2011). *Caring for veterans with deployment-related stress disorders.* Washington, DC: American Psychological Association.

Ryan, R. M., & Deci, E. L. (2000). Self–determination theory and the facilitation of intrinsic motivation, social development, and well-being. *The American Psychologist, 55*(1), 68–78.

Ryan-Wenger, N. A., Sharrer, V. W., & Campbell, K. K. (2005, July-August). Changes in children's stressors over the past 30 years. *Pediatric Nursing.*

Rymer, R. (1994). *Genie: A scientific tragedy.* New York, NY: Harper Paperbacks.

Sabbagh, M. A., Bowman, L. C., Evraire, L. E., & Ito, J. M. (2009). Neurodevelopmental correlates of theory of mind in preschool children. *Child Development 80*(4), 1147–1162.

Sachs, J. (2009). Communication Development in Infancy. In J. B. Gleason (Ed.), *The Development of Language* (7th Ed., pp. 40–60). Columbus, OH: Allyn & Bacon.

Sack, R. L., Auckley, D., Auger, R. R., Carskadon, M. A., Wright Jr., K. P., Vitiello, M. V., & Zhdanova, I. V. (2007). Circadian rhythm sleep disorders: Part I, basic principles, shift work and jet lag disorders: An american academy of sleep medicine review. *Sleep: Journal of Sleep and Sleep Disorders Research, 30*(11), 1460–1483.

Sackett, P. R., & Shen, W. (2010). Subgroup differences on cognitive tests in contexts other than personnel selection. In J. L. Outtz (Ed.), *Adverse impact: Implications for organizational staffing and high stakes selection* (pp. 323–346). New York: Routledge/Taylor & Francis Group.

Sacks, O. (1985). The man who mistook his wife for a hat and other clinical tales. New York, NY: Touchstone.

Sadeh, A., Mindell, J. A., Luedtke, K., & Wiegand, B. (2009). Sleep and sleep ecology in the first 3 years: A web-based study. *Journal of Sleep Research, 18*(1), 60–73.

Sadler, J. Z., Hulgus, Y. F., & Agich, G. J. (1994). On values in recent American psychiatric classification. *Journal of Medical Philosophy, 19*(3), 261–277.

Sadler, M. S., Lineberger, M., Correll, J., & Park, B. (2005). Emotions, attributions, and policy endorsement in response to the September 11th terrorist attacks. *Basic and Applied Social Psychology, 27*(3), 249–258.

Sadler, P., & Woody, E. (2010). Dissociation in hypnosis: Theoretical frameworks and psychotherapeutic implications. In S. J. Lynn, J. W. Rhue & I. Kirsch (Eds.), *Handbook of clinical hypnosis (2nd Ed.)* (pp. 151–178). Washington, DC: American Psychological Association.

Sadock, B. J., & Sadock, V. A. (2007). *Synopsis of psychiatry: Behavioral sciences/clinical psychiatry (10th Ed.).* Philadelphia, PA: Wolters Kluwer/Lippincott Williams & Wilkins.

Sadock, V. A., & Kaplan, H. I. (2008). *Kaplan & Sadock's concise textbook of clinical psychiatry.* (Third Ed). Philadelphia, PA: Wolters Kluwer Health.

Safdar, S., Friedlmeier, W., Matsumoto, D., Yoo, S. H., Kwantes, C. T., Kakai, H., et al. (2009). Variations of emotional display rules within and across cultures: A comparison between Canada, USA, and Japan. *Canadian Journal of Behavioural Science, 41*(1), 1–10.

Safer, D. L., Telch, C. F., & Agras, W S. (2001). Dialectical behavior therapy for bulimia nervosa. *American Journal of Psychiatry, 158*(4), 632–634.

Saggino, A. (2000). The big three or the big five? A replication study. *Personality and Individual Differences, 28,* 879–886.

Saggino, A., & Kline, P. (1996). The location of the Myers-Briggs Type Indicator in personality factor space. *Personality & Individual Differences, 21,* 591–597.

Sahoo, F. M., Sahoo, K., & Harichandan, S. (2005). Five big factors of personality and human happiness. *Social Sciences. International, 21*(1), 20–28.

Sahraie, A., Hibbard, P. B., Trevethan, C. T., Ritchie, K. L., & Weiskrantz, L. (2010). Consciousness of the first order in blindsight. *PNAS Proceedings of the National Academy of Sciences of the United States of America, 107*(49), 21217–21222. doi: 10.1073/pnas.1015652107

Sakurai, T., Cai, G., Grice, D. E., & Buxbaum, J. D. (2011). Genomic architecture of autism spectrum disorders. In E. Hollander, A. Kolevzon & J. T. Coyle (Eds.), *Textbook of autism spectrum disorders* (pp. 281–298). Arlington, VA: American Psychiatric Publishing, Inc.

Sales, E., Baum, M., & Shore, B. (1984). Victim readjustment following assault. *Journal of Social Issues, 40*(1), 117–136.

Salkovskis, P. M. (1999). Understanding and treating obsessive-compulsive disorder. *Behavioral Research and Therapy, 37*(Suppl. 1), S29–S52.

Salkovskis, P. M. (1985). Obsessional-compulsive problems: A cognitive-behavioural analysis. *Behavioral Research and Therapy, 23,* 571–584.

Salkovskis, P. M., Thorpe, S. J., Wahl, K., Wroe, A. L., & Forrester, E. (2003). Neutralizing increases discomfort associated with obsessional thoughts: An experimental study with obsessional patients. *Journal of Abnormal Psychology, 112*(4), 709–715.

Samelson, F. (1980). J. B. Watson's Little Albert, Cyril Burt's twins, and the need for a critical science. *American Psychologist, 35,* 619–625.

SAMHSA (Substance Abuse and Mental Health Services Administration). (2010). Mental health and mental disorders. In NIMH (National Institute of Mental Health), *Healthy people 2010.* Washington, DC: Department of Health and Human Services.

SAMHSA. (Substance Abuse and Mental Health Services Administration) (2008, June 16). *National survey on drug use and health.* Washington, DC: Department of Health and Human Services.

SAMHSA (Substance Abuse and Mental Health Services Administration). (2002). *National Survey on Drug Use and Health, 2002.* Washington, DC: Author.

Sanberg, C. D., Jones, F. L., Do, V. H., Dieguez Jr., D., & Derrick, B. E. (2006). 5-HTla receptor antagonists block perforant path-dentate LTP induced in novel, but not familiar, environments. *Learning & Memory, 13*(1), 52–62.

Sanderson, C. A. (2010). *Social psychology.* Hoboken, NJ: John Wiley & Sons.

Sanford, A. J., Fay, N., Stewart, A., & Moxey, L. (2002). Perspective in statements of quantity, with implications for consumer psychology. *Psychological Science, 13,* 130–134.

Sankupellay, M., Wilson, S., Heussler, H. S., Parsley, C., Yuill, M., & Dakin, C. (2011). Characteristics of sleep EEG power spectra in healthy infants in the first two years of life. *Clinical Neurophysiology, 122*(2), 236–243.

Santerre, C., & Allen, J. J. B. (2007). Methods for studying the psychophysiology of emotion. In J. Rottenberg & S. L. Johnson (Eds.), *Emotion and psychopathology: Bridging affective and clinical science.* Washington, DC: American Psychological Association.

Santostefano, S. (2010). Developmental psychopathology—Self, embodiment, meaning: A holistic-systems perspective. In W. F. Overton & R. M. Lerner (Eds.), *The handbook of life-span development,vol. 1: Cognition, biology, and methods* (pp. 792–836). Hoboken, NJ: John Wiley & Sons.

Sapir, E. 1921. *Language.* New York: Harcourt, Brace & Co.

Sarbin, T. R., & Allen, V. L. (1968). Role theory. In G. Lindzey & E. Aronson (Eds.), *Handbook of social psychology* (2nd Ed., Vol. 1. pp.488–567). Reading, MA: Addison–Wesley.

Sareen, J., Afifi, T. O., McMillan, K. A., & Asmundson, G. J. G. (2011). Relationship between household income and mental disorders: Findings from a population-based longitudinal study. *Archives of General Psychiatry, 68*(4), 419–426.

Sassi, R. B. (2011). Got a raise? Thank your kindergarten teacher. *Journal of the American Academy of Child & Adolescent Psychiatry, 50*(1), 2.

Saucier, D. M., & Elias, L. J. (2001). Lateral and sex differences in manual gesture during conversation. *Laterality, 6,* 239–245.

Saucier, G., Hampson, S. E., & Goldberg, L. R. (2000). Cross-language studies of lexical personality factors. In S. E. Hampson (Ed.), *Advances in personality psychology, Vol. 1* (pp. 1–36). Hove, England: Psychology Press.

Saxvig, I. W., Lundervold, A. J., Gronli, J., Ursin, R., Bjorvatn, B., & Portas, C. M. (2007). The effect of a REM sleep deprivation procedure on different aspects of memory function in humans. *Psychophysiology, 45*(2), 309–317.

Scarr, S. (1991). Theoretical issues in investigating intellectual plasticity. In S. E. Brauth, W. S. Hall, & R. Dooling (Eds.), *Plasticity of development.* Cambridge, MA: MIT Press.

Schacter, D. L. (2001). The seven sins of memory: How the mind forgets and remembers. NY: Houghton.

Schachter, S., & Singer, J. (1962). Cognitive, social, and physiological determinants of emotional state. *Psychological Review, 69,* 379–399.

Schalock, R. L, Borthwick, S. A., Bradley, V. J., Buntinx, W. H. E., Coulter, D. L., Craig, E. M., Gomez, S. C., et al. (2010). *Intellectual disability: definition, classification, and systems of supports (11th Ed)*. Washington, D.C.: American Association on Intellectual and Developmental Disabilities.

Schienle, A., Ebner, F., & Schafer, A. (2011). Localized gray matter volume abnormalities in generalized anxiety disorder. *European Archives of Psychiatry and Clinical Neuroscience, 261*(4), 303–307.

Schienle, A., Schäfer, A., & Vaitl, D. (2008). Individual differences in disgust imagery: a functional magnetic resonance imaging study. *Neuroreport, 19*, 527–530.

Schiffman, H. R. (1996). *Sensation and perception* (4th Ed.). New York, NY: John Wiley & Sons, Inc.

Schildkraut, J. J. (1965). The catecholamine hypothesis of affective disorders: A review of supporting evidence. *American Journal of Psychiatry, 122*(5), 509–522.

Schiller, D., Levy, I., Niv, Y., LeDoux, J. E., & Phelps, E. A. (2008). From fear to safety and back: Reversal of fear in the human brain. *The Journal of Neuroscience 28*(45), 11517–11525.

Schlenger, W. E., Caddell, J. M., Ebert, L., Jordan, B. K., Rourke, K. M., Wilson, D., et al. (2002). Psychological reactions to terrorist attacks. *Journal of the American Medical Association, 288*(5), 581–588.

Schmidt, G. L., DeBuse, C. J., & Seger, C. A. (2007) Right hemisphere metaphor processing? Characterizing the lateralization of semantic processes. *Brain and Language, 100*(2), 127–141.

Schmidt, M. V., Sterlemann, V., & Müller, M. B. (2009). Chronic stress and individual vulnerability. *Stress, neurotransmitters, and hormones: Neuroendocrine and genetic mechanisms* (pp. 174–183). New York, NY: New York Academy of Sciences, Wiley-Blackwell.

Schmitt, D. P., Allik, J., Mccrae, R. R., & Benet-Martínez, V. (2007). The geographic distribution of big five personality traits: Patterns and profiles of human self-description across 56 nations. *Journal of Cross-Cultural Psychology, 38*(2), 173–212.

Schmitt, F. F., & Lahroodi, R. (2008). The epistemic value of curiosity. *Educational Theory, 58*(2), 125–149.

Schmukler, M. A. (1995). Self-knowledge of body position: Integration of perceptual and action system information. In P. Rochat (Ed.), *The Self in Infancy: Theory and Research*. Elsevier.

Schnabel, J. (2010). Secrets of the shaking palsy. *Nature*, S2–S5. doi:10.1038/466S2b

Schneider, K. J., & Krug, O. T. (2010). *Existential–humanistic therapy*. Washington, DC: American Psychological Association.

Schneider, T. A., Butryn, T. M., Furst, D. M., & Masucd, M. A. (2007). A qualitative examination of risk among elite adventure racers. *Journal of Sport Behavior, 408*, 330–337.

Schon, J. (2003). Dreams and dreaming: Perspectives over the century. *Psychoanalytic Psychotherapy in South Africa, 11*(2), 1–23.

Schooler, C. (2001). The intellectual effects of the demands of the work environment. In R. J. Sternberg & E. L. Grigorenko (Eds.), *Environmental effects on cognitive abilities* (pp. 363–380). Mahwah, NJ: Lawrence Erlbaum Associates Publishers.

Schredl, M., Blomeyer, D., & Gorlinger, M. (2000). Nightmares in children: influencing factors. *Somnologie, 4*, 145–149.

Schuel, H., Burkman, L. J., Lippes, J., Crickard, K., Mahony, M. C., Guiffrida, A., et al. (2002). Evidence that anandamide-signalling regulates human sperm functions required for fertilization. *Molecular Reproduction and Development, 63*, 376–387.

Schuller, R. A., & Ogloff, J. R. P. (2001). *Introduction to psychology and law: Canadian perspectives*. Toronto: University of Toronto Press.

Schulz, K. (2004, August 22). Did antidepressants depress Japan? *New York Times*.

Schultz, L. T., Heimberg, R. G., & Rodebaugh, T. L. (2008). Social anxiety disorder. In M. Hersen & J. Rosqvist (Eds.), *Handbook of psychological assessment, case conceptualization, and treatment,* Vol. 1: *Adults* (pp. 204–236). Hoboken, NJ: John Wiley & Sons.

Schultz, L. T., Heimberg, R. G., Rodebaugh, T. L., Schneier, F. R., Liebowitz, M. R., & Telch, M. J. (2006). The appraisal of social concerns scale: Psychometric validation with a clinical sample of patients with social anxiety disorder. *Behavior Therapy, 37*(4), 393–405.

Schultz, W., Dayan, P., & Montague, P. R. (1997). A neural substrate of prediction and reward. *Science, 275*, 1593–1599.

Schulze, T. G., & McMahon, F. J. (2009). The genetic basis of bipolar disorder. In C. A. Zarate Jr. & H. K. Manji (Eds.), *Bipolar depression: Molecular neurobiology, clinical diagnosis and pharmacotherapy* (pp. 59–76). Cambridge, MA: Birkhauser.

Schwanenflugel, P. J., Akin, C., & Luh, W. (1992). Context availability and the recall of abstract and concrete words. *Memory & Cognition, 20*(1), 96–104.

Schwarting, R. K. W. (2003). The principle of memory consolidation and its pharmacological modulation. In R. H. Kluwe, G. Lüer, & F. Rösler (Eds.), *Principles of learning and memory* (pp. 137–153). Cambridge, MA: Birkhäuser.

Schwartz, B., Ward, A., Monterosso, J., Lyubomirsky, S., White, K., & Lehman, D. R. (2002). Maximizing versus sacrificing: Happiness is a matter of choice. *Journal of Personality and Social Psychology, 83*, 1178–1197.

Schwartz, C. E., Snidman, N., & Kagan, J. (1999). Adolescent social anxiety as an outcome of inhibited temperament in childhood. *Journal of the American Academy of Child and Adolescent Psychiatry, 38*, 1008–1015.

Schwartz, M. F., Saffran, E. M., & Marin, O. S. M. (1980). The problem of word order in agrammatism: Comprehension. *Brain and Language, 10*(2), 249–262.

Sclafani, A., & Springer, D. (1976). Dietary obesity in adult rats: Similarities to hypothalamic and human obesity syndromes. *Physiology and Behavior, 17*, 461–471.

Scott, C. L. (2010). *Handbook of correctional mental health*. Arlington, Virginia: American Psychiatric Publishing.

Scott, W. B., & Milner, B. (1957). Loss of recent memory after bilateral hippocampal lesions. *Journal of Neurological Neurosurgery Psychiatry, 20*(1), 11–21.

Sealy, P., & Whitehead, P. C. (2004). Forty years of deinstitutionalization of psychiatric services in Canada: an empirical assessment. *The Canadian Journal of Psychiatry*. Retrieved from http://ww1.cpa-apc.org:8080/publications/archives/cjp/2004/april/sealy.asp.

Seeck, M., Mainwaring, N., Ives, J., Blume, H., Dubuisson, D., Cosgrove, R., Mesulam, M. M., & Schomer, D. L. (1993). Differential neural activity in the human temporal lobe evoked by faces of family members and friends. *Annals of Neurology, 34*, 369–372.

Segal, N. L. (2010). Twins: The finest natural experiement. *Personality and Individual Differences, 49*(4), 317–323.

Seligman, M. E. P. (2007). Coaching and positive psychology. *Australian Psychologist, 42*(4), 266–267.

Seligman, M. E. P. (1992). Power and powerlessness: Comments on "cognates of personal control." *Applied & Preventive Psychology, 1*(2), 119–120.

Seligman, M. E. P. (1975). *Helplessness: On depression, development, and death*. San Francisco: W.H. Freeman.

Seligman, M. E. P., & Steen, T. A. (2005). Positive psychology progress: Empirical validation of interventions. *American Psychologist, 60*(5), 410–421.

Seligman, M. E. P., Weiss, J., Weinraub, M., & Schulman, A. (1980). Coping behavior: learned helplessness, physiological change and learned inactivity. *Behavioral Research Therapy, 18*, 459–512.

Seligman, M. E. P., & Csikszentmihalyi, M. (2000). Positive psychology. *American Psychologist, 55*, 5–14.

Seligman, M. E. P., Rashid, T., & Parks, A. (2006). Positive psychotherapy. *American Psychology, 61*, 774–788.

Seligman, M. E. P., & Maier, S. F. (1967). Failure to escape traumatic shock. *Journal of Experimental Psychology, 74*, 1–9.

Selkoe, D. J. (2002). Alzheimer's disease is a synaptic failure. *Science, 298*(5594), 789–791.

Selkoe, D. J. (2000). The origins of Alzheimer's disease: A is for amyloid. *Journal of the American Medical Association, 283*(12), 1615–1617.

Selkoe, D. J. (1991). Amyloid protein and Alzheimer's disease. *Scientific American, 265*, 68–78.

Selye, H. (1993). History of the stress concept. *Handbook of stress: Theoretical and clinical aspects (2nd Ed.)* (pp. 7–17). New York, NY: Free Press.

Selye, H. (1956). Stress and psychobiology. *Journal of Clinical & Experimental Psychopathology, 17*, 370–375.

Selye, H. (1956). *The stress of life*. New York, NY: McGraw-Hill.

Selye, H. (1936). A syndrome produced by diverse nocuous agents. *Nature, 138*, 32.

Semendeferi, K., Lu, A., Schenker, N., & Damasio, H. (2002). Humans and great apes share a large frontal cortex. *Nature Neuroscience, 5*(3), 272–276.

Sénéchal, M., & LeFevre, J. (2002). Parental involvement in the development of children's reading skill: A 5-year longitudinal study. *Child Development, 73,* 445–460.

Sénéchal, M., & LeFevre, J. (2001). Storybook reading and parent teaching: Links to language and literacy development. In P. R. Britto & J. Brooks-Gunn (Eds.), *The role of family literacy environments in promoting young children's emerging literacy skills: New directions for child and adolescent development* (pp. 39–52). San Francisco, CA: Jossey-Bass.

Senechal, S. (2009). *Dogs Can Sign, Too. A breakthrough method of teaching your dog to communicate to you.* Random House/Crown/TenSpeed Press.

Senior, J. (2006). Some dark thoughts on happiness [Electronic version]. *New York Magazine,* 17 July.

Seta, J. J., Seta, C. E., & McElroy, T. (2002). Strategies for reducing the stress of negative life experiences: An average/summation analysis. *Personality and Social Psychology Bulletin, 28,* 1574–1585.

Sewards, T. V., & Sewards, M. A. (2000). The awareness of thirst: proposed neural correlates. *Conscious Cognition, 9*(4), 463–487.

Seyfarth, R. M., & Cheney, D. L. (2003). Meaning and emotion in animal vocalizations. In P. Ekman, J. J. Campos, J. J. Davidson, R. J. de Waal, & B. M. Frans (Eds.), *Emotions inside out: 130 years after Darwin's: The expression of the emotions in man and animals* (pp. 32–55). New York, NY: New York University Press.

Sgoifo, A., Braglia, F., Costoli, T., Musso, E., Meerlo, P., Ceresini, G., & Troisi, A. (2003). Cardiac autonomic reactivity and salivary cortisol in men and women exposed to social stressors: Relationship with individual ethological profile. *Neuroscience and Biobehavioral Reviews, 27*(1–2), 179–188.

Shackelford, T. K., & Larsen, R. J. (1997). Facial asymmetry as an indicator of psychological, emotional and physiological distress. *Journal of Personality and Social Psychology, 72,* 456–466.

Shadish, W. R., & Baldwin, S. A. (2005). Effects of behavioral marital therapy: A meta-analysis of randomized controlled trials. *Journal of Consulting and Clinical Psychology, 73*(1), 6–14.

Shaffer, D. R., Rogel, M., & Hendrick, C. (1975). Intervention in the library: The effect of increased responsibility on bystanders' willingness to prevent a theft. *Journal of Applied Social Psychology, 5*(4), 303–319.

Shafir, E., & Tversky, A. (2002). Decision making. *Foundations of cognitive psychology: Core readings* (pp. 601–620). Cambridge, MA: MIT Press.

Shafran, R. (2005). Cognitive-behavioral models of OCD. In J. S. Abramowitz & A. C. Houts (Eds.), *Concepts and controversies in obsessive-compulsive disorder.* New York: Springer Science + Business Media.

Shah, D. B., Pesiridou, A., Baltuch, G. H., Malone, D. A., & O'Reardon, J. P. (2008). Functional neurosurgery in the treatment of severe obsessive compulsive disorder and major depression: Overview of disease circuits and therapeutic targeting for the clinician. *Psychiatry, 5*(9), 24–33.

Shah, N. (2007). *Obstructive sleep apnea is associated with an increased risk of coronary artery disease and death.* Presented at the International Conference of the American Thoracic Society, San Fransisco.

Shamay-Tsoory, S., Tomer, R., Berger, B. D., Goldsher, D., & Aharon-Peretz, J. (2005). Impaired "affective theory of mind" is associated with right ventromedial prefrontal damage. *Cognitive and Behavioral Neurology, 18*(1), 55–67.

Sharf, R. S. (2012). *Theories of psychotherapy & counseling: Concepts and cases* (5th Ed.). Pacific Grove, CA: Brooks/Cole.

Sharf, R. S. (2008). *Theories of psychotherapy and counseling: Concepts and cases* (4th Ed.). Belmont, NY: Thomson Brooks Cole.

Shargorodsky, J., Curhan, S. G., Curhan, G. C., & Eavey, R. (2010). Change in prevalence of hearing loss in US adolescents. *Journal of the American Medical Association, 304*(7), 772–778.

Shariff, S. (2005). Cyber-dilemmas in the new millennium: School obligations to provide student sfety in a virtual school environment. *McGill Journal of Education, 40,* 467–487.

Sharma, A., Nash, A. A., & Dorman, M. (2009). Cortical development, plasticity and re-organization in children with cochlear implants. *Journal of Communication Disorders, 42,* 272–279.

Shaw, P., Eckstrand, K., Sharp, W., Blumenthal, J., Lerch, J. P., Greenstein, D., Clasen, L., Evans, A., Giedd, J., & Rapoport, J. L. (2007). Attention-deficit/hyperactivity disorder is characterized by a delay in cortical maturation. *Proceedings of the National Academy of Sciences USA, 104,* 19649–19654.

Shaw, P., Greenstein, D., Lerch, J., Clasen, L., Lenroot, R., Gogtay, N., Evans, A., Rapoport, J., Giedd, J. (2006, March 30). Intellectual ability and cortical development in children and adolescents. *Nature, 440*(7084), 619–620.

Shaw, P., Kabani, N. J., Lerch. J. P., Eckstrand, K., Lenroot, R., Gogtay, N., Greenstein D., Clasen, L., Evans, A., Rapoport, J. L., Giedd, J. N., & Wise, S. P. (2008). Neurodevelopmental trajectories of the human cerebral cortex. *Journal of Neuroscience, 28*(14), 3586–3594.

Shayer, M., & Adhami, M. (2010). Realizing the cognitive potential of children 5–7 with a mathematics focus: Post-test and long-term effects of a 2-year intervention. *British Journal of Educational Psychology, 80*(3), 363–379.

Sheikh, A. A., Ramaswami, S., & Sheikh, K. S. (Eds.). (2007). *Healing with death imagery. Imagery and Human Development Series.* Amityville, NY: Baywood Publishing Co.

Sheldon, K. M., Ryan, R. M., Deci, E. L., & Kasser, T. (2004). The independent effects of goal contents and motives on well-being: it's both what you pursue and why you pursue it. *Personality and Social Psychology Bulletin, 30*(4), 475–486.

Sheldon, S. A. M., & Moscovitch, M. (2010). Recollective performance advantages for implicit memory tasks. *Memory, 18*(7), 681–697.

Shepard, T. H., & Lemire, R. J. (2004). *Catalog of teratogenic agents (11th edition).* Baltimore, Maryland: Johns Hopkins University Press.

Shepperd, J. A. (1995). Remedying motivation and productivity loss in collective settings. *Current Directions in Psychological Science, 4,* 131–134.

Shepperd, J. A. (1993). Productivity loss in performance groups: A motivation analysis. *Psychological Bulletin, 113,* 67–81.

Sheppird, S. F. (2009). *100 Questions & answers about anorexia nervosa.* Burlington, MA: Jones & Bartlett Learning.

Sher, L. (2003). Daily hassles, cortisol, and depression. *Australian and New Zealand Journal of Psychiatry, 37*(3), 383–384.

Sherman, J. W., Stroessner, S. J., Conrey, F. R., & Azam, O. A. (2005). Prejudice and stereotype maintenance processes: Attention, attribution, and individuation. *Journal of Personality and Social Psychology, 89*(4), 607–622.

Sherry, A., & Whilde, M. R. (2008). Borderline personality disorder. In M. Hersen & J. Rosqvist (Eds.), *Handbook of Psychological Assessment, Case Conceptualization, and Treatment, Vol 1: Adults* (pp. 403–437). Hoboken, NJ: John Wiley & Sons Inc.

Sherry, D. F., & Schacter, D. L. (1987). The evolution of multiple memory systems. *Psychological Review, 94*(4), 439–454.

Sherwood, A. (1993). Use of impedance cardiography in cardiovascular reactivity research. *Cardiovascular reactivity to psychological stress & disease* (pp. 157–199). Washington, DC: American Psychological Association.

Shin, L. M., Orr, S. P., Carson, M. A., Rauch, S. L., Macklin, M. L., Lasko, N. B., Peters, P. M., Metzger, L. J., Dougherty, D. D., Cannistraro, P. A., Alpert, N. M., Fishman, A. J., Pitman, R. K. (2004). Regional cerebral blood flow in the amygdala and medial prefrontal cortex during traumatic imagery in male and female Vietnam veterans with PTSD. *Archives of General Psychiatry, 61,* 168–176.

Shmuelof, L., & Zohary, E. (2007). Watching others' actions: Mirror representations in the parietal cortex. *The Neuroscientist, 13,* 667–672.

Shoda, Y., & Lee Tiernan, S. (2002). What remains invariant?: Finding order within a person's thoughts, feelings, and behaviors across situations. In D. Cervone & W Mischel, *Advances in Personality Science, 1,* 241–270.

Shors, T. J. (2009). Saving new brain cells. *Scientific American, 300*(3), 46–52, 54.

Shubin, N. (2008). *Your inner fish: a journey into the 3.5-billion-year history of the human body.* Random House Books: Toronto.

Shultz, D. P., & Schultz, S. E. (2008). *A history of modern psychology 9th edition.* Cengage Learning.

Shultz, D. P., & Schultz, S. E. (1987). *A history of modern psychology 4th edition.* Harcourt Brace Jovanovich.

Sidhu, M., Malhi, P., & Jerath, J. (2010). Intelligence of children from economically disadvantaged families: Role of parental education. *Psychological Studies, 55*(4), 358–364.

SIECCAN. (2009). Sexual health education in the schools: Questions and answers (3rd edition) *The Canadian Journal of Human Sexuality, 18*(1–2), 47–60.

Siegel, B., & Ficcaglia, M. (2006). Pervasive developmental disorders. In M. Hersen & J. C. Thomas (Series Eds.) & R. T. Ammerman (Vol. Ed.), *Comprehensive handbook of personality and psychopathology, Vol. 3: Child psychopathology*. Hoboken, NJ: Wiley.

Siegel, G., Albers, R. W., Brady, S., & Price, D. (2006) *Basic neurochemistry 7th Ed*. Elsevier.

Siegel, J. (2009). Sleep viewed as a state of adaptive inactivity. *Nature Reviews Neuroscience, 10*, 747–753.

Siegel, J. M. (2005). Clues to the functions of mammalian sleep. *Nature, 437*, 1264–1271.

Siegel, L. S. (1992). An evaluation of the discrepancy definition of dyslexia. *Journal of Learning Disabilities, 25*, 618–629.

Siegel, S. (2005). Drug tolerance, drug addiction, and drug anticipation. *Current Directions in Psychological Science, 14*(6), 296–300.

Sigel, E. (2008). Eating disorders. *Adolescent Medicine: State of the Art Reviews, 19*(3), 547–72, xi.

Sikstrom, S., & Soderlund, G. (2007). Stimulus-dependent dopamine release in attention-deficit/hyperactivity disorder. *Psychological Review, 114*(4), 1047–1075.

Silvera, D. H., & Laufer, D. (2005). Recent developments in attribution research and their implications for consumer judgments and behavior. In F. R. Kardes, P. M. Herr, & J. Nantel (Eds.), *Applying social cognition to consumer-focused strategy* (pp. 53–77). Mahwah, NJ: Lawrence Erlbaum Associates Publishers.

Silverman, K., Evans, S. M., Strain, E. C., & Griffiths, R. R. (1992). Withdrawal syndrome after the double-blind cessation of caffeine consumption. *New England Journal of Medicine, 327*(16), 1109–1114.

Silverman, M. S., McCarthy, M., McGovern, T. (1992). A review of outcome studies of rational-emotive therapy from 1982–1989. *Journal of Rational-Emotive & Cognitive Behavior Therapy, 10*(3), 111–186.

Simeon, D. et al, (2000), Feeling unreal: A PET study of depersonalization disorder. *American Journal of Psychiatry, 157*, 1782–1788.

Simon, H. A. (1990). Invariants of human behavior. *Annual Review of Psychology, 41*, 1–20.

Simon, H. A. (1957). *Models of man*. New York: John Wiley & Sons, Inc.

Simon, J., Braunstein, G., Nachtigall, L., Utian, W., Katz, M., Miller, S., et al. (2005). Testosterone patch increases sexual activity and desire in surgically menopausal women with hypoactive sexual desire disorder. *The Journal of Clinical Endocrinology and Metabolism, 90*(9), 5226–5233.

Simonton, D. K. (2010). Research notes: The curious case of Catharine Cox (Miles): The 1926 dissertation and her Miles-Wolfe (1936) follow-up. *History of Psychology, 13*(2), 205–206.

Simpson, P. A., & Stroh, L. K. (2004). Gender differences: Emotional expression and feelings of personal inauthenticity. *Journal of Applied Psychology, 89*, 715–721.

Singer, J. L. (2003). Daydreaming, consciousness, and self-representations: Empirical approaches to theories of William James and Sigmund Freud. *Journal of Applied Psychoanalytic Studies, 5*,461–483.

Singer, T., & Kimbles, S. L. (2004). *The cultural complex: Contemporary Jungian perspectives on psyche and society*. New York, NY: Brunner-Routledge.

Singh, D. (1995). Female judgement of male attractiveness and desirability for relationships: Role of waist-to-hip ratio and financial status. *Journal of Personality and Social Psychology, 69*, 1089–1101.

Singh, D. (1994). Ideal female body shape: Role of body weight and waist-to-hip ratio. *International Journal of Eating Disorders, 16*, 283–288.

Sizemore, C. C. (1991). A mind of my own: The woman who was known as "Eve" tells the story of her triumph over multiple personality disorder. New York, NY: William Morrow.

Skaret, E. Raadal, M., Kvale, G., & Berg, E. (2000) Factors relating to missed and cancelled dental appointments among adolescents in Norway. *European Journal of Oral Sciences, 108*(3), 175–183.

Skinner, B. F. (1958). Diagramming schedules of reinforcement. *Journal of the Experimental Analysis of Behavior, 1*, 67–68.

Skinner, B. F. (1957). *Verbal behavior*. New York, NY: Appleton-Century-Crofts.

Skinner, B. F., & Morse, W. H. (1958). Fixed-interval reinforcement of running in a wheel. *Journal of the Experimental Analysis of Behavior, 1*, 371–379.

Skodol A. E., Williams, J. B., Spitzer, R. L., Gibbon, M., & Kass, F. (1984). Identifying common errors in the use of DSM-III through diagnostic supervision. *Hospital and Community Psychiatry, 35*(3), 251–255.

Slater, A., & Morrison, V. (1991). Visual attention and memory at birth. In M. J. S. Weiss & P. R. Zelazo (Eds.), *Newborn attention: Biological constraints and the influence of experience*. Norwood, NJ: Ablex.

Sloan, D. M. (2004). Emotion regulation in action: Emotional reactivity in experiential avoidance. *Behaviour Research and Therapy, 42*, 1257–1270.

Sloan, D. M., Bradley, M. M., Dimoulas, E., & Lang, P. J. (2002). Looking at facial expressions: Dysphoria and facial EMG. *Biological Psychology, 60*(2–3), 79–90.

Slobin, D. (1986). *The cross-linguistic study of language acquisition*. Mahwah, NJ: Earlbaum.

Slovic, P. (1990). Choice. In D. N. Osherson & E. E. Smith (Eds.), *An invitation to cognitive science: Vol. 3: Thinking*. Cambridge, MA: MIT Press.

Smart, R. G., Stoduto, G., Adlaf, E. M., Mann, R. E., & Sharpley, J. M. (2007). Road rage victimization among adolescents. *Journal of Adolescent Health, 41*(3), 277–282.

Smith, A. B., Taylor, E., Brammer, M., Halari, R., & Rubia, K. (2008). Reduced activation in right lateral prefrontal cortex and anterior cingulate gyrus in medication-naïve adolescents with attention deficit hyperactivity disorder during time discrimination. *Journal of Child Psychology and Psychiatry, and Allied Disciplines, 49*, 977–985.

Smith, C. (2006). Symposium V—Sleep and learning: New Developments. *Brain and Cognition. 60*(3), 331–332.

Smith, C. (1996). Sleep states, memory processes and synaptic plasticity. *Behavioural Brain Research, 78*(1), 49–56.

Smith, D. (2004). Love that dare not squeak its name. *The New York Times*. Retrieved from http://www.nytimes.com/2004/02/07/arts/07GAY.html.

Smith, J. C., Nielson, K. A., Woodard, J. L., Seidenberg, M., Durgerian, S., Antuono, P., . . . Rao, S. M. (2011). Interactive effects of physical activity and APOE-ε4 on semantic memory activation in healthy elders. *NeuroImage, 54*(1), 635–644. doi: 10.1016/j.neuroimage.2010.07.070

Smith, L. B. (2010). More than concepts: How multiple integrations make human intelligence. In D. Mareschal, P. C. Quinn, & S. E. G. Lea (Eds.), *The making of human concepts* (pp. 335–363). New York: Oxford University Press.

Smith, L. D., Peck, P. L., & McGovern, R. J. (2004). Factors contributing to the utilization of mental health services in a rural setting. *Psychological Reports, 95*(2), 435–442.

Smith, M. L., & Glass, G. V. (1977). Meta-analysis of psychotherapy outcome studies. *American Psychologist, 32*(9), 752–760.

Smith, M. L., Glass, G. V., & Miller, T. I. (1980). *The benefits of psychotherapy*. Baltimore, MD: Johns Hopkins University Press.

Smith, R. A., & Weber, A. L. (2005). Applying social psychology in everyday life. In F. W. Schneider, J. A. Gruman, & L. M. Coutts (Eds.), *Applied Social Psychology: Understanding and Addressing Social and Practical Problems* (pp. 75–99). Sage Publications.

Smith, S. M. (1984). A comparison of two techniques for reducing context-dependent forgetting. *Memory & Cognition, 12*(5), 477–482.

Smith, T. W., & Gallo, L. C. (2001). Personality traits as risk factors for physical illness. In A. Baum, T. A. Revenson, & J. E. Singer (Eds.), *Handbook of health psychology* (pp. 139–173). Mahwah, NJ: Erlbaum.

Smyth, J. M., & Pennebaker, J. W. (2001). What are the health effects of disclosure? In A. Baum, T. A. Revenson, & J. E. Singer (Eds.), *Handbook of health psychology* (pp. 339–348). Mahwah, NJ: Erlbaum.

Snarey, J. R. (1985). Cross-cultural universality of social-moral development: A critical review of Kohlbergian research. *Psychological Bulletin, 97*, 202–232.

Snyder, W. V. (1947). *Casebook of non-directive counseling*. Boston, MA: Houghton Mifflin.

So, J. K. (2008). Somatization as cultural idiom of distress: Rethinking mind and body in a multicultural society. *Counselling Psychology Quarterly, 21*(2), 167–174.

Sokal, M. M. (2010). Scientific biography, cognitive deficits, and laboratory practice. James McKeen Cattell and early American experimental psychology, 1880–1904. *Isis, 101*(3), 531–554.

Solanto, M. V., & Arnsten, A. F. T. (2001). *Stimulant drugs and ADHD: Basic and clinical neuroscience*. New York, NY: Oxford University Press.

Solms, M. (2007). Freud returns. In F. E. Bloom (Ed.), *Best of the Brain* from *Scientific American* (pp. 35–46). Washington, D.C.: Dana Press.

Solms, M. (2007). The interpretation of dreams and the neurosciences. In L. Mayes, P. Fonagy, & M. Target (Eds.), *Developmental science and psychoanalysis: Integration and innovation. Developments in psychoanalysis*. London, England: Karnac Books.

Somers, J. M., Goldner, E. M., Waraich, P., & Hsu, L. (2004). Prevalence studies of substance-related disorders: A systematic review of the literature. *Canadian Journal of Psychiatry, 49*(6).

Soorya, L. V., Carpenter, L. A., & Romanczyk, R. G. (2011). Applied behavior analysis. In E. Hollander, A. Kolevzon, & J. T. Coyle (Eds.), *Textbook of autism spectrum disorders* (pp. 525–535). Arlington, VA: American Psychiatric Publishing.

SoRelle, R. (2000). Nearly half of Americans with severe mental illness do not seek treatment. *Circulation Electronic Pages, 101,* e66. Retrieved from http://circ.ahajournals.org/content/101/5/e66.full

Sørensen, T. I., Holst, C., Stunkard, A. J., & Skovgaard, L. T. (1992). Correlations of body mass index of adult adoptees and their biological and adoptive relatives. *International Journal of Obesity and Related Metabolic Disorders: Journal of the International Association for the Study of Obesity, 16*(3), 227–236.

Soto, D., Hodsoll, J., Rotshtein, P., & Humphreys, G. W. (2008). Automatic guidance of attention from working memory. *Trends in Cognitive Sciences, 12,* 342–348.

Soussignan, R. (2002). Duchenne smile, emotional experience, and autonomic reactivity: A test of the facial-feedback hypothesis. *Emotion, 2,* 52–74.

Spain, J., Eaton, L., & Funder, D. (2000). Perspectives on personality: The relative accuracy of self versus others in the prediction of emotion and *behavior. Journal of Personality, 68,* 837–867.

Spanos, N. P., Mondoux, T. J., & Burgess, C. A. (1995). Comparison of multi-component hypnotic and non-hypnotic treatments for smoking. *Contemporary Hypnosis, 12*(1), 12–19.

Spencer, R. M. C., Zelaznik, H. N., Diedrichsen, J., & Ivry, R. B. (2003). Disrupted timing of discontinuous movements by cerebellar lesions. *Science, 300,* 1437–1439.

Sperling, G. (1960). The information available in brief visual presentation. *Psychological Monographs, 74*(11), 29.

Sperry, R. W. (1998). A powerful paradigm made stronger. *Neuropsychologia, 36*(10), 1063–1068.

Sperry, R. W. (1982). Some effects of disconnecting the cerebral hemispheres. *Science, 217*(4566), 1223–1226.

Sperry, R. W., Gazzaniga M. S., & Bogen, J. E. (1969). Interhemispheric relationships:the neocortical commissures; syndromes of hemisphere disconnection. In P. J. Vinken, G. W. Bruyn (editors), *Handbook of clinical neurology* (pp. 273–290). Amsterdam: North Holland.

Spiegel, H., & Spiegel, D. (2004). *Trace and treatment: clinical uses of hypnosis.* Arlington, VA: American Psychiatgric Publishing.

Spiegler, M. D., & Guevremont, D. C. (2003). *Contemporary behavior therapy*. Belmont, CA: Thomson/Wadsworth.

Spielberger, C. D. (1985). Anxiety, cognition, and affect: A state-trait perspective. In A. H. Tuma & J. Maser (Eds.), *Anxiety and the anxiety disorders*. Hillsdale, NJ: Lawrence Erlbaum.

Spielberger, C. D. (1972). Anxiety as an emotional state. In C. D. Spielberger (Ed.), *Anxiety: Current trends in theory and research* (Vol. 1). New York, NY: Academic Press.

Spielberger, C. D. (1966). Theory and research on anxiety. In C. D. Spielberger (Ed.), *Anxiety and behavior*. New York, NY: Academic Press.

Spitzer, R. L., Skodol, A., Gibbon, M., & Williams, J. B. W. (1983). *Psychopathology: A case book*. New York, NY: McGraw-Hill.

Spitzer, R. L., Skodol, A., Gibbon, M., & Williams, J. B. W. (1981). *DSM-III case book* (1st Ed.). Washington, DC: American Psychiatric Press.

Spokas, M., & Heimberg, R. G. (2009). Overprotective parenting, social anxiety, and external locus of control: Cross-sectional and longitudinal relationships. *Cognitive Therapy and Research, 33*(6), 543–551.

Spooren, W., Lesage, A., Lavreysen, H., Gasparini, F., & Steckler, T. (2010). Metabotropic glutamate receptors: Their therapeutic potential in anxiety. In M. B. Stein., & T. Steckler (Eds.), *Behavioral neurobiology of anxiety and its treatment* (pp. 391–413). New York: Springer Science + Business Media.

Sports City. (2011). *Toronto Maple Leafs player salaries.* Retrieved from http://www.sportscity.com/NHL/Toronto-Maple-Leafs-Salaries

Sprenger, J. (2011). Hypothetico-deductive confirmation. *Philosophy Compass, 6,* 497–508.

Springer, S., & Deutsch, G. (1993). *Left brain, right brain.* New York: Freeman.

Sprinkle, R., Hunt, S., Simonds, C., & Comadena, M. (2006). Fear in the classroom: an examination of teachers' use of fear appeals and students' learning outcomes. *Communication Education, 55*(4), 389–402.

Squire, L. R., & Schacter, D. L. (Eds.) *Neuropsychology of memory (3rd Ed.) (2002)*. New York, NY: Guilford Press.

Squire, L. R., Stark, C. E., & Clark, R. E. (2004). The medial temporal lobe. *Annual Review of Neuroscience, 27,* 279–306.

Squire, P. (1988). Why the 1936 Literary Digest poll failed. *Public Opinion Quarterly, 52*(1), 125–133.

Sriram, T. G., & Silverman, J. J. (1998). The effects of stress on the respiratory system. In J. R. Hubbard & E. A. Workman (Eds.), *Handbook of stress medicine: an organ system approach.* New York, NY: CRC Press.

Sritharan, R., & Gawronski, B. (2010). Changing implicit and explicit prejudice: Insights from the associative-propositional evaluation model. *Social Psychology, 41*(3), 113–123.

Srivastava, A. S., Malhotra, R., Sharp, J., & Berggren, T. (2008). Potentials of ES cell therapy in neurodegenerative diseases. *Current Pharmaceutical Design, 14,* 3873–3879.

Srivastava, S., John, O. P., Gosling, S. D., & Potter, J. (2003). Development of personality in early and middle adulthood: Set like plaster or persistent change? *Journal of Personality and Social Psychology, 84,* 1041–1053.

Stacey, C. P. (1985), *A Very Double Life: The Private World of Mackenzie King,* Amazon.ca: C. P. Stacey: Books.

Stanovich, K. E. (2008). *How to Think Straight about Psychology* (8th Ed.). Boston, MA: Allyn & Bacon.

Stanton, A. L., Parsa, A., & Austenfeld, J. L. (2002). The adaptive potential of coping through emotional approach. *Handbook of positive psychology* (pp. 148–158). New York, NY: Oxford University Press.

Stanton, A. L., Sullivan, S. J., & Austenfeld, J. L. (2009). Coping through emotional approach: Emerging evidence for the utility of processing and expressing emotions in responding to stressors. *Oxford handbook of positive psychology (2nd Ed.)* (pp. 225–235). New York, NY: Oxford University Press.

Statistics Canada. (2011). *Family violence in Canada: A statistical profile*. Statistics Canada, Canadian Centre for Justice Statistics. Retrieved from http://www.statcan.gc.ca/pub/85-224-x/85-224-x2010000-eng.pdf.

Statistics Canada. (2010). *Canadian Internet use survey*. The Daily, Monday, May 10, 2010.

Statistics Canada. (2007). *Family portrait: continuity and change in Canadian families and households in 2006, 2006 census.* Retrieved from http://www.samesexmarriage.ca/docs/FamilyCensus2006.pdf.

Statistics Canada. (2006). *Census of population.* Statistics Canada catalogue no. 97-559-XCB2006012.

Statistics Canada. (2006). *Child care in Canada.* Catalogue no. 89-599-MIE–No. 003. Retrieved from http://www.statcan.gc.ca/pub/89-599-m/89-599-m2006003-eng.pdf .

Statistics Canada. (2005). *General Social Survey, Cycle 18 overview: Personal safety and perceptions of the criminal justice system.* Ottawa: Statistics Canada, Cat. No. 85-566-XIE. Retrieved from http://www4.hrsdc.gc.ca/.3ndic.1t.4r@-eng.jsp?iid=59.

Statistics Canada. (2004). *Health reports supplement: how healthy are Canadians? Annual report. Alcohol and illicit drug dependence.* Retrieved from http://www.statcan.gc.ca/pub/82-003-s/2004000/pdf/7447-eng.pdf.

Stehlin, I. B. (1996). Inside FDA: office of women's health. *FDA Consumer Magazine, 30*(8).

Stein, D. J. (2008). Classifying hypersexual disorders: Compulsive, impulsive, and addictive models. *Psychiatric Clinics of North America, 31*(4), 587–591.

Stein, D. J., & Fineberg, N. A. (2007). *Obsessive-compulsive disorder*. Oxford, England: Oxford University Press.

Stein, D. J., & Williams, D. (2010). Cultural and social aspects of anxiety disorders. In D. J. Stein, E. Hollander, & B. O. Rothbaum (Eds.), *Textbook of anxiety disorders* (2nd Ed., pp. 717–729). Arlington, VA: American Psychiatric Publishing.

Stein, R., Gossen, E., & Jones, K. (2005). Neuronal variability: noise or part of the signal? *Nature Reviews Neuroscience, 6*(5), 389–397.

Steiner, I. D. (1972). *Group process and productivity*. New York: Academic Press.

Steinhausen, H. (2002). The outcome of anorexia nervosa in the 20th century. *American Journal of Psychiatry, 159*, 1284–1293.

Steinhausen, H. C., Blattmann, B., & Pfund, F. (2007). Developmental outcome in children with intrauterine exposure to substances. *European Addiction Research, 13*, 94–100.

Stephens, R., Atkins, J., & Kingston, A. (2009). Swearing as a response to pain. *NeuroReport: For Rapid Communication of Neuroscience Research, 20*(12), 1056–1060.

Stephure, R. J., Boon, S. D., MacKinnon, S. L., & Deveau, V. (2009). Internet initiated relationships: associations between age and involvement in online dating. *Journal of Computer-Mediated Communication, 3*, 658–681.

Steptoe, A. (2000). Health behavior and stress. In G. Fink (Ed.), *Encyclopedia of Stress, Vol. 2* (pp. 322–326). New York: Academic Press.

Stern, R. (1995). *Mastering phobias—cases, causes and cures*. London, UK: Penguin.

Sternberg, R. J. (2010). Teaching for creativity. In R. A. Beghetto & J. C. Kaufman (Eds.), *Nurturing creativity in the classroom* (pp. 394–414). New York: Cambridge University Press.

Sternberg, R. J. (2007). Intelligence and culture. In S. Kitayama & D. Cohen (Eds.), *Handbook of cultural psychology* (pp. 547–568). New York: Guilford Press.

Sternberg, R. J. (2007). Who are the bright children? The cultural context of being and acting intelligent. *Educational Researcher, 36*(3), 148–155.

Sternberg, R. J. (2004). A triangular theory of love. In H. T. Reis & C. E. Rusbult (Eds.), *Close relationships: Key readings* (pp. 213–227). Philadelphia, PA: Taylor & Francis.

Sternberg, R. J. (2003). Biological intelligence. In R. J. Sternberg & E. L. Grigorenko (Eds.), *The psychology of abilities, competencies, and expertise* (pp. 240–262). New York, NY: Cambridge University Press.

Sternberg, R. J. (2003). A broad view of intelligence: The theory of successful intelligence. *Consulting Psychology Journal: Practice and Research, 55*(3), 139–154.

Sternberg, R. J. (2003). WICS: A model of leadership in organizations. *Academy of Management Learning & Education, 2*(4), 386–401.

Sternberg, R. J. (2003). *Wisdom, intelligence, and creativity synthesized*. New York, NY: Cambridge University Press.

Sternberg, R. J. (1987). Liking versus loving: A comparative evaluation of theories. *Psychological Bulletin, 102*, 331–345.

Sternberg, R. J. (1986). A triangular theory of love. *Psychological Review, 93, 119–135.*

Sternberg, R. J., Conway, B. E., Ketron, J. L., & Bernstein, M. (1981). People's conceptions of intelligence. *Journal of Personality and Social Psychology, 41*(1), 37–55.

Sternberg, R. J., & Grigorenko, E. L. (2004). Why cultural psychology is necessary and not just nice: The example of the study of intelligence. In R. J. Sternberg and E. L. Grigorenko (Eds.), *Culture and competence* (pp. 207–223). Washington, DC: American Psychological Association.

Sternberg, R. J., & Grigorenko, E. L. (2001). Unified psychology. *American Psychologist, 56*, 1069–1079.

Sternberg, R. J., Jarvin, L., & Grigorenko, E. L. (2011). *Explorations in giftedness*. New York: Cambridge University Press.

Sternberg, R. J., Wagner, R. K., Williams, W. M., Horvath, J. A., et al. (1995). Testing common sense. *American Psychologist, 50*(11), 912–927.

Sternberg, R. J., & Weis, K. (2006). *The New Psychology of Love*. New Haven, CT: Yale University.

Stetter, F., & Kupper, S. (2002). Autogenic training: A meta-analysis of clinical outcome studies. *Applied Psychophysiology and Biofeedback, 27*(1), 45–98.

Stewart, A. E. (2005). Attributions of responsibility for motor vehicle crashes. *Accident Analysis & Prevention, 37*(4), 681–688.

Stewart, M. E., Ebmeier, K. P., & Deary, I. J. (2005). Personality correlates of happiness and sadness: EQP-R and TPQ compared. *Personality and Individual Differences, 38*, 1085–1096.

Stickgold, R. (2011). Memory in sleep and dreams: The construction of meaning. In S. Nalbantian, P. M. Matthews & J. L. McClelland (Eds.), *The memory process: Neuroscientific and humanistic perspectives* (pp. 73–95). Cambridge, MA: MIT Press.

Stoleru, S., Gregoire, M. C., Gerard, D., Decety, J., Lafarge, E., Cinotti, L., et al. (1999). Neuroanatomical correlates of visually evoked sexual arousal in human males. *Archives of Sexual Behavior, 28*, 1–21.

Stone, J. V., Hunkin N. M., & Hornby, A. (2001). Predicting spontaneous recovery of memory. *Nature, 414*(6860), 167–168.

Stone, T. H., Winslade, W. J., & Klugman, C. M. (2000). Sex offenders, sentencing laws and pharmaceutical treatment: A prescription for failure. *Behavioral Sciences & the Law, 18*(1), 83–110.

Storms, M. S. (1973). Videotape of the attribution process: Reversing actors' and observers' points of view. *Journal of Personality and Social Psychology, 27*, 165–175.

Stout, D., & Chaminade, T. (2012). Stone tools, language and the brain in human evolution. *Philosophical Transactions of the Royal Society B: Biological Sciences, 367*(1585), 75–87.

Strack, F., Martin, L. L., & Stepper, S. (1988). Inhibiting and facilitating conditions of the human smile: A non-obtrusive test of the facial-feedback hypothesis. *Journal of Personality and Social Psychology, 54*, 768–777.

Stranahan, A. M., Khalil, D., & Gould, E. (2007). Running induces widespread structural alterations in the hippocampus and entorhinal cortex. *Hippocampus, 17*, 1017–1022.

Stranahan, A. M., Khalil, D., & Gould, E. (2006). Social isolation delays the positive effects of running on adult neurogenesis. *Nature Neuroscience, 9*, 526–533.

Strauss, B. (2002). Social facilitation in motor tasks: A review of research and theory. *Psychology of Sport and Exercise, 3*(3), 237–256.

Streita, W. (2006). Microglial senescence: does the brain's immune system have an expiration date? *Trends in Neurosciences, 29*(9), 506–510.

Strelau, J. (2010). How far are we in searching for the biological background of personality? In T. Maruszewski, M. Fajkowska, & M. Eysenck. (Eds.), *Personality from biological, cognitive, and social perspectives: Warsaw lectures in personality and social psychology*. Clifton Corners, NY: Eliot Werner Publications.

Stricker, E. M., & Zigmond, M. J. (1986). Brain monoamines, homeostasis, and adaptive behavior handbook of physiology: Intrinsic regulatory systems of the brain (pp. 677–696). Bethesda, MD: American Physiological Society.

Strümpfel, U. (2006). *Therapie der gefühle: For-schungsbefunde zur gestalttherapie*. Cologne, Germany: Edition Huanistiche Psychologie.

Strümpfel, U. (2004). Research on gestalt therapy. *International Gestalt Journal, 27*(1), 9–54.

Stuart, H. (2010) Mental disorders and social stigma: Three moments in Canadian history. In J. Cairney, & D. L. Streiner (Eds.*), Mental disorder in Canada: An epidemiological perspective* (pp. 304–330). Toronto, ON: University of Toronto Press.

Stuart, T. D., & Garrison, M. E. B. (2002). The influence of daily hassles and role balance on health status: A study of mothers of grade school children. *Women & Health, 36*(3), 1–11.

Stuss, D. T., Gallup Jr., G. G., & Alexander, M. P. (2001). The frontal lobes are necessary for "theory of mind." *Brain: A Journal of Neurology, 124*(2), 279–286.

Sue, D. W., Capodilupo, C. M., Torino, G. C. (2007). Racial microaggressions in everyday life: Implications for clinical practice. *American Psychologist, 62*, 271–286.

Sugita, M. (2006). Taste perception and coding in the periphery. *Cellular and Molecular Life Sciences, 63*, 2000–2015.

Sullivan, R. M., Landers, M., Yeaman, B., & Wilson, D. A. (2000). Good memories of bad events in infancy. *Nature, 407*, 38–39.

Sulloway, F. J. (1996). Born to rebel: Birth order, family dynamics and creative lives. New York, NY: Pantheon.

Sun, M. (Ed.). (2007). *New research in cognitive sciences*. Hauppauge, NY: Nova Science Publishers.

Super, C. M. (1976). Environmental effects on motor development: The case of african infant precocity. *Developmental Medicine & Child Neurology, 18*(5), 561–567.

Super, C. M., & Harkness, S. (2002). Culture structures the environment for development. *Human Development, 45*, 270–274.

Super, C. M., & Harkness, S. (1972). The infant's niche in rural Kenya and metropolitan America. In L. Adler (Ed.), *Issues in cross-cultural research*. New York, NY: Academic Press.

Sutton, S. K., & Davidson, R. J. (2000). Prefrontal brain electrical asymmetry predicts the evaluation of affective stimuli. *Neuropsychologia ,38*(13), 1723–1733.

Sutton, S. K., Ward, R. T., Larson, C. L., Holden, J. E., Perlman, S. B., & Davidson, R. J. (1997). Asymmetry in prefrontal glucose metabolism during appetitive and aversive emotional states: An FDG-PET study. *Psychophysiology, 34*, S89.

Swain, J. E., Lorberbaum, J. P., Kose, S., & Strathearn, L. (2007). Brain basis of early parent-infant interactions: Psychology, physiology, and in vivo functional neuroimaging studies. *Journal of Child Psychology and Psychiatry, and Allied Disciplines, 48*(3–4), 262–287.

Swap, W. C. (1977). Interpersonal attraction and repeated exposure to rewarders and punishers. *Personality and Social Psychology Bulletin, 3*, 248–251.

Sweatt, J. D. (2010). *Mechanisms of memory (2nd Ed.)*. San Diego, CA: Elsevier Academic Press.

Swinkels, A., & Giuliano, T. A. (1995). The measurement and conceptualization of mood awareness: Monitoring and labeling one's mood states. *Personality and Social Psychology Bulletin, 21*(9), 934–949.

Symons, D. (2004). Mental state discourse and theory of mind: Internalisation of self-other understanding within a cognitive framework. *Developmental Review, 24*, 159–188.

Taanila, A. Murray, G. K., Jokelainen, J., Isohanni, M., & Rantakallio, P. (2005). Infant developmental milestones: a 31-year follow-up. *Developmental Medicine and Child Neurology, 47*(9), 581–586.

Tager-Flusberg, H. (2001). Putting words together: morphology and syntax in the preschool years. In J. Berko Gleason (Ed.), *The development of language* (5th Ed., pp. 116–212). Boston, MA: Allyn and Bacon.

Tajfel, H. (1981). *Human groups and social categories*. Cambridge: Cambridge University Press.

Tajfel, H., & Turner, J. C. (2004). The social identity theory of intergroup behavior. In J. T. Jost, & J. Sidanius (Eds.), *Political psychology: Key readings in social psychology* (pp. 276–293). New York, NY: Psychology Press.

Takahashi, J., Takagi, Y., & Saiki, H. (2009). Transplantation of embryonic stem cell-derived dopaminergic neurons in MPTP-treated monkeys. *Methods in Molecular Biology, 482*, 199–212.

Takano, K., & Tanno, Y. (2009). Self-rumination, self-reflection, and depression: self-rumination counteracts the adaptive effect of self-reflection. *Behaviour Research and Therapy, 47*, 260–264.

Talarico, J. M., & Rubin, D. C. (2009). Flashbulb memories result from ordinary memory processes and extraordinary event characteristics. In O. Luminet, & A. Curci (Eds.), *Flashbulb memories: New issues and new perspectives* (pp. 79–97). New York, NY: Psychology Press.

Talarico, J. M., & Rubin, D. C. (2007). Flashbulb memories are special after all; in phenomenology, not accuracy. *Applied Cognitive Psychology, 21*(5), 557–578.

Talarico, J. M., & Rubin, D. C. (2003). Confidence, not consistency, characterizes flashbulb memories. *Psychological Science, 14*(5), 455–461.

Talwar, R., Nitz, K., & Lerner, R. M. (1990). Relations among early adolescent temperament, parent and peer demands, and adjustment: A test of the goodness of fit model. *Journal of Adolescence, 13*, 279–298.

Talwar, V., & Lee, K. (2008). Social and cognitive correlates of children's lying behavior. *Child Development, 79*(4), 866–881.

Talwar, V., Gordon, H. M., & Lee, K. (2007). Lying in the elementary school years: verbal deception and its relation to second-order belief understanding. *Developmental Psychology, 43*(3), 804–810.

Tamminga, C. A., Shad, M. U., & Ghose, S. (2008). Neuropsychiatric aspects of schizophrenia. In S. C. Yudofsky & R. E. Hales (Eds.), *The American Psychiatric Publishing textbook of neuropsychiatry and behavioral neurosciences* (5th Ed.). Washington, DC: American Psychiatric Publishing.

Tanaka-Matsumi, J. (2001). Abnormal psychology and culture. In D. Matsumoto (Ed.), *The handbook of culture and psychology* (pp. 265–286). New York, NY: Oxford University Press.

Tang, C. Y., Eaves, E. L., Ng, J. C., Carpenter, D. M., Mai, X., Schroeder, D. H., & Haier, R. J. (2010). Brain networks for working memory and factors of intelligence assessed in males and females with fMRI and DTI. *Intelligence, 38*(3), 293–303.

Tatzer, E., Schubert, M. T., Timischl, W., & Simbruner, G. (1985). Discrimination of taste and preference for sweet in premature babies. *Early Human Development, 12*(1), 23–30.

Taube-Schiff, M., & Lau, M. A. (2008). Major depressive disorder. In M. Hersen & J. Rosqvist (Eds.), *Handbook of psychological assessment, case conceptualization, and treatment, Vol. 1: Adults* (pp. 319–351). Hoboken, NJ: John Wiley & Sons.

Tavris, C. (2003). Uncivil rights—the cultural rules of anger. *Violence and society: A reader* (pp. 3–14). Upper Saddle River, NJ: Prentice Hall/Pearson Education.

Tavris, C. (1991). The mismeasure of woman: Paradoxes and perspectives in the study of gender. In J. D. Goodchilds (Ed.), *Psychological Perspectives on Human Diversity in America* (pp. 87–136). Washington, D.C.: American Psychological Association.

Tavris, C. (1989). *Anger: The misunderstood emotion (rev. Ed.)*. New York, NY: Touchstone Books/Simon & Schuster.

Taylor, B., Miller, E., Farrington, C. P., Petropoulos, M., Favot-Mayaud, I., Li, J., & Waight, P. A. (1999). Autism and measles, mumps, and rubella vaccine: no epidemiological evidence for a causal association. *The Lancet, 353*(9169), 2026–2029.

Taylor, D. A., Gould, R. J., & Brounstein, P. J. (1981). Effects of personalistic self-disclosure. *Personality and Social Psychology Bulletin, 7*, 487–492.

Taylor, I., & Taylor, M. M. (1990). *Psycholinguistics: Learning and using language*. Prentice Hall.

Taylor, J., Iacono, W. G., & McGue, M. (2000). Evidence for a genetic etiology of early-onset delinquency. *Journal of Abnormal Psychology, 109*, 634–643.

Taylor, S. E. (2010). Health. In S. T. Fiske, D. T. Gilbert, & G. Lindzey (Eds.), *Handbook of social psychology*, Vol. 1 (5th Ed., pp. 698–723). Hoboken, NJ: John Wiley & Sons.

Taylor, S. E. (2010). Health psychology. In R. F. Baumeister & E. J. Finkel (Eds.), *Advanced social psychology: The state of the science* (pp. 697–731). New York: Oxford University Press.

Taylor, S. E. (2008). From social psychology to neuroscience and back. *Journeys in social psychology: Looking back to inspire the future* (pp. 39–54). New York, NY: Psychology Press.

Taylor, S. E. (2007). Social support. *Foundations of health psychology* (pp. 145–171). New York, NY: Oxford University Press.

Taylor, S. E. (2006). *Health psychology (6th Ed.)*. New York, NY: McGraw Hill.

Taylor, S. E. (2006). Tend and befriend: Biobehavioral bases of affiliation under stress. *Current Directions in Psychological Science, 15*(6), 273–277.

Taylor, S. E. (2004). The accidental neuroscientist: Positive resources, stress responses, and course of illness. In G. G. Berntson & J. T. Cacioppo (Eds.), *Essays in social neuroscience* (pp. 133–141). Cambridge, MA: The MIT Press.

Taylor, S. E., Lerner, J. S., Sherman, D. K., Sage, R. M., & McDowell, N. K. (2003). Are self-enhancing cognitions associated with healthy or unhealthy biological profiles? *Journal of Personality and Social Psychology, 85*, 605–615.

Teicher, M. H., Andersen, S. L., Navalta, C. P., Tomoda, A., Polcari, A., & Kim, D. (2008). Neuropsychiatric disorders of childhood and adolescence. *The american psychiatric publishing textbook of neuropsychiatry and behavioral neurosciences (5th Ed.)* (pp. 1045–1113). Washington, DC: American Psychiatric Publishing, Inc.

Temoshok, L. R. (2003). Congruence Matters: A Consideration of Adaptation and Appropriateness. *Advances in Mind-Body Medicine, 19*, 10–11.

Temoshok, L. R., Waldstein, S. R., Wald, R. L., Garzino-Demo, A., Synowski, S. J., Sun, L., & Wiley, J. A. (2008). Type C coping, alexithymia, and heart rate reactivity are associated independently and differentially with specific immune mechanisms linked to HIV progression. *Brain, Behavior, and Immunity, 22*(5), 781–792.

Temple, S. (2001). The development of neural stem cells. *Nature, 414*, 112–117.

Temrin, H., Buchmayer, S., & Enquist, M. (2000). Step-parents and infanticide: New data contradict evolutionary predictions. *Proceedings of the Royal Society of London B, 267*, 943–945.

Tennen, H., & Affleck, G. (2009). Assessing positive life change: In search of meticulous methods. *Medical illness and positive life change: Can crisis lead to personal transformation?* (pp. 31–49). Washington, DC: American Psychological Association.

Tennen, H., & Affleck, G. (2002). Benefit-finding and benefit-reminding. *Handbook of positive psychology* (pp. 584–597). New York, NY: Oxford University Press.

Tennen, H., Affleck, G., & Armeli, S. (2005). Personality and daily experience revisited. *Journal of Personality, 73*(6), 1465–1484.

Tennov, D. (1999). *Love and limerence: The experience of being in love* (2nd edition). Chelsea, MI: Scarborough House.

Thagard, P. (2001). How to make decisions: Coherence, emotion, and practical inference. In E. Millgram (Ed.), *Varieties of practical inference* (pp. 355–371). Cambridge, MA: MIT Press.

Thakkar, M. M., & Datta, S. (2010). The evolution of REM sleep. In P. McNamara, R. A. Barton & C. L. Nunn (Eds.), *Evolution of sleep: Phylogenetic and functional perspectives* (pp. 197–217). New York, NY: Cambridge University Press.

Thelen, E. (1989). The (re)discovery of motor development: Learning new things from an old field. *Developmental Psychology, 25*, 946–949.

Thelen, E., & Smith, L. B. (2006). Dynamic systems theories. In R. M. Lerner (Ed.), *Handbook of child psychology, Vol. 1: Theoretical models of human development* (6th Ed., pp. 258–312). Hoboken, NJ: Wiley.

Theodorou, S., & Haber, P. S. (2005). The medical complications of heroin use. *Current Opinions in Psychiatry, 18*(3), 257–263.

Thigpen, C. H., & Cleckley, H. M. (1957). *The three faces of Eve*. New York: McGraw-Hill.

Thomas, A. K., Hannula, D. E., & Loftus, E. F. (2007). How self-relevant imagination affects memory for behaviour. *Applied Cognitive Psychology, 21*(1), 69–86.

Thompson, R. A. (1994). Emotion regulation: A theme in search of a definition. *Monographs of the Society for Research in Child Development, 59*, 25–52.

Thompson, R. F. (2000). *The brain: A neuroscience primer (3rd Ed.)*. New York, NY: Worth Publishers.

Thompson, S. C., Sobolew-Shubin, A., Galbraith, M. E., Schwankovsky L., & Cruzen, D. (1993). Maintaining perceptions of control: Finding perceived control in low-control circumstances. *Journal of Personality and Social Psychology, 64*(2), 293–304.

Thorndike, E. L. (1933). A proof of the law of effect. *Science, 77*, 173–175.

Tillmann, B., Peretz, I., & Samson, S. (2011). Neurocognitive approaches to memory in music: Music is memory. In S. Nalbantian, P. M. Matthews & J. L. McClelland (Eds.), *The memory process: Neuroscientific and humanistic perspectives* (pp. 377–394). Cambridge, MA: MIT Press.

Time. (1982, October 25). *The 27 faces of 'Charles.'*

Time. (1980). Let's fall in limerence. *Time Magazine*. Retrieved from http://www.time.com/time/magazine/article/ 0,9171,952554-1,00.html.

Tinghitella, R. M., & Zuk, M. (2009). Asymmetric mating preferences accommodated the rapid evolutionary loss of a sexual signal. *Evolution, 63*, 2087–2098.

Toates, F. (2009). An integrative theoretical framework for understanding sexual motivation, arousal, and behavior. *Journal of Sex Research, 46*(2). 168–193.

Todorova, I. L., Falcon, L. M., Lincoln, A. K., & Price, L. L. (2010). Perceived discrimination, psychological distress and health. *Sociology of Health & Illness, 32*(6), 843–861.

Tolman, E. C., & Gleitman, H. (1949). Studies in spatial learning; place and response learning under different degrees of motivation. *Journal Experimental Psychology, 39*, 653–659.

Tomasello, M. (1999). *The new psychology of language: cognitive and functional approaches to language structure*. Mahwah, NJ: Lawrence Erlbaum.

Tomes, Y. I. (2010). Culture and psychoeducational assessment: Cognition and achievement. In E. García-Vásquez, T. D. Crespi, & C. A. Riccio (Eds.), *Handbook of education, training, and supervision of school psychologists in school and community, vol. 1: Foundations of professional practice* (pp. 167–183). New York: Routledge/Taylor & Francis Group.

Tomkins, S. S. (1992). Affect, imagery, consciousness, vol. 4: Cognition: Duplication and transformation of information. New York, NY: Springer Publishing Co.

Tomkins, S. S. (1980). Affect as amplification: Some modifications in theory. In R. Plutchik & H. Kellerman (Eds.), *Emotion: Theory, research and experience* (pp.141–164). New York: Academic.

Tomkins, S. S. (1962). *Affect, imagery, and consciousness*. New York, NY: Springer Publishing.

Tonigan, J. S., Toscova, R., & Miller, W. R. (1995). Meta-analysis of the literature on Alcoholics Anonymous: Sample and study characteristics moderate findings. *Journal of Studies on Alcohol, 57*(1), 65–72.

Torrey, E. F. (2001). *Surviving schizophrenia: A manual for families, consumers, and providers* (4th Ed.). New York: HarperCollins.

Toth, K., & King, B. H. (2010). Intellectual disability (mental retardation). In M. K. Dulcan (Ed.), *Dulcan's textbook of child and adolescent psychiatry* (pp. 151–171). Arlington, VA: American Psychiatric Publishing.

Tourangeau, R., Smith, T. W., & Rasinski, K. A. (1997). Motivation to report sensitive behaviors on surveys: Evidence from a bogus pipeline experiment. *Journal of Applied Social Psychology, 27*, 209–222.

Tousignant, M. (1984). Pena in the Ecuadorian Sierra: A psychoanthropological analysis of sadness. *Culture, Medicine, and Psychiatry, 8*, 381–398.

Townsend, F. (2000). Birth order and rebelliousness: Reconstructing the research in *Born to Rebel. Politics and the Life Sciences, 19*(2), 135–156.

Tramo, M. J., Loftus, W. C., Stukel, T. A., Green, R. L., Weaver, J. B., & Gazzaniga, M. S. (1998). Brain size, head size, and intelligence quotient in monozygotic twins. *Neurology, 50*(5), 1246–1252.

Tramontin, M., & Halpern, J. (2007). The psychological aftermath of terrorism: The 2001 World Trade Center attack. In E. K. Carll (Ed.), *Trauma psychology: Issues in violence, disaster, health, and illness* (Vol. 1). Westport, CT: Praeger Publishers.

Tranel, D., & Damasio, A. R. (1993). The covert learning of affective valence does not require structures in hippocampal system or amygdala. *Journal of Cognitive Neuroscience, 5*(1), 79–88.

Trawick-Smith, J., & Dziurgot, T. (2011). "Good-fit" teacher–child play interactions and the subsequent autonomous play of preschool children. *Early Childhood Research Quarterly, 26*(1), 110–123.

Treanor, M. (2011). The potential impact of mindfulness on exposure and extinction learning in anxiety disorders. *Clinical Psychology Review, 31*(4), 617–625.

Treisman, A. M., Kanwisher, N. G. (1998) Perceiving visually presented objects: recognition, awareness, and modularity. *Current Opinions in Neurobiology 8*, 218–226.

Trembath, D., Balandin, S., Stancliffe, R. J., & Togher, L. (2010). Employment and volunteering for adults with intellectual disability. *Journal of Policy and Practice in Intellectual Disabilities, 7*(4), 235–238.

Trenholm, C., Devaney, B., Fortson, K., Quay, L., Wheeler, J., Clark, M., et al. (2007). *Impacts of Four Title V., Section 510 abstinence education programs*.

Triandis, H. C. (2001). Individualism-collectivism and personality. *Journal of Personality, 69*(6), 907–924.

Triandis, H. C. (1989). Cross-cultural studies of individualism and collectivism. In J. Berman (Ed.), *Nebraska Symposium* (pp. 41–130). Lincoln, NE: University of Nebraska Press.

Triandis, H., Botempo, R., Villareal, M., Asai, M., & Lucca, N. (1988). Individualism and collectivism: Cross-cultural perspectives on self in group relationships. *Journal of Personality and Social Psychology, 54*, 332–336.

Triandis, H. C., McCusker, C., & Hui, C. H. (1990). Multimethod probes of individualism and collectivism. *Journal of Personality and Social Psychology, 59*, 1006–1020.

Triplett, N. (1898). The dynamogenic factors in pace-making and competition. *American Journal of Psychology, 9*, 507–533.

Troyer, J. M. (2006). Post-bereavement experiences of older widowers: A qualitative investigation. ProQuest Information & Learning: US. *Dissertation Abstracts International Section A: Humanities and Social Sciences, 66*(8), 3051.

Truett, K. R., Eaves, L. J., Walters, E. E., et al. (1994). A model system for analysis of family resemblance in extended kinships of twins. *Behavior Genetics*, 24(1), 35–49.

Tsukiura, T., Sekiguchi, A., Yomogida, Y., Nakagawa, S., Shigemune, Y., Kambara, T., . . . Kawashima, R. (2011). Effects of aging on hippocampal and anterior temporal activations during successful retrieval of memory for face–name associations. *Journal of Cognitive Neuroscience, 23*(1), 200–213. doi: 10.1162/jocn.2010.21476.

Tsuruga, K., Kobayashi, T., Hirai, N., et al. (2008). Foreign accent syndrome in a case of dissociative (conversion) disorder. *Seishin Shinkeigaku Zasshi, 110*(2), 79–87.

Tulving, E. (1974). Recall and recognition of semantically encoded words. *Journal of Experimental Psychology, 102*(5), 778–787.

Tulving, E., & Thomson, D. M. (1973). Encoding specificity and retrieval processes in episodic memory. *Psychological Review, 80,* 352–373.

Turati, C., Di Giorgio, E., Bardi, L., & Simion, F. (2010). Holistic face processing in newborns, 3-month-old infants, and adults: Evidence from the composite face effect. *Child Development, 81*(6), 1894–1905.

Turiel, E. (2010). The development of morality: Reasoning, emotions, and resistance. In W. F. Overton, & R. M. Lerner (Eds.), *The handbook of life-span development,* vol. 1: *Cognition, biology, and methods* (pp. 554–583). Hoboken, NJ: John Wiley & Sons.

Turkington, C., & Harris, J. R. (2009). *The Encyclopedia of the brain and brain disorders (3rd edition).* New York, NY: Facts on File/Infobase Publishing.

Turkington, C., & Harris, J. R. (2001). *The Encyclopedia of memory and memory disorders (2nd edition).* New York, NY: Facts on File/Infobase Publishing.

Tversky, A. (1972). Elimination by aspects: A theory of choice. *Psychological Review, 79,* 281–99.

Tversky, A., & Kahneman, D. (1993). Probabilistic reasoning. In. A. I. Goldman (Ed.), *Readings in Philosophy and Cognitive Science* (pp. 43–68). Cambridge, MA: MIT Press.

Tversky, A., & Kahneman, D. (1981). The framing of decisions and the psychology of choice. *Science, 211*(4481), 453–458.

Tversky, A., & Kahneman, D. (1974). Judgment under uncertainty: Heuristics and biases. *Science, 185,* 1124–1131.

Twemlow, S. W., Fonagy, P., & Sacco, F. C. (2003). Modifying social aggression in schools. *Journal of Applied Psychoanalytical Studies, 5*(2), 211–222.

Uchino, B. N., & Birmingham, W. (2011). Stress and support processes. In R. J. Contrada & A. Baum (Eds.), *The handbook of stress science: Biology, psychology, and health.* New York: Springer Publishing Co.

Ulrich, R. S. (1984). View through a window may influence recovery from surgery. *Science, 224,* 420–21.

Underwood, B., & Moore, B. (1982). Perspective-taking and altruism. *Psychological Bulletin, 91,* 143–173.

Ungerleider, L. G., & Haxby, J. V. (1994). What and where in the human brain. *Current Opinion in Neurobiology, 4,* 157–165.

Urcuyo, K. R., Boyers, A. E., Carver, C. S., & Antoni, M. H. (2005). Finding benefit in breast cancer: Relations with personality, coping, and concurrent well-being. *Psychology of Health, 20*(2), 175–192.

Urry, H. L., Nitschke, J. B., Dolski, I., Jackson, D. C., Dalton, K. M., Mueller, C. J., Rosenkranz, M. A., Ryff, C. D., Singer, B. H., & Davidson, R. J. (2004). Making a life worth living: neural correlates of well-being. *Psychological Science, 15*(6), 367–372.

Ursano, R. J., McCarroll, J. E., & Fullerton, C. S. (2003). Traumatic death in terrorism and disasters: The effects on posttraumatic stress and behavior. *Terrorism and disaster: Individual and community mental health interventions* (pp. 308–332). New York, NY: Cambridge University Press.

U.S. Census Bureau. (2011). The national data book. *The 2011 Statistical Abstract: International Statistics.* Retrieved from http://www.census.gov/compendia/statab/cats/international_statistics.html

U.S. Census Bureau. (2004). *Statistics by country for narcolepsy.* US Census Bureau International Data Base. Retrieved from http://www.wrongdiagnosis.com/n/narcolepsy/stats-country.htm.

USDE (United States Department of Education). (1977). Definition and criteria for defining students as learning disabled. *Federal Register, 42*(250), 65083. Washington, DC: U.S. Government Printing Office.

USDHHS (U.S. Department of Health & Human Services). (2011). *About the Office of Head Start.* Washington, DC: Author.

USDHHS (US Department of Health & Human Services). (2011). *Head Start impact study and follow-up, 2000–2011.* Washington, DC: Author.

Usher, J. A., & Neisser, U. (1993). Childhood amnesia and the beginnings of memory for four early life events. *Journal of Experimental Psychology: General, 122,* 155–165.

Uziel, L. (2007). Individual differences in the social facilitation effect: A review and meta-analysis. *Journal of Research in Personality, 41,* 579–601.

Valenstein, E. S. (2010). *Great and desperate cures: the rise and decline of psychosurgery and other radical treatments for mental illness.* Create Space.

Van Ameringen, M., Mancini, C., Patterson, B., & Boyle, M H (2008). Post-traumatic stress disorder in Canada. *CNS Neuroscience and Therapy, 14*(3), 171–181.

Van Cauter, E., Leproult, R., & Plat, L. (2000). Age-related changes in slow-wave sleep and REM sleep and relationship with growth hormone and cortisol levels in healthy men. *Journal of the American Medical Association, 284,* 861–868.

van den Berg, H., Manstead, A. S. R., van, der Pligt, J., & Wigboldus, D. H. J. (2006). The impact of affective and cognitive focus on attitude formation. *Journal of Experimental Social Psychology, 42*(3), 373–379.

Van der Werf, Y. D., Jolles, J., Witter, M. P., & Uylings, H. B. M. (2003). Contributions of thalamic nuclei to memory functioning. *Cortex, 39,* 1047–1062.

Van der Werf, Y. D., Witter, M. P., & Groenewegen, H. J. (2002). The intralaminar and midline nuclei of the thalamus. Anatomical and functional evidence for participation in processes of arousal and awareness. *Brain Research Reviews, 39,* 107–140.

van Duijvenvoorde, A.C., Zanolie, K., Rombouts, S.A., Raijmakers, M.E., Crone, E.A. (2008). Evaluating the negative or valuing the positive? Neural mechanisms supporting feedback-based learning across development. *Journal of Neuroscience, 28,* 9495–9503.

van Eck, M., Nicolson, N. A., & Berkhof, J. (1998). Effects of stressful daily events on mood states: Relationship to global perceived stress. *Journal of Personality and Social Psychology, 75*(6), 1572–1585.

Van Wagner, K. (2007). Phobia list: An A to Z list of phobias. *About.com.* Retrieved from http://psychology.about.com/od/.phobias/a/phobialist.htm.

Vasey, M.W, Crnic, K.A., & Carter, WG. (1994). Worry in childhood: A developmental perspective. *Cognitive Therapy Research, 18*(6), 529–549.

Vega, W. A., Ang, A., Rodriguez, M. A., & Finch, B. K. (2011). Neighborhood protective effects on depression in Latinos. *American Journal of Community Psychology, 47*(1–2), 114–126.

Verhaeghen, P. (2003). Aging and vocabulary score: A meta-analysis. *Psychology and Aging, 18*(2), 332–339. doi: 10.1037/0882-7974.18.2.332

Verheyden, S. L., Henry, J. A., & Curran, H. V. (2003). Acute, sub-acute and long-term subjective consequences of 'ecstasy' (MDMA) consumption in 430 regular users. *Human Psychopharmacology, 18*(7), 507–517.

Verheyden, S. L., Maidment, R., & Curran, H. V. (2003). Quitting ecstasy: an investigation of why people stop taking the drug and their subsequent mental health. *Journal of Psychopharmacology (Oxford),* 17(4), 371–378.

Verissimo, M., Santos, A. J., Vaughn, B. E., Torres, N., Monteiro, L., & Santos, O. (2011). Quality of attachment to father and mother and number of reciprocal friends. *Early Child Development and Care, 181*(1), 27–38.

Vermetten, E., et al. (2006). Hippocampal and Amygdalar volumes in dissociative identify disorder. *American Journal of Psychiatry, 163,* 630–636.

Verster, J. C., Brady, K., Galanter, M. & Conrond, P. J. (2011). *Drug abuse and addiction in mental illness: Causes, consequences and treatments.* Humana Press.

Vertes, R. P., & Eastman, K. E. (2003). The case against memory consolidation in REM sleep. In E. F. Pace-Schott, M. Solms, M. Blagrove, & S. Harnad (Eds.), *Sleep and dreaming: Scientific advances and reconsiderations.* New York, NY: Cambridge University Press.

Vessey, J. T., & Howard, K. I. (1993). Who seeks psychotherapy? *Psychotherapy: Theory, Research, Practice, Training, 30*(4), 546–553.

Vidal, F. (2011). Memory, movies, and the brain. In S. Nalbantian, P. M. Matthews & J. L. McClelland (Eds.), *The memory process: Neuroscientific and humanistic perspectives* (pp. 395–415). Cambridge, MA: MIT Press.

Viggiano, D., Ruocco, L. A., Arcieri, S., & Sadile, A. G. (2004). Involvement of norepinephrine in the control of activity and attentive processes in animal models of attention deficit hyperactivity disorder. *Neural Plasticity, 11,* 133–149.

Viswesvaran, C., & Ones, D. (1999). Meta-analysis of fakability estimates: Implications for personality measurement. *Educational and Psychological Measurement, 54,* 197–210.

Vohs, K. D., Glass, B. D., Maddox, W. T., & Markman, A. B. (2011). Ego depletion is not just fatigue: Evidence from a total sleep deprivation experiment. *Social Psychological and Personality Science, 2*(2), 166–173.

Volkow, N., & Fowler, J. (2000). Addiction, a disease of compulsion and drive: involvement of the orbitofrontal cortex. *Cerebral Cortex, 10,* 318–325.

Vollrath, M. (2001). Personality and stress. *Scandinavian Journal of Psychology, 42*(4), 335–347.

Volz, J. (2000). Successful aging. The second 50. *APA Monitor, 31,* 24–28.

Voss, J. L. (2009). Long-term associative memory capacity in man. *Psychonomic Bulletin & Review, 16*(6), 1076–1081. doi: 10.3758/PBR.16.6.1076

Vossekuil, B., Fein, R. A., Reddy, M. Borum, R., & Modzeleski, W. (2002). The final report and findings of the safe school initiative: Implications for the prevention of school attacks in the United States. Washington, D.C.

Vujanovic, A. A., Zvolensky, M. J., Bernstein, A., Feldner, M. T., & McLeish, A. C. (2007). A test of the interactive effects of anxiety sensitivity and mindfulness in the prediction of anxious arousal, agoraphobic cognitions, and body vigilance. *Behaviour Research and Therapy, 45*(6), 1393–1400.

Vygotsky, L. S. (2004). Imagination and creativity in childhood. *Journal of Russian & East European Psychology, 42*(1), 7–97.

Vygotsky, L. S. (1991). Genesis of the higher mental functions. In P. Light, S. Sheldon & M. Woodhead (Eds.), *Learning to think.*(pp. 32–41). Florence: Taylor & Frances/Routledge.

Vygotsky, L. (1978). *Mind in society: Development of higher psychological processes.* Cambridge, MA: Harvard University Press.

Wagner, U., Gais, S., Haider, H., Verleger, R., & Bom, J. (2004) Sleep inspires insight. *Nature, 427,* 352–355.

Wahlen, D. (2007). *The stigma associated with mental illness.* The Canadian Mental Health Association. Retrieved from www.cmhanl.ca/pdf/Stigma.pdf.

Waite, L. J., Laumann, E. O., Das, A., & Schumm, L. P. (2009). Sexuality: measures of partnerships, practices, attitudes, and problems in the national social life, health, and aging study. *The Journals of Gerontology. Series B, Psychological Sciences and Social Sciences.* Retrieved from: http://www.ncbi.nlm.nih.gov/ pubmed/19497930.

Wakefield, A., Murch, S., Anthony, A., et al. (1998). Ileal-lymphoid-nodular hyperplasia, non-specific colitis, and pervasive developmental disorder in children. *Lancet, 351*(9103), 637–641.

Wakin, A., & Vo, D. B. (2008). *Love-variant: The Wakin-Vo I.D.R. model of limerence.* Retrieved from http://www.inter-disciplinary.net/ptb/persons/pil/pil2/wakinvo%20paper.pdf.

Walker, E. F., & Diforio, D. (1997). Schizophrenia: A neural diathesis-stress model. *Psychological Review, 104*(4), 667–685.

Walker, L. (1980). Cognitive and perspective taking prerequisites for moral development. *Child Development, 51,* 131–139.

Walker, L. J. (2006). Gender and morality. In M. Killen & J. G. Smetana, (Eds), *Handbook of moral development* (pp. 93–115). Mahwah, NJ: Lawrence Erlbaum Associates.

Wall, T. L., Shea, S. H., Chan, K. K., & Carr, L. G. (2001). A genetic association with the development of alcohol and other substance use behavior in Asian Americans. *Journal of Abnormal Psychology, 110*(1), 173–178.

Wallace, H. M., Baumeister, R. F., & Vohs, K. D. (2005). Audience support and choking under pressure: A home disadvantage? *Journal of Sports Sciences, 23*(4), 429–438.

Wallace, V., Menn, L., & Yoshinaga-Itano, C. (1999). Is babble the gateway to speech for all children? A longitudinal study of children who are deaf or hard of hearing. *Volta Review, 100,* 121–148.

Wallerstein, R. S. (2006). The relevance of freud's psychoanalysis in the 21st century: Its science and its research. *Psychoanalytic Psychology, 23*(2), 302–326.

Wallis, C. (2005). The new science of happiness. *Time, 165(3),* A2–A9.

Walsh, W. B. (2007). Introduction: Special section on self-efficacy, interests, and personality. *Journal of Career Assessment, 15*(2), 143–144.

Walster, E., Aronson, E., & Abrahams, D. (1966). On increasing the persuasiveness of a low prestige communicator. *Journal of Experimental Social Psychology, 2,* 73–79.

Wampold, B. E., Hollon, S. D., & Hill, C. E. (2011). Unresolved questions and future directions in psychotherapy research. In J. C. Norcross, G. R. VandenBos, & D. K. Freedheim (Eds.), *History of psychotherapy: Continuity and change* (2nd Ed., pp. 333–356). Washington, DC: American Psychological Association.

Wan, C. Y., & Huon, G. F. (2005). Performance degradation under pressure in music: An examination of attentional processes. *Psychology of Music, 33,* 155–172.

Wang, M., & Jiang, G-R. (2007). Psychopathological mechanisms and clinical assessment of dissociative identity disorder. *Chinese Journal of Clinical Psychology, 15*(4), 426–429.

Wang, S. S. (2007, December 4). The graying of shock therapy. *Wall Street Journal Online.* Retrieved from http://online.wsg.com/public/article_print/SB119673737406312767.html.

Wang, X. (2005). Discovering spatial working memory fields in pre-frontal cortex. *Journal of Neurophysiology, 93*(6), 3027–3028.

Warziski, M. T., Sereika, S. M., Styn, M. A., Music, E., & Burke, L. E. (2008). Changes in self-efficacy and dietary adherence: The impact on weight loss in the PREFER study. *Journal of Behavioral Medicine, 31*(1), 81–92.

Was, C. A. (2010). The persistence of content-specific memory operations: Priming effects following a 24-h delay. *Psychonomic Bulletin & Review, 17*(3), 362-368. doi: 10.3758/PBR.17.3.362

Wason, P. C. (1960). On the failure to eliminate hypotheses in a conceptual task. *Quarterly Journal of Experimental Psychology, 12,* 129–140.

Waterfield, R. (2000). *The first philosophers: The Presocratics and the Sophists.* New York, NY: Oxford University Press.

Waterhouse, J. M., & DeCoursey, P. J. (2004). The relevance of circadian rhythms for human welfare. In J. C. Dunlap, J. J. Loros, et al. (Eds.), *Chronobiology: Biological timekeeping.* Sunderland, MA: Sinauer Associates, Inc.

Waterstrat, A., Oakley, E., Miller, A., Swiderski, C., Liang, Y., & Van Zant, G. (2008). Mechanisms of stem cell aging. In K. L. Rudolph (Ed.), *Telomere and telomerase in aging, disease, and cancer: molecular mechanisms of adult stem cell aging* (pp. 111–140). Berlin: Springer-Verlag.

Watkins, M. W. (2010). Structure of the Wechsler intelligence scale for children—Fourth edition among a national sample of referred students. *Psychological Assessment, 22*(4), 782–787.

Watson, D., & Tellegen, A. (1985). Towards a consensual structure of mood. *Psychological Bulletin, 98,* 219–235.

Watson, D., Clark, L. A., & Chmielewski, M. (2008). Structures of personality and their relevance to psychopathology: II. Further articulation of a comprehensive unified trait structure. *Journal of Personality, 76*(6), 1545–1586.

Watson, J. C., Goldman, R. N., & Greenberg, L. S. (2011). Humanistic and experiential theories of psychotherapy. In J. C. Norcross, G. R. VandenBos, & D. K. Freedheim (Eds.), *History of psychotherapy: Continuity and change* (2nd Ed., pp. 141–172). Washington, DC: American Psychological Association.

Watson, J. B., & Raynor. R. (1920). Conditioned emotional reactions. *Journal of Experimental Psychology, 3,* 1–14.

Watt, T. T. (2002). Marital and cohabiting relationships of adult children of alcoholics: Evidence from the National Survey of Family and Households. *Journal of Family Issues, 23*(2), 246–265.

Watts, R. E. (2000) Entering the new millenium: Is individual psychology still relevant? *Journal of Individual Psychology, 56*(1), 21–30.

Watts, S., & Stenner, P. (2005). The subjective experience of partnership love: A Q methodological study. *British Journal of Social Psychology, 44*(1), 85–107.

Waxman, S. R., & Medin, D. L. (2006). Core knowledge, naming and the acquisition of the fundamental (folk)biologic concept 'alive'. In N. Miyake (Ed.)., *Proceedings of the 5th International Conference on Cognitive Science* (pp. 53–55). Mahwah, NJ: Lawrence Erlbaum.

Weale, R. (1983). *Focus on vision.* Cambridge, MA: Harvard University Press.

Weaver, C. M., Borkowski, J. G., & Whitman, T. L. (2008). Violence breeds violence: Childhood exposure and adolescent conduct problems. *Journal of Community Psychology, 36*(1), 96–112.

Webster, R. (2001). *Neurotransmitters, drugs and brain function.* London: Wiley-Blackwell.

Wechsler, H., Lee, J. E., Kuo, M., Seibring, M., Nelson, T. F., & Lee, H. (2002). Trends in alcohol use, related problems and experience of prevention efforts among US college students 1993 to 2001: Results from the 2001 Harvard School of Public Health college alcohol study. *Journal of American College Health, 50*, 203–217.

Weekes-Shackelford, V. A., & Shackelford, T. K. (2004). Methods of filicide: Stepparents and genetic parents kill differently. *Violence Victims, 19*, 75–81.

Weeks, D., & James, J. (1995). *Eccentrics: A study of sanity and strangeness.* New York: Villard.

Weinberg, R. S., & Gould, D. (2003). *Foundations of sport and exercise psychology*. Champaign, IL: Human Kinetics.

Weinberger, D. R., & Harrison, P. (Eds.) (2011). *Schizophrenia 3rd Ed.* Wiley-Blackwell.

Weiner, I. B,. & Greene, R. L. (2008). *Handbook of personality assessment.* Hoboken, NJ: John Wiley & Sons, Inc.

Weinraub, M., Horvath, D. L., Gringlas, M. B. (2002). Single parenthood. In M. H. Bornstein (Ed.), *Handbook of parenting: Vol. 3. Being and becoming a parent (2nd edition)*. Mahwah, NJ: Erlbaum.

Weinstein, Y., & Shanks, D. R. (2010). Rapid induction of false memory for pictures. *Memory, 18*(5), 533–542.

Weiskrantz, L. (2009). Is blindsight just degraded normal vision? *Experimental Brain Research, 192*(3), 413–416. doi: 10.1007/s00221-008-1388-7

Weiskrantz, L. (2002). Prime-sight and blindsight. *Consciousness and Cognition: An International Journal, 11*(4), 568–581.

Weiskrantz, L. (2000). Blindsight: Implications for the conscious experience of emotion. In R. D. Lane & L. Nadel (Eds.), *Cognitive neuroscience of emotion*. London, England: Oxford University Press.

Weiss, J. (2000). To have and to hold: marriage, the baby boom, and social change. Chigago, IL: University of Chicago Press.

Weiss, J. M., & Glazer, H. I. (1975). Effects of acute exposure to stressors on subsequent avoidance-escape behavior. *Psychosomatic Medicine, 37*, 499–521.

Weiss, L. G. (2010). Considerations on the Flynn effect. *Journal of Psychoeducational Assessment, 28*(5), 482–493.

Weissman, M. M., Livingston, B. M., Leaf, P. J., Florio, L. P., & Holzer, C., III. (1991). Affective disorders. In L. N. Robins & D. A. Regier (Eds.), *Psychiatric disorders in America: The Epidemiologic Catchment Area Study.* New York: Free Press.

Wellman, H. M., Cross, D., & Watson, J. (2001). Meta-analysis of theory-of-mind development: The truth about false belief. *Child Development, 72*, 655–684.

Wellman, H. M., & Hickling, A. K. (1994). The mind's "I": Children's conception of the mind as an active agent. *Child Development, 65*, 1564–1580.

Wells, A. (2010). Metacognitive therapy: Application to generalized anxiety disorder. In D. Sookman & R. L. Leahy (Eds.), *Treatment resistant anxiety disorders: Resolving impasses to symptom remission* (pp. 1–29). New York: Routledge/Taylor & Francis Group.

Wells, G. L., & Loftus, E. F. (2003). Eyewitness memory for people and events. In A. M. Goldstein (Ed.), *Handbook of psychology: Forensic psychology, vol. 11* (pp. 149–160). Hoboken, NJ: John Wiley & Sons, Inc.

Wells, G. L., Small, M., Penrod, S., Malpass, R. S., Fulero, S. M., & Brimacombe, C. A. E. (1998). Eyewitness identification procedures: Recommendations for lineups and photospreads. *Law and Human Behavior, 22*(6), 603–647.

Wender, P. H., Reimherr, F. W., Marchant, B. K., Sanford, M. E., Czajkowski, L. A., & Tomb, D. A. (2011). A one year trial of methylphenidate in the treatment of ADHD. *Journal of Attention Disorders, 15*(1), 36–45.

Wenseleers, T., Helanterä, H., Hart, A., & Ratnieks, F. L. (2004). Worker reproduction and policing in insect societies: an ESS analysis. *Journal of Evolutionary Biology, 17*(5), 1035–1047.

Wenzel, A. (2011). Panic attacks. In *Anxiety in childbearing women: Diagnosis and treatment* (pp. 73–90). Washington, DC: American Psychological Association.

Wenzel, A. (2011). Social anxiety. In *Anxiety in childbearing women: Diagnosis and treatment* (pp. 91–102). Washington, DC: American Psychological Association.

Werker, J. F. (1989). Becoming a native listener: A developmental perspective on human speech perception. *American Scientist, 77*, 54–59.

Wertenbaker, L. (1981). *The human body-eye: Window to the world.* Washington, D.C.: U.S. News books.

West, R. L., Bagwell, D. K., & Dark-Freudeman, A. (2008). Self-efficacy and memory aging: The impact of a memory intervention based on self-efficacy *Aging, Neuropsychology, and Cognition, 15*(3), 302–329.

Westen, D. (2002). Implications of developments in cognitive neuroscience for psychodynamic psychotherapy. *Harvard Review of Psychiatry*, 10, 369–373.

Westen, D., Betan, E., & Defife, J. A. (2011). Identity disturbance in adolescence: Associations with borderline personality disorder. *Development and Psychopathology, 23*(1), 305–313.

Westen, D., Dutra, L., & Shedler, J. (2005). Assessing adolescent personality pathology: Quantifying clinical judgment. *British Journal of Psychiatry, 186*(3), 227–238.

Westen, D., & Harnden-Fischer, J. (2001). Personality profiles in eating disorders: Rethinking the distinction between axis I and axis II. *American Journal of Psychiatry, 158*(4), 547–562.

Whalen, P. J. (1998). Fear, vigilance, and ambiguity: Initial neuroimaging studies of the human amygdala. *Current Directions in Psychological Science, 7*(6), 177–188.

Whalen, P. J., Davis, F. C., Oler, J. A., Kim, H., Kim, M. J., & Neta, M. (2009). Human amygdala responses to facial expressions of emotion. In P. J. Whalen & E. A. Phelps (Eds.), *The human amygdala* (pp. 265–288). New York, NY: Guilford Press.

Whipple, R., & Fowler, J. C. (2011). Affect, relationship schemas, and social cognition: Self-injuring borderline personality disorder inpatients. *Psychoanalytic Psychology, 28*(2), 183–195.

Whisman, M. A., & McGarvey, A. L. (1995). Attachment, depressotypic cognitions, and dysphoria. *Cognitive Therapy and Research, 19*(6), 633–650.

Whitaker, R. (2002). Mad in America: Bad science, bad medicine, and the enduring mistreatment of the mentally ill. Cambridge, MA: Perseus.

White, B. J., & Madara, E. J. (Eds.). (2011). *Self-help group sourcebook online.* Retrieved from www.mentalhelp.net/selfhelp.

Whorf, B. (1956). *Language, Thought & Reality*. Cambridge, MA: MIT Press.

Whorf, B. (1940). Science and linguistics. reprinted in *Language, Thought & Reality*. Cambridge, MA: MIT Press.

Whyte, G. (2000). Groupthink. In A. E. Kazdin (Ed.), *Encyclopedia of Psychology, Vol. 4* (pp. 35–38). Washington, D.C.: American.

Wicherts, J. M., & Dolan, C. V. (2010). Measurement invariance in confirmatory factor analysis: An illustration using IQ test performance of minorities. *Educational Measurement: Issues and Practice, 29*(3), 39–47.

Wickwire, E. M., Jr., Roland, M. M. S., Elkin, T. D., & Schumacher, J. A. (2008). Sleep disorders. In D. Reitman (Ed.), *Handbook of psychological assessment, case conceptualization, and treatment: Volume 2—Children and adolescents*. Hoboken, NJ: John Wiley & Sons, Inc.

Wieser, H. G. (2003). Music and the brain. Lessons from brain diseases and some reflections on the "emotional" brain. *Annals of the New York Academy of Sciences, 999*, 76–94.

Wilde, D. J. (2011). *Jung's personality theory quantified*. New York: Springer-Verlag Publishing.

Wilkins , P. (2000) Unconditional positive regard reconsidered. *British Journal of Guidance & Counselling, 28*(1), 23–36.

Williams, K. D., Harkins, S. G., & Latane, B. (1981). Identifiability as a deterrent to social loafing: Two cheering experiements. *Journal of Personality and Social Psychology, 40*, 303–311.

Williams, P. G. (2004). The psychopathology of self-assessed health: A cognitive approach to health anxiety and hypochondriasis. *Cognitive Therapy and Research, 28*, 629–644.

Williams, P. G., Smith, T. W., Gunn, H. E., & Uchino, B. N. (2011). Personality and stress: Individual differences in exposure, reactivity, recovery, and restoration. In R. J. Contrada & A. Baum (Eds.), *The handbook of stress science: Biology, psychology, and health.* New York: Springer Publishing Co.

Williams, S. P. (1998). The serotonin transporter: A primary target for antidepressant drugs. *Journal of Psychopharmacology, 12*(2), 115–121.

Williams, T. (1986). The impact of television: A natural experiment in three communities. Academic Press.

Williams, T. J., Pepitone, M. E., Christensen, S. E., Cooke, B. M., Huberman, A. D., Breedlove, N. J., et al. (2000). Finger-length ratios and sexual orientation. *Nature, 404*, 455–456.

Wilson, D. A. (2001). Receptive fields in the rat piriform cortex. *Chemical Senses, 26*, 577–584.

Wilson, G. (1981). The Coolidge effect: An evolutionary account of human sexuality. New York: William Morrow.

Wilson, G. T. (2011). Behavior therapy. In R. J. Corsini & D. Wedding (Eds.), *Current psychotherapies* (9th Ed.). Florence, KY: CENGAGE Learning.

Wilson, G. T. (2008). Behavior therapy. In R. J. Corsini & D. Wedding (Eds.), *Current psychotherapies* (8th Ed.). Belmont, CA: Thomson Brooks/Cole.

Wilson, G.T., & Shafron, R. (2005). Eating disorders guidelines from NICE. *Lancet, 365,* 79–81.

Wilson, J. G. (2010). Repression: Psychoanalytic and sartrean phenomenological perspectives. *Existential Analysis, 21*(2), 271–281.

Wilson, K. A., & Hayward, C. (2005). A prospective evaluation of agoraphobia and depression symptoms following panic attacks in a community sample of adolescents. *Journal of Anxiety Disorders, 19*(1), 87–103.

Wimmer, F., Hoffmann, R. F., Bonato, R. A., & Moffitt, A. R. (1992). The effects of sleep deprivation on divergent thinking and attention processes. *Journal of Sleep Research, 1,* 223–230.

Wimmer, H., & Perner, J. (1983). Beliefs about beliefs: Representation and constraining function of wrong beliefs in young children's understanding of deception. *Cognition, 13*(1), 103–128.

Wincze, J. P., Bach, A. K., & Barlow, D. H. (2008). Sexual dysfunction. *Clinical handbook of psychological disorders: A step-by-step treatment manual (4th Ed.)* (pp. 615–661). New York, NY: Guilford Press.

Windholz, G. (1987). Pavlov as a psychologist. A reappraisal. *Pavlov Journal of Biological Sciences, 22,* 103–112.

Wing, L. (1976). Epidemiology and theories of aetiology. In L. Wing (Ed.), *Early childhood autism.* Oxford: Pergamon.

Winningham, R. G. (2010). *Train your brain: How to maximize memory ability in older adulthood* Amityville, NY: Baywood Publishing Co.

Witthoft, M., & Hiller, W. (2010). Psychological approaches to origins and treatments of somatoform disorders. *Annual Review of Clinical Psychology, 6,* 257–283.

Wixted, J. T. (2010). The role of retroactive interference and consolidation in everyday forgetting. In S. Della Sala (Ed.), *Forgetting* (pp. 285–312). New York, NY: Psychology Press.

Wixted, J. T. (2004). The psychology and neuroscience of forgetting. *Annual Review of Psychology, 55,* 235–269.

Wixted, J. T., & Squire, L. R. (2010). The role of the human hippocampus in familiarity-based and recollection-based recognition memory. *Behavioural Brain Research, 215*(2), 197–208. doi: 10.1016/j.bbr.2010.04.020

Woese, C., Kandler, O., & Wheelis, M. (1990). Towards a natural system of organisms: Proposal for the domains Archaea, Bacteria, and Eucarya. *Proceedings of the National Academy of Sciences USA, 87,* 4576–4579.

Wolberg, L. R. (1967). *The technique of psychotherapy.* New York: Grune & Stratton.

Wolf, S. (1969). Psychosocial factors in myocardial infarction and sudden death. *Circulation, 39,* 74–83.

Wolfson, A. R., & Richards, M. (2011). Young adolescents: Struggles with insufficient sleep. In M. El-Sheikh (Ed.), *Sleep and development: Familial and socio-cultural considerations* (pp. 265–298). New York, NY: Oxford University Press.

Wolitzky, D. L. (2011). Psychoanalytic theories of psychotherapy. In J. C. Norcross, G. R. VandenBos, & D. K. Freedheim (Eds.), *History of psychotherapy: Continuity and change* (2nd Ed., pp. 65–100). Washington, DC: American Psychological Association.

Wolman, B. (1979). *Handbook of dreams: research, theories, and applications.* Van Nostrand Reinhold.

Wolosin, S. M., Richardson, M. E., Hennessey, J. G., Denckla, M. B., & Mostofsky, S. H. (2009). Abnormal cerebral cortex structure in children with ADHD. *Human Brain Mapping, 30,* 175–184.

Wolpe, J. (1997). From psychoanalytic to behavioral methods in anxiety disorders: A continuing evolution. In J. K. Zeig (Ed.), *The evolution of psychotherapy: The third conference.* New York, NY: Brunner/Mazel.

Wolpe, J. (1997). Thirty years of behavior therapy. *Behavior Therapy, 28*(4), 633–635.

Wood, J. M., Garb, H. N., Lilienfeld, S. O., & Nezworski, M. T. (2002). Clinical assessment. *Annual Review of Psychology, 53*(1), 519–543.

Woods, S. C., Lutz, T. A., Geary, N., & Langhans, W. (2006). Pancreatic signals controlling food intake; insulin, glucagon, and amylin. *Philosophical transactions of the Royal Society of London. Series B, Biological sciences, 361*(1471), 1219–1235.

Wootton, J. (2008). Meditation and chronic pain. In J. F. Audette & A. Bailey (Eds.), Integrative pain medicine: The science and practice of complementary and alternative medicine in pain management. Contemporary pain medicine. Totowa, NJ: Humana Press.

Worley, L. L. M. (2010). Review of *Understanding postpartum psychosis: A temporary madness. Psychosomatics: Journal of Consultation Liaison Psychiatry, 51*(2), 181.

Worthington, E. L., Jr. (2011). Integration of spirituality and religion into psychotherapy. In J. C. Norcross, G. R. VandenBos, & D. K. Freedheim (Eds.), *History of psychotherapy: Continuity and change* (2nd Ed., pp. 533–543). Washington, DC: American Psychological Association.

Worthman, C. M. (2011). Developmental cultural ecology of sleep. In M. El-Sheikh (Ed.), *Sleep and development: Familial and socio-cultural considerations* (pp. 167–194). New York, NY: Oxford University Press.

Worthy, M., Gary, A. L., & Kahn, G. M. (1969). Self-disclosure as an exchange process. *Journal of Personality and Social Psychology, 13,* 59–63.

Wortman C. B., Sheedy, C., Gluhoski V., Kessler R. (1992). Stress, coping, and health: Conceptual issues and directions for future research. In H. S. Friedman (Ed.), *Hostility, coping, and health* (pp. 227–256). Washington, D.C.: American Psychological Association.

Wundt, W. M. (1883). *Philosophische studien.* Leipzig: Wilhelm Engelmann.

Wyatt, G. W., & Parham, W. D. (2007). The inclusion of culturally sensitive course materials in graduate school and training programs. *Psychotherapy: Theory, Research, Practice and Training, 22*(2, Suppl.), 461–468.

Wynn, K. (2002). Do infants have numerical expectations or just perceptual preferences?: Comment. *Developmental Science, 5*(2), 207–209.

Wynn, K. (1992). Addition and subtraction by human infants. *Nature, 358*(6389), 749–750.

Wynne, K., Stanley, S., & Bloom, S. (2004). The gut and regulation of body weight. *The Journal of Clinical Endocrinology and Metabolism, 89*(6), 2576–2582.

Yadav, R., Suri, M., Mathur, R., & Jain, S. (2009). Effect of ventromedial nucleus of hypothalamus on the feeding behavior of rats. *Journal of Clinical Biochemical Nutrition, 44(May),* 247–252.

Yahr, P. (1977). Social subordination and scent marking in male Mongolian gerbils (Meriones unguiculatus). *Animal Behavior, 25,* 292–297.

Yale Centre for Dyslexia. (2008). *Successful dyslexics A to Z.* Retrieved from http://dyslexia.yale.edu/successfuldyslexics.html.

Yalom, I. D., & Josselson, R. (2011). Existential psychotherapy. In R. J. Corsini & D. Wedding (Eds.), *Current psychotherapies* (9th Ed.). Florence, KY: CENGAGE Learning.

Yalom, I. D., & Leszcz, M. (2005). *The theory and practice of group psychotherapy* (5th Ed.). New York: Basic Books.

Yamamoto, K. (1979). Children's ratings of the stressfulness of experiences. *Developmental Psychology, 15,* 581–682.

Yehuda, R. (2009). Stress hormones and PTSD. *Post-traumatic stress disorder: Basic science and clinical practice* (pp. 257–275). Totowa, NJ: Humana Press.

Yehuda, R. (2001). Biology of posttraumatic stress disorder. *Journal of Clinical Psychiatry, 62,* 41–46.

Yehuda, R., Flory, J. D., Pratchett, L. C., Buxbaum, J., Ising, M., & Holsboer, F. (2010). Putative biological mechanisms for the association between early life adversity and the subsequent development of PTSD. *Psychopharmacologia, 212*(3), 405–417.

Yehuda, R., McFarlane, A. C., & Shalev, A.Y. (1998). Predicting the development of posttraumatic stress disorder from the acute response to a traumatic event. *Biological Psychiatry, 44*(12), 1305–1313.

Yela, C. (2006). The evaluation of love: Simplified version of the scales for Yela's tetrangular model based on Sternberg's model. *European Journal of Psychological Assessment, 22*(1), 21–27.

Yerkes, R. M., & Dodson, J. D. (1908). The relation of strength of stimulus to rapidity of habit-formation. *Journal of Comparative Neurology and Psychology, 18,* 459–482.

Yessine, A. K., & Bonta, J. (2009). The offending trajectories of youthful Aboriginal offenders. *Canadian Journal of Criminology and Criminal Justice, 51*(4), 435–472.

Yetiv, S. A. (2011). *Explaining foreign policy: U.S. decision-making in the Gulf Wars.* Johns Hopkins University Press.

Yetiv, S.A. (2003). Groupthink and the Gulf Crisis. *British Journal of Political Science, 33,* 419–442.

Yontef, G., & Jacobs, L. (2011). Gestalt therapy. In R. J. Corsini & D. Wedding (Eds.), *Current psychotherapies* (9th Ed.). Florence, KY: CENGAGE Learning.

Yoon, H. (2003). Factors associated with family caregiver's burden and depression in korea. *International Journal of Aging & Human Development, 57*(4), 291–311.

Yoon, I. Y., Kripke, D. F., Elliott, J. A., Youngstedt, S. D., Rex, K. M., & Hauger, R. L. (2003). Age-related changes of circadian rhythms and sleep-wake cycles. *Journal of the American Geriatrics Society, 51*(8), 1085–1091.

Yoon, T., Okada, J., Jung, M.W., and Kim, J.J. (2008). Prefrontal cortex and hippocampus subserve different components of working memory in rats. *Learning and Memory, 15*, 97–105.

Young, K. S. (2009). Assessment and treatment of internet addiction. *The praeger international collection on addictions, vol 4: Behavioral addictions from concept to compulsion* (pp. 217–234). Santa Barbara, CA: Praeger/ABC-CLIO.

Young, K. S. (2004). Internet addiction: A new clinical phenomenon and its consequences. *American Behavioral Scientist, 48*(4), 402–415.

Young, K. S. (1998). Internet addiction: The emergence of a new clinical disorder. *CyberPsychology & Behavior, 1*(3), 237–244.

Young, K. S. (1996). Psychology of computer use: XL. addictive use of the internet: A case that breaks the stereotype. *Psychological Reports, 79*(3), 899–902.

Young, L. R., & Nestle, M. (2007). Portion sizes and obesity: Responses of fast-food companies. *Journal of Public Health Policy, 28*(2), 238–248.

Yu, D. L., & Seligman, M. E. P. (2002). Preventing depressive symptoms in Chinese children. *Prevention and Treatment, 5*, No Pages.

Yuan, J. W., & Kring, A. M. (2009). Dysphoria and the prediction and experience of emotion. *Cognition and Emotion, 23*(6), 1221–1232.

Yule. W. (1973). Differential prognosis of reading backwardness and specific reading retardation. *British Journal of Education Psychology, 43*, 244–248.

Yutzy, S. H. (2007). Somatoform disorders. In S. C. Yudofsky, J. A. Bourgeois, & R. E. Hales (Eds.), *The American Psychiatric Publishing Board prep and review guide for psychiatry* (pp. 235–243). Washington, DC: American Psychiatric Publishing.

Zager, A., Andersen, M. L., Ruiz, F. S., Antunes, I. B., & Tufik, S. (2007). Effects of acute and chronic sleep loss on immune modulation of rats. *Regulatory, Integrative and Comparative Physiology, 293*, R504–R509.

Zajonc, R. B. (1980). Feeling and thinking: preferences need no inferences. *American Psychologist, 35*, 151–175.

Zajonc, R. B. (1965). Social facilitation. *Science, 149*, 269–274.

Zajonc, R. B., Murphy, S. T., & Inglehart, M. (1989). Feeling and facial efference: Implications of the vascular theory of emotion. *Psychological Review, 96*, 395–416.

Zanarini, M. C., Frankenburg, F. R., DeLuca, C. J., Hennen, J., Khera, G. S., & Gunderson, J. G. (1998). The pain of being borderline: dysphoric states specific to borderline personality disorder. *Harvard Review of Psychiatry, 6*(4), 201–207.

Zarit, S. H., & Gaugler, J. E. (2000). Stress and caregivers. In G. Fink (Ed.), *Encyclopedia of stress, Vol. 1* (pp. 404–407). New York, NY: Academic Press.

Zatorre, R. J. (2003). Absolute pitch: a model for understanding the influence of genes and development on neural and cognitive function. *Nature Neuroscience, 6*, 692–695.

Zawadzki, B., Strelau W., Oniszczenko, W., Roemann, R., & Angleitner, A. (2001). Genetic and environmental influences on temperament. *European Psychologist, 6*, 272–286.

Zelazo, P. D. (2004). The development of conscious control in childhood. *Trends in Cognitive Sciences, 8*, 12–17.

Zelazo, P. D., & Lee, W. S. C. (2010). Brain development: An overview. In W. F. Overton, & R. M. Lerner (Eds.), *The handbook of life-span development*, vol. 1: *Cognition, biology, and methods* (pp. 89–114). Hoboken, NJ: John Wiley & Sons.

Zentall, T. R., & Levine, J. M. (1972). Observational learning and social facilitation in the rat. *Science, 178*, 1220–1221.

Zhu, B., Chen, C., Loftus, E. F., Lin, C., He, Q., Chen, C., . . . Dong, Q. (2010). Individual differences in false memory from misinformation: Cognitive factors. *Memory, 18*(5), 543–555. doi: 10.1080/09658211.2010.487051

Zimbardo, P. (2006). A situationist perspective on the psychology of evil: Understanding how good people are transformed into pe+rpetrators. In R. Falk, I. Gendzier, & R. J. Lifton (Eds.), *Crimes of War: Iraq* (pp. 366–369). New York, NY: Nation Books.

Zimbardo, P. G. (2006). On rethinking the psychology of tyranny: The BBC prison study. *British Journal of Social Psychology, 45*(1), 47–53.

Zimbardo, P. G. (1972). Psychology of imprisonment. *Transition/Society*, 4–8.

Zimmer, C. (2001). *Evolution: The Triumph of an Idea*. HarperCollins Publishers: New York.

Zoccolillo, M., Price, R., Ji, T., Hyun, C., & Hwu, H.-G. (1999). Antisocial personality disorder: Comparisons of prevalence, symptoms, and correlates in four countries. In P. Cohen, C. Slomkowski, & L. N. Robins (Eds.), *Historical and geographical influences on psychopathology* (pp. 249–277). Mahwah, NJ: Lawrence Erlbaum Associates Publishers.

Zola, S. M. (1998). Memory, amnesia, and the issue of recovered memory: Neurobiological aspects. *Clinical Psychology Review, 18*(8), 915–932.

Zucker, K. J. (2005). Gender identity disorder in children and adolescents. *Annual Review of Clinical Psychology, 1*(1), 467–492.

Zucker, K. J. (2002). Intersexuality and gender identity differentiation. *Journal of Pediatric and Adolescent Gynecology, 15*, 2–13.

Zucker, K. J., & Bradley, S. J. (2005). Gender identity and psychosexual disorders. In J. M. Weiner & M. K. Dulcan (Eds.), *American Psychiatric Publishing Textbook of Child and Adolescent Psychiatry, 3rd edition*. Washington, DC: American Psychiatric Publishing.

Zuckerman, M. (2011). Trait and psychobiological approaches. In *Personality science: Three approaches and their applications to the causes and treatment of depression* (pp. 47–77). Washington, DC: American Psychological Association.

Zuckerman, M. (2007). Sensation seeking and risk. *Sensation seeking and risky behavior* (pp. 51–72). Washington, D.C.: American Psychological Association.

Zuckerman, M. (1995). Good and bad humors: biochemical bases of personality and its disorders. *Psychological Science, 6*, 325–332.

Text and Illustration Credits

Chapter 1

Figure 1-3: Figure 1, Ciccarelli, Saundra K.; White, J. Noland, Psychology, 2nd Edition, © 2009, p. 18. Reprinted by permission of Pearson Education, Inc., Upper Saddle River, NJ.; Figure 1-4: Based on College of Ontario Psychologists 2010; Figure 1-5: Ciccarelli, Saundra K.; White, J. Noland, Psychology, 2nd Edition, © 2009, p. 18. Reprinted by permission of Pearson Education, Inc., Upper Saddle River, NJ.

Chapter 2

Figure 2-3: Adapted with permission of John Wiley & Sons, Inc., from Carpenter, S., & Huffman, K. (2008). Visualizing Psychology. Hoboken, NJ: Wiley, p. 15.

Chapter 3

Figure 3-2: Adapted with permission of John Wiley & Sons, Inc., from Carpenter, S., & Huffman, K. (2008). Visualizing Psychology. Hoboken, NJ: Wiley, p. 230; Figure 3-5: Based on Weiten, W. (2007). Psychology: Themes and Variations (7th ed.). Belmont, CA: Thomson Higher Education. Adapted by permission from Macmillan Publishers Ltd: Nature, K. Wynn, Addition and subtraction by human infants, vol. 358, pp. 749–750, © 1992; page 88; Figure 3-8: Statistics Canada, Child Care in Canada: Children and Youth Research Paper Series, Bushnick, Tracey (2006) Catalogue no. 89-599-MIE2006003, April 2006, Figure 6, 2002-2003, page 14; Figure 3-12: Adapted by permission from BMJ Publishing Group Limited. Archives of Disease in Childhood, JM Tanner, RN Whitehouse, and M. Takaislu, vol. 41, pp. 451–471, 1966; Figure 3-13: Chandler, M.J. and Lalonde, CV. E. (2009) Cultural continuity as a moderator of suicide risk among Canada's first nations.

Chapter 4

Figure 4-5: Adapted with permission of John Wiley & Sons, Inc., from Huffman, K. (2010). Psychology in Action (9th ed.). Hoboken, NJ: Wiley, p. 64.

Chapter 5

Figure 5-2: Huffman 9e, Psychology in Action, Application: Sensation of Perception, part b, p. 129; Figure 5-10: Reprinted with permission of John Wiley & Sons, Inc., from Carpenter, S., & Huffman, K. (2008). Visualizing Psychology. Hoboken, NJ: Wiley, p. 107; Figure 5-14: M.C. Escher's "Convex and Concave" © 2011 The M.C. Escher Company-Holland. All rights reserved. www.mcescher.com; Figure 5-16: Reprinted with permission of John Wiley & Sons, Inc., from Kowalski, R., & Westen, D. (2009). Psychology (5th ed.). Hoboken, NJ: Wiley, pp. 143, 144.

Chapter 6

Table 6-2: Adapted with permission of John Wiley & Sons, Inc., from Carpenter. S., & Huffman, K. (2008). Visualizing Psychology. Hoboken, NJ: Wiley, p. 129.

Chapter 8

Figure 8-9: Reprinted from Bahrick, Bahrick, and Wittlinger. (1974). Those unforgettable high school days. Psychology Today.

Chapter 9

Figure 9-2: Adapted with permission from Fenson, Dale, Reznick, et al. (1994). Variability in early communicative development. Monographs of the Society for Research in Child Development, 59(5, Serial No. 173), Blackwell Publishers, based on Lilienfeld, S., Lynn, S., Namy, L., & Wolf, N. (2009). Psychology: From inquiry to understanding. Boston: Pearson/Allyn & Bacon, Figure 8-3, p. 325; Figure 9-4: Reprinted from Cognitive Psychology, 21, J.S. Johnson & E.L. Newport, Critical period effects in second language learning: The influence of maturational state on the acquisition of English as a second language, pp. 60-99, Copyright 1989, with permission from Elsevier.

Chapter 10

Figure 10-5: Sample items similar to those found in the Wechsler Adult Intelligence Scale, Third Edition (WAIS-III). Copyright © 1997 NCS Pearson, Inc. Reproduced with permission. All rights reserved. "Wechsler Adult Intelligence Scale" and "WAIS" are trademarks, in the US and/or other countries, of Pearson Education, Inc. or its affiliates; Figure 10-6: Sample items similar to those found in Raven's Progressive Matrices (Advanced). Copyright © 1976, 1947, 1943 NCS Pearson, Inc. Reproduced with permission. All rights reserved. "Raven's Progressive Matrices and vocabulary scales" are trademarks, in the US and/or other countries, of Pearson Education, Inc. or its affiliates; Figure 10-7: Adapted from Weiten, W. (2007). Psychology: Themes and Variations (7th ed.). Belmont, CA: Thomson Learning; Horgan, J. (1995). Get smart, take a test. Scientific American, 273(5), 1995, p. 14. Adapted with permission of Dmitry Schidlowsky Illustration.

Chapter 11

Figure 11-1: Adapted with permission of John Wiley & Sons, Inc., from Carpenter, S., & Huffman, K. (2008). Visualizing Psychology. Hoboken, NJ: Wiley, p. 285; Figure 11-6: "Figure 9.13 p. 361" from PSYCHOLOGICAL SCIENCE, 2ND EDITION by Michael S. Gazzaniga and Todd F. Heatherton. Copyright © 2006, 2003 by W.W. Norton & Company, Inc. Used by permission of W.W. Norton & Company, Inc.; Figure 11-7: Reprinted with permission from Masters, W. H., & Johnson V. E. (1966). Human sexual response. Boston: Little, Brown, p. 5. Copyright © 1966 by the Masters and Johnson Institute.

Chapter 12

Table 12-1: Adapted with permission of John Wiley & Sons, Inc., from Kowalski, R., & Westen, D. (2009). Psychology (5th ed.). Hoboken, NJ: Wiley, p. 361; data from Plutchik, R. (1980). Emotions: A psychoevolutionary synthesis. New York: Harper & Row; Practically Speaking Box (page 472): Reprinted with permission from Ed Diener and Robert Biswas-Diener, Happiness: Unlocking the Mysteries of Psychological Wealth (Malden, MA: Blackwell Publishing, 2008), pp. 237–239.

Chapter 13

Figure 13-2: Adapted with permission from Eysenck, H. J. (1976). The biological basis of personality, p. 36. Courtesy of Charles C Thomas Publisher, Ltd., Springfield, Illinois; based on Weiten, W. (2007). Psychology: Themes and Variations (7th ed.). Belmont, CA: Thomson Wadsworth; Figure 13-3: Adapted from Cattell, Personality pinned down. Psychology Today, July 1973; Figure 13-5: Adapted with permission From WEITEN. *ACP PSYCHOLOGY-THEMES AND VARIATIONS-FIU EDITION, 6E. © 2004 Wadsworth, a part of Cengage Learning, Inc. Reproduced by permission. www.cengage.com/permissions.

Chapter 14

Figure 14-2: Adapted with permission of John Wiley & Sons, Inc., from Kowalski, R., & Westen, D. (2009). Psychology (5th ed.). Hoboken, NJ: Wiley, p. 614; based on Festinger, L., & Carlsmith, J. M. (1959). Cognitive consequences of forced compliance. Journal of Abnormal and Social Psychology, 58, 203–210; Figure 14-3: Reginald W. Bibby, "Racial Intermarriage: Canada and the U.S." Project Canada Surveys, University of Lethbridge. Release #9, 2007; Figure 14-5: Adapted from Myers, D. G. (2002). Social Psychology (7th ed.). New York: McGraw-Hill, Figure 3-2; data from Jones, E. E., & Harris, V.A. (1967). The attribution of attitudes. Journal of Experimental Social Psychology, 3, 1–24; Figure 14-8: Adapted from Asch, S. E. (1955). Opinions and social pressure. Scientific American, 193(5), 31–35. © 1955 by Scientific American, Inc.; Figure 14-11: Adapted from Myers, D. G. (2002). Social Psychology (7th ed.). New York: Mc-Graw Hill, Figures 3-2 and 12-4; based on Darley, J. M., & Latane, B. (1968). Bystander intervention in emergencies: Diffusion of responsibility. Journal of Personality and Social Psychology, 8, 377–383.

Chapter 15

Table 15-1: Undergraduate Stress Questionnaire, Crandall, C. S., Preisler, J. J., & Aussprung, J. (1992). Measuring Life Event Stress in the Lives of College Students: The Undergraduate Stress Questionnaire (USQ). Journal of Behavioral Medicine, 15(6), 627-662; Table 15-2: Reprinted from Journal of Psychosomatic Research, Vol. 11; Holmes and Rahe: "The Social Readjustment Rating Scale," 213–218, 1967, with permission from Elsevier.

Chapter 16

Figure 16-1: Health Canada. A Report on Mental Illnesses in Canada. Ottawa, Canada 2002 © Health Canada Editorial Board Mental Illnesses in Canada Canadian Cataloguing in Publication Data ISBN H39-643/2002E Cat. No. 0-662-32817-5; Table 16-3: Reprinted with permission from the Diagnostic and Statistical Manual of Mental Disorders, Fourth Edition, Text Revision, (Copyright ©2000). American Psychiatric Association; Figure 16-4: Schizophrenia Genesis: The Origins of Madness, New York: W.H. Freeman, 1991, p. 96 © 1991 Irving I. Gottesman.

Chapter 17

Table 17-2: Reprinted with permission of John Wiley & Sons, Inc., from Kowalski, R., & Westen, D. (2009). Psychology (5th ed.). Hoboken, NJ: Wiley, p. 574.

Photo Credits

Before You Go On

Page 8: Suprijono Suharjoto/iStock; page 10: Shutterstock; page 16: Mark Anderson/Rubberball/Corbis; page 24: Shutterstock.

Chapter 1

Page 2: Jae Rew/Getty Images; page 4: CJG – Technology/Alamy; page 5: Stuart Freedman/Corbis; page 8: Chuck Stoody/CP; page 9 (top): ilker yüksel/iStock; page 9 (bottom): The Granger Collection; page 11 (top): The Art Archive/Down HouseKent/Eileen Tweedy/The Kobal Collection, Ltd.; page 11 (bottom): Robbie Jack/Corbis; page 12: Archives of the History of American Psychology, The Center for the History of Psychology- The University of Akron; page 14 (top): The Granger Collection; page 14 (bottom): Rune Hellestad/Corbis; page 16: Wide World Photos/AP; page 18 Nina Leen/Time & Life Pictures/Getty Images; page 19: Markus Botzek/zefa/Corbis; page 20: Roger Ressmeyer/Corbis; page 22: Karen Kasmauski/Corbis; page 23: Thefinalmiracle/Dreamstime/GetStock; page 24 (far left): Mitchell Kanashkevich/Getty Images; page 24 (left): Vitoria Blackie/Getty Images; page 24 (right): Theo Allofs/Masterfile; page 24 (far right): Daniel Milnor/Masterfile; page 27: Wide World Photos/AP; page 28: Clemens Bilan/AFP/Getty Images; page 30: © Michael Newman/Photo Edit; page 32: Ian Berry/Magnum Photos.

Chapter 2

Page 36: Pando Hall/Getty Images; page 38: Dreamstime/GetStock; page 39: Joe Raedle/Getty Images; page 42: Colin Hawkins/Getty Images; page 43 (top left): ER Productions/Brand X/Corbis; page 43 (top right): Joseph Lindau/Corbis; page 43 (bottom): China Foto Press/Getty Images; page 45: Courtesy of Dr. Stanley Coren; page 46 (top): David M. Dennis/Maxx Images; page 46 (bottom): John Henley/Corbis; page 48: Sergei Bachlakov/ZUMA Press/Corbis; page 50: Jeff Greenberg/PhotoEdit; page 52: Picture Partners/Alamy; page 56 (left): iStock; page 56 (right): Mike/Zefa/Corbis; page 57: Thinkstock/Getty Images; page 58: Image Source/Getty Images; page 60: Milena Boniek/PhotoAlto/Corbis; page 61: Dream Stock/Masterfile.

Chapter 3

Page 64: John Lund/Annabelle Breakey/Getty Images; page 66: Eric Bouvet/Gamma-Rapho/Getty Images; page 68: Monkeybusinessimages/Dreamstime/GetStock; page 70 (top): Nina Leen/Time & Life Pictures/Getty Images; page 70 (bottom): Robert van der Hilst/Corbis; page 74 (left): CNRI/Photo Researchers; page 74 (right): © Graham Dunn; page 75: Rubberball/Getty Images; page 77 (top right): Biophoto Associates/Photo Researchers; page 77 (bottom right): Petit Format/Nestle/Photo Researchers; page 78: Courtesy of Fasstar Enterprises www.fasstar.com; page 79: Spencer Grant/Photo Edit; page 83 (left & centre): Doug Goodman/Photo Researchers; page 83 (right): Laura Dwight/Photo Edit; page 85: Niderlander/Dreamstime/GetStock; page 90: Masterfile; page 91: Pat LaCroix/Getty Images; page 93: iStock; page 94 (left, centre, & right): Ellen B. Senisi/The Image Works; page 100 (top): John Giustina/Getty Images; page 104: Masterfile; page 105 (top left): Created by Graham Johnson of grahamj.com for the Howard Hughes Medical Institute/HHMI Bulletin ©2004; page 105 (top centre): The Image Works; page 105 (top right): ZoranMilich/Masterfile; page 105 (centre): Thomas Deerinck, NCMIR/Photo Researchers, Inc.; page 105 (bottom left): Masterfile; page 105 (bottom right): Thomas Deerinck, NCMIR/Photo Researchers, Inc.; page 106: Betsi van derMeer/zefa/Corbis; page 107: LookatSciences/Phototake; page 112 (top): Jessica Webb Sibley/AP; page 112 (bottom): Zach Gold/Corbis; page 117: Ariel Skeley/Getty Images.

Chapter 4

Page 118: G. Tompkinson/Photo Researchers; page 120: Courtesy Leigh Nystrom & Jonathan Cohen, Princeton University; page 122: Primary rat hippocampal neurons, courtesy of Dr. LLewelyn Roderick, Dr. Martin Bootman, and Dr. Paul Cuddon, The Babraham Institute, Cambridge, UK; page 123 (top): From Wikipedia, http://commons.wikimedia.org/wiki/File: Zwei_Verschiedene_Neurone .png; page 123 (bottom): Riccardo Cassiani-Ingoni/Photo Researchers; page 129: Dennis Kunkel/Phototake; page 131: Bob Pardue/Alamy; page 134: iStock; page 135: Courtesy of Thomas Deerinck, NCMIR, University of California, San Diego; page 136: Hola Images/Getty Images; page 137: Thomas Northcut/Getty Images; page 138 (bottom): Chad Slatterly/Getty Images; page 140: Asia Images/Getty; page 142 (top left): From the collection of Jack and Beverly Wilgus. Image from Wikipedia.org; page 142 (top right): Harvard Medical School/AP; page 142 (bottom): www.mindfreedom.org; page 143 (top): Mark Nielsen; page 143 (bottom): Masterfile; page 145: Courtesy of the University of Chicago; page 147 (top): Stapleton Collection/Corbis; page 148 (left): Michael Nicholson/Corbis; page 148 (right): Neilld/Dreamstime/GetStock;

page 149: Shawnhemp/Dreamstime/GetStock; page 151: Courtesy of Zazzle Inc; page 152 (left): Danielle Wooten/ Getty Images; page 152 (right): Michael Rosenfield/ Getty Images; page 153: Dana Hursey Photography/Getty Images; page 155 (top): Evan Agostini/AP; page 155 (bottom): Courtesy ReNeuron; page 159: Owen Franken/ Corbis.

Chapter 5

Page 160: Masterfile; page 164 (bottom): ER Productions/ Corbis; page 167: Steve Prezant/Corbis; page 168: Stockbroker/Age Fotostock; page 169 (top left): Courtesy of Drs. Hang Hu and Ariel Agmon, Sensory Neuroscience Research Center, West Virginia University School of Medicine; page 169 (top right): Neuroscience Research Center, West Virginia University School of Medicine; page 169 (centre): Masterfile; page 169 (bottom right): From Marco Tizzano et al., BMC Neuroscience, 2008, 9:110, Figure 5; ©2008 Tizzano et al; licensee BioMedCentral Ltd.; page 170 (top): Paul Taylor/Corbis; page 170 (bottom): iStock; page 171: Louie Psihoyos/Corbis; page 172: Patrick Sheandell O'Carroll/PhotoAlto/Corbis; page 174: Owen Franken/Corbis; page 176: Dreamstime/ GetStock; page 177: Robbie Jack/Corbis; page 178 (top): Stockbyte/Getty Images; page 178 (bottom): Jim Mone/ AP; page 182: Jose Luis Pelaez/Corbis; page 183 (top): George Steinmetz/Corbis; page 183 (bottom): Getty Images; page 184 (top): Gareth Brown/Corbis; page 184 (bottom): Mark Davis/Fox/PictureGroup/CP; page 185: Landov; page 188: Omikron/Photo Researchers; page 189 (top): Steven Senne/AP; page 191: Argument/iStock; page 193 (top): Margo Silver/Getty Images; page 193 (bottom left & right): Wasserman & Partners Advertising; page 194: Ron Watts/Corbis; page 195 (top): Field Museum Library/Getty Images; page 195 (bottom): Department of Tourism & Parks, New Brunswick, Canada; page 196: Billy Hustace/Getty Images; page 199: Londie Padelsky/ Monsoon/Corbis.

Chapter 6

Page 200: Ron Krisel/Getty; page 202 (top): Lisa F. Young/Shutterstock; page 202 (bottom): Damir Frkovic/ Masterfile; page 203: John Burcham/Getty Images; page 206: Charles Gullung/Getty Images; page 207: Arenacreative/Dreamstime/GetStock; page 210: Science Photo Library/PhotoResearchers; page 212 (top left): Life Boat/Getty Images; page 212 (top right): Jupiter Images/ Getty Images; page 213 (top): Eric Vandeville/Gamma-Rapho/GettyImages; page 213 (bottom): Stockbyte/Getty Images; page 214 (left & right): Hank Morgan/Photo Researchers; page 216: Gail Mooney/Masterfile; page 217 (top left): Image adapted from Neuron 54, 2007 (by Kurt Sailor, Guo-li Ming, and Hongjun Song at Johns Hopkins School of Medicine); page 217 (centre left): J. Livet, J.R. Sanes, J.W. Lichtman, Center for Brain Science—Harvard University; page 217 (right): Courtesy of Sebastien G. Bouret; page 217 (bottom): Masterfile; page 218: Harald Sund/Getty Images; page 219: PM Images/Getty Images; page 220 (top): Alistair Baker/Corbis; page 220 (bottom): Julia Klee/Corbis; page 223 (left & right): Louie Psihoyos/ Science Faction/Corbis; page 224: Francoise Sauze/Photo Researchers; page227: Masterfile; page 229: Darryl Dyck/ CP; page 230: Murat Taner/Corbis; page 231: Andrew Lichenstein/Corbis; page 232: Catherine Karnow/Corbis; page 234: Bob Thomas/Corbis; page 235: The Granger Collection; page 236: Carol and Mike Werner/Phototake; page 238: Jonathan Hayward/CP; page 243: Newmann/ Corbis.

Chapter 7

Page 244: Masterfile; page 246: Tetra Images/Corbis; page 247 (left & right): Nyul/Dreamstime/GetStock; page 248: Courtesy of Columbia University, New York. Image from Wikipedia, http://en.wikipedia.org/wiki/Aplysia_californica; page 249: Juniors Bildarchiv/Age fotostock; page 251: The Granger Collection; page 253: Janine Wiedel Photolibrary/Alamy; page 254: Courtesy of Benjamin Harris, University of New Hampshire; page 256: Alan and Sandy Carey/Photo Researchers; page 257 (left): Reprinted by permission of Elsevier from L. Goossen, et al., Amygdala Hyperfunction in Phobic Fear Normalizes After Exposure, *Biological Psychiatry, 62*(10), 1119–1125, Figure 1; page 257 (right): Serge Kozak/Corbis; page 258: blickwinkel/Alamy; page 263: UrbanZone/Alamy; page 265 (top): Dennis MacDonald/Alamy; page 265 (bottom): A. Witte/C. Mahaney/Getty Images; page 266: Getty Images; page 267: Dan McCoy/Rainbow/Corbis; page 268: Photograph by Frans de Waal from The Ape and the Sushi Master; page 269 (top & bottom): Courtesy of Albert Bandura; page 270:Thinkstock/Getty Images; page 271: Courtesy of the American Philosophical Society; page 272: David H. Wells/Corbis; page 274: Dan Hallman/Getty Images; page 275: LookatSciences/Phototake; page 276: Masterfile; page 277 (top left): From Michael Petrides, J. Neurosci. 2003 Jul 2; 23 (13):5945–5952; page 277 (top right and centre left): courtesy of Elizabeth Gould; page 277 (bottom): Masterfile; page 279: Olivier Voisin/ Photo Researchers; page 280: Chuck Burton/AP; page 283: Photodisc/Getty Images.

Chapter 8

Page 284: Chris Ryan/Age Fotostock; page 288: Digital Vision/Getty Images; page 289: Courtesy of World Memory Championships; page 290: Masterfile; page 292 (top):Thinkstock/Getty Images; page 292 (bottom): Kevin Lam photographer, www.kevinlamphoto.com, courtesy of Patty Ho; page 294: Tetra Images/Getty Images; page 295: Tomas Hajek/isifa/Getty Images; page 299 (left):

AAGAMIA/Getty Images; page 299 (right): iStock; page 301: Michael Newman/PhotoEdit; page 302: Roger L. Wollenberg/UPI/Landov; page 304: Todd Korol/Reuters/Landov; page 307 (left): Chip Somodevilla/Getty Images; page 307 (right): Jeff Hutchens/Getty Images; page 308: Thinkstock/Getty Images; page 310: Chuck Burton/AP; page 311: Oscar Sosa/AP; page 312 (top): PNC/Getty Images; page 312 (bottom right): Image Source/Stewart Cohen Pictu/CP; page 312 (bottom left): Heide Benser/Corbis; page 313 (top left): Courtesy of Elizabeth Gould; page 313 (top right): Roberto Cabeza, Duke University. From Cabeza, Cerebral Cortex, 2007, Figure 4. Reproduced with permission of Oxford University Press; page 313 (bottom right): J. Livet, J.R. Sanes, J.W. Lichtman, Center for Brain Science—Harvard University; page 313 (bottom left): Masterfile; page 314: From Edward T. Bullmore, Neuroimage 22(4), 1704-1714, Figure 5; page 316: Aurelie and Morgan Da/Maxx Images; page 318: Christiana Koci Hernandez/Corbis; page 320: Paul Chiasson/CP; page 321 (top): Science Source/Photo Researchers; page 321 (bottom left): ISM/Phototake; page 321 (bottom centre): Pasieka/Science Photo Library; page 321 (bottom right): Carolina Biological Supply Company/Phototake; page 322: Trappe/Alamy/GetStock; page 327: STOCK4B/Getty Images.

Chapter 9

Page 328: Masterfile; page 331: Hans Reinhard/Corbis; page 332: Paul Chiasson/CP; page 333: Laura Dwight/Corbis; page 335: Joe Bator/Corbis; page 336: David Young-Wolff/PhotoEdit; page 337: GENIE by RUSS RYMER. Copyright © 1993 by Russ Rymer. A portion of this book appeared in somewhat different form in The New Yorker magazine. Reprinted by permission of HarperCollins Publishers; page 338 (top): Joe Castro/AP; page 338 (bottom): Asia Images Group/Getty Images; page 339: Courtesy of Dr. Bill Vicars; page 340 (bottom): WDCN/Univ. College London/Photo Researchers, Inc; page 341 (top): Digital Vision/Getty Images; page 341 (bottom): AlaskaStock/Masterfile; page 342: Thinkstock/Getty Images; page 344 (centre): David Lyons/Alamy; page 344 (right): Peter Holmes/Age Fotostock; page 344 (bottom): Masterfile; page 345 (top left): From Yapeng Wang, Neuroimage 35(2):862-70, Figure 1, 2007; page 345 (top right): From K.L. Sakai, Science 310 (5749):815-9, Nov. 4, 2005, Figure 3; page 345 (bottom right): From D. Perani, Human Brain Mapping 19(3):170-82, Figure 2, 2003.; page 345 (centre): Masterfile; page 347: Interfoto/Alamy; page 350 (top left): Tom Grill/Corbis; page 350 (top right): Image Source/Corbis; page 350 (centre): Image Source/Corbis; page 351: JAGADEESH NV/epa/Corbis; page 355: Bryn Colton/Assignments Photographers/Corbis; page 356: Car Culture/Corbis; page 358: George Doyle/Getty Images; page 359 (top): Frans Lanting/Corbis; page 359 (bottom): Thinkstock/Getty; page 360: Tom Stewart/Corbis; page 361: Avec l'autorisation de la Fondation des maladies mentales; page 365: Gabe Palmer/Corbis.

Chapter 10

Page 366: Influx Productions/Getty Images; page 370: AFP/Getty Images; page 371 (top left): Tim Mosenfelder/Getty Images; page 371 (top centre): Fred Thornhill/Corbis; page 371 (top right): Justin Sullivan/Getty Images; page 375 (top): © Warner Brothers/Courtesy Everett Collection/CP; page 375 (bottom): CBC/George Stroumboulopoulos Tonight; page 376 (left): Bruno Morandi/Getty Images; page 376 (right): Paul Barton/Corbis; page 377: Rene Johnston/GetStock; page 380: Bettmann/Corbis, Archives de la Société Binet-Simon; page 381: Damian Dovarganes/AP; page 385: James Shaffer/PhotoEdit; page 387: Bob Daemmrich/PhotoEdit; page 389 (left): eyetrigger Pty Ltd/Corbis; page 389 (right): Richard Schultz/Corbis; page 391: Rick Gershon/Getty Images; page 393 (top): Marcus Mok/Getty Images; page 393 (bottom): Hoang Dinh Nam AFP/Getty Images; page 394 (top): Lester Lefkowitz/Getty Images; page 394 (bottom): Stefan Berg/Getty Images; page 395: Romeo Gacad/AFP/Getty Images; page 397: Jim West/PhotoEdit; page 398: Valuavitaly/Dreamstime/GetStock; page 399: Masterfile; page 400: John MacDougall/AFP/Getty Images; page 401 (top & bottom): From J. Duncan, Science, 289 (5478):457-460, July 21, 2000, Figures a and b; page 402 (left): Peet Simard/Corbis; page 402 (right): Kristy-Anne Glubish/Design Pics/Corbis; page 403 (left): Markus Moellenberg/Corbis; page 403 (left): Hayley Madden/Redferns/Getty Images; page 404: AFP/Getty Images; page 405: The Tennessean, Rex Perry/AP; page 409: Hill Street Studios/Getty Images.

Chapter 11

Page 410: Thomas Barwick/Digital Vision/Getty Images; page 412: Krystle Wright/Aurora Open/Corbis; page 413 (top): Jennie Woodcock/Reflections Photolibrary/Corbis; page 413 (bottom): Denny Allen/Getty Images; page 414: Shalom Ormsby/BlendImages/Corbis; page 415: Courtesy of Canada's Wonderland; page 416 (left): Massimo Borchi/Corbis; page 416 (right): Thierry Dosogne/Getty Images; page 417: Jorge Rios iPhoto Inc./Newscom; page 420: Courtesy of Philip Teitelbaum; page 421 (top): Eye - CNImaging/Newscom; page 421 (bottom): Greg Ceo/Getty Images; page 422: Sodimages/Dreamstime/GetStock; page 423 (top): Gary Salter/Corbis; page 423 (bottom): Mark Peterson/Corbis; page 424: Tim Boyle/Getty Images; page 425: Stephen Ferry/Liaison/Getty Images; page 426: David Gray/Reuters; page 428 (top): Jonathan Hayward/CP; page 428 (bottom): Don Hammond/Design Pics/Corbis; page 430 (top): Shuttlecock/Dreamstime/GetStock; page 430 (bottom): choja/iStock; page 431: Courtesy of Lucy L. Brown, Albert Einstein College of Medicine;

page 432: Belinda Images/Superstock; page 435 (left): Charla Jones/Toronto Star/CP; page 435 (right): Tony Bock/Toronto Star/CP; page 436: Orange-Melody/iStock; page 437: Sunset Boulevard/Corbis; page 438: QMI Agency; page 439: Mark J. Terrill/AP; page 440 (top): Bob Krist/Corbis; page 440 (bottom): Lee Mason; page 441: Mascarucci/Corbis; page 442: AIC/Age Fotostock/MaxxImages; page 443 (top left): Nancy Kedersha/UCLA/Science Photo Library/Photo Researchers; page 443 (top right): Courtesy of Elizabeth Gould; page 443 (bottom right): S. Small, et al., Proc Natl Acad Sci USA:104(13):5638-43, 2007; page 443 (bottom left): Masterfile; page 444: Brampton Ontario 1900, National Archives NPA-164911; page 447: Odilon Dimier/Photo Alto/©Corbis.

Chapter 12

Page 448: Glow Images/Age Fotostock; page 450: Darren Calabrese/CP; page 451: Mike Kemp/Getty Images; page 452 (all): Courtesy of P. Ekman, Human Interaction Lab, University of California, San Francisco; page 454: Tom Stewart Photography; page 455: Dann Tardif/Corbis; page 456: Dreamstime/GetStock; page 459: Diego.cervo/Dreamstime/GetStock; page 461 (left): Photo by Wendy J Photography, www.wendyjphotography.com; page 461 (right): Kempter/iStock; page 463 (top left & right): David Young-Wolff/Photoedit; page 463 (bottom left & right): Courtesy of Karen Huffman; page 464: Masterfile; page 466: Stretch Photography/Blend Images/Getty Images; page 469 (left): Jack Goldfarb/Design Pics/Corbis; page 469 (right): Masterfile; page 470: David Woods/Corbis; page 473: Corbis; page 474: Stockbyte/Getty Images; page 475: Edward Bock/Corbis; page 477 (left): Kin Cheung/Reuters/Corbis; page 477 (right): Jens Buettner/epa/Corbis; page 478: Elfenbein, Beaupré, Lévesque, and Hess, 2007; Dr. David Matsumoto; Lévesque, and Hess, 2007; page 479: Ashley Cooper/Corbis; page 480: Erica Shires/Corbis; page 481 (far left): Albert L. Ortega/PictureGroup/CP; page 481 (left): Alik Keplicz/CP; page 481 (right): Courtesy of Oscar Lopez.com; page 481 (far right): Dave Hogan/Getty Images; page 485: John Lund/Drew Kelly/Blend Images/Corbis.

Chapter 13

Page 486: Digital Vision/Getty Images; page 488: James Woodson/Digital vision/Getty Images; page 490: Masterfile; page 492 (top): Monkeybusinessimages/Dreamstime/GetStock; page 492 (bottom left): Image Source/Corbis; page 492 (bottom right): Jose Luis Pelaez, Inc./BlendImages/Corbis; page 493 (top): Anna Peisl/Corbis; page 493 (bottom): Michael Macor/San Francisco Chronicle/Corbis; page 494: Cancan Chu/Getty Images; page 495 (left): Dinodia Photos/Getty Images; page 495 (right): Alexander Raths/iStock; page 500: Baerbel Schmidt/Getty Images; page 501: Ableimages/Getty Images; page 504: Peter Byrne/PA Wire/AP/Wide World Photos; page 505: T.K. Wanstal/The Image Works; page 507: Bettmann/Corbis; page 510: Michaeljung/Dreamstime/GetStock; page 511: Roger Ressmeyer/Corbis; page 512: Tim Pannell/Corbis; page 514 (top left): Creasource/Corbis; page 514 (top right): Tokyo Space Club/Corbis; page 514 (bottom): Nancy Honey Cultura/Newscom; page 516: Leah Hennel/*Calgary Herald*; Reprinted with permission of *The Calgary Herald*; page 518: Ryan Remiorz/CP; page 519: Image Source/Corbis; page 521 (left): Index Stock/Photolibrary; page 521 (right): Vincent McIndoe/Stock Illustration Source/Getty Images, Inc.; page 525: Image Source/Corbis.

Chapter 14

Page 526: Masterfile; page 528: Nick Procaylo/Vancouver Sun; page 529: Jose Luis Peleaz/Blend Images/Corbis; page 531: Spencer Grant/PhotoEdit; page 532: Michele Constantini/Photo Alto/Corbis; page 534 (left): Dave Martin/AP; page 534 (right): Chris Graythen/Getty Images; page 537 (left): Jay Directo/AFP/Getty Images; page 537 (right): Tetra Images/Getty Images; page 541: Christine Schneider/Corbis; page 544 (top): Richard T. Nowitz/Corbis; page 544 (bottom): Image Source/Getty Images, Inc.; page 545: Philip G. Zimbardo, Inc.; page 546: Jose Luis Pelaez/Getty Images; page 549 (left & right): ©1968 by Stanley Milgram. © renewed 1993 by Alexandra Milgram. From the film OBEDIENCE, distributed by Penn State Media Sales; page 552: Masterfile; page 553: Lou Cypher/Fancy/Firstlight; page 554: Getty Images; page 556: Albert Gea/Corbis; page 557 (top): Ann Cutting/Getty Images; page 557 (bottom): Digital Vision/Getty Images; page 559: Sergio Dionisio/Getty Images; page 561: Corbis; page 565: Jonas Ekstromer/AP; page 567: Silvia Morara/Corbis; page 571: Jasper White/Getty Images.

Chapter 15

Page 572: Bloom Image/Getty Images; page 574: Corbis; page 575: Brendan McDermid/Reuters/Landov; page 577: QMI Agency; page 578 (top): Carmen Taylor/AP; page 578 (bottom): Maverick/Dreamstime/GetStock; page 581 (top): Stockphoto4u/iStock; page 581 (bottom): Digital Vision/Getty Images; page 583: Jim Young/Reuters/Landov; page 584 (top): ZUMAPress/Keystone; page 584 (bottom): Kevin Dodge/Corbis; page 587 (top): Geoff Howe/CP; page 587 (bottom): Medioimages/Photodisc/Thinkstock; page 588: Jessica Teft/Keystone; page 589: Mike Kapusta; page 591 (left): © JEVGENIJA/Alamy; page 591 (centre): Rob Marmion/Dreamstime/GetStock; page 591 (right): © amana images inc./Alamy; page 592: Masterfile; page 593 (top left): Courtesy Jason J. Radley, University of Iowa; page 593 (top right): Courtesy Elizabeth Gould; page 593 (bottom left): Image provided by Casper Hoogenraad (Erasmus Medical Center

Rotterdam, The Netherlands; c.hoogenraad@erasmusmc.nl) and Harm Krugers (SILS-CNS, University of Amsterdam, The Netherlands, h.krugers@uva.nl); page 593 (bottom right): Masterfile; page 595: Richard Heathcote/Getty Images; page 597: Susana Vera/Reuters/Corbis; page 598: Jerzyworks/Masterfile; page 599: Xinhua Press/Corbis; page 601: age fotostock/MaxxImages; page 602 (top): Fotodesign/Dreamstime/GetStock; page 602 (bottom): Jean Claude Revy/ISM/Phototake; page 604: Chris Arend/Getty Images; page 605: Shannon Stapleton/Reuters/Corbis; page 606: Wolfgang Rattay/Reuters; page 607: QMI Agency; page 608: Chris Hondros/Getty Images; page 611: Stockbyte/Getty Images.

Chapter 16

Page 612: Justin Horrocks/iStockphoto; page 614 (left): Burstein Collection/Corbis/©2009 The Munch Museum/The Munch-Ellingsen Group/Artists Rights Society (ARS), NY; page 614 (right): Bettmann/Corbis; page 615: Corbis; page 616: Rajesh Nirgude/AP; page 617: Stewart Cook/Rex Features/CP; page 619: SukreeSukplang/Reuters/Corbis; page 621: M. Spencer Green/AP; page 622: The Charlotte Observer, Christopher A. Record/AP; page 623: epicurean/iStock istock-photo-2403667; page 624 (top): Monalyn Gracia/Corbis; page 624 (bottom): Radius Images/Corbis; page 625: Romeo Ranoco/Reuters/Landov; page 626: Steve Woods/epa/Corbis; page 628: Aflo Relax/Masterfile; page 629: Digital Vision/Getty Images; page 631: Image Source/Corbis; page 633: Thinkstock/Getty Images; page 634: Thinkstock/Getty Images; page 637: Image Source/Corbis; page 638: Nal_ha/iStock; page 639: Infinityphoto/Dreamstime/GetStock; page 640: Javier Pierini/Corbis; page 642 (left): Printed by permission of Random House Canada; page 642 (right): Todd Korol/Reuters/Landov; page 644: Roy McMahon & Wieger Poutsma/Corbis; page 646: Grunnitus Studio/Photo Researchers; page 650: Ariel Skelley/Corbis; page 651: Michaeljung/Dreamstime/GetStock; page 652: Getty Images; page 654: Chris Leschinsky/Getty Images; page 661: Corinne Boutin/Getty Images.

Chapter 17

Page 662: Dreamstime/GetStock; page 664: age fotostock/MaxxImages; page 666: tunart/iStock; page 667: United Artists/Fantasy Films/The Kobal Collection; page 669: Bigtexphoto/Dreamstime/GetStock; page 670: Michael A. Keller/Corbis; page 671: (top left) From Paul Keedwell, *Journal of Psychopharmacology 23*(7):775-88, Figure 3, 2009, Sage Publications. ©2009 British Association for Psychopharmacology; page 671 (bottom left): MedioImages/Photodisc/Getty Images, Inc.; page 671 (bottom right) Courtesy of Charles Nicholson, New York University School of Medicine; page 672 (top): Will & Deni McIntyre/Photo Researchers, Inc; page 673 (left): Bonnie Weller/MCT/Landov; page 673 (right): Winfried Rothermel/AP; page 674 (left): Zephyr/Science Photo Library; page 674 (right): Tim Vernon, LTH NHS Trust/Photo Researchers; page 675: Photonica/Getty Images; page 676 (top): Iconica/Getty Images; page 676 (bottom): Konstantin Binder/Wikipedia Creative Commons; page 679 (top): Piotr Marcinski/Shutterstock; page 679 (bottom): David Young-Wolff/PhotoEdit; page 680 (top): Aspenphoto/Dreamstime/GetStock; page 680 (bottom): Cynthia Dopkin/Photo Researchers; page 682: Masterfile; page 685 (top): David Woods/Corbis; page 685 (bottom left & right): Pascal Preti/Getty Images; page 687 (left): Robin Nelson/PhotoEdit; page 687 (centre): Richard T. Nowitz/Corbis; page 687 (right): Comstock/Getty Images; page 688: Lisa F. Young/Shutterstock; page 689: M. Spencer Green/AP; page 692: Jedd Cadge/The Image Bank/Getty Images; page 693: Chuck Stoody/AP; page 697: Images.com/Corbis.

Name Index

C

D

E

F

I

J

K

L

M

N

O

Subject Index

B

C

D

E

F

M

N

P

Q

R

T

U

V